Comparative Politics at the Crossroads

Contributors

Ervand Abrahamian
BARUCH COLLEGE

Adigun Agbaje
UNIVERSITY OF IBADAN

Christopher S. Allen
UNIVERSITY OF GEORGIA

Joan DeBardeleben
CARLETON UNIVERSITY

Maria do Carmo Campello de Souza
COLUMBIA UNIVERSITY

Shigeko N. Fukai
OKAYAMA UNIVERSITY

Haruhiro Fukui
UNIVERSITY OF TSUKUBA

Merilee S. Grindle
JOHN F. KENNEDY SCHOOL OF GOVERNMENT, HARVARD UNIVERSITY

Richard A. Joseph
THE CARTER CENTER AT EMORY UNIVERSITY

William A. Joseph
WELLESLEY COLLEGE

Mark Kesselman
COLUMBIA UNIVERSITY

Atul Kohli
PRINCETON UNIVERSITY

Joel Krieger
WELLESLEY COLLEGE

Scott D. Taylor
EMORY UNIVERSITY

Comparative Politics at the Crossroads

General Editors

Mark Kesselman
COLUMBIA UNIVERSITY

Joel Krieger
WELLESLEY COLLEGE

William A. Joseph
WELLESLEY COLLEGE

D. C. Heath and Company
Lexington, Massachusetts   Toronto

Dedication
MK—for Ishan and Javad
JK—for Lucille, Philip, and Al
WAJ—for Abigail, Hanna, and Rebecca

Address editorial correspondence to:

D. C. Heath and Company
125 Spring Street
Lexington, MA 02173

Acquisitions: Paul Smith
Development: Valerie Aubry
Editorial Production: Kathleen Deselle
Design: Jan Shapiro
Photo Research: Linda Finigan
Art Editing: Prentice Crosier
Production Coordination: Dick Tonachel
Permissions: Margaret Roll

Published simultaneously in Canada.

Printed in the United States of America.

International Standard Book Number: 0–669–33200–3

Library of Congress Catalog Number: 95–79140

10 9 8 7 6 5 4 3 2 1

Preface

These are exciting—yet daunting—times to teach comparative politics. After years in which the contours of the subject matter were quite familiar, the field's geographical, national, and intellectual boundaries are now very much in flux.

We have designed *Comparative Politics at the Crossroads* to help students come to terms with the quick pace and sheer scope of political changes throughout the world today, to examine the challenges each country faces, and to understand where countries may be headed politically once they move beyond the current crossroads. At the same time, we have kept the needs of instructors—for clear and readable prose, for comparative analysis focused on countries and political systems, for comprehensive treatment of institutions, political behavior, political economy, and the policy-making process—very much in mind.

The text presents eleven country studies written by leading specialists and drawn from the industrial democracies (Britain, France, Germany, and Japan), communist and post-communist states (Russia and China), and Third World polities (India, Mexico, Brazil, Nigeria, and Iran). A chapter is devoted to each country. Within each chapter are five sections that treat the historic formation of the modern state, the political economy of past and current national development, the major institutions of governance and policy-making, the processes of representation and participation, and the major issues that confront the country and are likely to shape its future as we approach the end of the twentieth century.

In *Comparative Politics at the Crossroads,* we emphasize historical patterns of state formation, political economy, domestic politics, and the politics of collective identities within the context of an international system. The most innovative feature of the book is the use of four comparative themes to frame our presentation of each country's politics. We explain the themes in the Introduction and present an intriguing puzzle for each. These themes—treated in each country study—focus attention on the continuities and contrasts among the eleven country studies:

- **A World of States** highlights the importance of state formation and the interstate system for political development.

- **Production and Exchange on a Global Scale** analyzes state strategies for governing the economy, and stresses the effects of economic globalization on domestic politics.
- **The Democratic Idea** explores the challenges posed by citizens' demands for greater control and participation in long-established democracies, transitional democracies, and authoritarian regimes.
- **The Politics of Collective Identities** considers the political consequences of race, ethnicity, gender, religion, and nationality, and their complex interplay with class-based politics.

Through our four themes, the methods of comparative analysis come alive as students examine specific similarities and differences among countries and within—and between—political systems. This thematic approach offers timely and comprehensive analysis of the historical continuities and contemporary challenges that locate each state at the crossroads of change.

Comparative Politics at the Crossroads strikes a balance between the richness of national political development and a more general comparative analysis. The Introduction explains the comparative method, analyzes the four key themes of the book, and describes the distinguishing features of industrial democracies, communist and post-communist systems, and Third World states. Each country study presents a clear and thorough treatment of political institutions and their relation to socioeconomic, cultural, and transnational influences.

Several special features assist in the teaching and learning process. At the beginning of each chapter, students will find a page of basic demographic, social, economic, and political information to aid in comparing countries. An appendix provides comparable data on the United States. Throughout the chapters a host of maps, tables, charts, photographs, and political cartoons enliven the text and present key information in clear and graphic ways. Each country study features sidebars that highlight interesting and provocative aspects of politics—for example, a critical political development or the biography of an especially important political leader. Key terms are set in boldface when first introduced and are defined in the Glossary at the end of the book. Students will find that the Glossary defines many key concepts that are used broadly in comparative politics.

In *Comparative Politics at the Crossroads,* we combine an innovative thematic approach and comprehensive coverage of political institutions and processes. We hope that it serves as a stimulating and accessible introduction to the field of comparative politics for your students.

We are grateful for the advice and critical comments of many colleagues, including Alfred P. Montero for his assistance in the preparation of the chapter on Brazil, and Ms. Rehnuma Shehabuddin for her research assistance in preparing the chapter on India. We are especially indebted to those who reviewed portions of the manuscript:

John Bailey, Georgetown University; **Amrita Basu,** Amherst College; **Mark Beissinger,** University of Wisconsin; **Linda Dolive,** Northern Kentucky University; **Jean Doyle,** University of Massachusetts at Dartmouth; **Jerrold Green,** Rand Corporation; **Joyce Kallgren,** University of California at Davis; **Roger Kangas,** University of Mississippi; **Randall Kindley,** University of Minnesota; **Jeffrey Kopstein,** University of Colorado at Boulder; **D. M. Kurtz,** University of Southwestern Louisiana; **Hong Yung Lee,** University of California at Berkeley; **Scott Mainwaring,** University of Notre Dame; **Paul Marantz,** University of British Columbia; **Carol Mershon,** University of Virginia; **Neil J. Mitchell,** University of New Mexico; **Joyce Mushaben,** University of Missouri at St. Louis; **David J. Myers,** Pennsylvania State University; **Jorgen Rasmussen,** Iowa State University; **Jeffrey Ringer,** Brigham Young University; **Richard J. Samuels,** Massachusetts Institute of Technology; **W. Rand Smith,** Lake Forest College; **Gale Stokes,** Rice University; **Kaare Strom,** University of California at San Diego; **Frank Tachau,** University of Illinois at Chicago; and **Donald C. Williams,** Western New England College.

Finally, our thanks to the talented and professional staff at D. C. Heath: Paul Smith, acquisitions editor; Valerie Aubry, development editor; Leah Strauss, editorial assistant; Kathleen Deselle, production editor; Jan Shapiro, designer; Margaret Roll, permissions editor; and Dick Tonachel, production coordinator.

M. K.

J. K.

W. A. J.

Brief Contents

Contents

Tables

Comparative Politics at the Crossroads

CHAPTER 1

*Comparative
Politics
at the
Crossroads*

Part 1

Introduction

CHAPTER 1

Comparative Politics at the Crossroads

The Global Challenge of Comparative Politics

We are living in extraordinary times. Since the mid-1980s, politics throughout the world has been rocked by dramatic and unpredictable developments. The revolutions of 1989 in Central and Eastern Europe marked the disintegration of much of the communist world. One after another, in Poland, Hungary, and Czechoslovakia, hard-line leaders resigned, free elections were held, and political power was transferred democratically. When the Berlin Wall—which divided East and West in both physical and symbolic terms—was dismantled brick by brick beginning in November 1989, the architecture of Europe was forever recast. Within a year, Germany was unified after nearly a half-century of **Cold War** division, and by the end of 1991, the Soviet Union, once a formidable superpower, had collapsed into fifteen troubled republics, including a much humbled Russia. By the middle of the decade, Nelson Mandela was transformed from prisoner to president of a newly democratic South Africa. An awkward handshake on the White House lawn between Yasir Arafat and Yitzhak Rabin in 1994 launched the Palestine Liberation Organization and Israel on a fitful and uncertain peace process in the Middle East. The unbelievable mixed with the unthinkable.

Beyond the unforgettable images captured in front-page news photos, these developments mark a fundamental political crossroads for our world. They reflect a shift in historical epochs that creates exciting opportunities for human progress, but also increases the risks of instability and conflict.

As the world has painfully learned in recent years, freedom, peace, and a reasonable standard of living cannot be built on hopes alone. It is desperately hard to make such dreams a reality. Removing dictatorial regimes often proves less difficult than building new democracies. In many countries, the rush to democracy awakens new and restless constituencies with demands that neither the government nor the economy can easily meet.

Post–Cold War political changes and the transformation of the global balance of power have produced new forms of international cooperation and competition—and new sources of international tension and violence. The grim but predictable bipolar world of superpower rivalry between the United States and the Soviet Union, reinforced by their respective NATO and Warsaw Treaty Organization (Warsaw Pact) alliances, has been replaced by the uncertainties of a more fragmented map of global power. During the Cold War, the rivalry between the Soviet Union and the United States was often fought out and contained in the **Third World,** as in the Vietnam War or the Middle East conflicts. But now with no superpower standoff to channel and contain conflicts, increasing economic, religious, and ethnic divisions create tension and crises in every corner of the world. We have witnessed a surge of brutal clashes between and within countries, along with a quieter dynamic of fierce competition and a rash of serious trade wars among professed allies.

It is not surprising that in the flash of newspaper headlines and television sound bites, these upheavals and changes may make politics look chaotic beyond comprehension. Although the study of **comparative politics** can help us understand current events in a rapidly changing world, it involves much more than snapshot analysis or Monday-morning quarterbacking. *Comparative Politics at the Crossroads* describes and analyzes in detail the government and politics in eleven different countries and identifies common themes in the development of these countries that can explain longer-term causes of both changes and continuities. The book provides cross-national comparisons and explanations based on four themes that we believe are central for understanding how our world has reached such a crucial political crossroads. The four key themes are these:

• The interaction of states within the international order.

• The role of states in economic management.

• The pressures for more democracy and the challenges of democratization.

• The political impact of diverse sources of social identity, including class, gender, ethnicity, and religion.

This cartoon captures some of the trends and tensions of comparative politics at the crossroads. It depicts a triumphant and rich, but economically fragile, "First World" (the capitalist industrial democracies), a defeated "Second World" (the Soviet bloc) led to ruin by misguided policies (that's Stalin's head being cut off), and a deprived and neglected "Third World." The venomous snake of "nationalism" threatens all parts of the world with ethnic, religious, and other types of communal conflict.
Source: © 1991 WittyWorld International Cartoon Magazine. Reprinted with permission.

technology, mass communications and culture, immigration and travel—as well as politics—forge deep connections among people worldwide. It is particularly urgent that we adopt a truly global perspective as we explore both the unique politics of different countries and regions and their growing interdependence.

There is an added benefit: by comparing political institutions, values, and processes in countries around the world, the student of comparative politics acquires analytical skills that can be redeployed at home. After you study comparative politics, you begin to think like a comparativist. As comparison becomes almost automatic, you look at the politics of your own country differently, with a wider focus and new insights.

For example, you may be surprised to discover that the sharing of authority between the central government and state or local governments *(federalism)* has more dramatic impact on public policy in the United States than in just about any other country. In the United States, public education, the welfare program that provides direct aid to families with dependent children (AFDC), and land use or zoning are largely decided at the state and local levels. The significance of federalism in the United States grows when viewed in comparative terms. You may have thought that it is perfectly natural for major public policies to have very different local outcomes. But you will soon discover that the diversity in local implementation of public policy in the United States is highly unusual. This larger comparative context may help you evaluate American public policy, as you weigh the benefits of greater local participation in decision making against the disadvantages of local inequalities.[1] Thus, comparative politics can put U.S. politics—or the politics of whatever country you call home—into a much richer perspective.

The contemporary world provides a unique laboratory for the study of comparative politics and gives unusual significance to the subject. We hope that you share our sense of excitement and join us in the challenging effort to understand comparative politics at the crossroads. We begin by first exploring what comparative politics actually compares and how comparative study enhances our understanding of politics.

We also expect that these four themes will be useful for identifying where the countries covered in this book may be heading politically once they move beyond the crossroads. Moreover, the themes illustrate what a valuable intellectual tool comparative politics offers for making some sense of even the most tumultuous times. The closing years of the twentieth century present an extraordinary challenge to those who study comparative politics, but the study of comparative politics also provides a unique opportunity for understanding this uncertain era.

Contemporary politics presents a demanding agenda for the student of comparative politics. In order to appreciate the complexity of politics and political transitions in countries around the world, we must look beyond our own immediate experiences. Today, business and trade, information

SECTION 2

What—and How—Comparative Politics Compares[2]

To "compare and contrast" is one of the most common exercises, whether in the classroom study of literature or politics or animal behavior—or in selecting dorm rooms or listing your favorite movies. In the observation of politics, the use of comparisons is very old, dating at least from Aristotle, who categorized Athenian city-states in the fifth century B.C. according to their form of political rule: rule by a single individual, rule by a few, or rule by all citizens. He added a normative dimension (a claim about how societies *should* be ruled), by distinguishing ("contrasting") good and corrupt versions of each type. The modern study of comparative politics refines and systematizes the age-old practice of evaluating some feature of *X* by comparing it to the same feature of *Y* in order to learn more about it than isolated study would permit.

The term *comparative politics* refers to a subject matter, a field or specialty within the academic study of politics (that is, political science), and a method or approach to the study of politics. The subject matter of comparative politics is the domestic politics of countries or peoples. Within the study of political science, comparative politics is one of four areas of specialization. In addition to comparative politics, most political science (or government) departments in U.S. colleges and universities include courses and academic specialists in three other fields—political theory, international relations, and American politics.

There is no logical reason why study of the United States should not be included within the field of comparative politics. In fact, important studies in comparative politics—and quite a few courses—have integrated the study of American politics with the study of politics in other countries. However, because it is widely believed that students living in the United States should study American politics intensively and with special focus, the two fields remain separate. The pattern of distinguishing the study of politics at home from politics abroad is also common elsewhere, so students in Canada may be expected to study Canadian politics as a distinctive specialty, and Japanese students would likewise be expected to master Japanese politics.

The comparative method or approach to understanding relies principally on analysis designed to identify the similarities and differences between political institutions and processes, by focusing on selected features or developments. Students of comparative politics (we call ourselves comparativists) believe that we can't be sure about most political observations by looking at only one case. We often hear statements such as: "The United States has the best health care system in the world." Comparativists immediately wonder what kinds of health care systems exist in other countries, what they cost and how they are financed, who is covered by health insurance, and so on. Besides, what does "best" mean when it comes to health care systems? Is it the one that provides the widest access? the one that is the most technologically advanced? the one that is the most cost-effective? the one that produces the healthiest population? We wouldn't announce the "best movie" or the "best car" without considering other alternatives or deciding what specific factors enter into our judgment.

Comparativists often analyze political institutions or processes by looking at two or more cases deliberately selected for their mix of common and contrasting features. The analysis then involves actually comparing similar aspects of politics in more than one country—for example, the executive branches of government in the United States, Britain, and Canada.[3] Some comparative political studies take a thematic approach and draw on many different countries to analyze broad issues, such as what causes revolutions.[4]

Comparative politics can also include *single-country* case studies when they are conceptualized *comparatively.* The usual method here is for a political scientist to analyze the politics of a single country within the framework of the more general type of political system in which that country's politics best fits. For example, detailed studies of Chinese politics are written within the comparative framework of communist political systems even when explicit comparisons with other communist regimes are not made.

A single-country study can also be comparative when a second case is well known and supplied intuitively by the reader based on direct experience. A classic example of this approach comes from the 1830s when French aristocrat Alexis de Tocqueville traveled to the relatively young United States to study a political system based on the principles of popular sovereignty and majority rule, which at that time in history were very revolutionary ideas. Tocqueville's book, *Democracy in America,*[5] reflected his admiration for the high degree of liberty and the remarkable progress toward equality in the United States. But he also included a cautionary note about American democracy. Tocqueville was concerned about what he called the "tyranny of the majority," which he believed threatened the values and rights of minority opinion. Writing for a French audience grappling with a transition from monarchy to a democratic form of government, Tocqueville understood that his readers would naturally fill in the comparisons with their native France.

Comparisons can be very useful for political analysis at several different levels. Political scientists often compare developments in different cities or at the level of regions, provinces, or states. Comparative analysis can also focus on specific institutions and processes in different countries, such as the legislature, executive, political parties, social movements, or court systems. The organization of *Comparative Politics at the Crossroads* reflects our belief that the best way to begin the study of comparative politics is at the level of **countries.** Countries, which are also sometimes referred to as **nation-states,** can be thought of as distinct, politically defined territories that encompass political institutions, cultures, economies, and ethnic and other social identities.

Although often highly divided internally, countries historically have proven to be the most important source of a people's collective political identities and the major arena for organized political action in the modern world. Therefore, countries are the natural unit of analysis for many domestic political variables and processes. These include **political institutions** (the formal and informal rules and structured relationships that organize power and resources in society), **political culture** (attitudes, beliefs, and symbols that influence political behavior), and **political development** (the stages of change in the structures of government).

Within a given country, the **state** is generally the most powerful cluster of institutions. But just what *is* the state? The way the term is used in comparative politics is probably unfamiliar to many students. In the United States, it usually refers to the states in our federal system. But in comparative politics, the state comprises a country's key political institutions that are responsible for making, implementing, enforcing, and adjudicating important policies in that country. The most important state institutions are the national executive, notably, the president and/or prime minister and **cabinet,** along with the army, police, administrative **bureaucracy,** the legislature, and courts. In casual usage, the terms *state* and *government* are sometimes used interchangeably. However, in comparative politics, government often does not refer to the permanent administrative or bureaucratic agencies but to the key partisan officials and offices whose fates are linked by election or appointment to the president or prime minister and who direct major administrative agencies. The use of the term *government* in comparative politics—as in the phrase, "the government of Prime Minister John Major in Britain"—is very similar to the term *administration* in American politics—as in the "Clinton administration."

States claim, usually with considerable success, the right to issue rules—notably, laws, administrative regulations, and court decisions—binding for people within their borders. Even democratic states, in which top officials are chosen by procedures that permit all citizens to participate, can survive only if they can preserve enforcement (or coercive) powers both internally and with regard to other states that may pose challenges. There are examples of countries with highly repressive states whose political survival depends largely on military and police powers. But even in such states, long-term stability requires that the ruling regime have some measure of political **legitimacy;** that is, a significant segment of the citizenry must believe that the state acts with some moral authority. Political legitimacy is greatly affected by the state's ability to "deliver the goods" through satisfactory economic performance and an acceptable distribution of economic resources. Moreover, in the contemporary period legitimacy seems to require that states represent themselves as democratic in some fashion, whether or not they are in fact. Thus, this text looks particularly closely at, first, the state's role in governing the economy and, second, the pressures exerted on states to develop and extend democratic participation.

The fact that states are the fundamental objects of analysis in comparative politics does not mean that all states are the same. Indeed, the organization of state institutions varies widely, and these differences have a powerful impact on political and social life. Hence, each country study in this book devotes considerable attention to variations in institutions of governance, participation, and representation and their political implications. Each country study begins with an analysis of how the institutional organization and political procedures of the state have evolved historically. This process of **state formation** fundamentally influences how and why states differ politically.

Because countries are the basic building blocks in politics and because states are the most significant political organizations and actors, these two become the critical units for comparative analysis. The comparativist looks at similarities and differences among countries or states and tries to develop *causal theories*—hypotheses that can be expressed formally in a causal mode: "If *X* happens, then *Y* will be the result." Such theories include factors (the *independent variables,* symbolized by *X*) that are believed to influence some outcome and the outcome (the *dependent variable,* symbolized by *Y*) that is to be explained. For example, it is commonly argued that if a country's economic pie shrinks, conflict among groups for resources will intensify. This hypothesis suggests what is called an *inverse correlation* between variables (as *X* varies in one direction, *Y* varies in the opposite direction). As the total national economic product *(X)* decreases, then political and social conflict over economic shares *(Y)* increases. Even when the explanation does not involve the explicit testing of hypotheses (and often it does not), comparativists try to identify similarities and differences among countries and to identify significant patterns.

It is important to recognize the limits on just how "scientific" political science—and thus comparative politics—can be. In laboratory sciences such as physics or chemistry (often called *natural* sciences), experimental techniques can be applied to isolate the contribution of distinct factors in promoting an outcome. It is possible to change the value or magnitude of a factor that influences an outcome—for example, the force applied to an object—and to measure how the outcome has consequently changed. Physicists or chemists can manipulate factors, or variables, when their variation is expected to have interesting consequences. However, political scientists and comparativists like other *social* scientists—for example, economists or sociologists—rarely have the opportunity to apply such experimental techniques.

In the real world of politics, unlike in a laboratory, variables cannot easily be isolated or manipulated. Some political scientists employ techniques that attempt to identify the specific causal weight of a variable in explaining a political outcome. But it is very difficult to measure precisely how, for example, a person's **ethnic identity, gender,** or income influences her or his choice when casting a ballot. Nor can we ever know for sure what exact mix of factors—conflicts among elites, popular ideological appeals, the weakness of the state, the organizational capacity of insurgents, or the discontent of the masses—precipitates a successful revolution.

Despite these difficulties and limitations, the study of comparative politics involves the search for just the right balance in an explanation between the specifics of individual cases and the search for universal patterns. One common goal of comparativists is to develop what is called **middle-level theory.** Such a theory explains phenomena found in a limited range of cases, which in comparative politics means a specific set of countries with given characteristics, political institutions, or processes. If we go too far to one extreme and study only the politics of individual countries without any comparative framework, then comparative politics becomes merely the study of a series of isolated cases. It would be impossible to recognize what is most significant in the collage of political characteristics we find in the world's many countries. As a result, the understanding of patterns of similarity and difference among countries would be lost, along with an important tool for evaluating what is and what is not unique about a country's political life.

If we go too far to the other extreme and try to make universal claims that something is *always* true in *all* countries, we either stretch the truth or neutralize all the interesting differences and obscure the most fascinating patterns of variation. For the political world is incredibly complex, shaped by an extraordinary array of factors and an almost endless interplay of variables. Indeed, after a brief period in the 1950s and 1960s when many comparativists tried—and failed—to develop a "grand theory" that would apply to all countries, most comparativists now see the attempt to develop middle-level theory as the most promising.

For example, comparativists have worked hard to analyze the efforts in many countries to replace (or attempt to replace) authoritarian forms of government, such as military **dictatorships** and one-party states, with more participatory and democratic **regimes.** In studying this important phenomenon of *democratic transitions* comparativists do not treat each national case as unique nor look to a universal pattern that ignores all differences. Applying middle-level theory, we attempt to identify the influence on the new regime's political stability of specific variables such as institutional legacies, political cultural heritage, levels of economic development, the nature of the regime before the transition, and the degree of ethnic conflict or homogeneity. Explanations seek to identify patterns associated with the emergence and consolidation of democratic regimes in southern Europe in the 1970s (Greece, Portugal, and Spain) and compare them to developments in Latin America, Asia, and Africa

since the 1980s, and in East-Central Europe since the revolutions of 1989.

The study of comparative politics involves many challenges, including the complexity of the subject matter, the fast pace of change in the contemporary period, and the impossibility of manipulating variables or replicating conditions for the study of politics. What can we expect when the whole political world is our laboratory? When we put the method of comparative politics to the test and develop a set of themes derived from middle-level theory, we discover that it *is* possible to find explanations and discern patterns that make sense of a vast range of political developments and link the experiences of states and citizens throughout the world.

SECTION 3

Comparative Politics at the Crossroads: Themes

We began this introduction by emphasizing the extraordinary importance and fluid pace of the global changes currently taking place. Next, we explained the subject matter of comparative politics and described some of the tools of comparative analysis. This section describes the four themes by which we organize the large volume of information on political institutions, processes, conflicts, policy, and changes presented in the eleven country chapters in *Comparative Politics at the Crossroads.* These themes will help explain continuities and contrasts among countries and demonstrate what patterns apply to a group of countries—and why—and what patterns are specific to a particular country. We will also suggest a way that each theme highlights some puzzle in comparative politics.

Before we introduce the themes, a couple of warnings are necessary. First, our four themes cannot possibly capture all the infinitely varied experience of politics throughout the world. Our framework in *Comparative Politics at the Crossroads,* built on four core themes, provides a guide to understanding many features of contemporary comparative politics. But we urge students (and rely on instructors!), who through study and experience know the politics of the United States and many other countries, to challenge and augment our interpretations. Secondly, we want to note that a textbook builds from existing theory but does not construct or test new hypotheses. That task is the goal of original scholarly studies. The themes then are

intended to crystallize some of the most significant findings in the field of contemporary comparative politics.

THEME 1: A WORLD OF STATES

The theme that we call *a world of states* reflects the fact that, since the beginning of the modern era several centuries ago, states have been the primary actors on the world stage. For better or worse, it is state officials who send armies to conquer other states and territories, states whose legal codes make it possible for business firms to operate within their borders and beyond, and states that regulate the movement of people across borders through immigration law. Courses in international relations focus primarily on interaction among states, whereas courses in comparative politics put more stress on what goes on within a country's borders. In *Comparative Politics at the Crossroads* we emphasize one key feature of the international arena: the impact on a state's domestic political institutions and processes of its relative success or failure in competing economically and politically with other states.

No state, even the most powerful such as the United States, is unaffected by influences originating outside its borders. One element of the transition occurring today in comparative politics is the heightened importance of various cross-national influences. A wide array of general and specialized international organizations and treaties, including the United Nations, and regional organizations and/or trade blocs like the **European Union,** the Organization of American States, the North American Free Trade Agreement, and countless others, challenge the sovereign control of national governments within their borders. Transnational corporations, international banks, and currency traders in New York, London, and Tokyo affect countries and people throughout the world. A country's political borders do not protect its citizens from environmental pollution or infectious diseases that come from abroad. More broadly, developments linked to technology transfer, the growth of an international information society, immigration, and cultural diffusion have a varying but undeniable impact on the domestic politics of all countries. For example, thanks to the relatively recent global diffusion of radio, television receivers, and the Internet, people everywhere are remarkably informed about international developments. This knowledge may fuel popular local demands that governments intervene in humanitarian efforts in faraway Bosnia, Rwanda, or elsewhere. And this global awareness may make citizens more ready to hold their own government to internationally recognized standards of human rights.

As we near the year 2000, nations are experiencing intense pressures from an expanding and increasingly complex mix of external influences. In all countries, politics and policy-making are shaped in important ways by influences that come from outside their borders. But international political and economic influences do not have the same impact in all countries; nor do all states equally shape the institutional form and policy of international organizations in which they participate. It is likely that the more advantaged a state is, as measured by such factors as level of economic development, military power, and resource base, the more it will shape global influences. Conversely, the policies of less advantaged countries are more extensively molded by other states, by international organizations, and by broader international constraints.

The theme we identify as a world of states includes a second important focus: similarities and contrasts among countries in state formation. We study the ways that states develop historically, diverse patterns in the organization of political institutions, the processes—and limits—of democratization, the ability of the state to control social groups in society and sustain power, and the state's economic management strate-

gies and capacities. We observe the linkage between state formation and the relative position of different states in the international order. Certain countries, such as Britain and India, are connected by **colonial** histories; others, like China and Russia, share developmental patterns that for decades were shaped by communist ideologies, political structures, and approaches to economic organization.

A puzzle: To what extent do states still remain the basic building blocks of political life? Increasingly the politics and policies of states are shaped by external actors. At the same time, many states face increasingly restive constituencies who challenge the power and legitimacy of central states. In reading our eleven country case studies, try to assess what impact pressures from both above and below—outside and inside—have had on the role of the state in carrying out its basic functions and in its relationship to its citizens.

THEME 2: PRODUCTION AND EXCHANGE ON A GLOBAL SCALE

The success of states in maintaining their authority is greatly affected by their ability to assure that an adequate volume of goods and services is produced to satisfy the needs of their populations. Certainly, the inadequate performance of the Soviet economic system was an important reason for the rejection of communism and the disintegration of the Soviet Union. How a country organizes production and exchange is therefore one of the key elements in its overall pattern of political as well as economic development. It is very important to analyze, for example, how countries differ in the balance between agricultural and industrial production in their economies, how successful they are in competing with other countries that offer similar products in international markets, and the relative importance of market forces versus government control of the economy.

An important goal of all countries in the contemporary world is to achieve durable economic development. In fact, effective economic performance is near the top of every state's political agenda. The term **political economy** refers to how governments affect economic performance—and how economic performance in turn affects a country's political processes. We accord great importance to political economy in *Comparative Politics at the Crossroads* because we believe that politics in all countries is deeply influenced by the relationship between government and the economy, in both domestic and international dimensions.

A puzzle: What political factors foster successful national economic performance? This is a question that students of political economy have long pondered—and to which there are no easy answers. Take, for example, this apparently straightforward question: Are democratic states more or less able to pursue effective developmental strategies? A detailed study of the question, "Does democracy in the political realm foster or hinder economic growth?" concludes that there is no clear answer.[6] Some democracies, notably Germany and Japan (at least until a recession in the 1990s), have been outstanding economic success stories; others, including the United States and Britain (at least until a recent upswing), have experienced declining competitiveness during much of the last few decades. Some states have effectively mobilized private economic interests to achieve remarkable records of development despite having an authoritarian government; the Republic of Korea (South Korea) exploded economically in the 1960s and 1970s, and China has enjoyed the highest growth rate in the world in recent years. Other authoritarian states have suffered badly in economic terms; an example is Zaire, where the state preys on the society. As you read the country studies, try to reach your own conclusions about what factors—such as level of democracy and approaches to economic management—lead to economic success and whether any consistent patterns apply across countries.

THEME 3: THE DEMOCRATIC IDEA

Our comparative case studies reveal a surprising level of complexity in the seemingly simple fact of the rapid spread of democracy throughout much of the world in recent years. First of all, they show clearly the growing global appeal of the *democratic idea,* by which we mean the claim by citizens that they should, in some way, exercise substantial control over the decisions made by their states and governments. Nevertheless, the cases also show that there is still a lot of **authoritarianism** in the world; that is, there remain many states based on arbitrary and unchecked political power in which citizens cannot exercise free choice in the selection of leaders and cannot openly oppose the government or question the decision of rulers.

But as authoritarian rulers have recently learned in diverse settings, such as the former Soviet Union,

Brazil, Nigeria, and China, once persistent and widespread pressures for democratic participation develop, they are hard (although not impossible) to resist. A good indication of the near universal appeal of the democratic idea is that even authoritarian regimes proclaim their attachment to democracy—usually asserting that they embody a superior form to that prevailing elsewhere. For example, leaders of the People's Republic of China claim that their brand of "socialist democracy" represents the interests of the vast majority of citizens more effectively than do the "bourgeois democracies" of capitalist societies.

Second, the case studies draw attention to diverse sources of support for democracy. Democracy has proved appealing for many reasons. In some historical settings, it may represent a standoff or equilibrium among political contenders for power, in which no one group can gain sufficient strength to control outcomes alone.[7] Democracy may appeal to citizens in authoritarian settings because democratic regimes often rank among the world's most stable, affluent, and cohesive countries. Another important pressure for democracy is born of the widespread popular desire for dignity and equality. Even when dictatorial regimes appear to benefit their countries—for example, by promoting economic development or nationalist goals—citizens are still likely to demand democracy. Although authoritarian governments can suppress demands for democratic participation for a long period, the domestic and (in recent years) international costs of doing so are high.

Third, as we show in the country chapters of *Comparative Politics at the Crossroads,* democracies vary widely in concrete historical, institutional, and cultural dimensions. We pay substantial attention to different electoral and party systems, to the distinction between parliamentary and presidential systems, and to differences in the values and expectations that shape citizens' demands in different countries.

Fourth, we emphasize the potential fragility of democratic transitions. The fact that popular movements or leaders of moderate factions often displace authoritarian regimes and then hold elections does not mean that democratic institutions will prevail or endure: a wide gulf exists between a *transition* to democracy and the *consolidation* of democracy. Historically, powerful groups have often opposed democratic institutions because they fear that democracy will threaten their privilege. On the other hand, disadvantaged groups may oppose the democratic process because they see it as unresponsive to their deeply felt grievances. As a result, reversals of democratic regimes have occurred in the past and will doubtless occur in the future. The country studies do not support a philosophy of history or theory of political development that identifies a single (democratic) end point toward which all countries will eventually converge. One important study, published in the early phase of the most recent democratic wave, captured the tenuous process of democratization in its title: *Transitions from Authoritarian Rule: Tentative Conclusions about Uncertain Democracies.*[8] Some suggest that it is far easier for a country to hold its first democratic election than its second. Hence, the fact that the democratic idea is so powerful does not mean that all countries will adopt or preserve democratic institutions.

Finally, our democratic idea theme suggests the incompleteness of democratic agendas even in countries with the longest and most developed experiences of representative democracy. In virtually every democracy in recent years, many citizens have turned against the state when their living standards were threatened by high unemployment and economic stagnation. At the same time, antagonistic social movements have targeted the state because of its actions or inactions in such varied spheres as environmental regulation, reproductive rights, and race or ethnic relations. Comparative studies confirm that the democratic idea fuels political conflicts no matter how long-established the democracies because, usually, a large gap separates democratic ideals and the actual functioning of democratic political institutions. Thus, even in countries with impressive histories of democratic institutions, citizens may invoke the democratic idea to demand that their government be more responsive and accountable.

A puzzle: Democracy and stability. Comparativists have intensely debated whether democratic institutions contribute to political stability or, on the contrary, to political disorder. On the one hand, democracy by its very nature permits political opposition: one of its defining characteristics is competition among those who aspire to gain high political office. Political life in democracies is turbulent and unpredictable. On the other hand, the fact that political opposition and competition are legitimate in democracies appears to deepen support for the state even among opponents of a particular government. And history reveals far more cases of durable democratic regimes than durable authoritarian regimes in the modern world. In your country-by-country studies, look for the stabilizing and destabilizing consequences of democratic transitions and the challenges faced by long-standing democracies.

THEME 4: THE POLITICS OF COLLECTIVE IDENTITY

How do individuals understand who they are in political terms, and on what basis do groups of people come together to advance common political aims? In other words, what are the sources of *collective political identity?* At one point, social scientists thought they knew. Observers generally held that age-old loyalties of ethnicity, religious affiliation, race, gender, and locality were being dissolved and displaced by economic, political, and cultural modernization. Comparativists thought that **social class**—solidarities based on the shared experience of work or, more broadly, economic position—had become the most important source of collective identity. And they believed that most of the time groups would pragmatically pursue their interests in ways that were not politically destabilizing.[9] We now know that the formation and interplay of politically relevant collective identities are far more complex and uncertain.

In the industrial democracies, the importance of identities based on class membership has declined, although class and material sources of collective political identity remain significant in political competition and economic organization. By contrast, contrary to earlier social science predictions, in many countries nonclass identities have assumed growing, not diminishing, significance. These affiliations develop from a sense of belonging to particular groups based on language, religion, ethnicity, race, nationality, or gender.

The politics of collective political identity involves struggles to define which groups are full participants in the political community and which are marginalized or even ostracized. It also involves a constant tug-of-war over the relative power and influence—both symbolic and substantive—among groups. Issues of inclusion and priority remain pivotal in many countries, and they may never be resolved. One reason why conflict around this question can be so intense is that political leaders in the state and in opposition movements often seek to mobilize support by exploiting ethnic, religious, racial, or regional rivalries.

Identity-based conflicts are found in long-established countries, such as Britain, where the "Irish question" serves as a painful reminder of how difficult it is to resolve ethnic-nationalist and religious tensions, particularly when these divisions are reinforced by differences in power and privilege. (The Protestants who support continued union with Britain are the "haves," and the Catholics who usually support Irish nationalism in one form or another are the "have-nots" in Northern Ireland.) These conflicts are often particularly intense in postcolonial countries, such as Nigeria, where in the period after World War II colonial powers forced ethnic groups together in order to carve out a country, and borders were drawn with little regard to preexisting collective identities. This process of state formation by the imposition of external will sowed seeds for future conflict in Nigeria and elsewhere, and threatens the continued survival of many postcolonial countries.

A puzzle: Collective identity and distributional politics. Once identity demands are placed on the political agenda, can governments resolve them by distributing resources in ways that redress the grievances of the minority or politically weaker identity groups? Collective identities operate both at the level of symbols, attitudes, values, and beliefs and at the level of material resources. However, the contrast between material versus nonmaterial-based identities and demands should not be exaggerated. In practice, most groups are animated *both* by feelings of loyalty and solidarity *as well as* by the desire to obtain material benefits for their members. But the analytical distinction between material and nonmaterial demands re-

mains useful, and it is worth considering whether the nonmaterial aspects of the politics of collective identities make political disputes over ethnicity or religion or language or nationality especially divisive and difficult to resolve.

In a situation of extreme scarcity, it may prove nearly impossible to reach any compromise among groups with conflicting material interests and demands. But if an adequate level of resources is available, such conflicts may be easier to resolve because groups can "split the difference" and get a share of resources that they find at least minimally satisfying. Since this process refers to who gets what or how resources are distributed it is called *distributional politics*. However, the demands of ethnic, religious, and nationalist movements may be difficult to satisfy by a distributional style of politics. The distributional style may be quite ineffectual when, for example, a religious group demands that its religious values be imposed on the whole society or a dominant linguistic group insists that a single language be used in education and government throughout the country. In such cases, political conflict tends to assume an "all-or-nothing" quality, making conciliation difficult. The country studies will examine a wide range of conflicts involving collective identities. It will be interesting (and possibly troubling) to ponder whether or not and under what conditions they are subject to the normal give-and-take of political bargaining.

These four themes provide our analytic scaffold. With an understanding of the method of comparative politics and the four themes in mind, we can now discuss how we have grouped the country studies that comprise *Comparative Politics at the Crossroads* and how the text is organized for comparative analysis.

SECTION 4

Political Systems in a World in Transition

Most textbooks and courses in comparative politics have traditionally been organized according to categories that distinguished between *industrialized* (or developed), *communist,* and *Third World* (or developing) countries. This categorization was based, in part, on distinctive economic features that helped characterize **political systems,** a term that applies to broad patterns of interaction among state institutions, economic coordination, and political culture.

Economic organization and performance both affected and reflected the realities of politics in these different systems: the capitalist (or market) economies and high standards of living in North America, Western Europe, Japan, and a few other countries; the socialist (or planned) economies of countries ruled by a communist party, such as the Soviet Union and China; and the low level of economic development and widespread poverty characteristic of the

Third World, which included most of the countries of Asia, Africa, and Latin America.

Democracy was another dividing line in this way of looking at the nations of the world. The capitalist industrialized countries not only were wealthy, but also were stable, well-functioning (if not untroubled) democracies; communist systems were unquestionably dictatorial; and Third World nations had either personal despotisms, one-party rule, military regimes, or—at best—democracies marred by high levels of social and political violence.

One of the consequences of our world in transition is that these economic and political dividing lines among types of countries are no longer so obvious. The collapse of most communist regimes since 1989 has shrunk to a handful the number of countries in what was once among the clearest categories of regime types used in the study of comparative politics. Moreover, sharp differences in economic growth rates among developing countries in recent years make it difficult to generalize with confidence about the Third World.

Perhaps most important from the viewpoint of political science and the major themes of this book, the spread of democracy in recent decades has blurred our conventional way of looking at the world. Not that the distinction between democracy and dictatorship is less clear: no one confuses the democratic character of the French or Indian governments with the dictatorial rule of the Chinese Communist Party or Nigeria's military leaders. But fifteen or twenty years ago democracies made up only a small minority of nations; today, in contrast, democracy—whether long-established or newly realized, whether relatively stable or shaky, whether strongly rooted or shallow—is the world's most common form of government. Most of the countries that once made up the so-called communist world (from Albania to Mongolia) and much of the Third World (from Bangladesh to Paraguay) now have democratic governments or are in the midst of a transition from dictatorship to democracy.

These recent economic and political trends challenge and complicate the way comparativists categorize the world's countries. But because no clear or compelling alternative framework for comparative analysis at the introductory level has yet emerged, we have chosen to group the countries covered in this book according to the categories of "Industrial Democracies," "Communist and Post-Communist States," and "Politics in the Third World." As we discuss below, the countries in each category share many characteristics that distinguish them in important ways from the countries in other categories.

THE INDUSTRIAL DEMOCRACIES

In addition to Britain, France, Germany, and Japan, which are covered in this text, other industrial democracies include the United States, Canada, Australia, New Zealand, Israel, and most of the countries of Western Europe. The defining characteristics of these countries can be understood by analyzing the words in the category name: "Industrial" and "Democracies."

By "Industrial" we mean that these countries have the world's most developed and technologically advanced economies; they also have the highest standards of living as measured by average income and by the health and educational levels of their populations. Even the less affluent industrial nations like Ireland and New Zealand have a standard of living estimated to be three or four times higher than some of the more prosperous developing nations such as Brazil and Mexico. The richest industrial democracies (like France and Japan) have a standard of living that by some calculations is fifty or sixty times that of the world's poorest countries (such as China, India, and Nigeria).

Indeed, many industrialized countries have moved beyond being "industrialized" in that more of their labor force works in the "services" (for example, government, communications, commerce, banking, and education) than in industry. In these countries—which are sometimes called postindustrial—the economy is dominated by the service and industrial sectors, while agriculture plays a very small (though often politically significant) role. Some developing countries, including Brazil, Iran, Mexico, and Nigeria, have relatively large service sectors (often a sign of a bloated bureaucracy in the Third World), but agriculture and manufacturing based on unskilled labor still play a much larger role in their economies than is the case in the industrialized democracies (see Figure 1).

The second label, "Democracies," means that these countries have political institutions and procedures that put into practice the core value of democracy: that the citizens of a country should be able to control their government. Comparativists generally agree that to qualify as a democracy a country must have the following political characteristics:

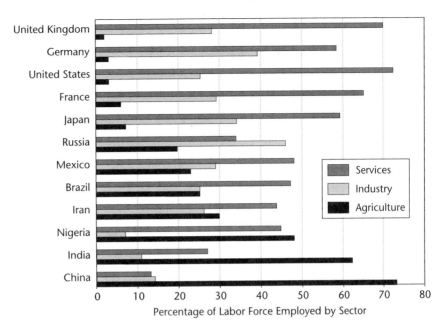

Figure 1 Industrialization in Comparative Perspective
One way to measure the level of industrialization in a country is to look at where people work in the major sectors of the economy. This chart shows the percentage of the labor force in services, industry, and agriculture for all the countries in this textbook and, for comparison, the United States. Source: *United Nations Human Development Report,* 1994.

• *Political accountability.* There must be formal procedures by which those who hold political power are chosen by and held accountable to the people of the country. The key mechanism for such accountability is regular, free, and fair elections in which the voters may elect or defeat candidates for office.

• *Political competition.* Political parties must be free to organize, present candidates for office, express their ideas, and compete in fair elections. The winning party must be allowed to take office, and the losing party must relinquish power through legal and peaceful means.

• *Political freedom.* All citizens must possess political rights and civil liberties. These include the right to participate in the political process; freedom of assembly, organization, and political expression (including the right to criticize the government); and protection against arbitrary state intrusion into their private lives. A judiciary not subject to direct political control is a common institutional means for safeguarding these freedoms.

• *Political equality.* All citizens must be legally entitled to participate in politics (by voting, running for office, or joining an interest group), and their votes must have equal weight in the political process. Mem-

bers of political, ethnic, or other minority groups must have equal rights as citizens.

While these four points are useful as a general checklist of the political prerequisites of democracy, several qualifications need to be added. First, no government has ever fully lived up to these standards, and all democratic governments have, at various points in their histories, violated them to a greater or lesser extent. For example, the United States did not extend voting rights to women until 1920 and did not effectively protect the rights of racial minorities until the 1960s (and by some important measures still has not fully done so).

Second, these ideals are limited, not absolute, in actual practice. All democracies have laws restricting views, actions, and organizations that are judged to threaten national security or public safety. Such laws place limits on political freedom and sometimes on political competition (as when a "subversive" political party is banned).

Third, the methods for interpreting and implementing these ideals are often debatable and sometimes become very contentious political issues. For example, the debate over gun control in the United States involves sharply differing perspectives on the meaning of freedom: Some Americans see any ban on

weapons or a registration requirement as an infringe-
ment of their constitutional right to bear arms, whereas
others believe that the government must restrict gun
ownership in the name of public safety. In most every
other industrial democracy, gun control is not even an
issue: Few citizens question the state's authority to
limit the possession of weapons.

Fourth, even in democracies economic inequalities load the political deck. Wealthier citizens, interest
groups, and parties can use their more substantial resources to increase their chances of winning an election or influencing public policy. This power creates a
tension, to a greater or lesser degree, in all industrial
democracies between the formal political procedures
(such as voting) in which all are equal, and the actual
situation in which the affluent are "more equal than
others" because of their greater ability to influence
political outcomes and public policy.

The tension between citizens' economic inequalities and their equal right to participate in elections and
to try to affect policies is manifest in all industrial
democracies—indeed, it is a perpetual source of political division. Varying political coalitions have sponsored very different governmental policies in key
areas depending on the social groups who succeed in
electing officials responsive to their interests. Three
key areas of policy difference involve

- *The distribution of taxes.* Although all governments
levy taxes on citizens and businesses to support their
activities, who pays how much is often a source of
intense political debate.

- *Governmental economic priorities.* Should economic policy be directed above all toward restraining
inflation (a particular concern for the affluent or elderly because inflation reduces the value of their assets
and savings) or toward reducing unemployment
(which traditionally has harmed working people
most)?

- *The extent of governmental spending for social programs.* Typical benefits include the public provision of
health care, unemployment compensation, old-age
pensions, and assistance to the needy.

There are dramatic variations in governmental
policies in different industrial democracies in these
policy areas. Consider social expenditures, which includes programs for and payments to the elderly, disabled, and unemployed, often grouped under the term

welfare state. Although many factors influence policy
outcomes, in some countries where moderate or conservative parties have ruled for long periods, including
Japan and the United States, welfare state expenditures constitute around 10 percent of the gross national
product (GNP). In many Western European countries,
on the other hand, where labor movements have been
politically influential within ruling coalitions, social
spending may be three times as high. These differences obviously have an important impact on what it
means to live in these societies.

Finally, although all democracies share the core
political attributes of accountability, competition, freedom, and equality, they vary widely in their political
institutions. A common classification of democracies is
based on differing relationships between the executive
and the legislature. In presidential systems, such as in
the United States, the chief executive (the president)
and the national legislature (Congress) are chosen in
separate elections, and there is a clear separation of
powers between the executive branch and the legislature. This is actually an unusual form of democracy.
Most of the world's democracies (including Britain,
Germany, and Japan) have parliamentary governments
in which executive and legislative powers are fused
rather than separated. In these systems, the chief executive (the prime minister) and the cabinet are themselves
legislators who remain members of the legislature even
when serving in the executive branch.

The formal and informal "rules of the game" for
reaching and exercising power are very different in
presidential and parliamentary systems. In presidential
systems, members of the legislature jealously preserve
their autonomy. The legislature, elected separately
from the president, is constitutionally entitled to set its
own agenda, initiate policy proposals, and defy presidential directives. Presidents may have many resources to persuade the legislature to support the
administration's agenda, but even when the same party
controls both the presidency and the legislature, the
key word is *persuade.*

In parliamentary systems, short of the rare occasion when a rebellion within the ranks of the majority
party in parliament brings down the cabinet or forces a
change in the prime minister, the legislature may serve
as a forum for dramatic policy debate. But it neither
represents a significant source of policy initiatives nor
poses a decisive obstacle to the government legislating
its own proposals.

So what? you may ask. Good question! Ponder what difference it makes as you review parliamentary and presidential systems in this book. And as you do, note how rare presidential systems are—a point that may be surprising for those who assume that the U.S. presidential system is universal.

The distinction between presidential and parliamentary systems hardly exhausts the range of institutional variation within industrial democracies. You will discover that France's hybrid semipresidential system is quite different from both. France has a dual executive, with both a directly elected president and an appointed prime minister. As you will discover in this text, these differences raise the kinds of questions that are at the heart of comparative politics: How do different political institutions and procedures give concrete expression to the same democratic values? What consequences do these differences have for the effectiveness of government and the distribution of resources?

Despite these qualifications about the nature of democracy, the prerequisites of democracy—accountability, competition, freedom, and equality—are still useful tools in the study of comparative politics. Not only do they provide a demarcation between democratic and dictatorial political systems, they also serve as standards against which democracies themselves can be measured and compared. It may be impossible for comparativists to decide whether, for example, France is more or less democratic than Germany. But it is possible (and we hope interesting!) to compare how different democracies fulfill common democratic prerequisites by asking how presidential and parliamentary democracies differ in keeping executives and legislators accountable to the electorate. Such standards can also help us measure (though not precisely) the successes and shortcomings of established democracies in living up to democratic ideals and the process of democratization in post-communist and Third World nations.

What makes the countries in this part of the text distinctive is the combination of their long experience with democracy (extending for at least a half-century) and their highly developed economies. None of the countries in the other two categories meet *both* of these criteria. For example, India has been democratic for as long as Japan and Germany, but with a predominantly agricultural economy, extreme inequality, and extensive poverty, India is far from being industrial-

ized. Similarly, Russia could be considered by some measures to be as industrialized as France, but it is a new and very fragile democracy. Democratic durability and relative affluence are the foundations of politics in Britain, France, Germany, Japan, and the world's other industrial democracies.

COMMUNIST AND POST-COMMUNIST SYSTEMS

Part III, "Politics in Communist and Post-Communist States" includes one country (China) still ruled by a communist party and one country (Russia) in transition to a *post*-communist system. Although China now has far less in common with Russia than it had with the former Soviet Union, it still makes sense, in terms of comparative political analysis, to group Russia and China together for several reasons.

First, Russian political and economic development in the 1990s is very strongly influenced by the legacy of the Soviet system that was in power for more than seventy years; thus Russia's transitions *to* democracy and a market economy must first and foremost be analyzed as a transition *from* communism to **post-communism.** Second, one of the most intriguing questions for students of comparative politics is this: Why did communism collapse in the Soviet Union, but not in China? To begin to answer this question, one must first understand the origins and nature of the communist system in both countries.

As recently as the late 1980s, there were about twenty-five countries governed by a communist party or a party strongly influenced by communist ideology. This "communist world" accounted for a significant proportion of the globe's area, population, economic might, natural resources, and military power. For nearly half a century, the major issue in international politics was the confrontation between the United States (and its allies) and communism in its many and often conflicting national forms, including Soviet, Chinese, Cuban, and Vietnamese. Then beginning in 1989, the communist regimes of East-Central Europe (Albania, Bulgaria, Czechoslovakia, the German Democratic Republic [East Germany], Hungary, Poland, and Romania) collapsed, and in 1991, the Soviet Union disintegrated, giving way to post-communist Russia and fourteen other successor states. Most of the world's other communist systems suffered a similar fate.

Presently, there are only a few countries in which a communist party remains in power: China, Vietnam, Laos, the Democratic People's Republic of Korea (North Korea), and Cuba. Yet, communist systems still deserve attention in the study of comparative politics. Communist-led states have had a decisive impact on the course of history and have been one of the most distinctive types of political systems in the modern world. Post-communism also deserves our attention because the breakdown of communist regimes and the political and economic challenges that follow are surely among the most interesting and important phenomena of the late twentieth century.

Communist Party-States

Communist-led countries have always differed from one another in important ways. They have included some of the world's poorest countries (for example, Ethiopia) and some highly industrialized countries (such as East Germany). Communist countries have even quarreled with one another (and sometimes gone to war) over matters ranging from the meaning of communism (Yugoslavia and the Soviet Union in the 1950s) to the regional balance of power (Vietnam and Cambodia in the 1970s). Nevertheless, communist regimes past and present do have enough in common to be classified as a distinctive type of political system. We emphasize three common features of communist systems: Marxism-Leninism; party leadership; and the command economy.

Marxism-Leninism   The most distinctive characteristic of a communist political system is the ruling party's claim to be guided by an ideology called Marxism-Leninism. "Marxism" refers to ideas of Karl Marx, the nineteenth-century revolutionary German philosopher, social scientist, and political activist. Marx's extensive writings criticized capitalism for what he saw as its inevitable and extreme exploitation of workers (the proletariat) by factory owners and other capitalists (the bourgeoisie). He also condemned the competitiveness, greed, and inequality that resulted from capitalism's emphasis on private property and profits. Marx believed that socialism, a system in which the proletariat controlled the economy and the state and in which the needs of society took precedence over the quest for private profit, would be more humane and more productive than capitalism. Marxism and its belief in the superiority of socialism is the core of the formal ideals of communist-led political systems.

The second pillar of communist ideology, "Leninism," is based on the ideas of V. I. Lenin, a follower of Marx who was the leader of the Russian Revolution of 1917 that led to the founding of the Soviet Union. Like Marx, Lenin criticized the evils of capitalism (including its imperialist exploitation of the Third World) and defended the ideals of socialism. But, first and foremost, Leninism is a theory of how a communist party should be organized to seize state power and achieve socialist goals after the revolution. Lenin stressed that only the most committed revolutionaries should be admitted to membership in the party. He developed the concept of *democratic centralism,* a system of organization that allows open discussion before an issue is decided ("democracy"), but in practice delegates supreme power to the top party leadership ("centralism"). Countries ruled by communist parties are often said to have Leninist political systems because they all more or less follow Lenin's basic approach to organizing power.

Marx and Lenin both saw socialism as the first stage in the transformation of society after the revolutionary overthrow of capitalism. In the socialist stage, private property would be abolished and the state would be reorganized to serve the interests of the workers. At some future point, society would be ready to make the transition from socialism to communism, an even more advanced and radical stage of human development in which material goods would be distributed more equally, people would work more selflessly, and the state would "wither away" with power being exercised directly by all citizens.

No communist state has ever claimed to have reached the stage of communism. In fact, the phrase "communist state," although a convenient shorthand, is misleading because all such countries have described themselves as only in the process of "building socialism." Thus derives the distinction between the Union of Soviet *Socialist* Republics (the formal name of the former Soviet Union) and the *Communist* Party of the Soviet Union.

Communist parties, particularly those headed for a long time by a very powerful leader, often add their own local interpretation of Marxism-Leninism to the country's official ideology. For example, the ideas of Mao Zedong in China, Fidel Castro in Cuba, and Kim Il Sung in North Korea all became central elements of communist doctrine in those countries. Communists have often disagreed strongly and sometimes even violently over the "true" meaning of Marxism-Leninism. Such ideological disputes have been a major factor in conflicts between communist countries (as in the Sino-Soviet conflict of the 1950s and 1960s) and in power struggles within communist parties (witness the struggle between Stalin and Trotsky for leadership of the Soviet Communist Party in the 1930s).

Marxism-Leninism has the status of an official and exclusive ideology in a communist-led political system. The state promotes the spread of Marxism-Leninism, for example through schools and newspapers; other ideologies are branded as "subversive" or "counterrevolutionary." Not everyone in these countries believes in Marxism-Leninism. Indeed, as the collapse of the Soviet Union revealed, most citizens may be quite cynical about official communist ideology. But Marxism-Leninism defines the framework of formal political life in communist systems and sets the boundaries of what, in the view of the ruling communist party, is permissible in politics.

Party Leadership   In communist systems, all state institutions, such as the national legislature, the bureaucracy, and the military, are subordinate to the communist party. There are no institutional checks on party power and no meaningful political competition between the communist party and other political organizations.

There is a formal distinction between the *state* and the communist *party* in such systems; for example, the People's Republic of China is the *state* ruled by the Chinese Communist *Party*. The communist party makes policy while the state (or the government) carries out the party's policies. But the communist party maintains close supervision over the government to make sure that party policies are implemented correctly so that, in practice, the distinction between party and state is often an artificial one. We will use the term **communist party-state** to convey the pervasiveness of party leadership in this type of political system.

Ruling communist parties claim the right to exercise a "leading role" (to use the phrase that often appears in the constitution of countries governed by a communist party) not only over the state, but throughout society. The principle of party leadership is applied to the educational system, the media, and organizations such as labor unions and professional associations. The claim to this leading role is based on the party's view that it alone can represent the best interests of all the people. The communist party sees itself as a "vanguard party" because of its superior grasp of Marxism-Leninism, which it believes the nation must follow in order to achieve its domestic and international goals.

Despite Marxism-Leninism's emphasis on the masses and its rhetoric about giving power to the people, communist parties allow only a small percentage of the population in the countries they govern to become party members. Unlike political parties in democratic systems, most of which are open to participation by any interested citizen, communist parties have very restrictive procedures for joining. Even at the height of communist power in the Soviet Union, just 7 percent of the population belonged to the party. Only rarely have communist parties made up more than 10 percent of the total population; among the exceptions are North Korea (16 percent) and Romania (15 percent).

As self-proclaimed guardians of the people's interests, communist party-states have also assumed the right to decide when an individual, an organization, or even an idea becomes a threat to the people and to take whatever steps deemed necessary to suppress the threat. According to Marxism-Leninism, this type of political system is **"dictatorship of the proletariat,"** which implies that the communist party, acting on behalf of the working class, exercises complete control over the enemies of socialism.

Communist party-states are often called totalitarian because of the total control that the party exercises—or at least tries to exercise—over nearly every aspect of the life of the citizens of the country that it governs. The use of the totalitarian model by political scientists to explain politics in communist systems has been strongly criticized by some scholars. Such critics say that it attributes too much power to the party and too easily dismisses other sources of political influence (such as the bureaucracy); they also contend that the totalitarian model is unable to account for the rise of leaders like Mikhail Gorbachev in the Soviet Union or Deng Xiaoping in China who try to reform the communist system in very fundamental ways. Nevertheless, the term **totalitarianism** accurately captures the essence of politics in a system whose ruling party allows no opposition, insists on a single ideology for the whole nation, and seeks to control or monitor all social organizations.

Command Economy   The third important characteristic of a communist party-state is its distinctive economic system. This system is often called a **command economy** because government decisions (commands) rather than market mechanisms (such as supply and demand) are the major influences in the economy. In a command economy, the government uses **central planning** to set production targets and then allocates responsibility for meeting the targets to various economic enterprises under state control. The government also coordinates the flow of energy sources and raw materials, closely regulates trade and commerce, and determines prices for most commodities. Within the economy, priority is given to heavy industries such as steel, which are seen as the key to rapid modernization and a strong national defense. Most economic enterprises—from banks and large industries to farms and mines to restaurants and retail shops—are "publicly owned." In practice, however, public ownership means that the enterprise is run by the government or a collective rather than by private owners.

A command economy is often called a centrally planned economy because government planning is such a prominent feature of the model, or a Stalinist economy because the Soviet Union under Stalin in the 1930s was the first country to put such a system into place. It is also sometimes referred to as state socialism because of the extensive role of the government, which some observers believe is contrary to Marx's socialist vision of workers controlling their workplaces and the government.

Although all communist party-states have used some form of central planning and placed significant restrictions on private property, in practice command economies have ranged from the Soviet Union's highly centralized system to the Yugoslav model of decentralized worker management. China's market-oriented reforms, which began in the late 1970s, have reduced though not eliminated the role of the command economy. But the growth of private businesses and foreign investment in China (and more recently in Vietnam) has stretched even further the kind of mixed economic system that can be incorporated within a communist party-state.

Post-Communist States

The very notion of a post-communist state is a relatively new one. In the seven decades between the founding of the world's first communist party-state in the Soviet Union in 1917 and the chain-reaction downfall of communist regimes in East-Central Europe in 1989, no ruling communist party was ever removed from power and replaced by a noncommunist leadership. Social scientists have only recently begun to study the radical political and economic changes involved in the transition from communism to post-communism.

Politically, post-communism means dismantling the party-state and replacing it with a more democratic system. Post-communist democracies were established almost immediately in the aftermath of the sudden collapse of communist rule and in countries that, for the most part, had little if any previous experience with democracy. In the short run, these democracies have survived, but they face serious problems and their long-term prospects are far from certain. Several of the countries that emerged from the former Yugoslavia have been torn by genocidal ethnic conflict. Authoritarianism still has a strong following in Russia, where many citizens blame social ills (like crime) and economic problems (like inflation) on the weakness of the democratically elected government. In a few post-communist states, the old communist party (usually renamed to deter unfavorable associations with the past) has attracted popular support. In some cases (Poland, Bulgaria, and Hungary), these parties have even won elections and taken a share of power through democratic means.

At the same time that post-communist states are attempting to make the transition from dictatorship to democracy, they also face the difficult challenge of making the transition from a command to a market economy. This transformation involves many complicated steps, including privatizing state-owned enterprises without creating massive unemployment, attracting foreign investment, encouraging entrepreneurs to start businesses, training profit-driven managers to replace plan-driven bureaucrats, and making prices responsive to supply and demand without provoking ruinous inflation. Shortcomings in meeting the material expectations of their peoples and the failure to develop internationally competitive economies were major reasons for the collapse of communist party-states. The political fate of the new post-communist states and especially their efforts to attain or sustain democracy will also depend largely on their economic records.

In a take-off on *The Wizard of Oz*, this cartoon shows that many people who celebrated the collapse of communism in East-Central Europe and elsewhere were not aware of or prepared for the many difficulties involved in making the transition to a capitalist economy.
Source: © Kevin Kallaugher, Cartoonists & Writers Syndicate.

POLITICS IN THE THIRD WORLD

The term *Third World* was coined by French authors in the 1950s to draw attention to the plight of the world's poorer nations, which they believed to be of as much global importance as the headline-grabbing Cold War and its superpower adversaries. To make their point, they adapted terminology from the French Revolution: in the mid-twentieth century, a long-neglected and oppressed Third World was struggling for recognition and power just as the Third Estate of the common people had done against the privileged and powerful clergy (the First Estate) and the nobility (the Second Estate) in the 1780s. Some people criticize the label as suggesting a numerical order in which the Third World ranks behind the First World (the industrial democracies) and the Second World (which once applied to the former Soviet Union and Eastern European communist party-states).

But in its original sense, Third World was meant to embody the struggle of poor nations for empower-

ment in the international system and a fairer share of global wealth. For many, the term remains a powerful symbol of common purpose and determination and is still widely used to describe the developing countries of Asia, Africa, and Latin America. We believe that Third World remains a valid and important concept to use in the study of comparative politics. We will also use other terms, such as "developing" and "less developed" interchangeably with Third World. This is a good place to note that China is often considered (and considers itself) to be part of the Third World. Although we have placed it in our "Communist and Post-Communist Systems" category, comparativists analyze China as both a communist party-state and a developing nation.

When reading about the Third World, you also may encounter the term "South" as a way of referring collectively to developing nations in contrast to the developed nations of the "North." Like Third World, South has achieved a certain symbolic importance by conveying the fact that there are enormous differences

---

TABLE 1   Diversity in the Third World

Country	Location	Political System	Economy	Selected Comparative Themes
Brazil	South America	New democracy	Capitalist upper-middle income	Transition from military rule to democracy
China	East Asia	Communist party-state	Socialist, low income with high growth	Why communist power survived
India	South Asia	Established democracy	Mixed, low income with moderate growth	Democracy, poverty, and religious conflict
Iran	Middle East	Islamic Republic; theocracy	Lower-middle income, heavily dependent on a single export (oil)	Rise and spread of Islamic populism
Mexico	Northern Central America	Single-party dominant semidemocracy	Capitalist upper-middle income	Peasant rebellion, political violence, and democratization
Nigeria	West Africa	Military regimes	Low income, heavily dependent on a single export (oil)	Politics in a multiethnic state and military resistance to democracy

---

between the rich and poor nations of the world. Granted, South is geographically somewhat misleading since there are developed nations in the southern hemisphere (like Australia) and less developed nations in the northern part of the globe (like Afghanistan).

The terms Third World and South are applied to countries that are all economically poorer than the industrial democracies. But it is very important to recognize that these countries (which contain about 75 percent of the world's population) are very diverse geographically, economically, politically, and culturally. Some observers have asserted that there is such great diversity in the Third World that the concept is outdated because it implies too much similarity in the challenges facing the developing nations and too much unity in their international policies. They point to the enormous differences in levels of economic development among countries usually considered part of the Third World. They question whether a country like Bangladesh with its extreme poverty and overwhelmingly rural population has much in common with the economically booming and highly urbanized **"newly industrializing countries" (NICs)** such as South Korea, which are usually still considered to be part of the Third World. Others argue not for abandoning the term Third World, but for taking account of such differences by adding the concept of a "Fourth World" to refer to very poor countries with deteriorating economies.

This book acknowledges the rich diversity of the Third World. In fact, the countries included in Part IV were chosen, in part, to reflect this variety, as well as to illustrate important themes in the study of comparative politics. Table 1 indicates the multiformity of the developing nations (including China) that are covered in this text.

The Development Gap

If there are such extensive differences among developing nations, what gives coherence to the concept of the Third World? Simply put, Third World nations are poorer, their peoples have a lower standard of living, and their economies are not as modernized as the industrialized countries: in other words, they are less developed. A few examples should make the realities of this development gap between the Third World and the industrialized countries clearer (see Figure 2).

The World Bank, a major international organization providing financial assistance to the Third World, divides developing countries according to their *annual* gross national product (GNP) per capita into three groups: low-income (average $380), lower-middle income (average $1,590), upper-middle income (aver-

Figure 2   The Development Gap
This graph shows the global distribution of several important indicators of economic activity in the early 1990s. The world's population (by country) is divided into equal fifths (20 percent), as represented by the horizontal bands. The "champagne glass" depicts what share of the world's gross national product, trade, savings, and investment each one-fifth gets. The gap between the rich and poor nations of the world remains one of the most significant features of comparative politics at the crossroads.
Source: *United Nations Human Development Report*, 1994.

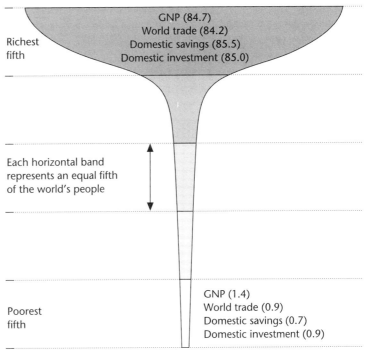

Distribution of economic activity, 1991
(percentage of world total)

Richest fifth

GNP (84.7)
World trade (84.2)
Domestic savings (85.5)
Domestic investment (85.0)

Each horizontal band represents an equal fifth of the world's people

Poorest fifth

GNP (1.4)
World trade (0.9)
Domestic savings (0.7)
Domestic investment (0.9)

age $4,370). The industrialized (high-income) countries have an average GNP per capita of over $23,000 per year.

Generally speaking, a country's GNP per capita reflects both its level of modernization and its relative power in the international economic system. But GNP per capita figures also reflect the ability of a country to meet the material needs of its people. Thus, lower average standards of living and greater poverty also distinguish less developed from more developed nations.

The stark contrasts in the statistics used to measure a country's overall **"physical quality of life"** **(PQLI)** give some sense of what such poverty means in terms of people's lives.

· • **Life expectancy** in the low-income countries averages only 62 years, in the middle-income developing countries it is about 68, and in the high-income developed countries a person can expect to live 77 years on average. In some of the poorest countries, such as Uganda and Afghanistan, life expectancy is about 45 years.

• The **infant mortality rate** (which measures how many children die between birth and age one) in low-income countries is 64 per 1,000 live births, and in the very poorest countries it reaches well over 100 per 1,000; in the middle-income countries infant mortality is 39; in contrast, in the world's richest countries, the infant mortality rate is only 7 per 1,000 live births.

• **Illiteracy** among adults (people over fifteen who cannot read or write) averages 41 percent in the low-income countries (up to 70–80 percent in some) and 15–20 percent in the middle-income countries; in the developed countries, illiteracy is generally well under 5 percent.

It is important to recognize that there are vast differences in the PQLI statistics among Third World countries that have similar levels of GNP per capita. For example, China, India, and Nigeria are all ranked as low-income countries by the World Bank with very comparable levels of GNP per capita ($490, $300, and $300, respectively); but China's life expectancy of 69 is considerably higher than India's (61) and Nigeria's

How Is Development Measured?

One frequently used measure of a country's level of economic development is its **gross national product (GNP)** per capita. This figure is an estimate of a country's total economic output (including income earned from abroad) divided by its total population. Such estimates are made in a country's own currency, such as pesos in Mexico or rubles in Russia.

In order to make comparisons of GNP per capita across countries, it is necessary to convert them to a common currency, usually the U.S. dollar. This is done using **official international currency exchange rates,** which, for example would tell you how many pesos or rubles it takes to buy $1 U.S. But many economists believe that an estimate of GNP per capita in dollars based on official exchange rates doesn't give a very accurate sense of the real standards of living in different countries because it doesn't tell what goods and services (such as housing, food, and transportation) people in a particular country can actually buy with their local currencies.

An alternative and increasingly popular means of comparing per capita GNP levels and levels of economic development across countries is to use exchange rates based on **purchasing power parity (PPP).** PPP-based exchange rates take into account the actual cost of living in a particular country by figuring what it costs to buy the *same* bundle of goods in *different* countries; for example how many pesos does it actually take to buy a certain amount of food in Mexico or rubles to pay for housing in Russia? Many analysts think that PPP provides a more reliable (and revealing) tool for comparing standards of living among countries.

The data boxes that are part of each country unit in this text give both GNP per capita at official exchange rates and GDP per capita figures computed using purchasing power parity. (GDP stands for gross domestic product and is quite similar to gross national product, although it excludes foreign sources of income.) As you will see, the differences between the two calculations can be quite dramatic, especially for developing countries. China's GNP per capita in 1993, for example, was estimated to be only $490, whereas its PPP-based GDP per capita in the same year was estimated at $2,330!

Because income comparisons based on either GNP per capita or purchasing power parity do not provide a complete picture of a country's level of development, the United Nations has introduced another concept that is useful in making socioeconomic comparisons among nations: the **Human Development Index (HDI).** Based on a formula that takes into account the three factors of *longevity* (life expectancy at birth), *knowledge* (literacy and average years of schooling), and *income* (according to PPP), the UN assigns each country of the world for which there is enough data a Human Development Index decimal number between 0 and 1; the closer a country is to 1, the better its level of human development.

Out of 174 countries ranked according to HDI by the United Nations in 1995, Canada (.950) was at the top followed by the United States (.937). Niger (.207) was ranked last. Among the countries included in this book, Japan (3), France (8), Germany (15), Britain (18), Russia (52), Mexico (53), and Brazil (63) scored as having "high human development;" Iran (70) and China (111) had "medium human development," and India (134) and Nigeria (141) were ranked as having "low human development."

---

(51); China also has much lower levels of infant mortality and illiteracy than do India and Nigeria. The case studies in this book analyze how such differences reflect important contrasts in the historical experiences and government policies of various nations.

The use of national averages also tends to mask class, gender, and racial inequalities *within* countries. Although this is true in all countries, developing or developed, the disparities are particularly acute in the Third World. For example, in the northeast African nation of the Sudan the overall adult literacy rate is an already "low" 27 percent—but among women it is a dismal 12 percent! Some people have even suggested that poor women in low-income countries (the Fourth World) should be called the "Fifth World" because they are, indeed, the poorest of the world's poor.

Many developing nations have seen significant progress over the last few decades. A few, such as China, have experienced tremendous economic growth, and infant mortality rates in the low-income countries have dropped by more than 40 percent since 1970. Similar trends are apparent in the other figures that are used to measure poverty in the less developed countries.

Nevertheless, many developing countries have very low and sometimes even negative economic growth rates. Others may be experiencing increases in production but have populations that are growing at a rate that literally swallows up the gains of increased output and makes real economic expansion impossible. Ghana's economy, for example, grew by an average of 3.5 percent per year in the period

1980–1993, but its population grew by 3.3 percent per year during the same period. The result? Per capita income in Ghana hardly grew at all. Thus, the enormous socioeconomic gap that separates most of the Third World from the industrialized nations (which have very low population growth rates) is at best closing very slowly—and, in some cases, is even widening—and remains one of the most important ways of categorizing the world's countries.

Third World States

There are many types of political systems in the Third World; as Table 1 indicates, the countries presented in this book include an established democracy (India), a new democracy (Brazil), a semidemocracy (Mexico) that has only very recently begun to permit real political competition, an authoritarian military regime (Nigeria), a communist party-state (China), and a theocracy (Iran) in which supreme political power is held by the religious elite. Despite these variations, there are several ways in which politics in the Third World in general is very different from politics in industrialized countries.

First, politics and government in all Third World countries are shaped by the basic facts of scarce resources, extensive poverty and inequality, and a relatively weak position in the international economic system. Political leaders in less developed countries simply have fewer options available in responding to problems or to demands from various groups for a bigger piece of the national economic pie. Economic conflicts therefore are more likely to lead to violence or repression in Third World states; for example, peasants may rebel in their quest for more land or the government may violently suppress labor unions striking for higher wages. Corruption is also a very serious problem in much of the Third World because officials personally profit from the state's control over the limited economic opportunities. Resistance to democratization in the Third World has often come—as it also did during earlier stages in the political development of Europe and North America—from elites who fear that greater popular control of the government will jeopardize their economic privilege as well as their political power.

Second, the political legitimacy of many Third World states is very weak; in other words, most citizens do not have much faith in their political leaders or perhaps even in the very nature of the political system of their country. They may obey the law, they may even vote. But they do not see the government as being very relevant to their lives or as being able to do anything about their most serious concerns. They may even regard the government as having a negative impact on their lives, and their citizenship in the state may be negligible as a source of their political identity.

There are various causes of weak state legitimacy in the Third World. The populace may see the government as serving the interests of one ethnic, religious, or economic group more than others, or even actively discriminating against some groups. Economic failure, political repression, extreme corruption, and military defeat may cause people to lose faith in the government. New democracies—which are now quite common in the Third World—simply have not had enough time to establish legitimacy in the eyes of their citizens. Whatever the cause, states with weak legitimacy are particularly prone to political violence, radical and sudden changes (such as military **coups d'état**), and government paralysis.

Third, the effective power of governments in the less developed countries is often very limited. The state may have little real ability to exert its authority much beyond the capital city and a few urban centers. In the rural areas and small towns where much or most of the population lives, political life is frequently based more on the relationship between powerful and usually wealthy individuals ("patrons") and those they control ("clients") by dispensing favors or instilling fear. In much of the Third World, the formal aspects of government such as laws, parties, and elections are less important than the nonformal politics of patron-client relationships.

There are significant variations in how governments in the developing countries face the political struggle over scarce resources, weak legitimacy, and the influence of **patron-client politics.** But, to one degree or another, they all experience these problems in ways that make the Third World state a distinctive and important entity in the study of comparative politics.

Organization of the Text

The core of this book consists of case studies of eleven countries selected for their significance in terms of our comparative themes and to provide a reasonable cross-section of types of political systems and geographic regions. Although each of the country studies makes some important comparative references, they are primarily intended to provide detailed descriptions and analyses of the politics of individual countries. At the same time, the country studies have common section and subsection headings to help you make comparisons and explore similar themes across the various cases. The following are brief summaries of the main issues and questions covered in the major sections and subsections that appear in each of the country studies.

Section 1: The Making of the Modern State

The purpose of this section is to provide an overview of the forces that have shaped the particular character of the state. We believe that an understanding of the contemporary politics of any country requires some familiarity with the historical process by which its current political system was formed. "Politics at the Crossroads" uses a specific event to illustrate an important political transition in that country's recent history and to highlight some of the critical political issues it now faces. "Critical Junctures" looks at some of the major stages and decisive turning points in state development. This discussion should give you an idea of how the country assumed its present geographic shape and political order and a sense of how relations between the state and the society it governs have developed over time. Several of the text's core themes are used to analyze the making of the modern state: How was the country's political development affected by its place in the world of states? What has been the country's experience with the democratic idea? What are the important bases of collective identity in the country, and how do these relate to the people's image of themselves as citizens of the state? "Implications for Contemporary Politics" shows how the past pattern of state development continues to shape the country's current political agenda and highlights the significance of this case for the study of comparative politics.

Section 2: Political Economy and Development

This section traces the country's recent and contemporary economic development. It explores the issues raised by the core theme of production and exchange on a global scale and analyzes how economic development has affected political change. The placement of this section near the beginning of the country study reflects our belief that an understanding of a country's basic domestic and international economic situation is essential for analyzing politics in that country. "State and Economy" discusses the basic organization of the country's economy, with an emphasis on the role of the state in managing economic life and on the relationship between the government and other economic actors in the country. This section also analyzes the state's social welfare policies, such as health care, housing, and pension programs. "Society and Economy" examines the social and the political implications of the country's economic situation. It asks who benefits from economic change and looks at how economic development creates or reinforces class, ethnic, gender, regional, or ideological cleavages in society. "The International Political Economy" considers the country's global role: How have patterns of trade and foreign investment changed over time? What is the country's relationship to regional and international organizations? How have international economic issues affected or reflected the domestic political agenda?

Section 3: Governance and Policy-Making

Here we describe the state's major policy-making institutions and procedures. The section on the "Organization of the State" lays out the fundamental principles—as reflected in the country's constitution, its official ideology, and its historical experience—on which the political system and the distribution of political power are based. It also sketches the basic structure of the state, including the relationship between different levels and branches of government. "The Executive" encompasses whatever key offices (for example, presidents, prime ministers, communist party leaders) are at the top of the political system, focusing on those who have the most power, how they are selected, and how they use their power to make policy. It looks at the national bureaucracy and its relationship to the chief executive(s) and the governing party and its role in the policy-making. The military is also covered in this section. "Other State Institutions" generally include the judiciary and the legal system, state-run corporations, and subnational government. "The Policy-Making Process" summarizes how state policy gets made and implemented. It not only draws on the information about formal institutions and procedures presented in the previous subsections, but also emphasizes nonformal aspects of policy-making, such as patron-client relations and interest group activity.

SECTION 4: REPRESENTATION AND PARTICIPATION

The relationship between the state and society it governs is the topic of Section 4: how different groups in society are organized to further their political interests, how they participate and are represented in the political system, and how they influence policymaking. Given the importance of the U.S. Congress in policy-making, American readers may expect to find the principal discussion of "The Legislature" in the previous section on "Governance and Policy-Making" rather than here. But the United States is rather exceptional in having a legislature that is very nearly a co-equal branch of government with the executive in the policy process. In most political systems, the executive clearly dominates the policy process—even when it is ultimately responsible to the legislature, as in a parliamentary system. In most countries other than the United States, the legislature functions primarily as an institution that *represents* and *provides a forum* for the political expression of various interests in government; it is only secondarily (and in some cases, such as a communist party-state, only very marginally) a policy-making body. Therefore, although this section does describe and assess the legislature's role in state policy-making, its primary focus is on how the legislature represents or fails to represent different interests in society. "The Party System and Elections" both describes the overall organization of the party system and reviews individual parties. It also discusses the election process and its significance (or lack of significance) as a vehi-

cle for citizen participation in politics and in bringing about changes in the government. The section on "Political Culture, Citizenship, and Identity" examines how people perceive themselves as members of the political community: the nature and source of political values and attitudes; who is considered a citizen of the state; how different groups in society understand their relationship to the state. The topics covered may include political aspects of the educational system, the media, religion, and ethnicity. "Interests, Social Movements, and Protest" discusses how various groups in society pursue their political interests outside the party system: When do they use formal organizations (such as unions) or launch movements (such as "Green" environmental movements)? What is the relationship between the state and such organizations and movements? When and how do citizens engage in acts of protest that may take them beyond the boundaries of the law? And how does the state respond to such protests?

SECTION 5: POLITICS AT THE CROSSROADS

In Section 5, each country study returns to the book's focus on the major challenges that are reshaping our world and the study of comparative politics. The goal is to give you a sense of the most important contemporary issues and tensions in the country that may shape the direction of future political change. The section begins with a mini–case study of an event or situation that captures the essence of those issues and tensions. "Political Challenges and Changing Agendas" lays out the major unresolved political challenges facing the country and assesses what issues are likely to dominate in the near future. "Politics in Transition" focuses on how the nature of politics in the country may change as the state responds (or fails to respond) to unresolved challenges and new issues; in some cases, this section lays out some possible alternatives for political change in the country. The final section presents a "Comparative Perspective" by highlighting what this particular case study tells us about politics in other countries that have similar political systems or that face similar kinds of political challenges.

SPECIAL FEATURES

At the beginning of each case study, there is a page of basic geographic, demographic, economic, social, and political information* that we hope will not only provide you with some important facts about that particular country, but also will help you make some interesting comparisons among different countries. We include an Appendix that provides comparable information about the United States. This should help place the data from other countries in a familiar context.

Throughout each case study numerous maps, charts, graphs, tables, photographs, and other visual aids amplify or illustrate important points made in the text. We have included a number of political cartoons, most often from the press in the country itself. Because such cartoons usually express a strong opinion, we think they are a good way to see how some people view important political figures, issues, or events. Key terms in each chapter are boldfaced and defined in the Glossary at the end of the text.

Each country study also has several feature boxes that present additional interesting information about some aspect of politics in the country; for example, a sidebar might contain a biography of a major political leader, background on a decisive event, or an elaboration of a concept, policy, organization, or region that will help you better understand the country's politics.

It is quite a challenge to understand the contemporary world of politics. We hope that the timely information and thematic focus of *Comparative Politics at the Crossroads* both prepares you and inspires your interest to explore further the endlessly fascinating terrain of comparative politics.

Key Terms

Cold War	political development
Third World	state
comparative politics	cabinet
country	bureaucracy
nation-state	legitimacy
political institutions	state formation
political culture	

---

* The data for these features are compiled from Encyclopedia Britannica, *Book of the Year, 1995* (on-line version); Central Intelligence Agency, *World Factbook, 1994* (on-line version); Broderbund, PC Globe Map 'N' Facts (computer program); United Nations, *Human Development Reports, 1994 and 1995;* and World Bank, *World Development Report, 1995.* Unless otherwise noted, all statistics are from the early 1990s.

ethnic identity (ethnicity)	newly industrializing countries (NICs)
gender	physical quality of life (PQLI)
middle-level theory	life expectancy
dictatorship	infant mortality rate
regime	illiteracy
European Union	gross national product (GNP)
colonial(ism)	
political economy	official international currency exchange rates
authoritarianism	
social class	
political systems	purchasing power parity (PPP)
post-communism	
communist party-state	Human Development Index (HDI)
dictatorship of the proletariat	coups d'état
totalitarianism	patron-client politics
command economy	
central planning	

Suggested Readings

A World of States

Downing, Brian M. *The Military Revolution and Political Change: Origins of Democracy and Autocracy in Early Modern Europe.* Princeton: Princeton University Press, 1992.

Esping-Andersen, Gosta. *Politics Against Markets: The Social Democratic Road to Power.* Princeton: Princeton University Press, 1985.

Evans, Peter, Dietrich Rueschemeyer, and Theda Skocpol, eds. *Bringing the State Back In.* Cambridge: Cambridge University Press, 1985.

Geddes, Barbara. *Politician's Dilemma: Building State Capacity in Latin America.* Berkeley: University of California Press, 1994.

Migdal, Joel S., Atul Kohli, and Vivienne Shue, eds. *State Power and Social Forces: Domination and Transformation in the Third World.* Cambridge: Cambridge University Press, 1994.

Skocpol, Theda. *States and Social Revolutions.* Cambridge: Cambridge University Press, 1979.

Production and Exchange in a Global Context

Bates, Robert C. *Beyond the Miracle of the Market: The Political Economy of Agrarian Development in Rural Kenya.* Cambridge: Cambridge University Press, 1989.

Callaghy, Thomas M., and John Ravenhill, eds. *Hemmed In: Responses to Africa's Economic Decline.* New York: Columbia University Press, 1993.

Haggard, Stephan. *Pathways from the Periphery: The Politics of Growth in the Newly Industrializing Countries.* Ithaca, N.Y.: Cornell University Press, 1990.

Hall, Peter A. *Governing the Economy: The Politics of State Intervention in Britain and France.* New York: Oxford University Press, 1986.

Hart, Jeffrey. *Rival Capitalists: International Competitiveness in the United States, Japan, and Western Europe.* Ithaca, N.Y.: Cornell University Press, 1992.

Przeworski, Adam. *Democracy and the Market: Political and Economic Reforms in Eastern Europe and Latin America.* Cambridge: Cambridge University Press, 1991.

Wade, Robert. *Governing the Market: Economic Theory and the Role of Government in East Asian Industrialization.* Princeton: Princeton University Press, 1990.

The Democratic Idea

Diamond, Larry, and Marc F. Plattner, eds. *The Global Resurgence of Democracy.* Baltimore: Johns Hopkins University Press, 1993.

Diamond, Larry, Juan J. Linz, and Seymour Martin Lipset, eds. *Democracy in Developing Countries.* 4 vol. Boulder, Colo.: Lynne Rienner, 1988–1989.

Huntington, Samuel P. *The Third Wave: Democratization in the Late Twentieth Century.* Norman: University of Oklahoma Press, 1991.

O'Donnell, Guillermo A., Philippe C. Schmitter, and Laurence Whitehead, eds. *Transitions from Authoritarian Rule.* 4 vol. Baltimore: Johns Hopkins University Press, 1986.

Putnam, Robert, with Robert Leonardi and Raffaella Y. Nanetti. *Making Democracy Work: Civic Traditions in Modern Italy.* Princeton: Princeton University Press, 1992.

Rueschemeyer, Dietrich, Evelyne Huber Stephens, and John D. Stephens. *Capitalist Development and Democracy.* Chicago: University of Chicago Press, 1992.

Collective Identities

Anderson, Benedict. *Imagined Communities: Reflections on the Origins and Spread of Nationalism.* Rev. ed. London: Verso, 1991.

Breuilly, John. *Nationalism and the State.* 2d ed. Chicago: University of Chicago Press, 1994.

Connor, Walker. *Ethnonationalism: The Quest for Understanding.* Princeton: Princeton University Press, 1994.

Greenfield, Liah. *Nationalism: Five Roads to Modernity.* Cambridge: Harvard University Press, 1992.

Inglehart, Ronald. *Culture Shift in Advanced Industrial Society.* Princeton: Princeton University Press, 1990.

Katznelson, Ira, and Aristide R. Zolberg, eds. *Working Class Formation: Nineteenth Century Patterns in Western Europe and the United States.* Princeton: Princeton University Press, 1986.

Tarrow, Sidney. *Power in Movement: Social Movements, Collective Action and Politics.* Cambridge: Cambridge University Press, 1994.

Endnotes

[1] See James Q. Wilson, *American Government: Brief Version* (Lexington, Mass.: D. C. Heath, 1994), 33–56.

[2] See Philippe Schmitter, "Comparative Politics," in *The Oxford Companion to Politics of the World,* ed. Joel Krieger (New York: Oxford University Press, 1993), 171–177. This essay provides a comprehensive and insightful discussion of the methods of comparative politics and its evolution, and several elements of the discussion here are drawn from it.

[3] See, for example, Colin Campbell, *Governments Under Stress: Political Executives and Key Bureaucrats in Washington, London, and Ottawa* (Toronto: University of Toronto Press, 1983).

[4] See, for example, Theda Skocpol, *Social Revolutions in the Modern World* (Cambridge: Cambridge University Press, 1994).

[5] Alexis de Tocqueville, *Democracy in America,* ed. J. P. Mayer, trans. George Lawrence (New York: Anchor Doubleday, 1969).

[6] Adam Przeworski and Fernando Limongi, "Political Regimes and Economic Growth," *Journal of Economic Perspectives* 7, no. 3 (Summer 1993).

[7] This view has been developed well by Adam Przeworski, *Democracy and the Market: Political and Economic Reforms in Eastern Europe and Latin America* (Cambridge: Cambridge University Press, 1991).

[8] Guillermo O'Donnell, Philippe Schmitter, and Laurence Whitehead, eds. *Transitions from Authoritarian Rule: Tentative Conclusions about Uncertain Democracies* (Baltimore: Johns Hopkins University Press, 1986).

[9] For a survey of political science literature on this question, see Mark Kesselman, "The Conflictual Evolution of American Political Science: From Apologetic Pluralism to Trilateralism and Marxism," in *Public Values and Private Power in American Democracy,* ed. J. David Greenstone (Chicago: University of Chicago Press, 1982), 34–67.

Part 2

Politics in Industrial Democracies

CHAPTER 2

Britain

U N I T E D   K I N G D O M   O F   G R E A T   B R I T A I N   A N D   N O R T H E R N   I R E L A N D

Land and Population

Capital	London
Total Area (square miles)	94,525 (slightly smaller than Oregon)
Population	58 million
Annual Projected Population Growth Rate (1993–2000)	0.3%
Urban Population (% of total)	89%

Ethnic Composition		
National Identity	English	81.5%
	Scottish	9.6%
	Irish	2.4%
	Welsh	1.9%
	Ulster	1.8%
	Other	2.8%
Ethnic Minority (% of total)	5.5%	
Major Language	English	
Major Religions	Anglican	47%
	Catholic	16%
	Muslim	2%
	Other and Nonreligious	35%

Economy

Domestic Currency	Pound Sterling
GNP (US$)	$1.05 trillion
GNP per capita (US$)	$18,060
Purchasing Power Parity GDP per capita (US$)	$17,210
Average Annual GDP Growth Rate (1980–1993)	2.5%

Structure of Production (% of GDP)	Agriculture	2%
	Industry	33%
	Services	65%
Labor Force Distribution (% of total)	Agriculture	2%
	Industry	28%
	Services	70%
Women as % of Total Labor Force	39%	

Income Distribution (1988)	% of Population	% Share of Income or Consumption
	Richest 20%	44.3%
	Poorest 20%	4.6%
Total Foreign Trade (exports plus imports) as % of GDP	45%	

Society

Life Expectancy	Female	79
	Male	74
Population per Doctor	710	
Infant Mortality (per 1,000 live births)	7	
Adult Literacy	99%	
Average (Mean) Years of Schooling (of adults 25+)	Female	11.8
	Male	11.6
Communications (per 100 people)	Radios	114
	Televisions	43
	Telephones	48
1995 Human Development Index (1 = highest)	Ranks 18 out of 174	

Political Organization

Political System   Parliamentary Democracy/Constitutional Monarchy

Regime History   Long constitutional history, origins subject to interpretation, usually dated from the seventeenth century or earlier.

Administrative Structure   Unitary state with fusion of powers. Parliament has supreme legislative, executive, and judicial authority.

Executive   Prime Minister, answerable to House of Commons, subject to collective responsibility of the cabinet; member of Parliament who is leader of party that can control a majority in Commons.

Legislature   Bicameral. House of Commons elected by single-member plurality system with no fixed term but a five-year limit. Main legislative powers: to pass laws, provide for finance, scrutinize public administration and government policy. House of Lords, unelected upper house: limited powers to delay enactment of legislation and to recommend revisions; specified appeals court functions.

Judiciary   Independent but with no power to judge the constitutionality of legislation or governmental conduct. Judges appointed by Crown on recommendation of PM or lord chancellor.

Party System   Two-party dominant, with regional variation. Principal parties: Conservative and Labour; a center party (Liberal Democrats); and national parties in Scotland, Wales and in Northern Ireland.

SECTION 1

The Making of the Modern British State

In an era of dramatic upheavals and dangerous political transitions around the world, it is easy to think of Britain as an exception because its political system has endured for so many centuries. In fact, Britain's privileged position in comparative politics textbooks—it almost always comes first—seems to follow naturally from the important historical "firsts" it has enjoyed. Britain was the first nation to industrialize and, for much of the nineteenth century, the British Empire was the world's dominant economic, political, and military power, with a vast network of colonies throughout the world. Britain was also the first nation to develop an effective parliamentary democracy (a form of representative government in which the executive is drawn from and answerable to an elected national legislature). As a result of its vast empire, Britain had tremendous influence on the form of government introduced in countries around the globe. For these reasons, British politics is often studied as a model of representative government. Named after the building that houses the British legislature in London, the **Westminster model** of government emphasizes that democracy rests on the supreme authority of a legislature, in Britain's case the Parliament, and the accountability of its elected representatives. Traditionally, the Westminster model and the values of consensus-building and stability on which it rests have served as one standard (the American political system has been another) for countries struggling to construct democratic political systems. Finally, Britain has served as a model of gradual and peaceful evolution of democratic government in a world where transitions to democracy are often turbulent, interrupted, and uncertain.

It appears, however, that Britain has been declining as a power for over a century. At the height of its power in 1870, the British Empire's trade represented nearly one-quarter of the world total and its people enjoyed perhaps the highest per capita income in the world. The decline in this enviable competitive position began with the growth of mass production heavy industry during the "second Industrial Revolution" in the late nineteenth century and accelerated in the twentieth century. By the early 1990s, its share of world trade had shrunk to about 9 percent and its per capita income had fallen to eighteenth in the world, with fourteen Western European countries enjoying higher average incomes. In terms of economic strength and political influence in the world of states, it now lags behind industrial democracies such as the United States, France, Germany, and Japan. Not surprisingly, this long period of decline has tarnished Britain's reputation as a model democracy and made it more difficult for British governments to gain support for their policies at home and abroad.

Britain's decline needs to be understood in context. When the price levels of basic products in different countries are taken into account and purchasing power is considered, Britain is far down the list of

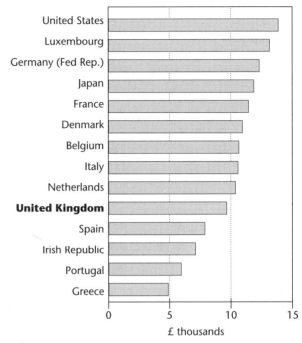

Figure 1   Gross Domestic Product per Capita: International Comparison, 1991
Although the comparisons are in British currency (sterling), the calculations use purchasing power parities (PPP) and therefore take into account the different price levels of commodities in each country.
Source: Eurostat, from *Social Trends* 24, © Crown Copyright 1994.

industrial democracies in Europe and its major trading partners, but only slightly below a group of middle-income European countries. Figure 1 indicates how tightly clustered the economies are. The chart also shows that the United Kingdom (U.K.) has approximately 70 percent of the gross domestic product (GDP) per head of the United States, but that people in Britain enjoy nearly twice the average buying power of people in Greece.

Given its past dominance, Britain was humbled when its applications for membership in the European Community (EC) were rejected in 1963 and again in 1967 at the hands of the French. Worse, since its admission in 1973, Britain's participation in the EC (since November 1993, the European Union or EU) has tended to underscore its declining power. Many Britons remain skeptical about the advantages of Britain's political and economic integration with Europe and are uneasy about the loss of sovereign control that results from membership in an increasingly powerful regional organization. Thus, Britain's reluctant participation in the EU reflects its isolation from Europe, an isolation that begins with its geography (the British Isles, after all, lie off the European coast).

Britain's position in the world seems more curious every year. Is it a world power or a middle-of-the-pack country in Western Europe? It appears to be both. As a legacy of its imperial might and the position it enjoyed as a victorious ally at the close of World War II, Britain sits as a permanent member in the United Nations Security Council, a position denied much more powerful countries such as Germany and Japan. Yet Britain has slipped in economic competitiveness and remains a relative outsider in the European Union.

Before its relative decline in economic power and international influence, Britain's leadership and its list of firsts defined how and why we studied its politics. Its relative decline has changed that rationale, but its study remains important for different reasons. How it handles (or mishandles) decline will provide lessons for many countries grappling with the challenge of mobilizing consensus and developing effective and stable government in a context of great economic uncertainty.

This chapter on Britain will provide ample information about its position in world politics, the domestic and international pressures it faces, and the development of its political institutions and processes. In addition, it will analyze British politics as framed by the four themes introduced below. In Section 5, we review these critical themes and return to the questions raised here about the durability of the Westminster model and the challenges it faces.

The first theme of this chapter is that a state's relative position in the world of states influences its ability to manage domestic and international challenges. This theme suggests that a weaker international standing makes it more difficult for a country to control international events, shape the policy of powerful international organizations, or insulate itself from external pressures. British postwar governments, both Labour and Conservative, have certainly learned that Britain is no exception to this rule. How well has Britain adjusted to its diminished influence and international standing? A second theme is the potent political influence of the democratic idea, the universal appeal of core values associated with parliamentary democracy as practiced first in the United Kingdom.

The Westminster model (as it has evolved and changed) and a set of cultural norms and institutions that encourage moderation and tolerance endow Britain with a certain resiliency in the face of significant challenges. Does Britain still offer an appealing and distinctive model of democracy—one of its few world class exports—or has it become a democracy in decline? In addition, this chapter will analyze strategies of economic governance in Britain and compare the success of its "less-is-more" laissez-faire approach to the more directive state-centered models of France, Germany, and Japan. A third theme involves collective identities, or how individuals define who they are politically and come together to pursue political goals. The chapter will assess how well ethnic minority communities have fared in Britain and consider how the politics of ethnicity and race has influenced politics in postcolonial Britain.

Much of this first section will analyze critical moments in British **political development** that have shaped contemporary Britain. Before reviewing these critical junctures, we present a brief overview of the key features of British politics, past and present, and outline the major characteristics of the current **regime.**

Britain at the Crossroads

Britain's process of adjustment to its profound decline has been unsettling and leaves unresolved important questions about its national identity, its role in the international order, and the viability of its long-established democratic institutions.

In international terms, Britain's reluctance to participate fully in the European Community's agenda for economic and political integration has deepened the perception that the United Kingdom is an outsider within Europe. Britain's commitment to the **Commonwealth** (an association of some fifty independent states which were once part of the British Empire) and to a "special relationship" with the United States based on common language and shared values have done little in recent years to offset a general decline in global influence. As a result, questions of British national identity and, in particular, its relationship to the European Union have remained divisive for Britons. Finally, successful struggles for independence by former colonies have brought ethnic and racial minorities to the United Kingdom from the Caribbean, South Asia, Africa, and elsewhere. Decolonization contributed to the creation of a multiracial society in Britain,

Margaret Thatcher

Born in 1925 in Grantham, a small city in the commercially minded east Midlands, the daughter of a shopkeeper, Margaret Thatcher was the first woman prime minister in a major Western European country. She studied chemistry at Oxford and was later trained as a barrister (a lawyer who pleads cases in court) before winning a seat in Parliament for the North London district of Finchley in 1959. She held the seat continuously until her retirement from the Commons in 1992. After winning the top party post as a surprise challenger for the leadership of the Conservative Party in 1975, she wasted little time in launching a set of bold policy initiatives that, with characteristic forthrightness, she began to implement after the May 1979 election in which the Conservatives returned to power with Thatcher as prime minister. Margaret Thatcher served longer without interruption than any other prime minister during this century, never losing a general election (she won as the incumbent in 1983 and 1987).

Not content simply to govern, she worked to transform British political life. She was convinced that collectivism had sapped British industry, permitted powerful and self-serving unions to hold the country ransom, and contributed to Britain's decline. In an attempt to reverse Britain's relative economic decline, Thatcher sought to jump-start the economy by cutting taxes, reducing social services where possible, and using government policy to stimulate competitiveness and efficiency in the private sector.

Beyond changes in economic policy and approach, Thatcher helped crystallize a powerful alternative vision of politics grounded in an ethic of reduced government management of the economy and the so-called Victorian values that England upheld during the age of Queen Victoria, 1819–1901, a period associated with vitality and the height of Britain's international influence. *Thatcherism* (the term coined to characterize Thatcher's distinctive leadership style, economic and political strategies, and cultural values) prized individual responsibility, commitment to family, frugality, and an affirmation of the entrepreneurial spirit.* These values combined nostalgia for the past, a rejection of permissiveness and disorder, and an appeal to a new civic morality. Taken together, they stood as a reproach and an alternative to collectivism and were referred to as the *enterprise culture*.† Her leadership, moral agenda, and approach to economic policy helped inspire a **new right** alternative to collectivism, both in Britain and abroad (most notably in the United States during Ronald Reagan's presidency from 1980 to 1988 and in the success of conservative Republicanism that gained control of Congress after the 1994 elections).

---

*For an excellent treatment of the moral dimension of Thatcherism, see: Peter Jenkins, *Mrs. Thatcher's Revolution: The Ending of the Socialist Era* (London: Pan Books, 1987), 66–77.

†See: Kent Worcester, "Ten Years of Thatcherism: the 'Enterprise Culture' and the Democratic Alternative," *World Policy Journal* 6, no. 2 (Spring 1989), 297–320.

---

leaving an aftermath of ethnic and racial tensions. These divisions are an unsettling legacy of Britain's imperial past that present important challenges today.

In domestic terms, for more than three decades after the end of World War II, Britain's two major parties (Conservative and Labour) nurtured a collectivist consensus. *Collectivism* is the term coined to describe the consensus that drove politics in the harmonious postwar period when a significant majority of Britons and all major parties agreed that the state should take expanded responsibility for economic governance and provide for the social welfare in the broadest terms. They accepted as a matter of faith that governments should work to narrow the gap between rich and poor through public education, national health care, and other policies of the **welfare state,** and accepted state responsibility for economic growth and full employment. Equally important, the policy process and instruments applied were collective, in the sense that government mobilized the mass support of powerful make-or-break constituencies. Collectivism brought class-based actors (representatives of labor and management) inside politics, and forged a very broad consensus about the expanded role of government.[1]

From Collectivism to the Enterprise Culture

Beginning in the 1970s, stagnating economic growth and the declining competitiveness of key British industries in international markets fueled industrial strife and kept underlying class-based tensions near the surface of politics. As a stagnating economy increased the discontent of groups throughout society, no government appeared equal to the tasks of economic management. Each party failed in turn. First, the Conservative government of Edward Heath (1970–1974) could not resolve either the economic problems or the political tensions that resulted from the previously unheard-of combination of increased inflation and reduced growth (stagflation). Then, the 1974–1979 Labour government of Harold Wilson and James Callaghan were unable to improve conditions. As trade unions became increasingly disgruntled, the country was beset by a rash of strikes throughout the

With characteristic aplomb, Prime Minister Margaret Thatcher greets the annual Conservative Party Conference at the seaside resort of Bournemouth in October 1986. Source: © Stuart Franklin, Magnum Photos, Inc.

winter of 1978–1979 (dubbed the "winter of discontent"). Labour's inability to discipline its trade union allies hurt their chances badly in the election just a few months later in May 1979. The traditional centrist Conservative and Labour alternatives within the collectivist mold seemed exhausted, and many Britons were ready for leadership which would advance a new policy agenda.

In many ways, the period of Margaret Thatcher's leadership as prime minister (1979–1990) marks a critical dividing line in postwar British politics. Until a leadership challenge within Thatcher's own Conservative Party caused her sudden resignation in November 1990, she set the tone and redefined the goals of British politics like few before her.

As the vignette that follows shows, Thatcher's ouster was swift, sharp, and memorable. More impor-

tant, it raised some crucial issues about British politics concerning changes in the **political culture,** Britain's role in Europe, the significance of leadership style, and how difficult it is for citizens to control government.

Thatcher's Demise

Against the advice of her most senior and trusted cabinet ministers, Thatcher refused full British participation in the European Community's monetary and economic integration. A growing chorus of critics blamed high rates of inflation on Thatcher's anti-European stance. They painted a picture of growing isolation: of Thatcher within her party and of Britain within Europe.

Thus, the House of Commons was hushed, poised for a historic speech when Geoffrey Howe rose to his feet in November 1990 to explain his resignation as deputy prime minister. If Britain was shocked by the departure of Howe, the last remaining member of Thatcher's initial 1979 cabinet, it was positively astounded by his speech in Commons. Labeled by the press, "the most damning indictment of a prime minister by a senior colleague in living memory," Howe's attack on Thatcher's anti-EC stance was the beginning of the end for Thatcher.

"The tragedy is . . . that the Prime Minister's perceived attitude towards Europe is running serious risks for the future of our nation," noted Howe in the speech that is widely credited with inciting Conservative members of Parliament (MPs) to rebel against her leadership. "It risks minimising our influence and maximising our chances of being once again shut out. We have paid heavily in the past for late starts and squandered opportunities in Europe. We dare not let that happen again."

In Britain the leader of the party that controls the majority in Parliament becomes the prime minister. Within days of Howe's fiery indictment of Thatcher, the unthinkable occurred! Rebellious former ministers for the first time used the routine procedure for selecting a party leader—of the venerable Conservative Party, no less—against a sitting prime minister. Unable to gain enough support from Conservative Party MPs to win on the first ballot, Thatcher resigned as leader and subsequently as prime minister. By the end of the month, the forty-eight-year-old John Major, a chancellor of the exchequer (finance minister) little known outside parliamentary circles, was Britain's head of government, elected by the Conservative Party's 372 members of the House of Commons.

Margaret Thatcher's fall from power in an unprecedented coup led by the inner ranks of her own Conservative Party underscores some critical issues about British politics. First, it indicates in dramatic fashion that the deference, respect for authority, and gradualism long associated with British political culture can no longer be taken for granted. Partly as a result of Thatcherism and partly as a consequence of much older historical legacies, party politics has become more contentious, and party loyalty and discipline have eroded. Second, it is worth emphasizing the policy areas that triggered the rebellion. Thatcher was removed over British policy toward Europe, and in particular her reluctance to link British economic policy to plans for economic integration within the EC. This shows just how powerful external pressures on domestic politics have become. In this regard, it is useful to consider the extent to which political success hinges on economic policy, and the success of economic policy in turn hinges on the ability of a state to harmonize its national policy with powerful regional power brokers (such as the European Union).

Third, Thatcher's removal from office raises important questions about leadership style. Thatcher mixed conviction with an abrasive and high-handed style, often overriding the objections of her cabinet. Her admirers argued that firm and decisive leadership was needed to forge a new policy direction. Her detractors claimed that she weakened important safeguards, such as the **collective responsibility** of the cabinet, a system that required formal cabinet approval for government policy. (This contrasts with the role of the cabinet in the United States, where the president is at liberty to override the cabinet, which serves more as an informal sounding board for policy.) Did the dismissal eliminate the one leader in a generation who had the strength and conviction to lead Britain back from retreat or a leader who weakened democratic governance? Observers disagree, but either way the removal stands as an important commentary on the risks of a decisive and uncompromising leadership style in a democracy.

Finally, there is much talk about how difficult it is to build democratic institutions that make it possible for citizens to control their governments in the countries of East-Central Europe or the Third World. Thatcher was the first British prime minister to win

Standing in front of 10 Downing Street, John Major addresses Britain for the first time as prime minister. Source: AP/Wide World Photos.

three successive general elections since the early nineteenth century. Her leadership style may have poisoned relationships among her closest political allies, but she was never turned out by the electorate. Margaret Thatcher's overthrow reveals how difficult it has become for ordinary citizens to exercise political control even in a classic Western democracy and how wide a gap has emerged between the often obscure preoccupations of political elites and the concerns of voters. Studied for the questions it raises about these critical issues, Thatcher's dramatic departure helps identify themes to which we will return throughout this section.

Although the circumstances and timing of Major's accession to the office of prime minister were certainly not to Thatcher's liking, he was her handpicked successor. Indeed, he represents quite a success story of his own. As the son of a one-time circus performer and someone who grew up in a two-room apartment, left school at the age of sixteen, and rose to the top of the banking profession before entering politics, Major is a legendary success story and a symbol of the enterprise culture.

Not unexpectedly, his premiership has been framed by Thatcher's legacy and the long shadow she casts. Her considerable success in shifting the terms of debate in Britain, challenging collectivism, streamlining and modernizing British industry, and weakening the power of trade unions, created opportunities for the like-minded Major to advance the enterprise culture. At the same time, he inherited divisions in the Conservative Party over Thatcher's leadership style and policy on Europe and faced the inevitable challenge posed by her international celebrity and scale of accomplishments. By any standard, Thatcher was a tough act to follow.

We have emphasized the place of Margaret Thatcher in British political development because her policies and force of character made her premiership an important watershed in postwar British politics. In addition, Thatcherism has had great influence outside Britain. Building on the special relationship between Britain and the United States, and on natural ideological affinities, Thatcher inspired President Ronald Reagan, who invoked many of the values of the enterprise culture and fought against the American version of collectivism associated with New Deal liberalism. Thus, Thatcherism provides an important lens for viewing British politics. It also provides an important point of comparison for interpreting developments in the United States.

Before considering John Major's premiership and contemporary British politics, we must place Britain's challenges in a broader historical context. Our study begins with a look at the historic development of the modern British state. History shapes contemporary politics in very important ways. Once in place, institutions leave powerful legacies and the mythic interpretations of battles lost and won assume the force of tradition. In addition, issues placed on the agenda in one period, but left unresolved, present challenges for the future.

CRITICAL JUNCTURES

In looking at the main turning points or critical junctures that have shaped Britain's political institutions, processes, and values, we will first discuss how the United Kingdom was initially formed as a modern state. We will then track the state's development in light of two especially important influences and themes of this chapter: Britain's changing position in the world of states and the evolution of its democracy.

Finally, we will examine the influence of two world wars in expanding the role of the British state in economic governance and the provision of social welfare.

The Formation of the United Kingdom

In many ways Britain is the model of a unified and stable state with an enviable record of continuity and resiliency. Nevertheless, the history of state formation reveals how complex and open-ended the process can be. Some issues that plague other countries, such as religious divisions, were settled long ago in Britain. Yet others, such as multiple national identities, remain on the historical agenda.

For the sake of simplicity, we have been using the term *Britain* as shorthand for the United Kingdom of Great Britain and Northern Ireland (U.K.). In law, the term *Great Britain* encompasses England, Wales, and Scotland, but not Northern Ireland. Covering an area of approximately 94,000 square miles, Britain is roughly two-thirds the size of Japan or approximately half the size of France. To put this once immensely powerful country in perspective, it is slightly smaller than Oregon. Although outsiders may sometimes use *England* as shorthand for *Britain* or the *U.K.*, the British **state** (a unified political entity) is comprised of four culturally distinct **nations** (a political community with common historical and cultural characteristics that inhabits a clearly defined territory). How did a single **nation-state** emerge?

Britain is known for its gradual evolution rather than for radical change, a process that began with the consolidation of the British state from among different, even hostile, nations. On the surface, the making of the state involved the unification of kingdoms or crowns (hence the literal significance of the name United *Kingdom*). After Duke William of Normandy defeated the English in the Battle of Hastings in 1066, the monarchy established by the Normans increasingly extended its authority throughout the British Isles. Wales was politically assimilated to England after the accession of the Welsh ruler Henry VII to the English throne in 1485 and the signing of the Act of Union of 1535. The unification of the Scottish and English crowns occurred when the Protestant James Stuart was accepted to the English throne as James I after Elizabeth I died in 1603. Thereafter, England, Scotland, and Wales were known as Great Britain. Scotland and England remained divided politically, however, until the Act of Union of 1707. Henceforth, a common Parliament of Great Britain replaced the two separate parliaments of Scotland and of England and Wales.

At a deeper level, beneath the unification of kingdoms and royal families, the making of the British state in the sixteenth and seventeenth centuries involved a complex interplay of forces: religious conflicts, national rivalries, and struggles over authority between monarchs and the fledgling Parliament. These conflicts erupted in the Civil War of the 1640s, culminating in the beheading of Charles I and the subsequent forced abdication of James II in 1688. The bloodless political revolution, since then known as the Glorious Revolution, confirmed the power of Parliament over the monarchy. It also marked the "last successful political coup d'état or revolution in British history."[2] The outbreak of war with France's Louis XIV in 1689, who sheltered James II, forced the hand of the new Protestant king, William of Orange. He had no choice but to turn to Parliament to secure financing and support for challenging Western Europe's foremost power. In exchange, Parliament required him to meet with it annually and to agree to regular parliamentary elections. This contrasted dramatically with the arrangement enjoyed by Louis XIV, who was gaining power at the expense of the French nobility, and operating without any constraint from commoners.

By the end of the seventeenth century, the framework of a constitutional or limited monarchy—which would still exercise flashes of power into the nineteenth century—was established in Britain. For more than 300 years, Britain's monarchs have been answerable to Parliament, which has held the sole authority for taxation and the maintenance of a standing army.

The Civil War of the 1640s also involved bitter religious conflict between Catholics and Protestants until the removal of the Roman Catholic James II restored a Protestant to the throne and ensured the dominance of the Church of England (or Anglican church). To this day, the Church of England remains the established (official) religion and enjoys advantages over other religions, including the designation of some two dozen of its leading clerics (bishops and archbishops) as members of the House of Lords (Lords Spiritual).

Thus, by the end of the seventeenth century, an embryonic form of parliamentary democracy had emerged and the problem of religious divisions, which continue to plague countries throughout the world, was settled. Equally important, these seventeenth-

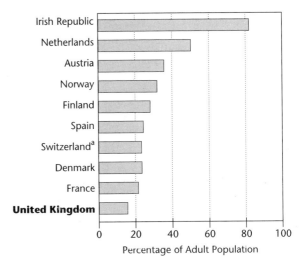

ªFrench speaking area.

Figure 2   Active Church Membership: European Comparison, 1990
Source: Christian Research Association, from *Social Trends 26*, © Crown Copyright 1994.

century developments became a defining moment for how the British perceive their history to this day. However divisive and disruptive the process of state-building may have been originally, its telling and retelling have contributed significantly to a British political culture that celebrates democracy's continuity, gradualism, and tolerance.

As a result of settling its religious differences early, Britain has taken a more secular turn than most countries in Western Europe. The majority of Britons do not consider religion a significant source of identity and, as Figure 2 shows, active church membership in Britain is very low in comparison to other selected Western European countries. In Britain, religious identification has less political significance—in voting behavior or party loyalties—than in many countries. By contrast to France where devout Catholics display a significant tendency to vote right of center, there is relatively little association between religion and voting behavior in Britain (although Anglicans are a little more likely to vote Conservative). Unlike party politics in Germany or Italy, for example, conservative politics in Britain is secular. No parties have denominational (religious) affiliation, a factor that has helped foster the success of the Conservative Party, one of the most unified and impressive right-of-center parties in Europe.

As a consequence, except in Northern Ireland where religious divisions continue, the party system in the United Kingdom has traditionally emphasized economic and social class distinctions and remains free of the pattern of multiple parties (particularly right-of-center parties) that occur in countries where party loyalties are divided both by class and religion.

Britain has not enjoyed the same success when it comes to national identities. The enduring themes of Scottish and Welsh nationalism which flared in the 1970s and the problems associated with Northern Ireland make clear that the multinational character of the British state remains an open-ended problem. Despite the longevity of its constitutional order (dating from the late seventeenth century) and the stability of the British state, distinct national identities remain a powerful and sometimes divisive force in contemporary Britain.

Britain in the World of States

Britain's role in the international order has been critically shaped by three processes: (1) the Industrial Revolution and growth of empire, (2) the loss of empire and the resulting reconfiguration of Britain's international position, and (3) its uneasy relationship with Europe. We now look in turn at each of these critical junctures.

Industry and Empire   Although the British state was consolidated by the seventeenth century, its form was radically shaped by the timing of its industrial development and the way that process transformed Britain's role in the world. The Industrial Revolution in the mid-eighteenth century involved rapid expansion of production and technological innovation.[3] It also involved monumental social and economic transformations. Externally, England used its competitive edge to transform and dominate the international order. Internally, the Industrial Revolution helped shape the way the British state developed, and change forever the British people's way of life.

The consequences of the Industrial Revolution for the generations of people who experienced its upheavals can scarcely be exaggerated. The transformation of English social and economic life was both fundamental and wide-ranging. The typical worker was turned "by degrees . . . from small peasant or craftsman into wage-labourer," as historian Eric Hobsbawm observes. Cash and market-based trans-

actions dominated, as industrialization was tied to commercialization.[4]

Despite a gradual improvement in the standard of living in the English population at large, the effects of industrialization were often profound for agricultural laborers and particular types of artisans. With the commercialization of agriculture, many field laborers lost their security of employment and cottagers (small landholders) were squeezed off the land in large numbers. The mechanization of manufacturing, which spread furthest in the cotton industry, upset the traditional status of the pre-industrial skilled craft workers and permanently marginalized them. During the period of early industrialization, the traditional means of scratching out subsistence—using wood from a common area for fuel, keeping a cow, taking what was left unharvested from the master's land—were destroyed. In "village after village, common rights [were] lost, and the landless and—in the south—pauperised labourer [was] left to support the tenant-farmer, the landowner, and the tithes of the Church"[5] by succumbing to conditions of highly exploited labor.

Equally important, the Industrial Revolution established production and exchange on a global scale for the first time, with particular consequences for the making of the British state. Cotton manufacture, the driving force behind Britain's growing industrial dominance, not only symbolized the new techniques and changed labor organization of the Industrial Revolution but also represented the perfect imperial industry. It relied exclusively on imported raw materials and, by the turn of the nineteenth century, already depended on overseas markets for the vast majority of its sales of finished goods. Growth depended on foreign markets rather than on domestic consumption. This export orientation fueled an expansion far more rapid than an exclusively domestic orientation would have allowed, making the empire both possible and necessary.

With its leading industrial sector dependent on overseas trade, Britain's leaders worked aggressively throughout the eighteenth century to secure markets and expand the empire. Toward these ends, Britain defeated European rivals in a series of military engagements, culminating in the Napoleonic Wars (1793–1815), which confirmed Britain's commercial, military, and geopolitical preeminence. The Napoleonic Wars also secured a balance of power on the European continent favorable for largely unrestricted international commerce (free trade). Propelled by the

TABLE 1   **World Trade and Relative Labor Productivity**

	Proportion of World Trade (%)	Relative Labor Productivity[a] (%)
1870	24.0	1.63
1890	18.5	1.45
1913	14.1	1.15
1938	14.0	0.92

[a]As compared with the average rate of productivity in other members of the world economy.

Source: Robert O. Keohane, *After Hegemony: Cooperation and Discord in the World Political Economy* (Princeton: Princeton University Press, 1984), 36.

formidable and active presence of the British navy, international trade helped England take full advantage of its position as the first industrial power. Many scholars suggest that Britain had the highest per capita income in the world (it was certainly among the two or three highest), and in 1870 at the height of its glory, its trade represented nearly one-quarter of the world total and its industrial mastery ensured highly competitive productivity in comparison to trading partners (see Table 1).

By the reign of Queen Victoria (1837–1901), the British Empire was immensely powerful and encompassed fully 25 percent of the world's population. Britain presided over a vast formal and informal empire, with extensive direct colonial rule over some four dozen countries, including India and Nigeria, and a huge network of independent states economically dependent on England. Britain ruled as the **hegemonic power,** the state that could control the pattern of alliances and terms of the international economic order, and often could shape domestic political developments in countries throughout the world.

Overall, the making of the British state observed a neat symmetry. Its global power helped underwrite industrial growth at home. At the same time, the reliance of domestic industry on world markets, beginning with cotton manufacture in the eighteenth century, prompted the government to project British interests as forcefully as possible overseas. The international orientation of the British economy from the mid-eighteenth century is also reflected in the unique

250-year history of the City of London (the financial district in London, like Wall Street in New York). To this day a premier world financial center, it helped orient the British economy toward overseas investment and international commercial transactions, long after the decline of the British Empire. The prestige of the City of London and the strength of the British currency (sterling) continued to symbolize the status of Britain as a great power, even after the process of decolonization and the emergence of the United States and the Soviet Union as superpowers shrunk British influence in global terms in the post–World War II period.

Decolonization Another defining moment in Britain's relationship to the world of states, the process of decolonization, began in the interwar period (1919–1939) with the independence of the "white Dominions" of Canada, Australia, and New Zealand. In Britain's Asian, Middle Eastern, and African colonies the pressure for political reforms leading to independence deepened during World War II and in the immediate postwar period. Beginning with the formal independence of India and Pakistan in 1947, an enormous empire of dependent colonies more or less dissolved in less than twenty years (although the problem of white-dominated Rhodesia lingered until as Zimbabwe it achieved independence in 1980). The process of decolonization ended any realistic claim Britain could make to be a major player in world politics. In addition, through the immigration of its former colonial subjects to the U.K., decolonization helped create a multicultural society in Britain. As we will see, issues of race and cultural identity have challenged the long-standing British values of tolerance and consensus.

Britain and Europe Finally, in the postwar period, Britain's role in the world of states has been complicated by its uneasy relationship with its Western European counterparts. Viewing British entry into the European Community as a threat to France's grand designs, Charles de Gaulle blocked U.K. membership in 1963 and again in 1967. In addition, because Britain was not a founding member, key areas of policy and procedure were locked in place when it joined in 1973. Both the humiliation and the late entry itself have done little to encourage Britain to embrace a European destiny. In fact, Britain has remained divided in its attitudes toward Europe and the European Union. Its wariness with integration, as illustrated in dramatic fashion in the Howe-Thatcher controversy, seems to reinforce its geographical condition as a European outsider.

For analytical purposes, we have concentrated thus far on the particular relationship between industry and empire in Britain, and on the international aspects of the processes that helped orient state policy from the eighteenth century through the post–World War II period. In tandem with these developments, British state institutions were shaped by the centuries-old struggles of its citizens to advance democratic political control over the state. We turn now to the story of how democratic rights were expanded and parliamentary democracy modernized, a second critical aspect of British state formation.

The Democratic Idea

In Britain, the struggle for sovereign authority by a representative body over the monarchy was fought and won early by Parliament in the seventeenth century. The expansion of control by citizens over the government nearly stalled, however, when it came to the crucial matter of extending voting rights and permitting broad political participation by the mass of citizens.

The Struggle for Voting Rights   The first critical juncture in the long process of democratization began in the late 1820s, when the "respectable opinion" of the propertied classes and increasing popular agitation pressed Parliament to expand the right to vote (franchise) beyond a thin band of men with substantial property, mainly landowners. With Parliament under considerable pressure, the Reform Act of 1832 extended the franchise to a section of the (male) middle classes.

The Industrial Revolution had shifted economic power from landowners to men of commerce and industry. In principle, this social transformation was confirmed politically by the 1832 Reform Act, which gave new urban manufacturing centers, such as Manchester and Birmingham, more substantial representation. However, the massive urban working class created by the Industrial Revolution and populating the cities of Charles Dickens's England remained on the outside looking in. In fact, the reform was very narrow and defensive. Before 1832 less than 5 percent

of the adult population was entitled to vote—and afterward, only about 7 percent!

In extending the franchise so narrowly, the reform underscored the strict property basis for political participation, and inflamed class-based tensions in Britain. Following the Reform Act, a massive popular movement erupted in the late 1830s to secure the program of the People's Charter which included demands for universal male suffrage and other radical reforms intended to make Britain a much more participatory democracy. The *Chartist movement,* as it was called, held huge and often tumultuous rallies, and organized a vast campaign to petition Parliament, but failed to achieve any of its aims.

Expansion of the franchise proceeded very slowly. The Representation of the People Act of 1867 increased the electorate to just over 16 percent but left cities significantly underrepresented. The Franchise Act of 1884 nearly doubled the size of the electorate, but it was not until the Representation of the People Act of 1918 that suffrage included nearly all adult men and women over thirty. How slow a process was it? The franchise for men with a specified level of income dated from the fifteenth century, but all women between the ages of twenty-one and thirty were not enfranchised until 1928! The voting age for both women and men was lowered to eighteen in 1969. Except for some episodes during the days of the Chartist movement, the struggle for extension of the franchise took place without violence, but its time horizon must be measured in centuries. This is British gradualism—at its best and worst (see Figure 3 on the following page).

The Making of the Interventionist State   With the matter of the franchise finally settled, in one sense the making of the British state as a democracy was concluded. But in another important sense, the modernization of the state was just beginning in the twentieth century with the expansion of the state's direct responsibility for management of the economy and provision for the social welfare of its citizens. The making of what is sometimes called the *interventionist state* was spurred by the experience of two world wars.

The state's involvement in the economy increased in Britain to a significant degree during World War I. For example, the state took increasing control of a number of industries, including railways, mining, and shipping. It also set prices and restricted the flow of capital abroad, and channeled the country's resources

Figure 3   Expansion of Voting Rights
Source: Jorgen S. Rasmussen, *The British Political Process,* p. 151, Copyright © 1993 Wadsworth Publishing Company. Reprinted with permission of the publisher.

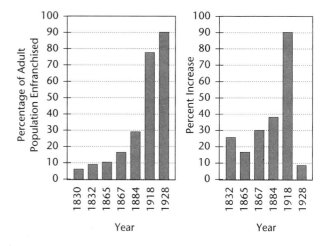

into production geared to the war effort. "In fact between 1916 and 1918 Britain was forced to evolve a first incomplete and reluctant sketch of the powerful state-economy of the Second World War," notes historian Eric Hobsbawm. "It was dismantled with unseemly haste after 1918. . . . Nevertheless, nothing could be quite the same again."[6]

After World War I, the state remained active in the management of industry in a rather different way. When unemployment skyrocketed at the end of the postwar boom—from 2 percent in 1919–1920 to 12.9 percent in 1921–1922[7]—industrial tension erupted in a set of highly charged showdowns. A Triple Alliance of powerful unions (railway workers, miners, and transport workers) challenged the government's decision to ignore the recommendation of a royal commission that the coal industry be taken over, or nationalized, by the state. In 1921, the coalition government of Lloyd George invoked emergency powers amid threats of a general strike and won capitulation from the miners. Five years later the general strike of 1926 confirmed the intensity of class divisions in Britain. It also revealed the capacity of the state—now deeply enmeshed in industrial management—to wield its power to fragment the trade union movement and resist any working-class agenda for a socialist Britain.

This considerable government manipulation of the economy openly contradicted the policy of laissez-faire (minimal government interference in the operation of economic markets). When the economic downturn of the 1930s arrived, however, it was clear that a new era had begun. The wartime experience transformed the British political-economic culture and

policy framework in a crucial way. Laissez-faire gave way to active state intervention into the economy; that is, the state actively regulated certain market processes and in some cases replaced private with public ownership of industries. During the interwar years, state intervention involved, among other things, the rationalization of industry through the creation of larger production units and the regulation of prices, the creation of cartels (industrial syndicates formed to control prices and output), and the application of duties on imported goods to protect domestic industry.

After World War II, the British state extended and diversified its responsibilities for the conduct of the economy and the provision of social benefits, as did other Western European states. The leading political parties and policy-making elites agreed that the state must take an active role in regulating the economy through the strategic manipulation of fiscal instruments (taxation, borrowing and spending) and monetary instruments (the determination of interest rates and exchange rates, the supply of money and credit). The state accepted the responsibility to secure full employment, maintain a steady rate of growth, keep prices stable, and achieve desirable balance of payments and exchange rates. It took responsibility for the social welfare of its citizens by building extensive public housing, providing pensions, and instituting a national health service.

These expanded responsibilities were thrust on the state for several reasons. A general association between the excesses of free-market capitalism—notably the Great Depression beginning in 1929—and the causes of World War II led to a broad consensus that

TABLE 2 Prime Ministers, 1945–Present		
Name	Party	Years in Office
Clement Attlee	Labour	1945–1951
Winston Churchill	Conservative	1951–1955
Anthony Eden	Conservative	1955–1956
Harold Macmillan	Conservative	1956–1963
Alec Douglas-Home	Conservative	1963–1964
Harold Wilson	Labour	1964–1970
Edward Heath	Conservative	1970–1974
Harold Wilson	Labour	1974–1976
James Callaghan	Labour	1976–1979
Margaret Thatcher	Conservative	1979–1990
John Major	Conservative	1990–

governments must act to flatten out the business cycle and ensure that a cycle of depression followed by war would not be repeated. In addition, the requirements of reconstruction made greater state intervention necessary to ensure efficient retooling and expansion of the economy to meet peacetime requirements.

In addition, the war transformed the fortunes of the Labour Party, which although formed in 1906, had never led a majority government. The first postwar election in 1945 gave Labour its greatest victory ever (before or since) in terms of its share of seats in Parliament and a mandate for significant social change (see Table 2). Demands to reduce capitalist control over how the economy would be run and resources distributed and to expand the working-class share of what society produced were now louder and harder to ignore. The fear of depression and the burst of pent-up yearnings for change helped transform the role of the state.

In this context of shared victory and common misery (almost everyone suffered terrible hardships immediately after the war), reconstruction took priority over ideological conflict. This broad culture of reconciliation and a determination to rebuild and improve the conditions of life for all Britons helped forge the thirty-year collectivist consensus of the postwar period.

Throughout this period (from the end of World War II to the mid-1970s) there was a remarkable unity among electoral combatants, as the Labour and Conservative mainstream endorsed the principle of state responsibility for the collective good in both economic and social terms. Although modest in comparative European terms, the broad commitment to state management of the economy and provision of social services marked a new era in British politics. Nothing could dramatize the change in temperament from the collectivist consensus to the era of the enterprise culture more than the Conservative challenges by Thatcher and Major, not only to the costs, but to the principles, of the welfare state.

IMPLICATIONS FOR CONTEMPORARY BRITISH POLITICS

The processes that met in these historical junctures continue to influence the present in powerful and complex ways. Long-settled issues about the constitutional form and unity of the state have reemerged with unexpected force in recent decades. Can the interests of England, Wales, Scotland, and Northern Ireland be reconciled within a single, unitary nation-state? How well can a state constructed for empire adjust—economically, politically, and institutionally—to a century-long decline? Do the centuries-old traditions of gradualism and consensual politics provide durable resources for meeting contemporary challenges or leave Britain caught in the starting blocks when a rapid adjustment to change is needed? We will expand on these questions here and return to them frequently throughout this chapter.

The Resurgence of National Identities

A stagnating economy in the 1970s deepened the pattern of uneven development in national and regional terms, in which England prospered by comparison to

Scotland and Wales. The discovery of vast oil reserves off the north shore of Scotland increased demands for more extensive national self-determination. At the same time, culturally based nationalism flared in Wales. The 1970s witnessed powerful movements for *devolution*—the shifting of specified powers from the British Parliament to national parliaments in Scotland and Wales. At the same time, the growth of nationalist parties in Scotland (the Scottish National Party) and in Wales (the Plaid Cymru) seemed to signal a weakening of two-party (Conservative and Labour) dominance in party competition, and a remapping of party competition with more regional dimensions.

The "Irish question" remains among the most enduring conflicts over sovereignty and self-determination in the contemporary world. Historically, the making of the British state has involved the coerced inclusion of what is today Northern Ireland into a United Kingdom with England, Scotland, and Wales. Unresolved conflicts between a native Irish Catholic majority and a British settler-colonial Protestant minority led to a failed nationalist uprising in 1916 known as the Easter Rebellion. Soon thereafter, Westminster partitioned Ireland following the Government of Ireland Act of 1920: The six northern counties of Ireland were divided administratively from the remaining twenty-six counties. The twenty-six counties (the Irish Free State and, later, the Republic of Ireland) became an independent nation-state within the Commonwealth in 1922 and surrendered all formal ties to the United Kingdom when it ended Commonwealth affiliation in 1949. The six northern counties became Northern Ireland, a partitioned fourth nation within the United Kingdom called Ulster and dominated in economic and political terms by the Protestant descendants of English and Scottish settlers. Approximately 950,000 of Ulster's 1.6 million people are Protestant, and most of them support the continued union of Northern Ireland with Great Britain (hence they are called *unionists*). The remaining residents of Northern Ireland, descendants of the original Irish inhabitants, are predominantly Catholic (like the overwhelming majority of citizens of the Republic of Ireland). Many of them are Irish nationalists who oppose U.K. ties and support reunification with the Republic of Ireland (they are referred to as *republicans*).

After a civil rights movement calling for Catholic political and economic equality helped provoke Prot-

estant riots in the summer of 1969, the British government sent troops to Northern Ireland to quell violence and preserve British political control. The strife that began in 1969 has resulted in over 3,000 deaths in sporadic but seemingly never-ending violence. However, a series of initiatives to begin negotiations between the Northern Irish communities, the United Kingdom, and Ireland, including the 1985 signing of the Anglo-Irish Agreement between Britain and Ireland, helped facilitate a series of on-again, off-again talks beginning in the spring of 1991. By the fall of 1994, the announcement of a cease-fire by the Irish Republican Army (IRA) was quickly matched by the Unionist paramilitary forces. The cease-fire raised hopes that the political deadlock in Northern Ireland might be broken through negotiations, which resulted in an apparent breakthrough in February 1995. The prospects for a negotiated peace in Ireland and the implications for British politics will be discussed in Section 5.

Whatever the prospects for peace, Northern Ireland remains a constant reminder that even in powerful and secure states with centuries-old constitutional arrangements, union can be highly contentious in the face of complex nationalist, religious, and economic divisions. As our theme about collective identities suggests, it will not be easy to resolve the Irish question which involves age-old feelings of marginalization and fear of attack on all sides. It will be quite a challenge to settle the conflict by economic means (improving the investment climate and enhancing the position of Catholics in Northern Ireland) or even by the redistribution of political resources through power-sharing arrangements.

The Decline in International Influence

The loss of its role as a great power has created foreign policy dilemmas for Britain. It has tried to reconcile three foreign policy orientations: (1) as a European state with middling influence on regional and world affairs; (2) as a postcolonial power with cultural and economic ties to the former colonies in the Commonwealth (who increasingly chafe at Britain's sometimes high-handed behavior in the organization); and (3) as an unequal partner in a special relationship with the United States. The balancing act is very difficult to sustain.

Despite Britain's troubles in adjusting to an often secondary role in international affairs, at times it was

Source: Courtesy Chris Riddell, from *The Economist.*

able to turn opportunities to advantage. In the Falklands/Malvinas War in 1982, for example, in which Britain soundly defeated Argentina in a war over disputed territory in the South Atlantic, Britain was able briefly to relive the glory of an imperial power. With the government at a low point in popular support at home, military victory and the projection of power abroad helped solidify Thatcher's hold on office. Moreover, as the most senior head of government in Europe and one who could claim both a kinship with Reagan and a good business-like relationship with Gorbachev, for a time Thatcher emerged as an important player in international affairs.

On balance, however, Britain's foreign policy record suggests a decline in global influence. Britain's efforts to maintain its role as a postcolonial global power led to a humiliating defeat in the Middle East in 1956. A failed military effort with France and Israel to reassert control of the Suez Canal by seizing it from Egypt shocked Britain into withdrawing its military presence east of Suez, and confirmed U.S. dominance in the region. Moreover, the high-profile but "second fiddle" role of the United Kingdom beside the United States as the most determined advocate of the war that erupted in the Persian Gulf in January 1991, confirms both its special role and its status as junior partner in American-led foreign policy initiatives. By contrast to the mutual support offered during kindred Republican and Conservative administrations in the United States and the United Kingdom, the relationship between the Clinton and Major administrations, which

enjoy no ideological kinship, has been testy at times. But on balance both partners seem very reluctant to criticize each other publicly, even when there are apparent policy differences, for example, over the many ineffectual initiatives to bring peace to Bosnia. The contrast with French–U.S. relations, which were far more contentious in the mid-1990s, suggests that the notion of a special relationship may have some real value.

In contrast to his predecessor, John Major has not achieved any special standing in the international community during an uncertain and tumultuous time. More specifically, he faces a significant policy challenge in the British commitment to preserve democracy in Hong Kong, a small, commercially vibrant British colony off the southern tip of China, while observing its treaty commitments to return the territory to China in 1997. Whether in the conflict in the South Atlantic with Argentina, the often acrimonious negotiations with China over the fate of Hong Kong, its relations with Commonwealth countries, or its ambivalence about Europe, Britain's imperial legacy continues to cloud its participation in the world of states. In addition, as our theme about the world of states suggests, the ability of a state to manage the domestic impact of external forces and to shape its external environment depends on its international position and Britain is no exception. With declining power comes reduced influence.

Race, Ethnicity, and Empire

Problems about democratic ideals and practices in Britain are another legacy of empire. Britain has adjusted poorly to the creation of a multiracial society following decolonization. Minority communities in the United Kingdom are predominantly made up of citizens who were born in (or whose parents were born in) the former colonies. Britain's ethnic minorities comprise approximately 5.5 percent of the population (see Figure 4). These include some half-million Afro-Caribbeans and some 1.5 million individuals of South Asian descent (India, Pakistan, and Bangladesh).

Racial and ethnic minorities have faced considerable discrimination and cultural isolation, and persons hoping to immigrate from the Commonwealth have found barriers to entry increasing as the end of steady growth in Britain's economy reduced demand for labor. A set of immigration and nationality acts have institutionalized a preference for white immigrants,

Figure 4   Ethnic Minority Population

Breakdown of Ethnic Minorities

Black Caribbean	500,000
Black African	212,000
Black Britons	178,000
Indian	840,000
Pakistani	467,000
Bangladeshi	162,000
Chinese	156,000
Other Asian	197,000
Other African, Iranian, Arab	290,000

Source: Centre for Research into Ethnic Relations (1991 Census), from Philip Allan, John Benyon, and Barry McCormick, eds., *Focus on Britain 1994* (Chicago: Fitzroy Dearborn Publishers, 1994), 196.

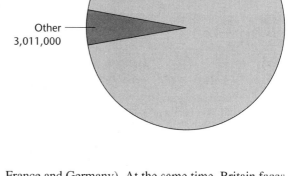

and in 1979, the Conservative victory that made Margaret Thatcher the prime minister was in part due to her ability to exploit issues of race. Thus, the problems of racism are another legacy of the making of modern Britain, with roots in empire.

In addition, Britain has experienced a resurgence in racism directed at blacks and Asians. In 1992, 7,780 racial assaults were recorded (up from 4,383 in 1988), and it was estimated that only one in ten assaults was documented. A 1992 survey indicated that as many as 10 percent of ethnic minority households had experienced racial abuse, threats, or physical attacks.[8] The issues of xenophobia and empire have come together in a complicated and troubling manner.

The United Kingdom has a rich history of relations with countries throughout the world and presents a complicated and sometimes contradictory image to the outside. Britain is linked to some countries by the profound connections of its colonial past (e.g., India, Nigeria, and Iran) and to others by complicated ties of regional cooperation and rivalry (e.g.,

France and Germany). At the same time, Britain faces a contest of wills and world views in its relations with China, as Hong Kong reverts to China's control in 1997.

As suggested by Thatcher's removal following a difference over Britain's EC policy, domestic politics can be influenced dramatically by a country's international role—and by difficult transitions and dilemmas concerning that role. The ability of British governments to present a political and social vision to the citizenry and sustain support for their policies is limited by uneven economic performance. Likewise, politics is made more complex by the overlap, proliferation, and collision of collective identities, as Britain wrestles with the meaning and political significance of class, gender, race, ethnicity, and nationality. In a world of narrowing resources and reduced international influence, Britain's resiliency will be tested by a host of pressures in the years ahead. To understand the interplay of these critical themes, it is necessary to examine the defining features of Britain's political and economic development in the postwar period.

SECTION 2
Political Economy and Development

The timing of industrialization and of a country's introduction into the world economy are important variables in explaining how and how successfully the state intervenes in economic governance. Both the specific policies chosen and the relative success of the economic strategy, in turn, have significant political repercussions. Economic developments often deter-

mine political winners and losers, influence broad changes in the distribution of resources and opportunities among groups in society, and affect a country's international standing. In this section, we analyze the politics of economic management, beginning with a historical overview of Britain's economic development. Then we consider in turn the principles of Brit-

TABLE 3   **Economic Performance, 1993**

	Increase in GDP (%)	Inflation Rate[a] (% per year)	Unemployment Rate (% of workforce)	Change in Unemployment Rate[b]
United States	2.9	2.8	6.8	−0.6
United Kingdom	1.9	1.7	10.4	−0.2
Japan	0.1	1.9	2.4	+0.4
Italy	−0.3	4.4	11.0	+0.9
France	−0.8	2.2	11.5	+1.6
Germany	−2.1	4.2	8.2	+1.8

[a]Consumer prices at mid-year.
[b]Change in unemployment rate from December 1992 to December 1993.

Sources: OECD and British national sources, in Philip Allan, John Benyon, and Barry McCormick, eds., *Focus on Britain 1994* (Chicago: Fitzroy Dearborn Publishers, 1994), 104.

ish economic management, the social consequences of economic developments, and political repercussions of Britain's position in the international economic order.

In addition to its claim as the first industrial nation, Britain is also the country with the longest experience of economic decline. In a way, the country was a victim of its own success and approach to economic development. From the eighteenth century onward, Britain combined its naval mastery and the dominant position created by the Industrial Revolution to fuel expansion based on the foreign supply of raw materials and markets. With plenty of profits available from this traditional overseas orientation, British entrepreneurs became complacent about keeping up with the newest industrial techniques and investing in machinery at home. Secure in the advantages of empire and the priority of international trade over domestic manufacturing, the government stuck to its belief in free trade (low tariffs and removal of other impediments to open markets) in the international realm and a hands-off approach at home. With low investment in the modernization of industrial plants and little effort to enhance efficiency by grouping small-scale firms into cartels and trusts as the Americans and Germans were doing, Britain slipped behind its competitors in crucial areas: technological innovation, investment in domestic manufacturing, the scale of production facilities.

By the 1890s, Britain's key export in the nineteenth century, textiles, was slipping, and the international position of the machine-tool industry, which Britain also had dominated, was collapsing even more rapidly. Both Germany and the United States had overtaken Britain in steel production, the key indicator of competitiveness in the period, and the gap was widening. By the time Andrew Carnegie sold out to J. P. Morgan's U.S. Steel in 1901, Carnegie alone was producing more steel than all of England![9] Thus, for more than a century, Britain has been concerned about relative economic decline—or, as it is commonly called in the United Kingdom, "the British disease." Throughout the twentieth century, the political fortunes of governments have risen and fallen with the application of alternative, and mostly inadequate, remedies.

Has the trend reversed? By 1987, the date of Margaret Thatcher's last victory in a general election, heady optimism about the British economy led to talk of an economic miracle and raised hopes that a strong dose of Thatcherism had cured the British disease. A downturn from mid-1990 to mid-1992, characterized by increased inflation and falling industrial investment and production made it clear that talk of economic miracles was unrealistic. However, by the mid-1990s, the British economy was performing better than most of its major competitors, including its European neighbors who were mired in recession. As Table 3 shows, among major developed economies, only the United States enjoyed a greater decline in unemployment and stronger growth.

TABLE 4   **Average Annual Growth Rates (percentage)**

	1957–1967	1967–1978	1980–1988	1988–1992
Japan	10.4	7.2	3.4	2.9
United States	4.1	3.0	1.9	0.2
Germany	5.5	3.8	1.7	2.3
France	5.6	4.4	1.4	1.4
Britain	3.1	2.3	1.7	0.6
All OECD	**4.8**	**3.8**	**2.0**	**1.0**

Sources: P. Whiteley, "Economic Policy," in *Developments in British Politics 3*, ed. Patrick Dunleavy et al. (London: Macmillan, 1990), 193; OECD Main Economic Indicators.

Since the end of the recession in 1992, British inflation has remained low, and reduced interest rates have spurred consumer buying. Unemployment is down (though still very high in historical terms), and there has been convincing (although unspectacular) evidence of growth. Cost competitiveness in exports is improving due in part to devaluation (British goods were cheaper to buy in foreign currencies) and in part to improved productivity and low wage settlements, "a favourable legacy of Thatcherism, based on better industrial relations and greater competition."[10] But the historic weak spot in British economic development—investment in and modernization of industrial plants—has remained weak. In addition, economic policy is still motivated too much by short-term political pressures for tax cuts or increases in social spending, particularly before elections. More broadly, economic policy cannot seem to escape abrupt reversals in strategy (what the British call "stop-go" policy cycles). Will the pattern of respectable growth and low inflation continue? Has Thatcherism cured the British disease?

Even beyond the predictable partisan disagreements, prospects remained clouded. "The Conservatives got lucky in September 1992, following the *debacle* of Black Wednesday," noted one observer, referring to Britain's withdrawal from the EC effort to harmonize exchange rates among member states and its decision to go it alone with a radical devaluation of the British currency. "They have not yet shown that they can take full advantage of their new opportunity. Further re-balancing of the economy, towards investment and exports and away from consumption and government spending, is needed if 'stop-go' cycles are to be consigned to the economic history books."[11] It is not surprising that the issues of economic management and alternative prescriptions to cure the British disease continue to preoccupy governments and voters alike. How can we understand the political significance—both the underlying causes and the contemporary consequences—of Britain's historic economic decline and contemporary uncertainty?

STATE AND ECONOMY

Whereas late industrializers, like Germany and Japan, relied on powerful government support during their industrial take-off period, England's Industrial Revolution was based more on laissez-faire, or free-market, principles. When the state intervened in powerful ways, it did so primarily to secure free markets at home and open markets for British goods (free trade) in the international sphere. More than in all its principal trading partners (and competitors) except the United States, British economic management began with a laissez-faire emphasis, and it has continued in the same vein.

With regard to our production and exchange theme, some scholars suggest that states that have institutionalized effective relationships with organized economic interests (such as France, Germany, and Japan) enjoy more consistent growth and enhanced economic competitiveness. Table 4 provides corroborating evidence that Britain's annual growth rates have generally been lower than those of Japan, Germany, and France.

Rather than institutionalizing a dense network of relationships among government agencies, business, and labor, Britain preserves arms-length relationships between the state and key economic actors. With British political culture trumpeting the benefits of free-market individualism, and the stamp of Thatcherism on economic policy, the state provides little direct strategic steering of the economy. The advantages of the enterprise culture and the legacies of hands-off, laissez-faire economics have become a source of considerable controversy today. Does this core ingredient in Britain's political culture make it more difficult to compete with countries that can effectively apply the institutions of the state to the problems of economic competitiveness? Alternatively, have Thatcher's and Major's support for entrepreneurship, competition, and industriousness in the private sector helped provide the basis for newly efficient growth? If Thatcher and Major have finally cured the British disease through a laissez-faire approach, then the advantage of more institutionalized relationships with economic interests is dubious. Thus, the British model becomes a critical test case for our production and exchange theme and for the commonplace wisdom that countries such as Germany and Japan can outperform Britain or the United States, where the approaches to economic governance are more hit-or-miss and shallower. An assessment of this central issue in British politics requires a deeper understanding of the state's role in shaping the British economy during the post–World War II period, including the limits and political implications of that role.

In Section 1, we discussed the growth of the interventionist state beginning with the control of crucial industries during World War I, and the active management of industry by the state in the interwar years. After World War II, the sense of unity inspired by the shared suffering of war and the need to rebuild a war-ravaged country helped crystallize the collectivist consensus. In common with other Western European states, the British state both broadened and deepened its responsibilities for the overall performance of the economy and the well-being of its citizens. The leading political parties and policy-making elites agreed that the state should take an active role in regulating the economy through the strategic manipulation of fiscal instruments (taxation, borrowing and spending) and monetary instruments (the determination of interest rates and exchange rates, the supply of money and credit).

The state also accepted the responsibility to secure low levels of unemployment (referred to as a policy of "full employment"), expand social services, maintain a steady rate of growth, keep prices stable, and achieve desirable balance of payments and exchange rates. The approach was characterized by what has come to be called **Keynesian demand management,** or **Keynesianism** (after the British economist John Maynard Keynes). State budget deficits were used to expand demand in an effort to boost both consumption and investment when the economy was slowing. Cuts in government spending and a tightening of credit and finance were used to cool demand when high rates of growth brought fears of inflation or a deficit in balance of payments. Taken together, this new agenda of expanded economic management and welfare provision, sometimes referred to as the Keynesian Welfare State (KWS), directed government policy throughout the era of the collectivist consensus.

Despite broad political agreement and cultural support for the Keynesian Welfare State, economic performance significantly influenced the terms of the new postwar agenda. During the first two decades of the postwar years, Britain and other European industrial democracies experienced a very favorable set of economic conditions unlikely to be seen again in such combination. Increasing worker productivity encouraged a solid rate of domestic investment. At the same time, Britain enjoyed low inflation, virtually full employment, and a steady rate of growth. In comparison with the interwar period, Britain's postwar economic growth rate of 2.8 percent represented a record of solid achievement. However, this was far short of the much-vaunted "miracles" of economic growth that occurred elsewhere during the same twenty-year period—6.7 percent in West Germany, 6.0 percent in Italy, and 4.5 percent in France.

It is likely that the scale of Britain's postwar boom was limited by the continuing pattern of weak investment in domestic industry, magnified by relatively low investment in the research and development (R&D) of new production technologies. British competitiveness was weakened further by the higher proportion of outdated plants and equipment (owing to the longevity of British manufacturing and the fact that factories were left relatively undamaged by war, compared to Germany's or Japan's). In addition, the country endured a relatively abrupt adjustment to the end of empire, with the loss of all the commercial advantages that it entailed.[12] With respectable but unspectacular growth rates, British policymakers faced less room for maneuver than their European counter-parts, a factor that reenforced their natural caution in developing welfare state policies and in considering new proposals for economic governance. Two central dimensions—economic management and welfare pol-icy—capture the limited scale and scope of the state's role in economic and social life.

Economic Management

Like all states, whatever their commitment to free markets, the British state intervenes in economic life, sometimes with considerable force. When some states intervene, they exercise strategic control over the economy to guide it and enhance competitiveness. When the British state intervenes most decisively (es-pecially in the period since 1979), it does so to shift the balance of power: from the public to the private sector through **privatization** of industries, and from labor to management by limiting the disruptive capac-ities of unions and affirming management authority. To this day the British have not developed the more pro-active or institutional capacities for state-sponsored economic **planning** or **industrial policy** enjoyed by some of their competitors, like France, Germany, or Japan. In France the *Commissariat du Plan* (Planning Commission) has been used as an in-strument to shape leading sectors of the economy and enhance competitiveness. The German Social Market Economy advances competitiveness through a com-prehensive strategy of coordination between the pub-lic and private sectors, with critical strategic roles played by the banks (led by Germany's central bank, the *Bundesbank*), trade unions, and employer and industry organizations. In Japan the Ministry of In-ternational Trade and Industry (MITI) has played a powerful role in shaping a superbly competitive economy based on mass-produced, high-value-added industries (such as automobiles and consumer electronics) that rely on cutting-edge organizational innovations and production technologies.

By contrast, the shallow British equivalent, the National Economic Development Council (NEDC or, more colloquially, "Neddy"), introduced under the Conservative government of Harold Macmillan in 1962, was never equipped to provide strategic coordi-nation of the economy. It was viewed with suspicion by the Treasury, hamstrung by disagreements between its business and trade union members, and trapped by the inconsistent direction of government policies. The

NEDC was never intended to intrude too much upon free-market initiatives and had little effect on eco-nomic performance. It was abolished by John Major in 1992, ending a thirty-year tradition of tripartite con-sultations between representatives of business, labor, and government over economic policy (referred to as **corporatism**).

The Limits of Macroeconomic Policy   The effective-ness of economic policy in Britain has been limited by a lack of cohesion. There has been little effort to con-nect policies aimed at national economic performance with particular industrial sectors. In France, Germany, and Japan, economic policy instruments are designed to harmonize and coordinate macroeconomic policy (intended to shape the overall economic system at the national level by concentrating on policy targets such as unemployment, inflation, or growth) with industrial policy (aimed at enhancing competitiveness through strategic attention to particular industrial sectors and the relationship among them). Apart from its manage-ment of nationalized industries, the British state has limited its role mainly to broad policy instruments de-signed to influence the economy generally (macro-economic policy) by adjusting state revenues and expenditures.[13] One of the foremost disappointments of postwar British economic policy has been its failure to make links between these two levels. Macroeco-nomic policy has dominated economic policy, and since 1979 attention to inflation has crowded out all other policy goals.[14]

Macroeconomic policy, with its focus on the Treasury and the Bank of England, has been reactive and sometimes skittish. It responds to fluctuations in the business cycle and is sensitive to short-term politi-cal calculations that abruptly shift policy agendas. As a result, state involvement in economic management has been relatively ineffectual. An ongoing stop-go cycle of reversals has plagued policy, which has had relatively little effect on natural business cycles and was unable to prevent recessions, most recently, dur-ing 1979–1981 and 1990–1992.

The generally reactive and minimalist orientation of economic management strategies in Britain bridges the two eras of postwar politics in Britain—the earlier period until 1979 characterized by the collectivist con-sensus and broad support for the Keynesian Welfare State and the contemporary period (the Thatcher and Major governments) marked by staunch defense of free-market economics, disavowal of the principles of the welfare state, and the rejection of Keynesianism.

The End of Consensus   Before Thatcher, Conservative leaders in Britain generally accepted the terms of the collectivist consensus. Their traditional belief in a hierarchical society and their historic concern for the permanent interests of society linked to property made them Conservatives. They were Conservatives, too, in their unquestioned "commitment to authoritative leadership as a permanent social necessity"[15] and in their paternalism. But these Conservatives were also modernizers, and they were prepared to manage the economy in a way consistent with the Keynesian approach and to maintain the welfare state and guarantee full employment.

Economic decline only made the situation for mainstream Conservatives and, indeed, for any government, more complex and difficult. By the 1970s public officials no longer saw the world as one they understood and could master: it had become a world without economic growth and with growing political discontent. Edward Heath, the Conservative centrist who governed from 1970 to 1974, was the first prime minister to suffer the full burden of recession and the force of political opposition from both traditional business allies and resurgent trade union adversaries. Operating in an era marked by increased inflation and reduced growth (stagflation), Heath could never break out of the political constraints imposed on him by economic decline.

Heath accepted the terms of the collectivist consensus: the welfare state, the mixed economy of private and public enterprises, and the effort to secure full employment. But recession meant confrontations with trade unions and reduced investment by entrepreneurs. There were strikes by workers from dockers, to municipal employees, to mineworkers, and strikes by investors (who chose to make their investments overseas), which proved especially frustrating to Heath. In the end, Heath had little room for successful maneuver, but his failure represented only the first act in a deepening drama of defeat for Britain's tradition of political consensus.

From 1974 to 1979, the Labour government of Harold Wilson and, after his resignation in 1976, James Callaghan, reenforced the impression that governments could no longer control the swirl of events. The beginning of the end came when trade unions became increasingly restive under the pinch of voluntary wage restraints pressed on them by the Labour government. Frustrated by wage increases well below inflation rates, the unions broke with the government in 1978. The number of unofficial work stoppages increased, and official strikes followed, all fueled by a seemingly endless series of leapfrogging pay demands which erupted throughout the winter of 1978–1979 (the "winter of discontent"). Figure 5 on the following page shows how dramatic the spike in work stoppages was in 1978–1979. There is little doubt that the industrial unrest that dramatized Labour's inability to manage its own allies—the trade unions—contributed mightily to Thatcher's election just a few months later in May 1979. If a Labour government couldn't manage its trade union allies, whom could it govern? More significantly, the winter of discontent helped write the conclusion to Britain's collectivist consensus, and discredit the Keynesian Welfare State.

The Post-Consensus Policy Orientation   In policy terms, the economic strategies of Thatcher and Major reflect a growing disillusionment with Keynesianism, a process begun under the Labour government of 1974–1979. In its wake, **monetarism** emerged as the new economic doctrine. Keynesian demand management assumed that the level of unemployment could be set and the economy stabilized through decisions of government (monetary and fiscal or budgetary policy). By contrast, monetarism assumed a "natural rate of unemployment" determined by the labor market itself. By implication, government spending to run up budgetary deficits was ruled out as a useful instrument for stimulating the economy. On the contrary, governments could contribute to overall economic efficiency and growth by reducing social expenditure and downsizing the public sector, by reducing its workforce or privatizing nationalized industries.

In fact, monetarism reflected a radical change from the postwar consensus regarding economic management. Not only was active government intervention considered unnecessary, it was seen as undesirable and destabilizing. Monetary and fiscal policy should be passive, and intervention limited (so far as this was possible) to a few rules that would help foster appropriate rates of growth in the money supply and keep inflation as low as possible.

Differences in the strict theoretical meanings of Keynesianism and monetarism are not what mattered

Figure 5   Work Stoppages, 1970–1991

Source: Data from Butler and Butler (1986, p. 373); *Guardian*, 12 March 1992, from Bill Coxall and Lynton Robins, *Contemporary British Politics*, 2d ed. (London: Macmillan, 1994), 90. Reprinted by permission of *Guardian Weekly*.

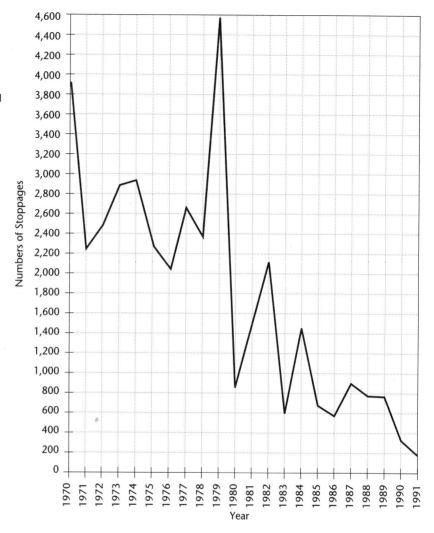

most in policy terms. In fact, British governments have never followed any economic theory consistently in the making of economic policy, and by the mid-1980s monetarism was quietly abandoned. Since then, economic policy has focused almost exclusively on controlling inflation. The political consequences of economic orientations are more significant: each economic doctrine helped to justify a broad *moral and cultural vision* of society, provide motives for state policy, and advance alternative sets of values. Should the government back off and allow the market to function competitively and thereby promote entrepreneurship, competitiveness, and individual autonomy? Or should it intervene, work to reduce inequalities through the mildly redistributive provisions of the welfare state, and sustain the ethos of a caring society? In this way, economic management strategies are closely linked to social or welfare policy.

Social Policy

Observers have noted that the social and political role of the welfare state depends as much on policy goals and instruments as on spending levels. Does the state provide services itself or offer cash benefits that can be used to purchase services from private providers? Are benefits limited to those who fall below an income threshold (means-tested) or universal? Are they designed to meet the temporary needs of individuals or to help redistribute resources between the more and less prosperous in society?

The expanded role of government during World War II and the increased role of the Labour Party during the wartime coalition government led by Winston Churchill prepared the way for the development of the welfare state in Britain. The 1943 Beveridge Report provided a blueprint for an extensive but, in comparative European terms, fairly shallow set of provisions. The welfare state in Britain offers relatively few comprehensive services, relies more on subsidies for private provision than on direct state provision of services, and stresses means-tested "safety-net" programs over universal provision. In general, welfare state provisions interfere only reluctantly in the workings of the market, and policymakers do not see the reduction of group inequalities as the proper goal of the welfare state. Although the National Health Service (NHS), for example, has provided comprehensive and universal medical care, much emphasis is placed on means-tested and relatively ungenerous assistance when compared to other Western European countries. The principle means-tested program is social security, a system of contributory and noncontributory benefits to provide financial assistance (not services directly) for the elderly, sick, disabled, unemployed, and others similarly in need of assistance.

Support for the policies of the welfare state runs high, but so does public dissatisfaction with the services provided. In a 1979 report, a group of public sector employees who worked on state-sponsored projects to improve services in inner cities captured the contradictory and limited character of British welfare services:

> Somehow what we get is never quite what we asked for. It is not just that state provision is inadequate, under-resourced and on the cheap. The way it is resourced and administered to us doesn't seem to reflect our real needs.

The report concluded with a widely shared sentiment: "State provision leaves a bad taste in our mouths."[16]

Ironically, these sentiments by social activists reenforced the criticism of Conservatives that the welfare state was inefficient, bureaucratized, and too expensive. As a result, by the time the 1970s brought heightened budgetary pressures, reduced provisions, and the growth of the British new right, the welfare state had few stalwart defenders. It was ripe both for ideological attack and for institutional and budgetary retrenchment.

The Welfare State Under Thatcher and Major   The record on social expenditure by Conservative governments since 1979 is mixed and, in a sense, less dramatic than the antiwelfarist stance (particularly of the Thatcher governments) would lead one to suppose. Against a backdrop of continued public support for public provision of education, pensions, and health care, Conservative governments have attempted more limited welfare reform than many at first anticipated. They have encouraged private provision alongside public provision in education, health care (insurance), and pensions, worked to increase efficiency in social services, reduced the value of some benefits by changing the formulae or reducing cost-of-living adjustments, and "contracted out" some services (purchased them from private contractors rather than providing them directly). In addition, in policy reforms reminiscent of "workfare" requirements for AFDC recipients that are now in place in many American states, the British have tried to reduce dependency by denying benefits to youths who refuse to participate in training programs.

Table 5 on the next page shows that in the period from 1979 to 1990, the commitment to reduced spending could not be easily sustained, partly because recession triggered rises in income support and unemployment benefits (included under the "Social Security" heading). In addition, there are some expenses that no government can easily contain. For example, the cost of health care provision has risen dramatically in the industrial democracies, no matter how the system is organized or what policy preferences the government chooses, because costs are linked to such nonpolicy factors as the increasing age of the population. The political scientist Paul Pierson has observed that through the 1980s "the relative size of the public sector has largely tracked the business cycle, rising in the early 1980s but then falling as the economy recovered."[17] Figure 6 shows British social expenditures for 1980 and 1990 in comparative perspective. Aggregate expenditures in Britain on social services as a proportion of gross domestic product (GDP) are relatively low by Western European standards, although much higher than those of the United States and Japan. The increase in the 1980s tends to parallel roughly the EC rate of increases in expenditure. Therefore, looked at in broad aggregates, government convictions about the welfare state do not seem as significant as one might suspect (see Figure 6).

TABLE 5   Government Spending, 1979/80, 1989/90

	1979–1980	1989–1990
Housing		
% of total	7.3	2.9
% of GDP	2.7	0.9
Defense		
% of total	11.9	11.7
% of GDP	4.7	4.0
Social Security		
% of total	25.9	29.7
% of GDP	9.6	10.2
Education and Science		
% of total	14.5	14.6
% of GDP	5.4	5.0
Health		
% of total	12.1	13.8
% of GDP	4.5	4.7
Law and Order		
% of total	4.1	5.6
% of GDP	1.5	1.9

Source: Data from the *Guardian,* 12 March 1992; derived and recalculated from Public Expenditure Analyses to 1994–1995, HM Treasury, in Bill Coxall and Lynton Robins, "Government Spending, 1979–1990" in *Contemporary British Politics,* 2d ed. (London: Macmillan, 1994), 482. Reprinted by permission of *Guardian Weekly.*

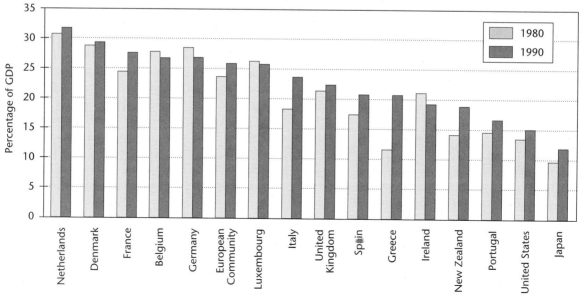

Figure 6   Social Protection Expenditure
Expenditures include health, social services, social security, and pensions.
Source: OECD, Eurostat, from Philip Allan, John Benyon, and Barry McCormick, eds., *Focus on Britain 1994* (Chicago: Fitzroy Dearborn Publishers, 1994), 177.

To a degree, however, this aggregate expenditure pattern masks specific and, in some cases, highly charged policy changes both in expenditure and in the institutionalized pattern of provision. In housing, the changes in state policy and provision were the most extensive, with repercussions both in electoral terms and in changing the way Britons think about the welfare state. Early on, Thatcher's housing policy became a major test case of her vision of society, as she emphasized private ownership and responsibility over public provision. Even before she was prime minister, Thatcher made housing a high-profile issue. During the 1979 campaign, she promised to give all tenants in council (public) housing the opportunity to buy their homes at up to 50 percent below market value.

She kept her promise. By 1990 more than 1.25 million council houses were sold—particularly the attractive single-family homes with gardens (quite unlike American public housing). Two-thirds of the sales were to rental tenants. In addition, Thatcher's housing policy was significant in political-electoral terms, beginning with her victory in the 1979 general election. As one observer noted, housing "was electorally crucial in dividing a working class movement, deeply disillusioned by the apparent inadequacies of the Welfare State and politically embittered by the economic policies pursued by the Labour government after 1976, by its populist appeal to the anti-bureaucratic, individualist and self-sufficient ideology of home ownership."[18] Electoral data supports this observation: By one calculation, between 1979 and 1983 there was a swing (change in the percentage of vote received by the two major parties) to the Conservative Party of 17 percent among those who bought their council houses.[19] By 1987, the swing by new buyers from Labour to Conservative was down to just 2 percent over the national trend, however. As the rise in adjustable mortgage rates (some 6 percent in 1988–1989 alone!) fueled a steep increase in monthly mortgage payments, the housing issue no longer worked to the advantage of the Conservative Party; it may have started cutting the other way.[20]

British Attitudes About the Welfare State   Despite great Conservative success in the campaign to privatize housing, a strong majority of Britons remain stalwart supporters of the principle of collective provision for their basic needs. Thus, limits are imposed on the ability of governments to alter policy. For example, Thatcher-era reforms to introduce market practices into the National Health Service (NHS) in 1989 raised objections by professional associations in the health care sector such as the British Medical Association (BMA). There was widespread concern that the creation of an "internal market"—with general practitioners, for example, managing funds and purchasing hospital care for their patients—would create incentives for doctors or hospitals to cut corners and reduce services to those with the fewest options. Many voiced fears that the internal market reforms would create a two-tier system of provision for rich and poor.

Thereafter, despite efforts by the Major government to demonstrate that it had spent more on health care than ever before and improved services, the health issue hurt him substantially in the 1992 election. Labour gained a commanding lead over the Conservatives on the health issue—a majority of two to one judged it the best party to run the NHS.[21] By the mid-1990s, much of the hostility to the reforms had faded, however, and Labour made it clear it had no intention to reverse the reforms if it came to power. The broad commitment to budgetary constraint and public sector efficiency represents an important element of an emerging new consensus at the pragmatic center of British politics in the mid-1990s. (We will return to this important theme in Section 5.)

Nevertheless, the political damage was done. Major has worked to distance himself from Thatcher's perceived disregard for the plight of the less fortunate. The government has increased welfare spending, in part, to persuade the electorate that the Conservatives could be trusted on the "caring" issues. Characteristically, and with some quiet success, Major has taken a pragmatic nonideological turn in welfare policy, looking for cuts and improvements at the same time, within a general framework that prefers means-tested to universal benefits. However, as Table 6 on the following page shows, Major has a long way to go in persuading the electorate that key social policies, such as health care and education (which also endured extensive "internal markets" reforms in the late 1980s), are safer in Conservative hands. As Table 6 indicates, confidence in Major's handling of the health service and state education has fallen since the 1992 election and remains very low.

TABLE 6   Social Policy Opinion Poll

Health Service
"The NHS is safer in Mr. Major's hands."

	1993	1992	1991	1990	Men	Women	Conservative	Labour	Liberal Democrat
Agree	13	27	30	18	14	13	43	4	6
Disagree	75	53	49	68	76	75	40	91	85
Difference	-62	-26	-19	-50	-62	-62	+3	-87	-79
Neither	8	11	13	9	7	8	12	3	6
Don't know	4	9	8	5	3	4	5	2	2

State Education
"State schools are safer in Mr. Major's hands."

	1993	1992	1991	1990	Men	Women	Conservative	Labour	Liberal Democrat
Agree	18	33	36	22	19	16	51	6	8
Disagree	69	47	44	61	69	70	31	89	79
Difference	-57	-14	-8	-39	-50	-54	+20	-83	-71
Neither	8	10	12	11	7	9	14	3	8
Don't know	5	10	9	6	5	5	4	3	5

Source: ICM "State of the Nation" poll published in the *Guardian*, 17 September 1993, in Bill Coxall and Lynton Robins, "Public Opinion Poll," in *Contemporary British Politics*, 2d ed. (London: Macmillan, 1994), 482. Reprinted by permission of *Guardian Weekly*.

TABLE 7   **Distribution of Marketable Wealth, 1976, 1989**

Percentage of Population	Percentage Owned of Marketable Wealth		Percentage Owned of Marketable Wealth plus Occupational and State Pension Rights	
	1976	1989	1976	1989
1	21	18	13	11
5	38	38	26	26
10	50	53	36	38
25	71	75	57	62
50	92	94	80	83

Source: *Social Trends* 22 (HM Stationery Office, 1992), 101, in Philip Norton, *The British Polity,* 3d ed. (New York and London: Longman, 1994), 19.

SOCIETY AND ECONOMY

It is at this juncture, where the attitude about and the conduct of economic and social policy converge, that the legacies of a long string of Conservative governments can best be seen. What are the *distributional effects*—the consequences for group patterns of wealth and poverty—of the economic and social policies of Thatcher and Major? How has government policy influenced the condition of minorities and women? It is impossible to distinguish fully the social consequences of government policy agendas from the consequences of economic performance (independent of policy preferences). The evidence is clear, however, that economic inequality has grown in Britain since the mid-1970s, and that ethnic minorities and women continue to experience significant disadvantages in economic and social terms.

Economic performance since the mid-1970s has increased economic inequality. Table 7 indicates that an already deeply unequal distribution of wealth in Britain in 1976 was further skewed by 1989. Although the share of marketable wealth (the value of assets such as stocks, cash, bank accounts, consumer durables, land, buildings, and houses) owned by the top 1 percent declined from 21 percent to 18 percent, the share owned by the top one-quarter rose from 71 percent to 75 percent. By the end of the 1980s, the more wealthy half of the population owned fully 94 percent of all national wealth, and the redistributive effects of assets linked to old-age pensions (and private pensions) had diminished.

As British journalist Peter Jenkins observed, a host of Thatcher-era policy outcomes—high unemployment, changes in tax policy that increased the tax burdens of the poor relative to the rich, the reduction in the real value of welfare benefits—led to increased inequality. In the 1980s there was much talk in Britain of "two nations" (rich and poor) and a frequent (usually critical) characterization of Thatcher, accordingly, as a "two-nation Tory." Jenkins takes the analysis a step further, suggesting that the upward pressure on the top end of the economic scale and the downward pressure on the bottom end have created a three-tiered society of "the haves, the have-nots, and the have-lots."

Policy initiated during the period of Conservative Party leadership beginning in 1979 tended to deepen inequalities, as poverty and diminished opportunity disproportionately characterized the situation of women in female-headed households and blacks (a term applied in Britain to peoples whose origins extend to Africa and the Caribbean, and also to South Asia, for example India or Pakistan).

Inequality and Ethnic Minorities

Britain has adjusted slowly and, by most accounts, poorly to the realities of a multiracial society. The postwar period has witnessed the gradual erosion of racial and religious-ethnic tolerance in Britain. Blacks, particularly youths, are subject to unequal treatment by the police and considerable physical harassment. With the general tightening of labor demand and high unemployment, ethnic and racial minorities have

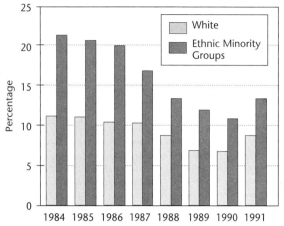

Figure 7   Unemployment Rates by Ethnic Origin, 1984–1991
Economically active persons of working age, measured in
Spring of each year.
Source: Labour Force Survey estimates, from Philip Allan,
John Benyon, and Barry McCormick, eds., *Focus on
Britain 1994* (Chicago: Fitzroy Dearborn Publishers, 1994),
198.

experienced cultural isolation as well as marginalization in the educational system, job training, and the
labor market. In addition, several developments in the
1980s and 1990s have combined with the downward
pressure of reduced welfare benefits and high unemployment to deepen the racial, ethnic, and religious
divisions in Britain.

During the Thatcher era, discussion of immigration and citizenship rights was used for partisan political purposes, and assumed a distinctly racial tone. In a
curious way, the Falklands/Malvinas War in 1982
deepened the cultural isolation of minorities. Many
expressed concerns that white Britons appeared to feel
more kinship or shared identity with white settlers
8,000 miles away in the South Atlantic than with ethnic minorities at home.[22]

The sense of cultural isolation within the ethnic
minority communities seems strong and these perceptions have deepened ethnic and racial—as distinct
from British—identities. "In defining ourselves we
sometimes say we are English or Welsh or Indian or
Jamaican," observed the Afro-Caribbean social theorist and cultural critic Stuart Hall. "Of course this is to
speak metaphorically. These identities are not im-
printed in our genes. However, we do think of them
as if they are part of our essential natures.[23] Few in
the minority communities are apt to identify them-

selves simply as part of a national culture—as
English—without reference to their subnational minority identity.

Poor rates of economic success reenforce the
sense of isolation and distinct collective identities.
Figure 7 indicates that a distinct gap remains between
the job opportunities available to whites and to ethnic
minorities in Britain, with unemployment highest
among people of Pakistani, Bangladeshi, or Afro-
Caribbean descent. It is important to note that this employment trend has continued despite evidence that
minority ethnic youths stay in school longer than
white students and that a higher proportion of Afro-
Caribbean women (37 percent) successfully complete
the course work necessary for university admission (A
levels) than do their white counterparts (31 percent).
In the mid-1990s, it seemed that "many of the better
educated minority ethnic people were denied employment on the basis of their background, and that people
of Pakistani and Bangladeshi origin constituted a
highly disadvantaged underclass."[24]

Inequality and Women

Women's participation in the labor market in Britain
is still disproportional in many respects. Both the
Thatcher and the Major governments have made clear
that management flexibility in hiring part-time workers and lowering labor costs would take priority over
efforts to reduce gender inequality in the workforce.
Of the 10.1 million jobs occupied by women in
1993, fully 4.6 million (more than 45 percent) were
part-time. In addition, women received on average
75 percent of men's earnings for the same job. The pay
differential compounded the effect of reduced status,
pension rights, opportunities for advancement, and
employment protection associated with part-time jobs.

As government policy encouraged management
flexibility in the assignment of work, the proportion of
working women in part-time (less secure, lower paid)
employment increased. Thus, in a context of welfare
state cutbacks in provision for those needing home
care, employment policy tended to "confirm the old
ideas that women worked only for pin money (money
to spend for nonessentials) or should stay at home and
care for their husbands, children and sick or elderly
relatives."[25] In addition, government policy tended to
worsen the often precarious situation of female heads
of household when the eligibility for income maintenance was tightened, the value of benefits was re-

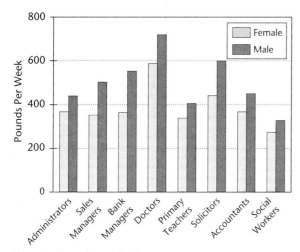

Figure 8 Comparison of Earnings
Source: Income Data Services, from Philip Allan, John
Benyon, and Barry McCormick, eds., *Focus on Britain 1994*
(Chicago: Fitzroy Dearborn Publishers, 1994), 195.

duced, and full-time work was replaced by part-time
work. Finally, as Figure 8 shows, even when women
were able to move up the job ladder, they encountered
serious problems: women in management positions
earned 25 percent less than their male counterparts and
54 percent of working women reported receiving "unwanted attentions" from men at work.[26]

BRITAIN AND THE INTERNATIONAL POLITICAL ECONOMY

From the period of the Industrial Revolution (discussed in Section 1) to the contemporary period, Britain has been more dependent than most countries on
international commerce for the creation of wealth in
all major facets of its economy, including production,
trade, finance, and investment. Because Britain's
economy is more interdependent with the global economy and therefore more exposed than most leading
industrial powers, it faces considerable external pressures on its economic policy. In this context, political
choices have significant economic consequences and
choices about economic policy become highly political. Either way, the consequences can be significant.
Two quite different but important cases—oil production and European integration—illustrate the interplay
between economics and politics in an era of global
interdependence.

Choices About North Sea Oil

For a relatively brief period, roughly coinciding with
the Thatcher years, Britain's oil production in the
North Sea helped shape the British economy in significant ways. On the one hand, at their peak in 1985–
1986, oil revenues cushioned the economy from other
sources of competitive decline, boosted state revenues, improved balance of payments, and counted for
about one-fifth of visible exports. On the other hand,
North Sea oil tended to increase the exchange rate of
sterling (the British currency) and therefore hurt British exports (by making them more expensive), and
weakened manufacturing industries more generally.
Moreover, the Thatcher economic approach called
for reduced public spending and taxation. Therefore, rather than using the oil revenues to increase
investment in industry to improve competitiveness,
the revenues were used to balance the books. This
controversial political decision had dire economic
consequences: just as oil revenues were peaking, the
tables were turned on Britain as for the first time since
the Industrial Revolution, British imports for manufacturing goods exceeded exports!

The Dilemmas of European Integration

After a period when the movement toward European
integration languished, and in large part as a response
to the pressure exerted by United States and Japanese
economic competition, the members of the EC ratified
the Single European Act which went into effect in
1987, and provided for a considerable deepening of
the process of European economic unification. They
selected December 31, 1992, as the date when physical barriers (such as passport controls), technical barriers (such as professional credentials or standards for
product safety), and fiscal (budgetary) barriers to free
economic relations within EC member states were to
be dismantled.

As difficult in economic and political terms as this
policy goal proved to be (the program was not fully
accomplished on schedule), the process of integration
was complicated further by the requirements of the
European Monetary System (EMS) introduced in
1979. The EMS fixed the values of the exchange rates
among member currencies (referred to as the Exchange Rate Mechanism or ERM), and permitted only
limited fluctuation above or below an agreed upon
band of exchange rates. Intended to stabilize European

economies and promote trade among members, its success depended on the willingness of member states to pursue compatible economic strategies—and on their ability to maintain similar growth rates and levels of inflation. In retrospect, this plan seems highly unrealistic. How likely were Spain, Portugal, Greece—or even Britain—to keep pace with Germany? But there was tremendous pressure to complete the process of integration rapidly before political disagreements or recession could close the window of opportunity.

Throughout the 1980s, Thatcher held firm in her opposition to British participation in the ERM, insisting on British sovereign control over its economic policy. However, a domestic policy focused overwhelmingly on keeping inflation to a bare minimum was not working. By 1990, "inflation rates were exploding towards 10 percent, thereby undermining many of the hard-won gains of the early 1980s and revealing Thatcher's claims of an economic miracle to be delusory."[27] In this context, Thatcher's anti-EC stance pitted her against senior ministers and leaders of Britain's EC partners as well as against the bulk of the British business community. It seemed that everyone but Thatcher thought participation in European integration would ease inflation in Britain and enhance its competitiveness.

In the end, Thatcher succumbed to the pressure to give up a measure of economic sovereignty, in effect, to Germany and its central bank (the *Bundesbank*), whose decisions would force Britain to follow in lockstep. She permitted Britain to join the ERM in October 1990, and, ironically, one month later she was toppled from office by a coup led by those in her own party who most deeply resented her handling of European policy.

For the new government of Prime Minister Major, participation in the ERM held enormous symbolic and political significance. As chancellor of the exchequer he had quietly pressed Thatcher to join, and as prime minister, he staked his reputation and bet the country's economic policy on its success. It was the cornerstone of his government's economic policy in the middle of an enduring recession: participation would stabilize European trade and was the key to his anti-inflationary strategy.

In September 1992, the European Monetary System shattered under the impact of downward pressures in the British economy and the strains of German unification. Under mounting debt from the expenses of absorbing the former German Democratic Republic (GDR), Germany raised interest rates to attract investments. This locked the United Kingdom into a high interest rate strategy, far from its own choosing, which contributed to a deepening recession. A desperate effort to prop up the value of sterling and keep Britain in the ERM by raising interest rates 5 percent in a single day failed. Britain suspended its participation in the ERM, sending the international money markets—and EC economic policy—skittering. The prime minister's reputation was badly damaged, and the momentum behind growing economic unity among EC countries was abruptly stalled. Neither support for John Major nor plans for economic integration in the EU have yet been put back on track. Remarkably, a single European policy (the ERM) led to Thatcher's downfall and has politically haunted John Major. The implications of Europe and European integration will be discussed further in Section 5.

As our world of states theme suggests, the introduction of a country into the global economic order diminishes national sovereign control and, as a consequence, raises unsettling questions in even the most established democracies. Amid complicated pressures, both internal and external, do state institutions retain the capacity to administer policy effectively? How much do the growth of powerful bureaucracies at home and complex dependencies abroad limit the ability of citizens to control policy ends? In Section 3, we turn to these questions.

SECTION 3

Governance and Policy-Making

An understanding of British governance begins with consideration of its constitution, which is notable for two significant features: its form and its antiquity. Britain lacks a formal written constitution in the usual sense, that is, a single unified and authoritative text that carries special status above ordinary law and can be amended only by special procedures. Rather, the British constitution is a combination of statutory law (mainly Acts of Parliament), common law, convention, and authoritative interpretations. Although it is often said that Britain has an unwritten constitution, this is not accurate. Authoritative legal treatises are written, of course, as are the much more significant Acts of Parliament that define fundamental elements of the British political system. These include acts that define the powers of Parliament, its relationship with the Crown, the rights governing the relationship between state and citizen, the relationship of constituent nations to the United Kingdom, the relationship of the United Kingdom to the European Union, and many others. Thus, it is probably best to say that "what distinguishes the British constitution from others is not that it is unwritten, but rather that it is part written and uncodified."[28]

More than its form, however, the British constitution's antiquity raises questions. It is hard to know when conventions and Acts of Parliament with constitutional implications began, but they can certainly be found dating back to the seventeenth century, notably with the Bill of Rights of 1689, which helped define the relationship between the monarchy and the Parliament, if not before. "Britain's constitution presents a paradox," observed a British scholar of constitutional history. "We live in a modern world but inhabit a premodern, indeed, ancient, constitution."[29] For example, several industrial democracies, including Spain, Belgium, and the Netherlands are constitutional monarchies, in which policy-making is left to the elected government and the monarch fulfills largely ceremonial duties. In fact, Western Europe contains the largest concentration of constitutional monarchies in the world.[30] However, Britain, alone among Western democracies, permits *two* unelected hereditary institutions—the Crown (the monarchy) and the House of Lords—to participate in governing the country (in the case of the Lords, sometimes quite significantly).

More generally, in many areas the structure and principles of government have been accepted by constitutional authorities for so long that appeal to convention has enormous cultural force. Thus, widely agreed-upon rules of conduct and conventions, rather than law or American-style checks and balances, set the limits of governmental power. Most of the time these rules constrain state officials from overstepping generally accepted boundaries and prevent any state institution from achieving undue concentration of power.

For example, after a general election the Crown (since 1952, Queen Elizabeth II), whatever her likes or dislikes for the individual or her private political preferences, will invite the leader of the victorious party to form a government. Similarly, that leader (now serving as prime minister) will surely ask the Crown to dissolve Parliament within five years, thereby introducing a new general election. Neither activity is required by statute nor specified in a written constitutional document, but no one in Britain harbors the least doubt that governments will be formed and parliaments dissolved as required by the constitution, that is, by binding custom.

Nevertheless, the absence of a single document of binding authority means that rules of conduct may be less than clear when a condition lacks sufficient precedent. For example, if no party is quite victorious after a general election—that is, if none has a clear-cut majority by itself in the House of Commons (a condition known as a "hung Parliament")—the conventions that govern the formation of a new government are not terribly clear.

As a leading constitutional authority recently observed, if the expectation that a general election would deliver a majority government no longer held, "[t]he Crown would presumably have to decide what the conventions were, and since party agreement is only one element in the make-up of conventions such an agreement might not be conclusive. . . ."[31] It may seem odd that such a *venerable* constitution is also *vulnerable* in such a basic matter as the formation of a government, but it is nonetheless.

This underscores an important observation about the principles of British government: *absolute* principles of British government are few. At the same time, those that exist are widely encompassing and central to governance, policy-making, and patterns of representation. We turn now to a brief discussion of the organization of the state and the relationships among the branches of government in Britain.

ORGANIZATION OF THE STATE

What are the central organizing principles of the British state? First, the core constitutional principle of the British political system and cornerstone of the Westminster model is **parliamentary sovereignty.** Parliament can make or overturn any law without recourse by the executive, the judiciary, or the throne. Only Parliament can nullify or overturn legislation approved by

Parliament. In a classic parliamentary democracy, the prime minister is answerable to the House of Commons (the elected element of Parliament) and may be dismissed by it.

Second, by contrast to the federal systems of Germany, India, Canada, or the United States, where power is shared between the central government and state or regional governments, Britain is a **unitary state.** By contrast to the United States, where powers not delegated to the national government are reserved for the states in accordance with the Tenth Amendment to the Constitution, no powers are reserved constitutionally for subnational units of government in the United Kingdom.

Third, Britain operates within a system of **fusion of powers** at the national level: Parliament is the supreme legislative, executive, and judicial authority and is comprised of the monarch as well as the House of Commons and the House of Lords. The fusion of legislature and executive is also expressed in the function and personnel of the cabinet. Whereas American presidents can direct or ignore their cabinets, which have no constitutionally mandated function, the British cabinet bears enormous constitutional responsibility. Through its collective decision making, the cabinet—and not an independent prime minister—shapes, directs, and takes responsibility for government. Cabinet government stands in stark contrast to presidential government, and is perhaps the most unique feature, certainly the center, of Britain's system of government, because it is in this body, where the executive and legislature overlap, that control of government rests.

Finally, sovereignty rests with the Queen-in-Parliament (the formal term for Parliament). Britain is a constitutional monarchy: the position of head of state passes by hereditary succession, but nearly all powers of the Crown must be exercised through officers selected and bound by convention and law. Taken together, parliamentary sovereignty, parliamentary democracy, and cabinet government form the core elements of the Westminster model and the central principles of British government, which many consider a model democracy and the first effective parliamentary democracy. How well has the British model of government stood the test of time—and radically changed circumstances?

The absence of legally enforceable limits to the exercise of power raises questions about the gap between democratic ideal and political reality in Britain. Can a willful prime minister overstep the generally agreed limits of the collective responsibility of the cabinet and achieve an undue concentration of power? Has the fusion of branches of central government in a unitary state led to an overconcentration of power at the top and a threat to the ability of citizens below to exercise control over their government? Do age-old conventions and the legacies of premodern institutions limit the capacity of the British state to manage fast-paced contemporary affairs in an era of powerful new institutions like the European Union?

These questions underscore the problems faced even by the most stable democracies. They also help identify important comparative themes, because the organizing principles of the British state contained in the Westminster model were, with some modifications, adopted widely by former colonies ranging from Canada, Australia, and New Zealand to India, Jamaica, and Zimbabwe. So British success (or failure) in maintaining the core values of control by citizens over their government have far-reaching implications well beyond the British Isles. We begin our discussion of British state institutions of governance and policy-making with the executive, focusing on cabinet government in both theory and practice.

THE EXECUTIVE

The commonplace characterization of British government as *cabinet government* leaves much unsaid about the operations of the executive (or policy-making and implementing) part of the British state. In fact, the executive extends from ministries (departments) and ministers to the civil service in one direction, and to Parliament (as we shall see in Section 4) in the other direction. However, the expression *cabinet government* is useful in emphasizing the key functions it exercises: responsibility for policy-making, supreme control of government, and coordination of all government departments.

Cabinet Government

After a general election, the Crown invites the leader of the party which emerges from the election with control of a majority of seats in the House of Commons to form a government and serve as prime minister. That process begins with the prime minister's selection of approximately twenty ministers to constitute the cabinet (the number can vary). In 1994, John Major's cabi-

---

TABLE 8 The Conservative Cabinet in April 1994

Prime Minister	John Major
Lord Chancellor	Lord Mackay of Clashfern
Foreign Secretary	Douglas Hurd
Home Secretary	Michael Howard
Chancellor of the Exchequer	Kenneth Clarke
Lord Privy Seal and Leader of the House of Lords	Lord Wakeham
Chancellor of the Duchy of Lancaster	William Waldegrave
Environment	John Gummer
Defence	Malcolm Rifkind
Education	John Patten
Lord President of the Council and Leader of the House of Commons	Tony Newton
Transport	John MacGregor
Employment	David Hunt
Trade and Industry	Michael Heseltine
Social Security	Peter Lilley
Health	Virginia Bottomley
Agriculture	Gillian Shephard
Northern Ireland	Sir Patrick Mayhew
Wales	John Redwood
Scotland	Ian Lang
National Heritage	Peter Brooke
Chief Secretary to the Treasury	Michael Portillo

Source: Bill Coxall and Lynton Robins, *Contemporary British Politics,* 2d ed. (London: Macmillan, 1994), 133.

---

net included twenty-two members (see Table 8). The most significant assignments include the foreign office (equivalent to an American secretary of state), the home office (Ministry of the Interior), and the chancellorship of the exchequer (a more powerful version of a treasury secretary).

Constitutional convention requires that members of the cabinet be selected mainly from the House of Commons, although a few members of the House of Lords are often included. A combination of political prudence and convention ordinarily dictates that cabinet members represent diverse political tendencies within the prime minister's party. In general, technical expertise in the affairs of a particular ministry is less important than national reputation and the need to balance different "wings" of the party in selecting ministers.

The responsibilities of a cabinet minister are immense. "The Cabinet, as a collective body, is responsible for formulating the policy to be placed before Parliament and is also the supreme controlling and directing body of the entire executive branch," notes S. E. Finer. "Its decisions bind all Ministers and other officers in the conduct of their departmental busi-

ness."[32] In contrast to the French Constitution, which prohibits a cabinet minister from serving in the legislature, British constitutional tradition *requires* overlapping membership between Parliament and cabinet. Unlike the informal status of the U.S. cabinet, its British counterpart enjoys considerable constitutional privilege and is a powerful institution with enormous strategic significance for both the political and administrative success of the government.

The cabinet system is a complex patchwork of conflicting obligations and potential divisions. Each cabinet member who is a departmental minister has responsibilities to the *ministry* that he or she must run; and, unless he or she is a member of the House of Lords, a cabinet member is also linked to a *constituency,* or electoral district (as an elected member of Parliament or MP), to the *party* (as a leader and, often, a member of its executive board), to the *prime minister* (as an appointee who shares in the duties of a plural executive), and to a *political tendency* within the party (as a leading proponent of a particular social vision).

Because of the prestige and significance of the cabinet, and given the independent reputations and standing of its members, the cabinet room at Number 10 Downing Street (the prime minister's official residence) is a place of intrigue as well as collective deliberation. There is an old maxim about British politics: "Where there is death, there is hope." And short of death, there is always the chance that the prime minister will fail. Either way, almost inevitably, the prime minister's successor as party leader and potential prime minister will emerge from the ranks of the cabinet (or former cabinet members). From the perspective of the prime minister, the cabinet may appear as a collection of ideological combatants, potential challengers for party leadership, and parochial advocates for ministerial advantages that often run counter to the overall programmatic objectives of the government.

Against this background of drama and high-stakes scheming, the convention of collective responsibility normally assures the continuity of government by unifying the cabinet on matters of policy. The principle of collective responsibility requires that all ministers are bound to support any action taken by an agency in the name of the government, whether or not the action was discussed in the cabinet or known to the minister in advance. This makes the probability of parliamentary support extremely high. In principle, the prime minister must gain the support of a majority of the cabinet for a range of significant decisions, notably the budget and the legislative program. The only other constitutionally mandated mechanism for checking the prime minister is through a defeat by a vote of no confidence in the Commons (discussed in Section 4), which is rarely used because it results in the collective resignation of cabinet or dissolution of Parliament and a new general election. Thus, except for these radical and uncommon gestures of defiance, the potential for the cabinet to constrain the action of the chief executive remains the only routine check on prime ministerial power. Collective responsibility is therefore a crucial aspect of the Westminster model of democracy.

Insofar as collective responsibility is a fluid principle, its interpretation is subject to the discretion of the prime minister, thereby making it a political resource. By contrast to her more pragmatic Labour predecessors who generally sought consensus in cabinet, Thatcher more often attempted to galvanize loyalists in cabinet and either marginalize or expel detractors with her strong ideological convictions. Therefore, controversial issues (such as the proposed reorganization of health provision in 1988–1989) were often decided by hand-picked members of cabinet in combination with personal advisers and senior civil servants. In this way, Thatcher often avoided full cabinet scrutiny of critical policies.

In addition, she was increasingly accused of intimidating opponents within the cabinet by shuffling cabinet posts and threats of dismissal. By keeping cabinet members off guard and casting out those who challenged her leadership, Thatcher reduced the variety of opinion represented in the cabinet and limited its classic functions as a powerful instrument of collective deliberation. Thatcher even went so far as to refer to the cabinet as her "political advisers," and they were "made to feel their major responsibility lay upwards to Downing Street rather than outwards to parliament and country."[33] The use of personal advisers outside the cabinet to circumvent the responsible cabinet minister came to a flash point in October 1989 when one of Thatcher's longest serving and most respected ministers, Chancellor of the Exchequer Nigel Lawson, resigned in a dispute over the role of the prime minister's personal economic adviser. In the end, Thatcher's treatment of the cabinet stretched British constitutional conventions.

Many observers of Thatcher's government thought the British cabinet was losing its vital role as a check on the prime minister and becoming more advisory and less independently powerful like its American counterpart. Thatcher's treatment of the cabinet is an interesting test case for the elasticity of a "part written and uncodified" constitution. She may have overstepped the boundaries of prime ministerial power, and her treatment of the cabinet undoubtedly contributed to her downfall. Major has returned to a more consultative approach, in keeping with the classic model of cabinet government.

Alongside collective responsibility, members of the cabinet assume explicit individual ministerial responsibility for personal or private misconduct and, more importantly, for administrative or political misjudgment. Responsibility is taken seriously: it means resignation. Since 1900, more than one hundred ministers have resigned, although far more often for personal misconduct or to avoid being fired than out of high political principle or to take responsibility for an administrative error committed within their departments.

The Thatcher and Major governments witnessed sixteen resignations through 1993 that fell, at least

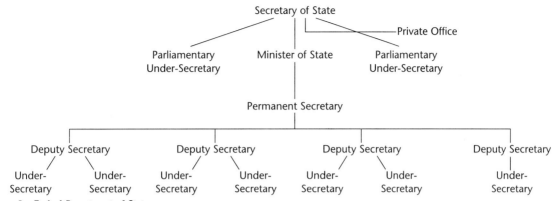

Figure 9   Typical Department of State
Source: Bill Coxall and Lynton Robins, *Contemporary British Politics*, 2d ed. (London: Macmillan, 1994), 148.
Reprinted by permission of the Macmillan Press Ltd.

partly, under the principle of individual responsibility. In a classic illustration of this rule (and its political use to insulate the prime minister), the foreign secretary, Lord Carrington, and two colleagues resigned after the Argentine invasion of the disputed Falkland/Malvina Islands in 1982 for failing to anticipate the invasion, perhaps the only postwar instance of strict resignation for bungled ministerial responsibilities. Most typical have been resignations over sexual misconduct or public relations blunders—from terrifying the populace over salmonella-poisoned eggs to excessively pointed criticism of Germany in the run-up to unification. Since 1994, there have been a rash of scandals and resignations both of cabinet members and MPs, and the growing concern over the "sleaze factor" in John Major's government will be discussed in Section 5.

On balance, cabinet government and the fusion of legislature and executive represent a durable and effective formula for governance. There is no Washington-style gridlock (the inability of legislature and executive to agree on policy) in London! On the contrary, if there is a problem at the pinnacle of national power, it is not the separation of powers, but the potential for excessive concentration of power by a prime minister who is prepared to manipulate cabinet and blunt the force of collective responsibility.

Bureaucracy and Civil Service

Viewed from 10 Downing Street, the policy-making functions of the state may appear to be increasingly concentrated in the prime minister's hands. At the same time, viewed from Whitehall (the London nerve center of the civil service), the executive may appear to be dominated by its vast administrative agencies. The expanded range and tremendous complexity of state policy-making mean in practice that the cabinet's authority must be shared with a vast set of unelected officials. Figure 9 illustrates the structure of a typical department of state.

In organizational terms, ministers (a generic term for holders of high executive office) who are in charge of government departments (and therefore cabinet members) will have the formal title *secretary of state for X*, where *X* designates the ministry, such as Defense or Employment. Alternatively, they may have a special title such as chancellor of the exchequer (equivalent to a finance minister or secretary of the treasury). To help bridge the closely linked functions of policy-making and the administration and implementation of policy, each secretary has a few political assistants (appointed by the prime minister in consultation with the secretary). These *ministers of state* may take responsibilities for specific policy areas and often assume some discretionary authority over policy. *Junior ministers* act as intermediaries with the nonpolitical bureaucracy of the civil service and may also assume responsibility for particular departmental duties.

Because ministers of state and junior ministers are nearly always MPs (or occasionally Lords), the fusion of legislature and executive is expressed in the daily management of departments. These political appointments are highly sought as the inside track to subsequent cabinet membership, and they are paid positions. Ministers of state and junior ministers are considered to be part of the government and, together with the members of the cabinet, may number roughly one hundred. Because ministers even below the level of cabinet are bound by the principles of collective responsibility, and their career path probably depends on loyalty to their superiors, the government begins every debate in the Commons with a large, absolutely solid voting bloc. "The crucial core of support," notes one scholar of British politics, "is referred to somewhat derisively as the payroll vote."[34]

How is the interaction between the civil service and the cabinet ministers (and their political assistants) coordinated? A very senior career civil servant, called a *permanent secretary,* has chief administrative responsibility for running a department. The permanent secretaries are assisted, in turn, by other senior civil servants, including deputy secretary and under secretary (the top three grades of senior civil servants number some 650). There are approximately 77,000 senior executives a few rungs down from the level of interaction with ministers and junior ministers. In addition, the minister reaches into his or her department to appoint a *principal private secretary,* an up-and-coming civil servant, who assists the minister as gatekeeper and liaison with senior civil servants. In 1992, the total number of civil service personnel was just over 400,000, down from a high of some 730,000 in 1979.

Although "permanent secretaries are the main filter through which departmental business is purified, reduced and made palatable for ministerial consumption," the interface between the politicians and administrative officials is somewhat more diffuse.[35] Because policy-making and policy implementation or administration are intertwined, successful policy requires translation of policy goals into actual policy instruments. With nearly all legislation introduced on behalf of the government and presented as the policy directive of a ministry, civil servants do the work of conceptualizing and refining legislation that is done by committee staffers in the U.S. Congress. In practice, civil servants more than ministers assume operational duties and, despite a certain natural level of mutual mistrust and incomprehension, the two must work closely together. To the impartial, permanent, and anonymous civil servants, ministers are too political, unpredictable, and temporary—and they are tireless self-promoters who may neglect or misunderstand the

needs of the ministry. To a conscientious minister, the permanent secretary may be protecting "his" or "her" department too strenuously from constitutionally proper oversight and direction. Without a sharp delineation between the responsibilities of ministers and civil servants, there is no choice but to execute policy in tandem.

The roughly 400,000 civil servants are engaged in a wide range of state activities. Approximately half are involved in delivering services—from the welfare state provisions of sickness benefits or pensions to the staffing of prisons. Fully one-quarter work for the Ministry of Defense. The remaining quarter are involved in various policy and central administrative duties and a range of services such as Inland Revenue (the equivalent to the Internal Revenue Service in the United States).

Like ministers, civil servants are servants of the Crown, but are not part of the government. A change of minister or government, whatever the cause, does not involve a change in departmental staffs. Civil servants are highly respected for their traditional anonymity and political neutrality, and for the technical expertise and continuity they contribute to policy-making. The structure and behavior of the British civil service is often considered a model of politically insulated, efficient administration, free of the partisanship, insider dealing, and corruption found in many bureaucracies, particularly in postcommunist, post-authoritarian, and postcolonial regimes. When policy-making is discussed below, this characterization is revealed as only partly accurate.

The significant—and growing—influence of civil servants (and the size of the bureaucracy) raises important questions about the proper role of unelected officials in a democratic polity. Indeed, the civil service has been assaulted from many directions. Since the early 1980s, the pace of change at Whitehall has been very fast, with governments looking to cut the size of the civil service, streamline its operations, and enhance its accountability to citizens. Beyond these pressures, the frustration of civil servants was deepened by Thatcher's effort to reduce their number and make the civil service more efficient in management terms—and by her evident impatience with the time-worn customs of impartiality and red tape that hindered her aggressive policy agenda.

In addition, the reinvigoration of parliamentary select committees has complicated the civil service role. Traditionally, ministers serve as the political heads of departments—not the civil servants—and take responsibility for policy and face scrutiny in Parliament. Constitutionally, civil servants have no responsibility or role distinct from their minister. The system assumed that civil servants were not answerable for policy, and would keep the operations of their department (embarrassing to a minister or otherwise) confidential. Although tradition requires senior civil servants to testify on behalf of their ministers, the more aggressive stance of select committees in recent years has, for the first time, pressed them to testify, in effect, *against* their ministers, if need be to satisfy parliamentary concerns about misconduct or poor judgment (this will be discussed in Section 4).

The Secretary of the Cabinet (who oversees the conduct of cabinet business under the direction of the prime minister) observed in 1993 that in the last decade the civil service had faced "restructuring, the delegation of management, market testing, open competition for appointments and greater openness of information."[36] He remained optimistic about the continued cohesiveness and shared ethic and values of the civil service, and about its future, despite all the pressures. Not all share his view, as some describe a situation of crisis, loss of morale, and uncertainty about their position. With day-to-day operational responsibility for the affairs of state, civil servants know that ministerial responsibility is often a fiction, but they are worried about the unpredictable scrutiny they now face.

Nationalized Industries

The nationalization of basic industries was a central objective of the Labour government's program in the immediate postwar period. Between 1946 and 1949, the Bank of England was nationalized, and coal, iron and steel, gas and electricity supply, and the bulk of the transport sector became public corporations. By 1960, the nationalized industries accounted for about 18 percent of total fixed investment, produced about one-tenth of the national income, and employed some 8 percent of the U.K. workforce.[37] Table 9 on the next page lists the major nationalized industries in 1975.

With nationalization, the British state added *market-replacing* functions to its economic policy instruments. Replacing private entrepreneurs and acting through publicly constituted boards of directors for each industry, the state now hired, bargained with, and

fired workers; paid the bills; set pricing policies; and invested, planned, and presided over a vast industrial empire. It appeared the ability of private entrepreneurs to control the economy had been dealt a stunning blow. Or had it? A closer look at the public sector reveals a different picture. Given the woeful condition of many of these basic industries in 1945, some comprehensive state intervention was necessary for reconstruction. Compensation to the displaced stockholders and capitalist owners was high, and the new governing boards were dominated by people whose ideology and social background led them to trust professional management and preserve its traditional powers against unions and workers. Many directors were the captains of industry from the days of private ownership.

Nationalization involved the creation of state monopolies backed by public financing that could operate more effectively than the smaller undercapitalized firms they had replaced. The state takeover of industries was designed to ensure the cheap and reliable provision of essential fuel supplies and transport, to facilitate a modicum of central coordination of personnel and investment planning, and to improve productive efficiency.

The nationalized industries have operated by principles that give all of the advantages and none of the risk to private capitalists—for example, "buy dear" (at a high price) from the private sector and "sell cheap." Private firms made a profit from selling materials and equipment and saw their costs of production drop with the steady and relatively cheap supply of basic fuel and energy, for example. In addition, statutory guidelines required publicly owned enterprises to break even on the average of good and bad years until 1967, and stricter targets for profitability were introduced thereafter. During the 1970s and especially since Thatcher's rejection of the collectivist consensus began in 1979, the boards of the nationalized industries have practiced increasingly hard-edged industrial relations strategies to defeat public sector unions in both political and industrial terms.

Since the 1980s, a high-profile and ideologically driven campaign begun by Thatcher and continued by Major has urged the privatization of publicly owned industries and the reduction of the size of the public sector (which had already been shrinking). Nearly a million workers transferred from public to private sector employment, and by 1995 the output of the nationalized sector was less than half the percentage of

TABLE 9 **Major Nationalized Industries**

	Shares in Total U.K. Economy in 1975 (% of total)			
	Output	Employment	Investment	Domestic Market
Nationalized Before 1945				
Post Office & Telecommunications[a] (1635–1710)	2.8	1.8	4.5	100
Electricity Board (1926)	1.5[b]	0.7[b]	2.9[b]	100[c]
British Airways[d] (1939)	0.3	0.2	0.4	76
Nationalized 1945–1964				
National Coal Board (1946)	1.5	1.2	0.9	96[c]
British Railways Board (1947)	1.2	1.0	1.0	8[e]
National Bus Company (1947)	0.2	0.3	0.1	34
National Freight Corporation (1947)	0.2	0.2	—	10
British Gas Corporation (1948)	0.8	0.4	1.7	100[c]
British Steel Corporation (1951, 1967)	0.8	0.9	2.0	56
Nine Major Nationalized Industries	9.2	6.7	13.6	
Other Nationalized Industries	0.4	0.2	0.8	
All Nationalized Industries	9.6	6.9	14.4	
Other Public Corporations	1.4	1.1	4.6	
All Public Corporations	11.0	8.0	19.0	

NOTE: The following were nationalized after 1970: Rolls Royce (1971), British Leyland (1975), British National Oil Corporation (1976), British Shipbuilders (1977), British Aerospace (1977).
[a]British Telecommunications became a separate corporation in 1981 and was privatized in 1984.
[b]England and Wales only.
[c]In 1975, gas accounted for 22%, coal 19%, electricity 13%, and oil (then still imported) 46% of final consumption of energy.
[d]British Overseas Airways Corporation formed 1939; British European Airways 1946; merged 1972–1974.
[e]Of total passenger/km: 47% of freight tonne/km.

Source: Colin Leys, *Politics in Britain: From Labourism to Thatcherism* (London: Verso, 1989), 326.

GDP it had been in 1975. Table 10 shows the major privatizations from 1979 to the present. The privatization campaign had important cultural and political implications as part of Thatcher's effort to advance the enterprise culture of competitiveness and business initiative, and to forge new electoral identities. The implications of privatization will be discussed in Section 4.

Nondepartmental Public Bodies

Along with nationalized industries and formal government departments, processes of state policy-making in the past thirty years have encouraged the transfer of a growing set of administrative functions to a new generation of quasi-nongovernmental organizations (quangos). There are three kinds of nondepartmental public bodies: executive bodies, tribunals, and advisory bodies or agencies. *Executive bodies* operate within broad ministerial guidelines, but with considerable latitude. Examples include the Arts Council and the Commission for Racial Equality. *Tribunals* are judicial bodies that often have a regulatory function and that operate outside the formal court system. Important examples are industrial tribunals, which consider claims of unfair dismissal and pay discrimination on gender or racial lines; other tribunals review rent increases, social welfare benefits appeals, decisions concerning immigration, and similar matters. Many governmental departments have *advisory bodies or agencies,* usually appointed by the responsible minister charged with assisting departments by making specific policy recommendations.

TABLE 10   **Major Privatizations, 1979–1994**

Industry	Date of Sale
British Petroleum	1979/1981/1983/1987
British Aerospace	1981/1985
Cable & Wireless	1981/1983/1985
Amersham International	1982
National Freight Consortium	1982
Britoil	1982/1985
Associated British Ports	1983/1984
Enterprise Oil	1984
Jaguar	1984
British Telecom	1984
British Gas	1986
British Airways	1987
Royal Ordnance	1987
Rolls Royce	1987
British Airports Authority	1987
Rover Group	1988
British Steel	1988
Water Companies (10)	1989
Electricity Companies (12)	1990
National Power/Powergen	1991
Scottish Electricity Companies	1991
British Telecom	1993
British Coal Corporation	1994

Source: Based on T. Butcher, "Rolling Back the State," *Talking Politics* 4, no. 2 (Winter 1991/2), in Bill Coxall and Lynton Robins, *Contemporary British Politics,* 2d ed. (London: Macmillan, 1994), 176.

The early Thatcher years witnessed "quango-hunting." Like the campaign to reform the civil service, it was part of a drive to enhance efficiency and accountability of the public sector, and cut its size wherever possible. However, the nondepartmental public bodies enjoy considerable administrative and political advantages. They take responsibility for specific functions and can combine governmental and private sector expertise. At the same time, ministers can distance themselves from controversial areas of policy, such as race relations, arms sales, or aspects of health care delivery during the phasing in of internal market reforms.

By the early 1990s, the process of eliminating quangos had been refined, and a new generation of powerful, broadly defined, and well-funded quangos replaced the smaller-scale quangos of the past. A survey in 1990–1991 revealed that quangos were spending three times as much as they had in 1978–1979. The growth was particularly significant in locally appointed agencies, including bodies charged with responsibility in education, job training, health, and housing. By 1994, quangos were responsible for one-fifth of all public spending and more than three-quarters of local government spending. Key areas of public policy that had previously been under the political and budgetary authority of local government were now being controlled by quangos, which are nonelected bodies. Across the political spectrum, some have expressed concern that principles of democratic control are compromised by the power of quangos which are not clearly responsible or accountable to the electorate. In addition, some see the growth of local quangos as contributing to the increased concentration and centralization of power, in which agencies appointed by ministers displace functions of local government. We will return below to consider local government in Britain, but we move now to a discussion of the military and police.

The Military and Police

From the local bobby to the most senior military officer, those involved in security and law enforcement have enjoyed a rare measure of popular support in Britain. Public opinion polls show the army and the police scoring one and two, respectively, in a ranking of institutions in which Britons have confidence. Constitutional tradition and professionalism distance the British police and military from politics—they harbor virtually no political ambitions and have traditionally steered clear of partisan use. Nevertheless, in recent decades both institutions have been placed in more politically controversial and exposed positions.

In the case of the military, British policy in the post–Cold War period remains heavily focused on a gradually redefined set of NATO commitments. Ranked among the top five military powers in the world, Britain retains a global presence, and the Conservative governments of Thatcher and Major have deployed forces in ways that have enhanced their political positions and maximized Britain's global influence. In the Falklands/Malvinas conflict in 1982, Britain soundly defeated Argentina in a war over disputed territory in the South Atlantic. In the Persian Gulf War of 1991, Britain deployed a full armored division in the UN-sanctioned force arrayed against Iraq's Saddam Hussein. Only the United States made a greater military commitment. In the mid-1990s, after quite heroic but unavailing diplomatic efforts by former Foreign Secretary David Owen on behalf of the EU, the British tried to support a diplomatic settlement in the bloody war raging in Bosnia by committing forces under United Nations mandate.

The popularity and success of these missions (except for Bosnia) must be measured, however, against the more controversial role of the military in the dispute in Northern Ireland. After a civil rights movement calling for Catholic political and economic equality helped provoke Protestant riots in the autumn of 1969, the British government sent troops to Northern Ireland. At least until the cessation of paramilitary activities in 1994, it was hard to disassociate the British army from the brutality and deadly violence on all sides. Caught amid the brutal political violence between the paramilitary organizations of the unionist and republican communities, the British army was subject to grim accusations that it violated the human rights of detainees and was used as a partisan political instrument to repress Irish nationalism. Few recruits—Britain has an all volunteer army—were able to avoid a tour of duty patrolling the streets of Belfast.

As for the police, which traditionally operate as independent local forces throughout the country, the period since the 1980s has witnessed growth in government control, centralization, and level of political use. The coal miners' strike of 1984–1985, the longest and most violent in postwar Britain, raised significant questions about the political roles forced on the police (and, as we shall see, the judiciary) by the Thatcher government. In practice, police operated to an unprecedented—and perhaps unlawful—degree as a national force coordinated through Scotland Yard (London police headquarters). Police menaced strikers and hindered miners from participating in strike support activities. This partisan use of the police to support government policy in an industrial dispute flew in the face of constitutional traditions and offended some police officers and officials. Moreover, a pattern of hostile behavior by police in minority communities—which helped provoke riots in the London neighborhoods of Brixton and Toxteth in the summer of 1981—has focused public attention on the political implications of policing in Britain. During the 1990s, there has been increased concern about police/community relations including race relations, corruption, and the interrogation and treatment of people held in custody.

The entire criminal justice system, including the police and the judiciary, has received harsh scrutiny in recent years. As the authoritative British newsweekly, *The Economist,* observed, the system has spawned "a long list of miscarriages caused by faulty, fabricated or withheld evidence, uncorroborated confessions, biased comments by judges, police misbehaviour and the reluctance of the Court of Appeal to overturn jury verdicts."[38] In July 1993, the Royal Commission on Criminal Justice proposed 352 recommendations for overhauling criminal justice. Because British culture so strongly identifies the police with the smiling local bobby, there is relatively little tolerance for police misconduct, which is comparatively low. The report left few satisfied and underscored growing concerns that problems abound.

OTHER STATE INSTITUTIONS

As the preceding discussion outlined, given the expanded responsibilities of the state in the postwar period, British public administration extends well beyond its tradition focus on finance or foreign affairs or law and order, although these policy areas remain critical. In this section, we turn our focus to the judiciary and local government.

The Judiciary

The function of the British judiciary has been far more limited than that of its significant continental (French, German) or U.S. counterparts. In the United States, for instance, the Supreme Court used the 1803 *Marbury* v. *Madison* decision to secure its right to decide the constitutionality of actions by the executive and legislative branches of government, thereby limiting their power through **judicial review.** In Britain, however, the principle of parliamentary sovereignty has limited the role of the judiciary. Courts have no power to judge the constitutionality of legislative acts; they can only determine whether policy directives or administrative acts violate common law or an Act of Parliament.

Because it is not mandated to set policy on controversial issues (such as a woman's right to abortion or the limits of affirmative action), the British judiciary is generally less politicized and influential than its American counterpart. In recent decades, however, governments have pulled the courts into political battles over the conduct of public policy concerning the rights of local councils, the role of police and trade unions in industrial disputes, and the activities of police in urban riots. For example, the courts played a controversial role in the 1984–1985 miners' strike discussed above. They interpreted the new Employment Act of 1982 very broadly, freezing the entire assets of the miners' union, a decision that helped tip the balance in the dispute toward the government. Moreover, in a decision that confounded many, the Court of Appeal rejected an unusual application by the local police authority in Northumbria to compel the home secretary (the cabinet minister responsible for the administration of justice) to withdraw instructions for the aggressive use of a powerful tear gas and plastic bullets to disperse the miners. At a stroke, the decision showed the new and controversial political role of the courts, advanced the centralized cabinet-level (hence political) control over policing, and affirmed an ancient royal prerogative against the local police authorities.

Jurists have also participated in the wider political debate outside of court, as when they have headed royal commissions on the conduct of industrial relations, the struggle in Northern Ireland, and riots in Britain's inner cities. Some observers of British politics are concerned that governments have used judges in these ways to secure partisan ends, displace criticism, and weaken traditions of parliamentary scrutiny of government policy and conduct by taking the inquiries out of Parliament and giving them to blue-ribbon commissions handpicked by ministers.

The fact that newly activist and politicized courts (by British, if not by American, standards) are increasingly called into the breach when the normal interplay of party, interest organization, and institutional politics cannot resolve contemporary disputes raises serious questions about British democracy. Should nonelected officials, as are all senior judges, be granted such a powerful role in resolving disputes among interests in society and, indirectly, in social and economic policy formation?

Another type of involvement has been forced on British courts by the United Kingdom's extranational entanglements. Parliament passed the European Communities Act in 1972 to seal Britain's entry into the European Community, with the provision that existing European Community (now European Union, or EU) law be binding on the United Kingdom. In any conflict between British law and EU law, EU law prevails. The act specifies that British courts must adjudicate any disputes of interpretation that arise from EU law. In addition, the Treaty of Rome (the treaty that established the EC, to which the United Kingdom is bound by the terms of its membership) specifies that cases reaching the highest domestic appeals court—the House of Lords—be sent to the European Court of Justice (ECJ) for final ruling.

Moreover, as a signatory to the European Convention on Human Rights, Britain is required to comply with the rulings of the European Court of Justice on Human Rights (ECJHR) in Strasbourg. Interestingly, a set of extremely embarrassing decisions by the ECJHR concerning Britain's interrogation procedures in Northern Ireland resulted in some procedural changes; recently, in September 1995, the court ruled that Britain unlawfully killed three IRA members in a 1988 action by undercover soldiers in Gibraltar. In addition, two decisions by the ECJ led to the enactment of the Sex Discrimination Act of 1986 because previous legislation did not provide the full guarantees of women's rights in employment mandated to all members by the EC's Equal Treatment Directive. The pace of supranational influences on Britain, in legal as in other policy areas, will probably increase throughout the 1990s as EU economic and political integration proceed. Politically, the binding nature of EU laws and regulations is likely to fuel the fear that Britain is losing sovereign control, whether to jurists in Strasbourg or to bureaucrats in Brussels.

Subnational Government

Because the British political framework is unitary, not federal, no formal powers devolve to states or regions as in the United States, India, or Germany. Although no powers are constitutionally reserved to local governments, they historically had considerable autonomy in financial terms and discretion in implementing a host of social service and related policies. In the 1950s and 1960s, local government was irrelevant in national policy debates. Suddenly, Britain woke up in the 1970s to the political and administrative significance of local government. For example, an administrative reorganization of the National Health Service gave local government (councils) greater participation in implementing policies for health care and medical provisions.

In the early 1980s, councils began to pursue experimental and often contrasting policies. Conservative councils introduced the practice of contracting out (and thereby privatizing) services to private enterprise. Labour councils attempted a range of socialist or progressive initiatives, including the promotion of local job opportunities, the creation of nuclear-free zones, the reduction of fares for public transportation, and the funding of community groups.[39] A growing struggle between left-wing Labour councils and the right-wing national administration bent on significant reductions in welfare provision and firm budgetary administration began to push the role of local councils to the forefront of British political debate.

Before 1975, elected local governments set their own spending and taxation levels through the setting of *rates,* or local property taxes. In the context of increased fiscal pressures that followed the 1973 oil crisis, the Labour government introduced the first check on the fiscal autonomy of local councils by introducing *cash limits* (ceilings on spending imposed by the central government) beginning in fiscal year 1976–1977. Beginning in 1980, with the newly elected Thatcher government's Local Government, Planning

and Land Act, the fiscal constraints on the autonomy of local government increased. The act created a new (and quite complicated) system of local finance in which the central government determined local needs and disbursed central grants (called *block grants*) to local authorities, who would be penalized for spending outside central guidelines, even if the "extra" expenditures—for school meals, for example—were financed out of local rates. In 1982, the central government tightened political control by setting a ceiling on the local rates (a rate cap). The outright abolition of London's progressive and multiculturally-oriented city government (the Greater London Council, or GLC) and a group of metropolitan councils in March 1986, completed the political onslaught on local autonomy.

Riots in a host of British cities in 1981 and 1985, and the much-vaunted Battle for London—the campaign of resistance to the GLC's abolition—provoked some of the most hard-edged debates about democracy in recent British history. With the GLC's emphasis on ethnic minority cultural initiatives and campaigns for equal opportunity and political access, the struggle also highlighted the racial dimension of British politics.

In 1989, riots greeted the introduction of the poll tax (equal per capita levy for local finance to replace the age-old system of *rates,* or property taxes). This radical break with tradition, which shifted the burden of local taxes from property owners and businesses to individuals irrespective of income (and taxed rich and poor alike), was monumentally unpopular. The poll tax proved a tremendous political liability, maintained the local edge to national politics, and helped lead to Thatcher's departure. As in other areas of public policy, Major has tried to depoliticize local government, while continuing the controversial elements of Thatcher-era reforms. He quickly replaced the poll tax with a new local tax linked to the value of properties but has kept policies in place that centralize and control local finance.

THE POLICY-MAKING PROCESS

As already discussed, parliamentary sovereignty is the core constitutional principle of the British political system. However, when it comes to policy-making and policy implementation, the focus is not on Westminster, but rather on Whitehall (the London street that once housed government ministries and whose name still connotes the world of ministers and civil servants and the apex of the British executive). In many countries, such as Japan, India, and Nigeria, personal connections and informal networks play a large role in both policy-making and in the implementation of policy. How different is the British system?

The interaction between the Cabinet Secretary and his or her junior ministers and their counterparts among the career civil servants, notably the permanent secretary, deputy secretary, and under secretary reveals much about the policy-making process. Policy-making emerges primarily from within the executive—from the combined and interactive efforts of what is sometimes called the *partisan executive* (the ministers) and the *merit executive* (the career civil servants who are duty-bound to turn policy goals into instruments, then implement the executive orders and Acts of Parliament that result).[40]

Unlike the American system, in which policy-making is concentrated in Congress and myriad committees in each house, Parliament plays a symbolic role but has little direct participation in policy-making.[41] Britain preserves centralized decision making for the corridors of Whitehall. However, the decision-making process and the implementation of policy involve much more than just a collaboration between high-flying junior ministers and anonymous mandarins (a term originally referring to officials in Imperial China and used colloquially to describe top civil servants).

Stressing the separation of ministers despite the constitutional mandate of collective responsibility, observers have characterized the British cabinet as "sprawling fence posts."[42] It is a useful metaphor for emphasizing that each minister stands a good distance from his or her colleagues, in a sense isolated by separate policy and administrative concerns. In this context, decision making and implementation are strongly influenced by *policy communities,* informal networks with very extensive knowledge, access, and personal connections to those responsible for policy. In this "private, specialized, and invariably 'closed' world," civil servants, ministers, and members of the policy communities (sometimes referred to as *subgovernments*) trade expertise and mutual recognition of authority. This is the make-or-break context of policy decision making, in which mutually satisfactory outcomes are reached.

A cooperative style, even a coziness, develops as the ministry becomes an advocate for key players in its policy community, and as civil servants come perhaps to overidentify the public good with the advancement of policy within the area of their particular responsibility. For example, some accuse the Ministry of Agriculture, Fisheries and Food of defending farmers and manufacturers in their effort to boost food prices and profits. In a similar vein, classic **patron-client relations** develop, in which "sponsor departments" advance the interests of the sectors affected by their policies. This describes, for example, the typical relationship between the Department of Health and Social Security and the medical establishment or between the Department of Education and Science and teachers and their associations and unions. By the late 1980s, however, efforts by the Conservative government to introduce unpopular internal market reforms in health care and education broke the cooperative policy styles and sent both doctors and teachers rushing into the Commons and the committee rooms to battle legislation they had been unable to rewrite or block through the normal functioning of their policy communities.[43]

As will be discussed further in Section 4, the breakdown of the collectivist consensus transformed politics at many levels, from the policy-making process to the organization of interests and the broad dynamics of representation and political participation, to which we now turn.

SECTION 4

Representation and Participation

An analysis of policy-making institutions reveals that the traditional characterization of the executive in Britain as *cabinet government* leaves unstated the importance of unelected officials (the civil service) or the ability of the prime minister to shrink collective responsibility. Similarly in discussing the institutions of representation in Britain, it will quickly become evident that the expression *parliamentary sovereignty* does not quite reveal the limited powers of a House of Commons (or simply Commons, as the lower body with the main legislative power is often called). In addition, it does not capture the surprising resurgence of the House of Lords as an active oppositional body. In this section, we also investigate contemporary currents in British political culture and national identity and assess broader patterns of political participation linked to class, race, gender, and ethnicity.

THE LEGISLATURE

As discussed in Section 3, parliamentary sovereignty is the core constitutional principle defining the role of the legislature and, in a sense, the whole system of British government. No Act of Parliament can lawfully be set aside by any act of the executive or judiciary, nor is any Parliament bound by the actions of any previous Parliament. Is Parliament still as sovereign in practice as it remains in constitutional tradition?

In the mid-nineteenth century, from roughly the 1830s to the 1880s—after monarchical control of government ended but before the formation of modern mass-membership parties—the House of Commons was vastly more powerful than it has ever been since. During this Golden Age of Parliament, it collaborated in the formulation of policy and members amended or rejected legislation on the floor of the House. Contemporaries even referred to Parliament's "elective function" because of its frequent role in the seating and unseating of governments and ministers.[44] From the period of the Reform Act of 1867 onward, with the growth of mass-membership parties, functions that Parliament had exercised during the Golden Age were transferred elsewhere. The function of selecting the government moved *downward* to the electorate at large. At the same time, the legislative and policy-making function tended to move *upward* to the cabinet and government.[45] As a result, today the Commons does not so much legislate as assent to government legislation because (with rare exceptions) the governing party has a majority of the seats and requires no cross-party voting to pass bills. Moreover, in the postwar period, the enormous range of economic and social welfare responsibilities and the sheer complexity of policies have meant that in Britain (as elsewhere) the balance of effective oversight of policy has shifted from the legislature to executive agencies.

We will discuss in order the House of Commons, the House of Lords, parliamentary proceedings, and recent reforms and pressures for change.

Proceedings

Legislative proceedings are conducted according to time-honored customs and procedures. A law begins in draft form as a parliamentary bill. There are private bills that concern matters of individual or local interest. But most bills are public bills sponsored by the government, and the most important of these have generally passed through an elaborate consultative process before they reach the floor of the house.

To become law, bills must be introduced in the House of Commons and the House of Lords, although approval by the latter is not required. The procedure for passing a public bill is quite complex. According to tradition, in the House of Commons, the bill usually comes to floor three times (referred to as *readings*). The bill is formally read upon introduction (the *first reading*), printed, distributed, debated in general terms, and after an interval (from a single day to several weeks), given a *second reading,* followed by a vote. The bill is then usually sent for detailed review to a standing committee of between sixteen and fifty members chosen to reflect the overall party balance in the House. It is then subjected to a report stage during which new amendments may be introduced. The *third reading* follows; normally, the bill is considered in final form (and voted on) without debate.

After the third reading, a bill passed in the House of Commons follows a parallel path in the House of Lords. There the bill is either accepted without change, amended, or rejected. According to custom, the House of Lords passes bills concerning taxation or budgetary matters without alteration, and adds technical and editorial amendments to other bills (which must be approved by the House of Commons) to add clarity in wording and precision in administration. After a bill has passed through all these stages, it is sent to the Crown for royal assent (approval by the queen or king, which is only a formality), after which it becomes a law and is referred to as an Act of Parliament.

The House of Commons

In constitutional terms, the House of Commons, the lower house of Parliament (with 651 members at the time of the 1992 election), exercises the main legislative power in Britain. Along with the two unelected elements of Parliament, the Crown and the House of Lords, the Commons has three main functions: (1) to

A historic view of proceedings at the House of Commons.
Source: © Fox/Hulton Deutsch.

pass laws, (2) to provide finance for the state by authorizing taxation, and (3) to review and scrutinize public administration and government policy.

Elections Parliament usually has a maximum life of five years, with no fixed term. General elections are held after Parliament has been dissolved by the Crown at the request of the prime minister. However, for strategic political reasons the prime minister may ask the Crown to dissolve Parliament at any time. Thus, the ability to control the timing of elections becomes a tremendous political asset for the prime minister. As a result, general elections are often held after three or four years, but there is no fixed minimum. In 1974, there were two general elections.

British elections are exclusively for legislative posts. The prime minister is not directly elected. He or she is elected only as an MP from a single constituency (electoral district) with approximately 67,000 eligible voters. After a general election, the leader of the party who can control a majority in Commons is invited by the Crown to form a government. Likewise, the inability of the government to maintain a majority in the Commons leads in principle (but no longer clearly in practice) to the dissolution of Parliament and a new general election. The role of the legislature in

making and potentially unmaking the government is a core principle of a parliamentary system of government. This contrasts sharply with that of a presidential system, characteristic of the United States, with direct election of the chief executive—and no guarantee (quite the contrary) that the president can command a majority in the Congress.

Election for representatives in the Commons (who are called members of Parliament, or MPs) is by a "first past the post" (or winner-take-all) principle in each constituency. Referred to more formally as a *single-member plurality system,* the candidate who receives the most votes is elected, as in the voting for Congress in the United States. There is no requirement of a majority and no element of **proportional representation** (a system in which each party is given a percentage of seats in a representative assembly roughly comparable to its percentage of the popular vote). Table 11 on the following page shows the results of the general elections from 1945 to 1992.

This "winner-take-all" electoral system tends to exaggerate the size of the victory of the largest party over other parties, and reduce the influence of regionally dispersed lesser parties. Thus, it tends toward stable single-party government, but raises questions about representation and fairness in the electoral

TABLE 11 General Elections, 1945–1992

	Percentage of Popular Vote					Seats in House of Commons					
	Conservative	Labour	Liberal[a]	National Parties[b]	Other	Conservative	Labour	Liberal[a]	National Parties[b]	Other	Government majority
1945	39.8	48.3	9.1	0.2	2.5	213	393	12	0	22	146
1950	43.5	46.1	9.1	0.1	1.2	299	315	9	0	2	5
1951	48.0	48.8	2.5	0.1	0.6	321	295	6	0	3	17
1955	49.7	46.4	2.7	0.2	0.9	345	277	6	0	2	60
1959	49.4	43.8	5.9	0.4	0.6	365	258	6	0	1	100
1964	43.4	44.1	11.2	0.5	0.8	304	317	9	0	0	4
1966	41.9	47.9	8.5	0.7	0.9	253	363	12	0	2	95
1970	46.4	43.0	7.5	1.3	1.8	330	288	6	1	5	30
Feb. 1974	37.8	37.1	19.3	2.6	3.2	297	301	14	9	14	−34[c]
Oct. 1974	35.8	39.2	18.3	3.5	3.2	277	319	13	14	12	3
1979	43.9	37.0	13.8	2.0	3.3	339	269	11	4	12	43
1983	42.4	27.6	25.4	1.5	3.1	397	209	23	4	17	144
1987	42.3	30.8	22.6	1.7	2.6	376	229	22	6	17	102
1992	41.9	34.4	17.8	2.3	3.5	336	271	20	7	17	21

[a]Liberal Party 1945–1979; Liberal/Social Democrat Alliance 1983–1987; Liberal Democrat Party 1992.
[b]Combined vote of Scottish National Party (SNP) and Welsh National Party (Plaid Cymru).
[c]Following the February 1974 election, the Labour Party was 34 seats short of an overall majority. It formed a minority government until obtaining a majority in the October 1974 election.

Source: Anthony King, et al., *Britain at the Polls 1992* (Chatham, N.J.: Chatham House, 1993), 249.

TABLE 12   **Women Elected to Parliament, 1945–1992**

	Conservative	Labour	Liberal[a]	PC/SNP	Others	Total Women	% Total MPs
1945	1	21	1	0	1	23	3.8
1950	6	14	1	0	0	21	3.4
1951	6	11	0	0	0	17	2.7
1955	10	14	0	0	0	24	3.8
1959	12	13	0	0	0	25	4.0
1964	11	18	0	0	0	29	4.6
1966	7	19	0	0	0	26	4.1
1970	15	10	0	0	1	26	4.1
1974	9	13	0	1	0	23	3.6
1974	7	18	0	2	0	27	4.3
1979	8	11	0	0	0	19	3.0
1983	13	10	0	0	0	23	3.5
1987	17	21	2	1	0	41	6.3
1992	20	37	2	1	0	60	9.2

[a]Liberal until 1983, then Liberal Social Democratic Alliance to 1987, then Liberal Democrat.

Source: FWS Craig British Parliamentary Facts 1832–1987, in Pippa Norris, Elizabeth Vallance, and Joni Lovenduski, "Do Candidates make a Difference? Gender, Race, Ideology and Incumbency," *Parliamentary Affairs* 45, no. 4 (October, 1992), 512.

system. Questions may also be raised about the relative homogeneity of the elected MPs. In 1992, sixty women were elected as MPs out of 650 seats (9.2 percent), an increase from forty-two members in 1987 (6.3 percent) (see Table 12). Six ethnic minority candidates were elected, up from four in 1987, the first time since before World War II that Parliament included minority members.

What Parliament Does and Doesn't Do   The preeminence of the executive and the power of political discipline in voting by MPs tend to limit the effectiveness of Parliament in controlling the government. In practical terms, the Commons has a very limited legislative function, but it nevertheless serves a very important democratic function. It provides a highly visible and culturally unique arena for policy debate and the partisan collision of political worldviews. The House comes alive during the debate on the government's legislative program, which is prepared by the cabinet but read by the Crown at the beginning of a session (the *queen's or king's speech*). It is at its best when party-motivated challenges to the government spark debates over legislation, and in the scrutiny of

cabinet members. During *question time,* an hour each afternoon from Monday through Thursday, ministers give oral replies to questions submitted in advance by MPs and offer off-the-cuff responses to follow-up questions and sarcastic asides (often to the merriment of all in attendance). Two fifteen-minute periods on Tuesday and Thursday are allotted as prime minister's question time, when the prime minister and the leader of the opposition are involved in highly charged verbal combat. The exchanges create extraordinary theater and can make and unmake governments and careers: the ability to handle parliamentary debate with style and panache is considered an important prerequisite for party leadership.

The high stakes and the flash of rhetorical skills bring drama to the historic chambers, but one crucial element of drama is nearly always missing: the outcome in these debates is seldom in doubt. Deeply ingrained traditions of strict party discipline lessen the significance of legislative debates. The likelihood that the Commons will invoke its ultimate authority, to defeat a government, is very small. MPs from the governing party who rebel against their leader (the prime minister) are understandably reluctant actually to vote against their government in a close and critical vote and to force a general election—which would place their jobs in grave jeopardy. Only once since the defeat of Ramsay MacDonald's government in 1924 has a government been brought down by a defeat in the Commons (in 1979). At the same time, contemporary constitutional conventions seem to provide a good deal of "wiggle room" for the government. It was once taken for granted that defeat of any significant motion or bill would automatically result in cabinet resignation or a dissolution of Parliament. However, it is now likely that only defeat on a motion that explicitly refers to "confidence in Her Majesty's government" still mandates dissolution. For now, the balance of institutional power has shifted from Parliament to the governing party and the executive.

The House of Lords

The House of Lords (or Lords) is a wholly unelected second chamber, whose membership includes all hereditary peers (nobility of the rank of duke, marquis, earl, viscount, or baron), life peers (appointed by the Crown on the recommendation of the prime minister), and law lords (appointed to assist the House in its judicial duties and who become life peers). The Lords also includes the archbishops of Canterbury and York and two dozen senior bishops in the Church of England. The House of Lords is the final court of appeal for civil cases throughout Britain and for criminal cases in England, Wales, and Northern Ireland. In 1994, there were roughly 1,200 members of the House of Lords, but there is no fixed number, and membership changes with the appointment of peers. Not surprisingly, the Conservatives have a considerable edge in party allegiance in the upper house with just over one-half of peers, and Labour runs a distant second at some 12.5 percent. It is interesting that a significant percentage (approximately 30 percent) are *crossbenchers,* or independents.

In modern times, the Lords has served mainly as a chamber of revision, providing expertise in redrafting legislation. Since the introduction of life peers in 1959, and particularly since the 1970s, the Lords' activities have greatly increased. Government "defeats" (adverse votes) have generated considerable interest and sometimes encouraged compromises. During the Thatcher years, the House of Lords took on a highly visible and surprisingly adversarial role. The members of the upper house consider one of their central func-

tions to be a stewardship of the constitution. Ironically, although they sit in an unelected body and are themselves a vestige of hereditary rule and monarchical sovereignty, the Lords are inclined to be wary of changes in representative institutions. As a body, they remain ill-disposed toward what they view as a weakening of the rights of political participation. When Thatcher challenged traditional Tory values, the government experienced open rebellion among Conservative peers. For example, they became the focus of opposition to the government's plans to control the revenue raising powers of local government (rate capping) and resisted aspects of the plan to abolish the Greater London Council (GLC) and six metropolitan county councils. From 1979 to 1992, the Lords voted against the Conservative governments on 179 occasions (7.9 percent of the time). Although the Lords does not serve as a serious impediment to the government, it can slow down legislation and encourage modifications. The House of Lords attracts a variety of opinions. Some MPs on the Labour left (and others) persistently call for its abolition as an undemocratic body. Others view it, like the Crown, with a tolerant affection. Remarkably, some have begun to take the Lords seriously, and some scholars have begun to ask whether the Lords has become more independent than the Commons.

Recent Reforms in Behavior and Structure

It is a sign of the contemporary decline of the Commons that constitutional commentators stress the independence of the Lords. But the more significant development is the shift in power toward the executive and especially the cabinet: "Supposedly, Parliament, Lords no less than Commons, checks and controls the executive. In practice it is the other way around."[46] How significant are contemporary changes in the House? How far will they go to stem the tide in Parliament's much-heralded decline?

Behavioral Changes: Backbench Dissent   In recent years, as the ability of parties to control the votes of their MPs has weakened, important changes in the *behavior* of MPs have been observed. Since the 1970s, backbenchers (MPs of the governing party who have no governmental office and rank-and-file opposition members) are markedly less deferential and prefer to participate more directly in policy formation. It used to be that a *three-line whip* (the strongest appeal to

TABLE 13　**Backbench Attitudes**

	Agree (%)	Disagree (%)
"I would never vote against my party on a three-line whip."	8.4	83.6
"My primary loyalty is to my party."	51.1	37.8
"My electors expect me to use my judgment on issues."	87.6	4.6

Source: Paul Silk, *How Parliament Works* (London: Longman, 1987), 52.

party discipline in a vote before the House, neglect of which once carried a clear threat of reprisal or ouster from the party) would result in very nearly unanimous obedience. Today, the loyalty of MPs and their obedience to party line can no longer be taken for granted. A survey of backbenchers shows how extensive the behavioral change has been (see Table 13). As we shall see in Section 5, the Major government has experienced very significant backbench rebellion, most critically on Britain-EU policy, which has assaulted the prestige of the prime minister and contributed to his historically low approval ratings.

Structural Changes: Parliamentary Committees
In addition to the standing committees that routinely review bills during legislative proceedings, in 1979 the Commons revived and extended the number and "remit" (i.e., responsibilities) of *select committees.* These committees help Parliament exert control over the executive by examining specific policies or aspects of administration.

For Americans accustomed to powerful and quite independent committees in the Congress, the strengthening of the select committee system in the British Parliament may not seem a very dramatic development. But in the context of a century of decline in parliamentary influence, the revitalization of select committees is considered a serious structural reform— so serious, in fact, that the government and the executive have done their best to undermine the committees' powers.

The most controversial select committees are more independent "watchdog" committees that monitor the conduct of the major departments and ministries. Select committees hold hearings, take written and oral testimony, and question senior civil servants, ministers, and other interested parties to public policy.

They then issue reports that often include strong policy recommendations at odds with government policy. How significant has the 1979 reform in select committees been in practice? On balance, the committees have been extremely energetic. Power is another issue, however, because their direct influence on legislation and their ability to hold executive departments or the government accountable is limited. For the most part, when the committees have been effective it is because they have served to publicize and critically evaluate government policy. They serve as magnets to attract otherwise scattered criticisms and give them the visibility and prestige of a parliamentary audience. Radical changes in procedure, political culture, and tradition would be necessary to make select committees powerful watchdogs.

THE PARTY SYSTEM AND ELECTIONS

Like the term *parliamentary sovereignty,* which conceals the reduced role of Parliament in legislation and the unmaking of governments, the term *two-party system,* which is commonly used to describe the British party system, is somewhat deceiving. It is true that since 1945, leaders of either the Labour or Conservative parties have exclusively occupied 10 Downing Street as prime minister. From 1945 through the 1992 election, the Conservative Party had won eight general elections and the Labour Party six. It is also true that throughout the postwar period, these two parties have routinely divided among themselves 90 percent or more of the seats in the House of Commons. But a variety of other parties—centrist, environmental, nationalist, and even neofascist—have complicated the picture of party competition. In addition, an increasingly visible "North-South divide" in the pattern of party competition further muddies the picture. A significant distinction has begun to emerge between party representation in Parliament (which remains predominantly two-party) and electoral support at elections (in which one-fifth of the electorate chooses third or minor parties). We discuss, in turn, the parties themselves, and then recent developments in the party system and patterns of electoral behavior.

The Conservative Party

The pragmatism, flexibility, and organizational capabilities of the Conservative Party, which dates back to the eighteenth century, have made it probably the most successful political party in Britain. In contrast to some leading conservative parties in Italy and Germany, it has been a secular party wholly committed to democratic principles, free of the association with fascism during World War II that has tainted the others. In fact, the British Conservative Party is one of the most successful and, at times, innovative center-right parties in Europe.

Although the association of the Conservative Party with the economic and social elite is unmistakable, it is also true that Conservatives in Britain are associated historically with the birth of the modern welfare state during the government of Prime Minister Benjamin Disraeli (1874–1880). The creation of a "long-lasting alliance between an upper-class leadership and a lower-class following"[47] has made possible Conservative Party dominance in modern British politics and guaranteed for the Conservatives electoral support from a minimum of about one-third of the working class throughout the postwar period.

Several ideologies of governance have developed within the Conservative Party, and there is no consensus about their relative significance. Some scholars stress a strong division between hierarchical and paternalistic attitudes on the one side, and individualistic free-enterprise traditions, on the other. By this analysis, Heath and Thatcher represent the same free-enterprise tradition (and, by implication, the wave of the future), in contrast to their predecessors as Conservative prime ministers (Alec Douglas-Home and Harold Macmillan) who shared a more elitist, paternalistic vision. Others argue that the Conservative Party represents the interests of one class (the bourgeoisie or property-owning class) and not the nation as a whole, and that ideological currents and factions within the party can be largely explained by the divisions of interest among different capitalist elements (for example, financial versus manufacturing interests or domestic versus internationalist interests).[48] The analysis here, by contrast, tends to emphasize the shift, starting with Thatcher, away from the principles of the collectivist consensus—Keynesianism, the welfare state, public ownership of some key industrial sectors, the integration of the working class and its allied trade unions into national political life—that Labour and Conservative elites had shared for three decades.

Although the institutional changes of the welfare state are ideologically associated with center-left parties in Western Europe generally, and with the 1945–1951 Labour government of Britain in particular, both cross-party and interclass consensus were a crucial part of the postwar settlement. The period from the late 1940s to the mid-1970s represents the high-water mark of interparty consensus during which traditional Tories (as Conservatives are often colloquially called) were clearly committed to collectivist goals: expanded welfare provision; state intervention to neutralize the consequences of unchecked market forces; and consistent government efforts to secure full employment.[49]

Thatcher broke with this consensus tradition, deepening divisions within the party. Today, the party is split between mainstream Conservative modernizers who urge pragmatism, moderation, and consensus building and those committed to the reform project inaugurated by Thatcher. The latter are more ideological and determined to cut back the welfare state, rekindle entrepreneurial spirit, and return to a more laissez-faire tradition. Under Major's more pragmatic approach, which attempts to heal the rift, the significance of this division has been reduced. However, it has been replaced by another damaging divide that pits supporters against opponents of Britain's participation in a more fully integrated European Union. The implications of this fundamental division for the Conservative Party and for Britain will be discussed in Section 5.

The Labour Party

As one of the few European parties with origins outside electoral politics, the Labour Party was launched by trade union representatives and socialist societies at the start of the twentieth century. From its inception in a labor representation committee, supporters sought to advance working-class political representation and to further specific trade unionist demands. In the years preceding World War I, the party expanded its trade union affiliation but made only weak progress at the polls. Although Labour secured only 7.1 percent of the vote in 1910, the radicalizing effects of the war and the expansion of the franchise in 1918 nearly tripled its base of support. In 1918, it received 22.2 percent, even with a shift of emphasis from the defense of trade union rights to explicitly socialist appeals. Its landslide 1945 victory promoted a party with deep working-class roots and a socialist ideology to major player status in British politics. At the same time, Labour began moderating its ideological appeal and broadening its electoral base.

Early in the postwar period, it was clear that Labour Party *fundamentalism,* which stressed state ownership of industry and workers' control of production, would take a back seat to the more moderate perspective within the Labour Party, which advocated the projects of the collectivist consensus (referred to by contemporaries as *revisionism* or *Labourism*). During the height of Labourism (roughly 1945 to the mid-1970s), party identification and electoral behavior displayed a strong correlation with occupation. In the 1950s and early 1960s, those not engaged in manual labor voted Conservative three times more commonly than they did Labour; and more than two out of three manual workers, by contrast, voted Labour. During this period Britain conformed to one classic pattern of a Western European party system: a two-class/two-party system.

The period since the mid-1970s has been marked by basic changes in the party system and by a growing disaffection with even the moderate social democracy associated with the Keynesian Welfare State and Labourism. The party suffered from divisions between its trade unionist and parliamentary elements, constitutional wrangling over the power of trade unions to determine party policy at annual conferences, and disputes over how the leader (a potential prime minister) would be selected. In 1981, a centrist breakaway of leading Labour MPs further destabilized the party.

Divisions spilled over into foreign and defense policy issues as well. Although generally internationalist, persistent voices within Labour challenged participation in the European Community on the grounds that EC policy would advance the interests of business over labor and damage the standard of living of working Britons. However, by 1987, as the period of Conservative dominance continued, and there was widespread talk that Britain was turning into a one-party dominant system with the Conservatives running

the show, Labour began to look to the European Community as a means of offsetting its weakness at home. In particular, the EC consideration of the Social Charter to extend workers' rights and protections helped turn Labour into a pro-EC party.

In addition, there was a strong pacifist and an even stronger antinuclear sentiment within the party. Between 1981 and 1986, the party conferences repeatedly passed motions by lopsided majorities that opposed the siting of cruise missiles with nuclear warheads on British soil and that supported the removal of American nuclear bases from Britain. Nevertheless, the support for unilateral nuclear disarmament (the reduction and elimination of nuclear weapons systems with or without comparable developments on the Soviet side) was a decisive break with a national consensus on security policy, which contributed to its losses in 1983 and 1987; unilateralism was then scrapped. The party's stance did nothing to enhance its prestige with NATO allies (especially the United States), damaged its credibility as a potential governing party, and forged another area of division between the more progressive grassroots members of the party and the more conservative leadership.

The 1980s and 1990s have witnessed a period of relative harmony within the party, with moderate trade union and parliamentary leadership agreeing on major policy issues. Recent party leaders—Neil Kinnock (who served from 1983 until Labour's defeat in the March 1992 election), John Smith (who replaced Kinnock and served as leader until his death in May 1994), and Tony Blair (who was quickly selected to replace him)—have abandoned socialism and led the party in a new pragmatic direction.

An important policy review, initiated after Labour's loss in the 1987 election, confirmed its more moderate electoral orientation. The review stressed the need to support improvements in the competitiveness of British industry over the need to support social justice in economic policy. In addition, it emphasized support for a European Community that would advance women's rights, protect the environment, and enhance social protections. It carefully avoided proposing much in the way of new programs or specific refinements, for fear of being labeled a "tax and spend" party. Fighting the 1992 general election on the terms set out in the policy review, the party was not able to galvanize an alternative to the Conservatives or consolidate a new set of values to replace the old

Tony Blair, the well-spoken, pragmatic leader of the Labour Party, waits in the wings for his chance to govern Britain. Source: Reuters/Bettmann Archive.

Labourite themes of collectivism, class identity, and enhancing equality between the haves and have-nots. Through the 1992 election, which nearly everyone expected them to win, Labour has lost four elections in a row, its worst string of losses in the postwar period.

Eclipse of a Two-Party System?

Since the 1970s—the "decade of dealignment"[50]—any description of British party politics as a two-party system neglects a number of important factors. First, there has been an upswing in the active competition and agenda-setting ability of a range of so-called third parties (a term used in the United Kingdom to refer to almost *any* significant party challenging Labor and Conservative). In the 1970s, the nationalist parties pressed the attack on two-party dominance. They were led by the Scottish National Party (SNP), which dates from 1934, and its Welsh counterpart, the Plaid

Cymru, founded in 1925. In addition, the activity of minor parties picked up. The National Front (formed in 1967)—a far-right, neofascist, anti-immigrant party—won seats on local councils and entered candidates (unsuccessfully) for Parliament. After the National Front faded in the late 1970s, the British National Party (formed in 1983) emerged as the most visible far-right party. Finally, Northern Ireland is home to a set of parties with distinctive perspectives and platforms. In 1992, three predominantly Protestant, pro-English parties (Ulster Unionist, Democratic Unionist, and Ulster Popular Unionist) won a total of thirteen parliamentary seats; the predominantly Catholic Social Democratic and Labour Party, which seeks the reunification of Ireland through political negotiations, won four seats. In addition, the Alliance Party (with no connection to the British SDP/Liberal Alliance which contested the 1983 and 1987 elections) is a nonsectarian party which works to build bridges between the Protestant unionist and Catholic republican communities. It has never won a seat.

Third Parties   Since the 1980s a changing roster of centrist parties have posed the most significant threat to two-party dominance. The Alliance was an electoral amalgamation of two such parties, the Liberals (a governing party in the pre–World War I period and thereafter the traditional centrist third party in Britain) and the Social Democratic Party, or SDP (a 1981 breakaway from the Labour Party). At the height of the collectivist consensus, the appeal of center parties was blunted because the Labour and Conservative parties were themselves united in moderate and consensual policy approaches. However, the renewal of ideological conflict gave a new opening to the Liberals and subsequently the SDP and the Alliance. They were able to defend a middle ground between the Conservatives and Labour on both foreign and domestic policy fronts. In foreign and defense policy they emphasized a "less nuclear" (but not unilateralist) policy and sought to explore opportunities to advance cooperation with the Soviets. On domestic policy, they pledged to keep some of the Thatcher-era constraints on trade unions, such as the requirement of secret ballots for trade union elections, but pledged to increase pensions and investments in education.

The strength of centrist parties in the mid-1980s led to expectations of a possible Alliance-led government (which did not occur), and observers of British politics began to talk about a party system with "four major national parties" (Conservative, Labour, Liberal, and SDP).[51] After the Conservative victory in the 1987 general election, the "shake out" among centrist parties and factions continued. Early in 1988, the Liberal Party and most of the SDP merged to form the Social and Liberal Democratic Party (now called the Liberal Democrats, or the LD). A small rump of the SDP hung on as an independent organization until disbanding in June 1990.

As a group, third parties have weakened the electoral support of the Labour and Conservative parties. Since February 1974, with the exception of 1979, the third parties—centrist and nationalist combined—have received between one-fifth and one-fourth of the vote in every general election.

What are the political implications of third-party ascendancy? Support for the center party alone (not including the national parties) declined slightly in the 1992 election (down to 17.8 percent from 22.6 percent of the popular vote). But as Major's popularity declined much faster and further after the 1992 election, and as Labour failed initially to catch hold, the Liberal Democrats started winning by-elections (elections held between general elections to fill vacancies) by wide margins. Once again, talk of a breakthrough by the Lib Dems gathered steam (although by mid-decade the surging popularity of Tony Blair's Labour Party turned expectations toward a Labour government by 1997).

Another party, the Greens (formed in 1973 by environmentalists, the oldest Green Party in Europe) surprised everyone (themselves included) by achieving a 15 percent third-place showing in the June 1989 elections to the European Parliament (but winning no seats). With public opinion surveys ranking "pollution and the environment" as the third-most-common concern,[52] the major parties hustled to acquire a greenish hue. But the Green Party failed to capitalize on its 1989 showing. By the mid-1990s, party membership declined and the commitment of environmentalists spread to a wide range of grassroots initiatives.

Regional Trends Recent general elections have deepened geographic and regional fragmentation on the political map. British political scientist Ivor Crewe has referred to the emergence of *two* two-party systems,[53] in which competition between the Conservative and Labour parties dominates contests in English urban and northern seats, and Conservative–center party competition dominates England's rural and southern seats. It is now difficult to find a common two-party pattern of electoral competition throughout Britain. In addition, Labour–nationalist party competition dominates the Scottish contests, with the ruling Conservative Party attracting barely one-quarter of the popular vote.

The Gap Between Votes and Seats Finally, elections since the 1970s have displayed a striking gap between continuing two-party (and through 1992 Conservative) dominance at the parliamentary level and the strong tendency toward a multiparty system in terms of the votes cast. In 1979, the Conservatives were elected with far less than a majority (43.9 percent) of the popular vote, and they have received a *lower* percentage of the vote—42.4 percent in 1983, 42.3 percent in 1987, and 41.9 percent in 1992—in each of their subsequent victories. The winner-take-all electoral system preserves two-party dominance in Parliamentary representation and the Conservatives and Labour have continued to share over 90 percent of the seats in the House of Commons. But the popular vote tells a different story: between 1974 and 1992 the combined share of the popular vote for Conservative and Labour averaged 75 percent.[54] This is another indication that talk of a two-party system hardly reveals the true measure of disaffection and weakening partisan support for the two leading parties, nor does it take into account important contemporary undercurrents in political culture and public opinion.

POLITICAL CULTURE, CITIZENSHIP, AND IDENTITY

In their classic study of the ideals and values that shape political behavior, political scientists Gabriel Almond and Sidney Verba wrote that the civic (or political) culture in Britain was characterized by trust, deference to authority and competence, pragmatism, and the balance between acceptance of the rules of the game and disagreement over specific issues.[55] Many have considered these characteristics the model for active, informed, and stable democratic citizenship.

Viewed retrospectively, the 1970s appear as a crucial turning point in British political culture and group identities. During that fateful decade, the long slide of economic decline culminated in actual economic reversals in the standard of living for many Britons.

Also for many, historic bonds based on occupational and social class grew weaker. Union membership declined with the continued transfer of jobs away from the traditional manufacturing sectors. More damaging, unions lost support as they appeared to bully society, act undemocratically, and neglect the needs of an increasingly female and minority workforce. At the same time, a growing number of conservative think tanks and the powerful voice of mass-circulation newspapers—which are overwhelmingly conservative—worked hard to erode the fundamental beliefs of the Keynesian Welfare State. Weakening class identification and the appeal of Scottish and Welsh nationalism shook up party politics, and **new social movements** (such as feminism, antinuclear activism, and environmentalism) challenged basic tenets of British political culture. Identities based on race and ethnicity, gender, and sexual orientation gained significance. Thus, a combination of economic strains, ideological assaults, and social dislocations helped foster political fragmentation and, at the same time, a shift to the right in values and policy agendas.

Thatcher's ascent to power reflected these changes in political culture, identities, and values. It also put the full resources of the state and a bold and determined prime minister behind a sweeping agenda for change that would go far beyond the specifics of policy or economic doctrine. As a leading British scholar put it, "Thatcher's objective was nothing less than a cultural revolution."[56] Most observers agree that she fell considerably short of that aim. There were, of course, continuities with the previous consensus era and limits placed on the Thatcher Revolution in strict policy terms. For example, the welfare state was not dismantled because support for key policies such as health care provision and pensions remained extremely high, and growing unemployment actually led to increased social expenditures. Nevertheless, Thatcherism cut deep. It touched the cultural recesses of British society, helped recast political values, and redefined national identity.

To the extent that the Thatcherite worldview took hold (and the record is mixed), its new language and ethos helped transform the common sense of politics and redefined the political community. Monetarism (however modified) and the appeal to an enterprise culture of competitive market logic and entrepreneurial values fostered individualism and competition—winners and losers. It rejected collectivism, the redis-

tribution of resources between rich and poor, and state responsibility for full employment. Thatcherism considered individual property rights more important than the social and universal rights owing to all citizens in the welfare state. This ideological change at the top helped weaken the Labour Party's hold on its natural working-class base and eroded the force of its underlying collectivist appeals.

However, data from opinion polls suggest a far less decisive legacy in social and economic terms. Thatcherite ideals have overtaken collectivist ideals in some dimensions, but not others. For example, in the late 1980s, respondents narrowly preferred a market-driven society "which allows people to make and keep as much as they can" to an egalitarian society which "emphasizes similar incomes and rewards for everyone." But they dramatically preferred (by a five-to-one ratio) a society in which "caring for others" is more highly rewarded than "the creation of wealth."[57]

Thatcher's reform agenda included both positive and negative appeals. There were rhetorical appeals to individualism, self-reliance, and private ownership and specific policies that advanced the new ethos. These included the cut-rate sale of council houses to tenants and the privatization of nationalized industries (most notably British Telecom) with share offers structured to attract investments by small investor-citizens—and give them immediate profits. But the negative appeals of Thatcherism must also be acknowledged. A review of Thatcher's first general election reveals the repoliticization of race. She promised tougher nationality legislation to restrict immigration, expressed sympathy for those who harbored "fear that [England] might be swamped" by nonwhite Commonwealth immigrants, and associated minorities with lawlessness. In a similar vein, during the 1984–1985 strike, she cast the miners as the "enemy within" by way of comparison to the external Argentine enemy during the Falklands/Malvinas war of 1982.

Thatcher embraced some groups and symbolically expelled others—ethnic minority communities and the unrepentant miners—from the national community. In this way, Thatcherism involved an attempt to redefine national identity in Britain. As political scientist Benedict Anderson has observed, national identity involves the belief in an "imagined community" of belonging, shared fates, and affinities among millions of diverse and actually unconnected citizens.[58] Since the 1970s, the cultural isolation of racial,

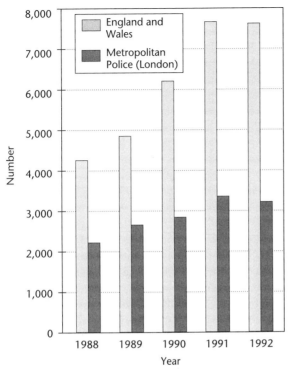

Figure 10   Reported Racial Incidents, 1988–1992
Source: Home Office, from Philip Allan, John Benyon, and Barry McCormick, eds., *Focus on Britain 1994* (Chicago: Fitzroy Dearborn Publishers, 1994), 197.

productivity. Labour Party failure was blamed both on its commitment to these ideals and on the unions' considerable power within the party.

The imagined community of Britain fragmented into smaller communities that existed side by side but not necessarily in amiable proximity. An appeal to England or Britain took on a patriotic and partisan tone— but in a way that excluded many. In defining themselves, some might say they were Scottish or Pakistani or Jamaican or Muslim.[59] But they didn't feel very British in the 1970s, and they felt even less British later.

The cultural legacy of Thatcherism is powerful, but ambiguous. Issues of race, ethnicity, and immigration—which preceded Thatcher but were sharpened during her premiership—remain politicized and divisive. With concern about the political fallout from this inheritance, and with his more conciliatory nature, Major has tried to humanize Thatcherism. But it is a sign of Thatcher's cultural legacy that it seems highly unlikely—whatever emerges in the realm of party competition—that any collectivist consensus will soon be seen on the political horizon in Britain.

INTERESTS, SOCIAL MOVEMENTS, AND PROTEST

Given the two-party/two-class model that has traditionally dominated British politics, the most effectively organized and influential interests have been those linked to class and industrial interests. During the period of consensus that framed politics from the end of World War II until the 1970s, business interests and trade union organizations vied for influence over both economic and social policy. Equally important, governments worked very hard, often without success, to gain the cooperation of these interests in the formulation and implementation of policy.

Throughout the postwar period until Thatcher's administration, British governments worked hard (some would say desperately) to reduce the frequency and duration of often crippling strikes, constrain the political power of trade unions, and limit wage increases in both the public and private sectors. They tried two somewhat contradictory policy approaches. On the one hand, governments sought to legally restrict trade union rights (for example, by the 1972 Industrial Relations Act of the Heath government). On the other hand, they tried to expand the involvement of

religious, and ethnic communities has actually deepened. The politicization of immigration in the 1979 election and an increase in racially motivated attacks underscore the resentment white Britons direct against minority communities who insist on maintaining their own religious beliefs and cultures (see Figure 10). At the same time, the significance of national divisions within the United Kingdom has deepened, as seen in the growth of national parties in Scotland and Wales, and in the deepening pattern of uneven economic development. By the mid-1990s however, the increased prospect of a negotiated settlement in Northern Ireland offered the hope that discord over national identity may be reduced in that area.

In addition, working-class identity and politics were stigmatized when the behavior of unions was sharply criticized. The traditional values of "an honest day's work for an honest day's pay," resistance to cutbacks in wages or changes in work assignments, and solidarity among coworkers in industrial disputes were characterized as "rigidities" that resulted in poor the national association of trade unions—the Trades Union Congress (TUC)—in the design and implementation of policy. Why not "turn the poacher into the gamekeeper" and involve trade union leaders in the enforcement of voluntary wage restraints? For example, the 1974–1979 Labour government negotiated a series of highly visible Social Contracts with the TUC initially, and subsequently with individual trade unions. When these agreements fell apart, strikes erupted in the 1978–1979 winter of discontent, leading to Thatcher's victory the following May. Labour and Conservative governments alike tried both approaches with only fleeting success.

Since the new juncture in British politics marked by the election of Margaret Thatcher in 1979, governments have held class-based interests more at arms length. In particular, trade unions have "been the target of a series of measures designed to reshape their activities and curb their power."[60] A formidable combination of legislated constraints on union rights to strike, internal affairs, and broad political agendas; trade union defeats in industrial disputes, and massive unemployment (particularly in the traditionally unionized manufacturing sectors) helped crystallize a continuing pattern of decline in union membership, militancy, and power.

How has the contemporary arms-length approach influenced the ability of business to advance its interests? Medium-scale manufacturing industries, which provide much of the constituency-level leadership of the Conservative Party, are organized politically through the Confederation of British Industry (CBI). It has not been as influential as one might expect under recent Conservative governments. After very public criticisms of Thatcher's economic management early in her premiership—which was viewed by manufacturing as disruptive and skewed toward financial interests—the CBI quickly lowered its profile. In general, Thatcher remained aloof from interest pleading, and the role of interest organizations such as the CBI has diminished in favor of such institutions as the Institute of Directors, which more closely mirrored Thatcher's policy convictions.[61] As a result, organizations like the CBI that traditionally operated upon the executive developed closer relations with Parliament when the traditional policy communities lost their ability to influence policy directions effectively from the inside. In general, the work of interest groups and lobbyists in the Commons has increased considerably in recent years.

The influence of financial interests continue. Section 1 discussed the historical significance of the financial interests of the City of London (the capital's financial district). Today, City influence over economic policy and Conservative politics remains considerable: senior treasury officials move back and forth freely between government and private firms in the City and are widely believed to influence policy (such as the deregulation of the London Stock Exchange in 1986).

At the same time, the emergence of new social movements (NSMs) has changed the landscape of politics in Britain since the late 1960s, as they have elsewhere in the industrial world. By contrast to the traditional interest-group–oriented social movements, the NSMs tend to be more fluidly organized and democratic, less oriented to immediate payoffs for their group, and more focused on fundamental questions about the values of society. To note one example, the British feminist movement has emphasized consciousness raising, self-help, and life-style transformations. Its adherents have worked with considerable success to gain funding and maximize influence by working closely with Labour councils and local authorities in urban settings. The movement has spawned dozens of action groups, ranging from health clinics to battered women's and rape crisis shelters, to feminist collectives and black women's groups, to networks of women in media, law, and other professions. The women's movement in Britain has kept a radical edge, remaining decentralized and activist-oriented, and less involved than the American women's movement, for example, in legislative lobbying or coalition politics.[62] In the 1970s and 1980s, activists in the women's peace movement protested Britain's participation in NATO nuclear defense strategies and organized a string of mass demonstrations. These activities, like the broader efforts of the Campaign for Nuclear Disarmament (launched in 1958), were radical in message but almost reassuring in style: they seemed to tap a traditional strain of popular symbolic political resistance in Britain.

Simultaneously, the subcultures and countercultures of black Britain have been a vital source of NSM activity, often expressed in antiracist initiatives. "Rock Against Racism" concerts in the 1970s brought reggae and skinhead bands together in public resistance to the National Front; today, lower profile efforts are made to sensitize local councils to the cultural needs of ethnic minorities and to publicize their potential political clout. As a consequence, some councils (mostly Labour) work actively to win support in black communities by preserving social services and supporting the cultural activities of diverse communities. Like the women's movement, such movements are decentralized, activist, and culturally engaged. They are much less focused on legal challenges, legislation, or coalition building than comparable movements in the United States.

Taken together, the breakdown of traditional channels for class-based interest bargaining and the growth of influential NSMs in Britain underscore the complexity and relative uncertainty of contemporary politics. How will Britain face the future? In Section 5, we reflect on the challenges ahead.

British Politics at the Crossroads

"In the wake of the 1992 general election," noted one observer, the consensus among mainstream commentators seemed to be that Britain was finally 'on the mend.' "[63] A broad spectrum of political elites agreed that after more than a decade of Thatcher's aggressive campaign for change, it was time to preserve the best of her reforms and abandon her hard-edged style with its resulting turmoil. The new centrist consensus included support for what many viewed as positive Thatcher-era reforms, including a more efficient export-oriented economy, renewed attention to efficiency in both the public and the private sectors, an ethos of personal responsibility and government accountability, and a less "bloody-minded" (aggressive and arrogant) trade union movement. But it also supported a return to traditional British values of pragmatism, compromise, and a more genial acceptance of disagreement. Many were ready to believe less could be more: less confrontation with citizens (over the poll tax), trade unions (in collective bargaining), cabinet ministers (over their independence), and the European Union (over almost everything), could bring more beneficial results in both economic and political terms.

When unexceptional policies and programs of the collectivist era were considered in pragmatic rather than ideological terms, there was much worth preserving, at least when modified policies mixed with a solid measure of fiscal constraint. If the state should not guarantee full employment, at least it should try to boost employment and increase the skill base and training opportunities for new workers. If the state could not spend its way out of problems, it could and should modernize, reform, and support a first-class National Health Service.

This new post-Thatcher moderate consensus included more accountability by government to the citizens (this was a major goal of a signal initiative of the Major government called *citizen's charters*). It also promised a return to some constitutional basics and enhanced democratic participation, with a more collaborative style that revitalized collective responsibility in cabinet, and a healthy respect for process, deliberation, and consultation in decision making that would reassure both citizens and policy communities. Finally, it called for Britain to situate itself very differently with regard to EU policy by working to preserve its sovereign control over policy, for example, by opting out of the Social Charter, while contributing constructively to negotiations regarding increased integration.

The new consensus allowed for an appropriate range of disagreement about issues such as the level and character of state intervention, the pace of European integration (and the place of workers' rights within that process), and both the generosity of social service provisions and the degree to which they should react to cost accounting and compete with private providers. John Smith, the pragmatic Scottish solicitor who took over Labour's leadership soon after the 1992 election, and Paddy Ashdown, the leader of the Liberal Democrats, could readily sign on to this "pro-market, pro-Europe consensus of sensible moderation."[64] It also served as the ideal launching pad for Tony Blair (who succeeded Smith as Labour leader after his death in 1994).

POLITICAL CHALLENGES AND CHANGING AGENDAS

The country's choice of John Major for prime minister was the right one for the job of consolidating this new mix of Thatcher-era reforms, moderate welfare state

Citizen's Charters

In the late 1970s, a critically minded constitutional reform group called Charter 88 began to press for the expansion and protection of rights, freedom of information, more grassroots democracy, and decentralization of power (to include Scottish and regional authorities with legislative and taxing powers). As an organization with ties to the left of the Labour Party, Charter 88 helped influence the Labour Party's important policy review after its 1987 defeat, which included the call for expanded democratic rights. In his own way, John Major tried to address some of these concerns through the introduction early in his premiership of citizen's charters which set standards for government accountability and stressed more open government.

Along with the "back to basics" campaign, the concept of *citizen's charters* was an initiative of John Major intended to demonstrate his political vision and help identify the distinctiveness of his administration. By redefining the relationship between the citizen and the state (emphasizing that citizens are consumers of services), Major hoped to turn dissatisfaction with state services to political advantage and extend the notion of democracy to include more control by citizens over governmental services. The change in language ("citizens" became "clients" or "customers") bespoke an effort to bring to the public sector the kind of accountability and efficiency associated with the private sector business world.

Central principles of the citizen's charters included
• Openness and communication
• Clearly stated guidelines and standards for public service
• Complaints procedures and legal remedies for redress
• New standards for courtesy and assistance
• Emphasis on efficiency and budgetary constraints
• Clear performance guidelines and quality standards

More than thirty different charters were issued, and ceremonies were held in which the prime minister awarded "Charter Marks" for outstanding achievement. Many welcomed the initiatives, which seemed to extend the principles of the enterprise culture into government, and encourage more efficient use of resources by the state, and friendlier, more respectful interaction. To a limited degree, the citizen's charter campaign extended the concept of rights in a new direction. The campaign, however, suffered from extremely high expectations. Citizen's charters did not result in constitutional reform (as John Major's supporters had led many to believe) and, as one observer noted, "public services remained largely unloved."*

———
*Peter Madgwick, "Government at the Centre," in *Focus on Britain 1994,* ed. Philip Allan et al. (Chicago: Fitzroy Dearborn, 1994), 40. See Madgwick for a fuller explanation of the citizen's charters on which this analysis is based.

goals, consensual values, and cautious European initiatives. After the Conservative electoral victory in the spring of 1992, there was widespread, if cautious, optimism despite a deepening recession. Ironically by the mid-1990s, heady claims that the U.K. economy was outperforming the rest of Europe notwithstanding, the Conservatives were well behind Labour in opinion polls and losing badly in by-elections. Norman Lamont, a former Conservative chancellor of the exchequer, said openly what many were thinking, that the Major government was still in office, but it was no longer in power. What had gone wrong? The answer can be summarized in a few words: "back to basics" and Europe.

Back to Basics

In an appeal familiar to Americans, the government tried to take the political offensive in 1993 by inaugurating a "back to basics" campaign that reasserted traditional family values and decried permissiveness in society. Unfortunately for a shocked John Major, an

uncanny rash of scandals involving Tory MPs, Lords, and ministers quickly followed. The episodes were magnified by government appeals to personal responsibility and individual morality, and by Major's reluctance to take decisive action in dismissing his misbehaving ministers. There were scandals to suit almost every taste: illegal speculation in the housing market by a parliamentary private secretary; support by a minister for a bankrupt tycoon facing charges of fraud; a variety of sex-related scandals; evidence that large sums of money were donated to the Conservative Party in return for special favors. There was even a charge brought against Margaret Thatcher's son Mark that he benefited financially from commissions paid to him for helping to promote an arms deal with Saudi Arabia while his mother was prime minister. By the fall of 1994, 61 percent of respondents to a Gallup poll agreed that the Tories appear "very sleazy and disreputable," and a *Financial Times* editorial concluded that "standards of public life in Britain have fallen too far."[65] The scandals contributed to a growing sense that John Major's administration was losing its capacity to govern.

Britain and Europe

As the discussion in Section 1 of the inner-party coup against Margaret Thatcher made clear, prime ministers can pay dearly for unresolved tensions about Britain's role in the European Union. An extraordinary sequence of backbench revolts and the high drama of a vote of confidence in the House of Commons in July 1993 proved that John Major's problems in managing Britain's relations with Europe were still growing. Will Europe scuttle the careers of two Conservative prime ministers in a row? What deeper significance do the divisions in the Conservative Party and the crisis over Europe have for the challenges facing Britain in the last years of the twentieth century?

From the moment he became prime minister, Major worked hard to refocus U.K.–EU relations. He inherited a party divided over Europe and with little standing among European allies who resented Thatcher's intrusive and highly visible series of assaults on EC initiatives. Major faced a very tough balancing act. How could he shelve Thatcher's anti-European stance without antagonizing her (and his) supporters, accept the trend of deepening cooperation, and at the same time preserve the necessary margin of British autonomy? At the beginning, to nearly everyone's surprise, he appeared to pull off the miracle.

At one of his first summit appearances with his European counterparts, Major performed brilliantly in the small Dutch town of Maastricht in December 1991, during negotiations for the Treaty on European Union (often called the Maastricht Treaty). The treaty, which required separate approval in each of the member states, represented a bold agenda for economic and monetary union, and for deeper cooperation on foreign policy and security matters. Maastricht also established a plan to phase in a single EC currency and control of national monetary policy by an EC central bank (the Eurofed) by 1999. In addition, Maastricht gave treaty status to the "Community Charter of the Fundamental Social Rights of Workers," or Social Charter as it is commonly called (except by the British who call it the Social Chapter).

The Social Chapter, which was originally accepted at the Strasbourg summit of the EC in 1989 by all governments except Britain, is a fairly loose declaration of mainly employment-related social rights. These include principles on such issues as the free movement of labor throughout the Community, workplace health and safety, fair pay (minimum wage), equal pay for men and women, and workers' rights to information, consultation, and participation in workplace affairs.[66] The Social Chapter was vehemently opposed by most Conservative MPs and many in the business community. Moreover, other central elements of the Maastricht Treaty were also hard to implement and politically unacceptable to British "Eurosceptics." Few in Britain could countenance a common EC currency in place of sterling (the British currency), a symbol of empire and national autonomy, or accept direct control over monetary policy by a European central bank.

Unlike Thatcher, Major positioned himself as pro-Europe and was solicitous of his allies. But he also stood his ground on the two proposals he could not accept. Negotiating well, thereby gaining the respect of his fellow leaders, he secured crucial opt-out (or as Major called them, opt-in) clauses for Britain. The United Kingdom would not be bound by the provisions of the Social Chapter or by any single currency plans when the treaty achieved formal adoption. "It's game, set, and match for Britain," the prime minister exulted after the Maastricht summit. "We surrendered nothing. We lost nothing. I am delighted. It is a good day for Britain and a good day for Europe." Unfortunately for Major, political contests unlike tennis matches are seldom so decisively won.

The Thatcherite anti-Maastricht hard core never accepted the victory Major claimed to have won and dug in against Major on the key issues of economic and monetary union. At the same time, the Labour opposition supported the expansion of workers' rights as a matter of principle—and gleefully saw in the backbench Conservative rebellion an opportunity to embarrass, and possibly defeat, the Major government. The rebels were clever enough to hold their fire until after the March 1992 election when, as it turned out, a safe 102-seat government majority was slashed to a dangerously small twenty-one-seat majority. The pause did not last much longer. In June, Denmark sent shock waves throughout the EC by rejecting the treaty in a referendum. Then, in September, the government was sent reeling when it had to take Britain out of the Exchange Rate Mechanism (ERM)—an arrangement to harmonize economies and stabilize the value of one currency against another by limiting exchange rate fluctuations.

With high interest rates in Germany consuming investment and Britain experiencing a deepening recession, a tidal wave of selling pressed the value of the pound downward. Despite heroic efforts, Major could not save the British currency from fluctuating below the 6 percent limit set by the ERM. Black Wednesday (September 16, 1992), the day Britain was forced to abandon the ERM, was a sharp blow to Major's government. It at once wiped out the core European and domestic economic policies on which Major staked his leadership and symbolized in unmistakable terms that Britain's economy could not keep step with Germany or France. The lid blew off the opposition, as Tory rebels and Labour repeatedly attacked the prime minister and assailed his leadership. For very different reasons, Conservative critics and the Labour opposition intrigued to derail Maastricht, as the treaty went through a series of preliminary debates, committee and report stages, and its three readings in the Commons.

Because the Social Chapter dominated debate, Labour managed to tack on a very unusual amendment—immediately dubbed the "ticking time-bomb"—requiring that the Commons would face a separate vote on the Social Chapter *after* the government's Maastricht bill (which excluded the Social Chapter) became law. After more than a year of trench warfare, the Commons approved the Maastricht bill over the continued opposition of forty-one Conservative Eurosceptics in the Commons. Then the Lords easily passed the Maastricht bill, and on Tuesday, July 20, 1993, it received the royal assent and became law. Two days later, the timebomb exploded. Amid extraordinary anger and confusion, the government barely squeaked through on the first of two motions, by defeating a Labour motion calling on the government to abandon the opt-out from the Social Chapter. But then the almost unthinkable occurred—Tory rebels (who opposed Maastricht on any terms) joined forces with the Labour and Liberal Democratic opposition to defeat a government motion for authority to ratify the treaty.

Facing calls for his resignation, the prime minister immediately raised the stakes. Major took the extraordinary step—never before taken in recent history—of introducing a confidence motion by the gov-ernment (ministers dubbed it the "nuclear option") and demanded a vote the very next night. Having staked his future on Maastricht, Major forced the twenty-three rebels who voted against him to face a somber choice. If they voted against him in the vote of confidence, the government would fall, he would dissolve Parliament, and the Conservatives would face a general election under the worst possible circumstances. Opinion polls showed Major's approval rating at about 20 percent, and the Conservatives in third place behind Labour and the Liberal Democrats. In addition, the rebels would likely be banished from the party. On Friday night, the Conservative opposition dissolved, and Major survived the confidence motion by a comfortable forty-vote margin. What is the significance of the Maastricht episode for John Major's premiership and for British politics?

The Implications of Maastricht

The repercussions of Maastricht run deep and will help shape the challenges that the government and the country face in the years ahead. At one level, Maastricht absorbed the political agenda of the Major administration for more than a year, crowding out other issues. It focused party politics and defined leadership. Innocuous as the Social Chapter provisions seemed to many, Conservative MPs and many in the business community argued that its provisions would raise labor costs, hamstring business, and reduce British competitiveness. Beyond the specific consequences of the provisions, it held great symbolic significance. "The Social Chapter has grown out of all proportion to its true costs or benefits," noted Peter Riddell. "For the Tories, it is the symbol of their rejection of Brussels [European Union] interference and centralisation, around which all the party can unite."[67]

For John Major, the seemingly endless backbiting and rebellion over the Social Chapter and Maastricht hijacked his premiership. British-EU relations have tested—and weakened—his hold on party and office and have undermined his leadership from the earliest days through the mid–1990s. Not surprisingly, Conservative divisions over Europe, which extend into his cabinet, have increased Major's vulnerability to other problems, notably the embarrassment of his "back to basics" campaign. For Labour, the Social Chapter symbolizes a critical opportunity to offset the reduction in workers' rights and social benefits which occurred during the Thatcher and Major years. If implemented seriously, the provisions would go a long way toward raising British standards to a continental norm. Therefore, Labour MPs and supporters were solid on the Social Chapter, but the Party gained little support in the country with its reliance on tactical parliamentary maneuvers and its failure to emphasize the real significance of policy differences.

At another level, the Maastricht intrigues helped crystallize evolving constitutional practices, with important consequences for democratic ideals in Britain. When push came to shove, Major was able to win a vote of confidence—of his own making—and keep his government intact after losing a very significant motion in the Commons. These developments reenforce the pattern of declining parliamentary sovereignty. Even a weak and unpopular prime minister, it seems, with a sudden taste for political hardball can survive. In a system of fusion—not separation—of executive and legislature, significant questions may be asked about what remains of the democratic check on the exercise of prime ministerial power except at election time.

It should be noted, however, that in his conduct during the Maastricht crisis, Major reverted to a more traditional constitutional approach. By contrast to Thatcher, who bypassed the cabinet in many critical decisions, Major consulted the cabinet extensively, hatched the confidence vote strategy with senior ministers, and ratified it in the cabinet. Thus, both the underlying Europe policy and the parliamentary gambit were clearly stamped by collective responsibility. One constitutional principle (parliamentary sovereignty) was weakened, while another (the collective responsibility of the cabinet) was reaffirmed.

There is yet a deeper level of politics at play in the Maastricht intrigues that divided parties and deepened the fault line in British politics over Europe. Because Maastricht became a lightening rod for attacks on an untested prime minister, it became painfully obvious that the Conservative Party is deeply split over Europe. But so, too, is Labour. Some party supporters and as many as one hundred MPs oppose critical elements in the program (notably the creation of an independent European central bank). Maastricht offends them with its emphatic pro-business approach, notably its preoccupation with creating a European trading bloc to rival North America's NAFTA and an East Asian bloc led by Japan. Nor is the issue as simple as one might expect for the generally pro-Europe Liberal

Democrats. They are perceived as shifting, not gaining, ground on key issues such as the Social Chapter, pushing against the positions of the two leading parties, rather than firmly fixing their own. "The divisions inside British political parties are at least as deep as over any previous issue," observed the normally staid *Financial Times* in a morning-after editorial.[68] The remark points to the deep connection between international affairs and domestic politics and underscores the significance of our world of states theme. Far weaker than Germany in economic terms and isolated from the French political and diplomatic initiatives within the EU that have driven the pace of economic and political integration, Britain has been unable to manage the domestic impact of European policy.

BRITISH POLITICS IN TRANSITION

The trouble that EU policy has caused Thatcher and Major, and its role as a lightening rod for political opposition, are graphic illustrations of the interplay between "Europolitics" and domestic politics in Western Europe. Thus in France, President François Mitterrand of the Socialist Party was deeply hurt by a divisive referendum on the Maastricht Treaty that squeaked by in 1992 by less than 1 percent, despite the support of all major parties. In Germany, Chancellor Helmut Kohl's perceived leadership in foreign policy in Europe (his deft handling of unification and his control over EU economic policy) helped secure him a very narrow victory over the Social Democrats in October 1994. In both cases, European issues partly overlapped and partly displaced conventional left-right disagreements over resource allocation (distributional politics).

The Remapping of Politics?

It could well be that divisions over the European Union and the broader challenges of reconciling national interests and supranational ideals will contribute to a partial remapping of politics in much of Western Europe. It would not be surprising to find such disputes absorbing political agendas and differentiating political parties when a pragmatic consensus over economic and social policy reduces the level and intensity of traditional class or distributional politics. Although it is unusual for foreign policy concerns to shape domestic politics, the policy agenda of the EU affects domestic policy significantly by threatening Britain's national sovereignty over its economic, and potentially social and foreign, policy. In fact, this assault on national sovereignty is the principal reason European integration is so controversial and divisive.

The Maastricht agenda for increased economic and monetary union will fundamentally influence Britain's ability to compete internationally in economic terms. It will have dramatic consequences, therefore, on the standards of living and the distributional politics—the battles between social groups over their shares of the economic pie—at home. Mastering intra-EU diplomacy and policy-making may well become a litmus test of a party's and a government's credibility and electability, as the ability to run the economy and maintain the support of unions and business was in the past. It is likely, therefore, that the Europe issue will continue to bedevil British governments. To become Europeans—and not the most influential of EU countries at that—requires an adjustment to reduced standing and, for many, a weakening of national identity. Public opinion surveys suggest a sizeable gap in interest and conviction between political and economic elites who gradually accept the practical necessity of a pro-European stance and the voters who remain unconvinced and remarkably uninterested.

When interviewed, plainspoken Britons in Christchurch, a small, extremely conservative town on England's south coast, indicated their frustrations. They had heard enough about Maastricht and Europe and were fed up with the preoccupations of their representatives and leaders. One person said that she didn't know where Maastricht was; another remarked caustically that it was pensions that worry him, not Europe; a third said he couldn't stand the "silly games" in Parliament.[69] The citizens of Christchurch—who had voted Conservative in every election since 1910—weakened Major further by voting massively for the Liberal Democrats in a by-election (a special election for a vacated parliamentary seat) just after the Maastricht votes.

The Gap Between Government and Citizens

The attitudes expressed in Christchurch seem to reflect a much broader schism between the preoccupations of Parliament and the concern of Britons. In a sampling of public opinion taken shortly before the Maastricht intrigues in the Commons, respondents were asked to identify "the most important issue facing Britain" and

"other important issues." Only 9 percent identified Europe/EC as an important issue, compared to 69 percent for unemployment and 37 percent for National Health Service (NHS)/Health Care.[70] Closing this gap between the concerns of government and of the governed may be the greatest challenge ahead for British governments, whatever their political hue.

Ironically, British politics became preoccupied with Maastricht just when circumstances raised urgent questions about the prospects for European integration. Will the treaty's program ever be fully implemented? After the ERM was shaken once again in the summer of 1993 by currency speculation directed at the French franc and several other currencies, the timing and credibility of the Maastricht plan for economic and monetary union were jeopardized. At the same time, the plan for greater foreign policy coordination and a new post–Cold War security role for Europe lost credibility as the devastating war in Bosnia continued, despite high-profile efforts by the European Union to find a solution. More generally, the EU countries were increasingly troubled by recession, rising unemployment (an EU average of over 10 percent), and a loss of leadership and initiative—not to mention a troubling upsurge in anti-immigrant violence. By the mid-1990s, the spirit of Maastricht was spent, and the future of European integration uncertain.

There is a second irony about Britain and Maastricht. An unexpected transition in both economic fortunes and regional influence may be underway. Notwithstanding the dire political repercussions for the Major government, once Britain left the ERM in September 1992, it appeared to prosper in economic terms. By mid-1993, the United Kingdom reported increased growth, relatively low inflation rates, and falling unemployment—in short, healthy signs of economic recovery that made Britain the best-performing European economy at mid-decade. Politically, the French and Germans, among others, clung to the ERM and the Maastricht plan. But it began to dawn on political leaders and business elites on the continent, whose national economies were suffering a deepening recession, that there might be an alternative. After years of ridicule, the British approach to economic management and EU policy—a mix of deregulation, greater national autonomy, and expansion of EU ties with the East—was at least gaining a quiet audience. To the extent that policy failures and post–Cold War complications slowed (or derailed) the pace of economic and monetary integration, the British approach might gain greater support. If so, British influence in the EU might expand, and the ostracism and recriminations of the Thatcher era might be relegated decisively to the past.

The International Dimension

In another policy area, however, Britain's international relations may become more, rather than less, contentious as Britain grapples with its obligations to the residents of the crown colony Hong Kong. After lengthy negotiations completed in 1984, Britain and the People's Republic of China agreed that the territory would revert to Chinese sovereignty in 1997. Britain's policy options in China are complicated by the postcolonial legacy of divisions over race and immigration, combined with international pressures—to maintain positive relations with China as a growing economic power, but to pressure it to permit democracy and preserve market freedoms in Hong Kong.

The Tiananmen Square massacre in 1989 dramatically increased fears among Hong Kong residents of a repressive regime after the transfer of power. In July 1990, after rancorous debate, the British Parliament approved a plan to grant the right of British residence to 50,000 "key people" and their family members (up to a total of 225,000). Because it favors selected elites, this policy satisfies almost no one (certainly neither the majority of Hong Kong residents nor the Chinese government, which fears a brain drain). Moreover, it raises important questions about the linkage between citizenship rights and specific credentials or economic circumstances.

As the date of transfer approached, negotiations with China were strained and generally unproductive as Britain pressed for democratic reforms in Hong Kong against China's wishes. In an era when the United States granted China most-favored-nation status (an agreement that Chinese products can enter U.S. with the fewest possible barriers), how far is the U.K. prepared to press China, and risk the wrath of a huge economic power?

Constitutional Questions

Not only in China or in other Third World countries, but even in Britain, issues about democratic governance and citizen participation remain unresolved (although, of course, to a lesser degree). Because the traditionally sacrosanct royal family has been rocked

by scandal and improprieties, questions about the undemocratic underpinning of the British state are asked with greater urgency. "Why is the House of Commons not sovereign?" wondered one observer somewhat caustically. "Why does it have to share sovereignty with other, unelected institutions?"[71] Few reject the monarchy outright, but there is more grumbling than ever before about the role the Crown might have in the formation of a government when no party had won a clear-cut majority after a general election. Also, in a time of cutbacks and budgetary pressures, and particularly after a fire at Windsor Castle brought the issue of royal finances to the fore, the cost to taxpayers of the expensive and battered monarchy raises questions for many. Perhaps most significantly, questions about the role of the monarchy helped place on the agenda broader issues about citizen control over government and constitutional reform.

The balance of power among constitutionally critical institutions remains a major issue of contemporary political debate. One well-respected observer of the British constitution recently noted,

> At the moment, the Commons is hobbled. It is constricted on one level by strong, oligopolistic political parties. On another, it is virtually neutered by a modern executive whose reach (vis-à-vis its own policy) far exceeds that of any other executive in the Western world.[72]

Add to these concerns, the secrecy afforded the British government (there is no equivalent to a Freedom of Information Act) and the absence of a Bill of Rights, and it seems appropriate to raise questions about the accountability of British government to its citizens, despite the reforms embodied in the citizen's charters.

Northern Ireland

In the fall of 1994, cease-fire declarations made by the IRA and the Protestant paramilitary organizations renewed hope for a peace settlement in Northern Ireland. Then in a dramatic new development in early spring 1995, a Framework Agreement jointly issued by British Prime Minister John Major and Irish Prime Minister John Bruton inspired mounting optimism about a political settlement. The key proposals in this agreement included a new Northern Ireland assembly;

Source: Courtesy Chris Riddell, from *The Economist.*

an all-Ireland body of elected representatives from the Northern Ireland assembly and the Irish parliament with executive as well as consultative powers; an end to the Irish constitutional claim to Northern Ireland; and a guarantee that no settlement would be imposed by London or Dublin (rather, that any settlement would be subjected to separate referendums in the Republic of Ireland and, more significantly, in Northern Ireland).

The document judiciously balanced the unionist and republican concerns. Nevertheless, its challenge to the status quo that favors those who want Northern Ireland to remain part of the United Kingdom enflamed the unionist community and gave new force to the idea that a political settlement requires close collaboration between Northern Ireland and the Irish Republic. Although it appeared in 1995 that John Major was winning a high-stakes gamble on a settlement in Northern Ireland, his short-term political risks were considerable, especially since he

needed unionist votes in the Commons to control a majority.

The Pragmatic Center

Remarkably, by the mid-1990s, Northern Ireland was John Major's one bright spot. But for that unlikely source of optimism, Major remained on the defensive, engulfed in the rush of scandals and continued backbench rebellion over Europe. Two years after the parliamentary crisis over Maastricht—and that much closer to a general election mandated for no later than early April 1997—nothing was settled. Hoping to outmaneuver the Eurosceptics who continued to plague his premiership and threaten to mount a leadership challenge, Major forced the issue by abruptly resigning as party leader in June 1995. In the hasty ballot for leader that followed early in July, Major prevailed in the first round over a low-profile former cabinet member, the Welsh secretary, John Redwood. By winning the high-stakes gamble against a lesser candidate, Major saved himself from a more bruising contest against a more formidable challenger later, and probably secured the right to lead the party into the next general election.

Major was buoyed by the victory and by a successful effort to bring into the fold a far more significant potential challenger, Michael Haseltine, by appointing him Deputy Prime Minister after the leadership vote. Nevertheless, the fact that approximately one-third of the Conservative MPs refused to vote for the prime minister on the first ballot was ample testimony that divisions over Europe were not healed and that the Major premiership was unlikely to ever free itself from attack by the Eurosceptics.

At mid-decade the Major government seemed ill-equipped to lead the country or to consolidate a new moderate consensus. If given the chance, the young, telegenic and popular leader of the Labour Party, Tony Blair, characterized as "idealistic without being ideological," would help move British politics to a pragmatic pro-market, pro-Europe center. And opinion polls decisively suggested that his chance would come.

Of course, distributional issues remain on the agenda from Britain's classic two-class/two-party system. Inequality and differences of perspective (not to mention partisan politics) mean that consensus can never be fully achieved on issues such as benefit levels for social services, wage levels and commitments to full employment, and the role of the state in governing the economy or leaving it to private interests. Nevertheless, it appears that Britain is prepared to leave behind both the collectivist consensus and the Thatcherite alternative.

BRITAIN IN COMPARATIVE PERSPECTIVE

For many reasons, both historical and contemporary, Britain represents a critical case in comparative terms and a useful basis for examining comparative politics at the crossroads. The British case remains unusually instructive, even if Britain is no longer a leading power, because of its record of "firsts," the influence of the Westminster model on its former colonies throughout the world, and the high-profile pro-market model of individualism and competition advanced powerfully by Margaret Thatcher and John Major.

As the first industrial nation, Britain took the lead in establishing production and exchange on a global scale. It also was the first country to construct an innovative model of democracy based on parliamentary sovereignty and supported by a political culture that prized moderation, respect for disagreement, and toleration. The leading power in the nineteenth century, Britain has experienced the domestic political dislocations of decline far longer than any other country. Does it still offer a distinctive and appealing model of democracy? How well have three uninterrupted centuries of constitutional government and a culture of laissez-faire capitalism prepared Britain for a political and economic world it has fewer resources to control? How well has it handled decline—and what general lessons can be drawn from its successes and failures?

For example, we have asked how well a model of government formed in a very different era has stood the test of time and radically changed conditions. Sparked initially by criticisms of the monarchy, many voices in Britain, representing a surprising spectrum of political opinion, answer that substantial constitutional changes are needed to enhance accountability and democratic control by its citizens. A recent editorial in *The Economist* stressed that in terms of constitutional revision there are bigger issues than the monarchy to address: excessive power of the Commons and, therefore, of the cabinet; an electoral system that permits strong majority government to be elected by a minority of voters; the absence of both a

court authorized to engage in judicial review and a Bill of Rights; and a constitutionally protected lack of accountability to the country by the vast unelected agencies of government. The editorial concluded that the case for constitutional change is "irresistible."[73]

As we have discussed, the core constitutional concept *parliamentary sovereignty* does not capture the reality of executive-dominated government, secured almost always by single-party majorities in the Commons and MPs unwilling to exert their ultimate authority by forcing an early election. Nor does the concept of *cabinet government* reveal the potential for prime ministerial dominance, on the one hand, or the power of a vast unelected bureaucracy, on the other. Nevertheless, it should be emphasized that the shift from parliamentary to executive authority is a pattern common to all industrial democracies, as the scale and complexity of policy make parliamentary scrutiny unworkable and an extensive professional corps of officials necessary.

If the British feel themselves removed from day-to-day control over the affairs of government, they are hardly alone! And despite the questions Britons raise about the rigidities built into their quite ancient institutional architecture, others—in Nigeria, Russia, Japan, or even the United States—see the Westminster model as an enduring testament to representative democracy, stability, tolerance, and the virtues of a constitutional tradition that balances a competitive party system with effective government at the center.

Although the relatively small scale of the ethnic minority community limits the political impact of the most divisive issues of collective identity, it is probably in this area that rigidities in the British political system challenge tenets of democracy and tolerance most severely. With a single-member, simple-plurality electoral system and no proportional representation, minority representation in Parliament is very low, governments are unresponsive to concerns about cultural isolation, and racially motivated violence is rising. Cuts in the value of benefits, and the tightening of eligibility requirements for some benefits, and weak employment prospects for minorities (a result of both labor market pressures and prejudice) deepen the marginalization of religious, ethnic, and racial minority communities. The British experience reflects a global trend of rising ethnic tensions within industrialized and developing countries in the 1990s. The

British case suggests the importance of the collective identities theme, and the tendency for marginalization of minority communities through the loss of employment opportunities and the narrowing of social services.

What implications does the British case have for our world of states theme? In Chapter 1, we discussed the expectation that a declining power, even in European terms, would encounter difficulty in managing the domestic impact of decisions by regional blocs, and here the British case is no exception. Britain did better than expected in shaping EU policy at Maastricht however, and this should remind us to consider such intangibles as leadership, negotiating skill, and historic (as distinct from contemporary) power in analyzing international relations. Britain is no longer a world power and cannot rival Germany or even France in European terms, but it is possible to view its policy as a stalwart and reasonably successful effort to shape its external environment in accordance with its goals.

Finally, we come to the theme of production and exchange. It has become an axiom of comparative politics and knowledgeable commentary, more generally, that the world's economic success stories—Japan, Germany, and the newly industrializing countries of east Asia such as Taiwan, the Republic of Korea, and Singapore—rely on sophisticated interventionist strategies of economic governance by the state and a dense network of reciprocal relationships with private interests. Some comparativists argue that strategic interaction between the state and key economic and social interests advances the prospects for innovation and international competitiveness and increases the likelihood of coherent policy and consistent economic performance. Very true, but the United Kingdom has escaped the recession plaguing the rest of Europe, and (one of the best kept secrets of comparative politics) has enjoyed higher growth rates than Germany throughout much of the 1980s and 1990s! The causes for Britain's success and its economic prospects for the future continue to fuel partisan debate. Did Britain get lucky in September 1992, when it was forced to change course after the debacle of Black Wednesday? Or is Britain's "less is more" approach to economic management an important and timely alternative to the more state-centered and interventionist strategies of Germany, France, or Japan?

Agreement on this highly charged issue is unlikely, but the economic performance of Britain, like its efforts to secure a powerful independent voice in international relations and renew the debate about long-settled constitutional questions, has repercussions far beyond the tiny British Isles. Is Britain outmoded or resilient? In this era of uncertain democratic transitions and experimentation with diverse models of economic management, Britain's response to contemporary challenges will be closely watched for important clues.

Key Terms

Westminster model	Keynesianism
political development	privatization
regime	planning
Commonwealth	industrial policy
new right	corporatism
welfare state	monetarism
political culture	parliamentary
collective	sovereignty
responsibility	unitary state
state	fusion of powers
nations	judicial review
nation-state	patron-client relations
hegemonic power	proportional
Keynesian demand	representation
management	new social movements

Suggested Readings

Section 1

Hobsbawm, E. J. *Industry and Empire.* Harmondsworth: Penguin/Pelican, 1983.

Ingham, Geoffrey. *Capitalism Divided? The City and Industry in British Social Development.* London: Macmillan, 1984.

Landes, David S. *The Unbound Prometheus: Technological Change and Industrial Development in Western Europe from 1750 to the Present.* Cambridge: Cambridge University Press, 1969.

Maitland, F. W. *The Constitutional History of England.* Cambridge: Cambridge University Press, 1931.

Thompson, E. P. *The Making of the English Working Class.* New York: Vintage, 1966.

Section 2

Beer, Samuel H. *Britain Against Itself: The Political Contradictions of Collectivism.* New York: Norton, 1982.

Middlemas, Keith. *Politics in Industrial Society: The Experience of the British System since 1911.* London: Andre Deutsch, 1979.

Panitch, Leo. *Social Democracy and Industrial Militancy: The La-bour Party, the Trade Unions and Incomes Policy, 1945–1974.* Cambridge: Cambridge University Press, 1965.

Shonfield, Andrew. *Modern Capitalism: The Changing Balance of Public and Private Power.* Oxford: Oxford University Press, 1965.

Titmuss, Richard. *Social Policy.* New York: Pantheon, 1974.

Wilson, Elizabeth. *Women and the Welfare State.* London: Tavistock, 1977.

Section 3

Ashford, Douglas E. *Policy and Politics in Britain: The Limits of Consensus.* Oxford: Basil Blackwell, 1981.

Drewry, Gavin, and Tony Butcher. *The Civil Service Today.* Oxford: Basil Blackwell, 1988.

Greenwood, John, and David Wilson. *Public Administration in Britain.* London: George Allen and Unwin, 1984.

Gyford, John. *Local Politics in Britain.* 2d ed. London: Croom Helm, 1984.

Hall, Peter A. *Governing the Economy: The Politics of State Intervention in Britain and France.* New York: Oxford University Press, 1986.

Marshall, Geoffrey. *Ministerial Responsibility.* Oxford: Oxford University Press, 1989.

Rush, Michael, ed. *Parliament and Pressure Politics.* Oxford: Clarendon Press/Oxford University Press, 1990.

Section 4

Drucker, Henry, et al. *Developments in British Politics.* Vol. 4. New York: St. Martin's Press, 1993.

King, Anthony, et al. *Britain at the Polls, 1992.* Chatham, N.J.: Chatham House, 1993.

Marshall, Geoffrey. *Constitutional Conventions: The Rules and Forms of Political Accountability.* Oxford: Clarendon Press/Oxford University Press, 1986.

Norton, Philip, ed. *Parliament in the 1980s.* Oxford: Basil Blackwell, 1988.

Särlvik, Bo, and Ivor Crewe. *Decade of Dealignment: The Conservative Victory of 1979 and Electoral Trends in the 1970s.* Cambridge: Cambridge University Press, 1983.

Section 5

Allan, Philip, et al., eds. *Focus on Britain 1994.* Chicago: Fitzroy Dearborn, 1994.

Barnet, Anthony, et al., eds. *Debating the Constitution: A New Perspective on Constitutional Reform.* Cambridge: Polity, 1993.

Gilroy, Paul. *'There Ain't No Black in the Union Jack' : The Cultural Politics of Race and Nation.* Chicago: University of Chicago Press, 1991.

Hall, Stuart, and Martin Jacques, eds. *The Politics of Thatcherism.* London: Lawrence and Wishart, 1983.

Riddell, Peter. *The Thatcher Decade.* Oxford: Basil Blackwell, 1989.

Endnotes

[1] For the classic treatment of collectivism, see Samuel H. Beer, *British Politics in the Collectivist Age* (New York: Knopf, 1965).

The book was published in Britain with the title *Modern British Politics: A Study in Parties and Pressure Groups,* and a new edition was subsequently introduced in 1982 in the United States with that title.

[2] Jeremy Black, *The Politics of Britain 1688–1800* (Manchester and New York: Manchester University Press, 1993), 6. Black locates the Glorious Revolution of 1688 very well within the context of seventeenth-century British politics.

[3] David S. Landes, *The Unbound Prometheus: Technological Change and Industrial Development in Western Europe from 1750 to the Present* (Cambridge: Cambridge University Press, 1969), 41–123.

[4] E. J. Hobsbawm, *Industry and Empire* (Harmondsworth: Penguin/Pelican, 1983), 29–31.

[5] E. P. Thompson, *The Making of the English Working Class* (New York: Vintage, 1966), 168. This discussion more generally follows closely from Thompson, especially pp. 189–233.

[6] E. J. Hobsbawm, *Industry and Empire* (Harmondsworth: Penguin/Pelican, 1983), 13.

[7] Keith Middlemas, *Politics in Industrial Society: The Experience of the British System Since 1911* (London: Andre Deutsch, 1979), 154.

[8] Philip Allan, John Benyon, and Barry McCormick, eds., *Focus on Britain 1994* (Chicago: Fitzroy Dearborn, 1994), 197.

[9] See Paul M. Kennedy, *The Rise and Fall of British Naval Mastery* (London and Atlantic Highlands, N.J.: Ashfield Press, 1992), 186–189.

[10] Nick Crafts, "Economic Profile," in *Focus on Britain 1994,* ed. Philip Allen, John Banyan, and Barry McCormick, (Chicago: Fitzroy Dearborn, 1994), 101.

[11] *Ibid.,* 103.

[12] For a useful summary of the causes of economic decline in Britain see Bill Jones and Dennis Kavanagh, *British Politics Today* (Manchester and New York: Manchester University Press, 1994), 190–194.

[13] Peter A. Hall, "Patterns of Economic Policy: An Organizational Approach," in *The State in Capitalist Europe,* ed. Stephen Bornstein, et al. (London: George Allen and Unwin, 1984), 34–39.

[14] See Stephen Wilks, "Economic Policy," in *Developments in British Politics 4,* ed. Patrick Dunleavy, et al. (New York: St. Martin's, 1993), 222–223.

[15] Samuel H. Beer, *Britain Against Itself: The Political Contradictions of Collectivism* (New York: Norton, 1982), 175.

[16] Community Development Project, *In and Against the State* (London: CDP, 1979), 6.

[17] Paul Pierson, "Taking the Jewel From Labour's Crown? Mrs. Thatcher's Assault on the British Welfare State," Department of Government and Center for European Studies Working Paper, Series no. 27 (Cambridge, Mass.: Center for European Studies, Harvard University, 1990), 6.

[18] Michael Jones, *Marxism Today* (May 1980): 10.

[19] Ivor Crewe, "Labor Force Changes, Working Class Decline, and the Labour Vote: Social and Electoral Trends in Postwar Britain," in *Labor Parties in Postindustrial Societies,* ed. Frances Fox Piven (New York: Oxford University Press, 1992), 34. See also David Marsh and R. A. W. Rhodes, "Implementing Thatcherism: Policy Change in the 1980s," *Parliamentary Affairs* 45, no. 1 (January 1992): 34–37.

[20]Joel Krieger, "Class, Consumption, and Collectivism: Perspectives on the Labour Party and Electoral Competition in Britain," in Piven, *Labor Parties in Postindustrial Societies,* 58–63.

[21]Kenneth Newton, "Caring and Competence: The Long, Long Campaign," in *Britain at the Polls 1992,* ed. Anthony King (Chatham, New Jersey: Chatham House Publishers, 1993), 147.

[22]See Paul Gilroy, *'There Ain't No Black in the Union Jack': The Cultural Politics of Race and Nation* (Chicago: University of Chicago Press, 1991), 51–59.

[23]Stuart Hall, "The Question of Cultural Identity," in *Modernity and Its Futures,* ed. Stuart Hall, David Held, and Tony McGrew (Cambridge: Polity, 1992), 291.

[24]Ian Forbes, "Gender, Race and Inequality," in *Focus on Britain 1994,* 199.

[25]Bob Jessop, Kevin Bonnett, Simon Bromley, and Tom Ling, *Thatcherism* (Cambridge: Polity Press, 1988), 48.

[26]Forbes, "Gender, Race and Inequality," 193–196.

[27]Wilks, "Economic Policy," 224.

[28]Philip Norton, *The British Polity,* 3d ed. (New York and London: Longman, 1994), 59. See Norton for a useful discussion of the sources of the British constitution.

[29]Stephen Haseler, "Britain's Ancien Regime," *Parliamentary Affairs* 40, no. 4 (October 1990): 415.

[30]Philip Norton, "Constitutional Monarchy," in *The Oxford Companion to Politics of the World,* ed. Joel Krieger (New York: Oxford University Press, 1993), 190–191.

[31]Geoffrey Marshall, *Constitutional Conventions: The Rules and Forms of Political Accountability* (Oxford: Clarendon Press/Oxford University Press, 1986), 220–222. The discussion of conventions associated with a hung parliament follows closely from Marshall's account.

[32]S. E. Finer, *Five Constitutions* (Atlantic Highlands, N.J.: Humanities Press, 1979), 52.

[33]Donald R. Shell, "The British Constitution in 1984," *Parliamentary Affairs* 38, no. 2 (Spring 1985): 131.

[34]Jorgen S. Rasmussen, *The British Political Process* (Belmont, Calif.: Wadsworth, 1993), 84. Consult Rasmussen for a clear and useful explanation of the organization of the executive and the relationship between ministries and civil service.

[35]Gavin Drewry and Tony Butcher, *The Civil Service Today* (Oxford: Basil Blackwell, 1988), 21.

[36]Andrew Gray and Bill Jenkins, "Public Administration and Government 1992–3," *Parliamentary Affairs* 47, no. 1 (January 1994): 8.

[37]Simon Mohun, "Continuity and Change in State Economic Intervention," in *Restructuring Britain: Politics in Transition* (London: Sage, 1989), 73.

[38]"Still Under Suspicion" *The Economist,* July 10, 1993, 47.

[39]John Gyford, *Local Politics in Britain* (London: Croom Helm, 1984), 284.

[40]For a discussion of this terminology, see Jorgen S. Rasmussen, *The British Political Process,* 87.

[41]See David Judge, "Parliament and Interest Representation," in *Parliament and Pressure Politics* (Oxford: Clarendon Press, Oxford University Press, 1990), 31–38.

[42]A. G. Jordan and J. J. Richardson, *Government and Pressure Groups in Britain* (Oxford: Clarendon Press, Oxford University Press, 1987), 8. The metaphor was originally applied to the Norwegian cabinet.

[43]David Judge, "Parliament and Interest Representation," in *Parliament and Pressure Politics,* ed. Michael Rush (Oxford: Clarendon Press, Oxford University Press, 1990), 34–35.

[44]Philip Norton, *The Commons in Perspective* (Oxford: Basil Blackwell, 1985), 11–26. For a discussion of the historic decline of Parliament, see in addition Norton, "Introduction: Parliament in Perspective," in *Parliament in the 1980s,* ed. Philip Norton (Oxford: Basil Blackwell, 1988), 1–19; Dennis Kavanagh, *British Politics: Continuities and Change* (New York: Oxford University Press, 1988), 222–224.

[45]Norton, *Parliament in the 1980s,* 4.

[46]*The Economist,* November 5, 1983, 64.

[47]Samuel H. Beer, *The British Political System* (New York: Random House, 1973), 157.

[48]See Colin Leys, *Politics in Britain: From Labourism to Thatcherism,* rev. ed. (London: Verso, 1989), 193–212.

[49]Bob Jessop, et al., "Authoritarian Populism, Two Nations and Thatcherism," *New Left Review,* no. 147 (September/October 1984): 39.

[50]See Bo Särlvik and Ivor Crewe, *Decade of Dealignment: The Conservative Victory of 1979 and Electoral Trends in the 1970s* (Cambridge: Cambridge University Press, 1983).

[51]Henry Drucker and Andrew Gamble, "The Party System," in *Developments in British Politics 2,* rev. ed., ed. Drucker, et al. (London: Macmillan, 1988), 60.

[52]Market and Opinion Research International (MORI), *British Public Opinion* xiii, no. 6 (July 1990): 4.

[53]Ivor Crewe, "Great Britain," in *Electoral Change in Western Democracies,* ed. I. Crewe and D. Denver (London: Croom Helm, 1985), 107.

[54]Rasmussen, *The British Political Process,* 186.

[55]See Gabriel A. Almond and Sidney Verba, *The Civic Culture: Political Attitudes and Democracy in Five Nations* (Princeton: Princeton University Press, 1963); Almond and Verba, eds., *The Civic Culture Revisited* (Boston: Little, Brown, 1980); and Beer, *Britain Against Itself,* 110–114.

[56]Ivor Crewe, "The Thatcher Legacy," in *Britain at the Polls 1992,* ed. Anthony King, et al. (Chatham, N.J.: Chatham House Publishers, 1993), 18.

[57]*Ibid.,* 18–25.

[58]Benedict Anderson, *Imagined Communities,* rev. ed. (London and New York: Verso, 1991).

[59]See Stuart Hall, "The Question of Cultural Identity," in *Modernity and Its Futures,* ed. Stuart Hall, et al. (Cambridge: Polity Press, 1992), 273–316.

[60]Wyn Grant, "The Erosion of Intermediary Institutions," *The Political Quarterly* 60, no. 1 (January 1989): 12.

[61]David Judge, "Parliament and Interest Representation," in *Parliament and Pressure Politics,* ed. Michael Rush (Oxford: Oxford University Press, Clarendon Press, 1990), 33–34.

[62]Joyce Gelb, "Feminism and Political Action," in *Challenging the Political Order: New Social and Political Movements in Western Democracies,* ed. Russell J. Dalton and Manfred Kuechler (New York: Oxford University Press, 1990), 140–144.

[63]Kent Worcester, "The Follies of John Major," *New Politics* (Summer 1994): 47. Worcester offers a very useful review of the goals and problems of the Major government, from which several points in this introductory section are drawn.

[64]*Ibid.*

[65]*Financial Times,* October 12, 1994.

[66]See Clive Archer and Fiona Butler, *The European Community: Structure and Process* (New York: St. Martin's, 1992), 107–113.

[67]Peter Riddell, "Confident Major Goes on Offensive," *The Times,* July 23, 1993, 2.

[68]*Financial Times,* July 24, 1993, 8.

[69]David Butler, "Sideshow Waits Patiently for Its Moment in the Spotlight," *Financial Times,* July 24/25, 1993, 4.

[70]*British Public Opinion Newsletter,* July 1993, 2.

[71]Haseler, "Britain's Ancien Regime," 418.

[72]Haseler, 420.

[73]"An Idea Whose Time Has Passed," *The Economist*, October 22–28, 1994, 15–16.

CHAPTER 3

France

Land and Population

Capital	Paris
Total Area (square miles)	211,208 (more than twice the size of Colorado)
Population	57.5 million
Annual Projected Population Growth Rate (1993–2000)	0.4%
Urban Population (% of total)	73%

Ethnic Composition National Origin	French-born	93%
	Other European	3%
	North African	2%
	Other	2%
Major Language	French	
Major Religions	Catholic	79%
	Secular	16%
	Protestant	2%
	Muslim	1%*
	Jewish	1%

Economy

Domestic Currency	Franc
GNP (US$)	$1.09 trillion
GNP per capita (US$)	$22,490
Purchasing Power Parity GDP per capita (US$)	$19,000
Average Annual GDP Growth Rate (1980–1993)	2.1%

Structure of Production (% of GDP)	Agriculture	3%
	Industry	29%
	Services	68%
Labor Force Distribution (% of total)	Agriculture	6%
	Industry	29%
	Services	65%
Women as % of Total Labor Force	40%	

Income Distribution (1989)	% of Population	% Share of Income or Consumption
	Richest 20%	41.9%
	Poorest 20%	5.6%

Total Foreign Trade (exports plus imports) as % of GDP	37%

Society

Life Expectancy	Female	81
	Male	73
Population per Doctor	350	
Infant Mortality (per 1,000 live births)	7	
Adult Literacy	99%	
Mean Years of Schooling (of adults 25+)	Female	12.1
	Male	11.9
Communications (per 100 people)	Radios	89
	Televisions	40
	Telephones	61
1995 Human Development Index (1 = highest)	Ranks 8 out of 174	

Political Organization

Political System   Unitary republic

Regime History   Semipresidential system; popularly elected president, popularly elected parliament, and prime minister and government appointed by president and responsible to National Assembly.

Administrative Structure   Unitary, with 22 regions and 100 departments

Executive   Dual executive: president (seven-year term); PM appointed by president, generally leader of majority coalition in National Assembly, and responsible to National Assembly.

Legislature   Bicameral: Senate (upper house) has power to delay legislation passed by lower house. National Assembly (lower house) can pass legislation and force government to resign by passing a censure motion.

Judiciary   A nine-member independent Constitutional Council named for nonrenewable nine-year terms; president of republic names three members, president of each house of parliament names three. They exercise right of judicial review.

Party System   Multiparty. Principal parties: Rally for the Republic (RPR), Union for French Democracy (UDF), and Socialist Party (PS); minor parties: Communist Party (PCF), National Front (FN), and Green Party.

* This figure refers only to the proportion of Muslims among French *citizens*. Howerver, there are many immigrants from North Africa living in France who are Muslims and who are not naturalized French citizens. If they are included, Muslims are estimated to make up as much as 7% of France's total population.

SECTION 1
The Making of the Modern French State

FRANCE AT THE CROSSROADS

In order to understand how much France has changed since the 1980s, one might compare the celebration that occurred on May 10, 1981, the night that François Mitterrand was elected the first Socialist president in the Fifth Republic, with the one that occurred on May 7, 1995, following Jacques Chirac's election as president to succeed Mitterrand.

The Place de la Bastille, presently a large plaza in the center of Paris, was the site of the feared and despised Bastille prison under the French monarchy. The beginning of the French Revolution is often dated from the storming of the Bastille by an angry mob on July 14, 1789, an event that marked a new era in French, and possibly world, history. Bastille Day—July 14—is the equivalent of July 4 in the United States, the country's festive national holiday. The Place de la Bastille continues to be revered as the site where "the common people" triumphed over their oppressors more than two centuries ago.

A crowd at the Place de la Bastille, Paris, celebrates François Mitterrand's election as the first Socialist president of the Fifth Republic, May 10, 1981.
Source: Vincent/Rapho.

On the evening of May 10, 1981, after the election returns indicated that François Mitterrand had defeated his conservative rival to win the presidential election, a crowd gathered at the Bastille in a driving rainstorm. Thousands danced and sang to celebrate "the tranquil revolution" that Mitterrand had called for in his election campaign. The event symbolized the shift from a tired, stale, conservative government, which had governed France ever since the Fifth Republic was created in 1958, to a vibrant socialist movement eager to transform France.

It did not take long, however, for the passions that were ignited by the Socialist Party's 1981 program and that promised to produce a new society to fade. During the Socialists' long period in office—Mitterrand occupied the Élysée, the presidential palace, from 1981–1995, longer than any previous French president—a fundamental shift occurred in France's political economy and political culture. The change was a product of what did *not* occur while the

Socialists governed France. Contrary to Mitterrand's ambitious list of 121 proposed changes and his bold campaign slogans of 1981—"the tranquil revolution," "change life", and so on—the Socialists failed to create an egalitarian, radically democratic regime. But the considerable continuity in French politics before and after 1981 was itself highly significant for two reasons. First, it promoted the "normalization" of political alternation in France. The change from one governing coalition to another has lost the dramatic character that it had in 1981, and most French no longer expect that political alternation will produce important change. Second, because the Socialists cruelly extinguished the hopes that they had kindled, many French citizens became disillusioned with the very possibility of achieving social progress by political means. Such skepticism is a break with past tradition in a country where, for generations, people relied heavily on the state for help.

Newly elected President Jacques Chirac rides down the Champs Élysées, Paris, to his inauguration ceremony, May 17, 1995. Source: © Pool Passation de Pouvoir Mitterand-Chirac/Gamma.

In the mid-1990s, the exuberant certainties of 1981 gave way to doubt and confusion. When Jacques Chirac, mayor of Paris and leader of France's largest conservative party, succeeded Mitterrand as president in 1995, he carefully refrained from enumerating campaign promises, and his program was not much different from that of Socialist Party candidate Lionel Jospin, Chirac's principal rival. In the 1995 presidential election, a large proportion of French citizens abstained from voting or chose parties opposed to the major established parties that have governed since the beginning of the Fifth Republic. Chirac's supporters tried to copy Mitterrand's example by sponsoring an election-night celebration. But it was a poor imitation of the one that had occurred fourteen years earlier. It was held at the Place de la Concorde, a square in central Paris with no particular political symbolism, and turnout was small.

The flight from political engagement that began relatively soon after Mitterrand's election in 1981 may well mark the end of a period in French, and even world, history that began on July 14, 1789. Now, at the dawn of the twenty-first century, France is at a crossroads. Long-established practices and beliefs can no longer be taken for granted, including the central role of the French state, France's role in the world, and the very meaning of French democracy and national identity.

France was once a leading power, probably the most powerful country in the world in the seventeenth and eighteenth centuries. Yet, since the nineteenth century, France's claim to international preeminence has rested less on superior economic performance, military might, and political influence—the usual measures of international stature—and more on cultural leadership. Ever since the Revolution of 1789, the French have prided themselves on championing values that are distinctively French yet also hold universal appeal, notably, rationalism, modernity, **democracy,** and nationalism. At the same time, the Revolution produced a troubled legacy, for many French citizens rejected the revolutionary heritage, with its attack on the Catholic church and social privilege. The turbulence following the Revolution produced frequent changes in regime. Indeed, since the Revolution, France has experienced a change of regime, on average, every twenty years: five republics, two monarchies, two empires, and the **authoritarian** Vichy **regime** (see Table 1 on the following page).

The two-century cycle of political instability ushered in by the French Revolution may be ending. On the one hand, the Fifth Republic, created in 1958 during a period of great turmoil, eventually developed wide support. The political stability of recent decades contrasts strongly with the turbulence of French

---

TABLE 1 **Major French Constitutional Regimes**

Ancien régime (Bourbon monarchy)	Until 1789
Revolutionary regimes	1789–1799
Constituent Assembly, 1789–1791	
(Declaration of Rights of Man, Aug. 26, 1789)	
Legislative, 1791	
Convention, 1792–1795: Monarchy abolished and	
First Republic established, 1792	
Directory, 1795–1799	
Consulat and First Empire (Napoleon Bonaparte)	1800–1814
Restoration	1814–1830
July Monarchy	1830–1848
Second Republic	1848–1851
Second Empire (Louis Napoleon)	1852–1870
Paris Commune	1870
Third Republic	1870–1940
Vichy regime	1940–1944
Fourth Republic	1946–1958
Fifth Republic	1958–Present

---

politics throughout the nineteenth and early twentieth centuries. On the other hand, France's newfound stability may prove quite fragile, more a product of widespread ideological fatigue and anxiety about the future than an indication of political maturity. French citizens have become less certain of what is distinctive about their culture, less proud of their cultural heritage, and less secure about France's place in the world. Although some key values that the French claim as their own—for example, democracy—now enjoy near universal support, by that very token they are no longer distinctively French. Other values, including reason, progress, and modernity, are increasingly challenged by groups within France and elsewhere on the grounds that they represent a disguised form of cultural imperialism.

For generations, the French prided themselves on their nation's cultural uniqueness and superiority. This belief was combined with hostility toward American cultural values, often rejected as vulgar and materialistic. An important part of the recent shift in values is the embracing of American culture. Indeed, American popular culture—television programs, movies, cuisine, music, and clothing—has taken France by storm. After generations of French sneering at American culinary habits, Tex-Mex restaurants are now all over Paris. Even the French language is being "invaded" by English words, in a mixture that the French call

Franglais (a combination of *Français* [French] and *anglais* [English]). Yet, along with this new cultural openness, one can detect anxiety about the meaning of French national identity. French governments have recently fought to preserve French culture and identity by passing regulations that limit the use of English words in advertising and other public communication, and that limit American-produced programs on French television networks.

The French must not only reexamine what is distinctive about their political community and national identity. They must also confront challenges linked to France's relationship to Europe [given the strengthening of the European Union (EU), or European Community (EC) before 1995], global economic competition, and acute social and economic problems. Ironically, these challenges have developed at the very moment when, for the first time in generations, the Fifth Republic, which was created in 1958, has provided a stable and widely accepted political framework.

This political-institutional framework is quite unusual. The Fifth Republic's **semipresidential system** is a hybrid form of democratic regime, neither a fully **presidential system** nor fully a **parliamentary system.** The executive is by far the dominant power; the president and government direct the powerful bureaucracy and keep a tight rein on the legislature. The president is popularly elected, and some observers have described the regime as an elected monarchy because of the president's long term (seven years) and enormous power. What makes the regime semipresidential is the existence, alongside the president—who is the supreme head of the executive—of a government or cabinet headed by a prime minister chosen by the president. The government answers to a popularly elected parliament and governs on a day-to-day basis.

France's Socioeconomic Setting

France is among the world's favored countries, thanks to its temperate climate, large and fertile land area, relatively low population density, and high standard of living. With a population of over 57,000,000 inhabitants, France is one of the most populous countries in Western Europe, but its large size—221,000 square miles—means that its population density is low. The gross national product (GNP) of over $1 trillion and the per capita income of $20,000 place France among the most affluent countries in the world. Because images of bucolic village life still persist, many people do not realize how technologically advanced the French economy is. In recent decades, France pioneered in such varied fields as telecommunications, high-speed rail transportation, and atomic energy.

Thanks to rapid economic growth in the 1950s–1970s, France has become fully equipped with modern consumer conveniences. Most families own a television, a VCR, a telephone, and an automobile. Half own their own home. France ranks eighth among the 174 nations in the world in overall quality of life, according to the United Nations Human Development Index.

France has a modern economy, and the bulk of the population work in the industrial and service sectors. However, agriculture continues to occupy a significant place in the economy and, because the country was predominantly rural until quite recently, an even stronger place in the country's collective memory. Heightening the importance of the countryside is the fact that France is relatively underpopulated and has a relatively small urban population. No other French city comes close to rivaling Paris, the capital, in size and influence, and, other than Lyons and Marseilles—the next largest French cities—there are few large cities in France.

Although many countries confront socioeconomic and political challenges more acute than

France's, there are particular reasons why French politics is at a crossroads. When we analyze the critical junctures, or historical turning points, that have influenced the making of the modern French state, we find that the state has played a key role in forming and steering France's economy and society. In the present period, however, the French **state,** as is true of states throughout the world, has been less able to retain a commanding position. In France, as elsewhere, the balance has shifted toward greater freedom for private enterprise. However, it is doubtful that relying on market competition will offset declining state capacity in providing France with cohesion and leadership.

CRITICAL JUNCTURES

The Ancien Régime

"No other nation in the world entertains with the State as dense and passionate a relationship as does France."[1] This observation has been made countless times, for the French have historically displayed toward the state both enormous respect and intense resentment. France was created by monarchs in the premodern period who laboriously knit together the diverse provinces of what is present-day France but whose actions provoked periodic protest. The pattern of vigorous state activity and a popular backlash persisted until recently.

The development of the modern French state administrative system in the seventeenth and eighteenth centuries represented a breakthrough in Western political engineering. From the middle of the seventeenth century, Louis XIV sponsored the creation of a relatively efficient state bureaucracy, separate from the Crown's personal domain and the feudal aristocracy. France began to be administered according to a legal-rational code in which standardized regulations were applied throughout the country. But, alongside the modernizing state, there remained a complex and burdensome system of inherited feudal privileges. Furthermore, the monarchy collected taxes not only to finance a modern legal and administrative system but also to support the wasteful court at Versailles. Another cause of the popular resentment that eventually produced the French Revolution of 1789 was the Catholic church, a large landowner, tax collector, and ally of the feudal authorities.

In order to understand the modern French state, one must also understand France's relationship to the international political and economic arena. Dominant throughout Europe in the seventeenth century, France began declining when its principal rival, England, achieved an economic breakthrough as a result of improvements in agricultural techniques. An important cause of the French Revolution, the second moment in the emergence of the French state, was the domestic repercussions from France's inability to compete with England.

The Revolution[s]

Shortly after a crowd burst through the gates of the Bastille on July 14, 1789, freeing the prisoners, the French monarchy and entire **ancien régime** (old order) were abolished and a new era began in French and world history. France was the first European nation in which a **revolution** abolished the monarchy and established a **republic** based on the belief that all citizens, regardless of social background, were equal before the law. It is difficult to overestimate the impact of the revolution on people's thinking, in France and elsewhere. Historian Lynn Hunt observes:

> The chief accomplishment of the French Revolution was the institution of a dramatically new political culture. . . . Revolution in France contributed little to economic growth or to political stabilization. What it did establish, however, was the mobilizing potential of democratic republicanism and the compelling intensity of revolutionary change.[2]

Inspired by the ideas of the eighteenth-century Enlightenment philosophers Voltaire, Diderot, and others, the actions of the French revolutionaries suggested that ordinary men and women, and not kings and queens, could make history. Seeking to understand its significance, historian François Furet suggests that the revolution was the moment when

> the masses had broken in on the stage of history. . . . That is why, in a sense, everything indeed "began" there: 1789 opened a period when history was set adrift.[3]

The revolution was at the same time a *national* revolution, which affirmed the people's right to choose their own political regime; an *international* revolution, which inspired national uprisings elsewhere in Europe and sought to expand French revolutionary values internationally (often through military means); a *liberal* revolution, which championed the value of individual liberty in the political and economic spheres; and a *democratic* revolution, which gave rise to the notion that a nation's identity and the political regime's legitimacy derive from all citizens participating in choosing the government. These provocative ideas have since been diffused on a global level.

Yet the significance of the revolution did not lie simply in its democratic message. Far from destroying the centralized administrative apparatus created by French monarchs, the revolution freed the state from the centuries-old patchwork of feudal particularism that had hindered state action. Alexis de Tocqueville, a French aristocrat in the nineteenth century who was a brilliant student of French and American society, was the first to emphasize that the revolution not only produced a rupture with the ancien régime of the monarchy, but also promoted a major aim pursued by French monarchs: strengthening state institutions. Some important examples: Napoleon Bonaparte, the popular general in the revolutionary army who seized power and proclaimed himself emperor in 1802, created the system by which state-appointed officials called prefects administer localities; the Conseil d'État (State Council), which supervises the central administration; the École Polytechnique, which trains top civil servants; and the Napoleonic Code of civil law, an elaborate legal framework. These innovations persist to the present day.

What was absent—both during the period of the monarchy and during the revolution itself—was wide support for liberal values, notably, respect for limited government, political pluralism, loyal opposition to the prevailing government, an independent judiciary, and individual rights. This absence characterized—and plagued—French political culture until the 1980s, when a fundamental shift toward liberal values and political practice apparently occurred in French political development.

It is useful to contrast France with its neighbor across the English Channel. As political theorist Mark Lilla points out, "[French history] is littered with republics, restorations, revolutions, and empires, [but] the spirit of liberalism in the English and American sense never really took hold."[4] One can identify two dominant traditions in modern-day French political thought and practice, neither of which was friendly to liberalism. The first, originating in the absolute monarchy of the seventeenth century, accords the state a central role in creating and directing the French nation. The second has roots in the French Revolution and insists that citizens should decide their fate directly. The conflict between the statist and the democratic traditions produced a typical pattern of French politics, which political scientist Stanley Hoffmann has described as "[the coexistence of] limited authoritarianism and potential insurrection against authority."[5]

Since the revolution, French politics has often revolved around the question of how to reconcile state autonomy—the state's independence from pressure coming from groups within society—with democratic participation and decision making. Both tendencies flourish in France—but the two conflict. The French state, with its long tradition of independence, succeeded in developing the capacity to regulate the most important as well as the most trivial areas of social life. For example, the Ministry of Education controls the curriculum that shall be taught in all public schools; and, until quite recently, the Ministry of the Interior kept close watch on the names that local governments assigned to city streets and vetoed proposed changes it disliked. Regimes with sharply divergent orientations may succeed each other, but the state has pursued its own solitary course. And yet, at the same time—and partly because of the reaction provoked by the high-handed state—the democratic and confrontational legacy of the French Revolution has remained influential as well.

Rapid Regime Change, Slow Industrialization

France spent much of the nineteenth and early twentieth centuries digesting and debating the legacy of the revolution. The succession of regimes and revolutions during the two centuries after 1789 can be interpreted as varied attempts to resolve the key issue that the revolution posed but did not satisfactorily resolve: how to reconcile state autonomy and direction with democratic participation and decision making. Following the Revolution of 1789, there were frequent uprisings, revolutions, and regime changes. The First Republic was created in 1792 during the revolution, when Louis XVI was removed from power and the monarchy was abolished. The republic was undermined when Napoleon Bonaparte declared himself

emperor in 1802. The Bourbon monarchy, restored to power in 1814 following Napoleon's defeat by a coalition of European powers, was soon overthrown in a popular uprising and replaced by the Orleans monarchy during the revolution of July 1834. In 1848, another revolution produced yet another regime, the short-lived Second Republic. Napoleon III, the nephew of Napoleon Bonaparte, overthrew the republic after three years and proclaimed himself emperor. When France lost the Franco-Prussian War of 1870, the Second Empire was swept away by a revolutionary upheaval, which produced the Paris Commune. The Commune was quickly crushed, to be succeeded by the Third Republic, created in 1870 under the shadow of military defeat and civil war. The Third Republic, which lasted from 1870–1940, turned out to be France's most durable regime in the modern era. In a famous phrase by nineteenth-century sociologist Ernest Renan, the republic was described as that regime "which divides us [French] least."

The succession of regime changes dating from the Revolution of 1789 is extremely important in that it highlighted the existence of sharp cleavages and the absence of political institutions capable of regulating conflict. However, in sharp contrast with the dizzying pace at which regimes came and went, the rate of economic change in nineteenth- and early twentieth-century France was quite gradual. Compared to Germany, its dynamic neighbor to the northeast, France chose economic stability over modernization. The slow pace of industrialization—in a way, the *opposite* of a critical juncture—resulted, in part, from the fact that the political institutions of the Third Republic dispersed political power and prevented decisive political leadership.

The explanation for France's relatively poor economic performance also lies in the realm of cultural values. Stanley Hoffmann has characterized nineteenth- and early twentieth-century France as a *stalemate society*. Powerful social groups, rooted in small-town and rural France, clung to the established order for fear that changes associated with economic modernization, including urbanization, industrialization and, especially, the growth of an industrial working class, might produce social and political upheaval. The state was closely linked to the stalemate society and directed its efforts toward the conservative goal of maintaining law and order, rather than seeking to promote economic modernization. Slow economic growth did not prevent political conflict. But it did contribute to France's humiliating defeat by the Nazi regime in 1940.

Vichy (1940–1943) and the Fourth Republic (1946–1958)

World War II was one of the bleakest periods in French history. When France was overrun by Germany in 1940, the Third Republic collapsed and Marshal Philippe Pétain, an aged military hero, signed an armistice with the Nazi regime, dividing France in two. The north was under direct German occupation; the south was controlled by a puppet regime, presided over by Pétain, whose capital was at Vichy. The Vichy government collaborated with the Nazi occupation by providing workers and supplies for the German war machine and sending tens of thousands of Jews in France to their destruction in Nazi concentration camps. France was even more dishonored by the fact that, as historians have clearly demonstrated, the Vichy regime committed some of the worst crimes on its own initiative and not at the dictate of the Nazis. This perhaps helps explain why even today the French continue to find it so difficult to take responsibility for the Vichy era.

Although the vast majority of French quietly accepted France's defeat and meekly complied with the Vichy government's directives, a small, armed resistance movement developed within France. Charles de Gaulle, a prominent general, publicly broke with Vichy and assumed leadership of resistance forces. Although France actually contributed little to the Allied victory, de Gaulle's skillful actions enabled France to gain acceptance as a member of the victorious coalition and to obtain one of the five permanent membership seats on the United Nations Security Council following the war.

In 1945, at the war's end, de Gaulle sought to sponsor a new regime that would avoid the errors that, in his view, had weakened France, contributed to its moral decline and military defeat by Germany, and enabled the puppet Vichy regime to reach power. De Gaulle was strongly opposed to the institutional design of the Third Republic, in which the executive was completely dependent on parliament. Because many parties were represented in parliament and weak party discipline prevailed, stable coalitions rarely emerged to provide durable support for the govern-

ment. As a result, governments were toppled often, making effective leadership virtually impossible. De Gaulle charged that this situation encouraged party politicians to pursue their personal careers at the expense of public interests. He proposed creating a regime in which the government was independent and powerful.

De Gaulle failed to achieve the institutional reforms he desired. Having just overthrown the authoritarian Vichy regime, the French opposed strong executive leadership in the newly created republic. De Gaulle abruptly resigned as leader of the provisional regime drafting a constitution for the Fourth Republic and mounted an unsuccessful opposition campaign to the new republic. The constitution of the newly created Fourth Republic was, in fact, very similar to that of the Third Republic.

Despite some constitutional gimmicks intended to strengthen the government against the legislature, the Fourth Republic, which existed from 1946–1958, embodied an extreme form of parliamentary rule and weak executive. The constitution gave parliament a near monopoly of power, which it exercised in a quite destructive fashion: governments were voted out of office an average of once every six months! This situation resulted from the fact that many parties were represented in parliament, partly as a result of the system of proportional representation used to elect deputies to the National Assembly (the powerful lower house of parliament). As in the Third Republic, rapid shifts in party alliances, as well as a lack of discipline within parties, meant that governments lacked the cohesion and authority to make tough decisions and develop long-range policy. Although the Fourth Republic was often described as highly unstable, the situation might better be described as one of political stalemate.

Neither the Vichy regime nor the Fourth Republic satisfactorily combined state direction and democratic participation. By their opposite excesses, they underlined the need for devising an adequate constitutional framework to permit stable, democratic rule.

Despite some important achievements, notably, setting France on the road to economic expansion and modernization, the Fourth Republic was so internally divided that it failed to take decisive action in many important spheres. The regime was severely handicapped by the fact that powerful political forces, notably the Communist Party and de Gaulle's political movement, were well-represented in parliament and

"What!?? The president's a Socialist and the Eiffel Tower is still standing!??" "Incredible!"
Source: Courtesy Plantu, from *Le Monde*, May 1981.

strongly opposed one government after another. What finally destroyed the Fourth Republic was the agonizing war mounted by the Algerian independence movement to free Algeria from French colonial domination. This stalemate provided Charles de Gaulle with the opportunity to regain power. By threatening to direct a military takeover, he pressured parliament to authorize him to scrap the constitution of the Fourth Republic and propose a new constitutional framework, with a vastly strengthened executive and a weakened parliament.

The Fifth Republic (1958–Present)

The contrasting institutional designs of the Fourth and Fifth Republics provide a textbook case of how institutions shape political life. The Fourth Republic could be unkindly but accurately described as all talk and no action. While parliament debated endlessly, and voted to make and unmake governments, elected political leaders did little to address the nation's pressing problems. On the other hand, the Fifth Republic created institutions in which leaders could act decisively but (at least in the early years) were hardly accountable to parliament or public opinion.

It is unlikely that the French would have tolerated such an imbalanced regime for long. What made it acceptable in the short run was the extraordinary

personality of Charles de Gaulle, who served as first president of the Fifth Republic. Resistance hero, commanding presence, and one of the political giants of the twentieth century, de Gaulle was able to persuade the French to support a regime in which democratic participation was strictly limited. However, although de Gaulle commanded wide popularity, he also provoked bitter opposition both to his own leadership and to the centralized institutions of the Fifth Republic. For example, in May 1968, the high-handed attitude of the regime provoked students and workers to launch the largest general strike in Western history. For weeks, protesting workers and students occupied factories, offices, and universities, and the regime's very survival hung in the balance. Although de Gaulle regained control of the situation, he was discredited by the May events. He resigned from office the following year, after a referendum he sponsored to reorganize political institutions was defeated. Yet popular support for the Fifth Republic has gradually increased over time, in part because political institutions have become more responsive. (The functioning of political institutions is described in Sections 3 and 4.)

The Fifth Republic was severely tested in 1981, when François Mitterrand was elected president and Mitterrand's Socialist Party allies replaced conservative governments that had ruled since the beginning of the regime. At this time, many feared that Fifth Republic institutions would crumble under the impact of the shift from right to left in the political spectrum. But, on the contrary, the political alternation helped to consolidate support for the Fifth Republic. Socialist rule did not produce political chaos but, instead, strengthened political stability by demonstrating that the political institutions of the Fifth Republic provide an adequate framework for organizing political competition and change.

Most scholars now agree that the regime reflects a fairly adequate balance between state autonomy and democratic participation—possibly for the first time in French history. However, the fate of the French state has also been heavily influenced by France's relation to the international order, and, currently, new strains have developed from France's relation to the world of states.

FRANCE IN A WORLD OF STATES

France's relationship to Europe and other regions of the world, particularly Asia and Africa, has, to a large extent, shaped state formation. For over a century following France's defeat by an international coalition after the French Revolution, the country displayed an inward-oriented, isolationist orientation. For example, France erected high tariff barriers throughout the nineteenth century and the first half of the twentieth century to minimize international trade. France's colonial conquests in the nineteenth century were far smaller than Britain's.

France's relationship with Germany, against whom France fought three costly wars since 1870, has weighed heavily on state development. The fact that the two countries developed cordial relations after World War II, in part thanks to the mutually beneficial expansion of the world economy, has provided France with a vastly increased measure of security.

Although no longer in the first rank militarily, France remains an important player on the world stage. Unlike most countries, the French state can significantly influence its external environment and minimize the ways in which external forces shape domestic politics. Consider, for example, international negotiations in 1993 to revise the General Agreement on Tariffs and Trade (GATT), which regulates trade worldwide. Despite opposition from virtually all countries in the world, French negotiators succeeded in protecting French interests in the sphere of agricultural exports and in film and television production. And in the face of bitter international opposition, France conducted a series of underground nuclear tests in 1995–1996.

THE DEMOCRATIC IDEA

France has had an intense and complex relationship with the democratic idea. On the one hand, as described above, France's deeply rooted statist tradition is quite hostile to democratic participation and decision making. On the other hand, France is home to two very different democratic currents, both of which give high priority to the value of popular sovereignty. The first current, direct democracy, which dates back to eighteenth-century philosopher Jean-Jacques Rousseau, has been highly influential in France and throughout the world. The theory of direct democracy is hostile to political representation and intermediate associations, on the grounds that citizens should participate directly in political decisions, rather than merely choosing leaders who monopolize political power. In the nineteenth and twentieth centuries, the

tradition of direct democracy inspired the socialist movement in France and elsewhere. Closely linked to workers' struggles against their harsh treatment, the socialist movement (heavily influenced by Karl Marx's radical critique of capitalism) had a vibrant history, although it rarely succeeded in gaining control of the state. However, the Socialist Party's victory in presidential and legislative elections in 1981 ushered in over a decade of Socialist rule.

Although the conception of "strong democracy" contains much of value, it may not accord high priority to the rights and liberties of individuals and dissenting minorities. A related danger, as Tocqueville warned over a century ago, is that a demagogue may manipulate the institutions of direct democracy in order to become a popular dictator. Examples of this tendency include Napoleon Bonaparte, after the French Revolution, and his nephew Louis Napoleon, who destroyed the Second Republic in 1851.

The second powerful democratic current in French political culture emphasizes the dangers of direct democracy and stresses the value of representative democracy. Many who opposed de Gaulle's high-handed actions after World War II and following his return to power in 1958 criticized him for violating the representative democratic tradition and assuming *le pouvoir personnel*—"personal power." The parliamentary tradition opposes anything that smacks of direct democracy. It advocates, instead, delegating power to the people's elected representatives in parliament.

Despite their great differences, the two democratic traditions share with each other and with the statist tradition an important feature, one that was considered a central pillar of French political culture until recently. All three influential political currents have traditionally opposed the concept of a written constitution, interpreted by an independent judiciary, limiting state power. The French have rarely viewed a constitution with the reverence displayed by many Americans toward the U.S. Constitution. And they have even more vehemently opposed an independent judiciary limiting the executive and legislature. A fundamentally important change in French political culture since the 1970s has been the development of widespread support for the Constitution of the Fifth Republic and the right of the Constitutional Council to strike down governmental decisions as contrary to the constitution. The result has been the development of greater bal-

TABLE 2   **Proportion of French Citizens Identifying Themselves as Members of a Social Class**

	December 1976	March 1983	April 1987
Total	68%	62%	56%
Occupation of Respondents			
Higher executives, professionals	68	67	60
Middle executives, school teachers	57	66	63
Office workers	64	62	59
Manual workers	74	71	50

Source: *L'Expansion,* March 20 to April 27, 1987 in Louis Dirn, *La Société française en tendances* (Paris: PUF, 1990), 63.

ance between democratic institutions and the statist tradition.

NATIONAL IDENTITY

French national identity is closely linked to state formation. The monarchy, based in Paris and the surrounding area known as the Île de France, often used military force to subdue independent provinces to form modern-day France. The Revolution of 1789 further contributed to the idea that what binds the members of a political community together is core political values. The revolution championed the idea that anyone could become French if they accepted republican values. The French approach to citizenship and national identity encourages immigrants to become French citizens on the condition that they accept dominant cultural and political values. Such an approach closely resembles the American idea of the melting pot, in which immigrants of diverse origins are "melted" into a single political community. The French approach to citizenship stresses shared political values rather than common racial or ethnic, that is, inherited, characteristics. France has successfully integrated large immigrant populations from Italy, Poland, and Portugal. However, the dominant approach discourages immigrants from publicly affirming their own separate identity and values.

In the past, French institutions—especially the educational system, conscription in the armed forces, and the media—fostered the republican values of liberty, equality, and fraternity, which, in the official view, made France distinctive. Conflicts existed, of course, such as those between members of different

social classes and those between the religiously observant (usually Catholics) and the opponents of organized religion. Since the 1950s, there has been a rapid decline of religious observance, and several decades of economic growth have reduced class and ideological conflict, as shown in Table 2.

If class cleavages have diminished, however, conflict has been fueled recently by ethnic differences. In recent years, many first- and second-generation immigrants of Algerian origin have affirmed their pride in being Algerian and Muslim, demanding cultural autonomy and the right to be different when it comes to dress, food, religious practice, and the like. Conversely, many French citizens have reacted by seeking to exclude these groups from the French political community.

STATE-SOCIETY RELATIONS

One can identify three long-standing characteristics of state-society relations in France. First, as explored above, the French state has traditionally been quite strong; conversely, France has traditionally had a weak civil society, that is, diverse voluntary associations formed by citizens that could promote autonomous action separate from the state. Second, this pattern of state autonomy and weak civil society has periodically been challenged by the members of protest movements, who oppose the state yet call for state action to satisfy their demands. Since the target of protest movements is the state, and the result of protest is often increased state intervention, this rich tradition of protest has by and large not promoted autonomous conflict regulation but has, on the contrary, reinforced the pattern of a strong state and weak civil society. Third, the conflict between France's statist and democratic traditions has been made manifest in two ways: within the state, there has been an opposition between a strong administration and a turbulent parliament; and, through time, as we reviewed above, there has been a succession of political regimes, very different from one another but equally unable to reconcile the contending currents.

When the Fifth Republic was created by Charles de Gaulle in 1958, it appeared to be yet another example of an imbalanced and ephemeral regime tipping toward statist dominance at the expense of democratic participation and representation. However, as a result of changes in the sphere of political institutions and society, described in Sections 3 and 4, a fairly adequate balance has developed between state autonomy and democratic participation. And yet, as discussed in the beginning of this chapter, new and daunting challenges have developed.

IMPLICATIONS FOR CONTEMPORARY FRENCH POLITICS

As a result of the critical junctures that shaped French state formation, the state possesses some important assets to help the country confront current challenges—but these same patterns of state formation have also produced particular handicaps. On the positive side, the French state is a powerful, capable instrument that can help the country adapt to the challenges posed by global economic competition. In recent years, the state skillfully promoted internationally acclaimed industrial projects, including high-speed rail travel (the high-speed train, or TGV), an efficient European air carrier (the Airbus) in which France played a major role, an electronic telephone directory and data bank (the Minitel), and relatively safe and cheap nuclear power generating plants.

Consider France's neighbor across the English Channel. Britain's long economic decline is in significant measure due to the fact that the state was ill-equipped to manage a modern industrial economy as a result of the different historical pattern of British state development.

France's statist tradition served it well at some points in French history, but it has proven to be an increasingly heavy liability in the current period. As a result of increased global economic integration and

competition, as well as citizens' demands for more autonomy, the characteristically French style of state regulation is under siege, and there has been some adaptation. For example, the state no longer seeks to regulate in as far-reaching a manner, and the state itself has been decentralized. But it remains the case today, as Tocqueville lamented well over a century ago, that in the sphere of the economy, education, and community life, private groups have not learned to manage their common affairs because the state assumes responsibility for doing so. In the present period, it is more difficult yet more important than ever to develop the capacity for autonomous problem solving.

New Cleavages

Although we analyzed how traditional bases of collective identity have declined, important new sources of conflict have developed.

First, conflict has arisen from the economically excluded citizens. In the past, social class was an important dimension differentiating winners and losers in French society. Recent patterns of economic change divide citizens in new ways. With structural employment at record levels, whole regions devastated as industries have closed down, declining numbers of jobs available, and young people seeking their first job at a particular disadvantage, a major new cleavage is access to stable employment. Although there is some correlation between class lines and the cleavage between the stably employed and the excluded, the two are not identical. For example, public-sector employees, even those without much training, are relatively protected. On the other hand, managers and technicians in private firms may find themselves among the ranks of the economically and socially excluded.

Second, new conflicts have arisen over differing conceptions of citizenship. Within the past several years, increasing numbers of native-born French citizens have made immigrants and their children the scapegoats for economic stagnation and record levels of unemployment. As a result, a more restrictive and exclusionary conception of citizenship and French identity is developing.

A third new area of conflict is environmental protection and bureaucracy. As in many other countries, an alliance of private firms and state administrators in France has accorded higher priority to industrial expansion than to the quality of the social and natural environment. Several green parties have challenged the dominant pro-growth orientation of the major parties. They have also made the state bureaucracy the target of criticism, by proclaiming the need for citizens to be associated more closely with decisions affecting their daily life. This argument has particular appeal, given France's long statist tradition. President Chirac, himself the product of an elite civil service training school, was able to strike a popular chord in the 1995 presidential campaign by criticizing the bureaucracy.

France's relationship to Europe, especially the European Union—the organization of Western European nations whose principal goal is to create economic integration and unity among member states—is a fourth new source of conflict. In a referendum held in 1992, French citizens split evenly on the question of whether to support a treaty negotiated at Maastricht, Holland, strengthening European Union institutions and integrating more fully the economies of the EU member states.

In brief, France is currently at a crossroads. The democratic idea and the traditional orientation of the French state are challenged by new socioeconomic and cultural conflicts involving economic change, immigration, and France's role in the international economic and political order. The acceleration of technological change, international economic competition, and supranational institutions, especially the EU, challenge France's statist form of regulation and national identity. Economic stagnation and restructuring have produced high unemployment and severe social tensions, which have overburdened France's system of extensive state provision of social services. At an even deeper level, there is confusion about the core values uniting the French political community.

We begin analyzing French politics at the crossroads by examining France's political economy in a global context, for the way that a country organizes production and consumption within the world economy deeply influences the functioning of its political system.

SECTION 2
Political Economy and Development

STATE AND ECONOMY

The French state has long played a key role in shaping the country's economy. For well over a century—far more than was true for Britain, the world's first industrializer—the French state fostered industrial growth while seeking to maintain the privileged position of the small business and agricultural sectors. These patterns developed after the French Revolution, when a large proportion of the population were small farmers, independent producers, and shopkeepers. They used the political power and control of the state that derived from their numbers and standing to prevent social and economic change. Although a drastic shift occurred in the state's relation to the economy following the upheaval of World War II, elements of the traditional situation persist to the present day. For example, in 1993, France nearly caused an international economic crisis when it opposed a trade agreement negotiated by the United States and the European Union that required the French state to reduce its subsidies to farmers. France succeeded in gaining a compromise solution

that preserved the possibility of granting farmers favored treatment.

The Leading Role of the State

In a tradition dating back to Jean-Baptiste Colbert, the powerful finance minister to Louis XIV in the seventeenth century who directed the creation of a French merchant marine, the state has often played an important role in sponsoring large-scale economic projects. For example, in the 1860s, under Napoleon III, the state consolidated several small railroad companies, encouraged the formation of the Crédit Mobilier, an investment bank to finance railroad development, and guaranteed interest rates on bonds sold to underwrite railroad construction. This tradition continued through the 1970s, when the state acted vigorously to sponsor the creation of large industrial firms, into the early 1980s, when the Socialist government extended the statist tradition by nationalizing many leading private firms in key industrial and financial sectors. But, in a shift of far-reaching significance, the Socialists sponsored a substantial reversal beginning in 1983. Since then, the state has withdrawn from one economic sector after another. Although the state remains far more intimately involved in economic decision making than other comparable countries like Britain or Germany, the state's retreat from active involvement is an important feature of the new French political economy.

During the long initial period of industrialization in Western Europe from the late eighteenth century through the nineteenth century, the French state pursued a quite distinctive goal compared to the British and German states. Along with the United States, these nations were the world's leading economic powers in the nineteenth century. In Britain, the first industrialized power, the state sought to remove restrictions on the free operation of market forces. In Prussia (which consolidated neighboring states to form Germany in 1866), the state fostered industrialization from above. The French state, by contrast, aimed to "maintain an equilibrium among industry, commerce, and agriculture and attempt[ed] to insulate France from the distress and upheaval that had struck other nations bent upon rapid economic advance."[6] Consequently, France had among the world's highest tariff barriers throughout the nineteenth and early twentieth centuries. The reason for shielding French firms from foreign competition was not to enable them to compete effectively internationally, but to enable small producers (farmers, manufacturers, and artisans) to survive free of unwelcome competition from abroad.

The French excelled at manufacturing luxury products, such as silks, lace, fine wearing apparel, Limoges china, and wine. Skilled workers and artisans were needed to produce these goods. Thus, it was difficult to use modern machinery and recruit an extensive unskilled labor force. In the United States, Britain, and Germany, on the other hand, manufacturers mechanized production and recruited many unskilled workers to produce commodities for mass consumption.

The Stalemate Society—and Economy

As a result of these cultural, technical, and economic factors, France was not among the leaders of the enormous industrial expansion of the nineteenth and early twentieth centuries. According to Stanley Hoffmann, France could be characterized as a "stalemate society" until after World War II, resulting from the fact that the French economy could be considered a "halfway house between the old rural society and industri-alization."[7] Hoffmann suggests that the peasantry (small farming population), small business owners, shopkeepers, and professionals sought to prevent change. They were a large group to begin with, and their influence was further increased through electoral institutions. For example, rural overrepresentation in drawing legislative district boundaries gave these groups disproportionate political influence. Conversely, urban groups, especially workers, were underrepresented.

This situation could last only as long as the state was able to protect French industry and the nation from external threat. However, this became increasingly difficult and eventually proved impossible. France was severely weakened by its participation in World War I (1914–1918). It adopted an isolationist stance in the 1920s and 1930s, which would have been comic if it had not proved tragic. Because France feared the rise of German militarism, it constructed, at enormous cost, the Maginot Line, an armed fortification running along the several-hundred-mile border between France and Germany. There was only one flaw in the plan: the Maginot Line did not extend to France's border with Belgium. When Germany invaded France in 1940 for the second time within living memory, after rapidly overcoming Belgium's tiny army, its armed forces swept through France's unprotected northern flank and quickly reached Paris. The Third Republic collapsed and Marshal Pétain signed a humiliating armistice with the Nazi regime, signifying France's total defeat.

France learned the hard way that there was no sanctuary. The lesson was that for state action to be effective, it had to have positive aims—notably, strengthening the French economy—rather than the defensive goal of preserving the status quo. After the Allied powers defeated the Nazi regime, and the Fourth Republic was created in France, an important transformation occurred in the state's relationship to the economy. "After the war," historian Richard Kuisel observes, "what was distinctive about France was the compelling sense of relative economic backwardness. This impulse was the principal stimulus for economic renovation and set France apart from other countries."[8]

The New French Revolution

From the nineteenth century through World War II, the state had aimed to ensure an equilibrium among the social forces that formed the republican synthesis. In the new scheme, the state was used to foster a modernized capitalist economy based on large, productive firms using advanced technology to invest, expand, and export.

As a result of its long-standing statist tradition, France was especially well equipped to develop the institutional capacity to steer the economy. Kuisel describes the French state's approach as follows:

> France resembled other capitalist countries in developing an arsenal of institutions for managing the economy. . . . Yet France found its own way to perform these tasks. It lodged responsibility in new public institutions and staffed them with modernizers. It relied heavily on state intervention and planning. . . . The result was a Gallic style of economic management that blended state direction, corporatist bodies, and market forces.[9]

Along with other Western European nations, such as Britain and Germany, France experienced a remarkable economic boom in the years after World War II. However, France stood out in three major respects: (1) the extent and durability of economic growth was unusually great; (2) the state played a key role in restructuring the economy; and (3) organized labor was underrepresented in the new arrangements. Two French scholars highlighted the importance of the shift in striking fashion:

> The last thirty-five years have witnessed a new French Revolution. Although peaceful, this has been just as profound as that of 1789 because it has totally overhauled the moral foundations and social equilibrium of French society.[10]

The new French revolution consisted of a change in attitudes, the economy, and social practices. After a century of economic and demographic stagnation, France grew in terms of its population and economic base. The republican synthesis crumbled as people accepted—indeed, enthusiastically supported—change. They were acutely aware that the old ways had produced economic, political, and moral devastation. But, on the positive side, they were confident that, for the first time in generations, change would produce an improvement, not a decline, in the situation of France and its citizens.

Key to the new situation was a change in the role of the state, from guardian of the established order (the republican synthesis) to sponsor of social and economic progress. Postwar policymakers used the state to modernize France's inefficient and backward economy. In addition, under pressure from leftist forces, which had played a leading role in the resistance to the Vichy regime during World War II, many sectors of the economy were nationalized. Furthermore, the state sponsored a wide array of social services associated with the modern welfare state, including family subsidies, day-care facilities, old-age pensions, public health care, unemployment insurance, and public housing. In time, France was providing among the most extensive array of cradle-to-grave social programs of any country in the world.

The state exercised its new role through what the French called **indicative planning,** in which the Planning Commission, composed of administrators appointed by the government, developed national economic and social priorities in a four- or five-year plan. The plan set broad goals for the economy through a process in which public and private officials participated in modernization commissions establishing targets to be given priority in the next several years. Examples included economic growth rates, specific industries and regions that were considered key and, in later plans, social goals such as educational targets.

Perhaps more important than the particular targets set was the fact that planning contributed to a change in political culture. In place of the attempt to preserve the status quo at all costs, which characterized the stalemate society, it fostered the belief that change was to be welcomed because of the improvements it would provide. Thus, planning played a key role in transforming the stalemate society.[11]

Planning developed broad support in part because it was not imposed in a heavy-handed fashion. The planning agency was staffed by a small group of young, dynamic problem solvers. Unlike Soviet-style planning, French plans were not legally binding but represented an informal consensus reached by public and private officials. They provided a way of sharing information and, through a process of informal coordination, streamlining the process of economic decision making. State planners, administrators, and politicians made the final decisions regarding the economic and social priorities contained in the various plans. But they did so after discussing alternatives with business officials and other qualified private citizens.

The planning process did not represent all interests. In particular, industry—especially the modern corporate sector—and organized farm interests were given a privileged role. In fact, key to the success of the planning process was the formation of a close alliance between the state and dynamic producer interests—above all, large, technologically advanced firms seeking to compete in world markets. In the period before World War II, during the heyday of the stalemate society, this segment of French business was in a marginal position. Thanks to what one scholar called the "complicity" that planning fostered between big business and the state in the postwar period, big business came into its own.

On the other hand, organized labor and consumer interests were kept at arm's length in the planning process. Opponents charged, quite correctly, that planning was undemocratic because decisions were made behind closed doors and important voices were excluded from the process. Although the fruits of economic growth trickled down to many sections of French society, planning fueled political tensions and contributed to narrowing the scope of democratic decision making. It is no accident that, despite substantial economic growth in the postwar period, France had one of the highest industrial strike rates of any industrialized democracy.

Although state-guided modernization and growth began in the Fourth Republic, the first steps were halting and uncertain. Vigorous leadership at the top by the executive was needed to overcome the conservative forces opposing change and to assure full-scale commitment to economic modernization. Such leadership was provided after 1958 when Charles de Gaulle, the most influential politician in twentieth-century France, regained power and created the Fifth Republic.

Gaullist-Style Modernization

De Gaulle was a complex, controversial, and contradictory figure. On the one hand, he was a faithful representative of traditional France, deeply attached to the values of order and hierarchy, which earned him the enmity of the left. On the other hand, de Gaulle's personal leadership and the republic that he created provided the force to undermine the republican synthesis and restructure the French political economy.

Stephen Cohen captures the irony that de Gaulle and the Gaullist movement functioned to hold "traditional France in place politically while building a new France."[12] Thus, at the same time that de Gaulle was closely linked to the traditional social forces of rural and small-town France, the policies that he sponsored to rationalize French capitalism severely undermined these groups.

General de Gaulle's return to power in 1958 ushered in a period of state-led industrialization and growth based on a distinctive pattern of indicative planning, state steering of cheap credit toward favored sectors and firms, and state action to promote the creation of large firms in key industrial sectors—what came to be called economic champions. The labor movement played a relatively marginal and often oppositional role. A number of national unions, loosely tied to political parties, competed with each other for members and refused to engage in unified action. The result was to give French employers a free hand to squeeze wages. But frequent strikes were a vehicle for workers to demand higher wages and better working conditions.

The French described their system of relations between the state and the economy as **dirigiste** (directorial), which highlights the state's importance in steering the economy. Many key economic decisions were made in governmental ministries, especially the ministries of finance, economy, and industry, as well as the planning agency. The state compensated for the relatively weak role played by private entrepreneurs by acting directly as well as by closely regulating private firms.

Consistent with the *dirigiste* approach, the French state pursued the most active industrial policy of all the Western European nations. Four key elements can be identified. First, like other nations, French macroeconomic policies, including monetary, income, and fiscal policies, price regulation, public investment, and vocational training, all influenced industrial development. However, in contrast to other nations, the French state coordinated policy-making in these spheres through the planning process and the government, the Ministry of Finance, and other agencies.

Secondly, the state developed fiscal policies, including subsidies, tax write-offs, and loans, to achieve its economic goals, such as industrial concentration, specialization in new fields, and technological innovation. For example, for several decades after World War

TABLE 3   **Changes in the Occupational Structure**

	1954	1962	1975	1982	1990
Farmers	21%	15.5%	7.5%	6.5%	4%
Artisans, shopkeepers, small business operators	13	10.5	8	8	8
Higher executives, professionals	3	4.5	7	8	12
Middle executives, schoolteachers	9	11.5	17	18	20
Office workers	17	18.5	24	26.5	27
Manual workers	37	39.5	36.5	33	29
Total	100	100	100	100	100

Source: INSEE, Enquêtes "Emploi et recensements," in Louis Dirn, *La Société française en tendances* (Paris: PUF, 1990), 160.

II, the bulk of capital for new investment was provided by state grants and loans to industry. In addition, the state regulated interest rates and set quotas on private bank loans to steer investments toward priority sectors. Third, the state developed specific sectoral plans, for example, in steel, machine tools, and paper products, to restructure these industries. The ministry of industry pressured medium-size industrial firms in these sectors to merge in order to create large private firms (national champions) able to compete in world markets. A fourth element—and the state's most vigorous intervention within industrial development—consisted of direct creation, development, and management of new industries. Thus, the state created and ran the major firms in such key fields as armaments, nuclear energy, high-speed railroads, aeronautics, space development, and telecommunications. While these firms enjoyed a certain measure of independence, their chief executives were appointed by the state, state administrators often intervened to dictate company decisions, and the firms were totally dependent on the state for capital. In the French economic model, the state was a (indeed, *the*) chief economic player.[13]

France's Economic Miracle

During the period that French economist Jean Fourastié designated as "the thirty glorious years" (1945–1975), the planners and their allies within the bureaucracy and private sector were remarkably successful in their efforts.[14] Whereas defenders of the stalemate society had succeeded in maintaining a balance between agriculture and industry throughout the nineteenth and early twentieth centuries, there was an intense movement off the land and into cities in the postwar period. The proportion of the labor force engaged in farming was 60.0 percent in 1850, 41.8 percent in 1901, and 38.4 percent in 1946. By 1962, it had dropped to less than half the 1946 level, and it has continued to fall steadily since then (see Table 3).[15] At the same time, according to historian Gordon Wright, there was a "rural revolution in agriculture" as a result of the mechanization of agricultural production, a drastic reduction in the number of traditional family farms, by consolidating them into large, commercially viable units.[16]

The drastic decline of the rural population was matched by the rapid rise of the urban population. In 1946, 53.2 percent of the French lived in urban areas and 46.8 percent lived in rural communes, or "localities"; but by 1962, 63.5 percent of the French were city dwellers and 36.5 percent lived in rural areas. The gap between the urban and rural populations thus increased from 6.4 to 27.0 percent in less than two decades. Urban growth was especially rapid in mid-sized cities, with populations between 50,000 and 100,000: while the French population as a whole during this period increased by one-tenth, the number of French living in cities over 50,000 doubled.[17]

After nearly a century of slow population growth, France grew at a comparatively rapid rate. In the fifteen years following the end of World War II, the French population grew by 5 million—as much as in the eighty years preceding the war.

The newly urbanized population helped to swell the ranks of the industrial working class: the proportion of the labor force engaged in manufacturing increased from 35.3 percent in 1944 to 43.3 percent in

TABLE 4	Average Growth Rates in Gross National Product, 1958–1973
Japan	10.4%
France	5.5
Italy	5.3
West Germany	5.0
Belgium	4.9
Netherlands	4.2
Norway	4.2
Sweden	4.1
United States	4.1
United Kingdom	3.2

Source: Bela Belassa, "The French Economy under the Fifth Republic, 1958–1978," in *The Fifth Republic at Twenty,* ed. William G. Andrews and Stanley Hoffmann (Albany: State University of New York Press, 1981), 209.

1962. An even greater increase occurred in the service sector, notably teaching, health, and the state bureaucracy. Between 1944 and 1962, the service sector increased from 26.2 to 37.1 percent of the labor force. The French economy was rapidly transformed from a balanced agrarian and small-manufacturing economy like that of other southern European countries, to an industrial and service-based economy characteristic of northern Europe.

Restructuring the French economy became considerably easier once economic growth produced substantial benefits. During France's "economic miracle," as it was called, the country's economic growth was highest of all the European nations and second only to that of Japan (see Table 4). Note the contrast with the 1930s, when the French economy declined at the rate of 1.1 percent annually.[18]

The fruits of economic growth were quickly transformed into higher living standards. In effect, wages were linked to price and productivity increases, so that workers had an incentive to support modernization. The shared fruits of economic growth made for general stability despite the grievances of particular groups and the persistence of political divisions. The average French citizen's annual income nearly tripled between 1946 and 1962, increasing from $511 to $1,358 in constant dollars.[19] This was reflected in a wholesale transformation of consumer patterns as French citizens began to enjoy the benefits of industrialization. For example, between 1946 and 1962, the proportion of homes with running water increased

from 36.9 to 80.9 percent. The number of automobiles registered in France increased from 4.5 million in 1959 to 14 million in 1973. The number of housing units completed annually increased from 290,000 to 500,000 during the same period. In sum, after a century of economic stagnation, France enjoyed a sharp surge of economic expansion and leapfrogged into the twentieth century.

May 1968: The Shattering of the Gaullist Dream

During the 1950s and 1960s, the economy was growing, purchasing power was increasing, and France was benefiting handsomely from the expansion of the world capitalist system. De Gaulle's strong leadership provided a solid framework of stability, which encouraged the state-business alliance to flourish. And yet, despite dramatic economic growth, the appearance of political stability proved misleading. Conservative forces were relatively satisfied, but following an initial period in which about one-third of workers supported de Gaulle, most workers became opposed to the Gaullist government.

Political opposition was provoked by dilemmas within the planning process. As Peter A. Hall points out, "The reorganization of production to attain greater efficiency tends to intensify the social conflict that planning is also supposed to prevent."[20] This was especially true given labor's meager role in influencing economic change. As a result, economic expansion increased class inequalities. The most dramatic evidence of the regime's fragility occurred in the May 1968 uprising that followed several years of turbulence, including government-imposed wage restraint, the reduction of trade union representation on the governing boards of the Social Security (public health) system, and the rapid extension of universities with inadequate provision of facilities and guidance for students. The May uprising, "the nearest thing to a full-blown revolution ever experienced in an advanced industrial society," was in part the product of rapid economic growth without social adaptations to soften France's rigid system of authority and hierarchy.[21]

Beginning with university occupations at Nanterre and the Sorbonne and a characteristically harsh government response, the May movement quickly sparked a general strike throughout France. Thousands of factories, offices, and universities were

Students and workers unite in a mass demonstration on the Left Bank of Paris, May 27, 1968.
Source: AP/Wide World Photos.

occupied by striking workers and students. At the height of the uprising, half of France's workers and a larger proportion of students were on strike. Before 1968, the highest number of workdays lost from strikes in any one year in the postwar period was 5 million (in 1959); in May 1968 alone, 150 million workdays were lost to strikes. With factories, offices, schools, theaters, and political institutions paralyzed as strikers convened in nonstop meetings to debate the shape of the desired new society and to design its institutions, the fate of the Fifth Republic hung in the balance. De Gaulle and his prime minister, Georges Pompidou, eventually regained control of the situation by outmaneuvering the leftist opposition and offering workers substantial concessions (including an increase of 35 percent in the minimum wage and increased protection for labor unions). But de Gaulle's authority was badly shaken by the uprising, and when a referendum that he sponsored in 1969 (in large part to restore his tarnished

legitimacy) was defeated, he resigned from the presidency.

Economic Crisis and Political Conflict in the 1970s

Although the beginning of social, economic, and political crisis can be dated from May 1968, it was not until the mid-1970s, with the slowdown of French economic growth, that the crisis became acute. Indeed, May 1968 at first proved quite beneficial for French business: The government-decreed wage hike meant a substantial increase in purchasing power, which fueled business expansion; the government provided business firms with additional subsidies and tax incentives in order to assist them in paying wage increases; and a devaluation of the franc in 1969 (which lowered the price of French goods for foreign consumers) stimulated French exports.

Yet May 1968 also signified a new militancy of French labor and a refusal to accept workplace

Figure 1 Women in the Labor Force
Source: INSEE, in Louis Dirn, *La Société française en tendances* (Paris: PUF, 1990), 108.

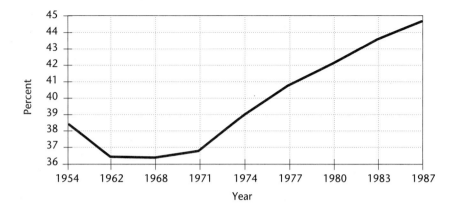

discipline and hierarchy in return for wage increases. Strikes in the early 1970s were frequent and often involved highly militant tactics, such as seizing factories, sequestering managers, and even organizing production directly. Rather than seeking to improve wage levels (the characteristic cause of earlier strikes), workers also challenged harsh authority in the workplace, speedups in the pace of work, and technological innovations that increased workplace hazards.[22] A rapid increase in female employment, beginning in the early 1970s, also produced some important strikes when women protested against employers attempting to provide them with fewer benefits than men (see Figure 1).

As a result of their militance, workers gained increased rights and benefits, and the state and employers' associations sought to achieve stability through organizing collective bargaining at industrywide and national levels. For example, legislation and bargaining agreements in 1969 and 1973 codified procedures for laying off workers, granted state labor inspectors a limited veto power over layoffs, and specified that workers be given advance notice of layoffs as well as severance pay; unemployment benefits were increased, amounting to 90 percent of a worker's wage in many cases; collective-bargaining agreements were concluded on an industrywide level in the petroleum, chemical, and textile industries; and, within the public sector, a network of management-union agreements included provisions for automatic wage increases. These were all attempts to restore stability and to continue on the path of economic growth forged in the earlier period. However, two developments prevented a return to the past: a political challenge from the left, and a widening economic crisis.

In the political sphere, the two largest left-wing opposition parties, the Communist Party (PCF) and the Socialist Party (reformed and renamed the PS in 1969), forged a coalition in 1972 that promised to bring them to power in the near future. The alliance, named the Union of the Left, accepted the institutional framework of the Fifth Republic but advocated substantial economic and social changes, notably nationalization of industry, labor law reform, and a sharp increase in social welfare spending.

There were severe economic strains in the 1970s. First, France began to exhaust the benefits that derived from its relative backwardness of the earlier period. As the substantial shift of workers out of agriculture and from rural to urban areas ended, gains in productivity began to slow.

France benefited from international economic expansion in the postwar period, but was damaged by changes in the 1970s. The country was heavily dependent on imported petroleum, which left it vulnerable when petroleum prices increased sharply in the 1970s. The restructuring of international capitalism in the 1970s damaged French industry in two ways. On the one hand, newly developing nations, such as Taiwan, the Republic of Korea (South Korea), and Brazil, began to outcompete France in such basic industrial sectors as textiles, steel, and shipbuilding. French firms not only began to be less competitive internationally but also lost substantial shares of the domestic market to foreign competition. Hundreds of thousands of jobs were eliminated in these three industries alone (for example, more than one-third of all steelworkers were permanently laid off at this time), and entire regions were devastated by deindustrialization. Demographic trends also contributed to the squeeze on employment:

Unemployment

Following the mid-1970s, unemployment steadily increased in France until it reached among the highest levels of industrialized capitalist countries. Probably more than any other single factor, joblessness was responsible for the political alternations that have occurred in recent decades. The Socialist Party reached office in 1981 by criticizing President Valéry Giscard d'Estaing and his conservative political allies for failing to stem the rise of unemployment. Similarly, the conservatives gleefully quoted the Socialists' criticisms in the 1980s when unemployment continued to rise under Socialist governments. Jacques Chirac, in turn, made the battle against unemployment his major campaign theme in his victorious 1995 presidential bid.

Why are governments of both left and right helpless in the face of unemployment? Economists have identified several reasons:

1. *Demographics.* There are more young people who begin a search for jobs each year than there are elderly workers who retire.

2. *Structural weaknesses.* French firms entered the fierce competition to penetrate export markets relatively recently, compared to such countries as Japan and Germany. For much of the postwar period, French firms produced solely for the sheltered markets of France and her colonies in Africa and Asia. The result was that, with the increasing international economic competition generated by lower trade barriers and the European Union, French firms lost domestic market shares to foreign firms yet did not compensate sufficiently by increasing exports.

3. *Rigidities of economic and social institutions.* France is at a disadvantage because of an extensive system of social protection—high minimum wage, unemployment insurance programs, early retirement, generous paid vacations—on the one hand and, on the other, a system of job training less developed than that of its competitors and more authoritarian workplace relations.

at the same time that France was losing jobs, there were 230,000 new jobseekers (mostly young people) each year.

On the other hand, the French economy was battered in the 1970s by the development of a new generation of advanced technology. France was not large

C'EST QUAND MÊME BEAU À VOIR, TOUS CES DIPLÔMES !

ANPE

PLANTU

"It's touching to see all these graduates." (ANPE is the employment office.)
Source: Courtesy Plantu, from *Le Monde*.

enough to be a world leader in such growth industries as microelectronics, bioengineering, and robotics. U.S. and Japanese producers rapidly captured the newly created French markets in these fields. Thus, French industry was squeezed by the dual movement. Just when the country needed to generate increased export earnings to finance the increased costs of petroleum, basic industries were losing export markets to the fastest-growing Third World nations, where wage costs were low, and were importing high technology from advanced capitalist leaders. And, as the international economic boom slowed in the 1970s, the French economy suffered further, along with other Western European nations.

The new trends were linked to a crisis in the French model of development, based on the state-sponsored creation of large national champions. The postwar approach worked well when France could shield its economy from international competition and crash programs were needed for industrial reconstruction and modernization. Beginning in the 1970s, however, it became more urgent to adapt rapidly, decentralize economic decision making, and compete with foreign firms. The traditional approach, involving extensive state direction, proved less effective in new fields, which were often dominated by smaller, flexible firms, financed by venture capital, and in close geographic proximity to university research laboratories and other firms that provided parts and markets. Success in these conditions is achieved by creative breakthroughs, not emulation. This has been a central political and economic challenge in the last two decades, one that the French political economy is less well equipped to meet than the challenges of the postwar years.

French Socialism in Practice—and Conservative Aftermath

When the conservative governments of the first decades of the Fifth Republic failed to meet the economic challenges of the 1970s, the left gained the chance to try. A new era began in 1981, when the Socialist and Communist parties—until that point permanent minorities in the Fifth Republic—gained power after twenty-three years of opposition. François Mitterrand soundly defeated incumbent President Valéry Giscard d'Estaing in the 1981 presidential elections. Immediately upon gaining office, Mitterrand dissolved the conservative-dominated National Assembly. The Socialist Party gained an absolute majority of seats in the elections and were well positioned to enact their sweeping reform agenda.

The Socialist government initially sponsored a program responsive to the left's traditional demands for a substantial increase in welfare state benefits and a larger economic role for the state, notably through extensive nationalization of industrial firms and banks. Many French citizens benefited from the government's redistribution policies. But these failed to stimulate the new period of economic growth that the Socialists had promised, in large part because private business executives in France and international investors distrusted the government and exported capital, a move known as **capital flight.** With France's currency reserves rapidly being exhausted in 1983–1984, the government was forced either to pursue even more radical policies or to pull back. Rather than gamble on the riskier course, the government engaged in an about-face and adopted a conservative approach involving support for private enterprise. The crisis cruelly demonstrated just how limited the margin of maneuver was for a medium-rank power like France.

The Socialist government continued to provide substantial financial assistance to ailing industries in the 1980s, and the French economy became far stronger under Socialist rule. But, beginning in the mid-1980s, the Socialists replaced the statist orientation prevailing during the four decades following World War II with an approach that relied on market forces.

Today, the French state continues to play an important role in the economy. But since the mid-1980s, the balance of power in France, as in most nations throughout the world, has shifted from state to market forces. However, the new orientation has not been a satisfactory replacement for the former pattern of state direction, for it has been associated with persistently high levels of unemployment and slow economic growth. As a result, a large number of French citizens have been deprived of the fruits of full participation in French society, generating a new cleavage between the majority of French and the group that the French designate as "the excluded."

SOCIETY AND ECONOMY

French political culture has traditionally placed low priority on entrepreneurship and economic efficiency. An aristocratic tradition, rooted in the period before capitalist industrialization began in the eighteenth and nineteenth centuries, and a socialist critique of capitalism that originated during the period of capitalist industrialization have shared a distaste for core capitalist values of profit and efficiency. It has been widely believed that the state should regulate market competition in order to limit social dislocation. The French have placed service to the state above economic gain. The most prestigious schools of higher education exist to train top civil servants, not business executives, lawyers, or doctors (see Section 3). However, in a world of increasingly intense economic competition, France has often been at a disadvantage.

One problem area that has hindered economic performance in France is relations between management and labor. Consider the cases of Germany and Japan. In these countries, in quite different ways, the labor movement has accepted the value of cooperating with management within the firm and at higher levels of the economy in order to maximize output. In return, it has demanded, and generally received, a share of the benefits produced by economic growth. By contrast, the most powerful French trade unions have traditionally been highly suspicious of management, and for good reason: business executives have generally sought to weaken labor unions and exclude them from a role in the firm.

Workers have more often gained benefits by contestation and political action rather than by cooperation

Socioeconomic Changes

In the last several decades, despite the economic difficulties described in the text, France has continued to modernize at a brisk pace. Since the 1970s, France has entered the age of mass consumption. Among many examples: Whereas nearly half of all houses and apartments lacked indoor toilets in the early 1970s, fewer than one-tenth do today. The number of households with washing machines was 15 percent in 1973; twenty years later it was 94 percent. The number of automobiles in France has doubled in the same period, as has the number of books published, the number of visits to museums, and the number of French who take winter vacations. Even more dramatic, only 5 million French homes and businesses had telephone service in 1973, but 30 million were connected by the 1990s.

Socioeconomic changes have not all been positive, however. For example, in 1973, thirteen French died from an overdose of drugs; more than 400 succumbed two decades later. Nearly double the number of French were in prison in 1993 than in 1973. Simultaneously, the proportion of unemployed persons soared. And although the French have always been known for outspoken criticism of their condition, recent years have witnessed substantial increase in books published on "the French disease" (as one author put it)—that is, analyses of a crisis in French society.

with their employers. It took the May 1968 uprising for labor unions to gain the right to organize plant-level locals. Until the Socialist government sponsored labor reforms in the early 1980s, including the obligation of French employers to bargain collectively over wages and hours, French workers did not enjoy benefits that workers in northern European nations had gained decades earlier. And, during the current period of economic crisis and restructuring, the French labor movement has suffered especially severe declines in membership. At present, less than 10 percent of the wage-earning population belong to a labor union.

Despite labor's weakness within the economy and the generally weak position of leftist political forces in the postwar period until 1981, France has created extensive programs of social protection. These gains often occurred after workers resorted to direct protest (May 1968 is the most dramatic example). In part, conservative governments granted concessions in order to prevent a left-wing electoral victory. And, when a Socialist government was finally elected in 1981, it substantially extended social benefits. Thus, much of France's housing stock is built and managed by public agencies. France also has extensive family subsidies, with eligibility not tied to income. In 1988, the Socialist government passed legislation guaranteeing a minimum income to all citizens. Because citizens are entitled to state-financed medical benefits, the public health system is enormously popular—although, in France, as elsewhere, the health care system has been jolted by rising costs and a decline in resources as a result of high unemployment and a decline in the proportion of the population that is of working age. Moreover, although state welfare programs remain highly

popular, there is growing opposition to paying the increased taxes needed to finance the system. In the short run, the problem has been addressed by raising taxes and cutting back on benefits. But the crisis of the welfare state has not been resolved.

FRANCE AND THE INTERNATIONAL POLITICAL ECONOMY

France has historically sought to shield itself from international economic competition as a result of its reluctance to put a high priority on industrial growth. Nonetheless, France remained a powerful and affluent nation because it was large, with ample natural resources, skilled workers, and a large internal market. But what was possible when France was a dominant power in Europe, and Europe the dominant region in the world, has become impossible in the current era. France remains one of the most powerful nations in the world: it holds one of the five permanent seats on the United Nations Security Council, possesses nuclear weapons and, along with Germany, is a leading European power. But France is in the second rank of the world's military powers, trailing far behind the United States. And, unlike the United States, Japan, or Germany, France cannot claim to exercise world economic dominance even though its economy is in the second tier, not far from the economic frontrunners. Perhaps France's greatest dilemma in the sphere of economic performance has been that the evolution of the international economy threatens the distinctive manner in which France achieved economic success. In a world of intense economic integration, France's characteristic style of state-managed growth is no longer possible.

In the nineteenth century, France engaged in colonial conquest on a smaller scale than Britain. But, unlike Britain, it continued to maintain close relations with its former African colonies (until recently). This proved to be a mixed blessing for the French economy. A large share of France's production was absorbed by the internal market or was exported to France's former colonies, who remained closely integrated with France through governmentally negotiated arrangements. As a result, because French industry was in the comfortable position of not having to outperform firms in the other major industrialized nations, French firms did not have to remain in the technological vanguard. When, beginning in the 1980s, it became less possible to protect markets from international competition, France was less well positioned.

One important reason for intensified international competition has been France's participation in the EU. In the postwar period, France took the lead in creating supranational European institutions. But France's primary goal was to prevent Germany's economic resur-gence from leading to political dominance. Several decades of economic growth produced greater optimism in France about the value of international cooperation, especially because Germany did not challenge French political leadership in Europe throughout much of the postwar period. By the mid-1980s, French president François Mitterrand proposed strengthening European Union institutions. However, many French oppose participation in the EU, resenting the transfer of power from the French state to EU institutions and the fact that intensified international competition buffets inefficient firms and sectors. Bitter conflict about the EU erupted in 1992, when a referendum was held on the Maastricht Treaty, which proposed accelerating European monetary and economic unity. Maastricht split France evenly in two and produced a new fault line in French politics linked to France's insertion in the international economy. Conflicts about the shape of the EU and the benefits that France derives from participation rank high on the agenda of current issues in French politics in transition to be discussed in Section 5.

SECTION 3
Governance and Policy-Making

ORGANIZATION OF THE STATE

Despite frequent changes of constitutional regimes in France within the past several centuries, three important characteristics of the French state remained nearly constant—at least until recently. The fact that all three have changed substantially in the past decade suggests the importance of the transition presently occurring in French politics.

First, for centuries there has been nearly universal agreement on the desirability of a unitary state. It would be hard to conceive of federalism in a nation with such a strong statist tradition. Since the French Revolution, subnational governments have been regarded as an administrative arm of the state based in Paris; their primary reason for existence was to help implement national policy. Although the French remain united on the desirability of a unitary state, an important change occurred in the 1980s when the Socialist government transferred substantial powers to local governments. A new spirit of local autonomy is evident in the 1990s, representing a significant contrast with French tradition.

Second, for generations, there has been a near consensus among French citizens that the state should play a central role in directing social affairs. Although one can identify an anarchist, or antistatist, current in France, a far more powerful tradition has been suspicious of the private sphere of civil society. The dominant tradition of *dirigisme,* which was reviewed in Section 2, claims that the state should play an active role in making the decisions affecting the nation. This tradition, too, has been challenged widely within recent years, with the fundamental shift beginning under Socialist governments in power from 1981–1993. For a variety of reasons, including soaring tax burdens, economic recession, changes in political culture, and France's linkage to the international sphere, *dirigisme* has declined and civil society has become less subject to state direction.

These changes in the underlying principles of the French state point to a shift in the balance between the state and society. The transition has been conflictual and troubled; the change is far from total. Compared to most other industrialized capitalist nations, including Britain and Germany, the French state remains highly active and interventionist. (The closest parallel to France is Japan.) But the extent of change within such a brief period is quite astonishing.

The third change involves limits that have developed on state action from within the state itself. It may be surprising to learn that a nation that places heavy emphasis on the importance of formalized legal codes and that, along with the United States, boasts the modern world's first written constitution, has, until recently, not considered that the constitution should be scrupulously respected. This approach was linked to the weak position of the judiciary within the French political system. Unlike the judiciaries in established democracies such as Britain or Germany, which have great independence and power to check the executive and legislature, judges in France have traditionally enjoyed little autonomy and, indeed, have been considered part of the executive branch. This too has changed in the recent past. The Constitution of the Fifth Republic has generally come to be regarded as the key source for allocating power among political institutions; the judiciary has gained the vital power to interpret the constitution and thereby check the legislature and executive.

Principles of Constitutional Power

Given the importance of the unitary state in France, it is especially important to understand how power is distributed among political institutions. There has been intense controversy over this issue throughout recent French history. Three approaches to organizing state power have been in conflict: popular sovereignty exercised through direct democracy; legislative dominance, guided by the principle that the people's elected representatives are exclusively qualified to embody the people's will; and executive rule, which rests on the assumption that the bureaucracy is rational, disinterested, and competent—the qualities needed to exercise power wisely. No French regime has been able to achieve an adequate balance among the three contending principles, and successive constitutions have tended to reflect a fairly extreme form of one of the three. In its early years, the Fifth Republic resembled earlier regimes in its imbalanced character, and it re-

mains quite imbalanced. But, as the result of several developments, the Fifth Republic has evolved to achieve somewhat greater balance among the three contending approaches to organizing power. This shift helps explain why the Fifth Republic has become one of the most stable and widely accepted regimes in French history.

The Constitution of the Fifth Republic distributes powers in an unusual fashion, usually described as a semipresidential system, which combines elements of presidential and parliamentary systems. In a wholly presidential system, such as in the United States, the executive and the legislature are chosen separately and neither is answerable to the other. In a parliamentary system, as in Britain, the executive and legislature are fused, not separated, and both institutions have important powers over the other. The government, that is, the cabinet, which controls the executive, is accountable to parliament, which means that the government must resign if parliament passes a motion of no-confidence. At the same time, the government has substantial control over the parliamentary agenda and can dissolve parliament, thereby provoking new elections. In a presidential system, by contrast, the legislature and executive have independent powers and neither controls the agenda of the other. Moreover, both institutions have fixed terms in office and neither the government nor the legislature can force the other to resign and face new elections.*

France is considered a semipresidential system; the "semi" refers to the fact that there is not as complete a separation between the legislature and the executive as there is in a "pure" parliamentary system. The system is called semipresidential, not semiparliamentary, because the executive, and especially the president, dominates parliament, not the other way around. In all those cases where the political system of the Fifth Republic deviates from being purely parliamentary or purely presidential, the result is a strengthening of the executive—primarily the president—not parliament. This is because, in the Fifth Republic, as

---

* There is one exception to this generalization in presidential systems. The legislature can impeach the president in the very unusual case when it deems that the president has committed treason. Once impeached, the French president is judged by a High Court composed of members of parliament. However, this procedure has never been used in the Fifth Republic.

in parliamentary systems (but unlike the situation in a presidential system), the executive closely controls the legislature and can, if it so chooses, dissolve parliament to provoke new elections. There is thus a *fusion* of executive and legislative powers characteristic of parliamentary regimes with respect to the procedure that strengthens the executive. But there is a *separation* of powers in the constitution concerning a key provision that, in parliamentary regimes, enables parliament to control the executive. The Constitution of the Fifth Republic follows the practice of presidential regimes by rendering the president independent of parliament: Parliament cannot vote a censure motion forcing the president to resign.

Political arrangements are further complicated in the Fifth Republic by the existence of a government appointed by the president yet answerable to parliament. As in parliamentary systems, the French National Assembly (the more powerful house of parliament) can force the government to resign by voting a motion of censure.

Despite criticism that the executive is unduly powerful, the Fifth Republic has become one of the most stable regimes in French history. A 1991 poll found that 61 percent of the French judged that political institutions have functioned well in the Fifth Republic. An overwhelming majority of 89 percent supported popular election of the president—a controversial innovation when it was introduced in 1962—and 91 percent supported use of the referendum.[23] Although there are many proposals to reform particular features of political institutions, especially the seven-year presidential term, for the first time in modern French history political conflicts are now played out within a widely accepted institutional framework.

Since the beginning of the 1980s, the Constitution of the Fifth Republic has survived two important kinds of political tests, and the regime has emerged even stronger: first, a shift in political control ("alternation") from one political coalition to another; and second, **"cohabitation,"** as it is called by the French, or power-sharing, when opposing political coalitions control the presidency and parliament.

Alternation first occurred in 1981, when the rightist coalition that ruled since the beginning of the Fifth Republic in 1958 was defeated at the polls by the Socialists. Contrary to widespread predictions that the shock would destabilize the regime, the institutions of the Fifth Republic proved quite adequate to the challenge. Indeed, subsequent political swings, such as the shift to the right in 1993–1995, when the conservatives regained power, have become a normal feature of French political life.

Cohabitation can occur because elections for the presidency and National Assembly occur at different times. For many years, the French judged that if opposing forces were to control the executive and legislature, political stalemate—or worse—would occur. In fact, when the unthinkable finally did occur in 1986, and Socialist President Mitterrand was confronted by a newly elected conservative majority in the National Assembly, the event proved to be the mouse that roared. Mitterrand appointed Jacques Chirac, leader of the conservative parliamentary coalition, prime minister, and the two found workable solutions to governing together. The first period of cohabitation ended in 1988, when President Mitterrand was reelected, dissolved the National Assembly, and succeeded in sweeping a Socialist plurality into power in elections to the National Assembly. When a new period of cohabitation began in 1993, following a conservative victory in legislative elections, the rules of the game for conducting government in such a situation were firmly in place.

Three reasons might be advanced why political institutions were able to overcome both challenges. First, the ideological distance between left and right had declined *prior* to alternation and cohabitation, which reduced the intensity of political conflict. The gap further diminished after the Socialist government moderated its policies in 1983–1984, two years after alternation occurred in 1981. Second, the Constitutional Council, the nation's highest court, effectively maintained a balance (equilibrium) among institutions. Finally, during both tests, public opinion strongly favored institutional stability: In 1981, even most opponents of the Socialists recognized their right to govern following their electoral victories; during the two periods of cohabitation, most French citizens wanted the experiment to succeed. These developments signify a profound change in French political culture, involving the decline of French exceptionalism and the rise of a more moderate, pragmatic type of politics.

The Triple Executive

Aside from Russia, France is the only major country with a semipresidential system. In parliamentary regimes, the chief of state—either a president or a monarch—exercises purely ceremonial duties, while the bulk of executive power, that is, the power to direct the administration in order to implement policy, is concentrated within the government. In France, the president is not only head of state, the symbolic and ceremonial leader of the country, but also possesses substantial policy-making and executive power.

The president is far from all-powerful, however, since he or she shares executive and policy-making powers with the government, that is, the prime minister and other cabinet ministers. Particularly during periods of cohabitation, which occurred in 1986–1988 and 1993–1995, the government's independent constitutional and political powers sharply limit presidential leadership. Although the president names the prime minister and other members of the government, the National Assembly (the lower house of parliament) can force the government to resign by voting a motion of no-confidence. Thus, when the National Assembly is controlled by a majority hostile to the president, as occurred in 1986–1988 and 1993–1995, the president must bow to political realities and appoint a government representing opposing political forces. In this situation, the government, not the president, controls most major decisions. Whether the president can count on the support of a parliamentary majority or not thus makes a vital difference. As Mitterrand's presidency demonstrates, the same president can shift from commanding enormous power—when in control of a parliamentary majority—to being confined to a quite modest role when forced to confront a hostile parliamentary majority.

To describe France as having a dual executive, as many do, obscures the power of the bureaucracy, a third key element within the executive apparatus. The three pillars of the executive provide the motor force of the French state.

The President   As long as a single party controls both the executive and the legislature, the powers of the French president are immense. The president combines the independent powers of the U.S. president—notably, command of the executive establishment and independence from legislative control—with the powers that accrue to the government in a parliamentary regime—namely, control over parliament's agenda and its day-to-day activity, and the ability to dissolve parliament and force new legislative elections. Moreover, as will be described in the next section, the

government—usually under the president's direction—controls parliament more tightly than other democratic regimes do. The result is a greater degree of executive dominance within the French political system than in virtually any other democratic nation. And the president occupies the office at the very top of this commanding edifice.

The presidency has become so powerful for three reasons: (1) the towering personalities of the two most powerful Fifth Republic presidents, Charles de Gaulle, the founder and first president of the Fifth Republic (who was president between 1958 and 1969), and François Mitterrand, the Socialist president who held office from 1981 to 1995; (2) the ample powers conferred on the office by the Constitution of the Fifth Republic; and (3) the political practices of the Fifth Republic.

1. *Presidential personalities.* Charles de Gaulle was unquestionably the most influential French politician in the twentieth century. He first achieved this position by his bold and courageous actions in leading the resistance forces in France during World War II in opposition to the Vichy regime, allied with the Nazi occupation. After de Gaulle succeeded in toppling the Fourth Republic in 1958, he set out to design political institutions for the Fifth Republic that would enable political leaders to rise above party rivalry and legislative interference in order to sponsor ambitious projects for France. As first president in the Fifth Republic, de Gaulle was the cornerstone of the regime until he resigned in 1969.

Although when François Mitterrand was a youthful leader in the resistance during World War II he was an ally of de Gaulle, the two became lifelong rivals after the war. Mitterrand led a coalition of political forces that squarely opposed de Gaulle during the early years of the Fifth Republic. Mitterrand charged that the Fifth Republic was undemocratic and that de Gaulle created a presidential office permitting him to exercise power in an arbitrary and authoritarian manner. In the 1960s and 1970s, Mitterrand helped direct the minority leftist forces opposing de Gaulle personally, de Gaulle's policies, and the Constitution of the Fifth Republic. During this period, Mitterrand twice ran for president, losing both times. However, he succeeded in remaking the Socialist Party into a major alternative to the Gaullist coalition and finally obtained the supreme prize. In 1981, in his third presidential bid, he defeated incumbent president Valéry

General Charles de Gaulle (top) was reelected president of the Republic in December 1965 after a challenge from the candidate of the left, François Mitterrand, who would be elected President in 1981.
Source: © Dalmas/Sipa Press.

TABLE 5   Presidents of the Fifth Republic

President	Term
Charles de Gaulle	1958–1969
Georges Pompidou	1969–1974
Valéry Giscard d'Estaing	1974–1981
François Mitterrand	1981–1995
Jacques Chirac	1995–Present

tutions of the Fifth Republic weren't created with me in mind, but they suit me fine!'' The commanding personalities of de Gaulle and Mitterrand, both of whom dominated the periods in which they governed, helped make the presidency the supreme political prize in the Fifth Republic.

2. The Constitutional Presidency. The Constitution of the Fifth Republic endows the president with the ceremonial powers of head of state, the role occupied by the president in previous regimes. However, to these symbolic functions it adds important political powers that belonged to the prime minister and government in the past, as well as new powers not previously exercised in previous republics. Thus, the president both symbolizes the unity and majesty of the state and actively participates in political decision making. (Table 5 lists the Fifth Republic's presidents and their terms of office.)

The president, the only official chosen in a nationwide election, is elected for a seven-year term, an extremely long period, which in itself bolster's presidential power. In order to be nominated to run for president, a candidate must obtain the signatures of local elected officials throughout France. The requirement is not too demanding, however, and in all elections there are many candidates—usually more than five. In reality, since the 1970s, only candidates nominated by the three major parties (reviewed in the next section) stand a serious chance of winning. But candidates from smaller parties may receive a significant share of the vote. For example, when National Front candidate Jean-Marie Le Pen, running on an anti-immigrant platform, won 15 percent of the vote in the 1988 and 1995 presidential elections, it was an ominous sign that many citizens judged the major parties incapable of dealing effectively with France's economic and cultural challenges.

Giscard d'Estaing and began what became the longest presidential term in the history of the Fifth Republic.

At the same time, while Mitterrand and the left edged closer to gaining power within the institutions of the Fifth Republic, they gradually came to accept the legitimacy of the Fifth Republic. The supreme irony is that, as president, Mitterrand ruled in a manner strikingly similar to that of his archrival, de Gaulle. Many of the same charges that he had leveled at de Gaulle's exercise of power could well be applied to Mitterrand: He was solitary, capricious, and monarchical in his governing style. As he humorously remarked soon after taking office in 1981, ''The insti-

A two-ballot election system is used for presidential elections. In order to be elected at the first ballot, a candidate must obtain an absolute majority of votes at the first ballot, that is, over 50 percent of those voting. If no candidate receives more than half the votes at the first ballot, a runoff election is held between the two front-runners. Since many candidates compete in a presidential election, it is unlikely that any candidate can gain an absolute majority at the first ballot. In all six presidential elections thus far held by universal suffrage in the Fifth Republic, a runoff ballot has been necessary.

As it does in the United States, a presidential election produces the most intense political excitement and passion in France's political life. The system of direct election provides the president with powerful personal support and probably bolsters the legitimacy of the entire regime.

Currently, presidents are eligible for reelection, and François Mitterrand did serve two full seven-year terms. Given the enormous powers of the presidential office, many have proposed amending the constitution, either by reducing the presidential term to five years or by limiting presidents to a single seven-year term.

The constitution grants the president vital political powers, including the right to

• name the prime minister and other cabinet officials, as well as high-ranking civil, military, and judicial officials.

• preside over meetings of the council of ministers (the government). [Note that it is the president, not the prime minister, who is charged with this responsibility.]

• conduct foreign affairs (through the power to negotiate treaties, as well as to name French ambassadors and accredit foreign ambassadors to France).

• direct the armed forces.

• dissolve the National Assembly and call for new elections. [However, if the president has dissolved the assembly, he or she cannot do so again during the newly elected assembly's first year.]

• appoint three of the nine members of the Constitutional Council, including its president, and refer bills passed by parliament to the council to determine if they conform to the constitution.

Four other constitutional grants of power are especially important in strengthening the president's position. Article 16 authorizes the president to assume emergency powers when, in his or her judgment, the institutions of the republic, the independence of the nation, the integrity of its territory, or the execution of France's international (treaty) commitments are threatened.

Article 89 authorizes the president, with the approval of the prime minister, to propose constitutional amendments. An amendment must be approved by a majority of both houses of parliament and then ratified by either a national referendum or a three-fifths vote of a congress composed of both houses of parliament meeting in joint session.

The amendment procedure has been used several times. Two amendments were passed in 1993. One, at President Mitterrand's initiative, reformed the procedure for promoting judges and trying cases in which cabinet ministers are accused of crimes. The second, sponsored by the conservative government elected in 1993, overturned a decision of the Constitutional Council which invalidated a law sponsored by the government limiting the conditions under which political refugees could gain asylum in France.

Article 11 authorizes the president to sponsor a referendum, ratify proposed treaties, as well as approve proposed changes in the constitutional powers of political institutions. By creating a direct link between the president and French citizens, the constitution sharply broke with French parliamentary traditions and practice, which dictated that the president be a distant and largely ceremonial political figure in order to minimize the risk of a demagogue endangering democracy. The referendum played a key role in the early years of the Fifth Republic. Perhaps the most dramatic occasion was in 1962, when de Gaulle proposed that the constitution be altered to provide for popular election of the president. With the exception of his own loyal allies, de Gaulle was opposed by politicians from throughout the political spectrum, who feared that the president's powers would be strengthened at the expense of parliament and the political class. De Gaulle won the face-off and demonstrated the formidable power that skillful use of the referendum could provide.

But use of the referendum is a double-edged sword. When voters rejected a referendum that de Gaulle called in 1969 to approve his proposal to restructure the Senate and create regional governments, he resigned from office, on the grounds that he had lost popular confidence.

Later presidents have been reluctant to use the referendum procedure. President Pompidou sponsored one referendum; President Giscard d'Estaing, none. President Mitterrand sponsored two. Although both were approved, the "victories" probably caused the president more harm than good. In 1988, Mitterrand held a referendum providing for self-determination for New Caledonia, a French colony in the Pacific. Although three-quarters of those voting supported the measure, only one-third of all voters bothered to go to the polls, and the high level of abstentions proved damaging to Mitterrand. The second referendum that Mitterrand proposed may have harmed him even more.

In 1992, he called a referendum to provide for French ratification of the Maastricht Treaty enlarging the powers of the European Union. At first, it was widely expected that the referendum would be approved by a large margin. But as the vote drew near, the campaign became heated. Although voters approved Mitterrand's proposal, the outcome was extremely close. This result weakened Mitterrand and highlighted how widespread was the opposition to a project that Mitterrand strongly favored. No doubt, future presidents will be extremely cautious in sponsoring a referendum.

Presidential power has been greatly bolstered by Article 5, which directs the president "to ensure, by his arbitration, the regular functioning of the governmental authorities, as well as the continuance of the State. He shall be the guarantor of national independence, of the integrity of the territory, and of respect for Community agreements and treaties." Because the president is the sole official charged with arbitrating and guaranteeing national independence, the constitution confers on the president enormous legitimacy and power over the state machinery.

The Constitution of the Fifth Republic creates a powerful president on paper. However, to be effective, a president must translate these formal powers into the actual exercise of influence.

3. *The Political President.* Among the most important institutional changes in the Fifth Republic, and one that permanently altered the character of the presidency, was a reform sponsored by de Gaulle in 1962 to elect the president by universal suffrage. In the first years of the Fifth Republic, the president had been elected by local officials, mostly mayors and town councilors. After a bitter struggle with politicians, including Mitterrand, who argued that the reform would further strengthen an office that was already too powerful, de Gaulle succeeded in gaining majority support for his proposal when he submitted it to a popular referendum. As a result, the president is the only official elected by the entire nation. The mantle of democratic legitimacy provides a powerful weapon that can be used against the opposition as well as the president's own political associates. It helps explain why, most of the time, the prime minister defers to the president's wishes.

De Gaulle and successive presidents have used their formal and informal powers to the hilt. In addition to the constitutional power to designate prime ministers, presidents have successfully claimed the ability to dismiss them as well, thus making the government responsible not only to the National Assembly, as specified in the constitution, but also to the president. Except during the two periods of cohabitation, prime ministers have accepted the fact—nowhere specified in the constitution—that they serve at the president's pleasure. Presidents have also assumed the power, formally delegated by the constitution to the government, to develop policy and intervene in virtually any domain that they choose (again except during periods of cohabitation). As a result of the president's long term and the extensive powers of the presidency, French presidents have often been compared to the monarchs of the ancien régime!

A good example is provided by President Mitterrand's sponsorship, on his own initiative, and with quite little consultation, of twelve major projects that transformed the landscape of Paris. They include the glass pyramid that serves as the entrance to the Louvre museum, a new opera at the Bastille, a museum of science and technology, and the largest library in the world. Many of the projects provoked major controversy, because of their large costs and unusual architectural features, but Mitterrand was successful in seeing every one through to completion before he left office.

Yet, even the most forceful president is not all-powerful. The key to understanding the complexities of policy-making in France is the relation between president and prime minister. In brief, when the same political coalition controls both offices, the president's

Of Presidents and Prime Ministers

The relationship between the president and the prime minister is of central importance in the Fifth Republic. Typically, the president and prime minister are political allies. (In the text, we describe the periods of cohabitation, in which the two were political opponents.) Charles de Gaulle dramatically illustrated his conception of presidential primacy by naming as his second prime minister Georges Pompidou, an obscure, former high administrator and banker who had never held elected office. However, the tradition was soon established that presidents appointed as prime ministers senior party officials. The reason is that a prominent prime minister can provide the president with important political assets: parliamentary support for the government's policies, skill in gaining sympathetic media treatment, and experience in directing the state bureaucracy.

The reverse side of the coin, however, is that the same qualities that make a prime minister a valuable presidential ally are also a source of tension. Prime ministers are constantly tempted to stake out a position independent of their president. Prime ministers have their own power bases and personal ambitions, and most nurture the hope that one day they will move from the Matignon to the Élysée. In order to do so, a prime minister must be more than a president's lapdog.

In general, whatever tensions may exist between a president and prime minister are concealed from public view—although they are the stuff of media gossip. On rare occasions, hints of open conflict are unmistakable. Although Jacques Chirac played a key role in getting Valéry Giscard d'Estaing elected president in 1974—and was rewarded with the post of prime minister—Chirac constantly blocked Giscard's policy initiatives. For years after he was elected president in 1981, François Mitterrand refused to appoint Michel Rocard, his principal rival for leadership of the Socialist Party, as prime minister. He finally did so in 1988—only after there were no other obvious prospects he could tap. However, perhaps the most dramatic instance of tension occurred under President Pompidou. His first prime minister, Jacques Chaban-Delmas, made an important speech in which he proposed, on his own initiative, an ambitious reform program; in short order, Pompidou dismissed him from office. In the subtle tug-of-war between a president and a prime minister, a president can never allow the prime minister to gain the upper hand.

power is much greater. In this situation, which has prevailed most of the time in the Fifth Republic, the president chooses as prime minister a close political ally, who accepts playing second fiddle to the president. On those rare occasions, however, when the president's political opponents gain a majority in the National Assembly, and the president is forced to work with their leaders to form a government, the president's power shrinks. During the periods of cohabitation (1986–1988 and 1993–1995), conservative coalitions hostile to Mitterrand controlled the National Assembly and the government. Mitterrand exercised a leading role only in the fields of foreign affairs and defense, which the constitution explicitly places under presidential control, and retreated to the Élysée Palace, prudently refraining from engaging in major clashes with the government.

The Government and Prime Minister

Although the government has deferred to the president during most periods of the Fifth Republic, the constitution designates the government, not the president, as the preeminent policy-making institution. Article 20 specifies that the government "shall determine and direct the policy of the nation. It shall have at its disposal the administration and the armed forces." Govern-

ments usually follow the president's lead in the Fifth Republic because of political dynamics rather than constitutional directives. Although the constitution charges the president with presiding over meetings of the council of ministers (the formal designation of the government), the periods of cohabitation amply demonstrate that the government can choose to defy the president's wishes—when the government commands a parliamentary majority opposed to the president. But when the president has led the dominant parliamentary coalition, to which the prime minister and other cabinet ministers belong, there has never been a major case in the Fifth Republic where the government has not accepted presidential leadership.

The Cabinet   The cabinet (also known as the government) is a collective body under the prime minister's direction. The constitution specifies that the president appoints the prime minister, who is usually a major figure in the dominant parliamentary coalition. In turn, the prime minister nominates and the president appoints other members of the cabinet. After the president and prime minister, cabinet ministers are the most powerful members of the executive. They direct the bureaucracy and participate in developing specific policy initiatives that, after receiving the approval of the government and president, constitute the legislative agenda.

Although the president appoints the government, the constitution specifies that it is responsible only to the National Assembly. A government must resign when a censure motion, moved by at least one-tenth of all deputies, is voted by an absolute majority of all deputies in the National Assembly. The constitution is silent about whether the government is also responsible to the president, that is, whether the president can dismiss the cabinet. In practice, however, save for the two periods of cohabitation, all prime ministers have accepted the president's right to dismiss them and appoint a new prime minister and government.

The Constitution of the Fifth Republic is extremely confusing in regard to the division of responsibilities between the president and the government. It provides a brief catalog of the government's powers and specifies some powers that are shared with the president, but there are important areas of overlap and, therefore, potential conflict. Whereas Article 21 states that the prime minister is "responsible for national defense," the president is designated as "commander of the armed forces," and is responsible for presiding over key military policy-making committees. Similarly, Article 21 directs the prime minister to "ensure the execution of the laws," which overlaps with the directive to the president (Article 5) to ensure the regular functioning of governmental authorities. Article 21 grants the prime minister authority to make appointments to civil and military posts, yet Article 13 delegates this same power to the president!

For nearly thirty years, from 1958 to 1986, when cohabitation began, every president exercised virtually unchallenged dominance over the government, and therefore the precise division of responsibilities between the two institutions did not produce open political conflict. In practice, presidents assumed responsibility for the most important decisions in key policy areas, while the prime minister and government developed policy in areas of lesser importance, translated the president's overall orientation into specific policies, directed the implementation of policy, and carried on the day-to-day business of governing. The issue became important only during periods of cohabitation.

Although the presidency is clearly the supreme political office in the Fifth Republic, the prime minister is the second most powerful position. Most prime ministers have been prominent politicians, and the office is considered a stepping-stone to the presidency. Thus far, two prime ministers—Georges Pompidou and Jacques Chirac—subsequently became president. Being named prime minister singles out a prominent politician and makes him or her a natural potential candidate for president.* For example, until he was appointed prime minister in 1993, Edouard Balladur was not regarded as a major presidential contender. Although he was a prominent figure in the Gaullist party, the leader of the party, Jacques Chirac, was widely considered the Gaullist party's standard-bearer. However, when Balladur proved a popular prime minister, he quickly emerged as a major potential presidential candidate and a rival to Chirac. In the 1995 presidential elections, Balladur initially enjoyed the favored position in public opinion polls, far ahead of Chirac. However, Chirac's greater experience and command of the party machine enabled him to eclipse Balladur and win the election.

During the typical political situation, that is, outside the exceptional periods of cohabitation, an informal division of political labor prevails between the president and the prime minister. The president develops the administration's overall policy orientation; the prime minister develops specific policy proposals, directs the government and bureaucracy, shepherds the government's proposals through parliament, keeps a tight rein on parliament thanks to the measures provided by the constitution, and shields the president from criticism. Cabinet ministers are generally named from among the ranks of senior politicians in the ruling parliamentary coalition. The constitution prohibits cabinet ministers from serving in the legislature, so that deputies and senators appointed to the cabinet must resign their parliamentary seat. De Gaulle sponsored this provision to prevent politicians from maneuvering when in parliament to gain ministerial office. However, in practice, the prohibition has had little effect. When a minister leaves the cabinet, it has become common practice to hold a by-election (that is, an election in one district, as opposed to a general election, in which contests are held in all districts). In such cases, the former minister usually regains a seat in the National Assembly.

---

* Thus far, there has been one female prime minister in the Fifth Republic: Edith Cresson, who served from 1991–1992.

The cabinet as a collective body has little real power. Presided over by the president, its meetings are largely ceremonial. The details of policy are hammered out at higher levels—at the Élysée—and in interministerial committee meetings, which bring together representatives of ministries to develop details of specific proposals. Although a member of the *president's* staff attends ministerial meetings, a member of the *prime minister's* staff presides over them. This symbolizes the fact that the president generally confines attention to the most important policy decisions, whereas the prime minister is responsible for the actual conduct of government.

There are substantial differences in the power of various cabinet positions and ministerial departments. The Minister of Finance has great power over other government ministries. Other important departments are defense, external affairs, and interior.

The Bureaucracy

The French bureaucracy is generally regarded as one of the most competent and efficient in the world. Positions at the top of the administration are among the most powerful in France, given the country's *dirigiste* tradition. The French bureaucracy intervenes more extensively and is more powerful than is true in most comparable nations. For example, despite the growth of European Union institutions and the new political economy, in which market forces play a prominent role, administrators continue to make many important choices regarding particular firms (even those formally within the private sector), industries, and the entire economy. The bureaucracy enjoys unusually great autonomy because the constitution severely restricts the number of fields in which parliament can legislate and authorizes the bureaucracy to issue binding regulations in all other fields.

Special mention should be made of ministerial *cabinets,* or personal staffs.* Members of the minister's staff are not, strictly speaking, part of the administration. Rather, they advise cabinet ministers on policy and partisan matters, and informally supervise the minister's department in the minister's name. Most members of the *cabinets* are recruited from the ranks

of talented rising young administrators, who often return to the regular administration when they leave the *cabinet.* Compared, for example, to British ministers, who lack a personal staff and depend for information and advice on the bureaucracy they are charged with directing, French ministers have considerable power over the line bureaucracy thanks to the help provided by their *cabinets.*

Most choice bureaucratic posts are reserved for graduates of the *grandes écoles,* selective educational institutions whose purpose is to train higher civil servants. At the top of the French academic pyramid are the École Nationale d'Administration (ENA), a public institution that trains top administrators and managers in the public sector, and the École Polytechnique (informally known as "X") and the École des Mines, which provide engineering and technical training for future civil servants. Students who graduate at the head of their classes in the top *grandes écoles* are offered positions in *grands corps,* small, specialized, highly cohesive, elite networks of civil servants. The most powerful *corps* are the finance inspectorate, *Conseil d'État,* diplomatic corps, and *Corps des mines,* whose members have colonized key positions in particular ministries and extended their reach throughout the administration. Thus far in the Fifth Republic, two presidents—Valéry Giscard d'Estaing and Jacques Chirac—have been members of *grands corps.*

The French bureaucracy has enormous power and autonomy, defining policy objectives behind closed doors and pursuing them with a grand indifference to criticism. Although the bureaucracy is widely respected for its honesty, efficiency, and nonpartisan character, it has been criticized as rigid, aloof, and antidemocratic. The Constitution of the Fifth Republic reinforced this preexisting tendency by severely limiting the legislative domain and expanding the area in which the bureaucracy could issue binding regulations without need for parliamentary approval.

In all countries, the army and the police are key executive agencies that provide the coercive force to enforce state decisions. In some countries, the armed forces play an important role in shaping policy and directing the state. In France, the army has traditionally played a minor role in politics. However, in some exceptional but important cases, the army has played a vital role, most recently in 1958, when it helped topple the Fourth Republic and return de Gaulle to power.

---

* In order to distinguish the *cabinet,* or personal staff, from the cabinet that is composed of government ministers, we italicize *cabinet* when referring to the personal staff.

The police do have considerable freedom on a day-to-day level, however. The "forces of order," as they are called in France, have a reputation for committing extensive abuses of power, including illegal surveillance, arbitrary actions, and torture. The judiciary or high executive officials have rarely acted vigorously to restrain the police.

Semipublic Agencies

During the period since World War II, France has had an important array of semipublic agencies, including public sector enterprises in the fields of basic industry, transportation, energy, telecommunications, and services. Furthermore, the state controlled many investment decisions, both directly, through state-owned industrial firms, and indirectly, as a result of the credit policies of state-controlled banks and the Ministry of Finance. An intricate network of state financial agencies also exercised tight control over credit and investment policy.

The Socialist government elected in 1981 further expanded the nationalized sector in order to deal with the economic crisis. Many large banks were already in the public sector as a result of reforms enacted after World War II; most private banks that remained were nationalized in 1982. At that time, large firms were nationalized in the steel, aluminum, electronics, and aeronautics industries. The measure provoked intense controversy, in part because it went squarely against the dominant trend in the 1980s toward increasing the autonomy of private market forces.

The Socialists' experiment, however, proved to be quite short-lived. Since 1983, the trend has been in the opposite direction. At that point, the Socialists abruptly reversed their statist course after a financial crisis erupted that could have produced economic chaos. The government allowed some of the public sector firms to sell assets to private investors. It deregulated financial markets, shifting control of investment decisions to private individuals.

When the right gained office in 1986 and again after 1993, it privatized many firms that the Socialists had nationalized, as well as firms that had been nationalized after World War II. Key public sector firms, including Elf Petroleum, the Rhône-Poulenc chemical firm, and several major banks and insurance companies, were privatized in 1993–1994. Pressure for the change came from conservative political forces within France. Downsizing the state's industrial and financial

sector, as well as deregulating credit, has drastically reduced the formerly commanding role of the state and represents an enormous change within the French political system.

OTHER STATE INSTITUTIONS

There are countless state agencies that could be described here. We focus on those designated by the Constitution of the Fifth Republic, notably, the Constitutional Council, the State Council, the Economic and Social Council, and local governments.

The Judiciary and the Constitutional Council

Traditionally, the French judiciary had little autonomy and was considered an arm of the executive. In the past two decades, however, this has dramatically changed. Since the founding of the Fifth Republic, possibly no political institution in France has gained more power than the Constitutional Council. Originally designed to be an instrument that the executive could use to restrain the legislature, it has become, instead, a source of executive restraint. One study of the council observes, "Originally an obscure institution conceived to play a marginal role in the Fifth Republic, the Constitutional Council has gradually moved toward the center stage of French politics and acquired the status of a major actor in the policy-making system."[24]

Access to the council has been broadened considerably. At first, only the president of the republic and the presidents of the two houses of the legislature could bring cases to the council. As a result of a constitutional amendment passed in 1974, however, sixty deputies or sixty senators can also bring suit. The result is that the council is now asked to rule on most important legislation.

In addition, the Constitutional Council's jurisdiction has been broadened. The council was not originally designed to exercise the power of judicial review, that is, the power to invalidate legislation that in its opinion violates the constitution. The change occurred as a result of skillful maneuvering by the council, followed by broad public acceptance of the council's new role. Although this development is unprecedented in French history, the council now routinely exercises the sweeping power in a bold and continuous fashion. If the primary innovation of the Fifth Republic in its first few years was to consolidate the dominance of the executive over the legislature, the primary development since then has been to consolidate the primacy of the constitution, as interpreted by the Constitutional Council, over both the legislature and the executive. The change has involved a substantial expansion of the powers of the council and a greater equilibrium of powers within the regime. For example, in addition to the increased powers of the Constitutional Council, a constitutional amendment passed in 1993 made judges more independent of the president and the executive branch.

The French judicial system of Roman law, codified in the Napoleonic Code and other legal codes (for example, those governing industrial relations and local government), differs quite substantially from the pattern prevailing in the United Kingdom, the United States, and other nations inspired by the common law system. Courts accord little importance to judicial precedent; what counts is existing legislation and the codification of legislation in specific subfields. French judges also play an active role in questioning witnesses and recommending verdicts to juries. Responsibility for preparing the case is delegated to a judicial authority, the *juge d'instruction*. Criminal defendants enjoy fewer rights against the prosecution than in the American or British systems of criminal justice.

State Council

The French administrative system includes a system of administrative courts. The highest is the *Conseil d'État* (State Council), which hears cases brought by individuals alleging that administrative regulations violate their rights. The State Council also advises the government in drafting new legislation. This body is not empowered to consider the wisdom of regulations, but merely their procedural regularity, and the government can overrule the council. Nonetheless, its opinions command great respect. A State Council ruling that had an important impact on French political life declared that European Union treaty provisions and regulations take precedence over French legislation, ministerial directives, and regulations. (This principle was later enshrined in a constitutional amendment in 1992.) The State Council plays the role of watchdog on the executive, an especially important function in the French political system, where the executive has such great autonomy.

The Economic and Social Council

The Economic and Social Council is a consultative body composed of representatives of various interests, including business, agriculture, labor unions, social-welfare organizations, and consumer groups, as well as leading citizens from cultural and scientific fields. Although it has issued some widely respected reports on matters pending in parliament, it is generally unknown to most French citizens and has no formal legislative or administrative role and little political power.

Local Government

Until the 1980s, responsibility for regulating local affairs was centered in the hands of national administrators stationed in the provinces to oversee local government, principally the prefect, supervisor of civil engineering, and top financial officer. French local governments were quite weak and had little legal autonomy, financial resources, or political power. Furthermore, the local governmental structure was extremely fragmented: There are over 36,000 village and city governments in France, more than the combined total of local governments in the other major Western European nations.

The Socialist government's first major reform measure after gaining power in 1981 was a thorough overhaul of the local government system. The decentralization reform has been one of the left's most successful achievements. It has transferred substantial authority to subnational authorities, including newly created regional governments. Although many major leftist reforms were reversed following the right's electoral victories in 1986 and 1993, the decentralization reform has taken firm root and, except for some minor aspects, is widely supported by citizens, politicians, and local officials of both right and left.

THE POLICY-MAKING PROCESS

Throughout the Fifth Republic—except during periods of cohabitation, when the president's power was vastly reduced—a nearly hierarchical chain of command has linked the president, government, administration, and parliament. The president, along with a small staff of advisers, has formulated major policy initiatives. The prime minister and other cabinet ministers have also proposed policies, but those of any importance have required presidential approval. The government, assisted by the formidable bureaucracy, has been responsible for developing detailed legislative proposals as well as administrative regulations for implementing policy. The government has normally been highly successful in obtaining legislative approval for proposed policies.

The way that policy is implemented has generally reinforced the preeminent position of the executive. Although often forced to bargain with interest groups for their support in order to implement policy, the bureaucracy usually has the upper hand. The bureaucracy is itself often divided by competition among ministerial services; and administrators safeguard their own interests when they implement decisions from above. Thus, one cannot predict the details of policy *outcomes* merely by knowing the content of policy *decisions*. Yet, compared to virtually all other countries in the world, the French bureaucracy is more honest, better trained, more efficient, and more politically neutral. As a result, policy-making and implementation are generally quite cohesive and effective.

The basic problem regarding policy-making in France is not the difficulties in policy formulation and implementation but the relatively few channels available for political participation, debate, and opposition. In particular, as the next section describes, parliament has precious little autonomy. Although the Constitutional Council has begun to act as a counterweight to the executive, the constitution so fully enshrines executive dominance at the expense of the legislature and popular participation that the balance has not shifted much. A good illustration was provided in 1995 when President Chirac announced that France was planning to conduct a series of nuclear tests in the South Pacific. Despite intense opposition from a large majority of French citizens, as well as from citizens and governments in most European and other countries, France held the tests as scheduled.

By focusing exclusively on relations among the president, the government, the bureaucracy, and the parliament, the impression may be conveyed that the French executive is well-nigh all-powerful. Such a view, however, fails to accord adequate weight to important sources of influence on policy-making outside the state. First, divisions within the governing coalition may influence policy-making. Consider Giscard d'Estaing's presidency, 1974–1981. Although Giscard led one of the coalition partners that dominated parliament, the largest party in the coalition (the Gaullist party led by Jacques Chirac) delighted in sniping at the president.

A second counterweight to executive dominance is the streets. On several notable occasions in the Fifth Republic, governments have been forced to change direction after popular protest. For example, both the Socialist government in 1984 and the conservative government in 1986 withdrew proposed educational reforms following huge demonstrations. A third source of influence outside the executive is market forces within and outside France. In 1983, President Mitterrand and his Socialist government were bluntly reminded, regardless of what the constitution specified, that they did not have complete autonomy to make policy. The government was forced to carry out an agonizing reappraisal of its fundamental policy orientation after France began to teeter on the edge of economic chaos as a result of lagging private investment and capital flight to safe havens outside France's borders. The vastly increased integration of international currency markets in recent years means that the French executive can no longer develop policy in majestic isolation.

Many changes have produced greater political stability in France in the recent period than during much of the nineteenth and early twentieth centuries. Above all, the political institutions of the Fifth Republic are effective and popular. Trends in the party system have also buttressed stability, as has the reduction of intense ideological conflicts. Yet, the following two sections make clear that new political identities, parties, and conflicts pose large challenges to the French political system.

SECTION 4

Representation and Participation

The Constitution of the Fifth Republic grants the executive an astonishing array of powers and severely limits participation, representation, and legislative activity. These arrangements were inspired by Charles de Gaulle, the principal architect and first president of the Fifth Republic. De Gaulle believed that, in the

Third and Fourth Republics, political parties and parliament had overstepped their proper roles of representing interests and keeping government accountable by trying to take over the functions of policy-making and administration. The Constitution of the Fifth Republic was designed to assure the independence of the executive and to limit the influence of political parties, organized interests, and parliament.

De Gaulle fully succeeded in limiting parliament's influence. But paradoxically, his regime stimulated the growth of mass-based parties for the first time in France. Prior to 1962, all political parties—with the notable exception of the French Communist Party (PCF)—were highly decentralized organizations. Their main goal was to attempt to capture local and parliamentary offices. Once the presidency emerged as a powerful and attractive stake, and especially once the president was chosen by popular election, parties were forced to become highly centralized to maximize their chances of winning the all-important nationwide contest for the presidency.

Yet traditional patterns of popular protest against state authority within French political culture, reinforced by current strains around collective identities and citizenship in France, mean that political stability and acceptance of executive direction can never be taken for granted. As we will see, the French tradition of political protest is alive and well.

The Legislature: The Truncated Parliament

In the semipresidential system of the Fifth Republic, the French parliament is probably the weakest parliament of any democratic regime. The constitution apparently assumes that parliament should be seen but not heard. Parliament lacks the autonomy and separation from the executive that legislatures enjoy in presidential systems; yet, because it cannot pass a motion of no-confidence in the president, it cannot hold the executive accountable as legislatures can in parliamentary systems. The French parliament does not provide a forum for important national debates, adequately represent conflicting interests, or check governmental abuses of power. With that said, parliament has gradually gained somewhat greater importance since the early years of the Fifth Republic.

The French parliament is bicameral, the two chambers being the National Assembly and the Senate. Until 1958, when the Fifth Republic was created, the National Assembly was regarded as the sole voice of the sovereign people. It could make and unmake governments, legislate on any subject it chose, and intervene in any aspect of French government and administration. (The Senate was much weaker in the Fourth Republic and remains so in the Fifth Republic.)

Under the Fifth Republic, the National Assembly was stripped of many powers. No longer the seat of sovereignty, the constitution strictly limits the areas within which parliament is authorized to act. At the same time, the executive is granted extensive powers independent of parliament, as well as numerous opportunities to control parliamentary activity.

To begin with, the constitution limits the number of normal parliamentary sessions to two per year, each about three months long. The prime minister can convene special sessions for specific purposes, and the practice has become quite common given the government's full legislative agenda. Although parliament can request that it meet in special session, the executive can refuse. As in other parliamentary regimes, the government can choose to dissolve the National Assembly before its normal five-year term ends. (The government cannot dissolve the Senate, but, as described below, the Senate's powers are limited in any event.) The only check on the government's power of dissolution is that, once the National Assembly is dissolved, the government cannot dissolve it again for a year.

Article 34, which defines parliament's legislative jurisdiction, represents a minor revolution within French constitutional law. Rather than having the power to legislate in all areas except those ruled off-limits by the constitution, parliament is authorized to legislate only in those areas enumerated in the constitution. Outside these areas, the executive can issue legally binding regulations. Even within the areas in which parliament is given lawmaking power, Article 38 authorizes the government to request parliament to delegate its legislative power. This may happen, for example, if the government wishes to save time, avoid long parliamentary debate on its proposals, or minimize the risk of unwelcome amendments. If parliament votes to empower the government, as has happened on some matters of vital importance, the government can issue ordinances with the force of law. The referendum procedure provides yet another means for the executive to bypass parliament.

Outside the constitutionally specified areas of lawmaking, the constitution has created a category, termed *regulation,* over which parliament has no power at all. Within this vast domain, the executive issues rules and decrees with the force of law.

Even within the constricted area of lawmaking, the constitution grants the government far more extensive powers to control legislative activity than is the case in comparable parliamentary systems. The government establishes the parliamentary agenda, while the parliamentary opposition has few rights in this matter, and governmental texts are accorded priority over proposals from members of parliament. As in other parliamentary regimes, most legislation coming before parliament is initiated by the government, not backbenchers. The government is empowered to restrict amendments and debate.

The government's control over parliament is bolstered by several unusual measures. Under Article 44, the government can call for a single vote—known as the *vote bloqué* ("blocked vote")—on all or a portion of a bill. The government can select from among the amendments to the bill those that will be included with the text. Governments have used—or, according to the opposition, abused—this power to restrict debate on many key legislative texts.

The government can further curb parliament by calling for a confidence vote either on its overall policies (Article 49, Clause 1) or on a specific legislative text (Article 49, Clause 3). This provision applies only to the National Assembly, since the Senate cannot vote censure, that is, bring down a government. (In any event, as described below, the government has other means of ensuring passage of legislation despite senatorial opposition.)

When the government calls for a confidence vote on a text, the bill is considered approved unless opposition deputies (members of the National Assembly) succeed in passing a censure motion within twenty-four hours. The government can also call for a confidence vote on a general policy declaration or on its entire program. If a censure motion passes, on the other hand, the government must resign from office. The constitution requires that, for a censure motion to pass, an absolute majority of all deputies must vote in favor of it. Thus, deputies who are absent or who abstain from voting are really supporting the government. In other parliamentary regimes, the government is defeated on a confidence

motion if a plurality of the legislature opposes the government.

Articles 34, 38, 44, and 49 provide the government with powerful means to limit parliament that exceed those possessed by governments in virtually all other democratic regimes. When a government relies on these powers to overcome parliamentary resistance, which occurs frequently and on important legislation, a loud outcry is heard from the opposition. However, since governments of both left and right have found these measures highly useful—especially when they have a slim parliamentary majority, are internally divided, or seek to legislate an ambitious agenda quickly—it has been impossible to abolish them.

Deputies can also submit censure motions on their own initiative. Such a motion must be signed by one-tenth of all deputies in the National Assembly. A censure motion is passed in the same way that a motion of no-confidence is passed. Deputies who sign a censure motion under this procedure cannot sign another one during the same parliamentary session. Since deputies belonging to the governing majority would not, of course, sign a censure motion, there are never more than four censure motions yearly initiated by the opposition.

Given the fact that the government normally commands majority support in the National Assembly, it need not worry about being forced to resign by a vote of censure. In fact, only one censure motion has ever passed since the creation of the Fifth Republic in 1958. In 1962, the majority of parliament was enraged when President de Gaulle convened a referendum to approve his initiative to elect the president by popular vote. Unable to vote censure of de Gaulle (because the constitution does not make the president accountable to parliament), the National Assembly vented its spleen by censuring de Gaulle's prime minister and close associate, Georges Pompidou. However, parliament emerged weaker from the combat since, following the censure vote, de Gaulle promptly dissolved parliament and called new elections. When the Gaullist coalition won the legislative elections that followed, de Gaulle sealed his victory by again designating Pompidou to head the new government.

Parliament has limited control over the budgetary process. Members of parliament are prohibited from introducing amendments to the budget that raise expenditures or lower tax revenues. Furthermore, unless parliament approves the budget within seventy days after the government submits it, the government is authorized to enact the budget by decree (although this has never occurred within the Fifth Republic).

In some parliamentary systems, parliamentary committees or, as the French term them, commissions, play a vital role. But not in the Fifth Republic. There are six permanent commissions, whose jurisdictions include foreign policy; finances and economy; defense; constitutional changes, legislation, and general administration; cultural, family, and social affairs; and production and exchange.* Commissions are responsible for reviewing proposed legislation. Although they may propose important changes, their role is quite limited—a far cry from the formidable powers wielded, for example, by committees in the U.S. Congress. Furthermore, there have been few independent parliamentary commissions of inquiry or control, and they have been wholly ineffective in investigating government misconduct.

In sum, parliament's limited autonomy severely restricts representative processes in France. Granted, popular election of the president provides an important mechanism for popular participation and representation. Yet this arrangement further reinforces executive dominance and keeps parliament on a short leash. As a result of this imbalanced situation, popular discontent in France often takes the form of direct protest.

In recent years, parliament has modestly increased its power in three ways.

1. Because of procedural changes, members of parliament have more opportunity to question cabinet ministers, and opposition deputies can now select questions to ask ministers.

2. Members of parliament have exploited the right to amend government-sponsored bills to increase their leverage. When especially controversial legislation is proposed, the opposition (and occasionally the government's own supporters) may propose literally thousands of amendments.

3. Parliament's informal power has increased in two kinds of situations. First, rank-and-file deputies

count for more when the government does not have a solid majority in parliament, as occurred during the first period of cohabitation (1986–1988), and when Socialist prime ministers had only a plurality, not a majority, in the National Assembly during 1988–1993. Second, during periods of cohabitation, divided control of the executive creates space for parliamentary maneuvering.

Unequal Bicameralism

Within parliament, the National Assembly is by far the more powerful chamber. Only the assembly possesses the power to censure the government. And the National Assembly has the decisive role in passing legislation.

A bill can be introduced in either house. If passed in identical form by the two, it becomes law. If, however, the two houses vote different versions or the Senate rejects a text, the government may ask the National Assembly to override the Senate. When the two houses have voted differing texts twice, and are therefore deadlocked, the government may convene a joint commission composed of seven representatives from each house to reconcile their differences. (The government is authorized to convene a joint commission after one reading by each house if it designates the bill as urgent.) If the joint commission reaches agreement and the government approves the text, it is submitted to both houses for a vote. If passed by both, it becomes law. However, if the joint commission is deadlocked or reaches agreement on a text that is passed by the National Assembly but rejected by the Senate, the government can submit the text to the National Assembly for a final vote. If passed, the bill becomes law despite the lack of senatorial approval.

The National Assembly and Senate may adopt different positions because members of the two houses are elected by different procedures. Members of the National Assembly are chosen from single-member districts for five years (unless the government dissolves the chamber before the end of its normal term). There are currently 577 seats in the National Assembly; thus, there are 577 districts. A two-ballot procedure is used, similar to the one used for presidential elections. A candidate must receive an absolute majority of votes in order to be elected at the first ballot. If no candidate obtains a majority—the usual situation—a runoff election is held the following week. Unlike the presidential election, in which only the two

---

* Special commissions may also be appointed to examine particularly important legislation, as occurred during the Socialist government's nationalization reform in 1981.

front-running candidates may compete at the runoff, any candidate receiving at least 12.5 percent of the vote at the first ballot can compete in the runoff. Typically, however, parties on the left and those on the right negotiate alliances in which each party to the agreement agrees to support the best-placed candidate from the alliance in each district (and therefore to withdraw less-well-placed candidates in the coalition, even if they obtain over 12.5 percent of the vote). There are powerful incentives to negotiate such an agreement, since candidates nominated by a party outside an alliance are isolated at the second ballot. Because minor-party candidates rarely obtain enough votes to remain in the runoff, it is unusual for more than two candidates to compete at the runoff ballot in most districts.

Since alliances follow the left-right divide, the electoral system used to elect the National Assembly has an important polarizing effect on French politics. Thus, despite quite bitter opposition on the left between the Socialist and Communist parties much of the time, as well as conflict between the center-right parties, at election time the left-right cleavage is usually resurrected.

The major effect of the electoral system used for the National Assembly is to maximize the chances of a stable majority emerging in parliament. It is for this reason that political scientist Jean Charlot claims that the two-ballot, single-district system "has proved . . . one of the most solid underpinnings of the Fifth Republic. The electoral law . . . weakens or even neutralizes the natural tendency of the French and their parties toward division."[25] Stating this in a slightly different way, because the two-ballot system that is used to elect deputies maximizes the chances for a majority to emerge in parliament, it has proved to be an important source of political stability in the Fifth Republic.

While the two-ballot system gives a bonus to large parties, the other side of the coin is that it penalizes small, isolated parties that cannot form agreements with major parties. In recent years, the Communist Party, the National Front, and the Green Party have obtained far smaller proportions of parliamentary seats than of popular votes. For example, in the 1993 parliamentary elections, FN candidates obtained over 12 percent of all popular votes but, because its supporters were spread throughout France and the FN could not ally with a large party, it failed to

TABLE 6	Popular Vote and Parliamentary Seats, 1993 Legislative Elections	
Party	Popular Vote (%)	National Assembly Seats (%)
PCF	9	4
PS	19	10
Greens	11	0
UDF	19	37
RPR	20	45
FN	12	0
Independents	10	4
Total	100	100

Source: Ministry of the Interior.

elect a single deputy. As a result, the diversity of French public opinion is not reflected in the distribution of parliamentary seats.

The 1993 parliamentary elections were an extreme case illustrating the possible distortions that can occur when the two-ballot, single-member procedure is used in a multiparty system. Although the 39 percent of the vote that the center-right coalition received was far greater than that of any other single party or coalition, it was considerably less than the 82 percent of parliamentary seats that the center-right obtained. What explains the difference between the popular vote and parliamentary seats is the fact that no other party or coalition came close to gaining pluralities in many districts (see Table 6).

The 322 senators are chosen for nine-year terms by an electoral college composed of mayors and town councillors from each *département* (the one hundred administrative districts into which mainland and overseas France is divided).* Rural interests are substantially overrepresented in the departmental electoral colleges: Although one-quarter of the population live in villages of under 1,500, 40 percent of delegates from departmental electoral colleges represent these communes (localities); the 23 percent of citizens living in communes of over 30,000 elect only 10 percent of the delegates who choose senators.[26] The Senate is thus particularly zealous in defending the interests of small towns and villages.

---

* Twelve senators are elected by nonresident French citizens.

Throughout the Fifth Republic, with the important exception of the two periods of cohabitation, a high degree of cohesion has existed among state institutions. However, contrary to the expectations of the Fifth Republic's founders, the reason for unity at the top is not the intricate procedures that limit parliamentary initiative. Rather, it is because the same coalition usually wins both the presidential and the parliamentary elections.

THE PARTY SYSTEM AND ELECTIONS

We have suggested that, despite de Gaulle's opposition to political parties on the grounds that they nurture division, instability, and paralysis, the emergence of powerful political parties has played a key role in buttressing cohesion, stability, and leadership within the Fifth Republic. An important development in the Fifth Republic has been the emergence of governing coalitions of political parties. Moreover, there has been a powerful tendency for parties to coalesce into two opposing coalitions, facing each other across the left-right divide. This outcome is a product of the historical divisions in France, whose roots go back to the Revolution of 1789 and before, and of electoral dynamics in the Fifth Republic, notably the popular election of the president and the majority-based influence of the two-ballot electoral law for presidential and legislative elections.

The formation of rival political coalitions has strengthened the legitimacy and stability of the Fifth Republic by making possible political alternation in office. Popular support and political stability increase when elections represent a choice between alternative political coalitions. Yet, in recent years, the decline in ideological distance between the center-left and the center-right means that which coalition wins is less significant. At the same time, many French citizens feel unrepresented by *both* of the two established choices.

From 1958 to 1981, the center-right controlled the presidency and the government. Left opposition parties initially regarded the Fifth Republic as illegitimate but eventually contributed to political stability. Especially after the May 1968 uprising, leftist parties provided a vehicle for the expression of grievances in a relatively orderly fashion. The left made an even greater contribution to the republic's stability after the 1981 elections by accepting the legitimacy of the Fifth Republic, working within established institutions to promote change, and sponsoring overdue reforms. The

left has organized and integrated social forces that might otherwise have opposed the republic. Thus, the party system helped structure both government and opposition in a nation where, in the not-so-distant past, government was subject to continual challenge. Yet the major parties have proved increasingly unable to represent the spectrum of political interests and demands, as evidenced by the rise of the National Front and Green parties in the 1980s and 1990s and the persistence of the Communist Party.

Evolution of the Party System

When de Gaulle proposed electing the president by popular vote in 1962, he hoped to reduce presidential dependence on political parties, whose local leaders formed the electoral college that elected the president until 1962. Instead, parties have become essential vehicles for mobilizing popular support in the all-important presidential contest. The change contributed to the emergence of a new kind of party system in France, in which major parties are generally allied in coalitions confronting each other across the left-right divide.

Popular election of the president produced the *polarization* and *"presidentialization"* of the party system and French politics in general. Polarization describes the tendency for the electorate to divide into two camps as a result of the procedures used to elect the president. As with the election of deputies to the National Assembly, the two-ballot system used for presidential elections encourages parties to form two broad competing alliances, each united under the banner of one of the two standard-bearers who compete in the runoff ballot of the presidential election. Presidentialization means that parties give priority, in terms of their program, internal organization, alliance strategy, and leadership, to winning the next presidential election. Parties are organized to be efficient electoral vehicles, and the process rewards leaders who project an appealing image and perform well on television. The party shapes its program to capture the widest possible audience, which produces a tendency toward ideological moderation. As French parties have moved in this direction, some observers see French politics becoming "Americanized," for the tendencies we have just identified are most evident in U.S. elections.

Counterpressures, however, constantly challenge the trend toward polarization and presidentialization. In particular, because the major parties seek to develop broad alliances and appeal to the ideological center, they have neglected groups who feel that the system does not serve their interests. Thus, in recent years, the tendency toward polarization has been offset by the countertendency toward fragmentation within the party system. Small parties have achieved significant levels of support in elections for the European Parliament, National Assembly, and presidency.

In the present French party system, three major parties vie for dominance, each of which has held top offices within the Fifth Republic. The Movement for the Republic (RPR) and the Union for French Democracy (UDF) are the two major parties on the center-right, and the Socialist Party (PS) is the major center-left party. In addition, we review three smaller parties: the Communist Party, the National Front, and the Greens.

The Major Parties

The RPR   French parties on the right of the political spectrum have traditionally been numerous and fragmented. Under de Gaulle's leadership, a new party was created, which dominated the Fifth Republic in the early years. The RPR, as it is presently known, never had a precise program. It was originally created to support de Gaulle's personal leadership and his somewhat vague program of championing France's national independence, providing decisive political leadership within France, and modernizing French society and economy while preserving France's distinctive cultural heritage.

When de Gaulle resigned as president in 1969, following his defeat in a referendum to reorganize the state, his former prime minister, Georges Pompidou (who was also leader of the Gaullist party), won the election to fill the vacant presidential office. However, when Pompidou died in office in 1974, the RPR lacked a dominant leader and lost control of the presidency. Valéry Giscard d'Estaing, the victorious candidate in the presidential election that year, led a party allied with the RPR, but he did not belong to the Gaullist movement. From 1974 until 1995, the RPR no longer controlled the presidency. Thus, although it remained one of France's "big three" parties, it did not dominate French politics the way it had in the first years of the Fifth Republic.

Since 1974, the RPR has been led by Jacques Chirac, who unsuccessfully ran for president twice (in

1981 and 1988) before finally winning the presidential race in 1995 on his third try. To win, however, Chirac had to vanquish Edouard Balladur, a member of the RPR and a close associate of Chirac's. Balladur became prime minister in 1993, with Chirac's blessing, when the conservative parties won the 1993 parliamentary elections. A resounding success as prime minister, Balladur could not resist the temptation to announce his own candidacy when the 1995 presidential campaign began. However, with Chirac firmly in control of the RPR party machine, Balladur was unable to maintain his early lead and came in third at the first ballot, behind Socialist candidate Lionel Jospin and Chirac. Chirac went on to win the runoff ballot, and the RPR finally regained control of the Fifth Republic's supreme prize. Chirac immediately appointed Alain Juppé, his principal adviser and leader of the RPR, to be prime minister, thereby consolidating the party's dominance over the executive.

In part because of de Gaulle's own complex legacy, the RPR is not a classic **conservative** party. For example, it has advocated the need for social reforms if they are in the general interest. When his supporters were asked in a public opinion poll why they voted for Chirac in 1995, two-thirds responded that the reason was to promote needed reforms.

Nonetheless, the social base of the RPR generally reflects its conservative orientation. Business executives, professionals, the highly educated, and the affluent are more likely to favor either the RPR or the second conservative party, which we review below. In the runoff ballot of the 1995 presidential elections, 67 percent of respondents in a public opinion poll who identified themselves as affluent chose Chirac. (A large majority of those identifying themselves as having low income voted for Chirac's opponent, Lionel Jospin.)

The UDF   Created in 1978, the UDF is an umbrella organization grouping several small parties on the center-right that opposed de Gaulle and his political movement in the early years of the Fifth Republic. The party's major leader has been Valéry Giscard d'Estaing, elected president in 1974 and defeated for reelection by François Mitterrand in 1981. Other prominent UDF leaders include Raymond Barre and François Léotard.

Although the parties united under the UDF banner nominate joint candidates for legislative and other elections, they maintain a separate organizational existence, and there is much rivalry among them. The UDF has positioned itself toward the center of the political spectrum, reflecting Giscard d'Estaing's opinion that the French wish to be governed from the center, and that they oppose the left-right polarization so often evident in French politics. The risk of adopting a centrist position, however, is that it may displease voters on both sides of the political divide because they view it as too close to the other side!

In the early years of the Fifth Republic, the reason for two major center-right parties was self-evident. The two differed sharply on whether to support or oppose de Gaulle, support or oppose European integration, and favor state economic regulation or free enterprise. Recently, however, the rationale for two parties has virtually disappeared. De Gaulle is long gone and disagreements over other issues do not so much pit the parties against each other as divide them internally. The RPR and the UDF ally during most election campaigns—often running common candidates in legislative elections—and they formed a coalition government after winning the 1986 and 1993 parliamentary elections. The UDF did not run a candidate in the 1995 presidential elections. But the RPR and the UDF remain distinct and often rival organizations. The reason has been the presidential ambitions of their respective leaders—in particular, Chirac and Giscard d'Estaing. After 1995, with Chirac in the Élysée and the aging Giscard d'Estaing beginning to withdraw from political activity, the dividing line between the two parties became ever more blurred.

The Socialist Party (PS)   The PS is one of the major success stories in contemporary France. Few could have predicted in the 1960s that a party of aging notables and schoolteachers would become the vanguard of a new France in 1981, when it swept presidential and parliamentary elections. For over a decade after 1981, the Socialist Party dominated French politics. By 1995, after it suffered a stinging electoral defeat in the 1993 parliamentary elections and its presidential nominee, Lionel Jospin, lost the 1995 runoff presidential election to Jacques Chirac, the PS again found itself as the political opposition. But the PS profoundly shaped present-day France, both by its general policy orientation and by the specific reforms it sponsored while governing in the 1980s and early 1990s.

The PS reached power in 1981 by advocating substantial, even radical, changes, and it kept its promises by sponsoring a whirlwind of reforms in its first years in office. However, as reviewed in Section 2, the government soon encountered severe economic and political difficulties in pursuing its reform agenda. When President Mitterrand reluctantly decided on a dramatic about-face in 1983–1984, French **socialism** lost its bearings. For decades, the PS had advocated a radical reformist course, and its first actions in office were inspired by this vision. When, after 1984, the Socialist government pursued the very same policies of economic austerity and support for private enterprise that the PS had opposed for years, the party was incapable of defending its new course. Although the PS remained in office for a decade after its right turn, contributing by its policies to the modernization of French industry and by its ideological moderation to the "normalization" of French politics, it never succeeded in forging a new vision to replace the one it had abandoned in the mid-1980s.

The electoral decline of the PS in the late 1980s and 1990s had other causes. Although PS governments helped revitalize the French economy, unemployment remained at record levels. Some leading PS party leaders and cabinet ministers were convicted of corruption, as a result of illegally diverting funds to finance the party and for their personal use. Other PS government ministers were tried on charges of allowing government stocks of blood contaminated with the HIV virus to be distributed to patients, causing them to contract AIDS.

The party was also damaged after the late 1980s by the fact that its fortunes were narrowly tied to François Mitterrand, its most gifted leader. As Mitterrand began to become unpopular and fade from the political scene, PS leaders devoted less energy to forging a new direction for the party than to competing with each other to succeed Mitterrand. Given the party's severe internal divisions and lack of a new vision, it was no surprise that voters began to desert the PS in droves.

The low point of the party's fortunes was the 1993 legislative elections. The PS share of the popular vote declined by half from the level of the 1988 legislative elections and, from enjoying a relative majority in the National Assembly and control of the government, the PS was reduced to a small opposition force. After Lionel Jospin, the party's presidential candidate in 1995, produced a surprisingly fine showing and lost to conservative candidate Chirac by only a small margin, the PS might have been on the road to recovery. (The PS repeated its strong showing in local and senatorial elections later in 1995.) Nonetheless, the PS has not yet developed an attractive program to replace the one it abandoned in the 1980s, and fierce conflicts persist among party leaders. The difficulties of the PS are part of the larger crisis of the left in Western Europe and elsewhere.

Small Parties

Although three political parties dominate the French political system, they do not command universal support. Especially as their programs become increasingly alike, many voters believe that none of the major parties is responsive to their concerns. As a result, there is significant support for several small parties that now represent a significant political force, though they are not serious contenders for power. However, because the small parties differ so much among themselves and are all so critical of the major parties, the result is greater fragmentation within the French political system.

The Communist Party (PCF)   In the period from World War II until the 1980s, the PCF was among the largest political parties in France. It presented itself as the heir to the French revolutionary tradition, proud of its close links both to the French working class—whose electoral support was key to the party's strong position—and to the Soviet Union, which the PCF generally supported as a desirable socialist model and as the major progressive force in the world.

Like orthodox **communist** parties elsewhere, the PCF's internal organization was based on the concept of democratic centralism, which in practice meant that the distribution of power within the party was long on centralism and short on democracy. The party's top leaders, especially its secretary general and his closest associates in the secretariat, chose lower-level party officials and decided the party's general orientation. Even the mildest criticism of the party's position or its leaders by rank-and-file members was considered equivalent to treason. Critics from within the party's ranks were usually quickly isolated and expelled from the party.

The PCF was a powerful and divisive force within French politics. For decades, it was the major opposition force to established parties of both the right and

the moderate left. Its opposition to the Fourth Republic, coupled with the fact that it was among the largest parties represented in parliament, was an important reason for the fragility of the regime. The PCF also opposed the Fifth Republic at first, although it gradually came to accept the regime while contesting the governmental policies. Yet the PCF's impact was not simply destabilizing. By acting as a tribune for the unrepresented, the PCF helped to integrate workers and other excluded citizens into political and social life. As political scientist Martin Schain observes, "[PCF] opposition to the [Fifth] republic was progressively converted into opposition within the republic."[27] The irony is that this sowed the seeds for the PCF's eventual decline.

The PCF's identity was shaped during the grim period of the Great Depression, World War II, and the Cold War. It adapted too little and too late to the political, social, and economic changes that transformed France beginning in the 1960s. Wave after wave of dissidents challenged party leaders to reject the cherished Soviet model, promote more open debate within the party, and modernize the party's discourse and program. But the party leadership, under Georges Marchais, who led the party from the 1970s until 1994, adapted too little and too late, and party support dwindled. From commanding over 20 percent of the vote in elections in the postwar period, the PCF vote fell to under 10 percent by the 1980s. Many of its former supporters, especially in the working class, eventually drifted to the National Front, both because of the party's anti-immigrant message and its more dynamic—and coarse—opposition to the established parties. With the PCF no longer a major influence in French politics, the entire political spectrum shifted toward the right in the 1980s.

Nonetheless, the PCF survived the disintegration of the Soviet Union, proclaimed the need for internal reform, and stabilized its support. In the 1990s, it is nearly alone among the world's surviving communist parties to proclaim itself communist, and by obtaining nearly 10 percent of the vote in the 1995 presidential elections it remains a significant political force.

The National Front (FN)   The National Front has existed for decades, but the rapid rise in its support base in the 1980s was produced by high unemployment, fears about increased crime, and the choice of a handy scapegoat—immigrant workers and their families, especially those from Algeria, France's former North African colony. The FN is one of the first openly racist political parties in Western Europe in the contemporary period. Many such parties flourished in France and elsewhere in Western Europe before World War II, but were discredited by the widespread revulsion toward the Nazi regime during and after the war.

The National Front's slogan is "France for the French," meaning that immigrants, especially those who are not white, should be expelled from France. The FN exploits the insecurity of native-born French citizens (and white immigrants to France from France's former North African colonies and elsewhere).

The personality of FN leader Jean-Marie Le Pen powerfully contributes to the FN's success. He is a dynamic, articulate orator, and thus a dramatic contrast to the lackluster leaders often found in other parties. In both the 1988 and 1995 presidential elections, Le Pen received 15 percent of the vote, which placed him just behind the major candidates, and FN candidates obtained an average of 12 percent in the 1993 parliamentary elections.

The FN's greatest impact is on public opinion. For the first time since World War II, a French political party openly insults members of an ethnic minority and advocates racist and authoritarian measures. The FN's propaganda has borne fruit. For example, a poll after the 1995 presidential elections indicated that one-third of all voters and 43 percent of pro-Chirac voters hoped "that the ideas proposed by the National Front [would] be taken seriously into account by the newly elected president."[28]

The Greens   A revealing clue to the success of the Green Party *(les Verts)* is the fact that, while the major political parties have paid little attention to environmental issues, French citizens now rank ecology fourth in importance among their preoccupations.[29] The state's relative indifference to environmental concerns provides the potential for a green movement in France. For example, France has the largest nuclear power program in Western Europe. The state-controlled nuclear power agency and the electric power agency are often described as states within the state because of their isolation and overbearing approach.

In the 1989 elections, the Green Party, which had been on the political scene for years, achieved a major breakthrough by receiving 10.6 percent of the vote,

coming in fourth behind an RPR-UDF ticket, the PS, and the National Front, and ahead of the PCF. In the 1993 legislative elections, the Greens' 11-percent share of the vote represented a substantial advance, although internal divisions and the two-ballot electoral law prevented the Greens from electing any deputies.

The Greens' recent breakthrough may have been linked to the "new look" that the party adopted in the late 1980s, which appeals to young, well-educated voters—who provide the bulk of support for the Greens. The party abandoned its New Left orientation in 1988 when it selected as leader Antoine Waechter, an environmental engineer from Alsace who stressed the party's "serious" (that is, technocratic) approach. Waechter sought to appeal to voters of diverse ideological sympathies by asserting that the party was "neither right nor left."

No less than most other French political parties—in fact, more so than other parties—the Greens have been divided by the personal ambitions of their leaders. In the 1993 parliamentary elections, Brice Lalonde, former minister of the environment in a Socialist government, mounted his own party, which ran candidates in opposition to Waechter's Green Party. The Greens have been badly damaged by their internal divisions, and the single Green candidate in the 1995 presidential elections received a meager 3 percent of the vote.

Electoral Behavior and Partisan Trends

French voters go to the polls nearly every year, to vote in a referendum or in elections for municipal, departmental, or regional councillor, deputy to the European Parliament or National Assembly, or president. Despite rapid shifts in electoral support from one election to the next, there are broad continuities that can be discerned over time. Electoral studies have demonstrated astonishing similarities in the political orientation of regions over periods of time—sometimes as long as a century in duration—although the political parties that represent a given ideological position may change (see Table 7 on the following page).

In the 1980s and 1990s, however, important changes have occurred, most notably, the decline of the PCF and the radical option that it represented. For the first time in two centuries, the far-left is not a major force in French politics. A key to its decline is the massive desertion of young voters, who traditionally

TABLE 7 **Electoral Results, Elections to National Assembly, 1958–1993 (percentage of those voting)**

	1958	1962	1967	1968	1973	1978	1981	1986	1988	1993
Far Left	2%	2%	2%	4%	3%	3%	1%	2%	0%	2%
PCF	19	22	23	20	21	21	16	10	11	9
Socialist Party/Left Radicals	23	21	19	17	22	25	38	32	38	21
Ecology	—	—	—	—	—	2	1	1	1	12
Center parties	15	15	18	10	16	{21	{19	{42	{19	{19
Center-Right	14	14	0	4	7					
UNR → RPR	18	32	38	44	24	23	21		19	20
Far Right	3	1	1	0	3	0	3	10	10	13
Abstentions	23	31	19	20	19	17	30	22	34	31

Note: Percentages of parties do not add to 100 because of minor-party candidates and rounding errors.

Sources: Françoise Dreyfus and François D'Arcy, *Les Institutions Politiques et Administratives de la France* (Paris: Economica, 1985), 54; *Le Monde,* March 18, 1986; "Les élections législatives," *Le Monde,* 1988; Ministry of the Interior, 1993.

TABLE 8   **Eighteen- to Twenty-four-Year-Old Voting Preference, Legislative Elections**

	1978	1981	1986	1988	1993
Far-Left	9	2	4	2	1
Communist	28	18	7	10	9
Socialist	25	44	33	40	18
Greens	4	2	2	1	12
Gaullist	34	33	40	32	36
Far-Right	—	1	14	15	18
Independent	—	—	—	—	6
	100	100	100	100	100
(Total Right)	(34)	(34)	(54)	(47)	(54)

Source: *SOFRES/Nouvel Observateur—post-électoral,* in Jean Charlot, *La Politique en France* (Paris: Editions de Fallois, 1994), 160.

were especially likely to vote for the Communist and other far-left parties. Whereas 37 percent of young voters supported the far-left in the late 1970s, 20 percent did so in the early 1980s, with a further sharp decline occurring later in the decade and continuing through the early 1990s.[30]

The rapid pace and magnitude of the shift in French voting patterns can be seen by charting changes in voting patterns among youth in the past two decades (see Table 8). One can also identify somewhat parallel shifts among major socioeconomic groups in the same period (see Table 9 on the following page).

Some scholars describe the shift as the "normalization" of French politics, in that French political patterns increasingly resemble politics in northern Europe and the United States. The declining ideological distance between political parties, as a result of the PCF's decline and the Socialist Party's greater moderation beginning in 1982, has contributed to this normalization. For example, 57 percent of the electorate report that they see little difference between the Socialist Party and the center-right parties.[31] Another contributing factor has been alternation between parties of the center-left and center-right. Such alternation, which occurred four times between 1981 and 1993, seemed unthinkable only a few years earlier. Alternation has become so routine because political conflict has become so moderate, at least among the major parties.

These changes represent a fundamental restructuring of the French party system and political life. Yet, before concluding that the new era signifies political health, we should note some disturbing trends. Indeed, scholars have identified a crisis of political representation and the party system due, in part, to four major trends.

First, support for those parties not part of the "club" of governmental parties has climbed in the past few years. The combined vote total of so-called peripheral candidates in the 1995 presidential elections was 38 percent, and to this should be added the 3 percent of voters who spoiled their ballots at the first round, as well as some of the 22 percent of nonvoters. Thus, over half of the electorate failed to vote for candidates from the major parties of center-left and center-right.

Second, there has been increased volatility in voting patterns, as evidenced by greater vote switching among parties, suggesting a decline of voters' party loyalty.

Third, the level of abstentions and deliberately spoiled ballots has increased within the recent past, further evidence of citizens' discontent with the choices that parties offer them. Nearly 10 percent of voters turned out to cast a blank or spoiled ballot in the 1993 legislative elections; 6 percent did so in the 1995 presidential elections. As the major parties move closer together, citizens become skeptical that parties

---

TABLE 9   Political Parties' Social Base, 1993 Legislative Elections (percentage)

	PC	PS	UDF/RPR	FN	Other[a]
Farmers					
1978[b]	9	17	67	—	7
1981	6	32	60	—	2
1993	4	13	59	14	10
Artisans, Shopkeepers					
1978	14	23	58	—	5
1981	10	35	53	2	—
1993	5	14	56	18	7
Higher Executives, Professionals					
1978	9	15	67	—	9
1981	7	38	50	—	5
1993	3	24	53	6	14
Middle Executives, Office Workers					
1978	18	29	42	—	11
1981	16	45	34	1	4
1993	12	23	32	12	21
Workers					
1978	36	27	31	—	6
1981	24	44	30	—	2
1993	12	19	37	15	17

[a]Note that "Other" includes ultra-left, ecology, and independent candidates.
[b]In this table the *rows* total 100, not the columns.

Source: *SOFRES/Nouvel Observateur—post-électoral,* in Jean Charlot, *La Politique en France* (Paris: Editions de Fallois, 1994), 163.

---

can make a difference, and fewer citizens bother casting a useful ballot.

Finally, virtually every major political party, and most of the minor ones as well, are wracked by internal dissension. The causes may differ—hostility to leadership rigidity within the PCF; a succession struggle within the PS; a stalemate among UDF leaders—but beyond particular factors, existing parties seem ill-equipped to confront the social, economic, and cultural changes sweeping France. This helps explain the success of the National Front and the Greens in restructuring the political agenda.

POLITICAL CULTURE, CITIZENSHIP, AND IDENTITY

French public opinion is divided, confused, and angry. On the one hand, socioeconomic problems, population movements, and France's changing relation to the in-

ternational order pose severe challenges. On the other hand, ideological maps, party organizations, and collective loyalties inherited from the past offer little help in confronting the new challenges. An important example is the decline of class identities, one of the major elements by which French citizens have traditionally defined their place in the **society.** There has been a rapid drop in the numbers of those identifying themselves as members of social classes, and the erosion of working-class self-identification has been especially great.

Similarly, the ideological markers that French citizens have traditionally used to define their identities are of little help in the present period. Witness the crisis of Marxist and socialist theory, which helps explain the ideological and political difficulties of the Socialist and Communist parties. The dramatic decline in Catholic religious observance has also weak-

Local elections: "Next Sunday, I'm counting on your support." "What's happening Sunday?"
Source: Courtesy Plantu, from *Le Monde.*

ened the social networks that formerly promoted the right's social cohesion. In addition to ideological and social disorientation, we have emphasized how recent economic difficulties, notably, the high level of unemployment, have disoriented French citizens.

INTERESTS, SOCIAL MOVEMENTS, AND PROTEST

Most scholars agree that the overbearing French state has typically tended to limit possibilities for **social movements** and private interests to organize and regulate their own affairs. The Fifth Republic reinforced this tendency by further strengthening the executive. But the May 1968 insurrection illustrated that civil society was alive and kicking. Even if the state prevented interests from managing their own affairs, it could not prevent citizens from taking to the streets to protest against this situation. Moreover, organized interests are not wholly excluded from playing a significant role. In some sectors, interests compete with each other in **pluralist** fashion. In others, the state has associated interests in state decision making through **neocorporatist** arrangements.

Although the French bureaucracy is generally considered exceptionally resistant to outside pressures, scholars have provided conflicting assessments of the overall influence of organized interests in France and the manner in which interests are linked to the bureaucracy. Some scholars believe that French **interest groups** have little impact on policy-making,

with barks much worse than their bites. Many interest groups have loudly protested government decisions, for example, by marching in the streets to mount demonstrations, but the result is usually negligible. Yet other scholars highlight the close relations between the bureaucracy and private interests. This may occur in an informal fashion, as when particular interest groups lobby an administrative agency. It may also take a neocorporatist form when the administration designates particular interest groups as official representatives of their constituency. In these cases, interest groups are given state subsidies, and their leaders sit on advisory commissions or even participate in administrative decisions.

Scholars probably differ so much about the character and extent of interest group influence because relations between administrative agencies and organized interests vary so much from one sector to another. For example, at one extreme, the peak agricultural organization, the Fédération Nationale des Syndicats d'Exploitants Agricoles (National Federation of Farmers' Unions, or FNSEA), exercises immense power. Its representatives serve on administrative commissions that set levels of agricultural prices and subsidies. In some respects, it is difficult to distinguish where the bureaucracy ends and the FNSEA begins. This example is far from unique. Trade associations and labor unions play an important part in administering the far-flung public health system, as well as the state-financed vocational training programs. A state institution, the Economic and Social Council (described in Section 3), is an advisory body on which representatives of interest groups serve.

At the other extreme of interest representation, French labor unions are terribly weak. Unlike the FNSEA, which speaks with a single voice, labor unions are highly divided. There are four major trade unions claiming to represent workers throughout the economy, as well as independent unions in specific sectors (such as teachers). For years, the labor movement could not persuade the state to legislate even minimal protection for union officials in the face of arbitrary employer actions. Unions have had little say in formulating and implementing policies of direct concern to workers and unions. Under these conditions, they have typically been forced to express their demands by direct protest—a more dramatic, but often less effective, means than behind-the-scenes meetings with administrative officials.

French farmers, protesting provisions of the GATT on agriculture, block the entrance of Euro Disney, a symbol of American interference in French affairs. The sign reads "Wheat is life."
Source: © Brian Palmer/Impact Visuals.

Which of the two situations is typical? Probably neither. We have intentionally selected cases at the extremes to illustrate how varied are relations between the state and private interests and to suggest that there is probably no "typical" pattern of interest intermediation in France.

Women, the largest "minority"—in reality, a 51 percent majority—are highly underrepresented in the French political system. At the highest level of state institutions, there has never been a female president of the republic and there has only been one female prime minister—Edith Cresson, who served a brief and unsuccessful term under President Mitterrand. Although women rarely gain significant representation in the government, Prime Minister Alain Juppé, Jacques Chirac's first prime minister, appointed a record number of female cabinet ministers in 1995.

State policy has often been unresponsive to women's particular concerns, partly as a result of their meager political representation. Contraception, for ex-

ample, was illegal in France until 1967, and abortion was wholly illegal until 1974, when legislation was passed authorizing abortion until the tenth week of pregnancy.

Protest as Politics

Those groups who do not entertain close relations with the bureaucracy resent their second-class status. Even groups with a privileged relationship, such as farmers, may calculate that their interests are better served by direct action—street demonstrations, strikes, and the like—than by peaceful collaboration with the state. France has a long tradition of direct protest. Throughout the nineteenth century, regimes were toppled by mass opposition in the streets. More recently, in May 1968, the Fifth Republic was the target of widespread protest when millions of workers and students brought the economy and the entire society to a halt with demonstrations and factory occupations. Although President de Gaulle subdued the May movement, it struck a

Newly appointed Prime Minister Edith Cresson during a television appearance in 1991.
Source: AP/Wide World Photos.

mortal blow to his claim to represent all French and he resigned from office the following year.

France's historically high strike rate is linked to the tradition of direct action. Strikes have been frequent and turbulent. In recent years, however, the overall rate of strikes has drastically declined as a result of high unemployment, for workers fear losing their jobs if they strike. But although labor unions now hesitate to organize strikes, spontaneous strike movements, led by strike-coordinating committees not directly under union control, periodically erupt without warning. More generally, in the current period, farmers, fishing interests, postal workers, high school students, truck drivers, health care workers, tax collectors, electric and gas workers, and immigrants and their offspring—to provide only a partial list—have mounted disruptive protests. These diverse groups are united only by the angry claim that government policies serve their interests poorly.

The Fifth Republic erected sturdy institutions to facilitate state action but provided few legitimate channels by which private interests could be heard. Although there has been some liberalization of French institutions, procedures for effectively representing interests have not been devised.

SECTION 5
French Politics at the Crossroads

POLITICAL CHALLENGES AND CHANGING AGENDAS

What a distance separates French politics in the 1990s from politics even a few years earlier. Political conflict in the 1970s and 1980s—as well as the major political parties—were arrayed quite neatly along a left-right ideological continuum linked to social class divisions. In the 1970s, attention was riveted on the opposition between the Union of the Left alliances of the Communist and Socialist parties, based on a radical reformist program, and the conservative center-right parties. In the early 1980s, Socialist government reform initiatives dominated the news. When the center-right gained a parliamentary majority in 1986, its first priority was to roll back many Socialist reforms.

As the decade ended, however, a strange calm began to prevail in French politics—strange when viewed from the perspective of the political combats of the immediate past. The major political parties on the center-left and center-right virtually abandoned reformist ambitions and defended their claim to rule on the basis of technical steering capacity. If the challenges that the parties faced were immense, their pretensions—and divergences—were modest. Unlike the situation in some countries, established political parties shared a commitment to preserving France's welfare state, although they agreed that cost-saving measures needed to be devised because of budget deficits and inflationary pressures. There was a general consensus that many key Socialist government reforms should be preserved, including the decentralization measures that transferred powers to local governments, reform of the media (which bolstered their independence from the government), and labor law reform designed to reduce conflict in the workplace. Above all, the Socialist measures contributed to creating a more modest role for the French state, reversing many decades of state growth. This goal was further strengthened by the two periods of cohabitation, when conservative governments rolled back state control over the economy, for example, by privatizing many state-owned firms.

By the early 1990s, it appeared that significant ideological controversy over organizing the economy had ended. The result was broad acceptance of France's mixed economy, consisting of the coexistence of a strong role for the state but also heavy reliance on private market forces. This consensus may explain why over two-thirds of respondents in a 1988 public opinion poll agreed that "notions of left and right no longer make sense."[32]

Does the end of intense debate over the overall organization of the economy signify that political conflict has ended in France? Certainly not. First, although the major political parties are ideologically closer, this does not mean that their relations are harmonious. If only to achieve "product differentiation" in the political marketplace, each party emphasizes what distinguishes it from the others. Thus, competition between center-left and center-right parties continues to generate conflict in the 1990s. Second, new political issues have emerged, which often cut across existing partisan lines. Whereas earlier conflicts concerned contending political-economic approaches, new conflicts often revolve around group loyalties and cultural styles, such as the meaning of French citizenship.

A third source of new political conflicts in the 1990s—partially related to the second—derives from the surge of political parties, such as the Greens and the FN, that challenge the consensus forged by the major parties. Together these developments signify that French politics is at a crossroads.

Some of the new issues confronting French politics can be highlighted by reviewing the 1992 referendum to ratify the Maastricht Treaty, which produced a major political controversy. The referendum campaign suggests the existence of a new fault line in French politics, linked to France's relationship to the international arena (in particular, the European Union) and to the changing world economy. It illustrates the existence of conflicts, such as those generated by the costs of economic modernization and international integration, that the major parties wish to ignore. The results of the Maastricht referendum suggest the existence of issues and challenges—either quite new or submerged

for a long period—linked to France's relationship to the international economic and political order, French national identity, and the social base of the major political parties.

Maastricht: A New Fault Line in French Politics?

One of the political nonevents of 1992 appeared to be in the offing when President François Mitterrand announced that the government was planning to sponsor a referendum to seek popular approval of the Maastricht Treaty. The treaty was negotiated by the member states of the European Union to accelerate the process of economic and social integration in Western Europe. A long and complex document, which even lawyers found difficult to understand, it hardly seemed the stuff of popular controversy. Moreover, since all established parties supported the treaty, the referendum campaign promised to be brief and boring. Cynics suggested that Mitterrand proposed the referendum as a way in which to write the final chapter in his long presidency, for the constitutional changes required to ratify the treaty could have been voted by parliament, thus avoiding the cumbersome process of a nationwide referendum.

And yet, voters came within a hair of rejecting the Maastricht Treaty. Less than 51 percent voted in favor of it, and over 49 percent opposed the treaty. Analyzing the political cleavages revealed by the results of the Maastricht referendum reveals important new challenges that have recently emerged on the French political agenda.

The results reflected popular disgust with the incumbent Socialist coalition, including President Mitterrand and the ruling Socialist Party and government, and thus foreshadowed voters' desertion of the Socialist Party in the 1993 parliamentary elections and the 1995 presidential elections. Opposition to the Socialist Party was understandable: After holding office for a decade, the party was internally divided, ideologically exhausted, and tarnished by charges of corruption. Moreover, as public opinion polls repeatedly demonstrate (see Table 10), unemployment is the major issue that preoccupies French citizens—and in this vital domain, Socialist governments failed badly. Although the Socialist Party gained election in 1981 because the incumbent conservative government could not stem unemployment, the numbers of unemployed mounted

TABLE 10 Citizens' Concerns

"Which of the following problems do you judge most pressing?"

	Percent[a]
Welfare system	55
Immigration	38
Reforming political institutions	8
Constructing Europe	30
French foreign and defense policy	10
The struggle against unemployment	92
Improving the moral level of public life	16
Reforming education	27
The struggle against exclusion	37

[a]Answers exceed 100 percent because those questioned could provide up to four responses.

Source: *Le Monde*, May 11, 1995.

steadily throughout the Socialists' reign. It was no surprise that, in his victory speech after being elected, three years after the referendum on the Maastricht Treaty, Jacques Chirac declared, "Our battle has a name: the struggle against unemployment." The fate of Chirac's presidency depends, to a considerable extent—as did that of Mitterrand's presidency—on the outcome of this battle.

The unemployment problem has specific causes, including the frequent international recessions of recent decades. But it has deeper roots as well, linked to changes in the character and pace of technological change. Few governments of industrialized capitalist countries have devised satisfactory policies to counter the tendency toward high levels of structural unemployment. In this regard, the results of the Maastricht referendum and the elections that brought the conservative coalition back to power in the 1990s reflect popular discontent but do not point the way toward a solution. Perhaps the basic dilemma here is that a medium-rank power such as France is far less able today than in the past to regulate its economy to assure balanced economic growth. Given France's long-standing tradition of state-sponsored growth, the problem is especially acute there.

Maastricht was a referendum on the entire French political establishment. Most leaders of the established center-right parties joined the Socialist government in urging voters to ratify the treaty. Only the

National Front and the PCF were officially opposed. Thus, half the electorate rejected the advice of leaders from the established parties.

The specific question asked in the referendum provides an important reason for the near defeat of the referendum over Maastricht. The PCF charged that Maastricht involved a capitalist conspiracy to construct an economic framework to maximize its interests; the National Front charged that strengthening EU ties would further dilute France's national identity. Although couched in exaggerated (for the PCF) and racist (for the FN) language, these charges were not wholly false. Moreover, ratifying the Maastricht Treaty has not only failed to resolve these challenges but has made them more acute. Thus, fully half the French apparently judged that their interests were poorly served by transferring power from Paris to Brussels. The sad irony is that those who voted no were *already* served badly by existing arrangements. Most opponents came from declining regions and socioeconomic categories: unskilled workers, the poor, small shopkeepers, and small farmers. But if they exaggerated the importance of the EU in producing the past erosion in their situation, they may have been correct in fearing that their already precarious situation might be further weakened by closer international economic integration.

Maastricht represented a massive warning to established political leaders and institutions. Voters signaled that established political parties were incapable of commanding the support of large numbers of French citizens. What has been the response since 1992? Generally, business as usual. Despite the erosion of support for established parties that was demonstrated by the vote over Maastricht and the 1993 and 1995 elections, the traditional political class has maintained its monopoly of power. The major conservative politicians who replaced the Socialists were the same familiar faces whom the Socialists had replaced in the early 1980s! (Recall that President Chirac served as prime minister in the 1970s.)

But playing political musical chairs will not, by itself, bridge the deepening gap between popular discontent and the response offered by established institutions. The problems of the recent past—namely, ailing economic growth, high unemployment, the relation of France to the international order, and questions of national and social identity linked to the above tensions—will continue to generate conflicts in the future. In brief, the major axis that structured the party system in the past—that between left and right—has been partially replaced by a new and less defined axis of conflict—that between relatively privileged groups and excluded groups.

Although the established parties continue to monopolize control of France's highest political offices, this does not mean that the fracture revealed by the referendum has disappeared. For example, in the 1995 presidential elections, those opposed to ratifying the Maastricht were nearly twice as likely to support candidates from peripheral political parties, that is, those other than the "big three" established parties.[33]

New-Style Political Conflict

Since the mid-1980s, the big three parties continue to jockey for advantage, but they are driven less by ideological passion than by the more mundane quest for the spoils of office. Their spirited attempt, especially around election time, to mobilize support by warning voters that the fate of France is at stake is generally unconvincing.

The diminution of ideological passion has been accompanied by a substantial change in French political culture and values. No longer is the state considered the source of all good, while private interests are considered suspect. There has been a shift in the sphere of philosophy and culture toward a recognition of the value of liberalism, pragmatism, and compromise.

Does the new political-cultural climate signify belated political maturity? In part, yes. In French politics, melodrama has often been as evident as drama: Marx was writing about France when he observed, in *The Eighteenth Brumaire,* that history often repeats itself, the first time as tragedy, the second as farce.

However, this view implies both that previous clashes on competing visions of society were foolish and that important political issues and problems no longer exist. Neither is true. French society is presently rife with economic problems, and the political system neither represents the excluded nor seems able to resolve the problems that produced the fracture in the first place. The reason parties do not conflict on economic policy is not that there is an absence of economic problems, but that there is a lack of effective solutions. Thus, for many French, what prevails is more resignation than satisfaction. As one official

study commission observed, "France is doing better than she thinks but worse than she could."[34]

Moreover, conflicts do abound in French politics and society—but they have sources other than class antagonisms or conflicting conceptions of how to organize the economy. Indeed, the emergence of new issues has split existing parties and given rise to new ones.

New Issues and Sources of Partisan Conflict

The change in the social and political climate in France in recent years is suggested by the fact that, in 1993, when the center-right gained control of the government, there was more controversy over its proposal to change the procedures for naturalizing French citizens than over its proposal to privatize a large share of state-controlled enterprises. France has experienced substantial waves of immigration within the past several decades. When, during the boom years of the 1960s and early 1970s, few native-born French would accept unskilled industrial positions at low wages, French businesses made an active effort to lure immigrant workers to France. After the onset of economic stagnation in the 1970s, these workers and their families became a convenient scapegoat, and the government ended most further immigration in the late 1970s. The total number of immigrants currently in France has been estimated at 6–8 percent of the total population.[35]

France has traditionally attracted significant numbers of immigrants. Indeed, in 1930, France had a higher proportion of immigrants than did the United States, a country known as a major destination for emigrants.[36] In the past, tensions often ran high between native-born French and immigrants arriving from Poland, Italy, and Portugal, for example. But two factors in the recent past have intensified conflicts around the issue of immigration. The first involves cultural conflict. Sociologist Rogers Brubacker has emphasized the traditionally close link in France between nationhood, citizenship, and common cultural values.

> In the French tradition, the nation has been conceived in relation to the institutional and territorial frame of the state. . . . Yet while French nationhood is constituted by political unity, it is centrally expressed in the striving for cultural unity. Political inclusion has entailed cultural assimilation, for regional cultural minorities and immigrants alike.[37]

An ethnically diverse Paris neighborhood.
Source: © Harvey Finkle/Impact Visuals.

Whereas in the postwar period, the bulk of immigrants were from Italy, Spain, and Portugal, most immigrants since the 1970s have come from North Africa, especially Algeria. Muslim, Arab, and dark-skinned, they are often resented by native-born French, most of whom are Catholic and white. Moreover, many immigrants have begun to assert the right to preserve their cultural and religious traditions, rejecting the demand to abandon their heritage and assimilate dominant French values.

Second, conflict has been intensified in the current period by economic stagnation and soaring unemployment. Immigrants were grudgingly tolerated when there were not enough native-born French workers to perform necessary jobs like building roads, homes, and automobiles. Recently, however, the shift to a service-based economy, as well as lagging economic growth, has reduced the demand for unskilled and semiskilled jobs, and there is now a surplus, not a shortage, of workers.

This explosive mix has stimulated the growth of new parties and movements. At the start of the 1980s, National Front leader Jean-Marie Le Pen failed to gain the minimum number of signatures from local elected officials on a nominating petition to run for president. By the early 1990s, the National Front was the fourth-largest party in France. Their slogan of "France for the French" does not answer the question: Who (and what) is French? But the NF's simplistic and racist approach has helped reshape the structure of ideological conflict and public opinion. For example, it is tempting to believe the graffiti that the FN sprays in prominent places—"3 million immigrants = 3 million unemployed"—which falsely implies that the way to solve France's unemployment problem is to deport all immigrants (many of whom, it should be noted, are French citizens).

The FN has polarized public opinion around the issue of immigration and moved the center of political gravity toward the right on this issue. In an attempt to undercut the National Front's support, political parties often vie with each other to appear "tough" by prohibiting further immigration and expelling undocumented immigrants. In 1993, the conservative government of Prime Minister Edouard Balladur sponsored a measure restricting the right of immigrants' children born on French soil to obtain French citizenship automatically.

On the opposite side of the new political axis, which can be designated as identity politics, immigration and the struggle against racism have stimulated the formation of progressive social movements in France. The best-known example was S.O.S.-Racisme, created in the early 1980s to protest racist attacks on immigrants. The organization became widely known when it coined the slogan, *"Touche pas à mon pote"* ("Hands off my pal"), which was printed on millions of badges worn by sympathizers of the movement, and sponsored free rock concerts in Paris to dramatize the cause of antiracism. Nonetheless, S.O.S.-Racisme's popularity did not succeed in ending assaults on immigrants, especially Arabs, who have been the primary target of racist wrath. There have been numerous instances of racially motivated crimes in recent years.

The growing importance of a united Europe has further jostled French national identity. Although France has been a vigorous supporter of European integration, there has been growing unease over the precise meaning and consequences of a stronger European Union. As the controversy over the Maastricht Treaty described above suggests, the issue of European integration splits existing parties and produces an unconventional balance of political forces.

Note that the two new issues identified here circumvent the French state in opposite fashion: one from below and one from above. The role of the state is increasingly being questioned as new social movements develop within civil society and at the regional local levels. Yet, at the same time, national sovereignty and autonomy are being eclipsed by the growth of European institutions. Although these tendencies are not peculiar to France, they pose an especially acute problem for a nation where the state has played such a central role. As we have seen, basic patterns of French political culture are being challenged, including the state's leading role in eco-

nomic management, social regulation, and cultural definition.

One political-cultural trait remains constant: The state remains the target of traditional, as well as newly emergent, demands. In terms of traditional protest, influential social groups, including workers, farmers, civil servants, and professionals, have continued to demand—often by mounting disruptive actions—that the state intervene to assure favorable treatment. Regarding new issues, the Green Party has seized the opportunity offered by state inaction to dramatize a popular cause neglected by the established parties. Like the issue of cultural identity and racism, environmental protection does not fit neatly into the traditional left-right ideological categories and is not rooted in social class antagonism. Some version of a Green Party has existed in France since the 1970s. But the recent success of the Greens is due both to the greater salience of the issue, along with its continued studied neglect by other parties, and the strategy developed by Antoine Waechter, who led the party between 1988–1993, to promote a "green" program that was not linked to a leftist ideological position. (However, the Greens' poor showing in elections in the early 1990s led to Waechter's replacement by a more leftist-oriented leader in 1993.)

FRENCH POLITICS IN TRANSITION

French politics has entered a new era. On the one hand, traditional ideological conflicts have waned and established political parties have moved closer together. The center-left Socialist Party has drained much of the support that in the past made the PCF one of France's largest parties. The two major center-right parties uneasily coexist. Furthermore, ideological struggles over how to organize the economy have given way to a kind of centrist, pragmatic managerialism, with widespread acceptance of a mixed economy consisting of state regulation and market competition. Political institutions have surmounted some key challenges and, although the executive remains overbearing and there are inadequate channels for popular participation, somewhat greater balance has developed in the present period between popular participation and representation, on the one hand, and policy formulation and execution, on the other.

Yet, as we have seen, this appearance of stability may be deceptive. Established parties are severely divided and command ever-smaller levels of support. Citizens are voting with their feet—by supporting dissident political parties or not voting at all. The issues around which the major parties have traditionally organized are less salient, and the new issues divide and disarm established parties.

Nor does the end of intense debate over competing economic projects mean that France's economic problems are resolved. In fact, France is especially poorly equipped to compete in the **neoliberal** framework of the European Union. The French have excelled at state-directed promotion of large firms that produce projects for captive markets at home and abroad (the latter negotiated with foreign states), as well as at crash programs of industrial development (such as rail and road transport, aerospace, and telecommunications). In the new situation, victory in the economic race goes not to the large but to the flexible; and state-direction becomes a handicap, not an advantage. Moreover, the cost of industrial innovation in many new spheres now exceeds the capacity of a medium-size power such as France. Thus, fundamental patterns of French political economy are under stress.

French cultural identity is also being challenged by groups within France and by the increasing importance of the European Union. The state and cultural identities are squeezed both from below, as groups in civil society demand more autonomy, and from above, as material and cultural production and consumption are conducted on a European and even global scale. An advisory commission of intellectuals and concerned citizens appointed within the framework of French planning to reflect on "The State and French Society in the Year 2000" observed that France is more poorly equipped than comparable nations to confront the future for two reasons. First, the important place occupied by the French state relative to civil society is under challenge. Second, French national identity has traditionally reflected the comforting notion that France has a particular mission to dramatize the values of liberty, equality, and fraternity stemming from the French Revolution. Yet, as these values become more universally shared, they are regarded as less specifically French. The authors of the report ask,

"Will the road toward democratic maturity, within the context of the globalization of values and a reduced role for national states, be more arduous in France than in other nations?"[38]

FRANCE IN COMPARATIVE PERSPECTIVE

France provides an interesting case for comparative analysis through its many attempts at state- and regime-making. By comparing the Fourth and Fifth Republics, we can study the impact of institutions on political outcomes. The same country was governed in two dramatically different ways within a short time. Unfortunately, the experiment teaches what to avoid rather than what to emulate. The Fourth Republic demonstrates the excesses that can occur with a fragmented multiparty system, undisciplined parties, and a parliamentary regime with a weak executive. The Fifth Republic demonstrates the danger of an isolated and unduly powerful executive. Yet the Fifth Republic has taken halting steps toward developing more balanced institutions, including a larger role for the Constitutional Council, stronger local governments, and independent media. The results suggest that France's semipresidential system may prove attractive to countries seeking lessons in political-institutional design.

On the level of political culture, France has prided itself on its universalist, yet distinctive, role in history, deriving from its revolutionary heritage of liberty, equality, and fraternity. But while they have become increasingly accepted, both within France and on a global scale, these values are less able to promote cohesion among French citizens. There is much to learn from how well France adjusts to the process of abandoning its claims to preeminence among the countries of the world. It will also be interesting to see if France learns how to reconcile a centralized state with democratic values, as well as how it melds presidential and parliamentary forms. (On the latter point, the Fifth Republic's constitution has influenced such diverse countries as Poland, Nigeria, and Brazil.) Similarly, France is not alone in seeking to reconcile the conflicting claims of maintaining national cohesion in the face of extensive internal diversity with increasing integration in the international economic and political system. Thirty years after the youthful French protesters chanted in May 1968, "The struggle continues," the words have lost none of their relevance.

Key Terms

democracy	capital flight
authoritarian regime	cohabitation
semipresidential system, or regime	conservative
	socialism
presidential system	communist
parliamentary system	society
state	social movements
ancien régime	pluralist
revolution	neocorporatist
republic	interest groups
indicative planning	neoliberal
dirigiste	

Suggested Readings

Section 1

Hoffmann, Stanley. *Decline or Renewal? France Since the 1930s.* New York: Viking, 1974.

Hunt, Lynn. *Politics, Culture, and Class in the French Revolution.* Berkeley: University of California Press, 1984.

Paxton, Robert O. *Vichy France: Old Guard and New Order, 1940–1944.* New York: Norton, 1972.

Tilly, Charles. *The Contentious French: Four Centuries of Popular Struggle.* Cambridge, Mass.: Harvard University Press, 1986.

Tocqueville, Alexis de. *The Old Regime and the French Revolution.* New York: Doubleday Anchor, 1955.

Weber, Eugen. *The Hollow Years. France in the 1930s.* New York: Norton, 1994.

Section 2

Adams, William James, and Christian Stoffaës, eds. *French Industrial Policy.* Washington, D.C.: Brookings Institution, 1986.

Hall, Peter. *Governing the Economy: The Politics of State Intervention in Britain and France.* New York: Oxford University Press, 1986.

Hayward, Jack. *The State and the Market Economy: Industrial Patriotism and Economic Intervention in France.* New York: New York University Press, 1986.

Howell, Chris. *Regulating Labor: The State and Industrial Relations Reform in Postwar France.* Princeton, N.J.: Princeton University Press, 1992.

Loriaux, Michael. *France after Hegemony: International Change and Financial Reform.* Ithaca, N.Y.: Cornell University Press, 1991.

Schmidt, Vivien A. *From State to Market? The Transformation of French Business and Government.* Cambridge: Cambridge University Press, 1996.

Section 3

Birnbaum, Pierre. *The Heights of Power: An Essay on the Power Elite in France.* Chicago: University of Chicago Press, 1982.

Levy, Jonas. *Tocqueville's Revenge: Dilemmas of Institutional Reform in Post-Dirigiste France.* Cambridge, Mass.: Harvard University Press, 1996.

Schmidt, Vivien A. *Democratizing France: The Political and Administrative History of Decentralization.* New York: Cambridge University Press, 1990.

Stone, Alec. *The Birth of Judicial Politics in France.* New York: Oxford University Press, 1992.

Suleiman, Ezra. *Elites in French Society: The Politics of Survival.* Princeton, N.J.: Princeton University Press, 1978.

———. *Private Power and Centralization in France: The Notaires and the State.* Princeton, N.J.: Princeton University Press, 1987.

Section 4

Bell, David, and Byron S. Criddle. *The French Socialist Party: The Emergence of a Party of Government.* 2d ed. Oxford: Oxford University Press, 1988.

Boy, Daniel, and Nonna Mayer, eds. *The French Voter Decides.* Ann Arbor: University of Michigan Press, 1994.

Duchen, Claire. *Feminism in France: From May '68 to Mitterrand.* London: Routledge and Kegan Paul, 1986.

Ireland, Patrick. *The Policy Challenge of Ethnic Diversity.* Cambridge, Mass.: Harvard University Press, 1994.

Keeler, John. *The Politics of Neo-corporatism in France: Farmers, the State and Agricultural Policymaking in the Fifth Republic.* New York: Oxford University Press, 1987.

Mendras, Henri, with Alistair Cole. *Social Change in Modern France: Towards a Cultural Anthropology of the Fifth Republic.* Cambridge: Cambridge University Press, 1991.

Wilson, Frank L. *Interest Group Politics in France.* New York: Cambridge University Press, 1987.

Section 5

Daley, Anthony, ed. *The Mitterrand Era: Policy Alternatives and Political Mobilization in France.* London and New York: Macmillan and New York University Press, 1995.

Godt, Paul, ed. *Policy-Making in France: From de Gaulle to Mitterrand.* New York: Columbia University Press, 1989.

Hall, Peter A., Jack Hayward, and Howard Machin, eds. *Developments in French Politics.* New York: St. Martin's Press, 1990.

Hollifield, James F., and George Ross, eds. *Searching for the New France.* New York: Routledge, 1991.

Keeler, John, and Martin A. Schain, eds. *Mitterrand's Legacy, Chirac's Challenge.* New York: St. Martin's Press, 1996.

Singer, Daniel. *Is Socialism Doomed? The Meaning of Mitterrand.* New York: Oxford University Press, 1988.

Endnotes

[1] Laurence Ménière, ed., *Bilan de la France, 1981–1993* (Paris: Hachette, 1993), 12.

[2] Lynn Hunt, *Politics, Culture, and Class in the French Revolution* (Berkeley: University of California Press, 1984), 15.

[3]François Furet, *Interpreting the French Revolution* (Cambridge: Cambridge University Press, 1981), 46.

[4]Mark Lilla, ed., *New French Thought: Political Philosophy* (Princeton, N.J.: Princeton University Press, 1994), 8. Lilla could have added that hostility to liberalism persisted in France until the 1980s.

[5]Stanley Hoffmann, "Paradoxes of the French Political Community," in *In Search of France,* ed. Stanley Hoffmann (New York: Harper Torchbook, 1965), 8.

[6]Richard F. Kuisel, *Capitalism and the State in Modern France* (Cambridge: Cambridge University Press, 1981), 15.

[7]Hoffmann, "Paradoxes," 7.

[8]Kuisel, *Capitalism,* 277.

[9]Kuisel, *Capitalism,* 248.

[10]Henri Mendras with Alistair Cole, *Social Change in Modern France: Towards a Cultural Anthropology of the Fifth Republic* (Cambridge: Cambridge University Press, 1991), 1.

[11]Peter A. Hall, *Governing the Economy: The Politics of State Intervention in Britain and France* (New York: Oxford University Press, 1986), chs. 6–7.

[12]Stephen S. Cohen, "Twenty Years of the Gaullist Economy," in *The Fifth Republic at Twenty,* ed. William G. Andrews and Stanley Hoffmann (Albany: State University of New York Press, 1981), 248–249.

[13]John Zysman, *Governments, Markets, and Growth: Financial Systems and the Politics of Industrial Change* (Ithaca: Cornell University Press, 1993), ch. 3; and Jeffrey A. Hart, *Rival Capitalists: International Competitiveness in the United States, Japan, and Western Europe* (Ithaca: Cornell University Press, 1992), ch. 3.

[14]Jean Fourastié, *Les Trentes glorieuses, ou la révolution invisible de 1945 á 1975* (Paris: Fayard, 1979), *passim.*

[15]William G. Andrews, "Introduction: The Impact of France on the Fifth Republic," in *The Fifth Republic at Twenty,* 3; Richard F. Kuisel, "Postwar Economic Growth in Historical Perspective," in *The Mitterrand Experiment: Continuity and Change in Modern France,* ed. George Ross, Stanley Hoffmann, and Sylvia Malzacher (New York: Oxford University Press, 1987); and Louis Dirn, ed., *La Société française en tendances* (Paris: PUF, 1990), 160.

[16]Gordon Wright, *Rural Revolution in France* (Stanford: Stanford University Press, 1964), *passim.*

[17]Kuisel, *Capitalism,* 264.

[18]*Ibid.*

[19]Andrews, *The Fifth Republic at Twenty,* 4. This section also relies on Cohen, "Twenty Years," 240–250.

[20]Hall, *Governing the Economy,* 163.

[21]Stephen Bornstein, "States and Unions: From Postwar Settlement to Contemporary Stalemate," in *The State in Capitalist Europe, A Casebook,* ed. Stephen Bornstein, David Held, and Joel Krieger (Winchester, Mass.: George Allen & Unwin, 1984), 64.

[22]Mark Kesselman and Guy Groux, eds., *The French Workers' Movement: Economic Crisis and Political Change* (Winchester, Mass.: George Allen & Unwin, 1984), *passim;* and Chris Howell, *Regulating Labor: The State and Industrial Relations Reform in Postwar France* (Princeton: Princeton University Press, 1992), chs. 3–4.

[23]Jean Charlot, *La Politique en France* (Paris: Editions de Fallois, 1994), 27.

[24]John T. S. Keeler and Alec Stone, "Judicial-Political Confrontation in Mitterrand's France: The Emergence of the Constitutional Council as a Major Actor in the Policy-Making Process," in *The Mitterrand Experiment: Continuity and Change in Modern France,* 176. Also see Alec Stone, *The Birth of Judicial Politics in France* (New York: Oxford University Press, 1992).

[25]Charlot, *La Politique en France,* 21.

[26]Françoise Dreyfus and François D'Arcy, *Les Institutions Politiques et Administratives de la France* (Paris: Economica, 1985), 79.

[27]Martin A. Schain, "The French Communist Party: The Seeds of Its Own Decline," in *Comparative Theory and Political Experience: Mario Einaudi and the Liberal Tradition* (Ithaca: Cornell University Press, 1990). See also Georges Lavau, *À quoi sert le parti communiste français?* (Paris: Fayard, 1981).

[28]*Libération,* May 9, 1995.

[29]Olivier Duhamel and Jérôme Jaffré, "Le mal-être de la gauche," in *L'État de l'opinion, 1990,* ed. Duhamel and Jaffré (Paris: Le Seuil, 1990), 9–20.

[30]Charlot, *La Politique en France,* 159.

[31]*Ibid.*

[32]Elisabeth Schweisguth, "L'Affaiblissement du clivage gauche-droite," in *L'Engagement politique, Declin ou mutation?* ed. Pascal Perrineau (Paris: Presses de la Fondation Nationale des Sciences Politiques, 1993), 228.

[33]*Le Monde,* May 10, 1995. Similarly, the unemployed and workers were especially inclined to support "peripheral" parties.

[34]Alain Minc et al., *La France de l'An 2000,* report to the prime minister (Paris: Éditions Odile Jacob, 1994), 9.

[35]Ménière, *Bilan de la France,* 188; and Gérard Mermet, ed., *Francoscopie, 1995* (Paris: Larousse, 1994), 47.

[36]Patrick Weil, *La France et ses étrangers* (Paris: Gallimard, 1991), 28.

[37]Rogers Brubacker, *Citizenship and Nationhood in France and Germany* (Cambridge, Mass.: Harvard University Press, 1992), 1.

[38]Bernard Cazes, Fabrice Hatem, and Paul Thibaud, "L'État et la société française en l'an 2000," in *Esprit,* no. 165 (October 1990): 95.

CHAPTER 4

Germany

Land and Population

Capital	Berlin*	
Total Area (square miles)	137,803 (slightly smaller than Montana)	
Population	80.7 million	
Annual Projected Population Growth Rate (1993–2000)	0.2%	
Urban Population (% of total)	86%	
Ethnic Composition Major Ethnic Groups	German	95%
	Turkish	2%
	Other	3%
Major Language	German	
Major Religions	Protestant	45%
	Catholic	37%
	Muslim	3%
	Unaffiliated or other	15%

Economy

Domestic Currency	Deutschemark	
GNP (US$)	$1.9 trillion	
GNP per capita (US$)	$23,560	
Purchasing Power Parity GDP per capita (US$)	$16,850	
Average Annual GDP Growth Rate (1980–1993)	2.6%	
Structure of Production (% of GDP)	Agriculture	1%
	Industry	38%
	Services	61%
Labor Force Distribution (% of total)	Agriculture	3%
	Industry	39%
	Services	58%
Women as % of Total Labor Force	40%	

Income Distribution (1988)	% of Population	% Share of Income or Consumption
	Richest 20%	40.3%
	Poorest 20%	7.0%

Total Foreign Trade (exports plus imports) as % of GNP	50%	

Society

Life Expectancy	Female	79
	Male	73
Population per Doctor	370	
Infant Mortality (per 1,000 live births)	6	
Adult Literacy	99%	
Mean Years of Schooling (of adults 25+)	Female	11.1
	Male	12.2
Communications (per 100 people)	Radios	90
	Televisions	57
	Telephones	59
1995 Human Development Index (1 = highest)	Ranks 15 out of 174	

Political Organization

Political System Parliamentary democracy

Regime History After Third Reich's defeat, Germany was partitioned and occupied by Allies in 1945. In 1949 the Federal Republic of Germany (FRG) was established in the west and the German Democratic Republic (GDR) was established in the east. The two German states unified in 1990.

Administrative Structure Federal, with 16 states. Germany does not have sharp separation between levels of government.

Executive Ceremonial president is the head of state, elected for a five-year term (with a two-term limit) by the Federal Convention. Chancellor is head of government and is a member of the *Bundestag* and a leader of the majority party or coalition.

Legislature Bicameral. *Bundestag* (663 members at 1994 federal election) elected via dual ballot system combining single-member districts and proportional representation. Upper house *(Bundesrat)* comprises 69 members who are elected and appointed officials from the 16 states.

Judiciary Autonomous and independent. The legal system has three levels: Federal High Court which is the criminal-civil system; Special Constitutional Court dealing with matters affecting Basic Law; and Administrative Court, consisting of Labor, Social Security, and Finance courts.

Party System Multiparty. Major parties are Christian Democratic Union (CDU), Christian Social Union (CSU), and Social Democratic Party (SPD), Free Democratic Party (FDP), and the Greens. Significant minor parties are Party of Democratic Socialism (PDS), and *Republikaner* (Rep).

* The capital of united Germany was moved from Bonn to Berlin in 1990, but Bonn will remain the base for many national administrative agencies until the tradition is complete in the year 2000.

SECTION 1
The Making of the Modern German State

Modern Germany's development has been more turbulent than that of most other European nations. Its current democracy emerged only in 1949 in the wake of World War II. From 1933 until 1945, Adolf Hitler and the Nazi Party sought to expand their **fascist** state into a global empire. Together with their allies Japan and It-

aly, the Nazis waged a world war that cost 60 million lives and radically transformed the international order. The Nazis alone killed six million Jews and millions of others—Slavs, Gypsies, and other non-German minorities, as well as homosexuals and political dissidents—who were deemed racially impure or illegitimate. The major Allied powers (Britain, France, the USSR, and the United States) ultimately defeated Germany and its collaborators and occupied the country from 1945 to 1949. But as the Cold War intensified between the Soviet Union and the three other powers, Germany became the dividing line between the two camps, and two Germanies emerged: the capitalist Federal Republic of Germany, or FRG* (West Germany), and the communist German Democratic Republic, or GDR (East Germany). This situation prevailed until the collapse of the East German government and its integration with West Germany in 1990.

The first modern German state formed late in 1871, when numerous German-speaking principalities were brought together under the principality of Prussia and its leader, Otto von Bismarck. The newly unified Germany proved fragile, and although Bismarck and those who succeeded him were able to attain world power at the expense of other industrialized countries, the authoritarian regime fell apart during World War I. The parliamentary democracy of the Weimar Republic, which came to power in 1918, was also short-lived. By 1933, weakened by economic and political instability, Weimar had collapsed, and the Nazis had seized power. The twelve tortuous years of Hitler's "Thousand Year Reich" brought Holocaust to the Jews, institutionalized terror to all Europeans, and ignominious shame to the German state itself. Though a stable democracy finally took hold in postwar West Germany, East Germany was pulled into the Soviet Union's sphere of influence, and was ruled by a highly repressive communist government until unification in 1990. In less than a century then, Germany has been ruled by a variety of governments: feudal, imperialist, fascist, communist, and parliamentary democratic.

Despite this turbulent history, postwar West Germany produced spectacular economic and political successes. Among its most significant achievements were:

• The **Economic Miracle** *(Wirtschaftswunder)* that produced rapid economic growth in the 1950s and 1960s, paving the way for the FRG to achieve global economic power alongside Japan and the United States by the 1970s. By the 1970s and early 1980s,

some analysts were suggesting that Germany and Japan—with their more cooperative relationships among business, labor, and government—were alternative capitalist models to that of the United States[1];

• Leadership in forging a European Union (EU), which promises to unify the entire continent economically and perhaps eventually politically. With its population of 80 million and its position as the strongest European country, Germany is poised to play a major role in the evolution of Europe's political economy;

• The establishment and solidification of a successful and legitimate multiparty parliamentary democracy. Contemporary Germany has five major political parties that represent a wide range of political opinion and produce electoral turnout rates of between 80 and 85 percent of the adult population; and

• The development of the **Social Market Economy** *(Sozialemarktwirtschaft),* combining generous welfare and labor provisions that have produced the world's highest-paid workforce and have created one of the world's highest standards of living while simultaneously retaining a competitive economy.

GERMANY AT THE CROSSROADS

Two conflicting images depict the rapid pace and complexity of late twentieth-century German politics. One is that of East and West Germans hugging each other and dancing on top of a crumbling Berlin Wall in November 1989 to celebrate their reunion after nearly thirty years of forced separation. The other is that of neo-Nazi skinheads setting fire to a hostel housing newly arrived immigrants while chanting *"Ausländer raus!"* ("Foreigners Out!") as local German residents look on without intervening.

Germany arrived at this crossroads somewhat unexpectedly. Almost no one predicted the collapse of the GDR's communist regime and the tearing down of the Berlin Wall that had divided Germany since 1961. Once the Wall was razed and East Germans could travel freely, the old East German regime could not prevent citizens from emigrating to the West in large numbers. When the trickle of emigrants became a flood in early 1990, the GDR became increasingly shaky as a nation-state. The communist economic system broke down under the East German clamor for higher quality western goods. As a stopgap, the West German government

---

* The FRG is also the name of the newly unified Germany because the former East Germany officially joined the FRG as five separate, new federal states.

Germans sing and dance on top of the Berlin Wall to celebrate the opening of East-West German boundaries in November 1989.
Source: AP/Wide World Photos.

allowed East Germans to exchange their increasingly worthless currency for the stronger West German deutschemark (DM) in the summer of 1990. The emigration west continued however, and the rush of East Germans to West Germany overwhelmed state and local governments. Politicians in both Germanies agreed that rapid reunification was the only solution. By October 1990, less than a year after the Berlin Wall was breached, the GDR was gone, its former territory incorporated as five new federal states *(Bundesländer)* in the expanded Federal Republic of Germany.

Unification has proved far more difficult than many observers had first anticipated. Before unification East Germany was considered the strongest of the Eastern European communist economies, but unification soon revealed that the East German economy was far more backward than most economists reckoned.

The communist planned economy (sometimes called a command economy) was not sensitive to market signals because production of goods was determined more by rigid government dictates than by consumer needs. The East German level of technology was decades behind that of the developed economies of the West. For example, simple telephone communication was usually crude, so the newly unified Germany had to spend billions of DM to rebuild communication networks. Open political discourse and expression had been discouraged, if not prohibited, in East Germany. Although people would meet and speak candidly among family or close friends, a liberal democratic political culture did not exist as it did in West Germany.

Other challenges confront the newly united German state as well. For over thirty years, West Germany has had a reputation for producing high-quality goods while offering high wages and providing generous social welfare benefits. European integration and competition from countries with lower social and economic standards threaten to produce economic strains in united Germany as it tries simultaneously to maintain high living standards and integrate the five new eastern states. The German birth rate, especially in the eastern states, is lower than the current death rate, a trend that threatens to put increased pressure on the welfare and pension system as the population ages. Germany's strong economy has attracted immigrants fleeing other countries, particularly those in former communist Eastern Europe. And the Federal Republic's liberal political asylum laws (in response to widespread human persecution by Nazis) were drastically curtailed in the early 1990s by Helmut Kohl's government. This action was partially in response to the increased physical violence against the influx of immigrants and foreigners by extreme right-wing groups, actions tolerated even by otherwise peaceful German citizens. These ultra-right groups represent a very small minority of the population, since no right-wing group or party has achieved the 5 percent of the vote necessary for representation in the German *Bundestag* (the lower house of the legislature). However, Germany's history of racial intolerance during the first half of the twentieth century makes both Germany and its allies especially sensitive to any such racial intolerance.

In the 1980s many observers thought West Germany's economically successful and politically democratic Federal Republic had subdued Germany's unstable and militarily aggressive past. However, the difficulty of unification and the racist attacks on ethnic minorities in recent years suggest to some that Germany is not the "model" sometimes portrayed.

In short, Germany finds itself at a crossroads. One path might lead to the consolidation of postwar successes and the achievement by former East Germans of the material prosperity and democratic political culture of their western countrymen. This could help Germany to become an anchor in the expanding European Union (EU) as a partner, not a conqueror, of its neighbors. The other path would be perilous—a Germany experiencing rising social conflict, weakened domestic institutions, uncertain international relations, and

difficulties in responding to international economic competition.

Comparative Themes

Why did the emergence of the modern German state differ so greatly from that of its neighbors? In this chapter, we examine the complex tensions that made German political development both more difficult and more precarious than that of most industrialized democracies. We also point out how the demise of the GDR and its assimilation into the FRG in less than a year suggests that the process of state formation should never be seen as a fait accompli. If anything, German unification should serve as a powerful reminder that state formation is an ongoing, dynamic process.

Throughout, we consider Germany's history and prospects in light of four comparative themes. One theme considers how a state and a nation's collective identities influence one another. In Germany, bitter religious, ideological, and regional conflicts were among the causes that delayed its unification and stable development. As a result, German-speaking principalities lagged several centuries behind other western powers in forming a modern state. Even before unification, however, German-speaking areas shared vibrant political and philosophical traditions (dating from the early-nineteenth-century writings of Johann Fichte and Georg Hegel) that favored a strong, centralized public authority. Though each German-speaking principality acted as its own subnational state before 1871, there was often strident competition among the larger principalities for primacy (e.g., Prussia and Bavaria). Even after unification, tension between competing identities and the desire for a strong nation-state persisted as evidenced by the pressure nationalist movements placed on German governments prior to World War I and during the Weimar Republic. Hitler finally succeeded in unifying the German nation and state from 1933 to 1945 through ruthless suppression of Germany's collective identities. Thus, it is this legacy of an aggressive, unified Germany that causes some to view rather warily the newly unified and expanded FRG of the 1990s.

A second theme considers how a state's position in the international system—measured in part by its resource base, its level of political and economic development, and its military power relative to other states—affects its ability to manage domestic and international pressures. By the time Germany embraced industrialization in the late nineteenth century, it felt compelled to catch up with an array of more advanced industrial states such as Britain, France, and the United States that had divided a large share of the world's primary resources and trade among themselves. Germany's intense effort to expand its industrial and military power at the expense of other states had significant, and adverse, consequences for its development.

Our third and fourth themes consider the significance of democracy and political economy for a state's ability to manage its challenges. In Germany, the delayed timing of capitalism and democracy proved crucial for its development. In Britain and the United States, democratic political institutions developed gradually in the late eighteenth century (at least for white male property owners), well before the process of industrialization began. When industrial capitalism emerged in the nineteenth century, it was able to develop in ways that did not threaten established democratic political forms based on individual rights. In Germany, industrial capitalism emerged much later in the nineteenth century, before full parliamentary democracy had been achieved. This enabled the forces pressing for democracy to fuse political and economic issues. The swelling ranks of German workers not only had no democratic economic rights in the workplace, but they also had few democratic political rights as citizens. By the early twentieth century, this merging of economic and political demands produced the strongest socialist political party and labor movement in Europe. Another result of this delayed political development was that the German state faced pressing social divisions and fierce international competition without the aid of established democratic institutions to help promote public debate and compromise. Without strong democratic restraints to hold them in check, authoritarian elites responded by suppressing dissent and leading the German people into two disastrous wars. When stronger democratic institutions, socialist parties, and labor unions emerged after World War II, they helped to mitigate the previously sharp tensions between capitalism and democracy. Finally, delayed industrialization may have proved beneficial once democratic institutions matured enough to hold the state accountable. In order to compete with more advanced industrial powers, the German state, like that of Japan, had to be directly involved in the industrialization process, over time developing close relationships with business and labor interests that would help promote economic growth in the postwar period. In contrast, Britain and the United States industrialized with little government intervention and their economies today rely much more on private market forces. (In Section 2, we consider the implications of Germany's economic strategy for its postwar development.) The remaining portion of this section examines several critical junctures in Germany's political evolution, followed by an analysis of their implications for contemporary German politics.

CRITICAL JUNCTURES

Unification in 1990 represented a great triumph for democratic Germany, but this milestone also forces us to examine *why* Germany was divided in the first place. By examining critical historical junctures from the eighteenth through the twentieth centuries, we can better appreciate Germany's dynamic evolution, including the upheavals that earlier German regimes caused both its neighbors and its own citizens. This discussion reviews the key periods that shaped modern Germany: nineteenth-century unification, empire building, two world wars, the Weimar Republic, the Nazi period, the postwar states of West and East Germany, and reunification.

Nineteenth-Century Unification of the German State

European history recounts many attempts to unify a German nation. The first was known as the Holy Roman Empire, founded by Charlemagne in A.D. 800 (and sometimes referred to as the "First" Reich). But this wide-ranging, loose, and fragmented empire bore little resemblance to a modern nation-state. For over 1,000 years, the area now known as Germany was comprised at times of as many as 300 sovereign entities. It was not until 1871, under the leadership of the Prussian* military leader Otto von Bismarck, that Germany was united as a nation-state. Bismarck called his

---

* Prussia no longer exists as a state or province, but it was an independent principality in what is now northeast and northwest Germany and part of Poland.

realm the Second Reich (1871–1918) because the name suggested a German state that was both powerful and rooted in centuries-old traditions.

Three main points characterize state formation in general, and the formation of the German state in particular.[2] First, state building requires an evolution of collective identity beyond the family, village, and local region to one encompassing a broader collection of peoples. Clear geographic boundaries may help define such an identity, as in the British Isles and in France, a region surrounded by rivers and mountains, both of which developed nation-states centuries ago. Germany, however, occupied central European plains with few natural lines of demarcation.

On the other hand, the development of a national identity can be hindered by religious, linguistic, or ethnic differences. The Protestant Reformation led by the German Martin Luther in 1517 not only split Christianity into two competing sects, it also divided many European societies in ways that profoundly affected the evolution of nation-states. Bitter religious wars broke out among advocates of each side in many parts of Europe. Britain and France settled these contests in favor of Protestantism and Catholicism, respectively, thereby resolving this decisive issue early. In Germany, neither sect prevailed, and the war's extensive casualties only deepened hostilities that lasted for centuries. Because the conflict was regarded as both a military and a spiritual war which needed forceful leadership, the development of **liberal** or democratic impulses in Germany was delayed. Though religious animosity subsided by the twentieth century, today northern Germany remains mostly Protestant, and the south is mostly Catholic.

Ethnic and linguistic divisions (which sometimes involved widely different forms of spoken German) also delayed unification. Nevertheless, the similarities were great enough to produce a common cultural identity before the nation-state emerged. In the absence of clear geographic boundaries or shared religious and political experiences, racial and cultural traits came to define Germans' national identity to a much greater extent than they did in other European states.

The second characterization of state formation is that nation-states can promote economic growth more easily than can fragmented political entities. Whereas Britain and France were already imperial powers, delayed unification and industrialization in Germany prevented it from embarking on the race for empire

and raw materials until the late nineteenth century. By the time Germany joined the global economy, it so lagged behind Britain and France in industrializing and securing access to the natural resources of the developing world, that it was forced to play catch-up.[3] In the nineteenth century, German leaders believed the country needed access to raw materials other than those contained within its own borders. This pursuit of fast economic growth combined with the awakened sense of German nationalism in the late nineteenth century produced an aggressive, acquisitive state in which economic and political needs overlapped.

A third characteristic of state formation is military strength, a basic tool used to shape and consolidate. In Germany, the rise of militarism and a corresponding authoritarian political culture were exaggerated for several reasons.[4] It is a country with many neighbors and few natural geographic barriers. Thus its exposed position in the central plains of Europe encouraged military preparedness in the nineteenth century because any of its neighbors could mount an attack with few constraints. In addition, the lack of a solid democratic or liberal political culture in the various German-speaking lands before unification in 1871 allowed Prussian militarism to exert an even greater influence over political and civic life.

The Emergence of Nationalism (1806–1871)

Nineteenth-century German nationalism had a long history and deeply rooted origins. Even before unification, a common language and culture in German-speaking areas helped to promote its growth. Other countries such as Britain and France had already established centralized states and had thereby become major world powers. Even the Netherlands, despite its size and geographic location, had enjoyed centralized political power for centuries and had grown to be an important nation in world trade from the sixteenth to the early nineteenth centuries. Prussian political elites noted this contrast between Germany and other states, with hopes of achieving similar world influence with a unified Germany. For many Germans in the early nineteenth century, this lack of political unity stood in sharp contrast to the strong influence of German culture in areas such as literature and religion. From the Reformation until the early nineteenth century, German literary and cultural giants such as Johann Wolfgang von Goethe and Friedrich von Schiller flourished. For many Prussians and other Germans, the discontinuity between cultural influence and political disunity would act as a powerful spur to nationalistic impulses during the remainder of the nineteenth century and into the first half of the twentieth century.

Prussia, which had been a major military force in German-speaking lands since the seventeenth century, had become Europe's greatest military power by the time of the Seven Years' War (1756–1763). Yet Prussia, and most of Europe, were overtaken by Napoleon in the early nineteenth century when the French emperor swept eastward into Russia. During this conquest, Napoleon consolidated many of the smaller German-speaking principalities, particularly those in what is now northwest and northeast Germany. With Napoleon's defeat in 1814, the Prussians, under the leadership of Friedrich Wilhelm III, conducted a "War of Liberation" against French forces and further consolidated German-speaking states, now under Prussian control.

The rise of Prussian influence in German-speaking areas continued through the first half of the nineteenth century with the spread of Prussian socioeconomic forces and political culture throughout what is now northern and central Germany. Prussian leaders were flush with military conquest and supremely confident that their authoritative, as well as authoritarian, leadership suited an awakening German-speaking population. Political and economic currents such as free-market capitalism and democracy did not find strong roots in the Prussian-dominant Germanic principalities. Rather, the outstanding features of Prussian rule were (1) a strong state deeply involved in economic affairs (an economic policy known as mercantilism), (2) a reactionary landowning group of feudal lords called *Junkers,* (3) a patriotic military, and (4) a political culture dominated by virtues such as honor, duty, and service to the state.

In 1848 German democrats and liberals ("liberal" in the original European sense of favoring free markets) tried to challenge Prussian dominance by attempting to emulate the democratic revolutionary movements in France and other European countries. The growth of free-market capitalism and the evolution of greater democracy in the United States and Britain served as catalysts in both France and Germany. Because the Prussian state and authoritarian political culture were so strong, however, free-market and revolutionary democratic movements in Germany were violently suppressed. Yet Prussia, and eventually a united Germany, were to experience a different kind of revolution, a "revolution from above"[5] as political sociologist Barrington Moore called it.

After the democratic revolution failed in 1848, Otto von Bismarck continued to forge unity among the remaining German-speaking independent principalities. Realizing that the spread of German nationalism required firm economic foundations, Bismarck saw Prussia's (and a united Germany's) need to industrialize and modernize its economy to compete with countries such as Britain, France, and the United States. After the suppression of the 1848 revolution ruled out a democratic and free-market approach, Bismarck united the unlikely and nondemocratic coalition of feudal *Junkers* in the northeast and the new industrial barons in the growing coal and iron ore industries of the northwestern Ruhr River valley. This alliance among grain-growing landowners and new-money industrialists under the guidance of a strong state was Bismarck's "revolution from above." It was a revolution not from the bottom up but from the top down: it relied on an alliance of elites rather than on a mobilization of democratic and/or working-class support, as had the French and American revolutions.

Bismarck's aggressive nationalism culminated in the unification of Germany into a second "empire," or Reich, in 1871. But the rise of nationalism and the formation of a united Germany from the divided German states were fraught with conflict. Militarism was a key component of Prussian nationalist political culture, and Bismarck used his armies to unite all German-speaking peoples under his influence. This aggressive nationalism produced three bloody conflicts in the 1860s as the Prussian armies defeated Denmark (1864), Austria-Hungary (1866), and France (1870) in short wars that established Germany's modern boundaries.

The Second Reich (1871–1918)

The Second Reich was an authoritarian regime with some of the symbols of a democratic regime, but very little of the substance. The failure of the democratic revolution in 1848 meant that undemocratic forces (industrial and landed elites) in the newly united Germany not only mobilized and controlled both political and economic power, but also constructed political institutions to retain this power. Bismarck's regime was only symbolically democratic in that the "Iron Chancellor" (a title derived from his military successes and his attacks on democratic forces) allowed for universal suffrage but retained real decision-making authority in nonelected bodies that he could control. The political dominance by nondemocratic forces was held by or was exercised through a bicameral legislature consisting of a lower house *(Reichstag)* and an upper house *(Landtag)*. The *Reichstag* was popularly elected, but real power lay in the hands of the *Landtag,* whose members were either directly or indirectly appointed by Bismarck. In other words, the *Reichstag* could pass legislation with little if any hope that it would become law.

For the first twenty years of its regime, the goal of the Second Reich was rapid industrialization supported by state power and a powerful banking system geared to foster large-scale industrial investment rather than by the trial-and-error methods of free markets. The Second Reich was so economically successful that Germany had become a leading industrial power by 1900. At the fore were such industries as coal, steel, railroads, dyes, chemicals, industrial electronics, and machine tools. The state emphasized the development of such heavy industries at the expense of those producing consumer goods. As a result, industrialists reaped large profits while the majority of Germans did not directly benefit from their country's economic growth. Lacking a strong domestic consumer goods economy, Germany had to sell a substantial portion of what it produced on world markets.

The rapid transformation of what had been a largely feudal society until the 1850s to an industrial one by the turn of the twentieth century created widespread social dislocation and growing opposition to the regime. A middle class of professionals and small business owners with rising expectations pressured the government to democratize and provide basic liberal (i.e., free-market) rights. Industrialization also promoted the growth of a blue-collar, manually skilled working class and the corresponding rise of a militant Social Democratic Party (SPD, or *Sozialedemokratische Partei Deutschlands*). The Social Democrats' primary goals were economic rights in the workplace and democratization of the political system. Greatly influenced by the writings and the active participation of the founders of socialism,* Karl Marx and Friedrich Engels, both of whom were Germans, the SPD grew as fast as the pace of German industrialization.

During much of his rule from 1871–1890, Bismarck alternately persecuted and grudgingly tolerated the democratic and socialist opposition. He banned the Social Democratic Party yet created the first welfare state as a way to blunt the effects of rapid economic growth. Social welfare benefits included health insurance and the first forms of state-sponsored old-age pensions. This combination of welfare with political repression (sometimes referred to as Bismarck's iron fist in a velvet glove) suggested that Bismarck was an astute politician who knew precisely how far to push the opposition and when to give ground in order to maintain long-term political control.

Bismarck was also skillful in balancing the very different interests of the grain-growing feudal *Junkers* in East Prussia and the expanding industrialists in the north and west of Germany. Sometimes referred to as the "marriage of iron and rye,"[6] these disparate social forces were united by mutual economic and political needs. The *Junkers* needed a way to get their crops to market and the industrialists needed a commodity (i.e., rye wheat) to ship on their expanding railroad system. The two groups also needed to stay united to stave off the clamoring democratic and socialist forces opposing them.

Bismarck applied his leadership skills to balance the divisive energy of nationalism against the need to maintain a coherent state policy. Invocation of nationalism enabled him to unite the diverse German-speaking peoples despite resentment by Bavarians and Rhinelanders (among others) toward the Prussian-dominated regime. In time, however, nationalism proved difficult to contain. The spirit unleashed by a newly unified and rapidly industrializing Germany produced a Pan-Germanic feeling of nationalism among German-speaking Europeans in Eastern Europe. This often took the form of militant anti-Semitism because some Germans perceived that Jews had enjoyed a disproportionate share of wealth and influence in Central Europe. In general, the Pan-Germanic movement espoused themes that the Nazis would later use to justify their claims of racial and cultural superiority.

Bismarck also significantly influenced German political culture by creating a strong and centralized German state. The ***Kulturkampf*** (cultural struggle) he

---

* Socialism advocates greater equality in economic and political conditions. Its philosophy argues that workers, who produce the goods and services in society, should receive a greater share of economic and political power.

initiated was a prime example of Prussian and Protestant dominance. Essentially a movement against the Catholic church, it sought to remove educational and cultural institutions from the church and confer them on the state. This action, which polarized the church and many Catholic Germans, left a powerful political legacy.

With the growth of the German economy in the latter part of the nineteenth century, German business and political leaders faced an immediate problem: How to obtain the necessary raw materials and access to world markets for their finished goods in order to sustain rapid economic growth? Although Germany possessed considerable iron and coal deposits, it had few other natural resources. Germany had neither the colonial possessions of Britain or France, nor the geographic advantages of the United States (a largely self-sufficient domestic market with plentiful natural resources). With little influence in either North America or Asia, Germany participated in what historian Geoffrey Barraclough has called "the scramble for Africa."[7] However, Germany was a latecomer on this continent and was able to colonize only in Southwest Africa and Togoland, whereas the British, French, and Belgians obtained colonies in African regions with more easily exploitable resources. From 1871 until World War I, Germany's foreign policy was primarily concerned with extending its colonial and economic influence, only to be repeatedly checked by other colonial powers. This inflamed German nationalists and pushed German leaders to invest in the rapid development of the shipbuilding industry to equip a commercial shipping fleet and a powerful navy that could secure German economic and geopolitical interests.

An undemocratic domestic political system, the lack of profitable colonies, an exposed geopolitical position on the central European plains with nine bordering nations, and increasingly inflamed nationalism heightened Germany's aggression toward other nations and ultimately prompted it to help launch World War I.

Originally envisioned by German leaders as a brief war to solidify the country's geopolitical position and maintain socioeconomic power for dominant elites, it accomplished neither. Before the war, Germany had felt threatened by an inability to expand its economic and military resources and had allied itself with the Austro-Hungarian Empire. When the Aus-

trian Archduke was assassinated by a Serbian nationalist, the Austro-Hungarian Empire attacked Serbia (which was allied with Britain and France) and the war was on. It turned into a protracted conflict which cost Germany both its colonial possessions and its imperial social order. The combination of weak leadership (Bismarck's successors were poor imitations of the original), lack of resources, and overconfidence in Germany's military prowess led to Germany's defeat, not only causing the collapse of the Second Reich, but also leaving a weak foundation for the country's first attempt to establish a parliamentary democracy.

The Weimar Republic (1918–1933)

The impact of Germany's military defeat in World War I on state formation and democracy was profound. When the ceremonial head of state, Kaiser (King) Wilhelm II, abdicated the throne following the resignation of the last wartime government, Germany was without either a head of government (**chancellor)** or head of state (Kaiser). This political vacuum was filled by the large but politically inexperienced Social Democratic Party (SPD), the only leading party of the Second Reich not discredited by Germany's defeat. In 1918, this new leadership proclaimed Germany's first democratic government, one later called "accidental" by some due to the SPD's unexpected assumption of power. It was born in defeat and lacked legitimacy in the eyes of many Germans, in other words it was a "republic without republicans."

The Weimar Republic, named after the town of Weimar where the constitution was drafted, was a procedural democracy in the sense that it held regular elections and comprised multiple parties. The German Reichstag appeared to function like many other democratic parliaments at the time, such as those in Britain and France. It contained a broad spectrum of political parties from the far left to the far right. Yet its fatal flaw was that the many right-wing political parties and social forces—as well as the Communists on the left—refused to accept the legitimacy of democratic government and actively tried to destabilize and undercut its legitimacy.

From the beginning, the SPD leadership was on shaky ground. The military establishment and the industrialists who had so strongly encouraged Germany's aggressive nationalism were never held accountable for their actions. Not only did they suffer no criminal or political sanctions for leading Germany

Weimar National Assembly: 1932 Nazi-led vote banned the Communist Party (KPD). Within two years all democratic parties were banned.
Source: © Ullstein Bilderdienst.

into a destructive war, but the Republic's first government turned to the military to help it restore order during late 1918 when the newly formed Communist Party (KPD) and various leftist groups challenged its authority. By asking the undemocratic army to defend democracy, the SPD undercut its ability and authority to make major changes in German society.

The outcome of the war further intensified the nationalist impulses of many conservative and reactionary Germans. Many in the military believed that cowardly democratic politicians had betrayed Germany at the signing of the Treaty of Versailles following the German surrender to the Allies on November 11, 1918. The treaty demanded the demilitarization of the Rhineland, a region bordering on France, and huge financial reparations from Germany to the victorious Allies to pay for the costs of the war. German nationalists branded the Weimar leaders as "Jews, democrats,

and Socialists" who had sold out Germany's honor. By controlling various right-wing newspapers and magazines, the nondemocratic right kept up a steady drumbeat of poisonous rhetoric that eventually crippled the regime.

A severe economic crisis in 1923 (largely brought on by Germany's attempt to deal with the reparations payments to the Allies after World War I) further strengthened the nationalists' cause. Because the German economy had been weakened by mobilization for World War I, the burden of the reparations payments made a bad economic situation even worse. The government's solution was to keep printing more money, rationalizing that a cheaper *Reichsmark* (the name of the currency then) would reduce the real costs of the reparations. This caused inflation to reach astronomical proportions (e.g., $1.00 = approximately 12,000,000 *Reichsmarks*) by 1923. Individual Germans were intensely affected in many ways. At the height of the inflationary wave, people had to receive their paychecks twice a *day,* once in the morning and once in the evening after work. The cost of basic foodstuffs rose hourly, so that people who waited to buy goods after work (instead of shopping on their lunch break), would find these late-day goods much more expensive. Simple bank deposits also reached ludicrous proportions, with some individuals carrying wheelbarrows of near-worthless *Reichsmarks* to the bank. To the nondemocratic right wing, this was a concrete example of a democratic government unable to supervise a stable economy.

In the early 1920s, Adolf Hitler, a little-known, Austrian-born, former corporal in the World War I German army, founded the Nazi Party (Nazi is a German acronym for National Socialist German Workers' Party). Although this sounds like a left-wing party name, the word *national* is key for understanding the party's right-wing character. Hitler used nationalism as a weapon to attack both leftist parties, the Social Democrats and the Communists (SPD and KPD, respectively), thereby undercutting the movements' German roots. Taking advantage of a deepening economic crisis and a weakened democratic opposition, the Nazis mobilized large segments of the population by preaching hatred of the left, of "internationalism" (the key philosophical underpinning shared by both the SPD and KPD), and of "inferior, non-Aryan" races. Hitler unleashed powerful racist social forces antagonistic to democracy, which ultimately undermined it and caused its destruction.

After the Great Depression began in 1929, Germany became even more unstable with none of the major parties of Weimar (Communists, Social Democrats, Catholic Center, Democrats, Liberals, Bavarian People's Party, Nationalists, Conservatives, or Nazis) able to win a majority or even form durable government coalitions. All had fundamentally different views on how Germany should be governed, and many were not even committed to the idea of democracy. In the wake of this political instability, the early 1930s witnessed numerous inconclusive elections. The last several months of the Weimar Republic (1932–1933) witnessed no fewer than six elections, all resulting in minority governments. At no time did the Nazis ever receive a majority. The most support they received in free and fair elections was 229 seats out of 609 in the fall 1932 vote. This was the last election

without violent intimidation by Nazis toward other political parties.

Nevertheless, the Nazis relentlessly pressed for political power from a population that continued to underestimate Hitler's real intentions and viewed his hate-filled speeches as merely political rhetoric. The Nazis were rewarded when in early 1933 Hitler outmaneuvered Weimar's aging (84) and ill President Hindenburg, a World War I general, to award the Nazis cabinet positions in the last Weimar government. Hitler immediately demanded, and received, from President Hindenburg the chancellorship on January 30, 1933. Under the Weimar Constitution, as in many parliamentary systems, the head of state (president or constitutional monarch) must choose the next head of government (chancellor or prime minister) if no one party or coalition has received a majority of the seats. Once in power, the Nazis arranged for a fire at the *Reichstag* that they tried to blame on the Communists. Hitler then forced President Hindenburg to grant, by emergency decree, sweeping powers to the Nazi-dominated cabinet, thereby rendering the *Reichstag* irrelevant as a representative political body.

Thus the parliamentary democracy of the Weimar Republic was short-lived. From its shaky beginnings in 1918, the very stability of the state was mortgaged to forces bent on its destruction. Ironically, the constitutional structure of the Weimar regime was relatively well designed. The two significant exceptions were the emergency provisions allowing for greater executive power in crises and the lack of a mechanism to form and maintain stable governing coalitions among the various political parties. A more fundamental problem with Weimar, however, was that not enough political parties and social forces were committed to democracy. The Republic's critics included the military, many unemployed former soldiers, the Prussian aristocracy, elements of both the Catholic and Protestant churches, and large segments of big business. In addition, the Communist Party of Germany (KPD) criticized the Weimar Republic from the left. Unlike stable multiparty political systems in many other countries, the Weimar Republic was plagued by a sharp and increasing polarization of political parties. Even parties expected to have at least some ideological affinities (the Communists and Social Democrats, for example) were mortal enemies during Weimar. The Weimar Constitution was an elegant document, but without

Hitler strides triumphantly through a phalanx of Nazi storm troopers (SA) in 1934.
Source: © Ullstein Bilderdienst.

broad-based popular support, the regime itself was continually under attack from within.

The Third Reich (1933–1945)

After the Nazis had obtained the chancellorship, establishing social control was their next major priority, and the initial step was the systematic banning of political parties. The first party to be outlawed was the Communist Party, next the Social Democrats and their trade union allies, and after that almost all remaining democratic political parties. Even civic institutions such as clubs, neighborhood organizations, and churches were subject to Nazi control, influence, or restrictions on independent action.

Ultimately, the Nazis employed propaganda, demagoguery, and the absence of a democratic opposition to mobilize large segments of the German popula-

tion. Using mesmerizing speeches and a relentless propaganda ministry led by his aide Josef Goebbels, Hitler exercised total control of political power and the media to reshape German politics to his party's vision. This vision allowed no opposition, not even within the party. For example, after establishing power, the Nazis turned on their own foot soldiers, the brown-shirted storm troopers (*Sturmabteilung,* or SA). The SA was a large, but rag-tag group of street fighters whom the party used in the 1920s and early 1930s to seize and burn opposition newspapers, as well as to loot and destroy businesses owned by Jews, foreigners, and other opponents of the Nazis. However, once the Nazis had established control and political opposition had been neutralized, the storm troopers became a major liability. The SA and its leader, Ernst Röhm, believed that such valiant service should propel the SA to a level equivalent or superior to that of the army. But to the ears of the Nazi leadership, including the generals who had embraced Hitler, this was mutiny. The Nazis dispensed with the SA in 1934 with the grisly murder of Röhm and the entire SA leadership in a predawn raid by Hitler's elite guard (*Schutzstaffeln,* or SS) on a storm trooper barracks in Berlin, an event now known as the "Night of the Long Knives."

Domestic policy during the first few years of Nazi rule was concentrated in two major areas: (1) the consolidation and institutionalization of centralized political power; and (2) the rebuilding of an economy devastated by the monetary chaos of the 1920s and the depression of the early 1930s. The Nazis chose to centralize all political authority in Berlin by subjecting regional and local authorities to tight, autocratic control. This departed from past German practice of allowing moderate political autonomy to regional and local governments, a tradition based partly on the independence that German regions had enjoyed prior to unification. The main purpose of this top-down system was to ensure that Nazi policy regarding the repression of political opposition, Jews, and other racial minorities was carried out to the most minute detail. Such political centralization also enabled Goebbels's propaganda ministry to spread relentlessly the Nazi "virtues" of submission to authority, racial superiority, intolerance, and militarism.

The Nazis' economic program was also autocratic in design and implementation. Because free-trade unions had been banned, both private and state-run industries forced workers, including slave laborers during World War II, to work long hours for little or no pay. The program emphasized heavier industries (coal, steel, chemicals, machine tools, and industrial electronics) that required massive investment from the large manufacturing cartels, from the banking system, and from the state itself. Although some segments of big business had initially feared Hitler before he took power, once free-trade unions were suppressed, most of German industry endorsed Nazi economic policies. The Nazis also emphasized massive public works projects, such as building the *Autobahn* highway system, upgrading the railroad system, and constructing grandiose public buildings to reflect Nazi greatness. These projects did employ large numbers of workers, but only under very repressive conditions. The emphasis on heavy industry and transportation clearly favored military production and expansion. Almost all of the industries that the Nazis favored had direct military application, and the *Autobahn* was built more for easing military transport than for encouraging pleasure driving.

During the Third Reich (1933–1945), Hitler fanned the flames of German nationalism by glorifying the warrior tradition in German folklore and exulting in imperial Germany's conquering of rival armies in the mid-nineteenth century. In calling for a return to the mythically glorious and racially pure German past, he made scapegoats out of homosexuals, and ethnic minorities such as Poles, Danes, Alsatians, and especially Jews. In fact, the Nazis' strident anti-Semitism helped bolster their party's growth in other European countries during the 1920s and 1930s. Anti-Semitism proved a powerful political force that allowed nationalist leaders such as Hitler and Italy's Benito Mussolini to blame any political problems on an "external," international minority and to target them as an enemy of nationalism to be relentlessly persecuted and suppressed.

On international issues, the Nazis refused to abide by the provisions of the Treaty of Versailles that the Weimar government had signed in 1918. One provision called for severe restrictions on German military activity. After 1933, however, Nazi Germany began producing armaments in large quantities, remilitarized the Rhineland (the area of Germany closest to France), and sent aid to Francisco Franco's fascist army as it fought to overthrow the democratically elected Spanish republic from 1936–1939. The Nazis also rejected the territorial divisions of World War I, as Hitler claimed that a growing Germany needed increased "space to live" (*Lebensraum*) in Eastern Europe. He ordered the forced union (*Anschluss*) with Austria in March 1938 and the occupation of the German-speaking Sudetenland section of Czechoslovakia in September 1938. The Third Reich's attack on Poland on September 1, 1939, finally precipitated World War II.

Hitler's grandiose visions of German world domination were dramatically heightened by the conquests of first Poland and then the rest of Europe. By the summer of 1941, he began to turn his attention to the only other continental power that stood in the way of his goal of total European domination: the Soviet Union. Hitler assumed that the defeat of the USSR would happen as easily as his other conquests. Therefore, he embarked on a direct attack on the Soviet

Union in the summer of 1941, thereby violating the Nazi/Soviet Nonaggression Pact. The attack not only ended German military successes, it also began the defeat of the Third Reich, a process which would grind on for almost four more years. Yet even as defeat loomed for Germany in May 1945, Hitler preferred to see it totally destroyed rather than to have its national honor besmirched by total surrender.

Clearly the most heinous aspect of the Nazi movement was the systematic execution of 6 million Jews and millions of other civilians in the concentration camps throughout Germany and occupied Central and Eastern Europe. Hitler explicitly stated in his book *Mein Kampf (My Struggle)* that the Germans were the master race and all non-Aryan races, especially the Jews, were inferior. As they had with much of his rhetoric during his rise to power, many Germans chose to ignore the implications of this hatred or thought it was simple political exaggeration. However, the magnitude of the Nazi plans for other races became apparent after Hitler came to power, and they were continued until Germany's defeat in 1945.

The Nazis began their suppression by imposing severe restrictions on freedom for Jews and other persecuted peoples. Then property was confiscated and destroyed, culminating in the 1938 *Kristallnacht* (night of broken glass) when Jewish stores, synagogues, and homes were systematically ransacked. Last, concentration and extermination camps were systematically constructed and filled with Jews and other minorities. The Nazis placed most of the extermination camps in occupied countries like Poland; the most infamous one in Germany was Dachau, just outside of Munich.

The Nazi period had a profound impact on German state formation during the post–World War II years. It served as an antimodel of what any postwar democratic political system should avoid at all costs. Unfortunately, the Nazi legacy has also served as a model for the various neo-Nazi groups that have sprung up in FRG, both in the mid-1960s and especially in the postunification years of the 1990s. Although today constitutional prohibitions denounce and penalize neo-Nazi activities, numerous outlaw groups, and their quasi-legal sympathizers, still admire the horrors of the Third Reich. The number of active members in these groups is small, perhaps a few thousand at most, but some studies of public opinion show support for the goals, if not the tactics of such groups

at near 10 percent of the population. We examine these forces more closely in Section 4.

Occupation and a Divided Germany (1945–1949)

Germany's legacy of conquest and domination led the victorious Allied powers to treat it differently from the other Axis powers, Japan and Italy. Unlike the latter two countries, Germany was occupied by the four victorious Allied powers from 1945 to 1949. A Cold War intensified in the late-1940s as tensions grew between the USSR and the other three Allied powers. In the process, Germany became the dividing line between the two camps. Just how long the country would stay occupied, and how long it would remain divided were unknowns during 1946 and 1947. With the arrival of the Cold War, however, many of the immediate postwar expectations for Germany's future changed. The transformation of the Soviet zone of occupation into the GDR and its inclusion into the Soviet-led Warsaw Pact, as well as the birth of the FRG and its inclusion in NATO, preempted indefinitely any discussion of reunification.

Several important constraints imposed by both German and Allied officials in the postwar occupation years were continued with the FRG. The first reduced the powers of the central state in domestic politics, which were partially assumed by strong regional governments. The second limited the FRG's role as an international political power. Because Germany had waged aggressive war, the Allied occupation authorities prevented the German military from holding legal independent status until the mid-1950s, after which time it was closely monitored and controlled by the Western Allies and eventually by NATO. A third reformed the party system, helping to create parties with more broad-based interests and ideological considerations. Perhaps the most significant political development was the merger in 1946 of Catholic and Protestant interests into the Christian Democratic Party unlike Weimar, when the Catholics had their own, often uncooperative party.

Nation-statehood was restored to the two Germanies in 1949. But the ensuing lack of German sovereignty has left an enduring legacy. Specifically, during the period from 1949–1990, neither Germany possessed the political responsibilities that sovereign nation-states assumed for themselves. The Federal Re-

---

Critical Junctures in Germany's Development

1871–1918	Unification, Second Reich
1919–1933	Weimar Republic
1933–1945	Third Reich
1945–1949	Occupation
1949–1990	Division into German Democratic Republic (GDR) and Federal Republic of Germany (FRG)
1990–Present	Unification; GDR incorporated into FRG

---

public deferred to the United States in matters of international relations as did the GDR to the Soviet Union. Both the United States and the USSR felt it was necessary to constrain independent and international German political activity. This constraint on the Federal Republic created an economic giant/political dwarf syndrome that only began to change in the 1990s.

The Two Post–World War II German States (1949–1990)

With the founding of the Federal Republic in 1949, a more stable, democratic form of government emerged in West Germany. The Federal Republic has generally practiced a procedural democracy, characterized by constitutional provisions for free elections, civil liberties, and individual rights, and an independent judiciary. Its main political institutions are

• A bicameral parliamentary system with a lower house *(Bundestag)* and an upper house *(Bundesrat).* The lower house is directly elected; the upper house comprises delegates selected by the sixteen federal states *(Länder);*

• A chancellor (head of government) and a president (head of state). The chancellor is similar in power to the British prime minister and attains office by virtue of being the leader of the majority party or coalition, whereas the largely ceremonial president is similar to constitutional monarchs such as Queen Elizabeth;

• A multiparty system consisting of five major parties that cover a wide political spectrum and provide representation for diverse, democratic political opinions;

• An independent judiciary that respects the rule of law; and

• A comprehensive state that provides generous benefits to German citizens and works closely with private sector interests to maintain economic strength.

The Federal Republic's democratic system developed in three general phases. The first phase took place under the leadership of chancellors Konrad Adenauer (1949–1963) and Ludwig Erhard (1963–1966), leaders of the newly formed Christian Democratic Union (CDU). A former mayor of Cologne in the Weimar years, Adenauer was known as *Der Alte,* "the old man." His paternalism struck a responsive chord among a majority of voters at a time when the FRG was rebuilding from the devastation of the war. His successor in the CDU, Ludwig Erhard, had been

Chancellor Konrad Adenauer (right) greets his successor, Ludwig Erhard, in 1963.
Source: UPI/Bettmann

economics minister under Adenauer and was widely credited with formulating the policies that produced the economic miracle of the 1950s and early 1960s. As chancellor from 1963 to 1966, Erhard was much less effective than Adenauer, however. He not only failed to respond to a slight recession in 1965, but he also lacked Adenauer's decisiveness. His political weaknesses, and those of his successors, led to the electoral victory of the CDU's opposition in 1969. This first phase witnessed the establishment of a new parliamentary regime, an extensive system of social welfare benefits, a politically regulated market economy, and the reestablishment of strong state governments *(Länder),* which assumed responsibilities formerly handled by the central government.

The second phase was ushered in by the 1969 election, in which the Social Democratic Party (SPD) became the dominant coalition partner, a position it retained until 1982. The SPD's thirteen-year tenure was largely due to the strong leadership of chancellors Willy Brandt (1969–1974) and Helmut Schmidt (1974–1982). As leaders of the SPD, both were adept at brokering conflicts between the left-wing of the party and the centrist Free Democratic Party (FDP) coalition partner. Formerly West Berlin's mayor during the 1960s, Brandt emphasized *Ostpolitik* **(eastern policy),** which entailed encouraging relations with the GDR and the rest of the Soviet bloc, a policy continued by his successors. This period saw a consolidation of full employment and a large increase in social services, which were followed by moderate cutbacks in social services and increased unemployment in the late 1970s and early 1980s. Unlike many Western capitalist countries in the 1980s, the FRG's postwar welfare state retained many of its services and most of its public support.

During the third phase, the Federal Republic emerged from a period of "Eurosclerosis" to its position as the leading nation in the process of European integration and its unification with the former East Germany. Since the 1982 election, the FRG has once again been led by the Christian Democrats, this time in the person of Chancellor Helmut Kohl, who has consistently been underestimated by his critics. It has been the Kohl center-right coalition that has enthusiastically embraced the concept of the single European market and pragmatically moved to consolidate the former GDR into the FRG. The opposition (both the SPD and the Greens) has been much slower to em-

brace either of these developments, to their political detriment.

The strongest adherents of the viability of the Federal Republic's democratic traditions since 1949 praise Germany's commitment to parliamentary democracy and political stability. Forces on the democratic left (the SPD and Greens, as well as the trade unions) have also strongly emphasized democratizing material resources, specifically via legally-mandated in-plant works councils and firm-wide co-determination (i.e., trade union participation on company boards). For most of the post–World War II period, this "rank-and-file" democratic participation, often called democratic corporatism,[8] helped alleviate much of the social tension that had plagued Germany before 1945. To be sure, the treatment of immigrant workers within German industry has not been without antagonism. Certain illiberal elements of German political culture have stigmatized and attacked racial and ethnic minorities, often accompanied by less than thorough prosecution of these crimes by the state. Some observers of German democracy have also been troubled by the Federal Republic's banning of both communist and neo-Nazi parties during the 1950s and 1960s, and by its purges of the civil service in the early 1970s, presumably to root out radicals who were alleged to have obtained positions in the bureaucracy. The stresses placed on democratic institutions (both procedural and substantive) in the wake of German unification and European integration have renewed such concerns and caused many observers to reexamine German democracy in a more critical light in the 1990s.

The lack of democracy in the German Democratic Republic of East Germany (a "people's democracy" in communist parlance) did not change throughout the GDR's history from 1949–1990. During the 1950s, many East Germans who wished to flee communism would travel to Berlin, which was under the control of the four World War II Allied powers (Britain, France, the United States, and the USSR). Once in the free western sectors of Berlin, they could then travel to the FRG and receive immediate citizenship. Hundreds of thousands of East Germans used this route to migrate west, causing a labor shortage and a brain drain from the GDR. Finally, in August 1961, the GDR erected the Berlin Wall, making escape to the West impossible. The GDR called this an "antifascist" barrier, but all Germans—both in the east and west—realized that it cemented what many feared was the permanent division of Germany.

Chancellor Willy Brandt (left) meets his East German counterpart, Willi Stoph in 1970 at the outset of Brandt's *Ostpolitik* (eastern policy), which initiated the first official dialogue between the two German states.
Source: © Ullstein Bilderdienst/Bundesbildstelle.

The GDR was a one-party state under the control of the communist political party known as the Socialist Unity Party (SED or *Sozialistiche Einheits Partei*). Although the state provided full employment, housing, and various social benefits to its citizens, it was a rigid, bureaucratic, Stalinist regime which tightly controlled economic and political life under the leadership of party chairmen Walter Ulbricht, then Willi Stoph, and finally Eric Honnecker. The GDR assumed a universal consensus about the correctness of communism and suppressed all public democratic dissent as deviationist and undermining the true path of socialism. In fact, East Germans caught trying to flee to the West were subject to execution on the spot. Those escapees who were shot are honored by numerous memorials along the site of the former Berlin Wall. Many observers have argued that the anti-foreigner attacks of the mid-1990s, which have been strongest in the former East Germany, can be partially attributed to the lack of a genuine democratic tradition of dialogue, tolerance, and public discourse.

For more than forty years, Germany's role in the international family of nations was limited. Not only did Allied and NATO restrictions prevent German political unilateral action, the German **Basic Law** (the term to designate the FRG constitution) prevented German troops from being used outside of NATO (i.e., largely Western European) areas. Furthermore, the country was likely to remain divided for the foreseeable future, which meant that the political role of the two German states was intentionally circumscribed by each of their alliance partners. Not only was the GDR restrained by the Soviet Union, so too was the Federal Republic limited, in turn, by the Western Allies, NATO, and the presence of a seemingly permanent garrison of foreign military forces. Even as the West German economy grew stronger during the *Wirtschaftswunder* (Economic Miracle) years of the 1950s, becoming the leading Western European economy by the 1960s, its political role remained much more limited. The GDR also had a similar pattern. It apparently became the strongest of the Warsaw Bloc's economies, although the massive rebuilding required in eastern Germany since unification has challenged the depth of the former GDR's economic "strength."

Germany's unification in 1990 took place rapidly, surprising West and East Germans alike. When the Berlin Wall was opened in November 1989, the two German states envisioned a slow process of increased contacts and cooperation while maintaining separate sovereign states for the short term. But when the initial slow flow of East Germans moving West turned into a deluge, the Kohl government was forced to take action to stem the influx of eastern Germans. One step was to provide a currency exchange whereby former East German currency could be exchanged for valuable West German deutschemarks, but this move only fueled the migration westward in the summer of 1990 as GDR citizens sought to consume the more valuable West German goods. After hurried negotiations in the late summer, the former GDR was incorporated into the Federal Republic of Germany as five new FRG states *(Länder)*.

Thus, through unification in 1990, the role of the German state in the international arena remained muted. The supposedly settled international political landscape that the Cold War afforded, in which a divided Germany was taken for granted, vanished with the destruction of the Berlin Wall and the break-up of the USSR. For better or for worse, Germany as a single, powerful nation-state had made a rapid reappearance onto the international stage. We will consider the implication of this major change throughout the remaining discussion.

Before continuing, we need to address the concept of the so-called German Model, a term often used in political science literature to describe the Federal Republic of Germany's distinctive political/

The Unshakable Helmut Kohl

During the early years of the Helmut Kohl chancellorship, the CDU leader was roundly criticized as colorless, provincial, and lacking in strategic vision. Following the urbane and worldly Helmut Schmidt was a difficult task for the career politician from the city of Ludwigshafen in the state of Rhineland-Palatinate. Unlike Schmidt, Kohl does not speak English in public and often seems ill at ease at ceremonial functions. He is a physically robust man, who is said to typify to non-Germans the avuncular and *gemütlich* (jovial) characteristics that seem more appropriate for German travel posters than for a federal chancellor.

Kohl's most important task has been holding the governing coalition together. The FDP's critical swing position in the Federal Republic's political system as the CDU/CSU's small coalition partner has often produced independent and high-profile politicians such as Otto Graf Lambsdorff and Hans-Dietrich Genscher. Managing that relationship has been Kohl's most immediate responsibility. Not far behind in his list of tasks as chancellor has been the management of the relationship with the CDU's sister party, the Bavarian-based CSU. For many years, until his death in 1988, the CSU was led by the larger-than-life figure, and Kohl's rival for the CDU/CSU chancellorship candidacy in the elections of 1976 and 1980, of Franz-Josef Strauss. Kohl handled this relationship carefully and purposefully, realizing that any disturbance could produce disaster for his leadership.

When Strauss was alive, coalition meetings among Strauss, Kohl, and former FDP-leader Martin Bangemann—large men, all of them—were often characterized in the German press as the "Elephants' Waltz." However, Kohl saw that the culmination of such meetings always concluded with none of the elephants trampling any innocent bystanders, or each other!

In recent years, however, Chancellor Helmut Kohl's center-right CDU/FDP government clearly has misjudged both the economic as well as the political costs of German unification. By mid-1992 Kohl finally acknowledged what had been apparent to others for several years: namely, that the successful integration of the eastern economy into the western one would cost much more than originally predicted and require a longer period of time. The amount budgeted in the 1993 *Bundestag* budget for reconstruction in Germany was DM 92 billion ($60.5 billion), approximately 20 percent of the entire FRG budget. In addition, funds from private firms, regional governments, and other subsidies amounted to another DM 50 billion, still not enough to smooth the assimilation process. These policy missteps caused the CDU/CSU to consider seriously whether to replace Kohl as chancellor before the fall 1994 elections. Kohl persevered, however, and led his coalition to victory in the 1994 elections just as he did the ones in 1983, 1987, and 1990.

socioeconomic features.[9] More than other democratic countries, German society is organized in the sense that political institutions, social forces, and the patterns of life in civic society place more emphasis on collective action than on the individualism characteristic of Anglo-Saxon countries. This should not imply that citizens have reduced freedoms compared to those in other western democracies, nor that there is no conflict in Germany. It means, however, that political expression, both in the state and in civil society, revolves around group representation and articulation of a cooperative spirit in public action.

IMPLICATIONS FOR CONTEMPORARY GERMAN POLITICS

The organization of the German state is similar to that of other western democracies in terms of its political institutions, organization of participation, and rotation in office. The Federal Republic, even after the addition of the five states from former East Germany, remains a parliamentary democracy anchored within the European Union (EU, formerly the EC). Its government is based on a multiparty political system in which coalitions between and among major and minor parties are necessary and the political pendulum, in terms of governing coalitions, has swung from moderately center-right (1949–1966), to moderately center-left (1969–1982), and back again (1982–present).

Despite the surface similarities between Germany and some European states, it also differs from them in substantial ways. The most significant difference between Germany on the one hand, and England and France on the other, is that Germany is a federal state and the others are unitary. This German federalism has produced economic and political patterns quite different from its two European neighbors.

Another important difference is Germany's later industrialization, which produced a strong though unbalanced economic growth until after World War II. Combined with nationalism and militarism in the late nineteenth and early twentieth centuries, Germany was feared by its neighbors, and with good reason.

A third difference is Germany's delayed development of democratic forms of representation until the

Weimar Republic. Once it was destroyed by the Third Reich, parliamentary democracy was not resumed until the founding of the Federal Republic in 1949.

The most significant difference between Germany and other Western European states, of course, is the Nazi period and the destruction that the Third Reich wrought. Many observers from the post–World War II period may have thought this difference had declined in significance. However, the racist attacks on foreigners by neo-Nazi forces in the 1990s have caused many to rethink whether the evils of the Nazi period are confined entirely to the past. Such concerns are somewhat allayed, however, by the general stability of Germany's postwar development, a stability supported by its alliance with Western industrialized states, the successful development of its democratic institutions, and a political economy characterized by a highly organized business community and active worker participation within a strong labor movement.

Unification with the former communist East Germany (GDR) is another obvious difference between Germany and its neighbors. The economic, political, cultural, and physical strains of uniting two disparate societies have placed greater strains on the Federal Republic's politics and institutions than any other event since the state's founding in 1949. Although post–World War II Germany has manifested most of the features of a stable capitalist democracy, these peculiarities and their legacies create and maintain significant tensions within society.

Last, Germany's role in the European Union (EU) presents both opportunities and challenges to Germany and its neighbors. As the strongest European power, Germany has many economic and political advantages in integrating Europe. However, it must deal with the suspicions that its twentieth century history has aroused among its neighbors and confront the question of whether its post–World War II political institutions, so well suited to Germany, will also fit other Europeans in the EU.

As Germany faces its major contemporary challenges, the following questions stand out:

1. How to rebuild and solidify the nation-state's collective identity in the face of ethnic tensions, racist violence, and the economic strains caused by unification? That is, what does it mean to be German at the close of the twentieth century? What values and identities provide the most solid foundation?

2. How to institute and maintain the democratic idea in the five new federal states of former East Germany, fight the racist violence against foreigners that has surfaced throughout Germany, and retain commitment to civil rights and democracy? Is a stronger enforcement presence needed to safeguard rights, or should there be a greater emphasis on civic education?

3. How to adapt a high-wage, high-welfare state country like Germany to an increasingly competitive world economy? Can the hitherto impressive vocational education and apprenticeship training systems continue to integrate the workers from the new *Bundesländer* and provide adequate employment for all?

4. How to deal with its role in the single market of the European Union? Will Germany continue to be the leading European power as "nation-state Germany," or will it find its primary political expression among the collective EU institutions? How does Germany reconcile three orientations: looking inward, the better to surmount the strains of unification; looking toward Western Europe, as the economic, and increasingly, the political leader of the EU; looking toward East-Central Europe, as opportunities and challenges beckon from this direction?

SECTION 2

Political Economy and Development

Some comparativists suggest that, to enjoy sustained economic growth, a state should have a balanced relationship with social and economic interests, and between the means of production and exchange. The state should promote an independent economic strategy, yet work closely with influential economic sectors within society, whether financial institutions, trade unions, or business elites in order to make more informed decisions. This theory suggests that neither state nor market interests in society should overpower the other. The Federal Republic of Germany comes closer than most states in approximating this model; it has taken a development path that emphasizes cooperative interaction with a dense interest group network made up of key social and economic participants. In this way, post–World War II Germany has avoided the imbalances that plague many nation-states: (1) when powerful private interests (typically the leaders from one sector of the economy) may capture or dominate state policy; and (2) when the state dominates or captures private interests. As we suggest in this chapter, its unique forms of organized capitalism combined with a Social Market Economy have spared Germany the imbalance of state economic strategies subject to unpredictable changes and boom/bust cycles.

STATE AND ECONOMY

Germany is an organized capitalist country in which two groups, representing industry generally and employers specifically, are powerful and coordinated. Rather than emphasizing individual entrepreneurship and small business as the defining characteristics of its economy, Germany has relied on an organized network of small and large businesses working together. In addition, the banking system and financial community are directly involved in private investment and engage in little of the financial speculation characteristic of Wall Street brokers. Their primary role is to provide long-term investments to support the internationally competitive manufacturing industries that are the foundation of the economy. For example, unlike their American counterparts, German banks are legally allowed to develop close financial ties with firms in other industries, including owning the stock of such firms, granting them long-term loans, having representatives on their boards of directors, and voting as stockholders or on behalf of third-party investors. The end result is private investment based on long-term relationships among familiar partners rather than the short-term deals common among banks, investors, and firms in the United States.

Government economic policy is indirect and supportive rather than heavy-handed and overregulatory. Although the government sets broad guidelines, it encourages the formation of voluntary associations that are empowered to coordinate negotiations among organized interests such as employers, banks, trade unions, and regional governments in order to reach the government's policy objectives. This does not mean the government is not involved in economic policy-making; it just does so more flexibly. This flexibility is produced in two ways.

First, German regulation establishes a general framework for economic activity, rather than detailed standards, an approach more common in other countries. The government sets rigorous, yet broad licensing and performance standards for most professions and industries. For example, German banks must possess greater capital reserves than internationally accepted minimums and their officers must demonstrate competence to hold their positions to a semipublic institution, the Federal Bank Supervisory Office. Government policymakers believe that, once their core requirements are met and their general objectives known, private actors can be trusted to achieve government goals without detailed regulation. Failure to uphold government standards can result in fines, or, in some criminal cases, imprisonment. Supervision of the banking system, for example, is guided by a few general regulations, but very few specific ones. This gives considerable power to the Federal Bank Supervisory Office and entrusts private banks with autonomy and responsibility (via self-regulation) in implementing policies affecting their industry. In contrast, the United States has no such core requirements, but over time issues many layers of detailed regulations in the wake of banking failures and abuses.

Second, among the major European economies, Germany has the smallest share of industry in government hands. This is accomplished by a cooperative federalism that delegates to the states *(Länder)* the administrative powers of laws and regulations passed at the federal level. Both characteristics are integral parts of Germany's Social Market Economy *(Sozialemarktwirtschaft)* which is discussed in more detail later.

Unlike Britain and the United States, Germany did not experience the kind of trial-and-error capitalism that characterized much of the early nineteenth century. By the time that it was unified in 1871, Germany was forced to compete with a number of other countries that had already developed industrialized capitalist economies. German business and political elites realized that a gradual, small-firm-oriented economy would face ruinous competition from countries such as Britain, France, and the United States. To be competitive, the German state became a significant and powerful force in the German economy. This meant building on the foundations established by the formerly independent and autonomous states such as

Prussia, Bavaria, and other regions, that became part of a united Germany in 1871.

The autonomy of regional governments in the years before unification produced a tradition of strong public sector involvement in economic growth and development. In the fragmented Germany of the late eighteenth and early nineteenth centuries, states had to develop governmental systems that could provide for the material and social needs of their populations without relying on a centralized national state to deliver such programs. Regional governmental actors worked both directly and indirectly with private economic interests, thus blurring distinctions between state and market.

The economic powers assumed by the modern states *(Länder)* of the Federal Republic are also derived from their century-long involvement in promoting industrialization. The most common metaphor for analyzing industrial growth in Germany during the nineteenth century has been Alexander Gershenkron's late industrialization thesis.[10] Gershenkron maintains that Germany's transformation from a quasi-feudal society to a highly industrialized one during the latter two-thirds of the nineteenth century was characterized by a process of explicit coordination among big business, a powerful universal banking system (universal because banks, then as now, handle all financial transactions and are not segmented into savings and commercial branches, for example), and government. This progress has often been called rapid German industrialization, although a more accurate account would call it rapid Prussian industrialization because it was Bismarck's vision and mobilization of Prussian interest groups that proved the dominant force.

The foundations for economic growth and the most spectacular early leaps of industrial modernization happened before Germany's unification in 1871. The creation of the customs union **Zollverein** in 1834 from eighteen independent states with a population of 23 million people propelled industrial modernization. This process was led by Prussia, and the dominant symbol for Prussia's hegemonic position has been Bismarck's role in brokering the interests of grain-growing *Junkers* in the east with those of the coal and steel barons in the Ruhr. Bismarck used the development of the railroads as a catalyst for this "marriage of iron and rye."[11] He astutely realized that although railroads were a primary consumer of coal and steel, they also provided an effective way to transport the *Junk-*

ers' grain from the relatively isolated eastern part of Germany to market.[12] The image of Prussian-led, rapid, state-enhanced industrial growth is important, but the opening of trade among these independent principalities did not dislodge the distinct patterns of modernization that the less powerful states had developed on their own. Small-scale agricultural production remained in many parts of the southern states, particularly in Bavaria, and small-scale craft production continued in Württemberg, as well as in many other regions where feudal craft skills were adapted to the patterns of industrial modernization.

Because each of the states had different material needs and social circumstances, their regional governments may have done a more effective job than a central state could in fulfilling needs. Certainly, Bismarck's welfare-state measures brought economies of scale to those programs that needed to be implemented on a national basis. However, the strong role of the regional governments in the provision of certain specific needs continued, especially during the Second Reich (1871–1918). Later, when the Weimar regime was succumbing to the Third Reich, regional governments tried unsuccessfully to resist the Nazi state's goal of massive centralization of policy.

After the horrors of the Third Reich between 1933 and 1945, when the state worked hand-in-glove with German industry to suppress workers, employ slave labor, and produce military armaments, drastic change was needed. Postwar policymakers avoided a strong role for the state in the Federal Republic's economic life. Unlike either the French or Japanese states, which have been much more economically interventionist, the German state has evolved a rather unique relationship between the public and private sectors. Rather than creating a state-versus-market relationship, the German public and private sectors have evolved a densely interpenetrated association that avoids the kind of state planning that marks post–World War II Japan or France. Germany has avoided the opposite pattern as well, namely the antigovernment, free-market policies of Britain and the United States in the 1980s.

The key concept here is that the relationship between state and market in Germany is neither free-market nor state-dominant. Rather the state sets clear general ground rules, acknowledged by the private sector, but then allows market forces to work relatively unimpeded within the general framework of

The Social Market Economy

The Social Market Economy *(Sozialemarktwirtschaft)* is the term used to describe the set of economic policies in the post–World War II Federal Republic. Its intellectual origins derive from the Economics Department of the University of Freiburg during the 1920s and 1930s as well as from Christian social and economic teachings characteristic of the European Catholic church. The most well-known Freiburg School theorists and practitioners of the Social Market Economy were Wilhelm Röpke, Walter Eucken, Egon Tuchtfeldt, Ludwig Erhardt, and Alfred Müller-Armack. The Social Market Economy is often considered the linchpin in the rapid economic growth of the Federal Republic during the 1950s and early 1960s, the period also known as the Economic Miracle *(Wirtschaftswunder)*. These social market principles continued to shape German economic policy during the 1970s, 1980s, and 1990s.

The Social Market Economy is sometimes referred to as simply a combination of a free market economy with a considerable layer of social benefits. In reality, this set of economic policies is more complex, so just situating it on a continuum between laissez-faire and state-centered policies does not do justice to this concept. Its authors wanted a set of economic policies that sidestepped the shortcomings of Naziism, communism, laissez-faire, and the post–World War II Keynesian policies. Specifically, the primary principle behind the Social Market Economy is the market system, but one embedded within a comprehensive framework *(Rahmenbedingungen)* that encourages the interpenetration of private and public institutions. The working out of these framing policies produces a stable set of outcomes that is organized and implemented by coordination among public and private sector participants *(Ordnungspolitik)* to improve, not impede, economic competitiveness. The Social Market Economy does not lie halfway between state and market but represents a qualitatively different approach.

The social component of the Social Market Economy also differs from that of other countries. Although the Federal Republic has always been generous with its benefits, they serve more than just distributive income transfer purposes. For example, two of the most important provisions, government savings subsidies to individuals and a comprehensive vocational education system, have direct and positive benefits for the competitiveness of the entire German economy.

government supervision. Since the time of the first postwar chancellor, Christian Democrat Konrad Adenauer, the Germans have referred to this approach as the Social Market Economy *(Sozialemarktwirtschaft)*. Basically, the concept refers to a system of capitalism in which fundamental social benefits are essential, not antagonistic, to the workings of the market. Among the social components of the German economy are: health care, workers' rights, public transportation, and support for the arts. In some respects, these benefits are similar to those provided by the Japanese and French governments. However, the provision of some public benefits through organized private interests (the quasi-public sickness funds that provide for health insurance, for example) make the German Social Market Economy a blend of public and private action that supports and implements public policies. Thus, the Social Market Economy does not lie halfway between state and market, but represents a qualitatively different approach.

The social component of the Social Market Economy is unique to Germany. Although the Federal Republic has always been generous with welfare benefits, these benefits serve more than just to redistribute income. For example, two of the most important provisions—government savings subsidies to individuals

and a comprehensive vocational education system— have direct and positive benefits for the competitiveness of the Germany economy. They provide a stable pool of investment capital and create a deep pool of human capital that enables Germany to produce high-quality goods.

The German system of **framework regulation** is best explained in the words of economist Wilhelm Röpke, one of the shapers of post–World War II economic policy:

> [Our program] consists of measures and institutions which impart to competition the framework, rules, and machinery of impartial supervision which a competitive system needs as much as any game or match if it is not to degenerate into a vulgar brawl. A genuine, equitable, and smoothly functioning competitive system can not in fact survive without a judicious moral and legal framework and without regular supervision of the conditions under which competition can take place pursuant to real efficiency principles. This presupposes mature economic discernment on the part of all responsible bodies and individuals and a strong impartial state.[13]

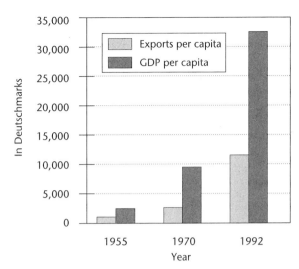

Figure 1   German Economic Growth
Source: International Herald Tribune special section
"Germany," in *Deutschland Magazine* 1, February 1995.

This system has enabled German economic policy during the post–World War II period to avoid the sharp lurches between laissez-faire freedom and state-led economic policy that have characterized its European neighbor Britain.

Germany is a prime example of a high-wage, high-welfare nation that has maintained its competitive world position far better than other advanced industrialized states since the oil crisis of 1973 (see Figure 1). Its success in combining strong competitiveness with high wages and social spending has surpassed even that of Japan. An emphasis on high skills in key export-oriented manufacturing industries is the specific path that German economic policy has taken to maintain its competitive position. An elaborate vocational education system combined with apprenticeship training underlies this policy. It is implemented through the works councils elected by every worker in all German firms with five or more employees. This system of advanced skill training has enabled Germany to resist the siren song of the postindustrial, service-sector-oriented world that countries such as the United States and Britain have tried. Relying extensively on this elaborate apprenticeship training program, Germany has maintained competitive positions in such traditional manufacturing industries as automobiles, chemicals, machine tools, and industrial electronics. By stressing the value which its highly skilled work force adds to raw materials, Germany has

for over twenty years defied predictions that its industrial economy will erode as has happened in many formerly manufacturing-oriented economies. Despite a lack of natural resources (like most of Europe), Germany maintains a surplus balance of trade and still has a large working-class population that historically has spurned protectionism. With one in every three jobs devoted to exports (one in two in the four industries above), protectionism for German unions would be self-defeating. The skills of its workers help German industry overcome the costs of acquiring resources and paying high wages; in fact, Germany industry has emphasized that high quality and high productivity offset these costs.

Germany's research and development strategy has enhanced these economic policies. Rather than push for specific new breakthroughs in exotic technologies or invent new products that might be years from the market, it chooses to adapt *existing* technologies to traditional sectors and to refine already competitive sectors. This is the exact opposite of the United States' research and development strategy, for example. During the postwar years, this policy has enabled Germany to maintain a favorable balance of trade and a high degree of competitiveness. However, European integration and German unification have forced German industry and policymakers to examine whether this model remains appropriate or needs some modification. Depending on others to make core discoveries and then quickly applying the technology to production are delicate tasks that require coordinated policies among all producer groups. Trying to institute the western German policy among former GDR workers raised in a different industrial culture has begun to prove difficult.

Other than the government, the German institution most responsible for shaping economic policy is the very independent *Bundesbank*. Although the *Bundesbank* will be discussed in depth in Section 3, its central role in shaping economic policy deserves mention here. This institution is both the "Bankers' Bank," in that it sets interest rates, and the agency that determines the amount of money in circulation. This second point has proved especially contentious during the 1980s and early 1990s. The *Bundesbank* prefers low inflation, both because this is a traditional demand of all central bankers and because of Germany's history of ruinous inflation during the Weimar Republic. The relevance for economic policy is that when the government wishes to expand the economy through increased spending or through reduced taxes, the *Bundesbank* always prefers policies that favor monetary restrictions over fast economic growth. In other words, the government and the *Bundesbank* can disagree on economic policy, as they have repeatedly in the years since unification.

This organized capitalist model is not considered a complete success by all Germans. Both the Greens, the ecologically-oriented, small-is-beautiful, political party that first won *Bundestag* seats in 1983, and the small, free-market-oriented sector feel that the organized, and perhaps closed, nature of the producer groups favors those that are inside the system (such as industry organizations, employer groups, and the banking community) and excludes those outside. Moreover, the Greens criticize many business policies as not being sufficiently protective of the environmental consequences of progrowth economic policies. The primary complaint of the small business sector is that the organized nature of large-firm-dominant capitalism is not sufficiently flexible in the creation of new products and industries. However, neither the Greens nor advocates of a more laissez-faire approach to economic policies have dislodged the dominant position of German organized capitalism in the shaping of economic policy.

In the early 1990s a sharp, three-pronged attack was launched against the idea of a smoothly functioning German economic juggernaut. First, the Kohl government badly misjudged the costs of unification and the institutional resources necessary to integrate the five new *Bundesländer.* By mid-1992 Kohl finally acknowledged what had been apparent for several years, namely that the successful integration of the eastern economy into the western one would cost much more and require a longer period of time than originally predicted. Second, the structural challenges that the German political economy faced in the mid-1990s were far more extensive than any the Federal Republic had experienced since the 1950s. The amount budgeted in the early 1990s for reconstruction in Germany was approximately 20 percent of the entire FRG budget. In addition, funds from private firms, regional governments, and other subsidies amounted to another DM 50 billion, yet even these huge sums were not enough to help smooth the assimilation process, and today a large gap in productivity levels exists between the two regions. Third, the western German integrated

institutions (even when working well) became difficult to transfer as a model to eastern Germany. For example, the Treuhand (the government reconstruction agency) privatized some 7,000 of the total of 11,000 firms that it had inherited from the former GDR. One of the most significant costs of this transition from state to private ownership was the high unemployment in the former eastern sector. Some 1.2 million workers were officially unemployed, and another 2 million enrolled in a government-subsidized short-time program combined with job training (this program's funds were slashed as part of an austerity budget).

In short, the magnitude of the problems in eastern Germany threatened to overwhelm the institutional capacity to handle them. Some pessimistic observers began to suggest that these stresses placed the German political economy in a precarious position. Germany's economic prowess has depended on certain manufacturing industries that produce eminently exportable goods, but whose technologies must constantly be upgraded and whose labor costs continue to rise.

Although the German Model of economic growth has proved remarkably durable through most of the post–World War II period, the specific and demanding requirements of unification at home and integration with Europe have confronted it with unusual pressures. Among these are weaning eastern German workers from a communist industrial culture and extending the German Model to a European-wide stage. The huge demands of unification, in terms of funding the transformation of a region that had lived for more than forty years under communist rule is daunting enough. But complicating the demands on Germany's economic institutions is the obligation to align Germany's economic policies with those of its European neighbors. The future of this model will be examined more closely in Section 5.

WELFARE PROVISION

Welfare policies can be described as the social part of the Social Market Economy. The Federal Republic's social-welfare expenditures are consistent with historically generous Western European standards. Although they are not as extensive as those in some of the small European countries such as the Netherlands and Scandinavia, public services in the Federal Republic since the 1950s have dwarfed those of the United States, for example. From housing subsidies, to savings subsidies, to health care, to public transit, to the rebuilding of the destroyed cities and public infrastructure, the Federal Republic is still remarkably generous in its public spending. Even under the moderately conservative rule of the CDU-led Adenauer coalition, there was a strong commitment to providing adequate public services. This strategy recalls Bismarck's efforts to use public services to forestall radical demands in the late nineteenth century. For example, in the early 1880s, Bismarck introduced elaborate social-welfare measures to provide a degree of relief for the most adverse effects of industrial growth. From health insurance to social security, Bismarck's government established the first modern welfare state. He did so, not against the wishes of the industrialists, but on their behalf and with their support, because most realized that economic growth required a cooperative workforce. For nondemocratic conservatives like Bismarck and for democratic conservatives like Adenauer, such comprehensive welfare benefits were not philanthropic but were a direct response to the demands of the Social Democratic Party (SPD) and the trade unions. Thus, welfare in Germany has never been a gift but a negotiated settlement, often after periods of conflict, between major social forces that have agreed to compromise based on positions of strength.

The development of welfare services has been tremendously enhanced as well by the European Christian social tradition—a major force in the CDU/CSU coalition. Both Catholic and Protestant churches espouse a belief in public spending for services as a responsibility of the strong for the welfare of the weak. Similarly, the unions' and the SPD's demands for increased public spending ensured that the Left was incorporated into the political order during the 1950s and early 1960s.

During the mid-1970s, when unemployment grew from 1 or 2 percent to roughly 4 percent, and when some social welfare measures were capped (but not reduced), citizens of the Federal Republic spoke of the crisis of the welfare state. Yet non-German observers were hard pressed to find indications of crisis. Clearly, contraction of substantial welfare state benefits in no way approximated those cutbacks of the United States and Britain in the 1980s and 1990s.

In the 1980s, continued high unemployment (by German standards) and the costs of support for workers who had depleted their benefits, presented difficult

dilemmas for the welfare state. German jobs tend to be highly paid, so employers try to avoid creating part-time jobs, preferring to wait on hiring until the need for employees is sustainable. During times of recession, the number of new jobs created can be miniscule. A factor that compounded this problem was the ***Gastarbeiter* (guestworker)** issue. Under this plan, temporary workers were recruited from southern Europe in the 1960s with the stipulation that they would return to their native countries if there was an increase in unemployment. However, the economic boom lasted so long that by the time the economy did turn down in the mid-1970s, it was difficult for these so-called guests to return to homes in which they had not lived for a decade or more. And as semipermanent residents, they were eligible for welfare benefits. These foreign workers produced heightened social strain in the 1970s and 1980s, at a time of increasing unemployment. Because German citizenship was not granted to either the guest workers or their children, the problem remained unresolved. Although not as severe as in the Second Reich, the clash between German and *Gastarbeiter* cultures increased in intensity into the 1980s, particularly in areas where Turkish workers were highly concentrated.

Uncertain economic conditions in the early 1980s cost the Social Democratic coalition led by Chancellor Helmut Schmidt considerable support. It was replaced in 1982 by a Christian Democratic–Free Democratic (CDU/CSU–FDP) coalition government, led by Christian Democrat Helmut Kohl, that shouldered the cost of sustaining the long-term unemployed through general welfare funds. However, a more serious structural problem lay beyond the immediate issue of cost: How could the Federal Republic's elaborate vocational education and apprentice system absorb all the new entrants into the labor market? This problem could have undermined one of the strengths of the German economy, the continued supply of skilled workers. Despite these threats in the mid-1980s, both the unemployment compensation system and the vocational education and apprenticeship system survived under the Kohl government. However, this issue has resurfaced with the large increase in the unemployment rate following unification in 1990, particularly in the eastern German states.

The costs of the "social" market economy, as witnessed by the costs of unification, stressed the upper limits of Germany's capacity to pay for them.

Massive budget cuts became imperative by spring 1993. The completion of the EU's Single Market, supposedly the grand culmination of a post–Cold War spirit of German and European unity, has proved ephemeral. Its alleged immediate benefit will likely only strengthen the trends toward decentralization and deregulation already begun in Western Europe. More significantly for the German regime, union will potentially disturb the organized capitalism of its small and large businesses which features an intricate, mutually reinforcing pattern of government and business self-regulation. In addition, the apparent deregulation in European finance threatens Germany's distinctive finance/manufacturing links, which depend on long-term relationships between the two parties, not short-term deals. Thus the trend toward Europeanization, on a path that challenges Germany's preeminent position, may be incompatible with the highly consensus-oriented and coordinated nature of Germany's adjustment patterns.

Tensions have also flared up between the former East and West Germans. The GDR economy was considered strong by communist standards: It provided jobs for virtually all people, but many of these jobs evaporated when the communist countries collapsed. GDR industry, as in most former communist countries, was inefficient by Western standards, and most firms were not able to survive the transition to the western German capitalist system. Among the most serious problems were overstaffing and inadequate quality control. Consequently, many easterners lost their jobs. For a time, they were generously supported by western subsidies, but the recovery in the five new eastern states lagged much more than the Kohl government originally anticipated. Easterners resent the slow pace of change and high unemployment, and western Germans are bitter about losing jobs to easterners and paying, through increased taxes, for the clean-up of the ecological and infrastructural disaster inherited from the former East German regime.

SOCIETY AND ECONOMY

During the boom years of the mid-twentieth century, German economic growth provided a sound foundation for social development. The Social Market Economy of the Christian Democrats was augmented by governments led by Social Democrats from 1969–1982, when the supportive social programs of the 1950s and 1960s were extended and enhanced. This growth, with its corresponding social policies, helped Germany to avoid the kind of occupational and regional conflict common to many other countries. Although divisions exist in German society and in the economy, the strong role of trade unions and the unwillingness (perhaps the result of trade union strength) of the employers to confront workers on wage and workplace issues, have minimized stratification of the society and workplace.

The most controversial issues for German society in the 1990s have been race and ethnicity, with profound implications for both Germany's ideology and its political culture. Racist attacks have forced Germans to confront the possibility that forty years of democracy have not tamed some of the xenophobic aspects of Germany's political culture. The issue of ethnic minorities affected the economy and society during the 1980s and has been exacerbated in the 1990s by unification and European integration. The most pressing concerns lie in the areas of nationalism and ethnicity. The population of the GDR was raised in a society that did not celebrate, or even value, toleration or dissent and in which official unemployment did not exist. East Germany was a closed society, as were most communist regimes, and many GDR citizens had little contact with foreign nationals prior to 1989. In contrast, since the 1960s, West Germany has encouraged the migration of millions of guestworkers *(Gastarbeiter)* from southern Europe. The FRG has also provided generous provisions for those seeking political asylum, in an effort to overcome—to some degree at least—the legacy of Nazi persecution of non-Germans from 1933–1945.

Thus when unification arrived, with a flood of different ethnic minorities into both the former East and West Germany, few former GDR citizens were able to respond positively to these momentous changes. First, the former GDR citizens were expected to embrace, completely and immediately, the western democratic ideals of debate and toleration of diversity. Second, they were expected to deal with a labor market that did not always supply an adequate number of jobs. Gone was a world of guaranteed lifetime employment and in its place was one where structural unemployment claimed as much as 25 percent of the workforce. Third, they were confronted with a much more open and ethnically diverse society than they had ever known, so that immigrants and asylum seekers became the scapegoats for the lack of employment. Consequently, those German citizens who were falling through the cracks of the German welfare state were also susceptible to racist propaganda from demagogues blaming ethnic minorities for all the major changes that had occurred so rapidly.

Another significant issue has been the role of women in German society. The increase of women in the labor force has created tension in an area where men had traditionally dominated all positions of authority in both management and the union movement. The union movement has made greater strides than management in providing women with expanded opportunities for responsibility and authority. In areas outside the formal workplace, the differences between the laws of the former GDR and those of preunification FRG have created a firestorm of controversy. In the former East Germany, women had made far greater social and economic progress (relatively speaking) and received more government support for such services as child care and family leave than their West German sisters. Today, one of the most heated controversies in Germany has been over the reduction of the East German brand of benefits to women (including abortion) in favor of the more conservative and restrictive ones of the Federal Republic.

GERMANY AND THE INTERNATIONAL POLITICAL ECONOMY

Germany's relationship to the regional and international political economy is shaped by two factors: the European Union (formerly the European Community, or EC) and Germany's political role on the world stage. The EU was embraced by most Germans and by the political and industrial establishment, especially in the first few years after unification. As Europe's leading economic power, Germany should benefit greatly from a successful European integration because its position of strength will likely be enhanced by wider market opportunities. Many actions and policies that might once have been viewed as German domination by its neighbors become more acceptable when seen as Germany's active participation as a member of the larger European Union.

Several difficult issues confront Germany's international position in the mid-1990s. One concern is whether successful, German-specific institutional arrangements—such as its institutionalized system of worker (and union) participation in management, its

tightly organized capitalism, and its elaborate system of apprenticeship training—will prove adaptable or durable in a wider European context. What may work well for Germany may be derived from indigenous institutional, political, and/or cultural patterns that will not successfully transfer beyond the Federal Republic. Another concern involves Germany's political role on the world stage. After the momentous events of German unification and European integration, many observers in Europe, Japan, and North America assumed that Germany would take on greater political responsibility based on its position of economic strength and its newfound political unity. However, indecision and inaction in world affairs by the Kohl regime in the 1990s suggests that Germany is unwilling or incapable of assuming the responsibilities of a world power. Examples of this inaction can be seen in the failure of leadership in areas such as the Gulf War, Somalia, and especially Bosnia. Perhaps Germany does remain a political dwarf, at least in a geopolitical sense.

Germany is being pressed to take greater political responsibility, both within the EU and as a sovereign nation-state, based on its economic resources and its political power as the leading European nation. Yet its first foray into the post–Cold War arena of Eastern Europe demonstrated Germany's lack of diplomatic skill. The country's initial inaction regarding Bosnia and the appropriate policies for Germany and Europe toward the former Yugoslavia have literally paralyzed German (and European) foreign policy. In addition, Germany's impulsive recognition of Slovenia and Croatia followed by legitimating Bosnia's separatist claims made the creation of a purposeful European response more difficult. This position was opposed by other Western powers, and it in fact precipitated much of the violence when the former Yugoslavia distintegrated.

If Germany assumed more leadership, a united Europe might be able to develop a region-wide geopolitical policy. But leadership requires working with one's allies and not simply taking an independent position diametrically opposed to their interests. Future military issues are closely tied to this question of leadership in the European Union. Whether the UN, NATO, or the European Union itself are to take military responsibility for Europe remains uncertain. This uncertainty is prolonged by Germany's own ambivalence about its international political role. In their defense, the Germans continue

Problems with a too-strong DM.
Source: *Frankfurter Allgemeine Zeitung.*

to stress the strains and huge costs of unification as well as the difficulty of dealing with the political asylum issue. However, great nations find ways to do extremely difficult things when it is not convenient. As yet, Germany has not developed the skills necessary to meet the obligations of political responsibility.

Other issues such as trade, economic competition with Japan, monetary policy for the European Union, and the general pace of economic integration remain major areas of concern, though less serious than the ones just discussed. With the passage of the Uruguay Round of the General Agreement on Tariffs and Trade (GATT) in December 1993, some of the more contentious trade issues are no longer areas of potential conflict. To its credit Germany, as a goods-exporting nation, has always favored an open trading

system. Management and unions realize that exports represent both profits and jobs and that seeking refuge in protectionism would be self-defeating. The Japanese economic threat has receded somewhat in the mid-1990s, as the Japanese experienced the recession that had beset both Europe and North America earlier in the 1990s. Germany's strategy to deal with the Japanese economic challenge differed from that of other Western nations. Instead of giving up older manufacturing industries in the face of the Japanese competitive onslaught, as did Britain and the United States, the Germans felt that these industries could remain competitive with a high-skill, high-value-added approach. This approach has largely succeeded and may give the German economy some breathing room as Japan struggles with its own recession.

As for how quickly European integration proceeds, countries that might consider emulating German institutions require not just strategies, but also the means of implementing them. The lack of a cohesive European-wide institutional framework would severely hinder efforts to develop strategies appropriate to meeting the domestic and international challenges of European unification. Most other European nations can identify their goals, namely a highly skilled workforce able to compete in international markets on some basis other than a combination of low labor costs and high-tech production strategies. But whether they can or want to follow Germany's example remains to be seen, especially in light of recent German economic difficulty. The preoccupation of Germany with its immediate domestic issues, plus the German-specific nature of the institutions of its political economy, has partially diminished the luster of German-style policies for the New Europe.

SECTION 3

Governance and Policy-Making

The governing principles of the Federal Republic have emerged phoenix-like from the ashes of the catastrophic experiences brought on by previous regimes in Germany. When the Federal Republic was established in 1949, the primary goals of its founders were to work toward eventual unification of the two Germa-

nies and, more importantly, to avoid repeating the failure of Germany's only other experiment with democracy, the Weimar Republic. When unification was blocked indefinitely, the founders instituted the Basic Law *(Grundgesetz)* as a compromise. They preferred to wait until Germany could be reunited before using the term *constitution (Verfassung).** Their other primary goal, insuring a lasting democratic order, presented a more complicated problem. Two fundamental institutional weaknesses had undermined the Weimar government: (1) provisions for emergency powers enabled leaders to arbitrarily centralize authority and suspend democratic rights; and (2) the fragmentation of the political party system prevented stable majorities from forming in the *Reichstag.* This second weakness, instability, encouraged the implementation of the first, the use of emergency powers to break legislative deadlocks.

Under the strong urgings of the Allied occupation authorities, the builders of the postwar government sought to remedy the abuse of centralized power by establishing a federal system in which the *Länder* were given considerable powers, particularly administrative powers. It is paradoxical that a constitution that owes so much to the influence of foreign powers has proved so durable. Under the Basic Law of the Federal Republic, many functions that had formerly been centralized during the imperial, Weimar, and Nazi periods, such as the educational system, the police, and the radio networks, now became the responsibility of the states. Although the federal *Bundestag* (lower house) became the chief lawmaking body, the implementation of many of these laws fell to the *Länder* governments. Moreover, the *Länder* governments sent representatives to the *Bundesrat* (upper house), which was required to approve bills passed in the *Bundestag.*

There was little opposition from major actors within the Federal Republic to this shift from a centralized to a federal system. The Third Reich's arbitrary abuse of power with respect to Jews, political parties, trade unions, and human rights in general had created strong sentiment for curbing the state's repressive capacities. In addition, political leaders, influenced by advisers from the United States, were inclined to support a federal system. Further, the development of a federal system was not a departure, but a return to form. Prior to the unification of Germany in 1871, the various regions of Germany had formed a decentralized political system with such autonomous

institutions as banks, universities, vocational schools, and state administrative systems.

Several methods were used to surmount party fragmentation and the inability to form working majorities. The multiplicity of parties characteristic of the Weimar Republic was partially controlled by the institutionalization of the 5 percent rule. This measure required a political party to receive 5 percent of the popular vote in an election to obtain seats under the system of proportional representation used in elections for the *Bundestag* or for any *Land* or municipal government. In the late Weimar period, sharp conflict among parties opened the door for the Nazi rise to power; however, under the 5 percent rule, smaller parties tended to fade, with most of their members absorbed by the three major parties until the rise of the Greens Party in the early 1980s. In the 1990 federal election, only the Party of Democratic Socialism, or *Partei Demokratische Sozialismus* (PDS, comprised of the former East German Communists, or SED) and *Bündnis '90* (an alternative/ecological party now merged with the western German Greens Party) gained seats in the *Bundestag* as new parties in 1990. Both were successful in attaining representation in 1994 as well. The extreme right-wing party, the *Republikaner,* flirted with the 5 percent hurdle in several regional elections and threatened to exceed the threshold in the 1994 federal elections but ultimately failed, receiving less than 2 percent of the popular vote.

The *Bundestag* is more likely to achieve working majorities than the Weimar government did for several other reasons. Election laws require that the interval between elections be four years (except under unusual circumstances). This gives an elected government the opportunity to implement its electoral goals and to take responsibility for success or failure. The electoral system (explained later in the section on the *Bundestag*) was also changed from an unstable proportional representation system under the Weimar government to a combination of proportional representation and single member electoral districts. New constitutional provisions limited the possibility for the *Bundestag* to vote a government from office. Under the Weimar constitution, negative majorities often garnered enough votes to unseat the chancellor but did not provide a mandate to install a replacement. In the Federal Republic, a *constructive vote of no-confidence* is required, meaning that any action to vote out one

---

* Yet, after unification in 1990, the term *Basic Law* has been retained because most Germans rightly associate what was used as a temporary term with the country's longest and most successful experience of democracy.

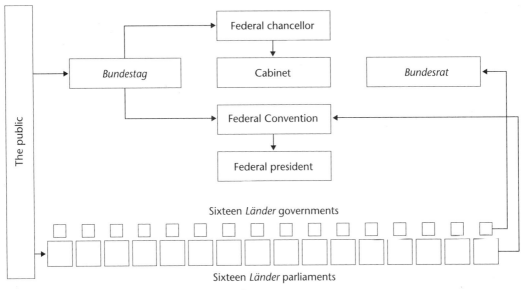

Figure 2   Constitutional Structure of Germany's Federal Government

chancellor must also simultaneously vote in another. In addition, the chancellor's powers are now more clearly defined. As the leader of the dominant party or coalition of parties, the chancellor now has control over the composition of the cabinet, so that the federal president is merely the ceremonial head of state. Under the Weimar constitution, the president could be called on to wield emergency powers. Hitler invoked this rule to manipulate the system under the aging President Paul Hindenburg in 1932 and 1933. In the Federal Republic, the president has been stripped of such broad power.

The principles of the Federal Republic's government contained in the Basic Law give the nation a solid foundation, one that appeared capable of assimilating the five *Länder* of the former GDR when unification occurred in 1990. After surviving for more than forty years, it is clear the most important goals of the Federal Republic have been fulfilled. However, in the 1990s, threats of neo-Nazi movements and racist violence have surprised many observers who thought these sentiments had long since been purged from German politics. Political scientist Ralf Dahrendorf has stated in his book *Society and Democracy in Germany* that until the arrival of the Federal Republic, Germany had been a premodern country. From 1949 until unification, it appeared much more like other western industrialized countries. After unification in

1990, with the difficulties in integrating the two regimes and the uncertainties regarding European integration, some of the more optimistic assumptions about a reformed, more democratic Germany have been challenged. The remaining portions of this section examine the dominant political institutions of the Federal Republic.

ORGANIZATION OF THE STATE

The German state is organized as a federal system, with sixteen *Länder,* each with considerable powers independent of the federal government (see Figure 2). The most important powers provide the right to raise revenue independently and the right to own and operate firms, usually in partnership with private industry. As a parliamentary democracy, the functioning of the German government resembles the parliamentary systems of Britain and France; namely, there is a fusion of powers in that the chancellor, the executive or head of government, is also the leader of the leading party (or coalition) in the *Bundestag*. This contrasts with the separation of powers system used in the United States in which the president cannot simultaneously serve in the Congress, nor can cabinet officials. Generally the executive dominates the legislative in the Federal Republic, but this authority derives from the chancellor's role as party leader and a high level of party discipline. Most members of the governing parties support the

Helmut Kohl addresses the first parliament meeting of the united Germany in the Berlin *Reichstag* on October 4, 1990.
Source: Reuters/Bettmann.

chancellor at all times, as their own positions depend on successful government. This loyalty diffuses the lone ranger syndrome, so common in the U.S. House and Senate, where individual members of Congress or the Senate often act as independent political entrepreneurs.

The Federal Republic's legislature is bicameral, with the 663-member *Bundestag* as the lower house and the 69-member *Bundesrat* as the upper house. Unlike the U.S. Senate and the British House of Lords, the *Bundesrat* is comprised of elected and appointed officials from the sixteen *Länder* (states) of the Federal Republic. In this way, Germany's constitutional system allows more governmental institutional overlap than countries that are either unitary (France, Britain) or that have a sharp separation of powers within the federal government and a separation of powers between federal and state governments (United States). The *Bundestag* members are elected in a basi-

cally PR system (explained in Section 4), in which the leader of the major party, who is usually the leader of the largest party in a two- or three-party coalition, is the chancellor. As in most parliamentary systems, the chancellor must maintain a majority for the government to survive.

THE EXECUTIVE

The division between the head of government (the chancellor) and the head of state (the president) is firmly established in the Federal Republic, with major political powers delegated to the chancellor. Responsibilities and obligations are clearly distinguished between the two offices. For example, the chancellor can be criticized for the government's policies without the criticism being perceived as an attack against the state itself. This division of power in the executive branch was essential to establish respect for the new West German state at a time when most of its neighbors were suspicious of Germany's past. After all, it was Chancellor Hitler who outmaneuvered President Hindenburg in 1934 to increase the powers of the chancellor. When Hindenburg died shortly thereafter, Hitler fused the offices of chancellor and president, creating the position of Fuhrer!

The chancellor is elected by a majority of the members of the *Bundestag*. In practice, this means that the chancellor's ability to be a strong party leader (or leader of a coalition of parties) is essential to the government's success. A government is formed after a national election, or, if the chancellor leaves office between elections, after a majority of the *Bundestag* has nominated a chancellor in a constructive vote of no confidence. The new leader consults with other party (and coalition) officials to make up the cabinet. These party leaders have considerable influence in determining which individuals receive ministries. In the event of a coalition government, party leaders often earmark, even before the election, leaders of their party who will receive certain ministries. Negotiations on which policies a coalition will pursue can often become heated, so the choice of ministers for particular ministries is made on policy as well as personal grounds.

From their party or coalition, chancellors select members of the cabinet who can best augment and support the executive branch. The most significant cabinet ministries are those of finance, economics, justice, interior, and foreign policy (the Foreign

Ministry). Decision making within the cabinet meetings is often quite formalized, with many of the important deliberations conducted prior to the official cabinet meetings. In many cases, chancellors rely on strong ministers in key posts, but some chancellors have often taken ministerial responsibility themselves in key areas such as economics and foreign policy. Helmut Schmidt and Willy Brandt, respectively, fit this pattern. The economics and finance ministries always work closely with the *Bundesbank,* the powerful independent central bank mentioned in Section 2.

Once the cabinet is formed, however, the chancellor has considerable authority to govern, due to the power of the Federal Chancellery *(Bundeskanzleramt).* This office is the "first among equals" of all the cabinet ministries, thus enabling the chancellor to efficiently oversee the entire government as well as mediate conflicts among the other ministries. It is a kind of super-ministry that has wide-ranging powers in many areas.

The office of the chancellor (an office essentially equivalent to prime minister) has played a pivotal role in the Federal Republic. The clearly defined role of the chancellor within the federal framework has resulted in an office far more effective than was the case in the Weimar period. Requiring that the chancellor be the head of the majority party or coalition, the Federal Republic has avoided the opportunity for a chancellor such as Hitler to manipulate a president such as Hindenburg to attain power for himself. One drawback of this change is that the chancellor's more limited role within the context of a federal system has constrained the ability of the central government to take sweeping action. To many Germans, this limitation of centralized executive power is a welcome improvement.

Perhaps the most significant source of the chancellor's powers is a constitutional provision called the constructive vote of no-confidence. To avoid the weakness of the cabinet governments of Weimar, the Federal Republic's founding fathers added a twist to the practice followed in most other parliamentary systems in which a prime minister is brought down on a vote of no confidence. In most such countries, if prime ministers lose such a vote, they are obliged to step down or to call for new elections. In the Federal Republic, however, such a vote must be "constructive," meaning that a chancellor cannot be removed unless the *Bundestag simultaneously* elects a new chancellor

(usually from one of the opposition parties). This constitutional provision strengthens the chancellor's power in at least two ways: (1) chancellors can more easily reconcile disputes among cabinet officials without threatening their own position; and (2) the opposition must come up with concrete and specific alternatives to the existing government, thus preventing confrontation just for the sake of opposition.

Chancellors also face significant limits on their power. As will be discussed in Section 4, the *Bundesrat* (upper house) must ratify all legislation passed in the *Bundestag* (lower house), unless overridden by a two-thirds vote. In addition, the *Bundesrat* generally implements most legislation passed in the *Bundestag* so it is necessary for chancellors to consider the position of the upper house on most issues.

The German president is the head of state, a much weaker position than that of the chancellor. Like constitutional monarchs in Britain, for example, German presidents stand above the political fray, which means that their role is more ceremonial than political. However, if there was a political crisis affecting the chancellor, the president would remain as an overseer of the political process, thus providing continuity in a time of national calamity.

> As head of state, the president represents Germany in international affairs, concluding treaties with other countries and receiving the credentials of foreign ambassadors and envoys. He or she formally appoints and dismisses federal civil servants, federal judges, and officers of the Federal Armed Forces and may exercise the right of presidential clemency. He or she participates in the legislative process through the promulgation of laws, the dissolution of the *Bundestag,* and the formal proposal, appointment and dismissal of the federal chancellor and the ministers. The political system of Germany assigns the president a non-partisan role, often of a ceremonial nature, with powers that rest largely on the moral authority of the office rather than on political power. An exception is the occurrence of a parliamentary crisis when no candidate can command the support of an absolute majority of *Bundestag* members. In this case, the president can decide whether the country is to be governed by a minority

administration under a chancellor elected by a plurality of deputies or whether new elections are to be called.[14]

In July 1994, Roman Herzog was elected president by the Federal Convention *(Bundesversammlung),* an assembly of all *Bundestag* members and an equal number of delegates elected by the state legislatures according to the principle of proportional representation (the equivalent of an electoral college). The presidential term is five years, with a limit of two terms. Herzog replaced former president Richard von Weizsäcker.

The Bureaucracy

An essential component of the executive is the national bureaucracy. In Germany it is very powerful and protected by long-standing civil service provisions. During the Second and Third Reichs, German **civil servants** *(Beamten)* had a reputation for inflexibility and rigidity in the performance of their duties. Even though the bureaucracy has been under democratic supervision, there are certainly inefficiencies in the Federal Republic's public sector, just as there are in all public and private bureaucracies. Yet civil servants maintain the conviction that their work is a profession, not just a job.

Surprisingly, only about 10 percent of civil servants are employed by the federal government, with the remainder employed by the various state and local governments. In the years before the founding of the Federal Republic, most civil servants were recruited from the families of the reactionary nobility, but today most come either from major German universities and/or from positions within the political parties. The federal bureaucrats are primarily policymakers who work closely with their ministries and the legislature. The bureaucrats at the state and local levels are the predominant agents of policy implementation because the states *(Länder)* must administer most policies determined at the national level. This overlapping of national, regional, and local bureaucracies is supported by the belief that certain functions can only be performed by the public sector and that it is their mandate to perform these duties well. The ongoing institutionalized relationship among the various levels of the bureaucracy has produced a more consistent and effective public policy than is found in other countries where federal and state governments are often at odds with one another.

Overlapping responsibilities, or **policy** *(Politikverflechtung),* make it difficult to separate the institutions of federalism from the national to the regional level, and from the regional to the local levels as well. For example, the cities of Bremen and Hamburg, which have been members of the Hanseatic League specializing in foreign trade, remain city-states. Even today they have overlapping municipal and *Land* governments. The newly unified Berlin city government fits into this category too.

Renowned for being officious, rigid, and unfriendly, the German bureaucracy has high, if grudging, political respect from the population. It is generally seen as efficient, although sometimes arcane. The selection of some bureaucrats is based on party affiliation, following the traditional German pattern of proportionality, in which all major political groupings are represented in the bureaucracy. However, as we mentioned in Section 1, the 1970s witnessed attempts to purge the bureaucracy of suspected radicals, a move that tarnished its reputation for impartiality and fairness. Those who are chosen based on party politics, usually top federal officials, are in the minority. Selection to the status of civil servant *(Beamte)* is generally based on merit, with elaborate licensing and testing for those who advance to the highest professions. German bureaucrats enjoy a well-deserved reputation for competence, especially when compared to the bureaucracies of most developed states.

The Military

From the eighteenth century (when it was the Prussian military) through World War II, the German military was powerful and aggressive. During this two-century period, it was responsible for many wars and major acts of aggression. After World War II, however, the German military was placed completely under civilian control and tightly circumscribed by law and treaty. Germany's armed forces have been legally proscribed from extranational activity, first by the allied occupation and later by the German Basic Law. Under the provisions of the Basic Law, the German military is to be used only for defensive purposes within Europe, and then in coordination with NATO authorities. One of the most contentious issues regarding military affairs in the early 1990s was whether German forces should go to Somalia under UN auspices. The Kohl

CDU/CSU–FDP government favored amending the constitution to allow such action, but the opposition SPD and Greens resisted. Only very limited military activity under tightly reined approval (e.g., via NATO) has altered the general prohibition.

Since World War II, two generations of Germans have been educated to deemphasize the military and militarism as solutions to political problems. The irony is that it is now politically—and until recently, constitutionally—difficult for Germany to commit troops to regional conflicts, even under UN auspices. The dilemmas intensify when the issues of Bosnia, Serbia, and the catastrophe of the former Yugoslavia are overlaid on this set of policy proscriptions. The SPD and Greens argue that, because of the Third Reich's aggressive military expeditions to the east in World War II, it is impossible for the German military, either under UN or NATO auspices, to play a constructive role in Eastern Europe. Yet, how is Germany to take on more geopolitical responsibility? This is not an easy issue, and vacillating political leadership has not made it any easier.

Semipublic Institutions

Semipublic institutions are powerful, efficient, and responsible for much national policy-making. The most influential include the *Bundesbank,* the Sickness Funds that administer the national health care system, and the vocational education system (which encompasses the apprenticeship training system). These are part of an integrated corporatist system in which national (and regional) governments delegate much policy-making authority to them. These institutions generally operate from a principle of including all relevant participants in the policy community and engaging in continuous dialogue until appropriate policies are found.

In countries that had a feudal guild system of representation—such as Germany—an inclusionary, often corporatist, form of representation is common. Semipublic institutions combine aspects of both representation and implementation.* The corporatist inter-

---

* The semipublic institutions differ greatly from pluralist representation in countries such as the United States where interest groups petition public authority for redress of grievances while keeping at arm's length from the implementation process. See Robert Dahl, *Dilemmas of Pluralist Democracy: Autonomy vs. Control* (New Haven: Yale University Press, 1982).

est groups are also very much intertwined with the Federal Republic's semipublic agencies, which this discussion argues are institutions crucial for the functioning of the German political economy. A gray area encompassing both public and private responsibilities, these institutions are an apparent seamless web that shapes, directs, implements, and diffuses German public policy.

In the late 1940s, the idea of a strong central state in Germany was discredited for two reasons: the excesses of Nazism and the American occupation authorities' strong affinity for the private sector. West German authorities faced a dilemma. How would they rebuild society if a strong public sector role was prohibited? The answer was to create modern, democratic versions of those nineteenth-century institutions that blurred the differences between the public and private sectors. These institutions have played a crucial role in the German political economy, one that has long been unrecognized.

Political scientist Peter Katzenstein has written extensively about the semipublic agencies, calling them detached institutions. He sees them as primarily mediating entities that reduce the influence of the central state.[15] Katzenstein finds that they have tended to work best in areas of social and economic policy, but not as well in their interaction with the university system. Among the most important semipublic agencies are the Chambers of Industry, the Council of Economic Advisors (known colloquially as the Five Wise Men), and the institutions of worker participation (codetermination and the works councils). Even areas of the welfare system are semipublic because the distribution system for welfare benefits is often administered by organizations not officially part of the state bureaucracy. The most significant example of this are the **health insurance funds** *(Krankenkassen),* which bring all major health interests together to allocate costs and benefits via an elaborate system of consultation and group participation.

Another important set of semipublic institutions that implement policy are unions involved in industrial relations. This is in sharp contrast to Anglo/American patterns and is known as the system of **codetermination** *(Mitbestimmung).* This group of institutions is discussed here because industrial relations in Germany help shape public policy.

Co-determination provides that workers, including union members, participate on the supervisory

Co-Determination

Co-determination is an institutional relationship between organized labor and business that gives labor movements the opportunity and right to participate with their employers in major decisions that jointly affect their firm and industry. Found in northern Europe, including the Netherlands, and Scandinavia, but best known in the Federal Republic of Germany, co-determination *(Mitbestimmung)* allows representatives of workers and trade unions to obtain voting seats on the supervisory board of directors *(Aufsichtsrat)* of firms with 2,000 or more employees.

The roots of co-determination lie in the guild structures of feudal Europe: Handicraft traditions encouraged the transmission of worker skills in a master-journeyman-apprentice system that deeply embedded participatory traditions among skilled workers. More modern roots of co-determination stem from a resurgence of worker participation during the Weimar Republic in Germany (1918–1933) when workers demanded increased rights in a newly democratic society. Partially eroded by increasingly conservative governments in the 1920s and cut short by the Nazis' suppression of independent worker representation, co-determination in its present form did not reappear until the formation of the Federal Republic of Germany in 1949.

German co-determination has two official forms, one for the coal and steel industries *(Montanmitbestimmung)* and one for all other industries. The former provides full parity for worker reprsentatives in all decisions on the supervisory board *(Aufsichtsrat)*, whereas the latter provides nearly full parity between worker and employer representatives, because a representative of management always has the tie-breaking vote. Post–World War II roots of co-determination sprang from the anger of German workers toward the complicity of German industrialists with the Nazi war machine.

This was especially true of the coal and steel barons, hence the full parity in those industries. Thus, after World War II, the idea of placing workers and union representatives on the boards of directors of these firms was seen by many as an opportunity to ensure increased accountability from German capitalism.

The laws governing co-determination, first passed in the early 1950s and expanded in the 1970s, reflect the powerful role of the trade unions in the politics of the postwar Federal Republic. They give the workers—and indirectly, their unions for those firms so organized—a form of institutionalized participation via membership on the supervisory board *(Aufsichtsrat)* of German firms. This participation, rather than making German firms uncompetitive, actually has had the opposite effect. Workers and unions can comprehend, if not unilaterally determine, corporate decisions regarding investment and the introduction of new technologies. Co-determination has allowed German workers a broader and deeper knowledge of the goals and strategies of the firms for which they work.

Co-determination has not been conflict-free in the Federal Republic. In 1976, at the time of the broadening of some of the unions' powers, the Constitutional Court ruled that worker reprsentatives could never attain majority representation on the supervisory board. The court argued that such a provision could compromise private property in the Federal Republic. This ruling caused the unions to break away from a more structured process of consultation on macroeconomic policy, known as Concerted Action, with the government and organized business. Despite this residual tension however, co-determination has provided substantial benefits to German business, workers, and the entire society.

---

boards of directors of all medium and large firms, thus giving unions an inside look at the workings of the most powerful firms in the Federal Republic. Unions can thus understand, if not control, how and why major corporate decisions are made on such issues as investment and application of technology. Based on laws passed in the early 1950s and expanded in the 1970s, co-determination gives workers (and unions) up to one-half of the seats on these company boards. The unions' problem in challenging management positions on contentious issues is that (with the exception of the coal and steel industries) the laws always provide management with one additional, and hence, likely tie-breaking vote.

An additional institutional structure represents German workers and gives them access to the policy implementation process: the **works councils** *(Be-*

triebsräte). In notable contrast to the trade unions' external role of representation, these internal bodies of workers represent all shopfloor and plant level affairs. The trade unions have historically addressed collective bargaining issues whereas the works councils have concentrated on social and personnel matters. With the current trend to more flexible workplaces, however, these lines of demarcation have been blurred since the late 1980s and early 1990s.

The unions' legitimation derives from a country-wide, multi-industry representation of a large number of diversified workers. The works councils, on the other hand, owe their primary allegiance to their local plants and firms. The distribution of power between these two distinct and separate bodies causes rivalries, periodic rifts, and competing spheres of interest. Despite an 85 percent overlap in personnel between unions and works councils, and despite a structural entanglement between these two major pillars of labor representation in the Federal Republic, these divisions can produce tensions among organized labor. A period of general flux and plant-related, management-imposed flexibility in the middle and late 1980s exacerbated these tensions. Specifically, the centrifugal nature of this dual system of representation generated mini-corporatist tendencies that partially undermined the large-scale, all-embracing solidarity claimed by the unions. The unions have successfully avoided the proliferation of any serious plant-level divisions among workers in the 1990s.

OTHER STATE INSTITUTIONS

In addition to the chancellor, the bureaucracy, the military, and para-statal organizations, the judiciary, and subnational governments are essential institutions for governance and policy-making.

The Judiciary

The German judiciary is an autonomous and independent institution whose rulings are generally consistent with accepted constitutional principles. It remains outside the political fray on most issues, although a ruling in 1993 limiting access to abortion for many women, in direct opposition to the former law on abortion in the GDR, was a clear exception to the general pattern. The judiciary has also been criticized in the 1990s for showing too much leniency toward perpetrators of racist violence.

The judiciary has always played a major role in German government because of the state's deep involvement in political and economic matters. As we have discussed, the central state in Germany was deeply involved in industrialization, necessitating an extensive body of law to define its wide-ranging powers. Thus the German state has historically been supported by a strong legal system. The extremely close relationship between the state administration and the judiciary during the 1871–1945 period engendered many abuses. During the Second Reich, the court was used to safeguard the privileged position of those in power; for example, its failure to rule against the *Reichstag* voting system allowed a small number of landowning Prussian estate owners to hold the majority of power. During the Weimar period, the court frustrated the progress of democracy when it ruled against the workers councils' demands for increased power

within the workplace. Hitler abused the court system extensively during the Nazi regime, inducing it to make a wide range of antidemocratic, repressive, and actually criminal decisions. Among these were banning non-Nazi parties, allowing the seizure of Jewish property, and sanctioning the deaths of millions.

The Federal Republic's founders were most concerned that the new judicial system avoid these earlier abuses. One of the first requirements was that the judiciary explicitly safeguard the democratic rights of individuals, groups, and political parties, stressing some of the individual freedoms that had long been associated with American, British, and French legal systems. In fact, the Basic Law contains a more elaborate and explicit statement of individual rights than exists in either the U.S. Constitution or in British Common Law.

However, the Federal Republic's legal system differs from the Anglo-Saxon legal tradition. The Anglo-Saxon legal system is characterized by adversarial relationships between contending parties, in which the judge (or the court itself) merely provides the arena for the struggle. What emerges from these proceedings is an ad hoc system of laws. In these countries, the courts are essentially only a neutral arbiter. In continental Europe, including Germany, the legal system is based on a more codified legal system with roots in Roman law and the Napoleonic code.

In the Federal Republic, this translates into a judiciary that is an active administrator of the law rather than solely an arbiter. Specifically, judges have a different relationship with the state and with the adjudication of cases. This judicial system relies on the concept of the "capacity of the state" (as political sociologist Theda Skocpol terms it) to identify and implement certain important societal goals.[16] And if the task of the state is to create the laws to attain these goals, then the judiciary should safeguard their implementation. In both defining the meaning of very complex laws and in implementing their administration, German courts go considerably beyond those in the United States and Britain, which supposedly have avoided political decisions. The German court's role in shaping policy has been most evident in its ruling on whether to allow the unions to obtain increased co-determination rights in 1976. The court allowed the unions to obtain near parity on the boards of directors but stated that full union parity with the employers would compromise the right of private property.

The court system in the Federal Republic is three-pronged. One branch consists of the criminal-civil system, which has as its apex the Federal High Court *(Bundesgerichtshof)*. Because it is a unified rather than a federal system, it is not subject to the *Länder* governments' control. In fact, it tries to apply a consistent set of criteria to legal issues in the sixteen *Länder*. As a court of appeals, it addresses cases that have been appealed from the lower courts. the *Bundesgerichtshof* handles the range of criminal and civil issues common to most industrialized states, passes judgment on disputes among the *Länder*, and makes decisions that would be viewed in some countries as political.

The Special Constitutional Court *(Bundesverfassungsgericht)* deals with matters directly affecting the Basic Law. A postwar creation, this branch of the judiciary was founded to safeguard the new democratic political order. Precisely because of the Nazis' abuses of the judiciary under the Third Reich, the founders of the Bonn Republic (Bonn was the capital of West Germany) added an additional layer to the judiciary, basically a judicial review, to ensure that the democratic order was maintained. The most notable decisions of the Constitutional Court in the 1950s were the banning of both the ultra-right Socialist Reich Party and the leftist Communist Party as forces hostile to the Basic Law. During the early 1970s when the Radicals Decree was promulgated, the Constitutional Court ruled that several individuals who had lost their jobs were "enemies of the constitution." During the brief terrorist wave of the late 1970s when several prominent individuals were kidnapped and/or killed by the ultra-radical Red Army Fraktion (RAF), this court again was asked to pass judgment on the undemocratic actions of the terrorists. At that time, it also sanctioned a wide, indiscriminate sweep for all those who might be supporters of the RAF. In a state that claimed to be an adherent of western-style liberalism, and in one ruled by the SPD-led government, such far-reaching action alarmed many who were concerned about individual freedoms and due process.

The **Administrative Court** *(Bundesverwaltungsgericht)* is the third branch of the court system. Consisting of the Labor Court, the Social Security Court, and the Finance Court, the Administrative Court has a much narrower jurisdiction than the other two branches. Whereas the *Bundesrat,* with its regional divisions, concerns itself with the implementation of the law within geographical boundaries, the Administrative Court system concerns itself with the implementation of the law within functional boundaries. Because the state and its bureaucracy have such a prominent place in the lives of German citizens, this level of the court system acts as a corrective balance to the arbitrary power of the state bureaucracy. Compared to Britain and France, where much public policy is determined by legislation, German public policy is more often determined by the administrative actions of the bureaucracy. Through this court, citizens can challenge bureaucratic decisions—for example, if authorities improperly take action with respect to labor, welfare, or tax policies.

In the 1990s the courts have come under great pressure to resolve the intractable policy issues that unification and European integration have brought about. As they are being drawn deeper and deeper into the political thicket, they are under much more scrutiny regarding their decisions. Clandestine searches for terrorists in the late 1970s left many observers believing that the democratic rights of citizens who were unaffiliated with any terrorist organizations had been compromised. Many critics wish that today's courts would show the same diligence and zeal in addressing the crimes of neo-Nazis as the courts did in the 1970s when Germany was confronted with violence from small ultra-leftist groups. The courts' responses to the violence of the 1990s has not shown the same resolute action it did in the 1970s.

Subnational Government

There are sixteen *Länder* in the Federal Republic, eleven of which comprised the old West Germany and five the former East Germany (GDR). Among the most well-known regions are Bavaria, the Rhineland including the industrial Ruhr River valley, the Black Forest area in the southwest, and the city-states of Hamburg and Bremen. Unlike the weakly developed regional governments of Britain and France, the *Länder* of the Federal Republic enjoy both considerable autonomy and significant independent powers. Each state has a regional assembly *(Landtag),* which functions much like the *Bundestag* does at the federal level. The governor *(Minister-Präsident)* of each *Land* is the leader of the largest party (or coalition of parties) in the *Landtag* and forms a government in the *Landtag* in much the same way as does the chancellor in the *Bundestag*. Elections for each of the sixteen state elections are held on independent, staggered four-year cycles, which generally do not coincide with federal elections and only occasionally coincide with elections in other *Länder*. Like the semipublic institutions, subnational governments in Germany are powerful, significant, and responsible for much national policy implementation.

Particularly significant is Germany's marble-cake federalism in which policies developed in the *Bundestag* are often explicitly implemented by *Länder* governments. A good way to show how Germany's functional federalism works is to cite the example of industrial policy. Regional governments are much more active than the national government in planning and targeting economic policy, and therefore have greater autonomy in administering industrial policy. Precisely because the *Länder* are constituent states, they are able to develop their own regional versions of **industrial policy** *(Ordnungspolitik).* Because the different regions have different economic needs and industrial foundations, these powers are seen as legitimate and appropriate by most voters.

The *Land* governments encourage banks to direct investment and loans to stimulate industrial development in the respective *Länder*. They also encourage cooperation among regional firms, many in the same industry, to spur international competition. This coordination avoids violation of the Cartel Law of 1957 because it does not impede domestic competition. *Land* governments also invest heavily in vocational education to provide the skills needed for manufacturing high-quality goods, the core of the German economy. Organized business and organized labor also have a direct role in shaping curricula to improve worker skills via the vocational education system. These *Land* governments have enhanced industrial adaptation by qualitatively shaping the framework for adaptation, rather than adopting a heavy-handed regulatory posture.

However, the states do not pursue identical economic policies, and there have been various models of government involvement in economic policy and industrial adjustment in these regions. The specific patterns identified have included the organized yet flexible specialization of Baden-Württemberg, the twentieth-century late industrialization of Bavaria, and the managed decline and adjustment of North-Rhine Westphalia.

In the Federal Republic, state politics are organized on the same political party basis as the national parties. This does not mean that national politics dominate local politics, but instead voters are able to see the connection among local, regional, and national issues in ways that enhance both unity and diversity in the political system. Because the parties take positions and establish platforms for state and city elections, voters can discern the ideological differences between parties and not be swayed on the basis of personalities. This does not mean that personalities do not play a role in German regional politics. Rather, the nature of the party system in the Federal Republic encourages national political figures to begin their careers with service at local and regional party and government levels. Because regional and local party members' political careers are tied closely to the national, regional, and local levels of the party, there is affinity between actions taken at the various political levels. This connection in the Federal Republic among national, regional, and local politics may be one reason why voter turnout in German state elections far exceeds that of equivalent U.S. elections.

Local governments in the Federal Republic can raise revenues by owning enterprises, and there is a wide degree of local government ownership of revenue-generating enterprises. This has partly resulted from the historical patterns of public sector involvement in the economy but also from the assumption that these levels of government are the stewards of a collective public good. From the maintenance of art museums, theater companies, television and radio networks, recreational facilities, and adequate housing complexes, to various direct and indirect subsidies to citizens, these measures are seen as necessary to maintain the quality of life in modern society. Even during the recessions of the early 1980s and the early 1990s, there were remarkably few cutbacks in ownership of public enterprises or in these various types of social spending.

THE POLICY-MAKING PROCESS

Policy-making is primarily determined by the chancellor and the cabinet, but the executive does not wield arbitrary power in this area. Despite the strong executive role, the policy-making process in Germany is largely consensus-based, with contentious issues usually sharply and extensively debated within various public, semipublic, and private institutions. Although the legislature has a general role in policy-making, the primary driving force is the respective cabinet depart-ment and the experts on whom these institutions call.

If policy-making is shaped mainly through the ex-ecutive, then policy implementation is more diffuse. Along with corporatist interest groups and various semipublic organizations, the *Bundesrat* (upper house) plays a significant role in policy implementa-tion throughout the Federal Republic. Policy imple-mentation occurs in a wide range of areas, among which the most significant are vocational education, welfare, health care, and worker participation.

Many observers misunderstand exactly why and how institutions support the Federal Republic's eco-nomic policy-making process. The role that these institutions have played in the process of flexible ad-aptation to competitive pressures has enabled the Ger-man economy to outperform the economies of most other industrialized countries for most of the post–World War II period. At first glance, it seems these institutions are merely regulatory agencies that inhibit economic freedoms. A closer examination, however, reveals that German institutions regulate not the min-ute details, but the general framework. Because all economic actors are clear on the general parameters, German regulatory policy is remarkably free of the microregulations common to other countries. More-over, many policies, especially in the banking and manufacturing industries, are reinforced by industry self-regulation that makes heavy-handed government intervention unnecessary.

What components of this policy-making process actually create economic policy? First of all, corporat-ism is a *system* and not just a collection of firms and/or discrete policies. In this system, business, labor, and the government work together from the outset of the process and develop consensual policy solutions to na-tional, regional, state, and local issues. The Germans

have spoken of their "social" (not "free") market economy because of the deeply entrenched belief that business must share in the responsibility to provide a stable order, both for the economy and, indirectly, for society.

German business, labor, and government's sup-port for the framework regulations has produced a system that is often called externally rigid (in the sense of prohibiting easy entrance and exit with re-spect to firms and industry) but internally flexible (in the sense that large institutions and firms are often, to American observers, surprisingly flexible in adapting applied technologies to produce specialized goods). In short, this system regulates not the details, but the general rules of the game under which *all* actors must play.

Some would criticize such a system as being too cumbersome and inflexible. However, the Germans see a great advantage to their system in that it gener-ally produces agreement on major policy direction without major social dislocation. Once agreement has been informally worked out among all of the major parties, it is easier to move forward with specific legis-lation. This process is generally less conflict-oriented than in Britain because the German parliamentary sys-tem takes more deliberate steps to include wider sup-port among major interest groups.

This consensual system, however, has been greatly challenged recently by the extraordinary nature of unification issues, which have put this in-formal style of policy-making under tremendous pressure. Among the issues that have proved most intractable are the noneconomic issues of political asylum, racist violence, and scandals that have tar-nished reputations of major public figures, both within the political system and within major interest groups.

SECTION 4

Representation and Participation

In the aftermath of unification and European inte-gration, Germany continues to search for a synthesis between democratic participation and extraparlia-mentary opposition that is neither exclusionary nor an-tidemocratic. In short, the nation still struggles with issues surrounding collective identities. The issue of

resocializing disparate political cultures when respect for dissent and dialogue is not deeply ingrained is a dilemma for any society. However, the key issue for Germany in this regard is how to develop a system of democratic participation that encompasses both ex-trainstitutional groups and specific organized political institutions. This section examines how the Germans have attempted to reconcile these issues.

THE LEGISLATURE

The legislature occupies a prominent place in the political system with both the lower house *(Bundestag)* and upper house *(Bundesrat)* holding significant and wide-ranging powers. The Federal Republic is similar to other parliamentary regimes that have a fusion of power in which the executive branch derives directly from the legislative branch. In other words, there is not a sharply defined separation of powers between cabinet and legislature.

The electoral procedures for choosing members of the two houses differ substantially. For example, the *Bundestag* elects its members directly via the ballot in which voters choose both individual district representatives and the political parties that represent their interests. The *Bundesrat*'s members, on the other hand, are comprised of officials who are elected and/or appointed to the regional *(Länder)* governments. Both branches of the legislature are broadly representative of the major interests in German society—although some interests such as business and labor are somewhat overrepresented while ecological and noneconomic interests are somewhat underrepresented.

The executive branch introduces specific legislative proposals according to the Basic Law, which requires that legislation regarding the federal budget and taxation be initiated by the executive. Although most bills are initiated in the cabinet, this does not diminish the influence of *Bundestag* or *Bundesrat* members. In fact, because the chancellor is the leader of the major party or coalition of parties, no sharp division exists between the executive and legislative branches. There is generally strong consensus within parties and within coalitions about both the input and output of the legislative process because parties are generally ideologically coherent. Parties and coalitions that depend on party discipline to sustain majorities place a high value on agreement regarding major legislation.

When the chancellor and the cabinet propose a bill, it is sent to a relevant *Bundestag* committee. Most of the committee deliberations take place privately so that the individual committee members can have considerable latitude to shape details of the legislation. The committees will call on their own expertise, as well as that of relevant government ministries and testimony from pertinent interest groups. To some this

may appear to be a kind of insiders club, and perhaps to some degree it is. However, the committees generally call on a wide range of groups, both pro and con, that are affected by the proposed legislation. By specifically consulting the corporatist interest groups, a more consensus-oriented outcome is achieved. In contrast, countries with a more pluralist (that is, less inclusive) form of lobbying, such as Britain, experience legislative sessions that are more likely to be contentious and less likely to produce overall agreement. Under pluralism it is relatively easy for groups to articulate issues; however, lacking a uniform system of access, policy-making is more haphazard.

After emerging from committee, the bill has final readings in the *Bundestag*. Although the major parameters have already been defined, the debate in the *Bundestag* will often produce considerable criticism from the opposition and sharp defense by the governing coalition parties. The primary purpose of the debate is to educate the public about the major issues of the bill. Following passage in the *Bundestag,* a bill must be approved by the upper house, the *Bundesrat,* whose assent includes the determination of how a particular law will be implemented at the regional level.

The social composition of the legislature has been mostly male and of professional and/or middle-class orientation (even among the supposedly working-class SPD, which in the 1950s had a much greater proportion of blue-collar workers elected to the *Bundestag*). From the 1950s to the 1970s there were few women lawmakers, though this pattern began to change in the 1980s and 1990s, particularly because the Greens elected an increased number of female *Bundestag* members.[17] The addition of newer parties—such as the worker-oriented ex-communist Party of Democratic Socialism (PDS) and the continued presence of the Greens with their self-described *alternativ* life-styles—has increased the variety of backgrounds among party members. If these newer parties maintain representation in the legislature, the tendency of *Bundestag* members to share a common middle-class professional profile will diminish.

The Bundestag

Until unification, the lower house of the legislature, the *Bundestag,* consisted of 496 seats—248 elected in single-member districts and 248 elected by proportional representation from lists compiled by the political parties. After unification, owing to the representatives of the five new *Länder,* the number of seats was expanded to 663. This number, which exceeds the number of representatives in the British Parliament, caused a strain on the facilities in Bonn, because the *Bundestag* chamber was not originally built to accommodate such a large number.

The Germany parliamentary system represents a synthesis between the British and American traditions of a single legislator representing one district and the European tradition of proportional representation in which a number of party members represent a given region according to the percentage of the party's vote in that region. This unusual combination of two systems resulted from a compromise between the British and American preference for single-member districts and the prevailing German practice of multiparty representation. Single-member district voting systems tend to produce a two-party system, and Germany wanted to ensure that all major parties were represented, not just two. In practice, the German hybrid system, known as personalized proportional representation, requires citizens to cast two votes on each ballot: the first one for an individual member of a political party (usually, but not always) from the district; and the second one for a list of national/regional candidates grouped by party affiliation. This system has the effect of personalizing list voting because voters have their own representative but also can choose among several parties. To insure that only major parties are represented, only those that get 5 percent of the vote or that have three candidates who directly win individual seats, can gain representation in the *Bundestag.*

Allocation of seats by party in the *Bundestag,* however, functions more like proportional representation. Specifically, the percentage of total seats won per party corresponds strongly with the party's percentage of the popular vote (providing the party receives the 5-percent minimum to attain seats). For example, if a party's candidate wins a seat as an individual member, the candidate's party gains one less candidate from the list. In practice, most of the district seats are won by the two large parties, the Social Democrats and the Christian Democrats, because the district vote is winner-take-all. The smaller parties' representatives, however, are almost always elected through the party lists. Thus, the list system creates stronger, more coherent parties. In countries with fragmented, individualistic parties it is often difficult to gain and hold effective majorities. In contrast, Willy Brandt's SPD-

FDP coalition governments (1969–1974) had such extremely narrow margins that only strong party discipline enabled Brandt to remain in power.

Although political parties are discussed later, it is necessary to mention their general ideological coherence because each *Bundestag* member almost always votes with fellow party members. This party unity contributes to consistency in the parties' positions over the course of a four-year legislative period and enables the electorate to identify each party's stance on a range of issues. Consequently, all parties and their representatives in the *Bundestag* can be held accountable by voters based on their support for their party's positions on the issues. This party discipline, in turn, helps to produce more stable governments.

One direct result of the party discipline is that the Federal Republic has high electoral participation (80 to 90 percent at the federal level). Some observers have argued that German citizens vote in such high numbers out of habit or duty.[18] Given the remarkable stability or the voting patterns of the three main postwar parties, with little deviation in each party's electoral outcome from election to election, it is more likely that high electoral participation is due to clear party ideology. The newer parties, with similar kinds of ideological coherence, appear to confirm this. For nearly fifty years in the FRG, voting participation rates have matched or exceeded those in all other Western European countries.

The tradition of strong, unified parties in the *Bundestag* has had some drawbacks, however. The hierarchy within parties relegates newer members to a comparatively long apprenticeship as backbenchers. (Senior party members sit in the front benches of the *Bundestag,* as in other European legislatures, leaving the rear seats for newly elected members.) Some of the most prominent postwar politicians at the national level in the Federal Republic built up their visibility and political skill through long service in *Land* or local government service before launching a bid for national political power. For example, former SPD Chancellor Willy Brandt was mayor of Berlin in 1961 when the Berlin Wall was constructed; former SPD Chancellor Helmut Schmidt was mayor of Hamburg; and Helmut Kohl was for many years the dominant CDU regional official in his home *Land* of Rhineland-Palatinate.

This system educates younger members into party ideology, but it also frustrates particularly ambitious young legislators, who may become even more impatient when their party is in power because the dominance of the party elders increases at that time. The Federal Chancellery, an administrative unit comprised of the chancellor's top appointed officials, often controls the *Bundestag* by setting legislative agendas and making key policy decisions. As mentioned earlier, most bills originate with the Chancellery and the ministries, rather than with the *Bundestag* or *Bundesrat.* Thus party discipline tends to channel committee discussion well within the broad position that the party itself has taken, and the structure of the *Bundestag* discourages individual actions by legislators.

The chancellor and the party leadership can easily lose touch with the backbench members of their party. For example, Helmut Schmidt took positions—refusing to stimulate the economy and allowing the stationing of additional U.S. missiles on German soil—to which the majority of his SPD were strongly opposed in the early 1980s. Thus, when the FDP attacked Schmidt on economic issues, his own party's rank and file also criticized him. Ultimately, any leadership of a governing party that fails to respond to its parliamentary membership, its voters, or both, will likely be forced to resign or will lose in the next election.

The Bundesrat

As the upper house of the legislative branch, the *Bundesrat* occupies a position quite different than either the U.S. Senate or the British House of Lords. The *Bundesrat* is the mechanism that makes the federal system work. It is responsible for the distribution of powers between national and state levels and grants to the states the rights to implement federal laws. It is the point of intersection for the national and the state governments and is made up of members from the sixteen *Länder* governments (the eleven original ones from West Germany and the five new ones from the former GDR). The total number of seats is sixty-nine, an increase from forty-five prior to unification, with each *Land* sending at least three representatives to the *Bundesrat,* depending on its population. States with more than 2 million residents have four votes, and states with more than 6 million people have five votes.

The political composition of the *Bundesrat* at any given time is determined by which parties are governing the *Länder.* Each of the sixteen *Länder* cast their votes in a bloc, depending on the views of the party or coalition in control of the state government at the time.

Consequently, the party controlling the majority of *Länder* governments can have a significant effect on legislation passed in the *Bundestag.* And because *Länder* elections usually take place between *Bundestag* electoral periods, the *Bundesrat* majority can shift during the course of a *Bundestag* legislative period. For example, in the two years before the 1994 federal elections, the states governed by the SPD had a majority in the *Bundesrat,* making it difficult for the Kohl government to implement all of its policies.

The *Bundesrat* must approve all amendments to the constitution, as well as all laws passed in the *Bundestag* that address the fundamental interests of the *Länder,* such as taxes, territorial integrity, and basic administrative functions. It also enjoys a suspensive veto; that is, if the *Bundesrat* should vote against a particular bill, the *Bundestag* need only pass the measure again by a simple majority to override the *Bundesrat*'s veto. If, however, a two-thirds majority of the *Bundesrat* were to vote against a bill, the *Bundestag* must pass it again by a two-thirds margin. In usual practice, however, the *Bundesrat* has not acted to obstruct. When the legislation is concurrent—that is, when the state and national governments jointly share administrative responsibilities in implementation of the particular policy—there is almost always easy agreement between the two houses. Also if a party or coalition achieves a stable majority in the *Bundestag,* then any possible obstruction by the *Bundesrat* can be overcome. For example, during most of his term as chancellor, Social Democrat Willy Brandt faced a *Bundesrat* that had a one-vote majority of Christian Democrats. However, because his SPD-FDP coalition also had a slim but firm majority in the *Bundestag,* he was able to overcome the opposition on many issues and never lost a key vote.

The *Bundesrat* introduces comparatively little legislation. More bills are introduced in the *Bundestag,* though the majority of laws originate from the government itself (through one or another of the ministries). However, the *Bundesrat*'s administrative responsibilities are considerable. Most of the members of the *Bundesrat* are also *Länder* government officials who are well experienced in the implementation of particular laws. Their expertise is frequently called upon in the committee hearings of the *Bundestag,* which are open to all *Bundesrat* members. This overlapping *(Politikverflechtung)* is a unique feature of the Federal Republic. Many Americans make the mistake

---

TABLE 1   **Political Parties**

Christian Democrats (right)
   Christian Democratic Union (CDU)
   Christian Social Union (CSU)
Free Democratic Party (FDP) (center)
Social Democratic Party (SDP) (left)
Greens/*Bündnis '90* (environment)
Democratic Socialism (PDS) (formerly communist)
Republikaner (far-right)

of equating German and American federalism. However, *Politikverflechtung* provides a qualitatively different relationship between national and state governments. The Federal Republic avoids the problems of administrative jurisdiction that sometimes plague other decentralized, federal countries because many of the laws passed in the *Bundestag* are implemented at the *Land* level. As already discussed, this approach enables the national government to use fewer employees than would be the case without *Politikverflechtung,* an extremely significant contribution of German federalism.

The *Bundesrat*'s strong administrative role is a key component of the government. In different ways, this system avoids the shortcomings of both the fragmented legislative practices of the United States and the overly centralized policies of previous German governments. Because the *Bundesrat* is concerned with implementation, its role is more purposeful than that of the U.S. Congress, where laws that overlap or contradict previous legislation are frequently passed. For example, the *Bundesrat* coordinates the link between regional and national economic policies, vocational education systems, and a major television network (ARD). The *Bundesrat* tends to be closer to the concerns and needs of the entire country and provides a forum for understanding how national legislation will affect each of the sixteen *Länder.*

Although the *Bundesrat* was originally envisioned to be more technocratic and less politically contentious than the popularly elected *Bundestag,* debates in the *Bundesrat* became strongly politicized in the 1970s and 1980s. The most common occurrence was the conflict that emerged when regional elections caused a change in control of the *Bundesrat,* especially when this change gave more influence to the party, or group of parties, that was in opposition to the *Bundestag.*

THE PARTY SYSTEM AND ELECTIONS

Political Party System

Germany has a multiparty system that has proved quite stable for most of the post–World War II period. Until the early 1980s, Germany had a "two-and-a-half" party system, comprised of a moderate left Social Democratic Party (SPD), a moderate right Christian Democratic grouping (CDU in most of the FRG, CSU in Bavaria), and a small, centrist Free Democratic Party (FDP). The ideological distance between these parties was not wide. The SPD broadened its base from its core working-class constituency to include more middle-class supporters beginning in the late 1950s. The CDU/CSU is a political grouping that includes both Catholics (mostly from the Bavarian-based CSU) and Protestants. The FDP is liberal in the European sense and favors both free-market solutions to economic problems and extensive personal freedoms for individuals. With only 5–10 percent of the electorate, it is a pragmatic party and almost always chooses to ally itself with one of the two large parties to form a government. During their time as the only parties on the political landscape (1949–1983), these groups presided over a stable, growing economy with a widely mixed public/private sector agreement on economic and social policies.

During the 1980s and 1990s, three new parties emerged to challenge the "two-and-a-half" major parties (see Table 1). Their entrance into the political fray has begun to complicate Germany's comparatively tidy political landscape, and this condition promises to continue in the late 1990s. These parties are (1) the Greens/*Bündnis '90,* generally of the left and favoring ecological, environmental, and peace issues; (2) the Party of Democratic Socialism (PDS), which is the former Communist Party of East Germany; and (3) the Republicans (*Republikaner*), a sharply right-wing party, much more conservative than the CDU/CSU, which has emphasized nationalism and aggression toward immigrants and ethnic minorities. Figure 3 on the following page shows the current distribution of the parties in the legislature.

The Greens/*Bündnis '90* entered the political scene in 1979 and have won seats at national and regional levels ever since. Because of the 5-percent rule

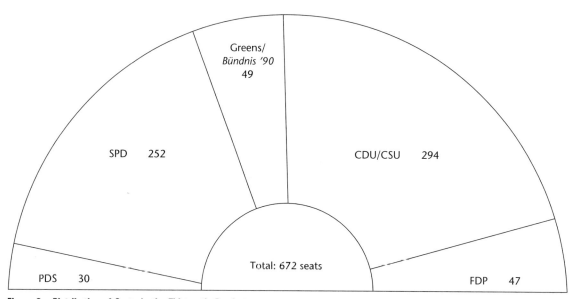

Figure 3   Distribution of Seats in the Thirteenth *Bundestag*
The Thirteenth German *Bundestag* was elected on October 16, 1994. Presently, 663 deputies represent the Federal Republic of Germany's 60.2 million voters.

(requiring parties to obtain at least 5 percent of the vote for membership in any parliamentary body), the *Republikaner* are not represented in the *Bundestag,* although the party has won seats in some local and regional bodies. The PDS is regionally concentrated in the five *Länder* of the former GDR, and while it has received as much as 20 percent of the vote in some regional and local elections, it draws well under the 5-percent mark in the states of the former West Germany.

Germany has often been called a party democracy because its parties are so important in shaping state policy. However, criticism of the major parties surfaced in the late 1980s and early 1990s due to several financial and political scandals involving members of all three of the major parties. For example, one major CDU state official was found dead in a hotel bathroom under suspicious circumstances, and former FDP officials have been subject to financial investigations. Such developments have provided increased opportunities for the new parties and could possibly disturb the relatively "tame" political party landscape.

The Christian Democrats   The Christian Democrats combine the Christian Democratic Union (CDU, in all *Länder* except Bavaria) and the Christian Social

Union (CSU, the affiliated Bavarian grouping).[19] Unlike the older parties (SPD and FDP) of the Federal Republic, the CDU/CSU originated immediately following World War II, when most nonleftist parties worked to avoid the bickering and divisiveness of the Weimar period and establish a counterweight to the SPD. The moderate leaders of the nonleftist parties feared that after the war the SPD would represent a partially united left, whereas the forces of the right were both fragmented and discredited due to the close ties between the Nazi Party and some of these conservatives. Consequently, several of the moderate conservatives proposed the creation of a Christian party grouping, which would finally unite Catholics and Protestants in one confessional (Christian) party and also serve as a catchall party of the center-right, incorporating the various nonleftist elements (including "rehabilitated" ex-Nazis).

Programmatically, the CDU/CSU stressed the *Sozialemarktwirtschaft,* Social Market Economy. The Social Market Economy favored neither a social democratic state (such as contemporary Sweden) nor a pure market economy (as expounded by the Reagan and Bush administrations in the United States and the Thatcher and Major governments in Britain). Rather, it blended elements of both forms to create a society that was capitalist, but with a paternalistic sense of social responsibility, thereby synthesizing the interests of a wide range of party supporters. The most active supporter of the market side of the equation was Adenauer's economics minister for most of the 1950s (and later chancellor), Ludwig Erhard. Favoring the social side were the Christian trade unionists whose ideology derived from a Catholic tradition that celebrated the value of human work and the Protestant work ethic.

After the SPD and FDP established their center-left coalition in 1969, the CDU/CSU spent thirteen years as the opposition party. During this period, the popularity of SPD policies and the unpopularity of the CDU/CSU leadership prevented the Christian Democrats from mounting a strong challenge to the SPD–FDP coalition. It was not until the SPD–FDP coalition collapsed in 1982 over economic policies that the CDU/CSU returned to power in coalition with the FDP. Political pundits called this *Die Wende,* the turnaround, but the Christian Democrats' return had more to do with the failings of the SPD to manage the economy, and its coalition with the FDP, than with any new ideological tendency.

Despite the electoral rhetoric about change and turnarounds, the first CDU-led Kohl government (1983–1987) made no dramatic program overtures. In fact, many observers were predicting that the stolid and colorless Kohl would either lose the next election or be challenged within his party for the chancellorship. Kohl was not an ideologue as were Margaret Thatcher in Britain and Ronald Reagan in the United States, and as a result many criticized him for his plodding, pragmatic style. How then was he able to maintain his leadership of both the CDU/CSU and the center-right coalition? It is important to stress that the nature of the German party system—in fact *any* parliamentary system—places a premium on the leader's ability to manage the party as an institution. In this task, Helmut Kohl has been the consummate CDU leader. Kohl reputedly knows the name of every Christian Democratic mayor *(Bürgermeister)* in the entire Federal Republic. It is by the mastery of such allegedly pedestrian skills as this that he maintained and reinforced his leadership of the Christian Democrats. There is, of course, nothing pedestrian about winning four consecutive federal elections.

During the mid-1980s, two additional factors helped Kohl and the CDU to retain power: one was the lack of a clear alternative position by the SPD opposition that could challenge the center-right coalition; the

other was the strong CDU/CSU position in support of strengthening European integration. Taken together, both factors enabled the Christian Democrats and Chancellor Kohl to become the dominant political forces in the Federal Republic during the early years after unification.

The problems of the 1990s have renewed some of the criticisms heard earlier about Kohl. Among those are his apparent overselling of unification and his lack of leadership to face the challenges of resurgent racism and identifying Germany's geopolitical position after the Cold War. With the end of the Cold War and the tensions surrounding European integration and German unification, some party divisions have surfaced as well. One position originates from the Bavarian CSU, led by Finance Minister Theo Waigel, and supports a more conservative policy toward immigrants and minorities. The second is a more independent position in favor of government intervention that originates in the regional CDU branches of eastern Germany. After the 1994 elections, there has been concern within the governing coalition (CDU/CSU–FDP) because the FDP only narrowly achieved the 5 percent of the vote necessary for representation. Although some Christian Democrats began to consider another Grand Coalition with the SPD, this alliance did not appear to be a realistic option by the mid-1990s.

The Free Democratic Party   The philosophy of the FDP comes closest to the individualistic ideals of British and American liberal parties.[20] (It must be emphasized again that *liberal* is used in the European context to mean an emphasis on the individual as opposed to an activist state tradition. It does *not* mean liberal in the American context, which has come to be associated primarily with an extensive welfare state.) The FDP's major influence is its role as a swing party because it has allied with each of the two major parties (SPD and CDU/CSU) at different periods since 1949. In fact, it has been included in the governing coalition for almost the entire history of the FRG. Clearly, the influence of the FDP has been disproportionate to its electoral strength of 5–10 percent of the voters. The primary reasons for the party's key position are the discrediting of the central state after the Nazi abuses, the role of the U.S. occupation forces and their preference for free-market economic arrangements, and the effects of the Cold War. These factors increased the influence of nonleftist parties among the Allied powers and the citizens of the Federal Republic, a role the FDP was happy to play.

The FDP's perspective encompasses two ideologies, broadly characterized here as economic liberalism and social liberalism. During the postwar period, the FDP has relied on two philosophies to align itself with the two major political groupings, the CDU/CSU and the SPD. In fact, the FDP has been shut out of the cabinet only twice since 1949: during the CDU/CSU majority from 1957–1961, and during the Grand Coalition from 1966–1969. Moreover, the FDP has almost always held either the Economics Ministry and/or the Foreign Ministry in the various coalition governments.

The FDP has carefully nurtured its centrist position by utilizing one or another of its political leanings to soften the ideological profile of the major party with which it is allied at the time. For example, during the latter years of the center-left Schmidt governments in the late 1970s and early 1980s, the FDP acted as a strong counterweight to the leftist economic demands made by many of the SPD's rank and file for more public spending. In fact, many of these SPD members described the FDP as the "tail that wagged the (SPD) dog." Conversely, during the center-right Kohl government after 1983, the FDP resisted the CDU/CSU's demand to increase the government's surveillance capacities over individual citizens of the Federal Republic.

By adopting a strategy of coalescing with first one major party and then the other, the FDP has occasionally been accused of lacking strong political convictions. Critics view the FDP as a small collection of notables who affiliate with the party to gain important cabinet posts. Each time this accusation is made, usually after a change of government, it seems that the FDP will so disillusion its members as to fall below the 5 percent necessary for representation in the *Bundestag*. During the early and mid-1980s, the FDP failed to reach the 5-percent minimum in several *Land* elections; however, the Federal Republic's voters have generally been reluctant to give either of the two large party groupings an absolute majority. This occurred only from 1957–1961. Voters have been induced to turn to the FDP again today as a buffer against the ideological extremes of the SPD and the CDU/CSU. Many individuals have predicted the demise of the FDP for years, but the party continues to frustrate

these predictions as evidenced during the late 1980s and early 1990s, when it took leading and forceful positions (largely thanks to the efforts of Hans-Dietrich Genscher) on European integration and German unification. By the 1994 election, the FDP was dropping badly in the preelection polls. Under the leadership of Klaus Kinkel, it survived the election with 6.9 percent of the vote, achieving the minimum necessary for representation. Yet, the FDP's electoral drop from 1990 (11 percent) was very troubling for the FDP, as well as the CDU/CSU, because the Christian Democrats needed the FDP for the governing coalition.

The Social Democratic Party As the leading party of the left in Germany, the *Sozialdemokratische Partei Deutschlands* (SPD) has had a long and durable history. The SPD was founded in the 1860s in response to rapid German (and Prussian) industrialization, survived Bismarck's attempts in the 1880s to outlaw it, and grew to be the largest party in the *Reichstag* by 1912. The party was badly split by World War I, however, with the more evolutionary wing supporting the war and the imperial German government. The revolutionary wing saw the war as an opportunity to defeat capitalism in all countries; to them, support of bourgeois governments' war efforts represented a fundamental betrayal of the international working class.[21] Following World War I, the evolutionary socialists who controlled the SPD helped it to become the leading party of the Weimar Republic during its early years. The revolutionary socialists joined either the *Kommunistische Partei Deutschlands* (KPD, Communist Party) or the short-lived independent socialists (USPD), a party that lasted only until the early 1920s. Such splits among the left-wing parties proved fatal for the SPD in the Weimar period. The lack of a united left prevented a clear response to the growing economic and social turmoil, and thereby indirectly helped the Nazis find a path to power.

When the SPD reemerged after 1945, it was initially in a strong position to play a dominant role in rebuilding Germany. Industrialists and the conservative Weimar parties had been discredited due to their relationships with the Nazis, and the SPD had retained its evolutionary commitment to both democracy and socialism. In the immediate postwar years the SPD, under the leadership of Kurt Schumacher, led the call for nationalization of industry under democratic control, the provision for a vast array of state welfare measures to rebuild the country, and a return to participatory workplace structures (i.e., the workers councils) that had been curtailed by the early Weimar governments.

Despite strong influence in postwar Germany from 1945–1948, the SPD was only able to obtain about 30 percent of the popular vote from 1949 until the early 1960s. Some critics of the SPD observed that the party's inability to achieve wider influence resulted from its continued emphasis on its working-class origins and reliance on a Marxist-based ideology. Observers more sympathetic to the SPD believed that the Cold War, the communist GDR just to the east, and the economic miracle of the 1950s all helped to reduce the party's influence. In any event, the SPD was politically marginal in the 1950s. The party formed municipal governments in a few of the major cities and regional governments in several traditionally strong northwestern *Länder* but exercised little national influence.

In an attempt to broaden its constituency, the SPD altered its party program at a 1959 party conference in Bad Godesberg. Abandoning its solid stance on Marxism, its new goal was to become what political scientist Otto Kirchheimer has called a "catchall party."[22] The SPD neither relinquished Marxism completely nor ceased to be a party representing the working class, but it began to seek and attract support from groups outside the traditional blue-collar working class. Among these were service sector workers, elements of the middle class, professional employees, and defectors from the Free Democrats or Christian Democrats. The Bad Godesberg conference transformed the SPD into a party similar to other Western European social democratic parties.

The SPD finally won a place as the leading member of a majority coalition in 1969. It increased its share of the vote to 42.7 percent and could thus propose a new coalition government with the FDP, which had received 5.8 percent of the vote. (Although the two parties together had less than 50 percent of the popular vote, they attained a bare majority of the apportioned *Bundestag* seats after the smaller parties with fewer than 5 percent of the vote were discounted). The center-left SPD–FDP coalition appeared shaky at first (it had a slim majority until its reelection in 1972), but it was able to stay in power for thirteen years.[23] The SPD brought to the coalition a

concern for increased welfare and social spending, partially because of pressure by the APO (the extraparliamentary opposition), and the FDP brought its support for increased individual freedom of expression at a time when youths in all industrialized societies were seeking a greater voice. The principal factor cementing the interests of these two dissimilar parties for such a long time was the strong performance of the Federal Republic's economy. In fact, the coalition did not break up until the early 1980s when an economic recession prevented the increased social spending demanded by the SPD left. The downturn also induced the FDP to define individualism less in terms of free expression and more in terms of an antistatist, free-market economic position.

During the 1980s and 1990s when the SPD was out of power, it failed to (1) formulate clear alternative policies to make itself attractive to its members, supporters, and voters; (2) forge a durable coalition with the Greens to challenge the center-right coalition; (3) develop positions on European integration that would induce supporters to turn in the party's direction; or (4) take advantage of the opportunity to capture support in the former GDR during and after the unification process. After the 1994 *Bundestag* elections, the SPD remained uncertain about what kind of party it was. It continued to agonize over whether to reemphasize its working-class roots and perhaps garner support from the PDS in the east, or find some new synthesis of positions that could blunt the Greens' rising support. Its electoral support remained stuck in the upper 30-percent range. Options for the SPD seemed limited. They could attempt to reach out to either the Greens or the PDS, but then the Christian Democrats would accuse them of moving left. On the other hand, some suggested the idea of another Grand Coalition with the Christian Democrats, but, as in the late 1960s, that option might generate greater support for the smaller parties because they would be the only opposition to such a Grand Coalition. Both alternatives seemed unworkable by the mid-1990s.

The Greens   The Greens Party (now merged with the former East German *Bündnis '90*) is a heterodox party that first drew support from several different constituencies in the early 1980s: urban-based **Citizens Action Groups** *(Bürgerinitiativen);* ecological activists; rural farmers; anti–nuclear-power activists; the remnants of the peace movement; and small bands of

The New and the Old Left: The Greens and the SPD

Greens parties concerned with environmental protection have sprung up in the past ten to fifteen years in all industrialized countries, particularly those of Western Europe. In most countries they emerged to challenge Social Democratic and Labor parties for support of the democratic left. In general, the Greens are less concerned with working-class material issues than with "post-material" ones. The most famous of the Green parties has been Germany's and, not surprisingly, it has had an uneasy relationship with the larger left-wing party, the SPD.

Green Party activists and members come from disparate roots, but all share the belief that the dominant left-wing SPD has become too bureaucratic and unwilling to address the concerns of the rank-and-file members of the party. Some ex-members of the SPD resented the removal of left-wing activists from the civil service in the early 1970s under the SPD chancellorship of Willy Brandt. Brandt later regretted this action and often referred to the Greens as the "SPD's lost children," meaning that their rank-and-file activism was lost to the SPD. Brandt felt this loss denied the SPD the vitality it badly needed to challenge the Christian Democrats more effectively as the leading party in Germany.

Yet the Greens have not faded from the political scene, and after their political uncertainty in the immediate post-unification period, they have found new support among the population. By the mid-1990s they had emerged as the third-largest party in the Federal Republic, achieving between 10–12 percent in opinion polls while the traditional "third" party, the centrist FDP, has struggled with the 5 percent electoral threshold for representation in German parliamentary bodies.

The relationship between the Greens and the SPD is important because if there is to be an alternative to a center right coalition under Christian Democratic leadership, it most certainly would have to include these two parties.

The Greens continue to see the SPD as too bureaucratic and wedded to a belief in economic growth without sufficient concern for ecological issues. Most members of the SPD view the Greens as a rag-tag group of people pursuing "alternative life-styles" with little understanding of the responsibility required to govern the largest Western European country.

There have been several attempts to form a Red-Green coalition at the *Land* (state) level, the most long-lasting being the coalition in the state of Hesse, where Frankfurt is the largest city. This coalition fell apart on the issue of economic growth versus ecology, and many observers feel that a coalition between the Greens and the SPD at the national level would struggle between these sometimes incompatible goals.

Can advanced industrialized states combine a strong economy with environmental sensitivity? The Greens and the Social Democrats of Germany are a good test case to observe.

Marxist-Leninists. After overcoming the 5-percent hurdle in the 1983 *Bundestag* elections, the party went on to win seats in most *Länder* in subsequent regional elections by stressing noneconomic, quality-of-life issues. The electoral successes of this "anti-party party" generated a serious division within the party, between the *realos* (realists), and the *fundis* (fundamentalists). In the mid-1980s, the realists, who pragmatically believed it was important to enter political institutions to gain access to power, won the upper hand over the fundamentalists who opposed any collaboration with existing parties, even if the allegiance meant some Greens' goals could be attained.

Even though the realists were more pragmatic, there was still no guarantee of long-term success for the Greens because all of the other parties began to include environmental and qualitative issues in their party programs. They were successful in continuing to win seats in regional and local elections. Moreover, with the *Bündnis '90* merger, making the 5 percent hurdle in federal elections seemed assured for the foreseeable future. However, the Greens' position and direction remained uncertain in the 1990s. Like the SPD, the Greens were caught off guard by the process of European integration and especially by the rapid move toward German unification during 1990. Many Greens Party members were opposed to both of these developments, and the party lost strength as the twin processes of unification proceeded.

Until the merger with the *Bündnis '90*, the Greens' position looked bleak. The party's squabbling about *fundi* or *realo* positions undercut their credibility among potential new voters. Its inability to grasp the seriousness of unification and thus develop positions to deal with the end of the two German states made the party appear unwilling to deal with reality. The ability of other parties to address what had formerly been labeled "Green" issues, such as the environment, made their specific appeal less distinctive. Last, the Greens' failure to motivate its own core constituency ultimately proved the party's undoing. As shown in Table 2 on pages 214 and 215, electoral turnout for general elections in the Federal Republic has averaged between 84 and 90 percent for every election between 1953 and

1987. However, electoral turnout for the 1990 federal election reached only 78 percent and in 1994 was up slightly to 79 percent. Several postelection analyses found that a disproportionate share of the nonvoters were previously Greens' supporters. A further embarrassment to the party in 1990 was the success of *Bündnis '90* in attaining seats by virtue of obtaining 6.0 percent of the vote in the former GDR *Länder.* Before the general election, the western Greens had spurned an offer from *Bündnis '90* to run a joint ticket. Had the Greens done so, the Green alliance would have won 5.1 percent of the vote on an all-German basis, enough for representation in the *Bundestag.* It was this embarrassment for the Greens Party that eventually led to its merger with *Bündnis '90.*

The persistent ecological problems of the five *Länder* from the former GDR have presented the Greens a tremendous opportunity to gain strength. With the merger of the Greens and *Bündnis '90* in 1993, a Green alternative appeared certain to have a position in parliament for the foreseeable future. In the 1994 elections, however, the Greens attained a somewhat disappointing 6 percent of the vote after preelection polls had placed them closer to 10 percent. Still, 6 percent gave the party a firm base, and it is likely to remain a permanent fixture in the German *Bundestag.*

The Party of Democratic Socialism—PDS   The PDS (the former Communist Party in the GDR, known as the SED, *Sozialistische Einheits Partei,* or Socialist Unity Party) is a new party concentrated in the former GDR, even though in fact it has had a long and volatile history. It sprang from the *Kommunistische Partei Deutschlands* (KPD), which was founded after World War I, during the stage of the Russian Revolution when all socialist and labor parties split on the issue of evolutionary or revolutionary socialism. The Communist Party (KPD) split from the Social Democratic Party (SPD) in 1919 following the success of the Russian Revolution and continually attacked the SPD until both were outlawed and suppressed by the Nazis.

Following World War II, the KPD reappeared only briefly in West Germany and eventually disappeared in 1956, banned by the Constitutional Court. Several factors were responsible for its demise. Prior to Hitler's rise to power in 1933, a major area of the KPD's support was in the northeastern part of Germany. After World War II, this area became the Ger-

man Democratic Republic. The newly defined West Germany supplied a much smaller constituency for the KPD. In addition, the onset of the Cold War in the late 1940s seriously eroded the KPD's support in West Germany, although the party did receive 5.7 percent of the vote in the Federal Republic's first election in 1949. However, the intensity of the postwar anticommunist thrust was particularly damaging to the KPD in West Germany. West German leaders took advantage of anticommunist feelings to propagandize against communism and the party's support diminished continually until banned by the Constitutional Court.

After the ban, some members of the KPD organized themselves as the German Communist Party (DKP, or *Deutsche Kommunistische Partei),* but the new Communist Party received even less support than the KPD. In 1968 the ban on the KPD was lifted, and its name was appropriated by Maoists and the "new left." It had a brief period of influence during the social turbulence of the late 1960s. The new KPD split in the early 1970s, and a Marxist-Leninist KPD also appeared. By the late 1970s, there were numerous tiny communist parties and sects, none of which came close to achieving even 5 percent of the electoral vote (although most of these tiny parties regularly contested elections). By the early 1980s, many of the sects had officially disappeared, with many former members gravitating to the Greens and occupying a minority wing within that fledgling party.

In the GDR, on the other hand, the KPD had a very different history. In the late 1940s, the KPD flourished in the Soviet zone and under USSR acquiescence forced a merger with the SPD, which had also sprung up after the war in an area of traditional party strength. The name of the merged Communist party was the SED. This party, which dominated all aspects of life in the GDR under the leadership of Walter Ulbricht, Willi Stoph, and Erik Honnecker, was considered the most Stalinist and repressive of the Soviet client Communist parties. During the 1980s, elements in the SED favored establishing a dialogue with elements of the SPD in the Federal Republic.[24] Some of the rapprochement built on the legacy of Willy Brandt's *Ostpolitik* forged in the 1970s, but such attempts to broaden SED contacts and appear less repressive ultimately proved unsuccessful. Thus in 1990 as the process of unification continued, the SED quickly changed its name to the PDS. Under the leadership of Gregor Gysi, the PDS showed considerable

TABLE 2   **FRG Election Results, 1949–1994**

Year	Party	% of Vote	Government
1949	CDU/CSU	31.0	CDU/CSU-FDP
	SPD	29.2	
	FDP	11.9	
	Others	27.8	
	Voter Turnout	78.5	
1953	CDU/CSU	45.2	CDU/CSU-FDP
	SPD	28.8	
	FDP	9.5	
	Others	16.7	
	Voter Turnout	86.0	
1957	CDU/CSU	50.2	CDU/CSU
	SPD	31.8	
	FDP	7.7	
	Others	10.3	
	Voter Turnout	87.8	
1961	CDU/CSU	45.3	CDU/CSU-FDP
	SPD	36.2	
	FDP	12.8	
	Others	5.7	
	Voter Turnout	87.8	
1965	CDU/CSU	47.6	CDU/CSU-SDP
	SPD	39.3	(The Grand Coalition)
	FDP	9.5	
	Others	3.6	
	Voter Turnout	86.8	
1969	CDU/CSU	46.1	SPD-FDP
	SPD	42.7	
	FDP	5.8	
	Others	5.4	
	Voter Turnout	86.7	
1972	SPD	45.8	SPD-FDP
	CDU/CSU	44.9	
	FDP	9.5	
	Others	16.7	
	Voter Turnout	86.0	
1976	CDU/CSU	48.2	SPD-FDP
	SPD	42.6	
	FDP	7.9	
	Others	0.9	
	Voter Turnout	90.7	

immediate strength in the five *Länder* of the former GDR, winning between 9 and 15 percent of the vote during the October 14, 1990 *Landtag* elections and 11.1 percent of the vote in these same *Länder* for first all-German elections on December 2, 1990. The new PDS was plagued, however, by the legacy of corruption and wasteful extravagance under the Honnecker regime, and the secret transfer of millions of DM to the Soviet Union *after* unification had occurred in October 1990.

Year	Party	% of Vote	Government
	TABLE 2	**FRG Election Results, 1949–1994 (continued)**	
1980	CDU/CSU	44.5	SPD-FDP
	SPD	42.9	
	FDP	10.6	
	Others	0.5	
	Voter Turnout	88.6	
1983	CDU/CSU	48.8	CDU/CSU-FDP
	SPD	38.2	
	FDP	7.0	
	Greens	5.6	
	Others	0.5	
	Voter Turnout	89.1	
1987	CDU/CSU	44.3	CDU/CSU-FDP
	SPD	37.0	
	FDP	9.1	
	Greens	8.3	
	Others	1.3	
	Voter Turnout	84.3	
1990	CDU/CSU	43.8	CDU/CSU-FDP
	SPD	33.5	
	FDP	11.0	
	Greens	3.8	
	PDS	2.4	
	Bündnis '90	1.2	
	Others	3.5	
	Voter Turnout	78.0	
1994	CDU/CSU	41.5	CDU/CSU-FDP
	SPD	36.4	
	FDP	6.9	
	Greens	7.3	
	PDS	4.4	
	Others	3.5	
	Voter Turnout	79.0	

Source: German Information Center, 1990 and 1994.

By the mid-1990s the difficulties of unification had helped to renew the strength of the PDS. In regional and local elections in eastern Germany, it attained over 20 percent of the vote and won four directly elected seats in the 1994 federal election. The winning of four individual seats on the first ballot gave the party representation in the *Bundestag* even though its overall voting percentage on the second ballot fell just under the 5 percent threshold. Thus the PDS has remained a strong force in German politics. During 1994 it formed a coalition government with the SPD in the *Land* of Saxony (a phenomenon that has caused the Christian Democrats to resurrect some of their anticommunist rhetoric of the 1950s and 1960s). The adverse economic conditions of Saxony combined with PDS strength would seem to prevent this "red socks" coalition, as it is called in the German press, from ever serving as a model for a national coalition. To some observers, the most interesting development regarding the PDS is that it is not a "communist" party any more. Rather it has become a regionally based party beseeching the national government for greater resources. In this sense, it seems to be a left-wing, eastern German mirror image of the right-wing, Bavarian-based CSU.

Stimmzettel

für die Wahl zum Deutschen Bundestag im Wahlkreis 136 Kreisfreie Stadt Wiesbaden am 2. Dezember 1990

Sie haben 2 Stimmen

hier 1 Stimme
für die Wahl
eines / einer Wahlkreis-
abgeordneten

Erststimme

hier 1 Stimme
für die Wahl
einer Landesliste (Partei)
- maßgebende Stimme für die Verteilung der
Sitze insgesamt auf die einzelnen Parteien -

Zweitstimme

	Erststimme			Zweitstimme	
1	**Rönsch,** Hannelore Angestellte **CDU** Christlich 6200 Wiesbaden Demokratische Carl-von-Ossietzky-Str. 38 Union Deutschlands	○	○	**CDU** Christlich Demokratische Union Deutschlands Dr. Alfred Dregger, Hannelore Rönsch, Dr. Christian Schwarz-Schilling, Dr. Heinz Riesenhuber, Bernhard Jagoda	1
2	**Wieczorek-Zeul,** Heidemarie Lehrerin Sozialdemokratische 6200 Wiesbaden **SPD** Partei Walkmühlstraße 39 Deutschlands	○	○	**SPD** Sozialdemokratische Partei Deutschlands Heidemarie Wieczorek-Zeul, Rudi Walther, Dr. Dietrich Sperling, Uta Zapf, Karsten Voigt	2
3	**Koch,** Ulrich Friedrich Sozialarbeiter 6200 Wiesbaden **GRÜNE** DIE GRÜNEN Feldstraße 27	○	○	**GRÜNE** DIE GRÜNEN Ulrike Riedel, Hubert Kleinert, Marina Steindor, Dietrich Wetzel, Freya Klier	3
4	**Dr. Funke-Schmitt-Rink,** Margret Studienrätin Freie 6200 Wiesbaden **F.D.P.** Demokratische Sonnenberger Straße 3 Partei	○	○	**F.D.P.** Freie Demokratische Partei Dr. Hermann Otto Prinz zu Solms Hohensolms-Lich, Hans-Joachim Otto, Dr. Gisela Babel, Ekkehard Gries, Dr. Heinrich Kirff	4
			○	**DIE GRAUEN** DIE GRAUEN Initiiert vom Senioren-Schutz-Bund „Graue Panther" e.V. („SSB-GP") Ludwig Neise, Sibylle Schönig, Karl Roth, Dr. Hildegard Mulert, Arno Hildebrandt	5
6	**Langer,** Herbert Prokurist 6200 Wiesbaden **REP** DIE REPUBLIKANER Sonnenberger Str. 27	○	○	**REP** DIE REPUBLIKANER Gert Feldmeier, Herbert Langer, Brigitte Kleinert, Peter Munch, Günter Hamer	6
7	**Deubert,** Ernst Wilhelm Rentner National- 6000 Frankfurt/Main 60 **NPD** demokratische Bergerstraße 234 Partei Deutschlands	○	○	**NPD** Nationaldemokratische Partei Deutschlands Winfried Krauß, Dons Zutt, Hans Schmidt, Dieter Fuhrmann, Volker Sachs	7
			○	**ÖDP** Ökologisch-Demokratische Partei Gerhard Mahnke, Waltraud Schunck, Monika Zickwolff, Dr. Wolfgang Günther, Rolf-Dewet Klar	8
			○	**PDS/ Linke Liste** Partei des Demokratischen Sozialismus/Linke Liste Manfred Coppik, Angela Knol, Heike Schmuser, Manfred Alter, Reinhold Rückert	9

Figure 4 1990 *Bundestag* Election Ballot
With their "first vote," voters from the Bonn electoral district can choose a candidate by name from the lefthand column. The "second vote" in the righthand column is cast for a party list at the federal level.

The Republikaner The *Republikaner* Party was formed in the late 1980s when increasing numbers of non-Germans began arriving in Germany at the start of European integration. There had been various splinter group right-wing parties throughout the Federal Republic's history, but with the exception of the National Party of Germany (NPD) which received 4.3 percent of the vote in 1966, they had never seriously threatened to win seats in the *Bundestag*.[25] The *Republikaner*'s strength in local and regional elections in 1989 suggested that this right-wing party might finally break through the 5 percent threshold.

But the pace at which the Kohl government had conducted the unification process in the early 1990s had a devastating impact on the far-right *Republikaner* and its leader, former Nazi SS soldier Franz Shön-

huber. In effect, Kohl's speedy and comparatively pragmatic process of unification had stolen the very essence of the *Republikaner* appeal. Much the way the Greens complained that the other parties were stealing their issues—that is, embracing Green issues within their own party platforms—the *Republikaner* found their primary goals of curtailed asylum and restrictions on immigration had already been achieved without their input or influence. However, as the difficulties of European integration and German unification intensified in the mid-1990s, the *Republikaner* became a safe political outlet for the neo-Nazi sentiments that people did not publicly admit. In elections during 1992 and 1993, the *Republikaner* continually surpassed its preelection predictions because some of the party's voters did not tell pollsters how they would actually vote.

In the mid-1990s this far-right party threatened to achieve the 5 percent threshold necessary for *Bundestag* representation. The ongoing difficulties of unification present a major advantage to the *Republikaner* because one of the party's primary appeals is to citizens in both the eastern and the western parts of the Federal Republic who support a resurgent German nationalism to counter the rising tide of internationalism represented by European integration. Prior to the 1994 elections, the party seemed to be taking advantage of Kohl's drift and indecisiveness on issues such as political asylum, immigration, racism, and taming the renewed nationalist impulses. Because the Kohl government was perceived as lacking direction in the 1990s, most observers felt the *Republikaner* could be a serious threat to Kohl and the Christian Democrats. However, the 1994 elections were a disaster for the *Republikaner:* They garnered less than 1.7 percent of the vote. Once again another party had underestimated Helmut Kohl's ability to undercut its positions.

Electoral Procedure and Results

As mentioned in the section on the *Bundestag,* Germany has two ballot electoral systems requiring voters to cast ballots for individual members in their district and also to cast ballots for the party list of their choice at the federal level (see Figure 4). Seats are awarded in a proportional representation system corresponding to the percentage of the votes as long as parties attain a minimum of 5 percent of the popular vote, or win at least three seats on the first ballot, as the PDS did in 1994. This system has produced two significant outcomes. First is a coherence among the parties because the electoral system, as well as the constitutional system, specifically supports the parties as essential institutions for political democracy. Second, the 5 percent hurdle ensures that only parties that command sufficient support attain seats in the *Bundestag*. This has helped Germany avoid the wild proliferation of parties that plagues some democracies, such as Italy and Israel, and that has made coalition formation extremely difficult.

As Table 2 suggests, Germany has been a country without volatile electoral swings. There have been three major periods of party dominance since 1949: CDU/CSU (with FDP) from 1949–1966; Grand Coalition interregnum (1966–1969); SPD-led coalition (1969–1982); and CDU/CSU–led coalition (1982–present). However, with the proliferation of three new parties in the past ten years, this might change significantly in the late-1990s.

POLITICAL CULTURE, CITIZENSHIP, AND IDENTITY

With political parties representing such a broad ideological spectrum, there is wide-ranging political debate in Germany. This diversity is reflected in the media, where newspapers have a similarly wide ideological reach in their appeal to a broad spectrum of political opinion. The major print media range from the mass-market tabloid *Bild Zeitung* (literally, picture newspaper) on the right, to more conservative and liberal broadsheet newspapers such as *Die Welt* of Hamburg, the *Süddeutscher Zeitung* of Munich, and the *Frankfurter Allgemeine Zeitung,* to the *Frankfurter Rundschau,* which is close to the SPD in its editorial positions, to the *TAZ* of Berlin, which is closest to the Greens in its editorial positions. There is now a wide variety of private TV cable channels, but the three main networks are public channels and they are careful to provide a proportional balance of major party positions. The prevailing pattern on the public channels during the two-month electoral campaigns until recently has been to prohibit paid TV campaign commercials. Instead the networks present one- or two-hour-long roundtable discussions in which all parties participate in debates. This approach has prevented the bigger and richer parties from buying a larger share of the popular vote, although recently some parties have advertised on the private channels.

This wide variety of public opinion has helped dispel the view that Germany's high voting turnout rate was due to a sense of duty and not to any real commitment to democracy.[26] Perhaps during the Weimar years, and certainly during the period of the Second Reich (1871–1918), the commitment to democracy in Germany was suspect. However, the post–World War II period contains examples that sharply challenge the perceptions that Germans participate in politics only out of a sense of duty. A close look within German society reveals evidence of a strong participatory ethic among the democratic left in the form of various opportunities for participation at the workplace such as corporatism, co-determination, and the works councils that exist in virtually all firms. Moreover, one of the primary appeals in the formation of the Greens has been its emphasis on increased **grassroots democracy**—that is, rank-and-file democratic participation (called *Basisdemokratie* in German).[27] The strength of the Greens—and now the PDS and *Republikaner*—has forced the traditional parties to develop more focused attempts to mobilize their supporters and potential supporters.

Germany's educational system has also changed since the Federal Republic was created, particularly in terms of the socialization of German citizens. The catalyst was the student movement in the university system during the 1960s. At that time, the university system was elitist and restrictive and did not offer sufficient critical analysis of Germany's bloody twentieth-century history. Not only did the student mobilizations of the 1960s open up the educational system to a wider socioeconomic spectrum, it also caused many of the so-called '68 Generation (1968 was the year of the most significant demonstrations) to challenge their parents about attitudes shaped by the Nazi period and before. Even in the 1990s, many critics of the German educational system argue that some of the older attitudes toward non-Germans remain and that the educational system should increase its efforts to build an educated and tolerant citizenry.

Attitudes toward Germany's Social Market Economy also enjoy broad acceptance among most Germans, with the possible exceptions of isolated minority positions on the extreme left and right. The Social Market Economy provides benefits to almost all segments of the population, including public transit, subsidies for the arts, virtually free higher and vocational education, among many others. Thus there is a general tolerance for a wide variety of political and artistic opinion and very little of the squabbling and acrimony over public funding of the arts that is common in some other countries.

Some of the optimistic views that Germany has become a typical parliamentary democracy have been challenged by anti-ethnic and anti-immigrant violence in the late 1980s and early to mid-1990s. The attacks on foreign immigrants, including guestworker *(Gastarbeiter)* families who have lived in Germany for more than thirty years, have raised questions among some observers regarding the degree of German toleration. Owing to Germany's repressive history toward Jews and all non-Germans during the first half of the twentieth century, such concerns must be taken extremely seriously. Even more disturbing to many is the Kohl government's lack of leadership and the apathy, in some cases enthusiasm, of some in not attacking the intolerant violence of the 1990s. Although Germany is not alone among industrialized nations in racist violence, its history brings German citizens the burden to confront and overcome any display of intolerance if it is to gain the world's respect as a decent nation.

The nature of citizenship, democracy, and participation in Germany remains problematic. As discussed in Section 1, Germany has chosen a restrictive position on immigration. Although immigrant workers have generally fared better in German society than those non-Germans outside the protection of organized worker representation and the political parties of the democratic left, this workplace representation does not address the citizenship issue. Unlike many other European nations, Germany makes it difficult for nonethnic Germans to be naturalized, no matter how long they have lived in the country, and denies citizenship to children of noncitizens born on German soil. This policy has become exacerbated by the end of the Cold War and the demise of the USSR. For example, ethnic Germans whose ancestors had not lived in Germany for centuries were allowed to enter Germany legally and assume citizenship rights immediately. Yet the *Gastarbeiter* who had lived in Germany for decades, some at the express invitation of the German governments of the 1960s, were denied such opportunities for instant citizenship.*

Perhaps the most contentious citizenship/identity issue has surrounded the political asylum question, a theme introduced in the first section. Following World War II, Germany passed one of the world's most liberal political asylum laws, in part to help atone for the Nazis' political repression of millions. With the end of the Cold War and the opening up of Eastern European borders, the trickle of asylum-seekers turned into a flood in the minds of some Germans. This influx drove the Kohl government to curtail drastically the right of political asylum, a step that questioned whether German democracy was as mature and well developed as it claimed during the stable postwar period. Germany's commitment to democratic rights appeared to contain some new conditions, and many of them involved a definition of identity that looked remarkably insular in a Europe that was in other respects becoming more international.[28]

INTERESTS, SOCIAL MOVEMENTS, AND PROTEST

In regard to the organization of interests, social movements, and the politics of collective identity, Germany remains a country of organized collectivities. This is true of the major economic producer groups, the political parties (in which real, participatory membership is high), and social groups. Germany has never been a country with a strong individualistic ethos.

From the descriptions of organized business and organized labor in the previous section, it is clear that interest groups in Germany operate differently than they do in Anglo-Saxon countries. In the Federal Republic, interest groups are seen as having a societal role and responsibility that transcend the immediate interests of their members. Germany's public law traditions, which derive from Roman and Napoleonic legal foundations, specifically allow private interests to perform public functions, albeit within a clearly specified general framework. Thus interest groups are seen as part of the fabric of society and are virtually permanent institutions. This view places a social premium on their adaptation and response to new issues. To speak of winners and losers in such an arrangement is to misunderstand the ability of existing interest groups to make incremental changes over time.

---

* Turkish *Gastarbeiter* are disadvantaged because if they accept German citizenship, they generally surrender property rights in Turkey.

Strikes and demonstrations on a wide range of economic and noneconomic issues do occur, but rather than being seen as signs of a failure of the institutions, they should be counted as evidence of success. Political institutions sometimes are mistakenly seen as fixed structures that are supposed to prevent and/or repress dissent or controversy. A more positive way to analyze such conflicts is to take a new institutionalist approach. This theory argues that political organizations shape and adapt to social and political protest and channel such action in ways that are not detrimental to democratic participation, but in fact represent its essence.[29]

This distinction has direct implications for the role of interest groups in the Federal Republic. Rather than encouraging fractious competition, this system creates a bounded framework within which interest groups will struggle tenaciously, yet eventually come to an agreement on policy. Moreover, because they are encouraged to aggregate the interests of all members of their association, their policy total (the general interest of the group as a whole) will be greater than the sum of its parts (the aggregated concerns of individual members). By their structural integration into the fabric of society, interest groups have an institutional longevity that surpasses the duration of interest groups in most other industrialized countries. But how does the German state mediate the relationship among interest groups?

Peter Katzenstein observes that in the Federal Republic, "the state is not an actor but a series of relationships," and these relationships are solidified in what he has called "para-public institutions."[30] The para-publics encompass a wide variety of organizations, among which the most important are the *Bundesbank,* the institutions of co-determination, the labor courts, the social insurance funds, and the employment office. Under prevailing German public law, which is rooted in pre-1871 feudal traditions, they have been assigned the role of "independent governance by the representatives of social sectors at the behest of or under the general supervision of the state." In other words, German organizations, seen as mere interest groups in other countries, are combined with certain "quasi-government agencies" to fill a "para-public" role in the Federal Republic.

Employer associations and trade unions are the key interest groups within German soci-

ety.* Other, less influential, groups include the Protestant and Catholic churches, the Farmers Association *(Deutscher Bauernverband,* or DBV), the Association of Artisans *(Handwerk Verein),* the Federal Chamber of Physicians *(Bundesaerztekammer),* and the now nearly defunct League of Expelled Germans *(Bund der Vertriebenen Deutschen,* or BVD), which has represented the interests of emigrants from the GDR and Eastern Europe. Each of these groups has been tightly integrated into various para-public institutions to perform a range of essential social functions that in other countries might be performed by state agencies. These organizations must assume a degree of social responsibility, via their roles in policy implementation, which goes beyond what political scientist Arnold Heidenheimer has called the "freewheeling competition of 'selfish' interest groups."[31]

For example, through the state the churches assess a church tax on all citizens born into either the Protestant or Catholic churches. This provides the churches with a steady stream of income, assuring them institutional permanence while compelling them to play a major role in the provision of social welfare and aid to the families of *Gastarbeiter* (guestworkers). The Farmers Association has been a pillar of support for both the FDP and the CDU/CSU and has for decades strongly influenced the agricultural ministry. It has also resisted the attempts by the European Union to lower the agricultural support provided by the Common Market to European farmers in the form of direct subsidies as part of the EU's common agricultural policy. The Association of Artisans is a major component of the DIHT (the German Chamber of Commerce, to which all firms in Germany *must* belong), and the Chamber of Physicians has been intimately involved with the legislation and implementation of social and medical insurance (i.e., social security and general welfare).

These interest groups and the para-public agencies within which they function attempt to limit social

---

* German industry is represented by the BDI (Federal Association of German Industry) and employers are represented by the BDA (Federal Association of German Employers). The former addresses issues pertaining to industry as a whole, whereas the latter focuses specifically on issues of concern to employers. German workers are represented by sixteen different unions, organized by industry, which belong to the DGB (German Trade Union Confederation).

Demonstration in Solingen after the firebombing of a single-family house in which five Turkish women and children were killed. The sign says, "Yesterday it was the Jews, today it is the foreigners, will we be it tomorrow?"
Source: © Ullstein Bilderdienst.

conflict by means of multiple, small-scale corporatist institutions. The Federal Republic's corporatist variant in the 1980s was much more regionalized and industry-specific and much less centralized than earlier national-level manifestations of corporatism. This interest group/para-public system is subject to the same problems that have plagued macrolevel corporatism in other, more centralized industrial societies such as Sweden and France; that is, it must express the concerns of member organizations, channel the conflict, and recommend (and sometimes implement) public policy. If the system fails and conflict is allowed to go unresolved, the effectiveness of the institutions is questioned and some elements of society may go unrepresented. A partial failure of certain interest groups and institutions led to the rise of a series

of social movements during the 1960s and 1970s, particularly around university reform, wage negotiations, and foreign policy. The very existence of the Greens Party in the 1980s and 1990s is a prime example of a movement that responded to the inability of existing institutions to address, mediate, and solve certain contentious issues.

Until recently, extrainstitutional participation and protest have left few outside the political arena. Those who are outside belong to political groups that fail to meet the 5-percent electoral threshold. The *Republikaner* belongs in this category as well as other right-wing groups. Likewise the substantial Turkish population, comprising 2.3 percent of Germany's inhabitants, might be included here. Many have now resided in Germany for decades after first arriving as guestworkers. Unlike *Gastarbeiter* from EU countries (like Italy and Spain), Turkish residents have fewer rights in Germany. Finally, the once-active leftist community of revolutionary Marxists still retains a small presence, mostly in large cities and university towns. Some of these left-wing parties contest elections, but they never get more than 1 percent of the vote.

Since the student mobilizations of the late 1960s, Germany has witnessed considerable protest and mobilization of social forces outside the established channels of political and social representation. Among the most significant social forces in the postwar FRG have been feminists, the peace movement, and the antinuclear movement. All three groups, in different ways, challenged fundamental assumptions about German politics and the inability of the institutional structure to respond to the needs and issues represented by these groups. From opposition to a restrictive abortion law in the 1970s, to demonstrations against the stationing of nuclear missiles on

German soil in the 1980s, and regular protests against nuclear power plants since the 1970s, the spirit of direct action has animated German politics in ways that were not possible in the years before the late 1960s.

The 1990s, however, have witnessed less protest from the left than from the right. Illegal neo-Nazi groups have been responsible for racist attacks. Significantly, all of these attacks by the right-wing fringe have been met with spontaneous, peaceful marches of anywhere from 200,000 to 500,000 people in various cities. This reaction suggests that social protest, as a part of an active democratic political discourse, has matured in the face of this new threat from the right. As we stated in the beginning of this section, the challenge for German politics is to maintain a system of democratic participation that encompasses both extra-institutional groups and specific organized political institutions in a way that enhances democracy rather than destroys it.

SECTION 5
German Politics at the Crossroads

It will now be instructive to review the two images of German politics described in the first section. Is contemporary Germany best represented as a revitalized democracy, exemplified by the celebration and joy for increased freedoms unleashed by the destruction of the Berlin Wall? Or is Germany again becoming a place hostile to foreigners and any who do not appear German, as suggested by the firebombs thrown at a hostel housing immigrants? An accurate picture of contemporary German politics lies between these two extremes. Nevertheless, *both* vignettes represent aspects of modern Germany, and it remains a political challenge for all German citizens to cultivate the spirit of freedom for all while discouraging the outrages of xenophobia.

Which path German politics takes will be determined by the resolution of the four core issues identified in Section 1. The more optimistic direction would take the form of the continued integration of eastern Germany into the fabric of the Federal Republic as a whole; however, mutual suspicions between eastern and western Germans remain high. The former resent the so-called elbow society of the West, in which material goods appear high in the order of societal goals,

while the latter resent the huge costs, meaning increased taxation, required to rebuild the eastern *Länder.* Yet for successful economic, political, and social integration to occur demands patience and a sound institutional foundation. Once these domestic transitions are accomplished, Germany can then devote more attention to the larger issue of European integration.

The more pessimistic direction may mean a less than robust economy with consequential social tensions and conflict. There are now five political parties in Germany's political landscape rather than the three of the period from the late 1940s to the early 1980s. Can Germany's organized society *(Organizierte Gesellschaft)* and institutional political structure sustain the increased cooperation necessary to maintain a vibrant democracy? And what of Germany's economic giant/political dwarf syndrome? Can Germany assume the political responsibility that accompanied its economic stature? Do its European neighbors really want it to do so? And what of Germany's high-wage and welfare structure in the face of increased economic competition from lower-wage countries in East Asia and elsewhere? Negative outcomes to any of

A cynical western German view of money spent to rebuild
eastern Germany.
Source: *Frankfurter Allgemeine Zeitung.*

these questions could produce a much less satisfactory
outcome both for Germany and its neighbors.

POLITICAL CHALLENGES
AND CHANGING AGENDAS

For many years Germany was presented as a model for
other institutionalized societies to emulate. In the years
since unification, however, racial intolerance has intensified as the country's formerly vaunted economic
strength has partially eroded. What is the state of German democracy in the face of racist attacks and rising
intolerance, and what is the state of the German economy in the face of the structural challenges?

There has been a significant change in the nature
of political conflict in Germany since unification.
Clearly the model Deutschland of the 1970s and 1980s
is much less appropriate. In the previous sections, the
theme of democratic tolerance and respect for the
views of other individuals and groups has been examined. The question remains: Can Germany evolve
peacefully and democratically in a region where increased integration will become more likely? The expansion of the EU in the early 1990s has enabled more

European citizens to live and work outside their home
countries. What happens to German collective identity
given this fluidity? Can the elaborate and, for forty
years, effective institutional structure that balances
private and public interests be maintained and supported? Will the EU augment or challenge Germany's
position in Europe? Will these challenges threaten
Germany's enviable position in the face of increased
competition from the newly industrializing countries
(NICs)?

GERMAN POLITICS IN TRANSITION

The future of German politics depends greatly on how
the country addresses the four primary themes identified in this analysis of the Federal Republic: collective
identities, democracy, political economy, and a state's
position in the international system. For much of the
post–World War II period Germany enjoyed a spiral of
success that enabled it to confront these issues with
more confidence and resolve. For example, problems
of collective identities were handled in a much less
exclusionary way as women, ethnic groups, and newer
political parties and movements all began to contribute to a stable and healthy diversity in German politics
that had been lacking for most of the country's history.
Democratic institutions balanced participation and
dissent more effectively, thereby offsetting the country's turbulent and often racist past by almost fifty
years of a stable multiparty democracy. Even while
Germany was governed during most of this period by
a moderate-conservative Christian Democratic party,
it supported one of the most powerful and respected
Social Democratic parties in the world. Germany's
economic success has been significant and unique:
The country is both a stronghold of advanced capitalism, yet it supports an extensive state welfare and
government-mandated programs of worker/trade
union/works council participation in managerial decision making. Moreover, these economic and political
successes have helped Germany to participate more
effectively on the international scene. For much of the
post–World War II period, however, Germany's growing international economic prowess was not accompanied by a similar level of international political
responsibility. In the 1980s and 1990s, this has improved as Germany has confidently—and with the
support of its neighbors and allies—taken a leading
role in European integration. It is firmly anchored in
Western Europe, but it is uniquely positioned to assist

in the transition of the former communist Central and Eastern European states toward economic and political modernization.

However, close examination of all these four major themes, reveals Germany at a crossroads. Can the country continue to succeed in all four areas, or will tensions and difficulties undermine its success and produce a period of economic, political, and social instability?

In the area of collective identities Germany faces numerous unresolved challenges. For example, the country's guestworkers, of whom many are Turkish, remain essential to Germany's economy but often are denied or discouraged from seeking German citizenship. The opening up of the former communist Central and Eastern Germany in the late 1980s produced an influx of refugees and asylum-seekers that has placed great strains on a country that paradoxically has had generous political asylum laws and at the same time severe restrictions on non-German citizenship. Are some groups intentionally or unintentionally excluded from Germany's corporatist institutional structure? These issues have helped to produce increased ethnic tensions as German nationalism, which has been suppressed since the end of World War II, has shown some signs of resurgence. Two generations after the end of World War II, some younger Germans are asking what being German actually means. Although this search for identity can be healthy, its dark side is manifested by various extremist groups, which though still small preach exaggerated nationalism and hatred of foreigners and minorities. Such tendencies are incompatible with Germany's desire to play a leading role in European integration.

Democracy in Germany appears well established after nearly fifty years of the Federal Republic. It features high voter turnout, a stable and responsible multiparty political system, and a healthy civic culture.[32] Many observers now believe that broad-based political participation is part of the fabric of German political life. However, several issues present challenges as Germany's political institutions try to assimilate the five new *Länder*. One challenge concerns how well eastern Germans understand and practice democracy after years of authoritarian communist rule. For many East Germans, dissent was not political participation, it was treason. Likewise, can eastern Germans who have lost jobs and benefits in the transition to capitalism understand that ethnic minorities are not

the cause of their plight? Can tolerance and understanding develop while a right-wing fringe is preaching hatred and searching for scapegoats to blame for the costs of unification? Also is the legacy of a bureaucratic state that as recently as the 1970s, under a Social Democratic–led government, purged individuals who appeared to have radical tendencies completely gone? In other words, if social tensions continue to grow in the 1990s, how will the German state respond?

Germany's economy has also been touched by transitional challenges in the late 1990s. For many years it has been characterized as "high everything"[33] in that it has combined high-quality manufacturing with high wages, high fringe benefits, high worker participation, and high levels of vacation time (six weeks per year). Since the first oil crisis in the 1970s, critical observers have insisted that such a system could not last in a competitive world economy.[34] For the more than twenty years since then, however, the German economy has remained among the world's leaders. But recently, the huge costs of unification have caused many of the old criticisms about an extended and overburdened economy to surface again.

Pessimistic observers began to suggest that the stresses of the 1990s placed the German political economy in a precarious position. This "anti-German Model" consisted of several related arguments.[35] First was that Germany's economic prowess has resided in certain manufacturing industries whose goods were exportable but whose technologies were decidedly "low" (such as automobiles and machine tools). However, wage costs in these sectors continued to rise. Second, the costs of the Social Market Economy, as witnessed by the costs of unification, pressed on the upper limits of Germany's capacity to pay for them. In addition, economic tensions remain at the heart of conflict between the former East and former West Germans. While easterners resent the slow pace of change and high unemployment, western Germans are bitter about losing jobs to easterners and paying for the clean-up of the ecological and infrastructural disaster inherited from the former East German regime.

The completion of the single market of the European Union (EU) has also complicated Germany's relationship with other states. Although the EU was supposedly the grand culmination of a post–Cold War spirit of German and European unity, it has proved more difficult to establish than first anticipated. Its first immediate outcome has only strengthened the trends toward decentralization and deregulation already underway in Western Europe rather than enhancing integration. More significantly for the German economy, such deregulatory tendencies, if spread throughout Europe, could potentially disturb the organized capitalism of Germany's small and large businesses. In addition, the apparent deregulation in European finance threatens Germany's distinctive finance/manufacturing links. In short, the trend toward Europeanization may be incompatible with the highly consensus-oriented and coordinated nature of Germany's adjustment patterns. Moreover, as Europe becomes more open to the world economy, how well will Germany's "high everything" system be able to withstand increased economic competition from Asia and elsewhere? Politically, can Germany emerge from its dwarf status and play a leadership role in integrating Central and Eastern European states into a wider European Union?

GERMANY IN COMPARATIVE PERSPECTIVE

Germany offers important insights for comparative politics in several respects. First is the role of organized capitalism. Germany offers a model for combining state and market in a way that is unique to many advanced industrialized nations. Many models of political analysis choose to emphasize the distinctions between state and market. Debates about whether nationalized industries should be privatized, whether welfare should be reduced in favor of private charity, for example, are symptomatic of the conflict between state and market that animates the politics of most developed countries. Germany's organized capitalism, together with its Social Market Economy, has effectively blurred the distinction between the public and private sectors. It has refused to see public policy as a stark choice between these two alternatives, preferring to emphasize policies in which the state and market work together. Within the general framework of the model of production and exchange (outlined in the introduction), the German state effectively pursues development plans that benefit from its cooperative interaction with a dense network of key social and economic participants. Despite Germany's prominence as a powerful, advanced industrialized economy, this model remains

surprisingly understudied. Regardless of Germany's current economic difficulties, largely brought about by unification, it is a model worthy of comparative analysis.

The second insight concerns Germany's evolution of the principle of democratization and participation in a collectivist democracy. In many developed states, democracy is approached from an individual rights position, often taking the form of a series of individual choices much as a consumer would choose to buy one product or another in a supermarket. Germany, on the other hand, has evolved a different model, which—while sometimes underplaying a more individualistic democracy—does offer insights for participation and representation in a complex society. German democracy has emphasized participation within different groups. In other words, it has stressed the role of the individual not as a consumer in isolation from the rest of society, but as a citizen in a wider set of communities, organizations, and parties that must find ways of cooperating if the nation-state is to maintain its democracy. It is clearly within this complex of policies that Germany is wrestling with its treatment of different groups within the Federal Republic.

Germany offers a third insight regarding the issues of tolerance and respect for civil rights for ethnic minorities. Can Germany's group-oriented democratic practices include opportunities for former, longtime *Gastarbeiter* to participate and make a meaningful and significant contribution to German democracy? Can ethnic tensions be resolved in a way that enhances democracy rather than undermines it? Clearly, the issue of collective identities offers both powerful obstacles and rich opportunities to address one of the most crucial noneconomic issues that Germany faces in the last half of the 1990s.

A fourth insight asks whether Germany can remake its political culture in the wake of the Nazi past? Many had hoped so for the first forty years of the FRG, but now some are less certain. To what extent have the educational system, civil service, and the media addressed the Nazi past? To what extent do they bear some responsibility for today's rise of right-wing violence? Have the reforms in the educational system since the 1960s provided a spirit of critical discourse in the broad mainstream of society that can withstand burgeoning right-wing intolerance? Can judges effectively sentence those who abuse the civil rights of ethnic minorities? Will the news media continue to express a wide range of opinion and contribute to a healthy civic discourse? Or will strident, tabloid-style journalism stifle the more reasoned debate that any democracy must have to survive and flourish?

Fifth, what is the role of a middle-rank power as the potential leader of a regional world bloc of some 400 million people? To some extent this issue also confronts Japan, as it struggles to take on political responsibilities commensurate with its economic successes. In the late 1990s Germany not only faces intense pressures from within its borders, such as conflict among ethnic groups, but also from a complex mix of external influences. Germany's role as both a Western and an Eastern European power pulls at the country in different ways. Does the country emphasize the Western-oriented EU and build a solid foundation with its traditional post–World War II Allies? Or does it turn eastward to step into the vacuum created by the demise and fragmentation of the former USSR? Can Germany's twentieth-century history allow either its western or eastern neighbors to let it begin to play the geopolitical role that its low-profile postwar political status has only postponed? To some extent the political cover of the EU will allow Germany to do more as the leading country in a powerful international organization than it ever could do as a sovereign nation-state with its unique twentieth-century political baggage.

Last, Germany's historical importance on the world political stage during the past 150 years means that understanding its transition is essential for comparative purposes. It was late to achieve political unity, and it was a country that was late to industrialize. These two factors eventually helped produce a catastrophic first half of the twentieth century for both Germany and the whole world. Yet the country's transition to a successful developed economy with an apparently solid democratic political system would seem to suggest that other countries, particularly those in the Third World, may be able to learn from the successes—and failures—of countries such as Germany as they also attempt to achieve economic growth and to develop a political democracy.

Key Terms

fascist	*Gastarbeiter*
Economic Miracle	(guestworker)
Social Market	civil servants
Economy	overlapping
liberal	responsibilities
Junkers	(policy)
Kulturkampf	health insurance funds
chancellor	co-determination
Ostpolitik (eastern	works councils
policy)	Administrative Court
Basic Law	industrial policy
Zollverein	Citizens Action
framework regulation	Groups
	grassroots democracy

Suggested Readings

Section 1

Craig, Gordon. *The Politics of the Prussian Army.* Oxford: Oxford University Press, 1955.

Eley, Geoff. *Reshaping the German Right: Radical Nationalism and Political Change after Bismarck.* New Haven, Conn.: Yale University Press, 1980.

Moore, Barrington. *Social Origins of Dictatorship and Democracy.* Boston: Beacon Press, 1965.

Shirer, William. *The Rise and Fall of the Third Reich.* New York: Simon and Schuster, 1960.

Tilly, Charles, ed. *The Formation of National States in Western Europe.* Princeton: Princeton University Press, 1975.

Section 2

Braunthal, Gerard. *The Federation of German Industry in Politics.* Ithaca, N.Y.: Cornell University Press, 1965.

Gerschenkron, Alexander. *Bread and Democracy in Germany.* 2d ed. Ithaca, N.Y.: Cornell University Press, 1989.

Kemp, Tom. *Industrialization in 19th Century Europe.* 2d ed. London: Longman, 1985.

Piore, Michael, and Charles Sabel. *The Second Industrial Divide.* New York: Basic Books, 1984.

Rueschemeyer, Dietrich, Evelyn Huber Stephens, and John D. Stephens. *Capitalist Development and Democracy.* Chicago: University of Chicago Press, 1992.

Section 3

Dahrendorf, Ralf. *Society and Democracy in Germany.* Garden City, N.Y.: Anchor, 1969.

Evans, Peter B., Dietrich Rueschemeyer, and Theda Skocpol. *Bringing the State Back In.* Cambridge: Cambridge University Press, 1985.

Hesse, Joachim Jens. "The Federal Republic of Germany: From Cooperative Federalism to Joint Policy-Making." *West European Politics* 10, no. 4 (October 1987): 70–87.

Katzenstein, Peter. *Policy and Politics in West Germany: The Growth of a Semi-Sovereign State.* Philadelphia: Temple University Press, 1987.

Schmidt, Manfred G. "West Germany: The Politics of the Middle Way." *Journal of Public Policy* 7, no. 2 (1987): 135–177.

Section 4

Braunthal, Gerard. *The German Social Democrats since 1969: A Party in Power and Opposition.* 2d ed. Boulder, Colo: Westview Press, 1994.

Inglehart, Ronald. *Culture Shift in Advanced Industrial Society.* Princeton, N.J.: Princeton University Press, 1990.

Markovits, Andrei S. "Political Parties in Germany: Agents of Stability in a Sea of Change." *Social Education* 57, no. 5 (September 1993): 239–243.

Schmitter, Philippe C., and Gerhard Lembruch, eds. *Trends Toward Corporatist Intermediation.* Beverly Hills, Calif.: Sage, 1979.

Rein, Taagepera, and Matthew Soberg Shugart. *Seats and Votes: The Effects and Determinants of Electoral Systems.* New Haven, Conn.: Yale University Press, 1989.

Section 5

Hager, Carol. "Environmentalism and Democracy in the Two Germanies." *German Politics* 1, no. 1 (April 1992): 95–118.

Hirschman, Albert O. *Exit, Voice, and Loyalty.* New Haven, Conn.: Yale University Press, 1970.

Rusciano, Frank Louis. "Rethinking the Gender Gap: The Case of West German Elections." *Comparative Politics* 243 (April 1992): 335–358.

Endnotes

[1]Andrei S. Markovits, *The Political Economy of West Germany: Modell Deutschland* (New York: Praeger, 1982); and Ezra Vogel, *Japan as Number One: Lessons for America* (Cambridge: Harvard, 1979).

[2]Charles Tilly, ed., *The Formation of National States in Western Europe* (Princeton: Princeton University Press, 1975).

[3]Tom Kemp, *Industrialization in 19th Century Europe*, 2d ed. (London: Longman, 1985).

[4]Gordon Craig, *The Politics of the Prussian Army* (Oxford: Oxford University Press, 1955).

[5]Barrington Moore, *Social Origins of Dictatorship and Democracy* (Boston: Beacon Press, 1965).

[6]Alexander Gerschenkron, *Bread and Democracy in Germany*, 2d ed. (Ithaca: Cornell University Press, 1989).

[7]Geoffrey Barraclough, *An Introduction to Contemporary History* (Baltimore: Penguin, 1967).

[8]Philippe Schmitter and Gerhard Lembruch, *Trends Toward Corporatist Intermediation* (Beverly Hills: Sage, 1979).

[9]William E. Paterson and Gordon Smith, *The West German Model: Perspectives on a Stable State* (London: Cass, 1981).

[10]Alexander Gerschenkron, *Bread and Democracy in Germany*, 2d ed. (Ithaca: Cornell University Press, 1989).

[11]Gerschenkron, *Bread and Democracy.*

[12]Colleen A. Dunlavy, "Political Structure, State Policy and Industrial Change: Early Railroad Policy in the United States and Prussia," in Sten Steinmo, Kathleen Thelen, and Frank Longstreth, eds., *Structuring Politics: Historical Institutionalism in Historical Perspective* (New York: Cambridge University Press, 1992), 114–154.

[13]Wilhelm Röpke, "The Guiding Principle of the Liberal Programme," in H. F. Wünche, ed. *Standard Texts on the Social Market Economy* (Stuttgart and New York: Gustav Fischer Verlag, 1982), 188.

[14]German Information Office, May 20, 1994.

[15]Peter Katzenstein, *Policy and Politics in West Germany: The Growth of a Semi-Sovereign State* (Philadelphia: Temple University Press, 1987).

[16]Peter Evans, Dietrich Rueschemeyer, and Theda Skocpol, *Bringing the State Back In* (Cambridge: Cambridge University Press, 1985).

[17]Frank Louis Rusciano, "Rethinking the Gender Gap: The Case of West German Elections," *Comparative Politics* 24, no. 3 (April 1992): 335–358.

[18]Ralf Dahrendorf, *Society and Democracy in Germany* (Garden City, N.Y.: Anchor, 1969).

[19]Aline Kuntz, "The Bavarian CSU: A Case Study in Conservative Modernization" (Ph.D. diss., Cornell University, 1987).

[20]Andrei S. Markovits, "Political Parties in Germany: Agents of Stability in a Sea of Change," *Social Education* 57, no. 5 (September 1993): 239–243.

[21]Carl E. Schorske, *German Social Democracy, 1905–1917: The Development of the Great Schism* (Cambridge: Harvard University Press, 1983).

[22]Otto Kirschheimer, "The Transformation of the Western European Party System," in Roy C. Macridis, ed., *Comparative Politics: Notes and Readings,* 6th ed. (Chicago: Dorsey Press, 1986).

[23]Gerard Braunthal, *The German Social Democrats Since 1969: A Party in Power and Opposition,* 2d ed. (Boulder, Colo: Westview Press, 1994).

[24]Ann Phillips, "Seeds of Change in the German Democratic Republic," *American Institute for Contemporary German Studies,* Research Report #1, December 1989.

[25]Geoffrey K. Roberts, "Right-wing Radicalism in the New Germany," *Parliamentary Affairs* 45, no. 3 (1992): 327–345.

[26]Ralf Dahrendorf, *Society and Democracy in Germany.*

[27]Carol Hager, "Environmentalism and Democracy in the Two Germanies," *German Politics* 1, no. 1 (April 1992): 95–118.

[28]Joyce Marie Mushaben, "A Search for Identity: The 'German Question' in Atlantic Alliance Relations," *World Politics* 40, no. 3 (April 1988): 395–418.

[29]Sten Steinmo, Kathleen Thelen, and Frank Longstreth, eds., *Structuring Politics: The New Institutionalism in Comparative Perspective* (New York: Cambridge University Press, 1992).

[30]Peter Katzenstein, *Policy and Politics in West Germany: The Growth of a Semi-Sovereign State.*

[31]Arnold J. Heidenheimer, *Comparative Public Policy: The Politics of Social Choice in America, Europe and Japan,* 3d ed. (New York: St. Martin's Press, 1990).

[32]Gabriel A. Almond and Sidney Verba, eds., *The Civic Culture Revisited* (Newbury Park, Calif.: Sage Publications, 1989).

[33]Lowell Turner, *Democracy at Work: Changing World Markets and the Future of Labor Unions* (Ithaca: Cornell University Press, 1991).

[34]Bruce Nussbaum, *The World After Oil* (New York: Simon and Schuster, 1983); and Michael Moran, "A State of Inaction: The State and Stock Exchange Reform in the Federal Republic of Germany," in Simon Bulmer, ed., *The Changing Agenda of West German Public Policy* (Brookfield, Vt.: Gower, 1989), 110–127.

[35]Peter Neckermann, "What Went Wrong in Germany After the Unification?" *East European Quarterly* 26, no. 4 (1992): 447–470.

CHAPTER 5

Japan

JAPAN

Land and Population

Capital	Tokyo
Total Area (square miles)	145,882 (slightly smaller than California)
Population	124.5 million
Annual Projected Population Growth Rate (1993–2000)	0.2%
Urban Population (% of total)	77%

Ethnic Composition

Major Ethnic Groups	Japanese	99.4%
	Other (mostly Korean)	0.6%
Major Language	Japanese	
Major Religions	Observe Shinto and	
	Buddhism	57%
	Shinto only	16%
	Christian	1%
	Other	6%
	Unaffiliated	20%

Economy

Domestic Currency	Yen	
GNP (US$)	$3.9 trillion	
GNP per capita (US$)	$31,490	
Purchasing Power Parity GDP per capita (US$)	$20,850	
Average Annual GDP Growth Rate (1980–1993)	4.0%	
Structure of Production (% of GDP)	Agriculture	2%
	Industry	41%
	Services	57%
Labor Force Distribution (% of total)	Agriculture	7%
	Industry	34%
	Services	59%
Women as % of Total Labor Force	38%	

Income Distribution (1989)	% of Population	% Share of Income or Consumption
	Richest 20%	31.6%
	Poorest 20%	10.9%

Total Foreign Trade (exports plus imports) as % of GDP	16%

Society

Life Expectancy	Female	83
	Male	76
Population per Doctor	610	
Infant Mortality (per 1,000 live births)	4	
Adult Literacy	99%	
Mean Years of Schooling (of adults 25+)	Female	10.7
	Male	10.9
Communications (per 100 people)	Radios	91
	Televisions	62
	Telephones	56
1995 Human Development Index (1 = highest)	Ranks 3 out of 174	

Political Organization

Political System   Parliamentary democracy/Constitutional monarchy

Regime History   Current constitution written during post–World War II Allied Occupation and adopted in 1947.

Administrative Structure   Unitary state; 47 units of intermediate-level subnational government called prefectures and 3,236 lower-level units (as of 1993) called city, town, or village.

Executive   Prime minister selected by legislature; a cabinet of about 20 ministers appointed by prime minister.

Legislature   Bicameral; members of upper house (House of Councillors) are elected partly by single nontransferable vote from 47 multiple-seat prefecture-wide districts and partly by party-list PR from the nation at large. Members of lower house (House of Representatives) are elected (since 1994) partly by plurality vote from 300 single-seat districts and partly by party-list PR from 11 regions.

Judiciary   Supreme Court has 14 judges appointed by the cabinet, except chief judge who is nominated by the cabinet and appointed by the emperor; all eligible to serve until 70 years of age, subject to popular review.

Party System   One-party dominant from the mid-1950s to early 1990s; competitive multiparty since. Principal parties: Liberal Democratic Party, New Frontier Party (Shinshintō), Social Democratic Party of Japan, Democratic Socialist Party, Clean Government Party (Kōmeitō), and Japan Communist Party.

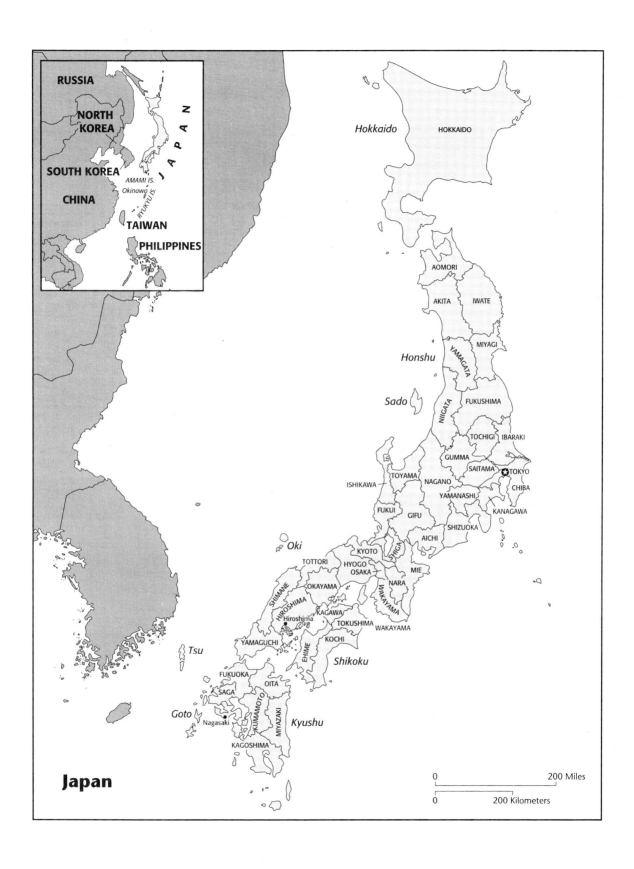

RUSSIA

NORTH KOREA

SOUTH KOREA

CHINA

TAIWAN

PHILIPPINES

JAPAN

AMAMI IS.
Okinawa
RYUKYU IS.

Hokkaido HOKKAIDO

AOMORI

AKITA   IWATE

Honshu   YAMAGATA   MIYAGI

Sado   NIIGATA   FUKUSHIMA

TOCHIGI   IBARAKI

GUMMA
SAITAMA
TOYAMA   ✪TOKYO
ISHIKAWA   NAGANO   CHIBA
YAMANASHI
KANAGAWA
FUKUI   GIFU
SHIZUOKA
AICHI

Oki
KYOTO
TOTTORI   SHIGA
HYOGO   MIE
OSAKA
OKAYAMA   NARA
SHIMANE
WAKAYAMA
HIROSHIMA   KAGAWA
Hiroshima   TOKUSHIMA   WAKAYAMA
YAMAGUCHI   KOCHI

Tsu   EHIME   *Shikoku*

FUKUOKA
OITA
SAGA
Goto   KUMAMOTO
Nagasaki   MIYAZAKI   *Kyushu*

KAGOSHIMA

Japan

0   200 Miles

0   200 Kilometers

The Making of the Modern Japanese State

Contemporary Japan is one of the few stable democracies in Asia. It also has one of the most productive and dynamic economies in the modern world. Japan's parliamentary democracy is similar in many respects to European parliamentary democracies, yet distinctive because of its uninterrupted rule by one dominant party from the mid-1950s until recently. In fact, the one-party rule appeared to be so well established that most observers assumed it would be a permanent feature of contemporary Japanese government. That impression, however, was proven wrong by a sequence of events in the late 1980s and early 1990s that caught everyone by surprise and, in retrospect, marked a turning point in post–World War II Japanese politics.

JAPAN AT THE CROSSROADS

In the late 1980s, Japanese politics entered a period of great instability and uncertainty not experienced since the early post–World War II years. The Liberal Democratic Party (LDP), which had ruled the nation since its founding in 1955, lost its majority in the upper house of Japan's bicameral parliament (National Diet) in 1989 and then in the lower house in 1993, for the first time in both cases.

The LDP government's downfall was brought about, in part, by a series of major corruption scandals involving its highest officials. In one of the most widely publicized cases, a number of politicians, including Prime Minister Kakuei Tanaka, and allied business leaders were charged in 1976 with conspiring to help a U.S. aircraft manufacturer, the Lockheed Corporation, sell its planes to a Japanese airline company, All Nippon Airways, in exchange for bribes.[1] Soon thereafter, Tanaka was forced to resign as prime minister over charges of other illicit fundraising activities and was subsequently indicted for allegedly receiving some ¥500 million (about $1.5 million) from Lockheed for his role in the scandal.

In another case, more than a dozen LDP politicians, including former Prime Minister Yasuhiro Nakasone, and several opposition politicians were charged in 1988 with buying pre-issue stocks of a real estate company and later selling them at as much as three times the original price. The transactions, obviously intended to win influential political friends for

the upstart company, led to resignations of several cabinet members, including then finance minister (and later prime minister), Kiichi Miyazawa.

In a more recent and even more explosive case, Shin Kanemaru, who was known as the LDP kingmaker for his pivotal role in the selection of several recent prime ministers, faced a criminal charge in the summer of 1992 for having received on the eve of the 1990 general election an illegal political contribution of ¥500 million (about $3.3 million) from a large and thriving express parcel service company. When he resigned as a result of the scandal, he was LDP vice president, leader of the largest LDP faction, and a twelve-term member of the lower house. Moreover, the investigation led to revelations about Kanemaru's involvement in the late 1980s with a well-known organized crime syndicate, allegedly on behalf of former Prime Minister Noboru Takeshita. These and other lesser scandals seriously damaged the LDP government's image and sowed the seeds of a widespread voter revolt and a nationwide political reform movement that eventually defeated the LDP government at the polls.

These developments were all the more remarkable because, from the mid-1950s to the late 1980s, Japanese government and politics were among the most stable and predictable in the world. As a conservative catchall party, the LDP won one Diet election after another and dominated both houses without a break, while five other national parties—a socialist party, a communist party, and three centrist parties— split the remainder of the seats in each house and together constituted a permanent opposition.

This extraordinary political stability was the result of a fortuitous combination of factors. The first, and perhaps most important, factor was Japan's record economic growth under the LDP's continuous rule, which rapidly raised the average voter's standard of living to an unprecedented level. This track record earned the LDP a reputation as a uniquely gifted and reliable custodian of the affairs of the state. Its leadership successfully boosted this image by deliberately avoiding tackling unpopular or controversial political issues—such as the revision of the Japanese constitution adopted during the post–World War II Allied Oc-

Japan New Party leader and Prime Minister-to-be Morihiro Hosokawa campaigning on the eve of the July 1993 House of Representatives general election.
Source: Reuters/Bettmann Archive.

cupation, rearmament, and involvement in military peacekeeping actions abroad—and concentrating instead on economic development and social welfare policies. This strategy not only deprived the opposition of salient issues around which to rally voters against the LDP at election time, but also paved the way for unofficial but effective compromise and cooperation between the LDP and the noncommunist opposition on most policy issues and bills debated in the Diet. The thriving economy and the LDP's prudent strategy thus contributed importantly to the political stability Japan enjoyed for more than three decades until the late 1980s.

The second factor was that Japan's election system seriously overrepresented rural voters and underrepresented urban ones. This gave unfair advantage to the parties of the right, particularly the LDP, which drew much of their support from rural constituencies, while disadvantaging parties of the left whose supporters were largely urban. Japan's peculiar electoral rules also forced a party intent on winning the majority or plurality of parliamentary seats to run two or more rival candidates in the same election district. Sharing similar opinions on most policy issues, such candidates tended to compete with each other in terms of the amount of pork barrel delivered and the number of personal favors done for their constituents. This, in turn, led them to spend, and therefore raise, very large amounts of campaign funds. This reliance on money as the primary means of winning votes bred political corruption and favored the conservatives who had access to the wealthiest and most generous business contributors. Since the economy was booming and incomes were rising, few voters seemed to mind the political effects or moral implications of what would later become known as "money politics."

Third, the opposition parties, sharply divided among themselves both ideologically and in terms of the social and economic interests they represented, came to accept their opposing role by the late 1960s and ceased even to try to defeat the LDP at the polls. This political passivity helped the LDP hold firmly onto the reins of government for as long as it did.

Fourth, the electorate was divided into well-defined, effectively organized, and mutually recognized partisan blocs, although the number of unattached, or "floating," voters increased substantially over the years. These divisions were so well fixed that candidates of different parties seldom trespassed on each other's bailiwicks within an election district. This tended to intensify competition among candidates of the same party, especially the ruling LDP, thereby contributing further to money politics; but it also helped stabilize relationships among the parties and nurture informal interparty coordination in both electoral and legislative actions.

Finally, the LDP managed to maintain a high degree of intraparty cohesiveness by rewarding its rival factions with shares of party and government offices roughly proportional to their size. This system of proportional representation within the party satisfied all factions and their members, just as electoral proportional representation satisfied most parties by guaranteeing them at least some seats in parliament.

As we will discuss in detail in later sections, these stabilizing conditions ceased to exist by the end of the 1980s. The annual, double-digit growth rates of the late 1950s and 1960s fell to 5 percent during the 1970s, 4 percent during the 1980s, and finally to virtually 0 percent in 1992 amid the worst recession Japan had experienced in twenty years.

In the meantime, the partisan blocs among Japanese voters that appeared nearly frozen for three decades began to loosen by the mid-1980s, due partly to defections by increasing numbers of their members and partly to changes in the blocs' political agendas. In light of their shrinking membership rolls and an economy characterized by low economic growth and increasing international competition, public and private sector labor unions merged at the end of the 1980s. The new 7.5-million-member labor federation set out to bring together Japan's two socialist parties, a centrist party, and potential defectors from the LDP and form an anti-LDP coalition able and willing to challenge the increasingly discredited and vulnerable ruling party at the polls.

While organized labor was thus redefining its political goals and strategies, organized business leaders and farmers also began to reconsider their unfailing support of the LDP. Well known for its financial support of the LDP, big business came under fire for its role in the rise of money politics and the spread of political corruption. Big business became increasingly sensitive to foreign, especially American, criticism of its collusive relationship with the ruling party and the government bureaucracy. This collusion was blamed for Japanese trade protectionism and the perpetuation of a trade imbalance between Japan and its major trading partners. At the same time, the end of the Cold War made the ideological antagonism between the capitalist LDP and the socialist parties irrelevant and made many business leaders and their organizations increasingly in favor of a change of government and formation of a non-LDP cabinet. Farmers, too, began to drift away from the LDP, mainly because of their dissatisfaction with the LDP government's removal of nontariff barriers against many foreign agricultural and dairy products.

Even the balance of power among the LDP factions began to show strains in the 1980s. The faction led by Kakuei Tanaka, which he continued to control even after being removed as prime minister in 1974, began to monopolize the party. The emergence of a hegemonic faction caused rancor among rival LDP factions and undermined the cohesiveness of the ruling party. Moreover, the Tanaka faction's aggrandizement of power was financed by huge amounts of money collected mainly from businesses (especially construction companies) and liberally dispensed to buy new recruits, largely from the pool of newly

水準の低さに閑口

"Scandal"
(On the flag) Political Great Power, Economic Great Power. "Their standards are so low."
Source: Mr. Kiyoshi Ichimura, *The Weekly Toyo Keizai,* January 2, 1993.

elected and still unattached LDP candidates in each Diet election. The growth of the Tanaka faction was thus accompanied by the growth of "money politics" and the spread of political corruption.

Money politics not only continued to thrive but reached new heights in the 1980s, spawning the spate of scandals in which virtually all top LDP leaders were implicated. In response to growing public disillusionment and protest, some LDP members left the party to start new "reform" parties. These new parties helped defeat the LDP government and end its thirty-eight-year-long monopoly of power in the summer of 1993. The result was the formation of the first non-LDP coalition government in Japan since the 1940s and the dawn of a period of great change in Japanese politics.

Despite the uncertainty of current Japanese politics, however, the stability of Japanese democracy is not in question, as it was before World War II. Understanding how Japan emerged from a vulnerable position as a developing nation, a troubled authoritarian past, and a devastating defeat in World War II to become one of the world's most prosperous industrialized democracies is a central focus of this chapter. In examining such questions, we will consider four themes of special importance in the development of the modern Japanese state: the state's changing power relative to other nations, beginning with its late and sudden entry into the world of states; its policy of state-led industrialization; its prewar and postwar approaches to democracy; and its evolving relationship with Japan's collective identities.

CRITICAL JUNCTURES

Emergence of the State

The chain of islands off the coast of the Eurasian landmass known today as Japan was inhabited by tribes of hunters and gatherers as early as 2000 B.C.[2] and possibly earlier. Surrounded by seas, the island domain had fairly well-defined natural borders from the beginning, separating it from Korea and China to the west and southwest and Russia to the northwest. This gave rise to a strong ethnic identity among its early inhabitants.

By the middle of the third century A.D., a modest state had emerged in the island domain. Broader control was established by a tribal chief who probably had ancestral roots in Korea and claimed to be a "heavenly king" descended from a mythical Sun Goddess. The early rulers of this small, insular state frequently sent embassies to Korea and the Chinese imperial court, who returned with advanced, continental cultural notions—notably letters, religion, and architecture. Among such early imports were the teachings of an ancient Chinese sage, Confucius (551–479? B.C.), about the moral foundations of political order and social harmony based, above all, on filial piety and submission to authority. Originally imported to Japan in the late third century A.D., Confucianism would make a profound and enduring impact on Japanese culture. Buddhism, with its ancient origins in India, reached Japan via China and Korea in the mid-sixth century A.D. Thereafter, it thrived among Japanese rulers and populace alike, though in a number of competing sects. Together with a native cult of nature and ancestor worship known as *Shinto* ("ways of the spirits"), Confucianism and Buddhism continue to shape everyday life in Japan today.

For more than fifteen centuries, Japan—known by its present Japanese name, Nihon or Nippon, and by its original Chinese name, Jihpen (from whence came "Japan") since the beginning of the eighth century A.D.—has remained a unified and politically independent state, except for several years during the Allied Occupation following World War II. During the greater part of its classical period up to the late twelfth century, the state was ruled first by shifting coalitions of tribal groups, and then by tribal descendants claiming the title of heavenly emperor and their regents. The latter founded the longest surviving monarchy in history, which continues to thrive in the last decade of the twentieth century. However, during Japan's medieval era, which began in the late twelfth century, the monarchy survived but yielded real power to a succession of military leaders or Shoguns. The last and most successful of these military leaders founded a durable dynasty known as the Tokugawa Shogunate (1603–1867). This dynasty survived for two and a half centuries in deliberate isolation from the world, until it was overthrown in a mid-nineteenth-century revolution known as the Meiji Restoration.

The Japanese developed a sense of national identity early in their history—as early as, if not earlier than, most European peoples. This was due partly to their racial homogeneity and partly to the effective dissemination of an ideology of loyalty and obedience to national authority. Both were largely a measure of Japan's insular position, which ensured considerable physical and cultural isolation before the advent of modern transportation and communication. The precocious development of a national identity, in turn, tended to suppress the growth of local and regional collective identities.

In Tokugawa Japan, the majority of those who belonged to the ruling warrior class, known as **bushi** or, more popularly, *samurai,* shared a well-defined sense of national identity. This warrior class was a relatively large group, accounting for about 8 percent of the total population, or about ten times the proportion of knights in the population of medieval England or France. As a rule, boys from warrior-class families—and increasingly those from wealthier merchant and farmer families and even some girls—had access to education offered by a large number of primary-level schools throughout the country.[3] A few of these schools were funded and controlled by the central government, some were sponsored by governments of the 300 or so local feudal domains, and the rest were run by nearly 10,000 Buddhist temples and Shinto shrines. In addition to the basic skills of reading, writing, and simple mathematics, children were taught the idea of Japan as a state separate from but equal to any other state. They were taught, above all, the Confucian virtues of unquestioning loyalty and obedience to parental authority in the family and state authority outside the family.

Tokugawa Japan was thus a feudalistic but centrally controlled regime with a sizable educated and literate ruling class and expanding ranks of better-off farmers and merchants sharing a similar educational experience and a collective identity. The ideology of the ruling class pervaded popular culture. Tales told in numerous and colorful versions of the failed Mongolian invasions of the late thirteenth century and, especially, of how "divine winds" (typhoons) caught and sank most of the invading ships off Japan's coast helped mold a myth of a unique nation created by gods and ruled eternally by their descendants. In later centuries, this myth would be elaborated upon and exploited to fuel popular support for a national drive toward military and economic parity with, if not superiority to, the Western powers.[4]

Class lines in Tokugawa Japan were rigidly drawn and strictly observed. Under the official classification system there were five classes—warriors, farmers, artisans, merchants, and outcastes—although the last category was often omitted from official mention. There was also a minuscule class of nobles at the imperial court in Kyoto, which had long since lost all of its political power to the samurai rulers but had survived as a traditional source of political legitimacy in a nation founded on the myth of the divine origin of its monarchs. In the nation at large and in each of its local feudal domains, members of the several classes lived and worked separately, each within an officially demarcated neighborhood.

One type of class-based segregation that continues to the present day is that imposed on Japan's outcaste group.[5] Since their origin in traditional class-based segregation, these outcastes have been condemned to a pariah status associated with particular residential areas, known in recent years as "special hamlets," and types of work once regarded as unclean, such as disposing of carcasses and working hides and leather. The Japanese caste system, of which the outcaste group is a product, is not as complex and elaborate as the Hindu caste system, but is very similar to systems found in early medieval Europe and, especially, in premodern and early modern China and Korea. As in China and Korea, the system has been legally abolished, but the prejudice nurtured under it for centuries has not completely disappeared.

Under the influence of the Confucian doctrines that ordered political and social relations in Tokugawa

Japan, women were treated as inherently inferior and subordinate to men and were denied participation in public affairs even at the village level.[6] An adult woman's role was strictly within the family, as her man's faithful and obedient wife, his children's loving and caring mother, and his household's selfless, hardworking servant. The ethnic, class, and gender divisions were effectively maintained and enforced by the absolutist Tokugawa regime by the use or threat of physical force reinforced by the indoctrination of a broad segment of the population with the Confucian principles of unquestioning deference and loyalty to authority.

The Meiji Restoration

The revolt that toppled the autocratic and isolationist Tokugawa regime in 1867, known as the Meiji Restoration, resulted partly from growing political tension within Japan caused by gradual but profound socioeconomic changes. It also resulted from rising pressure exerted by a number of Western powers to open and integrate the hermit nation into a rapidly expanding global economic system dominated by the Western nations. Most immediately, however, the revolution was brought about by the forced entry of a small flotilla of American warships into the Tokyo Bay in 1853 and 1854 in defiance of the centuries-old ban on the entry of unauthorized foreigners into Japanese territory.[7] The breach of the ban by Commodore Matthew C. Perry's small squadron and the Shogun's capitulation to his official demand from the U.S. government that Japan open its ports to American naval and merchant ships gave the Shogun's domestic enemies an excuse to revolt against the military autocracy.

The young and fiercely nationalistic revolutionaries who overthrew the Tokugawa regime and founded modern Japan quickly consolidated their position as a new ruling clique consisting almost exclusively of revolutionaries from four western domains. Those from the western provinces of Satsuma and Choshu dominated the group, and their leaders soon constituted a tightly knit inner circle. They derived their legitimacy to govern from their role as the official agents of the emperor, whom they claimed to have restored to his long-lost position as Japan's divine ruler. In the next half century, this oligarchy would spearhead a "revolution from above," which would transform the backward feudal nation into one of the major industrial and military powers of the early twentieth century.[8]

By the late nineteenth century, all states in South and Southeast Asia had been invaded, conquered, and claimed as colonies by one Western power or another. Closer to home, China appeared to be on the verge of succumbing as well. The oligarchs of Meiji Japan—known also as the "elder statesmen" *(genro)*—believed that, to survive in an age of imperialism, Japan needed a modern military and a strong industrial economy equal to those of the Western powers. Japan, however, lacked both sophisticated technology and virtually all of the raw materials essential to modern industries. To import such resources from abroad, Japan had to export what it could produce at home—mainly yarn and fabrics made of silk and cotton in the nineteenth century, then increasingly more sophisticated manufactures such as steel, ships, machinery, and chemicals after the turn of the century. Modern Japan was thus a trading nation from its very beginning. It imported a far greater portion of the raw materials its industry required and exported a greater portion of the manufactured goods it produced than most other nations did at a comparable stage of economic development.

While committed in theory to a capitalist economic system based on profit and the principles of private property, the Meiji state nonetheless assumed an aggressively interventionist role in the management of the national economy and society. It did so in the name of a perpetual national crisis, which certainly had the ring of truth during the heyday of Western imperialism in Asia.

From its beginnings, the Meiji state was engaged in a struggle to have the "unequal treaties" that were concluded between Japan and a dozen Western powers since the last years of the Tokugawa Shogunate renegotiated. These treaties contained two types of "unequal" clauses. One provided for "extraterritoriality," or the right of foreign diplomats to try and sentence citizens of their countries who committed offenses on Japanese territory. The other provided for denial of Japan's "tariff autonomy" and gave foreign governments the right to veto changes in Japanese tariff rates. The protracted and frustrating negotiations over these issues did not end until the extraterritoriality provisions were expunged from one treaty after another in the last decade of the nineteenth century and tariff

autonomy was restored to the Japanese government in the first decade of the twentieth century.

The Democratic Idea

After the Meiji revolution, Japan was thus no longer a nation deliberately and effectively isolated from the rapidly expanding world of modern capitalism and colonialism. In fact, the "opening" of Japan was both sudden and complete. The new government not only let foreigners visit the country for diplomatic, commercial, and other purposes, it also sent Japanese abroad, especially to the United States and Western Europe, to bring home the best means by which to modernize the nation as quickly as possible. In seeking to learn from the most economically advanced and powerful nations of the late nineteenth and early twentieth centuries, Japan imported a wide array of Western institutions, ideas, and practices.[9] In a particularly interesting example of this government-initiated effort to learn from the West, a fifty-member delegation was sent to the United States and Europe in 1871. Known as the Iwakura Mission after the name of its leader, Senior Minister Tomomi Iwakura, the group spent eighteen months abroad, visiting a great variety of institutions in a dozen different countries, ranging from government offices and military academies to shipyards, factories, banks, and chambers of commerce. Upon their return to Japan in the summer of 1873, leading members of the group, such as Hirobumi Itō who later became Japan's first prime minister and Privy Council president, spearheaded Meiji Japan's national drive for building "a rich country with a strong army" by following in the footsteps of the Western powers.

Meiji Japan imported not only economic models from abroad, but political ideas as well. By the 1880s, both John Stuart Mill's *On Liberty* and Jean Jacques Rousseau's *The Social Contract* had been translated and published in Japan, along with a dozen works by Japanese authors that were either based on or inspired by Western writers' works. The spread of the democratic idea gave rise to a "freedom and people's rights" movement led by two proto-political parties, one known as the Liberal Party and an advocate of French-style radical liberalism, and the other as the Reform Party and an advocate of British-style reformism. Led by former members of the early Meiji oligarchy who had left the government as a result of an internal power struggle and disagreement over policy issues, both parties stood for parliamentarism and other democratic ideas as a means of strengthening government legitimacy and power by mobilizing the entire nation in pursuit of national goals. The government finally responded to their call in 1889 by issuing a Western-style constitution modeled after the Prussian prototype and instituting a bicameral national legislature modeled after the British Parliament.

By the last decade of the nineteenth century, Japan was thus formally a constitutional monarchy with a partially elected parliament and highly vocal political parties. Its government was faced with the persistent popular demand for more democracy and popular participation in government. However, it was more the idea of democracy than the actual practice of democracy that appealed to most Japanese of the late nineteenth and early twentieth centuries. In reality, pre–World War II Japan was a nation far more determined to carry out a program of rapid industrialization and military buildup than one of democratization. The actual impact of the democratic idea on Japanese politics and society before the war was therefore very limited, though not insignificant, as seen in the Meiji Constitution, which is discussed below. Nor was Japan before World War II a nation committed to social and economic equality among its people.

In pre–World War II rural Japan, a small class of landlords dominated the agricultural economy and society at the expense of a vast class of tenant farmers, while in urban Japan, a handful of giant conglomerates, known as *zaibatsu*, dominated the industrial and financial sectors largely at the expense of myriad small businesses. The national bureaucracy, which acted as the primary agent of the ruling oligarchy, was dominated by graduates of a single national university created as the incubator of able and obedient servants of the autocratic state. Despite the superficial westernization of its political, social, and economic institutions following the Meiji Restoration, modern Japan was thus not fundamentally different from Tokugawa Japan, as far as the vast majority of common Japanese people were concerned. The only significant difference was that they or their children now had legal access to free and compulsory primary school education, which helped some of them climb out of the lower class into the middle class, though almost never into the upper class.

In its effort to unite and mobilize the nation in a single-minded drive for military and economic parity with the Western powers, the Meiji government replaced the five-class system of the Tokugawa period with a three-class system by retaining the warrior class, consolidating the farmer, artisan, and merchant classes into a single "commoner" class, and renaming the outcaste class the "new commoner" class. The change of names, however, did not lead to a significant change in either the social status or the economic conditions of members of the outcaste class until their leaders founded a national organization, called the Leveling Society in obvious emulation of the Levelers' Movement of mid-seventeenth-century England, and launched a vigorous campaign for attainment of equality for its members in the early 1920s.

Women's status and role in Japanese society and politics began to change only after the Meiji Restoration and, even then, only very slowly until after World War II. While Japan's first women's liberation movement emerged on the eve of World War I, it was not until after the next world war that women were recognized as men's equals, at least in law, and given the vote.

Conflicts arising from these social divisions were effectively kept under control before World War II by an ideology of national unity and cooperation, which was propagated through a centrally controlled education system and a conformist press. The ideology focused the attention and energy of the entire nation on a drive to catch up with the Western powers.

The Meiji Constitution

The governing role of the Meiji oligarchy was formalized by the 1889 Constitution of the Great Empire of Japan. It guaranteed civil rights and freedoms to the emperor's subjects "subject to the limitations imposed by law" and required every law to be enacted with the consent of the bicameral parliament, the Imperial Diet. But it was the emperor who had the prerogative to sanction and promulgate all laws; open, close, or adjourn the Diet; and, in his capacity as the supreme commander of the armed forces, declare war, make peace, and conclude international treaties.

In practice, the emperor's sovereign powers were delegated to his representatives, the ruling oligarchs of the Meiji government, who often exercised their powers in contempt of his subjects' expressed wishes. The emperor's representatives dominated the powerful nonelective institutions of government, such as the Privy Council, the House of Peers, which was the upper chamber of the Imperial Diet, and, above all, the civil and military bureaucracies. The representatives of the emperor's subjects spoke, by and large, ineffectually, if not always deferentially, through the only elected institution, the Diet's lower chamber, the House of Representatives, and a few legal political parties. Members of the House of Representatives could block legislation they did not approve of, but the oligarchy could then bully those members into changing their minds or, if that did not work, simply legislate by imperial decree.

Of particular importance for the elite's power was the establishment of the Army General Staff Office in 1878 and the Naval General Staff Office in 1886. These offices were invested with exclusive control over the armed forces, subject only to the will of the throne, and thus placed the military as a whole effectively beyond the control of the civilian government. The extraconstitutional prerogatives eventually led the military to practice what amounted to its own diplomacy, often at cross purposes with the civilian government's, and even to dominate decision making on critical domestic and foreign policy issues.

The House of Representatives did have some notable successes in liberalizing and democratizing the fundamentally authoritarian regime, especially in the latter half of the 1910s through the 1920s. This era, known as **Taisho Democracy,** however, was short-lived. As Japan's economy became more deeply mired in a protracted post–World War I recession, then devastated by the Great Depression in the early 1930s, the advocates of democracy at home and peace abroad came under increasingly savage and effective attack by the military and right-wing groups within and outside the civilian bureaucracy, who blamed them for all of Japan's woes.

The military began to take over the Japanese government and dictate its policy at the end of the 1920s, when an army general named Giichi Tanaka was appointed prime minister.[10] His government decided to bring northeastern China, known as Manchuria, under effective Japanese control in order to stem the tide of rising Chinese nationalism against Japanese influence there and secure a regional market that accounted for 70 percent of Japan's exports at that time. Tanaka's policy encouraged Japanese army units in Manchuria to take matters into their own hands and expand their operations against local Chinese forces without prior authorization from the government in Tokyo. One result was the assassination in 1928 of a Chinese warlord, Zhang Zuo Lin, an event that intensified the Chinese opposition to Japanese interference in China.

The events in Manchuria forced Tanaka to resign, and he was succeeded by a liberal civilian, Osachi Hamaguchi. Under Hamaguchi's direction, Japan participated in the 1930 Naval Disarmament Conference in London and agreed to limit the tonnage, and thus the fighting capacity, of its warships to less than that of the United States and Britain. The acceptance of these limitations by the Japanese delegation to the conference caused an uproar among the military and right-wing groups at home and led to Hamaguchi's assassination in 1930. Thereafter, the military steadily consolidated its control of the Japanese government with the emperor's acquiescence, if not overt support. It silenced its critics by propaganda, blackmail, and use or threat of force.[11]

While Hamaguchi's successors throughout the 1930s were either civilians or moderate military leaders, they failed to control radical younger officers bent on conquering northeastern China and, eventually, the rest of China and Southeast Asia as a vast resource base for Japanese industry and armed forces. In an unsuccessful coup attempt in May 1932, a band of young naval officers attacked several government offices and shot the prime minister to death. In another similar attempt in February 1936, army troops led by radical officers invaded a number of government offices, murdered the finance minister and several other government leaders, and occupied the central part of Tokyo for four days.[12] Neither action succeeded in installing a military government, but both helped to intimidate and silence opponents of the military not only in the government but also in business circles, academia, and the mass media.

When the League of Nations condemned the Japanese invasion of northern China in 1933, the Japanese government, already under strong military and right-wing pressure, chose to withdraw from the League, an action followed by Nazi Germany later that year. As the international criticism of Japanese action in China intensified, Japan entered into an ostensibly anticommunist military alliance with Nazi Germany in 1936, which was joined by fascist Italy the following year. When the United States terminated its trade agreement with Japan in 1939, thus blocking

Foreign Minister Mamoru Shigemitsu signs instrument of surrender on the deck of the U.S.S. *Missouri*, while General Douglas MacArthur looks on, September 2, 1945.
Source: AP/Wide World Photos.

Japan's access to its major source of petroleum and raw materials, the government in Tokyo decided to seek an alternative source of supplies in Southeast Asia and moved its troops into French Indochina. This move, in turn, led Washington to impose an immediate embargo on the export of scrap iron to Japan and, by the summer of 1941, to ban the sale of petroleum and aviation gasoline to Japan and freeze Japan's assets in the United States.

Faced with the prospect of exhausting its limited fuel and raw material reserves following the imposition of an international embargo in 1941, the Japanese government, led by General Hideki Tojo, made the fateful decision to start a war against the United States

and its allies.[13] On December 7, 1941, Japanese naval air units executed a carefully planned and spectacularly successful surprise attack on the major U.S. naval base at Pearl Harbor in Hawaii. President Franklin D. Roosevelt immediately declared war against Japan.

Japan enjoyed some notable successes in the early phase of the war, but within less than a year began to lose one major battle after another in the Pacific. By late 1944, Japan's cause was reduced to a desperate defense of its major cities from increasingly frequent and destructive air raids by American bombers. In August 1945, Japan's last-ditch resistance was brought to an end by the nearly total destruction of two major cities, Hiroshima and Nagasaki, by the first and only atomic bombs ever used in war. By then, virtually all major Japanese cities, including Tokyo, had been reduced to rubble by a series of American bombing raids.

The Allied Occupation

The Allied Occupation of Japan that followed World War II transformed a fundamentally autocratic state into a fundamentally democratic one.[14] The Occupation, which lasted from 1945 until 1952, was formally a joint operation by the victorious Allies, including the United States, Great Britain, the Soviet Union, and China. In practice, however, it was an American occupation, led almost single-handedly by General Douglas MacArthur, who was appointed **Supreme Commander for the Allied Powers (SCAP).**

During the first year and a half of the Occupation, SCAP made a determined effort to achieve the twin goals of the Occupation, namely, the thorough demilitarization and democratization of Japan. The Japanese armed forces were swiftly dismantled, troops were demobilized, military production was halted, and wartime leaders were purged. Almost as swiftly, Japanese workers' right to organize was recognized, women were given the vote for the first time, many family-controlled conglomerates (*zaibatsu*) were dissolved, and virtually all other important political, legal, economic, and social institutions and practices were subjected to close scrutiny for their militaristic or antidemocratic flaws. Many were abolished or extensively reformed.

By far the most important step taken for the democratization of Japan by General MacArthur was the thorough revision of the 1889 Meiji Constitution. Based on a draft prepared by a handful of American lawyers at General MacArthur's behest in 1946, thereafter known as the "MacArthur Constitution," the new constitution was intended to legitimize and perpetuate the effects of the various Occupation-sponsored demilitarization and democratization measures. It was thus a radically democratic and pacifist document, which reflected its American authorship in its overall tone and language, especially in its preamble.

The MacArthur Constitution relegated the emperor to a purely symbolic and ritual role while mak-

Department-store display of destruction resulting from dropping of atom bomb on two Japanese cities.
Source: © Kitamura/Gamma Liaison.

ing the Japanese people the sovereign of the nation. It made all members of both chambers of the Diet directly elected by the people and elevated the Diet to the status of the state's highest and sole lawmaking organ. In a provision unprecedented and unique in the history of constitutions, the Japanese constitution forbids Japan to maintain any form of military power or to engage in acts of war in order to settle international disputes. In practice, the spirit if not the letter of the provision has long since been violated by the creation in the early 1950s of the so-called **Self-Defense Forces (SDF),** which have grown into one of the largest and best-equipped military forces in today's world. The spirit of pacifism that the provision represents, however, lives on in the minds of the majority of Japanese half a century after the document was written by Americans.

Party politics was promptly revived following the war, with SCAP's blessing and encouragement. Japan had political parties as early as the 1870s, predating the founding of the Imperial Diet by a decade and a half.[15] During the period of Taisho Democracy, from the mid-1910s to the early 1930s, two conservative parties, the Friends of Constitutional Government Party and the Constitutional Democratic Party, alternately formed a government through electoral competition.[16] All prewar Japanese parties had been disbanded around the time of the Japanese attack on Pearl Harbor in December 1941, either voluntarily or by government order. No sooner was the war over, however, than all the prewar parties were quickly reestablished.

The offspring of the prewar Friends of Constitutional Government Party was renamed the Japan Liberal Party (despite its conservative ideology) and dominated Japanese politics for much of the occupation period. The Liberals' major rival was the Japan Socialist Party. The Socialists won a slim plurality in the Diet elections in 1947 and formed a coalition government with another conservative party, the Japan Progressive Party, which later became the Democratic Party. The Socialist-led coalition government lasted for only a little over a year and a half before the Liberals returned to power and began to consolidate their hold on the Diet. The conservative domination of Japanese government became even firmer after the Liberals merged with the Democrats in 1955 to form the Liberal Democratic Party (LDP).

The LDP held a majority or plurality in the Diet, and thus nearly monopolistic control of the government, from 1955 to 1993. While there were no legal obstacles to the assumption of power by an opposition party or parties, the LDP managed to win every Diet election, though not necessarily a majority of its seats in recent years. This prevented alternation of parties in office and turned Japan into a stable predominant-party system. The long era of LDP rule, however, was not an uneventful period in the history of postwar Japanese politics. One of the most important turning points came in 1960 when a major political crisis erupted over the revision of the Mutual Security Treaty that had been signed between Japan and the United States in 1952 at the end of the Occupation.

The LDP government's proposal to revise the treaty provoked fierce opposition not only on the floor of the Diet but also in the streets of Tokyo and other major cities. Hundreds of thousands of protesters joined Socialist-led rallies and marches against Prime Minister Nobusuke Kishi and his cabinet for their action that would allegedly make Japan a military ally of the United States and an enemy of both the People's Republic of China and the Soviet Union. The government eventually railroaded the revised treaty through the Diet, but the event caused such violent public reaction that President Eisenhower was forced to cancel his planned visit to Japan and Prime Minister Kishi and his cabinet were forced to resign in its aftermath.

The experience of the 1960 political crisis led Kishi's successors to avoid tackling controversial foreign and security policy issues and concentrate on eco-

Demonstrators against renewal of U.S.-Japanese Mutual Security Treaty in front of the Diet Building in Tokyo, May 1960.
Source: AP/Wide World Photos.

nomic issues. This change in the LDP's attitude ushered in an era of political stability and economic dynamism in Japan. That era, however, ended in 1993 when the fall of the LDP government signaled the arrival of an unprecedented period of coalition governments and political volatility, as Japan began to prepare for the end of an eventful century.

In a little over one century, Japan has thus changed from a vulnerable developing country into an advanced industrial nation, from an authoritarian state into a stable democracy, from a militaristic, imperialist culture into a pacifist one, and from an economic oligarchy into a more egalitarian society. The Japanese experience is of great interest to many developing countries in today's world, especially those making the transition to democracy. In seeking to understand the true dimensions and meanings of this great transformation, we have considered how Japan joined the modern world of states, how Japanese people formed their collective identities, how the democratic idea was introduced into Japan, and how Japan entered the international political economy. Let us summarize the main points of the foregoing discussion.

First, Japan, in a weak economic and military position, joined the modern world of states after two and a half centuries of self-imposed isolation, but with its formal political independence and sovereignty intact. Interestingly, this happened at about the same time that Germany joined the modern world, and with some of the same problems, such as a territory poorly endowed with natural resources, a rigidly stratified feudal society, and a largely agrarian economy. Both Japan and Germany found themselves in competition with far more advanced industrial nations that controlled most of the world's primary resources. At the beginning of their modernization, both nations thus had little assurance of gaining access to the resources they needed for their military security and economic development.

Second, the imperatives of nationbuilding and of maintaining independence in this difficult and generally hostile international environment led Meiji Japan's leaders to focus on the creation of a new national identity among its people using a family-state analogy with the emperor as the father of the nation. Like Germany, modern Japan's national identity thus had a distinctive racial and ethnic overtone. Their national drives to catch up with more advanced industrial powers both promoted and were spurred on by a strong sense of national identity and solidarity.

Modern Germany and modern Japan subsequently continued to share similar political and economic problems both at home and in their relations with the world. Both experienced democratization of government and politics, especially in the 1920s, but in the 1930s, the process was derailed in both countries by the impact of the Great Depression. In the wake of that depression, and faced with growing conflicts with advanced industrial nations, Japan entered World War II as an ally of Nazi Germany. After that war, Japan, like West Germany, was transformed into a contemporary democratic state by an occupying power, the United States.

Third, modern Japan initially grafted democratic symbols and forms onto an oligarchic, authoritarian state. A trend towards more pluralistic government and politics soon set in and accelerated in the 1920s but was cut short by the Great Depression and the economic polarization into which the world plunged in the wake of the depression. As in Germany, a much more thorough and durable democratization process

began during the postwar Allied Occupation. The process continues today.

Fourth, and last, Japanese leaders embarked on an intensive state-led program of industrialization in order to catch up with the Western industrial nations as quickly as possible. This produced rapid economic growth and new collective identities without a state equipped to negotiate conflicts democratically. Gross inequalities in the distribution of income, wealth, and power among classes and regions hindered the development of a large and vigorous domestic market for industrial goods and thus discouraged economic growth. This was an important factor in Japan's decision to embark on an aggressively expansionist foreign policy that eventually brought the nation into conflict with the Western powers and led to the Pacific-based war.

IMPLICATIONS FOR CONTEMPORARY JAPANESE POLITICS

The historical experience of Japan's entry into the world of states in the nineteenth century and its relationship with that world since then colors Japan's contemporary perceptions of and attitudes toward that world. To most Japanese, the world is a hierarchy made up of powerful, often imperious, self-aggrandizing states on the one hand, and powerless, often conquered and humiliated states on the other. It is thus very much an anarchic world that is depicted in the so-called realist literature on international politics. In order to survive in such a world, a state and its people must be vigilant and find a way to protect themselves either independently, if possible—by equipping themselves with strong armed forces and developing a highly productive industrial economy that can support such forces, as prewar Japan attempted to do—or by forming an alliance with a powerful and friendly ally, such as the postwar United States.

There is thus an underlying element of anxiety and wariness in the Japanese attitude toward the world. However, after their experience in World War II, especially the "atomic baptism," most Japanese don't believe that an independent military force is a viable means of national defense in the age of nuclear weapons. To them, the only feasible and sensible way to ensuring their nation's survival in today's world is through alliance, or at least cooperation, with other nations, particularly the most powerful. A nation as poor in natural resources as Japan must gain access to resources abroad through world trade and negotiation rather than force.

In short, the way it has joined and interacted with the modern world of states since the mid-nineteenth century, and especially since World War II, makes contemporary Japan an international trader, but with a degree of fatalism and cynicism in its fundamental view of international relations. This element of cynicism often makes the Japanese appear to the world to be selfish and even treacherous, and leads them into frequent disputes with their allies and economic competitors.

The Japanese people's national identity, formed very early in their history and deliberately molded into a strong sense of national unity and solidarity by the Tokugawa rulers and their Meiji and post-Meiji successors, makes them one of the best-integrated and most unified peoples in the contemporary world. It is unlikely that the Japanese nation and state will ever disintegrate into two or more contending nations and states and thus follow in the footsteps of the former Soviet Union, Yugoslavia, or Czechoslovakia.

Their own strong, well-defined national identity, however, makes it difficult for many Japanese to understand and sympathize with other peoples of the world who lack, for a variety of reasons, such a strong national identity. Although the Japanese are generally willing contributors to various international programs designed to help poorer, developing countries around the world, they are not particularly cooperative when it comes to helping others cope with problems related to multinationalism, multiculturalism, and multilingualism—as, for example, in a number of African nations. As we will discuss in Section 4, the same kind of indifference toward and intolerance of cultural diversity has often been displayed by Japanese in their treatment of domestic minorities. While their attitudes toward minorities in general, and in Japan in particular, are gradually changing, it remains difficult for many Japanese to grasp the full moral significance of the minorities' problems.

Democracy has become fully accepted both ideologically and institutionally in Japan only since the end of World War II and the Allied Occupation. Nonetheless, the experiment with the democratic form of government in prewar Japan, however half-hearted and ultimately unsuccessful it may have been, helped the Japanese accept the idea of democracy and actually practice it in the postwar period. In this regard, Japan is unique not only in Asia but in most parts of the world except for Western Europe, North America, and Oceania. The history of democracy in Japan makes this form of government more stable and reliable than in most parts of the world, outside of the regions mentioned above. Candidates and their supporters in Japanese elections may make liberal use of money, as do those in U.S. elections, but tampering with ballot boxes or refusal to accept the result of an election, both of which are commonplace in many developing nations, is very rare in postwar Japan.

Finally, Japan has also experimented with a method of developing an advanced industrial economy in a nation that lacks both the natural resources and the modern technologies essential to successful industrialization. The method involves regular, extensive intervention by the state in the management of the national economy, known as **industrial policy.** As we will see in the next section, this method has worked quite well in both prewar and postwar Japan, and has been studied and copied by Japan's Asian neighbors and, increasingly, by other developing nations as well. Success is an irresistible precedent to follow, and Japan is likely to follow the success of its own industrial policy. Whether it will continue to work well in the rapidly changing post–Cold War world remains to be seen. As will be explained in Section 5, it is doubtful that the method will work as well as it did in the past or will be accepted by Japan's trading partners as readily as it was during the Cold War era.

SECTION 2
Political Economy and Development

STATE AND ECONOMY

Contemporary Japan is one of the wealthiest and most advanced industrial nations in the world. Until the early 1990s, it boasted one of the highest gross national products (GNPs) per person, one of the highest and most stable annual GNP growth rates, and consistently the lowest inflation rate among the world's richest industrial economies. Moreover, as Table 1 shows, its income distribution is among the most egalitarian. Japan also has the world's lowest infant mortality rate and the longest life expectancy at birth. Enrollments of school-age children in Japan's primary and secondary schools are among the highest in the world, and its workforce is one of the most productive. Finally, Japan is one of the safest nations in the world with, by far, the lowest crime rate among the advanced industrial nations (see Table 2 on the following page).

In light of the devastating physical and psychological damage Japan suffered during World War II, the swift recovery, followed by the spectacular expansion, of its postwar economy impresses many people around the world. Its economic performance has been called a miracle and inspires both governments and citizens in many developing nations, especially in Asia. Like the legendary Rome, however, Japan's industrial economy was not built in a day; its history is as long and as complex as the histories of most European nations.

Economic Development in Prewar Japan

Japan's strategy of economic modernization was started by the Meiji state at its founding in the mid-nineteenth century. The new government started and, for a while, operated munitions factories, mines, railroads, telegraph and telephone companies, and textile mills. Within a decade and a half, however, most of these enterprises were sold to private entrepreneurs, some of whom subsequently built huge conglomerates known as *zaibatsu*. As economist Alexander Gerschenkron has pointed out, an effort to develop a national economy under strong government leadership is both logical and commonly seen in many late-developing nations.[17]

During the next seven decades or so, but especially in the first three decades of the twentieth century, these formidable, and increasingly transnational, corporate empires dominated the modern industrial sector of the Japanese economy and spearheaded its rapid expansion in tandem with an ambitious, disciplined, and highly nationalistic government bureaucracy. The bureaucracy systematically encouraged and

---

TABLE 1   Inflation, Income Distribution, Infant Mortality, and Life Expectancy in 1990

	Inflation Rates (1980–1990)	Income Distribution		Infant Mortality (per 1,000 live births)	Life Expectancy (at birth)
		Lowest 20%	Highest 10%		
France	6.1	(1979) 6.3	25.5	7	77
Germany	2.7	(1984) 6.8	23.4	7	76
Italy	9.9	(1986) 6.8	25.3	9	77
United Kingdom	5.8	(1979) 5.8	23.3	8	76
United States	3.7	(1985) 4.7	25.0	9	76
Japan	1.5	(1979) 8.7	22.4	5	79

Source: The World Bank, *World Development Report 1992* (Oxford: Oxford University Press, 1992); Table 1: "Basic indicators," 218–19; Table 13: "Money and interest rates," 242–43; Table 28: "Health and nutrition," 272–73; Table 30: "Income distribution and ICP estimates of GDP," 276–77.

TABLE 2 **Felony and Arrest Rates, 1989 (per 100,000 population)**

	Felony	Arrest
France	5,831	38.8%
West Germany	7,031	47.2
United Kingdom	7,355	33.6
United States	5,741	21.1
Japan	1,358	46.2

Source: Mariko Bando, ed., *Zusetsu: Sekai no naka no nihon no kurashi* [An illustrated evaluation of life in Japan by world standards], rev. ed. (Tokyo: Ministry of Finance Printing Office, 1992), 118–19.

guided the development of the national economy by providing a variety of incentives to industries and major firms, especially the *zaibatsu* conglomerates.[18] These included direct subsidies, tax breaks, tariff protection against foreign competition, and construction at public expense of industrial infrastructure, such as roads, railroads, port facilities, and communications networks. Japan became an outstanding example of a state that works with, rather than against, the most powerful economic groups in its society in a concerted effort to bring about rapid but controlled economic development.

Japan's economy grew by about 3 percent a year on average throughout this period, the pace quickening to over 5 percent a year during the 1930s.[19] World War I provided a windfall for Japanese businesses. Taking advantage of the war's disruption of Europe's global trade networks, especially of European nations' access to Asian markets, Japanese textile, steel, machine tool, chemical, and shipping industries quickly expanded. The wartime boom brought Japan's trade balance into the black for the first time in the nation's history.[20] In 1905, 65 percent of Japan's labor force still worked in agriculture, with only 12 percent working in the industrial (manufacturing and mining) sector. By 1940, however, the agricultural sector had declined to 44 percent and the industrial sector had grown to 24 percent of the labor force. In the thirty-five years between 1905 and 1940, factory output rose from 6 percent to 29 percent of net domestic product.[21] By the eve of World War II, Japan had one of the world's fastest growing and most competitive economies.

The pre–World War II Japanese economy, however, suffered from a number of serious problems. Internally, an extremely uneven distribution of income and wealth among its citizens not only generated considerable social tension but also prevented rapid growth of a domestic market for its industrial products. The worldwide depression triggered by the stock market crash in New York in 1929 hit the Japanese economy as hard as it hit the U.S. and European economies. The crisis lasted until mid-1933, when government policy began to turn the economy around.

Prewar Japan's handful of *zaibatsu* took the lion's share of industrial profits by squeezing both the working class and small businesses, many of which served as their subcontractors. Labor unions were not tolerated by most employers.[22] The unionization rate never reached 8 percent of the total urban workforce, and most unorganized workers were paid wages barely adequate for subsistence, especially in the small business sector that employed the overwhelming majority of such workers. There were frequent, bitter disputes between employers and both organized and unorganized employees over wages and working conditions. In the latter half of the 1920s through the end of the 1930s, for example, more than 1,000 such disputes were reported each year, involving hundreds of employers and tens of thousands of workers.

The rural economy in prewar Japan was characterized by similar problems. Throughout the late nineteenth and early twentieth centuries, land ownership in rural Japan became increasingly concentrated and the ranks of landless tenant farmers had risen to nearly 30 percent of all farmers by the late 1930s.[23] This gave rise to frequent, often violent, landlord-tenant disputes over such issues as land titles and rents, involving well over 30,000 landlords and 100,000 tenants a year in the period between the mid-1920s and the mid-1930s.

The great poverty of most farmers and urban workers was reflected in the frequency and intensity of disputes with their landlords and employers. Low incomes effectively deprived the majority of Japanese of the means to purchase many of the manufactures produced in rapidly growing quantities by domestic industry. This severely limited the growth potential of Japan's domestic market, drove its industry to seek markets abroad, and deepened the trade dependence of its economy. Since Japan had few natural resources within its own borders and had to import the bulk of raw materials needed by its industry, an increase in its exports meant an increase in its imports. Moreover, it increasingly depended on imported foodstuffs to feed its rapidly growing population. As a result, Japan's imports exceeded its exports for most of the period before World War II. Japan's dependence upon overseas markets and imports propelled its quest for colonies—first in Korea and China and later in Southeast Asia and the Pacific—in the effort to establish what was euphemistically called the "Greater East Asia Co-Prosperity Sphere," but what was really a vastly expanded Japanese empire.

Japan's economic development in the first decades of the twentieth century created a significant class of industrial workers and increasingly frequent and acrimonious labor disputes. According to one Japanese study, the total number of industrial disputes doubled between 1925 and 1931, from about 800 to nearly 1,500, and those involving job action, including strikes, work stoppages, work to rule, and so forth, more than tripled, from about 300 to nearly 1,000.[24] Moreover, the external expansion eventually brought Japan into a direct confrontation with the European colonial powers, especially Great Britain, France, and the Netherlands, who had long since staked out their spheres of control in Asia and the Pacific, and the United States, who had begun to claim its own share of the colonial pie in Asia and the Pacific since the mid-nineteenth century.[25] The steady expansion of Japanese control in China met with particularly stiff opposition from the United States, which had insisted for decades on the "Open Door" (equal opportunity) policy in China for all nations. The confrontation between Japan and the West culminated in the Japanese attack on Pearl Harbor in December of 1941, which began the Pacific-based part of World War II.

Japan's Postwar Economic Recovery

Japan's total defeat in the war and unconditional surrender in 1945 transformed not only its relationships with its Asian and Pacific neighbors and the Western powers but also its domestic political, social, and economic institutions and practices. Under the formal rule of a joint occupation authority of the Allied powers and the actual rule of United States military forces, Japan was disarmed and democratized almost overnight. The Occupation-sponsored reforms paved the way for a dramatic recovery and subsequent expansion of Japan's domestic economy and foreign trade.

The democratization reforms considerably reduced the concentration of economic wealth and power in Japan by dividing the assets and managerial control of some of the largest *zaibatsu* conglomerates into several new and independent firms, unionizing a significant portion of urban labor, and redistributing most of the landlord-owned farmland among tenants and small farmers. The control of the giant conglomerates by members of their founding families came to an end, although most of the conglomerates themselves survived the reform and subsequently acquired even greater wealth and power. The rate of unionization reached about 55 percent of Japan's urban workers at the end of the 1940s, although it steadily declined in subsequent years. The **land reform** reduced the tenant population from nearly 30 percent of Japan's farmers to about 5 percent, while boosting the owner-farmer population from about 33 percent to 62 percent.[26] This transformed an important source of prewar rural radicalism into one of the most stable blocs of electoral support for conservatives in postwar Japan. These changes had a combined effect of drastically reducing income differences based on social and economic status among Japanese citizens, substantially raising urban workers' and small farmers' standard of living, and thus creating a vast new domestic market for the goods and services soon to be supplied in increasing quantities by the nation's rapidly reviving industry.

The demilitarization program forced Japan not only to give up its existing armed forces and arms but, more important, to stop manufacturing and investing in the manufacture of arms. This provision, in effect, freed Japan from the heavy burden of military spending that had taken about a third of the nation's total budget in the early 1930s, three-quarters of it at the beginning of the Pacific-based war, and as much as 85 percent of it at the end of the war. Henceforth, Japan concentrated not only capital but also labor and its highly sophisticated military technology on the production of goods and services for civilian consumption at home and abroad. This shift soon led to Japan's reemergence as one of the most prosperous nations in the postwar world.

The Japanese economic "miracle" was also the result of a change in U.S. Occupation policy in response to the emerging Cold War. By 1948, the primary objectives of the Occupation shifted from demilitarization and democratization to swift economic recovery and the incorporation of Japan into the anticommunist bloc led by the United States. After China came under communist rule in 1949 and the Korean War broke out in 1950, Japan's new role as a key ally of the United States in Asia became ever more evident. This role gave Japan privileged access to vast export markets and advanced industrial technologies abroad, especially in the United States, and developed its own economy into a formidable export machine with large trade surpluses after the mid-1960s.

The United States helped Japan begin rebuilding its war-devastated economy by providing goods, including food, worth about $1.8 billion, between 1947 and 1951. From late 1948 through 1949, the U.S. Occupation also helped the Japanese government overcome postwar economic chaos, especially rampant inflation, by balancing the government budget, raising taxes, imposing price and wage freezes, and resuming limited foreign trade. After the Occupation ended and Japan regained its independence in 1952, the United States continued to help by opening its markets to Japanese exports and granting Japanese firms access to advanced industrial technology developed by U.S. firms. The United States also supported Japan's admission to various postwar international organizations, such as the United Nations, the International Monetary Fund (IMF), the World Bank, and the General Agreement on Tariffs and Trade (GATT). Membership in such international organizations helped Japan gain access to wider sources of raw materials, merchandise and capital markets, and advanced industrial technology and scientific information around the globe.

The Japanese economy grew at extraordinarily high and sustained rates during the next two and a half decades. The Korean War turned out to be a windfall for Japanese business, triggering a series of long economic booms during the next two decades. Japanese factories became the main source for the massive goods and services needed by the U.S. military. By the time the war-initiated boom came to an end in the early 1970s, Japan had become the second-largest market economy in the world after the United States.

Japan's Industrial Economy

Immediately following the end of the Allied Occupation in 1952, the Japanese government began to implement economic policies aimed at sustaining the country's postwar economic growth. These programs, known as industrial policies, provided investment funds, tax breaks, foreign exchange, and imported foreign technologies to specific "strategic" industries such as electric power, steel, transportation, and coal mining. In the 1960s, the government also encouraged, through an informal but effective system of advising known as **administrative guidance,** business mergers and cartelization—that is, agreement between two or more firms on matters such as prices, production, and distribution—in order to reduce counterproductive competition between firms. Over the years, the targets of industrial policy shifted to automobiles, computers, and other high-tech industries, while the forms of assistance also shifted to tariff and nontariff barriers against foreign imports, public funds for research and development activities in the private sector, and promotion of public-private collaboration in the development of cutting-edge technologies.[27]

As Japan's economy grew, and as its trade balance with such major trading partners as the United States began to record chronic surpluses after the mid-1960s, Japanese protectionist policies began to draw increasingly vocal foreign criticism. Many Japanese manufacturers and traders had by then grown strong enough not only to survive but to win international competition without as much government help as before. The combination of these two developments led to a gradual liberalization of the Japanese economy after the mid-1960s. It soon began to resemble the advanced industrial economies of Western Europe and North America in its operational principles. Compared with the most market-oriented among them, such as the United States', however, Japan's economy still remains more extensively and

Japan's Economic High Command

Outside Japan, the Ministry of International Trade and Industry (MITI) is far better known than the Ministry of Transportation. MITI has been credited with the bureaucratic leadership responsible for the phenomenal growth of the Japanese economy before and, especially, after World War II.

MITI is headed by a minister and composed of, as most other Japanese ministries are, the offices of an administrative vice minister, two parliamentary vice ministers, a minister's secretariat, several "staff" bureaus, and several "operating" bureaus. The staff bureaus are concerned with policy initiation and development in the areas of international trade policy, international trade administration, industrial policy, and industrial location and environmental protection. The operating bureaus are responsible for policy implementation in the areas of basic industries (for example, iron and steel, nonferrous metals, and chemicals), machinery and information industries (for example, industrial machinery, electronics, automobile, aircraft, and ordnance), and consumer industries (such as textiles, paper and pulp, ceramics, and home appliances).

Despite its reputation as the mastermind of the Japanese economic miracle, MITI is a ministry of relatively modest size as far as its shares of the official government budget and personnel of Japan's central government are concerned. In the early 1990s, for example, the ministry's share of the official budget of the Japanese central government was only slightly over 1 percent, and its share of the central government personnel was slightly over 1.5 percent. The ministry ranked eighth in terms of the official budget and sixth in terms of personnel among the twelve ministries.

MITI's power is thus based not on its share of the official government budget and personnel but on its licensing and permit-giving authority, its liberal and effective use of administrative guidance, and its share of an unofficial government budget called the **Fiscal Investment and Loan Program (FILP).** In the early 1990s, the range of activities over which MITI wielded regulatory authority was one of the widest, second only to the Ministry of Transportation's (1,915 versus 1,966 in 1992). MITI has also been known as one of the most skillful and aggressive users of administrative guidance, or informal pressure and coercion, in guiding the behavior of Japanese firms and industries. The ministry has used Japan's "other budget," FILP, as skillfully and aggressively for the same purpose.

FILP channels funds that accumulate in government-operated trusts and in pension, insurance, and postal savings programs into a variety of public works projects, such as highway construction and housing development, and selected areas of the private sector economy, such as high-tech industries, small businesses, agriculture, and so on. The Japanese government spending under FILP in the early 1990s amounted to nearly two-thirds of the official budget (¥45.7 trillion versus ¥72.3 trillion in 1993). MITI's share of this unofficial budget was about 19 percent.

effectively controlled and supported by the central government bureaucracy.[28] At the core of this government bureaucracy are half a dozen ministries with jurisdiction over specific sectors of the economy, such as the Ministries of Finance (MOF); International Trade and Industry (MITI); Construction (MOC); Transportation, Posts and Telecommunications; Agriculture, Forestry and Fisheries; and the Economic Planning Agency (EPA).

Each ministry's mandate as defined by law and by practice typically includes both regulatory and protective powers over individuals, corporations, and a variety of other social groups. Regulatory power is exercised mainly through the enforcement of legal and quasi-legal requirements for a license, permit, or certificate for virtually every kind of activity with actual or potential effects on the public interest. The protective power is used to provide various types of public assistance to private citizens and groups, such as subsidies and tax exemptions for particular industries, especially those with close ties to influential politicians or bureaucrats. This has contributed to the pervasive political corruption that erupted into sensational scandals at almost regular intervals during the LDP's one-party rule. Both types of power are based partially on formal laws and partially on the informal system of administrative guidance, which a ministry routinely uses to augment its formal powers. Each ministry regulates from a few dozen to nearly 2,000 types of citizens' social and economic activities.

The ubiquity of bureaucratic red tape is an important aspect of contemporary Japanese economy and society. For example, as of 1993, every buyer of a new car in Japan was legally required by the Ministry of Transportation to have the vehicle inspected and certified three years after purchase, then every two years, then annually after the car's eleventh year. (After 1995, the revised law requires eleven-year-old cars to be inspected every two years.) In addition to these required inspections, the ministry required, by means of administrative guidance, every car to be inspected every six, twelve, or twenty-four months, each longer interval doubling the number of parts to be inspected. A regular, legally required inspection of an average-size car costs the owner only about $12 in 1994. An informally required, semiannual inspection, however, costs about $950.

Many Japanese car owners complied with this informal requirement for fear that failing to do so might make their vehicle liable to detection of defects at the next legally required inspection and to repair work even more expensive than an informal inspection. This official racket forced many people to buy a new car every few years. Moreover, the 19 million or so inspections made each year by the nationwide network of licensed service stations generated an enormous income, part of which may have ended up in the campaign coffers of politicians with close ties to the ministry and the industry.

The private industrial sector of the Japanese economy is characterized by the interdependence of a vast number of small firms on the one hand and a small number of giant firms on the other. In the manufacturing sector, more than 95 percent of nearly half a million Japanese firms are small businesses with less than 100 employees. On the other hand, most of the few big businesses are affiliated with six huge conglomerates, known as **keiretsu** (business groups). Each *keiretsu* is composed of a major bank and several large manufacturing, trading, shipping, construction, and insurance companies. It is a group of firms of comparable size and capability that are horizontally linked with one another. There are also seventeen similar but smaller groups, including those built around the major automobile manufacturers, such as Toyota and Nissan. These, too, are often called *keiretsu,* but they are characterized more by vertical ties that link several large firms to numerous smaller ones. The latter serve as subcontractors to the former.

The Mitsubishi Group is an example of a horizontally organized (that is, functionally diverse) *keiretsu.* Mitsubishi is a descendant of a pre–World War II *zaibatsu* group with the same name; but today's Mitsubishi Group is no longer controlled by a single family, the Iwasakis. The contemporary Mitsubishi Group is composed of about thirty formally independent, co-equal corporations whose presidents form an informal executive committee called the Friday Club, which, as its name suggests, meets once a week. Each of these member corporations is a leading firm in its own line of business, as exemplified by Mitsubishi Bank, Mitsubishi Heavy Industries, Mitsubishi Chemical Industries, Mitsubishi Motors, Mitsubishi Estate, Mitsubishi Electric, and Mitsubishi Corporation, which is a trading company. About a dozen other firms, including Mitsubishi Atomic Energy Industries and Mitsubishi Space Software, are more loosely affiliated with the group.

By contrast, the Toyota Group, led by Toyota Motor Corporation, represents a vertically organized (that is, functionally related) business group. Under the automobile maker's direct control is a *keiretsu* group of a dozen large corporations, including Toyota Trading, Aichi Steel Works, and Towa Real Estate. Each member of this group has subcontracting relationships with about 250 smaller firms, which take orders from the group as a whole. In turn, many of these 250 or so subcontractors hand down some of their work to even smaller firms. In other words, the Toyota Group is a huge pyramid made up of several hundred legally independent but functionally interdependent firms.

The subcontracting system provides the small businesses with jobs and access both to markets for their products and to some of the advanced technologies in the possession of the big businesses within their group. The big businesses, however, benefit even more from the system because it enables them to avoid keeping certain kinds of workers on their regular payroll by using subcontractors' employees on a need-only basis. During an economic downturn, the big firms protect themselves financially by quickly reducing orders placed with their subcontractors or by delaying payment for orders already filled.

Small businesses in Japan hire large numbers of temporary and part-time workers, the overwhelming majority of whom are women. Women earn, on average, only about half as much as men for roughly the same quality and quantity of work, even after an equal employment opportunity law was enacted in 1985. The wage differentials between the largely male regular employees and the female temporary and part-time employees help businesses keep production costs down and profits up. This **dual-structure,** or double-deck, **system** also contributes to the international competitiveness of Japan's major export companies. The savings that big firms gain from it are, in part, passed on to some of their employees in the form of guaranteed employment and **seniority-based wages** that rise with the length of employment almost independently of employees' performance. This same system, however, takes advantage of the vulnerable part-time employees, especially women in small businesses.

Another salient characteristic of the contemporary Japanese economy is the close, and normally cooperative, relationships most labor unions maintain with management. At the end of the 1980s, Japan's various labor federations merged into a single organization known as the General Confederation of Japanese Labor, or Rengo. This merger was a result, not of a growing strength, but of a growing weakness, of the labor movement and the opposition parties it supported. For one thing, the proportion of unionized labor in Japan's total industrial workforce had declined from well over 50 percent in the late 1940s to less than half that figure by the end of the 1980s. The decline was caused by several factors, such as increased mechanization in industries with high unionization rates, notably textiles and shipbuilding, a rising proportion of employees in service industries where unionization rates were traditionally low, and a substantial increase in the number of temporary and part-time employees who tended not to become union members.

For another thing, leaders of many surviving unions had lost much of their control over their rank-and-file members' votes in elections. In the 1970s and 1980s, it became increasingly difficult for union leaders to deliver blocs of loyal members' votes to candidates of either socialist party, as they did in the 1950s through much of the 1960s. Moreover, union leaders, especially those of private sector unions, became increasingly willing to cooperate with management and moderate their prosocialist partisanship as well as wage and other job-related demands. While many larger unions continue to participate in the annual wage negotiations coordinated by the national leadership, known as the **spring labor offensive,** the radicalism and militancy that once characterized labor's position in such negotiations have greatly diminished, as have the number of strikes (see Table 3 on the following page).

The rapid growth of the Japanese economy in the 1950s and 1960s was to a large extent driven by the availability of relatively low-cost fuels, especially oil from the Middle East, other industrial raw materials, and advanced industrial technologies from the United States. But Japan's rapid growth also brought serious environmental problems and heavy dependence on imported oil. By the end of the 1960s, pollution had assumed crisis proportions and the Diet was forced to pass a series of laws aimed at discouraging and restricting the use of pollution-causing industrial equipment and practices. The destruction of the environment by industry was largely brought under control by the early 1970s. The costs of heavy dependence upon foreign-sourced fuels and raw materials became evident in the 1970s, when the Organization of Petroleum Exporting Countries (OPEC) engineered a sharp increase in the price of oil worldwide. In 1973, the Japanese government implemented policies aimed at forcing both industries and ordinary citizens to reduce the consumption of energy, especially oil. This effort was successful enough to spare the country another debilitating energy crisis.

Welfare and Social Policy

In sharp contrast to rapid industrial and military growth, a publicly funded system of social security developed very slowly and haphazardly in prewar Japan. A modest and partially government-funded health insurance program was created by law in the mid-1920s and evolved into a national program for voluntary subscribers by the late 1930s. From then through World War II, several other programs, including workers' compensation, assistance to soldiers, protection of single-parenting mothers and their children, and workers' pension insurance, were created. However, it was not until after World War II that the Japanese government began a systematic, sustained effort to provide a minimum level of social security to all citizens.

The development of a comprehensive national social security system in postwar Japan was mandated by an article in the 1947 constitution that states, "In all spheres of life, the State shall use its endeavors for the promotion and extension of social welfare and security, and of public health." During the four decades following the Allied Occupation, a

---

TABLE 3   **Industrial Disputes**

		Japan	U.S.	U.K.	West Germany	France
1965	1[a]	1,542	3,963	2,354	—	1,674
	2	1,682	1,550	876	6,250	1,237
	3	5,669	23,300	2,925	48,520	980
1970	1	2,260	5,717	3,906	—	3,319
	2	1,720	3,305	1,801	184	1,160
	3	3,915	66,413	10,980	93	1,742
1975	1	3,391	5,031	2,282	—	3,888
	2	2,732	1,746	809	36	1,827
	3	8,016	31,237	6,012	69	3,869
1980	1	1,133	3,873	1,330	—	3,542
	2	563	1,365	834	45	501
	3	1,001	33,389	11,964	128	1,674
1985	1	627	54	903	—	1,901
	2	123	324	791	78	23
	3	264	7,079	6,402	34	727
1990	1	284	44	630	—	29
	2	84	185	298	252	56
	3	145	5,925	1,903	264	166

[a]Note: 1 = number of industrial disputes with work stoppages;
2 = number of workers involved in thousands;
3 = number of man-days lost in thousands.

Sources: International Labour Office, *Year Book of Labour Statistics* (Geneva: International Labour Office), annual; Solomon B. Levine, "Labor," *Kodansha Encyclopedia of Japan,* vol. 4 (Tokyo: Kodansha, 1983), 349, Table 1.

---

number of state-sponsored and wholly or partially state-financed social security programs were created by law. But in the wake of the 1973 oil crisis, the government began to attempt to shift the major burden of financing the rapidly expanding social security system to the private sector. This "Japanese-style welfare society" failed to contain the growth of public or private welfare expenditures in subsequent years.

As Table 4 shows, the Japanese ratio of social security expenditure to gross domestic product (GDP) in the mid-1980s still remained lower than those of most other advanced industrial nations. Nonetheless, public and private social welfare programs today cost Japan roughly half a trillion dollars per year, or a little over 15 percent of GNP; and government welfare spending costs about $150 billion per year, or a little

over 20 percent of the national budget. Social security claims a larger share of the annual government budget than any other budget category except grants-in-aid to local governments and interest payments on public bonds.

The annual social welfare expenditures of half a trillion dollars are divided among a variety of programs, including health care for the elderly; public health, such as prevention of epidemic diseases and maintenance of health-related facilities; assistance to the handicapped, elderly, orphans, and indigent; and pension payments for former military personnel. The lion's share of the total social security spending, or about 85 percent, however, goes to four types of social insurance programs, namely, pension, medical, unemployment, and workers' compensation. These programs provide all Japanese citizens with at least some

TABLE 4	**Social Security Spending as Percentage of GDP, 1985**				
Japan	United States	United Kingdom	West Germany	France	Italy
11.1%	12.0%	19.4%	23.2%	27.3%	10.0%

Source: Somucho tokeikyoku [Office of the Prime Minister, Statistics Bureau], *Kokusai tokei yoran (1992/93 ban)* [Handbook of international statistics, 1992/93 edition] (Tokyo: Ministry of Finance Printing Office, 1992), 210–11.

medical insurance and all eligible citizens with some retirement income.

Japan's social security system has been criticized in recent years for the unevenness of the costs borne and benefits enjoyed by different groups. The employees of a small number of very large and thriving firms generally pay less and receive more than those who are either employees of small businesses or not gainfully employed. Efforts have been made since the mid-1980s to standardize the costs and benefits across all existing programs and eventually to unify them into a single system, but no specific steps have been taken so far to achieve either goal in the immediate future.

Today (in the mid-1990s), the average Japanese taxpayer pays roughly 25 percent of his or her annual income in national and local taxes. Japanese taxes are divided into direct and indirect taxes. The former include income, corporate, inheritance, and land-value taxes, whereas the latter include a much wider variety, such as consumption (sales), alcohol, tobacco, petroleum, and stock-exchange taxes. A capital gains tax was first introduced in 1989 and is considered an income tax. The average Japanese taxpayer pays somewhat more of his or her income in taxes than the average U.S. taxpayer but considerably less than the average Western European taxpayer. On the other hand, the average Japanese does not enjoy as many tax-supported social welfare benefits and public amenities as the average Western European does.

SOCIETY AND ECONOMY

The succession of conservative LDP governments that governed Japan for nearly the entire postwar period concentrated on building infrastructural support for industry rather than providing facilities and services for the general public. This has led to conspicuous imbalances in the physical and social environments in which many Japanese live.

In today's Japan, virtually all urban and rural families own an assortment of what were considered luxury items barely two decades ago: color televisions, washing machines, vacuum cleaners, refrigerators, and, increasingly, automobiles. The Japanese have roughly as many automobiles per 1,000 people (467 in 1990) as Britons (405), Germans (511 for West Germans), French (500), and Italians (477 in 1988), though considerably fewer than Americans (754 in 1989).[29] The same may be said about telephones and a wide range of other consumer durables.

Japanese workers earn wages comparable in absolute amounts to those earned by American and Western European workers, though in somewhat different ways. The typical Japanese wage consists of a relatively low basic monthly pay, several allowances of variable amounts, and substantial semiannual bonuses. Allowances are paid, for example, for dependents, housing costs, commuting costs, and so forth, while the two bonuses, paid in midsummer and at the end of the year, often amount to nearly half of the basic annual wage. Retirement benefits for most employees consist of a lump-sum severance pay equal to about thirty-five months' pay and, if one satisfies the age and length-of-service requirements, a contribution-based pension. Many employees of large firms are provided with company-subsidized housing and the privilege of using company-owned recreational and sporting facilities.

Housing conditions in urban Japan are generally poor. The floor space of the average Japanese housing unit is roughly half the size of its American counterpart, although not substantially smaller than the average in most European nations. Moreover, a rampant,

TABLE 5   **Japanese Trade with the World and the United States (in U.S.$ millions)**

	1965	1970	1975	1980	1985	1990	1993
Exports to World	8,332	19,316	54,734	121,413	174,015	280,374	351,292
Imports from World	6,431	18,880	49,706	132,210	118,029	216,846	209,778
Balance with World	1,901	436	5,028	−10,797	55,986	63,528	141,514
Exports to U.S.	2,479	6,015	11,149	31,649	65,278	90,322	105,405
Imports from U.S.	2,366	5,565	11,608	24,448	25,793	52,369	55,236
Balance with U.S.	113	450	−459	7,201	39,485	37,953	50,169

Sources: Keizai kikakucho chosakyoku [Research Bureau, Economic Planning Agency], ed., *Keizai yoran (Heisei 6-nen ban)* [Economic handbook, 1994 edition] (Tokyo: Ministry of Finance Printing Office, 1994), 188–89, 192–93; Statistical Bureau, Management and Coordination Agency, ed., *Japan Statistical Yearbook,* 43d ed. (Tokyo: Japan Statistical Association, 1993), 411, 413, 428.

speculation-driven inflation of urban land and home prices in the late 1980s made it impossible for the average working couple to purchase even a modest apartment in a metropolitan area in their lifetime. In 1990, the average nominal price of residential land in Tokyo was about 90 times the price in New York, 30 times that in London, and 25 times that in Frankfurt. Public parks are even scarcer and more overcrowded in Japanese cities. Tokyo, for example, has about one-tenth as much park area per population as Chicago or Berlin, and considerably less than one-tenth as much as London or Bonn.

Moreover, the prices of most consumer goods have been between 18 percent and 50 percent higher in Japan than in the United States or most Western European countries in recent years. As a result, average Japanese citizens, especially those in the nation's major cities, do not enjoy the standard of living that their country's very high statistical GNP per person would suggest. For example, while Japan's nominal GNP per capita in 1990 (about $19,000) was higher than the United States' (about $17,400), the average Japanese citizen's income in terms of its estimated purchasing power (about $14,000) was substantially lower than the United States', which was about the same as its nominal GNP per capita (or $17,400).

Growing awareness of unreasonably high consumer prices, an inferior and deteriorating urban environment, and the unfair distribution of costs and benefits in a rapidly changing economy bred widespread disillusionment and dissatisfaction among Japan's urban voters. Reports of an endless series of

scandals at the top levels of the nation's political and corporate worlds ignited this smoldering public anger into widespread voter revolts against the ruling party at the end of the 1980s and in the early 1990s.

During those decades, Japan experienced significant economic and social changes as well. As its economy continued to grow through the 1970s at steady rates, the demand for young and cheap labor also continued to grow in the manufacturing and service sectors. On the other hand, birth and population growth rates, which had already begun to taper off in the mid-1950s, began to decline in the mid-1970s. The main causes of this change included a steady decrease in the absolute number of women of childbearing age, a rising average age of marriage, and a decreasing number of children per married couple. The results were a perennially tight labor market and an unemployment rate of only 2.1 percent in 1991, compared to France's 9.3 percent, Great Britain's 8.1 percent, the United States' 6.6 percent, and West Germany's 6.3 percent.

The protracted recession of the late 1980s and the early 1990s, however, has brought about important changes in Japanese employment patterns and practices. In the early 1990s, the number of new university graduates exceeded the number of job openings for the first time in many years. Many firms abandoned the security of employment and age-based pay systems, and many employees were forced to retire early to become contract workers or to move to other affiliated firms. Increasing numbers of people of all ages now worked on a part-time, consulting, work-on-call, or work-at-home basis.

Japanese automobiles waiting on docks to be shipped abroad in mid-1980s.
Source: AP/Wide World Photos.

JAPAN AND THE INTERNATIONAL POLITICAL ECONOMY

Modern Japan's economic development has been based on export-led industrialization. Such a strategy seeks rapid industrialization initially by exporting relatively cheap products of labor-intensive industries, such as textiles, and then by exporting higher value-added products of more capital-intensive industries, such as iron and steel, shipbuilding, and machinery. If implemented successfully, this strategy makes it possible for a nation with few natural, financial, and technological resources and a small home market, such as Meiji Japan, to industrialize by importing resources from abroad and paying for them with foreign exchange earned by its own exports. Since the 1960s, a number of developing countries have successfully followed this strategy. The best known examples are the newly industrializing countries (NICs) or economies (NIEs) of East Asia, including South Korea, Taiwan, Hong Kong, and Singapore, which are sometimes called the "New Japans." By the early 1990s, these four Asian countries had become Japan's serious competitors in a number of industrial sectors, including steel, shipbuilding, and electron-

ics. In the meantime, other Southeast Asian countries, such as Thailand, Malaysia, and Indonesia, as well as China, have begun to follow in the footsteps of the New Japans and appear bound to become Japan's new competitors in the near future.

For Japan, the export-led strategy proved spectacularly successful both before and after World War II. By the mid-1970s, Japan had emerged as an economic superpower second only to the United States, and by 1990 had equaled or surpassed the United States as the world's banker, aid donor, and investor in the Asia-Pacific region. By 1990, Japan had become the world's second-largest exporter, after the United States, of high-technology manufactures, such as aerospace products, precision machinery, computers, electronic and communications equipment, and pharmaceuticals (see Table 5).

Nearly 90 percent of Japan's $340 billion in exports in 1992 consisted of heavy industrial goods, such as machinery, automobiles, and electrical and electronic goods, while nearly three-quarters of its $233 billion in imports in the same year consisted of fuels, industrial raw materials, and foodstuffs. In other words, Japan imports raw materials, turns them into industrial products, adding substantial value to them in

Victors in the automobile war
[The flag on Iwojima].
Source: Courtesy Bill Deore,
Dallas Morning News.

the process, and sells them back to the world, often at large profit margins.

On the other hand, Japan remains a net importer of scientific discoveries and inventions that are useful to industry, as reflected in newly registered industrial patents and copyrights. While it sells more industrial patents and copyrights than any other industrial nation except the United States and Germany, it also buys more than any except Germany. Thus, Japan combines a chronic surplus in "goods" trade with a chronic deficit in "knowledge" trade.

Today's Japan appears to be intent on exporting more than it imports so as to generate a trade surplus and amass foreign exchange at the expense of its trade partners. As post–Cold War nations become increasingly concerned with economic issues, rather than military or ideological ones, Japan's image as a ruthlessly competitive, expansionist trader and its burgeoning trade surplus have, in fact, led the country into recurrent and increasingly acrimonious disputes with its major trading partners, most notably the United States.

In the 1950s, Japan was accused of adhering to protectionist trade policies implemented through high tariff barriers against foreign manufactured goods. After the tariffs were substantially lowered in the 1960s, the criticism shifted to a variety of nontariff barriers, such as import quotas, discriminatory application of safety and technical standards against imports, and a government procurement policy favoring domestic products.[30] More recently, Japan has been accused of deliberately creating or maintaining "structural impediments" to imports and foreign investment, such as an impenetrably complex domestic distribution system, collusive business practices among *keiretsu* companies, and exorbitant land and housing costs in metropolitan areas. According to U.S. critics, these policies or practices make it very difficult, both financially and operationally, for foreign companies to enter Japan's domestic markets and successfully compete with entrenched Japanese producers.

Japanese companies have also been charged with engaging in "predatory" trade practices abroad, such as dumping (selling goods at prices lower than those charged at home). Whether accurate or not, such charges often lead the United States to take punitive actions against Japanese imports and threaten to put an end to the free access to American markets that has fueled Japan's economic miracle. Japan has also had large, chronic trade surpluses with virtually all Western European and Asian countries, except for a few oil exporters such as Indonesia, Malaysia, and Brunei, and recurrent, often bruising, disputes with them over who or what is to be blamed for the perennial and worsening trade imbalances.

Japan had better balanced trade relations with the former Soviet Union and Eastern European nations, but the amounts of goods traded with them were very small—only about 1 percent and 0.25 percent, respectively, of Japan's total exports and imports in 1990. In part, this reflects the legacy of the Cold War. More recently, Japan's relationship with the Soviet Union's successor states has been burdened with a long-standing dispute over the ownership of several islands off the coast of Japan's northernmost prefecture, Hokkaido, that were occupied by the Soviet Union at the end of World War II. The dispute has so far prevented conclusion of a peace treaty to end the legal state of war that has existed between the two countries since 1945 and makes Japan reluctant to commit itself to a large-scale economic aid program, especially for Russia, which has inherited those islands. Finally, the amounts of Japanese private investments in the former Soviet Union and Eastern Europe remain negligible given the continuing uncertainty about their economic futures.

The growing international criticism of Japan's allegedly protectionist and "predatory" trade behavior has left significant marks on the Japanese economy, the Japanese government's economic policy, and Japanese companies' and citizens' attitudes and behavior. Over the years, Japan has become more sensitive and responsive to foreign criticism, has removed or reduced many of the once impenetrable tariff and nontariff import barriers, and has corrected many of the "predatory" trade practices abroad. By the early 1990s, the Japanese government and the majority of Japanese citizens accepted the need to lift the total ban on the import of foreign-produced rice that had been rigidly maintained for nearly half a century to protect Japanese farmers.

There was growing realization among Japanese both within and outside the government that Japan, as a trade-dependent nation, not only had benefited enormously from the post–World War II system of free trade but could not continue to prosper without it. This realization has made them increasingly willing to abandon most of the protectionist policies and practices that served them well in the past but have begun to threaten their long-term economic success.

The Japanese government and people have also begun to understand that Japan's unenviable reputation as a selfish, self-aggrandizing nation derives not only from its economic policy and conduct but also from its refusal to play a more substantial and visible role in international politics, especially in global activities of the United Nations, in areas such as disarmament and arms control, peacekeeping operations, protection of the environment, and assistance to refugees. This understanding led Japan in the early 1990s to seek and gain admission to the Conference on Security and Cooperation in Europe (CSCE); to participate in peacekeeping operations in Afghanistan, Iran, Iraq, Namibia, Mozambique, and Cambodia; and not only to attend the multilateral conference on peace in the Middle East but to host meetings of its working group on the environment. The Japanese government has also begun to seek a more substantial role in the United Nations, including a permanent seat on its Security Council.

The Japanese government's global economic policy and the Japanese people's attitude toward the outside world have thus been changing. But to many outside observers, the change has been too slow and too small. Such impatience clashes with the Japanese belief that it would be imprudent to move faster in adjusting their international behavior. An overwhelming majority of Japanese have consistently opposed, and continue to oppose, both a significant increase in either the current force level of the Self-Defense Forces or in the annual defense budget and Japanese involvement in any military action abroad. This public opinion effectively binds the hands of the Japanese government and makes it impossible for Japan to play a significantly more active international role in areas other than economic or cultural. The Japanese government's passive posture, which reflects the climate of domestic opinion, is often regarded abroad as deliberate, selfish foot dragging.

SECTION 3
Governance and Policy-Making

ORGANIZATION OF THE STATE

Under the MacArthur Constitution, which was promulgated in 1947 in occupied Japan and has since remained intact, Japan is a constitutional monarchy and a parliamentary democracy, very much like, for example, Britain and Sweden. Thus, in theory, the people are sovereign, while the emperor is the symbol of the nation and the unity of its people.

Japan is a unitary state with a long tradition of rule by a strong central government and weak local autonomy. It differs from most other industrial democracies in that it has had a long, uninterrupted rule by a single party. The LDP ruled the country continuously from 1955 to 1993; and from 1948 to 1955 power was held by the two conservative parties that eventually formed the LDP. This record does not necessarily make Japan less of a democracy, but a different kind of democracy.

Labeled "uncommon democracy" by some scholars, because democracy is more commonly identified as a political system in which voters "throw the rascals out" fairly regularly and frequently, the long rule by a single party has given rise to a lively debate among scholars over the democratic character of government and politics in postwar Japan. While uncommon, however, Japan's is by no means the only democracy that has experienced a long rule by the same party. For example, Norway was governed by the Labor Party for 20 years from 1945–1965, India by the Congress Party for 30 years from 1948–1977, and Sweden by the Social Democratic Labor Party for 44 years from 1932–1976.

According to a recent comparative study of such "uncommon" democracies, one-party rule is cyclical and bound to come to an end despite its use of government offices to maintain its power.[31] The dominant party may prolong its rule by abandoning original support groups in favor of new and more vital ones or by electing to represent emerging interests while paying ideological lip service to original support groups. According to this logic, then, balancing old against new interests and making appropriate and timely policy shifts are key to the perpetuation of a dominant party's

rule. By adroitly maintaining such balance in keeping with the shifting ideological climate in society, and thus broadening its support base, a ruling party may create a virtuous circle to prolong its rule. However, that is not an easy act to perform, and failure to perform it skillfully often spells the end of one-party dominance. The fall of the LDP government in 1993 was brought about by a combination of specific circumstances, as pointed out at the beginning of this chapter. It may also have signaled the end of a cycle of one-party dominance.

The Japanese people exercise their sovereignty through their elected representatives, who work at the national level through the highest organ of the state and its sole lawmaking body, the National Diet. The Diet designates the prime minister who, in turn, appoints other members of the cabinet. By law, at least half of the cabinet must be members of the Diet; in fact, all but a very few have been ruling party members of the Diet. Laws enacted by the Diet are implemented by the executive branch of government, which is led by the cabinet and operates through the national bureaucracy. The cabinet is constitutionally subordinate and collectively answerable to the Diet. The national bureaucracy operates under the direction of the cabinet and is therefore indirectly answerable to the Diet.

The constitution endows the Diet with the power to enact laws, approve the government budget, ratify international treaties, and audit the financial transactions of the state. The Diet is bicameral, consisting of an upper chamber, the House of Councillors, and a lower chamber, the House of Representatives. Both houses consist exclusively of popularly elected members. The lower house is the larger and more powerful of the two, with the power to override the opposition of the upper house on votes concerning the budget and ratification of international treaties. The Diet also has the power to investigate any matter of public interest and concern, whereas the prime minister and the cabinet have the obligation to report to the Diet on the state of the nation and its foreign relations. In fulfilling this obligation, cabinet ministers regularly attend meetings of Diet committees and answer legislators' questions.

World's Oldest Monarchy

Crown Prince Naruhito and Masako Owada in a dress rehearsal for their wedding in 1993. Source: AP/Wide World Photos.

Japan is the oldest surviving monarchy in the world. The present occupant of its Chrysanthemum Throne, Akihito, is the 125th in an unbroken line of emperors and empresses, according to legend. His ancestors were Japan's actual rulers in the period from the mid-sixth through the early tenth century and thereafter remained the nation's theoretical rulers until shortly after the end of World War II. Under the Meiji Constitution (1889–1947), the emperor was not only Japan's sovereign ruler but a demigod whose person was "sacred and inviolable." The MacArthur Constitution, however, relegated the emperor's constitutional status to one of the symbol of the Japanese state whose new sovereign was its people. Akihito's father, Hirohito (1901–1989), was thus the sovereign head of the Empire of Japan during the first half of his long reign but the mere figurehead of the democratized Japan during the last half of his life.

Unlike his aloof and enigmatic father, who led Japan into and out of the disastrous war, and whose role in that war remains controversial, Akihito is a modern, cosmopolitan, and eminently approachable monarch. An eleven-year-old boy at the war's end, he lived through the austere early postwar years as an impressionable young man, mingled freely with classmates from ordinary middle-class families, learned English from an American Quaker woman, and chose to marry a businessman's daughter (née Michiko Shoda).

Of their three children, the two sons, Crown Prince Naruhito and Prince Fumihito, both studied at Oxford after graduating from a Japanese university and both married commoners' daughters. The youngest child, Princess Sayako, is still single. She, too, has graduated from a Japanese university and visited England. Prince Fumihito's marriage to his college sweetheart, Kiko Kawashima, in 1990 was the year's biggest media event in a country where the imperial family remains an object of intense and abiding popular interest, though no longer of awe and reverence. Crown Prince Naruhito's wedding in 1993 caused an even greater sensation, partly because the prince's apparent difficulty in finding a suitable and willing spousal candidate had been a hot topic in the tabloids for several years and partly because the bride, Masako Owada, was a young diplomat who had studied at Harvard and Oxford as well as their Japanese equivalent, the University of Tokyo. Apart from the festivity of the occasion, the event also raised some political and ideological issues.

While few objected to the wedding itself, some did object to the government's financial and other involvement as a violation of the constitutional principle of the separation of state and religion. Others were disturbed by Owada's decision to give up her promising professional career and the opportunity to help break the "glass ceiling" that perpetuates women's inferior status in male-dominated professions, in favor of housewifery in one of the most old-fashioned and rigidly controlled families on earth. Still, public opinion polls showed that an overwhelming majority of Japanese, young and old, approved of Owada's decision and hoped that she would use her new position as Japan's crown princess and future empress to reform and modernize the hidebound imperial institution at home and assist Japanese diplomacy abroad.

The world's oldest monarchy thus appears destined to survive for many more years to come.

In theory, the prime minister and the cabinet (the "government") serve only as long as they have the confidence of the Diet. Indeed, if the House of Representatives passes a non-confidence motion against a cabinet or refuses to pass a motion of confidence in a cabinet, the government must either dissolve the lower house within ten days or resign en masse. This leads either to the formation of a new cabinet or to new general elections. For example, in 1993, a non-confidence motion against the LDP cabinet of Prime Minister Kiichi Miyazawa passed with the support of a dissident LDP faction. This led to a split in the ruling party and the birth of two splinter parties, which, in turn, led to the LDP's historic defeat in the general election that followed and formation of the first non-LDP coalition government since 1948.

Constitutional theory notwithstanding, however, it is the cabinet rather than the Diet that has initiated most legislation and in effect made laws in the past. This has been due largely to the fact that members of the Diet have virtually no legislative staffs of their own, whereas cabinet ministers, even though they have no more substantial staffs, enjoy much greater access to the staff and other resources of the national bureaucracy. During the LDP's long one-party rule, it was bureaucrats in the various ministries who drafted the majority of bills. Most of these bills were then passed with the unanimous support of ruling party members. By comparison, bills introduced by individual Diet members, especially those sponsored by opposition members alone, were few in number and far less frequently passed. Of the relatively few bills introduced by individual members during the period of LDP dominance, only those receiving non-partisan support enjoyed a good chance of success.

It is still too early to predict the nature of governance and policy-making that may emerge following the fall of the LDP in 1993. The discussion that follows is therefore based mainly on extrapolations from precedents set and experiences gained during the era of LDP rule, with a few observations on the changes since the 1993 general election.

THE EXECUTIVE

As suggested above, the executive branch, led by the cabinet rather than the Diet, has been the actual source of most legislative and administrative initiatives in postwar Japan. Moreover, the long dominance of the Diet by a single party has made the position of the cabinet virtually unassailable.

The cabinet is headed by a prime minister who is elected by the Diet. Each house separately elects a candidate for prime minister by a simple majority vote during a plenary session. If different candidates are elected by the two houses, the one elected by the lower house becomes prime minister. If no candidate wins an absolute majority, a runoff election is held between the two with the largest numbers of votes. During the LDP's one-party dominance, the Diet invariably elected the leader (or president) of the LDP to be prime minister. The LDP rules provided for selection of the party's president by election. In practice, however, LDP presidents were chosen as often by back-room negotiation as by the ballot.[32] Eight of the fifteen LDP presidents who became prime ministers in the period from 1955 to 1993 were former ministry bureaucrats; the remainder came from the ranks of party politicians, business executives, and journalists. They were also usually leaders of the major LDP factions, and LDP presidential elections were notorious for the huge sums of money spent by various factions to recruit new members and, in effect, buy votes for their presidential candidate.

Once elected, the prime minister has nearly absolute legal authority to appoint or dismiss any cabinet member. The appointment of members of an LDP cabinet was dictated mainly by the prime minister's desire to maintain a balance of power among the several party factions in order to preserve the unity and stability of the party and to prolong his own prime ministerial tenure.

The prime minister has the constitutional power to submit bills to the Diet in the name of the cabinet; report to the Diet on the state of the nation and its foreign relations; exercise control and supervision over the national bureaucracy; approve all laws and cabinet orders; and, in rare cases, suspend a cabinet member's constitutionally guaranteed immunity against legal action during his or her tenure. The prime minister is also the nation's commander-in-chief under the Self-Defense Forces Law and has the power to declare a state of national emergency under the Police Law. If a prime minister resigns or otherwise ceases to hold his office, the cabinet as a whole must also resign.

The executive powers and responsibilities of the Japanese cabinet are wide-ranging. In addition to those common to the executive branch of government in most other industrial democracies, they include advising and taking responsibility for any of the emperor's actions that are of concern to the state (such as promulgation of laws and treaties, convocation of the Diet, dissolution of the House of Representatives, and receiving of foreign ambassadors and ministers); designating the chief justice of the Supreme Court, who is formally appointed by the emperor; appointing all other judges of the Supreme Court and those of the lower courts; calling the Diet into an extraordinary session and the upper house into an emergency session; and approving expenditure for the state's reserve funds.

The Bureaucracy

Each member of the cabinet has the title of minister and is assigned supervisory responsibility for a particular ministry or one or more agencies (see Table 6). Agencies are generally newer and smaller than ministries. Some agencies, such as the Economic Planning, Environment, Science and Technology, and National Land agencies, are represented in the cabinet by their own ministers, but many are not. There are currently twelve ministries and eight cabinet-rank agencies. Including the prime minister, a deputy prime minister (appointed by the prime minister), the chief cabinet secretary, and an occasional minister in charge of a special policy or project, the cabinet typically consists of twenty-two or -three members.

While in theory a minister supervises the work of an entire ministry or agency or sometimes two or more lesser agencies, his or her supervisory power and responsibility are often more nominal than real. This is largely because a minister is chosen, not on the basis of ability or record of performance in a given policy area, but on the basis of seniority in the ruling party or parties or in an LDP faction. Such seniority is determined mainly by the number of times one has been reelected to the Diet. As a result, many cabinet ministers are inexperienced in the particular policy areas to which they are assigned and are at the mercy, rather than in command, of the career civil servants who are his or her subordinates in a given ministry or agency.

In making cabinet appointments, a prime minister has always paid a great deal of attention to harmony and happiness among his political supporters in the

TABLE 6 **Cabinet Posts (February 1994)**
Prime Minister
Deputy Prime Minister
Minister of Justice
Minister of Foreign Affairs
Minister of Finance
Minister of Education
Minister of Health and Welfare
Minister of Agriculture, Forestry, and Fisheries
Minister of International Trade and Industry
Minister of Transportation
Minister of Posts and Telecommunications
Minister of Labor
Minister of Construction
Minister of Home Affairs
Special Minister for Political Reform
Director-General of the Management and Coordination Agency
Director-General of the Hokkaido Development Agency
Director-General of the Defense Agency
Director-General of the Economic Planning Agency
Director-General of the Science and Technology Agency
Director-General of the Environment Agency
Director-General of the Okinawa Development Agency
Director-General of the National Land Agency
Chief Cabinet Secretary

intraparty factions that made up LDP cabinets in the past and the several parties that have made up the post-1993 coalition cabinets. For example, the coalition cabinet formed in June 1994 by the LDP, the Social Democratic Party of Japan (SDPJ), and the New Party Harbinger (NPH) consisted of thirteen LDP ministers, six SDPJ ministers, and two NPH ministers.

Since every LDP faction and every coalition party has a long waiting list of its own candidates for cabinet posts, a prime minister is under great pressure to reshuffle the cabinet and replace incumbents with new people at frequent intervals. The result has been an average ministerial tenure of barely one year under the LDP's rule and six months under the two coalition cabinets formed immediately following the end of the LDP's monopoly of power in 1993. The short tenure denies a cabinet minister the time needed to learn the ropes of his or her ministry, which reinforces the minister's dependence on career bureaucrats to discharge even routine ministerial duties, including answering questions in the plenary sessions and committee meetings of the Diet.

For these reasons, a ministry or agency is run, in practice, by its own senior officials, led by the administrative vice minister and one or two deputy vice ministers who are career civil servants with many years of experience in the organization. Each ministry also has one or two appointed parliamentary vice ministers to assist the minister in dealings with the Diet. The parliamentary vice minister is a Diet member and has little real power in the ministry. A ministry or an agency is thus a bureaucracy with considerable autonomy and discretionary power of its own, particularly with regard to its internal organization and personnel decisions.

Ministerial autonomy often verges on isolationism and discourages cooperation with other ministries. In the aftermath of the devastating earthquake that hit Kobe City and its vicinity in January 1995, ministerial sectionalism was widely blamed for long delays, often with tragic consequences, in the Tokyo government's response to the crisis. As an editorial writer of a national daily observed at that time, whenever disaster strikes, each government ministry holds its own meetings, dispatches its own fact-finding teams, and implements its own relief measures.[33] The first priority is always coordination within each ministry rather than cooperation, much less coordination, with other ministries.

The cabinet usually meets twice a week, although prime ministers may call additional meetings on their own initiative or at the request of other ministers. The director-general of the Cabinet Legislation Bureau and two deputy chief cabinet secretaries are also usually present at these meetings. However, the agenda of a cabinet meeting is reviewed, and most outstanding issues are settled, in advance at a meeting of administrative vice ministers of all ministries and cabinet-rank agencies, held the day before the cabinet meeting.

Alone among prewar Japan's major political institutions, the central government bureaucracy survived the Occupation-sponsored postwar reform almost intact. The only notable casualty was the Home Ministry, which was divided into several smaller ministries and agencies. The national bureaucracy as a whole actually became stronger, rather than weaker, after the reform and played a leading role in the postwar recovery and development of the Japanese economy and society.

Before World War II and during most of the postwar period, the autonomy and discretionary power of career civil servants, combined with reasonable pay and security of employment, gave enormous prestige to Japan's national bureaucracy. The prestige, in turn, attracted a large number of university graduates to the annual public service entrance examinations and ensured that only the best performers in this rigorous selection process were appointed to fast-track positions in the most prestigious ministries, such as the MOF, MITI, and Ministry of Foreign Affairs (MFA). As the Japanese economy grew richer, the prestige and attractiveness of careers in the private sector, especially in one of the conglomerate-affiliated giant corporations, rapidly rose, while the popularity of public service careers declined. During the last half of the 1980s, for example, the number of applicants taking the highest level public service entrance examinations declined by nearly one-third. Still, the competition for a fast-track job in a ministry remains stiff, and only about one out of fifteen applicants passes the entrance examination.

By custom, though not by law, Japan's national public servants retire at a relatively young age, usually about fifty-five, with fairly modest retirement benefits. This forces most public service retirees to seek new jobs in either the private or public sector, and many do find high-paying jobs as officials of large, private companies or "para-statals" (public or semipublic business enterprises, such as the Japan Development Bank under MOF's jurisdiction, the Japan National Oil Corporation under MITI, and the Japan Highway Public Corporation under the Ministry of Construction). This postretirement career pattern is known as ***amakudari***, or "descent from heaven." The "descent" is usually arranged in advance between the government ministry ("heaven") from which a senior official retires and a private or semipublic company with which the ministry has a close relationship.

By international standards, Japan's national bureaucracy is modest in size, employing in 1990 about half a million people, or less than 8 percent of Japan's total workforce, and spending in 1991 about 16 percent of the nation's GNP, as compared to the United States' 25 percent, former West Germany's 32 percent, Great Britain's 38 percent, and France's 44 percent. Although it is difficult to compare the capabilities or efficiencies of different nations' public bureaucracies, it is reasonable to call the Japanese national bureaucracy lean, thrifty, and elitist.[34]

The Military

Japan's military establishment was totally dismantled at the hands of the Allied Occupation forces in the aftermath of World War II. Article 9 of the postwar constitution renounces the idea of "war as a sovereign right of the nation" and declares that "land, sea and air forces, as well as other war potential, will never be maintained." By 1950, however, exigencies of the Cold War and especially the outbreak of the Korean War had led to a Japanese rearmament program at Washington's urging. Initially, a "police" reserve force was established, which was so named to avoid provoking controversy over its constitutionality. By 1954, this organization had evolved into three so-called Self-Defense Forces (ground, maritime, and air). In 1959, the Supreme Court ruled that Article 9 allows Japan to take necessary measures to defend itself as an independent nation.

By the early 1990s, these forces had a combined size comparable to the armed forces of most Western European nations and were supported by a comparable budget. This makes Japan by far the largest military spender in Asia. In 1990, for example, Japan spent roughly three times as much as either China or North Korea, two and a half times as much as South Korea, and twice as much as India. Even though Japan's figure ($16.3 billion in 1990) amounted to only about 1 percent of its own gross domestic product, as compared to North Korea's 4.4 percent, South Korea's 3.8 percent, India's 3.2 percent, and China's 1.7 percent, the money could buy very large amounts of advanced weapons and military technologies—a fact not lost on any of Japan's neighbors, many of whom have very bad memories of Japanese aggression earlier in this century.

From the point of view of the United States, on the other hand, Japan's defense spending has been paltry. In 1990, the United States spent about $250 billion, or more than fifteen times as much as Japan did, which amounted to 5.4 percent of the U.S. gross national product. Partly out of a growing frustration over the large trade deficits with Japan, U.S. leaders have kept demanding a larger defense effort by Tokyo, which they hope will lead to increased Japanese purchases of American military products. Japan has partly responded to the U.S. demand by increasing its share of the maintenance costs of the 46,800 U.S. troops (as of September 1994) and their bases in Japan.

Under the persistent pressure applied by Washington, the Japanese antipathy toward war and arms born of their harrowing experiences in World War II has gradually eroded. Even the new Socialist prime minister, Tomiichi Murayama, declared in his inaugural speech in the summer of 1994 that, contrary to his party's long-standing policy, his government recognized the constitutionality of the Self-Defense Forces and supported the U.S.-Japan Mutual Security Treaty. Like their predecessors and the overwhelming majority of Japanese citizens, however, Japan's new leaders remained firmly opposed to a significant increase in the nation's defense spending, the troop level of its Self-Defense Forces, and peacekeeping operations abroad that would involve the use of arms.

Semipublic Organizations

Now, in the mid-1990s, Japan has about sixty semipublic organizations, which may be divided into three broad categories. The first category consists of about two dozen nonprofit public financial institutions, including two government-owned banks (the Japan Development Bank and the Japan Export Import Bank). The rest of the first category are either funds or foundations. All are provided with their capital by the central government and, as a rule, make loans to a variety of organizations or individuals such as small businesses, farm and fishing families, construction companies in the country's less developed regions, house buyers, foreign governments (via the Japan Overseas Cooperation Fund), and foreign scholars (via the Japan Foundation). Their budgets and expenditures are subject to approval and audit by the Diet.

The second category includes about thirty public corporations funded either exclusively by the central government or jointly by the central and local governments. Some are involved in large public works projects, such as conservation and development of natural resources, and construction and management of roads, railroads, or airports, while others are in charge of more specialized types of projects, such as support for nuclear and space sciences, social welfare programs, livestock farming, and small business pension funds.

The third category includes half a dozen joint-stock companies, which combine both public and private ownership. These include an airport construction company, two electric power companies, and two partially privatized, formerly government-run corporations, the Nippon Telegraph and Telephone Company

(NTT) and the Japan Tobacco Company (JT). Another major government monopoly, the Japan National Railways (JNR), has been divided into six private companies, collectively known as JR for Japan Railways.

The sale of government corporations in Japan has been driven by the global privatization trend of the 1980s and by domestic pressure to reduce large budget deficits by cutting back on government spending. It has gained considerable public and media support because most semipublic organizations have served as providers of lucrative postretirement *amakudari* employment and pay for senior ministry bureaucrats. This practice is viewed as giving ex-bureaucrats an unfair advantage over others in the postretirement job market, including most employees of private companies who also retire at comparable ages. But privatization means the elimination or downsizing of some semipublic companies and thus it is opposed by many bureaucrats and has so far achieved much less than the fanfare that has accompanied it would suggest. It has left the Japanese economy only slightly closer to the ideal free market envisioned by its most ardent advocates.

OTHER STATE INSTITUTIONS

The Judiciary

The judicial branch of the Japanese government operates according to rules and decisions made by the Supreme Court and is theoretically free from interference by either of the other two branches of government or any private interest group. The chief judge of the Supreme Court is nominated by the cabinet and appointed by the emperor, and all other judges are appointed by the cabinet. Supreme Court judges are subject to popular review and potential recall in the first House of Representatives general election following their initial appointment, and every ten years thereafter. Otherwise, judges on all types of courts may serve until the mandatory retirement ages of seventy for those on the Supreme Court and small claims courts and sixty-five for those on all other types of courts.

The Supreme Court, eight higher (regional) courts, and fifty district (prefectural) courts are invested with and occasionally use their constitutional power of judicial review. But the Supreme Court has been extremely reluctant to do so. For example, lower courts have twice found the Self-Defense Forces in violation of the war-renouncing Article 9 of the 1947 constitution and declared them unconstitutional—once in the late 1950s and again in the late 1970s. On each occasion, however, the Supreme Court reversed the lower court's verdict on the grounds that the issue was too political to be amenable to judicial review; in effect, this was a recognition of the constitutionality of the Self-Defense Forces. During the half century of its existence up to 1993, the Supreme Court upheld lower courts' prior verdicts of the unconstitutionality of existing laws in only five cases: two involving the Public Office Election Law, and one each involving the Criminal, Medical, and Forestry laws.

This passive posture of the Supreme Court helped sustain LDP domination of the Diet and the cabinet until the early 1990s. The court refused to order a fundamental redrawing of the country's election districts to reflect the massive postwar migration of the population from the countryside to the cities. As a result, the rural areas elected more Diet members *per voter* than did the urban areas. The Supreme Court acknowledged in 1976 and again in 1993 the unconstitutionality of such gross malapportionment, but on both occasions it rejected demands to declare the results of elections held under this system null and void.

The reluctance of Japanese courts to use their power of judicial review may be attributed to several factors. First, there is an influential legal opinion in the country that holds that the judiciary should not intervene in highly political acts of the legislative or executive branches of government, which represent the people's will more directly than the judiciary. Second, Japan has a much weaker case law tradition than either the United States or the United Kingdom. This makes judges less inclined to challenge constitutionality of new legislation on the basis of precedents. Third, most of the Supreme Court judges appointed by the succession of LDP cabinets tended to be conservative in their outlook. They were thus ideologically inclined to approve decisions made and actions taken by the conservative party in power. Fourth, judicial passivity may reflect the traditional reluctance of Japanese people in general to resort to litigation to settle disputes. Finally, Japan lacks a tradition of judicial review. Under the Meiji Constitution, the emperor was deemed above the law and the courts did not have the power to void executive acts taken in the emperor's name. The tradition continues to influence the attitudes and actions of contemporary Supreme Court judges.

Subnational Government

Decision-making power in contemporary Japan is virtually monopolized by the central government in all important areas of public policy, and very little is left to the discretion of either the 47 prefectures or the 3,250 or so municipalities. This lopsided distribution of power is sustained by the equally lopsided division of taxing power. The central government collects nearly two-thirds of the taxes raised by all governments and provides nearly two-thirds of local governments' expenditures through a system of grants-in-aid and subsidies. Moreover, most local public programs and projects are planned and funded by the central government and merely administered by local governments. In the early 1990s, the majority of Japan's prefectural governors were former officials of central government ministries.

The scope of local discretion has somewhat increased in recent years. However, the overwhelming power of the central government and the weakness of local autonomy are considered important factors impeding the realization of greater democracy in contemporary Japan. They discourage citizen participation in local government and politics and make the central government insensitive, even indifferent, to local interests and opinions.

THE POLICY-MAKING PROCESS

The majority of bills passed by the Diet originate in the national bureaucracy. Under the LDP's rule, the draft bills were reviewed and approved by the party's Policy Research Council before they were sent to the Diet. This policy review group in the LDP operated through seventeen standing committees, each of which corresponded to a ministry, such as Justice and Foreign Affairs, and seventy-five or so ad hoc committees. Some of these ad hoc committees were concerned with broad, long-term policy issues, such as the revision of the constitution, fiscal policy, and the educational system. Others were formed to deal with more specific issues, such as government assistance to depressed industries, treatment of foreign workers, and the control of drugs. The results of their deliberations were presented as recommendations to the executive committee of the Policy Research Council. If approved, these usually became LDP policies to be implemented through legislative actions of the Diet or administrative actions of the bureaucracy.

Most of these LDP policy committees were led by veteran Diet members who had been reelected half a dozen times or more and had become experts in specific policy areas. Over the years, they also formed close personal relationships with both senior bureaucrats and leaders of special interest groups. These LDP legislative bosses, who form among themselves what are popularly known as "tribes," formed informal policy-making networks with their bureaucratic and business allies. Such groups dominated policy-making in all major policy areas, including, among others, agriculture, construction, education, telecommunications, and transportation. Many of the bills drafted by bureaucrats and introduced in the Diet by an LDP cabinet originated in a tribe, as did many administrative measures implemented by a government ministry or agency.

Through such policy-making partnerships, or "iron triangles," special group interests were promoted by friendly politicians and bureaucrats, bureaucrats had their turfs protected and often enlarged by sympathetic politicians, and politicians had their campaign war chests filled with contributions from grateful interest groups. LDP tribes were thus also the principal agents of pork-barrel politics and major sources of political corruption and scandals. As a result, many policies pushed by LDP governments tended to be conservative and protectionist, their main purpose being to protect the well-organized, well-connected, and well-to-do special interest groups. Big manufacturers, small shop owners, farmers, realtors, builders, insurers, and doctors, among others, were all represented by their own tribes and protected against those who threatened their interests, whether they were Japanese consumers, insurance policyholders, or patients, or foreign producers, exporters, or providers of various services.

This process is well illustrated by the evolution of a 1991 bill to introduce a new land tax. The bill was proposed by the Ministry of Finance as a measure to curb skyrocketing land prices by imposing tighter controls on speculative land transactions. Before it reached the Diet, however, the bill went through a series of negotiations and compromises among several ministries, including MITI, the Ministry of Construction, Ministry of Home Affairs, Ministry of Agriculture, Forestry and Fisheries, and the National Land Agency, each representing the interests of a distinctive constituency. Regulatory provisions of the original bill were substantially watered down following these reviews. A number of additional exemptions for special interest groups were then written into the bill by LDP tribe members in party committees. For example, members of the agriculture and forestry tribe and the commerce and industry tribe added exemptions for agricultural land and land owned by small factories and offices, respectively. The bill eventually reached and passed the Diet, but it had been thoroughly gutted while making its way through the labyrinth of the tribe-dominated LDP policy review process.

As the term suggests, an "iron triangle" is a group characterized by strong member solidarity on the one hand and competitiveness and exclusiveness toward outsiders on the other. The whole policy-making process that revolved around dozens of such iron triangles was inevitably disjointed and incoherent. Decisions made and actions taken by one triangle in one policy area were seldom coordinated with decisions made and actions taken in another policy area. The medley of policies that often ran at cross-purposes were then introduced as new bills in the Diet and passed as new laws or simply announced as new government policies. As a result, there are numerous laws, regulations, and rules in contemporary Japan, but few comprehensive, coherent, long-term policies. Abstract

"visions" masquerade as such policies, as in the LDP's platform, which proclaims the party's determination to make Japan a "cultured democratic nation," a "self-reliant peace-loving nation," and a welfare state based on individual freedoms and comprehensive economic planning. Such empty platitudes turn most Japanese citizens into political cynics who pay hardly any attention to campaign slogans mouthed by individual candidates or party leaders at election time.

The coalition cabinets led, respectively, by Morihiro Hosokawa and Tsutomu Hata, which were formed after the LDP's exit from power in 1993, called for more deregulation and an end to the bureaucratic dominance in the policy-making process. Both cabinets fell, however, long before they had time to consolidate their power and address such controversial issues. The lack of experience and expertise on the part of the new non-LDP leaders may even have given the bureaucracy more, rather than less, freedom of action and actually increased its collective power. The third post-1993 coalition cabinet formed jointly by the LDP and the Socialists also promised to reform Japan's policy-making structure and process, but it is too early to tell how viable and effective a policy-making group this union of very odd political bedfellows will prove to be.

SECTION 4
Representation and Participation

THE LEGISLATURE

Even during the period of an LDP-dominated Diet, from the mid-1950s through the early 1990s, the national legislature played a central, indispensable role in the operation of democratic government in Japan as the most authoritative arena of public debates on important policy issues between the government and opposition. After all, the constitution declares that the Diet is the highest organ of state and that it decides the government budget, approves international treaties, elects the prime minister, and oversees the conduct of the cabinet. How the Diet is constituted and how it actually operates are therefore very important questions to consider in assessing the current state and future prospects of democracy in Japan.

The Diet

The House of Councillors, or the upper house of the bicameral Diet, has currently (mid-1990s) 252 seats. Upper-house members have a fixed term of six years, but, as is the case with U.S. Senators, their terms are staggered so that half of them are elected every three years. One hundred of them (50 in each triennial upper-house election) are elected by a nationwide system of proportional representation from party lists, while the remaining 152 (76 in each upper-house election) are elected from multiple-seat local constituencies, just as lower-house members were elected before the 1994 electoral reform.

Upper-house members are supposed to represent voters' opinions and interests somewhat differently than lower-house members. When the 1947 constitution was ratified, the upper house was expected to bring to parliamentary deliberations a broad, national perspective that was less constrained by parochial interests than the lower house. In practice, however, this distinction between the representational functions of the two houses has long been lost, and they are virtually indistinguishable.

The House of Representatives, or the lower house, currently has 500 seats. The full term of office for lower-house members is four years, but the actual term served by a member has been about two and a half years. This is because, unlike the upper house, the lower house may be dissolved by the cabinet when the House passes a motion of no-confidence against a cabinet or refuses to pass a motion of confidence in a cabinet. In either case, the cabinet must choose either to resign or to dissolve the lower house and call a new election. A cabinet may voluntarily choose to dissolve the lower house at other times as well. The constitution gives the emperor the right to dissolve the house with the advice and consent of a cabinet; in fact, he cannot refuse such a request from the cabinet. A cabinet would choose to dissolve the lower house if it believed that the ruling party would win the subsequent general election and thus strengthen its position.

A speaker and vice speaker preside in the lower house, and a president and vice president preside in the upper house. Unlike their counterparts in the U.S. Congress, the presiding officers of the Japanese Diet are expected to be nonpartisan in exercising their powers and discharging their duties. When a member of the Diet is elected to any of these four positions, the member nominally gives up any party affiliation and becomes an independent.

An ordinary session of the Diet sits for 150 days each year, beginning in December, subject to one or more extensions. An extraordinary session may be called any time by the cabinet or by a quarter of the members of either house. As in the U.S. Congress, a good deal of business is conducted in the standing and ad hoc committees of each house. Unlike members of the U.S. Congress, however, Japanese Diet members normally vote strictly along party lines, as do their counterparts in other parliamentary democracies. In the 1950s and early 1960s, the rigid enforcement of party discipline in Diet voting contributed to frequent confrontation between the LDP and the opposition, which sometimes even led to physical fights on the floor of the

Diet. When a nonpartisan consensus on policies designed to promote economic growth developed in the mid-1960s, the opposition replaced violent parliamentary tactics with delaying tactics such as repeated submissions of no-confidence motions against a cabinet. Since the early 1970s, parliamentary battles between the ruling party and the opposition have been increasingly ritualized. The opposition would first use a boycott or other means to stall Diet proceedings and kill a government proposal, but would eventually accept a settlement mediated by the Speaker of the House. The ruling party would reciprocate the opposition's cooperation by making limited concessions on other issues.

Nearly all Japanese legislators are male. Aside from casting ballots in elections, women participate very little in politics. While the female voter turnout has been consistently higher than that of male voters in local elections since the late 1950s and in Diet elections since the early 1970s, there are few female legislators either at the national or local level. Of the 511 lower-house members elected in the 1993 general election, for example, only 14, or 2.7 percent, were women, while 13 of the 127 elected to the upper house in 1992, or slightly over 10 percent, were women. Women thus play only a very limited role in Japan's national legislature, as they do in the executive and judicial branches of the national government and in prefectural and local governments.

The Diet has increasingly consisted of "second-generation" members in recent years. These are relatives—mainly sons—or aides of former Diet members who "inherit" their fathers' or bosses' Diet seats. In the early 1990s, nearly a quarter of all lower-house members and 40 percent of LDP lower-house members were such second-generation politicians. This made the Diet look more like a feudal club of aristocrats than a modern institution of democratic representation.

The passing of a Diet seat from an incumbent to a close aide or an offspring usually involves the passing of a local campaign machine, known as ***koenkai*** (support association), which plays a central role in a Diet election, especially for LDP candidates. It is very expensive to maintain an existing machine, but it is far more expensive to build a new one. Those who inherit an existing machine therefore have a great advantage over those who must create one from scratch. A machine is built by a politician on the basis of personal relationships with particular constituents and is transferable, in the manner of common property, from its founder to his or her heirs upon the legislator's retirement or death.

In the Japanese Diet, as in the U.S. Congress, committee deliberations, where special interests and pressure groups can exert their influence most effectively, play the central part in the legislative process. By comparison, plenary sessions seldom lead to substantial changes in the contents of a bill. While in most Western democracies bills are "read" three or more times by the entire membership of a house, there is only one reading of a bill in the plenary session of the Japanese Diet. As a result, entrenched special interests represented by their own tribes (and iron triangles) in committee deliberations are likely to have their cases heard far more effectively than newer and less organized interests, which are not so represented, such as those of urban residents, women, and youth.

The interests of the government bureaucracy are also effectively represented in the work of Diet committees. Bureaucrats are in a position to interpret laws almost as they please by issuing administrative orders, which are supposed to help implement a law but often have the effect of modifying or even replacing one. This is because Japanese laws tend to lack specific and detailed provisions, a fact that helps broaden the bureaucrat's discretion in interpreting them.[35] As a result, ministerial interests, as well as special private interests, tend to prevail over those of the broader public.

During the heyday of tribe politics under the LDP's one-party rule, the conflicts that often arose between ministries provided experienced tribe members with opportunities to enhance their power and reputation by mediating the conflicts. As the Japanese economy and society became increasingly complex and various policy issues became increasingly interrelated, the incidence of disputes between ministries rose, and so did the power of many a legislative tribe and its members.

THE PARTY SYSTEM AND ELECTIONS

The Party System

After years of stability, the Japanese party system is now in such great flux that it is hard to have any long-term confidence in it. Several new parties have been formed since 1993, most by groups that splintered from some older parties and then merged with each other and older parties. As of spring 1995, there are six national parties. One of these, the New Frontier Party (Shin-

shintō), was born in December 1994, when two new parties and two older ones merged. (Figure 1 shows the evolution of Japan's political parties.) Until the summer of 1993, when the LDP split and lost power, there were nine national parties, of which five—the Liberal Democratic Party (LDP), the Social Democratic Party of Japan (SDPJ), the Democratic Socialist Party (DSP), the Social Democratic Federation (SDF), and the Japan Communist Party (JCP)—were descended from prewar parties.[36]

The dominant LDP was formed in 1955 through the merger of two older conservative parties—the Liberal Party and the Democratic Party—which, in turn, had their origins in two prewar parties. The Socialist Party, or SDPJ (known in English as Japan Socialist Party [JSP] until the late 1980s), evolved from a prewar social democratic party founded in the mid-1920s. The two centrist parties—the DSP and SDF—were conservative JSP factions that left the JSP in 1960 and the late 1970s, respectively. Neither party won additional seats in either house of the Diet in subsequent years, but both survived as small centrist groups positioned between the conservative LDP and the socialist JSP (later SDPJ). The Japan Communist Party (JCP) is a direct descendant of the prewar JCP, banned upon its founding in the wake of World War I and rebuilt in 1945 by the prewar party's leaders, who were released from jail by order of General MacArthur.

Of the four parties of postwar vintage, the Komeitō or Clean Government Party (CGP) is the oldest. It was formed in the mid-1960s as the political arm of the Sōkagakkai, an organization of lay followers of a Buddhist sect founded by a thirteenth-century monk. Like the DSP and SDF, the CGP has carved out a middle-of-the-road position in Japanese politics. The LDP draws its core electoral and financial support from business and farmers, the SDPJ from public sector labor unions, the DSP from private sector unions, the CGP from a sectarian Buddhist organization, and the JCP from small but loyal groups of urban workers and intellectuals.

In the early 1990s, three splinter parties were formed by LDP defectors. The Japan New Party (JNP) was founded in 1992 by Morihiro Hosokawa, a former prefectural governor and LDP member of the upper house. The Japan Renewal Party (JRP), led by Tsutomu Hata and Ichirō Ozawa, and the New Party Harbinger (NPH), led by Masayoshi Takemura, were both formed only a few weeks before the 1993 lower-house general election. All three parties took issue

---

FIGURE 1   **The Lineage of Postwar Japanese Parties**

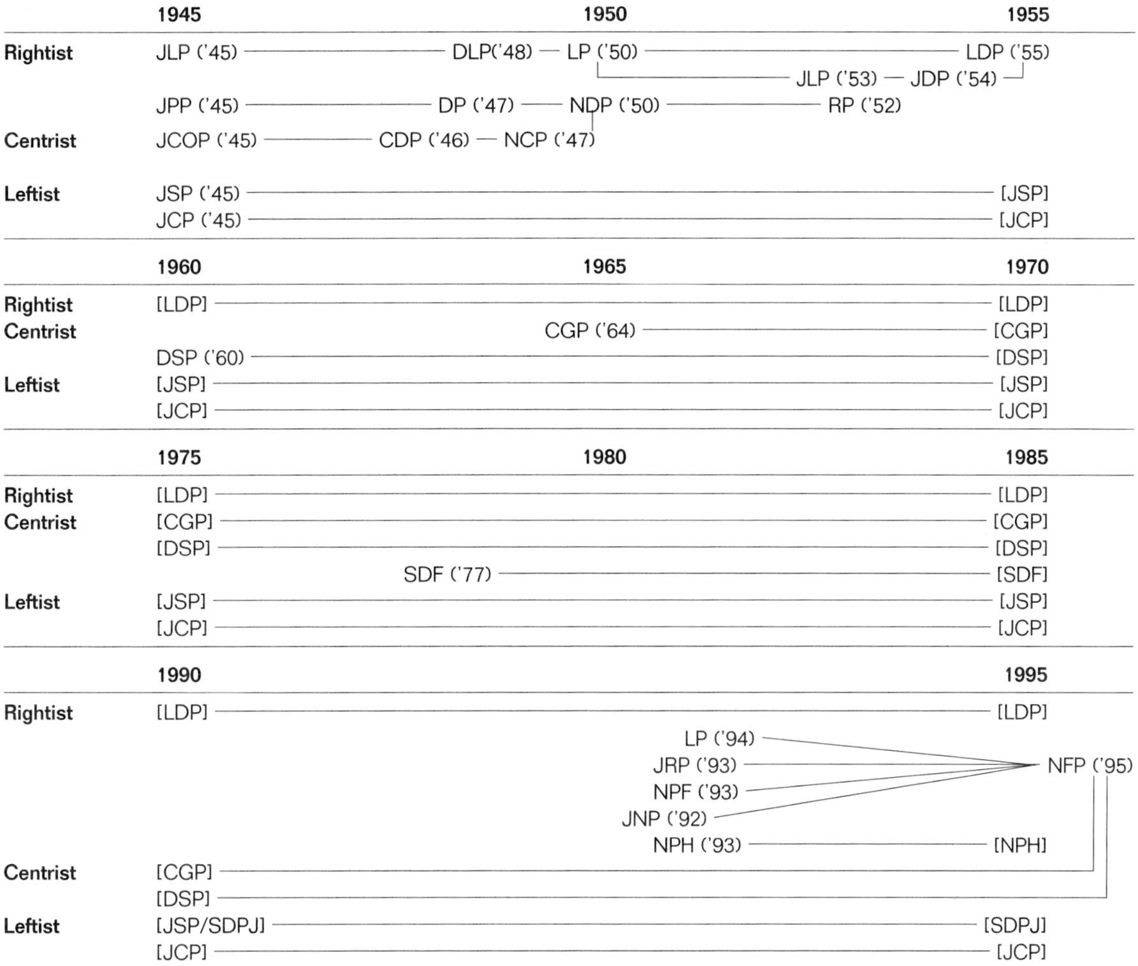

	1945	1950	1955
Rightist	JLP ('45) ——————————— DLP('48) — LP ('50) ———————————————— LDP ('55)		
	JLP ('53) — JDP ('54) ┘		
	JPP ('45) ——————————— DP ('47) —— NDP ('50) ———————— RP ('52)		
Centrist	JCOP ('45) —————————— CDP ('46) — NCP ('47)		
Leftist	JSP ('45) ———————————————————————————————————— [JSP]		
	JCP ('45) ———————————————————————————————————— [JCP]		

	1960	1965	1970
Rightist	[LDP] ————————————————————————————————————— [LDP]		
Centrist	CGP ('64) ——————————————————— [CGP]		
	DSP ('60) ——————————————————————————————————— [DSP]		
Leftist	[JSP] ————————————————————————————————————— [JSP]		
	[JCP] ————————————————————————————————————— [JCP]		

	1975	1980	1985
Rightist	[LDP] ————————————————————————————————————— [LDP]		
Centrist	[CGP] ————————————————————————————————————— [CGP]		
	[DSP] ————————————————————————————————————— [DSP]		
	SDF ('77) ——————————————————————— [SDF]		
Leftist	[JSP] ————————————————————————————————————— [JSP]		
	[JCP] ————————————————————————————————————— [JCP]		

	1990	1995
Rightist	[LDP] ————————————————————————————————————— [LDP]	
	LP ('94) ┐	
	JRP ('93) ———	
	NPF ('93) ———— NFP ('95)	
	JNP ('92) ┘	
	NPH ('93) ——————————————— [NPH]	
Centrist	[CGP] —————————————————————————————————————	
	[DSP] —————————————————————————————————————	
Leftist	[JSP/SDPJ] ————————————————————————————————— [SDPJ]	
	[JCP] ————————————————————————————————————— [JCP]	

Notes: ( ) = year newly established; [ ] = existing
Source: *Nihon keizai shinbun*, December 11, 1994, 3.

Acronyms Used in Figure 1

CDP	Cooperative Democratic Party	JSP	Japan Socialist Party
CGP	Clean Government Party	LDP	Liberal Democratic Party
DLP	Democratic Liberal Party	LP	Liberal Party
DP	Democratic Party	NCP	National Cooperative Party
DSP	Democratic Socialist Party	NDP	National Democratic Party
JCOP	Japan Cooperative Party	NFP	New Frontier Party
JCP	Japan Communist Party	NPF	New Party Future
JDP	Japan Democratic Party	NPH	New Party Harbinger
JLP	Japan Liberal Party	RP	Reform Party
JNP	Japan New Party	SDF	Social Democratic Federation
JPP	Japan Progressive Party	SDPJ	Social Democratic Party of Japan
JRP	Japan Renewal Party		

State of the Nation Speech by Prime Minister
Hosokawa. He is mumbling to himself, "I will ignore
some dissonance."
Source: Mr. Kiyoshi Ichimura, *The Weekly Toyo Keizai*,
September 4, 1993.

the two parties began to fight each other toward the end of the same decade, the progressive tide in local elections quickly receded until the conservatives recaptured most of the key governorships and mayoralties. Nonetheless, opposition members continued to outnumber LDP members in most big-city and ward assemblies.

The Diet, on the other hand, was dominated by the LDP from 1955 to the end of the 1980s.[37] Despite its overall success, from its inception, the party was divided into several well-defined rival factions, each led by a particularly influential party boss. The boss and his followers were bound by patron-client ties of mutual assistance and dependence: The boss supplied followers with campaign funds at election time and recommended them for appointment to Diet, cabinet, and party offices, while the followers reciprocated by pledging their support for the boss's actual or expected bid for the highest party office, the LDP presidency, which was virtually synonymous with the prime minister's position before 1993. A large factional following was therefore a very valuable asset for a boss with prime ministerial ambitions. The LDP factions thus evolved as intraparty campaign machines intent on aggrandizing themselves at each other's expense. They were not directly concerned with policy issues but did influence the policy-making process indirectly by virtue of the fact that all important Diet, cabinet, and party offices were allocated to individual LDP Diet members on the basis of their factional affiliation.

During the first quarter century of the LDP's existence, the personal role of the faction boss was particularly great, and the boss's death or retirement often resulted in splits or disintegration of the faction. After the late 1970s, however, the five surviving factions became increasingly institutionalized, so that the deaths or retirement of their bosses no longer necessarily threatened their continued existence. The faction once led by Masayoshi Ōhira (prime minister, 1978–1980) survived until 1994 under the leadership of Ōhira's successors, Zenkō Suzuki (prime minister, 1980–1982) and Kiichi Miyazawa (prime minister, 1991–1993); and the faction once led by Takeo Fukuda (prime minister, 1976–1978) similarly survived under his successors, Shintarō Abe and Hiroshi Mitsuzaka. Amid the complex party realignment process set off by the LDP's splits and fall from power in 1993, all LDP factions declared themselves dissolved by the end of 1994.

with the LDP leadership on how to deal with pervasive political corruption and how to reform the existing election system. On most other issues, however, they disagreed more with each other than with the LDP.

Divisions among opposition parties based on ideological or policy differences, competing organizational interests, personal conflicts among leaders, and historical rivalries helped keep the LDP in power for nearly four decades. Until the end of the 1980s, when the LDP began to lose control of, first, the upper house, and then the lower house, the role of the opposition in Japanese politics was largely marginal. However, where the opposition parties managed to bury their differences and unite against the LDP, they often succeeded in defeating it. In the mid-1970s, for example, effective electoral collaboration between the JSP and the JCP at the local level led to the election of "progressive" governors in 9 of the 47 prefectures, including the 2 most populous, Tokyo and Osaka, and mayors in 7 of the 10 largest cities. Conversely, when

TABLE 7   **Number of Seats and Percentage of Votes Won by Parties in 1990 and 1993 General Elections**

	Number of Seats		Percentage of Votes	
	1990	1993	1990	1993
Liberal Democratic Party	275	223	46.1	36.6
Social Democratic Party of Japan	136	70	24.4	15.4
Japan Renewal Party	—	55	—	10.1
Clean Government Party	45	51	8.0	8.1
Japan New Party	—	35	—	8.0
Japan Communist Party	16	15	8.0	7.7
Democratic Socialist Party	14	15	4.8	3.5
New Party Harbinger	—	13	—	2.6
Social Democratic Federation	4	4	0.9	0.7
Other parties	1	0	0.5	0.2
Independents	21	30	7.3	7.3
Total	512	511	100.0	100.2

Note: The number of seats in the House of Representatives was reduced by one between 1990 and 1993 as a result of the elimination of the one-seat island district (Amami Oshima).

Sources: *Asahi shinbun,* February 20, 1990, 4; July 19, 1993, 1; July 19, 1993, evening ed., 2.

Of the four parties in the parliamentary opposition until the early 1990s, only the SDPJ was host to factions as contentious as and, in some ways, more destructive than their counterparts in the LDP. While the LDP factions were concerned primarily with fund-raising and distribution of government and party offices among its Diet members, the SDPJ factions were primarily ideological and policy groups, some advocating a more radical version of socialism than others, some a more hostile policy toward the Self-Defense Forces and Japan's military alliance with the U.S., some a more critical attitude toward the middle-of-the-road parties, and so forth. The SDPJ factions were, however, sporadic and fragmented. Whereas virtually all LDP Diet members belonged to one or another faction in the party, less than half of the SDPJ Diet members did in recent years.

As Table 7 shows, the LDP lost its majority in the lower house in the 1993 general election. Following the election, eight of the nine opposition parties (all except the JCP) joined the coalition government.

This was an inherently unstable coalition with partners disagreeing among themselves, even more than with the LDP, on many key policy issues (see Table 8). There was virtual unanimity among all coalition parties on only two of the eight major election issues: All supported electoral reform and all opposed the import of foreign-grown rice. On the other six issues, there was disagreement among the parties, and a very serious split between three of them on whether Japan should seek a permanent seat on the United Nations Security Council. In short, the non-LDP coalition contained seeds of serious internal conflict on some of the most salient domestic and foreign policy issues of the times.

Not surprisingly, the Hosokawa coalition cabinet lasted only eight months before it resigned in April 1994. It was succeeded by another coalition cabinet led by the JRP leader, Hata. Hata's was an even weaker cabinet because the SDPJ, the largest non-LDP party in the Diet, and the NPH refused to join Hata's faction on ideological grounds and allied themselves with his opponents. Hata's cabinet lasted

TABLE 8   **Parties' Positions on Major Issues, July 1993**

Issues	LDP	SDPJ	JRP	CGP	JNP	DSP	NPH	SDF	JCP
Revision of the Constitution[a]	Yes[b]	No	Yes	Yes	Yes	Yes	No	No	NO
Electoral System: Single Seat/PR	N/C	YES	YES	YES	N/C	YES	YES	YES	NO
Campaign Contributions by Business and Unions	YES	No	Yes	No	Yes	No	Yes	NO	NO
Constitutionality of the Self-Defense Forces	YES	No	Yes	No	Yes	No	Yes	NO	NO
Participation in UN Peacekeeping Operations	YES	No	YES	Yes	No	YES	Yes	No	NO
Permanent Seat on UN Security Council	YES	No	YES	No	No	YES	NO	Yes	NO
Import of Rice	No	NO	No	No	N/C	NO	NO	No	NO
Nuclear Power for Industry	YES	No	Yes	N/C	Yes	YES	Yes	N/C	NO

[a]Proposals to revise the constitution involve a number of specific issues, including, among others, the status and functions of the emperor, the "peace clause" (Article IX), the organization of the Diet, the rights and duties of citizens, and the scope of local autonomy.
[b]Note: YES = strongly positive; Yes = moderately positive; NO = strongly negative; No = moderately negative; N/C = noncommittal.

Sources: *Mainichi shinbun,* July 6, 1993, pp. 12–13; *Asahi shinbun,* July 7, 1993, pp. 16–17.

only two months before it was replaced by an LDP-SDPJ-NPH coalition cabinet headed by the SDPJ leader, Tomiichi Murayama, in June 1994. In a strange partnership with its major opponent since the mid-1950s, the LDP thus returned to the cabinet less than a year after the end of its one-party rule.

Toward the end of 1994, four opposition parties (JRP, JNP, CGP, and DSP) merged and formed the New Frontier Party. This new party, a few remaining splinter groups, and the JCP opposed the ruling LDP-SDPJ-NPH coalition. A group in the SDPJ was attempting with considerable difficulty to form a new progressive-liberal party with members of other parties.

The party realignment under way in early 1995 is driven primarily by electoral calculations. To win in a single-member district system, it is better to run as a candidate of a larger party, which the system favors. In the 1992 House of Commons election in Britain, for instance, the Conservative Party won about 52 percent of the seats with 42 percent of the vote, and the Labour Party won about 32 percent of the seats with 42 percent of the vote, while the Liberal Democratic Party won only 3 percent of the seats with 17 percent of the vote. Simple electoral calculations thus should lead smaller parties and their members to join larger parties, as suggested by the formation of the New Frontier Party.[38] The plan of the group in the SDPJ to break away from the party was also prompted mainly by concern that SDPJ candidates had little chance of victory in the next lower-house election against competitors from the larger and better-organized conservative parties.

Campaigns and Elections

The House of Representatives election system was drastically changed by the 1994 electoral reform. Under the old system, all members of that house, as well as some members of the House of Councillors, were elected under a complex voting scheme, called the 'single nontransferable vote,'' or SNTV, system, that had been in effect since the mid-1920s and was nearly unique in the world. At the time of the 1993 lower-house election, for example, Japan was divided into 129 lower-house election districts, each of which elected between two and six members to that house. Because many candidates (including candidates from the same party) would run for a seat within each district, it was possible to win one of the available seats with as little as 10–15 percent of the vote. This system produced results very similar to those of a type of proportional representation, making it possible for smaller parties to win at least some seats.

The multimember system forced candidates of the same party to compete for votes in the same districts, which they did mostly by means other than highlighting their distinctive positions on policy issues. This tendency was particularly pronounced because all Japanese parties required their Diet members to support the official party line on all major policy issues. The most common and effective way to win the voters' favor was to offer them a variety of constituency services, ranging from helping them find jobs in local public offices or private companies to lobbying central government ministries on their behalf. The bulk of such constituency service activities were carried out by local campaign organizations, the *koenkai*.

These constituency-level campaign organizations turned members of local communities and organizations, such as agricultural cooperatives and merchant associations, into solid blocs of voters for particular candidates. It took enormous amounts of money and hard work to create and maintain *koenkai* both during and between elections—not so much to buy votes outright, but to rent campaign office space, pay staff salaries, and finance constituency services. The funds were provided mainly by businesses and business organizations. During their long uninterrupted rule, LDP politicians nurtured extensive, sturdy networks of patronage relationships, known as **clientelism,** with business organizations willing to raise huge amounts of political funds for conservative party candidates on the one hand and constituency organizations able to mobilize local voters in Diet and local elections on the other.

The LDP also owed its electoral success to a gross malapportionment of Diet seats among the election districts, which gave significant advantage to rural voters over their urban counterparts. The malapportionment had its roots in an early postwar census used to determine the original distribution of seats in the first Diet elections held in 1947 under the existing election law. The census was taken when the majority of Japanese lived in rural areas and major

cities were only sparsely populated after a series of devastating Allied air raids in the last months of the war. This apportionment has been only marginally adjusted to account for the enormous population shifts from rural to urban areas that occurred over the next fifty years. As a result, the LDP consistently championed farmers' interests, especially by maintaining a wartime system of price support for rice, and thus succeeded in turning rural Japan into a solid, and systematically overrepresented, bloc of staunchly pro-LDP voters.

The systematic bias in the election system, and the "money politics" that was blamed for the recurrent scandals involving top government and LDP leaders and business executives, raised serious doubts about the success of democracy in contemporary Japan. Many, including some LDP leaders, were calling for reform for nearly a quarter century. The determined opposition of those who benefited from the status quo, however, had effectively blocked any meaningful change. The dramatic reversal in the electoral fortunes of the LDP and the opposition in 1993, and the formation of a succession of coalition governments, at long last led to some serious attacks on the decades-old problems.

In early 1994, a set of four political reform bills were passed by the Diet in the hope that replacing the multiseat district system with a combination of single-seat district and proportional representation systems would help rid lower-house elections of money politics. The new system would replace the existing 129 multiseat districts that elected 511 lower-house members with 300 single-seat districts elected by the "first-past-the-post" rule and eleven regional districts (blocs) that would elect an additional 200 members by a party list–based proportional representation method. The first lower-house election under the new system is yet to be called at this writing, and it is impossible to predict whether the reform will actually lead to complete elimination or a substantial reduction of the influence of money in Japanese elections.

POLITICAL CULTURE, CITIZENSHIP, AND IDENTITY

Japan is a society with a Confucian fear of social conflict and a longing for order and harmony among and within all classes of people. As explained in Section 1,

Confucianism was originally imported from China in the third century A.D. and adopted as the official state ideology in Tokugawa Japan. Its emphasis on hierarchy, obedience, and orderliness was well suited to a feudal regime intent on perpetuating the existing political order and the social relationships underpinning it.

After the Meiji Restoration, Confucianism continued to be used by the rulers of modern Japan to mold a new nationalism based on emperor worship and a concept of the state as a big family under the rule of its benevolent emperor and his government. The ideology helped inculcate in the Japanese a belief in the virtues of hard work and frugality and in the uniqueness and superiority of their nation. This ideology was systematically transmitted to Japanese youth by compulsory systems of education and military service, both of which were introduced early in the Meiji period. Confucian teachings were reinforced by precepts of Shinto, originally a native cult of ancestor and nature worship, but then declared a new state religion, of which the emperor was the high priest.[39] These two ideologies helped turn many prewar Japanese leaders and citizens into true believers of the emperor cult and soldiers of fanatic nationalism.

Paternalistic practices still prevail in Japanese society, especially in the firm, which has replaced the state as the big family and as the new object of identity, loyalty, and dedication for most employees. This has political implications when, for example, the management and labor union of a firm join forces to mobilize all employees in support of particular candidates in a Diet or local election.

In contemporary Japan, as in prewar Japan, all important agents of political socialization, such as the family, the school system, and the mass media, tend to help perpetuate entrenched collectivist and conformist values. The most important function of the school in contemporary Japan, however, is to prepare students for entrance into either the job market or higher-level schools. Which school and, in particular, which university one graduates from in Japan determines to an important extent what kind of job one will hold after graduation. Some universities are believed to prepare students better than others to enter the most prestigious companies or government agencies, and therefore attract more and better-performing applicants to their entrance examinations.

The six-year elementary and three-year lower secondary school (junior high school) education is compulsory, and virtually all children finish it. Moreover, over 95 percent of lower secondary school graduates go to a three-year upper secondary school (high school), and over one-third of upper secondary school graduates go to a two-year college or a four-year university. The schools at these three levels are predominantly public, and private schools differ little from public schools in either organization or curriculum. The primary purpose of elementary and secondary schools is to prepare their pupils for entrance examinations for the next educational level; the primary purpose of upper secondary schools is to prepare students either for the job market, by training them in practical skills, or for college and university entrance examinations. This preparatory mission common to all Japanese schools absorbs the bulk of teachers' and students' time and energy, leaving little of either for education for any other purpose, such as acquiring knowledge for its own sake, learning to enjoy art, or developing critical faculties.[40]

This pervasive concentration on entrance examinations means that neither curriculum nor pedagogic approach varies much across schools. Moreover, all schools use very similar textbooks in all subject areas, thanks to the textbook certification system under which all drafts of textbooks must be submitted to the Ministry of Education for inspection, often extensive revisions, and certification before they are published and used in schools. This de facto censorship system continues to ensure that the textbooks are generally consistent with the opinions, preferences, and prejudices of Ministry of Education inspectors. As a result, the history and social studies textbooks used in Japanese schools tend to avoid touching on any controversial political issues. For example, they say little about the role of the Japanese throne in the rise and rampage of Japanese imperialism, the constitutionality of the Self-Defense Forces, the causes and consequences of money politics, and Japanese trade protectionism. In the early 1980s, the ministry inspectors went so far as to order changes in the descriptions of atrocities committed by the Japanese during their occupation of China and Korea before and during World War II. Protests by governments and people in both countries and many others subsequently led to some changes in the certification procedure.

On the other hand, the highly centralized and rigidly controlled educational system helps nurture a highly literate, hardworking, and dedicated labor force. Once out of school, most young Japanese become loyal employees of a firm, where their loyalty is reinforced by the activities of the **company union** and rewarded, in many cases, by the guaranteed security of **lifetime employment.** Japan has been called a "company state" or "company society," in reference to the company-centered lives of most blue-collar and white-collar workers. This largely closed life-style of typical Japanese employees further hinders the growth of broader political awareness and discourages active political participation and critical assessments of government policies.

This is the case despite the fact that contemporary Japan is one of the most media-saturated societies. It has only about one-tenth as many daily newspapers as the United States and half as many as Germany, but many of its papers have far larger circulations than their American or European counterparts. As a result, Japan boasts a larger total and per-person newspaper circulation than any other advanced industrial nation. This is also true for books and magazines: Some 45,000 new books per year, 2,400 monthly magazines, and 80 weekly magazines are published. Moreover, the average Japanese family owns two color televisions. Japanese are exposed daily to wide-ranging sources and kinds of information, but this deluge of information tends to reinforce conformism, rather than encourage a questioning attitude among the people.

For one thing, the major Japanese newspapers, especially the five with national circulation, have been either openly pro-LDP or critical of both the LDP and its opponents. The *Yomiuri,* with a daily circulation of nearly 15 million and the *Sankei,* with about 3 million, have been the most consistently pro-LDP. The other three—the *Asahi,* the *Nihon Keizai (Nikkei),* and, especially, the *Mainichi*—have generally been more critical of many of the LDP policies. But they have been equally or even more critical of the other parties. As a result, their criticisms of LDP policies failed until recently to move voters toward the opposition at election time and did not give rise to a political reform movement.

The Japanese press also tends to be conservative in its treatment of social and economic problems, largely because of its heavy financial dependence upon advertisers. This discourages the mass-circulation papers from publishing news that may embarrass or otherwise compromise the advertisers' interests or reputation. A company responsible for pollution of the environment, for example, may escape public attention thanks to deliberate silence on the part of one or more of the largest national papers that depend on that company's advertisements. For the same reason, a government agency with regulatory power over the offending company may escape a press report on its failure to enforce relevant laws.

Second, an entrenched institution known as the "press club" often leads to what amounts to self-censorship of its members. Such clubs, made up of a few reporters from each accredited news media, are found in nearly all important Japanese public and private organizations. A club is provided designated quarters in the given government or private organization, and its members gather information from the organization's official spokesmen. But information thus given is inevitably an official handout, and a reporter who ventures to seek unofficial information risks losing his or her good standing with the host organization and even his or her club membership. The system as a whole thus works to suppress publication of news critical of government or corporate policy or deeds.

The majority of the books and magazines published and television programs broadcast—increasingly dominant agents of socialization in Japan as in other industrialized societies—are devoted to entertainment, literature, arts, hobbies, sports, and natural sciences. If politics is discussed at all, it is usually in the form of preachy commentary by a handful of pundits in the mainstream press, in sensationalist and gossipy tabloid articles, or in comic strips. Very few well-informed, detailed, and critical discussions of politics and policy issues are readily available to ordinary citizens. This information vacuum contributes to the power of conformism and the weakness of dissident opinion in Japanese politics.

Japanese society thus appears conspicuously consensus-oriented and conformist. But the appearance of consensus and conformism is attributable partly to the fact that the vast majority of people have so far been generally satisfied with the existing state of affairs. Japan is not only an affluent country in which most of its citizens enjoy a high quality of life. It is a society in which income and wealth are distributed more evenly than in most other societies. This relative well-being encourages a certain amount of complacency and smugness among its citizens. It should be noted, however, that the postwar democratic reforms, including the promulgation of the MacArthur Constitution, have had a profound and pervasive impact upon the values and attitudes of the Japanese people. In addition, the rapid economic development and urbanization that followed have given rise to a host of divisive issues common to many industrialized societies.

The postwar rearmament of Japan has been one such issue. Throughout the forty or so years since the birth of the Self-Defense Forces (SDF), Japanese have been sharply divided over what role they should play in the event that Japan is attacked or invaded by a hostile foreign force and, especially, over how much larger the SDF should grow. In practice, apart from training exercises and recent participation in a few UN peacekeeping missions, the SDF's activity has been largely limited to domestic relief operations during natural disasters such as fires, earthquakes, and typhoon-caused flooding and landslides.

The status and relationship with government of the famous Yasukuni Shinto shrine in Tokyo has been another highly divisive issue. After the war, Shinto lost its privileged status as state religion, consistent with the principle of the separation of state and religion. Nonetheless, opinion has been sharply divided over the issue of whether high-ranking government officials, especially members of a cabinet, should or should not visit the shrine to pay respect to the spirits of some 2.5 million Japanese killed in all wars since the Meiji Restoration, including the seven leaders executed as war criminals at the end of World War II. In the late 1960s, the LDP leadership tried, with the support of organizations of the families of dead soldiers and strong nationalists, to pass legislation to make it possible for the government to provide financial assistance to the shrine, but the attempt failed in the face of widespread opposition. The opponents argued that government support of any religious establishment violates the principle of the separation of state and religion as well as the constitutional guarantee of the freedom of religion. Since the mid-1970s, however, some prime ministers and a number of other cabinet members have visited the shrine on the anniversary of the end of World War II (August 15) either privately or officially. In 1991, a higher court found government ties to the shrine unconstitutional, but the decision has not put an end to the protracted and highly emotional controversy.

INTERESTS, SOCIAL MOVEMENTS, AND PROTEST

There are a number of other contentious issues in contemporary Japan over which the interests and opinions of diverse groups clash. For example, the development and use of nuclear power by electric companies has been controversial in a country that was subjected to the first and, so far, only use of nuclear bombs in war. On the one hand, the electric power industry and the LDP leadership vigorously push the construction and operation of nuclear reactors as an ideal alternative to imported fuels, especially oil from the Middle East. Because of their dedication and persistence, Japan is today one of the world's major users of nuclear energy, with some forty reactors in operation (about 10 percent of the world's total) supplying more than a quarter of the nation's annual energy consumption. On the other hand, a number of local communities and governments around the country vigorously and uncompromisingly oppose construction of reactors in their own backyards. Alarmed particularly by the Three Mile Island nuclear accident in the United States in 1979 and the Chernobyl disaster in the Soviet Union in 1986, the opposition stiffened, forcing suspension of construction plans or operation of reactors at a number of sites from Hokkaido in the north to Shikoku and Kyushu in the south.

A variety of hazards to people's lives and health posed by the rapid industrialization of the economy and urbanization of society has also given rise to intense conflicts over a number of other environmental issues. In fact, a series of extremely severe cases of industrial pollution, including fatal mercury poisoning known as the **Minamata Disease** that first occurred in Minamata City in southern Kyushu and later in northern Honshu, cadmium poisoning in central Honshu, and asthma in southwestern Honshu, made the Japanese people one of the best-known and most frequently cited victims of environmental hazards resulting from a reckless industrialization drive in the 1950s and 1960s.[41] While a series of stiff antipollution laws passed in the early 1970s helped prevent recurrence of such devastating industrial accidents, citizens' concern about deterioration of the environment continues to spur battles in courtrooms and pro-

Against the State: The Narita Airport Incident

In 1965, the Ministry of Transportation decided to build a new international airport in Narita Town, east of Tokyo, without seeking the consent of the farmers who owned land in the area. This decision triggered one of the longest popular protests against a government action in modern Japanese history.

The protest initially involved about 3,000 local farmers, who were soon joined by groups of student radicals from Tokyo and other cities. Not only did the farmers refuse to sell their land to the government and leave the area, but they physically tried to prevent construction of the airport itself. They built obstructions in places earmarked for construction of important airport facilities and repeatedly fought battles with the police who had been sent in by the government to remove them. The often violent protest has now been going on for three decades, although most of the students have gone back to the universities and most of the farmers have settled for compensation payments from the government and quit the fight. Only a handful of defiant and militant protesters remain.

The protest has prevented the construction of a number of key airport facilities, including two of the three runways originally planned, and thus has kept Tokyo's main gateway to the world operating at far below its capacity. Tall wire fences still surround the entire airport, and round-the-clock security checks are enforced at every entrance. Over the years, some of the more violent clashes between government surveyors, builders, and police on the one hand, and protesting farmers and students on the other, have resulted in casualties on both sides, including several deaths.

The incident has thus taught the Japanese and, especially, the Japanese government, a simple but important lesson: citizens in today's democratic Japan, unlike their predecessors before World War II, will not defer to, but will fight, an arbitrary decision by public authorities. The LDP government was very slow to learn this lesson. Only in late 1989 did it finally acknowledge and officially apologize for its original mistake. And only in 1995 did the last few protesters agree to accept the government apologies and compensation and end the protest.

tests in the streets. Local citizens' opposition to noise, for example, often blocks or delays construction of new highways, railroads, and airports around the country.

These are usually controlled, nonviolent conflicts fought by law-abiding citizens and groups. However, Japanese society does have its share of violent and illegal conflicts as well. As a rule, they involve either leftist or rightist extremist groups who try to get their way by intimidating and, occasionally, physically harming their opponents in order to silence them. At one end of the political spectrum are the student and youth groups known since the early 1960s as the "new left," and called the Central Core, Revolutionary Marxist, Fourth International, and so on. The 12,500 or so members of these twenty-odd groups attack symbols of power and authority in the capitalist (and therefore, by definition, corrupt and dangerous) Japan. These targets range from the LDP headquarters and residences of members of the imperial family to airports and nuclear power stations.[42] Some of these groups engage in "urban guerrilla" actions with the use of high-tech weapons, such as sophisticated time bombs and remote-controlled missiles, which often result in considerable damage to property and occasionally in

human casualties. Their strength and effectiveness, however, have sharply declined in recent years, yielding to growing public hostility toward their extremist views and violent tactics and to their own internecine conflicts. The Red Army, which enjoyed considerable notoriety because of its links to international terrorism in the early 1970s, has been decimated by the arrest of virtually all of its leaders, and today only a rump group of a few dozen members barely survives.

The groups on the extreme right are far more numerous and better organized. There are 840 or so groups of this kind, with a combined membership of about 120,000. Most of them are vehemently chauvinist and anticommunist political organizations concerned—often more ostensibly than genuinely—about the future of the Japanese nation and its imperial tradition. Members of these groups often resort to violence to silence their opponents. Among the best known of such groups are Aikokuto (patriotic party), Kokusaku Kenkyukai (society to study national policies), and Yukoku Seiwakai (society of the pure and harmonious concerned about the nation). In 1987, a reporter of the liberal national daily *Asahi shinbun* was shot to death and another seriously wounded by a member of one of these groups, Sekihotai (red patriots' brigade).

And in 1990, the liberal mayor of Nagasaki City was wounded by another right-wing assassin for his remark on the last emperor's responsibility for the last war.

A cult group known as Aum Shinrikyo committed the most sensational violent act in recent times. Led by a Messianic leader and his apocalyptic messages, members of the group made well-coordinated attacks with a potent nerve gas, sarin, on several subway trains in central Tokyo in March 1995, killing 12 passengers on the spot and injuring 5,000 others. Subsequent investigations revealed that the cult, with some 10,000 Japanese and 30,000 Russian members, was assembling an arsenal of tanks, helicopters, and assault rifles, as well as poison gases, in preparation for an approaching Armageddon.

In addition to the cults, there are 350 or so crime syndicates, known as *yakuza,* with about 6,000 members. These groups make money from prostitution, gun running, drug smuggling, and other illegal and criminal operations. They also extract money from corporations, and cooperation from politicians and bureaucrats.[43]

There is a tradition of close association and mutual assistance between Japan's conservative politicians and right-wing groups, dating back to the Meiji period. The murky line separating bona fide political right groups from the *yakuza* has led to a series of political scandals involving top LDP leaders and *yakuza* groups. For example, in 1987, a right-wing organization called Kominto (party of the emperor's subjects) conducted a "harassment with praise" campaign against an LDP leader and later prime minister, Noboru Takeshita. A *yakuza* boss was reportedly involved in the attempts by Takeshita and other LDP leaders to get Kominto to stop the campaign.

Belying its stereotype as a homogeneous, consensus-governed society, contemporary Japan also has some serious issues of collective identity to contend with, although they are neither as widespread nor as intense as those in a number of other nations. Such issues are of great concern, particularly to the numerically minuscule but increasingly vocal ethnic minority known as the Ainu, the much larger and far more vocal minority of former outcaste people, and Korean and other resident foreigners.

The Ainu are descendants of the hunter-gatherers believed to have once inhabited the greater part of the northern half of the country. The traditional Ainu society had no system of private property, and most of their communally owned land was taken away from them and distributed among new settlers from southern areas in the land reform undertaken by the Meiji government. They were thus left only with the land on which they lived. They were also forced to abandon hunting by government decree. Most Ainu were quickly driven to extreme poverty. As the number of immigrants to Hokkaido from Japan's other islands grew, the number of intermarriages also increased. Today, about 17,000 Japanese are known to have some Ainu blood, but the number of full-blooded Ainu is estimated to be no more than about 200.

Since the Meiji period, the Ainu have ostensibly been protected by a "Law to Protect Former Natives of Hokkaido," but in practice little has been done to protect or help them. The entire Ainu community has long been afflicted with high incidence of alcoholism, tuberculosis, and venereal disease. These problems, and the plight of the Ainu in general, had been almost completely ignored, and largely forgotten, by both the Japanese government and the Japanese public until the mid-1980s, when a prime minister's characterization of Japan as a homogeneous nation provoked a public protest from leaders of the Ainu community. The prefectural government of Hokkaido has since recommended enactment of a new law aimed at the protection of Ainu human rights, improvement of their social and economic conditions, and preservation and promotion of their traditional culture. The national government has responded by appointing an interministry committee to study the issue and make a recommendation to the cabinet. A new law is likely to be enacted soon, and the long-ignored problem of the Ainu may be officially addressed for the first time. However, it will still be a long time before the effects of the centuries-old prejudice and neglect are corrected.

The movement for the liberation of former outcaste people (that is, descendants of those who were once forced to live in ghettos and follow occupations that were then seen as "unclean") and their residential neighborhoods picked up pace after World War II. In the 1970s, a series of laws were passed to help "liberate" the nearly 5,000 "special hamlets" that still existed, mostly in the southwestern half of the country, and "integrate" the well over a million people who lived there into the broader community. Considerable improvement has since been made in the economic conditions within former outcaste communities, but complete equality and integration in Japanese society at large, especially in areas such as employment and marriage, remain unfulfilled, elusive goals.

After the Meiji Restoration and, especially, after Japan annexed Korea as a colony in 1910, many Koreans began to immigrate to Japan. Initially, they came to Japan voluntarily. By the 1930s, however, they were increasingly brought by force to augment the ranks of a de facto corvée labor force in some of the nation's most poorly equipped and dangerous factories and mines. At the end of World War II, well over 2 million Koreans lived in Japan. The majority of them and their children have since returned to either South or North Korea, while a small minority have acquired Japanese citizenship.[44] Nearly 700,000, however, live in Japan as resident aliens, some by choice, but most because of Japanese immigration policy, which denies them citizenship. Their legal status, civil rights, and living and working conditions remain hotly disputed issues between them and the Japanese government and between the Japanese and Korean governments.

The most important and difficult issue raised by these minorities in contemporary Japan is not so much the physical hardships or material deprivation inflicted on them by deliberate government policy. In fact, many former outcaste communities have received generous financial assistance from both the national and local governments during the last quarter century and today enjoy greatly improved community facilities, including paved roads, schools, public libraries, and community halls. Many Korean residents own successful and profitable businesses, albeit mostly small businesses such as restaurants and game parlors. The core problem facing minorities in Japan is the informal social and cultural discrimination that they face in matters such as employment and marriage. Thus, affluent and democratic Japan, like many other countries, has a long way to go to solve this type of discrimination.

Contemporary Japan also shares with many other advanced industrial societies the problem of illegal foreign workers. About 300,000 such foreign workers, mainly from Asia and the Middle East, are believed to be employed in Japan in the mid-1990s and constitute the country's newest ethnic minority. These immigrants are a potential source of social tension and conflict over the issue of collective identity. They come to Japan in search of jobs, mostly menial, which pay many times the wages they could earn in their own countries. They are increasingly indispensable to many Japanese businesses suffering from chronic shortages of cheap, unskilled workers. As is happening in most other high-wage industrial nations of North America and Western Europe, however, the growing population of foreign workers is feared and resented by many Japanese who see them as a threat to their own wages, pensions, free medical care, and even jobs in a period of recession. While nearly all of these foreign workers are technically temporary visitors expected to return to their own countries in a few years, many stay much longer, and some become legal or illegal residents. The presence of this emergent ethnic minority poses a particularly troubling problem to Japan, which has long prided itself on racial purity.

A society long under the influence of Confucianism and viewing the state as a big family where order and harmony prevail and everybody not only knows but accepts his or her proper station has never been hospitable to modern class consciousness. As the society became increasingly affluent, what little class consciousness had developed among members of the working class during the harder times steadily diminished. A high degree of social mobility also contributed to the decline of class consciousness by blurring the boundaries between the classes. For all these reasons, by the early 1970s, about 90 percent of Japanese had begun to identify themselves consistently as part of the "middling class" between the very rich and the very poor in periodic public opinion surveys. Japan is thus often depicted as a classless society in which class distinctions have virtually disappeared in terms not only of income and wealth but also of consumption habits, lifestyles, levels of education, and basic values.[45]

In the mid-1950s, slightly more than half of white-collar and blue-collar workers supported the Japan Socialist Party, while only about a third supported the LDP; by the mid-1980s, the ranks of Socialist supporters had declined to about one-fifth of the total, while the ranks of LDP supporters had increased to well over half. Japanese business leaders, industrialists, and farmers have supported the LDP far more consistently. It is doubtful, however, that their partisanship results from their class consciousness. It is more likely based on their personal and organizational involvement with the LDP. Class has thus been a weak basis both for interest group organization and for political mobilization in contemporary Japan.[46]

Dissatisfaction has also not crystallized into organized citizen movements. Since the late 1960s, organized protests in Japan have been localized and have revolved mainly around environmental issues such as the controversial construction of a dam at the upper reaches of a river in central Honshu. However, these local activities seldom hit the headlines in the national press or attract the attention of major television networks. Apart from the noisy sound trucks of various rightist groups, bedecked with the national flag and seen fairly frequently in Tokyo and other major cities, today's Japan is a relatively quiet society whose citizens grumble privately rather than protest publicly.

SECTION 5

Japanese Politics at the Crossroads

POLITICAL CHALLENGES AND CHANGING AGENDAS

The importation of agricultural products from abroad has been the subject of an intense controversy among Japanese. Under rising foreign, especially U.S., pressure, both tariff and nontariff import restrictions have been gradually removed and Japan is today no more protectionist than most members of the European Union (EU) as far as trade in agricultural products is concerned. The road toward a freer market, however, has been anything but smooth. When the quotas on imported beef and oranges were significantly enlarged in response to U.S. demand in the 1980s, farmers and their allies in the Diet and the bureaucracy fiercely opposed the decision and were quieted only by substantial compensation payments. Their determined opposition kept Japan's 10-million-ton-a-year rice market almost totally closed until 1993, despite repeated and increasingly impatient U.S. demand for an opening of the market and sporadic calls for compromise heard from a few Japanese political and business leaders.

As illustrated by the rice import issue, Japan is struggling to restructure its political economy in order to adjust to the rapidly changing economic and political conditions both at home and abroad in the first decade of the post–Cold War era. In order to negotiate the transition successfully, the country will have to tackle two important and difficult tasks in particular. First, it must help devise a more effective division of labor with its major trading partners, especially in the Asia-Pacific region. Second, it must overhaul its domestic economy, especially its overregulated and notoriously inefficient agricultural and service sectors, so as to bring down the world's highest consumer prices through freer price competition and more active technological and managerial innovations. Seriously attacking these problems will represent a significant departure from the familiar methods and pattern of economic development in postwar Japan.

Since 1945, Japan has succeeded first in recovering from the devastation of its defeat in World War II, and then in building one of the world's most highly developed and dynamic economies, a stable and relatively conflict-free society, and an open and democratic polity. The dramatic transformation of the Japanese society and polity owed much to the even more dramatic transformation of its economy. This economic transformation, in turn, owed much to the availability of abundant and relatively cheap raw materials and advanced industrial technologies in accessible world markets. Japan paid for its huge imports with dollars earned by its thriving export trade. After the mid-1960s, this export-led developmental strategy was made possible by Japan's large surpluses with its major trading partners, especially the United States. To an important extent, Japan's postwar economic miracle was a product of its deliberate policy to maintain chronic export-import imbalances and invest its surpluses in the acquisition of advanced technologies from abroad and in research and development (R&D) to boost productivity at home.

Japan's mercantilistic trade policy was tolerated by the U.S. and, to a lesser extent, its European allies while they were preoccupied with the exigencies of the Cold War. However, following the end of the Vietnam War in the mid-1970s and especially after the collapse of the Soviet Union in 1991, the imbalance became an increasingly contentious issue between Japan and its trading partners. In the latest trade dispute between Tokyo and Washington, President Clinton

Opening Japan's Rice Market

In late 1993, the non-LDP government led by Morihiro Hosokawa decided to import a substantial amount of rice (about 2 million tons within a year) from abroad for the first time since the 1960s. The decision was made in order to deal with a critical shortage of domestic rice caused by an extremely poor harvest in the fall, a result of an unusually cold and wet summer.

The succession of LDP governments that had preceded Hosokawa's had steadfastly maintained a de facto ban on the import of foreign rice, mainly to protect Japanese farmers, who were among the most consistently partisan conservative voters in the country, and partly in deference to broader public support for the ban. This rigid exclusion of foreign-grown rice from the 10-million-ton-a-year Japanese rice market was made possible by a law enacted during World War II that aimed to ensure equitable distribution of scarce staple foodstuffs among all citizens. Under the Foodstuff Control System set up in 1942, all of the rice and other staple foodstuffs produced in a given year were sold to the government and then rationed for sale to citizens exclusively through government-appointed distributors. As the domestic supply of food caught up with, then surpassed, domestic demand in the quarter century after the end of the war, government control of distribution was gradually loosened. By the 1970s, consumers could choose to buy either government-distributed rice of generally inferior quality at controlled prices or better-quality rice at higher prices in the free markets.

By the 1990s, the Foodstuff Control System had long since ceased to play any meaningful role and had become very expensive for the government to maintain. Since the government bought rice from farmers at relatively high prices and then sold the same rice to citizens at relatively low prices, the government was bound to lose money. For example, in 1993, the government paid farmers about $150 per 60 kilograms (about 132 pounds) of unhusked rice and spent an additional $40 for its transportation and storage, for a total of $190. It then sold the same amount of unhusked rice to government-appointed distributors for about $165,

so that the distributors could make up to about $25 from the deal. In the process, the government—and thus the taxpayers—lost $25 per kilo. This carefully controlled price, which was also protected from foreign competition, was several times higher than the international price.

The Foodstuff Control System gave the Japanese government the legal power to ban sale of staple foodstuffs by Japanese farmers except by rules set up by the government. It also gave the government the power to ban the import of rice or any other staple foodstuffs. This system survived until 1993, thanks mainly to the sustained pressure of well-organized and vocal farmers, but partly also to broad public support for the ideal of self-sufficiency in the supply of staple foodstuffs. This public support reflects a genuine and deep concern among Japanese consumers about unforeseen consequences of excessive dependence upon foreign supplies for basic staples such as rice. This widespread concern is, in turn, based on the realization that Japan's level of self-sufficiency in food supply in general (68 percent in 1989) is considerably lower than that of any other major industrial nation, such as France (203 percent), the United States (172 percent), Great Britain (113 percent), and West Germany (98 percent). The sense of vulnerability (What if the U.S. suddenly stopped selling wheat or soybeans to Japan for whatever reasons, good or bad?) makes many urban Japanese willing to listen to warnings that opening Japan's rice market to foreign imports will place Japanese lives and health at the mercy of foreigners over whom the Japanese government has no control.

The 1993 decision of the Hosokawa government set an important precedent and most likely started a process of progressive liberalization of Japan's long-protected rice market. Given the Japanese farmers' political clout and, more important, the broad support for their position among Japanese consumers, the road to a wide-open market will be long and rugged. It may take several more cold and wet summers before Japanese make up their minds to travel the road as willingly and as fast as U.S. and other foreign rice farmers would like them to do.

announced in May 1995 a decision to impose 100-percent tariffs on virtually all Japanese luxury cars imported by the United States, unless Japan agreed to increase substantially the number of American cars and car parts imported by Japan. Japan thus found itself faced with new and formidable challenges to the foundations of its postwar economic success, social stability, and political democracy.

As suggested above, solving the trade problem will require a drastic overhaul of Japan's economic strategy. Such reorientation is bound to be very painful in an age of slow economic growth and a rapidly aging

population in Japan. As measured by GNP, Japan's miracle economy grew at the average real rate of 9.4 percent per year in the decade immediately preceding the 1973 oil crisis (1963–1972), at only 4.0 percent in the decade immediately following that crisis (1973–1982), and at 3.5 percent in the period from 1983 to 1990. Then, in the early 1990s, Japan experienced its first major recession in nearly two decades.

This recession was triggered by the bursting of the "bubble economy" that had grown on the low interest rates that had been deliberately maintained by the LDP government in the 1980s to offset the anticipated slowdown of the economy as the value of the yen rose sharply and Japanese exports became more expensive and less competitive abroad. The low interest rates failed to stimulate productive investment in plants and equipment by firms but encouraged both firms and individuals to invest in stocks and real estate for quick profits. This begot a huge speculative bubble. At the height of the speculative frenzy, the market value of the stock of a single Japanese corporation, Nippon Telegraph and Telephone, was inflated to more than the total value of the West German stock market, while the value of Japan's land as a whole was inflated to four times the value of all land in the United States. If the rise was as dramatic, the fall of the inflated stock market in 1990 was drastic and inflicted lasting damage to the economy and the morale of the Japanese people.

The sad state of the economy is not the only serious problem Japan faces in this, the last decade of the twentieth century. The state of Japanese society, too, is undergoing a transition with immediate and profound impacts on its economy and far-reaching implications for its future. One particularly important aspect of this transition is a dramatic demographic change, known as the "graying" of its population.

Japan's current crude birth rate of 11 per 1,000 is one of the lowest in the world, and its life expectancy of seventy-nine years at birth is the highest. Demographic projections based on these and related statistics predict that Japan will have the highest ratio of population over sixty-five years of age among the advanced industrial nations by the second decade of the twenty-first century. This will lead to a sharp rise in the costs of health care for the elderly and, at the same time, a significant fall in labor productivity, thus sapping the strength of the Japanese economy.

The record of low economic growth since the oil crisis of the early 1970s, combined with the anticipation of harder times to come, makes Japanese businesses and government more reluctant to undertake measures designed to reduce income derived from export trade. This reluctance is, in turn, bound to aggravate the recurrent trade disputes between Japan and its trading partners.

However, there are some factors at work that may help reduce the friction between Japan and its major trading partners. For example, there is a significant coincidence of interests between the foreigners who want Japan to increase imports by stimulating domestic demand and the Japanese consumers who would benefit from the lower prices and a wider variety of goods and services that would become available in more open domestic markets. Such changes would improve the living conditions of the average Japanese citizen. In fact, a number of Japanese leaders, as well as Japan's foreign critics, have been calling for a basic change in Japanese economic policy for nearly a decade. An astute Japanese government may finally be able to act boldly and take advantage of the coincidence that exists between the long-term needs of the international economy and those of the Japanese domestic economy.

Although the era of frenetic economic growth has ended, Japan has accumulated a very large stock of resources with which to finance measures to reduce its dependence upon exports, further deregulate and decentralize the economy, and upgrade the country's inadequate social infrastructure, such as the crowded housing and lack of public parks. The sharp rise of the yen in relation to foreign currencies has made Japanese exports more expensive in the world market and Japanese imports cheaper in yen terms. This should enable and encourage Japanese citizens to buy more imported goods and services and indirectly help reduce trade friction between Japan and its trading partners.

Rapidly growing Asian economies provide Japan with both promising new export markets and increasingly stiff competition for its exports. Moreover, the high yen is driving a growing number of Japanese manufacturers abroad, especially to those newly industrializing Asian countries that offer cheaper and generally well educated labor and buoyant markets. Japanese investment and technology transfer help accelerate the economic growth of the host countries, but also sow the seeds of more formidable competition for home-based Japanese industry to face in the future. In fact, Japan today imports from its Asian neighbors not only increasing amounts of goods but also increasingly diversified goods, including raw materials, textiles, steel, machinery, and electronics. A large proportion of such imports originate in the expatriate Japanese firms that have relocated abroad in the last decade or two. The situation stimulates debate among Japanese policymakers over potential incentives for businesses to stay in Japan, including improved financing facilities for venture businesses.

Japan also faces a troubling international issue of considerable political significance and delicacy. Despite the dramatic change in its international status and role in the last half of the twentieth century, Japan, along with its wartime allies, Germany and Italy, remains a pariah state in the text of the United Nations Charter. In 3 of its 111 articles, the document refers to these nations as "enemy" states, an expression Japan and the others have tried, so far in vain, to have removed.

Half a century after its defeat in World War II, many Japanese also support a larger role for Japan in the United Nations, including participation in peacekeeping operations throughout the world and accession to a permanent seat on the Security Council. By the early 1990s, Japan had, in fact, begun to participate selectively in peacekeeping operations.

Nonetheless, Japan's role in international politics, whether within or outside the United Nations, remains, and must remain, limited under its pacifist constitution. While there is a vocal minority of citizens who call for a revision of the constitution, especially its war-renouncing article, the majority of Japanese citizens still prefer to leave the original text of the document intact as a safeguard against involvement in another destructive war. In a July 1994 public opinion poll taken by a Japanese news agency, Kyodo Press, 55 percent of respondents wanted to leave it as it is, while 34 percent wanted to revise it. Another recent poll found about half of the respondents in favor of the Japanese government's effort to win a permanent seat on the United Nations Security Council, but without accepting any military role or obligations. Thus, Japan is likely to play only a very gradually expanding role in world politics in the immediate future.

Japanese people's identities are also changing, if only very gradually. Nationalism is not dead in today's Japan, but it no longer has the kind of bellicose racism and ethnocentrism associated with it that characterized prewar Japan. On the contrary, it has distinctively universalistic and globalist overtones, especially when it enters, consciously or unconsciously, discussions of Japan's international role. For example, it is expressed in the proposals made by the Japanese government or by individual Japanese citizens and nongovernmental organizations for contributions to such global causes as the development of Third World economies and the protection of the environment.

It is instructive in this regard to compare the way Japanese public agencies and private citizens treated foreigners, especially resident Koreans, in the wake of the great earthquake of 1923, which destroyed Tokyo and its vicinity, and the earthquake of 1995, which destroyed Kobe and its vicinity. In the former case, racist-inspired rumors led to a massacre of some 6,000 resident Koreans at the hands of both public officials and private citizens; in the latter, Koreans thanked Japanese for treating every victim of the disaster equally regardless of his or her nationality or ethnicity. It is very unlikely that Japanese nationalism will turn racist or virulently xenophobic again in the ever-shrinking world of states.

JAPANESE POLITICS IN TRANSITION

The movement for democracy in Japan was born in the throes of a mid-nineteenth century revolution that followed the opening of the country by threat of force from the United States. The movement, however, ultimately failed under the rule of a nearly absolutist monarchy installed during that revolution and formalized two decades later by a constitution modeled after the Prussian constitution. Following the end of World War II, the movement was revived with great fanfare during the Allied Occupation. Japan has since accomplished nearly all of the major goals of democracy—representation and accountability, participation, equality, and stability—at least in theory. In practice, however, Japan, like all other democracies, still falls far short of many democratic ideals. As discussed in previous sections, there is very wide political, economic, and social inequality between men and women, there is widespread discrimination against minority groups, and individual rights are sometimes trampled by the deeply ingrained influences of a traditional culture that stresses hierarchy and obedience. But it is the legacy of the more than four decades of rule by the LDP and its predecessor conservative parties that poses some of the most troubling questions and biggest challenges for Japanese democracy.

The LDP's one-party rule, which lasted for nearly four decades, helped Japan's economy grow at an unparalleled speed, but it also sowed the seeds of political disillusion and cynicism among a large segment of the nation's voters. Not only was there no alternation of power among the parties, a situation for which the majority of Japanese voters and the opposition parties were at least as responsible as the LDP, but the power of money, rather than opinion, ability, or performance, came to drive and dominate politics and policy-making.

Moreover, "money politics" begot political corruption and led to a seemingly endless series of political scandals involving the nation's highest political officeholders and their corporate supporters. These scandals led to a massive voter revolt against the LDP. The news of their elected representatives making and spending hundreds of millions of yen by fair means or foul may have merely raised the average voter's eyebrows in good times. But when harder times came in the early 1990s with a prolonged recession, and the average citizen was struggling to make ends meet, that news made many Japanese voters angry enough to vote against the party in power.

The many corrupt iron triangles that linked politicians, bureaucrats, and special interests (particularly big business), and that flourished under the LDP's prolonged rule, meant that Japanese policy-making was defined by those special interests, often at the expense of broader public interests. In effect, the one-party-dominated regime significantly depressed the level of representation and accountability in Japanese politics and blocked avenues for new policy initiatives required for meeting the rapidly changing needs of Japan's society and economy and its growing global integration. The ablest LDP policy tribe members were the products and agents of the entrenched special interests and were unable or unwilling to subject the status quo to a critical reexamination and lead it in much needed new directions. The growing realization of this systemic failure significantly contributed to the voter revolts of 1993 against the major beneficiaries of the old regime, the LDP, which was blamed for corrupting the system, and the SDPJ, which was blamed for letting the LDP do so with impunity.

While predictions are premature, given the volatility of the political situation in Japan in the mid-1990s, there are some indications that strong public pressure for a basic and long-term change in Japanese politics and policy-making is building. Recent political scandals and the resulting cynicism among Japanese voters have led increasing numbers of Japanese voters to elect candidates without ties to traditional bases of electoral support, such as an inherited campaign machine and a large campaign war chest. For example, only five of the thirty-five Japan New Party

candidates who won in the 1993 general election were heirs to a parent's seat. Widespread political corruption has also helped focus public attention on a basic flaw in the system: The nearly total control that the national government has over local governments, which many feel has been a major source of the abuse of power in Japan. All parties now call for a decentralization of both tax and policy-making authority, which is expected to increase citizens' interest and participation in local politics and nurture grassroots democracy. This nonpartisan consensus was behind the electoral reforms of 1994 and may eventually lead to the first fundamental change in the way Japanese government and politics have been organized since the Tokugawa era.

JAPAN IN COMPARATIVE PERSPECTIVE

Contemporary Japan is the only non-Western advanced industrial state and the only non-Western member of the small and exclusive group of the world's richest nations, the Group of Seven (G-7). Despite widespread criticism of Japan's aggressive trade policy, there is considerable respect and even admiration for its performance in economic and other areas.

Japan thus presents a model of state-led development that poses an interesting question: Why have Japan's national economic policies been so much more successful than those of other industrial democracies? One observer lists several characteristics of the Japanese model that have contributed to its success: the political stability provided by Japan's one-party dominant democracy for most of the postwar period; the ability of highly skilled government bureaucrats to devise and implement economic policies without political interference; the use of market forces to promote industrialization while controlling excessive competition through effective government intervention; the channeling of Japanese nationalism to support economic development; cultural values that give priority to the group rather than the individual; economic policies that favor producers yet preserve social harmony by recognizing the interests of other groups, such as labor; the inclination to save rather than consume; and an educational system "geared to making even the worst-trained students competent."[47]

In many parts of North America and Western Europe, as well as in Asia and other regions of the developing world, Japan is also depicted as a society characterized not only by rapid economic growth but also, and even more important, by a number of desirable cultural and institutional attributes, including high degrees of social cohesion and political stability, relatively egalitarian income distribution, mass literacy, universal access to high-quality education, effective crime prevention, and a capable and dedicated government bureaucracy. Such observations led a Harvard professor to write a book entitled *Japan as Number One,* which became a best-seller in the United States.[48] Japan is often cited as an example of a country that has succeeded in controlling the disruptive impact of modernization by preserving and utilizing many of its traditional cultural values and social institutions. However, Japan has certainly not been without its critics. Some writers have concluded that Japanese economic success has been achieved at the cost of a suffocating cultural conformity or seriously question just how democratic the Japanese political system is given the low priority given individual rights and the limited political influence of certain groups (such as women).[49]

In earlier times, the rise of modern Japan from the mid-nineteenth to the early twentieth centuries inspired many nationalist leaders in Asia, including Sun Yat-sen in China and Ho Chi Minh in Vietnam. The Japanese invasion and brutal occupation of much of Asia in the 1930s and 1940s, however, led to a shocking sense of betrayal and strong anti-Japanese sentiment. But the success of postwar Japan now inspires many Third World nations. The East Asian NIEs of South Korea, Taiwan, Hong Kong, and Singapore are seen as successful in following in Japan's footsteps in rapidly modernizing their economies through export-led growth.[50] Common to these and, increasingly, other members of the **Association of Southeast Asian Nations (ASEAN),** such as Thailand, Malaysia, and Indonesia, are priorities given to investment in the development of both physical and human capital, emphasis on basic primary and secondary, rather than university-level, education, deliberate policy-induced channeling of capital into strategic industries, export promotion, and a generally competent and incorruptible bureaucracy.

Contemporary Japan, at least during the LDP era, has also been cited as a model of so-called Asian-style democracy. Unlike the Western model, which emphasizes active citizen participation in independent interest groups and the periodic alternation of power between competing political parties, the Japanese model is said to justify a near monopoly of power by one party and the government's impunity to public opinion, particularly while the nation is intent on the task of economic development. Like Japan, many Third World countries place far greater emphasis on economic development and maintenance of political stability than on effective citizen participation in government or the protection of individual rights. This emphasis is particularly agreeable to those who believe in the Confucian ideal of an orderly, hierarchical, harmonious society governed by a wise and benevolent ruler with the support of a loyal and obedient citizenry. The model has often been used to justify repressive, authoritarian government in the name of rapid economic growth as, for example, in China under Deng Xiaoping.

The end of the LDP's domination in 1993, however, poses a serious challenge to the long-run viability of such a model of democracy. Where there are deep economic, social, or ideological divisions among the population, democracy inevitably gives rise to political contention. Japan experienced intense political conflict during the formative period (1947–1960) of its postwar democracy. In fact, it took a major political crisis caused by a massive popular protest against the undemocratic and high-handed conduct of government in the 1960 revision of the U.S.-Japanese Mutual Security Treaty to usher in the politics of compromise and consensus that are essential to democracy.

It thus took Japan a decade and a half of intense political conflict, and several more decades if one considers the struggle for democracy in prewar Japan, to learn to practice political democracy in peace. After the traumatic experience of 1960, the ruling LDP began not only to take seriously the opposition's opinion and policies but often to co-opt them. Many of the views and interests of organized labor, though not so much of unorganized workers or consumers at large, were incorporated into LDP policies and programs through informal consultation and deals between the LDP and the socialist-led opposition, if only to avert another political crisis.

Democracy did not get established in Japan in the absence of political conflict but rather in and through conflict, just as in Western Europe and the United States. The rupture of consensus and return of open conflict that led to the change of government in 1993 did not mean a breakdown of democracy in Japan. On the contrary, it reflected the strength and maturity of Japanese democracy by proving the ability of Japanese citizens to "throw the rascals out" of power. Moreover, this changing of the guard has given the opposition an opportunity to learn how to govern and the LDP an opportunity to learn how to oppose within the framework of democratic government. This reversal of political roles is an important step in Japan's transition from a one-party-dominant democracy to a true multiparty system.

The end of one-party dominance has helped make Japanese government more responsive to public opinion and less beholden to special interests. For example, when the Socialists became part of the coalition government that came to power in 1993, they remained as critical of the economic-growth-at-any-cost approach long followed by the LDP. In early 1994, the SDPJ minister of construction announced his decision to review a controversial plan to build a dam in a river in central Japan known as home to a number of increasingly endangered native fishes. This plan had originally been approved by the LDP government in the early 1970s but was strongly opposed by local fishermen and by all major environmentalist groups in the country. Later in the same year, the LDP-SDPJ-NPH coalition government led by a socialist prime minister also decided to make a substantial cut in the growth rate of defense spending: It proposed a 0.9 percent increase over the previous year's budget, as compared to a 1.9 percent increase approved by the LDP government in 1993. In the last decade of the twentieth century, Japan thus appeared poised to depart from the "uncommon" one-party model of democracy toward one more similar to the Western model in terms of responsiveness and accountability.

In one respect, however, contemporary Japan remains an uncommon nation: It continues to refuse to acquire a level of military power commensurate with its economic power. At least in theory, it is a uniquely pacifist state with a constitution that renounces the right to maintain armed forces or to engage in belligerent international acts. In practice, Japan maintains "self-defense forces" with a strictly limited operational mandate and devotes a much smaller portion of its gross national product to military spending than any other industrial or industrializing nation. Most Japanese leaders and people have been happy with and proud of this imbalance between their

"It's tough but if money does it." Additional contribution [to Gulf War], $10 billion.
Source: Mr. Kiyoshi Ichimura, *The Weekly Toyo Keizai,* February 2, 1991.

nation's economic and military power. Despite the persistent pressure from Washington to embark on a more ambitious rearmament program, the Japanese have so far refused to risk repeating their prewar mistakes, continuing to affirm the pacifism that has become an important part of the nation's identity.

The most important lesson we can learn from Japan at the crossroads is the way it has begun, albeit initially with considerable reluctance, to adapt to the dramatic changes under way in the post–Cold War international system by opening both its domestic economy and its domestic politics. In the process of this transition, many of its old policies and practices are being abandoned or drastically modified, while new ones are being explored and developed. There is a good chance that, when this transition is completed, Japan will be a more democratic, and an even more prosperous nation.

Key Terms

bushi

genro

zaibatsu

Taisho Democracy

Supreme Commander
  for the Allied Powers
  (SCAP)

Self-Defense Forces
  (SDF)

industrial policy

land reform

administrative
  guidance

Fiscal Investment and
  Loan Program (FILP)

keiretsu

dual-structure system

seniority-based wages

spring labor offensive

amakudari

koenkai

clientelism

company union

lifetime employment

Minamata Disease

Association of
  Southeast Asian
  Nations (ASEAN)

Suggested Readings

Section 1

Barnhard, Michael A. *Japan Prepares for Total War: The Search for Economic Security, 1919–1941.* Ithaca, N.Y.: Cornell University Press, 1987.

Borton, Hugh. *Japan's Modern Century.* 2d ed. New York: Ronald Press, 1955.

Dore, Ronald P. *Education in Tokugawa Japan.* London: Athlone, 1965.

Duus, Peter P., ed. *Cambridge History of Japan.* Vol. 6, *The Twentieth Century.* Cambridge: Cambridge University Press, 1988.

Gluck, Carol. *Japan's Modern Myths: Ideology in the Late Meiji Period.* Princeton, N.J.: Princeton University Press, 1985.

Section 2

Campbell, John Creighton. *How Policies Change: The Japanese Government and the Aging Society.* Princeton, N.J.: Princeton University Press, 1992.

Johnson, Chalmers. *MITI and the Japanese Miracle: The Growth of Industrial Policy, 1925–1975.* Stanford: Stanford University Press, 1982.

Lockwood, William W. *The Economic Development of Japan: Growth and Structural Change, 1868–1938.* Princeton, N.J.: Princeton University Press, 1954.

Nakamura, Takafusa. *The Japanese Economy: Its Development and Structure.* Trans. Jacqueline Kaminski. Tokyo: University of Tokyo Press, 1981.

Samuels, Richard J. *"Rich Nation, Strong Army": National Security and the Technological Transformation of Japan.* Ithaca, N.Y.: Cornell University Press, 1994.

Section 3

Campbell, John Creighton, *Contemporary Japanese Budget Politics.* Berkeley: University of California Press, 1977.

Hayao, Kenji. *The Japanese Prime Minister and Public Policy.* Pittsburgh: University of Pittsburgh Press, 1993.

Koh, B. C. *Japan's Administrative Elite.* Berkeley: University of California Press, 1989.

Upham, Frank K. *Law and Social Change in Postwar Japan.* Cambridge, Mass.: Harvard University Press, 1987.

Section 4

Abe, Hitoshi, Muneyuki Shindo, and Sadafumi Kawato. *The Government and Politics of Japan.* Trans. James White. Tokyo: University of Tokyo Press, 1994.

Allinson, Gary D., and Yasunori Sone, eds. *Political Dynamics in Contemporary Japan.* Ithaca, N.Y.: Cornell University Press, 1992.

Calder, Kent E. *Crisis and Compensation: Public Policy and Political Stability in Japan, 1949–1986.* Princeton, N.J.: Princeton University Press, 1988.

Krauss, Ellis S., Thomas P. Rohlen, and Patricia G. Steinhoff, eds. *Conflict in Japan.* Honolulu: University of Hawaii Press, 1984.

White, Merry. *The Japanese Educational Challenge: A Commitment to Children.* New York: Free Press, 1987.

Section 5

Ishida, Takeshi, and Ellis S. Krauss, eds. *Democracy in Japan.* Pittsburgh: University of Pittsburgh Press, 1989.

Lincoln, Edward J. *Japan's New Global Role.* Washington, D.C.: Brookings Institution, 1993.

Thurow, L. C. *Head to Head: The Coming Economic Battle among Japan, Europe, and America.* New York: William Morrow, 1992.

Vogel, Ezra F. *The Four Little Dragons: The Spread of Industrialization in East Asia.* Cambridge, Mass.: Harvard University Press, 1991.

Endnotes

[1] Terry MacDougall, "The Lockheed Scandal and the High Costs of Politics in Japan," in *The Politics of Scandal: Power and Process in Liberal Democracies,* ed. Andrei S. Markovits and Mark Silverstein (New York: Holmes and Maier, 1988).

[2] Conrad Totman, *Japan before Perry: A Short History* (Berkeley: University of California Press, 1981).

[3] Ronald P. Dore, *Education in Tokugawa Japan* (London: Athlone, 1965).

[4] Carol Gluck, *Japan's Modern Myths: Ideology in the Late Meiji Period* (Princeton: Princeton University Press, 1985).

[5] George De Vos and Hiroshi Wagatsuma, eds., *Japan's Invisible Race: Caste in Culture and Personality* (Berkeley: University of California Press, 1966); Frank K. Upham, *Law and Social Change in Postwar Japan* (Cambridge: Harvard University Press, 1987), Chapter 3.

[6] Gail Lee Bernstein, ed., *Recreating Japanese Women, 1600–1945* (Berkeley: University of California Press, 1991).

[7]Charles E. Neu, *The Troubled Encounter: The United States and Japan* (New York: John Wiley and Sons, 1975).

[8]Hugh Borton, *Japan's Modern Century,* 2d ed. (New York: Ronald Press, 1955).

[9]Sir George B. Sansom, *The Western World and Japan: A Study in the Interaction of European and Asiatic Cultures* (New York: Random House, 1949).

[10]James B. Crowley, *Japan's Quest for Autonomy: National Security and Foreign Policy, 1930–1938* (Princeton: Princeton University Press, 1966).

[11]Gordon M. Berger, *Parties Out of Power in Japan 1931–1941* (Princeton: Princeton University Press, 1977).

[12]Ben-Ami Shillony, *Revolt in Japan* (Princeton: Princeton University Press, 1973).

[13]Herbert Feis, *The Road to Pearl Harbor: The Coming of the War between the United States and Japan* (Princeton: Princeton University Press, 1950).

[14]Robert E. Ward and Sakamoto Yoshikazu, eds., *Democratizing Japan: The Allied Occupation* (Honolulu: University of Hawaii Press, 1987).

[15]Robert A. Scalapino, *Democracy and the Party Movement in Prewar Japan* (Berkeley: University of California Press, 1962).

[16]Peter Duus, *Party Rivalry and Political Change in Taisho Japan* (Cambridge: Harvard University Press, 1968).

[17]Alexander Gerschenkron, *Economic Backwardness in Historical Perspective* (Cambridge: Harvard University Press, 1960).

[18]Chalmers Johnson, *MITI and the Japanese Miracle: The Growth of Industrial Policy, 1925–1975* (Stanford: Stanford University Press, 1982).

[19]Hugh Patrick and Henry Rosovsky, "Japan's Economic Performance: An Overview," in *Asia's New Giant: How the Japanese Economy Works,* ed. Hugh Patrick and Henry Rosovsky (Washington, D.C.: The Brookings Institution, 1976), 7–9; Kazuo Yamaguchi, "Early Modern Economy (1868–1945)," *Kodansha Encyclopedia of Japan,* vol. 2 (Tokyo: Kodansha Ltd., 1983), 151–54.

[20]William W. Lockwood, *The Economic Development of Japan: Growth and Structural Change 1868–1938* (Princeton: Princeton University Press, 1954), 38–39.

[21]Kazushi Ohkawa and Henry Rosovsky, *Japanese Economic Growth: Trend Acceleration in the Twentieth Century* (Stanford: Stanford University Press, 1973), 80–81, 310, "Basic Statistical Table 15."

[22]Robert A. Scalapino, *The Early Japanese Labor Movement: Labor and Politics in a Developing Society* (Berkeley: Institute of East Asian Studies/Center for Japanese Studies, University of California, 1984).

[23]Ann Waswo, *Japanese Landlords: The Decline of a Rural Elite* (Berkeley: University of California Press, 1977).

[24]Mitsutoshi Takayanagi and Rizo Takeuchi, *Kadokawa nihonshi jiten* [Kadokawa dictionary of Japanese history], 2d ed. (Tokyo: Kadokawa shoten, 1974), 1288–1289, appended table.

[25]Michael A. Barnhart, *Japan Prepares for Total War: The Search for Economic Security, 1919–1941* (Ithaca: Cornell University Press, 1987).

[26]Ronald P. Dore, *Land Reform in Japan* (London: Oxford University Press, 1959).

[27]Daniel I. Okimoto, *Between MITI and the Market: Japanese Industrial Policy for High Technology* (Stanford: Stanford University Press, 1989).

[28]Peter J. Katzenstein, "Conclusion: Domestic Structures and Strategies of Foreign Economic Policy," in *Between Power and Plenty: Foreign Economic Policies of Advanced Industrial States,* ed. Peter J. Katzenstein (Madison: University of Wisconsin Press, 1978), 295–336.

[29]Data from International Road Federation, *World Road Statistics,* annual.

[30]Edward J. Lincoln, *Japan: Facing Economic Maturity* (Washington, D.C.: The Brookings Institution, 1988); Clyde V. Prestowitz, Jr., *Trading Places: How We Allowed Japan to Take the Lead* (New York: Basic Books, 1988).

[31]T. J. Pempel, *Uncommon Democracies;* Arend Lijphart, *Democracies—Patterns of Majoritarian and Consensus Government in Twenty-One Countries* (New Haven: Yale University Press, 1984).

[32]Kenji Hayao, *The Japanese Prime Minister and Public Policy* (Pittsburgh: University of Pittsburgh Press, 1993).

[33]Tadahiro Fujikawa, "Nature of Japanese Bureaucracy Hinders Ability to Conduct Coordinated Relief Effort," *Nikkei Weekly,* January 30, 1995, 7.

[34]B. C. Koh, *Japan's Administrative Elite,* (Berkeley: University of California Press, 1989).

[35]Hitoshi Abe, Muneyuki Shindo, and Sadafumi Kawato, *The Government and Politics of Japan* (Tokyo: University of Tokyo Press, 1994), 20–22.

[36]Ronald J. Hrebenar, *The Japanese Party System,* 2d ed. (Boulder, Colo.: Westview Press, 1992).

[37]Kent E. Calder, *Crisis and Compensation: Public Policy and Political Stability in Japan, 1949–1986* (Princeton: Princeton University Press, 1988).

[38]"Sea Change in Japan: The Country's Realignment Has Far-Reaching Implications," *Asiaweek* (December 14, 1994) 20.

[39]Helen Hardacre, *Shinto and the State, 1868–1988* (Princeton: Princeton University Press, 1989).

[40]Merry White, *The Japanese Educational Challenge: A Commitment to Children* (New York: The Free Press, 1987); Thomas P. Rohlen, *Japan's High Schools* (Berkeley: University of California Press, 1983).

[41]Norie Huddle and Michael Reich, with Nahum Stiskin, *Island of Dreams: Environmental Crisis in Japan* (New York: Autumn Press, 1975).

[42]David E. Apter and Nagayo Sawa, *Against the State: Politics and Social Protest in Japan* (Cambridge: Harvard University Press, 1984).

[43]David E. Kaplan and Alec Dubro, *Yakuza: The Explosive Account of Japan's Criminal Underworld* (Reading, Mass.: Addison-Wesley Publishing Company, 1986).

[44]Changsoo Lee and George De Vos, *Koreans in Japan: Ethnic Conflict and Accommodation* (Berkeley: University of California Press, 1981).

[45]Yasusuke Murakami, "The Japanese Model of Political Economy," in *The Political Economy of Japan,* Volume 1, *The Domestic Transformation,* ed. Kozo Yamamura and Yasukichi Yasuda (Stanford: Stanford University Press, 1987), 60.

[46]For an opposing view, see Rob Steven, *Classes in Contemporary Japan* (Cambridge, U.K.: Cambridge University Press, 1983).

[47]James Fallows' comment cited in Michael M. Mochizuki, "The Past in Japan's Future: Will the Japanese Change?" *Foreign Affairs* (September/October, 1994), 132.

[48]Ezra F. Vogel, *Japan as Number One: Lesson for America* (Cambridge: Harvard University Press, 1979).

[49]See, for example, Karel Van Wolferen, *The Enigma of Japanese Power: People and Politics in a Stateless Nation* (New York: A. A. Knopf, 1989); and *Democracy in Contemporary Japan,* ed. Gavan McCormack and Yoshio Sugimoto (Armonk, N.Y.: M.E. Sharpe, 1986).

[50]Ezra F. Vogel, *The Four Little Dragons: The Spread of Industrialization in East Asia* (Cambridge: Harvard University Press, 1991); and The World Bank, *The East Asian Miracle: Economic Growth and Public Policy* (New York: Oxford University Press, 1993).

Part 3

Politics in Communist and Post-Communist States

CHAPTER 6

Russia

RUSSIAN FEDERATION

Land and Population

Capital	Moscow
Total Area (square miles)	6,592,735 (about 1.8 times the size of U.S.)
Population	148 million
Annual Projected Population Growth Rate (1993–2000)	–0.3%
Urban Population (% of total)	75%

Ethnic Composition		
Ethnic-Linguistic Groups	Russian	82%
	Tatar	4%
	Ukrainian	3%
	Other	11%
Religions	Russian Orthodox	55%
	Muslim	18%
	Protestant	10%
	Catholic	7%
	Jewish	5%
	Other	8%

Economy

Domestic Currency	Ruble
GNP (US$)	$346 billion
GNP per capita (US$)	$2,340
Purchasing Power Parity GDP per capita (US$)	$4,573
Average Annual GDP Growth Rate (1980–1993)	–0.5%

Structure of Production (% of GDP)	Agriculture	9%
	Industry	51%
	Services	39%
Labor Force Distribution (% of total)	Agriculture	20%
	Industry	46%
	Services	34%
Total Foreign Trade (exports plus imports) as % of GDP	22%	

Society

Life Expectancy	Female	71
	Male	57
Population per Doctor	210	
Infant Mortality (per 1,000 live births)	26	
Adult Literacy	99%	
Average (Mean) Years of Schooling (of adults 25+)	9.0	
Communications (per 100 people)	Radios	33
	Televisions	37
	Telephones	17
1995 Human Development Index (1 = highest)	Ranks 52 out of 174	

Political Organization

Political System   Federal state, mixed presidential/parliamentary system

Regime History   Re-formed as an independent state with the collapse of communist rule in December 1991; current constitution since December 1993.

Administrative Structure   Federal system with 89 subnational governments including 21 republics, 55 provinces *(oblast', krai),* 11 autonomous districts or regions *(okrugs* or autonomous *oblast'),* and 2 cities of federal status.

Executive   Dual executive (president and prime minister). Direct election of president; prime minister appointed by the president with the approval of the lower house of the parliament (State Duma).

Legislature   Bicameral. Upper house (Federation Council) directly elected with two deputies from each of the 89 units of the federation. Lower house (State Duma) chosen by direct election, with half of the 450 deputies chosen through a proportional representation system and half from single-member constituencies. Powers include proposal and approval of legislation, approval of presidential appointees.

Judiciary   Independent constitutional court with 19 justices, nominated by the president and approved by the Federation Council, holding 12-year terms with possible renewal.

Party System   Fragmented multiparty system with changing party names and coalitions.

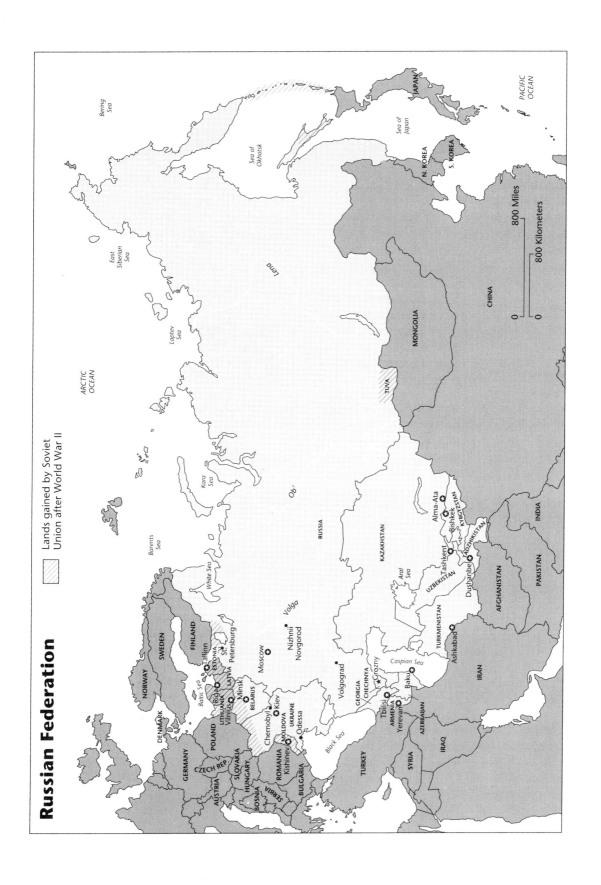

Russian Federation

Lands gained by Soviet
Union after World War II

ARCTIC
OCEAN

Bering
Sea

East
Siberian
Sea

Sea of
Okhotsk

Sea of
Japan

PACIFIC
OCEAN

JAPAN

N. KOREA

S. KOREA

Laptev
Sea

Lena

CHINA

800 Miles

800 Kilometers

Kara
Sea

Ob'

MONGOLIA

TUVA

Barents
Sea

RUSSIA

White Sea

KAZAKHSTAN

INDIA

Aral
Sea

Volga

Nizhnii
Novgorod

UZBEKISTAN

Alma-Ata
Bishkek
KYRGYZSTAN
TAJIKISTAN
Dushanbe
Tashkent

PAKISTAN

SWEDEN

FINLAND

NORWAY

Tallinn
ESTONIA
St.
LATVIA Petersburg
Riga
Moscow
LITHUANIA
Vilnius
Minsk
BELARUS
Chernobyl
Kiev
UKRAINE
MOLDOVA
Odessa
Kishinev

TURKMENISTAN

Ashkabad

AFGHANISTAN

DENMARK

GERMANY

POLAND

CZECH REP.

SLOVAKIA

AUSTRIA

HUNGARY

ROMANIA

Baltic Sea

Volgograd

GEORGIA
CHECHNYA
Crozny
Tbilisi
ARMENIA
Yerevan
AZERBAIJAN
Baku

Caspian Sea

IRAN

BOSNIA

SERBIA

BULGARIA

Black Sea

TURKEY

SYRIA

IRAQ

SECTION 1

The Making of the Modern Russian State

THE RUSSIAN FEDERATION
AT THE CROSSROADS

In December 1991, the Soviet Union ceased to exist. Each of the fifteen newly independent states that emerged in early 1992 entered the uncharted terrain of forming a new political entity. In this section we focus on the Russian Federation, the most important of these fifteen successor states, and still the dominant actor in the region. With a population of about 150 million, Russia is the largest European country both in population and size, and, in terms of territory, the largest country in the world. As a nuclear power, Russia also commands the attention of the West, although it can no longer rightfully be considered a superpower. What happens in Russia still greatly affects the course of events in the other post-Soviet states; the Russian state also has a vital interest in the welfare of the many Russians living in these countries, the "near abroad."

Russia's internal politics continue to be profoundly shaped by the legacy of the Soviet communist system. However, many political figures in the new Russia search for guidance in earlier Russian history. Still others, the Westernizers, look to North American and Western European approaches for direction. The mix and clash of these influences produce a baffling and intriguing political landscape. Winston Churchill's observation, made in 1939, is still valid: "[Russia] is a riddle wrapped in a mystery inside an enigma."

Today's Russia is often described as "in transition," but this depiction begs the question: transition to what? Some view Russia as a budding democracy and market economy, whereas others see the nation headed toward a new noncommunist form of authoritarian government, one in which basic democratic freedoms are repressed. Other questions involve the issue of Russia's identity. Will Russia even hold together as a single unit? Although it is officially a federation with eighty-nine constituent units, the relations between the center and the regions seem to be a hodgepodge of powers emerging on an ad hoc basis, depending on who can wangle a deal. Some wonder whether Russia, like the Soviet Union before, may gradually disintegrate into regional fiefdoms; still oth-

Sign: "To the market."
Comment: "The transition period—the most difficult moment."
Source: E. Vasil'eva, courtesy of *Trud (Labor)*.

ers consider coercive recentralization more likely. Although some foresee that the present economic transition could lead to the gradual, if painful, emergence of a viable market economy, others predict that the emerging market could drive the country toward economic anarchy, technological decay, bandit capitalism, and dangerous economic polarization, producing a spiral of further economic decline and disorder.

Each image of the new Russia is true in some way, for Russia today is a contradictory and complex place. Although pessimism and cynicism about government characterize large segments of the population, the beneficiaries of current trends expect that Russia could have a bright future, even though it may take a decade or more of turmoil. However, which factors will impel the country to one fate or another are unclear—neither experts nor politicians correctly anticipated the dramatic and rapid collapse of Soviet power; predicting the future of Russia is an equally uncertain endeavour.

Yeltsin, atop an armored tank, appeals to the people to resist the attempted coup d'état staged by opponents of Gorbachev's reform program in August 1991.
Source: AP/Wide World Photos.

Nothing symbolizes the contradictory nature of Russian politics better than the events which occurred in 1991 and 1993 outside the White House, the former seat of the Russian parliament in Moscow. In August 1991, the White House became a symbol of Russian democracy and self-determination. While the reform Communist leader Mikhail Gorbachev was held captive at his summer house *(dacha)* in the Crimea, the former party official and would-be radical, Boris Yeltsin, climbed atop a tank loyal to the reform leadership and rallied opposition to an attempted coup d'état intended to topple Gorbachev and reverse his liberalizing policies. The plotters wanted a return to the order and central control of the old Soviet system; Yeltsin declared himself the true champion of democratic values and Russian national interest.[1]

As events unfolded, the failed coup of August 1991 marked the beginning of the end for Gorbachev's moderate reform leadership and for Communist Party rule. By the end of 1991, the Soviet Union collapsed when Yeltsin, along with the leaders of the Ukrainian and Belorussian republics of the USSR, declared the formation of a loosely structured entity, called the Commonwealth of Independent States, to replace the Soviet Union. With no effective resistance to this action, Soviet rule was over, ushering a new period of escalating flux and uncertainty into this area of the world. This development marked the end of the Cold War era, when international politics were defined in terms of superpower competition and conflict. With the collapse of the Soviet superpower, the ideology of Soviet communism, which had restrained the region from integration into the global economic system, also gave way to a new ideology of global integration.

Just two years later the Moscow White House was the scene of a bloody political confrontation when Yeltsin was confronted with opposition to his Western-style program of market reform. On September 21, 1993, Yeltsin ordered the same Russian parliament that had stood by him in August 1991 to be disbanded, pending new elections in December. When some parliamentarians refused to vacate the White House, a crowd of demonstrators surrounded the building on October 2 to defend the old parliament. Encouraged by Russian vice president Alexander Rutskoi, part of the crowd proceeded to storm the nearby office of the Moscow mayor and the central television studio. The state's forces made no immediate response, but on the morning of October 4 military units supporting Yeltsin attacked the crowd and stormed the White House, forcing out the remaining hold-outs. Some protesters were arrested and estimates of death and causalities vary widely, but the number is probably in the hundreds. The facade of the Russian parliament building was blackened and singed by the fires of battle, a visible casualty of failed political compromise. While Yeltsin hailed the events as a victory of democracy over the communist and fascist reactionary forces

The White House, seat of the
Russian parliament, burns
while under assault from
troops loyal to President
Yeltsin during the confrontation
in October 1993.
Source: AP/Wide World
Photos.

opposing him, the public reaction was more critical
and cynical. As 1994 dawned, Russia seemed less
clearly headed down the path of democratization, economic prosperity seemed a far-off pipe dream, and
Russian nationalism was on the rise. The charred
White House, soon covered by white scaffolding,
came to symbolize the ambiguous meaning of democracy in Russia and the persistence of a tradition that
subordinated law to political power.

In this section, we elucidate the basic dilemmas,
challenges, and dynamics that face Russia as it seeks to
establish itself as a viable, stable, and prosperous political entity. First, however, some of the crucial turning
points in Russian and Soviet history that set the stage
for the dramatic events of the contemporary period.

CRITICAL JUNCTURES

Russia as Empire

By the late eighteenth century, Russia was an empire
encompassing vast expanses of land inhabited by peoples from more than 100 ethnic groups.[2] Unlike the
empires of Western Europe with their far-flung colonial possessions, Russia's empire bordered the historic
core of Russia. With its relatively unprotected location
between Europe and Asia, Russia had been repeatedly
invaded and challenged for centuries. This perceived
exposure to outside intrusion encouraged an expansionist mentality among the leadership. After nearly

250 years of domination by the Mongols that began in
the late 1400s, the principality of Moscow engaged in
expansion by conquest. By the seventeenth century,
the Russian empire extended east to the Pacific coast
in Siberia; by the time of the Bolshevik revolution in
1917, Russian influence extended to the Transcaucasian area, the Baltics, and what was later to become
Soviet Central Asia.

By the mid-nineteenth century it had become
clear to the tsar, the head of Russia's autocratic state,
that Russia was militarily inferior to the Western powers. The state's desire to remain an international force
compelled the regime to consider internal political reforms to help release the country's economic potential.
Serfdom, an economic and agricultural system that
tied the majority of the population (peasants) to the
land of the nobles whose land they worked, governed
rural life in Russia. The serfs were "emancipated" in
1861 in an effort to modernize Russia's economy, but
the traditional form of communal peasant organization
in the countryside, the *mir,* remained largely intact.
The freed peasants were still obligated to pay redemption fees to the state for forty-nine years to gain ownership of the land. Most of the peasants remained
bound to the *mir* which owned the land and was collectively responsible for the redemption payments.
Thus individual peasant farming did not develop in
Russia on a significant scale.

Meanwhile, an indigenous bourgeois or entrepreneurial class failed to develop in Russia as it had in Western Europe. Until 1762, Russian nobles were obliged to perform lifetime service in the military corps or state bureaucracy in exchange for the right to exploit land and labor. Even after these obligations ceased, most nobles showed little interest in manufacturing and trade. As a result, the key impetus for industrialization came from the state itself and from heavy injections of foreign (especially French, English, German, and Belgian) capital in the form of joint-stock companies and foreign debt incurred by the tsarist government. The dominant role of state and foreign capital resulted in the emergence of large factories alongside small private workshops. Trade unions were illegal until 1906, and even then their activities were carefully controlled. Under these conditions, worker discontent grew, culminating in the revolution of 1905 which involved widespread strikes in the cities and rural uprisings. Despite some transient reforms, the tsarist regime was able to retain control through increasing repression until its collapse in 1917.

The Bolshevik Revolution

In 1917 two revolutions occurred in Russia.[3] The March revolution threw out the tsar (Nicholas II) and installed a moderate provisional government. In November that government was overthrown by the Bolshevik Party, a faction of the Marxist party called the Russian Social Democratic Labor Party, subsequently to become known as the Communist Party of the Soviet Union (CPSU). This second revolution marked a major turning point in the history of Russia. Instead of trying to imitate Western European patterns of economic development, the Bolsheviks were committed to applying a dramatically different blueprint for economic, social, and political development.

The Bolsheviks were Marxists who believed their revolution reflected the political interests of a particular social class, namely the proletariat (working class).[4] Most of the revolutionary leaders, however, were not themselves workers but were from the more educated and privileged strata, commonly referred to as the intelligentsia. By 1917 broad social discontent enveloped the country, which the Bolsheviks were able to exploit. In addition, the country was suffering brutally under the impact of World War I, provoking strong sentiment among segments of the population

and army to simply withdraw. Shortages of bread affected the civilian population, and rural peasants wanted direct control over their land in order to till it and make a living. The Bolsheviks championed all of these causes with their slogan "Land, Peace, and Bread," thus appealing both to the working class and the discontented peasantry, which made up over 80 percent of Russia's population in 1917. With his keen political sense, Vladimir Lenin, the leader of the Bolshevik Party, was able to grasp the strategy and the proper moment for his party to seize state power.

The Bolsheviks formed a tightly organized political party based on their own understanding of democracy. Their strategy was founded on the notions of **democratic centralism** and vanguardism, concepts that differed significantly from the liberal democratic notions predominating in Western countries. Democratic centralism, which governed the internal party structure, combined participatory and hierarchical elements. Discussion of policy was to occur at all levels of the party, but the party itself was organized in a hierarchy. Top party leaders were elected from below based on this hierarchical structure. The party's leaders were theoretically accountable to those who elected them, but once a decision was taken, complete unanimity was required. In time, the centralizing elements of democratic centralism took precedence over the democratic elements, as the party tried to insulate itself first from informers of the tsarist forces and later from both real and imagined threats to the new regime on the domestic and international scene.

The concept of a **vanguard party** governed the Bolsheviks' (and later the Communist Party's) relations with broader social forces. Party leaders claimed to have a superior insight into social and political reality, and thus they claimed that they understood the interests of the working people better than the people did themselves. On this basis they could justify acting on behalf of the working class, even if their actions contradicted the expressed will or actions of the actual working class. It was democracy "for the people," not "by the people." In time, this philosophy was used to rationalize virtually all actions of the Communist Party and the Soviet state, which it dominated. Neither democratic centralism nor vanguardism emphasized democratic procedures or accountability of the leaders before the public. Rather, these concepts focused on achieving a "correct" political outcome that would reflect the "true" interests of the working class, as defined by the leaders of the Communist Party. In the short term, many of their actions imposed heavy costs on certain portions of the population.

Once in power the Bolsheviks soon learned that it is easier to criticize than to rule and felt compelled to take extraordinary measures to ensure the survival of the regime. The initial challenge was an extended Civil War (1918–1921) for control of the countryside and outlying regions. The Bolsheviks introduced War Communism to ensure the supply of materials necessary for the war effort. This involved increased state control of key economic sectors and forced requisitioning of grain from the peasants. Political controls also increased: The Cheka, the security arm of the regime, was strengthened, and restrictions were placed on other political groups, including other socialist parties. In 1921 attempts were made to control organized dissent within the party itself.

By 1921, the leadership recognized the potential political costs of the War Communism policy, which had effectively negated many of the benefits the peasants had gained from the revolution. The leadership feared that the peasants' resentment of the forced requisitioning of grain would continue to grow and ultimately undermine the very goals the regime was trying to pursue. The New Economic Policy (NEP, 1921–1928) brought concessions for the peasantry.[5] Forced grain requisitioning was abolished and replaced with a tax-in-kind, allowing the peasants to market above-tax production in the free market. In other sectors of the economy, private enterprise and trade were also revived. The state, however, retained control of large-scale industry and experimented with state control of the arts and culture.

Gradually throughout the 1920s the more authoritarian elements of Bolshevik thinking eclipsed the more democratic elements. The antidemocratic measures of the War Communism period were not reversed, providing a basis for further limitations on criticism and open opposition. Lacking a democratic tradition and bolstered by the vanguard ideology of the party, the Bolshevik leaders engaged in internecine struggles following Lenin's death in 1924. These conflicts finally culminated in the rise of Joseph Stalin and the arrest or exile of such prominent party figures as Leon Trotsky and Nikolai Bukharin. By 1929, all opposition, even within the party itself, had been eliminated. Political opponents were outlawed and forcibly oppressed to prevent challenges to party rule. Con-

flicts within the leadership were not open to public debate. Sacrifices of democratic procedure were justified in the name of protecting class interests. During the next critical juncture, the Stalinist revolution, the democratic aspects of Leninism were decisively squelched and the rights of society were subordinated to the state.

The Bolshevik revolution also initiated a period of international isolation for the new state. To fulfill their promise of "peace," the new rulers had to accept virtual surrender by granting important chunks of territory to Germany under the unfavorable Brest-Litovsk Treaty (1918). Only the defeat of Germany by Russia's former allies (the United States, Britain, and France) reversed some of these concessions. However, these countries were hardly pleased with internal developments in Russia. Not only did the Bolshevik revolution bring expropriation of foreign holdings and Russia's withdrawal from the Allied powers' war effort, it also represented the first successful challenge to the capitalist order. As a result, the former allies sent material aid and troops to oppose the new Bolshevik government during the Civil War. Even under the New Economic Policy, the Soviet Union did not receive significant Western investment or economic assistance.

Lenin had hoped that successful working-class revolutions in some developed Western countries, particularly Germany, would bolster the fledgling Soviet regime and bring it tangible aid. These revolutions did not occur, however, and the Soviet leaders had to rely on their country's own resources to build a viable economic structure. In 1923 Stalin announced the goal of building "socialism in one country." This implied that defending Soviet state interests was synonymous with the promotion of socialism, but it simultaneously set the Soviet Union on a course of economic isolation from the larger world of states. To survive in such isolation, the new Soviet leader, Joseph Stalin, felt compelled to pursue a policy of rapid industrialization and increased political control.

The Stalin Revolution

Beginning in 1929 until Joseph Stalin's death in 1953, the Soviet Union faced another critical juncture. During this time, Stalin consolidated his power as Soviet leader by establishing the basic characteristics of the Soviet regime that substantially endured until the collapse of the communist system in 1991.[6] Although many of these features were softened after 1953, they were firmly enough entrenched to produce deep obstacles to any fundamental change. Russia's problems since 1991 reflect the difficulties of extracting Russia from the features established during the Stalinist period.

The Stalin revolution brought radical changes to virtually every aspect of Soviet life to produce an interconnected system of economic, political, and ideological power. This painful and costly upheaval is sometimes called the "third revolution" (after the first two revolutions of March and November 1917). A policy of state ownership and control of the economy was adopted because Russia lacked a tradition of private property or market development, and Stalin argued that allowing the free development of private ownership would encourage the emergence of a capitalist class and negate the socialist goals of the regime. The historian Richard Pipes explains that before the 1917 revolution, Russia had a **patrimonial state,** that is, a state that not only ruled the country but also owned the land as well,[7] so that economic and political power were closely intertwined. A strong element within Bolshevik thinking viewed rapid industrialization as essential to realizing the precepts of communist ideology because industrialization would create the working class, which the party claimed to represent, and would assure the Soviet Union an economic basis for its own defense in the world of states dominated by capitalism. The Soviet leadership could not and did not want to rely on foreign capital to catch up with Western Europe's economic development. This obligated the state to use its power to accumulate the economic resources necessary for industrialization.

Under Stalin, the state thus became the engine for rapid economic development, with state ownership and control of virtually all economic assets (land, factories, housing, and stores). By 1935 over 90 percent of agricultural land had been taken from the peasants and placed under state control as state or collective farms. This **collectivization** campaign was justified as a means to prevent the emergence of a new exploitative capitalist class in the countryside, but it actually targeted the peasantry as a whole, evoked widescale resistance, and led to famine and loss of life. Those who showed resistance were placed under arrest or exiled to Siberia. In the industrial sector, a system of state ownership was extended to virtually all areas and a program of rapid industrialization was established,

with particular emphasis on the heavy industrial sectors (steel mills, hydroelectric dams, machine building). Economic control was exercised through a complex but inefficient system of central economic planning, in which the state planning committee (Gosplan) set production targets for every enterprise in the country. Likewise almost everyone became an employee of the state because factories, farms, and shops were all state run. The state's economic strategy dominated. Independent social groups or institutions were also brought under state control; thus input into the state's plan occurred only through the chaotic interplay of the state's own bureaucratic structures.

Five-year plans were introduced that set unrealistic production targets for industry and agriculture. Low-priority sectors, such as consumer goods production, were neglected. Although actual production often bore little relation to plan indicators, the Stalinist system's basic outlines for mandatory planning were retained until Gorbachev's reforms of the late 1980s. Stalin's economic campaigns did succeed in boosting industrial output and stimulated a massive migration of population from the countryside to the cities to meet the need for workers in the new industrial enterprises. Thus, the industrialization campaign was accompanied by social upheaval: People were uprooted from their traditional lives in the countryside and catapulted into the alienation and regimentation of urban industrial life. Under these circumstances, people were less able to organize themselves effectively to resist coercive state policies or to influence the political sphere.

In the early 1920s the Communist Party was the only political party permitted to function; and by the early 1930s opposition or dissent within the party itself had been eliminated. Gradually the party became subject to the personal whims of Stalin and his secret police: Party organs ceased to meet on a regular basis, and they no longer made important political decisions. Party ranks were periodically cleansed of potential opponents, and previous party leaders as well as citizens from many walks of life were violently purged (arrested, sentenced to labor camps, often executed). Open opposition was impossible, and the secret police, answerable to Stalin himself through his minister of internal affairs, replaced the party as the most powerful institution in Soviet society.

There were dramatic changes in the cultural and social spheres as well. Media censorship and state

Soviet Political Humor

Soviet citizens liked to tell jokes about their leaders, one of the few permitted forms of political commentary. Here are two jokes told about Brezhnev. In a lighter moment, Gorbachev dared to tell a joke about himself.

The foreign minister of the USSR, Andrei Gromyko, on returning to the USSR from a diplomatic visit to the United States, told the Communist Party leader Leonid Brezhnev that in the United States, applicants for government jobs are required to take a test. "Here is an example of a question," he said. "Who is my father's son but not me?"

Brezhnev hesitated and replied, "I don't know."

Gromyko said, "Well, it's my brother."

The next day Brezhnev was talking with fellow Politburo member Nikolai Podgorny. He repeated Gromyko's story and asked Podgorny the same question: "Who is my father's son but not me?

Podgorny hesitated and replied, "Your brother."

Brezhnev looked surprised and exclaimed, "No, it's Gromyko's brother!"

On Red Square in Moscow, a man shouts: "Brezhnev is an idiot!"

The militia seizes the man and puts him under arrest. He is sentenced on two charges: He is given fifteen days for hooliganism, and fifteen years for revealing a state secret.

Gorbachev tells a joke about himself:

"They say that Mitterrand has one hundred lovers. One has AIDS, but he doesn't know which one. Bush has one hundred bodyguards. One is a terrorist, but he doesn't know which one. Gorbachev has one hundred economic advisers. One is smart, but he doesn't know which one."

The *New York Times* reported that "the joke was warmly received by members of the Soviet Parliament who were listening."

Source: "The Humor of Gorbachev," *New York Times,* November 29, 1990, A20. Copyright 1995, Mikhail Gorbachev, for *La Stampa.* Distributed by The New York Times Special Features.

control of the arts stymied creativity as well as political opposition. The party/state became the authoritative source of truth, so anyone deviating from the authorized interpretation could be charged with treason. One outlet of expression for citizens, however, was the art of the political joke.

Under the Stalinist system of political, economic, and ideological control, social groups lost all autonomy: People could not form independent political organizations and public discussion about controversial issues was prohibited. A kind of psychological schizophrenia existed for the average citizen: Publicly one must avow loyalty and adherence to official state ideology and policy, but privately people often held completely different views. Forms of resistance, when they occurred, were evasive rather than active: peasants killed their livestock to avoid giving them over to collective farms; laborers worked inefficiently and absenteeism was high; in some cases citizens simply refused to vote for the single candidate offered in the elections, which were formalistic rituals rather than vehicles for the expression of public will. These forms of unorganized noncooperation could not be transformed into organized forms of political opposition. By 1930, even the Leninist version of democracy had died in the Soviet Union, and its rhetoric was retained only as window dressing for a tightly controlled political system.

Overall, an estimated 5 percent of the Soviet population was arrested at one point or another under the Stalinist system, usually for no apparent cause. The arbitrary and unpredictable terror of the 1930s left a legacy of fear in the population for years. The Stalinist model has often been labeled **totalitarian,** a term used to describe political systems in which the state seeks to penetrate all aspects of public and private life through an integrated system of ideological, economic, and political control.[8] Mechanisms to achieve this include complete control of the mass media, state ownership of the economy, an atmosphere of fear created by an arbitrary exercise of power by the secret police, and mobilization of the population to "participate" in a range of organizations and activities controlled from above. Some political scientists distinguish between authoritarian and totalitarian systems by defining an authoritarian state as one that demands political compliance from the population but allows people to live their private lives in peace. In a totalitarian system, the distinction between public and private life is nearly obliterated, as the scope of state authority expands to include every aspect of life. Thus, in the Stalinist period, children were even encouraged to inform authorities if they believed their parents engaged in behavior that might be deemed anti-system. Furthermore, many churches were closed, and expounding religious beliefs was tantamount to treason. The term *totalitarian* was coined not only to describe Stalinist Russia, but also to demonstrate its similarities to Nazi Germany. In reality, however, the scope of actual state control in the Stalinist period was less complete than the concept of totalitarianism suggests.

Isolation of the Soviet citizen from interaction with the outside world was a key tool of control for the Stalinist regime. Foreign news broadcasts were jammed, travel abroad was highly restricted, and contacts with foreigners brought citizens under suspicion. The economy was also highly autarkic—that is, isolated from interaction with the international economic system. Although this policy shielded Soviet society from the effects of the Great Depression of the 1930s that shook the capitalist world (indeed the decade of the 1930s was a period of rapid economic growth in the Soviet Union), it also allowed a highly inefficient and irrational system of production to survive in the USSR. Protected from foreign competition, the economy gradually fell behind in its capacity to keep up with the rapid pace of economic and technological transformation in the West.

During World War II, the Soviet Union was on the side of the victorious Allies and was a major force in the defeat of the Axis powers in Europe; this alliance was to have major consequences in the postwar period because it broadened the expansion of the USSR as well as its sphere of economic and political influence. The Western powers allowed the Soviet Union to absorb new territories into the USSR itself (these became the Soviet republics of Latvia, Lithuania, Estonia, Moldavia, and portions of western Ukraine). The USSR also extended its sphere of influence farther to the west. The Western Allies implicitly granted the USSR free rein to shape the postwar governments and economies in East Germany, Poland, Hungary, Czechoslovakia, Bulgaria, and Romania. Western offers to include parts of the region in the Marshall Plan were rejected under pressure from the USSR. Local communist parties in these countries, their legitimacy bolstered in some cases by their role in the anti-Nazi resistance, were the conduits for Soviet influence. With Soviet support these forces gained control of the coercive apparatus of the state and, by 1948, were able to subordinate other political groups to their control.

World War II also had a profound impact on the outlook of an entire generation of Soviet citizens. Soviet propaganda dubbed it the "Great Patriotic War,"

evoking images of Russian nationalism rather than of socialist internationalism—the sacrifices and heroism of the war period remained a powerful symbol of Soviet pride and unity until the collapse of communist power. The period was marked by support for more traditional values in family life and by a greater tolerance for religious institutions whose support Stalin sought for the war effort.

Among the social corollaries of the war effort were a declining birthrate and a long-lasting gender imbalance in society as a result of the large number of male casualties. A sort of "lost generation" of Soviet men resulted, not only because of the high casualty rate, but also because men who survived often missed opportunities to get a higher education and therefore did not rise to higher positions in the political sphere. The war also affected certain minority ethnic groups that were brought under suspicion for collaboration with the enemy during the war effort and were deported by the Stalinist regime from their homes to areas farther east in the USSR. These included Germans, Crimean Tatars, and peoples of the northern Caucausus regions such as the Chechens, Ingush, and Karachai-Balkar. Their later rehabilitation and resettlement caused renewed disruption and conflict, contributing to the ethnic conflicts of the post-Soviet period. In sum, the war experience had a profound influence on the development of postwar political elites, on demographic patterns in the country, and on ethnic relations in later periods.

Following World War II, the features of Soviet communism were largely replicated in those areas newly integrated into the USSR and in the countries of Eastern Europe. Economies were brought largely under state control (with a few notable exceptions, such as the failure of agricultural collectivization in Poland); Communist parties established a monopoly on political power; and efforts were made to isolate this region from Western Europe and to tighten its economic and political integration with the USSR. The Council for Mutual Economic Assistance (CMEA) and the Warsaw Treaty Organization (a military alliance) were formed for this purpose, thereby expanding the range of the USSR's international contacts and breaking its earlier isolation. But this enlarged Soviet bloc still remained insulated from the larger world of states. Some countries within the Soviet bloc, however, had strong historic links to Western Europe (especially Czechoslovakia, Poland, and Hungary), and in these states, domestic resistance to Soviet dominance forced some alterations or deviations from the Soviet model. Over time, these countries served not only as geographic buffers to direct Western influence on the USSR, but also as conduits for such influence. In the more Westernized Baltic republics of the USSR itself, the population firmly resisted assimilation to Soviet rule and eventually spearheaded the disintegration of the Soviet Union in the late 1980s.

Attempts at De-Stalinization

Stalin's death in 1953 triggered another critical juncture in Soviet politics. Even the Soviet elite realized that Stalin's system of terror could be sustained only at great cost to the development of the country. Even top leaders felt vulnerable under such a system; the terror stymied initiative and participation; and the unpredictability of Stalinist rule inhibited the rational formulation of policy. The period from Stalin's death until the mid-1980s saw a regularization and stabilization of Soviet politics, in contrast to the "revolutions from above" initiated by Stalin. Terror abated, but political controls remained in place, and efforts to isolate Soviet citizens from foreign influences continued.

Nikita Khrushchev succeeded Stalin as the party leader from 1955 until his removal in 1964 and embarked on a bold policy of de-Stalinization.[9] Although his specific policies were only minimally successful, the "thaw" in political and cultural control that he initiated planted the seeds which ultimately undermined the fundamental features of the Stalinist system. One basic feature of Khrushchev's de-Stalinization approach was a rejection of the terror that had been directed at the party itself as well as at the general population. According to Khrushchev, the party still embodied the positive Leninist values which had inspired the 1917 revolution—namely, the construction of an egalitarian and democratic socialist society that would protect the true interests of the working population. Khrushchev revived the Communist Party as a vital political institution able to exercise political, economic, and cultural authority throughout the country. The secret police (KGB) was made subordinate to party authority, party meetings were resumed on a regular basis, and the *nomenklatura* system was revived, under which the party itself governed the appointment of individuals to powerful positions in all areas of Soviet life. Internal party structures remained highly centralized. Formal elections to party office

took place according to the precepts of democratic centralism; however, these elections were uncontested and candidates were designated from above. Although Khrushchev tried to eliminate the worst abuses of the Stalinist system, the "democratic" kernel of Leninism remained subordinate to its centralizing and vanguard features, a pattern that continued until the late 1980s. In the cultural sphere, Khrushchev allowed sporadic liberalization, with the publication in the official media of some literature critical of the Stalinist system, but censorship continued and liberalization was at the whim of the top party leadership.

Leonid Brezhnev, Khrushchev's successor who headed the party from October 1964 until his death in 1982, partially reversed the de-Stalinization efforts of the 1950s and early 1960s. Controls were tightened again in the cultural sphere as individuals who tried to express dissenting views (members of the so-called dissident movement) through underground publishing or publication abroad, were harassed, arrested, or exiled. However, unlike in the Stalinist period, the political repression was predictable; people knew when they were transgressing permitted limits of criticism. In short, forms of political control came to resemble those typical of authoritarian regimes. Under Khrushchev and, later, Brezhnev the Soviet leadership was less intent on intruding into the private lives of its citizens through a systematic application of terror; rather it sought acquiescence and compliance with party/state directives. Particularly under Brezhnev, the regime could be described as primarily bureaucratic and conservative, seeking to maintain existing power structures rather than to introduce new ones. Reform efforts were half-hearted, halting, and eventually paralyzed by bureaucratic opposition and inertia. Although the population was encouraged to participate in a rather ritualistic way in various public campaigns and events, most people retreated into their private lives, abandoning politics to the 10 percent of the population who were members of the Communist Party.

During the Brezhnev era, a **tacit social contract** with the population governed state-society relations.[10] In exchange for political compliance, the population was granted job security; a lax work environment; low prices on basic goods, housing, and transport; free social services (medical care, recreational services); and minimal interference in personal life. Wages of the worst-off citizens (especially agricultural and industrial workers) were increased relative to those of the

TABLE 1 Provision of Urban and Rural Population with Various Goods at the End of the Year (total items per 1,000 persons)

	1970	1975	1980	1985	1989
Clocks	1,193	1,319	1,523	1,580	1,647
Televisions	143	215	249	293	316
Cameras	77	77	91	102	102
Refrigerators and freezers	89	178	252	275	276
Bicycles and mopeds	145	156	144	165	176
Sewing machines	161	178	190	190	185
Washing machines	141	189	205	205	216
Tape recorders	21	46	73	110	150
Radio sets	199	230	250	289	285

Source: Tsentral'noe statisticheskoe upravlenie SSSR (Central Statistical Administration of the USSR), *Narodnoe khoziaistvo SSSR 1983: statisticheskii ezhegodnik* (The Economy of the USSR in 1983: Statistical Yearbook) (Moscow: Iz. Finansy i statistika, 1984), 442; *Narodnoe khoziaistvo SSSR 1989: statisticheskii ezhegodnik* (The Economy of the USSR in 1989: Statistical Yearbook) (Moscow: Iz. Finansy i statistika, 1989), 121.

more educated and better-off portions of the population. For its part, the intelligentsia (historically Russia's social conscience and critic) was allowed more freedom to publicly discuss issues that were not of crucial importance to the regime. Even the political elite had a stake in the "social contract"—the violent Stalinist purges were halted and personnel changes were limited to maintain loyalty. The cost was an aging and increasingly lethargic leadership—Brezhnev was seventy-two when he died in office. In 1981 the average age of the all-male Politburo (the top party body) was sixty-nine.

From the late 1970s, the leadership was increasingly ineffective at addressing the mounting problems facing Soviet society. Brezhnev's preoccupation with foreign policy questions reinforced the tendency toward stagnation on the domestic issues. Economic growth rates declined and improvements in the standard of living were minimal (see Table 1). Further economic improvement would depend on introducing incentives to increase efficiency, but repeated attempts to tinker with the centralized planning system to achieve this end had failed. Many consumer goods were still in short supply, and quality was often mediocre. Meanwhile, modern communication and transportation systems made it difficult to isolate the population from information out of the West. As awareness of Western life-styles increased, popular expectations rose. As the economy stagnated, opportunities for upward career mobility declined. Low morale pervaded society because people perceived, on one hand, little opportunity for improving their standard of living and, on the other, a widening gap between the regime's promises of the good life and the reality.

To maintain the Soviet Union's superpower status and competitive position in the arms race, the best resources were diverted to the military sector, further gutting the capacity of the consumer and agricultural spheres to satisfy popular expectations. Russia's rich natural resources were being squandered, and the costs of exploiting new resource deposits (mostly in Siberia) were soaring. High pollution levels were beginning to visibly affect the quality of life and health in terms of morbidity and declining life expectancy. At the same time, liberalization in some Eastern European states and the telecommunications revolution made it increasingly difficult to shield the population from exposure to Western life-styles and ideas. Among a certain critical portion of the population, aspirations were rising just as the capacity of the system to fulfill them was declining. It was in this context that the next critical transition occurred.

Perestroika and Glasnost

Mikhail Gorbachev took office as CPSU leader in March 1985, at the relatively young age of fifty-three.[11] Gorbachev hoped to reform the system sufficiently to generate the initiative necessary to spur economic growth and political renewal, but without

Mikhail Gorbachev, expressing concern about Soviet-American relations at a post-summit press conference in 1985.
Source: Reuters/Bettmann.

undermining Communist Party rule or its basic ideological precepts. However, his policies were inadequately conceived and they produced unanticipated consequences that eventually led to the collapse of the Soviet system itself.

Four important concepts emerged as the basis of Gorbachev's reform program—perestroika, glasnost, *demokratizatsiia,* and "New Thinking." **Perestroika** (restructuring) involved decentralization and rationalization of the economic structure to enable individual enterprises (firms) to respond in a more dynamic and effective manner to the challenges of economic renewal. The central planning system was not to be disbanded but reformed. To counteract the resistance of entrenched central bureaucracies, Gorbachev enlisted the support of the intelligentsia, who benefited from his policy of glasnost. **Glasnost** (openness) involved the relaxation of controls over public discourse, the airing of diverse viewpoints, and the publication of previously prohibited literature.[12] Although glasnost did not at first completely lift media censorship, it awakened expectations that were impossible to si-

lence. *Demokratizatsiia* (Gorbachev's conception of democratization) described efforts to increase the responsiveness of political organs to public sentiments, both within and without the party. *Demokratizatsiia* did not endorse all of the precepts of Western liberal democracy, but it did place greater emphasis on procedural elements (competitive elections, a **law-based state,** freer political expression) than did the traditional Leninist approach. Thus it implicitly challenged both democratic centralism and vanguardism; it represented movement toward a conception of democracy "by the people" rather than simply "for the people." The party leadership was increasingly willing to acknowledge that citizens should be permitted to speak for themselves, rather than rely on a supposedly more enlightened elite to define the public's interests. Gorbachev also set the stage for a continuing debate about the true nature of democracy and how it is related to processes of economic reform involving a shift from state to private ownership.

Finally, "New Thinking" in foreign policy involved a rethinking of international power in nonmilitary terms; it emphasized the search for cooperative rather than confrontational interaction with the West.[13] Gorbachev recognized that the continuing arms buildup prevented the Soviet economy from responding to consumer expectations and the fundamental demands of economic renewal in the economy at large. Gorbachev's position was a direct step toward integration of the USSR into the world of states and the global economy. Rather than depicting the relationship between the Soviet Union and the West as one of ideological competition and class struggle, Gorbachev emphasized common challenges facing East and West such as the costs and hazards of the arms race and environmental degradation. Likewise, the economic reform process initiated by Gorbachev implied the beginnings of the Soviet Union's future integration into the global economic system.

Gorbachev's policies triggered a fundamental change in the relationship between state and society in the USSR. Citizens actively pursued their interests and beliefs through a variety of newly created organizations at the national and local levels. These included ethnonationalist movements in the various union republics, environmental groups, groups for rehabilitation of Stalinist victims, charitable groups, new or reformed professional organizations, more eclectic political clubs and movements, and many others. The entry of these groups into the sphere of active politics implicitly challenged the Communist Party's monopoly of political power and gradually created the possibility that alternative political parties might form. Within the Communist Party, splits emerged, marring the unanimity required by democratic centralism. The members of the group called the Democratic Platform wanted to push the reform process even further; many of its adherents left the party and formed new political organizations (later to become alternative political parties). In contrast, adherents of the so-called Marxist-Leninist platform wanted a return to genuine Leninist values. The new Russian branch of the Communist Party stood for a restoration of former patterns of Soviet rule. Gorbachev tried to accommodate these diverse strains by encouraging competitive elections within the party to revitalize its structure. A new party program was proposed to reflect the values of the reform agenda.

Gorbachev continued to assert his belief in true Leninism and in the notion of single-party dominance, arguing that the party could be sufficiently democratized to make it responsive to society, thereby avoiding the political fragmentation and chaos that might accompany multiparty competition. However, by March 1990, pressures from within and outside the party forced a retreat from this position. Article 6 of the Soviet Constitution, which affirmed the party's monopoly position, was rescinded by the Supreme Soviet (the Soviet parliament). Diverse political groupings began to form themselves into what were to become embryonic political parties, challenging the Communist Party's monopoly of political control. Gorbachev pushed for a restructuring of state institutions as well, and in the spring of 1989 the first contested elections since the 1920s were held for positions in the Soviet parliament. These were followed by elections at the republic and local levels in 1990, which elected new elites in some parts of the USSR (including Russia), more ready to push for more radical economic reform and for increased republic and regional autonomy.

The most divisive issues facing Gorbachev were economic policy and demands for republic autonomy. The Soviet Union was made up of fifteen **union republics,** each formed on the basis of an indigenous ethnic or national group, as only 50.8 percent of the Soviet population was ethnically Russian in 1989.[14] In several of these union republics, popular front organi-

zations formed, sometimes supported by a portion of the local communist leadership. First in the three Baltic republics (Latvia, Lithuania, and Estonia), then in other union republics (particularly Ukraine, Georgia, Armenia, Moldova [formerly Moldavia], and Russia itself) demands for national autonomy and, in some cases for secession from the USSR, became increasingly assertive. Ethnic background was an important basis of group identity for citizens in these regions, and although the Soviet authorities had emphasized class identity over national identity, they had also encouraged distinct national groups by retaining "nationality" as a category on the internal Soviet passport and by maintaining a federal structure built on ethnically based units.

Under glasnost, national traditions and memories of national oppression could be openly discussed by representatives of various ethnic groups; the Pandora's box of ethnic and national demands then proved impossible to close. Declining economic performance reinforced ethnic discontent when spokespersons of some ethnic groups expressed the belief that their union republics could do better on their own. Despite concessions to particular ethnic groups and union republics, Gorbachev's efforts to bring consensus on a new federal system uniting the fifteen union republics failed, as popular support and elite self-interest took on an irreversible momentum, resulting in a "separatism mania."

Gorbachev's economic policies failed as well. They involved half-measures that sent contradictory messages to enterprise directors, producing a drop in output and national income and undermining established patterns that had kept the Soviet economy functioning, albeit inefficiently. For example, under Gorbachev, enterprises were allowed to determine what they produced, but because many of them were monopoly producers of certain items, this sometimes resulted in a reduced quantity or quality of production of basic goods, aggravating shortages and consumer discontent. Inconsistencies and changes in central policy also prevented enterprises from taking real initiatives.

Gorbachev repeatedly hesitated to adopt a comprehensive program of economic transformation, because any such program would involve bitter consequences, either in the short or long term. A logical starting point for comprehensive reform might have been the agricultural sector, which had long encountered problems in meeting consumer demands, but the Soviet leadership failed to make any meaningful changes in this sector, preferring to focus more on industry, especially the machine-building sector. Even if successful, this approach would have produced few visible benefits for the Soviet citizen at a time when Gorbachev's reform rhetoric was evoking rising citizen expectations.

The economic downturn proceeded as perestroika progressed.[15] Money was issued with nothing to back it, so that too much money was chasing too few goods. Most prices were still subject to state control, so shortages of even basic goods were common. The economic decline reinforced demands by union republics for economic autonomy even as central policy appeared to shackle any real improvement. To protect themselves, regions and union republics began to restrict exports to other regions, despite planning mandates. "Separatism mania" was accompanied by "the war of laws," as regional officials openly defied central directives. Whereas previously the state had been able to enforce the basic outlines of its political and economic strategy, now its ability to implement its policies was rapidly declining. In response, Gorbachev issued numerous decrees; their number increased as their efficacy decreased.

Toward the end of the Gorbachev period, the wisdom of simultaneously trying to pursue *demokratizatsiia* and market economic reform was debated. Both processes implied a reduced state involvement in the affairs of the economy and society and could be mutually supportive. In reality, however, the two goals could not be achieved together, and by the end of 1991, the declining economy threatened to undermine democratic gains in the political sphere. For many people, "democracy" was associated mainly with deprivation and economic decline. At the same time, it seemed to be impossible to implement real economic reforms without liberalizing the political sphere; Gorbachev needed support from the intelligentsia and other social groups to overcome strong bureaucratic resistance to the economic reforms.

Glasnost proved to be a two-edged sword: It challenged the entrenched power of the economic bureaucracy but also immensely complicated the task of economic reform by requiring the leadership to gain broad-ranging support for economic measures that might increase economic and social inequality and involve short-term hardship for much of society. Once embarked upon, Gorbachev's commitment to glasnost

and *demokratizatsiia* was hard to retract; both policies generated new expectations among the Soviet population, especially in educated circles, that would be difficult to suppress by turning back the clock and reinstituting an authoritarian regime. Many Russians entered the 1990s somewhat cynical about "democracy" (thanks to the dubious benefits Soviet and Russian "democracy" had offered and the questionable integrity of some of the so-called democrats), but few were ready to return to the Soviet-style of top-down politics. The gap between democratic ideals (often poorly understood) and political institutions would breed further disillusionment, even resignation, in the 1990s; nonetheless, the notion that citizens should be able to exercise some control over their government had taken hold.

Gorbachev achieved his greatest success in the foreign policy sphere. Just as his domestic support was plummeting in late 1990 and early 1991, he was granted the Nobel Peace Prize, reflecting his esteemed international stature. Under the guidance of his "New Thinking," the military build-up in the USSR was halted, important arms control agreements were ratified, and many controls on international contacts were lifted. In 1989, Gorbachev informed local Communist leaders in the Eastern European countries that the USSR would not continue to prop up their unpopular governments. First in Hungary and Poland, then in the German Democratic Republic (East Germany) and Czechoslovakia, pressure from below pushed the Communist parties out of power, and a process of democratization and market reform ensued. More gradual transformations occurred in Bulgaria and Romania. Politicians in both East and West declared the Cold War over. To Gorbachev's dismay, however, the liberation of Eastern Europe fed the process of disintegration in the Soviet Union. Baltic nationalists were encouraged when the Berlin Wall fell in 1989 and when Soviet dominance and Communist Party rule were expelled in Warsaw, Prague, and Berlin. Why not also in the Baltic capitals of Tallinn, Riga, and Vilnius? Demands for autonomy and independence gained additional impetus, and Gorbachev's goal of pursuing reform without threatening the existence of the USSR was increasingly open to threat.

On August 19, 1991, a coalition of conservative figures attempted a coup d'état, temporarily removing Gorbachev from the leadership post to stop the reform initiative and prevent the collapse of the USSR. Rather

TABLE 2   **How Russians View Future Dangers (percent of respondents)**

Problem	Quite Likely		Unlikely	
	November 1993	April 1994	November 1993	April 1994
Mass unemployment	66	78	24	12
Economic collapse	*	64	*	19
Growth of the strike movement	55	58	28	23
Mass actions against the government	43	51	32	29
Mass hunger	30	36	56	49
Armed conflicts with former Soviet republics	27	36	50	40
Coup d'état	30	29	44	39
Civil war	*	28	*	46

*Not available

Source: Translated and adapted from VTsIOM Intertsentr (All-Russian Center for the Study of Public Opinion), Akademiia Narodnogo khoziaistva (Academy of the National Economy), *Ekonomicheskie i sotsial'nye peremeny: Monitoring obshchestvennogo mneniia: Informatsiunnyi biulleten'* (Economic and Social Variables: Monitoring of Public Opinion: Information Bulletin) 4 (July–August 1994), 9.

than restoring the old system, however, the failed coup was the death knell of the USSR and pushed the reform impetus in an even more radical direction. In December 1991, the Russian Federation stepped out as an independent country in the world of states. Its independent status (along with that of the other fourteen former union republics of the USSR) was quickly recognized by the major world powers. The USSR as superpower was history, and the new post-Soviet states, including Russia, would have to redefine their roles in the global economic and political system. Russia would try to establish itself as the successor to the USSR, thus retaining a central role in the world of states, but internal instability, economic decline, and reduced regional clout would make this task difficult.

Implications for Contemporary Russian Politics

Russia reemerged as an independent country under nearly the worst imaginable conditions. The economy was in shambles, and many traditional economic ties with other parts of the former Soviet Union and Eastern Europe were ruptured by the collapse of the Soviet system. Previous political institutions (the Communist Party and the institutions of the former Soviet state) were dismantled, and their functions had to be reassigned to new or ill-suited Russian political structures,

also remnants of the communist era. The Marxist-Leninist ideology that had prevailed for over seventy years was discredited, but there was little consensus on what should replace it. The country itself encompassed an ethnically diverse population and vast expanses of land that had proven, over the centuries, to be inherently difficult to govern.

The new Russian government, under the leadership of its popularly elected president, Boris Yeltsin, immediately proclaimed its commitment to Western-style democracy and market economic reform. The pattern of economic decline, regional self-assertion, and declining state authority continued under Yeltsin, who increasingly relied on presidential decrees to formulate policy, although the government was incapable of implementing these decrees. Extensive discussions about a new constitution for post-communist Russia became mired in conflict over the division of powers between the center and the regions, and between the various institutions of government. The failure to achieve a consensus among the political elite, particularly between the executive and legislative branches of the government, led finally to the showdown which occurred at the Russian parliament building in October 1993. The constitution subsequently adopted in a referendum in December 1993 instituted a strong form of presidential rule. It is unclear whether this strong executive authority will ultimately serve to undermine or to further democratize and stabilize the country.

While the central government has become increasingly unable to enforce its policy, the locus of power is shifting to the regions, although regional initiatives are frequently stymied by unclear or counterproductive policy directives from the central government. Regions, especially those rich in natural resources (for example, Tatarstan and regions in Western Siberia), have demanded more economic autonomy. Meanwhile the gap between rich and poor regions has widened, but the government's capability to establish an adequate system of social protection is minimal. Early on, Yeltsin committed himself to a relatively clear plan of economic transformation, but political pressures and fear of social unrest have restrained his government from single-mindedly pursuing its policy of radical economic reform. No coherent alternative policy has been presented either.

On the international front, the Russian leadership and population have had to accept the status of a failed superpower. For some, this national humiliation has intensified the bitter reality of economic decline. Like Gorbachev before him, Yeltsin seems to be constantly soliciting Western aid and accepting sometimes harsh conditions in return. The aid has been insufficient to begin addressing any of Russia's mammoth problems, and Russia's unstable economic and political position has hindered foreign investment. Meanwhile, on-and-off wars in neighboring states (in Georgia, Armenia and Azerbaijan, Tadzhikistan, Moldova, Yugoslavia) have sounded the alarm about the possible consequences of failed compromise in Russia. After failed attempts at a political resolution, in December 1994 the Russian government took forcible action to prevent the secession of one of its constituent units, Chechnya, thereby igniting a localized war within its own borders.

Russia's neighbors are skeptical of its motives and fear a resurgence of expansionist fervor. By the end of 1993, many Russian political figures were increasingly vocal in expressing support for Russian dominance in the region, or even for a reconstituted union of the former Soviet union republics. In response, Yeltsin began to voice concern about Russia's international status. The Russian leadership has sought to reassert Russia as a potential superpower by serving as a co-sponsor of Middle East peace talks, by taking over the Soviet Union's permanent seat on the UN Security Council, by reaffirming the importance of Russian–United States bilateral relations, and by taking a leading role in efforts to resolve the Bosnian crisis that emerged from the break-up of Yugoslavia. A resurgence of Russian nationalism is visible on the political landscape, and the Yeltsin team has responded by defending Russia's legitimate role as a regional power and its obligation to defend the rights of Russian minorities in the other former Soviet republics.

The main assets Russia possessed as independence dawned were a widespread rejection of the communist past, hope for a better future, and broad international support for the new regime. By 1994, all three of these resources were nearly exhausted. The Soviet Union's political collapse had contributed to economic collapse, regional wars, and declining international stature for the country. Over time, however, nostalgia for the security and the sufficiency of Soviet times has spread; the old system was disliked, but the new reality seems, in many ways, no better. Hope for the future has also declined, as many people have come to believe that their children will be worse off than themselves, and many see no credible exit from the multiple crises facing Russia. Finally, promises of Western aid have produced little visible effect, while the pursuit of a Western-style economic reform has been accompanied by hardship, inequality, and economic depression. The failed promises of Yeltsin's policy have elicited a growing skepticism toward the Western model and toward the motives or abilities of the so-called democrats. Society may have been liberated from the political controls of the communist period, but, many ask, to what end?

SECTION 2

Political Economy and Development

Imagine a Soviet bureaucrat traveling to London and observing that traffic there is less chaotic than in Moscow. The official concludes that the USSR should adopt the English system, and have people drive on the left-hand side of the road. Back in Moscow, traffic officials agree it is worth a try. But fearing public outrage, they first order only professional drivers (trucks and buses) to switch; ordinary drivers would be given time to adapt.[16] Well, you can imagine the result.

Some experts on post-communist economies liken the dangers of "half-reform" to the lesson of this anecdote. However, turning a highly centralized economy into a decentralized market structure is more complicated than reforming traffic patterns, and certainly has broader social and political consequences. The truth is, none of the so-called experts really know how to do it; and the politicians face a far more complex task than the economic experts; they not only need to know what to do, but also how to get others to comply. Meanwhile, large segments of the Russian economy appear to be in chaos. Is this the consequence of a flawed reform program? Has reform been too slow or too fast? Who are the winners and losers so far? In this chapter we will examine the roots of the present economic crisis and the nature of Russia's economic system as it is now developing.

STATE AND ECONOMY

As noted in the previous section, the tsarist state played the leading role in Russia's economic development until the Bolshevik revolution. After the Communists took power, the USSR became increasingly isolated from the world economy, both because of the West's hostility to the Bolsheviks' anticapitalist regime, but also because the Communists wanted to maintain control over their own social, economic, and political development. In the early years of Soviet rule, following the Civil War, the New Economic Policy (NEP, 1921–1928) represented a temporary retreat from a strong interventionist role by the state in the economy.[17] However, even during this period, large factories remained under state control and the state continued to play an important role in the purchase and distribution of agricultural output. In the late 1920s, a desire to accelerate industrialization and to prevent the formation of an agrarian capitalist class led party leader Joseph Stalin to shift the impetus for economic development back to the state. The isolation of the USSR from the global economy was, if anything, increased even further. The economic structure put in place in the 1930s, after the abandonment of the NEP, reinforced the dominant role of the state. The basic structures of that system were retained until the early 1990s. Therefore, to understand the dilemma of economic transformation in Russia, it is necessary to be familiar with Soviet economic practice and its social implications.

Many Soviet economic structures still function today in modified form, alongside new structures. Most of the personnel who occupy responsible positions in government and the economy were trained and socialized during the Soviet period and many hold similar posts now. Some of these people are highly capable and have proven themselves able to adapt to the new conditions; most are less flexible and are simply unable to respond in a dynamic and innovative way to the new challenges. A new generation of managers, now in their twenties or thirties, is gradually gaining more influence in private economic and state structures. Nonetheless, many behaviors and methods now utilized resemble the Soviet past. Old networks of personal contacts are particularly important for gaining access to materials, information, and benefits. There is much talk of "market economics," but few managers and bureaucrats comprehend how a market economy functions, and they lack the practical skills needed to operate in one.

The Soviet Economic System

In the Soviet period, land, factories, and all other important economic assets belonged to the state.[18] The complex Soviet structure operated through a system of powerful state ministries that oversaw various sectors of the economy (machine-building, light industry, grain products, and so on). Each was a large, hierarchically structured bureaucracy that extended down to the individual enterprises (firms). Gosplan (the state planning committee) was responsible for working out one-year and five-year economic plans to be implemented through the ministries. The one-year plans were operational, providing specific instructions as to what should be produced, by whom, and in what quantities. The plans had the force of law, although they were frequently too ambitious to be fulfilled. Enterprise directors learned various techniques (such as hoarding supplies and hiding capacities) to keep plan targets low and to avoid undue pressure from above.

In the agricultural sector, the *sovkhoz* (state farm) was the equivalent of the industrial enterprise. Some peasants worked on *kolkhozy* (collective farms), which theoretically were collectively run and owned by the peasants themselves. In practice the **kolkhoz** was included in the state plan and operated in much the same way as a state farm, although collective farm workers didn't receive all of the same social benefits as state farm workers. Since Stalin's rule, peasants had been permitted to till small private plots that were not included in the state planning system, yet provided families with food and supplementary income from sales at the peasant markets in the city. Production was more efficient here than on the state and collective farms. These were not, however, small, free-standing farms, because peasants needed resources from the state sector (equipment, seeds, fertilizers) to operate them. The peasant was able to look to the state or collective farm for a steady income, access to supplies, and social benefits.

The Soviet economy was unresponsive to consumer demands because production targets were determined by central bureaucrats rather than by consumer demand. Enterprises did not need to seek buyers for their goods, so what was delivered often did not meet the needs of other enterprises; retail stores piled up stocks of unwanted goods while goods in high demand (even some basic ones) were often unavailable. Both individuals and enterprises snatched up what they could, squirreling it away for trade or later use.

Prices were centrally controlled—they were set by the state and didn't rise when demand was high and supplies were limited, as in a market economy. Only in the peasant markets and the illegal black market did prices fluctuate in response to conditions of shortage or surplus. Thus producers had neither the incentive nor the resources to increase production of goods in short supply. As long as they met their state-set targets, it was not their concern whether the goods ultimately sold or not because enterprises were not motivated by the need to turn a profit. Indeed, if an enterprise was efficient and had excess income (above that needed to cover costs), most of this went back to the state budget anyway, just as deficits at the enterprise level were covered by the state budget. For the average citizen, the shortages meant waiting in line, even for basic items. Shops were most often organized so that a customer would have to wait in line several times at separate counters selling particular types of products; self-service stores were uncommon. This system added to the time required to find basic consumer goods and contributed to high absenteeism at work.

Environmental quality deteriorated under Soviet rule, which did not make environmental protection a priority.[19] Marxist-Leninist ideology saw technology as capable of mastering nature and counteracting any negative effects. Thus, large nature-transforming projects (hydroelectric dams, huge factory complexes) were glorified as symbols of Soviet power. At the same time, priority industries (metallurgy, machine building, chemicals, energy production) were highly polluting. On paper, Soviet standards for industrial emissions were in many cases impressive, but they were not enforced, partly because they were unrealistically ambitious. By the mid-1980s, air pollution levels in 100 Soviet cities exceeded maximum permissible standards tenfold. Inadequate technological safeguards and an insufficient regulatory structure led to the disastrous nuclear accident at Chernobyl (in Ukraine) in 1986, which contaminated immense areas of agricultural land in Ukraine and Belorussia and sounded the alarm about the drastic state of the Soviet environment and the inadequacy of state control. In highly polluted regions, the incidence of respiratory and other ailments was visibly higher; high nitrate levels and other contaminants in food, resulting from excessive use of chemical fertilizers and pesticides, were present in many areas of the USSR.

The Soviet Union, like Russia today, possessed a rich natural resource base, including natural gas and oil, precious metals, and mineral resources. When the most easily accessible deposits of natural resources in the Western part of the country approached depletion, Soviet authorities emphasized the development of rich deposits in Western Siberia, located far from major population centers in inclement climatic conditions. These resources are still critically important for the Russian state. Siberian development, however, has proved to be complicated and expensive: Costs are increased by permafrost conditions, transport distances, and the necessity of paying higher wages to attract workers. Technology has been insufficient to deal with many problems, resulting in a massive waste of resources and serious environmental problems, such as oil pipeline leaks.

Soviet Social Policy

Despite its inadequacies, the top-heavy Soviet system did allow the leadership to establish priorities; they were defined by the political elites with little input from society. Military production was one policy priority; the highest quality resources went to this sector. At the same time, through control of production and distribution, the state was able to enforce a set of social priorities that involved a kind of tacit social contract with the population. The party/state ensured security, fulfillment of basic social needs, and at least a minimal (and generally improving) standard of living in exchange for political cooperation and compliance by the population.

In this context, low-cost access to essential goods and services was made a regime priority; housing, transport, food supplies, cafeterias in the workplace, children's clothing, books, and cultural facilities were all heavily subsidized by the state. Citizens received many of these benefits (access to scarce goods and housing, subsidized meals, child care, and vacation facilities) through their place of employment, thus making the Soviet workplace a social as well as an economic institution. In many cases, however, even basic necessities were in short supply. Housing is a prime example. Housing was generally allocated through local state organs, trade unions, or the workplace; there was no open housing market because most housing was state-owned, in the form of high-rise apartment buildings in cities or developments constructed under Soviet rule. Housing shortages often meant that young married couples and their children continued to share a small apartment with parents; people would often wait years for housing, and housing difficulties greatly restricted geographical mobility.

A basic social safety net was provided by the Soviet government. Health care was free, even if its quality was at times dubious; sometimes under-the-table payments prompted better care. Although the number of physicians per capita was among the highest in the world in the late Soviet period, health care expenditure by the Soviet government, as a proportion of national income, was lower than in most Western countries.[20] Nonetheless considerable gains were made over the decades in reducing infant mortality rates and the incidence of infectious diseases. Alcoholism and health damage due to environmental pollution were significant problems in the Soviet period; life expectancy for Soviet men fell from 66.1 in 1964–1965 to 62.3 in 1980–1981, rising to only 63.8 in 1989.[21] Despite a commitment to equal treatment, regional differences characterized Soviet health care: Rural areas and the less developed non-Russian union republics (especially in Central Asia) suffered poorer levels of health care.

Under Soviet rule, mass education was a high priority and within the first decades after the revolution

virtually all segments of the population were provided access to primary and secondary schooling. The Soviet system did not allow private schools or private higher educational institutions (although private tutoring did go on), and the state provided education free of charge, with state stipends provided to university students. Following graduation, university graduates were assigned to particular jobs (sometimes in remote places) for a brief period as a sort of payment for the free education provided by the state. In theory, at least, the educational system was structured to provide training and knowledge to meet society's needs. In practice, however, the state found it difficult to match educational training to society's needs; therefore, many people were employed in jobs below their skill levels or in positions that did not match their formal training. A series of reforms in the Brezhnev period sought to resolve these problems, but with minimal success.

Other state benefits included the right to maternity leave (partially paid), child benefits, and disability pensions. Unemployment compensation, a mainstay of Western social protection systems, did not exist because the state was committed to a full-employment policy. The retirement age for women was fifty-five and for men sixty, although in the early 1980s about a third of the elderly continued to work after retirement age. Modest pensions were guaranteed by the state, assuring a stable but minimal standard of living for retirement.

After the Khrushchev era, agricultural and industrial employees grew accustomed to the security and social protection offered by the state-run system. The guarantee of job security was a core element of the tacit social contract—only in exceptional cases could an enterprise fire an employee. Participation in the labor market was high: Almost all able-bodied adults, men and women, participated in the workforce. People were usually permitted to seek employment for themselves, rather than assigned to a particular enterprise. Restrictions on labor mobility were usually the result of a chronic shortage of housing or of difficulties in gaining residency permits for particularly desirable locations such as Moscow.

An irony of the system was that labor in many sectors was nonetheless in constant short supply, reflecting the inefficient use of the workforce. Labor productivity was low, by international standards, and work discipline weak: Drunkenness and absenteeism were common phenomena. A Soviet saying of the time captured this element of the tacit social contract: "We pretend to work, they pretend to pay us." "Hidden unemployment" was widespread, that is, people were employed and paid, but did not work to capacity. Whereas the lax work atmosphere reduced the likelihood and frequency of labor conflicts, it also kept production inefficient.

Wage rates were centrally set; however, enterprise managers could make adjustments through reclassification of jobs to attract employees with needed skills. Pay rates in dangerous occupations or in difficult climatic conditions (such as in parts of Siberia) were set higher, to attract labor. Another feature of the system was the relatively low level of inequality, but at significantly lower levels of affluence than one might have expected from a superpower. As a matter of state policy, wage differentials between the best and worst paid were lower than in most Western economies. Because land and factories were state-owned, individuals could not accumulate wealth in the form of real estate, stocks, or ownership of factories. Any privileges that did exist were modest by Western standards. There was little "conspicuous consumption"; political elites did have special access to scarce goods, higher quality health care, travel, and vacation homes, but these privileges were hidden from public view and the private lives of the political leaders received virtually no attention in the media.

Russian Reform Efforts

Gorbachev equivocated on the state's role in the economy; he seemed particularly unwilling to give up the state's role in assuring full employment.[22] As noted in Section 1, the old planning system had largely ceased functioning in the late Gorbachev years. Although some enterprises still fulfilled "state orders," the increased autonomy offered to enterprises and the de facto appropriation of power by many regional and union republic authorities had disrupted the ties of supply that had been the basis of the Soviet economic system. Initially, some regional governments restricted the export of certain goods to assure supplies for the local population; a complex system of barter (nonmonetary) trade grew up, as a result of inadequacies in the banking system and rising inflation rates. Several proposed "reform" directions were discussed from 1989 to 1991 to deal with the economic decline, but the Gorbachev leadership failed to act decisively

and wavered between an apparent commitment to significant reform and a hesitancy about the likely disruption it would cause.

Only after the collapse of the Soviet Union did the Russian government commit itself to a path of radical **market reform,** sometimes referred to as **"shock therapy"** because of the radical rupture and disruption it implied.[23] This commitment marked a sea change in the broad sweep of Russian and Soviet history. The new Russian government staked its legitimacy on the market path, and affirmed it as a matter of principle. The basic notion underlying the reform was to take ownership of economic assets away from the state and place them in private hands; decision making about production, distribution of goods, and investment, to a large extent, was to be transferred from central planners to the new private owners. Enterprises would no longer receive state subsidies; they would be responsible for their own success or failure. Prices would be freed from central control, compelling producers to respond to consumer demand in making decisions about production and pricing. The rationale for this shock therapy approach was to jolt the Russian economy into a new mode of operation by introducing a range of radical changes. By definition, this strategy involved a breakdown of the tacit social contract forged during the communist period. The shock therapy would inevitably throw some sectors of the economy and of the population into a downward spin; it was hoped, however, that recovery would be relatively quick. The success of the policy would depend on instituting measures to stabilize the monetary system, especially strict controls both on state budget expenditures and on the issuance of money by the state bank. The final goal of the policy was to create a Western-type market economy, integrated into the global economic system, and capable of producing increasing domestic prosperity.

In practice, the Russian government has had difficulty in creating a market-driven economy. The social and political consequences of pursuing the policy in a comprehensive manner would include bankrupt enterprises, increasing social inequality, and high unemployment, with all the attendant social tensions and clashes. Despite the initial commitment of Yeltsin and his young Westernizing prime minister, Yegor Gaidar, to the shock therapy approach, the government was either unwilling or unable to push the reform to its conclusion. Political and social pressures have moder-

TABLE 3   Economic Indicators for the Russian Federation
(percent change from previous year, unless otherwise indicated)

	1990	1991	1992	1993	1994[a]
Economic growth[b]	−2.1%	−12.9%	−18.5%	−12.0%	−15.0%
Industrial production	−0.1%	−8.0%	−18.9%	−16.2%	−20.9%
Agricultural output	−3.5%	−4.5%	−9.0%	−4.0%	−9.0%
Consumer price inflation	5.0%	92.6%	1,354%	880%	320%
Population (in millions)	148.3	148.9	148.6	148.4	148.3
Students per 10,000 population[c]	—	190	186	178	171
Rubles per one U.S. dollar	16	30	220	930	2,500

[a]Preliminary est'mates by the Economist Intelligence Unit.
[b]Growth in real domestic product (controlled for inflation).
[c]For the academic years 1990–1991, 1991–1992, 1992–1993, and 1993–1994, respectively.

Source: Adapted from various issues of the Economist Intelligence Unit, *Country Report: Russia,* quarterly reports. In some cases, figures have been rounded or estimated from graph diagrams.

ated the pace of the program, and purity of the reform concept has been marred by a web of corruption and contacts, as former and new elites have scrambled to gain their share of the spoils from the dismantling of the state-ownership system. The lack of experience with individual entrepreneurship and private ownership has made the process more difficult in Russia than in parts of Eastern Europe, where market economies existed prior to the Communist takeover. In contrast to China, regional economic decentralization and self-reliance have weak roots in Russia. Even under relatively more propitious conditions, such as in Poland, where a radical shock therapy was adopted in 1990, the social and political consequences have been distressing.

Nonetheless, once Russia became an independent state, Boris Yeltsin quickly took some first steps to implement his commitment to radical market reform. In January 1992, price controls on most goods were loosened or lifted entirely; partial exceptions included some basic food items and energy resources, but here too dramatic price increases have been gradually allowed. The result has been high inflation fluctuating between 21 percent and 4 percent a month in 1994 and early 1995. Inflation has been fueled by a soft monetary policy pursued by the Central Bank of Russia; money is printed with nothing tangible to back it up. Large state budget deficits have also accumulated as subsidies to some enterprises continue to be provided

to prevent bankruptcy and the consequent unemployment. Not only Yeltsin's critics but some figures in his own government have been reluctant to risk the social upheaval associated with high unemployment. Strike threats in key industries and intermittent work stoppages have been used to protest delayed wage payments. At first the government responded with concessions, but it is now less influenced by such pressures because workers fear losing their jobs. To prevent a precipitous decline in living standards, the government has been forced to institute wage increases in state sector jobs, and to continually raise minimum wage and pension levels. Until 1994, wage increases did not keep pace with price rises, so that real wages, on average, declined by an estimated 50 percent between late 1991 and January 1993. In early 1994, overall, official statistics indicated some increases in real income compared to 1993, probably because many people took on second jobs. In early 1995, real income again began to fall; furthermore differences in income between the worst-off and the best-off have also increased dramatically.

The economic decline which began under Gorbachev intensified following the collapse of the USSR, and by 1994, Russia was in the grip of a severe depression (see Table 3). Although the exact extent of the decline is hard to specify (economic statistics are unreliable and official figures may understate actual levels of production), some estimates indicate that in

1993 gross national product and industrial output were about 60 percent of 1989 levels.[24] Industrial production and output and capital investment in 1994 were all about 25 percent lower than in 1993. In early 1995 the decline in industrial output slowed to 4.5 percent compared to a year earlier, but investment continued to slide more sharply. Although these figures may somewhat overstate the decline because some production may not be reported, the general downward trend is indisputable.

Particularly hard hit are core industrial sectors like machine-building, including production of agricultural machinery. The break-up of the USSR and the Council for Mutual Economic Assistance (the organization coordinating economic activities between the countries in the Soviet bloc) have fed the economic crisis; previous trade patterns were ruptured, and without controlled prices, supplies often became too expensive. "Inter-enterprise debt" levels have also risen to dramatic levels at times, as firms have been unable to pay for goods already received. This has led to nonpayment of wages, temporary layoffs, and demands on the state for subsidies to prevent plant closures.

A real market has not yet developed to provide the basis for a new supply system. Many enterprises are unable to continue producing the same goods, and many firms have lost their customers. The depression feeds on itself; declining capacity in one sector deprives other sectors of buyers or suppliers. Consumer purchasing power also dropped with the decline in real wages.

Regional conflicts have also been fueled by the attempted reform process. Regions rich in natural resources have demanded more economic autonomy, and some regions have even resisted transferring tax funds to the federal authorities. Regions making demands have often won concessions, and this has led other regions to claim unfair treatment and press for similar privileges.

Privatization has been a key component of the economic reform package pursued by the Yeltsin government. This has included the establishment of new private enterprises as well as the privatization of already existing state firms. Though new private firms have been encouraged since the early stages of perestroika, other aspects of state policy have prevented them from flourishing. Taxes are high, restrictions on use of hard currency have reduced incentives to export, and a poor infrastructure (transport, banking,

Russian citizens sell their personal possessions and other goods on a Moscow street in 1992, in order to supplement their declining incomes.
Source: MIR Photo Agency.

communications) has made survival difficult for new private enterprises. Many are appended to large state-run organizations; they make use of the latter's facilities, equipment, and space, but operate more efficiently and pay better wages. A symbiotic, mutually supportive relationship has developed between many small private firms and the state sector. **"Spontaneous privatization"** occurred in some state-owned enterprises in the late 1980s and early 1990s; existing managers or ministry bureaucrats transformed promising enterprises into privatized entities without a clear legal framework for doing so.

With the breakdown of the Soviet distribution system, trade is a lucrative business and the area in which the most successful private enterprises operate. These include not only the thousands of small kiosks operating on city streets, but behind-the-scenes middlemen who buy up large stocks of goods and resell them to other enterprises and organizations at inflated prices. Through use of contacts, savvy, and bribes, some of these "businessmen" are able to accumulate huge profits and deposit them in banks abroad. Less common is the entrepreneur who invests the profits in a factory that produces tangible products, for this is a more risky venture. Diverse methods of laundering money to avoid taxes and extract a profit from the remaining state-owned entities are also common; the decentralized but organized network of crime and corruption is widely referred to as the mafia.[25] Government officials, the militia (the police), and operators abroad are all part of this illegal network. Its existence also has fueled a rising crime rate; foreigners possessing hard currency and Russian bankers are particular targets, as are Russian journalists who expose crime and mafia operations. In March 1995 the popular Russian TV journalist, Vladislav Listyev, was murdered in front of his apartment after being appointed head of the Russian TV firm Ostankina. Some believe he was targeted because of his outspoken efforts to halt illegal siphoning of television advertising revenues. His murder produced an outpouring of public grief and outrage. Given the pervasiveness of corruption and crime, it is not surprising that the average Russian citizen views the country's young capitalism with considerable cynicism and apprehension.

Transforming large state enterprises into private property has been difficult in Russia, as elsewhere in the former Soviet bloc. Capital is scarce and buyers few. Although the Russian government encourages foreign investment, it has been reluctant to allow foreigners to buy a majority share in large state operations or in the potentially lucrative natural resource sectors. Many plants are pink elephants—technology is backward and the production profile unpromising without massive infusions of capital for restructuring. Government efforts to break up large enterprises that occupy a near monopoly position in their sector have been equally frustrating.

Three steps have been particularly important in the Russian government's privatization plan: (1) the distribution of **privatization vouchers** to all Russian citizens; (2) the adoption of a law on privatization (1991); (3) and various measures allowing private ownership of land. Each of these initiatives was controversial, and the effectiveness of each in achieving the goals of reform has been questioned.

In November 1992 each citizen of Russia (including children) was issued a voucher with a nominal value of 10,000 rubles (at that time approximately $10

"And this, dear, is all that remains for me from privatization."
Source: Aleksandra Markelova, courtesy of *Robochaia Tribuna (Labor Tribune).*

U.S.). These vouchers could be used in a variety of ways—to buy up shares in enterprises undergoing privatization, to sell for cash, or to invest through the intermediary of newly established investment funds. Many people viewed the vouchers as symbolic, representing the government's attempt to convince citizens that they were getting a share of the "people's" property during the privatization process. The government presented the vouchers as a mechanism to allow average citizens to participate in the privatization process. In practice, people were often confused about how to use the vouchers. In 1993, auctions selling shares in state enterprises sometimes occurred and private investment funds formed—firms offering to handle investment choices for voucher holders. Some workers bought shares in their own enterprises, a practice encouraged by the law on privatization (discussed below) and by enterprise managers. Because many vouchers were still unused by the end of 1993 (the deadline for their use), the government extended their period of validity until the summer of 1994. A new phase of privatization was to begin at that time in which firms could sell remaining unsold shares for cash or investment guarantees. This new stage was expected to add revenues to the state budget; however, by late 1995, this hope had not materialized to any significant extent.

The 1991 law on privatization mandated that most large state enterprises should be transformed into **joint-stock companies.** An important issue was how to distribute shares between present workers and managers ("insiders"), on the one hand, and outside buyers, on the other. The law established three variants for the formation of joint-stock companies, each involving a different scheme for the portion of insider and public shares. From 1992 to 1994 many state enterprises were "privatized" in this way, so that by early 1994 an estimated 80 percent of medium-size and large state enterprises in the designated sectors of the economy had been transformed into joint-stock companies;[26] by early 1994, a majority of Russian citizens were no longer state employees. Most Western experts agree that in many cases sufficient shares passed to the present managers and employees of former state enterprises to allow effective insider control, producing a pattern of **"insider privatization."**

The implications of this trend are as yet unclear. Some believe any real transformation in enterprise behavior will be hindered because the same personnel will be making decisions, and a network linking enterprise managers and state bureaucrats will continue to assure subsidies to protect inefficient firms from bankruptcy. In this view, the net effect will be the transfer of former state property into the private hands of the same elites. Other observers see insider privatization as an appropriately gradualistic form of economic transformation, preserving security and stability in the workplace, and giving employees and managers a personal interest in their work. It is equally unclear whether insider privatization was an intended effect of the Yeltsin reform package or an unintended consequence resulting from political compromises the government felt compelled to accept. In any case, it is clear that both enterprise and government officials have benefited from the trend and will be reluctant to disrupt it. Despite passage of a bankruptcy law in 1992, most unprofitable enterprises have not been forced to close. The official unemployment rate was still 7.4 percent of the economically active population in early 1995, but this figure hides short-term layoffs, workers still employed but only sporadically paid, or people shifted to partial employment. The real level of effective unemployment was estimated to be around 13 percent in early 1995.

The agricultural sector has been the Achilles heel of the Soviet economic system since Stalin's time.

Damage done by the collectivization campaign of 1929 and the early 1930s (loss of livestock, incentives, and morale) has never been fully repaired. Even with a renewed emphasis on agriculture under Khrushchev and increased investment under Brezhnev, this sector continued to function ineffectively with high rates of spoilage and crop loss.[27] Although Gorbachev in his early years gained a reputation as an innovator in agricultural policy, perestroika placed little emphasis on this sector. Perceiving the USSR to be an industrial giant and military superpower, the Soviet leadership most likely did not consider agricultural reform to be a high priority; improvements in the more advanced sectors of the economy were deemed more central in securing the USSR a viable position in the world economy. The Yeltsin regime expressed a commitment to agrarian reform, but it too was more deliberate in pursuing other dimensions of the economic reform package. It was hoped that lifting price controls in the agricultural sector, freeing trade, and privatizing land would stimulate more effective cultivation and high-quality crops. These policies have been slow to produce the desired effect—by early 1995 individual farmers owned only a small proportion of land, although most peasants continued to rely on their small private plots for family food supplies. Many state and collective farms have been transformed into joint-stock companies, but it is unclear to what extent this has changed their actual operations.

Change in this sphere has been slow partly because transformation of the agricultural sector poses special problems. Peasants have generally been reluctant to begin individual private farming and to give up the security offered by employment in the state sector or in the joint-stock farms created from the state sector. Legislation allowing privatization of land, passed in December 1991, was largely ineffectual. In late 1993 and early 1994, further restrictions on privatization of land were lifted by decree, but local political officials could still hinder formation of viable private farms. More technical problems also hinder rural transformation: poor roads, transport, and storage facilities; overuse of chemical fertilizers and pesticides; outdated equipment; and reliance on purchases by state agencies. Individual farmers have even fewer resources to resolve these problems than the state. Effective marketing structures for produce from small farms do not exist, so farmers often have to take their own goods to market in a nearby city, a time-

TABLE 4   **Russian Citizens' Evaluation of the Economic Reform Process**

Percentage of respondents who think that the economic reform is producing:

	August 1992	February 1993	May 1994
Positive results	6	3	8
No results	47	39	42
Negative results	33	37	39
Hard to say	11	18	12

Source: Adapted from Analytical Center of the Institute for Sociopolitical Research of the Russian Academy of Sciences, *Reformirovanie Rossii: Mify i real'nost' 1989–1994 (Reform of Russia: Myths and Realities 1989–1994)*, authors and compilers of the volume G. V. Osipov (head), V. K. Lavashov, V. V. Lokosov, and A. T. Klop'ev (Moscow: "Academia," 1994), 323.

consuming and inefficient method of distribution. In some cases, payoffs to the local mafia must be made to gain access to these more lucrative market outlets. State prices for some agricultural goods continue to be controlled, thus denying the agricultural sector the income needed to improve the infrastructure. Both private farmers and the new joint-stock farms need to find capital to finance their operations, and, as in Western countries, are subject to the uncertainties of the market and the weather.

A new Russian Agrarian Reform Law laid the groundwork in 1994 for a new phase of the land privatization program in several regions of Russia. This law established a framework for allowing collective and state farms to redistribute land and equipment to present employees of the organization. Under this plan, once the *kolkhoz* or *sovkhoz* has voted to implement the plan, each employee receives certificates based on length and type of employment on the existing farm; an auction is then held, at which certificates can be used to "buy" land or equipment from the collective. Although the program is in its early stages, it appears to be providing a mechanism for overcoming some of the difficulties of land privatization in certain regions.

Following the parliamentary elections in December 1993, the government's commitment to radical economic reform seemed to wane. The strong showing in the election of forces critical of the shock therapy approach (see Section 4) suggested widespread popular discontent (see Table 4). Key reform supporters resigned from the government. During 1994 and 1995, an issue of major contention was the state budget. Efforts to control inflation by curbing government

spending met with resistance from many quarters, including the military, which warned of possible unrest among troops if conditions were not improved. Pressures to bolster faltering industries and to provide subsidies to pay worker salaries also have prevailed in many cases. The government's inability to hold the line on spending has hindered economic stabilization. Payoffs, bribes, export of profits into private bank accounts abroad and other forms of corruption and illegal action by government officials, as well as private traders, are further obstacles to economic stabilization. In late 1994, renewed efforts to hold the line on state expenditures occurred following a sharp plunge (followed by a partial recovery) in the value of the ruble against the dollar. At this writing, it is unclear whether these efforts will be successful in controlling inflation and stabilizing the currency; side effects of the efforts at economic "stabilization" (such as rising unemployment and bankruptcies) could produce political destabilization.

The future of the state's role in Russia's economy remains in question. The state's capacity to influence economic behavior or economic performance is very limited. At the same time, independent interests interact in a seemingly chaotic and random manner. There is little evidence that the public has confidence that it can influence the shape and direction of economic policy or developments in the country. It seems that no one is in real control. The government is incapable of addressing any of the major economic dilemmas facing the country, and those in positions of power are believed to be corrupt and motivated by self-interest. This contrasts sharply with past perceptions that the

A comment on the October 1994 exchange rate crisis.
Source: Vadim Misjuk, courtesy of *Nezavisimaia Gazeta (The Independent Newspaper).*

state exercised virtually total control over the economy and that the system would assure security, if not affluence.

SOCIETY AND ECONOMY

Just as the Soviet state dominated the economy, so also did its political authorities attempt to define forms of collective identity for the Soviet citizenry. In principle, Marxist-Leninist ideology identified social class as the most important focus of social solidarity. The official position claimed that class antagonism had been overcome and that class divisions had no relevance in Soviet society; therefore, it was forbidden to organize independent organizations defined by class or group economic interests. Trade unions, for example, were subordinate to the party/state structure and

therefore could not themselves define the interests of workers vis-à-vis the state. It is not surprising that the population was somewhat cynical about official claims that class exploitation had been eliminated under Soviet rule, expressed in the following popular riddle: "What's the difference between capitalism and socialism?" (Answer: In capitalism man exploits man; in socialism it is just the opposite.)

Social tensions were officially muted, but simmered just below the surface. The party's rhetoric of social equality, along with traditional egalitarian values, reinforced intolerance of huge differences in wealth or income. Nonetheless, most Soviet citizens knew that the party elite had privileged access to goods, benefits, and services. With virtually everyone an employee of the state, however, people were not sure how their own economic interests differed or clashed with those of other social groups. Only in the 1990s did people begin to perceive how their position in the economic structure might define their political interests. In this context, a real foundation for collective identity based on common class or economic interests could begin to emerge. Groups such as entrepreneurs, private businesspeople, and top managers in the industrial structure now have a budding sense of group identity, but even this is only weakly reflected in political organizations.

Soviet ideology and policy produced significant unintended consequences for the way people thought about themselves, as shown by the emphasis on ethnicity or nationality after controls on public expression were lifted in the late 1980s. If Soviet authorities had downplayed the importance of ethnic identity, why did it assume such a powerful importance under glasnost? Despite official rhetoric, the Soviet administrative structure of the state and economy was based on fifteen union republics which were formed around and named for the particular national groups that inhabited them (the titular nationality). These ethnically based union republics, in turn, formed the basis for bureaucratic state structures; for example, many of the economic ministries were "union republic" ministries, meaning that for many sectors of the economy, operational planning and implementation occurred within the structure of these ethnically based units. Furthermore, elites in the union republics became advocates for the economic interests of their regions; so once Gorbachev allowed freer expression of such demands, these same elites sometimes claimed to represent the interests of their union republic's ethnic population.

Although efforts were made to pursue economic equality of the various union republics and regions, some parts of the USSR were clearly economically privileged (the large cities and Western regions of the country) and others were significantly more backward (for example, rural areas and Central Asia). The net effect of Soviet policy was to make the peoples of all union republics feel like the victims, rather than the beneficiaries, of central policy. For example, there was widespread sentiment in Russia that cheap energy and natural resources from Russia had subsidized other regions of the USSR. Furthermore, skilled Russian laborers often staffed key industries in non-Russian regions, providing essential expertise. Elites in other

union republics, on the other hand, claimed that the local economic structure had been distorted and skewed by mandates from the center, and that Soviet-imposed isolation from the larger global economy had imposed heavy costs. For example, Soviet autarky had prevented Latvia, Lithuania, and Estonia from forging closer links with the more developed—and neighboring—Scandinavian economies; thus the quality of production there dropped to the low level accepted in the USSR, rather than meeting the challenge of higher Western standards. In the eyes of the nationalist elites there, the standard of living did not rise as it might have if these countries had been allowed to develop freely. Furthermore, the Stalinist heavy industrial model of development brought polluting enterprises to these union republics, as well as Russian workers. As a result, the proportion of ethnic Estonians and Latvians in their own homeland declined rather dramatically under Soviet rule.

Grievances also emerged from Central Asia. The Soviet economic plan had decreed cotton to be the main crop, thereby producing a distorted economic structure; consequently, the region had to import many basic food items. In an effort to maximize cotton output, careless and excessive use of chemical pesticides, fertilizers, and irrigation schemes had produced a regional environmental catastrophe, with dramatically negative effects on the population's health. The Central Asian union republics remained less industrialized and urbanized, with lower levels of health care provision and education than the European regions of the USSR. In some ways, they resembled colonies rather than equal units in the Soviet federation. In comparison to some of their Middle Eastern neighbors (Iran, Iraq, Afghanistan, for example), economic and social development was, however, impressive. Nonetheless, by the late 1980s, elites at the union republic level began to express grievances about the relative deprivation of their regions; unwittingly Soviet policy had produced new national identifications, rather than an international "Soviet" identity.

The Soviet economic system affected gender identity as well. Women made impressive gains in the economic sphere under Soviet rule, but traditional gender role definitions continued to prevail. From the 1930s, the vast majority of working-age women were in the labor force under a Soviet regime that encouraged female employment for both ideological and economic reasons. Marxism-Leninism professed a commitment to gender equality; women were encouraged to gain an independent economic status as a foundation for equality in the family, society, and politics. Participation in the labor force was seen as a way to provide women the opportunity to participate equally with men in public life. For economic reasons, Stalin needed to mobilize all available resources, including female labor, to fuel the industrialization campaign.

Under Soviet rule, women did make considerable gains in the economic and educational spheres; however, economic structures were not responsive to their needs. Until the perestroika period, sanitary napkins and tampons were unavailable, and the primary method of birth control was abortion. Even in 1992, for every 100 births there were 225 induced abortions. Women carried the triple burden of employment outside the home, homemaker, and mother. Labor-saving devices (dishwashers, prepared foods, self-service stores, everyday services) were backward, reinforcing demands on women's time and energy. At the same time, commodities consumed in larger quantities by men (alcoholic beverages and cigarettes) seemed to enjoy a certain priority in the production system.

Economy and Society in Russia

Russian leaders inherited an array of social and economic patterns from the previous Soviet system; these helped define potential bases of collective identity, expectations about state policy, and grievances against the authority structure. This legacy has impeded efforts by the Russian state to carry through its economic program successfully. Since the collapse of the USSR, social and political factors have been critical in shaping Russia's attempts at economic reform. The attempted transition to market economics is producing winners and losers among the elite and in the general population. Furthermore, most elements of society suffer in the short term; and unless that suffering can be made tolerable, public protests, including strikes, demands for regional autonomy, and the formation of nondemocratic and antisystem parties or movements, will most certainly grow stronger.

The situation has been complicated by society's high expectations, inherited from the Soviet system, regarding the state's responsibility for the material welfare of its citizens. These expectations make the transition to market structures even more difficult because a market economy involves less direct state in-

volvement in securing that welfare. Budget constraints have produced cutbacks in state welfare programs at a time when there is a growing need for them. In addition, enterprises must be more responsive to competitive market pressures to reduce costs and increase work productivity. They have fewer resources for worker benefits, which presents a particularly pressing problem because so many social benefits have traditionally been channeled through the workplace, making it not merely a place of employment but an essential social institution as well. Many Russian citizens are still reluctant to accept inequality as legitimate; hence many view wealth as a sign of corruption, not of hard work and initiative. This attitude makes a significant portion of the population skeptical of new businesses and entrepreneurs. The negative stereotypes are reinforced by the pervasive nature of corruption in the new Russia, and because most new businesses are involved in trade (often viewed as "speculation," buying up goods at cheap prices and selling them dear) rather than in actual production.

Some groups have suffered more from the reform process than others, including children, pensioners, and the disabled. The number of homeless and beggars has skyrocketed, especially in large cities like Moscow, a magnet for displaced persons and refugees from war zones on Russia's perimeter. Alongside the "new poor" are the "new rich," probably less than 2–3 percent of the population who enjoy a standard of living luxurious by Western standards. These people, many of them multimillionaires with Western bank accounts, have been able to take advantage of their positions or skills to siphon off profits from state enterprises, trade, or foreign contacts. Between these two extremes, the mass of the Soviet population itself is affected by growing differentials in income. Dramatic declines in income have affected those without easily marketable skills, including unskilled laborers in low priority sectors of the economy and people working in areas of public service such as education. Wages for skilled workers in key economic sectors (oil and gas, for example) have risen quickly; individuals who have marketable skills (carpentry, plumbing, repairs) may also benefit; in addition, individuals with foreign-language skills can often earn higher incomes by working for foreigners. These increasing income differentials are becoming more and more visible.

Women continue to suffer many of the same hardships in Russia as they did in the Soviet period. They continue to carry the bulk of domestic responsibilities, including shopping, cooking, housework, and child-care. Child-care facilities still exist in many enter-prises and neighborhoods, and women are granted three-years maternity leave. Nonetheless, many women must rely on their mother or mother-in-law to help out. The father plays a relatively small role in childraising. In addition to domestic responsibilities, most women continue to work outside the home.

Other economic realities also burden Russian women. Higher prices mean that all possible sources of family income must be exploited. Some women might prefer to stay home with young children, but, as in the past, in most cases economic necessity prevails. Layoffs and unemployment are also hitting women harder than men. Employers are often reluctant to hire women of childbearing age who have certain rights to maternity leave which employers may view as disruptive or expensive to fulfill. Also, labor cutbacks in white-collar sectors, where women are more heavily employed, have been more severe than in traditionally male occupations. In 1993, about two-thirds to three-quarters of the registered unemployed were women.[28] On average, women have been losers in the economic transition process.

The birthrate in Russia is declining, continuing a trend begun under Soviet rule. This pattern has affected almost all industrialized countries, but in Russia the excessive demands placed on women by the dual bur-den of home and workplace have reinforced it. In addi-tion, many couples are reluctant to have children because of the daily hardships, rising costs, the declin-ing standard of living, and continuing housing short-ages—a line of thinking that reflects a dangerous demoralization of public life. Since 1992, the death rate has exceeded the birth rate. Today, contraceptive de-vices and sanitary products are more widely available than in the past, but the former are expensive if they are of reliable quality (usually Western imports). Women continue to rely on abortion as a primary means of birth control, even though unsanitary conditions and insuffi-cient regulation mean that abortion sometimes results in infertility, infection, or even death.

RUSSIA AND THE INTERNATIONAL POLITICAL ECONOMY

Right up to the end of the Soviet period, the economy remained relatively isolated from outside influences.

Most of the USSR's trade (53 percent of imports, 51 percent of exports, in 1984) was carried out with the countries of Eastern Europe.[29] The ruble, the Soviet currency, was nonconvertible, meaning that its ex-change rate was set by the state (at various levels for various types of exchange) and did not fluctuate freely in response to economic forces. Furthermore, the ruble could not legally be taken out of the country. All for-eign trade was channeled through central state organs, so individual enterprises had neither the possibility nor the incentive to seek external markets. Accounts in convertible Western currencies (so-called hard cur-rency) were under state control, although an under-ground market in hard currency also existed because hard currency allowed access to coveted Western goods (mainly on the black market). Russia's rich nat-ural resource base, particularly oil and gas, provided an important source of hard currency income and, in Soviet times, insulated the country from incurring a large hard currency debt.

Gorbachev sought to integrate the USSR more fully into the global economy by reducing interna-tional tensions, encouraging foreign investment, and reducing barriers to foreign contacts. The new Russia has pursued this policy even more aggressively. One long-term goal has been to achieve convertibility of the ruble, a policy that should eventually increase do-mestic confidence in the currency by linking its value to other currencies. Inside Russia today the ruble is freely convertible, although its export is still not al-lowed and it cannot be traded in international currency markets. Given high inflation rates and political insta-bility, some businesses and even individuals prefer to keep their monetary assets in U.S. dollars.

A kind of dual (ruble/dollar) economy developed in the early 1990s, with significant portions of internal trade being conducted in dollars; those with access to the dollar market (for example, waiters, taxi drivers, tour guides, interpreters, or employees in hotels cater-ing to Westerners) came to enjoy a privileged eco-nomic status. In an attempt to control this situation, Yeltsin issued a decree effective in January 1994 for-bidding domestic trade in hard currency. By artificially protecting the ruble in this way, the government may be hindering the country's progress toward convert-ibility. Nonetheless, one can change rubles for dollars at numerous small kiosks on the streets of downtown Moscow, as well as in banks and other locations in other cities.

Given Russia's dire economic situation, its political leaders have courted Western economic assistance. This has been a much debated topic in the West, and several governments, most notably Germany, have made fairly generous commitments of aid (at least on paper), mostly in the form of repayable credits. Various international agencies, most notably the World Bank, the International Monetary Fund, and the European Union, have also contributed economic assistance, although it has often come with strings attached. For example, release of money from a ruble stabilization fund established by the IMF is contingent on Russia pursuing a strict policy of fiscal and monetary control and lifting remaining price controls. The Russian government has had some difficulties in meeting these conditions, and thus the funds have been released intermittently and often in limited amounts.

Russia has also had problems attracting foreign investment. Although a large number of foreign-Russian joint ventures are legally registered, many are not operational. Most operate in the trade, tourism, or natural resource sectors, with fewer entering central areas of production. Continued uncertainty and instability regarding government policy toward joint ventures has reduced business confidence. For example, in the summer of 1993, the Russian government restricted export of oil and natural gas by joint ventures. This enraged the foreign investment community and further undermined investor confidence.

Russia's position in the international political economy remains undetermined. With a highly skilled workforce and an advanced technological base in certain (especially military) sectors, Russia has many of the ingredients necessary to be a competitive and powerful force in the global world economy. However, efforts to convert former military production facilities to civilian uses have so far had only sporadic success. Often the enterprises that receive government subsidies are the weakest rather than the most promising. Therefore, the technological base of production is deteriorating in the face of scarce investment funds and limited sources of credit. If this pattern continues, then Russia might be forced to rely even more on the export of natural resources (and foreign investment in those sectors) for hard currency income, and find itself in a position analogous to those Third World countries that are highly sensitive to fluctuations in raw material demand from the developed industrial countries. At the same time, its wealth in natural resources has given Russia advantages over its neighbors because expensive imports are not needed to supply industry with energy and basic raw materials. Russia can now demand hard currency payment for the export of oil and gas to other former Soviet union republics, although they are often unable to pay, leading to conflicts over debt payment and energy shortages in these countries. Russia has already been able to use oil exports as a way to gain trade concessions and political leverage with Ukraine, Belarus (formerly Belorussia), and the Baltic states. Petroleum is thus an important resource in the regional balance of power.

Ultimately, Russia's position in the global economy will depend on the ability of the country's political leadership to construct a politically viable approach to domestic economic problems. In the next section, we examine the political obstacles and assets available to Russia as it seeks a path out of economic crisis.

SECTION 3

Governance and Policy-Making

Political institutions in Russia, like everything else, are in flux; they are not established structures, but part of an evolving political environment. The institutional changes that have occurred since 1985 are nothing short of revolutionary. In 1985 Russia was a union republic in a nominally federal Soviet Union; now Russia is an independent state, experiencing political battles over the construction of a new federal structure within her own borders. In 1985, the Soviet system was dominated by one political party, with clearly formed structures capable of exerting authority over societal and state institutions; now, multiple, fluid institutions compete for power, producing a state largely incapable of governing.

SOVIET POLITICAL INSTITUTIONS

Before examining present political processes and the conditions that have shaped their formation, it is necessary to review the political institutions of the Soviet period.[30] In the post-Stalinist period preceding

Gorbachev's reforms, the dominant force was the Communist Party of the Soviet Union. Although we cover contemporary political parties fully in Section 4, in this section we include a brief depiction of the Communist Party as it functioned in the Soviet period because it is almost impossible to understand the nature of Soviet state institutions without considering their relationship to the Communist Party.

In the period before Gorbachev's reforms, top organs of the Communist Party decided the basic direction and outlines of policy. In addition, the party performed three other important political functions: (1) oversight of state bodies, to assure compliance with party directives; (2) ideological leadership, through control of the educational system and mass media; and (3) personnel selection for the most important posts in state institutions as well as in the media and culture. At every level of the system, there was a structure of parallel party and state organs and a high degree of overlap between personnel in state and party bodies.

The Communist Party was a hierarchical structure (see Figure 1 on the following page). Individual members formed primary party organizations at their place of work or study. Then, in accordance with the tenets of democratic centralism, these organizations selected delegates to higher party bodies, all the way up to the Party Congress, which met every five years and elected the top party bodies, including the Poltiburo and the Central Committee. Elections within the party were uncontested, and candidates for higher party posts had already been determined by top party organs.

The Politburo, a body consisting of fourteen full members in 1981 and eleven in early 1990, was the most powerful organ in the Communist Party. It considered all important policy issues and was the real decision-making center. A larger body, the Central Committee of the Communist Party (319 members in 1981), was made up of the most important and powerful figures in the country, including regional party leaders and representatives of various economic and social interests. In the Soviet period, although the Central Committee was a party body, in reality it was the closest thing in the political system to a real parliament (although a very tame parliament at that). It probably did not fulfill any important policy-making role. It did, however, serve to facilitate communication between the Politburo and the broader elite of the country. The bureaucracy of the Communist Party,

headed by the party Secretariat, was selected by and answerable to (at least in theory) the Central Committee. In the late 1970s an estimated 1,500 employees worked in the central party bureaucracy, but at lower levels of the party there were also full-time party workers, numbering perhaps close to 100,000.

Alongside the Communist Party was the structure of the Soviet state itself. Although state institutions resembled Western parliamentary structures in a formal sense, in reality decision-making power resided in the Communist Party: One could say that the party made policy, then the state institutions were to implement it. The Soviet state was a large bureaucratic structure with day-to-day responsibility in the political sphere and more importantly, in the economic sphere, which encompassed virtually all aspects of Soviet economic life. Although the state bureaucracy was considerably larger than the party structure, it was supposed to operate in subordination to the party's directives.

In theory, the state was governed by a constitution, the last of which was adopted in 1977. However, in practice, the constitution was of symbolic rather than operational importance, with many of its principles ignored. According to the constitution, the Soviet state had three branches of government—legislative, executive, and judicial. However, the concept of **separation of powers** was considered inapplicable to Soviet society. Because the Communist Party claimed to represent the interests of society as a whole, it was deemed unnecessary to institute artificial controls over its exercise of authority. In practice, persons holding high positions in all branches of government were appointed through the *nomenklatura* system, a mechanism that assured that the Communist Party was able to fill key posts with politically reliable individuals.[31] With the power of appointment firmly under party control, it made little sense to speak of legislative or judicial independence. When the constitution was violated (as it frequently was), the courts had no independent authority to protect its provisions.

The highest representative organ of the Soviet state was the Supreme Soviet. This body was elected directly by the population, but in uncontested elections in which the single candidate (not necessarily a party member) was chosen by Communist Party organs. The Supreme Soviet was essentially a rubber-stamp body whose sessions were short and decisions always unanimous. The body served a symbolic or ideological function to demonstrate the supposedly democratic

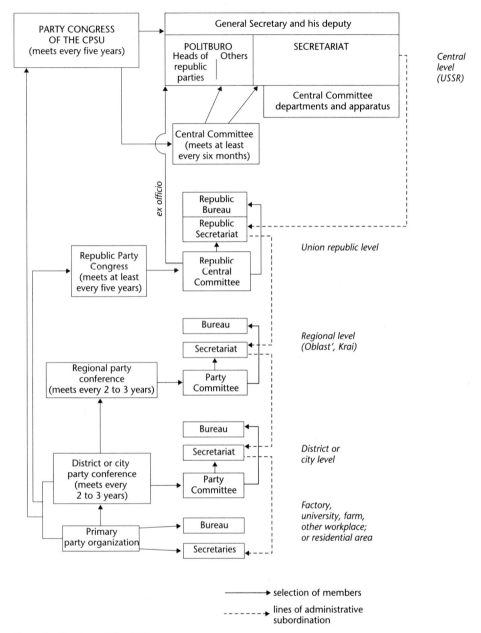

Figure 1   Structure of the CPSU
This chart shows party structures up until the Party's suspension on August 29, 1991. For clarity of presentation, some administrative levels are omitted (e.g., territories, autonomous republics and *okrugs*). Between 1989 and 1991 some variations from this scheme were introduced at the republic level and below.

character of the system. **Soviets** (or representative councils) at lower levels in the state hierarchy (the union republics, regions, cities, and rural districts) allowed many citizens to formally participate in public life, but these bodies also had only minimal impact on actual decision making, even at the local level.

Executive power resided in the Council of Ministers and a smaller Presidium of the same body. These bodies had much more power than the Supreme Soviet, as they included the heads of the powerful ministries and state committees which oversaw operation of the state-run economy. Ministers and other high state officials were approved through the party's *nomenklatura* system. The Council of Ministers was responsible for the day-to-day operation of the economy and it did exercise very real power, alongside the smaller party bureaucracy (called the apparatus). Under Communist rule, the judicial branch was subject to effective dominance by the party; "telephone justice" occurred in political cases, where judges would receive instructions from the party (by phone, in some cases).

The Soviet Union was designated a **federal system;** that is, according to the constitution certain powers were granted to the fifteen union republics (which have since become independent states). However, this was a type of "phoney federalism," in that all major aspects of life were overseen by a highly centralized Communist Party. Within the Russian Republic, now the Russian Federation, there were a number of so-called **autonomous republics,** each formed around a core non-Russian population group residing within Russia's borders. In the Soviet period, these autonomous republics were also given certain constitutional rights, which were largely unrealized in practice. In addition to the autonomous republics, the Russian republic was divided into regional administrative units, the *oblasts* and *krai,* which have no ethnic basis. So-called autonomous regions *(okrugs)* and autonomous districts also existed; like the autonomous republics these were ethnically based but had more limited formal powers.

A process of radical institutional change commenced under Gorbachev.[32] In 1988, Gorbachev initiated a process of constitutional and institutional restructuring which involved competitive elections, increased political pluralism, reduced Communist Party dominance, a revitalized legislative branch of government, and renegotiation of the terms of Soviet federalism. Although Gorbachev retained his post as general secretary of the Communist Party until August 1991, by March 1990 the locus of political leadership was shifting to the Soviet state, to assure a broader base of political legitimacy and support. The state's new authority was embodied in the newly created office of president, also occupied by Gorbachev. In the perestroika period, Gorbachev had initiated a process

to harmonize the constitution with political reality, and many constitutional amendments were adopted that altered existing political institutions. Together, these changes moved the political system slowly and unsurely in a vague direction resembling the liberal democratic systems of the West.

During the Gorbachev period, events surrounding the new political institutions elicited great public attention; in 1989 and 1990 citizens were often riveted to television broadcasts of the first genuine political debates in the new Soviet parliament, elected in 1989 on the basis of the first competitive elections these people had experienced. Before long, however, people became disillusioned with the new institutions as they seemed to be "talk shops" where much was said but little was resolved. Meanwhile, Gorbachev's institutional restructuring was interrupted by the failed coup d'état of August 1991. The attempted coup was intended to halt the democratization process and counter centrifugal tendencies pulling the USSR apart, but its consequences were just the opposite. The failed coup precipitated the USSR's collapse and ushered in even more radical political changes in the newly independent Russian Federation.

Changes in political institutions of the Russian republic itself began before the Russian Federation achieved independence in December 1991; before the demise of the USSR, these changes generally paralleled those made in central Soviet organs. A new post of president was also created for the Russian republic and on June 12, 1991, Boris Yeltsin was elected by direct popular vote as its first incumbent. This election gave Yeltsin an important base of popular legitimacy in his first two years in office.[33] By October 1993, it was clear that the new institutional structures were not functioning well; the October 1993 showdown ushered in a new stage in Russia's efforts to construct viable post-Communist political structures. However, the leadership of the independent Russian Federation faced a hornets' nest of problems in its attempt to adapt the muddled political institutions inherited from the Soviet period to the new challenges involved in trying to build a more democratic but stable system within Russia itself.

ORGANIZATION OF THE STATE

Since 1992, the Russian leadership has attempted simultaneous multiple "revolutions from above"—in the economic sphere, the political sphere, and the

TABLE 5   **Level of Trust in Various Institutions, May 1994 (percent of respondents)**

	Trust	Don't Trust
Army	38	28
President	20	50
Mass media	19	40
State Duma	16	41
Trade unions	16	45
Enterprise managers	15	41
Courts	14	46
Government	14	50
Regional leaders	13	43
Police	13	55
Federation Council	11	41
Banking and business circles	10	46
Political parties, movements	5	52

Source: Analytical Center of the Institute for Sociopolitical Research of the Russian Academy of Sciences, *Reformirovanie Rossii: Mify i real'nost' 1989–1994 (Reform of Russia: Myths and Realities 1989–1994),* authors and compilers of the volume G. V. Osipov (head), V. K. Lavashov, V. V. Lokosov, and A. T. Klop'ev (Moscow: "Academia," 1994), 358. This is a translation with some reordering of the institutions.

social sphere. This comprehensive upheaval has produced instability and uncertainty; political institutions are a battleground for playing out political conflicts. Often it seems that everything is in flux, as politicians clash not only over policy, but over the proper role of various institutions and processes in resolving policy issues. Political institutions in general suffer low levels of public respect and legitimacy (see Table 5), and their decisions are often ignored, contradicted, or contravened by citizens and public officials.

The weakness of Russia's political institutions is both a cause and effect of the economic crisis. Stalled reform in one sphere retards progress in others. The absence of strong and legitimate political institutions has hindered the state from effectively pursuing its economic agenda; at the same time, the economic crisis has hindered agreement about the shape of new political institutions. At this time, Russian political institutions are not permanent political fixtures, but at best temporary forums for the continuing struggle over fundamental interests and values.

Contested Principles of Governance

Agreement on the basic principles of governance has been one of the most difficult issues for the new Russia.

Because of the rapid and thoroughgoing change of the last five years, it has been difficult to build the foundation for a new consensus for politics. At the end of the Gorbachev period, the underlying values of the Soviet system had been questioned, challenged, and mostly rejected by the public and prominent political figures. But high expectations about the bright "post-Communist" future were soon dashed; even now, the struggle continues over which basic values should govern the new political system. A new Russian constitution, adopted in December 1993, embodies many of the basic ideas underlying Western presidential systems; however, it is unclear how these ideas will be interpreted, applied, and realized. Will the new constitution provide the basis for enduring political structures for the Russian state, or will it represent another transient phase in the process of political conflict and change? Indicative of the uncertainty is growing nostalgia among some leaders (military elites) and segments of the public (older age groups) for the Soviet past—for its stability, relative equality, and predictability. Concerns about Russian identity and interests are also increasingly evident as different political parties and leaders show support for diverse visions of Russia's future and the appropriate roles for various political institutions.

The lack of consensus regarding basic political principles is illustrated by the following examples. One important issue concerns the importance of honoring proper democratic procedures, regardless of whether the desired political outcome is achieved. As mentioned in Section 1, the Leninist notion of democracy emphasized outcomes rather than procedures. For the most part, this vanguard idea has been explicitly rejected by Russian political elites in favor of the more liberal ideals of democratic decision making and "rule of law." In theory, it is agreed that established procedures and legal provisions should be honored even if decisions reached do not always accord with the preferences of the political leadership. In practice, however, Russia's political leaders appear inclined to circumvent procedures of democratic decision making outlined in legal documents. Since 1992, Yeltsin has repeatedly issued presidential decrees to enact policies that assure his desired "outcome," an approach that became a point of contention between the president and the Russian parliament in October 1993. Initially, disputes over the legality of certain decrees were adjudicated by the new Russian Constitutional Court, but in October 1993 another presidential decree disbanded the court, leaving no route for legal resolution of such disputes until the court was reformed in early 1995.

Another contested issue is the relationship of order to liberty. The Russian population has long regarded the state as the guarantor of stability and security; Russian culture manifests a simultaneous attraction to and fear of anarchy. Some Russian commentators have described the present situation in Russia as one of disorder, given the decline in the state's capacity to govern and the unpredictability of economic and social life. In this context, can some undemocratic actions of the government be justified on the grounds that they contribute to order and stability? For example, following the 1993 October events, when Yeltsin disbanded and beseiged the old Supreme Soviet, some newspapers and political parties were temporarily banned and criticism of the proposed constitution was forbidden on Russian television. Provisions of the new Russian constitution also allow a similar curtailment of civil liberties if their enforcement threatens, among other things, the constitutional order, health, or state security. Although most liberal democracies have similar clauses in their constitutions, their application is governed by the political culture and norms affecting the political leadership. With its lack of a democratic tradition, weak norms of political tolerance, and traditional acceptance of strong state authority, solutions in Russia that emphasize order over liberty are very likely. In 1994 and 1995 the spate of murders of journalists who were investigating or had reported on government scandals and corruption suggests that there exists in Russia a deficiency of both order and liberty.

A similar ambivalence exists over the relationship between individual rights and social (communal) rights and obligations. The new Russian constitution guarantees protection of those individual civil liberties traditionally emphasized in liberal democracies (speech, thought, association), as well as the right to private ownership. At the same time, social rights—such as the right to housing, medical care, a decent environment, social security, and free education—are also guaranteed, suggesting a continuing commitment to communal responsibility for the welfare of the individual. But the relative importance of individual and communal rights is left undefined, even though they may often collide with each other. For example, when can individual property rights be restricted in the interests of assuring protection of the environment? Should governments be obliged to maintain a network of welfare programs even at the expense of economic stabilization? Furthermore, guarantees provided in the constitution may be too ambitious for the weak new state and economy to realize; the danger exists that they may again be paper rights rather than real ones. More broadly in Russia, there is continuing disagreement over the extent to which Russia should seek a unique path, as opposed to imitating Western models of development. Yeltsin's program initially embodied a Westernizing approach, but its disastrous economic consequences have increased political support for a specifically Russian approach to unique Russian problems.

Several concrete issues have been the focus of conflict over political institutions since 1991. The two most important and contentious issues involve (1) the balance of power between the legislative and executive branches and (2) the nature of Russian federalism. Although the new constitution adopted in December 1993 defines political institutions in each of these spheres on a formal level, only the continued political struggle will determine whether these definitions will be adequate to deal with the challenges ahead and whether the constitution itself will survive the next stages of the political battle.

The Executive and Legislative Branches at Loggerheads

Once Russia became independent in August 1991, the idea of separation of powers was, at least in theory, accepted and integrated into the new Russian state structures. Then conflicts between the branches of government gradually began to emerge and intensify. The support offered to Yeltsin by the Russian parliament in August 1991 when it stood united against the antireform coup plotters faded once Russia gained independence. The conflict came to involve not only important disputes about the pace and shape of the economic reform process, but also fundamental disputes about who should exercise power. By mid-1993, a stalemate had developed which seemed to immobilize the central government in its efforts to address the economic crisis; this paralysis of central state power encouraged political leaders at the regional level to claim more and more political power for themselves. It was in this context that the dramatic rupture of September/October 1993 occurred, when Yeltsin unconstitutionally disbanded the parliament and placed it under siege.

Amendments to the Russian constitution adopted in the late 1980s and early 1990s established a new structure of state institutions, including the Russian presidency and a new parliamentary body, the Congress of People's Deputies (CPD) and a smaller subgroup of it, the Supreme Soviet. In some ways the new institutions were altered versions of the old Soviet ones, but in other ways they were constructed on the basis of radically new principles such as competitive elections, a rejection of the single-party system, separation of powers, and judicial independence. By late 1990, it was evident that the changes already introduced required an entirely new constitution and that the newly established political institutions themselves needed to be examined in this context. Yet the process for negotiating and adopting a new constitution became an issue of intense political contest. In adopting a new constitution, these newly formed bodies would in effect be legislating themselves out of existence. Because the political stakes were high and experience with democratic decision making low, it is not surprising that the transition to a new constitutional order led to ruptures, polarization, and conflict.

After a period of discussion and debate, three main constitutional drafts emerged, including one from the president's office and one from a commission established by the Supreme Soviet (the smaller organ of the Russian parliament). The existing constitution gave the expanded parliament (the Congress of People's Deputies) legal authority to make constitutional changes. Since this unwieldy body was unlikely to agree on any single variant of the new constitution, discussion arose regarding alternative modes for adopting the document. Should a special constituent assembly be called? Or should a draft constitution be put to a referendum vote? If so, which draft should be presented for a vote? In short, controversy erupted not only about the possible content of the document, but also about procedures for adopting it. Increasingly, everything was up for grabs regarding the rules of the game, reflecting the lack of consensus and the high stakes involved.

On economic policy issues, Yeltsin complained that the parliament was holding back his market reform efforts. Indeed, the Supreme Soviet generally did take a more conservative position than did the president and his advisers. Representatives of the old Communist elite still had considerable representation there; the parliament may also have been more responsive to public anxieties about the possible social costs of the economic shock therapy. The parliamentary leadership was unhappy with the concentration of power in the president's hands through his use of the power of decree. An opposition coalition formed within the parliament, led by Vice President Aleksandr Rutskoi and the chair of the Russian Supreme Soviet, Ruslan Khasbulatov, both former Yeltsin allies. The Constitutional Court issued decisions regarding the constitutionality of various actions by the president and parliament, but increasingly the court's impartiality was drawn into question, because its head, Valerii Zorkin, seemed to issue judgments before examining all the facts.

In an effort to strengthen his position, Yeltsin called a referendum on himself and his reform program on April 25, 1993. Yeltsin won the vote, both for his personal leadership and his economic reform path. Nonetheless, he was unable to achieve a new momentum for pushing his reform forward. The economy continued to decline, and the Supreme Soviet continued to support policies representing a more gradualistic approach to the reform process. At the same time, the conflict over construction of a new constitution continued. The legislative and executive branches were locked in an apparently irresolvable conflict involving policy disagreements, personality clashes, and institutional rivalry. The deadlock at the center further undermined the state's ability to halt the downward economic spiral. Neither side seemed willing to compromise, leading to a dangerous polarization of political forces. The so-called centrists, those who sought to maintain a moderate position between the two extremes, were rebuffed by Yeltsin's forces. The inability of the leadership to resolve the conflict contributed to a continuing decline in the popular credibility and legitimacy of all political institutions.

The constitutional and political stalemate reached a dramatic outcome when Yeltsin illegally disbanded the parliament in September 1993. After the president's forces placed the seat of the parliament, the White House, under virtual siege, there was a violent showdown with supporters of the Supreme Soviet holding out in the building. Yeltsin then decreed that a constitutional draft should be put to a referendum vote; but only he and his advisers determined the exact content of the proposed document. According to Yeltsin's order, elections for a new parliament were to be held simultaneously with the referendum vote; however, the legal basis for those elections (determining the structure of the new parliament and the mechanisms of its selection) were outlined in the constitutional draft to be voted on at the same time. If the constitutional referendum failed to pass, the elections would have no legal foundation, leaving Yeltsin as the sole elected official still in place. Proponents of the constitutional draft could thus argue that rejecting the constitutional proposal would send the entire political system into a tailspin.

In charting this precarious course, Yeltsin's actions violated the existing constitution. He argued that a referendum itself was a mechanism of democratic decision making and therefore would assure a democratic outcome, even if specific provisions of the existing "rule of law" were circumvented. In addition to disbanding the Supreme Soviet and the constitutional court, Yeltsin placed restrictions on the press and media in the period leading up to the referendum vote, reinforcing doubts about the legitimacy of the process. A draft of the proposed constitution was published in the press, but time constraints limited public knowledge of its details. The population was skeptical about the honesty of the vote, especially because it seemed that central media coverage was slanted in favor of the president's position.

Despite these problems, the referendum was declared to have passed; 58 percent of those voting supported the draft, but turnout was reported to be only 54 percent (nonetheless, above the 50 percent mark required for passage). Widespread allegations of election fraud and misreporting of results were believed within Russia and abroad, but these were hard to prove, especially because precinct voting results were not released by the central electoral commission. Most opposition groups and critics finally accepted the referendum as quasi-legitimate because this represented the "lesser of the evils." If the vote were deemed unsuccessful, then Russia would, in effect, have no operative constitution and parliament, and this vacuum would potentially put even more power in the hands of the executive branch.

Some wonder whether Yeltsin's illegal actions of October 1993, which laid the groundwork for the December referendum, might not compromise the legitimacy of the new constitution itself. What would prevent the government, president, or some other force from suspending the new constitution in order to resolve any future political impasse? This scenario is not unlikely because by its own provisions, the new constitution is very difficult to amend and may not be flexible enough to respond to changing or unforeseen dilemmas. By overriding the "rule of law" in the name of higher goals (order, democracy, reform) Yeltsin may have undermined norms of civility, tolerance, and legality, and laid the groundwork either for an authoritarian path or for continued institutional instability.

Defining Russian Federalism

The collapse of the Soviet Union was precipitated by the demands of some union republics for more autonomy, and then finally independence. After the Russian Federation itself became an independent state, the problem of constructing a viable federal structure resurfaced. Some of Russia's constituent units, particularly the former autonomous republics and regions *(okrugs)* began to demand greater autonomy over their own affairs.[34] One of these units (Chechnya-Ingushetia) split into two new political entities; Chechnya declared independence from the Russian Federation, but the central

War Within Russia's Borders: The Chechnya Crisis

Despite its small size (it is estimated that the population in 1994 was 600,000), the "break-away republic" of Chechnya holds an important position on the southern border of Russia. Chechnya is also widely perceived as a safe haven for the mafia and criminal elements that operate in Russia. These facts, as well as fears that Chechnya's example might embolden other recalcitrant republics to pursue outright independence, in all likelihood motivated Russia to send troops into Chechnya on December 11, 1994, igniting a regional civil war.

Chechnya has long been a trouble spot for Russia and later the USSR. Prior to its incorporation into the Russian empire in 1859, and again after the Bolshevik revolution in 1917, local forces fought to maintain Chechnya's independence. In 1924 Chechnya was made part of the USSR and in 1934 was joined with an adjacent region, Ingushetia, to form a single, autonomous republic within the Soviet Union. During World War II, following an anti-Soviet uprising, Joseph Stalin deported hundreds of thousands of Chechens (along with other peoples from the Caucausus region) to Soviet Central Asia.

Taking advantage of the ongoing political upheaval in the USSR in October 1991, the newly elected president of the republic, Dzhokar Dudaev, declared Chechnya's independence from Russia. In 1992 Checheno-Ingushetia was officially recognized as two separate republics. Follow-

Chechnya and Region

ing its split from Ingushetia, Chechen leaders continued to pursue the republic's claim to independence. The Russian government staunchly rejected their claim. At the same time, internal political conflicts began to emerge in

government rejected the claim. The autonomous republics were renamed republics, and demanded special privileges, presented in a Federal Treaty signed by the heads of eighteen of the twenty republics and the central authorities in March 1992. This treaty elicited opposition from leaders of the *oblasts* and *krai,* who demanded an equal status in the federal structure with the republics. The issue became a major source of contention in the constitutional negotiations. In the draft constitution presented to the electorate in December 1993, concessions granted to the republics in the Federal Treaty were cut back somewhat, and *oblast'* and *krai* were given equal status with the republics. Leaders of the republics protested, arguing that their units should have a higher status and greater autonomy than the *oblast'* and *krai* which, under the Soviet system, had a lower status. It is significant that in twelve of the twenty republics of Russia, the referendum on the constitution either did not win a majority or turnout was less than the 50 percent needed, possibly indicating dissatisfaction with the powers of the republics, as defined in the new constitution.

Beyond the constitutional drama, many powers have in fact devolved to the subnational level since the early 1990s, often with an unclear or contested legal basis. The central government's limited capacity to govern and the deadlock between the central legislative and executive branches have allowed subnational authorities to assume more power. Specific areas of conflict involve regional control of valuable natural resources, retention of regional and municipal ownership of buildings or factories and the revenues they generate, division of tax revenues, responsibility for social welfare programs (which the center wishes to transfer to the regions), provision of central subsidies for local enterprises or for industrial restructuring, and issues of regional equalization.

Under the new constitution, the eighty-nine constituent units of the federation are represented in the upper house of the representative body, the Federation Council. However, many of the disputed issues between the regions and the center are not clearly resolved by the constitution, despite general statements about jurisdictions and shared responsibilities. Since

Chechnya. In 1993 the Chechen parliament voted to impeach Dudaev, who proceeded to dissolve the parliament. An opposition Provisional Council was formed in August 1994. Fighting then broke out between government (pro-independence) and opposition forces.

The Russian intervention in December 1994 evoked widespread opposition within the Russian Federation and its leadership circles, extending even to former Boris Yeltsin allies, such as Yegor Gaidar and other reform figures. Some opposed the military intervention completely and pressed for a political solution; others were primarily critical of the ineffective manner in which the war effort was carried out. The campaign was poorly organized and internal dissension within the army and among various security forces resulted in demoralized troops, inconsistent strategies, and finally the rampant use of brutal measures against civilians. Attempts to achieve a cease-fire and to set up an effective government of national revival were unsuccessful in the early months of 1995. On January 19 Russian troops captured the presidential palace of Grozny, the capital of Chechnya. The war continued to flare, however, and Russian soldiers found the fighting particularly difficult in the surrounding mountainous terrain.

On June 14, in a dramatic turn of events, Chechen fighters, facing near defeat elsewhere, took control of the Russian city of Budennovsk, which lies some 70 miles north of the Chechen border in the Russian province of Stavropol. They held some 1,500 hostages in the local hospital, graphically injecting the consequences of the war onto the Russian political stage. After Yeltsin's unsuccessful efforts to resolve the crisis and a failed attempt to storm the hospital to free the hostages (only about 150 escaped, others were killed), prime minister Viktor Chernomyrdin stepped in to seek a negotiated settlement. On June 17–18 he engaged in personal negotiations with the local Chechen commander, Shamil Basaev. The two sides finally reached an agreement which provided for the freeing of the hostages in exchange for a cease-fire on Chechen territory, the opening of peace talks with Dudaev (with whom the Russians had refused to negotiate earlier), and safe passage for the hostage-takers.

Chernomyrdin's compromise position evoked further dissension in Moscow, as the Duma mustered a successful vote of no-confidence in the government. Some of the opposition was in rejection of Chernomyrdin's concessions, while other sentiments applauded the return to a political route of resolving the issue. Ultimately, the Duma backed off after Yeltsin announced the dismissal of three ministers, thus placing responsibility on their shoulders for the botched policy which led to the Budennovsk fiasco.

The resolution of the hostage crisis led, at least in the short term, to renewed attempts to negotiate a settlement to the Russian-Chechen conflict and probably bolstered Chernomyrdin's status in Russia as a result. In an agreement signed on July 23, 1995, the Russians agreed to a prisoner exchange and some disarmament of the region. Both sides also agreed in principle to the holding of elections in Chechnya, but when these were undertaken in December 1995, renewed violence ensued.

1994, individual treaties have been negotiated with some of the more recalcitrant republics within the Russian Federation, such as Tatarstan and Bashkortostan. This process involves a continued reliance on an individualized ad hoc approach to constructing federalism, a process likely to engender continuing perceptions of favoritism and discrimination toward particular republics and regions. The likely results are an escalation of demands for regional privilege and a drop in the perceived fairness of central policy.

The most troublesome case for the Russian authorities proved to be Chechnya, a small republic in the southernmost part of the country that declared independence in 1991. Conflict escalated in December 1994 when the Yeltsin government attempted to oust the recalcitrant government of Chechnya (led by its elected president, Dzhokar Dudaev) by force, leading to an extended and bloody regional war that further undermined both the domestic legitimacy and international stature of the Russian government. The conflict was the second time (the first was Yeltsin's dissolution of the Russian parliament in September/October 1993) that failure to reach a political solution led to the use of violence on a scale shocking to the Russian public and, in the Chechnya case, the international community. The war in Chechnya continued in the mountainous terrain of the republic even after the Russian capture of the capital Grozny in early 1995, illustrating the unresolved nature of central/regional relations in Russia and the inability of the central government to enforce its position by political means.

THE EXECUTIVE

The new Russian constitution adopted in December 1993 shifts the balance of power decisively in the direction of the executive branch. The structures embodied in the new constitution resemble the French presidential system in many ways, but some critics in Russia call it an authoritarian constitution because it places so much power in the president's hands (see Figure 2 on the following page). As in France, the Russian constitution creates ample room for conflict between the legislative and executive branches. However, a combination of factors (including constitutional

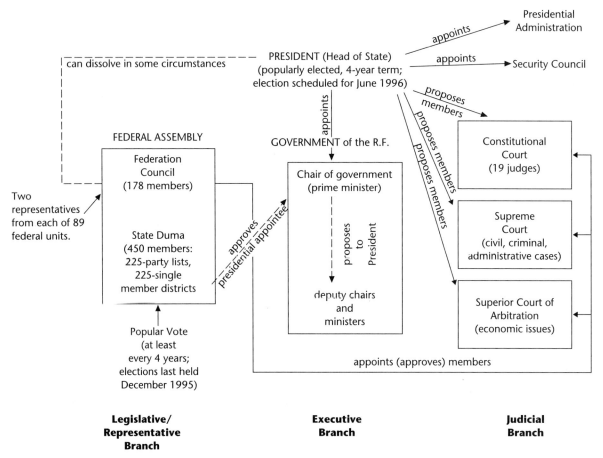

Figure 2   Political Institutions of the Russian Federation (R.F.), December 1993 to the Present

provisions, political culture, political party fragmentation, and regionalism) work to give more power to the Russian president than to the French president.

The constitution designates the president as the head of state, but unlike in Germany, the office is not a figurehead position. At the same time, the constitution places executive power in the government of Russia, which is headed by the prime minister. The president is elected directly by the population (every four years according to the constitution), as is the parliament (in completely separate elections, normally for four-year terms, but the 1993 vote was for two years). This structure encourages conflict between the president and the legislative branch because the president's party or supporters do not necessarily hold the balance of power in the parliament. The situation is complicated because the lower house of the parliament (the State Duma) must approve the president's nominee for

prime minister; if the Duma rejects the president's nominee three times, the president may dissolve the Duma, appoint an interim prime minister, and call new parliamentary elections. Likewise, although the Duma can issue a vote of no-confidence in the government (that is, the prime minister and cabinet), the incentive to do so is reduced because the vote must be successfully repeated again after three months, when the president can call new parliamentary elections, even though he would remain in office. Given this structure, if the parliament chooses to reject the president's choice of prime minister or issue a vote of no-confidence in the government, the move is tantamount to a suicide notice.

In practice, the new structures established in the constitution have produced a state in conflict with itself, but still surprisingly more stable than one might have expected. Following an electoral rebuff in the

December 1993 parliamentary elections, Yeltsin emerged with a parliament as potentially obstructive to his purposes as the one he had disbanded in September 1993. Support for Yeltsin's leadership declined further in the subsequent two years. The prime minister, Viktor Chernomyrdin, however, proved to be a fairly respected compromise figure, and several attempted votes of no-confidence failed to bring down his government.

The new constitution provides for a bicameral parliament known as the Federal Assembly. It consists of an upper house, the Federation Council, which represents Russia's constituent federal units, and a lower house, the State Duma, which represents the population through direct popular vote for candidates and parties. The constitution grants parliament certain powers in the legislative and budgetary areas that can be exercised effectively only if the body operates with a high degree of unity; in practice parliamentary powers can generally be overridden by the president. Both houses may establish committees, commissions, and hold legislative hearings to review draft laws submitted for consideration by its deputies, the executive branch, the president, and other organs specified in the constitution. Although most laws must be approved by both houses of the legislative body, the president may veto decisions of the parliament. To override the veto, two-thirds of the members of the Federal Assembly must support the original wording of the bill. Each house of parliament has the authority to confirm certain presidential appointees, in addition to the prime minister. For example, the State Duma also appoints the chair of the Central Bank of Russia, based on the president's nomination, and the Federation Council appoints federal judges on the same basis. In some cases, failure to approve the president's nominees has produced stalemate or prevented the offices under consideration from functioning.

One of the president's most useful powers is the authority to issue decrees, even those that concern contentious issues such as privatization, salaries of state workers, the running of the economy, and anti-crime measures. Presidential decrees have the force of law. In some cases, parliamentary decisions have been overridden by decrees; or failing to get parliamentary approval for his initiatives, the president can simply decree them law through his own power. The president's decision to launch the offensive in Chechnya was not brought before either house of the parliament, despite strong objections to it from a broad range of political groups. In September 1995 Yeltsin issued a decree delaying local elections until after the presidential elections scheduled for June 1996 despite the fact that just three weeks earlier he had signed a law on local government (passed by the Federal Assembly) which required municipal elections to be held by February 1996. The Federal Assembly appealed to the Constitutional Court to invalidate Yeltsin's action; however, the constitution does not provide clear guidance in such situations.

Other powers granted to the president include a right to call a state of emergency, impose martial law, grant pardons, call referendums, and temporarily suspend actions of other state organs if he deems them to contradict the constitution or federal laws. Some of these actions must be confirmed by other state organs (for example the upper house of the parliament, the Federation Council), however the constitution is vague on resolution of disputes over such actions. The president is commander-in-chief of the armed forces and heads a body called the Security Council, in charge of security matters broadly conceived. He conducts affairs of state with other nations. Impeachment of the president is a complicated process involving the Duma, the Federation Council, and the Constitutional Court.

The ministers of the government (other than the prime minister) do not need to be approved by the parliament; they are recommended to the president by the prime minister. Like the president, the government can issue decrees, but these can be overridden by presidential decrees. The government proposes the budget, proposes legislation (as does the president), and acts to ensure implementation of a unified state policy in areas such as economic policy, culture, education, defense, security, and protection of civil rights. The actual day-to-day work of drafting policy documents on major social and economic issues happens largely within the executive branch of government. Without disciplined parties in Russia, and none that link the executive and the legislative branches (as would exist in a "normal" parliamentary system), governmental proposals do not have a dedicated constituency in the parliament.

The future of the Russian presidency is unknown. Some wonder whether there are adequate limits on the power of the presidency to prevent either Yeltsin or a future incumbent from using the office as an instrument of authoritarian rule. New elections are formally scheduled for June 1996, but presidential hopefuls were already active in early 1995.

The National Bureaucracy

The new Russian government inherited a large bureaucratic apparatus from the Soviet state. Market reform reduces the role of the state in economic management; thus a decrease in the size of the state bureaucracy should follow. After the December 1993 elections, the number of ministries and state committees was reduced, but repeated efforts to downsize the executive bureaucratic apparatus have been only partially successful. Many agencies have reorganized, new ones have formed, former Soviet and Russian republic agencies have merged, old bodies have been renamed, and personnel has been shifted from one office to the other. In some cases, Russian ministries are essentially reincarnations of former Soviet ministries, but in most cases their functions have changed dramatically as their role in the actual operation of the economy has declined. In general, the economic ministries play an increasingly marginal role, one that is more regulatory, coordinating, or auxiliary in nature, rather than directive as during the Soviet era. During periods of restructuring, some agencies of the state virtually stop functioning.

The repeated reorganization of the state's bureaucratic structures partially reflects an attempt to redefine state functions in light of the restructuring of the economy; another factor involves bureaucratic and personalistic politics—that is, individuals trying to assure a secure position for their agencies, their clients or allies, and themselves under conditions of severe systemic upheaval. **Patron-client networks,** which were important in the Soviet period, still continue to play a key role. These linkages are similar to "old boys' networks" in the West (and they most often involve men in the Russian case); they underscore the importance of personal career ties between individuals as they rise in bureaucratic or political structures. New appointees often bring staff members from a previous post with them. The network of patron-client connections is more complex and less transparent now than it was in the Soviet period, but it is equally important. With the collapse of the old *nomenklatura* system for appointing government officials and the absence of a functioning system of civil service appointments, poli-

ticians and government officials look to people with whom they have past career links or whom they know and trust as they staff their organizations or develop alliances in other agencies.

Along with the state bureaucracy, the president is granted the power to establish a presidential administration, his personal staff, which is estimated at around 1,800 people. The president also uses outside consultants to advise his staff on particular issues. Finally, the president is empowered to appoint representatives at the regional level, and, until 1996, governors of the regions as well.

The Military

Historically, the military has not played a direct political role in Russian and Soviet politics.[35] Communist Party dominance over the military was never seriously challenged because the party controlled military appointments and gave preferential treatment to the military sector. At times, however, the military did assert its interests in conflicts between civilian leaders. Most notably, Khrushchev's loss of military support may have been an important factor in his removal from office in 1964. In post-Stalinist times, the military was almost always represented in the top decision-making body of the party, the Politburo. The military also formed a powerful lobby group during the process of resource allocation, and indeed generally those industries associated with military production and the military itself received access to the best resources available, producing a powerful military-industrial complex. In the late Soviet period, at least a quarter of the state budget was devoted to military expenditures.

In the late 1980s, several developments led observers to question whether the Soviet (and later the Russian) military might begin to intervene more actively in civilian political affairs. First, the threatened break-up of the USSR and the loss of superpower status alarmed most military officers. Following the collapse of the USSR, issues of concern to the military were high on the political agenda, including tensions between newly independent Ukraine and Russia over control of the Black Sea fleet; disputes over control of the nuclear arsenal located outside Russia; wars in former Soviet republics near Russia; removal of Soviet (now Russian) troops from other former Soviet republics, Germany, and other Eastern European states; and the large number of Russians (including military personnel) living in former Soviet republics. The military's goals are to maintain an integrated defense capacity and doctrine which would ensure Russia's regional dominance. These goals have not always coincided with positions of the civilian leadership, which has emphasized the diversion of resources to civilian economic sectors.

Both Gorbachev and Yeltsin oversaw a reduction in military expenditures. Reduced budget allocations can impede the military's ability to maintain a high technological standard, and they have a decided impact on living conditions for military personnel, which in some cases, have declined precipitously. Removal of former Soviet (Russian) forces from previously allied states in Eastern Europe and from former Soviet republics has increased the pressure on the military's capability to keep its troops happy. Some factories in the military-industry sector find it difficult to convert to civilian use, threatening layoffs on a large scale. Finally, beginning in the late 1980s, draft resistance increased under the influence of the liberal environment created by glasnost and continues to be a problem in Russia today.

Despite these tensions, thus far the military establishment has not directly intervened in civilian political affairs. It may not be sufficiently united to assume this role, but neither is there a tradition of military intervention in politics. During the August 1991 coup attempt, troops remained loyal to Yeltsin and Gorbachev even though the minister of defense was among the coup plotters; there were no orders to fire on Soviet citizens who took to the streets in defense of civilian government's reform course. Again in October 1993, despite some apparent hesitancy in military circles, military units defended the government's position, but this time fired on civilian protesters, shocking the country. Because Yeltsin depended on the military to quell the opposition, it appears that in subsequent months he felt pressured to take positions favorable to the military on several issues, for example opposition to NATO membership for former Eastern European allies, increased military expenditures, and more assertive expressions of support for Russians living in former Soviet republics. An indication of increasing politicization of the military occurred in late 1995: The minister of defense announced that over 120 candidates for the single-member-district races were being sponsored by the military. In addition, several prominent military officers or former officers figured in the leadership of electoral blocs and parties. For

A comment on Russia's military in the Chechnya crisis. Source: Vadim Misjuk, courtesy of *Nezavisimaia Gazeta (The Independent Newspaper)*.

example, Alexander Lebed, former commander of Russia's 14th Army and presidential hopeful took on a leading role in the electoral bloc, the Congress of Russian Communities; Boris Gromov, former commander of Russian troops in Afghanistan, played a leading role in the new "My Fatherland" bloc; and Alexander Rutskoi, also the former vice president of the Russian Federation, sought to further his political prospects through the creation of the "Great Power" *(Derzhava)* Party.

Throughout 1993, Yeltsin decreed pay raises for military personnel to calm discontent. In debates over the federal budget in 1994, a major issue of contention was the level of allocation to the military. Although allocations were increased as a result of military lobbying, there are claims they are inadequate to quell potential discontent. The possibility of splits within military ranks or on a regional basis have intensified concerns about the regional devolution of power. The dismal performance of the military in the Chechnya offensive, as well as debate within the military itself about that campaign and resistance by some field commanders to carrying out orders, raised serious questions not only about the military's capabilities, but also about the reliability of the command structure.[36] No doubt, the political leadership of Russia will be attentive to the interests of the military in the coming years, if only because instability and discontent within its ranks could destabilize society at large. The military has generally been highly regarded by the population, but its performance in the Chechnya conflict will likely lower its popular status to the same low rating as other state institutions.

Semipublic and Nonformal Aspects of Policy-Making

As noted previously, large state enterprises and ministries associated with the military-industrial complex, the energy sector, and heavy industry were powerful political actors under the Soviet system. These enterprises employ large numbers of workers and represent a large part of the country's productive capacity; therefore their managers remain a potent political force in contemporary Russia. Some of these enterprises continue to be state-run, while most have been privatized, that is, turned into joint-stock companies in which "insiders" often hold a controlling interest.

The strength of this "industrialist" lobby in the government is visible in Viktor Chernomyrdin, the prime minister since late 1992, who comes from this group. This is particularly significant, because political blocs and parties representing the **industrialists** (for example, the centrist force, the Civic Union) did not gain enough votes to win party representation in the parliament in the 1993 elections. Notwithstanding their electoral defeat, the power of the industrialists in the government derives from several factors. First, this group includes the managers or former managers of many of the country's largest industrial enterprises, those that employ large numbers of workers and, in some cases (like the energy sector), provide key resources for the economy as a whole. Because the failure or bankruptcy of these large enterprises could trigger major social or economic dislocations, when they lobby for continued subsidies for their plants (needed to pay wages or maintain at least minimum levels of production), they wield substantial bargaining power. Second, these managers can rely on their networks of old contacts to help them solve problems facing their firms (such as getting needed supplies, contracts, or privileged access to foreign markets). Finally, many of these individuals are competent and skilled in running their large firms. They have hands-on experience; they understand production in their industries; and they have survived thus far, indicating skills of adaptation and flexibility. In short, they "have

their feet on the ground," whereas, some allege, the pro-market economists in Moscow are ignorant about what really happens in the provinces and operate from a reform blueprint that bears little resemblance to reality.

In addition to the industrialists, other less formal forces influence the operations of government. One important force is patron-client relations discussed earlier. In general, even outside the ranks of the state bureaucracy, personal contacts continue to keep the Russian system going. A large proportion of high officials in all walks of life were former party members or held high posts before the end of Soviet rule; others forged their alliances during the perestroika period.

The influence of corruption is pervasive, both in and out of government. Special payments or favors are commonly received for issuing licenses, legal documents, or access to other goods and services needed to carry out economic activities. The Russian public is understandably cynical about the honesty of its politicians and government officials, an attitude that undermines the legitimacy of the new political institutions. Russians frequently refer to the **mafia,** a network of criminals who demand payoffs and protection money not only from private businesses but also from state organizations or public officials. Reasons for certain policy decisions are often hidden from public scrutiny, particularly if they concern the disposition of former state property, granting of special privileges or contracts, or other lucrative ventures. The Russian mafia is probably not a tightly organized national network, but it does operate effectively in certain regions and localities, and it has linkages abroad to assure avenues for gaining or exporting hard currency windfalls.

OTHER INSTITUTIONS

The Judiciary

Concepts such as judicial independence have no tradition either in prerevolutionary Russia or in the Soviet era. Under Soviet power, the courts were answerable to the Communist Party and judges were selected through the *nomenklatura* system of party appointment. Likewise, the principle of "rule of law" was poorly understood. Laws in the Soviet period often had more of an ideological than a legal function; they were intended to demonstrate the commitment of the authorities to certain widely proclaimed principles, but practice often deviated greatly from the norms and procedures set out in law. One notable example was the status of the Soviet constitution. The 1977 version of the document clearly gave union republics the right of secession from the USSR (Article 17), but this provision was never recognized in practice and became an issue of major political contention in the period before the collapse of the USSR. Various civil liberties such as freedom of the press, speech, and assembly were also guaranteed in the constitution (Article 125), but the guarantees had no real meaning. Gorbachev, however, did emphasize the importance of constructing a "law-based state," and he took several measures to make laws conform more closely with political practice. Notions of judicial independence and due process were widely accepted during this period; however, implementing them has proven to be a difficult and not wholly successful endeavor.

One step in this direction was the formation of the Soviet Committee of Constitutional Review in 1990. This body, however, could not issue binding decisions; its authority was limited to advising other political institutions on the constitutionality of various actions or laws. In Russia itself, a Constitutional Court was formed in 1991. Its decisions *were* to be binding, and in several cases even the president bowed to their authority in the early months of its operation. One controversial decision involved overriding Yeltsin's decree banning the further operation of the Communist Party. The court ruled parts of this action unconstitutional and mandated that while the central structure of the old Communist Party of the Soviet Union could be outlawed, the state could not forbid local communist organizations from forming or functioning. As the struggle between the executive and legislative branches heated up in 1992 and 1993, the court received repeated demands to rule on contentious issues between the legislature and executive branches. The impartiality of the court and its head (Valery Zorkin) were brought into question, particularly by Yeltsin supporters.

The controversy climaxed during the events of October 1993. Without the opportunity to consider the constitutionality of Yeltsin's decree disbanding the parliament, the court was unilaterally disbanded by another presidential decree. This action was unconstitutional, but no institution remained to make a judgment on the issue. The ideal of "rule of law" was, in practice, suspended in the period preceding the elections and referendum of December 1993. Both the na-

tional parliament and Constitutional Court had been struck down by the president's actions, removing any semblance of separation of powers, judicial oversight, or "rule of law."

The new constitution provides for a Constitutional Court with the power to adjudicate disputes regarding the compatibility of federal and regional laws with the constitution, as well as jurisdictional disputes between various political institutions. Only in early 1995 was agreement reached on the nineteen justices for the court, so until that time it was nonfunctional. The court's failure to provide an authoritative resolution of executive/legislative conflicts in the period before October 1993 raises concerns about its likely success in the future. Ultimately the court must rely on the legitimacy of its decisions or the power of the executive branch to assure compliance with its rulings. It remains to be seen whether the present law will provide a workable framework for the operation of the court; if not, then the system will be devoid of a mechanism for the judicial resolution of constitutional conflicts. The outcome of this issue may be a good test of how firmly the "rule of law" has penetrated Russia's political culture and system.

Subnational Government

Although the USSR was formally a federal state, in the Soviet period subnational governments had no independent authority; they were subordinated to central institutions charged with implementing directives emanating from the center. With no independent sources of revenue at their disposal, they were beholden to the ministries, the party, and the central state structures for carrying out their activities.

In independent Russia, subnational governments have gained increasing significance. The incapacity of central state organs to make and implement effective policy has produced a de facto transfer of power to the subnational governments. Thus, many Western experts argue that Russia's future will be fundamentally shaped by what goes on outside Moscow, even in some of the far-flung regions of the country.[37]

Case studies of politics in particular regions have become an important avenue for understanding Russian politics; these studies reveal that there is immense diversity between regions. In some cases, such as Moscow and Nizhnii-Novgorod, reformist governments have tried to push processes of market reform and privatization forward more assertively, whereas in other regions old structures of political power have remained more intact. In addition, differences between "rich" regions (such as Moscow and the oil/gas regions of Siberia) and "poor" regions (those with archaic industrial structures or weak agricultural sectors) have increased dramatically. Although local and regional governments have been saddled with new responsibilities for dealing with social and economic problems, they do not usually have adequate financial resources to do so, although they are permitted to collect certain types of taxes and receive a portion of other tax income. Nonetheless, regional and local governments often continue lobbying for special treatment or central support to deal with their problems; budgetary issues are negotiated by local officials and officials of the Russian Finance Ministry.

Although considerable political power has devolved to the regional and local level, stable political institutions at the subnational level have been slow to take shape. Local and regional politics have often reflected conflicts occurring in central state organs. In particular, the conflict between the legislative and executive branches at the central level has been replicated at the republic, regional, and local levels. Indicative of this was Yeltsin's dissolution of soviets at the city level and below in fall 1993. He depicted the soviets as holdovers from the Soviet period which were blocking the reform process. Repeated attempts by the center to interfere with the activities of regional and local organs suggest that local political organs are sometimes utilized as pawns in the power struggle at the center. In many cases, the structure and power of local and regional political institutions have become objects of political contest rather than mechanisms to resolve conflicts in society.

New elections to regional and local councils were held in various places in Russia throughout 1994 even though no standard legal framework for their selection and operation existed. In many of these elections, the refashioned Communist Party did better than expected, partly due to its strong organizational base at the local level. This development concerns reformist parties and suggests that conflict between legislative and executive organs is likely to continue at the regional and local level, especially because executive organs at the regional level have had closer links to the president and to central structures of the executive branch. The next elections at the local level are to be delayed until December 1996

according to a decree issued by President Yeltsin in the fall of 1995.

Since August 1991, presidential decrees have allowed the president to appoint presidential representatives at the regional level. In some regards these individuals are to fulfill a function similar to that of the regional party secretaries of the Communist Party under the communist system or the regional prefects in France, forming a network of personal linkages throughout the country. In addition, the president retained the power to appoint governors of the *oblasts* and *krai* until October 1995, when a presidential decree allowed for gubernatorial elections to go forward in a few regions in December 1996. The remaining governors are to be popularly elected before December 1996. The governors of the regions at times have found themselves subject to political cross-pressures, trying to respond simultaneously to local political pressures and to instructions from the center.

THE POLICY-MAKING PROCESS

The policy-making process in Russia in the mid-1990s is not as clearly defined as in most Western countries. The structures established under the new constitution provide a framework for policy-making that is roughly followed for major pieces of legislation. Legislation can be proposed by various participants including the government, the presidential administration, and individual parliamentary deputies. It is considered by committees and commissions of the parliament itself. After passage by the State Duma, it is usually considered by the parliament's upper house, the Council of the Federation; if passed, it is then submitted to the president for approval. Sometimes individual deputies in the parliament present draft laws for consideration, but these do not usually deal with major policy issues. Often expert consultants are drawn into the process, and much informal lobbying occurs, involving regional, industrial, and sectoral interests, but this occurs in a much less structured way than in many Western countries. The government's proposed budget has been a particularly contentious issue in recent years because efforts by the government to cut expenditures to reduce the high budget deficit have elicited loud protests from numerous sectors of society, including the military, trade unions, enterprise directors, and other government agencies. These pressures prevented the adoption of a budget for 1995 until the early months of that year, but the 1996 budget was adopted in December 1995. Participation by representatives of citizens' groups in budgetary or policy-making considerations is the exception, rendering policy-making the exclusive domain of the elite and the experts.

Many critical policy proclamations are made by presidential or governmental decrees, without formal consultation with the legislative branch. This decision-making process is much less visible and may involve closed-door bargaining rather than an open process of debate and consultation. A body known as the Security Council has taken on increasing prominence since October 1994 as a consultative organ for the president. Its fourteen members (in January 1995) include a representative from the State Duma and from the Federation Council; all but five are nominated by the president himself. The Security Council advises the president on the most important policy issues of the day. In some ways this body resembles the old Politburo that operated at the pinnacle of the political structure in the Soviet period, in that it includes representatives from various powerful political organs and is the ultimate collective organ for policy formulation. The exclusion of the public and even most parliamentary deputies from involvement in this aspect of policy-making means that presidential decrees often elicit strong criticism and cynicism from other parts of the political elite.

One difficulty in comprehending the Russian policy process is its ad hoc nature. Bilateral negotiations may be undertaken to establish policy toward a specific subnational region, producing a sense of arbitrariness and inequity. An even greater problem than policy-making is the inefficacy of policy implementation. Even in the Soviet period, when a hierarchical structure of party/state authority existed, implementation of central decisions was often spotty; policy goals were often ambitious, even grandiose, but they were rarely fulfilled

in practice. Referring to Russia's authoritarian past, a popular saying suggests that "the severity of Russia's laws is compensated by the laxity of their implementation." Russians have come to expect this laxity and thus have routinely developed strategies to circumvent regulations that obstruct their goals. The current Russian government has faced massive tax evasion, evasion of military conscription, and circumvention of a wide variety of regulations in spheres ranging from environmental protection to export of foreign currency. The network of corruption and payoffs that has penetrated the state security and police sector, as well as the underfunding of legitimate policing activities, has disabled enforcement. Furthermore, at the regional and republic levels, in many instances, local political authorities consciously and overtly have chosen to ignore federal laws and decrees, realizing that little can be done to enforce them. The Chechnya conflict provides a particularly striking example of this phenomenon, in that numerous positions by the central government countermanding Chechnya's declaration of independence were simply ignored by the republic's leadership.

Whereas under Communist rule, the party's control over political appointment and promotion enforced at least some degree of conformity to central mandates, now the fragmented and decentralized nature of political power gives even the president few resources to ensure compliance. Thus, in many ways, the president's extensive powers of decree have only limited impact on a political environment in which lawlessness dominates large areas of public activity. Reverting to coercion to enforce positions articulated by central political organs is a symptom of the breakdown of political order and legitimacy in the system as a whole.

The difficulty of clearly depicting the process of policy-making and implementation is rooted in the complexity of social and political relationships in the country as a whole. In the next section, we explore some of the social foundations for the disarray that plagues the political process.

SECTION 4

Representation and Participation

The upheaval underway in Russia since Gorbachev initiated perestroika and glasnost in the mid-1980s brought a dramatic change in the relationship between state and society. The communist political system was

driven by an impetus to control society; out of this stifling environment, glasnost breathed new life into autonomous social processes and sparked new public and private initiatives. Most restrictions on the formation of social organizations were lifted and a large number of independent groups appeared. Observers in the late 1980s began suggesting that **civil society** was emerging, that is, an autonomous sphere of social life that could act on but was not dependent on the state,[38] as seen through various groups that citizens organized to pursue particular interests.

By the mid-1990s, however, the Russian public, in many ways, seems to have become disoriented and confused. Clear definitions of collective identity, either for Russia as a whole or for various groups within the country, have not crystallized; and the democratic mechanisms that allow people to express their identities and interests seem to have failed to produce positive and concrete results. Cynicism, resignation, and apathy are on the rise, leading many people to retreat again into private life much as they did in the communist period. And yet compared to the communist era, during the glasnost period and in post-communist Russia, the public has gained an increased ability to express its interests and views. There are competitive elections, a freer media, and fewer controls on other forms of free expression. Whether these trends will blossom to produce a stable democracy is unpredictable. It may be that the present lapse in public confidence and self-assertion is a transient phase in the whole process of democratization; or it may be a step in a downward cycle toward renewed authoritarianism. By examining some of the mechanisms through which the Russian public is now able to express its interests and identities, we will understand better this "enigma" of Russian life.

THE LEGISLATURE[39]

The parliamentary elections of December 12, 1993, involved not only the election of a new set of deputies, but also the creation of a new legislative body. It will be unclear for some time, however, whether the new parliament will be an effective institution for representing various public views. Several factors limit parliament's ability to act in this capacity. First, as noted in the previous section, the current parliament is limited in its powers by the strong authority placed in the executive branch; in some ways, the parliament is still a "talk shop" where party leaders can express their views but have little impact on the affairs of state. Second, the blocs and parties represented in the parliament are isolated from the public at large and suffer low levels of popular respect. Many of the mechanisms that link parties and parliaments to citizens in Western democracies do not exist in Russia: interest associations to lobby the parliament are weak; party membership is low and party structures are poorly developed; public hearings on controversial issues are rare; and the political skills and economic resources necessary for effective organization are lacking in the public at large. Nonetheless, through the parliament, Russian citizens have had the opportunity to select deputies in truly competitive elections.

The new parliament, the Federal Assembly, is a bicameral body. Because the Federal Assembly was formed only in January 1994, the effectiveness of its actual operation is difficult to assess. The constitution leaves several aspects of its authority unclear; some of these points may be clarified by subsequent legislation or they may become focal points of future disputes between the branches of government.

The lower house of the Federal Assembly is called the State Duma, the name given the short-lived assembly formed by the Russian tsar following the 1905 revolution; the name emphasizes continuity with Russian (as opposed to Soviet) tradition. The 450 members of the State Duma are chosen by direct popular vote. (The republic of Chechnya did not participate in the elections in 1993, so its one deputy was missing.) The electoral system for the Duma resembles the one used for election of the German *Bundestag*, that is, it combines **proportional representation** with winner-take-all districts. Half of the 450 deputies are selected on the basis of party lists, and any party gaining 5 percent of the national vote is entitled to a proportional share of these 225 deputies in the State Duma. The remaining 225 deputies are elected in winner-take-all districts; these districts allow representation of local figures who can better reflect the interests of their particular constituencies.

Thirteen parties or blocs were on the ballot for the December 1993 elections to the State Duma. Blocs are coalitions of smaller parties that join together to increase their chances in the election. Of the thirteen electoral groupings, eight gained party representation in the State Duma by winning at least 5 percent of the popular vote. The structure of coalitions and parties in the State Duma that emerged following the elections was very fragmented, as some of the blocs have split or reorganized themselves. By early 1994 eleven factions (blocs of deputies) had formed in the parliament, and no bloc or coalition could easily form a majority.

Changing coalition patterns and conflicts between the deputy groups continued throughout 1994 and 1995. By early 1995, the various electoral groupings were jockeying for position in preparation for the December 1995 parliamentary elections.

The upper house of the Federal Assembly, the Federation Council, is specifically mandated to represent the 89 regions and republics comprising the Russian Federation. It serves a function analogous in some ways to the United States' Senate or the German *Bundesrat.* Its specific responsibilities include: alteration of borders, confirmation of presidential edicts on martial law, the use of armed forces outside the Russian Federation, and the appointment and removal of certain government officials.

The Federation Council includes two representatives (called deputies) from each of Russia's 89 constituent federal units (again, with the exception of Chechnya). In December 1993 the Federation Council was directly elected by the population in each region and consisted mainly of regional officials. Most deputies do not belong to a political party group, so party factions play no significant role, as they do in the Duma. However, the interests of the various regions represented in the Federation Council are highly diverse. The method of selection of new members for the Federation Council in December 1995 became a subject of dispute after the president vetoed a law passed by the Federal Assembly which provided that the Federation Council's members should again be directly elected. The president favored appointment or *ex officio* inclusion of regional officials in the Federation Council. A compromise reached in November 1995 provided *ex officio* inclusion of the heads of the executive and legislative branches of each regional government, with the proviso that all regional governors sitting in the Federation Council must have undergone popular election by December 1996.

A point of conflict emerged between the Federal Assembly and the president during the first weeks of its operation. The State Duma issued an amnesty for those citizens detained in connection with the August 1991 coup attempt and the October 1993 events in Moscow. The decision was immediately criticized by presidential advisers; However the constitution makes no provision for a presidential veto on such issues. The decision was allowed to stand, although the prosecutor general, who was obliged to implement it, resigned. However, the legislative body refused to

accept his resignation, which was subsequently retracted. A dispute ensued when President Yeltsin appointed a new prosecutor general, and the Federation Council refused to ratify the appointment in April and again in October 1994. Nonetheless, relations between the executive and legislative branches of government seemed less hostile after the December 1993 elections than they were previously.

Society's ability to affect particular policy decisions through the legislative process is fairly limited. This results from the poor organization of social interests, the relatively weak position of the legislative branch in the institutional structure, and the fragmented nature of the party/coalition system in the State Duma. Ways have not yet been found to integrate the views of the public into the policy-making process on a routine basis.

THE PARTY SYSTEM AND ELECTIONS

Perhaps the most important political change since the inception of perestroika in 1985 has been the gradual shift from a single-party system to a multiparty system. From the early 1920s until the 1990s, the Communist Party dominated political and economic life in the Soviet Union through its control of the political appointment process and political socialization (through the media, schools, and other social institutions), and through its ability to determine the structure and priorities of economic development.[40] The Communist Party used several methods to exercise these powers, including control over personnel appointments, parallel party and state structures in virtually all institutions of Soviet life, personnel overlap between state and party organs, and a set of centrally controlled public organizations to channel popular participation in the system.

The Communist Party provided the clearest path for upward career mobility for young Soviet citizens. Around 10 percent of the adult population were members of the party in the Brezhnev period, including those with the best positions in society and a disproportionately high number of individuals from the intelligentsia and educated groups. The party sought to co-opt the best and the brightest, both to use their skills for party work, but also to keep them from activities that might challenge the system. In addition, recruitment of working-class members was necessary to establish the party's legitimacy as representing the working people; nonetheless, in general, groups with lower status and less education, as well as women, were underrepresented.

Western writings have often depicted the Communist Party as a monolithic structure, but in fact, politicking, bargaining, and compromise occurred on a regular basis, reflecting the diverse regional, economic, and bureaucratic interests of various parts of the party structure.[41] The Communist Party of the Soviet Union served some of the functions generally carried out by political parties in the West: recruitment of political leaders, articulation of a political program and political ideology, political socialization, and a way to involve citizens in political activity. In other ways, however, the organization deviated from Western norms of political party activity: It did not engage in political competition and often hindered rather than facilitated the expression of popular interests.

Under Gorbachev's leadership, internal debate within the party expanded dramatically; separate political groupings were allowed to form within the party to advocate particular positions. Some of the fundamental precepts of Marxism-Leninism were opened to debate—for example, the notions of democratic centralism, party discipline, and the class nature of the party's program. Under Gorbachev's leadership the party limited its involvement in the day-to-day affairs of government, and the size of the party apparatus (the party's paid staff) was reduced. Communist Party branches in some of the union republics, particularly in the Baltic region, formed independent communist parties that aligned themselves with groups demanding greater autonomy for their union republics.

Throughout the late 1980s, Gorbachev continued to support the idea of a single-party system, but by 1991 came to accept the need for multiple political parties (under Communist Party leadership) to prevent a political explosion that could topple the entire communist system. Splits within the Communist Party then became more intense, and by early 1991, party members were handing in their party cards in increasingly large numbers.

Some of the defectors established alternative political blocs outside of the Communist Party. One of the most important of these new groups was the Democratic Russia movement, which formed the base of support for Yeltsin's leadership in Russia. Democratic Russia represented a broad coalition of forces, opposed to Communist Party dominance, which wanted Russia to gain enough autonomy to move more quickly in the direction of market reform and democratization, concepts that were still only vaguely defined at that time. Although Yeltsin refused to become formally associated with any political party or group (after giving up his Communist Party membership in 1990), Democratic Russia played a key role in his election campaign for president of Russia in 1991. Subsequently, the Democratic Russia movement split into several new political groupings, some of which became independent parties which ran candidates in the December 1993 parliamentary elections. Other political groupings also appeared in the late 1980s, particularly the national front organizations in the non-Russian union republics of the Soviet Union. These were broad-based movements uniting elements of the elite and population to press for greater autonomy (or independence) from Moscow. Within Russia, a variety of political organizations appeared, including nationalist, liberal, and neocommmunist movements and parties.

Although the first national competitive elections in the USSR were held in 1989, in the December 1993 elections, political parties were formal participants in a national electoral process for the first time in Russia. By late 1993, about 25 parties were registered; thirteen blocs or parties appeared on the ballot for the December 1993 parliamentary elections and 43 in December 1995. This proliferation of parties formed a confusing political landscape, making it difficult for the average citizen to develop a clear sense of the political spectrum.

Because Russian society and economy are in a state of extreme flux, it is difficult to construct a clear left-right spectrum in terms of political party positions. Some call the communist and social-democratic parties (traditionally considered to be on the left end of the political spectrum) rightist forces because they tend to favor slower change and because they support conserving some old structures. Those favoring a pro-capitalist position (traditionally considered to be on the right) may be called leftist because they favor radical change. The entire political spectrum in Russia, therefore, may seem to be turned on its head, sometimes making simple political discourse a confusing endeavor.

Political parties in Russia today have some peculiarities when compared to parties in Western democracies.[42] First, they generally have formed around a prominent individual and are commonly referred to by the names of their leaders. For example, the party led by

Vladimir Zhirinovsky is most often referred to as Zhirinovsky's party, although its formal name is the Liberal Democratic Party of Russia. The 1993 and 1995 ballots listed not only the names of the blocs and parties, but also the names of the leaders of each grouping. The importance of individual leaders in forming parties and party blocs has increased political fragmentation, because groups with similar programs often split along lines of personal loyalties. This may give the public the impression that politicians are motivated more by personal ambition than by political conviction.

Unlike some parties in the West, Russian parties generally do not have a firm social base or stable constituency. They have been relatively ineffective in outlining their programs to appeal to the economic and political self-interest of various social groups. While party platforms may express a general idea or sentiment, they are often less pragmatic than platforms of Western parties. Likewise, Russian parties tend to be loosely structured; organizational and decision-making structures are ill-defined (other than occasional party conferences). Finally, parties and electoral coalitions are fluid. Parties and blocs frequently splinter, join with others, and rename themselves, making it difficult for the public to hold parties and politicians accountable for their actions (or inaction) and to know whom to vote for (or against). Alternative policy approaches are not clearly articulated by a viable opposition party or coalition. As a result of all of this fragmentation and flux, many voters have become apathetic or confused. The weakness of political parties has also hindered the government's ability to develop a firm base of political support for its policies.

Three factors may account for the fragmented and weak party system in Russia. First, many Russian citizens are hesitant to join a political party from fear that strict party discipline or ideological conformity will be imposed by the new party, as it was by the Communist Party. Many citizens have also become increasingly wary of political activity in general, since it has produced few positive results in the past several years. Second, national elections before December 1993 were not held on the basis of party competition and thus political parties played only a marginal role in organizing political conflict, competition, and policy-making until that time. This is turn removed any incentive for parties to develop clear and unified positions or an effective organizational structure. Third, political parties may be weak because political interests are not clearly defined in society as a whole. Until recently, almost everyone was a state employee, sharing a set of common problems and grievances resulting from their government's policies. Now people are beginning to define their individual and group interests in relation to economic, social, and cultural issues. The general confusion in the country, lack of clear alternative ideologies, and weak formation of clear economic interests have made it difficult for political parties to define platforms to attract a definable and stable constituency. As the process of economic transformation proceeds, the interests of particular groups (for example, blue-collar workers, business entrepreneurs, or groups based on age, gender, or region) may well take on a more central role in the formation of parties.

The impact of the electoral system on party fragmentation is less clear. As discussed above, elections to the State Duma are based on a system that combines proportional representation and winner-take-all districts. Because existing parties and electoral blocs are so fluid and politics is so personalized, the proportional representation aspects of the electoral system may serve to both increase and decrease party fragmentation. Proportional representation gives parties a role in drawing up the candidate lists and the 5 percent threshold for representation does, to some extent, encourage the formation of electoral coalitions. On the other hand, proportional representation still allows fairly small parties to gain representation in the Duma and may discourage broader coalitions. The winner-take-all races may not bolster the chances of large parties as much as they do in established democracies because well-known local figures may win in these races without being associated with a particular party or bloc (see Table 6 on the following page).

Four parties/blocs running on a pro-market "reform" plank gained representation in the 1993 for the State Duma. Although there were some differences between the platforms of these four groupings, the range of differences could probably have been accommodated in one electoral bloc. Generally, the supporters of these parties were more likely to live in cities and had higher levels of education than average; they were also more supportive of the notion of market reform. As it was, the four parties split the reform vote. Had they joined forces, they would have won about a third of the party vote, a stronger showing than any other bloc. This inability to form a coalition evoked cynicism among

TABLE 6   **Composition of the State Duma Following the December 1993 Elections**

Party or Bloc	General Orientation of Party/Bloc	Party Leader	Percentage of Votes Cast[a]	Seats from PR Lists[b]	Seats from Single-Member Districts	Total Seats[c]	Percentage of Total Seats Elected
Liberal Democratic Party of Russia	Nationalist/Patriotic	V. V. Zhirinovsky	22.8	59	5	64	14.5
Russia's Choice	Pro-Market Reform	Ye. T. Gaidar	15.4	40	30	70	15.8
Yabloko	Pro-Market Reform	G. A. Yavlinsky	7.8	20	3	23	5.2
Russian Unity and Accord	Pro-Market Reform	S. M. Shakhrai	6.8	18	1	19	4.3
Movement for Democratic Reform	Pro-Market Reform	A. A. Sobchak	4.1	0	4	4	0.9
Women of Russia	Centrist	A. V. Fedulova	8.1	21	2	23	5.2
Civic Union	Centrist	A. I. Volsky	1.9	0	1	1	0.2
Democratic Party of Russia	Centrist	N. Travkin	5.5	14	0	14	3.2
Communist Party of the Russian Federation	Socialist	G. A. Zyuganov	12.4	32	16	48	10.9
Agrarian Party	Socialist	M. I. Lapshin	7.9	21	12	33	7.5
Other Parties					14	14	3.2
Independents					129	129	29.2
Total				**225**	**217**	**442**	

[a]Rounded to the nearest tenth of a percent.
[b]PR = Proportional Representation.
[c]Does not add up to 250 because races were declared illegal in some constituencies.

some potential supporters. In the December 1995 elections, several parties again split the pro-market "reform" vote, but the overall support they received from the electorate was substantially lower than in 1993 (see Table 7). Only the electoral union "Yabloko," headed by the reform economist Grigory Yavlinsky, surpassed the 5 percent barrier.

To the surprise of many observers, the Liberal Democratic Party of Russia (LDPR), headed by Vladimir Zhirinovsky, got the strongest support on the party ballot in 1993, winning almost 23 percent of the vote; this declined to 11 percent in 1995. Neither liberal nor particularly democratic in its platform, this party might more properly be characterized as nationalistic and populist. By "populist" we mean that Zhirinovsky's personal charisma elicits a strong emotional reaction from parts of the population; Zhirinovsky's campaign style was particularly effective in 1993 when he made better use of the mass media than other candidates. Many Russians believe he "speaks our language" and understands their concerns better than other politicians;

however, elements of democratic procedure and accountability are not well developed within the party.

Sociological surveys indicate that Zhirinovsky's 1993 electoral support was especially strong among working-class males and military personnel. Core supporters tended to be better educated and young, whereas those deciding to vote for the party at the last minute included older, less-educated workers. Concern with the breakdown of law and order seems to rank high among the priorities of Zhirinovsky supporters. The constituency of this party does not necessarily include those hardest hit by the economic depression. There is a significant anti-Western sentiment in the party's appeal, a response to the perceived humiliation Russia has suffered in its decline from superpower status and the government's perceived groveling for Western economic aid.

The 1993 campaign platform of this party stated its main task to be "the revival and strengthening of the Russian government . . . in the borders of the USSR in 1977." While the platform did not support a

TABLE 7   The December 1995 Parliamentary Elections[a]

Party or Bloc	Leader(s)	Popular Vote in 1993 Elections[b]	Comments	% in Dec. 1995 Vote[b]	Seats from Single-Member Districts	Total Seats in Duma[c]
Liberal/Reform						
Russia's Democratic Choice/United Democrats	Yegor Gaidar (former prime minister; supported shock therapy)	15.4%[d]	Coalition includes part of former Russia's Choice; party of former prime minister	3.9	9	9
Yabloko	Grigory Yavlinsky (an economist)	7.8%	Wants to accelerate economic reform; slogan is "Dignity, Order, Justice"	6.9 (31)	14	45
Party of Workers' Self-Government	Svyatislav Fyodorov (eye surgeon, business leader)	—	Supports market reform, with employee ownership	4.0	1	1
Centrist						
Russia Is Our Home	Viktor Chernomyrdin (prime minister)	—	Support from the cabinet, some regional governors; prime minister's party; includes leader of former Democratic Party of Russia	10.1 (45)	10	55
Women of Russia	Yekaterina Lakhova	8.1%	Concerned about family, women's issues	4.6	3	3
Communist/Social Democratic						
Communist Party of the Russian Federation	Gennady Zyuganov	12.4%	Favors price regulation; wants government of national salvation	22.3 (99)	58	157
Communist–Working Russia–For the Soviet Union	Viktor Anpilov	—	Radical communist; critical of the "revisionism" of the CPRF	4.5	0	0
Agrarian Party	Mikhail Lapshin	7.9%	Close to Communist Party	3.8	20	20
Power to the People	Nikolai Ryzhkov (former prime minister under Gorbachev)	—	Opposed to government; favors "prognosis planning"	2.1	9	9
Patriotic/Nationalist						
Liberal Democratic Party	Vladimir Zhirinovsky	22.8%	Favors a strong Russian state	11.2 (50)	1	51
Congress of Russian Communities	Yuri Skokov (former secretary of the Security Council); Aleksandr Lebed (army general)	—	Moderate nationalist; support from some heads of republics, in the military, veterans	4.3	5	5

[a]At this writing, "final preliminary" results are available; final results for 1995 may deviate somewhat from the tallies shown here. Figures may not add up to 100 percent or to the total numbers of deputies because votes for very small parties and for independents are excluded.

[b]Percentage of the total popular vote the party or bloc received on the proportional representation portion of the ballot in December 1993 and December 1995. A dash indicates that the party or bloc was not on that ballot or did not win a significant portion of the vote. Number in parentheses for 1995 is number of deputy seats won from the PR lists.

[c]Estimated. Included here are the number of seats won in the proportional representation races as well as the number won in the single-member district races.

[d]Participated in the 1993 elections as "Russia's Choice."

Vladimir Zhirinovsky
demonstrates his populist style
as he shakes hands with
supporters in Yugoslavia in
1994.
Source: AP/Wide World
Photos.

revival of the communist system, it described the creation of the new post-Soviet states (other than Russia) as illegal.[43] On the domestic front, the platform supported the creation of a presidential republic with strong executive power. In the economic sphere, the LDPR favors an economy with diverse property forms, including a strong state sector. An important feature of the party's appeal is its strong stance against crime and corruption; the platform supported limits on immigration from areas south of Russia (mainly Transcaucasia) which were identified as sources of criminal elements. In the foreign policy sphere the party supports a policy free of dependence on the West, in the pursuit of Russian national and geopolitical interests. In late 1994 and 1995, Zhirinovsky was one of the few prominent political figures who supported the government's offensive in Chechnya. While Zhirinovsky's rhetoric has often captured the cynical attitude of the public toward the government, it is ironic that on several concrete issues Zhirinovsky has, in practice, positioned himself closer to Yeltsin than most other politicians, demonstrating his political savvy.

The reaction to Zhirinovsky in the West and in Russia's "near abroad" (that is, the former Soviet republics) has been one of alarm. Some view him as a fascist and see certain analogies between Russia's present plight and Germany's following World War I, preceding Hitler's rise to power. Zhirinovsky's expansionist and sometimes racist rhetoric presents a special threat to the countries of the former Soviet Union and

Eastern Europe. Within Russia itself, there have also been strong negative as well as positive reactions to many of Zhirinovsky's statements, making it difficult to predict his political future.

Two other parties performed well in the 1993 elections, the Communist Party of the Russian Federation (CPRF) and a rural-based party closely associated with it, the Agrarian Party. Together they received 20 percent of the party list vote. These two parties represent a social democratic variant within the communist spectrum; they were the only communist-leaning parties to appear on the December 1993 ballot. The CPRF did even better in the 1995 parliamentary elections, winning almost 22 percent of the party list vote. This strong support reflects the CPRF's firm organizational base in particular localities (due to the communist legacy), and the widespread concern expressed by the CPRF about the social costs of the government's economic reform program.

Other parties gaining representation in the new State Duma in 1993 were the Democratic Party of Russia (a centrist formation), and the political movement "Women of Russia," a moderate group concerned with family issues and social welfare problems in the economic reform process. The Civic Union (a centrist political coalition close to Prime Minister Chernomyrdin), the ecological movement "Cedar," and the "Dignity and Compassion" group did not gain representation from the party list vote. In 1995 several new or re-formed

What Gorbachev Says About Yeltsin and Zhirinovsky

It's no coincidence that in this terrible military adventure [Chechnya] Vladimir Zhirinovsky, the ultranationalist leader, has been at Yeltsin's side. This proves, apart from anything else, that the alternative offered by Yeltsin to the West ("either me or Zhirinovsky") is a sham.

If Zhirnovksy didn't exist, Yeltsin would have invented him. Indeed, maybe he did.

From Mikhail Gorbachev, "Moscow turns to dictatorship: West must neither isolate Russia nor rationalize what it has done," *The Ottawa Citizen,* March 8, 1995, A15, distributed through *The New York Times* special features syndicate.

electoral blocs ran in the parliamentary elections, but of these only Prime Minister Chernomyrdin's bloc, Russia Is Our Home, gained representation through the proportional representation portion of the ballot.

Despite the important role of personalities and individuals in political party formation in Russia, President Yeltsin himself has insisted on maintaining a careful distance from any of the new parties. He apparently has wished to present himself as a representative of Russia, rather than to associate himself with a single partisan association. Some critics feel that Yeltsin's failure to develop a political party of his own (despite some moves in this direction in 1993) has reduced his ability to mobilize more broad-ranging support for his policies by denying himself a firm organizational base. Ironically, Yeltsin's behavior may be more consistent with the spirit of the old communist system than he acknowledges because the Communist Party also claimed to transcend particular interests in representing the people as a whole.

The other 225 members of the State Duma are selected in winner-take-all races in single-member districts. The results of these races greatly impact the final political composition of the State Duma. Although many of the candidates who run in single-member districts are associated with particular parties or blocs, many maintain a stance independent of all parties. This adds to the voters' difficulty in making a choice based on platform rather than personality. In 1995 candidates associated with the Agrarian Party and the Communist Party won many seats in the single-member district contests, but candidates from Zhirinovsky's party did poorly (see Table 7). The final balance of forces in the parliament is determined by the combined result of the party list vote and the single-member district votes.

A major fault line in terms of party positions forms around the pace of economic reform. All of the parties represented in the Duma favor privatization of some elements of the economy; differences center on the pace of reform, the exact nature of the privatization process (particularly the role that workers of enterprises themselves will play in the privatized enterprises), and the scope of continued state activity in the economy. Also at issue is the best way to stabilize the economy. Some parties and blocs (the communists, for example) have favored continued state subsidies to key economic sectors to limit unemployment and social disruption; the more pro-market parties have emphasized the need to limit government spending to reduce inflation and help stabilize the economy and the ruble.

Parties and blocs have also been divided on noneconomic issues, particularly those involving national identity, regional devolution of power within Russia, and Russia's search for a regional and global policy. Since the October 1993 events and the December 1993 elections, politicians across the political spectrum, including former Foreign Minister Andrei Kozyrev, have made stronger public assertions about Russian national interest, the defense of Russian interests in the former Soviet republics, and Russia's regional role. Some groups in the reform bloc, as well as the communists and nationalist forces, share a hope for the reconstitution of some kind of union of the former Soviet republics under the leadership of Russia. On other issues, however, their positions may differ radically. The Communist Party and the Agrarian Union continue to appeal to social class interests while the Zhirinovsky position emphasizes national identity.

Although 43 parties appeared on the ballot in the 1995 parliamentary elections, only four exceeded the 5 percent barrier needed to gain party representation in the State Duma. The winners in the 1995 elections were clearly the communists, winning more than one-third of the Duma's seats. Although Zhirinovsky's party came in second in the party list vote, this result represented a significant slide from 1993, particularly since the party did so poorly in single-member-district contests. Nonetheless, the CPRF and the LDPR are both clearly opposition parties, suggesting that popular support for the government's policy is weak. The elections represented a further set back for the course set by President Yeltsin and his pro-market reformers in 1992. The results of the election suggested broad public concern about the social consequences of the government's economic policy. But they also showed that the extreme nationalist appeal of the Zhirinovsky forces had declined. The public favored the more tempered and socially oriented nationalism expressed by Communist Party leader Gennady Zyuganov.

In third place in the party vote was "Russia is Our Home," a bloc formed under the leadership of Prime Minister Viktor Chernomyrdin in 1995. Representing the political establishment and a centrist political orientation, this bloc won about 10 percent of the party vote in 1995, putting the group in third place behind the Communist Party and the Liberal Democrats. The weak showing of the Yabloko group, winning just under 7 percent of the party vote, indicated the weak constituency for radical economic reform.

Given the weakness of the parliament and the continued party fragmentation in the State Duma, it might prove difficult for the CPRF to exert a strong influence on the direction of government policy. But the Communist Party's strong showing set the stage for the presidential elections of June 1995. A major question was whether the pro-market reformers and centrists would be able to unite around a single candidate (possibly Boris Yeltsin or Viktor Chernomyrdin) and whether the appeal of the Communists could be expanded to provide a real constituency for a communist presidency.

POLITICAL CULTURE, CITIZENSHIP, AND IDENTITY

Political culture can be a source of great continuity, even in the face of radical upheavals in the social and political spheres.[44] Indeed, in many ways, those Russian attitudes toward government that prevailed in the tsarist period seem to have endured with remarkable tenacity. These include acceptance of a wide scope of state activity, in both the economic and ideological spheres. In tsarist times, Orthodoxy, the variant of Christianity practiced in Russia, was a kind of state religion, just as Marxism-Leninism might be viewed as a state secular "religion" in communist times. Political autocracy has deep roots in Russia; thus censorship of the media and limits on civil liberties form part of the traditional pattern of Russian governance. Liberalism has had a weak political basis; values of individualism and private ownership have played a minimal role in Russian political culture. Patrimonialism (the state as owner of the

land and the political sovereign) played an important role in Russian history. The traditional peasant commune, the *mir*, in existence until Stalin's collectivization campaign, encouraged communal values and egalitarianism because it involved collective responsibility for periodic redistribution of land; it also reinforced conformity to group norms.

As this political portrait suggests, in many ways the Soviet period represented continuity with the pre-revolutionary period, in that it was consistent with some key aspects of traditional Russian political culture—autocracy, the broad scope of state authority, the articulation of a state ideology, state control and ownership of the economy, and an emphasis on egalitarianism and communalism. However, in other ways, the Soviet period represented a departure from elements of traditional Russian political culture. The Orthodox church was subject to severe restrictions during most of the period; atheism was the official doctrine. The peasant commune and other forms of traditional social life were destroyed by the Stalinist upheaval to be replaced by large state-run economic units such as collective and state farms. Simultaneously, society was catapulted into a process of industrialization and urbanization which imposed "modern" rationalist values on the traditional rural population. When communism finally collapsed in Russia in late 1991, a crisis of Russian national identity emerged, as elites, intellectuals, and ordinary citizens began to seek roots in the past.

Another dimension of the search for identity relates to what it means to be "Russian." The Russian language has two words for "Russian"—*russkii*, which refers to Russian as an ethnicity, and *Rossiiskii*, a broader concept referring to peoples of various ethnic backgrounds included in Russia as a political entity. In the USSR, just over 50 percent of the population was ethnically Russian; most of the major ethnic minorities now reside in independent states. The Russian Federation is considerably more ethnically homogeneous than was the USSR, but nonetheless nearly 20 percent of the population is of non-Russian ethnicity (the largest minority is the Tatars, a traditionally Muslim group residing primarily in Tatarstan, a republic of Russia). At the same time, some 25 million ethnic Russians reside outside of the Russian Federation in other former Soviet republics. Given this situation, it is significant whether one considers "Russianness" to be defined by ethnicity *(russkii)* or by citizenship *(Rossiiskii).* Politicians and groups that emphasize an ethnic definition tend to be more concerned with defending the interests of ethnic Russians in the "near abroad"; this in turn affects foreign policy toward neighboring countries. Treatment of Russians abroad could become a bargaining chip in foreign policy or trade negotiations; it could also, conceivably, become a pretext for forcible intervention in the affairs of neighboring states. In this context, it is understandable that Russia's neighbors may perceive Russian statements in support of Russians abroad as potentially threatening to their own state sovereignty. Another issue relates to the treatment of ethnic minorities within Russia. At present, although equal citizenship rights are granted to individuals from diverse ethnic groups, popular stereotypes greatly affect the way minority groups are treated in practice. For instance, politicians sometimes appeal to anti-Semitic sentiments or to negative stereotypes of Muslim minority groups.

National tensions within Russia have been accentuated by increasing refugee flows from some of the war-torn regions, particularly in the former Soviet republics of the Transcaucasian area (Georgia, Azerbaijan, and neighboring regions of southern Russia such as Chechnya and Ingushetia). Individuals from these regions play an important role in Russia's trade sector and are viewed by many Russians as speculators and crooks. Following the October events in 1993, in a popular move, Yeltsin decreed that illegal residents in Moscow should be expelled; implementation of this decree was directed especially at individuals of Transcaucasian background. Public opinion surveys indicate that a large proportion of the population, all across the political spectrum, think people from this region have too much power in Russia. The former head of the old Russian Supreme Soviet, Ruslan Khasbulatov, is himself a Chechen, a factor that reduced his popular appeal.

Religion also plays a role in shaping new conceptions of Russian identity. The traditional (prerevolutionary) role of the Russian Orthodox church is appealing to many citizens looking for a replacement for the discredited values of the communist system. A revival of religious practice has occurred in Russia, and in many localities citizen initiatives have focused on reconstructing or refurbishing churches, some of which were used for other purposes during the Soviet period. In general, the government of President Yeltsin has supported the revival of religion as a basis of Rus-

sian identity and social cohesion. To this point, however, the church has not played a major or direct role in the political process; attempts by figures in the Orthodox church to mediate the conflict between the parliament and the president in September/October 1993 were unsuccessful. A significant Muslim population, including the Tatars and groups in southern Russia (including the Chechens and Ingush), comprises one of the most assertive groups in demanding independence (in the case of Chechnya) or increased political and economic autonomy (in the case of Tatarstan).

In the Soviet period, the mass media, the educational system, and a variety of other social institutions played a key role in propagating the party's political values.[45] Under glasnost, these institutions were granted greater autonomy and no longer served simply as mouthpieces for official ideology. However, the Western concept of a free press is still not firmly grasped by Russian society. Although the print media represents a broad spectrum of political opinion and genuine opposition newspapers do publish, restrictions on their ability to function freely still exist.[46] First, financial constraints make their existence precarious. Many Russian citizens cannot afford to buy newspapers on a regular basis; therefore, readership has radically declined. A second factor affecting the ability of the press to give fair and complete coverage is the mafia. As already noted, courageous journalists have been a particular target of organized crime. Finally, the government itself has exerted pressure on the media to present issues favorably; rarely has this pressure taken the form of overt censorship (as occurred after the October 1993 events), but editors may endure considerable pressure to limit the publication of highly critical viewpoints, and some editors have been forcibly removed from their posts. Because the major newspapers receive financial subsidies from the government, pressure can be exerted in this way, as well as through government taxation policy and the price of newsprint.

The electronic media is even more subject to political pressure. The costs and limited availability of the technology needed to run television stations allow the state to more effectively maintain control over this sector. Central television has generally given favorable coverage to the government's positions, and in some cases debate has been overtly restricted. For example, during the campaign leading up to the referendum in December 1993, parties were given TV spots but were not allowed to criticize the proposed constitution on the air. It is not coincidental that Ostankino, the central television facility, was stormed by opposition forces in October 1993 and that the government used force to retain control of the station in order to shape public opinion. The continued political interference in media affairs is but one example of the difficult process involved in transforming political culture. For centuries, the state has exerted primary control over ideological and cultural policy; it is not surprising that a truly free press might be seen as a dangerous and divisive force.

INTERESTS, SOCIAL MOVEMENTS, AND PROTEST

In the Stalinist period, social organizations that served as intermediaries between state and society were, for the most part, either destroyed or brought under state control. New institutions were formed in the Stalinist and post-Stalinist periods to involve citizens in public life, but they were subordinate to the Communist Party and served as a conduit for ideological influence and political control. There was a type of controlled, or in some cases, mandated participation in public life. Examples of such groups included the various communist youth organizations (Octobrists, Pioneers, Komsomol), the trade unions, and various professional organizations for the intelligentsia (the Writers' Union, Cinematographers' Union, and the like).

The family was one of the few social institutions that survived communist rule somewhat shielded from direct political interference. Although many children attended day care at a young age, many were also cared for by grandparents or other relatives. As in other countries, industrialization has weakened the extended family, but in Russia, housing shortages often necessitate tight living quarters involving three generations. Family life has served as a place of retreat from public life, providing a reservoir of trust and shared confidences. Thus, while the family cannot be conceived of as a political association, its role in shielding people from the political sphere was an important feature of Soviet life.

Another sphere of semiautonomous societal activity in the Soviet period was the dissident movement, which became an important phenomenon beginning in the mid-1960s.[47] It included people pursuing a broad range of causes and interests, such as increased

rights for various national groups, religious freedom, and defense of civil liberties or artistic freedom. Although involving only a minuscule portion of the population, mainly intellectuals, dissident activities kept alive a sphere of independent political and social thought. Dissident groups were loosely organized and often functioned more as informal networks of committed individuals rather than as actual interest associations. People would meet secretly in apartments to discuss issues of interest or to share works of artistic creation not allowed dissemination in the communist-controlled media. Copies of manuscripts were typed by individuals (hence the term *samizdat*, or self-publication) and passed along from hand-to-hand, sometimes making their way into print abroad.

The dissident movement was able to appeal to the international community—the Helsinki Watch Group, a dissident group that monitored human rights violations in the USSR, was particularly important in this regard. Because the Soviet government wanted to be accepted in the international community, such appeals were sometimes successful in gaining concessions, particularly for prominent dissident figures. Also important in the dissident movement were the so-called refuseniks, Soviet Jews who had been refused permission to emigrate to Israel and who were often subject to sanctions and harassment in the USSR. Some dissidents, most notably the famous writer Aleksandr Solzhenitsyn, were expelled to the West to reduce their potentially disruptive impact in the Soviet Union. Interestingly, when Solzhenitsyn returned to Russia in 1994, his views elicited broad interest among the Russian public. Other former dissidents, like Andrei Sakharov, were allowed to remain in the USSR. From the time he was freed from internal exile in the city of Gorky (now renamed Nizhnii-Novgorod) in December 1986 until his death in 1989, Sakharov was able to participate freely in the reform process Gorbachev initiated; he commanded broad public respect both inside and outside the Soviet Union.

In the late 1980s, when glasnost permitted the formation of new and relatively autonomous social groups, the public life destroyed in the Stalinist and post-Stalinist periods had to be reconstructed. The process produced an outburst of public activity and many grassroots groups formed to express diverse interests and concerns. These included the national front organizations in the non-Russian republics, environmental groups, religious associations, political discussion clubs, and organizations devoted to a variety of particular causes such as rehabilitation of Stalinist victims, preservation of cultural monuments, and the interests of Afghan war veterans. It was this outburst of public activity that Gorbachev finally found so hard to control and that ultimately contributed to the collapse of communist power and control. People increasingly refused to allow Communist Party organizations to define their interests for them, but instead expressed their interests for themselves.

When the economy began to fall into a severe depression in the early 1990s, however, many people were diverted from the public arena to solving the increasingly arduous problems of everyday life. Many public associations and interest groups continue to be active all over Russia, but they generally have small memberships. Voter turnout has declined in general elections as well as in referendum votes that have been used extensively by governments at all levels to establish public support for their policies. Sporadic demonstrations and strikes characterize contemporary Russian politics, but they are generally smaller now than in the 1980s. Often on public holidays, such as May Day (traditionally celebrated as the day of worker solidarity), demonstrators gather around government buildings or in public squares. For the most part these demonstrations have remained peaceful or have involved only limited clashes with the police (militia).

Labor unrest is another form of social protest that sporadically affects various sectors of the economy.[48] Prior to glasnost, workers did not have the right to strike, although occasional strikes did occur. The authorities dealt with such instances through a combination of concessions, repression, and censorship. More often, workers expressed protest in more passive forms—by working inefficiently, drinking on the job, arriving late, or not showing up for work at all. Beginning in 1989, strikes have become more common. Most of these have been brief warning strikes, particularly in the energy sector.

In the early to mid-1990s new problems evoked labor discontent in other sectors as well. The depression and the crisis of the state budget has meant workers in both the state sector and in new joint-stock firms often fail to receive their full wages for long periods of time. This problem is exacerbated by the "inter-enterprise debt crisis," a vicious cycle of nonpayment of debts between enterprises, producing a massive tangle of debt defaults. In some cases, work-

ers are temporarily laid off; in other cases, they continue to work but receive at best only partial wages. So far the government has been unwilling to declare most failing enterprises bankrupt because so many enterprises would be affected (despite a bankruptcy law that would allow such action). To a greater degree than in most Western capitalist nations, workers address their protest to the state rather than to the firm employing them. Because the state often defaults on payments, workers perhaps rightly perceive that their own managers can do little to solve the problems. Furthermore, the traditional political attitude in Russia continues, as in the past, to accept a broad scope of state responsibility for assuring economic security. Political culture thus influences the way Russian workers define the problem and the adversary. The official trade unions established under Soviet rule have survived under the title Federation of Independent Trade Unions (FITU), although they are no longer an arm of the government or Communist Party. Still the largest union in Russia, FITU has lost the confidence of large parts of the workforce. In some sectors, new independent trade unions have formed, mainly at the local level.

Although worker unrest is significant in some sectors of the economy, a broad-based independent movement of workers has not developed. This may be the result of Soviet ideology that made workers cynical about the concept of social class power as well as a result of current economic insecurity that may prevent workers from protesting too assertively for fear of losing their jobs. A genuine sense of collective power does not seem to be widespread.

Which forms of collective identity will influence the future of Russian politics? It is difficult to say, because the population is struggling to define itself both as a nation and as individuals. Until now, ethnic conflict has been a focal point of social tension (particularly as it governed the lines of collapse of the Soviet Union); nationalism seems to be a growing source of political identity (even if as yet a confused political identity) for ethnic Russians. This may create growing tensions with Russia's ethnic minorities, foreshadowed by the conflict in Chechnya. Generational differences are also likely to shape social cleavages, as younger people are more flexible and adaptable in facing new conditions, but possibly less compliant in accepting deprivation.[49] To a lesser extent, gender differences may take on increasing prominence, evidenced by the relatively good showing of the Women of Russia party in the 1993 elections.

It may well be, however, that class conflict will generate the most pronounced collective identities, as it has in Russia's past. The present economic crisis continues to reinforce and make more visible the cleavages and differentials between various economic strata. Perhaps the collapse of Soviet communism will usher in a renewed phase of social class conflict played out on the weak scaffolding of capitalism that the reformers are trying to construct.

At this moment, one cannot, however, say that civil society has really formed in Russia, except perhaps among elements of the intelligentsia. Whatever forms of collective identity emerge, social forces do not, at this point, easily find avenues to exert constructive and organized influence on state activity. As Russian citizens awaken to political awareness, they seem to waver between activism and apathy, and the political system sways from near anarchy to renewed authoritarianism.

SECTION 5

Russian Politics at the Crossroad

POLITICAL CHALLENGES AND CHANGING AGENDAS

On April 28, 1994, 248 prominent public figures gathered in Moscow to sign the Civic Accord. The signatories included Russia's political leadership, heads of the regions and republics, and leaders of trade unions, political parties, movements, and religious organizations. On May 5, over 100 bankers and industrialists added their names to the accord as well. Standing aside in criticism of the project were a motley group of well-known leaders, among them the head of the Russian Communist Party (Gennady Zyuganov), former Vice President Aleksandr Rutskoi, reform figure Grigorii Yavlinsky, and the heads of two of Russia's regions. President Boris Yeltsin hailed the document as marking the end of decades of political upheaval initiated by the Civil War of 1918 to 1921; he presented the Civic Accord as a way to solve the deep conflicts that split Russian society.

According to the Civic Accord, all parties agreed to refrain from violence in pursuing their goals, not to call for early elections for the parliament and president, and to propose amendments to the constitution only in a conciliatory fashion. Bankers and industrialists agreed to deal honorably with workers, clients, and suppliers, as well as to avoid unnecessary production stoppages. The scene suggested a new phase of political compromise and accommodation, spearheaded by a president facing declining popularity, a recent electoral rebuff (in the December 1993 parliamentary elections), and a collapsing economic structure. At the time some questioned whether this initiative was a form of collusion between Russia's top elites in an effort to maintain their privilege and power in the face of systemic breakdown. Yeltsin claimed that it could usher in a period of real compromise and cooperation that would help Russia out of its crisis.

Some eight months later, Russia was mired in a civil war in one of the southern regions, which threatened to polarize and divide Russian society anew. Yeltsin's attempt to force the recalcitrant republic of Chechnya back into the federal fold had, by mid-April 1995, resulted in an estimated 1,518 deaths of Russian military personnel and many thousands of civilian casualties. The conflict's political cost multiplied as it became clear that the Civic Accord had been ruptured and that internal conflict resolution in Russia was anything but civil. Russian and international television showed images of the war's civilian victims, ruthless bombings of residential regions, and a disheveled and chaotic Russian army, thus shattering any vision of unity and accord. Yeltsin's former political supporters, including Yegor Gaidar (his former prime minister and architect of the shock therapy), became open critics of the president, along with the heads of the communist and centrist groups. Ironically, one of Yeltsin's staunchest supporters in the adventure was his erstwhile nemesis, Vladimir Zhirinovsky, whose support for Russian self-assertion seemed to have won the day.

During the height of the Chechnya crisis, some predicted that his unprecedented unpopularity would soon oust Yeltsin from office; others asked whether he had not already lost control of an anarchic military and state structure. Rumors about Yeltsin's poor health and alcoholism gained increasing credibility.

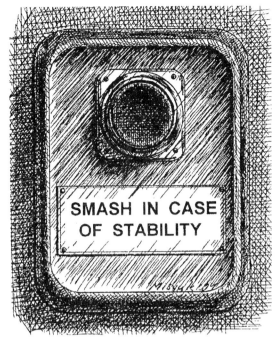

Smash in case of stability.
Source: Vadim Misjuk, courtesy of *Nezavisimaia Gazeta
(The Independent Newspaper)*.

By April 1995, it appeared that Yeltsin had more or less survived the crisis, that parliamentary elections would proceed in December 1995, and that an array of electoral opponents were lining up to challenge Yeltsin in the presidential elections scheduled for June 1996. The final outcome of the Chechnya war remained unknown, but some speculated that possible repercussions could include Russia's increasing isolation from the international community, unrest in other republics adjacent to Chechnya, an intensified economic decline as a result of the war's high costs, and a continuing fall in the legitimacy of state institutions, including the presidency and the military. One evident fact was that Yeltsin, like Gorbachev before him, was losing hold on the reins of power and was increasingly losing touch with the population and political reality. One of Yeltsin's critics called Chechnya the "harvest" of the illegitimate means by which Yeltsin achieved acceptance of his authoritarian constitution in late 1993. The extensive powers that Yeltsin managed to appropriate to himself through that document made possible his decision to embark on the Chechnya policy, leaving him politically isolated and ineffective.

Although it may appear that the Civic Accord was ruptured by the Chechnya war, Russia's basic political structures survived the crisis, perhaps indicating that Russia may be inching toward political stability. Distinguished political scientist Barrington Moore has suggested that formation of a cohesive group of political elites may be an important step on the path to democratization.[50] Key to this process is the emergence of a "loyal opposition," that is, some in the elite who may disagree with specific policies of the government, but nonetheless support the basic political order. Moore sees this as a crucial step in the development of competitive electoral politics, which will eventually involve alternation of various political groups in power and gradual expansion of the range of people able to participate actively and effectively in the political process. Thus, the combination of elite collusion and elite conflict evident in 1994 and 1995 may be indicative of an essential step in the process of constructing a stable political system based on political competition. For instance, much of the intense controversy surrounding the Chechnya conflict was not directed at the underlying goals of the policy (maintaining the territorial integrity of the Russian Federation by squelching separatist tendencies), but rather at its faulty implementation and the resulting loss of Russian lives.

One of the deficiencies underlying the Civic Accord, however, is what appears to be a weak consensus on the appropriate economic policy. One wonders whether disputes over bread-and-butter issues such as state subsidies, bankruptcies, regional economic equalization, and central/regional control of tax revenues will cause efforts at elite political consensus to fray at the edges and finally unravel. Not only elites, but above all, average Russians, are affected by the strains of the economic transition whose stakes are still very high. The process of privatization is incomplete; thus there is much to be gained or lost if one is not properly positioned to receive some of the power and property still to be distributed. For the population at large, proclamations of three or four hundred political and economic leaders may provide little solace when factories close, jobs evaporate, health conditions deteriorate, and prices continue to rise. Elite pacts may not be capable of maintaining the social consensus needed to survive such jolts.

At the same time, a significant portion of the public has grown apathetic about politics, as indicated by

According to this cartoon, the
Chechnya offensive puts
Russia on the precipice.
Source: Vadim Misjuk,
courtesy of *Nezavisimaia
Gazeta (The Independent
Newspaper).*

the levels of voter turnout. Allegations about election
fraud in the December 1993 elections led to the establishment of a special commission to study the charges.
The commission concluded that turnout for the constitutional referendum actually fell below the 50 percent
required to validate the result. Election turnout for local races in 1994 and 1995 was in many cases even
lower. The low turnout not only raises further questions about the legitimacy and legality of the new constitution and political institutions, but also suggests
that the Russian public is severely alienated from the
political process. However, an increase in voter turnout to about 65 percent in the December 1995 parliamentary elections suggested a possible revival of
interest in the political process.

Another basic issue relates to Russian identity.
Both Russian elites and citizens struggle with Russia's
economic decline, loss of empire, and fall from superpower status. The defense minister and other military
figures repeatedly warn that without higher budget allocations, even the military's basic needs cannot be
met. Discontent in military ranks, among the officer
corps and in key enterprises of the former military-
industrial complex, remains a very real concern and

aggravates instability and conflict. The large number
of Russians in countries of the "near abroad," some
alleging discrimination, also place pressure on the
political leadership to assert Russia's regional
dominance. Meanwhile, non-Russian refugees and
immigrants are perceived as threatening to Russia's
own stability. In short, not only is Russia's economy
and polity in crisis, but also its self-identity.

In early 1994, Russia's leaders requested that international aid be directed toward development of a
social safety network, and Western nations seemed
more inclined than earlier to focus efforts in this
area.[51] At the same time, Russia's leaders have insisted
on recognition as an equal partner with Western industrialized nations. Russia raised objections to requests
by Eastern European countries to be admitted to the
North Atlantic Treaty Organization (NATO, a security
alliance formed to counter the Soviet challenge after
World War II, but with an unclear mandate following
the end of the Cold War). In response, NATO established the Partnership for Peace program to permit
these countries to be associated with NATO's security
system without granting them full membership. Russia was also invited to join. Reactions to the proposal

Russia without leadership.
Source: Vadim Misjuk,
courtesy of *Nezavisimaia
Gazeta (The Independent
Newspaper)*.

in Russia reflected Russia's identity crisis: Support for joining the Partnership for Peace reflects Russian aspirations to be part of the Western community, but objections to equating Russia with the smaller countries of Eastern Europe reflect Russia's desire to be recognized as a major regional and world power, meriting a special status in such international organizations.[52]

Western nations are unlikely to feel comfortable with the increasingly frequent assertions made by Russian leaders about Russia's legitimate regional and global leadership role. With the Cold War just ended, some in neighboring states and in the West are still concerned about Russia's imperial aspirations. These concerns are reinforced by statements that may really be intended for domestic consumption.

RUSSIAN POLITICS IN TRANSITION

What awaits Russia? Only fools will confidently predict Russia's future. We can, however, suggest a range of possible scenarios, which can serve as a standard against which to measure real developments as they occur over the next several years.[53]

The Civic Accord evokes the image of the most positive outcome: that all parties to the political conflict will conduct themselves in a cooperative and conciliatory manner, producing political stability and a slow but sure progress toward marketization and democratization of the system. Although the Civic Accord involves voluntary restraints by its signatories, it

can be regarded as an accord of national emergency, maintaining the key features of a democratic path. While Yeltsin's original commitment to Western-style economics in Russia may have suffered a blow from continuing economic decline and the weak showing of the pro-Western forces in the 1993 and 1995 parliamentary elections, the successful conduct of those elections may suggest that politics can proceed in a relatively democratic manner. The Civic Accord may serve a useful function in projecting a common myth, even if the real path Russia follows is likely to be laced with numerous severe jolts, shocks, and conflict.

A second possible scenario involves the introduction of a more severe authoritarian rule in Russia—that is, a return to Russia's traditional political culture. This could be a benevolent and soft dictatorship (for example, under Yeltsin), introduced gradually, perhaps without great fanfare, but nonetheless involving increasing restrictions on personal freedom and independent political activity. Some steps in this direction are already evident: failure to dismantle some of the systems of control inherited from the Soviet era, which permits Russian authorities to maintain significant state control; controls on emigration; and increasing efforts to control the electronic media. "Soft" authoritarianism might involve indirect control of the media, allowing some critical positions to be published. Travel abroad and contacts with foreigners might be permitted, but within a broadening system of

What Gorbachev Says About Russia's Move Toward Dictatorship

The West wants a stable Russia. This is certainly understandable. An unstable Russia spells trouble for the whole world.

But the West can't go back to business as usual with Boris Yeltsin's Russia.

Not after Chechnya.

Not after Moscow's obvious turn toward dictatorship.

Not after the wanton destruction of the city of Grozny [Chechnya] also destroyed the pretence that responsible democracy is being fostered in Russia. . . .

Yeltsin's very politics are threatening Russia's stability. Stability can't be created by a president and a power that do not meet with public approval.

————

From Mikhail Gorbachev, "Moscow turns to dictatorship: West must neither isolate Russia nor rationalize wthat it has done," *The Ottawa Citizen,* March 8, 1995, A15, distributed through *The New York Times* special features syndicate.

government oversight and regulation; free artistic creation might be stifled by market pressures rather than overt repression. Erosion of democratic practice would be gradual and accompanied by continuing democratic rhetoric. The "hard" version of this authoritarian scenario could involve the actual suspension of constitutional rights in the name of defending the reform against "fascism," "reaction," and "communism." The mirror image variant would be a coup d'état by conservative, neofascist, or military figures, in the guise of defending Russia from disintegration and national humiliation.

Given developments over the past ten years, the softer variant of authoritarianism seems more likely than the harder variant. Although a full-blown civil society may not have emerged in Russia, much of the population now expects and demands a level of personal and political freedom unprecedented in Russian history. While cynical about "democracy" as it exists in Russia, they take as a given that governments *should* respond to public needs and demands. This is especially true for young people who never were socialized to accept limits imposed by the Soviet system. Furthermore, ever-broadening contacts with Western models and ideas have greatly expanded horizons and expectations. Finally, it should be noted that the transformation of the former Soviet Union has proceeded

with remarkable civility and peace, at least in the core regions (including almost all of Russia).

The disintegration of Russia into many small fiefdoms or individual states is another scenario often discussed in the Russian and Western media. Actually, political and economic decentralization has proceeded quite far already. In Russia there is much talk of possible national disintegration, but there is also a great awareness of the costs of such disintegration, including the further rupture of vital economic ties, consequent economic decline, ethnic wars, and vast refugee and migration flows. The Yugoslav case offers a graphic and visible warning. Unlike in the late Soviet period, demands within the Russian Federation for regional autonomy are generated mostly by economics as an assertion of ownership rights and control over natural resources and economic assets. Even in the Chechnya case, control of petroleum resources was an important impetus for the crisis. Less prominent are real concerns with establishing national sovereignty and independence. The break-up of Russia is, in this author's view, a less likely scenario; the Chechnya episode indicates that maintenance of Russia's territorial integrity remains a high priority for the Russian state. Although the weakening of central state power in some regions is probable, achievement of de facto independence will likely be the exception, not the rule.

The worst case scenarios for Russia's future include continuing severe economic decline, civil war, and military expansionism. Civil war could take a variety of forms. It could be contained on Russia's perimeters, involving skirmishes rooted in ethnic tensions, perhaps involving groups residing in neighboring countries. Or outbreaks of widespread labor strife in key economic sectors could further fuel economic decline and also lead to confrontations between the militia and demonstrators. The present government has evidenced an increasing willingness to use coercion to control opposition (first during the October 1993 events and then in Chechnya). If continuing economic concessions further aggravate Russia's economic decline by placing greater strains on the central budget, by increasing public debt, and by fueling inflation, then pressure to suppress labor unrest may be reinforced. A crucial factor will be the government's capability to create a functioning social safety network to protect the displaced, the weak, and the unemployed from the consequences of the economic transformations underway.

Military expansionism seems unlikely in the near future. The rhetoric and aspirations of some political leaders (most notably Zhirinovksy, but also individuals like Rutskoi) suggest a desire to reestablish Russian hegemony in part of the former USSR. However, the military capacity of the state is unlikely to support any such initiatives. Despite mandatory male conscription, actual recruits into the military have declined, causing the size of Russian's armed forces to fall below the 2 million mark (at 1.5 million in early 1994) considered necessary by the Defense Ministry; lack of resources makes it difficult to maintain, let alone upgrade, Russia's strategic arsenal or other military equipment. A far greater danger may be sale or leakage of military equipment or nuclear materials into the hands of irresponsible parties, possibly fueling regional conflicts elsewhere, raising levels of terrorism and criminality in Russia society itself, or facilitating global nuclear proliferation.[54]

RUSSIA IN COMPARATIVE PERSPECTIVE

Many countries in the world today are undergoing a process of transition from some sort of authoritarian regime to a more democratic political structure. The Russian experience is, however, unique in many regards. First, indigenous political traditions and political culture influence the nature of political change in any country. As noted in Section 4, such factors have presented obstacles to realization of the blueprint for change drawn by President Yeltsin in 1992 at the dawn of Russia's emergence as an independent state. Other unique features of the Russian situation, compared to other systems attempting democratization, are a more direct inheritance of the former communist system.

The Soviet Union is described by many historians as a totalitarian system in which the party/state attempted, especially in the Stalinist period, to extend the scope of its control to encompass the basic values and private lives of its citizens. A corollary was the total integration of economics, politics, and ideology in the Soviet model. The state was the owner of virtually all economic assets and nearly all citizens were employees of the state. The Communist Party, which controlled state structures, claimed a monopoly on the truth and tried to direct all of the major institutions of political socialization (schools, public organizations, the arts, and media). To maintain this system of control, society and economy were kept artificially isolated from the outside world.

The way in which politics, economics, and ideology were intertwined with one another in the Soviet period has profoundly affected the nature of political change there, and generally has made the democratization process more difficult. Altering the political structures has necessarily involved dismantling the entire foundation of the former Soviet system. In effect, four transition processes were begun at once: (1) liberalization and then attempted democratization of the political system; (2) dismantling state dominance of the economy; (3) a search for new forms of collective identity to replace those provided by the old communist ideology; and (4) a process of economic integration into the world of states and exposure to ideas and goods from the Western world.

Whereas other democratizing countries may have undergone one or two of these transitions simultaneously, several of the post-communist states, including Russia, have tried to tackle all four of them at once. This has made the stakes and the stress very high. The old political elites have no private wealth to fall back on; they may, therefore, be prepared to turn to corrupt or illegal methods to maintain former privileges and benefits under the evolving new system. Individuals, confronted with economic decline and an uncertain future, may be susceptible to nationalistic appeals, demogogic leaders, or antidemocratic movements. Value disorientation and confusion may affect large portions of the population, as the larger environment appears chaotic and unpredictable.

Another important factor should be mentioned here: Unlike processes of democratization and economic transformation in portions of the developing world, in Russia these changes are occurring in a highly industrialized country with a skilled and educated workforce. This high level of development, another legacy of Soviet rule, is associated with a host of contemporary problems: a heavily damaged natural environment; obsolescent industries; entrenched bureaucratic structures; a nuclear arsenal that must be monitored and controlled; and a public that expects the state to provide a stable system of social welfare. Unlike modernizing elites in the developing world, the Russian leaders must first de-construct these already modern structures before constructing new ones. This process of de-construction almost inevitably involves at least a temporary decline in economic performance and a rise in unemployment. For example, inefficient or highly polluting factories may need to be closed;

the military-industrial complex may be cut back; and the state may have to reduce social benefits. These problems, in turn, make it more difficult for the state to manage the domestic and international challenges it confronts.

So far we have discussed some of the unique aspects of democratization efforts in Russia and the other post-communist states.[55] Now let us consider how Russia is faring compared to some of the other post-communist systems.[56]

The nations of Eastern Europe and the former Soviet Union were all subjected to a remarkably similar system of economic, political, and ideological power during the period of communist rule. Despite efforts of the Soviet leadership to establish conformity throughout the region, national differences, however, did emerge. The countries of Eastern Europe had a history of closer ties and greater cultural exposure to Western Europe; ideas of liberalism, private property, and individualism were more widely adhered to in such countries as Czechoslovakia, East Germany, and Hungary than in regions farther east, including Russia. The Catholic church in Poland provided a focal point for national identity, and Poland's historical antipathy to Russia produced a stronger resistance to the imposition of the Soviet model there than in other Slavic countries of the region. Such cultural, geopolitical, and historical differences affected the shape that communist rule took in the various countries. In Poland collectivization of agriculture never succeeded and communist rule took a "softer" form; in Hungary a form of quasi-market reform began to emerge beginning in 1968; and in Czechoslovakia in 1968 a dramatic attempt to build "socialism with a human face" emerged from within the Communist Party elite itself and suffered defeat only at the hands of Soviet troops. Effects of Ottoman rule in Yugoslavia and Bulgaria produced yet a different cultural mosaic, and in several countries problems with ethnic minorities created unique tensions, even if their open expression was, for the most part, suppressed under communist rule. Within the Soviet Union too, considerable variation between the union republics existed. The Baltic republics of Latvia, Lithuania, and Estonia took a more experimental approach in many spheres of activity and had a more West European atmosphere; on the other extreme, the Central Asia republics retained aspects of traditional Muslim culture, preserved the extended family structure, and maintained within the construct of the Communist Party a greater prominence for links rooted in the clan system indigenous to the region. Only in Russia (and in China and Cuba) was communism largely an indigenous phenomenon rather than a pattern imposed by an outside force. In many ways Russia's culture helped to define the character of the communist system that it imposed throughout its sphere of influence.

All of the fifteen countries that gained independence after the collapse of the Soviet Union as well as the countries of Eastern Europe have experienced the collapse of the communist system of power since 1989. Given the diversity of nations that were subjected to the communist system, it is not surprising that paths of extrication from communist rule should also vary widely. How has Russia fared in the post-communist period compared to these other countries? We can, in sum, say, "not the best, but not the worst either." All of the post-communist states have shared common problems, but the elites have responded in different ways, and differences in traditional culture and the particular nature of the communist system in each country have affected the present condition of the post-communist polities and economies.

Russia has almost certainly suffered more severe economic dislocations than most of the countries of Eastern Europe (with the clear exception of Yugoslavia) in the post-communist period.[57] Poland has pursued the most radical variant of the shock therapy approach, at least until a communist-oriented coalition was voted back into power in 1992. In many regards it appears that Poland's post-communist economic strategy has been the most successful in terms of gross economic indicators. However, huge differentials in income and high unemployment rates have been costs of the approach. Russia's attempt to implement the radical reform strategy has been less successful than Poland's because internal political opposition has been more successful in moderating economic policy and indigenous culture is probably less conducive to market structures.

Russia has fared relatively well compared to neighbors like Ukraine, Belarus, the Transcaucasian region, and most of the Central Asian states. The leaders there have embraced market reform with considerably less commitment than the Russian government. For example, Ukraine and most of the Central Asian republics have embarked on only limited economic reform and the result has generally been a more severe

TABLE 8 **Changes in Gross Domestic Product per Capita Before and After Independence**[a]
(purchasing power parities)

	1986	1990	1991[b]	1992	1993	1994
Russia	95	111	100 ($6,962)	84	76	66
Ukraine	90	110	100 ($5,107)	85	75	59
Belarus	80	98	100 ($7,066)	92	84	68
Estonia	88	109	100 ($7,941)	81	82	88
Kazakhstan	85	110	100 ($5,334)	89	79	60
Kyrgyz Republic	78	103	100 ($3,460)	77	65	55
Uzbekistan	81	99	100 ($3,054)	90	89	82
Georgia	111	121	100 ($3,950)	59	37	24

[a]Adapted from purchasing power parities, based on gross domestic product per capita, provided in the Economist Intelligence Unit, *Country Report: Russia* (2d quarterly report, 1995), 48–49.
[b]1991 level = 100 for the country listed. Figure in parentheses is the U.S. dollar level for 1991.

Source: Adapted from Economist Intelligence Unit, *Country Report: Russia* (2d quarterly report, 1995), 48–49.

economic decline than has characterized Russia (see Table 8). Because Russia possesses rich deposits of natural resources (including energy resources), it has been able to cope with the ruptured economic ties resulting from the collapse of the Soviet Union better than some of the less well endowed new states. In addition, Belarus and Ukraine suffer from the severe economic and health effects of the Chernobyl accident, and the Central Asian states confront the disastrous effects of the cotton monoculture and associated environmental degradation (Aral Sea crisis). Furthermore, Russia has been the focal point of international economic assistance because of its large nuclear arsenal, its size, and its geopolitical importance. Although this aid has been insufficient to make a decisive difference in the success of the government's overall reform program, other parts of the former Soviet Union (with the likely exception of the Baltic states) have received even fewer benefits of international assistance, despite their weaker economic position.

In the political sphere, virtually all of the post-communist states claim to be pursuing some form of democratization, but in some cases this is more in name than in practice, particularly in Central Asia and parts of the Transcaucasian area. The attempt to construct democratic political institutions has everywhere been characterized by repeated political crises, weak representation of popular interests, executive-legislative conflict, faltering efforts at constitutional

revision, general immobilism, and corruption. These features exist in virtually all of the post-communist states, but they seem to be more marked in the more eastern ones. This may be the result of cultural differences between Russia and its more Europeanized western neighbors (particularly, Poland, East Germany, the Czech Republic, and Hungary) as well as to the shorter period of Communist Party rule in Eastern Europe, the Baltics, and some of the western portions of the former USSR (where the Communist Party took power only after World War II). The cultural and geographical proximity of Eastern Europe to the West has also meant less ambivalence on the part of the population and elite toward Western notions of political democracy. In Russia, on the other hand, there is considerable popular skepticism toward the wholesale adoption of a Western model of political development, and the political elites themselves, who mouth Western values, have to a large degree not understood or internalized them. The question might be asked whether the patrimonial, collectivist, and egalitarian thrust of Russian culture, as well some features of the cultures of Central Asia, Ukraine, and Belarus are really compatible with Western economic and political notions. Although the concept of democracy has a certain appeal in the region (partly because it has been associated with Western affluence), to much of the population in these countries it means, above all, personal freedom rather than support for notions of political accountability, "rule of law," or the civic role of the citizen.

Even though Russian politics have been highly contentious and the government operates at very low levels of efficacy and legitimacy, until recently Russia escaped major domestic violence and civil war, unlike Yugoslavia, Armenia, Azerbaijan, Georgia, Moldova, and the Central Asian state of Tadzhikistan. For all their problems, Russian politicians have conducted themselves in a relatively civil manner, and Yeltsin himself has rarely appealed to exclusivist definitions of Russian identity. Citizenship rights for all ethnic groups have been maintained, and state-sponsored racism has not been a major factor for evoking societal tension or civil strife. Some opposition figures have not been so restrained in their political rhetoric, but the Yeltsin government can be credited with avoiding marginalization of any major social groups.

Russia will undoubtedly continue to be a key regional force in Europe and Asia. Its vast geographical expanse, rich resource base, large and highly skilled population, and the legacy of Soviet rule will all assure this. Yet its former allies in Central Europe, especially the Czech Republic, Hungary, Poland, and to some degree the Baltic States, are gradually drifting into the orbit of Western European influence, both economically and politically. They are seeking, and to a degree have already achieved, closer economic and political ties to the European Union; their identity is increasingly defined by those ties. This could potentially leave Russia isolated and increasingly resentful of the loss of stature in both the regional and international world of states. Economic decline, deteoriation of military capacity, and the increasing infusion of foreign money and influence could also reinforce these tendencies. A rising sense of national humiliation could well make Russia a less tractable and more pugnacious force.

On Russia's eastern side, the former Central Asian republics (Turkmenistan, Uzbekistan, Tadzhikistan, and Kyrgystan) are being courted by the Middle Eastern states with whom they share linguistic, cultural, and religious ties. Here the pattern of economic and political transformation will be affected by traditions and cultures (including Islam) that play only a minimal role in the Christianized areas of the former Soviet bloc. And yet in many ways these regions, along with Kazakhstan, retain strong links to Russia, rooted in decades of economic and political interdependence. The states in the middle (Russia, Ukraine, Belarus, Moldova, Bulgaria, Romania) still lie, as historically, between East and West. Here, efforts to adapt a West European model of economy and polity have at times seemed tortured and incongruous with indigenous traditions and aspirations. The tradition of a strong state and weak society has not been reversed; cultural tendencies to egalitarianism, state paternalism, clientelistic networks, and communalism conflict with efforts to adopt Western market structures and legal regimes. And yet exposure to Western life-styles, affluence, and legal norms has instilled expectations and hopes, particularly in educated circles, for a more prosperous life-style, less encumbered by the bureaucratic control of the state. The global nature of politics and economics has made impossible the type of isolation that provided a bulwark for the legitimacy of the Soviet state for many decades. These states will likely continue to be torn between conflicting values and international pressures, with Russia both a feared but influential model (either to emulate or reject) for the neighboring countries.

Will Russia be able to find a place for itself in the world of states commensurate with the expectations of its educated and sophisticated population? Or will it forge its own destiny by adapting Western approaches to the uniqueness that is Russia? Analysts will be watching.

Key Terms

mir	privatization vouchers
democratic centralism	joint-stock company
vanguard party	insider privatization
patrimonial state	separation of powers
collectivization	soviets
totalitarian(ism)	federal system
nomenklatura	autonomous republics
tacit social contract	*oblast'*
perestroika	*krai*
glasnost	patron-client networks
demokratizatsiia	industrialists
law-based state	mafia
union republics	civil society
sovkhoz	proportional
kolkhoz	representation
market reform	political culture
shock therapy	
spontaneous	
privatization	

Suggested Readings

Section 1

Cohen, Stephen. *Rethinking the Soviet Experience: Politics and History Since 1917.* New York: Oxford University Press, 1985.

Getty, J. Arch. *Origins of the Great Purges: The Soviet Communist Party Reconsidered.* Cambridge: Cambridge University Press, 1985.

Pipes, Richard. *Russia Under the Old Regime.* London: Widenfelt & Nicolson, 1974.

Sakwa, Richard. *Gorbachev and His Reforms, 1985–1990.* London: Philip Allan, 1990.

Tucker, Robert C. *Stalin in Power: The Revolution From Above, 1928–1941.* New York and London: Norton, 1990.

Section 2

Cook, Linda J. *The Soviet Social Contract and Why It Failed.* Cambridge, Mass., and London: Harvard University Press, 1993.

Feshbach, Murray, and Alfred Friendly, Jr. *Ecocide in the USSR: Health and Nature Under Siege.* New York: Basic Books, 1992.

Gregory, Paul R., and Robert C. Stuart. *Soviet Economic Structure and Performance.* 4th ed. New York: Harper and Row, 1990.

Pryde, Philip R., ed. *Environmental Resources and Constraints in the Former Soviet Republics.* Boulder, San Francisco, and Oxford: Westview Press, 1995.

Section 3

Colton, Timothy, and Thane Gustafson, eds. *Soldiers and the Soviet State: Civil-Military Relations from Brezhnev to Gorbachev.* Princeton, N.J.: Princeton University Press, 1990.

Friedgut, Theodore H., and Jeffrey W. Hahn, eds. *Local Power and Post-Soviet Politics.* Armonk, N.Y.: M. E. Sharpe, 1994.

Hough, Jerry, and Merle Fainsod. *How the Soviet Union Is Governed.* Cambridge, Mass.: Harvard University Press, 1979.

White, Stephen, Alex Pravda, and Zvi Gitelman, eds. *Developments in Russian and Post-Soviet Politics.* 3d ed. London: Macmillan, 1994.

Section 4

Lewin, Moshe. *The Gorbachev Phenomenon: A Historical Interpretation.* Enl. ed. Berkeley: University of California Press, 1991.

Filtzer, Donald. *Soviet Workers and the Collapse of Perestroika: The Soviet Labour Process and Gorbachev's Reforms: 1959–1991.* Cambridge: Cambridge University Press, 1994.

Hajda, Lubomyr, and Mark Beissinger, eds. *The Nationalities Factor in Soviet Politics and Society.* Boulder, Colo.: Westview Press, 1990.

Millar, James R., ed. *Politics, Work, and Daily Life in the USSR: A Survey of Former Soviet Citizens.* Cambridge: Cambridge University Press, 1987.

Miller, Arthur, Vicki Hesli, and William Reisinger. "Reassessing Mass Support for Political and Economic Change in the Former USSR." *American Political Science Review* 88, no. 2 (June 1994): 399–411.

Urban, Michael. "The Politics of Identity in Russia's Post-Communist Tradition." *Slavic Review* 53, no. 3 (Fall 1994): 733–765.

Section 5

Bova, Russell. "Political Dynamics of the Post-Communist Transition: A Comparative Perspective." In *Post-Communist Studies and Political Science: Methodology and Empirical Theory in Sovietology,* edited by Frederic J. Fleron, Jr., and Erik P. Hoffman, 239–263. Boulder, San Francisco, and Oxford: Westview Press, 1993.

Dawisha, Karen, and Bruce Parrott. *Russia and the New States of Eurasia: The Politics of Upheaval.* Cambridge: Cambridge University Press, 1994.

Lapidus, Gail W. *The New Russia: Troubled Transformation.* Boulder, Colo.: Westview Press, 1994.

Przeworski, Adam. *Democracy and the Market: Political and Economic Reform in Eastern Europe and Latin America.* Cambridge: Cambridge University Press, 1991.

Endnotes

[1] For discussion of the events leading up to the collapse of the USSR, see Stephen White, *After Gorbachev* (Cambridge: Cambridge University Press, 1992); for an account of the coup itself, see Victoria Bonnell, Ann Cooper, and Gregory Freidin, *Russia at the Barricades: Eyewitness Accounts of the August 1991 Coup* (Armonk, N.Y.: M. E. Sharpe, 1994).

[2] On Russian history, see Michael T. Florinsky, *Russia: A History and an Interpretation* (New York: McMillan, 1953).

[3] On the revolutionary period and the 1920s, see Sheila Fitzpatrick, *The Russian Revolution 1917–1932* (Oxford and New York: Oxford University Press, 1984).

[4] On Lenin's version of Marxism, see Marcel Liebman, *Leninism Under Lenin* (London: Merlin Press, 1975). For a less sympathetic discussion of Leninism see Alfred G. Meyer, *Leninism* (New York: Praeger, 1957).

[5] On the developments of the 1920s and the New Economic Policy, see Stephen Cohen, *Bukharin and the Bolshevik Revolution: A Political Biography, 1888–1938* (Oxford: Oxford University Press, 1980).

[6] On Stalinism, see Robert C. Tucker, *Stalin in Power: The Revolution from Above, 1928–1941* (New York: Norton, 1990); for a revisionist interpretation see J. Arch Getty, *Origins of the Great Purges: The Soviet Communist Party Reconsidered* (Cambridge: Cambridge University Press, 1985).

[7] Richard Pipes, *Russia Under the Old Regime* (Harmondsworth, Middlesex, England: Penguin Books, 1974), 22–24.

[8] On the concept of totalitarianism, see Carl J. Friedrich and Zbigniew K. Brzezinski, *Totalitarian Dictatorship and Autocracy* (Cambridge, Mass.: Harvard University Press, 1965).

[9] On the Khrushchev period, see Carl Linden, *Khrushchev and the Soviet Leadership, 1957–1964* (Baltimore: Johns Hopkins University Press, 1966). See also Khrushchev's own memoirs, published in three volumes in the West: *Khrushchev Remembers* (Boston: Little, Brown, 1970); *Khrushchev Remembers: The Last Testament* (New York: Bantam, 1976); and *Khrushchev Remembers: The Glasnost Tapes* (Boston: Little, Brown, 1990).

[10] On the idea of the social contract, see Peter Hauslohner, "Politics Before Gorbachev: De-Stalinization and the Roots of Reform," in

The Soviet System in Crisis: A Reader of Western and Soviet Views, ed. Alexander Dallin and Gail W. Lapidus (Boulder, Colo.: Westview Press, 1991), 37–63; and Joan DeBardeleben, *Soviet Politics in Transition* (Lexington, Mass.: D. C. Heath and Co., 1992), 38–40.

[11]On the Gorbachev years, see Richard Sakwa, *Gorbachev and His Reforms, 1985–1990* (London: Philip Allan, 1990).

[12]On public discussion during the glasnost period, see Alec Nove, *Glasnost in Action: Cultural Renaissance in Russia* (Boston: Unwin, Hyman, 1989).

[13]See Mikhail Gorbachev, *Perestroika: New Thinking for Our Country and the World* (New York: Harper, 1987).

[14]On ethnic issues in the Gorbachev and pre-Gorbachev periods, see Lubomyr Hajda and Mark R. Beissinger, eds., *The Nationalities Factor in Soviet Politics and Society* (Boulder, Colo.: Westview Press, 1990).

[15]On economic decline in the perestroika period see William Moskoff, *Hard Times: Impoverishment and Protest in the Perestroika Years: The Soviet Union, 1985–1991* (Armonk, N.Y., and London: M. E. Sharpe, 1993).

[16]Adapted from Marshall I. Goldman, "Gorbachev and Economic Reform," *Foreign Affairs* (Fall 1985): 64.

[17]For a history of the Soviet economy, see Alec Nove, *An Economic History of the USSR, 1917–1991,* 3d ed. (London: Penguin, 1992).

[18]On the operation of the Soviet economic system, see Paul R. Gregory and Robert C. Stuart, *Soviet Economic Structure and Performance,* 4th ed. (New York: Harper & Row, 1990).

[19]On environmental problems in the USSR and Russia, see Murray Feshbach and Alfred Friendly, Jr., *Ecocide in the USSR: Health and Nature under Siege* (New York: Basic Books, 1992).

[20]See David Lane, *Soviet Society under Perestroika,* rev. ed. (London and New York: Routledge, 1992), 357–361.

[21]Feshbach and Friendly, *Ecocide in the USSR,* 4. (See Chapters 9–10 of this book for more on the health situation in the former USSR).

[22]On the early Gorbachev reform efforts, see Anders Aslund, *Gorbachev's Struggle for Economic Reform: The Soviet Reform Process, 1985–1988* (Ithaca, N.Y.: Cornell University Press, 1989).

[23]For discussion and debate of shock therapy, see Josef Brada, "The Transformation from Communism to Capitalism: How Far? How Fast?" *Post-Soviet Affairs* 9, no. 2 (1993): 87–100; and Peter Murrell, "What Is Shock Therapy? What Did It Do in Poland and Russia?" *Post-Soviet Affairs* 9, no. 2 (1993): 111–140.

[24]Vladimir V. Popov, "The Russian Economy in 1994: Forecasts and Annual Survey of 1993," CRCR Conference Report, no. 6 (Ottawa: Centre for Research on Canadian-Russian Relations, Carleton University, 1994), 3.

[25]See Stephen Handelman, *Comrade Criminal: The New Russian Mafia* (New Haven: Yale University Press, 1995).

[26]Radio Free Europe/Radio Liberty Daily Report (distributed by electronic mail) April 8, 1994, and May 17, 1994 (report by Keith Bush).

[27]See Stephen Wengren, "Rural Reform and Political Culture in Russia," *Europe-Asia Studies* 46, no. 2 (1994): 215–245.

[28]*Radio Liberty/Radio Free Europe Research Report,* vol. 3, no. 3, 28.

[29]Figures adapted from *EIU Quarterly Economic Review of the USSR,* 1985 Annual Supplement (London: Economist Intelligence Unit, 1985), 20.

[30]See Jerry Hough and Merle Fainsod, *How the Soviet Union Is Governed* (Cambridge, Mass.: Harvard University Press, 1979).

[31]On the *nomenklatura* system, see Michael Voslensky, *Nomenklatura: The Soviet Ruling Class,* trans. Eric Mosbacher (Garden City, N.Y.: Doubleday, 1984).

[32]See Stephen White, *After Gorbachev,* 4th ed. (Cambridge: Cambridge University Press, 1993).

[33]See the autobiography of Boris Yeltsin, *Against the Grain: An Autobiography* (New York: Summit, 1990); and Vladimir Solov'ev, *Boris Yeltsin: A Political Biography* (New York: Putnam, 1992).

[34]On center/periphery relations in Russia, see Richard E. Ericson, "Nationalism, Regionalism, and Federalism: Center-Periphery Relations in Post-communist Russia," in *The New Russia: Troubled Transformation,* ed. Gail W. Lapidus (Boulder, Colo.: Westview Press, 1994).

[35]See Timothy Colton and Thane Gustafson, eds., *Soldiers and the Soviet State: Civil-Military Relations from Brezhnev to Gorbachev* (Princeton, N.J.: Princeton University Press, 1990).

[36]See Benjamin S. Lambeth, "Russia's Wounded Military," *Foreign Affairs* (March/April 1995): 86–98.

[37]On the regional dimension of politics, see Darrell Slider, Vladimir Gimpel'son, and Sergei Chugrov, "Political Tendencies in Russia's Regions: Evidence from the 1993 Parliamentary Elections," *Slavic Review* 53, no. 3 (Fall 1994): 711–732.

[38]On the notion of civil society, see Moshe Lewin, *The Gorbachev Phenomenon: A Historical Interpretation,* enlarged edition (Berkeley: University of California Press, 1991); Gail W. Lapidus, "State and Society: Toward the Emergence of Civil Society in the Soviet Union," in *Politics, Society, and Nationality Inside Gorbachev's Russia,* ed. Seweryn Bialer (Boulder, Colo., and London: Westview Press, 1989), 121–147; and Michael Ignatieff, "On Civil Society: Why Eastern Europe's Revolution Could Succeed," *Foreign Affairs* (March/April 1995): 128–136.

[39]On the general problem, see Thomas Remington, ed., *Parliaments in Transition: The New Legislative Politics in the Former USSR and Eastern Europe* (Boulder, Colo.: Westview Press, 1994).

[40]For a history of the party, see Leonard Betram Shapiro, *The Communist Party of the Soviet Union,* 2d rev. ed. (New York: Random House, 1971).

[41]On politics within the Communist Party of the Soviet Union, see Jerry F. Hough, *The Soviet Prefect* (Cambridge, Mass.: Harvard University Press, 1969); and Jerry F. Hough, *The Soviet Union and Social Science Theory* (Cambridge, Mass. and London: Harvard University Press, 1977), 71–108.

[42]On the Russian party system and problems of its development, see Aleksandr Meerovich, "The Emergence of Russian Multiparty Politics," in *The Soviet System in Crisis: A Read of Western and Soviet Views,* ed. Alexander Dallin and Gail W. Lapidus (Boulder, Colo.: Westview Press, 1991), 161–173.

[43]"Liberal'no-Demokraticheskaia Partiia Rossii: Programmnye tezisy," published by the International Charitable Fund for Political-Legal Research "Interlegal," *Politicheskie partii i bloki na vyborakh (teksty izbiratel'nykh platform)* (Political parties and blocs in the elections [text of electoral platforms]) (Moscow, 1993), 47.

[44]On the political culture concept as applied to the region, see Archie Brown, "Ideology and Political Culture," in *Politics, Society, and Nationality Inside Gorbachev's Russia,* ed. Seweryn Bialer (Boulder, Colo.: Westview Press, 1989): 1–40.

[45]See Aryeh Unger, *The Totalitarian Party* (London: Cambridge University Press, 1974).

[46]On developments in the Russian mass media, see Julia Wishnevsky, "Manipulation, Mayhem, and Murder," *Transition: Events and Issues in the Former Soviet Union and East-Central and South-Eastern Europe,* 1994 in Review: Part II (February 1995), 37–40. (Published by the Open Media Research Institute, Prague.)

[47]See Ludmilla Alexeyeva, *Soviet Dissent: Contemporary Movements for National, Religious, and Human Rights,* trans. Carol Pearce and John Glad (Middletown, Conn.: Wesleyan University Press, 1985).

[48]On labor unrest, see Peter Rutland, "Labor Unrest and Movements in 1989 and 1990," *Soviet Economy* 6 (October–December 1990): 345–384; and Elizabeth Teague, "Perestroika and the Soviet Worker," *Government and Opposition* 25, no. 2 (1990): 191–211.

[49]See Deborah Adelman, *The "Children of Perestroika": Moscow Teenagers Talk About Their Lives and Future* (Armonk, N.Y.: M. E. Sharpe, 1991); and Deborah Adelman, *The "Children of Perestroika" Come of Age* (Armonk, N.Y.: M. E. Sharpe, 1994).

[50]Barrington Moore, Jr., "Liberal Prospects Under Soviet Socialism: A Comparative Historical Perspective," Columbia University, The First Annual W. Averill Harriman Lecture (November 15, 1989).

[51]On issues related to Western aid, see David Holloway and Michael McFaul, "Aid to Russia: What Difference Can Western Policy Make?" in *The New Russia: Troubled Transformation,* ed. Gail W. Lapidus (Boulder, Colo.: Westview Press, 1994).

[52]On Russia's relationship with NATO, see Douglas L. Clarke, "Uncomfortable Partners," *Transition: Events and Issues in the Former Soviet Union and East-Central and Southeastern Europe,* 1994 in Review: Part II (February 1995): 27–31.

[53]For perspectives on Russia's future, see Douglas W. Blum, ed., *Russia's Future: Consolidation or Disintegration* (Boulder, Colo.: Westview Press, 1994).

[54]On nuclear issues, see Thomas B. Cochran and Robert S. Norris, *Russian Nuclear Warhead Production* (Boulder, Colo.: Westview Press, 1995).

[55]For comparisons between the post-Soviet situation and democratization processes in Latin America, see, for example, Russell Bova, "Political Dynamics of the Post-Communist Transition: A Comparative Perspective," in *Post-Communist Studies and Political Science: Methodology and Empirical Theory in Sovietology,* ed. Frederic J. Fleron, Jr., and Erik P. Hoffman (Boulder, Colo.: Westview Press, 1993) 239–263; and Adam Przeworski, *Democracy and the Market: Political and Economic Reform in Eastern Europe and Latin America* (Cambridge: Cambridge University Press, 1991).

[56]See Sarah Meiklejohn Terry, "Thinking about Post-Communist Transitions: How Different Are They?" *Slavic Review* 52, no. 2 (Summer 1993): 333–337.

[57]On economic transitions in post-communist systems, see Robert W. Campbell, *The Postcommunist Economic Transformation: Essays in Honor of Gregory Grossman* (Boulder, Colo.: Westview Press, 1994).

CHAPTER 7

China

PEOPLE'S REPUBLIC OF CHINA

Land and Population

Capital	Beijing
Total Area (square miles)	3,705,386 (slightly larger than U.S.)
Population	1.2 billion
Annual Projected Population Growth Rate (1993–2000)	0.9%
Urban Population (% of total)	29%

Ethnic Composition		
Major Ethnic Groups	Han (Chinese)	92%
	Other	8%
Major Language	Chinese (various dialects)	93%
Major Religions	Nonreligious and atheist	71%
	Folk	20%
	Buddhist	6%
	Muslim	2%

Economy

Domestic Currency	Renminbi (People's Currency), also called yuan
Total GNP (US$)	$588 billion
GNP per capita (US$)	$490
Purchasing Power Parity GDP per capita (US$)	$2,330
Average Annual GDP Growth Rate (1980–1993)	9.6%

Structure of Production (% of GDP)		
	Agriculture	19%
	Industry	48%
	Services	33%

Labor Force Distribution (% of total)		
	Agriculture	73%
	Industry	14%
	Services	13%

Women as % of Total Labor Force	43%

Income Distribution (1990)	% of Population	% Share of Income or Consumption
	Richest 20%	41.8%
	Poorest 20%	6.4%

Total Foreign Trade (exports plus imports) as % of GDP	37%

Society

Life Expectancy	Female	71
	Male	68
Population per Doctor	730	
Infant Mortality (per 1,000 live births)	30	
Adult Literacy	Female	68%
	Male	92%
Average (Mean) Years of Schooling (of adults 25+)	Female	3.8
	Male	6.3
Communications (per 100 people)	Radios	18
	Televisions	3
	Telephones	1
1995 Human Development Index (1 = highest)	Ranks 111 out of 174	

Political Organization

Political System   Communist Party-State

Regime History   Established in 1949 after the victory of the Chinese Communist Party (CCP) in the Chinese civil war.

Administrative Structure   Unitary system with 22 provinces, 5 autonomous regions, and 3 centrally administered municipalities.

Executive   Premier (head of government) and president (head of state) formally elected by legislature, but only with approval of CCP leadership; the head of the CCP, the general secretary, is the country's effective chief executive.

Legislature   Unicameral National People's Congress; delegates elected indirectly from lower-level people's congresses for five-year terms. Largely a rubber stamp for Communist Party policies, although in recent years has become somewhat more assertive.

Judiciary   A nationwide system of people's courts which is constitutionally independent, but is, in fact, largely under the control of the Chinese Communist Party; a Supreme People's Court supervises the country's judicial system and is formally responsible to the National People's Congress, which also elects the court's president.

Party System   A one-party system, although in addition to the ruling Chinese Communist Party, there are eight politically insignificant "democratic" parties.

SECTION 1
The Making of the Modern Chinese State

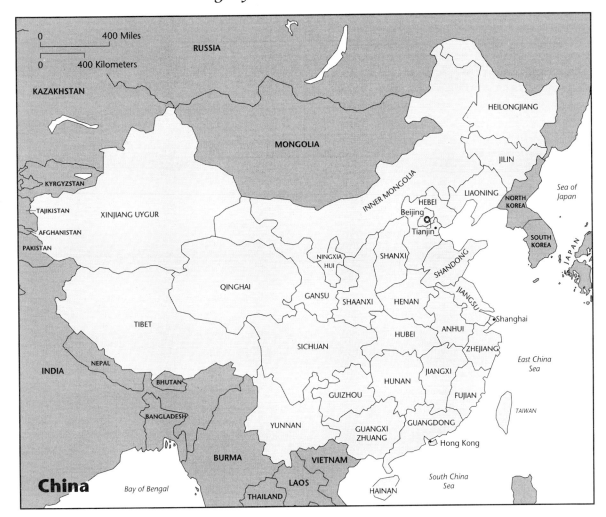

China

CHINA AT THE CROSSROADS

In the early morning hours of June 4, 1989, Chinese soldiers began the final stage of an assault to remove pro-democracy demonstrators from Tiananmen Square in the center of China's capital, Beijing. One of the protesters described what happened when he and others joined hands on the outskirts of the square to form a human barricade to halt the army's advance:

Then, without warning, the troops opened fire on us. People cursed, screamed and ran. In no time, seventy or eighty people had collapsed all around me. Blood spattered all over, staining my clothes.

At a nearby intersection, he recalls seeing "several hundred bodies, mostly young people." As the army continued to move toward the square, an angry crowd of over ten thousand surged forward to surround the troops. This time the soldiers turned on the people with even greater brutality. The fusillades from machine guns were loud and clear. Because some of the bullets used were the kind that explode within the body, when they struck, the victims' intestines and brains spilled out. I saw four or five such bodies. They looked like disembowcled animal carcasses.[1]

By the time dawn broke in Beijing, Tiananmen Square had, indeed, been cleared. Although many of the student protesters had been allowed to evacuate the area, several hundred people—perhaps as many as 2,000 according to some accounts—had been killed when soldiers took control of the square. Most had been killed by gunfire. Some had been run down by tanks or armored personnel carriers. Some had been immolated by flamethrowers. Others had been beaten to death after having been taken into custody.

In the days that followed, a wave of terror and repression spread throughout China. Thousands of Chinese citizens were arrested for their role in the demonstrations in Beijing and other cities, and there were several well-publicized executions of people charged with sabotage during the protests.

The demonstrations had begun in April when university students gathered in Tiananmen (literally, "Gate of Heavenly Peace") to protest widespread official corruption and to demand that the Chinese Communist Party (CCP) allow more democracy in China. The protesters had been emboldened by the fact that, under the leadership of Deng Xiaoping, the Chinese people were experiencing more economic and cultural freedom than at any time since the Communists had come to power in 1949. The students now wanted to extend the process of reform into the realm of government and politics.

Student demands were met with belligerent rhetoric from China's leaders, who denounced the protesters as conspirators and troublemakers intent on overthrowing the CCP. In response to the party's hard line and in the glow of international media attention, the demonstrations grew in size. Citizens from all walks of life in Beijing—teachers, artists, and writers, factory and office workers, business owners, retirees, and even government employees—came into the streets to show their support for the

Student demonstrators erected a statute called the "Goddess of Democracy" in Beijing's Tiananmen Square in late May 1989 to symbolize their demands for greater political freedom in China. In the background is an official portrait of former Chinese Communist Party leader, Mao Zedong. Chinese troops toppled and destroyed the statue after they occupied the square on June 4, 1989, a process that also resulted in the death of many protesters.
Source: AP/Wide World Photos.

students in the square. At one point, more than a million people were gathered in and around Tiananmen. Similar protests sprang up in dozens of cities across China.

Party intransigence and student insistence became locked into a deadly spiral of hostility and misunderstanding, and the stakes for both sides in the confrontation escalated to the point where neither would compromise or back down. The students declared a hunger strike; the government declared **martial law.** The students erected a 30-foot plaster statue of a "Goddess of Democracy," explicitly patterned after the Statue of Liberty; the government became more strident in denouncing foreign subversion as the source of the turmoil.

By early June, there were signs that the demonstrations were losing momentum, and it is likely that the crowds would have dispersed on their own accord in a matter of days. But China's Communist leaders ran out of patience. The order to move against the students and their supporters, and to do so with deadly force, was made by a handful of elderly party patriarchs, including Deng Xiaoping. Their motive was not just to clear the square and restore order in the city; they wanted to "kill the chicken to scare the monkey," an ancient Chinese political control strategy. The massacre was meant to send an unmistakable message throughout China that no challenge to the authority of the Chinese Communist Party would be tolerated and all necessary means would be used to crush any opposition.

How had China reached this point of political crisis in 1989 after more than a decade of tremendous economic progress and soaring hopes under the leadership of Deng Xiaoping? Deng had become China's most powerful leader in 1978 and had almost immediately launched the program of reforms that would fundamentally transform many aspects of the Communist regime in China. He had inherited a nation that had been dominated for nearly three decades by Mao Zedong, the man who had led the Communists to victory in 1949 after a long civil war, presided over the establishment of a Communist-led political system in China, and pushed the nation along a developmental path shaped by his fervent commitment to a particularly radical version of **Marxism-Leninism.** Mao had certainly accomplished a great deal in establishing China's independence after more than a century of humiliation and domination by foreign powers and in industrializing the country, but the legacy that Mao had bequeathed to Deng Xiaoping was basically one of political repression, social tension, cultural sterility, and economic underachievement. He also left Deng with the stewardship of a ruling Communist Party that, because of its harsh rule and radicalism, had squandered much of the genuine popularity and support it had enjoyed in its early years in power.

Deng's reforms were a profound break with the Maoist past. He introduced policies that reduced the role of the state and increased the role of the market in the economy. Agriculture was decollectivized and farm production returned to the control of individual families. He sanctioned the rapid expansion of private businesses in both city and countryside. The Chinese economy was opened to unprecedented levels of foreign investment.

On the cultural front, Chinese artists and writers saw most of the shackles of party dogma that had bound them for decades removed. Tens of thousands of Chinese students were sent abroad with the expectation that they would bring their new knowledge home to serve the nation. Deng took major steps to revitalize China's government by bringing in younger, better-educated officials. He promised an end to the bitter and divisive political struggles that had characterized the Maoist period. He proclaimed an era of social harmony in which the whole nation could concentrate its energies on the overarching goals of modernization and economic development.

The results of Deng's initiatives were, by any measure, astounding. After decades of stagnation, the Chinese economy experienced unprecedented growth. The winds of freedom and openness seemed to be blowing through every sector of life in China. Deng was named *Time* magazine's "Man of the Year" in 1979 and, again, in 1986 in recognition of both the boldness and the success of his efforts to change China.

Then came Tiananmen. There had been many warning signs. Deng had often said that the Communist Party and his version of communist doctrine would dictate the boundaries of reform. He had denounced earlier efforts to promote broader democratization in China as the result of "spiritual pollution" and "bourgeois liberalization" from the West, which would not be permitted to contaminate China's socialist system. He had authorized a crackdown on small-scale democracy movements in 1979 and 1987 and had purged one of his closest associates for being too soft on the issue of political reform. And, as a founding leader of the Chinese Communist regime, Deng had been Mao's junior partner in the establishment of one of the world's toughest dictatorships. Tiananmen was a shocking reminder that, for all the economic changes that had taken place under Deng, political life in China remained subject to strict regulation by the CCP.

Repression has relaxed considerably in the years since the Tiananmen massacre. Many political prisoners and dissidents have been released from custody, cultural restrictions have been loosened again, and

This cartoon captures the contradiction between economic reform and political repression that has characterized China under the leadership of Deng Xiaoping, especially since the Tiananmen crisis of 1989.
Source: © 1992, *The Boston Globe*. Distributed by Los Angeles Times Syndicate. Reprinted with permission.

people feel much freer to talk. Economic reform is being pursued more vigorously than ever before, with China embracing even more capitalist-like policies and moving even farther from its centrally planned economy and toward the market.

The specter of Tiananmen still haunts China, however, and a subtle but undeniable veil of terror that dissuades all direct opposition to Communist rule still hangs over the country. The People's Republic of China (PRC) is one of only a few countries still governed by a communist party. Its political system reflects the general characteristics of a **communist party-state,** including a communist party monopoly on political power, party control of all government and social institutions, and the existence of an official ideology that the party claims the nation must follow if it is to reach its domestic and international goals. The Chinese Communist Party was so dominated in the mid-1990s by a small number of elderly men in their eighties and nineties—including Deng, who turned ninety in 1994—that it was sometimes referred to as a **gerontocracy,** or "rule of the elderly." These party elders are desperately attempting to orchestrate the passing of power to younger leaders who share their view that China's development is best served by the combination of a vibrant economy and an **authoritarian** government. The rift between an oppressive party-state and an increasingly assertive society, which led

to the shedding of blood in Tiananmen in 1989, remains deep and ominous. How this conflict will be resolved in the years ahead is the biggest issue on China's political agenda as it approaches the twenty-first century.

The Chinese Communist Party governs a country that is slightly larger than the United States in land area, making it the second-largest nation in the world, after Russia. China has, by far, the largest population—about 1.2 billion in the mid-1990s—although India may surpass China sometime in the next century if current population growth trends continue in both countries. The PRC now has one of the fastest-growing economies in the world, averaging about 10 percent per year over the last decade or so. Despite such spectacular economic growth, China is still a developing nation in terms of both the structure of its economy and the economic realities of daily life for the majority of its people. Industrialization and urbanization have expanded significantly in recent years, but about 70 percent of China's people still live and work in rural areas. The incomes of most Chinese have gone up dramatically since Deng's reforms took hold, but they are still very low compared to the average North American, Japanese, or Western European income. By some measures of per capita income, China ranks among the poorest nations of the world, along with countries such as India and Nigeria. However, health and education statistics in China compare favorably with countries that are at a much higher level of economic development, such as Brazil and Mexico (see Table 1). This reflects the success of the party-state in both the Mao and the Deng eras in addressing some of the most basic needs of the Chinese people. Whether the CCP can manage the economy in a way that continues to yield significant improvements in living standards will also be a major factor in China's political future.

CRITICAL JUNCTURES

The People's Republic of China was founded in 1949. But understanding the formation of the modern Chinese state requires going back much further into China's political history. Broadly considered, that history can be divided into three periods: the imperial, or dynastic, period (221 B.C.–A.D. 1911); the republican period (1912–1949); and the communist period (1949 through the present).

TABLE 1   **China's Development in Comparative Perspective**

	GNP per capita ($)	Purchasing Power Parity GDP per capita ($)	Life Expectancy at Birth (years)	Infant Mortality (per 1,000 live births)	Adult Literacy Rate (%)
China	490	2,330	69	30	80
Brazil	2,980	5,370	67	57	82
India	300	1,220	61	80	50
Iran	2,410	4,670	68	35	56
Mexico	3,610	6,810	71	35	89
Nigeria	300	1,400	51	83	52

Sources: *World Development Report, 1995; Human Development Report, 1994.*

From Empire to Revolution

The Middle Kingdom   Modern China is heir to one of the world's oldest cultural and political traditions. The roots of Chinese culture date back more than 4,000 years, but the political entity that became the Chinese empire was established in 221 B.C., when a number of small kingdoms were unified by force under the Emperor Qin (or Ch'in, from which probably comes, via Latin, the name "China"). The Qin dynasty laid the geographic and institutional foundations of an imperial system that lasted for more than twenty centuries until its overthrow in 1911.

China's physical boundaries gradually expanded through time (reaching their approximate present scope in the eighteenth century), and the empire experienced tremendous political, economic, social, and cultural development in the course of more than a dozen different dynasties that ruled during the imperial period. Nevertheless, many of the core features of the imperial system remained remarkably consistent over time. This raises two fundamental questions: (1) Why did the Chinese empire endure for so long while other great empires of the ancient world, such as Egypt and Rome, disintegrated much sooner? and (2) Why did it collapse so suddenly and finally in the early twentieth century? Answers to these questions help us understand why modern state formation in China ultimately took such a radical turn, culminating in the capture of national power by the communists in 1949.

Several interrelated factors explain the durability of the Chinese empire. First, imperial China developed a sophisticated and effective system of national government long before the strong monarchical states of Europe took form in the seventeenth century.[2] At the pinnacle of this government was an all-powerful emperor and a small group of advisers and ministers in the capital. But the most distinctive feature of the Chinese political tradition was the civil service branch made up of scholar-officials (mandarins) chosen through a rigorous and highly selective examination process. These exams were, in theory, open to all adult males, but, in practice, largely accessible only to those who could afford the time and expense of the preparatory education. Although relatively few in number, imperial officials were stationed throughout the country and were the means by which the emperor exercised authority over the vast empire.

Second, the traditional Chinese economy was a source of great strength to the empire. Chinese farmers pioneered some of the premodern world's most productive agricultural techniques, including irrigation and multicropping. Commerce and transport were also highly developed for the times. Although China was and still is a country largely dominated by its rural areas, urbanization expanded in China much sooner and faster than it did in Europe. When the Italian traveler and trader Marco Polo journeyed to China in the thirteenth century, Hangzhou, with a population of over a million, was the largest and grandest city in the world.

Third, the structure of traditional Chinese society, especially in the million or more small villages that were its foundation, gave the imperial system great staying power. The vast majority of the population was made up of peasants, people who earned their living by working the land. Though some of them

A Very Brief Chinese Lesson

Chinese is spoken by more people than any other language in the world. Yet what we call "Chinese" really comprises many dialects, some of which are so different from one another that they are mutually incomprehensible and are often considered separate languages. Two of the major Chinese dialects are Mandarin, which is the form of Chinese spoken mainly in the northern part of the country, and Cantonese, which is spoken in the south.

Yet people who speak different Chinese dialects share the same written language. In other words, Mandarin and Cantonese speakers cannot understand each other in face-to-face conversations or over the telephone, but they can communicate by letter! This is because written Chinese is made up of *characters* rather than phonetic letters. These characters, which have evolved over time from symbolic pictures, represent meanings more than they depict sounds, so that speakers of various Chinese dialects may pronounce the same character very differently. There are more than 40,000 different Chinese characters, although basic literacy requires knowledge of about 4,000 because the vast majority of characters are ancient and have fallen out of common usage.

Chinese does not have an alphabet; both the meaning and the pronunciation of Chinese characters can only be learned by memorization. Like many of the world's other languages—including Arabic, Greek, Hebrew, Japanese, and Russian—that do not use the Roman alphabet on which English is based, Chinese characters must be "romanized" (or "transliterated") if English speakers are to have any idea how to pronounce them. The most common way of romanizing Chinese is the *pinyin* (literally, "spell sounds") system used in the People's Republic of China and by the United Nations. But because linguists have differed about how best to approximate distinctive Chinese sounds using Roman letters, there are still several alternative methods of romanizing Chinese.

This book and most other English-language publications generally use the *pinyin* romanization for Chinese names, places, and phrases. In most cases, a word in *pinyin* is pronounced as it looks. However, there are a few letters that appear in Chinese words in this chapter for which a pronunciation guide is helpful:

- "q" is pronounced "ch" as in Qing (Ch'ing) dynasty.
- "x" has no precise equivalent sound in English, but is close to a "sh" sound. Thus, Deng Xiaoping would be pronounced something like "duhng she-ow ping."
- "zh" is pronounced "j" as in Zhao (Jao) Ziyang.

One other important point: In China (as in Japan and Korea), the family name, or surname (for instance, Deng), comes before the personal, or given, name (for instance, Xiaoping). Some people interpret this as a reflection of the priority given to the family or the group over the individual in East Asian culture.

were relatively prosperous, most lived a precarious economic existence because of the small size of the average family farm and because they were bound in an exploitative relationship with landlords, who were the real source of power on the local level. The most powerful of the landlord families—the gentry—were those who had close ties to the imperial civil service. Most officials came from the gentry class, and it was the gentry who helped the imperial officials extend their reach down to the very basic level of Chinese society by carrying out many government functions, such as collecting taxes. The strong link between the local gentry and national officials was one of the major ingredients that held the empire together through the centuries.

Fourth, **Confucianism,** which is a social philosophy rather than a religion, provided the core of an official ideology that both legitimized and perpetuated the traditional order. This philosophy was based on the teachings of Confucius (c. 551–479 B.C.) and his later disciples and interpreters. It stressed social harmony and righteous behavior, deference to one's elders and

superiors (including the subordination of women to men), and the importance of family and education. Confucianism deeply influenced all aspects of life in traditional China and was preached by officials from the throne on down. It formed the content of the exams by which civil servants were chosen; it was the dominant influence in art and literature; and it was the basis of both family life and social organization. The strong cultural identity based on Confucianism also gave the sprawling Chinese empire a pervasive and durable sense of unity. Confucian teachings did contain an injunction—the "Mandate of Heaven"—that a ruler could be justifiably overthrown by the people if he did not govern benevolently, and Chinese history is full of rebellions against dynasties that were judged to have lost the heavenly mandate. Nevertheless, Confucianism was basically a conservative orthodoxy that served to justify and maintain an autocratic state, a patriarchal culture, and a stratified society.

Finally, the Chinese imperial system endured because, throughout most of its history, China was the dominant force in its known world. Not only was

China the overwhelming political and military power in the region, it also gave cultural values to its neighbors, including Japan, Korea, and Vietnam, which incorporated many aspects of Confucianism into their social systems. Foreign influences or peoples that could not be isolated or repelled by the Chinese empire, such as Buddhism from India or invaders from Mongolia (who actually conquered China in 1279), were absorbed, or "sinicized," by Chinese culture; in other words, they were changed more by China than they were able to change China.

The Chinese term for China, *zhongguo*, which literally means "Middle Kingdom," conveys an image of a country that stands at the moral and cultural center of the world. This belief in the preeminence of China contributed to a pervasive feeling among the Chinese that all non-Chinese were "barbarians" and that the Middle Kingdom could meet any challenge from outside without having to alter its basic way of life.

The End of the Empire   With such powerful forces for preservation, why did the imperial order start to disintegrate in the mid-nineteenth century? The sources of decline must be traced to unprecedented internal and external challenges that the Chinese empire eventually proved unable to meet.

In the 1800s, China was ruled by the Qing dynasty, which was founded in 1644 by Manchus, a non-Chinese ethnic group, who had been thoroughly "sinicized" after conquering China. Much of Qing rule had been characterized by political stability, economic prosperity, and cultural flourishing. But in the late eighteenth and early nineteenth centuries, the empire experienced an unprecedented population explosion and economic stagnation, along with a significant rise in official corruption, exploitation of the peasants by both landlords and the government, and social unrest.

Such internal problems would have challenged any government. But the Qing dynasty was further undermined by a fateful change in the Middle Kingdom's relations with the outside world caused by increased contacts and conflicts between China and the West.

The Chinese empire had had limited encounters with Europe for centuries, but by the end of the eighteenth century, the West, which by then had surged far ahead of China in terms of industrial development and military technology, began to press China to expand its trade and diplomatic relations. China showed little interest in such overtures and tried to limit the activities of Westerners in China. But Europe, most notably Britain, in the midst of its era of mercantile and colonial expansion, used its military supremacy to compel China to engage in "free" trade with the West. Qing efforts to stop Britain from selling opium in China to balance the huge British demand for Chinese tea led to military hostilities between the two countries. After suffering humiliating defeats in the Opium War (1839–1842) and other conflicts, China was literally forced to open its borders to foreign merchants, missionaries, and diplomats on terms dictated by Britain and other Western powers. The Middle Kingdom suddenly found itself thrust into a world of states in which its cultural power carried little weight against the superior firepower of Western cannons and in which it could no longer control the domestic impact of external forces.

Thus, in the second half of the nineteenth century, the Qing dynasty was under siege. Western ideas and peasant misery fed a massive internal revolt, the Taiping Rebellion (1850–1864), which took 20 million lives and nearly toppled the dynasty. China lost control of significant pieces of its territory to foreigners, including Hong Kong, which came under British rule through the "unequal treaties" imposed on the Chinese through military or diplomatic pressure. Important sectors of the Chinese economy had fallen into foreign hands, and even parts of the imperial government—such as the Chinese Maritime Customs agency, which controlled much of the country's foreign trade—were run by Westerners. There is considerable debate among scholars about how important Western **imperialism** was in bringing about the collapse of the Chinese empire, but there is no doubt that external forces gravely compounded the pressures on the Qing dynasty. Although China was never formally colonized, the circumstances of its entry into the modern world system were hardly conducive to independent national development.

There were many efforts to revive or reform the dynasty in the late nineteenth and early twentieth centuries. But, unlike Japan, where leaders who were committed to modernizing the nation in the face of Western encroachments took control of the country in the Meiji Restoration of 1868, power in China remained largely in the hands of staunch conservatives who resisted change. As a result, when change came, it came in the form of the Revolution of 1911, which not only overthrew the Qing dynasty, but also brought an end to the 2,000-year-old imperial system.

The Rise of the Chinese Communist Party   The Qing dynasty's fall in 1911 was due more to its own dead weight than to the planned action of revolutionaries. The empire was replaced by the Republic of China, with Sun Yat-sen, then China's best-known revolutionary and founder of its first political party, as president. Sun, a Western-educated doctor, believed that democracy had only limited applicability to China's situation and that the country would have to go through a period of tutelage in which the people would gradually learn about self-government while concentrating on the main tasks of national unity and modernization. But the Revolution of 1911 can be seen as the culmination of the first stirrings of the democratic idea in China and the first effort to establish a government in which citizens would have more say.

Sun Yat-sen was, however, quickly displaced as president of the Republic by Yuan Shikai, a powerful military leader who tried unsuccessfully to restore the imperial system. After Yuan's death in 1916, China fell into a lengthy period of conflict and disintegration known as the warlord era. Sun's Nationalist Party (the Guomindang) set about leading another **revolution** against the warlords who had taken power in the weak and fragmented Republic.

In 1921, the Chinese Communist Party (CCP) was established by a small group of intellectuals who had become disenchanted with the derailing of the republican movement and with continuing foreign intervention in China's government and economy. They had been inspired by the Bolshevik triumph in Russia in 1917 and by the anti-imperialism of the new Soviet Union to look for more radical solutions to China's most serious problems. In 1924, the small Communist Party, acting on Soviet advice, formed a united front with Sun Yat-sen's Nationalists with the common purpose of defeating the warlords. After some initial successes, the alliance came to a tragic end in 1927 when Chiang Kai-shek, a military leader who had become the head of the Nationalist Party after Sun's death in 1925, turned against his coalition partners and ordered a bloody suppression that nearly wiped out the Communists. Chiang then proceeded to unify the Republic of China under his personal rule largely by striking an

accommodation with some of the country's most powerful remaining warlords.

Ironically, the defeat of the CCP created the conditions for the eventual triumph of the man who would lead the party to nationwide victory. Mao Zedong, who had been one of the junior founders of the Communist Party, strongly advocated paying more attention to China's suffering peasants as a potential source of revolutionary support. "In a very short time," he wrote in 1927, "several hundred million peasants will rise like a mighty storm, like a hurricane, a force so swift and violent that no power, however great, will be able to hold it back."[3] Mao's views grew out of his own peasant background and his investigations of spontaneous uprisings against oppressive rural conditions. But his positive assessment of the revolutionary potential of the peasantry was at odds with the prevailing policy of the CCP, which held fast to the more orthodox Marxist-Leninist belief that a Communist-led revolution had to be urban-centered and based on China's then minuscule industrial **proletariat.**

But after the crushing suppression of the Communists by the Nationalists, the remnants of the party were forced to relocate to the countryside. Chiang Kai-shek's continued efforts to exterminate the CCP drove the party to undertake its fabled Long March in 1934–1935, an epic journey of 6,000 miles through some of China's roughest terrain to a refuge in Yanan in the remote northwest. In the meantime, however, the strategy of peasant revolution gained support in the party, and by the mid-1930s, Mao had risen to the top echelons of power in the CCP.

For more than a decade, China was embroiled in a fierce civil war that pitted Communists against Nationalists. In Yanan, the CCP greatly expanded its ranks. Mao consolidated his political and ideological leadership of the Communist Party (through sometimes repressive means) and was elected party chairman in 1943—a position that he held until his death in 1976. Mao further developed his ideas about **communism** and his strategy of **guerrilla warfare.** He also guided the effort to generate peasant support for the Communists through policies such as land reform and party-led "quasi-democratic" self-government in which, for the first time, peasants were given a direct role in running village affairs.[4] At the same time, the Republic of China, under Chiang Kai-shek, became a right-wing dictatorship closely allied with big business, foreign interests, and the rural elite. Although the

---

Critical Junctures in Modern China's Political Development

1911	Revolution led by Sun Yat-sen overthrows 2,000-year-old imperial system and establishes the Republic of China.
1912	Sun Yat-sen founds the Nationalist (Guomindang) Party to oppose warlords who have seized power in the new republic.
1921	Chinese Communist Party (CCP) founded.
1927	Civil war between Nationalists (now led by Chiang Kai-shek) and Communists begins.
1934	Mao Zedong becomes effective leader of the CCP.
1937	Japan invades China, marking the start of World War II in Asia.
1949	Chinese Communists win the civil war and establish the People's Republic of China.
1956–1957	Hundred Flowers Movement and Anti-Rightist Campaign
1958–1960	Great Leap Forward
1966–1976	Great Proletarian Cultural Revolution
1976	Mao Zedong dies.
1978	Deng Xiaoping becomes China's paramount leader.
1989	Tiananmen massacre

Nationalists did have some success in promoting economic modernization, the legitimacy of Chiang's government was severely undermined by corruption, mismanagement, and repression.

But international factors again proved decisive in determining China's destiny. The Japanese invasion of China in the late 1930s marked the start of World War II in Asia and not only brought horrible suffering to the Chinese people, but also greatly influenced the balance of power in China's civil conflict. Japan's assault pushed the Nationalist government deep into China's southwest and effectively eliminated it as an active combatant against Japanese aggression. On the other hand, the CCP base in Yanan was on the front line against Japan's troops in northern China, and Mao and the Communists successfully mobilized peasant resistance to the invaders. By the end of World War II, the vastly expanded CCP controlled much of the countryside in north China, while the Nationalist government was isolated and unpopular with many Chinese.

When the civil war resumed in earnest, the Communist forces won a decisive and surprisingly quick victory over the U.S.-backed Nationalists as the military acumen of Mao and his generals overwhelmed Chiang Kai-shek's serious battlefield blunders. In the fall of 1949, Chiang and more than a million of his supporters fled to the island of Taiwan, 90 miles off the Chinese coast. On October 1 of that year, Mao stood on a rostrum in Tiananmen near the entrance to the former imperial palace in Beijing and declared the founding of the People's Republic of China.

Communism in Power

Since 1949, there has been a basic stability in Chinese politics in the sense that there has never been any significant challenge to Communist power. China's leaders have remained firmly committed to Marxist ideology, and the basic Leninist structure of the political system has remained intact.

Such surface continuities, however, belie the tremendous political changes that have occurred in China while the CCP has been governing the country. In fact, the history of the PRC has been marked by extreme and disruptive political conflicts both between the Chinese party-state and its people and within the party itself. These conflicts have produced the dramatic swings in China's domestic and foreign policies that mark the critical junctures in the evolution of the modern Chinese state under Communist rule. The most important of these junctures during the Mao era were the **Hundred Flowers** movement (1956–1957), the **Great Leap Forward** (1958–1960), and the Great Proletarian **Cultural Revolution** (1966–1976).

State versus Society Conflicts between the Chinese Communist party-state and the society it governs have been a major source of political turbulence in the PRC. There have been times when state-society relations have been harmonious, especially when the party's economic and social policies have benefited large segments of the population. But at other times, and particularly in political matters, the pattern has been one of deep and sometimes violent conflict between state and society.

From the beginning of its rule, the CCP sought to extend and maintain its control of Chinese society. Time and time again, the coercive power of the state has been used to crush individuals and groups that have questioned party domination. Chinese Communist doctrine makes a sharp distinction between the "people," who support **socialism,** and the "enemies" of socialism (labeled rightists or counterrevolutionaries). The party leadership has always reserved for itself the power not only to define who fits into which category, but also to use whatever means are necessary to subdue the enemies of the people. The Tiananmen massacre was only the most recent in a long line of incidents in which the Chinese Communist state, acting in the name of the "people," has suppressed the people of China.

The relationship between state and society in the PRC started off on a more promising note. The Communists came to power in 1949 on the crest of an enormous wave of popular support because of their reputation as social reformers and patriotic fighters. The initial period of their rule was patterned on Mao's notion of a "New Democracy" based on a mixed socialist-capitalist economy and inclusive politics in which the CCP played a leading role, but also allowed for meaningful participation by noncommunists.

In a number of policies, "Chinese society was literally turned upside down in the early days of the People's Republic."[5] This bolstered the popularity of the new regime among large segments of the population in the early 1950s. For instance, a massive **land reform** campaign redistributed property from the rich to the poor and increased both equality and productivity in the countryside; highly successful drives literally eliminated opium addiction and prostitution from the cities; and a national law greatly enhanced the legal status of women in the family and allowed many women to free themselves from unhappy arranged marriages. Although the party moved swiftly and forcefully to install its authority throughout the land and did not hesitate to use violence to achieve its objectives and remove opponents, the Communists enjoyed widespread support and **legitimacy** during this "golden age" of the Maoist period.

The mixed economy of the New Democracy period was brought to an end and a decisive step was taken towards socialism with the **nationalization** of industry and the **collectivization** of agriculture, part of China's Soviet-style First Five Year Plan of 1953–1957. The end of inclusive politics also began around that time with the further strengthening of Communist domination of the political system. But the decisive political event of the times and the first major clash between the new state and society was the Hundred Flowers movement of 1956–1957.

The Hundred Flowers had its origins in Mao's perception that something had gone wrong with China's socialist development. Concerned that the CCP had lost some of its revolutionary zeal and that China's government was becoming too bureaucratic, Mao issued a call in 1956 to the citizens of China to "let a hundred flowers bloom, let a hundred schools of thought contend"; that is, to feel free to offer their frank opinions about how the Communists were running China. His goals were to shake up the bureaucrats and encourage broader participation in making public policy. But the outpouring of public criticism and a wave of large-scale industrial strikes revealed the fact that many people were harboring deep resentments about Communist policies and about the growing political dictatorship. Critics called into question the very premises of Communist rule in China, including the relevance of Marxism-Leninism to China's needs and the leadership of Mao himself.

Mao's reaction to the unexpectedly severe Hundred Flowers criticism was to order the Anti-Rightist Campaign of 1957, a vicious crackdown in which hundreds of thousands of people—particularly intellectuals—were accused of being traitors and punished by being demoted, fired, or sent to labor camps for reeducation. This campaign, which was supported by all of the CCP's major leaders, including Deng Xiaoping, stifled political debate in China and "destroyed the hope that China's 'transition to socialism' might proceed on the basis of some form of popular democracy and with some real measure of intellectual freedom. It reinforced . . . that the exercise of state power was a monopoly of the Communist Party."[6]

Many other examples of the party's determination to maintain its grip on society were seen during the more than thirty years that separated the Hundred Flowers suppression in 1957 from the Tiananmen massacre in 1989. Among the most dramatic were the brutal crushing of a rebellion against Chinese domination in Tibet in 1959, the dispersal of student groups who questioned party dictatorship in the mid-1960s, and the arrest of the leaders of pro-democracy movements in 1974–1975, 1978–1979, and 1986–1987. Under Deng Xiaoping, the CCP has clearly shifted its emphasis from **ideology** to modernization, but party domination of society has been maintained by a complex structure of control that still exists despite the political relaxation of recent years.

Power and Ideology   The political history of the People's Republic of China has also been shaped by a series of venomous conflicts within the Chinese Communist Party over the last forty years. Some of these conflicts have been power struggles among leaders jockeying for supremacy within the party hierarchy. Other conflicts have resulted from disputes over the meaning of Marxist-Leninist ideology and how it should be used to guide China's development. But most often the major conflicts that have torn the CCP have involved both a struggle for power and profound ideological differences, with individuals and factions seeking to gain positions that would allow them to implement policies reflecting their views of socialism and their interpretation of China's best interests.

In the aftermath of the Communist victory and what is called the Liberation of 1949, the CCP leadership was basically unified around the leadership of Chairman Mao Zedong. Initial agreement on the priorities of political stability, economic recovery, and remedying some of the country's most glaring social ills was followed by a consensus that China should adopt the Soviet model of rapid development through the extension of state control of the economy during the First Five Year Plan of 1953–1957. These policies yielded some impressive economic results, but they also created social inequalities, economic imbalances, and political conflicts that tore the party—and the country—apart over the next two decades.

In the mid-1950s, "three visions" of Chinese communism[7] began to surface within the CCP leadership in response to the results of the First Five Year Plan. One vision, that of the "bureaucratic communists," saw China as being on the right track in following the Soviet model of economic development with its emphasis on extensive government control of the economy through **central planning.** Party leaders who espoused this point of view were often labeled "conservatives" because of their preference for a more traditional or orthodox brand of communism.

A second vision, that of the "market communists," supported policies that combined central planning with capitalist-like market forces. The market socialists, often labeled "reformers" because they advocated reforming the Soviet model in the direction of less planning and more market, believed that China needed to go slowly in implementing socialist policies because of its poverty and technological backwardness. They were particularly concerned about the fast pace of collectivization in agriculture, which they feared would rob farmers of the incentive to work hard.

The third vision was that of Chairman Mao and the "radical communists." This group wanted to speed up the pace of building socialism in China, but in a way that broke dramatically with the Soviet model, which they saw as too bureaucratic. They also vehemently rejected the approach of the market communists, which they saw as backsliding toward **capitalism.** The radicals favored mobilizing the masses to achieve national goals, involving workers and peasants in factory and farm management, and promoting greater equality rather than simply pursuing economic growth.

In the storm of Chinese politics from the late 1950s through the mid-1970s, it was Mao and the radicals who prevailed for the most part, with profound and often devastating consequences for China's political and economic development. The radical vision, which is often called **Maoism,** put into practice the notion of "permanent revolution," that is, the effort to preserve communist spirit after the seizure of state power and keep China on the road to socialism through mass movements and "class struggle" against all those judged to be enemies of the revolution. In terms of national priorities, Maoism put social and ideological goals, such as minimizing inequalities and promoting communist values, ahead of economic development. At the heart of Maoism was a faith in the power of the masses to overcome any obstacles that history or nature might throw in their way (under the leadership of the Communist Party, of course) and a very idealistic view of human nature as basically selfless, cooperative, and boundlessly committed to the revolutionary cause. Much of Maoism grew out of the CCP's experience in mobilizing the masses to fight and defeat seemingly superior enemies such as the American-backed Nationalists and the Japanese during World War II.

Two events capture the essence of the radical policies and politics during the period of Maoist ascendancy in the PRC: the Great Leap Forward (1958–1960) and the Great Proletarian Cultural Revolution (1966–1976).

By 1957, Mao was very unhappy with the way in which China had developed since Liberation. There had been many achievements, to be sure, but also a loss of revolutionary enthusiasm, a growth of bureaucracy, and a deepening of socioeconomic inequalities, especially between the cities and the countryside. The Great Leap Forward was Mao's response to this situation and was meant to forge a distinctive pattern of socialist development based on mass mobilization as an alternative to the top-down methods of both the Soviet Union and China's own First Five Year Plan.

The Great Leap, which was launched in mid-1958, turned into "one of the most extreme, bizarre, and eventually catastrophic episodes in twentieth century political history."[8] It was a utopian effort to catapult the PRC into the forefront of industrial nations, but in a way that would also hasten the country's transition from socialism to the even more egalitarian stage of communism. The Leap aimed to harness both the labor and willpower of China's vast population in order to increase production rapidly. Industry and agriculture were reorganized in ways that assumed people would work harder for the goals of communism than for monetary rewards.

The Great Leap was a great flop. In the rural areas, irrational policies, wasted resources, poor management, and the lack of labor incentives combined with a streak of bad weather to produce the most widespread famine in human history, which directly or indirectly claimed between 20 and 30 million lives. An industrial depression soon followed the collapse of agriculture, causing a terrible setback to China's economic development.

The Leap was also a turning point in Chinese politics. Mao insisted on the removal of top leaders who sought to slow down the pace of the Leap when they first became aware that it was creating major problems in food production. This was a serious departure from the party's established practice of "collective leadership" in which differences of opinion were usually resolved through debate, not purges. It was a decisive step toward personalistic rule by Mao (and later Deng) within the CCP.

In the early 1960s, following the failure of the Great Leap Forward, Mao took a less active role in party decision making. Two of China's top leaders at the time, Liu Shaoqi and Deng Xiaoping, were among the chief proponents of a development strategy that rejected radicalism and drew from the bureaucratic (favored by Liu) and market (favored by Deng) visions of Chinese communism. Under their guidance, the emphasis of party policy shifted from mass mobilization, class struggle, and egalitarianism to bureaucrats, intellectuals, and material incentives.

By the mid-1960s, Mao had concluded that China and the CCP were both deviating from socialism and had, in fact, taken a turn down the "capitalist road." Using his unmatched political clout and considerable **charisma,** Mao put together a potent alliance of loyal army officers, radical ideologues, and student rebels to challenge anyone thought to be guilty of "revisionism," that is, betrayal of his version of Marxism-Leninism known as "Mao Zedong Thought."

This ideological crusade became the Great Proletarian Cultural Revolution, a movement launched by Mao to move China back in what he believed to be the direction of true socialism.[9] Like the Great Leap Forward, the Cultural Revolution was a campaign of mass mobilization and utopian idealism; but its methods were much more violent and its main objective was political purification of the party and the nation, not accelerated economic development.

In the movement's first phase (1966–1969), 20 million or so high school and college students, known as the Red Guards, responded to Mao's pronouncement that "It is right to rebel!" by going on a rampage that plunged the country into near **anarchy.** The Red Guards destroyed countless priceless historical artifacts considered to be remnants of the feudal past and harassed, tortured, and killed many thousands of people labeled as "class enemies." The Red Guards particularly targeted intellectuals, officials, and their families. Among their most prominent victims were Liu Shaoqi, who was then the president of the PRC and vice chairman of the CCP, and Deng Xiaoping, who was a vice premier (that is, deputy prime minister) of the PRC and a member of the party's highest ruling body. Both men were identified by Mao as "capitalist roaders" who were trying to subvert the CCP from the inside. Liu died in prison after sustained maltreatment, while Deng was sent to internal exile in the Chinese countryside. Deng's son was paralyzed for life after jumping out of a window at Beijing University while trying to escape from Red Guards.

In August 1966, Chinese Communist Party Chairman Mao Zedong greeted more than a million Red Guards gathered in Tiananmen Square during the Great Proletarian Cultural Revolution. In this picture, Mao is wearing a Red Guard armband in a gesture of support for the young rebels who were engaged in a vicious witchhunt for suspected enemies of communism. Source: UPI/Bettmann.

Some Red Guards and their radical adult patrons were motivated by revolutionary idealism or blind faith in Mao. The Mao cult was commonly symbolized by the wearing of "Mao badges" with portraits of the chairman on them and the memorization of *Quotations from Chairman Mao Zedong,* also known as "The Little Red Book" because of its small size and red plastic cover. Not everyone participated in the movement for political reasons, however; many joined simply for adventure or to get revenge against people they didn't like.

Once the alleged "capitalist roaders" had been removed from their positions of power, Mao and his radical allies introduced a wide range of policies aimed at making China a more purely socialist society. For example, art, literature, and drama, which were under the tight control of Mao's wife, Jiang Qing, were purged of all revisionist works and strictly limited to depicting revolutionary themes. When schools

were reopened in the early 1970s, procedures favoring applicants with worker or peasant backgrounds or with a record of political activism replaced grades and examinations as the principal basis for university admissions.

The next phase of the Cultural Revolution (1969–1971) was a period of military domination of Chinese politics that followed Mao's decision to use the army to stop Red Guard violence. Most of the young rebels were sent for several years to live and labor in the countryside, where they were supposed to be reeducated by the peasants. The military influence in politics was ended after some of its leaders allegedly attempted an abortive coup to seize power from Mao.

The last phase of the Cultural Revolution (1972–1976) involved intense conflict between the radical Maoist party leaders who wanted the nation to continue emphasizing class struggle and permanent revolution and a more moderate faction who felt it was time for China to shift attention to modernization and economic development. Deng Xiaoping was briefly "rehabilitated" politically in 1973 but was again sent into political exile in early 1976 by Mao and the radicals.

The CCP leadership also disagreed over which faction would control the succession to Mao Zedong, who was then in his early eighties and in seriously declining health. The leadership dispute was resolved when, a month after Mao's death at the age of eighty-two in September 1976, a coalition of relatively moderate leaders masterminded the arrest of the top radicals, the so-called Gang of Four, which included Mao's wife, Jiang Qing.

The arrest of the Gang (who were sentenced to long prison terms) and the subsequent purge of many of their radical followers was the final act in the decade-long Cultural Revolution. The full human toll of the Cultural Revolution is only now coming to light. Recent estimates put it at well over a million lives lost due to Red Guard violence and the radicals' reign of terror against their political opponents and personal enemies.

The arrest of the Gang also set in motion the process by which Deng Xiaoping made his way back to the center of power. The leaders who had arrested the Gang soon found that they needed Deng's experience and personal connections to help govern the country. After being restored to a party leadership post in 1977, Deng quickly consolidated power in his own hands by

"Dreaming of a Female Emperor." After the overthrow of the "Gang of Four" in October 1976, many cartoons appeared in the Chinese press criticizing Jiang Qing (Mao's wife) and her political allies for their lust for power, radical rhetoric, and lavish life-style. This cartoon shows Jiang (seated) being fanned, guarded, and trumpeted by the other members of the "Gang."

skillful political maneuvering. Soon thereafter he put China on the path of economic reform that has transformed the nation. Although Deng has never occupied the formal top offices in either the party or the government, he has been the real power behind the throne since 1978.

The Deng Xiaoping era has not put an end to the factional struggles within the Chinese leadership, although Maoist-style purges of "class enemies" are no longer used as an instrument of elite conflict. China's post-Mao leaders agree that the radical vision of Chinese communism has no role in China's future. But there are still very significant differences between conservative bureaucratic communists who want to maintain the primacy of central planning and reformers who want to push farther and faster in the direction of a market economy. Leaders have also been sharply divided over the question of political reform in China, and party officials considered to be too favorably disposed toward democracy have been purged. Thus, elite conflict has been among the most destructive political legacies of both the Mao and the Deng periods in China—and it is likely to continue, and perhaps intensify, in the power struggles that will almost inevitably follow the death of the elderly Deng Xiaoping.

China in a World of States From the Opium War of the mid-nineteenth century to the Japanese invasion of the 1930s, external forces and actors were instrumen-

tal in the revolutionary process that brought the Chinese Communists to power. International events have also shaped the People's Republic and greatly influenced the course of Chinese politics in the Communist period. Also, like its domestic politics, the foreign relations of the PRC have gone through some very dramatic changes in the last four decades.

In the first years of its existence, the PRC developed close ties with its communist ally, the Soviet Union. The Soviets were not involved to any significant degree in the Chinese civil war after the mid-1930s (and, in fact, were skeptical of Mao and his peasant army); but ideological affinity and the realities of the **Cold War** became the basis of a Sino (that is, Chinese)-Soviet alliance that resulted in a massive flow of economic aid and technical assistance to China and appeared to place the PRC firmly in the Soviet bloc.

The United States had backed Chiang Kai-shek's Nationalists with advice and weapons in China's civil war and had rebuffed several overtures for better relations by the CCP both before and after they came to power. Diplomatic hostility turned to military conflict when Chinese troops and U.S.-led United Nations forces fought each other in the Korean War of 1950–1953. China's ability to fight the United States to a stalemate in that war added to the new Communist regime's popularity among a population more accustomed to international humiliation and defeat and gave the PRC considerable prestige among Third World nations. But the Korean conflict was an economic hardship for the new state. It also "froze" the Chinese civil war by disrupting the CCP's plans to oust the Nationalists from their last stronghold on Taiwan. In response to the situation in Korea and as part of its emerging Cold War strategy to contain the spread of communism in Asia, the United States pledged to defend the Nationalist-led Republic of China on Taiwan.

The Sino-Soviet alliance began to come apart in the mid-1950s. The two communist powers found themselves differing on a wide range of issues including how to deal with the United States. The Soviets advocated "peaceful coexistence," while the Chinese insisted on confrontation and preparation for war. Strategic differences were compounded by a growing ideological rift. The Soviets, repelled by the Great Leap Forward's utopian policies and the Chinese claim that they would be the first to reach true communism, withdrew their advisers and technical support

The Republic of China on Taiwan

Despite the founding of the People's Republic of China on the Chinese mainland at the end of the civil war in 1949, the Republic of China (ROC) continued, and still continues, to function on the island of Taiwan, claiming to be a government-in-exile waiting to return to the mainland after the collapse or defeat of the Communist regime there. When Chiang Kai-shek and his supporters fled to Taiwan following the Communist victory in 1949, the island was already firmly under Nationalist control. The Nationalists had killed or arrested many of its opponents on Taiwan in the aftermath of a popular uprising in February 1947. The harsh dictatorship imposed by Chiang and the Nationalists deepened the sharp divide between "Mainlanders," who had come over to escape the Communists, and the native Taiwanese majority, whose ancestors had first settled on the island centuries before and who spoke a distinct Chinese dialect.

Economically, Taiwan prospered under Chiang's rule. With large amounts of American aid and advice, the Nationalist government sponsored a highly successful and peaceful program of land reform and rural development, attracted extensive foreign investment, and encouraged an export-led strategy of economic growth that made Taiwan a model **"newly industrializing country" (NIC)** by the 1970s. The government also invested heavily in the modernization of Taiwan's roads and ports and promoted policies that have given the island health and education standards that are among the highest in the world.

Political change, however, came more slowly to Taiwan. After his death in 1975, Chiang Kai-shek was succeeded as president of the ROC by his son, Chiang Ching-kuo, who most people expected would continue the repressive political policies of his father. Instead, the younger Chiang permitted some opposition and dissent and gave important government and party positions previously dominated by Mainlanders to Taiwanese. When he died in 1988, the presidency of the republic passed to the Taiwanese vice president, Lee Teng-hui, who also became head of the Nationalist Party. Under Lee Teng-hui, Taiwan has continued to make dramatic progress toward democratization. The laws

Taiwan

Land Area (sq. miles)	13,895 (about one-third the size of Virginia)
Population	21 million
Ethnic Composition	Taiwanese 84%, mainland Chinese 14%, aborigine 2%
GNP (US$)	$257 billion
GNP per capita (US$)	$12,070
Life Expectancy	Male, 72; Female, 79
Infant Mortality (per 1,000 live births)	5.6
Literacy	86%

used to imprison dissidents have been revoked, there are now free, multiparty elections for most local and national positions, and the press is free of all censorship. Since 1979, Taiwan and the People's Republic of China have developed extensive economic relations with each other, and millions of people from Taiwan have gone to the mainland to do business, visit relatives, or just sightsee.

In the legislative elections held in December 1992, the Nationalists won 53 percent of the vote, while the main opposition party won 31 percent, reflecting both the new openness of the political system and the credit that Taiwan's voters give the Nationalist Party for the island's progress. The most contentious political issue in Taiwan is whether the island should continue to aspire to reunification with the mainland or declare its independence as a separate Republic of Taiwan. Advocating Taiwanese independence used to be a treasonous act, often resulting in a long prison term. The fact that this issue can now be openly debated shows that Taiwan's political transformation in recent decades has been every bit as dramatic as its economic development.

---

from the PRC in the midst of the Leap. The Chinese, for their part, came to the conclusion that the Soviet Union under Khrushchev and Brezhnev had abandoned socialism and had even "restored capitalism," with party bureaucrats filling the role of the capitalists by their control of the economy and their privileged status in society. Mao's conclusions about the "restoration of capitalism" in the Soviet Union helped convince him that a Cultural Revolution was needed to prevent such an outcome in China.

The Sino-Soviet split shattered the myth of a monolithic world communism controlled by Moscow.

China saw both the Soviet Union and the United States as enemies during the 1960s. In 1969, the Chinese and the Soviets actually came into armed conflict over a border dispute, and China and the United States were engaged in indirect hostilities throughout much of the Vietnam War. Chinese foreign policy focused on rallying Third World opposition to Soviet and American "imperialism" and on encouraging revolutionary movements in many countries in Asia, Africa, and Latin America. China also pursued a policy of self-reliance in international relations, which meant economic **autarky** and diplomatic independence.

Beijing's radical view of the world was a reflection of the radicalism that also dominated Chinese domestic politics at the time.

In February 1972, U.S. President Richard Nixon visited China after several months of lower-level contacts and secret negotiations between the two countries. Nixon's meetings with Mao and other top Chinese leaders signaled the beginning of a Sino-American **détente** that brought a surprising end to more than two decades of antagonism between the United States and the PRC. The impetus for the reconciliation was each side's perception that the Soviet Union was its greatest enemy and that there was important strategic advantage in at least limited cooperation against this common threat.

Sino-American détente also had an effect on Chinese domestic politics. The United States–China relationship deepened throughout the 1970s and became part of a process of reengagement by the PRC in international organizations and the global economy. The turn toward moderation in foreign policy, initiated and approved by Mao and opposed by some of his even more radical associates, strengthened the hand of those in the Chinese leadership who favored renouncing the extremism of the Cultural Revolution. They believed that national development required international integration, not isolation, and their triumph in the struggle to succeed Mao paved the way for the pervasive globalization of the Chinese economy that has become a hallmark of China under Deng Xiaoping.

From the coming of the West in the early nineteenth century through the end of the Chinese civil war in the mid-twentieth century, China's destiny was deeply shaped by incursions and influences from abroad that it could do little to control. Since the 1950s, China's international stature has increased as its economic and military power have grown. Though still a relatively poor country by many per capita measures, the sheer size of the Chinese economy makes the PRC an economic powerhouse (see Table 2). The PRC is now a nuclear power with the world's largest conventional military force; it is an active and influential member of most international organizations, including the United Nations; and it is a major trading nation whose import and export policies have an important impact on the economies of many other countries. All in all, then, the PRC is a proud and independent nation that is clearly one

TABLE 2   China's World Ranking for Output of Major Industrial and Agricultural Products

Product	Rank[a]		
	1950	1978	1993
Steel	26	5	3
Coal	9	3	1
Crude oil	27	8	5
Electricity	25	7	3
Cement	8	4	1
Cotton cloth	3	1	1
Cereals	2	2	1
Cotton	4	3	1
Pork, beef, mutton	3	3	1

[a]Rank is based on total output. For example, in 1950 China ranked 26th worldwide in total steel output; in 1993 it ranked 3rd.

Source: *Beijing Review* 37, no. 40 (9 October, 1994): 22.

of the major players on the Asian and the global scenes.

IMPLICATIONS FOR CONTEMPORARY CHINESE POLITICS

In many ways, politics in China today bears the imprint of the country's long history. There are several striking parallels between the political system of imperial China and the Chinese communist party-state that have led some observers to emphasize the continuities between these two seemingly very different kinds of government. One scholar has even referred to China under the CCP as "The People's Middle Kingdom" to highlight the persistence of traditional influences well into modern times.[10]

For example, Deng, like Mao before him, is seen as acting like an emperor of old in his highly personalistic and absolutist style of leadership and his reliance on small cliques of advisers and political allies. The Mao cult during the Cultural Revolution also drew on the tradition of "emperor worship" that is deeply embedded in traditional Chinese **political culture.** Bureaucracy in the PRC is also reminiscent of the imperial civil service, especially the superior attitude of party-state officials who often act as "new mandarins" in their relations with ordinary citizens. Finally, despite profound differences between Confucianism in imperial China and Marxism-Leninism in the PRC, both doctrines have served as an official, state-sponsored ideology that dominated political life and provided the basis of legitimacy for the regime in power. Both ideologies also share the view that the needs of society should prevail over the rights of individuals, which has bolstered the claim of the Chinese state in traditional and modern times that it has the right to suppress dissent.

Chinese politics in the 1990s is also being shaped by the tortuous process of state formation in modern China and by the continuing influence of China's traditional political culture. In just the first half of this century, China experienced the collapse of both a long-established imperial system and a feeble republic, decades of national disintegration and ferocious civil war, and a brutal occupation of much of its territory by the Japanese during World War II. When the CCP came to power in 1949, most of its leaders had personally witnessed these traumatic events. They were also well aware that for much of the nineteenth century their country had suffered terribly from rebellions and foreign domination that were largely a consequence of China's weak government. These personal and historical memories of national disorder have amplified the age-old Chinese fear of "chaos" *(luan),* which many Chinese believe inevitably follows when the government loses control in such a vast land. Concerns about *luan* are deeply rooted in Chinese political culture and continue to shape the attitudes of China's leaders and people.

The consistent suppression of dissent by the CCP since 1949 can mostly be explained by its fierce determination to hold onto power at all costs. But it also reflects its fear that losing control could once again plunge the nation into a spasm of disorder. Deng Xiaoping and the other elderly leaders who ordered the Tiananmen crackdown acted as they did, in part, because of their very painful memories of what they and their families suffered during the chaos of the Cultural Revolution.

At a time when reform is causing significant economic power to shift from the central government to local areas and individuals, there is considerable apprehension about the flood of troubles that might be unleashed if the Communist Party were to give up or be forced from power too quickly. Many Chinese are skeptical about the suitability of democracy for their country and believe that the country needs a strong, authoritarian government to keep order and guide the nation's economic development.

However, there are also many who believe that the CCP has lost its right to govern because of its many blunders while in power. The party can take considerable credit for transforming China from a weak, impoverished country into a relatively powerful nation that appears to be well on its way to economic development and modernization. But it also bears responsibility for tragedies such as the Great Leap famine and the terrible violence of the Cultural Revolution. The scars of these traumas are still very visible in China, and the CCP and Chinese people as a whole have yet to come to terms with the full meaning of the Maoist era. As one journalist has noted, "Mao, unlike Stalin, did not target individuals for assassination, did not directly supervise any of the killing, and did not revel in it. And unlike Hitler, he did not select a whole people for extermination."[11] However, Mao's fanatical policies, his relentless pursuit of permanent revolution, his paranoia about class enemies, and his autocratic leadership directly or indirectly caused the deaths of tens of millions and left a legacy of divisiveness and alienation that still infects China's political life. China's economy and society under Deng has moved in very un-Maoist directions. Nevertheless, the Tiananmen massacre and continuing suppression of dissent have deepened the bitterness, cynicism, and apathy that many citizens feel toward politics and the party-state.

This situation raises serious questions about the future of communism in China. Can the CCP stay in power and somehow defy the trend set in motion by the collapse of communist regimes in Eastern and Central Europe that began in 1989? Under the leadership of Deng Xiaoping, the CCP has abandoned many basic socialist economic principles and embraced market reforms in order to stimulate modernization. The result has been a surge in China's economic growth, which the party hopes will help sustain it in power by enhancing its tarnished legitimacy (see Figure 1 on the following page).

However, Deng's reforms have also created a number of contradictions. China's view of its role in the world is changing. The country's new economic strength makes it an increasingly important actor in regional and global affairs, yet China still considers

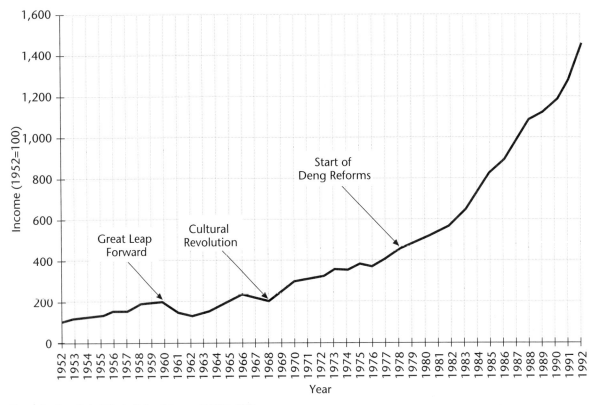

Figure 1   Growth in China's National Income,* 1952–1992
This chart shows the upsurge in China's economy since Deng's economic reforms began in 1978. It also shows the economic impact of Maoist radicalism in the Great Leap Forward (1958–1960) and the first phase of the Great Proletarian Cultural Revolution (1966–1969).
Note: The year 1952 is the base year, equal to 100. Annual changes are measured against that base.
Source: *China Statistical Yearbook, 1993.*
*National income is roughly equivalent to gross domestic product.

itself a Third World nation struggling against domination by richer and more powerful states. Although China has a strong sense of its cultural identity based on language, ethnicity, and traditions, reform and repression have undermined socialism as the basis of the nation's modern political identity. The Communist Party is trying to adjust communist ideology to make it more relevant to China's current situation; for many Chinese, however, what it means to be a citizen of a self-proclaimed socialist *People's Republic* of China is very much in doubt.

But it is the sharp disjunction between economic and political reform over the last decade or so that is the source of the deepest tensions in Chinese politics today. China's current leaders have sanctioned a remarkable degree of economic freedom in order to promote development, but they have not permitted any political reform that diminishes the Chinese Communist Party's essential monopoly on power. Yet modernization of the economy and society have produced pressures for political change, which the CCP has thus far been unwilling to accommodate. The relationship between economic reform and political change and how it may affect the prospects for democracy in China are the central themes on the pages that follow.

SECTION 2
Political Economy and Development

STATE AND ECONOMY

The growth of China's economy since the late 1970s has been called "one of the century's greatest economic miracles," which has, in turn, produced "one of the biggest improvements in human welfare anywhere at any time."[12] Such superlatives seem justified in describing overall economic growth rates that have reached as high as 13 percent per year at a time when the most developed countries in the world, such as the United States, have been growing less than half as fast. China's industrial output has been surging ahead at nearly 20 percent per year. National economic growth has also led to a noticeable improvement in the material lives of most Chinese. Average incomes have doubled or tripled since Deng's reforms were introduced; the consumption of poultry has risen by more than 400 percent; and annual production of televisions has gone from around half a million in 1978 to nearly 30 million in the early 1990s.

But China's economic transformation in recent years has involved much more than just quantitative growth. There has also been a profound redirection of the very nature of economic life in the PRC from what it had been during the Maoist era. Despite the many successes of Deng's reforms, economic policy, particularly the relative roles of the state and the market in promoting development, remains a bitterly divisive issue within the Chinese leadership.

The Maoist Economy

When the CCP came to power in 1949, the Chinese economy was suffering the cumulative effects of more than a hundred years of rebellion, invasion, political fragmentation, and bad government. The economy was racked by astronomical hyperinflation (prices rose 85,000 times in one six-month period in 1948!), trade and transport had been devastated, and production in both agriculture and industry was well below pre–World War II levels.

The first urgent task of China's new Communist rulers was stabilization and revival of the economy. These goals were achieved with rather rapid success through policies that, for the most part, emphasized moderation rather than revolutionary transformation. Although the property of some large industrialists, Nationalist supporters, and rural landlords was seized, much private ownership and many aspects of capitalism were allowed to continue in order to gain support for the government and get the economy going again.

Once production had been restored and the CCP had firmly established its political authority, the party turned its attention to promoting economic growth and "building socialism" in China by following the Soviet model of development with its emphasis on rapid industrial development. The essence of this model was a **command economy,** in which the state controls nearly all economic resources and in which government "commands" and central planning replace market forces as the principal determinant of economic activity. This type of economic system was in effect in China, with some important variations, from 1953 until the late 1970s when Deng Xiaoping began his market-oriented reforms.

The command economy in China was at its height during the First Five Year Plan of 1953–1957 when relations were still close between the PRC and the Soviet Union. Under this plan, both the nationalization of industry and the collectivization of agriculture were carried out, which effectively eliminated the private economy throughout the country. These policies yielded some impressive economic results, but they also created huge bureaucracies and new inequalities, especially between the relatively favored cities where industry was heavily concentrated and the investment-starved rural areas. These trends led Mao and his radical supporters to break with the Soviet model and fashion a distinctive Chinese road to socialism that would be more participatory and egalitarian. Both the Great Leap Forward and the Cultural Revolution embodied this Maoist approach to economic development.[13]

For example, in the Great Leap, more than a million "backyard furnaces" were set up throughout the country to prove that steel could be produced in every locality, not just in a few huge modern factories in the cities. In the Cultural Revolution, "revolutionary committees," controlled by workers and party officials, replaced the top-down management system in the running of industrial enterprises. Both of these Maoist experiments were less than successful: The backyard furnaces yielded great quantities of useless steel and squandered precious resources, and the revolutionary committees led to a politicization of factory life that hurt production. But for all of its radical innovations and more decentralized decision making, the Maoist strategy of development never really broke decisively with many of the basic precepts of the command system, such as the government domination of the economy and state-directed squeezing of the countryside to get the resources needed for rapid industrialization.

The economic legacy of Maoism is a mixed one. Though Maoism maintained a strong emphasis on the role of the state in economic development, populist campaigns like the Great Leap and the Cultural Revolution undermined the bureaucratic structure and technical expertise that are the lifeblood of a command system. The Maoists also ferociously attacked any vestiges of private economic activity as "capitalist weeds" that had to be expunged from socialist China, with the result that for most people there was little incentive to work hard. Maoist policies ultimately had very serious negative effects on the ability of the PRC to embark upon a path of sustained economic development. Growth rates, especially in agriculture, barely kept pace with population increase, and the scale of wasted resources due to poor management and ill-conceived investment schemes was truly staggering.

On the other hand, there were important economic achievements in China during the Mao years. Under Mao, the PRC "did accomplish, in however flawed a fashion, the initial phase of industrialization of the Chinese economy, creating a substantial industrial and technological base that simply had not existed before."[14] By the time of Mao's death in 1976, China's stock of industrial capital (factories and machinery, for example) was about twenty times greater than it had been in the early 1950s. Widespread experimentation, such as with varying degrees of central versus local control in economic management prevented the Chinese economy from becoming as bureaucratically stifled as that of the Soviet Union, although Maoist ideology did lead some experiments (like the Great Leap Forward) to get out of hand. Furthermore, there were very significant improvements in health and education during the Maoist era. The state, as part of its

socialist commitment to promote equality and reduce poverty, assigned a high priority to building schools and medical clinics throughout the country. By the time of Mao's death in 1976, the people of China were much healthier and more literate than they were in the early 1950s, and they were doing considerably better in terms of health and education than were most other Third World countries where the state took little initiative to address such issues.

China Goes to Market

Deng Xiaoping took China in a direction far different from that which the country had followed under Mao and far different from any that had ever been followed by a communist party-state anywhere. As one of the country's top leaders in the 1950s, Deng had backed the utopian Great Leap Forward, but by the early 1960s had come to the conclusion that China needed less ideology and more economic development, even if that required the use of some capitalist methods (such as the profit motive) to encourage production. Deng's pragmatic views were captured in his famous statement, "It doesn't matter whether a cat is white or black, as long as it catches mice," which meant that China should not be overly concerned about whether a policy was socialist or capitalist if it in fact promoted economic growth.[15]

After he became China's top leader in 1978, Deng concluded that drastic action was needed to get the Chinese economy moving after the Cultural Revolution and to adjust China's socialist system to the realities of an increasingly interdependent and competitive modern world. He spearheaded a program of far-reaching reforms that, in the course of less than a decade, literally remade the Chinese economy, touched nearly every aspect of life in the PRC, and redefined the very nature of socialism in China. Deng himself has referred to his economic reform program as China's "second revolution," comparing it in importance to the first revolution, which brought the Communists to power.[16] The upshot of these reforms has been to reduce the role of government commands while allowing the market mechanisms to operate in increasingly large areas of the economy. Thus, under Deng's leadership, China has developed an economy that is part socialist planning and part capitalist free market.

Since the early 1980s, there has been a significant degree of **decentralization** in the economy with au-

Workers in a shoe factory in the north China city of Tianjin sew leather boots destined for the U.S. market. Export-oriented factories like this one have been a major part of China's recent economic boom.
Source: AP/Wide World Photos.

thority for making economic decisions passing from bureaucrats to individual families, factory managers, and private entrepreneurs, all of whom are motivated primarily by the desire to make more money. Most prices are now set according to supply and demand, as in a capitalist economy, rather than by administrative decree, and in many sectors of the economy decisions about what to produce and how to produce it are no longer dictated by the state. Under the planned economy, state-owned industries and businesses had to turn all profits over to the state and were bailed out by the state if they ran into financial difficulty. Many state enterprises are now responsible for their own destiny; that is, if a company makes a profit, the workers and managers earn more income, and if it loses money, it may well go bankrupt and they may lose their jobs.

In addition to state ownership, the Chinese government now officially recognizes diverse forms of property rights, including private, semiprivate, and foreign ownership of factories, businesses, retail establishments, and housing. In many areas of the economy, government monopolies have given way to fierce competition between state-owned and nonstate-owned firms; for example, the government-run national airline, which was the country's *only* airline until 1985, now competes with more than twenty-five other provincial and private carriers. Several government-approved stock markets, which sell shares in enterprises

to private individuals, have been established, and many more ad hoc ones have sprung up in numerous locales. China still has more than 100,000 state enterprises with more than 100 million workers. State-owned factories produce a large chunk of China's total industrial output and continue to dominate critical sectors of the economy, such as the production of petroleum and steel, but their role is diminishing as private and local government-run collective industries expand and grow at a much faster rate (see Figure 2). But real **privatization,** in which the national government actually sells off many of its enterprises, has been much more limited in China than in the post-communist countries of East-Central Europe and many of the liberalizing economies of the Third World, such as Brazil and Mexico. In essence, extensive marketization of the economy—including competition, the profit motive, and setting prices according to supply and demand—has occurred in China (affecting even state-owned enterprises) without extensive privatization.

As a result of the reforms, people's economic lives are no longer characterized by the rationing of daily necessities or waiting in long lines to buy inferior products so typical of centrally planned economies that sacrifice consumer goods for the sake of industrial development. In the span of a decade, China has become a consumer society supported by an economy of relative abundance. To cite just one example:

Figure 2   China's Industrial Output by Type of Ownership, 1978–2000 (projected)

These charts show how the share of China's industrial output that comes from state-owned enterprises has declined steadily since the introduction of Deng Xiaoping's economic reforms in 1978. The category "Collective" consists mostly of town and village enterprises (TVEs), which are owned by local governments. "Private and Other" includes enterprises that are owned by individual entrepreneurs, industries that are full or partly foreign-owned, and various kinds of partnerships between state, collective, and private enterprises.

Sources: *China Statistical Yearbook, 1993; The New York Times*, October 19, 1992.

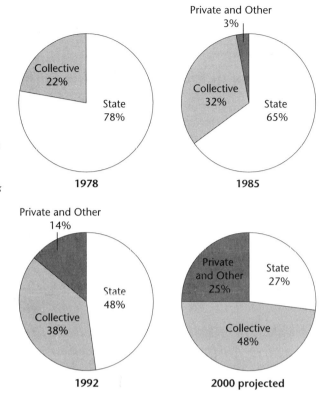

In 1981, there were only 0.02 refrigerators for each one hundred city households; by 1991, the number had jumped to fifty.

The success of the reforms can be attributed largely to the increased motivation to work hard and the new opportunities to invest created by the reduction of bureaucratic interference in the economy and the removal of many restrictions on private economic activity. As a Chinese saying that became popular in the 1980s put it, "To get rich is glorious!" Deng's China has given many people the chance to become much richer.

China's success in reforming its command economy stands in sharp contrast to the experience of the Soviet Union, where Gorbachev's reforms were met with ferocious resistance from both party-state officials and enterprise managers. The Soviet system of central planning was much older and, therefore, more extensive and deeply entrenched than the PRC's. Gorbachev's initial targets for reform were the heavily bureaucratized state-owned industries, while Deng's reforms began in the relatively less state-dominated countryside with the decollectivization of agriculture

and the return to family-based farming. This helped get China's reform process off to a dramatically successful start.

Industrial reform has also been more successful in China than it was in the Soviet Union, partly because Deng's policies have let even state-owned factories be more responsive to market forces. This has allowed managers and workers in these enterprises to share in the new prosperity, which has, in turn, made many of them enthusiastic supporters of reform. Furthermore, even though the Soviet Union was much more industrialized than China, the Soviet economy was notorious for its failures to produce internationally competitive products or enough domestic consumer goods to meet the Soviet public's needs. In contrast, by the late 1980s, Deng's reforms had created a vibrant export industry and had yielded a very impressive increase in both the quantity and quality of goods (both domestic and imported) available in the stores. As a result, the political legitimacy of China's communist party-state was strengthened by the country's economic performance. This was in sharp contrast to Gorbachev's situation, where even substantial politi-

Although China has become more industrialized and urbanized in recent decades, the vast majority of the Chinese people still live in rural areas, and many of them still earn their living through fairly traditional agricultural labor. In general, rural incomes are less than half those of the urban areas.
Source: AP/Wide World Photos.

cal change could not lessen public anger at the dismal state of the Soviet economy.

In fact, Gorbachev's efforts to mobilize popular support for his policies, by putting political reform **(glasnost)** ahead of economic reform **(perestroika),** undermined his ability to manage the process of change in the Soviet Union. The current Chinese leadership has concluded that too much rapid political change was the major reason for the collapse of Soviet communism, and they are determined not to make the same mistake.

China now says it has a "socialist market economy." This may sound like a contradiction in terms since a market economy is usually associated with capitalism. The idea of a socialist market economy can be seen as mere ideological window dressing to allow the introduction of capitalism into a country still ruled by a Communist Party. But from the official Chinese perspective, the term conveys the fact that China's economy now combines elements of both socialism and capitalism and also (in theory at least) the fact that the market remains subordinate to the plan.

The Chinese government claims that the socialist market economy is socialist because it will bring "common prosperity" to the entire Chinese nation. This is said to be fundamentally different from the capitalist goal of accumulating private wealth, even though the route to common prosperity in China certainly involves a big improvement in individual and family incomes.

As dramatic as some of the changes in the Chinese economy have been since the early 1980s,

Deng's policies have always reflected a "persistent statism that lay at the core of the reform program."[17] Command-based central planning in the PRC has been refined, not abandoned, and national and local bureaucrats still dominate crucial nodes in the production and distribution of goods, resources, and services. The extent of private property is still very restricted, while unproductive state enterprises continue to exert considerable drag on key economic sectors. And even though the market reforms have gained substantial momentum that would be hard to reverse, the Communist Party continues to wield the ultimate power to decide what direction economic reforms will take and whether or not they will continue. In summary, bureaucracy, politics, and ideology continue to tilt the balance of economic power in China decisively toward the party-state. China's socialist market economy still falls far short of the cooperative interaction between the government and private economic entities that characterizes the world's most dynamic economies, including Japan and Germany.

Remaking the Chinese Countryside

The changes in China under Deng Xiaoping have been particularly striking in the countryside, where about 70 percent of the Chinese people (over 800 million) still live and work. Although the PRC has more than thirty cities with a population of a million or more—the three largest being Shanghai (7 million), Beijing (6 million), and Tianjin (5 million)—China remains largely rural.

One of the first major efforts launched by the CCP after it came to power in 1949 was a land reform campaign that confiscated the property of landlords and redistributed it to the poorer peasants. This campaign, which gave ownership of land to individual peasant families, resulted in much greater equality and higher productivity in the countryside.

Beginning in the mid-1950s, farming was collectivized as part of China's transition to socialism, and by 1956, Chinese peasants lived on collective farms made up of several villages with about 250 families. The land now belonged to the collective, and production and labor were directed by local officials working in coordination with the state plan. Individuals were paid according to how much they worked on the collective land, while most crops and other farm products had to be sold to the state at low fixed prices. During the Great Leap Forward, collectives were merged into gigantic **people's communes** with several thousand families; although the size of the communes was scaled back following failure of the Leap, the commune system remained as the foundation of the rural economy throughout the rest of the Maoist period.

The system of collectivized agriculture proved to be one of the weakest links in China's command economy. The communes were able to deliver improved social services to the people in the countryside, and they undertook some large-scale construction projects (especially irrigation) that did benefit the rural areas. But they also seriously undermined peasants' incentives to work hard since much of the fruits of their labor went into the communal pot rather than into their own pockets or was bought by the state at low prices in order to feed the cities and fuel the factories. Per capita grain output in 1977 (the year after Mao's death) was at about the same low level as in 1957, a statistic that reflects serious economic problems in a country with a largely grain-based diet.

The first changes in the organization of agriculture in post-Mao China actually came in the late 1970s, not from the top leadership, but from the spontaneous actions of local leaders in Anhui province who were looking for ways to boost production. These local leaders moved to curtail the powers of the commune and allow the peasants more leeway in planting and selling their crops. Then, in the very early 1980s, Deng Xiaoping used his newly won political power to sanction this trend and moved to "bury the Maoist model once and for all" in the countryside by the

"massive dismemberment of the basic features of the former collectivized system."[18] The communes were dismantled and replaced by a **"household responsibility system"** in which farmland is contracted out to individual families who take full charge of the production and marketing of crops—functions that were previously tightly controlled by the commune. After paying—in cash or in kind—government taxes and contract fees to the village, which still owns the land, the family is largely free to consume or sell what it produces in its fields. In 1995, land contracts, which had been set at fifteen years, were extended for another thirty years in order to give farming families more stability in planning their production and investment. There has, however, been no serious discussion of actually selling the land to individual families, that is, real privatization of agriculture.

The freeing of rural labor from the constraints of the communal system led to a sharp increase in agricultural productivity; in the 1980s, agricultural production grew at the very impressive rate of just over 6 percent a year. This growth has led to a big improvement in the living standards of China's farmers and has also generated a surplus that has helped sustain the country's efforts to expand and modernize industrial production.

Nothing has contributed more to the remaking of the Chinese countryside, however, than the spread of a rural industrial revolution that, in speed and scope, is probably unprecedented in the history of the modern world. Although the foundations of rural industrialization were laid during the Maoist period, "township and village enterprises" (TVEs) have expanded enormously under Deng's reforms. These relatively small-scale rural factories are generally run by local governments and exist entirely outside of the state plan. TVEs employ nearly 100 million people—about 40 percent of China's industrial workforce. They are the fastest-growing sector of the Chinese economy (sometimes reaching annual growth rates of around 50 percent), produce 75 percent of the nation's clothes, and account for more than 25 percent of the country's total industrial output. Many families in the countryside now earn most of their incomes from nonagricultural employment related to the TVEs, and in some parts of China more rural dwellers work off the farm than in the fields.

The transformation of the Chinese countryside has not been without serious economic problems. The

China's "One-Child" Policy

The following comparative statistics may be helpful in understanding China's population dilemma.

- China and the United States are roughly equal in geographic size, yet China's population is about *five* times larger than that of the United States.
- China has a population density of about 320 people per square mile; in the United States, it is about 70.
- China has about 22 percent of the world's population but only 7 percent of the world's arable land.

The precarious balance between people and the land needed to feed them has been a dilemma for China for centuries, but only in the last couple of decades has the Chinese government had the political will and the technical means to begin to address the problem of population growth.

Mao Zedong did not see a reduction of China's population growth rate as an important national priority. On the contrary, he viewed vast amounts of human labor and the revolutionary enthusiasm of the masses as precious national resources. As a result, little was done to promote family planning in China during most of the Maoist era.

By the mid-1970s, cutting the birthrate and reducing the size of the overall population came to be seen as major prerequisites to modernization and economic development. Under Deng Xiaoping, the PRC has implemented a stringent population control policy that has used various means to encourage or even force couples to have only a single child. These means have included intensive media campaigns lauding the virtues and benefits of small families, the monitoring of contraceptive use and women's fertility cycles by workplace medics or local doctors, positive incentives such as more land or preferred housing for couples who have only one child, and negative sanctions such as fines or demotions for those who violate the policy.

The one-child campaign, the growing and modernizing economy, and a comparatively strong record in improving educational and employment opportunities for women have all played a role in the PRC's ability to bring down its population growth rate from around 2 percent per year in the 1970s to a projected annual average growth of only 0.9 percent in the period 1993–2000. This figure is very low for a country at China's level of economic development. India, for example, has also had some success in promoting family planning, but its projected annual population growth rate between now and the end of the century is 1.8 percent, while Nigeria's is 2.9 percent. These might not seem like big differences, but consider this: At present growth rates, it will take 78 years for China's population to double, whereas India's population will double in 39 years and Nigeria's in just 24 years!

There have, however, been some serious problems with China's population policy. Farmers have evaded the one-child policy—for example, by not registering births—because the return to household-based agriculture has made the quantity of family labor an important determinant in income. In some parts of rural China, female infanticide and the abandonment of female babies have increased dramatically because of the belief that male children will grow up to contribute more to the family, economically speaking. The compulsory, intrusive nature of China's family-planning program and the extensive use of abortion as one of the major means of birth control has led to some international criticism of the PRC's population policies, criticism that Beijing has rejected as interference in its domestic affairs.

Partly in response to rural resistance, the Chinese government has relaxed its population policies somewhat. Rural couples are now often allowed to have two children. In the cities, where there has been more voluntary compliance with the policy because of higher incomes and limited living space, the one-child policy is still basically in effect.

common practice of TVEs being run by local governments and Communist Party leaders has led to corruption and a situation where "local officials often behave more like business tycoons than public servants."[19] There have also been concerns about maintaining an adequate supply of some basic foodstuffs to the cities. Now that the state no longer commands farmers to give priority to grain production, farmers often choose, instead, to raise more lucrative cash crops such as flowers and vegetables. In fact, China has recently had to import fairly large quantities of grain. The government has also provoked considerable unhappiness and even sporadic violent resistance among some farmers in response to taxation and the failure of the state to pay promptly for agricultural products for which it contracts (at market prices). Economic factors, such as the need for larger families in situations where income is dependent on household labor, have also contributed to peasant efforts to circumvent China's controversial "one-child" population control policy.

The Political Impact of Economic Reform

Deng's efforts to transform the Chinese economy through market-style policies have had a major impact on domestic politics in the PRC. First of all, the market reforms have, at times, met with significant opposition from other powerful individuals and factions within the CCP. The so-called reformers want to put more emphasis on the market part of the socialist market economy and open the country even more to foreign trade and investment. "Conservatives," on the other hand, fear that further market reforms will cause the party to lose control of the economy and society and blame the country's ills, including growing corruption, on capitalist influences at home and from abroad. They prefer a system where the market is, as one leading party conservative (Chen Yun, who died at the age of eighty-nine in April 1995) put it, a "caged bird" in which central planning is the cage that keeps the bird within acceptable bounds. With Deng's strong backing, the reformers gained the upper hand in China's government in the mid-1990s and the conflict between the factions became muted. But it may well emerge again in the **succession** struggle that is likely to follow Deng's death.

Second, the decentralization of economic decision making, which has been an important factor in the success of Deng's reforms, has greatly increased the economic autonomy of provincial and local governments. Some observers have even spoken of the appearance of "economic warlordism" in China as regions compete with one another by erecting tariff and other trade barriers between provinces and defy the authority of the central government by, for example, going ahead with extensive construction projects without the approval of Beijing. Such seepage of power from the central to local levels of government poses serious questions about the ability of the party-state to maintain political control in the country. Beijing is especially concerned about its control over the provinces of southern China, such as Guangdong, which have become both more prosperous and more economically independent of the central authorities than other regions.

The decentralization of economic decision making has also undermined the central government's power to collect the taxes it needs to pay for its own operations and for things like defense, education, and infrastructure construction (roads, railways, ports, and so forth). In the command economy, the major source of national revenue was state-owned industry, which was compelled to turn *all* of its profits over to the government. This system was reformed in the 1980s so that factories now pay taxes on only a set percentage of their profit and retain the rest to distribute to employees as bonuses or invest in the expansion or modernization of their facilities. The objective was to encourage enterprises to increase their productivity and profits.

This desired effect has been achieved in the state sector, but overall tax policy in the PRC is still too centralized and has not been adjusted to reflect the enhanced power of local governments and the rapid growth of the private and semiprivate sectors of the economy. Beijing can no longer demand compliance and meets substantial resistance and even outright defiance from local governments who want to keep more of the revenue for their own use.

As a result of these trends, there has been a sharp decline over the last decade and a half in central government revenue as a percentage of GNP (from 35 percent to under 20 percent), which puts a damper on the funding of government activities. At the same time, the government is unwilling to cut its spending significantly for fear of slowing China's economic boom or antagonizing workers by reducing the subsidies used to keep some food prices low in the cities. This has produced large budget deficits that have fueled inflation in the urban areas and caused financial shortfalls that, from time to time, have led the government to give IOUs rather than cash to farmers who sell some of their produce to the state. Such trends could well create—among large segments of the population—unrest that would have obvious and ominous political implications for China and the CCP.

The CCP wants the Chinese people to believe that continuing economic growth depends on continuing party leadership. Deng, after all, undertook his program of bold reform not only to promote economic development in China, but also to bolster the legitimacy of the Chinese Communist Party, and he has remained committed to retaining the party's control over society. CCP leaders hope that growing prosperity will leave most people satisfied with the Communist Party and reduce pressures for political change. But economic development inevitably brings social change, which, in turn, creates new pressures on the political system and new challenges to the Chinese Communist Party.

SOCIETY AND ECONOMY

Market Reforms and Social Change

Market reforms have eroded state domination of the Chinese economy and shifted considerable economic power to private and semiprivate enterprises, households, and individuals. This new economic power has strengthened parts of Chinese society and made them less subject to control by the state. The CCP still claims the right to maintain its leading role over all social forces and reacts swiftly to stamp out or control potential sources of opposition. Nevertheless, economic reform has created groups and interests that must be allowed freer rein if the party wants to sustain the economic boom.

Among the new social groups created through the process of economic reform are the entrepreneurs—the driving force in the revitalized private sector. Under Mao, the private sector was almost entirely obliterated, but Deng's reforms have breathed new life into it. Although it is still a relatively small part of the Chinese economy and remains subject to certain restrictions and ambiguities (for example, the extent of private ownership allowed for certain types of property like land and corporations), the private sector has become the most dynamic part of the socialist market economy. The entrepreneurs who make up the private sector range from multimillionaire executives who preside over quasi-government conglomerates to owners of small factories in both city and countryside, and from youthful founders of profitable high-tech firms to the proprietors of mom-and-pop shops and food stalls. This group is too diverse and unorganized, too apolitical, and still too dependent on government officials in conducting their businesses to be considered, in any real sense, a counterforce to state power. Nevertheless, the emergence of a vigorous private business class raises important questions about the party's ability to control the very social forces that its own policies have unleashed. Some urban entrepreneurs were very visible in Tiananmen Square in 1989, protesting government corruption and even providing financial support for the student demonstrators.

Economic reform has also had a major impact on rural society in China. The shift of rural labor from agriculture to nonfarm occupations mentioned above has been one important transition. Reform has also opened China's cities to a flood of rural migrants. Under Mao, internal population movement was strictly controlled by a system of food ration cards and residence permits. This kept peasants in the countryside, which was an effective means of social control, and was one reason Chinese cities never developed the kind of shantytowns and crushing urban poverty so pervasive in much of the Third World. The easing of these restrictions in the 1980s in response to a surplus of rural labor has created a "floating population" of well over 50 million people who have left the countryside in order to find better economic opportunities in the towns and cities. Most rural migrants do not have official permission to be in the urban areas and are technically considered transients. They are putting increasing pressure on urban housing and social services, and their presence in Chinese cities could become politically destabilizing if they find their ambitions and aspirations thwarted by a stalled economy or government policy.

Likewise, the more than 200,000 Chinese who have gone abroad to study since the early 1980s could become an influential force in the country's economic and political development. Developing countries often experience a **brain drain** when talented people do not return to their home country from foreign study. The PRC's brain drain was made much worse when a large number of Chinese studying abroad decided not to go back to China in the aftermath of the Tiananmen massacre. Many had been, and still are, involved in overseas components of the democracy movement; many others believed that their professional opportunities would be diminished under a more repressive government. The Chinese government has tried to lure them back with promises of no reprisals and good jobs, but with only limited success. However, in time, many are likely to return to China to assume important posts in education, the economy, and government. Their experiences in the United States and elsewhere will strongly influence their political attitudes, and they could become a potent and well-positioned force for democratization. In time, these and other emerging groups will certainly confront the regime with some fundamental questions about the nature of Communist Party rule in China.

Reform and Its Discontents

Deng's reforms have undoubtedly yielded tremendous economic benefits for the nation and most of the Chinese people. But they have also prompted social discontent and growing political restiveness. The more open economy and society have also led to a sharp increase in crime, prostitution, drug use, and other social problems. Such social ills were almost nonexistent in the tightly controlled Maoist era, and even now are far less prevalent in the PRC than in many other countries.

Economic reform has also brought significant changes in China's basic system of social welfare, which have caused serious dislocations for many Chinese workers and farmers. The Maoist economy was characterized by what was called the "iron rice bowl." As in other command economies like the Soviet Union, this meant that employment, a certain standard of living (albeit, a low one), a pension, and basic cradle-to-grave social benefits were practically guaranteed to most of the urban and rural population. In China, the workplace has meant more than just a place to work and a salary; it has also provided its employees with housing, health care, day care, and other services. The reforms have deliberately sought to break this iron rice bowl, which reformers associated with poor work motivation and excessive costs for the government and economic enterprises. Income and employment are now no longer guaranteed, but are more directly tied to individual effort.

The "broken rice bowl" has increased productivity but has also led to a dramatic increase in unemployment (estimated to be as high as 200 million) as decollectivization makes much farm labor redundant, workers are laid off or fired, and factories go bankrupt. Workers in state enterprises still have rather generous health and pension plans, but employees in the rapidly expanding private sector usually have few benefits. In the countryside, the social services safety net provided by the communes has all but disappeared with the return to household-based farming. Many rural clinics and schools closed once collective financial support was eliminated, and the availability of health care, educational opportunities, disability pay, and retirement funds now depends on the relative wealth of families and villages, which has led to tremendous gaps between the prosperous and the poor areas of the country.

The anxieties of workers and farmers about the conditions of their employment and about access to social services is compounded by the negative side effects of China's rapid economic growth. The Chinese economy has been growing so fast that it is often regarded as "overheated"; that is, investment, construction, and expansion are proceeding irrationally, resulting in profiteering, speculation, energy and transportation bottlenecks, raw material shortages, and high inflation rates. Incomes may be rising rapidly for many Chinese, but there is widespread concern that any gains may quickly be swallowed up by soaring prices.

China's economic boom and decentralization have also created enormous opportunities for corruption. In fact, corruption by government and party officials was one of the main points of protest by students and others in 1989. In a country in transition from a command to a semi-market economy, officials still control a lot of resources and still have power over many economic transactions from which there are large profits to be made. Bribes are common in the heavily bureaucratized and highly personalized system. Because the rule of law is often weaker than "personal connections" *(guanxi),* nepotism and cronyism are rampant. There is particular concern about the growing economic and political influence of the children of high officials, the "princelings" who use their ties to the government for personal gain. The government has repeatedly launched much-publicized campaigns against official graft. Thousands of officials have been fired or jailed, and a few have even been executed for particularly massive embezzlement. But this has done little to stem the widespread feeling that the use of official power for private economic gain pervades the political system from top to bottom.

The benefits of economic growth appear to have spread throughout much of the country. The number of people living in absolute poverty, that is, below the line of minimal subsistence, has been reduced from 250 million in 1978 to about 80 million in 1993. China also still has less inequality than many other Third World countries.

Yet despite the significant growth of average rural incomes, decollectivization and industrialization have increased inequalities within villages and among different regions of the country. There is also still a large gap between the average living standards in the cities and those in the countryside. In the early 1990s, the average rural income was less than half that in the cities, and the per capita income of the richest cities was nearly seven times that of the poorest rural areas. Such income disparities are a source of both social unrest and conflict and are a concern to those in the leadership who fear that the PRC's quest for rapid economic development has led it to drift too far from the socialist commitment to equality.

Gender inequalities also appear to have increased in some ways since the 1980s. The situation of women in China has improved enormously since 1949 in terms of social status, legal rights, and employment and educational opportunities, and Chinese women have certainly benefited from the improved living standards that the reforms have brought. But the trend toward marketization has not benefited men and women equally. In the countryside, only male heads of households may sign contracts for land, and therefore men dominate household economic life. This is true despite the fact that farm labor has become increasingly feminized as many men move to jobs in rural industry or seek better economic opportunities in towns and cities. In the cities, as the iron rice bowl cracked and layoffs increased, "the reforms strengthened and in some cases reconstructed the sexual division of labor, keeping urban women in a transient, lower-paid, and subordinate position in the workforce."[20] Although nine out of ten Chinese city women work (giving China one of the highest female urban labor participation rates in the world), women make up only one-third of the employees in state enterprises, which are the most prestigious and most secure jobs in the urban sector.

Finally, the momentous economic changes in China have had serious environmental consequences. Under the old command system, China's environment suffered greatly, but the desecration of nature has gotten worse in the free-for-all atmosphere of the market reforms. Industrial expansion is fueled primarily by the use of polluting coal, which is still by far the major source of energy in China; soil erosion and deforestation are serious problems for the agrarian economy; and the dumping of garbage and hazardous wastes goes virtually unregulated. In one shocking case in mid-1994, the Huai River in north central China was inundated with toxic chemicals from dozens of factories, killing 26 million tons of fish, causing $15 million in economic losses, and making thousands of local residents severely ill. China's leaders have shown an increased awareness of the country's serious environmental problems and have enacted some environmental protection policies. However, "as is the case in most developing countries, the quest for economic development has superseded concern over environmental pollution. . . . [Therefore] China's environment is not likely to see much improvement during the decade of the 1990s."[21]

The prospects for labor, women's, or environmental movements that might push the government to include some of these social issues on the country's political agenda remain limited by the party's tight control of political life. Restrictions on the formation of autonomous interest groups in China are discussed in Section 4.

CHINA AND THE INTERNATIONAL POLITICAL ECONOMY

Deng Xiaoping's program for transforming the Chinese economy rests on two pillars: the market-oriented reform of the domestic economy and the policy of "opening China to the outside world." The extensive internationalization of the Chinese economy and the active diplomacy by the PRC in the last decade and a half contrasts sharply with the semi-isolationist policy of self-reliance pursued by Mao Zedong during much of his rule.

Trade and Investment in China

In 1978, when Deng came to power, the PRC was not a major trading nation. Total foreign trade was just a little over $20 billion (only about 10 percent of GNP) and foreign investment in China was minuscule, as the stagnant economy and heavy-handed bureaucracy were not attractive to potential investors from abroad.

In the early 1980s, China embarked upon a strategy of using trade as one important component of its drive for economic development, following in some ways the model of "export-led growth" pioneered by Japan and the "newly industrializing countries" (NICs) such as the Republic of Korea (South Korea). The essence of this model is to use low-wage domestic labor to produce goods that are in demand internationally and then to use the earnings from the sale of those goods to finance the modernization of the economy.

By the early 1990s, exports and imports were soaring. Foreign trade totaled nearly $200 billion (almost 40 percent of GNP), making China by far the largest trading nation in the Third World (see Figure 3 on the following page). In its trade with developed countries, China exports mainly textiles, light industrial goods, and agricultural products, while it imports mostly machinery, technology, and materials for industry. From the Third World, China largely imports primary commodities such as copper, zinc, phosphates, rubber, and timber, while it exports mainly manufactured goods to developing countries. Despite having large domestic sources of petroleum and significant untapped reserves, China became a net importer of oil for the first time in 1993 because of the huge energy demands of its economic boom.

Figure 3   China's Foreign Trade, 1978–1993
This graph shows the rapid rise of China's foreign trade since the beginning of Deng Xiaoping's "Open Policy" in 1978. By the early 1990s, China's total trade volume (imports and exports) was roughly equivalent to that of some industrialized nations such as Belgium and Canada, though still far less than the world's trading giants like the United States, Japan, Germany, France, and Britain. Source: *China Statistical Yearbook, 1994.*

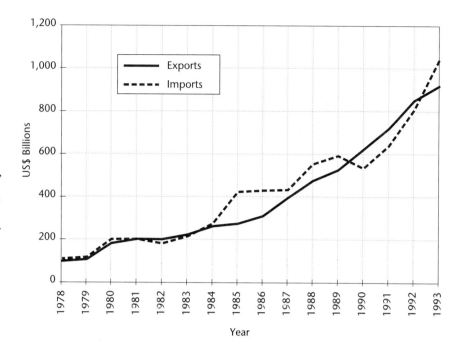

Most of China's trade is centered in Asia, particularly with Japan, Hong Kong, South Korea, and Taiwan, but the United States is China's largest export market (especially for clothing). By 1992, the U.S. trade deficit with the PRC was the second highest after (though still far behind) Japan's. This was increasing tensions in Sino-American relations, especially over the issue of U.S. complaints about restricted access to China's domestic market for American goods and the violation of American copyrights by Chinese firms that produce compact discs, video recordings, and computer software. Such pirating was estimated to cost U.S. businesses more than $1 billion per year in royalties. A trade war was avoided when China promised to crack down on copyright infringements, yet the Chinese government remains limited in its ability to control the far-flung local enterprises that are doing the pirating.

Foreign investment in China has also skyrocketed. By the end of 1992, the PRC claimed that $108 billion in foreign capital was either pledged or actually invested in 90,000 different enterprises. These enterprises range from small factories producing toys and clothing for export to large factories producing goods for the Chinese market, like Coca-Cola and Jeeps, to firms handling gigantic infrastructure projects such as ports.

Many of these foreign ventures are located in "special economic zones" (SEZs) set aside by the government to attract overseas investors through incentives such as tax breaks, modern infrastructure, and the promise of less bureaucratic red tape. The SEZs are even more free-wheeling and faster-growing than the Chinese economy as a whole and have also become hotbeds of speculation, corruption, and crime. The largest SEZ, Shenzhen (near Hong Kong), has been transformed in less than twenty years from a nondescript border town of 70,000 people into one of China's most modern cities with a population of over 2 million and one of the highest per capita incomes in urban China.

Much of the foreign investment in China comes from Hong Kong and, ironically, Taiwan, and a significant percentage of the PRC's trade is with these areas. Although the Republic of China on Taiwan and the PRC have not formally ended the civil war that has pitted the Nationalists against the CCP since the 1920s, extensive economic relations between the two have developed as a result of the opening of the mainland's economy. And Hong Kong, which will remain a British colony until 1997 when it reverts to Chinese control, is China's largest investor and trading partner.

Hong Kong: From China to Britain—and Back Again

Hong Kong became a British colony in three stages during the nineteenth century as a result of what the Chinese call the "unequal treaties" imposed on the Qing dynasty under military and diplomatic pressure. Two parts of Hong Kong were ceded permanently to Britain in 1842 and 1860, respectively, but the largest part of the tiny territory was given to Britain with a ninety-nine year lease in 1898. It was the anticipated expiration of that lease that set in motion in the 1980s negotiations between London and Beijing over the future status of Hong Kong. In December 1984, a joint declaration was signed by the two countries in which Britain agreed to return all of Hong Kong to Chinese sovereignty on July 1, 1997. The people of Hong Kong were not consulted in any meaningful way about the future of the colony.

Britain has ruled Hong Kong in a traditional, but benevolent, colonial fashion. A governor sent from London presides over a colonial administration in which foreigners rather than the local people exercise most of the power, although there is also a free press, a fair and effective legal system, and other important features of a democratic system. In recent years, there have been efforts to appoint more Hong Kong Chinese to higher administrative positions and to expand the scope of elections in choosing some members of the colony's governing and representative bodies. Efforts by the British governor of Hong Kong to implement even limited democratic procedures in the way Hong Kong is governed have met with threats from Beijing that after 1997 it will revoke any changes that do not have its approval. The British, who have controlled Hong Kong for over a century, have been criticized for taking steps toward democratization only on the eve of their departure from the colony. They have also allowed only a small number of Hong Kong residents to emigrate to the United Kingdom before the start of Chinese rule.

Hong Kong has flourished economically under the free-market policies of the British and has become one of the

Hong Kong	
Land Area (sq. miles)	401.5 (about six times the size of Washington, D.C.)
Population	5.8 million
Ethnic Composition	Chinese, 95%; Other, 5%
GNP (US$)	$90.8 billion
GNP per capita (US$)	$15,710
Life Expectancy	Male, 77; Female, 84
Infant Mortality (per 1,000 live births)	7
Literacy	91%

world's great centers of international trade and finance. The colony has the highest standard of living in Asia outside of Japan and Singapore. At the same time, Hong Kong is characterized by extremes of wealth and poverty. China has pledged to preserve Hong Kong's capitalist system for at least 50 years after 1997. Because of the growing integration of the economies of Hong Kong and southern China, the PRC has a strong motivation not to do anything that might destroy the colony's economic dynamism.

In mid-1997, Hong Kong will become a Special Administrative Region (SAR) of China. China will control Hong Kong's foreign and defense policies and have the right to station troops in Hong Kong, but the SAR has been promised a high degree of autonomy in its economic and internal political affairs. However, the SAR government will be responsible to Beijing and ultimately subject to its authority, leading those residents who would prefer independence for Hong Kong to feel that the end of British colonialism will mean the beginning of Chinese domination.

The growing economic integration of Taiwan, Hong Kong, and southern China, which is the most prosperous part of the PRC and often acts rather independently from the rest of the country, has led to the emergence of what is called "Greater China." In this informal, emerging economic community, China provides inexpensive labor while Hong Kong and Taiwan provide capital, know-how, and technology. Extensive investment has also poured into the region from the far-flung community of "overseas Chinese" in North America, Western Europe, and elsewhere. Greater China's share of world trade is already about the same as that of Britain or France. Given how fast the econo-

mies that make up Greater China are growing and their strong export orientation, many observers believe that this region is well on its way to becoming a powerhouse in the world economy.

China in the International System

China has emerged from the relative isolation of the Cultural Revolution period as an active and important player in international politics. In 1971, the People's Republic took over China's seat in the United Nations. Prior to that, the UN, acting in accordance with the wishes and veto power of the United States, had recognized the Nationalist-led Republic of China as the "legitimate" government of all of China, even though it controlled only the island of Taiwan after 1949. The PRC is now one of the five permanent members of the UN Security Council, and it acts there (and in the General Assembly and other UN-affiliated organizations) in a manner that reflects its dual status as both a major power and a developing nation. For example, the PRC did not use its veto power to block the Security Council's resolution that approved the use of force in response to Iraq's invasion of Kuwait in 1990. China abstained from that resolution (though it did vote for economic sanctions) and criticized the Western-led military buildup in the Persian Gulf as a provocative escalation of the crisis that precluded a peaceful resolution.

In many international forums, the PRC serves as a strong advocate of what it sees as Third World interests. At the 1992 United Nations Conference on the Environment and Development in Rio de Janeiro, China took the position that the developed nations bore the "main responsibility for global environmental degradation" and that since the Industrial Revolution they "have exploited the environment without heeding the consequences of their actions."[22] The PRC argued that it was unfair to ask the world's poorer nations to sacrifice economic growth for environmental reasons and called on the developed nations to take the lead in making the sacrifices necessary to halt pollution.

China has also challenged the developed nations on the issue of human rights. The PRC vehemently rejects Western criticism of its human rights record. It sees such criticism as interference in China's internal affairs, based on a narrow and ethnocentric definition of rights. A view of rights that stresses individual liberties above all else, they argue, is inappropriate to cultures like China's that emphasize social needs and responsibilities. China contends that the "right to development," as measured by economic growth and decent health and education standards, is the most basic human right and that on this score the PRC has done remarkably well compared to many nations. It points to homelessness, a high crime rate, and racism in the United States as human rights violations that belie U.S. criticisms of the policies of other nations.

Human rights became a subject of conflict in relations between China and the United States after the Tiananmen massacre when some members of the

U.S. Congress and groups like Amnesty International wanted to impose restrictions on Sino-American trade because of political repression in China. They argued that the United States should revoke China's most-favored-nation (MFN) status, an agreement between trading partners that guarantees that each will extend to the other the same favorable terms (for instance, low tariffs on imports) that it grants to any other country. However, many Americans believed that restrictions on U.S.-China trade would harm U.S. business and consumer interests, dampen Chinese economic growth, and hurt those in China, such as private entrepreneurs, who might become a force for democratization in the future. This was the position adopted by both the Bush and Clinton administrations, and China's MFN status has been repeatedly renewed since Tiananmen, with only minor and easily fulfilled human rights conditions attached.

The sale of weapons by China to other Third World nations has also become a point of contention in China's relations with the United States and other developed countries. The PRC has become a major international weapons dealer in the post–Cold War era, though it still ranks well behind Russia, the United States, Britain, and France in terms of total arms sales. China has been criticized for selling weapons to countries involved in conflicts with the West, such as Iran and Iraq, and for providing advanced missile technology to potential nuclear powers like Pakistan. China argues that the West's position on international arms sales is self-serving, although the PRC has agreed to abide by international conventions regulating weapons transfers.

China now has an important but rather contradictory position in the international system. On the one hand, its low level of economic and technological development compared to the industrialized countries makes it very much a part of the Third World. On the other hand, the total output and rapid expansion of its economy, its vast resource base (including its population), and its military strength make China a superpower—or at least a potential superpower—among nations. In the years ahead, China is certain to become an even more active participant in both the regional and world scenes. At the same time, international influences are likely to play an increasingly important role in China's economic and political development.

Governance and Policy-Making

ORGANIZATION OF THE STATE

"The force at the core leading our cause forward is the Chinese Communist Party," observed Mao Zedong in a speech given in 1954 at the opening session of China's legislature, the National People's Congress, which according to the constitution adopted at that meeting, was the "highest organ of state power."[23] Mao's statement was a blunt reminder to those present that the CCP was in charge of the national legislature and all other government organizations.

This same line was the very first entry in "The Little Red Book," the bible of Mao quotes used by the Red Guards, who ransacked the country in the name of ideological purity during the Cultural Revolution. Although many party members became targets of the Cultural Revolution, the prominence of this quotation reflected the fact that, even at the height of the movement's near anarchy, Mao and his supporters never intended to call into question the primacy of Communist Party rule in China.

Likewise, Deng Xiaoping, despite embracing economic liberalization and recasting some of the central tenets of Chinese socialism, has remained unshakably committed to the preservation of Communist power in China. In a speech in 1979 (a decade before Tiananmen), Deng rejected calls for more democracy and clearly spelled out his views on the role of the CCP in the Chinese political system:

> In the China of today we can never dispense with leadership by the Party and extol the spontaneity of the masses. Party leadership, of course, is not infallible and the problem of how the Party can maintain close links with the masses and exercise correct and effective leadership is still one that we must seriously study and try to solve. But this can never be made a pretext for demanding the weakening or liquidation of the Party's leadership.[24]

Since then, Deng has time and time again reaffirmed his belief that, without firm party leadership, China would stumble in its quest for economic development and degenerate into political and social chaos. And those most likely to succeed him, at least in the short run, appear to share this belief.

Despite many fundamental changes since the Maoist era, "party leadership" remains an inviolable principle of political life in China in the 1990s. Any analysis of governance and policy-making in China must begin with the power of the Communist Party.

China is one of the world's few remaining communist party-states, and the basic organization of the PRC reflects the defining characteristics of this type of political system, including Communist Party domination of all state and social institutions and the existence of an official and exclusive ideology. Party dominance in the PRC is based on the CCP's claim that, as the representative of the best interests of the entire nation, it has the right to exercise the "leading role" in the state and throughout Chinese society. The party's goal is to promote the building of socialism in China with the ultimate objective of creating a truly egalitarian and classless communist society.

The CCP also claims it has the right to lead the country because of its firm commitment to and superior understanding of communist ideology, which in China is referred to as "Marxism-Leninism–Mao Zedong Thought." The core of this ideology is said to be based on "universal truths" from the works of the founding fathers of communism, such as Marx's critique of capitalism and his definitions of socialism and communism and Lenin's theories on party organization and leadership. Mao's contributions to the ideology come from his adaptation of Marxism-Leninism to China's particular historical circumstances, including its economic underdevelopment and largely peasant society.

Many—perhaps most—people in China have lost faith in communist ideology because of the Communist Party's erratic and repressive leadership over the last several decades, and there are numerous other sources of beliefs and values in society, such as the family and religion. But Marxism-Leninism–Mao Zedong Thought still provides the framework for governance and policy-making and sets the boundaries for what, in the party's view, is permissible in politics.

The underlying political and ideological principles of party-state organization are clearly laid out in

China's constitution.[25] The preamble refers explicitly to "the leadership of the Communist Party of China and the guidance of Marxism-Leninism–Mao Zedong Thought." Article 1 defines the PRC as "a socialist state under the people's democratic dictatorship" and declares that "sabotage of the socialist system by any organization or individual is prohibited." Such provisions implicitly give the CCP the constitutional authority to exercise dictatorship over those opposed to socialism and the power to decide what kind of political participation is compatible with the country's socialist objectives and Communist leadership.

The People's Republic of China has had five very different governing documents since its founding: a "Common Program for China" adopted in 1949, which guided the early years of the PRC and was based on the "New Democracy" principles of a mixed economy and inclusive politics (see Section 1), and four constitutions (1954, 1975, 1978, and 1982). These documents have only marginally had the force of law. Rather, constitutional change (from amendments to total replacement) has reflected the shifting political winds in China. The character and content of the governing document in force at any given moment bears the ideological stamp of the prevailing party leadership. For example, in 1993 the current PRC constitution (adopted in 1982) was amended to replace references to the superiority of central planning and state ownership with phrases more consistent with economic reform, including the statement (Article 15) that China "practices a socialist market economy."

The People's Republic is administratively divided into twenty-two provinces, three "centrally administered cities" (Beijing, Shanghai, and Tianjin), and five "autonomous regions." The **autonomous regions** are areas of the country in which there is a high concentration of non-Chinese ethnic minorities. The PRC constitution specifies the structures and powers of subnational levels of government, but China is not a federal system (like Brazil, Germany, India, Nigeria, and the United States) in which subnational governments have considerable policy-making autonomy. Provincial and local authorities operate "under the unified leadership of the central authorities" (Article 3), which makes China a **unitary state** (like Britain, France, and Japan) in which the national government exercises a high degree of control over other levels of government.

THE EXECUTIVE

The government of the People's Republic of China is organizationally and functionally distinct from the Chinese Communist Party. For example, the PRC executive consists of both a premier (prime minister) and a president, whereas the CCP is headed by a general secretary. But because there is no alternation of parties in power in China and because the Communist Party controls government organizations and personnel through various mechanisms described below, it is the top leaders of the CCP, not the government, who hold real executive power when it comes to policy-making in China, while the government of the PRC acts as the administrative arm of the party. Nevertheless, to understand fully governance and policy-making in China, it is necessary to look at both the Chinese Communist Party and the government of the People's Republic of China.

The Chinese Communist Party

The constitution of the Chinese Communist Party (which is a separate document from the constitution of the PRC) specifies in great detail local and national party structures and functions, the distribution of authority among party organizations, the requirements for joining the party, the behavior expected of members, and procedures for dealing with infractions of party rules.[26] But the formality and specificity of this document belies the fact that individual power, factional maneuvering, and personal connections are ultimately more important than constitutional arrangements for understanding how the party works.

This point was never clearer than when Deng Xiaoping and other elderly leaders circumvented the entire formal structure of the party (and the government) in deciding how to deal with the Tiananmen demonstrations in 1989. Many of the men involved in those decisions were retired from their official positions. Deng, for all of his power, has never actually occupied any of the top offices in the political system (see Table 3). His highest formal positions have been: *vice* chairman of the CCP, *vice* premier of the PRC, and chairman of the party's military commission (his only formal post at the time of Tiananmen, but one that made him effectively the commander-in-chief of China's armed forces). In the mid-1990s, Deng's only remaining official position was as president of China's bridge association, reflecting his continuing enjoy-

---

TABLE 3   Who's Who in Beijing

CHINA'S TOP PARTY AND STATE LEADERS SINCE 1949

All of the following leaders were also members of the Standing Committee of the CCP Politburo, the party's most powerful decision-making body.

Person	Highest Positions	Years	Comments
Mao Zedong (1893–1976)	CCP Chairman PRC President	1943–1976 1949–1959	Became effective leader of the CCP in 1934–1935 during the Long March, although not elected chairman of the Politburo until 1943.
Liu Shaoqi (1898–1969)	PRC President	1959–1967	Also a CCP vice chairman. Purged as a "capitalist roader" during the Cultural Revolution.
Zhou Enlai (1898–1976)	PRC Premier	1949–1976	Also served for many years as China's foreign minister and top diplomat.
Lin Biao (1907–1971)	CCP Vice Chairman	1976–1980	Defense minister who was one of Mao's strongest supporters in the Cultural Revolution. Allegedly killed in plane crash after failure of attempted coup against Mao.
Hua Guofeng (1920–)	PRC Premier CCP Chairman	1976–1981	Became chairman after Mao's death and purge of Gang of Four. Removed from power by Deng Xiaoping who saw him as too much of a Maoist.
Deng Xiaoping (1904–)	PRC Vice Premier CCP Vice Chairman	1952–1966 1973–1976 1977–1980 1975–1976 1977–1987	Purged twice during Cultural Revolution. Despite giving up all official posts, still China's most powerful leader in the 1990s.
Hu Yaobang (1915–1989)	CCP Chairman[a] CCP General Secretary	1981–1982 1982–1987	Close protégé of Deng. Ousted for favoring too much political reform.
Zhao Ziyang (1919–)	PRC Premier CCP General Secretary	1980–1988 1987–1989	Another close Deng protégé. Ousted for being too sympathetic to pro-democracy demonstrators during Tiananmen crisis.
Li Xiannian (1909–1992)	PRC President	1983–1988	Veteran revolutionary and party leader rewarded with ceremonial post at end of career.
Yang Shangkun (1907–)	PRC President	1988–1993	Influential military leader and party elder. If he survives Deng, could be a key powerbroker in the succession struggle because of his military ties.
Jiang Zemin (1926–)	CCP General Secretary PRC President	1989– 1993–	A technocrat promoted by Deng Xiaoping after Tiananmen as a safe choice to carry out his policies.
Li Peng (1928–)	PRC Premier	1988–	One of China's most conservative leaders. Widely regarded as the real villain in the Tiananmen massacre.

[a]The position of CCP chairman was abolished in 1982 and replaced by general secretary as the official party leader. This move was widely interpreted as a symbolic effort to depersonalize the top party position, which had been held (and, in the view of many, abused) by Chairman Mao for more than three decades.

---

ment of a card game he learned while a student in France in the 1920s. Although Deng no longer played an active role in day-to-day governance, he was still consulted about important policy matters, and no major decision was made without his approval. In the Chinese media, he was regularly referred to as China's "paramount leader," the "chief architect" of the na-

tion's economic boom, and even as the country's "helmsman," a phrase that was often used to describe Mao at the height of his power. The sources of Deng's immense authority are his seniority as one of the founding leaders of the regime, his deep personal connections to other influential political and military leaders, and his longtime advocacy of now widely

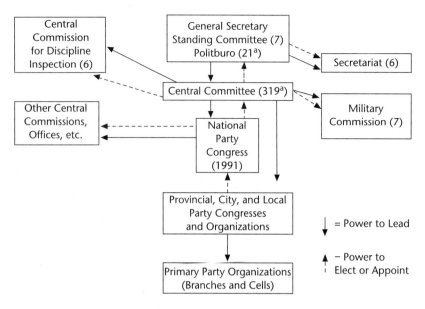

^aIndicates full and alternate members.

Figure 4   Organization of the Chinese Communist Party
Numbers in parentheses refer to the number of members as of the mid-1990s.

supported ideas about how China should develop into a strong and modern nation.

Despite the persisting influence of individual personalities and personal ties in Chinese Communist politics, the formal structures of power within the CCP are important in the routine operation of the party-state and are likely to become more so after the deaths of Deng and the other gerontocrats (that is, the CCP's elderly leaders).

According to the CCP constitution, the "highest leading bodies" of the party are the National Party Congress and the Central Committee (see Figure 4). The National Party Congress has broad constitutional powers, but it meets only once every five years (and in emergency circumstances). Its large size (about 2,000 delegates) also makes the Congress a relatively insignificant source of power within the party. Although there have been a few dissenting votes and limited debate at recent meetings, the essential function of the National Party Congress is to approve decisions already made by the top leaders and provide a showcase for the party's current policies.

The Central Committee is the next level up in the national pyramid of party power. It has about 300 full and alternate members (consisting of party leaders from around the country) and meets annually for about a week. It is elected by the National Party Congress by secret ballot votes, and there is some choice of candidates. Contending party factions may jockey to win seats, but the overall composition of the Central Committee is closely controlled by the top leaders to ensure compliance with their policies. People who study Chinese politics scrutinize the membership of newly elected Central Committees for clues about leadership priorities, the balance of power among party factions, and the relative influence of different groups in policymaking. The Central Committee elected in late 1992 was heavily weighted toward provincial and local officials, technocrats (bureaucrats with technical expertise), and others who strongly favor Deng Xiaoping's program of accelerated economic reform. Several prominent party figures who were considered to be antireform ran for, but were not elected to, the Central Committee.

The Central Committee has the power to direct party affairs when the National Congress is not in session, but its size and relatively short and infrequent meetings (called plenums) greatly limit its effectiveness. However, Central Committee plenums and its occasional informal work conferences, both of which are sometimes enlarged to bring in other important party members, can be significant milestones in Chinese Communist politics. The speeches made and documents issued at a Central Committee plenum may signal a major shift in party policy, as in late 1978 when Deng launched the first phase of his economic reform program. During periods of crisis or transition in China (such as the succession struggle likely to follow Deng's death), the Central Committee can, in fact, be a very important arena of political maneuvering and decision making.

However, most power in the Chinese party-state rests with the small "executive" bodies at the top of the CCP's pyramidal structure. The members of the Politburo (or Political Bureau) and its even more exclusive Standing Committee make up the real power elite in China's political system. These bodies are elected by the Central Committee from among its own members, but, again, under carefully controlled, if not completely orchestrated, conditions. The Politburo has ranged in size from 11 to 30, while the Standing Committee has had between 5 and 9 members since 1949; in the mid-1990s, the Politburo had 21 members (including 2 alternates), while the Standing Committee—the formal apex of power—had 7.

The Secretariat (currently 6 members) is another important central-level party organization, which manages the day-to-day work of the Politburo and Standing Committee and coordinates the party's complex and far-flung structure. The Secretariat has considerable authority in organizational and personnel matters, but is not a center of political or policy-making power.

The Politburo and Standing Committee, which are constitutionally responsible for carrying on the work of the Central Committee when it is not in session, are not accountable to the Central Committee or any other institution in any meaningful sense. The workings of these organizations are shrouded in secrecy. Their meetings are rarely announced and most of their work goes on, and many of the top leaders live, in a high-security compound adjacent to the former imperial palace near Tiananmen Square in Beijing. Observers of Chinese politics watch the composition of these top bodies closely in order to speculate about the balance of power among competing factions or policy tendencies within the party. The strong presence of Deng supporters and protégés on the Politburo and Standing Committee elected in 1992 indicated that party leaders favoring continued economic reform had won out (at least temporarily) over those who preferred to slow the pace of change.

The party's "chief executive"—and *formally* the most powerful position in the Chinese political system—is the general secretary, who presides over the Politburo, its Standing Committee, and the Secretariat and delivers the main speeches at the National Party Congress and Central Committee sessions. Prior to 1982, the top position in the Party was chairman, which was occupied by Mao Zedong for more than three decades until his death in 1976. The title of "chairman" was abolished in 1982 to symbolize a break with Mao's highly personalistic and often arbitrary style of leadership. But the formal authority that goes with the position of CCP general secretary still pales in comparison to the decisive influence of Deng Xiaoping and other "retired" party elders. Deng has masterminded the ouster of two general secretaries for being too soft on pro-democracy demonstrations, including Zhao Ziyang, who argued for compromise rather than confrontation with the Tiananmen protesters in 1989. Deng's handpicked successor to Zhao as general secretary, Jiang Zemin, is widely regarded as a capable, if cautious, administrator (he was previously the mayor and party leader of Shanghai). Jiang has been formally endorsed by Deng as the core of the leadership that is to carry on after he dies, but many observers of Chinese politics question whether Jiang can survive very long as China's top leader without Deng's personal clout to back him up.

Two other party organizations deserve brief mention. The Central Commission for Discipline Inspection and similar bodies on the subnational levels are responsible for monitoring the compliance of party members with the CCP constitution and other rules. It has the power to investigate and recommend punishment (including expulsion from the party) for violations of party discipline, and it may turn its findings over to judicial authorities if it thinks criminal proceedings are warranted. The commission has been used as a vehicle against thousands of party members accused of corruption, but it has also been used to enforce adherence to the party line and to punish, for example, those who supported the Tiananmen demonstrations.

The Central Advisory Commission (CAC) was abolished by the 1993 National Party Congress, but its existence was a reflection of the great power held by some of the party's oldest leaders. The CAC was established in 1982 as a consulting body to the Central Committee and was to be made up of a very select group of party veterans who met the requirement of

Figure 5 Organization of the Government of the People's Republic of China

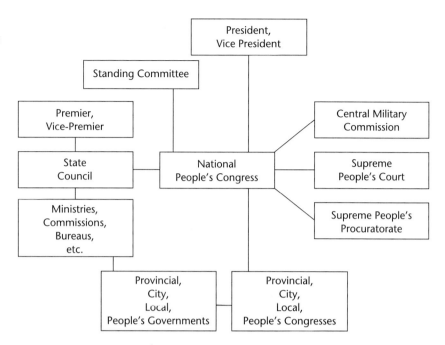

having been members of the CCP for more than forty years. Its purpose was to lure elderly officials into retirement by offering them positions on a body with some prestige and privileges, but with very little authority. In fact, the CAC became a source of great political influence for China's gerontocrats. When it became the center of opposition to Deng's plans for speeding up economic reform, he engineered its abolition to deprive his opponents of one of their major organizational bases.

The major organizational principle of the CCP is **"democratic centralism,"** a concept developed by Lenin in the early part of this century to ensure discipline, unity, and accountability in the communist movement during the Russian Revolution. The "democratic" component of the concept is supposed to allow for the expression of individual views and for rank-and-file input into leadership decisions, including the right of lower levels to elect officials at higher levels. The term "centralism" implies that lower levels of the party are subordinate to higher levels and individual members are subordinate to the organization. In Lenin's time, there was some vitality to the democratic part of the principle; but from Stalin on, centralism prevailed and intensified in the Soviet and other communist parties, including the CCP. The practice of democratic centralism created "a pseudo-

military command structure" in the CCP with authority flowing from the top down and in which a "higher authority could always encroach upon the jurisdiction of the lower level."[27] In other words, there is a lot more centralism than there is democracy.

The CCP is organized into several geographic layers that reach from the center of power at the national level down to "local party organizations"—a catchall term that includes provinces, cities, and counties—and finally down to more than 3 million "primary party organizations" (called branches and cells), which are found in workplaces, schools, urban neighborhoods, rural towns, villages, and army units. This structure, which extends party control throughout Chinese society, is highly centralized and hierarchical and is designed to ensure the subordination of each level of party organization to the next-higher level and to the central party authorities.

The Government of the PRC

Government authority in China is formally vested in a system of "people's congresses," which begins with a National People's Congress at the top and continues in hierarchically arranged levels down through provincial people's congresses, municipal people's congresses, rural township people's congresses, and so on (see Figure 5). In theory, these congresses (the legislative branch) are empowered to supervise the work of the "people's governments" (the executive branch) at the various levels of the system, but in reality, political executives (such as cabinet ministers, provincial governors, mayors, and so forth) are ultimately subject to party authority rather than to the congresses. Unlike the parallel system of *party* congresses, the *people's* congresses are supposed to represent *all* of the citizens at the relevant level, not just the minority who are members of the CCP. However, like the party congresses, the people's congresses play a politically limited, but symbolically important, role in policy-making.

The National People's Congress elects the president and vice president of the PRC. The president's term is concurrent with that of the Congress (usually five years) and is limited to two consecutive terms. Citizens must be forty-five or older to be eligible to serve as president. The position is largely ceremonial, though it has always been held by a senior party leader and has sometimes been used as a base for advancing one's personal power. In 1993, Jiang Zemin, who was also the general secretary of the CCP, was chosen as president of the PRC; Rong Yiren, a *non*-Communist business leader was selected as the country's vice president in a gesture that symbolized China's move toward a more market-oriented economy.

The premier, who is technically appointed by the president with the approval of the National People's Congress, presides over the actual workings of the government and has considerable authority over the government bureaucracy and in policy-making. In fact, the premier is in no way accountable to the president or the Congress and has always been a member of the Party Standing Committee selected to serve in that governmental capacity by the CCP leadership.

The premier directs the State Council, constitutionally "the highest organ of state administration" (Article 85). The State Council functions like the cabinet in a parliamentary system and is made up of the premier, the vice premiers, the heads of government ministries or their equivalents, a secretary-general (who manages the day-to-day work of the Council), an auditor-general (the financial administrator), and a few other top officials called "state councillors."

The size of the State Council varies as ministries and commissions are created, merged, or disbanded to meet changing policy needs. At times, it has included more than a hundred ministerial-level officials, but in

the early 1990s, it had only about fifty members, reflecting the decreased role of central planning and the administrative streamlining undertaken to make the government more efficient. The ministers and councillors run either functionally specific departments, such as the Ministry of Public Health, or organizations with more comprehensive responsibilities, such as the powerful State Economic and Trade Commission. Beneath the State Council and its constituent ministries and commissions are an array of support staffs, research offices, and other bureaucratic agencies charged with policy implementation.

State administration is based on two principles adopted from the Soviet system: "vertical rule" and "dual rule." Within vertical rule, central-level ministries and commissions under the State Council supervise the work of corresponding functional bodies at the lower levels of government. Within dual rule, government agencies are subject to control by the Communist Party as well as being subordinate to higher government bodies. Under vertical and dual rule, a county government, for example, would be subordinate to *both* the provincial government and to the county-level Communist Party organization. Such a system leads to complex and sometimes conflicting lines of authority within the Chinese bureaucracy, but it also reinforces two key aspects of governance and policy-making in China: centralization and party domination.

Since the 1980s, government administration in China has become increasingly decentralized as the role of central planning has been reduced, and more power has been given to provincial and local authorities, particularly in economic matters. Efforts have also been made to reduce party (that is, political) interference in administrative work. For example, the top party leader in a province (the secretary) is no longer allowed to serve simultaneously as the province's governor, its chief administrator. Nevertheless, China's bureaucracy remains a top-down system, subordinate to the power of the CCP.

China's bureaucracy is immense in size and expansive in the scope of its reach throughout the country. The total number of **"cadres"**—people in positions of authority who are paid by the state or party—in the PRC is in the range of 30 million. Of these, about 5 million are government officials. The remainder have authority in economic enterprises; schools; political, scientific, cultural, and other state-run institutions; and party organizations. Not all party members are cadres; in fact, most party members are just "ordinary" workers and farmers. And not all cadres are party members, though party cadres ultimately have power over nonparty cadres.

During the Maoist years, cadre recruitment and promotion standards often gave strong preference to people with good ideological credentials ("reds") over those who may have been more professionally qualified ("experts"), which seriously compromised the ability of the bureaucracy to do its job well. The balance has now clearly shifted to the experts, and there is much greater emphasis on having better-educated and more technically proficient personnel staffing the government bureaucracy. Economic reform has made a technocratically oriented bureaucracy an essential part of the policy process in China.

The Military

The military has never held formal political power in the PRC, but it has, in many ways and at many times, been a very important influence on politics and policy. Ever since the days of the revolution and the civil war, close ties have existed between the political and the military leaders of the CCP, with many top leaders (such as Mao and Deng) serving in both political and military capacities. One of the most famous quotes from Chairman Mao's writings, "Political power grows out of the barrel of a gun," conveyed his belief that the party needed strong military backing in order to win and keep power. However, the often overlooked second half of the quote, "Our principle is that the party commands the gun, and the gun must never be allowed to command the party,"[28] made the equally important point that the military had to be kept under civilian (that is, CCP) control. Although there have been a few periods when the role of the military in Chinese politics appeared to be particularly strong (and people speculated about the possibility of a **coup d'état**), the party has always been able to keep the "gun" under its firm command.

The height of military power in the PRC was during the Cultural Revolution. The People's Liberation Army (PLA), which encompasses all of the country's ground, air, and naval armed services, was one of Mao's closest institutional allies in launching his assault against alleged "capitalist roaders" in the party. National Defense Minister and PLA Marshal Lin Biao was among the chairman's most fervent ideological

and political supporters. In 1968, Mao ordered the army to stop Red Guard fighting and restore political order. The PLA subsequently filled the political vacuum during a period of paralysis in most state and party organizations, and, for a time, military officers were highly visible in the national, provincial, and local governments.

The military's political role ended when Lin Biao died in 1971, supposedly in a plane crash while attempting to flee China following an abortive attempt to overthrow Mao. Although some doubt the validity of this official account, it is certain that Mao and Lin had a serious falling-out that resulted in the death of Lin, a purge of his followers, and a retreat of the military from direct involvement in politics.

The PLA resumed a prominent political role during the Tiananmen crisis in 1989, when the army was ordered to recapture the square from the demonstrators and did so with brutal force. While some senior PLA officers opposed the intervention, in the end they ordered the troops in because the Chinese military "is a disciplined, professional army that takes orders from the Party leadership."[29] The PLA was rewarded for its loyalty in Tiananmen with increased military spending, which has increased more than 10 percent a year since 1989. The massacre greatly harmed the image of the PLA in the eyes of the Chinese public, who previously had a high regard for the military because of its incorruptibility and record of dedicated service in defense of the nation.

The PLA continues to play an important, if muted, role in Chinese politics. Military support remains a crucial factor in the factional intrigues that still figure prominently in inner-party politics. Deng's long-standing and extensive personal ties to many very senior PLA leaders were critical to his ability to outmaneuver party leaders who wanted to slow down the pace of his economic reform in the early 1990s. If Deng's death unleashes a fierce power struggle, the PLA could help decide who comes out on top.

Chinese Communist leaders have long been divided over the issue of what kind of armed forces the People's Republic of China needed. Mao was a strong advocate of equality between rank-and-file soldiers and officers, the use of guerrilla tactics ("people's war") even in modern warfare, the importance of ideological education within the military, and of the extensive use of the PLA in nonmilitary tasks such as the construction of public works projects and the training of citizen paramedics ("barefoot doctors"). Some of China's foremost military leaders believed just as strongly that the PLA ought to emphasize the discipline, professionalism, and modernization needed to defend the nation. Under Deng Xiaoping, the military leadership has been able to keep politics and ideology in the armed forces to a minimum and focus on making the PLA an effective, modern fighting force.

China's People's Liberation Army is the world's largest military force, with about 3 million active personnel. The PLA also has a formal reserve of another million or so and a backup "people's militia" of around 12 million, which could be mobilized in the event of war, although the level of training and weaponry available to the militia is generally minimal.

Despite the large size of the PLA, the Chinese military is, in fact, small in relation to China's total population. In 1991, the PRC had only 2.8 military personnel per 1,000 population, and ranked ninety-sixth in the world—far less than the U.S. ratio of 8.4 per 1,000, which was ranked forty-second. China's defense spending in 1991 equaled 3.3 percent of its GNP, or $44 per capita. In the United States, the comparable figures for defense spending were 4.9 percent of GNP, or $1,100 per capita.

In recent years, the PLA has climbed on the economic reform bandwagon in order to supplement its official budget by converting a number of its military factories over to the production of consumer goods such as refrigerators and motorcycles; running hotels and even discos; and opening up some of its previously secret facilities to foreign tourists in order to earn funds to supplement the formal defense budget. In the mid-1990s, it was estimated that the PLA ran more than 20,000 nonmilitary enterprises with 2.5 million workers.

The key organizations in charge of the Chinese armed forces are the PRC Central Military Commission (CMC) and the CCP Central Committee's Military Commission. On paper, these appear to be two distinct organizations, but, in fact, they overlap almost entirely in membership and function. The chair of the CMC is "elected" by the National People's Congress and is, in effect, the commander-in-chief of the PLA. This position is always held by a top party leader, for example, by Deng Xiaoping from 1983–1989 and since then by CCP general secretary Jiang Zemin. The CCP extends its control of the PLA through a system of party committees and political officers who are attached to all military units.

China exploded its first atom bomb in 1964 and has continued weapon development and above-ground testing since then. Its current nuclear stockpile is relatively small—450 strategic and tactical warheads (compared to 29,000 in Russia and 15,000 in the United States)—and its long- and medium-range delivery capabilities are quite limited. Nevertheless, the PRC is a formidable regional military power, and some of its neighbors are worried about the possibility of Chinese expansionism, especially if the government tries to use strident nationalism to supplement Marxism-Leninism as the country's unifying ideology. A potential hot spot in the region is the South China Sea, where the PRC claims a historical right to the Spratleys, a chain of hundreds of uninhabited islands and reefs that lie close to or even within the territorial waters of Vietnam, the Philippines, and several other southeast Asian nations. Already, there have been several small-scale military skirmishes between China and Vietnam in the South China Sea, and the dispute could escalate given the rich undersea oil and mineral deposits and fertile fishing grounds in the area.

The Police

China's police apparatus consists of several different organizations. The Ministry of State Security is responsible for combatting espionage and gathering intelligence both at home and abroad. The Ministry of Public Security is responsible for the maintenance of law and order, the investigation of crimes, and the surveillance of Chinese citizens and foreigners in China suspected of being a threat to the state. A 600,000-strong "People's Armed Police" guards public officials and buildings and is sometimes used to quell serious disturbances. The local branches of these various security organizations are under the command of central ministries in Beijing. So, in effect, China has a national police force stationed throughout the country.

Without making a formal charge, public security bureaus have the authority to detain indefinitely people suspected of committing a crime, and can use "administrative sanctions," that is, penalties imposed outside the court system, to levy fines or sentence detainees to up to three years in reformatories or prisons or to be supervised under a kind of house arrest. For people convicted of serious crimes, including political ones, the Ministry of Public Security maintains an extensive system of "labor reform camps." These camps, noted for their harsh conditions and remote locations, are estimated to have millions of prisoners and have been a human rights issue in U.S.-China relations because of claims that they use political prisoners as slave labor to produce millions of dollars worth of products (such as toys) that are then exported to U.S. and other foreign markets. China has agreed to curtail the export of prison-produced goods, but it maintains that productive work by prison inmates (common in many countries, including the United States) helps to rehabilitate prisoners and is an important and legitimate part of its penal system.

OTHER STATE INSTITUTIONS

The Judicial System

The judicial system of the PRC came under severe attack as a bastion of elitism and revisionism during the Cultural Revolution. The formal legal system pretty much ceased to operate during that period, and many of its functions were taken over by political or police organizations, which often acted arbitrarily in making arrests or administering punishments.

In recent years, China's legal system has been revitalized. Tens of thousands of judges and lawyers have been trained (some have even been sent abroad for legal education), and legal advisory offices have been established throughout the country to provide citizens and organizations with advice and assistance in dealing with the courts. Many laws and regulations have been enacted, including new criminal and civil codes, in the effort to regularize the legal system.

China has a four-tiered "people's court" system reaching from a Supreme People's Court at the top down through higher, intermediate, and basic people's courts located at the various administrative levels of the state. The Supreme People's Court supervises the work of lower courts and the application of the country's laws, but it hears few cases and does not exercise judicial review over government policies. A nationwide organization called the "people's procuratorate" serves in the courts as both public prosecutor and public defender and also has investigatory functions in criminal cases. Citizen mediation committees based in urban neighborhoods and rural villages also play an important role in the judicial process by settling a large majority of civil cases out of court.

In the day-to-day application of the law, "the legal system can render justice for ordinary citizens who do not threaten the authority of the state."[30] The courts provide a practical avenue of redress for a wide range of nonpolitical citizen grievances and have been extensively used to punish corrupt or abusive officials.

The criminal justice system works swiftly and harshly. Great faith is placed in the ability of an official investigation to find the facts of a case, and the outcome of cases that actually do come to trial is pretty much predetermined: Out of more than 2 million criminal cases tried n 1988–1993, only 0.4 percent were found not guilty. Prison terms for those convicted are long and subject only to cursory appeal. A variety of offenses in addition to murder—including, in some cases, rape and particularly serious cases of embezzlement and other "economic crimes"—are subject to capital punishment, which is carried out within days of sentencing. Hundreds—perhaps thousands—of people have been executed during the periodic government-sponsored anticrime campaigns, and China has been harshly criticized by human rights organizations such as Amnesty International for its extensive use of the death penalty.

Although the PRC constitution speaks of judicial and procuratorial independence, China's courts and other legal bodies remain under rigorous party control. The appointment of judicial personnel is subject to party approval, and the CCP can and does bend the law to serve its interests. Following the Tiananmen massacre, arbitrary arrests and detentions, beatings of prisoners, and secret "trials" were used as part of the crackdown against political dissidents, and legal officials who were considered too sympathetic to the pro-democracy movement were removed from their positions.

Recent legal reforms in China have not been designed to create a truly independent judiciary. They have been undertaken because the party knows that economic development requires detailed laws, professional judicial personnel, predictable legal processes, and binding documents (such as contracts). Like other government institutions in the PRC, the judicial system's basic purpose is to serve as an instrument of party rule. The scope of legality—the areas of society regulated by the legal system rather than the whims of officials or personal connections—has undoubtedly widened in China in the Deng era. But, all in all, the political system of the PRC in the 1990s is still one where the rule of individual leaders and of the Community Party prevails over the rule of law.

Subnational Government

There are several layers of state structure beneath the central government in China, including provinces, prefectures, cities, districts, counties, and rural towns, all of which are referred to as "local" in China's constitution. As noted above, each of these levels has a "people's congress" that is subordinate to higher-level authorities. Like the National People's Congress, these local congresses meet infrequently and briefly, though the standing committees of provincial- and county-level congresses are somewhat more active in managing local affairs.

Day-to-day administration at each subnational level is carried out by a "local people's government," which consists of an executive leader (for instance, a provincial governor, county head, or city mayor), various functional bureaus (such as education and industry), and judicial and procuratorial organs. According to China's constitution, the work of a local government is to be supervised by the local people's congress. But, in fact, the principles of vertical and dual rule discussed above make local officials more accountable to higher levels of state administration and to party organizations than to the local congresses.

Deng's reforms have led to a decentralization of decision making to lower levels of China's political system as provinces, cities, counties, and towns are now encouraged to take more initiative in promoting economic development in their areas. As a result, local governments are becoming increasingly vigorous in pursuing their own interests. Nevertheless, the central government still retains the power to intervene in local affairs when and where it wants. This power of the central authorities derives not only from their ability to set binding national economic priorities but also their control over such things as the military and the police, critical energy sources, and the construction of major infrastructure projects.

Beneath the formal layers of state administration are China's 800,000 plus rural villages that are home to the vast majority of the country's population. These villages are technically self-governing and are not formally responsible to a higher level of state authority; in reality, however, village autonomy is very limited.

In recent years, village leaders and village representative assemblies have been directly elected by local residents. Despite these democratizing trends, power in most Chinese villages tends to be highly personalistic and concentrated in a single individual, the village head, who is most often also the secretary (or leader) of the village Communist Party. The rural reforms described in Section 2 have given many villages more resources and more autonomy than they had under the Maoist commune system. But the reforms have also strengthened the role of the village head/party secretary who is often also the village's leading entrepreneur in establishing and managing the rural industries on which many areas now base their growing prosperity.

THE POLICY-MAKING PROCESS

At the height of Mao's power, many analysts described the policy process in China as a "Mao-in-Command" system in which the chairman and a few of his close lieutenants made the most important decisions and passed them along to be implemented by obedient party and government cadres. The Cultural Revolution led many scholars to conclude that policy outcomes in China were best understood as a result of factional and ideological struggles within the Chinese political elite. More recently, emphasis has shifted to analyzing the centrality of bureaucratic actors and institutions in the policy process and especially the ways in which subordinate bureaucratic units charged with implementing policy reshape the policies made by their superiors. Policy-making is still seen as highly authoritarian; but rather than portraying it as simply a matter of the party issuing orders from the top, this model of "fragmented authoritarianism" sees power as being dispersed among many bureaucratic agencies and policy outcomes as resulting from a process of conflict, competition, and bargaining among party and state organizations.[31]

Nevertheless, ultimate power in the Chinese political system and therefore control of the policy process at all levels belongs to the Chinese Communist Party. In China, the formal division of political labor is one in which the Communist Party makes policy and the government bureaucracy (headed by the premier and the State Council) implements it. This is superficially similar to other types of political systems where the political party in power controls policy-making and the bureaucracy carries out the policy decisions made by the governing party. For example, when the Conservatives are in power in

Britain or the Liberal Democrats are in power in Japan, they control the cabinet, which decides important policy matters, which, in turn, are implemented by the administrative arm of the government, the civil service. Of course, the crucial distinction in the case of China is that there are no opposition parties that have any chance of taking office, so the political power that undergirds policy-making remains the exclusive monopoly of a single political party, the CCP. Formal laws in China are enacted by government bodies like the State Council and the National People's Congress, but the policies behind those laws are made only by the Communist Party. Furthermore, public debate, media scrutiny, and the influence of organized interest groups play almost no role in the policy process in the Chinese party-state.

Like other ruling communist parties past and present, the CCP uses the weblike system of controls to supervise the government and to ensure that the bureaucracy remains compliant to the party's will in the policy process. Some of these control mechanisms, such as the fact that most key government leaders are also likely to be high-ranking members of the Communist Party, have already been mentioned. The CCP also exercises control over policy implementation through a variety of parallel and supervisory structures that oversee the work of government officials at every level of the political system. For instance, provincial governors work under the watchful eye of provincial party secretaries, and the Leading Group on Finance and the Economy is just one of numerous national-level party organizations with authority that cuts across many government ministries.

The CCP also maintains an effective presence inside every government organization, including ministries and bureaus, people's congresses, schools, state enterprises, military units, and so on. These organizations have a party branch or cell, which is made up of all the CCP members who work in that organization, and a party committee headed by a party secretary, who is usually the real source of authority even when technically outranked in that organization by a nonparty official. For example, Beijing University—China's premier institution of higher education—has both a president, who is the school's chief administrative and academic officer, and a party secretary, who is ultimately the most powerful person at the university. Some high-level government organizations also have a very powerful "Party Core Group" made up of three to five CCP members who also hold particularly important positions in the organization.

Finally, the CCP uses a "cadre list," or as it was known in the Soviet Union where the practice originated, the ***nomenklatura*** system to control the careers of millions of officials in the government and elsewhere (including, among others, newspapers, hospitals, banks, and trade unions). Any personnel decision involving appointment, promotion, transfer, or dismissal that affects a position on this extensive list must be approved by the party's Organization Department, whether or not the official involved is a party member. In recent years, the growth of nonstate sectors of the economy and administrative streamlining designed to improve efficiency have led to a reduction in the number of nonparty positions directly subject to party approval. Nevertheless, the *nomenklatura* list is still one of the major instruments by which the CCP tries to "ensure that leading institutions throughout the country will exercise only the autonomy granted to them by the party."[32]

Through these various mechanisms of political domination, the Chinese Communist Party has "not only controlled the government with a tight constant 'police patrol,' it actually substituted itself for the government"[33] in administering the state. In recent years, there has been much talk about drawing a sharper distinction between party and government functions and bringing more nonparty experts into the policy loop. And while some limited action has been taken, party domination and control remain the most salient features of the policy process in China.

Finally, no account of policy-making or implementation in China is complete without noting the importance of *guanxi* ("connections"), the personal relationships and mutual obligations based on family, friendship, school, military, professional, or other ties. The notion of *guanxi* has its roots in Confucian culture and has long been an important part of political, social, and economic life in China. One would expect that the Communists would have curtailed such a traditional practice after they came to power in 1949, but, on the contrary, "instead of declining in importance, *guanxi* may have increased as Chinese have experienced all the unsettling effects of revolution and social change" over the last several decades.[34] *Guanxi* count mightily in the highly personalized world of elite politics within the CCP where policy is made. They are also basic facts of life within the Chinese bureaucracy, where personal ties are often the key to getting things done. Depending on how they are used, *guanxi* can either help cut red tape and increase efficiency or bolster organizational rigidity and feed corruption.

In sum, the Communist Party is at the heart of the policy process in China. Party domination, however, "does not mean that politics operates in a monolithic way"; in fact, the system "wriggles with politics"[35] of many kinds, formal and informal. In order to get a complete picture of policy-making in China, one must look at how various influences, including bureaucratic interests, personal connections, ideological differences, factional conflicts, and social pressures, shape the decisions made by the Communist Party leadership.

SECTION 4
Representation and Participation

China's political system is officially described by the government of the People's Republic as a **socialist democracy,** which it claims is superior to democracy in a capitalist country. From the Chinese Communist Party's point of view, capitalist politics is profoundly influenced by the unequal division of private property and wealth. This, in turn, means that capitalist governments inevitably favor the rich and disadvantage the working classes even though workers may enjoy many political freedoms. The government of the PRC and the CCP, the argument goes, serve all the people, not just the privileged few. The official view is that the CCP "has no interests of its own and rules solely in the interests of the nation and the people. It follows that rule by the party's leaders is rule in the people's interest and by definition democratic."[36] Unlike the **social democracy** of some Western European political parties, such as the British Labour Party and the French Socialist Party, which is rooted in a commitment to competitive politics and political **pluralism,** China's socialist democracy is based on the unchallengeable leadership of the Chinese Communist Party.

Representation and participation play important roles in China's socialist democracy. There are legislative bodies, elections, and organizations like labor unions and student associations, all of which are meant to provide citizens with ways of influencing public policy-making and the selection of government leaders. But such mechanisms of popular input are strictly controlled by the Communist Party and are bound by the constitutional requirement that all Chinese citizens uphold the Four Cardinal Principles: the socialist road, the **dictatorship of the proletariat,** the leadership of the Communist Party, and the ideology of Marxism–Leninism–Mao Zedong Thought. In essence, then, representation other than that guided by the CCP is regarded as unnecessary or marginal. Participation other than that sanctioned by and supportive of the party is seen as subversive.

Some democratic content is imparted to party leadership by the concept of the mass line, which is supposed to guide the work of all cadres and keep them in close touch with the people. Developed initially by Mao Zedong in the 1930s, this concept means that officials are supposed to leave their offices and go among the masses to learn about their lives and problems and enlist their active participation in carrying out party policies. Although much of what Mao stood for has been rejected, the mass line ideal is still embraced by China's current leadership. The CCP's use of "campaigns" that mobilize citizens to help carry out party policies is an example of the mass line in action. Chinese leaders believe that if cadres continue to follow Mao's dictum "from the masses, to the masses" and stay in touch with the people, it will be possible to create a vibrant socialist democracy that reflects both party guidance and popular initiative.

In fact, as this section explains, there is a huge gap between the theory and the practice of the mass line in China, and little about the Chinese political system that is truly democratic. As ideology diminishes, repression persists, inequalities increase, interests diverge, and corruption abounds in the China of the 1990s, the concept of socialist democracy is losing even its theoretical force. But it still provides a powerful rationale for party dictatorship, at least in the eyes of China's rulers.

THE LEGISLATURE

Legislatures in communist party-states are often referred to as "rubber stamps," which implies that their main function is to give policies made by the party the

Campaigns, Chinese-Style

Campaigns are an important form of participation in the Chinese political system. When we speak of the role of campaigns in China, however, we do not mean the process by which candidates for office try to win votes. Although such election campaigns do occur, they are of limited significance in the political life of the nation.

In China, the term *campaigns* means *"mass campaigns,"* movements initiated and guided by the party leadership to get citizens to support or help realize a particular policy or political objective. Campaign methods include general directives issued by the top leadership, catchy slogans and eye-catching billboards, grassroots organizations, small group meetings, and public rallies. Campaigns involve *mobilized* participation, which originates from, and is directed from, the top down, rather than *autonomous* participation in which citizen involvement is self-initiated and voluntary.

Campaign-style political participation and policy implementation have their origins in the Communist bases during the civil war. The first major campaign after the CCP came to power was land reform, which mobilized peasants to take an active role in the struggle against landlords and the redistribution of farmland. Campaigns were used during the Maoist era to achieve important social goals such as eradication of opium addiction and improvement of public health standards. But they were also used for political ends, including ferreting out counterrevolutionaries and class enemies during the vicious Anti-Rightist Campaign of 1957. The Great Leap Forward and the Cultural Revolution were campaigns on a grand scale that Mao and his supporters hoped would realize their radical ideological objectives.

China's current leaders have renounced mass campaigns as instruments of political and class struggle, which they see as socially divisive and counterproductive to the goal of economic development. Furthermore, many leaders, including Deng Xiaoping, were targets of Mao's ideological campaigns. Nevertheless, the CCP still uses some campaign methods to generate public support for its policies, including family planning and crime prevention, and certainly shares the Maoist view that citizen participation should be mobilized or guided rather than autonomous.

---

appearance of being approved by representatives of the people. They may have some influence in important, though routine, state business (such as the formulation of the national budget), but the legislatures have very little substantive power when it comes to critical issues, and in no way provide a check on the authority of the party.

The label "rubber stamp" may be a bit extreme to describe China's legislature, the National People's Congress (NPC), but it does convey the fact that the Communist Party closely monitors every aspect of the NPC's operations to ensure that it is in compliance with the Four Cardinal Principles. Nevertheless, the NPC is a very visible part of the Chinese political system, and it is important to understand its structure and function and to gauge whether the legislature could become an active force for democratization in China.

The constitution of China grants the National People's Congress the power to enact and amend the country's laws, approve and monitor the state budget, and declare and end war. It is also empowered to elect (and recall) the president and vice president of the PRC, the chair of the Central Military Commission (the commander-in-chief of the armed forces), the head of China's Supreme Court, and the Procurator-General (something like the U.S. Attorney General),

and it has final approval over the selection of the premier and members of the State Council. China's legislature, then, is constitutionally more than just a coequal branch of government; it is the central branch of government, with supervisory authority over the executive and judicial branches. This is clearly different from the **separation of powers** between branches of government in the United States. The official Chinese view is that this is a very democratic system because it vests supreme power in the branch of government most closely connected to the people, but in fact these powers are exercised only in the manner allowed by the CCP.

The National People's Congress is a unicameral legislature. It is elected for a five-year term and meets annually for only about two weeks. Deputies to the NPC are not full-time legislators, but remain in their regular jobs and home areas except for the brief time each year when the Congress is in session. One of their responsibilities is to carry out the mass line through regular "inspection tours" of their local areas. The Chinese see this as an advantage of their system because it allows deputies to stay in touch with their constituents and keeps them from becoming professional politicians.

The precise size of the NPC is set by law prior to each five-year electoral cycle. The NPC elected in

China's legislature, the National People's Congress, meets once a year for about two weeks in the Great Hall of the People in Beijing. Although there are now some dissenting votes and more debate than in the past, the Congress still operates under the watchful eye of the Chinese Communist Party.
Source: AP/Wide World Photos.

1993 consisted of nearly 3,000 deputies chosen from China's various provinces, autonomous regions, and major municipalities, which makes it the largest legislative body in the world. Eighty percent of the deputies elected to this Congress were members of the Chinese Communist Party, with the remaining 20 percent either belonging to one of China's few noncommunist political parties or having no party affiliation.

Rather than emphasizing the party affiliation of NPC deputies, the Chinese government stresses their occupational and social backgrounds in order to show that the legislature represents people from all walks of life. For example, workers and farmers made up about a fifth of the deputies elected to the NPC in 1993; intellectuals and professionals made up another fifth; government and party cadres accounted for somewhat less than a third; and the remainder consisted of representatives of other occupational categories, such as soldiers and entrepreneurs. Women made up 21 percent of deputies. Eighty percent of deputies were under the age of 60, and 69 percent had at least a college education.

When the NPC is not in session, most of its powers are exercised by its Standing Committee (which is quite separate from the very powerful CCP Standing Committee described previously). The NPC Standing Committee meets once every other month; so, for

most of the year, it acts as the legislature of the PRC. The Standing Committee elected in 1993 had 134 members, 60 percent of whom belonged to the Chinese Communist Party, and several high-ranking party leaders in top positions.

The annual sessions of the NPC are hailed with great fanfare in the Chinese press as an example of socialist democracy at work. During these sessions, deputies discuss and decide upon legislation introduced by the government (that is, the State Council). Deputies may also make motions and suggestions to the Congress, which are sometimes enacted into law. In recent years, important legislation passed by the NPC has included major criminal and civil law statutes, laws governing foreign investment in China, and environmental regulations.

The NPC has permanent and temporary committees organized around issues such as education, foreign relations, minority affairs, and relations with overseas Chinese. These committees are limited in their ability to influence the legislative process and oversee the work of the relevant government agencies. They serve mainly as a forum for discussion and a means for leaders to hear the opinions of experts and specialists on pending policy matters.

Most of the work of the NPC is routine, such as listening to long reports by officials, and most

The Three Gorges Dam

The Three Gorges dam, which is being built on the Yangzi (Yangtze) River in China's Hubei province, will be the largest dam (over 600 feet high) and hydroelectric generating plant (84 billion kilowatt-hours per year) in the world when it is completed in the year 2009. The current budget for the project is $12 billion, but some estimates that take inflation into account foresee huge cost overruns and put the total at around $70 billion.

Proponents of the dam argue that the project is needed to meet the huge energy demands of economic development in central and southwestern China, and that hydroelectric power is much preferable to the polluting coal that is currently China's major energy source. They also say that the dam will control the Yangzi's periodic lethal flooding, which has killed more than 300,000 people in this century alone. It will also make it possible for large ships to navigate the Yangzi deep into China's interior, and thus help promote domestic commerce and foreign trade.

Opponents of the Three Gorges dam see the project as an environmental, human, and political nightmare. The dam will submerge some of China's most stunning scenery, along with thousands of hectares of fertile cropland, rice paddies, and orchards. Many experts also believe that it will threaten several endangered species, including the rare Chinese river dolphin. Hundreds of historical sites will be inundated, some containing artifacts more than 10,000 years old. More than 1.2 million people will have to be relocated from the villages and towns that will end up under the 400-mile-long artificial lake (longer than Lake Superior) created by the dam. Although the Chinese government is compensating and assisting those who need to move, critics of the project say that most of those who relocate will probably, in the long run, be poorer than before they moved. There are also serious questions about the dam's safety in the earthquake-prone region and about whether the project's energy output will ever justify the huge cost.

Opponents of Three Gorges also point out the completely undemocratic way in which the project was planned and implemented. The Chinese government, and especially Premier Li Peng (who is a Soviet-trained hydroelectric engineer), has made the Three Gorges project into a symbol of Chinese modernization and nationalism, and the authorities have attempted to silence people who have spoken out against the dam. Critics of the project have been purged from their party and state offices, and others have been forced into exile. The media is allowed to carry only positive assessments of the project. A collection of essays by scientists, journalists, and intellectuals opposed to the dam (available in English as *Yangtze! Yangtze!*, edited by Dai Qing, Toronto: Earthscan, 1994) was banned in China shortly after its publication in 1989. Citizen-based environmental groups are only now beginning to emerge in China and do not dare seriously challenge a state-backed megaproject such as the Three Gorges dam.

The fact that even under such repressive circumstances one-third of the National People's Congress voted against the Three Gorges project in 1992 or abstained from voting shows just how much doubt about the dam there must be in China. But, given the current political situation in China, there is little reason to believe that such doubt can be expressed in open public debate or could deter the Chinese government from moving ahead with the project.

---

legislation is passed by an overwhelming majority of deputies. But some debate and dissent do occur. For example, in 1992, about a third of the NPC deputies either voted against construction of the ecologically controversial Three Gorges dam project or abstained from voting. On rare occasions, government legislative initiatives are even defeated. But all NPC proceedings are subject to party scrutiny. The Congress never debates politically sensitive issues, and deputies, even though their right to speak and vote freely is protected by constitutional immunity, would be in serious political jeopardy if their actions were seen as a challenge to the principle of party leadership.

A number of things hamper the NPC's effectiveness as a working legislature: the size of the body, the infrequency and brevity of its meetings, and serious ambiguities in its operating procedures. But, more than anything else, the NPC is constrained by the watchful eye and strong arm of the party. The party monitors local elections to make sure that no outright dissidents are elected as NPC deputies, and the most important leadership positions in the NPC—including the members of its Standing Committee—are on the CCP's *nomenklatura* list, which means that they can only be filled by people who have the party's approval. Furthermore, key NPC leaders are always high-ranking party members. The party's top bodies decide behind closed doors who will get what position, and this is followed by a pro forma nomination and election process within the NPC. Some deputies do vote against party-endorsed nominees for government positions. In 1995, the two official candidates for vice premier were opposed, respectively, by 36 percent and 14 percent of the deputies for a variety of reasons, including questions about their qualifications, factional politics, and regional rivalries. Such protest votes may signal a somewhat more independent attitude on the part of some NPC deputies, but they do not yet add up to meaningful opposition to party-designated candidates.

The political impotence of the National People's Congress was dramatically illustrated during the Tiananmen demonstrations in 1989. About a third of the NPC Standing Committee signed a petition calling for an emergency meeting to defuse the crisis, but the petition was completely ignored by Deng and other party leaders, and the petitioners were denounced as conspirators. In the end, the NPC Standing Committee was convened only after the fact of the massacre to give the appearance of legality and legitimacy to the decisions made by the CCP leadership.

Still, as economics has replaced ideology as the main priority of China's leaders, the NPC has become a more important and lively part of the Chinese political system than it was during the Mao era. Many NPC deputies are now chosen because of their ability to contribute to China's modernization rather than simply on the basis of political loyalty, and therefore, they have become somewhat more assertive in expressing their opinions on some issues. The Congress also appears to have become one of the chief forums for the expression of provincial interests in national policy-making. At the 1995 NPC meeting, for example, provincial delegations were able to derail the central government's effort to get more control over the People's Bank (the state's major financial institution) by reorganizing its provincial branches along regional lines that cut across provincial boundaries.

Nevertheless, China's legislature clearly remains subservient to the CCP. However, in the Soviet Union and some Eastern European countries, legislatures that had long been dismissed as rubber stamps provided an important arena for loud and focused opposition during critical phases of the collapse of Communist rule. A major political crisis in China could provide a similar opportunity for the National People's Congress to emerge as a more truly representative and influential institution.

PARTIES, ELECTIONS, AND CAMPAIGNS

China is often called a one-party system because the country's politics are so thoroughly dominated by the Chinese Communist Party. In fact, China has *eight* political parties in addition to the CCP, but these parties neither challenge the basic policies of the CCP nor

play a significant part in running China's government. While the role of the noncommunist parties in the PRC will be examined below, any discussion of China's party system must focus primarily on the Chinese Communist Party.

The CCP: Who Joins? Why? and How?

At the time of the National Party Congress in 1992, the CCP had about 51 million members. The party has grown steadily since it came to power in 1949, when it had just under 4.5 million members. But there have been times over the last four and a half decades when large numbers of members have been expelled from the CCP through purges, as, for example, during the first and most violent phase of the Cultural Revolution. Unless criminal activities are involved in addition to political mistakes, being purged does not entail execution or imprisonment; it usually only results in being kicked out of the party and perhaps demoted. The CCP also carries out periodic "rectification campaigns" in which the records of all members are reviewed, and those whose behavior is found to have fallen short of party standards or whose views have differed too sharply with those of the dominant leaders are expelled or put on probation.

The Chinese Communist Party is certainly the largest political party in the world in terms of total formal membership. But, like all other former and current ruling communist parties, its members make up only a small minority of the country's population. CCP members are now only about 5 percent of China's population, or about 8 percent of those over eighteen, the minimum age for joining the party.

From the viewpoint of the CCP, the small percentage of Communists in Chinese society reflects the "vanguard" status and role of the party. Only those fully committed to the ideals of communism and willing to devote a great deal of time and energy to party affairs may join the CCP, and the process is long and arduous. The first step is to fill out a detailed application form, which includes recommendations by two party members, and submit it to the party branch in the organization where the applicant works. This begins a cycle of meetings, interviews, and investigations to ascertain whether the applicant is truly qualified to join the party. Applications approved by a party branch must then be approved by higher-level party organizations, and even if that step proceeds smoothly, the applicant is put on probationary status for a year, during which time the candidate member is not allowed to vote or run for office in party elections. Probationary members take an oath in which they swear allegiance to the party and vow to "fight for communism throughout my life, be ready at all times to sacrifice my all for the party and the people, and never betray the people" (Article 6 of the CCP constitution). After a year, a final decision (which, again, must be approved by a higher-level organization) is made to grant or deny the candidate full membership—or to extend probation for another year.

Deng's reforms have paved the way for a milestone transition in the backgrounds of both the party's leadership and its rank-and-file members. During the Maoist era, the CCP was led at all levels by "revolutionary cadres" whose careers depended on political loyalty and ideological purity; recruitment strongly favored the working classes and discriminated against intellectuals and other professionals. The CCP is now increasingly led by "party technocrats"—people "selected from the best educated segment of the Chinese population," with "academic training mainly in engineering and production-related fields," and careers largely made in the party-state bureaucracy.[37]

The social composition of the CCP's membership has also changed considerably in recent decades. "As China has modernized, the CCP has been transformed from an overwhelmingly peasant-based party to one in which all sectors of society are represented."[38] In the mid-1950s, peasants made up nearly 70 percent of the party, and although they are still the largest single group in the party, less than 40 percent of party members now come from the peasantry. Factory workers account for less than 20 percent of party membership. The fastest growing membership category consists of officials, intellectuals, technicians, and other professionals, who together constitute about 30 percent of the party. The remainder of the party is made up of various groups including military personnel, retired persons, and service workers. Women make up only 14 percent of the CCP as a whole and about 8 percent of the Central Committee. There are no women on the Politburo and its Standing Committee, the party's top decision-making bodies.

Despite the party's tarnished image since Tiananmen and what many Chinese feel is the increasing irrelevance of communist ideology to their lives and the nation's future, the CCP continues to recruit between 1 and 2 million new members each year. Some join because they believe in communist ideals; but many are motivated more by opportunism than by idealism. Party membership provides unparalleled access to influence and resources, especially given the current quasi-market nature of China's economy, and being a party member is still a prerequisite for advancement in many careers in China.

China's Noncommunist Parties

The eight noncommunist political parties in the PRC are collectively referred to as the "democratic parties," a designation that is meant to signify the role they play in representing different interests in the political process and lend some credibility to China's claim that it is a kind of democracy. Each democratic party draws its membership from a particular group in Chinese society. For example, the China Democratic League consists mostly of intellectuals, whereas the China Democratic National Construction Association draws members mainly from the business world.

The democratic parties have a total membership of only about 400,000 and operate within what is referred to in the preamble to the constitution as "a system of multiparty cooperation and political consultation under the leadership of the Communist Party." The noncommunist parties do not contest for power or challenge CCP policy. Rather, they view themselves as partners of the Communists in the task of building socialism in China. Their function is to provide advice to the CCP and generate support within their particular constituencies for CCP policies. Individual members of the parties may assume important government positions. But organizationally, these parties are relatively insignificant and function as little more than "a loyal non-opposition."[39]

The main forum through which the noncommunist parties express their views on national policy is the Chinese People's Political Consultative Conference (CPPCC). This body meets in full session once a year for about two weeks at the same time as the National People's Congress (NPC), which CPPCC members attend as nonvoting deputies. As its name suggests, the CPPCC is a consultative, not a legislative body, and its only role is to provide limited advice to the CCP and the NPC.

The majority of the 2,000 or so intellectuals and other leading figures from various spheres of national life who made up the CPPCC that convened in 1993 were noncommunists. But all the delegates were chosen through a process supervised by the CCP. Unlike the NPC, which is mostly organized along geographic lines with, for example, representatives from Guangdong province and Shanghai City, the CPPCC is structured to represent sectoral interests such as business or the arts. Its advisory role has increased in importance and visibility during the Deng era as the party finds these organizations to be useful sources of expertise in China's modernization effort. Most of the CPPCC's proposals have to do with the economy, science and technology, and education. Members sometimes speak out about national problems like corruption or low teachers' salaries, but they do not express serious dissent from the party line on any matter.

Elections

Elections in the PRC are basically mechanisms to give the party-state greater legitimacy by allowing large numbers of citizens to participate in the political process under very controlled circumstances. The CCP has what amounts to effective veto power over all candidates for office. It controls the commissions that run elections, and it reviews "draft lists" of proposed candidates to weed out those it finds politically objectionable. But the CCP rarely has to exercise its veto power over nominations or elections because few people dare to oppose the party openly.

Elections in China are both direct and indirect. In direct elections, all the eligible citizens vote for candidates for offices in a government body that serves that constituency. For example, all the voters in a rural county would vote for the deputies to serve at the county-level people's congress. In indirect elections, higher-level bodies are elected by lower-level bodies rather than directly by the voters at large. For example, deputies to the National People's Congress are elected by the provincial-level people's congresses, which, in turn, have been elected by county- or municipal-level people's congresses. All elections above the county level are still indirect, which means that there are no direct elections at the provincial or national levels.

Turnout for direct elections is heavy—usually over 90 percent of the eligible electorate. All citizens over the age of eighteen have the right to vote, except those who (as the Chinese constitution puts it) have been "deprived of political rights according to law"

(Article 34). This latter category may include the mentally ill, convicted criminals, and political prisoners.

For several decades after its founding, the PRC had a system in which only one candidate stood for a particular office, so the only choice facing voters was to approve or abstain. Since the early 1980s, many direct and indirect elections have had multiple candidates for each slot with the winner chosen by secret ballot. The nomination process has also become more open: Any group of more than ten voters can nominate candidates for an election. Most candidates in direct elections are now nominated by the voters, and there have been a significant number of cases where independent candidates have defeated official nominees, though even independent candidates are basically "party-approved."

The most significant progress toward democratic representation and participation in China in recent years has occurred in the rural villages. Laws implemented in the last decade or so have provided for directly elected village representative assemblies and the election, rather than the appointment from above, of village officials. The village assemblies are usually made up of one representative from every ten or so households and meet at least once every few months. Although the local Communist Party committee is still the most powerful organization in China's villages, these assemblies do have considerable authority over local finances and exercise some supervision over local officials.

Recent reforms in China have increased citizen representation and participation in government, but they have not undercut the basic fact of close CCP supervision of the electoral process. Chinese elections still cannot be considered a means by which citizens exercise effective control over the government. China's leaders have repeatedly rejected calls from both domestic and foreign critics for freer elections. They argue that multiparty elections would not work well in China because of the country's low level of educational and economic development (especially in the rural areas) and its relatively poor communications system. They express the fear that more democracy would only plunge the country into chaos—perhaps even civil war. Obviously, they also have reason to be apprehensive about the consequences of truly democratic elections for the party's hold on power.

POLITICAL CULTURE, CITIZENSHIP, AND IDENTITY

From Communism to Consumerism

Since its founding in 1949, the official political culture of the People's Republic of China has been based on communist ideology, and the party-state has made extensive efforts to make people's political attitudes and behavior conform to Marxism-Leninism–Mao Zedong Thought. But in those four and a half turbulent decades, this ideology has gone through severe crises and profound changes that have left its future in China seriously in doubt.

During the Maoist era, Mao Zedong Thought was hailed as holding the answer to all of China's problems in domestic and foreign policy. "The Little Red Book" of Mao quotes used during the Cultural Revolution referred to Mao Zedong Thought as "an inexhaustible source of strength and an infinitely powerful spiritual atom bomb." By the mid-1970s, however, the debacles of the Mao years had greatly tarnished the appeal of communism in China.

After Deng Xiaoping came to power in 1978, he set about trying not only to restore the legitimacy of the Communist Party through economic reforms, but also to revive communist ideology. As a first step, Mao's contributions to China and Mao Zedong Thought were reevaluated. There was no complete repudiation of Mao as there had been of Stalin in the Soviet Union in the 1950s, but Mao was judged to have made serious mistakes as well as great contributions. Those parts of Mao Zedong Thought, such as his views on the "mass line," that were considered useful in maintaining Communist rule were retained. Parts considered outmoded or counterproductive, such as the emphasis on class struggle, were jettisoned.

In the early 1990s, the CCP added Deng Xiaoping's theories to the official ideology by publishing a voluminous quantity of articles and books extolling the contributions of Deng Xiaoping Thought to China's development. Deng's views are generally referred to as the theory of "Building Socialism with Chinese Characteristics," a phrase now included in both the party and state constitutions. Deng's theories asserted that China is a poor country in the "initial stage" of socialism, rather than in an advanced stage as Mao had suggested, and therefore must use any means possible—even capitalist ones—to develop the economy. But Deng, like Mao, believes that only the Communist Party can lead China in this quest for development; without CCP leadership, the country would fall into chaos and drift away from its socialist goals, which are now defined vaguely as national development and common prosperity. In essence, Deng Thought is an ideological rationale for the combination of economic change and political repression that characterizes contemporary China. The campaign to extol "Building Socialism with Chinese Characteristics" is part of the effort by Deng Xiaoping and his potential successors to put their indelible mark on China's development well into the next century and to ensure the continuation of Communist Party rule in China.

The CCP tries to keep communist ideology viable and visible as the official political culture of the PRC by continued efforts to influence public opinion and socialization—for instance, by controlling the media and overseeing the educational system. Although China's media is much livelier than it was during the Maoist period, there is certainly no true freedom of the press, and reduced political control of the media has, to a large extent, meant only the freedom to publish more entertainment news, human interest stories, and local coverage. Newspaper articles may present contrasting views on matters such as economic policies, but true political discourse in the media remains limited by the unchallengeable principle of party leadership. There are a couple of thousand different newspapers in China, with a total circulation of hundreds of millions, but the largest share of this massive circulation is held by official "party organs," such as the *People's Daily,* which is run by the CCP Central Committee and has a circulation of over 5 million. Papers that stray beyond the proscribed boundaries are shut down, as happened to the popular pro-democracy *World Economic Herald* in 1989.

Schools are one of the main institutions through which states instill political values in their citizens. Educational opportunities have expanded enormously in China since the founding of the PRC in 1949. Today, primary school enrollment is close to 100 percent of the age-eligible (6–11) population, which helps to explain why China has such a high literacy rate (80 percent) for such a relatively poor country. However, enrollment rates drop sharply after primary school. Only about half of those between the ages of 12 and 17 are in secondary school (compared to about 90 percent in the United States), and only *about 2 percent* of the age-eligible population is in some type of college

A billboard in Beijing shows China's paramount leader, Deng Xiaoping, and announces a new documentary film (called "Historical Choice") that lauds his contributions to the nation's development.
Source: © Forrest Anderson/ Gamma-Liaison.

(compared to about 75 percent in the U.S.). Obviously, China is going to have to expand secondary and college education if its goals for economic modernization are to be met. At the same time, a more educated population could pose a potential threat to a regime intent on maintaining tight political control over its citizens.

Politics is no longer taught overtly in Chinese schools today. In the China of Mao Zedong, students at all levels spent a considerable amount of time studying politics and working in fields or factories, and teaching materials were often overlaid with a heavy dose of political propaganda. Now students are urged to gain skills and knowledge to help China modernize and to further their own careers. Yet schools are by no means centers of critical or independent thinking, and teachers and students are still closely monitored for political reliability. In the aftermath of the Tiananmen demonstrations, all college-bound high school graduates were required to undergo a year of military training and political indoctrination before actually enrolling in college. Although this requirement has been rescinded, it showed the determination of the party to keep the universities from becoming breeding grounds for political opposition.

The party's efforts to keep socialist values alive in China do not appear to be meeting with much success. Public confidence in the party and in communist ideology is very low, and "the CCP has become estranged from a rapidly changing Chinese society." For example, a survey in early 1989 revealed that nearly 62 percent of those polled had a negative image of the party—and that was before Tiananmen.[40]

Alternative sources of socialization are growing in importance, although these do not often take expressly political forms because of the threat of repression. In the countryside, there has been a resurgence of traditional customs and organizations. Peasants have replaced portraits of Mao and other Communist heroes with statues of folk gods and ancestor worship tablets, and the influence of extended kinship groups such as clans often outweighs the formal authority of the party in the villages. In the cities, popular culture, including gigantic rock concerts, shapes youth attitudes much more profoundly than do party messages about socialism. Throughout China, consumerism and the desire for economic gain, rather than communist ideals of self-sacrifice and the common good, provide the principal motivation for personal and social behavior. And religions of various kinds, once ferociously repressed by the Maoist party-state, are attracting an increasing (though still very small) number of Chinese adherents. Buddhist temples, Christian churches, and other places of worship operate more freely than they have in decades. However, the Chinese Catholic church is still prohibited from recognizing the authority of the Vatican, and clergy of any religion who are considered to be a political threat are still imprisoned.

Citizenship in China

The PRC constitution grants citizens extensive rights, including political rights, such as freedom of speech and assembly, and economic rights, such as the right to work and the right to health care and education. The constitution also proclaims that "Women in the

People's Republic of China enjoy equal rights with men in all spheres of life, political, economic, cultural and social, including family life" (Article 48).

The constitution also specifies the responsibilities or *duties* of China's citizens, including the duty to work, perform military service, pay taxes, and practice family planning. In addition, there are more general duties, such as "the duty to safeguard the security, honor and interests of the motherland" (Article 54). Such duties are vague enough to allow the authorities great leeway in interpretation and enforcement.

There is even an article in the Chinese constitution that clearly puts duties ahead of the rights of citizens, and that has been cited by party leaders as taking precedence over those articles that "guarantee" rights such as freedom of speech and assembly.

> The exercise by citizens of the People's Republic of China of their freedoms and rights may not infringe upon the interests of the state, of society and of the collective, or upon the lawful freedoms and rights of other citizens. (Article 51)

This provision gives the party-state constitutional grounds for suppressing dissent and opposition. Furthermore, the Criminal Law of the PRC contains a rather vague section on "crimes of counterrevolution," which gives the authorities broad powers to detain dissidents or others considered a threat to the regime.

National Identity in Flux

China in the 1990s is facing a profound crisis of national identity because of the wedge that the CCP's repressive policies and the excesses of communist ideology have driven between the Chinese party-state and its citizens. Moreover, the collapse of communism almost everywhere else in the world has left the People's Republic of China with a "national identity on the losing side of an emerging post–Cold War order."[41] For most people, socialism now does little in China beyond serving as a rationale for the continuing domination of political power by the Communist Party, which has become more a symbol of divisiveness and conflict than of national unity. Chinese feel great national pride in their country's achievements, including its recent economic progress, its stature in world organizations like the United Nations, and its impressive victories in international sports competitions. But such

pride is a reflection of the cultural identity that comes more from being Chinese and the inheritors of the world's oldest civilization than from loyalty to the Communist-led People's Republic of China.

The party realizes that most citizens view communist ideology as moribund or irrelevant, and it has turned increasingly to **nationalism** as a rallying point for the country. There is more official emphasis now on the greatness of the Chinese nation and its culture than on the People's Republic as a beacon of socialism in the global struggle against capitalism and imperialism. One reason that China tried so hard to land the Olympics in Beijing for the year 2000 was that the national glory and international prestige of staging the games would, it hoped, enhance the legitimacy of the government. When the International Olympic Committee voted instead to give the 2000 games to Sydney, Australia, because of concerns about human rights, environmental problems, and inadequate urban infrastructure in China, the government of the PRC announced immediately that it would redouble its efforts to get the 2004 Olympics for Beijing.

China's Non-Chinese Citizens

Although China is characterized by a high degree of cultural and racial homogeneity, creating a sense of nationalism that really unites the country will be a difficult task. "China today is what Europe would have been if the unity of the Roman Empire had lasted until now and there had not been the emergence of the separate entities of England, France, and the like."[42] It is a continental-size country with important regional, linguistic, and even ethnic differences.

China's crisis of national identity is most intense on the country's periphery, where the vast majority of the country's non-Chinese minorities live. In these areas, it is not just the failures of Communist rule that have alienated people from the government; ethnic differences create an even deeper sense of antagonism between the Chinese state and the non-Chinese society it governs.

China's ethnic minorities number more than 90 million, or about 9 percent of the total population of the PRC. There are fifty-five officially recognized minority groups in China, ranging in size from over 15 million (the Zhuang of southwest China) to just over 2,000 (the Lloba in the far west of the country). Among these minorities are at least 20 million Muslims, which gives China an Islamic population similar in size to that of Saudi Arabia and Iraq, but far smaller than India's, Iran's, or Nigeria's. China's minorities differ from the majority population (referred to as the "Han" people, after one of China's earliest dynasties) in several major ways, including race, language, culture, and religion. Most of these groups have come under the rule of China through the territorial expansion of the Chinese state over many centuries rather than through migration into China.

Minority peoples make up only a relatively small percentage of China's total population, but they are highly concentrated in the five autonomous regions of Guangxi, Inner Mongolia, Ningxia, Tibet, and Xinjiang, although only in the latter two do minority groups actually outnumber Han Chinese. These five regions are sparsely populated, yet they occupy about 60 percent of the total land area of the PRC. Some of these minority areas are resource-rich, and most are located in strategic border areas of the country, including the borders with Vietnam, India, and Russia. The autonomous regions are the equivalent of provinces in the administrative hierarchy of the PRC; within China's provinces, there are also autonomous counties and prefectures in small areas with high concentrations of minority people. The PRC constitution grants autonomous areas the right of self-government in certain matters, such as cultural affairs, but their autonomy is, in fact, very limited, and the minority regions are kept firmly under the command of the national government.

The government of the PRC has always insisted that the minority areas remain politically part of China. But state policy toward China's minority cultures has alternated between assimilation, which "involves the minorities being absorbed into the dominant group," and tolerant policies that let "the minorities retain their languages as well as large parts of their culture and traditional ways of behavior."[43] During the radical periods of PRC history, the emphasis was clearly on assimilating the minorities into a culture that was both Chinese and socialist. Assimilation was pursued by actively promoting Chinese migration into minority areas, the suppression of minority customs, and forced compliance with state policies even when that severely disrupted a traditional way of life. For example, the Mongol people were forced to abandon their nomadic economy and move into settled collectives and communes just prior to and during the Great Leap Forward, and many mosques were closed down in Muslim areas during the Cultural Revolution.

In contrast, minority peoples are now permitted to develop their local economies as they see fit, religious freedom is generally respected, and the use of minority languages in the media and literature is encouraged, as is bilingual education. In order to keep the already small minority populations from dwindling further, China's stringent family planning policy is applied much more loosely among minorities, who are often allowed to have two or more children per couple rather than the one child that is the prescribed limit for most Chinese.

The Chinese constitution guarantees that all minority groups have representation in the National People's Congress, and about 15 percent of the deputies and four out of nineteen vice chairs of the NPC elected in 1993 were minorities. The constitution further specifies that chairs of people's congresses and the administrative heads of autonomous areas must be members of the minority nationalities in that area. There has also been a concerted effort to recruit and promote minority cadres to run local governments in autonomous areas.

The impact of these positive political trends is, however, tempered by the fact that there are few minorities in the upper echelons of the party and military leadership and that, even in minority areas, the most powerful individual, the head of the regional or local Communist Party, is likely to be Chinese. Also despite significant progress in modernizing the economies of the minority regions, these areas remain among the poorest in China.

In some minority regions of China, ethnic tensions are very high. There has been increasing unrest in Muslim areas. Several clashes with Islamic separatists have caused the Chinese government to worry that pan-Islamic sentiments and activities may spread to western China from Afghanistan, Pakistan, and the Central Asian states that were once part of the former Soviet Union.

The most ethnically volatile area in China is Tibet, which first became subordinate to Chinese influence in the early eighteenth century. After the CCP came to power in 1949, Tibet was formally incorporated into the People's Republic. Although Tibet's ruler, a high Buddhist priest known as the Dalai Lama, was allowed to maintain some symbolic power, the CCP set about trying to transform what they considered to be brutal aspects of traditional Tibetan society, including an extremely exploitative system of serf labor. In 1959, a widespread revolt was viciously crushed by the Chinese army, and the Dalai Lama and many of his supporters fled to India. Since then Chinese political and military officials have kept a firm grip on Tibet. In recent years, Tibetans have been allowed more religious and cultural freedom, and the Chinese government has increased investment in Tibet's economic development. But the CCP still considers talk of Tibetan independence to be treason, and Chinese troops have suppressed anti-China demonstrations in various parts of the region.

To date, ethnic unrest in China has been limited, sporadic, and easily suppressed. China is basically a culturally and racially homogeneous nation, and its minority population is relatively small and geographically isolated. Therefore, the PRC has not had the kind of intense identity-based group political conflict experienced by countries with more pervasive religious and ethnic differences, such as India and Nigeria.

But improvements in the standard of living and the greater economic and cultural autonomy encouraged by Deng's reforms have reinforced ethnic identity in places like Tibet and the Muslim areas of the far west rather than strengthening their bonds to China. Prosperity has even led people in southern China to highlight their linguistic (Cantonese versus Mandarin) and other differences from the poorer north in a move interpreted by some as the reemergence of an ancient, and long latent, cleavage in China's collective identity. In the future, identity issues of various kinds could become more visible and important on China's national political agenda.

INTERESTS, SOCIAL MOVEMENTS, AND PROTEST

The formal structures of the Chinese political system are designed more to extend state control than to facilitate citizen participation in politics. Therefore, people make extensive use of their personal connections based on kinship, friendship, and other ties *(guanxi)* to help ease their contacts with the bureaucrats and party officials who wield such enormous power over so many aspects of their lives. Patron-client politics is also pervasive at the local level in China, as it is in many developing countries where ordinary people have little access to the official channels of power. For

example, a village leader (the patron) may help farmers (the clients) avoid paying some taxes by reporting false production statistics in exchange for their support to keep him in office. Such clientelism can be an important means by which local communities deflect the impact of state policies that they see as harmful to their interests.

Personal connections and patron-client networks are an important, but *unorganized,* way in which citizens pursue their interests in the Chinese party-state. *Organized* interest groups and social movements that are truly independent of party-state authority are not permitted to influence the political process in any significant way. Groups of citizens cannot effectively organize to promote their interests in the political arena. Rather, the communist party-state organizes and penetrates society in order to preempt the formation of autonomous groups and movements. The party uses "mass organizations" as its principal means of regulating socioeconomic interests and a variety of control mechanisms to monitor individuals and atomize society.

Mass Organizations

China has many mass organizations formed around social or occupational categories, with a total membership in the hundreds of millions. Principal among them are those that "represent" workers, youth, and women. In communist systems, mass organizations have traditionally been seen as "transmission belts" for communicating official policies to particular groups and for mobilizing public support for those policies. These organizations also implement the CCP's mass line by providing a means for interest groups to express their views on policy matters— within strict limits. The charters of these organizations place them explicitly under the leadership of the CCP; however, they do appear to be gaining influence in the policy process as China's leadership tries to enlist broad support for its development goals.

The vast majority of urban industrial workers in the PRC belong to the All-China Federation of Trade Unions, which is the umbrella organization for occupation-specific unions (such as the Textile Workers' Trade Union) and for workers' organizations in individual factories. Neither local nor national unions constitute an independent political voice for workers, but the national bodies do have some impact on economic policy and have pushed to get issues such as reducing the standard workweek from six to five days on the agenda of the National People's Congress. In addition, the factory-based unions often effectively represent workers in discussions or negotiations with management regarding their interests in wage, welfare, safety, and other issues.

China's young people are organized into a number of intersecting bodies. The Communist Youth League (CYL), with 56 million members as of 1993, is a vehicle for recruiting young people into the CCP and spreading communist values among older youth. Membership in the CYL is limited to "progressive youth"—that is, political activists—aged 15–28; and, like its parent organization, the CCP, only a minority of the eligible age group belongs to the Youth League. In contrast, more than 80 percent of Chinese aged 7–14 belong to the Young Pioneers, a less explicitly political group than the CYL, but one still designed to promote good social behavior, patriotism, and loyalty to the party among school children. Other mass organizations for young people include the All-China Students' Federation, for secondary and college students, and the All-China Youth Federation, which serves as an umbrella organization under the leadership of the CYL, for youth groups throughout the country.

The All-China Women's Federation is the exclusive national organization representing the interests of women in general. In recent years, it has emerged as perhaps the most active of China's mass organizations in voicing the concerns of its constituency. The federation—particularly some of its local branches—has become an effective advocate for women on issues ranging from domestic violence to economic rights. Nevertheless, the federation remains "a top-down, government-sponsored organization, rather than one independently formed by women. Moreover, most of its efforts on behalf of women [are] still undertaken in conjunction with state policy."[44]

The reform era has led to the spread of **nongovernmental organizations (ngos)** less directly subordinate to the CCP than the traditional mass organizations. These include local self-formed groups, like mutual support organizations for women called "friendly societies," charitable foundations, and hundreds of national professional groups such as the China Political Science Association. There are numerous nongovernmental organizations that draw members from the country's growing private business sector, including an association for owners of private businesses called the Self-Employed Laborers Association and the All-China Women's Entrepreneurs Association.

Most of these nongovernmental organizations have some latitude to operate within their functional areas of expertise without direct party interference. But many of them were established through state initiative, and all of them must register with the government. Thus, the Chinese political system appears to be evolving toward "socialist **corporatism**" in which the CCP, rather than overtly suppressing divergent social interests, co-opts them by allowing them some autonomy in exchange for their recognition of the ultimate authority of the party-state.[45]

The various organizations discussed above should not be dismissed as entirely irrelevant to politics and policy-making in the PRC. Although they remain subordinate to the CCP, the National People's Congress, the Chinese People's Political Consultative Conference, the democratic parties, and the mass organizations do "provide important access points between the Party and the organized masses, which allow the voicing of special interests in ways that do not threaten Party hegemony and yet pressure the shaping of policy."[46]

Mechanisms of Social Control

While China has certainly loosened up politically since the days of Mao Zedong, the party's mechanisms of control still penetrate to the basic levels of society and serve the CCP's aim to prevent the formation of groups or movements that could challenge its authority. In the rural areas, the small-scale, close-knit nature of the village facilitates control by the local party organization. But the major means of control used by the party-state in urban China, called the "unit" (or ***danwei***) system, is more complex. In the cities, almost everyone belongs to a unit, which is usually their place of work, be it a factory, office, store, or other institution like a school or hospital.

The unit is the center of economic, social, and political life for most urban residents. People depend on their units for jobs, income, and promotion, and larger units (like state-owned industries) may also provide housing, medical clinics, cafeterias, day-care centers, recreational facilities, and more. The unit is also the members' basic point of contact with the formal political system. They vote in their workplace; if they belong to the party, they do so through the branch in their unit; if there is a national campaign in progress, it is publicized through the unit and people may be mobilized to participate through the unit. For example, compliance with the national family-planning policy is usually monitored through a women's unit.

The unit holds meetings to discuss the official line on important policies or events. In the aftermath of the Tiananmen massacre, units were instructed to study and discuss documents portraying the demonstrations as a "counterrevolutionary rebellion" that was justifiably put down by the authorities. The personnel departments of units also keep a political dossier on every employee. The dossier contains a detailed record of the political activities and attitudes of the employee and his or her immediate family members—and if a person changes jobs, the dossier moves, too. In these and other ways, the unit acts as a check on political dissidence since unorthodox behavior would be unlikely to escape the attention of unit officials.

Residents' committees are another instrument of control in every urban neighborhood. These citizen organizations, which are often staffed by retired persons, housewives, or others not attached to a work unit, effectively extend the unofficial reach of the party-state down to the most basic level of urban society. The committees perform many positive functions that address neighborhood concerns like crime prevention and sanitation; but they also keep a semiofficial eye on who is doing what in the neighborhood, and suspicious doings are reported to the Public Security Bureau for further investigation. Foreign journalists in China have often found it difficult to meet with Chinese citizens in their homes because of the surveillance of the residents' committees.

As Chinese society continues to change due to the impact of economic reform, these control mechanisms are weakening. Rural industrialization and the breakdown of restrictions on migration to the cities have undermined party control in the villages. In the cities, the growth of private and semiprivate enterprises, increasing labor and residential mobility, and new forms of association (such as discos and coffeehouses) and communication (for example, cellular phones, e-mail, and fax machines) are just some of the factors that are making it harder for the party-state to monitor urban citizens as closely as it has in the past. The nervousness of the Chinese government over the potential political impact of new technologies is reflected in its

attempted ban on private-citizen ownership of satellite television dishes capable of receiving foreign programs. Such censorship is somewhat ironic in light of the PRC's efforts to earn money by leasing Chinese satellites to foreign companies to beam broadcasts *outside* of China.

Protest and the Party-State

Tiananmen showed the limits of protest in China. By sending in the army to remove the demonstrators forcefully, the party-state made it bloodily clear that economic reform was not to be accompanied by political liberalization. It was not just the fact that tens of thousands of individuals were demonstrating against the party that led to such a brutal crackdown in 1989. The leadership was perhaps even more alarmed at signs that a number of grassroots organizations, such as the Beijing Federation of Autonomous Student Unions and the Beijing Workers' Autonomous Union, were emerging from the protests. The party feared that autonomous citizen associations might become viable alternatives to the "transmission belt" mass organizations for the expression of social and political interests. The success of Solidarity, the independent Polish workers' movement, in challenging the power of the communist party in Poland in the late 1980s was much in the minds of China's leaders as they watched the Tiananmen protests unfold. Massive repression was their way of letting it be known that the "Polish disease" would not be allowed to spread to China and that neither open political protest nor the formation of autonomous interest groups would be tolerated.

There have been no significant political demonstrations in China since 1989, and pro-democracy groups have been driven deep underground. Known dissidents are continuously watched and harassed.

Take the case of China's most famous dissident, Wei Jingsheng. Wei, a twenty-nine-year-old electrician, was first arrested in 1979 after he publicly called for democratization to be given as high a priority as economic modernization in China and criticized the leadership of the CCP. He was convicted in a show trial on trumped-up charges of espionage and served more than fourteen years in prison, where he was often severely mistreated physically and mentally. He was paroled in September 1993 and almost immediately began speaking out on human rights issues, met with an American State Department official, and gave interviews to foreign journalists. He was arrested again in

April 1994, and, as of late 1995, was still being held without public charges and without being able to communicate even with his family.

Still, repression has not put an end to all forms of protest in the PRC. Individuals do find ways of protesting safely. In 1993, the hundredth anniversary of the birth of Mao Zedong, a "Mao fever" surged through China. Mao memorabilia (photos, T-shirts, buttons, and so forth), revolutionary songs from the Maoist era, and recordings of the late chairman's speeches became all the rage, especially among young people. Many who joined this craze were romanticizing the revolutionary idealism of the Maoist era, but they also appeared to be implicitly protesting the crass materialism and official corruption in the China of the 1990s.

Other forms of protest are more overt. As mentioned previously, ethnic protests occur sporadically on China's periphery. Labor unrest has been growing, with reports of hundreds of spontaneous strikes and other actions annually. There have been labor protests at some of the country's largest state-owned enterprises, where workers are angry about the ending of the iron rice bowl system of lifetime employment and guaranteed salaries. Many of the labor protests have been at foreign enterprises in China, where workers may feel somewhat freer to express themselves. For example, in February 1993, 700 women marched to the city hall in Tianjin to protest the sweatshop conditions at the South Korean–owned shoe factory where they worked. Such actions have remained limited in scope and duration, so the government has not cracked down on the protesters; nevertheless, it usually blames labor unrest on the influence of "subversives" who want to disrupt the Chinese economy.

There have also been significant protests in China's countryside, especially in poorer provinces away from the coast where much of the country's economic boom has been concentrated. In 1993, there were more than one hundred peasant riots in eleven different provinces. Farmers have attacked local officials and rioted over high local taxes and fees, corruption, and declining incomes. From time to time, the government, short of cash because of revenue shortfalls, has had to issue IOUs to farmers for state agricultural purchases, which has further fueled rural anger. These protests have remain localized and have focused on farmers' immediate material concerns, not grand-scale issues like democracy. Nevertheless, if the countryside is left too far behind in the process of economic development, rural discontent could spread and translate into more generalized anger against the regime.

The political situation in China as of the mid-1990s presented a rather contradictory picture. Although people are socially and economically freer than they have been in decades, political repression is still intense, and open political dissent is almost non-existent. But there are many signs that the Chinese Communist Party is losing some of its ability to control the movements and associations of its citizens and can no longer easily limit access to information and ideas from abroad. Some forms of protest also appear to be increasing and, in some places, may come to pose a serious challenge to the authority of the party-state.

SECTION 5

Chinese Politics at the Crossroads

POLITICAL CHALLENGES
AND CHANGING AGENDAS

Scenes from the Chinese Countryside in the 1990s[47]

Daiqiuzhuang, Hebei province: This is perhaps the most prosperous village in all of China, with a per capita income ($22,000 in 1993) nearly equal to that of the United States. Many villagers drive Mercedes-Benzes and other luxury cars, and all live in modern, brick, two-story houses—an unheard of level of comfort for most Chinese. Although the village is 45 miles from the northern Chinese city of Tianjin and was still only accessible via a bumpy dirt road in the early 1990s, the source of its phenomenal wealth is industry, not agriculture. The village has more than 200 factories and tens of millions of dollars in foreign investment. In addition to the 4,000 or so now-rich native residents, many of whom hold managerial positions, there are several thousand less well-off—some would say exploited—workers from elsewhere in China who provide most of the labor for the factories.

This picture, taken in Shanghai in the early 1990s, graphically captures how the modern and the traditional exist side-by-side in China. It also shows how the market-style reforms introduced by Deng Xiaoping have greatly increased disparities in wealth, a problem that could lead to growing social and political tensions in the future.
Source: Dan Habib/Impact Visuals.

Qibailong, Guangxi Zhuang Autonomous Region: This rural town is located in one of the areas known as "China's Third World" where persistent poverty rather than growing prosperity is still the common lot in life. There are no Mercedes here; most peasant families have a total income of less than $50 a year. Many of the children are hungry and half-naked, and most of the houses are little more than poorly constructed huts. Education, professional health care, and other social services are minimal or nonexistent. There is no industry, and the land barely supports those who work it. A few poor areas in China have been targeted by the government and international organizations for model poverty-relief programs, including start-up subsidization of small-scale industries to raise incomes. But towns and villages like Qibailong—and tens of millions of peasants—remain mired in poverty and have benefited little from either China's economic boom or state assistance.

Renshou, Sichuan province: In early 1993, a thousand or so angry peasants gathered in front of the county government headquarters in Renshou to protest burdensome taxes and fees imposed on farmers by local officials. Although the situation was defused when higher authorities promised to investigate the peasants' grievances, it exploded again a few months later because of government inaction. Traffic was blocked, local officials were beaten, police cars were burned,

and more than two dozen peasant leaders were arrested. The demonstrators let up only when the deputy governor of the province ordered that some of the taxes be refunded to the peasants with interest. The national government subsequently issued a directive that more than forty different rural taxes be abolished, including fees for land registration, rural toilet renovation, and rat extermination. In addition, steps were taken to limit peasant taxes to 5 percent of income.

Beiwang, Hebei province: In October of 1990, this village of 2,500 people elected its first representative assembly to supervise the work of local government officials. One of the first decisions made by forty representatives was to reassign the contracts for tending the village's 3,000 pear trees. After the rural communes were disbanded in the 1980s, each of the 500 or so families in the village was given six trees to look after under the new household responsibility system. The assembly, however, decided that it would be better to reassign the trees to a very small number of households who would care for them in a more efficient and productive manner. The local Communist Party branch objected to this on the grounds that the village might lose much of the revenue that it earned from signing contracts with many households, which was used to pay for various public works projects such as road maintenance. The party was probably also concerned about the ideological implications of a less egalitarian distribution of the village's trees and the income derived from them. Nevertheless, assembly representatives were able to generate strong support from their constituents for their proposal, and the party branch allowed the trees to be recontracted to just eleven households. In a short time, pear production zoomed. The new system proved to be economically beneficial not only to the few families who looked after the trees, but also to the village as a whole because of the government's share of the increased profits.

The varied scenes just described make several important points about Chinese politics today. First, they remind us not to lose sight of the central role that China's rural areas will play in the nation's future. Most foreign attention tends to be focused elsewhere: on protest and repression in large cities; on the plight of notable political prisoners and dissidents; on the booming economy of China's coastal region; on the policy pronouncements of top Communist Party leaders; and on China's relations with the world's major powers. But the fact remains that a large majority of Chinese still live in the countryside and China's political and economic fate will be greatly influenced by what goes on there.

These scenes also reflect the diversity of the political and socioeconomic situations in different parts of the Chinese countryside: prosperity and poverty, political protests and peaceful politics. It is very hard to generalize about such a vast and varied nation by looking at what is going on in only one small part of the country.

The scene from Beiwang reminds us that in China, as in other countries, not all politics is "high politics" involving matters of national or international significance. For many—perhaps most—Chinese, who looks after the village pear trees matters more than ideological disputes among party factions or pro-democracy demonstrations in the cities. The "victory" of the Beiwang representative assembly on the pear tree issue shows that sometimes, even in a communist party-state, the people prevail against the party and democracy works on the local level—as long as the basic principle of party leadership is not challenged.

The Qibailong and Renshou scenes reflect the trouble that is brewing in parts of the Chinese countryside. No one would deny the astonishing improvement

in the living standards throughout most of rural China brought about since the 1980s by decollectivization and industrialization. But huge pockets of severe poverty persist, especially in inland regions like Guangxi that are far removed from the more prosperous coastal regions. Most of rural China falls somewhere in between the conspicuous wealth of Daiqiuzhuang and the extreme poverty of Qibailong. In such in-between areas (like Renshou), the combination of new hopes brought about by economic improvements and the anger caused by blatant corruption, growing inequalities, stagnating incomes, and other frustrations may prove to be politically explosive. Social scientists have noted that such **"relative deprivation"**—the gap between soaring expectations and a declining capability to actually meet those expectations—is often more politically destabilizing than situations of "absolute deprivation" where both opportunities for advancement and expectations remain low.[48] Deng's economic reforms have yielded a better life and higher hopes for most of China's peasants. The CCP now faces the challenge of having to satisfy those hopes or risk the wrath of a social group that for decades has been the bedrock of the party's political support.

Economic Management and Political Legitimacy

The problems of China's rural areas are part of a larger challenge facing the country's leadership—namely, how to sustain and effectively manage the economic growth on which the CCP's legitimacy as China's ruling party is now largely based. The party is gambling that solid economic performance will literally buy it legitimacy in the eyes of the Chinese people and that most people will care little about democracy if their material lives continue to improve.

A serious economic crisis could have disastrous political consequences for the CCP and could raise serious questions about the future viability of communism in China. If the economy were to falter in a way that gravely affected the livelihood or dashed the expectations of a large segment of the population, the potential for social unrest and political upheaval would increase immeasurably and the party would be left with nothing but sheer coercion to sustain itself in power.

Despite the overall success of reform, the CCP faces a number of economic challenges that will affect

China's leaders face a difficult balancing act, as this cartoon suggests, between capitalism and communist ideology as they try to manage a "socialist market economy."
Source: © R. Lurie, Cartoonews International Syndicate, New York.

the party's political fortunes. Some of these problems—inequality, regionalism, and corruption—were discussed in Section 2. Failure to keep inequality—especially between city and countryside—under control or to continue providing opportunities for advancement for the less well-off could become a source of social instability and a liability for a political party that still espouses a commitment to socialist goals. The considerable autonomy gained by provinces and localities as a result of the decentralization of economic decision making has fostered a growing regionalism that poses a potentially serious threat to the political control of the central government. Corruption, which affects the lives of most people more directly than does political repression, has become so blatant and widespread that it may be the single most corrosive force eating away at the legitimacy of the Chinese Communist Party.

Deng's reforms have unquestionably spurred national economic growth and improved the material well-being of most Chinese. However, there are serious doubts about the ability of the CCP to continue to manage the economy effectively because of its reluctance to make even more fundamental changes. The PRC has moved sharply away from central planning, as reflected in the rapid expansion of nonstate sectors of the economy. But it has not moved far enough toward replacing government commands with the less intrusive kind of guidance, coordination, and consultation between the state and the private sector that is

generally considered essential for effective economic policy-making. Though the Chinese economy has, in many important ways, become more marketized, it is still constrained by heavy-handed bureaucratic institutions that impede the working of the market and the capacity of the government to respond constructively to serious economic problems.

This was clearly shown by the government's difficulties in dealing with China's "overheated" economy in the early 1990s, especially the inflation caused by explosive industrial growth rates. An effective response to such problems would require that reforms be extended to sectors of the economy that remain highly centralized, like banking and the production of steel and oil. But it is in just such crucial areas of economic policy that the Chinese Communist Party has been most reluctant to relinquish control. This reluctance stems partly from old habits and entrenched interests, but it also comes from fear of the political implications of dismantling the last strongholds of the command economy. To reduce even more the role of the party-state in managing the economy would further call into question the rationale for the CCP's continuing monopoly on political power.

China's economic development cannot continue at the pace or in the manner it has in recent years. Double-digit growth must be slowed down somewhat in order to control inflation, energy shortages, and environmental desecration. Some scenarios for the future predict a "soft landing" in which the country's leaders are able to manage effectively these and other problems through more market-type reforms and set the PRC on the path of sustained, if less dramatic, economic progress. Other scenarios suggest that a "crash landing" leading to a depression, massive unemployment, and increasing poverty is more likely because of the party's unwillingness or inability to make needed changes. Obviously, a soft landing and a crash landing would effect China's economic future and the political future of the Chinese Communist Party in very different ways.

Political Challenges

China in the 1990s has evolved toward a system of what one observer has called "Market-Leninism," a combination of economic openness and political rigidity under the leadership of a ruling party that adheres to a remodeled version of communist ideology.[49] The major political challenges now facing the CCP and the

This cartoon is meant to show the dilemmas of China's "half-reformed" economy, which seems, in many ways, caught between capitalist market-oriented reforms and socialist central planning.
Source: © R. Lurie, Cartoonews International Syndicate, New York.

country emerge from the sharpening contradictions and tensions of this hybrid system.

In the short run, the CCP gamble that the country's economic boom will divert the attention of most Chinese from politics to profits has paid off. Continuing repression has also contributed to political calm in China, because few dare openly defy the party. But sooner or later, the CCP will have to deal with the growing contradiction between increasing freedom in many aspects of Chinese society and the country's persistently rigid political system.

More than just the economy has opened up in China. Under Mao, nearly every aspect of life was subject to political intrusion. Today, although the party-state still intrudes in important "social" matters like family planning, it has basically abandoned its efforts to control the private lives of citizens as long as they steer clear of politics. Art or literature cannot be used as a medium of direct political dissent, but the party-state no longer insists on socialist realism that extols the glories of workers and peasants as the only legitimate art form. A wide variety of cultural mediums are thriving in China, ranging from traditional arts to avant-garde poetry and abstract painting. The Chinese film industry has produced a number of internationally acclaimed films in recent years, including the Academy Award nominee, *Farewell, My Concubine.*

There have been important political changes, too. The cumbersome bureaucracy inherited from the heyday of central planning has been streamlined, modernized, and, to some extent, depoliticized through staff reductions, organizational adjustments, and civil service reforms. There has also been an extensive effort to

recruit younger and better-educated officials to manage the country's economic development. The people's congresses, citizen organizations, and elections all play a more substantive role in the nation's political life than they did during the Maoist era. Yet the party has not wavered in its determination to limit political change and to maintain its political grip. Chinese leaders who embrace extensive reform of the socialist economy "have seemingly concluded that this requires construction of a more rationalized and tolerant—but still undemocratic—political system."[50] Indeed, politics seems to be the only part of Chinese society that remains tightly controlled by the party-state.

However, as the people of China become more secure economically, better educated, and more aware of the outside world through access to modern media and telecommunications, they are likely to become less politically complacent. Specific groups created or influenced by the course of economic development could become the source of pressures for political change. For instance, the rapidly expanding class of private entrepreneurs may want political clout to match their economic wealth; the intellectuals and specialists whose knowledge and skills are needed for the country's modernization drive may become more outspoken about the lack of political freedom; and the many Chinese citizens who travel or study abroad may find the political gap between China and the world's growing number of democracies to be increasingly intolerable. As China becomes more integrated with the global economy, the pressures from abroad for political change will also increase.

In sum, Deng's reforms have led to the stirrings in China of what is often called **civil society**—a sphere of public life and voluntary citizen association truly autonomous from party-state control, which, if allowed to thrive and expand, could provide fertile soil for future democratization. The growth of such a civil society, for example among workers in Poland and intellectuals in Czechoslovakia, played an important role in the collapse of communism in East-Central Europe in the late 1980s by weakening the critical underpinnings of party-state control of society.

Maoist policies successfully eliminated any sphere of independent social activity in China that might pose a challenge to party domination. Economic changes under Deng, however, have led to the rise of new social groups and influences that will not be easily contained by the Leninist framework on which the party's power depends.

The Tiananmen demonstrations of 1989 can be seen as a reflection of the growth of civil society in China. One of the most remarkable things about Tiananmen was the way in which divergent groups and individuals with different interests and agendas came together to express their dissatisfactions with the Communist Party. Students were at the core of the Tiananmen protests, but they were joined by workers, entrepreneurs, professionals, and other citizens from a broad cross-section of the Beijing population. Though in many ways the protests were disorganized and uncoordinated, independent citizen organizations did get the demonstrations going and more such organizations emerged as the protests gained momentum. The viciousness of the Tiananmen crackdown revealed the CCP's determination to crush civil society before it could seriously challenge Communist authority.

Yet as China continues to modernize, civil society will inevitably grow, and, with it, pressures for democratization will reemerge. The leaders of the Chinese Communist Party will again face the fundamental dilemma of whether to accommodate or repress these pressures. On the one hand, accommodation would require making some very basic changes in the Chinese political system, namely less party control and more meaningful citizen representation and participation. The party would have to abandon its claim to an exclusive "leading role" in Chinese society, something that no communist party has been able to do and still retain power. On the other hand, continued repression would strike at the heart of some of the groups and processes that are vital to the country's economic dynamism. This would have terrible costs for China and could also spell political trouble for the CCP.

In a sign of things to come, some of China's leading intellectuals and out-of-prison democratic activists in the spring of 1995 sent petitions to the party leadership calling for greater political openness and the release of people still imprisoned for taking part in the Tiananmen protest. Although these petitions were pretty much ignored by the party (and, in fact, some new arrests followed), they were widely interpreted as an effort by those favoring more democracy to influence those leaders who are seeking to succeed the elderly Deng Xiaoping and shape the political agenda of early post-Deng China.

CHINESE POLITICS IN TRANSITION

The Succession Question

The Chinese Communist Party is in the midst of an epochal, generational change in its leadership, which will have a major impact on the future of Chinese politics. The domination of Chinese politics by veteran revolutionaries who joined the communist movement in the 1920s is reaching its inevitable end as mortality catches up with Deng Xiaoping and the rest of the party's surviving old guard. Therefore, the first question to ask about the future of Chinese politics is, Who will succeed Deng Xiaoping and the other party elders as China's top leader or leaders?

Communist party-states are particularly vulnerable to power struggles when a leader dies because of the highly personalized nature of politics at the top and the weakness of institutionalized rules for determining succession. The inability to deal successfully with the issue of succession has been a major failing of Communist rule under both Mao Zedong and Deng Xiaoping. Mao Zedong twice turned against close political allies (Liu Shaoqi and Lin Biao) whom he had designated to succeed him as party leader when he concluded that they had betrayed him ideologically or politically. The result was a power struggle following Mao's death that ultimately paved the way for Deng Xiaoping to emerge as China's top leader.

Deng also has done poorly in preparing the way for a smooth transition of power after his death. Both Mao and Deng kept Chinese leadership politics highly personalized. Deng has facilitated the promotion of a younger generation of leaders to top positions in the CCP Standing Committee and Politburo, but by remaining the real power behind the scenes almost to his last breath, Deng has hampered the ability of these younger leaders to establish a political base of their own. He has also pushed aside two men—Hu Yaobang and Zhao Ziyang—who were being groomed to take over after him, largely because he thought they were too soft on the question of democracy.

Despite the uncertainty surrounding who exactly will succeed Deng, it seems unlikely that Chinese politics will again be dominated by a single person as it was during the Mao and Deng eras. No one remaining on the Chinese political scene has the combination of historical stature, charisma, and political connections accumulated over decades that allowed Mao and Deng to exercise such personal power. Thus, the passing of Deng is likely to mark a transition to a more collective style of leadership within the CCP.

Even when succession leads to a shift from personalized to collective party leadership, power still remains highly concentrated in communist party-states like China, and some leaders and factions are certain to emerge as more powerful and influential than others. Therefore, who comes out on top in the succession struggle that will follow Deng's demise will have a critical impact on China's political and economic development.

The major contenders for power in the immediate post-Deng period mostly come from a generation of party leaders born in the 1920s. CCP General Secretary Jiang Zemin has been designated by Deng Xiaoping as the "core" of the next generation of China's leaders. He is generally considered supportive of market reforms and has tried to portray himself as a tough opponent of corruption in order to gain popular support. Premier Li Peng prefers to maintain more bureaucratic control of the economy, though both he and Jiang are equally unlikely to support major political change. Li is very unpopular in China because of his very visible role as the regime's tough guy during the Tiananmen crisis.

Some analysts see Zhu Rongji, a party leader considered to be China's "economic czar" because of his broad authority in economic policy-making as the rising star of Chinese politics. His political future is likely to depend on how well he is able to manage some of the country's current economic problems. A dark-horse candidate to succeed Deng as China's top leader is Qiao Shi, a member of the CCP's elite Standing Committee and head of the PRC's National People's Congress. Qiao might be able to use the NPC's increasingly assertive role as a forum for the expression of provincial interests as a base to enhance his own political prospects.

It is possible that an advocate of greater political openness—a Gorbachev-type leader—could emerge as the dominant figure in China. Zhao Ziyang, the former CCP general secretary purged by Deng for being too conciliatory toward the Tiananmen demonstrators, remains very popular in some circles in China. He could reappear on the Chinese political scene after Deng dies, especially if, in the spirit of national reconciliation, there is an official reassessment of the correctness of Deng's decision to crush the Tiananmen protests with such force.

China's Uncertain Future

With China in the midst of so many major political and economic transitions, the only thing that seems certain about the future is change. It is impossible to predict with any confidence either the timing or source of that change, and a wide range of outcomes, some more likely than others, seems possible.

A sharp drop in economic growth brought about either by government mismanagement or international forces beyond China's control could lead to the sudden collapse of Communist power through an explosion of "people power" like that which toppled most of the party-states of East-Central Europe. A party whose legitimacy is further weakened by economic problems and leaders with less personal authority than Deng may not be able to use coercion to suppress a popular rebellion as effectively as the old guard did in Tiananmen.

Change might come not through an explosion of mass anger, but through the implosion, or collapse from within, of the Communist Party itself, as happened in the Soviet Union. Internal divisions, pervasive corruption, ideological irrelevance, deepening alienation from society, and loss of self-confidence may continue to eat away at the foundations of party power so that it falls virtually from its own deadweight rather than through an uprising from below.

Or perhaps change won't come rapidly from either a revolutionary explosion or implosion in the party-state but more gradually through evolution within the Communist Party. The succession could yield a leadership of able technocrats—officials more interested in efficiency than ideology—whose more flexible version of Marxism would allow for substantial political reform and greater accommodation with the interests of emerging social forces. One trend pointing toward a technocratic evolution in Chinese politics is that many of the individuals (including Jiang Zemin and Li Peng) poised to take over after Deng are not career revolutionaries like the party elders, but were trained as engineers before entering politics. They have now come to the edge of power on the tide of economic reform and have few ties to the ideological wars of the party's past.

In the short run, such a reign of the technocrats is likely to result in a more benign authoritarianism in China. Then, if economic progress continues, gradual democratization could take place under the party's guidance. These positive trends could revive the party's legitimacy and build a base of popular support for a new generation of leaders that would sustain the CCP—perhaps renamed to heal old wounds, as happened with many of the former communist parties in East-Central Europe—even in free elections.

Some bleaker outcomes are also possible. CCP "hard-liners" favoring the conservative bureaucratic communist approach could prevail in a post-Deng power struggle and impose a return to ideological orthodoxy, economic centralization, and efforts to exert party control over more aspects of social and cultural, as well as political life.

There are also circumstances which could lead China to disintegrate temporarily or permanently as a political entity. Serious disputes within the leadership or between the party and the people over the nation's future could provoke civil war. Economic troubles might also propel a splintering of China into regional blocs only nominally loyal to a central government in Beijing; this is particularly possible if the more prosperous areas of southern China should decide that it would be better off economically to go it alone rather than be dragged down by the poorer hinterland.

The unifying power of Chinese culture and the country's basic racial homogeneity make it unlikely that China will experience national fragmentation as happened to the former Soviet Union or ethnic warfare like that which followed the breakup of Yugoslavia. But if the power of the central government should be paralyzed by a crisis or seriously weaken for any other reason, separatist movements in Tibet and other minority areas could gain momentum and alter the political map of China.

The military—which is the strongest and most stable institution in China—is also likely to play an important role in determining the future of Chinese politics. A serious domestic or foreign crisis, political paralysis brought on by a protracted succession struggle, or an outbreak of widespread social disorder could provoke a military coup in the name of national security. This could usher in an era of even harsher dictatorship.

But it should not be automatically assumed that all of China's military leaders are antidemocratic. There are a number of cases in the Third World (for example, in Brazil) where the military initiated and supported the democratic transition. Some of China's most influential generals are known to have opposed the use of lethal force to stop the Tiananmen demonstrations, and they might look on the post-Deng era as a chance to blame the massacre on the politicians and to put the army on the side of the people by supporting successors who favor political change.

China and the Democratic Idea

What are the prospects that democracy will prevail in China?[51]

There are reasons to be both optimistic and pessimistic about the future of the democratic idea in China. On the negative side, China's long history of bureaucratic and authoritarian rule in both traditional and modern forms and the hierarchical values of still-influential Confucian culture seem to be mighty counterweights to democracy. And, even though its political legitimacy may be weak and some aspects of its social control have broken down, the coercive power of China's communist party-state remains formidable.

China's status as a Third World nation with a low general standard of living, large areas of extreme poverty, and poor communications also imposes some impediments to democratization. Neither are all segments of the population equally receptive to calls for democracy. The appeal of democratic values is most apparent among intellectuals and urban residents who still comprise a minority of the population. A large majority of the Chinese people are likely apathetic about national politics in general (preferring to focus on their immediate economic concerns) or fearful of the violence and chaos that radical political change might unleash.

On the positive side, the Confucian principle that the people are justified in overthrowing a tyrannical government suggests that the roots of Chinese political culture are not wholly antidemocratic. And, Third World though it may be, China still has a higher literacy rate, more extensive industrialization and urbanization, and less inequality than most countries at its level of economic development—all of which are conditions widely seen by social scientists as favorable to democracy.

Furthermore, as discussed above, economic reform is transforming China in a direction that is, in many ways, conducive to democratization, including the growth of civil society and more openness to the outside world. This trend could be accelerated if the post-Deng leadership is even more vigorous in pursuit of modernization. The spread of democracy around much of the globe in the 1980s and 1990s has also created an international trend that will be increasingly difficult for China's leaders to buck—though they showed no hesitation in doing so when they sent the troops into Tiananmen Square.

If democracy does come to China, it will not necessarily take a form familiar to Americans or other Westerners. Japan provides a comparative perspective for thinking about how a Chinese-style democracy might evolve. The Japanese constitution, electoral system, and parliamentary government are based on and sustain universal democratic principles such as citizen control of the government through fair and competitive elections. However, the cooperative relationship between government, business, and labor that is often credited with producing Japan's successful industrial policies draws on deeply rooted values of consensus-building and giving priority to the national good over special interests.

Similarly, a democratic China is likely to have institutions and procedures that both embody core values of democracy and reflect distinctive aspects of the nation's society and culture. Perhaps Chinese democracy will be more "collectivist," and less "individualist" than U.S. democracy by, for example, keeping a constitutional emphasis on citizens' duties to the state while also protecting citizens' rights and making the government truly accountable.

CHINA IN COMPARATIVE PERSPECTIVE

It is particularly useful to compare politics in China with the politics of other nations from two perspectives. First, the People's Republic of China can be compared with other communist party-states with which it shares or has shared many political characteristics. Second, China can be compared with other Third World nations that face similar challenges of economic and political development.

China as a Communist Party-State

One of the most interesting questions that China raises for students of comparative politics is, Why has the Chinese communist party-state so far proven more durable than the Soviet Union's and most of the other regimes of that type? A large part of the reason is that the PRC's successful economic development and the phenomenal rise in the living standards of most of the Chinese people over the last couple of decades has saved the CCP from the kinds of economic crises that greatly weakened most other communist systems.

The nature of the revolution that first brought the CCP to power also provides some clues about why communism has survived in China. As you will recall, the Chinese Communists came to power through an indigenous revolution in which the CCP did not depend on foreign support for its victory. This is very different from the situation in most of East-Central Europe, where the Soviet Red Army helped to install and maintain communist regimes, which never quite shed the image of having been imposed from the outside. Furthermore, due to their successes as both social reformers and patriotic fighters against the Japanese, the Chinese Communists were able to build a much larger and broader base of support—especially among the peasantry—than were the Soviet Communists, who came to power much more quickly through what was largely an urban revolution. Therefore, even though repression and corruption may be harming the popularity of the CCP, among some segments of the population the party still has a deep reservoir of historical legitimacy that has helped to sustain it in power.

China also has many things in common with other communist party-states, including the basic features of what is often called its totalitarian political system. **Totalitarianism** (a term which has also been applied to fascist regimes such as Nazi Germany) describes a system in which the ruling party prohibits all forms of meaningful political opposition and dissent and insists on obedience to a single state-determined ideology; such regimes also seek to bring all spheres of public activity (including the economy and culture) and many spheres of the private life of its citizens under the *total* control of the party-state in the effort to modernize the country and, indeed, to transform human nature.

Totalitarian systems are different in several important ways from authoritarian dictatorships, such as the military governments that presently rule Nigeria or ruled Brazil in the past. Like totalitarian states, authoritarian states suppress opposition and dissent; but they do not attempt to control or penetrate society in nearly as thorough a manner as do totalitarian states. Authoritarian governments generally allow a large "zone of indifference" in society where citizens are free to pursue their interests (such as in religion or the arts) without state interference as long as they steer clear of sensitive political issues.

The case of China sheds interesting comparative light on the nature of change in totalitarian systems. Partly because of their inflexibility, totalitarian regimes in Russia and East-Central Europe collapsed quickly and thoroughly, to be replaced by democracies—or at least efforts to democratize. The CCP appears to be trying to save communist rule in China by abandoning or at least moderating some of its totalitarian features.

In order to promote economic development, the CCP has relaxed its grip on many areas of life, resulting in a relatively large apolitical "zone of indifference" in the China of the 1990s. The PRC under Deng Xiaoping has clearly evolved from Maoist totalitarianism toward a less intrusive, but still dictatorial "consultative authoritarian regime" that "increasingly recognizes the need to obtain information, advice, and support from key sectors of the population, but insists on suppressing dissent . . . and maintaining ultimate political power in the hands of the Party."[52] Thus, China may be going through a type of post-totalitarian transition that is characterized by bold economic reforms in the communist party-state, but leads to (or at least through) another form of dictatorship rather than democratization.

China as a Third World State

The record of communist rule in China raises important issues about the role of the state in economic development. It also raises interesting comparative questions about the complex relationship between economic and political change in the Third World.

When the Chinese Communist Party came to power in 1949, China was a desperately poor country, with an economy devastated by a century of civil strife and world war. The nation had also been torn apart politically and socially and was in a weak and subordinate position in the post–World War II international order. Measured against this starting point, the PRC has made remarkable progress in improving its citizens' living standards and quality of life. The CCP has also enhanced China's global role and international prestige and has built a strong state that not only has the capacity to control and repress its people but can also carry out most of the necessary functions of a modern government from running schools to delivering the mail.

Why has China been more successful than many other Third World nations in meeting some of the major challenges of development? Many Third World states serve narrow class or foreign interests more than they serve the national interest and corrupt political leaders wind up being a drain on development rather than a stimulus. The result is that governments of Third World countries often become defenders of a status quo built on extensive poverty and inequality rather than agents of needed, fundamental change.

In contrast, the PRC's rulers have been quite successful in creating what social scientists call a **"developmental state"**[53] in which political leaders effectively use government power and public policy to promote economic growth. The Chinese Communist Party has been fiercely committed to preserving its own power and has not hesitated to use brutal force to achieve its ends, but it has also been unflinching in pursuit of China's national development and unafraid to undertake radical change (sometimes too radical in the Maoist era!) in pursuit of its developmental goals. The Chinese developmental state under Deng Xiaoping certainly has serious economic and social problems, but his policies of market reform and opening the country to the outside world have produced spectacular results that have made China one of the great economic success stories of the Third World in the last decades of the twentieth century.

While much of the Third World seems to be heading toward democracy without development (or at least very slow development), China seems to be following the reverse course of very fast development without democracy. As this chapter has stressed, there is a sharp and disturbing contrast between the harsh political rule of the CCP and its remarkable accomplishments in improving the material lives of the Chinese people. This contrast is at the heart of what one journalist has called the "riddle of China" today. The government of the PRC, he notes, "fights leprosy as aggressively as it attacks dissent. It inoculates infants with the same fervor with which it arrests its critics. Partly as a result, a baby born in Shanghai now has a longer life expectancy than a baby born in New York City."[54] This "riddle" makes it difficult to settle upon a clear evaluation of the overall record of Communist rule in China today. It also makes it hard to predict the future of the Chinese Communist Party since the regime's economic achievements could provide it with a source of legitimacy and support that may help keep the CCP in power despite its serious political shortcomings.

The CCP's tough stance on political reform is, in part, based on its desire for self-preservation. But in keeping firm control on political life while allowing the country to open up in other important ways, the Chinese Communist Party also believes it is wisely following the model of development pioneered by the newly industrializing countries (NICs) of East Asia such as South Korea, Taiwan, and Singapore.

The lesson that the CCP draws from the NICs' experiences is that only a strong government can provide the political stability and social peace required for rapid economic growth. According to this view, democracy—with its open debates about national priorities, political parties contesting for power, and interest groups squabbling over how to divide the economic pie—is a recipe for chaos, particularly in a huge and relatively poor country. Chinese leaders point out that democracy has not often been conducive to successful economic development in the Third World. In India, for example, a democratic, but weak government has been unable to respond effectively to internal ethnic strife and has been thwarted by entrenched interests in its efforts to alleviate poverty. Some Chinese who support both extensive free-market reforms and a further relaxation of the party's totalitarian features nonetheless

argue that, rather than democratization, what China needs—at least for the foreseeable future, is NIC-like "neo-authoritarianism," that is, a strong government that maintains both political order and promotes economic growth.[55] As discussed above, this, in fact, appears to be the way China's political development is heading in the mid-1990s.

But another of the lessons of the East Asian NICs, and one that most Chinese leaders are unwilling to acknowledge, is that economic development, social modernization, and global integration also create powerful pressures for political change from below and abroad. In both Taiwan and South Korea, authoritarian governments that had presided over economic "miracles" in the 1960s and 1970s were forced to give way to democratic forces in the 1980s. The dynamic expansion and transformation of the Chinese economy suggest that the PRC is in the early stages of a period of growth and modernization that may eventually lead it to NIC status. However, in terms of the extent of industrialization, per capita income, and the strength of the middle and professional classes, China's economic development is still far below the level at which democracy succeeded in Taiwan and South Korea. It is important to remember that "authoritarian governments in East Asia pursued market driven economic growth for decades without relaxing their hold on political power."[56] So, in the short run, the "neo-authoritarian" formula may work for China and for the CCP.

At some point, though, the Chinese Communist Party will again face the challenge of the democratic idea. Economic reform has already created groups and processes, interests and ideas that may become sources of pressure for more and faster political change; and the experience of the NICs and other developing countries suggests that such pressures are likely to intensify as the economy and society continue to modernize. In the past, the CCP has responded to pressures for political change with repression. Whether the next generation of China's leaders will respond differently to the challenge of the democratic idea is perhaps the most important and uncertain question about Chinese politics at the crossroads.

Key Terms

martial law

Marxism-Leninism

communist party-state

gerontocracy

authoritarian

Gross National Product
(GNP) (Table 1)

Purchasing Power
Parity (Table 1)

Confucianism

imperialism

revolution

proletariat

communism

guerrilla warfare

Hundred Flowers

Great Leap Forward

Cultural Revolution

socialism

land reform

legitimacy

nationalization

collectivization

ideology

central planning

capitalism

Maoism

charisma

anarchy

Cold War

newly industrializing
country (NIC)

autarky

détente

political culture

luan

command economy

decentralization

privatization

glasnost

perestroika

people's communes

household
responsibility system

succession

brain drain

guanxi

autonomous regions

unitary state (system)

democratic centralism

cadres

coup d'état

nomenklatura

socialist democracy

social democracy

pluralism

dictatorship of the
proletariat

separation of powers

nationalism

nongovernmental
organizations (ngos)

corporatism

danwei

relative deprivation

civil society

totalitarianism

developmental state

Suggested Readings

Section 1

Chang, Jung. *Wild Swans: Three Daughters of China.* New York: Simon and Schuster, 1991.

Dietrich, Craig. *People's China: A Brief History.* 2d ed. New York: Oxford University Press, 1994.

Fairbank, John King. *The Great Chinese Revolution, 1800–1985.* New York: Harper and Row, 1986.

Garver, John. *Foreign Relations of the People's Republic of China.* Englewood Cliffs, N.J.: Prentice Hall, 1993.

MacFarquhar, Roderick, ed. *The Politics of China, 1949–1989.* Cambridge: Cambridge University Press, 1993.

Spence, Jonathan D. *The Search For Modern China.* New York: Norton, 1990.

Section 2

Brugger, Bill, and Stephen Reglar. *Politics, Economy, and Society in Contemporary China.* Stanford: Stanford University Press, 1994.

Chan, Anita, Richard Madsen, and Jonathan Unger. *Chen Village Under Mao and Deng.* Berkeley: University of California Press, 1992.

Harding, Harry. *China's Second Revolution: Reform After Mao.* Washington, D.C.: Brookings Institution, 1987.

Mackerras, Colin, Radeep Taneja, and Graham Young. *China Since 1978: Reform, Modernization, and "Socialism" with Chinese Characteristics.* New York: St. Martin's Press, 1994.

Riskin, Carl. *China's Political Economy: The Quest for Development since 1949.* New York: Oxford University Press, 1987.

White, Gordon. *Riding the Tiger: The Politics of Economic Reform in Post-Mao China.* Stanford: Stanford University Press, 1993.

Section 3

Baum, Richard. *Burying Mao: Chinese Politics in the Era of Deng Xiaoping.* Princeton, N.J.: Princeton University Press, 1994.

Dreyer, June Teufel. *China's Political System: Modernization and Tradition.* New York: Paragon House, 1993.

Hamrin, Carol Lee, and Zhao Suisheng. *Decision-Making in Deng's China: Perspectives from Insiders.* Armonk, N.Y.: M.E. Sharpe, 1995.

Lieberthal, Kenneth. *Governing China: From Revolution Through Reform.* New York: Norton, 1995.

———, and Michel Oksenberg. *Policy Making in China: Leaders, Structures, and Processes.* Princeton, N.J.: Princeton University Press, 1988.

Wang, James C. F. *Contemporary Chinese Politics: An Introduction.* 5th ed. Englewood Cliffs, N.J.: Prentice Hall, 1995.

Section 4

Gilmartin, Christina, Gail Hershatter, Lisa Rofel, and Tyrene White, eds. *Engendering China: Women, Culture, and the State.* Cambridge, Mass.: Harvard University Press, 1994.

Goldman, Merle. *Sowing the Seeds of Democracy in China: Political Reform in the Deng Xiaoping Era.* Cambridge, Mass.: Harvard University Press, 1994.

Mackerras, Colin. *China's Minorities: Integration and Modernization in the Twentieth Century.* New York: Oxford University Press, 1994.

Oi, Jean. *State and Peasant in Contemporary China: The Political Economy of Village Government.* Berkeley: University of California Press, 1989.

Walder, Andrew G. *Communist Neo-Traditionalism: Work and Authority in Chinese Industry.* Berkeley: University of California Press, 1986.

Section 5

Kristof, Nicolas D., and Sheryl WuDunn. *China Wakes: The Struggle for the Soul of a Rising Power.* New York: Time Books, 1994.

Pei Minxin. *From Reform to Revolution: The Demise of Communism in China and the Soviet Union.* Cambridge, Mass.: Harvard University Press, 1994.

Schell, Orville. *Mandate of Heaven: A New Generation of Entrepreneurs, Dissidents, Bohemians, and Technocrats Lay Claim to China's Future.* New York: Simon and Schuster, 1994.

Terrill, Ross. *China in Our Time: The Epic Saga of the People's Republic from the Communist Victory to Tiananmen Square and Beyond.* New York: Simon and Schuster, 1992.

Endnotes

1. Wu Ming (pseud.), "I Witnessed the Beijing Massacre," cited in Timothy Brook, *Quelling the People: The Military Suppression of the Beijing Democracy Movement* (New York: Oxford University Press, 1992), 129.

2. For good descriptions of the political system of imperial China, see John K. Fairbank, *The United States and China,* 4th ed. (Cambridge, Mass.: Harvard University Press), ch. 5; and Albert Feuerwerker, *State and Society in Eighteenth Century China: The Ch'ing [Qing] Empire in Its Glory,* Michigan Papers in Chinese Studies, no. 27 (Ann Arbor: Center for Chinese Studies, The University of Michigan, 1976).

3. Mao Zedong [Mao Tsetung], "Report on an Investigation of the Peasant Movement in Hunan," March 1927, in *Selected Readings from the Works of Mao Tsetung* (Beijing: Foreign Languages Press, 1971), 24.

4. Brantly Womack, "The Party and the People: Revolutionary and Post-Revolutionary Politics in China and Vietnam," *World Politics* 39, no. 4 (July 1987): 479–507.

5. Vivienne Shue, "Powers of State, Paradoxes of Dominion: China 1949–1979," in *Perspectives on Modern China: Four Anniversaries,* ed. Kenneth Lieberthal et al. (Armonk, N.Y.: M.E. Sharpe, 1991), 208.

6. Maurice Meisner, *Mao's China and After: A History of the People's Republic* (New York: Free Press, 1986), 195.

7. See Dorothy J. Solinger, ed., *Three Visions of Chinese Socialism* (Boulder, Co.: Westview Press, 1984).

8. David Bachman, *Bureaucracy, Economy, and Leadership in China: The Institutional Origins of the Great Leap Forward* (Cambridge: Cambridge University Press, 1991), 2.

9. Several books by participants and victims of the Cultural Revolution give gripping and terrifying accounts of the movement. See, for example, Gao Yuan, *Born Red: A Chronicle of the Cultural Revolution* (Stanford: Stanford University Press, 1987); Liang Heng and Judith Shapiro, *Son of the Revolution* (New York: Vintage, 1984); and Nien Cheng, *Life and Death in Shanghai* (New York: Penguin, 1988).

10. John King Fairbank, "The People's Middle Kingdom," *Foreign Affairs* 44, no. 4 (July 1966): 574–86.

11. Daniel Sutherland, "Uncounted Millions: Mass Deaths in Mao's China," *The Washington Post,* July 17, 1994, A23.

12. "When China Wakes," *The Economist: A Survey of China,* November 28, 1992, 3, 15.

13. For a description of the Maoist model of economic development, see Carl Riskin, "Neither Plan nor Market: Mao's Political Economy," in *New Perspectives on the Cultural Revolution,* ed. William A. Joseph, Christine P. W. Wong, and David Zweig. Harvard Contemporary China Series: 8. (Cambridge, Mass.: Council on East Asian Studies, Harvard University, 1991), 133–152.

14. Barry Naughton, "The Pattern and Legacy of Economic Growth in the Mao Era," in *Perspectives on Modern China: Four Anniversaries,* 250.

15. Deng Xiaoping first expressed his "cat theory" in 1962 in a speech entitled "Restore Agricultural Production" in the aftermath of the failure and famine of the Great Leap Forward. In the original speech, he actually quoted an old peasant proverb that refers to a "yellow cat or a black cat," but it is most often rendered "white cat or black cat." See *Selected Works of Deng Xiaoping (1938–1965)* (Beijing: Foreign Languages Press, 1992), 293.

16. Deng Xiaoping, "Reform Is China's Second Revolution," March 28, 1985, in *Selected Works of Deng Xiaoping (1982–1992)* (Beijing: Foreign Languages Press, 1994), 119–120.

17. Dorothy J. Solinger, *China's Transition from Socialism: Statist Legacies and Market Reforms, 1980–1990* (Armonk, N.Y.: M.E. Sharpe, 1993), 277.

18. Kathleen Hartford, "Socialist Agriculture is Dead; Long Live Socialist Agriculture! Organizational Transformation in Rural China," in *The Political Economy of Reform in Post-Mao China,* ed. Elizabeth J. Perry and Christine Wong. Harvard Contemporary China Series: 2. (Cambridge, Mass.: Council on East Asian Studies, Harvard University, 1985), 55.

[19]Christine P. W. Wong, "China's Economy: The Limits of Gradualist Reform," in *China Briefing, 1994,* ed. William A. Joseph (Boulder, Colo.: Westview Press), 50.

[20]Emily Honig and Gail Herschatter, *Personal Voices: Chinese Women in the 1980s* (Stanford: Stanford University Press, 1988), 337.

[21]Baruch Boxer, "China's Environment: Issues and Economic Implications," in Joint Economic Committee of Congress, *China's Economic Dilemmas in the 1990s: The Problems of Reform, Modernization, and Interdependence,* vol. 1 (Washington, D.C.: U.S. Government Printing Office, 1991), 306–307. The above cited case of toxic dumping in the Huai River is described in Patrick E. Tyler, "A Tide of Pollution Threatens China's Prosperity," *The New York Times,* September 25, 1994, 3.

[22]"Environment and Development: A World Issue," in *Beijing Review* 35, no. 23 (June 8–14, 1992): 20.

[23]Mao Zedong, "Strive to Build a Great Socialist Country," September 15, 1954, in *Selected Works of Mao Tsetung [Mao Zedong],* vol. 5 (Beijing: Foreign Languages Press, 1977), 149.

[24]Deng Xiaoping, "Uphold the Four Cardinal Principles," March 30, 1979, in *Selected Works of Deng Xiaoping (1977–1982)* (Beijing: Foreign Languages Press, 1984), 178.

[25]A full text of the 1982 constitution of the People's Republic of China and its 1988 amendments can be found in Kenneth Lieberthal, *Governing China: From Revolution Through Reform* (New York: Norton, 1995), 355–381. The texts of the 1993 amendments to the constitution can be found in Foreign Broadcast Information Service, *Daily Report: China,* March 30, 1993 (FBIS-CHI-93-059), 42.

[26]The party constitution has also been completely rewritten or amended to reflect shifting political winds. Since coming to power in 1949, there have been five very different party constitutions (1956, 1969, 1973, 1977, and 1982). The 1982 CCP constitution was significantly revised in 1992 to incorporate Deng Xiaoping's ideas about economic reform and to legitimize the concept of the "socialist market economy." A full text of the 1992 constitution of the Communist Party of China can be found in Lieberthal, *Governing China,* 383–402.

[27]Hong Yung Lee, *From Revolutionary Cadres to Party Technocrats in Socialist China* (Berkeley: University of California Press, 1991), 194–195.

[28]Mao Zedong, "Problems of War and Strategy," November 6, 1938, in *Selected Works of Mao Tsetung [Mao Zedong],* vol. 2 (Beijing: Foreign Languages Press, 1972), 224.

[29]Ellis Joffe, "The Chinese Army: Coping with the Consequences of Tiananmen," in *China Briefing, 1991,* ed. William A. Joseph (Boulder, Colo.: Westview Press, in cooperation with The Asia Society, 1992), 42.

[30]Margaret Y. K. Woo, "Courts, Justice, and Human Rights," in *China Briefing, 1992,* ed. William A. Joseph (Boulder, Colo.: Westview Press, in cooperation with The Asia Society, 1993), 97.

[31]Kenneth Lieberthal and David Michael Lampton, eds., *Bureaucracy, Politics, and Decision-Making in Post-Mao China* (Berkeley: University of California Press, 1992).

[32]John P. Burns, *The Chinese Communist Party's Nomenklatura System: A Documentary Study of Party Control of Leadership Selection, 1979–1984* (Armonk, N.Y.: M.E. Sharpe, 1989), ix–x.

[33]Susan L. Shirk, "The Chinese Political System," in *Bureaucracy, Politics, and Decision-Making in Post-Mao China,* 65.

[34]Lucian Pye, *The Dynamics of Chinese Politics* (Cambridge, Mass.: Oelgeschlager, Gunn, and Hain, 1981), 139.

[35]Gordon White, *Riding the Tiger: The Politics of Economic Reform in Post-Mao China* (Stanford: Stanford University Press, 1993), 20.

[36]Andrew J. Nathan, *Chinese Democracy* (Berkeley: University of California Press, 1985), 124.

[37]Hong Yung Lee, *From Revolutionary Cadres to Party Technocrats in Socialist China,* 387

[38]Stanley Rosen, "The Chinese Communist Party and Chinese Society: Popular Attitudes Toward Party Membership and the Party's Image," *The Australian Journal of Chinese Affairs,* no. 24 (July 1990): 56.

[39]James D. Seymour, *China's Satellite Parties* (Armonk, N.Y.: M.E. Sharpe, 1987), 87.

[40]Stanley Rosen, "The Chinese Communist Party and Chinese Society," 85.

[41]Samuel S. Kim and Lowell Dittmer, "Whither China's Quest for National Identity?" in *China's Quest for National Identity,* ed. Samuel S. Kim and Lowell Dittmer (Ithaca, N.Y.: Cornell University Press, 1993), 258.

[42]Lucian W. Pye, "How China's Nationalism Was Shanghaied," *The Australian Journal of Chinese Affairs,* no. 29 (January 1993): 130.

[43]June Teufel Dreyer, *China's Political System: Modernization and Tradition* (New York: Paragon House, 1993), 361.

[44]Emily Honig and Gail Hershatter, *Personal Voices: Chinese Women in the 1980s,* 320.

[45]Margaret M. Pearson, "The Janus Face of Business Associations in China: Socialist Corporatism in Foreign Enterprises," *The Australian Journal of Chinese Affairs,* no. 31 (January 1994): 25–46.

[46]James R. Townsend and Brantly Womack, *Politics in China,* 3d ed. (Boston: Little, Brown, 1986), 271.

[47]The following scenes are extrapolated from: Nicholas D. Kristof and Sheryl WuDunn, *China Wakes: The Struggle for the Soul of a Rising Power* (New York: Times Books, 1994), *passim;* Agence France Presse English Wire Service, "Peasants Surviving on Less than 20 Dollars a Year," *China News Digest-Global* (on-line service), February 19, 1994; Chiang Chen-ch'ang, "A Study of Social Conflict in Rural Mainland China," *Issues and Studies* 30, no. 3 (March 1994): 35–50; and Susan V. Lawrence, "Democracy, Chinese-Style: Village Representative Assemblies," *The Australian Journal of Chinese Affairs,* no. 32 (July 1994): 61–68.

[48]Ted Robert Gurr, *Why Men Rebel?* (Princeton: Princeton University Press, 1970), especially chapter 2.

[49]Nicholas D. Kristof, "China Sees 'Market-Leninism' as Way to Future," *The New York Times,* September 6, 1993, 1, 5.

[50]Nina R. Halpern, "Economic Reform, Social Mobilization, and Democratization in Post-Mao China," in *Reform and Reaction in Post-Mao China,* ed. Richard Baum (New York: Routledge, 1991), 53–54.

[51]Many of the points in this section are based on Martin King Whyte, "Prospects for Democratization in China," *Problems of Communism* (May–June 1992): 58–69.

[52]Harry Harding, *China's Second Revolution: Reform After Mao* (Washington, D.C.: Brookings Institution, 1987), 200.

[53]For an early statement of the idea of the "developmental state," see Chalmers Johnson, *MITI and the Japanese Miracle* (Stanford: Stanford University Press, 1982). For an application of the concept to China, see Gordon White, *Riding the Tiger: The Politics of Economic Reform in Post-Mao China.*

[54]Nicholas D. Kristof, "Riddle of China: Repression as Standard of Living Soars," *The New York Times,* September 7, 1993, A1, A10.

[55]Barry Sautman, "Sirens of the Strongman: Neo-Authoritarianism in Recent Chinese Political Theory," *China Quarterly,* no. 129 (March 1992): 73–102.

[56]Nicholas Lardy, "Is China Different?: The Fate of Its Economic Reform," in *The Crisis of Leninism and the Decline of the Left,* ed. Daniel Chirot (Seattle: University of Washington Press, 1991), 147.

Part 4

Politics in the Third World

CHAPTER 8

India

Land and Population

Capital	New Delhi	
Total Area (square miles)	1,269,339 (slightly more than ⅓ size of U.S.)	
Population	898 million	
Annual Projected Population Growth Rate (1993–2000)	1.8%	
Urban Population (% of total)	26%	
Ethnic Composition		
Languages*	Hindi	39%
	Various dialects	56%
	Other	5%
Religions	Hindu	80%
	Muslim	14%
	Christian	2%
	Sikh	2%
	Buddhist, Jain, other	2%

Economy

Domestic Currency	Rupee		
GNP (US$)	$269.4 billion		
GNP per capita (US$)	$300		
Purchasing Power Parity GDP per capita (US$)	$1,220		
Average Annual GDP Growth Rate (1980–1993)	5.2%		
Structure of Production (% of GDP)	Agriculture	31%	
	Industry	28%	
	Services	41%	
Labor Force Distribution (% of total)	Agriculture	62%	
	Industry	11%	
	Services	27%	
Women as % of Total Labor Force	25%		
Income Distribution (1988–1990)	% of Population	% Share of Income or Consumption	
	Richest 20%	41.3%	
	Poorest 20%	8.8%	
Total Foreign Trade (exports plus imports) as % of GDP	17%		

Society

Life Expectancy	Female	61
	Male	61
Population per Doctor	2,440	
Infant Mortality (per 1,000 live births)	80	
Adult Literacy	Female	35%
	Male	64%
Average (Mean) Years of Schooling (of adults 25+)	Female	1.2
	Male	3.5
Communications (per 100 people)	Radios	8
	Televisions	3
	Telephones	1
1995 Human Development Index (1 = highest)	Ranks 134 out of 174	

Political Organization

Political System   Parliamentary democracy and a federal republic.

Regime History   Current government formed by the Congress Party under the leadership of Narasimha Rao, since 1991.

Administrative Structure   Federal with subnational government called state governments.

Executive   Prime minister, leader of the party with the most seats in the parliament.

Legislature   Bicameral, upper house elected indirectly and without much substantial power; lower house, the main house, with members elected from single-member districts, winner-take-all.

Judiciary   Independent constitutional court with appointed judges.

Party System   Multiparty system. Congress Party is dominant; major opposition parties include Bhantiya Janata Party (BJP), Janata Party, and the Communist Party of India, Marxist (CPM).

* Hindi is official language, but English is most important language for political, commercial, and other national-level communication.

SECTION 1
The Making of the Modern Indian State

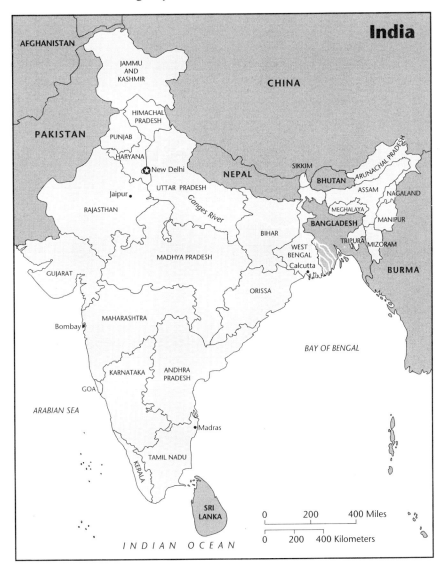

INDIA AT THE CROSSROADS

Referring to events in India on December 6, 1992, *The New York Times* reported this lead story the next day on its front page: "Thousands of Hindus stormed and destroyed an Islamic Mosque in a north-central city of India, Ayodhya." The impact of the event was chilling as many recalled the tumult when the modern Indian state emerged in 1947 amid considerable Hindu-

Muslim conflict. The destruction of a mosque thus suggested the possible resurgence of large-scale ethnic violence in the world's most populous democracy. Although the worst outcomes were avoided, this religious conflict was the culmination of a dispute that had been brewing in India for a few years, encouraged by one of India's prominent political parties, the Bharatiya Janata Party (Indian People's Party, or the BJP). The BJP is a religious, nationalist party that had

A crowd of Hindu fundamentalists listens to speeches by leaders around a disputed mosque in Ayodhya, a town in northern India, on December 6, 1992. The mosque was later torn down by belligerent volunteers, precipitating a major political crisis.
Source: Reuters/Bettmann.

been courting the electoral and political support of **Hindus,** India's largest religious group at over 80 percent of the country's population. BJP leaders argued that the Islamic mosque at Ayodhya—a place of worship for India's **Muslim** minority, who constitute nearly 14 percent of India's population—had been built on the site that the BJP claimed was the birthplace of the Hindu god Rama. They wanted to replace the mosque with a Hindu temple. When the national government, ruled by India's main centrist party, the Indian National Congress (or the Congress), refused to allow demolition of the mosque, the BJP mobilized Hindus throughout India in political protest.

The BJP's political mobilization was quite successful, especially in the short term. The political use of religious symbols touched a raw nerve in a multiethnic society in which religious conflict has a long history and in which stories and memories of communal hostility and suspicion are ever present. The other constant destabilizing ingredients in Indian society are widespread poverty and inequality; thus dissatisfied groups are always available for political mobilization. When the BJP leaders succeeded in generating support for their cause, some of the mobilized followers—especially poor young men from small towns who had few resources but much anger—raged out of control. Once mobilized, these followers continued to promote the conflict. The Congress-led national government presented an ambiv-

alent attitude toward the growing Hindu mobilization: On the one hand, the government needed to protect India's minorities and to maintain law and order, but on the other hand, it was afraid of alienating the Hindu majority group, whose electoral support was essential for winning future elections. As the national government hesitated and the BJP sustained its high level of mobilization, thousands of Hindus stormed and demolished the Islamic mosque at Ayodhya.

This incident highlights three important themes in contemporary Indian politics. First, political struggles in a relatively poor democracy are especially likely to be contentious. Given the multicultural nature of India, many of these struggles readily become ethnic conflicts; the lines of conflict are sometimes defined along religion, at other times, along language or territorial attachments. Second, the growing contentiousness among groups is political in the sense that mobilized groups seek to influence who rules and what the rulers do. In other words, numerous mobilized groups want more of what is valued in society, namely, wealth, status, and power, and expect the government to fulfill their demands. And third, although growing conflicts often push Indian politics to the brink, somehow India's democracy in the nearly fifty years since independence has managed to pull back, absorb the crises, and muddle through, albeit with a strained democratic system.

The Caste System

Originally derived from the Portuguese word *castas,* today the word *caste* inevitably evokes images of the rigid hierarchy that constitutes Indian society and is the overriding determinant of behavior by Indians. In reality, however, castes are less immutable and timeless categories than suggested by popular image.

Historically, the **caste system** compartmentalized and ranked the Hindu population of the Indian subcontinent through rules governing various aspects of daily life, such as eating, marriage, and prayer. Sanctioned by religion, the hierarchy of caste is based on a conception of the world as divided into realms of purity and impurity. Each hereditary and endogamous group (that is, a group into which one is born and within which one marries) constitutes a *jati,* which is itself organized by *varna,* or shades of color. The four main varna are: the ***Brahmin*** or priestly caste, the *Kshatriya* or

warrior and royal caste, the *Vaishyas* or trading caste, and the *Shudra* or artisan caste. Each of these *varna,* are divided into many *jatis* that often approximate occupational groups (such as potters, barbers, and carpenters). Those who were not considered to be members of organized Hindu society—because they lived in forests and hills rather than in towns and villages, or were involved in "unclean" occupations (such as sweepers and leather workers)—were labeled **untouchables,** outcastes, or scheduled castes.

Because each *jati* is often concentrated in a particular region, it is sometimes possible to change one's *varna,* when one moves to a different part of the country by changing names or adopting the social customs of higher castes—for example, by giving up eating meat. Some flexibility within the rigidity of the system has contributed to its survival across the centuries.

With a population of nearly 900 million (nearly the population of all African and Latin American countries combined), India is the world's largest democracy. It is also the oldest democracy among the developing countries of Asia, Africa, and Latin America. India has functioned as a democracy with full adult suffrage since the late 1940s when it emerged as a sovereign nation-state following the end of British colonial rule. The durability of Indian democracy is especially intriguing considering the diversity of Indian society. Some fourteen major languages and numerous dialects are spoken in India. Although Hinduism is the religion of most Indians, people subscribing to nearly every one of the world's great religions—Islam, Buddhism, Christianity, and Judaism—live in India. Furthermore, Indian society, especially the Hindu society, is divided into a myriad of castes. Although these are mainly occupation groups, they also tend to be "closed" social groups in the sense that people are born into, marry, and die within their caste.

Wealth and income present intense contrasts in Indian society. At the top are a small number of the incredibly affluent who have made their fortunes in business and industry. The personal wealth of the wealthiest of these—for example, Tatas and Birlas, two of India's largest business houses—rivals the wealth of business executives around the world. Below them, a much larger group, nearly 100 million Indians, are relatively well-off and have the same standard of living as "middle classes" in many de-

veloped countries. By contrast, India's lower middle classes, some 500 million Indians, are mainly small farmers or urban workers, relatively poor by global standards; they barely eke out a living. And finally, at the bottom of the class structure are about 300 million people who are extremely poor and are concentrated mostly in India's thousands of villages as landless laborers or as the urban unemployed in shabby city slums.

Another aspect of Indian diversity is the contrast between primitive and sophisticated technologies of production. Low levels of literacy, poverty, and primitive technology characterize a fair amount of India's rural society. At the other end of the spectrum, India has a very sophisticated, technologically developed industrial sector that produces a variety of consumer products, military technologies, nuclear energy, and computers. Last, India's diversity is organized into a federal system of government with twenty-two states and several other special political units. This social, economic, and political diversity provides a challenging context within which to comprehend the functioning of Indian democracy.

India is a parliamentary democracy designed on the British model. The parliament—in India known as the *Lok Sabha,* or the House of the People—is the most significant political body. The leader of the political party with the most seats in the *Lok Sabha* becomes the prime minister, who nominates a cabinet, mostly from the ranks of the other elected members to parliament. The prime minister and the cabinet, along with permanent civil servants, control much of the government's daily functioning.

The current government in India is formed by the Congress Party, which except for a few important interludes has ruled India continuously since the late 1940s. Congress governments during the 1990s have enjoyed only a very slim majority in the *Lok Sabha*. The main opposition party in the *Lok Sabha* is the right-leaning, Hindu-nationalist party, the BJP. Another significant opposition party is the left-leaning Communist Party of India (Marxist), or the CPM; although communist in name, it is mainly a reform-oriented party with support from peasants and workers. Both the BJP and the CPM are regionally concentrated, whereas the Congress is organized throughout the country.

During the last two to three decades, some of India's essential political institutions—such as political parties, the federal system, bureaucracy, and the judiciary—have not functioned very effectively, partly because of the unavoidable democratic demands from India's diverse and mobilized political groups. However, this ineffectiveness has also resulted from the actions of India's top political leaders who, when threatened, sought to block access that challengers may have to powerful positions. This is one reason why India's important political party, the Congress, has stopped conducting internal party elections for selecting party officers. Also, leaders below the national level, especially at the state level, have in recent years been appointed from above rather than elected from below. Those loyal rather than competent have similarly been favored for appointments in the bureaucracy and the judiciary. Such developments have contributed to the growing ineffectiveness of some of India's most important political institutions, further complicating the task of governing India's complex society.

With governments of precarious majorities in power, together with weakened political institutions and considerable political activism in the society, the political situation in contemporary India is not very stable. India's domestic troubles both reflect and influence its changing status in the world of states. The nation emerged from its long independence struggle against Great Britain to assume the leadership of the nonaligned bloc, a group of developing nations intent on remaining neutral in the Cold War contest between the United States and the Soviet Union. India also sought economic self-sufficiency through a policy of state-led industrialization focused on meeting the needs of its large internal market. This economic strategy has had mixed results and has done little to alleviate the country's terrible poverty. As with many other developing nations, India is having to adjust its economic strategy to meet the demands of increasingly competitive and interdependent global markets.

How this situation developed and where the country is headed are among the subjects discussed in this section on India. The central theme to consider is how a democratic government in India can simultaneously accommodate the demands of its diverse social groups and create a wealthier and more egalitarian society. If India succeeds in this task, it may join the East Asian examples of development success such as The Republic of Korea (South Korea); however, if India fails, it could join the ranks of the more troubled cases of Africa. India's most likely future path will be to continue performing somewhere between the out-of-control success cases of East Asia on the one hand and the sad development disasters of Africa on the other hand.

This section will provide a broad historical overview of the major turning points in Indian politics. The three following sections will explore various facets of the contemporary situation: political and economic development; governmental institutions; and the political struggles of various groups over participation and representation. We will return to the issue of likely future directions in the concluding section.

CRITICAL JUNCTURES

India is among the most ancient civilizations of the world, dating back to the third millennium B.C. The area where the countries of Pakistan, India, and Bangladesh now exist, the Indian subcontinent, has witnessed the rise and fall of many civilizations and empires, some vast, others more limited. Only the most recent legacies that have shaped the political present are reviewed here. Of these, three are especially significant. First is the impact of nearly 200 years of British colonial rule from the mid-eighteenth to the mid-twentieth century, out of which emerged, not only India's present political boundaries, but also a relatively stagnant economy and a nationalist movement committed to bringing both sovereignty and prosperity to a new nation. Second, in more recent times, is the Nehru era (approximately 1950 to 1964), when sovereign India was ruled by

---

Critical Junctures in India's Development

3000 B.C.–A.D. 1757	Precolonial period.
1526	Founding of Mughal dynasty.
1612–1690	British East India Company establishes trading stations at Surat, Bombay, and Calcutta.
1757–1857	Britain establishes informal colonial rule.
1857–1947	Britain establishes formal colonial rule in response to Sepoy Rebellion.
1885	Creation of Indian National Congress.
1947	India achieves independence from Britain; partition of India and Pakistan and founding of modern Indian state.
1947–1964	Jawaharlal Nehru is prime minister.
1966–1984	Indira Gandhi is prime minister except for a brief period from 1977–1980.
1984–Present	Contemporary period.

Jawaharlal Nehru, during whose rule India developed both a democratic and a federal system of government and a planned economy aimed at India's industrialization. Third is the Indira Gandhi era (approximately 1965 to 1984), when Nehru's daughter ruled India and when democratic politics became more populist and turbulent; her left-leaning rhetoric also failed to relieve India's considerable poverty.

The Colonial Legacy

Motivated by a combination of economic and political interests, the British started making inroads into the Indian subcontinent in the late seventeenth and early eighteenth centuries. Since 1526, large sections of the subcontinent had been ruled by the Mughal dynasty; the Mughals came to India originally from Central Asia and were Muslim by religion. As the power of the Mughal emperors declined in the eighteenth century, lesser princely contenders vied with one another for supremacy. In this environment, the British East India Company—a large English trading organization with commercial interests in India and strong backing for its ventures from the British Crown—was able to play off one Indian prince against another, forming alliances with some, subduing others, and thus managing to enhance its control by a policy of divide and rule. Growing control also enabled the British to sell their relatively cheap manufactured goods to Indians, with significant long-term economic consequences: indigenous manufacturing, especially of textiles, and a whole generation of Indian artisans were ruined by the forced opening of the Indian market.

This informal empire was replaced in the mid-nineteenth century with a more formal one. After a major revolt by an alliance of Indian princes against growing British power—an incident known in Indian history as the Sepoy Rebellion or the Mutiny of 1857—the British Crown assumed the direct control of governing India.[1] The ensuing ninety-year formal British rule over India—from 1857 to 1947—left important legacies for the future of Indian politics. India occupied a key place in Britain's global empire: as its largest colony, it was the "jewel in the crown" and of great psychological value to Britain's global ambitions. Like other colonies, India contributed to Britain's successful Industrial Revolution because it was a source of cheap raw materials and provided an outlet for both British manufactured goods and investment. British political control over the Indian subcontinent was also essential—it is no coincidence that India's independence from Britain in 1947 marked the beginning of the end of Britain as a major imperial world power. Colonial rule in India provided a model for subsequent British colonial ventures, for example, in Nigeria. Finally, India was a strategic resource: It provided raw materials and soldiers to help Britain during both world wars.

In order to consolidate its political and economic hold over India, the British entered into alliances with India's traditional ruling groups and eventually helped form a modern, central government.[2] The British created three main varieties of ruling arrangements within India. First, numerous small- to medium-sized states—as many as 500—covering an area equal to two-fifths of the subcontinent, continued to be ruled through the colonial period by traditional Indian princes, the ***Maharajas.*** In exchange for accepting British rule, these Indian princely states were allowed a relatively free hand within their realms. Second, in other parts of India, British "indirect rule" penetrated more deeply than in the princely states, for example, in the Bengal presidency (currently the states of Bihar, West Bengal, and Bangladesh). In these regions, the British transformed traditional Indian elites, who controlled much agricultural land, into legal landlords, the ***zamindars,*** in exchange for periodic payments to the colonial administration. Third, the British established "direct" rule in other parts of India, for example, in Bombay and the Madras presidencies (large areas around the cities of the same name), where British civil servants were directly responsible for collecting land taxes and for adjudicating law and order.

Although the British rule in India thus took a variety of forms, it seldom reached very deep into Indian society, especially rural society, which was organized into numerous, relatively self-sufficient villages. Within villages, social life was further divided into religiously sanctified caste groups, with some landowning castes dominating many other castes lower in the ritual hierarchy, occupation, and income scale. Diverse villages shared this basic organization, irrespective of whether they were located in princely states, in areas controlled by *zamindars,* or in areas controlled directly by civil servants.

At the top of this structure was an alien, colonial rule. A semblance of coherence to this British rule in India was achieved through the creation of a central government that could impose control over these various territories. The British thus helped create an all Indian civil service, police force, and army. Although at first only British nationals could serve in these institutions, especially as officers, the British gradually introduced modern educational institutions to India, and some educated Indians were incorporated into these governmental services. Unlike some other colonies, especially those in Africa, the British in India helped create a relatively effective state structure. When India emerged from British rule in 1947, the new Indian state basically inherited, maintained, and expanded these colonial institutions. Because the civil, police, and armed services in contemporary India continue to be organized along the principles established by the British colonialists in the last century, it is fair to suggest that the roots of the modern Indian state can be traced back to their colonial origins.

The Indian economy during British rule remained inefficient and largely stagnant.[3] The British did not colonize India to develop its economy; instead they ruled India for their own economic and political interests, with several long-term repercussions. For example, during the colonial period the Indian economy was largely agricultural, with hundreds of millions of poor peasants, living in thousands of small villages, tilling the land with primitive technology, and producing at a fairly low level the society's main source of wealth, namely, agricultural products. The British, along with Indian landlords, extracted extensive resources from Indian agriculture, mainly in the form of land revenues, land taxes, and tributes from Indian princes. However, they only reinvested a small portion of this surplus into improving agricultural production. Most resources were squandered through conspicuous consumption by Indian princes and landlords or used to run the expensive colonial government. The result of this mismanagement of resources was that Indian agricultural productivity—that is, the amount of wheat, rice, or other products produced from one unit of land—mostly stagnated in the first half of the twentieth century. Agricultural productivity in India was considerably lower in 1950 than in Japan or even China.

Some industry developed under colonial rule, but its scope was also limited. The British wanted to sell their own manufactured goods to India in exchange for Indian raw materials, and because the British economy was more advanced, it was difficult for Indians to establish manufacturing enterprises that could compete successfully. The British did not provide any real protection to Indian industry, and in any case most Indians were too poor to generate a substantial demand for industrial products. These factors made it difficult for Indians to enter manufacturing as viable competitors. The Indian economy at independence from Britain in 1947 was thus relatively stagnant, especially in agriculture, but also in industry. As a result, one of the central tasks facing Indian leaders since 1947 has been to stimulate the growth of this sluggish economy.

With the growth of commerce, education, and urban life, groups of urban, educated, Indian elites, often of high caste origin, emerged as the new Indian "middle classes." They both observed and closely interacted with their colonial rulers and often felt slighted by their treatment as second-class citizens next to British nationals within their own society. Some members of this new middle class attempted to reform the traditional Hindu Indian society, especially its more repugnant elements of a highly discriminatory caste system and poor treatment of women. Among these were early Hindu nationalists who believed that a reformed Hinduism could provide a basis for a new, modern India. Others were attracted to British liberal ideas and invoked these to seek greater equality with the British.

The century of British colonial rule witnessed growing intellectual and cultural ferment in India. The British colonial rulers and traditional Indian elites had become allies of sorts, squeezing from the poor Indian peasantry resources that were simultaneously used to maintain the colonial, bureaucratic state and to support the conspicuous life-styles of a parasitic landlord class. It was not long before Indian nationalists sought to oppose these arrangements, and an opposition political movement with long-term consequences emerged, namely, the Indian nationalist movement. The organization that represented this movement, the Indian National Congress (INC) emerged in 1885 in Bombay. Its aim was to right racial, cultural, and political wrongs of colonial rule. Over time, this organization grew from its limited elite origins to a full-blown, mass nationalist movement that demanded and eventually succeeded in establishing a sovereign Indian state.

The Nationalist Movement

In its early years, the INC was mainly a collection of Indian urban elites who periodically met and sent petitions to India's British rulers, invoking liberal principles of political equality, and requesting greater Indian involvement in higher political offices. Although the British made some concessions, they ignored most of these requests. In time, this neglect turned requests into demands and pushed some angry Indian elites into militancy and others into the nonviolent mobilization of the Indian masses.

World War I was an important turning point for Indian nationalists. After the war, as great European empires disintegrated, creating new sovereign states in Europe and the Middle East, the principle of self-determination for people who considered themselves a nation gained international respectability. Among the supporters of this principle was the American president, Woodrow Wilson. The Russian Revolution of 1917 also encouraged Indian nationalists because they interpreted the overthrow as a successful political movement against imperialism.

The man most responsible for helping transform the INC from a narrow, elitist club to a mass national-

ist movement was Mohandas Karamchand Gandhi, called Mahatma ("great soul") by his followers, one of the most influential—and admirable—leaders of the twentieth century. After becoming the leader of the INC in the 1920s, Gandhi successfully mobilized the Indian middle classes, as well as a segment of the Indian peasantry, into an anti-British movement that came to demand full sovereignty for India.[4]

Three characteristics of the nationalist movement greatly influenced state building and democracy in India. First, within what is now modern India, the INC succeeded in bringing together a wide variety of Indians in a relatively cohesive nationalist movement. Indians of different economic classes, castes, and ethnic backgrounds came to share some core political values, especially the value of national sovereignty and the related belief that a sovereign Indian state must be achieved and preserved. Because the INC became a powerful political organization, committed to establishing an Indian nation and an Indian state, many conflicts could play themselves out within the INC, as long as they did not threaten the cause of the Indian nation. The INC thus came to embody the principle of "unity within diversity," a principle that served India well in creating and maintaining a relatively stable political system.

Second, although a variety of Indians in their encounter with the British discovered what they had in common with each other—that is, their Indianness—they also recognized their differences, especially their different languages and their different gods. Even Hindus, India's majority population, are a highly diverse lot: There is no organized church in Hinduism; Hindus worship a variety of deities; and they are divided among themselves along different castes. As leaders of the INC—including Gandhi, Jawaharlal Nehru, and Vallabbhai Patel—sought to unite Indians against the British, some Indian groups became suspicious of other Indian groups. With much to gain by emphasizing the divisions among Indians, whenever the opportunity arose, the British favored one group over another, thus contributing to growing divisiveness.

Some of these divisions and conflicts, such as over language or caste-based ethnic identities, were relatively manageable over the long run, though they continue to fuel some ethnic strife and even violence in contemporary India. By contrast, religious conflict between Hindus and Muslims was much more intractable. A segment of the Indian Muslim elite refused

Mohandas Gandhi

Born in 1869 in western India, Mohandas Gandhi studied law in London for two years and worked in Durban, South Africa, as a lawyer and an activist for twenty-one years before returning home to join the Indian nationalist movement. His work among the different communities in South Africa helped him to develop the political strategies of nonviolence, or **satyagraha** (literally, "grasp of truth"). On his arrival in India in 1915, he set about transforming the Indian National Congress into a mass party by reaching out to the urban and rural poor, non-Hindu religious groups, and the scheduled castes, whom he called *Harijans* or Children of God.

Following the British massacre of unarmed civilians gathered in protest in the Punjab (at the Jallianwala Bagh, a location well known in Indian history) in April 1919, Gandhi and Nehru proposed a noncooperation movement. This required a boycott of British legal and educational institutions as well as merchandise and their substitution by indigenous or *swadeshi* varieties. (The image of Gandhi weaving his own cloth is familiar to many.) Gandhi believed that mass civil disobedience could succeed only if people were truly committed; the involvement of some Congress workers in a violent incident in 1922 greatly disturbed him, causing him to call off the noncooperation movement.

Gandhi was strongly opposed to the partition of India along religious lines in 1947, but because he had resigned from the Congress in 1934, his protests went unheard. Nevertheless, he dominated India's nationalist movement for more than two decades until he was assassinated in January 1948, five short months after India achieved its goal of self-rule, or *swaraj*. He is often referred to as the Mahatma, or "great soul."

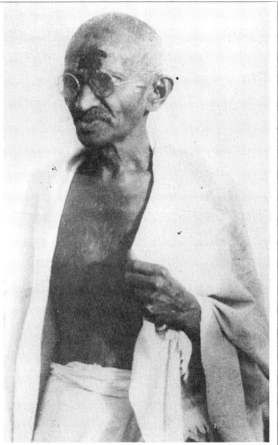

Mahatma Gandhi, the leader of India's Independence movement as he appeared at the head of a 200-mile march, staged in defiance of the statute establishing a government salt monopoly by the British colonial government in 1930.
Source: UPI/Bettmann.

to accept the leadership of Gandhi and the INC, demanded separate political rights for Muslims, and when the INC refused, demanded a separate Muslim state. The eventual, bloody division of the Indian subcontinent into the two states of India and Pakistan, and subsequent Hindu-Muslim hostilities within India (including those in the Indian state of Kashmir today) originated in the discovery of these differences.

And third, although the INC opposed British rule in India, it did so in a manner that was consistent with democratic norms. Many of INC's prominent leaders,

like Nehru, were educated in England and were committed democrats. Gandhi's mobilizational style was also largely nonviolent. Moreover, the INC participated in limited elections allowed by the British, ran democratic governments with limited powers in various British Indian provinces, and elected its own leaders through internal elections within the INC. These pre-independence democratic tendencies were valuable assets for the subsequent success of democracy in India.

During the 1920s and the 1930s, Gandhi, Nehru, and other leaders of the INC were increasingly suc-

Jawaharlal Nehru

Nehru, the first Prime Minister of the new government of India, salutes the flag during Independence Day ceremonies at Red Fort, New Delhi, August 15, 1947.
Source: AP/Wide World Photos.

tablished India as a socialist, democratic, and secular state—in theory if not always in practice—and on the international front, he helped found the nonaligned movement.

With the Soviet Union as his example, Nehru attempted to set India on a rapid road to industrialization by establishing heavy industry. His efforts to effect redistribution of wealth through land reform were countered by an equally strong commitment to democratic and individual rights, such as the right to private property. Upon his death, India inherited a large public sector and an intricate pattern of state control over the private sector.

Today, Nehru is criticized by many for having harbored unrealistic expectations of a secular Indian

Trained at elite British institutions, Jawaharlal Nehru was a staunch believer in liberal democratic principles. His aristocratic background and English education, however, hampered his efforts to extend the support base of his party, the Indian National Congress, to the ordinary people of British India—until Gandhi's arrival on the political scene. Upon India's independence in 1947, Nehru became prime minister as head of the Congress Party and retained that position until his death in 1964. During this period, he es-

state. At the time, however, he saw few alternative means for preventing a recurrence of the bloodshed and trauma that accompanied India's independence. He regarded religion as a source of conflict and religious attachments as both a function and a cause of backwardness. His claim that such affiliations would be worn down by economic progress has not proven true—there has been neither remarkable economic progress for the poorest strata of society nor a decline in the importance of communal ties.

cessful in mobilizing Indians in an anti-British nationalist movement for India's independence. The more successful the movement became, the more the British had to either repress the INC or make concessions, and they tried both. However, World War II consumed Britain's energies so that the government could not simultaneously deal with a major European war and insurgent colonies. In order to gain Indian support for its war efforts, the British promised Indians greater independence following the war, although Gandhi and others who supported full independence refused to cooperate and were jailed for the entire duration of the war. For all practical purposes, however, this final con-

frontation between the British and the INC marked the beginning of the end of British colonial rule in India.

The Nehru Era

India became a sovereign state in August 1947 when the British, weakened from World War II, decided to withdraw from the subcontinent. The resulting division of the subcontinent into two sovereign states—the Muslim state of Pakistan and the secular state of India—was a turbulent, bloody affair. Millions of Muslims rushed from India to Pakistan and millions of Hindus went the other way; over 10 million people migrated and nearly half a million died in communal violence. The euphoria of independence in India was thus tempered by the human tragedy that accompanied the subcontinent's partition.

Within India, Nehru, who was initially favored by Gandhi, emerged as the leader of the new nation. Soon thereafter Gandhi, who opposed the partition and later ardently defended Muslims within India, was assassinated by a Hindu fanatic. The other key Indian leader, Patel, also died within a few years after independence. By 1950, therefore, Nehru became the uncontested leader of a new India, a position he maintained until his death in 1964.[5] The years of Nehru's rule shaped the dominant patterns of India's future development.

Nehru's India had inherited an ambiguous legacy from the British rule: a relatively strong central government and a weak economy. Nehru was a committed nationalist and a social democrat; that is, he sought to strengthen India's independence and national power on the one hand, and to improve its economy and the lives of the Indian poor on the other. Nehru used the governmental machinery that India inherited to accomplish these new tasks.

Immediately after independence, India faced such major political problems as a massive inflow of refugees, a war with Pakistan over the disputed state of Kashmir, and the attempt to consolidate numerous Indian princely estates into a coherent, new national state. Concerned about India's capacity to deal with such problems, Nehru and other leaders, especially Patel, came to depend on and further strengthened the civil, police, and armed services that were a legacy of colonial rule. Although this facilitated India's political stability, it had other, less positive, long-term consequences. Most important, the new Indian state came to resemble the old British Indian state that Nehru and others had so vociferously opposed. The colonial state tended to favor traditional Indian elites and was constructed mainly to extract resources from Indian society and to maintain order within it. This conservative attitude from the colonial state carried over into the postindependence era.

After independence, India adopted a democratic constitution and established a British-style democracy with full adult suffrage. Because political power in this new system required winning elections, the INC had to transform itself from an oppositional, nationalist movement into a political party. This it did quite successfully, though not without costs. The INC, now the Congress Party, needed the electoral support of a majority of Indians, most of whom were poor, low-caste, village dwellers. Because they were new to the democratic system, most of these underprivileged, uneducated poor citizens tended in the early years to follow the political lead of village "big men"—local influentials in villages and often men of high caste and means. The Congress Party thus built its electoral network by establishing a patronage system with such "big men" across India; the "big men" would mobilize electoral support for the Congress Party during elections and, once in power, the Congress Party would channel governmental resources to these local influentials, further enhancing their local position and assuring their support. This patronage system (some call it machine politics) worked quite well for the Congress Party for nearly two decades. Even when electorally successful, however, this strategy bequeathed internal contradictions to the INC: The great, pro-poor Congress Party of India, with a socialist shell, came to be internally dominated by high-caste, wealthy Indians.

Another important change in the decade following independence was the linguistic reorganization of states. As in the United States, the Indian constitution defines India as a federal system. The contentious political issue in the 1950s was the criterion by which Indian political groups could demand a state within the federal union. With Indians divided by the languages they speak, one obvious way to create a federal system was around language groups. Hindi is the most common indigenous language of India; however, most of India's Hindi speakers are concentrated in the north-central part of the country. Those living in the south, east, and parts of the west are generally non-Hindi speakers. Concerned about domination by Hindi-speakers, many of these non-Hindi groups demanded a reorganization of Indian union into linguistically defined states. Nehru resisted this demand for a while, worried that linguistic states within a federation could turn secessionist and demand a sovereign country of their own. As demands for linguistic states mounted, however, especially from southern Indian groups, Nehru compromised in 1956 and the new Indian union was organized around fourteen linguistically defined states. Following subsequent changes, there are now twenty-three major states within India.

Major political changes instituted during the Nehru era put India firmly on a stable, democratic road. The powerful groups in the society—elite bureaucrats; landowning, wealthy groups; and leaders of well-organized, ethnic movements (not to mention businesspeople, who are discussed later)—were all accommodated within the new system. However, the poor and the unorganized did not fare as well. While Nehru and the Congress Party continued to maintain a pro-poor, socialist rhetoric, their capacity to delivery on their promises was limited. This was not a serious political liability in the 1950s because the poor masses could not readily challenge the narrow, elitist rule. In a few states, for example, Kerala, India's most literate state, the poor were organized and elected a communist state government. But India's poor remained relatively unorganized during the 1950s, mired in a centuries-old caste system, fragmented from one another, looking to their caste superiors for political guidance.

Two other legacies of the Nehru era are noteworthy. First, Nehru was an internationalist who wanted India to play a global role. However, as Nehru was consolidating power in India, the Cold War was unfolding globally, dividing the world into two blocs, one allied with the United States and the other with the Soviet Union. Nehru did not want India to join either bloc. Because India had won its independence after a prolonged nationalist struggle against the British, for Nehru, joining either bloc meant compromising hard won sovereignty. Together with postcolonial leaders of Asia and Africa, he initiated what became known as the nonaligned movement, which united those countries wishing to maintain a healthy distance from the two warring superpowers. The United States was suspicious of these nonaligned countries because they did not support what it viewed as the global struggle of the "free world" versus "totalitarianism." Having emerged from Western colonial rule, however, India and many other developing countries did not see the world in the same terms—for them, both Western capitalism and Soviet communism were problematic. Under Nehru India played a leadership role among other nonaligned developing countries while pursuing a "mixed" economy at home that was neither fully capitalist nor socialist.

During Nehru's rule India adopted a model of development largely based on private property, although the role of government ownership of firms and of government planning in guiding private economic activity was considerable. Nehru created a powerful planning commission that, following the Soviet model, made Five Year Plans for the Indian economy outlining the activities in which government investment would be concentrated. Unlike communist party-states, the plan also indicated priority areas for private entrepreneurs, who remained a powerful force in the Indian economy.

The Indian government also levied high tariffs on imports, arguing that new Indian industries, so long disadvantaged under colonial rule, required protection from foreign competitors. The government tightly regulated the start-up and expansion of private industries under the presumption that the government was a better safeguard of the public interest than private entrepreneurs. This government-planned private economy achieved mixed results: It helped India create an impressive industrial base but did not do much to help the poor; and even the protected industries turned out to be quite inefficient by global standards.

The Indira Gandhi Era

When Nehru died in 1964, the party divided over the choice of a successor party leader and prime minister. The second tier of Congress leaders hurriedly selected mild-mannered Lal Bahadur Shastri, who subsequently died of a heart attack in 1966. Once again, the Congress elites were divided over the choice of a successor. This time, they found a compromise candidate in Nehru's daughter, Indira Gandhi. Two reasons favored her choice: (1) as Nehru's daughter, she would be helpful in elections; and (2) she was perceived by the Congress leaders as a weak female who could be manipulated by competing factions within the Congress. Congress leaders were right about the first point, but they could not have been more wrong about the second.

The Congress Party lost considerable popular support in the 1967 national elections. Nehru's death, a relatively divided Congress, and food shortages resulting from bad weather created dissatisfaction and contributed to this decline in popularity. This state of affairs weakened many old, established Congress leaders. In the aftermath, Indira Gandhi moved swiftly to consolidate her position by pushing out the old Congress Party leaders who opposed her and creating a new Congress Party in her own image. Subsequently, Indira Gandhi depicted the old Congress elite as standing for the status quo and preventing her from helping the poor and implementing progressive policies. Indira's populist rhetoric won her immense popularity among India's poor and the underprivileged. By 1971,

Indira Gandhi

Indira Gandhi became prime minister of India shortly after the death of her father, Jawaharlal Nehru, and dominated the Indian political scene until her assassination in 1984. Her years in power strengthened India's international position, but her domestic policies weakened the organizational structure of the Congress Party. Her tendencies toward centralization and the personalization of authority within the Congress and the concomitant use of populist rhetoric in electoral campaigns contributed to the institutional erosion of the Congress Party over the past thirty-odd years. In a desperate bid to maintain diminishing electoral support, she introduced populist tactics through the use of *Garibi Hatao* ("alleviate poverty") slogans to mobilize the electorate.

When confronted by escalating opposition to her authoritarian tendencies, Indira Gandhi suspended democracy for the first time in the history of independent India in 1975 by declaring a state of emergency. Eighteen months later she called elections, in which she and the Congress Party were voted out of power—again, for the first time since independence—and replaced by the Janata Party.

On her return to power in 1980, Gandhi increasingly resorted to the use of Hindu symbols: She presented regional conflict in the Punjab and problems with Pakistan as Hindu-Sikh and Hindu-Muslim issues. Her decision to send troops into the holiest of the holy Sikh temples in Amritsar deeply alienated Sikhs, a small but important religious group in India. The ensuing bloodshed culminated in her assassination by her Sikh bodyguards in 1984.

Indira Gandhi, 1968
Source: UPI/Bettmann.

she dominated Indian politics as much as Mahatma Gandhi or her father Nehru ever had; she continued to be the central figure of Indian politics until 1984, when she was assassinated for political reasons.

Indira Gandhi was India's prime minister from 1966 to 1984, except for the brief period, 1977 to 1980.[6] During this time she was not only India's prime minister but a powerful, controversial, leader. Her rule left several long-term legacies for contemporary Indian politics. First, Indian politics during Indira's rule became more personal and populist than during Nehru's era. By the time Indira Gandhi assumed power in 1966, India's old Congress Party had begun to lose its political sway and anticolonial nationalism was fading. The spread of democratic politics had mobilized many poor, lower-caste citizens who depended less and less on village "big men" for political guidance. As a result, numerous regional parties started

challenging Congress's monopoly on power. Weather-related food shortages in the mid-1960s also hurt the Congress Party in the 1967 elections. Indira Gandhi sought to reverse the decline in Congress's electoral popularity through mobilizing India's vast majority, the poor, by promising "alleviation of poverty" as the core of her political program. This promise struck a popular chord, propelling Indira Gandhi to the top of India's political pyramid.

An additional factor that helped Indira Gandhi's popularity was the way she reignited Indian nationalism. India's neighbor, Pakistan, always evokes considerable hostility among many Indians. During the late 1960s, the political situation within Pakistan became turbulent when the Bengali-speaking eastern half of that country—which was separated from its western half by nearly 1,000 miles of Indian territory—demanded sovereignty. As violence escalated within

Pakistan and refugees from East Pakistan began pouring into India, Indira Gandhi ordered Indian forces to intervene on the side of East Pakistan, which led to the creation of the sovereign state of Bangladesh. Because the United States sided with Pakistan in that conflict (and the Soviet Union backed India), Indira Gandhi was able to mobilize Indian nationalist sentiment against both Pakistan and the United States. This war-related victory only added to Indira Gandhi's growing personal popularity. This popularity among nationalists of various hues and among India's poor and underprivileged groups, freed Indira Gandhi from the old Congress leaders who tried to block or challenge her growing hold on power. She used her newly acquired power to squeeze most of them out of significant positions, replacing them with those loyal and beholden to her. These loyal minions, in turn, appointed yet others who were loyal to them at lower levels.

A second important legacy of Indira's rule now emerges: Slowly but surely, India's political system acquired a "top-down" quality. Whereas during the Nehru era, local elites helped select higher political office holders, in the 1970s a highly popular Indira Gandhi chose to appoint these same officeholders at both the national and regional levels. Although this strategy helped Indira Gandhi to consolidate her power rapidly, over time the same political strategy led to such negative consequences for governing as growing centralization of decision making in the nation's capital, Delhi, and the erosion of the local leaders' legitimacy in the outer reaches of India.

A third important legacy of Indira Gandhi's rule was her failure to translate populist rhetoric into real gains for India's poor. She was neither able to redistribute agricultural land from large landowners to those who worked the land, nor to generate employment, provide welfare, or improve access to education and health for the really poor. The reasons for these failures are complex and controversial. Some analysts argue that she was never sincere in her commitment to the poor; they contend that her populism was mainly a strategy for enhancing electoral popularity, and this argument has some merit. Even if Indira Gandhi had really wanted to improve the lot of India's poor, however, she would have encountered many obstacles, given India's enormous numbers of poor, especially in relation to its wealth. Although some reallocation of national resources to the poor would have been possible, the means to achieve such a goal were not available. For example, India's conservative bureaucracy would have been a logical but unlikely agent to implement such pro-poor policies, mainly because lower-level Indian bureaucrats often side with the wealthy and harbor little sympathy for the poor. Political parties might have been another avenue for policy implementation, but after the split of the Congress Party in 1969, the new party under Indira Gandhi's direction did not reach into the villages, where most of the poor reside. Thus, even if Indira Gandhi had really wanted to redistribute some of India's scarce resources to its poor, the lack of the institutional capability would have made it impossible.

During Indira Gandhi's tenure, Indian politics became more and more turbulent. And this is a fourth legacy, with long-term significance, of her rule. As her popularity soared, so did her opposition. The old Congress elite started coalescing into a loosely knit but coherent opposition. They denounced Indira's populist political style, arguing that her government was corrupt from top to bottom, and that India needed a total revolution both to oust her from power and to cleanse the government. This opposition, led by an old, credible follower of Mahatma Gandhi, Jai Prakash Narain, began organizing mass demonstrations and strikes to press its political case. During 1974 the political situation in India became volatile, with the opposition organizing general strikes and Indira Gandhi threatening massive state repression. When Narain called on the Indian armed forces to mutiny, Indira Gandhi declared a national "Emergency," suspended many democratic rights, and arrested most of the opposition leaders. This **Emergency** lasted for nearly two years, the only period since 1947 when India was not a full democracy.

When the prime minister rescinded the Emergency, hoping to reestablish her popularity by calling new national elections in 1977, she was rudely surprised. She was voted out of power and for the first time since independence, a non-Congress government came to power in India. Various groups that had opposed Indira Gandhi joined together in a loosely and hastily organized party (the Janata Party) and won power. The party won, in part because Indira Gandhi's authoritarian measures during the Emergency were unpopular, but also because the Janata momentarily united India's fragmented opposition groups (a united opposition has a better chance of winning in India's electoral system). However, the Janata Party was a loose coalition and soon after the elections, top Janata leaders started bickering for positions. Factionalism at the top became so unwieldy that the Janata government collapsed, providing a new opportunity for Indira Gandhi to return to power in the 1980 parliamentary elections.

To summarize, a personal and populist political style, a more and more top-down political system, failure to implement antipoverty policies, and growing political turbulence, were the most important legacies of Indira Gandhi's rule in the 1970s. Although much of this continued after she regained power in 1980, she slowly introduced two important sets of changes that have also had long-term significance. The first of these was in the realm of the economy. During much of the 1970s, India's industry grew relatively slowly for several reasons: the government was spending too much public money buying political support and not enough on investment; incomes of the poor were not improving and therefore demand for new products was limited; and excessive rules and regulations were counterproductive, both for domestic entrepreneurs and for integrating India into the world economy. With little means to rechannel government spending or to improve the spending capacity of the poor, Indira Gandhi started liberalizing the rules that governed India's economy. This process of **economic "liberalization"** (that is, moving toward less government intervention) is currently a major issue in Indian politics that will be analyzed in the next section.

The second important change concerns the strategy used to mobilize support for elections. Because poverty was not diminishing, it was clear that continuing appeals to poverty alleviation would not provide a successful electoral strategy. Moreover, economic policy was moving toward liberalization, whereas rapid progress toward poverty alleviation would have required greater government involvement. With the loss of populist promises as a strategy to win support, the prime minister needed a new appeal—at this point, religion returned to Indian politics. From the 1950s onward, Nehru and Indira Gandhi in her early years as prime minister argued for socialism and secularism. Beginning in the early 1980s, however, Indira Gandhi started experimenting with a different theme: using religious appeals to mobilize India's majority religious group, the Hindus. Although the early efforts were subtle and veiled, one dramatic implication was that Indira's Congress did not want to appear soft, or to be

pandering to India's minorities. Thus, religious conflicts reentered Indian politics in the early 1980s, as illustrated by the growing conflict between the **Sikh** religious minority, based in the Punjab, and the national government. During this conflict, Indian security forces attacked Sikh militants hiding inside the holiest of the holy Sikh shrines, the Golden Temple in the city of Amritsar. The resulting alienation of Sikhs from Indira Gandhi peaked with her assassination by one of her Sikh bodyguards in 1984. Her death ushered in the contemporary period whose political system, institutions, policies, and social conflicts will be analyzed in subsequent sections.

IMPLICATIONS FOR CONTEMPORARY INDIAN POLITICS

Father and daughter, Jawaharlal Nehru and Indira Gandhi, dominated Indian politics for over three decades and left enduring legacies for contemporary Indian politics. During the Nehru era, Indian politics was relatively elitist and stable. In this early period, the Indian masses were not highly mobilized, anticolonial nationalism provided a powerful political glue for the politically active groups, and the shrewd decisions of Nehru and his colleagues, especially concerning the accommodation of the powerful in Indian society, established India on a firm democratic footing. However, because the powerful were accommodated and the masses were not organized, the socialist and egalitarian commitments of the Congress Party were hardly implemented.

Over time, the spread of democratic politics helped to mobilize India's diverse poor masses. As the old nationalist and elitist style of Congress politics lost sway, Indira Gandhi revamped Congress's sagging popularity by turning populist. Because the institutional capacity to implement antipoverty policies was missing, Indira Gandhi's radical posturing brought turbulence to Indian democracy, damaged the economy, and never provided real benefits to the poor. Ever since her assassination in 1984, Indian politics has been searching for a new center of gravity. Several leaders have come and gone in India since 1984 (see Table 1). Indira Gandhi's son Rajiv Gandhi was prime minister from 1984 to 1988. Following that, several short-lived governments came to power, culminating in the Congress government of Narasimha Rao, who won elections in 1991.

TABLE 1 **Prime Ministers**

	Years in Office	Party
Jawaharlal Nehru	1947–1964	Congress
Lal Bahadur Shastri	1964–1966	Congress
Indira Gandhi	1966–1977	Congress
Morarji Desai	1977–1979	Janata
Charan Singh	1979–1980	Janata
Indira Gandhi	1980–1984	Congress
Rajiv Gandhi	1984–1989	Congress
V. P. Singh	1989–1990	Janata
Chandra Shekhar	1990–1991	Janata (Socialist)
Narasimha Rao	1991–	Congress

Below the national government, many different parties govern India's twenty-three states. The federal system allows for this political diversity, though not without political conflict between the central and state governments. Political power at both the national and state levels is held by the leader of the party with a majority of parliament seats. These leaders formulate policies that are implemented by a permanent bureaucracy (details of these and other institutions of Indian politics will be developed in Section 3). The quality of government below the national level is often poor, contributing to flaring regional and ethnic conflicts.

Contemporary Indian politics poses major questions. For example, what political strategies can help create a successful and durable formula for winning elections? Can appeals to religion provide such a formula? Then, if appeals to the dominant religion provide electoral dividends, what are the implications for India's religious minorities? Can India's democracy cope with numerous religious and other identity-based political conflicts? In other words, democracy and identity politics have become intricately linked in contemporary Indian politics. Will liberalization of India's state-controlled economy provide a basis for increased wealth in that poor country? And finally, what, if any, political and economic strategies will help India's poor millions? These are among the most serious challenges that face Indian leaders and observers who are concerned about the future of this continental-sized, poor democracy.

The central challenge of contemporary Indian politics is how to establish a coherent, legitimate government while using the power of this government to facilitate economic growth and equitable distribution. The former requires forming durable electoral coalitions without exacerbating political passions and ethnic conflicts. The latter, in turn, requires careful experimentation with policies that simultaneously help entrepreneurs produce goods and ensure a fair distribution of the growth in production. How India is coping with these contemporary challenges is discussed in subsequent sections.

SECTION 2
Political Economy and Development

STATE AND ECONOMY

India at the time of independence was largely a poor, agricultural economy. Although it still has a very large agricultural sector today and considerable poverty continues, India of the 1990s also has a fairly substantial industrial base and a vibrant middle class. The current Congress government under Narasimha Rao has listed liberalization of India's economy as one of its main priorities. Before discussing what liberalization entails, why it has become a main priority, and some of its implications for Indian politics, it is important to review the development of the Indian political economy.[7]

As noted in Section 1, the Indian economy at the time of independence was not dynamic. Production in agriculture was controlled by a variety of traditional landlords and was generally stagnant. The larger of these landowning elites had been allies of the colonial government and were often political adversaries of the new nationalist rulers of India. By contrast, a small but significant group of Indian industrialists and business-people worked closely with India's emerging national-ist politicians because the views and the interests of the two elites converged: Nationalists like Nehru, even when socialist in rhetoric, wanted self-sufficient and rapid industrialization of India and thus needed the cooperation of indigenous industrialists; Indian indus-trialists, in turn, eagerly viewed the large Indian mar-ket as a place to sell their products and needed the nationalist politicians to raise tariffs and create quotas to protect the Indian market from British and other foreign goods.

Nehru and the Congress leaders created a series of Five Year Plans for India's industrialization. National-ist in temperament, these leaders were suspicious of involving foreign investors in India's economic devel-opment. If Indian investors were to be encouraged, however, they needed support from the government and protection from the more advanced foreign com-petitors. Indian government thus undertook a series of coordinated economic activities: It made significant public sector investments to create such heavy indus-tries as steel and cement; it provided protection to in-digenous entrepreneurs from foreign competition; where possible, it further subsidized these producers; and finally, it created elaborate rules and regulations controlling the activities of private producers. The combined result was that India rapidly developed a substantial industrial base over the next few decades. This rapid progress, however, was not without prob-lems. First, given the lack of competition, much of this industry was inefficient by global standards. Second, the elaborate rules and regulations controlling private economic activity encouraged corruption as entrepre-neurs bribed bureaucrats to get around the rules and proceed. And third, the focus on heavy industry di-rected a substantial portion of new investment into buying machinery rather than creating jobs.

To improve India's agriculture, Congress's lead-ers promised the redistribution of land from land-owners to tillers. Their rationale was that such a move would simultaneously weaken the former supporters of colonial government and improve the incentives of those who till the land to increase production. Al-

though some of the largest landowners were indeed eliminated in the early 1950s, the poor tenants and agricultural laborers received very little land. Unlike the communist government in China, India's national-ist government had neither the will nor the capacity to undertake radical property redistribution. Instead, most of the land remained in the hands of medium- to large-sized landowners. As stated earlier, many of these became part of the Congress machine when that party sought to win elections in the countryside. This development further weakened Congress's capacity to side with the poor in the countryside, and diluted its socialist commitments to the point of ineffectiveness.

The failure of land reforms led to a new agricul-tural strategy in the late 1960s known as the **green revolution** strategy. Instead of addressing land redis-tribution, this strategy sought to provide those who owned land with improved seeds and access to subsi-dized fertilizer. However, because irrigation was es-sential for this strategy to succeed, and because irrigation was only assured to larger farmers in some parts of India, the success of the green revolution was spotty. Production increased sharply in some parts of India, such as the Punjab, but in other regions the poorer farmers often got left behind. Nevertheless, In-dia grows enough food to feed its population, even exporting some, and has avoided the worst scenarios of mass starvation and famines.

Between 1950 and 1980, the Indian government facilitated what is best described as state-led eco-nomic development. The nationalist rulers hoped to strengthen India's international position by promoting self-sufficient industrialization. To a great extent the Indian government succeeded in achieving this goal (see Figure 1). Even though it is a poor country, by 1980 India was a major industrial power that produced its own steel, airplanes, automobiles, chemicals, mili-tary hardware, and most consumer goods. On the agri-cultural side, although land reforms failed, a revised agricultural strategy improved food production.

This pattern of state-led development insulated the Indian economy from the dynamics of global pro-duction and exchange while allying the Indian state with its business and landowning classes. This strat-egy resulted in modest economic growth: not as im-pressive as that achieved in such countries as Brazil, Mexico, or the Republic of Korea (South Korea), but better than the performance of such African countries as Nigeria. The main beneficiaries of this economic

Figure 1   Relative Proportions of Economic Sectors
Note: Figures from the mid-1990s are approximate.

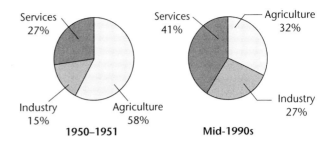

Services 27%
Industry 15%
Agriculture 58%
1950–1951

Services 41%
Agriculture 32%
Industry 27%
Mid-1990s

growth were business classes, medium and large land-owning farmers, and political and bureaucratic elites. A substantial urban middle class also developed during this phase. However, growth in industrial jobs was very modest; for a poor country, India directed too much of its investment into buying machinery rather than into creating jobs. In addition, poor tenant farmers and landless laborers failed to gain much from this pattern of growth. As a result, a large proportion of India's population—as much as 40 percent—did not share the fruits of this growth. Also, population continued to increase throughout this period, so the number of very poor people living in India increased substantially during these decades.

Since 1984, various Indian governments have been more or less committed to the liberalization of India's economy.[8] Liberalization has both a domestic and an international component. The government has sought to dismantle its own controls over private sector economic activities, especially in industry, and to improve the economic performance of the relatively large public sector (see Figure 2 on the following page). With respect to the global economy, the attempt has been to attract more foreign investment and to buy and sell more products from other countries, especially Western countries.

A number of global and national level changes moved India in this new economic direction. Throughout the 1980s, socialist models of development came under attack globally; India did not escape this worldwide trend. Within India, the political and economic elites were increasingly dissatisfied with India's relatively sluggish economic performance, especially in comparison to dynamic East Asian economies; for example, while India's economy during the 1970s grew at the rate of 3.4 percent per year, that of South Korea grew at 9.6 percent. This new elite, less nationalist and socialist than its 1950s counterparts, interpreted India's slow economic growth as a product of too many

governmental controls and of India's relative insulation from the global economy. India's business and industrial classes had grown during the intervening decades; now they increasingly found government intervention in the economy more of a hindrance than a help. Last, the elites were realizing that increased production would have to be sold to buyers abroad because India's poor did not have enough income to consume the new products.

India's economy did relatively well during the 1980s—growing at nearly 5 percent per year—especially in comparison to the dismal performance of many debt-ridden Latin American and African economies, such as Brazil and Nigeria, during the same period. Some of this improved performance resulted from the economic liberalization that integrated India more and more into production and exchange on a global scale. However, a large part of it was not very sound because it was based on increased borrowing from abroad, which followed a shift away from a fairly conservative fiscal policy. An expansionary fiscal policy, largely funded by foreign loans, was harmful because India's exports to other countries did not grow very rapidly—for example, India's exports during the 1980s grew at approximately 6 percent per year in comparison to 12 percent per year for both South Korea and China. As a result, the need to pay back the money borrowed from others in foreign currency grew and put enormous pressure on the government toward the end of the decade. India was forced to borrow even more foreign currencies from such international agencies as the International Monetary Fund (IMF), which generally lend money only on condition that a government dismantles protection and other forms of economic regulation. The Indian government entered into an agreement with the IMF in 1991 to further liberalize India's economy. This external pressure was the last of the forces that have propelled India to shift its economic direction.

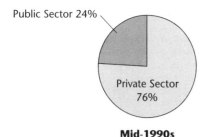

Mid-1990s

Figure 2   Economic Share of Private and Public Sectors
Note: Private sector includes agriculture. Figures from the mid-1990s are approximate.

Despite these external and internal changes, Indian government's efforts to liberalize the economy have not been consistent, perhaps because it is difficult to make sharp policy changes in India's large, cumbersome democracy. India's leaders are often worried about the impact these policy changes will have on their future electoral prospects. For example, the liberalization package involved reduction in government spending, but many groups in society who benefit from government spending reacted negatively to this planned reduction. So when Rao's government sought to reduce subsidies on fertilizer in 1992, farmers across India protested and the government made a hurried policy retreat. Other policy changes also affect specific groups adversely. Organized Indian labor, for example, reacted negatively to governmental efforts to improve the efficiency of the public sector, an effort that is likely to involve significant layoffs. This reaction has made the Indian government hesitant to sell public sector companies to private buyers. Even Indian business resisted certain aspects of the government's 1993 economic program, especially those parts aimed at encouraging foreign investors and goods that Indian industrialists find threatening.

The liberalization program affects India's industry more directly than its agriculture. During the 1980s, India's agricultural production made steady and modest progress. Weather patterns, especially the timeliness of seasonal rains (the monsoons), continue to have significant bearing on Indian agriculture. Government policy also matters, but during the 1980s it was of secondary importance. Agricultural production in India is dominated by medium- and small-sized peasant farmers. (Even the largest landowners in India

are small by global standards; any one who owns 40 to 50 acres of land is considered a large landowner.) The majority of the land is cultivated by farmers owning between 5 and 30 acres of land. Medium-sized and even some small farmers tend to use tenants or hired laborers to till the land. Scattered across different regions of India, millions of these peasant farmers are themselves divided by language and local culture, and even within the same region, they often belong to different castes, live in dispersed villages, and lack frequent communication with each other. As a result, India's peasant farmers are not readily organizable as a distinct and cohesive national-level political force. When their political presence is felt at the national level, it is through the indirect means discussed below. More often, landowning agriculturalists tend to be a powerful political force in state and local governments.

As a result of the green revolution, the largest landowning peasant farmers have in the recent years become quite well-off in some states of India, notably the Punjab and Haryana. Increased wealth has also enabled these peasant farmers to become a political force. When the national government attempts to implement policies that may affect these groups adversely—as, for example, the removal of fertilizer subsidies—they express their opposition through mass protests and demonstrations. In this way, although they are not a well-organized political force, these peasant farmers can block the implementation of government policies. Moreover, because of their large numbers, most political leaders must consider the interests of these well-off peasants to attract their electoral support.

Below the national level, landowning peasant farmers play an influential political role in most Indian states, especially in the green revolution states. In some other states, the landowning peasant status tends to overlap with caste status; for example, in parts of Uttar Pradesh and Bihar, medium-sized agriculturalists are often members of the "backward castes," or a caste status that is intermediate, somewhere between the high-caste Brahmins and the lowly untouchables. This overlap between middle-level economic and caste positions strengthens the identity of members of this group, who often vote as a bloc and thus become a significant political force. For example, in the state elections held in Uttar Pradesh in 1993, the backward castes in alliance with the scheduled castes elected a

The water buffalo provides several uses: pulling a plough during cultivation; as a dairy animal; and for pulling carts. Source: © Robert Nickelsburg/ Gamma-Liaison.

state-level government from their numbers and thus displaced Brahmins and other elite castes from ruling positions. (This alliance came undone in 1995.)

Within India, governmental and bureaucratic elites, business and industrial classes, and large and medium landowning farmers are generally the privileged groups.[9] Considering that India is a very poor country, many of these privileged groups are not that affluent by global standards. Moreover, these groups constitute India's ruling strata, and although there are differences and conflicts among them, for most purposes, they manage to work together. They share many more interests and views with each other than they do with the bottom half of India's poor, lower caste groups.

Social Welfare Policy

India's poor are a diverse, heterogeneous, and enormous social group comprising nearly half of that country's population. Most of India's population lives in villages, so it is not surprising that most of these poor also live in villages. (This doesn't mean that there isn't substantial urban poverty; rather, their relative numbers are small. Those who have steady jobs in the cities, such as factory labor, especially labor that is organized in unions [more on this later], tend not to be all that poor by Indian standards.)

The truly poor of India tend to be peasant farmers who own little land, agricultural tenants, landless labor-

ers in villages, and those without regular jobs in cities who eke out a living on society's margins, often hoveled into shanty towns, or living on the streets of cities like Calcutta or Bombay. Although most of these poor remain politically disorganized, their political weight is felt in several ways. First, their sizable numbers impel many Indian politicians to adopt populist or socialist electoral platforms. Second, because many of the poor share a lower-caste status (especially within specific states), their group identity and united electoral behavior can have considerable impact on electoral outcomes. In some states such as West Bengal and Kerala, there is a long history of radical politics; the poor in these states are well organized by communist or socialist parties and they have periodically helped elect left-leaning governments to power. Third, the anger and frustration of the poor probably provides the raw material for many contemporary "movements of rage" within India. Although it is difficult to illustrate exactly how poverty leads the poor to participate in demonstrations, riots, or religious and other ethnic movements, the fact is that the participants in many incidents of political violence are the young and the poor.

The last point to be made in this discussion of the state and economy concerns government policies aimed at improving the lot of the poor.[10] Over the years, Indian governments have tried different programs aimed at poverty alleviation, some of which have been successful, although most have not. Given the breadth of poverty in India, it is nearly impossible for any government to attempt a comprehensive welfare program. Redistribution of agricultural land to the poor was attempted but was mostly a failure compared to countries like China, where radical land redistribution was a key component of a successful assault on poverty. As a communist dictatorship, however, China could use government coercion to implement property redistribution. In some Indian states, such as West Bengal and Kerala, elected communist governments have also had some success in land redistribution. Overall, however, land reforms have proved to be nearly impossible in India's democracy.

India has very few Western-style welfare programs such as unemployment insurance, comprehensive public health, or guaranteed primary education. Some of these programs exist on paper but are not effective in practice. The size of the welfare problem is considerable and would tax the energy of any government. And it is scandalous that no Indian government has ever attempted to provide universal primary education, although under pressure from both Western and Indian observers, there may be some policy movement in this area in the near future.

The one set of welfare-enhancing programs that has had modest success in India are public employment programs. These programs enable the national and state governments to allocate a portion of the public budget to such projects as the construction of roads or bridges, or the cleaning of agricultural waterways. Because the poor in villages are often unemployed for nearly half the year when there are no agriculture-related jobs, public employment programs become their off-season source of employment and income. Many surveys have demonstrated that such programs do help the poor, though the impact is not sufficient to improve their living conditions beyond the short run. In recent years, however, under the impact of liberalization policies, government budgets have been under considerable pressure, creating a squeeze on public investments, especially in such areas as public employment.

SOCIETY AND ECONOMY

So far the focus of this section has been on the state, social classes, and economy of India. In addition, the following issues need to be discussed to understand India's political economy: the growing size of the population; the status of women and children; the role of caste; and the role of intellectuals and the media in public life.

India's large population continues to grow at a relatively rapid pace. For better or for worse, in the early part of the next century India will become the largest country in the world, surpassing China. This suggests that India's population is growing at a faster rate than that of China. Some observers argue that high rates of population growth are not a problem for countries like India and China because more people provide more labor and labor is an economic asset. However, most demographers do not accept this position. Countries like India already have more labor than they can use productively, thus rapid population growth hinders economic growth. Simply put, the more people there are, the more mouths there are to feed, and the more food and economic products must be produced to maintain society's standard of living, not to mention improve it.

Why should India's population continue to grow at such a rapid pace? The underlying causes are rather complex. The comparison with China again helps. The communist-led government of China has pursued very strict birth control policies—one child per family—since the late 1970s. In part, coercion was used to implement these policies, which did succeed in bringing down birthrates. India's democratic government, by contrast, has found it difficult to implement population control. Rates of population growth in some Indian states have slowed. For example, whereas the national rate of population growth is around 2.3 percent per year, the rate in Kerala is 1.4 percent, close to that in China in the early 1990s. This statistic has important implications; it suggests that governmental coercion is not necessary to control population growth rates. What has helped Kerala is one of the highest literacy rates, especially female literacy rates, in India. Whereas the national average female literacy rate in India is around 35 percent (for males, it is around 64 percent), Kerala's female literacy rate is 87 percent. It has thus been reasoned that, because literate women are more likely to adopt birth controls, female literacy is probably responsible for bringing down rates of population growth in states like Kerala. If true, an important policy implication is that the education of women plays a significant role in bringing down the rates of population growth in countries like India.

India has a large population of child laborers. The failure to require every child to be enrolled in a primary school contributes to this unfortunate practice.
Source: © Grosset-Spooner/Gamma-Liaison.

India has the world's largest population of child labor.[11] Children are employed widely, not only in agricultural labor, but also in such urban enterprises as matchmaking and rug weaving factories, and in numerous services such as selling tea or sweets at train stations. This is a problem, not only because children often work long hours, under difficult conditions, and at low wages, but because it deprives a segment of the population an opportunity to develop themselves through education and thus advance upward. The issue of child labor is closely related to the issue of India's failure to provide universal primary education. If school-age children were required to be in school, they could not be readily employed as full-time laborers. Many Indian elites argue that in their poor country, compulsory primary education is not an affordable luxury. However, this argument is not very persuasive; many poor African countries have higher rates of primary school enrollments than does India. The more likely obstacle to universal primary education is India's caste system. Many upper-caste elites do not readily see lower-caste children as potentially their equals, and thus they do not consider the issue of educating lower-caste children as a priority. The deep-rooted cultural inequalities of India thus lock children into wage labor and out of schools.

Caste issues pervade many other aspects of India's political and economic life. Not only does caste affect nearly all aspects of social life—social interactions, marriages, choice of occupation, social status, and political behavior—caste also influences India's political economy in several ways as well. First, by assigning people to specific occupations, it impedes the free movement of labor and talent. Although the link between caste and occupation has been weakening in India, especially in urban areas, it is nevertheless a very important principle on which employment is organized. And to the extent that caste inhibits the free movement of labor, it is an economic deficit for Indian society. Second, in the political arena, caste is a powerful force around which political groups and voting blocs coalesce. Although this is discussed in detail in Section 4, two side effects of this general tendency need to be mentioned here: because caste is usually a local category, to a large extent Indian politics takes on a local and segmented quality; and related to this, caste cuts across class, making it difficult for labor, business, and other economic classes in India to act in a politically cohesive manner. Third, Indian government often uses caste as a basis for reservations, the Indian version of affirmative action. The government reserves some jobs, admissions into universities, and similar privileges, for members of specific, underprivileged castes. This has become a highly contentious issue in Indian politics. And last, those who suffer the most in India's caste system are those at the bottom of the caste hierarchy, namely, the untouchables. Nearly 10 percent of India's population, or some 90 million people in India are categorized by the Indian census as untouchable. Notwithstanding considerable governmental efforts, the social stigma against members of this group runs deep in India. Because many untouchables are also poor, they suffer doubly: Poverty and social ostracism lead to a lack of dignity.

A variety of social injustices abound in India's political economy. Nevertheless, it is important to end this discussion by noting that there is widespread recognition of these injustices within India and that they

Figure 3   Major Trading Partners
India's main exports consist of textiles, handicrafts, and machinery and metal products. Imports include petroleum products, capital goods, precious stones, and chemicals. This data is from the early 1990s.

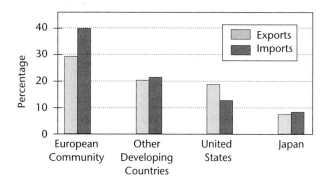

are discussed, debated, and challenged widely. India is a free and democratic country with a lively public culture. Although it is plagued by poverty, India has a significant middle class, many of whom are highly educated and politically active. India's media, especially its newspapers and magazines, are as free as any in the world. They endlessly debate what is wrong with India and its politicians and thus maintain the pressure for public action. This combination of a vocal intellectual stratum and a free press is a cherished one in India's democracy; its role, as well as the potential role of organized poor groups, sustains hope that pressures to address challenging social problems will be maintained within India. We will return to a more detailed discussion of caste-oriented and other types of identity politics in Section 4.

INDIA AND THE INTERNATIONAL POLITICAL ECONOMY

After a prolonged colonial experience, nationalist India in the 1950s shunned economic links with the outside world. Although India pursued an active foreign policy as a leader of the **nonaligned bloc,** it was defensive in its economic contacts. A prolonged and successful nationalist movement helps explain both the urge within India to play a global political role and to protect its economy from foreign influences. As mentioned earlier, India's political and economic elites favored protectionism in trade and sought to limit foreign investment. Although three decades of autarky of this type helped generate an industrial base and domestic capitalism within India, at the same time several new problems arose. Today India possesses a fairly diverse industrial sector but it is relatively inefficient by global standards. The recent efforts to liberalize and reintegrate the Indian economy into the world

economy are in part aimed at dealing with such nagging problems. And these new efforts have also run into some obstacles.

During the three decades of relatively autarkic development, powerful groups emerged that now have vested interests in maintaining the old order. To illustrate, many bureaucrats distorted the system of governmental controls over private economic activities for personal enhancement, often accepting bribes before releasing a government license to start a private business. Indian industry was often relatively inefficient because neither cheaper foreign goods nor foreign investors were readily allowed into India. Moreover, organized labor, especially in government-controlled factories, has a stake in maintaining the inefficient factories because jobs depend on them. These well-entrenched groups resist liberalization and threaten to throw their political weight behind opposition parties, making the ruling Congress government rather hesitant to undertake any decisive policy shift.

The other significant component of India's international political economy concerns its regional context. India is a giant among the other South Asian countries of Pakistan, Bangladesh, Sri Lanka, Nepal, and Bhutan, though its northern neighbor is an even bigger and more powerful giant, the People's Republic of China. Since 1947, India has experienced a fair amount of regional conflict: a war with China in 1962; three wars with Pakistan, the last of which was fought in 1971 and precipitated the break-up of Pakistan into the two states of Pakistan and Bangladesh; a military intervention into strife-torn Sri Lanka in the 1980s; and on-and-off troubled relations with Nepal. The net impact is that India has not developed extensive economic interactions with its neighbors. Figure 3 compares India's exports and imports with its major trading partners. As many nations look more and more to their neighbors for trade and investment, the pressure on India and its neighbors to put their mutual conflicts aside for increased economic contact is likely to grow. Some move in this direction was already evident in the first half of the 1990s, especially toward China, but there is still a long way to go before South Asia develops an integrated zone of economic activity.

SECTION 3

Governance and Policy-Making

ORGANIZATION OF THE STATE

India is a democratic republic with a parliamentary and a federal system of government.[12] The constitution adopted in 1950 created this system, and although there have been many profound changes since then in the distribution and the use of power, the basic character of India's political system has remained unchanged. Moreover, for much of this period India has been a stable, democratic country with mass adult suffrage and periodic elections at all levels—local, provincial, and national. This continuity and democratic stability are remarkable among developing countries. Note the contrast with such other countries as Brazil and Nigeria. To simplify a complex reality, the main explanation for this stability is that Indian democracy has accommodated many new power challenges, while successfully repressing the most difficult ones. This highlights the fact that India's democratic institutions, though always under pressure, have achieved considerable resilience and established their authority to effectively mobilize sufficient coercion that the most serious political threats to its integrity are contained.

India's constitution is a lengthy and, in contrast to the British one on which it is modeled, a written document that is periodically amended by legislation. Among its special features, three are worth noting. First, unlike many constitutions, the Indian constitution directs the Indian government to promote social and economic equality and justice. The constitution thus goes beyond stipulating formal procedures of decision making and allocating powers among political institutions to outlining substantial goals of politics and of the state. Although the impact of such constitutional provisions on governmental policies is limited, the provisions provide normative standards within which issues of welfare and social justice cannot be readily ignored as governmental responsibilities. Second, the Indian constitution, similar to the U.S. Constitution, provides for freedom of religion, thus making India a secular state. This is an especially controversial issue in contemporary Indian politics because one of the major political parties, the BJP, is committed to establishing Hinduism as a state-sanctioned religion. And third, the Indian constitution allows for the temporary suspension of many democratic rights under conditions of emergency. These provisions have been used, somewhat understandably, under conditions of a national security threat during wars with Pakistan or China, but more disturbingly to deal with internal political threats. The most dramatic example of the latter was the national Emergency from 1975 to 1977, when a politically vulnerable Indira Gandhi suspended many democratic rights and imprisoned her leading political opponents.

India's federal system of twenty-three states is relatively centralized. The central government controls the most essential government functions such as defense, foreign policy, taxation and public expenditures, and economic planning, especially industrial planning. State governments, by no means powerless, formally control such policy areas as agriculture, education, and law and order within the states. Because they are heavily dependent on the central government for funds in these policy areas, however, the power of states is limited.

The main institutions comprising India's central state are a president, a prime minister, a cabinet, two houses of parliament, and a permanent bureaucracy. The office of the president is largely ceremonial. By contrast, the prime minister is the linch-pin of the system because effective power is concentrated in that office, where most of the country's important policies originate. In periodic national elections, 544 members of *Lok Sabha,* the lower house of the bicameral parliament, are elected. *Lok Sabha* is much more politically significant than the *Rajya Sabha,* the upper house. The leader of the party with a majority (or in some circumstances, with the largest number of seats) in the *Lok*

Sabha usually becomes the prime minister, even though the prime minister is formally appointed by the president. The prime minister governs with the help of the cabinet, which periodically meets to discuss important issues, including any new legislation that is likely to be initiated. Individually, these cabinet members are the heads of various ministries—for example, the Ministry of Foreign Affairs or the Ministry of Industry—that direct the daily work of the government and make up the permanent bureaucracy.

THE EXECUTIVE

The president is elected indirectly by an electoral college, using a complex formula that ultimately involves elected representatives from both the national and state governments. In most circumstances, the president acts on the advice of the prime minister and is thus not a very powerful political figure in India. The presidency is a ceremonial office, symbolizing the unity of the country, and supposedly above partisan politics. Under exceptional circumstances, however, especially when the selection of a prime minister becomes a complex issue, the president can play an important political role. For example, in the early 1990s when no party had a clear majority in the *Lok Sabha,* the president had to decide whether to call new elections or to let the party with the most seats try to form a government.

The prime minister and the cabinet are the most powerful political figures in India. Because they represent the majority party in parliament, the passage of a bill is not always as complicated a process as it can be in a presidential system, especially one with a divided government. The prime minister and the cabinet also head various ministries, so that after legislation is passed, they oversee its implementation. In practice, the permanent bureaucracy, especially the senior and middle-level bureaucrats are truly responsible for policy implementation. Nevertheless, as in most parliamentary systems, such as those in Britain, Germany, and Japan, there is considerable overlap in India between the executive and the legislative branches of the government, creating a greater degree of centralization of power than at first seems evident.

The issue of who will become the prime minister has been a rather dramatic and infrequent issue in India's political life. Between 1950 and 1984, except for a few brief interludes, India had only two prime ministers: Nehru and Indira Gandhi. This is nearly unique among democracies; it underlines the powerful hold that the Nehru-Gandhi family had on India's political imagination, including the imagination of poor, illiterate Indians. Since then, however, India has had a more rapid turnover in prime ministers—four different leaders have ruled India since 1984. Rajiv Gandhi, Indira Gandhi's son, succeeded his mother after her assassination in 1984. When he lost power four years later, there were two attempts to form non-Congress governments under the leadership of V. P. Singh and Chandra Shekhar, respectively. Factionalism within the loose coalitions that comprised these non-Congress governments, however, curtailed these attempts. As Rajiv Gandhi campaigned in a bid to return to power, he too was assassinated. Subsequently, the Congress Party did win elections and again returned to power in 1990 with Narasimha Rao as prime minister.

The method of selecting a prime minister in India is fairly complex. The original choice of Nehru was a natural one, given his prominent position in the nationalist movement. The choice of Indira Gandhi was less obvious. She was chosen to head the Congress Party by a group of prominent, second-tier party leaders. Her choice reflected several considerations, the most important of which was her national name recognition and its ability to attract the popular vote. Although the process of passing power from a father to a daughter may appear rather feudal—which to some extent it is—there is valid electoral rationality for such a choice in India. A similar logic prevailed when Rajiv Gandhi was chosen by party elites to succeed his mother. The underlying logic was especially powerful: Rajiv Gandhi inherited all the political sympathy generated by his mother's assassination; his leadership enabled the Congress Party to return to power in 1984 with a handsome electoral majority.

Following Rajiv Gandhi's assassination, the Nehru-Gandhi family line had reached a natural end: Rajiv Gandhi was married to an Italian, Sonia Gandhi, and their children at the time were in college, too young to enter politics. The Congress Party was desperate enough that it attempted, unsuccessfully, to recruit Sonia Gandhi as its leader. Given the importance of the Nehru-Gandhi family in Indian politics, however, the eventual reemergence of Sonia Gandhi, or of her children, as leaders cannot be ruled out. The choice of Narasimha Rao was unusual, for he was about to retire from active politics. He was brought back as an "elder statesman," nonthreatening and ac-

"I have no ambitions. . . . My only aim is to serve the people—I'll serve them better if I become the Prime Minister."

A typical Indian politician couches his political ambitions in the idiom of public service.

Source: Keshav, courtesy *The Hindu*, Madras.

ceptable to competing factions within Congress. Narasimha Rao is the first prime minister from the south of India; all the previous heads of state have been from the north. In fact, but for one exception, they all had their political base in the most populous, north central, poor but politically significant, state of Uttar Pradesh.

After the leader of the ruling party, and thus the prime minister, has been selected, he or she chooses the cabinet, mostly from among the party's elected members to parliament. Seniority, competence, and personal loyalty are the top criteria that any prime minister takes into account when choosing the cabinet ministers. Regional and caste representation at the highest level of the government must also be considered in forming a government. During Indira Gandhi's rule, personal loyalty was critical in the choice of senior ministers. Rajiv Gandhi, by contrast, put a high premium on competence, which unfortunately he equated with youth and technical skills, at the expense of political experience. Narasimha Rao, an experienced politician, has put together an eclectic cabinet. With a narrow power base, he is less free than his predecessors to select a personally loyal cabinet. Rather, he has needed to include all those with power in one region or another of India, while taking into account issues of competence and caste balance, as well as ensuring that potential challengers are either co-opted or kept at bay.

The Bureaucracy

The prime minister and cabinet ministers run the government in close collaboration with senior civil servants. Each senior minister oversees what is often a sprawling bureaucracy, staffed by some very competent, overworked, senior civil servants and by many not so competent, underworked, lowly bureaucrats, well known for their long tea breaks while they stare at mounds of unopened files.

Because political leaders come and go, whereas senior civil servants stay, many civil servants possess a storehouse of knowledge and expertise that makes them very powerful. The higher-level civil servants in India reach their positions after considerable experience within the government. They enter the service, formally known as the **Indian Administrative Service (IAS),** at a relatively young age, usually in their early twenties, by passing a highly competitive general exam. Some of India's most talented young men and women were attracted to the IAS during the 1950s and the 1960s, underlining the prestige that service in national government used to enjoy in Indian society. This attraction of the IAS has declined, however, and many talented young people now also go into engineering or business administration or, if possible, leave the country for better opportunities abroad. Government services have become tainted as arenas of corruption have developed and the level of professionalism within the IAS has eroded, mainly because politicians prefer the criteria of loyalty over merit and seniority in promotions. Nevertheless, the IAS continues to recruit very talented young people, many of whom mature into dedicated senior civil servants, and who still constitute the backbone of the Indian government.

The IAS produces India's elite bureaucrats, those who occupy a critical but relatively thin layer at the top of India's sprawling bureaucracy. The competence of these elite bureaucrats is a central reason why India is moderately well governed. Below the IAS, unfortunately, the level of talent and professionalism drops rather sharply. Within each ministry at the national level, and in many parallel substructures at the state level, the bureaucracy in India is infamous for corruption and inefficiency. These problems contribute to the gap that exists in India between good policies made at the top and their poor implementation at the local level.

The Military and Police

The Indian military, with more than a million well-trained and armed men, is a highly professional organization that enjoys the respect of Indian society.[13] Unlike the militaries in many other developing countries—say, Brazil and Nigeria—the Indian military has never intervened directly in politics. This has as much, or more, to do with the fact that India has a relatively well-functioning democracy, as it has to do with the character of the Indian military. Over the years, however, the continuity of constitutional, electoral politics and a relatively apolitical military have come to reinforce and strengthen each other. Civilian politicians provide ample resources to the armed forces and, for the most part, let them function as a professional organization. The armed forces, in turn, obey the orders of democratically elected leaders and, although they lobby to preserve their own interests, for the most part they stay out of the normal tumble of democratic politics.

Since the 1980s, two factors have weakened this well-institutionalized separation of politics and military. First, during Indira Gandhi's rule, political agreement with and loyalty to political leaders became criteria for securing top military jobs. This policy tends to politicize the military and narrow the separation between politics and military. The second factor is the growing political problems within India, especially regional and ethnic demands for secession. (This issue will be discussed in greater detail in the next section.) As these demands became more intense in some states, notably the Punjab and Kashmir, and as those making the demands armed themselves, occasionally with the help of India's hostile neighbor Pakistan, the Indian government called in the armed forces. However, soldiers are not trained to resolve political problems; rather, they are trained to use armed coercion to force compliance from reluctant political actors. As a result, not only have democratic norms and human rights been violated within India, but the distance between politics and the military has further narrowed.

A similar trend toward politicization and deprofessionalization has occurred in India's sprawling po-

lice services, but with a difference. The Indian police organization was never as professionalized as the Indian armed forces, and the police services in India come under the jurisdiction, not of the central government, but of various state governments. Because state governments are generally less well run than the national government, the cumulative impact is that the Indian police are no longer apolitical civil servants. State level politicians regularly interfere in police personnel issues and police officers, in turn, regularly oblige politicians who help them. The problem is especially serious at lower levels where police officials interact with members of society. The image of the average police officer in most of India is not positive: The police are rightly viewed as easily bribed and often allied with criminals or politicians. In some states such as Bihar and Uttar Pradesh, police often take sides in local conflicts instead of acting as neutral arbiters or enforcers of laws. Thus they tilt the power balance in favor of such dominant social groups as landowners or upper castes or the majority religious community, the Hindus.

Between the regular armed forces and the state-level police forces, there are paramilitary forces of nearly half a million men. These troops are organized under various names and are controlled by the national government. As Indian politics has become more turbulent over the last two decades, these paramilitary forces have steadily increased; their expansion reflects the Indian government's growing concern over maintaining internal law and order. But because the national government calls on the regular armed forces only as a last resort in the management of internal conflicts and because the state-level police forces are not very reliable, these paramilitary forces are viewed as a way to maintain order, albeit a very expensive solution. A large, sprawling, and relatively ineffective police service continues to remain a problematic presence in Indian society. Also, as terrorists or "freedom fighters" have become better armed, especially in Kashmir, paramilitary forces have proven inadequate to contain them.

OTHER STATE INSTITUTIONS

The Judiciary

An independent judiciary is another component of India's state system. The main institution is the Supreme

Court, comprised of a chief justice and seventeen other judges, nominally appointed by the president, but as in most matters of political significance in India, only on the advice of the prime minister. Once appointed, the judges cannot be removed from the bench until retirement at age sixty-five. The caseload on the Supreme Court, as on much of the Indian legal system, is extremely heavy, with a significant backlog. The main political role of the Supreme Court is to ensure that legislation conforms with the intent of the constitution. Because the Indian constitution is very detailed, the need for interpretation is not as great as in many other countries. Nevertheless, there are real conflicts, both within the constitution and in India's political landscape, that often need to be adjudicated by the Supreme Court.

For example, the constitution protects private property but also urges the government to pursue social justice. Indian leaders have often promulgated socialist legislation such as requiring the redistribution of agricultural land. Legislation of this nature is necessarily considered by the Supreme Court because it potentially violates the right to private property. Many Supreme Court cases have involved the conflict between socialistically inclined legislation and basic constitutional rights. Cases involving other politically significant issues—for instance, rights of bonded labor, rights of religious minorities such as Muslims, and rights of women in society—also periodically reach the Supreme Court for decisions.

Like many other Indian political institutions, the Supreme Court has lost much of its autonomy over the last two decades. The process began during Indira Gandhi's rule when she argued that the court was too conservative and an obstacle to her socialist program. To remedy this shortcoming, she appointed many pliant judges, including a chief justice. The Supreme Court itself more or less succumbed to her wishes during the critical two years of Emergency (1975–1977), when the political and civil rights of many Indians were violated. Unfortunately, this episode cost the Supreme Court considerable prestige as a neutral arbiter in India's state system. No such dramatic instance of a politicized Supreme Court has reoccurred since the late 1970s. Nevertheless, India's highest court, although still a political institution of some significance, is by no means as independent an institution as the founders of India's state system may have

intended and as it was in the first decades following independence.

Local Government

Under its federal system, the balance of power between the central and state governments in India varies according to time and place. In general, the more popular the central government and the prime minister, the more the states feel obligated to the center. During Nehru's, and especially during Indira Gandhi's rule, the states were often quite constrained. By contrast, a weaker government at the center, as for example the Congress government that took office in 1991, enhances the room for state governments to maneuver. When state governments are run by political parties other than the national ruling party—and this is often true in contemporary India—there is considerable scope for center-state conflict. For example, a popular, communist government in West Bengal has in recent years often disagreed with the national government in New Delhi, charging it with "discriminatory" treatment in the allocation of finances and other centrally controlled resources.

The formal structure of the state governments parallels that of the national government. The chief minister of each state heads the state government; the office of the chief minister of a state thus parallels the office of the prime minister nationally. The chief minister is the leader of the majority party (or the party with most seats) in the lower house of the state legislature. As the prime minister does, the chief minister appoints a cabinet and these ministers, in turn, head various ministries staffed by a state level, permanent bureaucracy. In lieu of a president, each state has a governor, appointed by the national president. The governors, like the president, are supposed to serve on the advice of the chief minister, but in practice, they often become politically powerful, especially in states where the national government is at odds with the state government or where state governments are unstable. The governors can dismiss elected state governments and proclaim temporary presidential rule if they determine state governments to be ineffective. When this happens, the elected government is dissolved and the state is governed from New Delhi until fresh elections are called and a new government is elected. Although intended to be a sensible constitutional option, this provision is unfortunately often used by an intrusive national government to achieve political ends in one state or another. For example, following the Ayodhya incident that was described in Section 1, the Supreme Court ruled that the BJP had acted illegally, a decision that allowed Narasimha Rao to dismiss four state governments governed by the BJP. When new elections were held in these four states in November 1993, the BJP returned to power in only one of the four states, contributing to long-term acrimony between the BJP and the Congress.

The power struggle between the central government and the states is an ongoing one. With many Indian states inhabited by people who share different histories and cultures, including language, and with political parties in power at the center that differ from those in the states, the center-state conflicts become multidimensional, couched in the rhetoric of relative jurisdictions, but fueled by substantial political and ethnic conflicts. Although this issue will be discussed in the next section, we should note here that despite the formal division of power between the center and the states, India's central government is really quite powerful.

Below state governments are district, city, and village governments. Given India's size, it is not surprising that the specific forms, quality of personnel, and effectiveness of these local governments greatly varies. Usually, however, most local governments have both elected and bureaucratic personnel. None of these subgovernments are policy-making bodies; instead, policy is made at the national and state levels, with these lower levels responsible for implementation. Thus considerable resources pass through these institutions, and even though local governments seldom enjoy formal discretion over how these resources are allocated, there is ample room for misuse. Local political elites, bureaucrats, and other local "big men" often collude as they decide the location of projects, who gets a contract, or who gets jobs on public projects, all the time ensuring themselves a healthy share of the public money. This is why many local governments in India tend to be corrupt and ineffective. There are some exceptions to this abuse—for example, in the state of West Bengal, a reform-oriented, leftist government has helped improve the functioning of local governments—but for the most part, local governments in India languish and waste resources. As a result, city streets are not kept clean; potholes on paved streets do not get filled; irrigation canals in villages do not get desilted; tube wells are located in the backyards of village "big men"; and rural schools are so poorly built that they leak as soon as the monsoons start.

THE POLICY-MAKING PROCESS

Major policies in India are made at the highest level of the government, in New Delhi, the nation's capital. As mentioned earlier, the prime minister and the senior cabinet ministers are generally responsible for initiating new policies and related legislation. Behind the scenes, senior civil servants in each ministry, as well as in such specific cross-ministry offices as the prime minister's secretariat or the Planning Commission, play a critical role in identifying problems, synthesizing available data, and presenting alternate solutions and their various implications to political leaders. After decisions have been made at the highest level, many of them require new legislation. With the prime minister dependent on a majority in the parliament to remain prime minister, passage of most legislation through the parliament is not a significant political obstacle in India, except in extremely controversial areas. Rather, the real policy drama in India occurs both during the early process when major bills are under consideration and then during the process of implementation. To fully understand these processes, how interests get organized and find representation, needs to be explained.

Examples of several specific policies will help clarify these issues. First, let us take the example of "economic liberalization" policies. These policies represent a major economic change and they are decided at the highest level of government, involving only a handful of senior ministers and bureaucrats. To reach these decisions, however, a fairly complex set of political activities unfold. For example, the decision makers need to consult some of the most important interest groups, such as associations of Indian businessmen or representatives of such critical multinational organizations as the World Bank or the IMF. Others, including those who may be adversely affected, need to be heard; organized labor, for example, may call a one-day general strike (as they actually did) to warn the government that any attempt to privatize the public sector will meet considerable resistance. Newspapers, magazines, and intellectuals also express their support or opposition publicly. Sooner or later, political parties get into the act. Members of the ruling party, the Congress in this case, do not necessarily support the political thinking of their own leaders at the early stage; rather, they worry about the political implications of policies, both for intraparty power struggles, but especially for future elections. Opposition parties, in turn, worry about the interests of their constituencies and adopt a more or less principled stand toward the new policies under consideration—that is, for, against, or somewhere in between. All of these pulls and pushes modify the policy that the government eventually adopts.

After policies have been adopted, their implementation is far from assured. Again, continuing with the liberalization example, some aspects of the new policy package have proven easier to implement than others. Changing the exchange rate (the value of Indian rupee in relation to such currencies as the U.S. dollar) is relatively easy to implement because both the policy decision and its implementation require the actions of only a handful of political and bureaucratic elites. By contrast, the attempts to simplify the procedures for Indian or foreign business executives to create new business enterprises has proven more complicated. Implementation of such policies involves layers of bureaucrats, most of whom at one time benefited from the control they exercised over businessmen. Now, forced to relinquish this control, many of them drag their feet and, where possible, sabotage the newly simplified procedures.

Another example concerns policies aimed at improving the standard of living for the Indian poor; it outlines a related but different set of issues in the policy-making process, especially in the implementation process. For a few decades, the national government has attempted redistribution of agricultural land (land reforms) and provision of public works programs as two policies that may help India's rural poor. The main role of the national government has been to set broad outlines for land reforms and to allocate funds for public works programs. As both of these measures primarily influence rural and agricultural life, and because agricultural issues in India tend to be under the jurisdiction of state govern-

ments, a further refinement of these policies, as well as their implementation, was left to the states. However, state governments vary, both in terms of the class coalitions and political parties that rule within them, as well as in terms of the quality of their bureaucracies. The result is that the implementation of antipoverty policies within India has been quite uneven.

Land redistribution involves taking land from well-off and powerful landlords and redistributing it to poor tenants or agricultural laborers. This is a highly controversial process, requiring some combination of forceful actions by state governments and the organization of the poor beneficiaries. Generally, attempts at land redistribution have been relatively unsuccessful in most Indian states because the interests of landowning classes are well-represented and state-level bureaucrats often have close links to these landowning groups. Partial exceptions to these trends are found in the states of Kerala and West Bengal, where communist state governments and the well-organized poor have made some progress in land reform.

Attempts to generate extra employment for the rural poor through public works projects (such as road construction and canal cleaning) have been somewhat more successful than land redistribution policies because they do not involve any direct confiscation of property. The main issues in the implementation of these policies are the quality of projects chosen and how honestly they are completed. This, in turn, draws attention to the quality of local governments in implementing policies initiated at the national level. Because this quality varies—though rarely is it very high—considerable resources assigned to poverty alleviation programs are wasted. Nevertheless, the policies have been effectively implemented in the states of Maharashtra and West Bengal, where there is considerable political pressure from caste or class politics, and in some southern states, where the quality of local bureaucracy is somewhat better.

To review, the policy-making process in India, though relatively centralized, takes into account various interests and frequently produces well-developed policies. By contrast, the process of implementation is quite decentralized and relatively ineffective. What often start out as sound policy ideas and positive intentions do not always come to fruition, both because policies are diluted as they get redefined at the state level and because of lackluster implementation.

Representation and Participation

THE LEGISLATURE

A good place to begin the discussion of representation and participation in a democracy is with the legislature, one arena in which diverse groups seek representation. The *Lok Sabha* at the national level and the various legislative assemblies at the state level provide such arenas in India. With considerable overlap between the executive and the legislative branches of government, legislative bodies do not have either a direct or significant role in policy-making. Nevertheless, election to a legislature is still much sought after in India, for two reasons. First, because a prime minister or a chief minister of a state needs the support of a majority in the legislature to acquire and maintain a position of leadership, legislatures hold a significant place in the pyramid of power. Second, those who become members of this power structure, although unable to influence policies directly, achieve considerable status, personal access to resources, and influence over allocations within their constituencies.

Elections to the *Lok Sabha* are supposed to be held at least every five years but, as in other parliamentary systems, the prime minister may choose to call elections earlier. India is currently divided into 544 electoral districts of roughly equal population, each of which elects and sends one representative to the national parliament. Those who contest elections generally contest them as nominees of one of the major political parties; that is, they contest them on a party ticket, with the support of one of the parties. Elections in India are won or lost mainly by parties, especially by party leaders, so most legislators are beholden to party leaders for securing a party ticket. Success in elections, therefore, does not depend on an independent power base but on a party whose leader— or, occasionally, whose programs—appeal to the populace. When these victorious legislators reach the *Lok Sabha,* they often fall in line with the goals of the party leadership, especially if the leadership is strong (in other words, has proven its capacity to attract the popular vote in elections).

The main business of the *Lok Sabha* is to pass new legislation, as well as to debate the pros and cons of governmental actions. Most new legislation is introduced by the government, although there are opportunities for independent members to introduce bills. After the political and bureaucratic elite introduce new legislation, as in most parliamentary systems, the new bills are formally announced and then assigned to parliamentary committees for detailed study and discussion. The committees report the bills back to the *Lok Sabha* for debate, amendments, and preliminary votes. Then the bills go to the *Rajya Sabha,* the upper house. Most members of the *Rajya Sabha* are elected indirectly by state legislatures, and some are also nominated. This is not a very powerful body in India; it mostly accepts bills that have been passed by the *Lok Sabha.* After any final modifications, the bills come back for a third reading, after which they are finally voted on in both houses and eventually forwarded to the president for approval.

To understand why the *Lok Sabha* in India does not play a significant independent role in policy-making, keep in mind that (1) new legislation is generally introduced by a small group of government leaders; (2) most legislators, especially those belonging to India's main ruling Congress Party, feel politically beholden to party leaders; and (3) all parties in legislatures use party whips to ensure voting along party lines. One unfortunate implication of parliament's relative ineffectiveness is that its social composition does not have direct policy consequences. In other words, whether members of parliament are business executives or workers, men or women, members of upper or lower castes, is not likely to lead to dramatic policy shifts within India. The policy-making process is relatively centralized and various interest groups influence the policy process through channels other than the legislature. Nevertheless, dramatic shifts in social composition are bound to influence policy, and even if marginal shifts have little impact on policy, many groups in society derive satisfaction from having "one of their own" in the parliament.

TABLE 2   **Major Party Election Results**

	1989		1991	
	Percentage of popular vote	Seats	Percentage of popular vote	Seats
Congress(I)	39.5	197	37.3	225
BJP	11.4	85	19.9	119
Janata Dal	17.8	143	10.8	55
Communists[a]	—	45	—	48

[a]Includes both the CPM and the CPI.

Source: *India Today,* July 15, 1991, 40–55.

The typical member of parliament in India today tends to be a male university graduate between forty and sixty years of age. Over the years, there have been changes in the social composition along some criteria but not others. For example, an average legislator in the 1950s was likely to be a male of urban background, often a lawyer by training, and a member of the higher castes. However, nearly half the members of parliament now come from rural areas, and many have agricultural backgrounds. Members of the middle castes (the so-called backward castes) are also well-represented in the parliament of the 1990s. These changes reflect some of the broad shifts in the distribution of power in Indian society. By contrast, the proportion of women and of poor, lower-caste individuals in the parliament remains abysmally low.

THE PARTY SYSTEM AND ELECTIONS

Political parties and elections are areas where much of the real drama of Indian politics occurs. Parties in control of a majority of seats in the national or in provincial parliaments generally form the national or state government, respectively, and control government resources. Parties thus devote substantial political energy to contesting and winning elections. Since independence, the party system has evolved from one dominated by the Congress Party to one in which the Congress, though still the most powerful national party, is significantly challenged (see Table 2). What began as nearly a one-party system has evolved into a real multiparty system, with at least four potentially significant national parties and many regional parties

competing for power. The four parties with significant national presence are: the Congress(I); the Janata Party; the BJP; and the Communist Party of India (Marxist), or the CPM. Whereas the CPM is a left-leaning party and the BJP is a religious, right-leaning one, both Congress(I) and the Janata are more or less centrist parties. Since the mid-1980s, the electoral fortunes of these parties have risen and fallen, often dramatically.

The Congress(I), usually referred to as the Congress, is India's premiere political party. Many aspects of the Congress have already been discussed because it is impossible to analyze Indian politics without referring to the role of the Congress Party. To briefly summarize, the Indian National Congress, under the leadership of Mahatma Gandhi, Nehru, and others, spearheaded India's nationalist movement during the 1920s and 1930s. After independence, Congress, with Nehru at its helm, was the unquestioned ruling party of India. Over the years, especially since the mid-1960s, this hegemony came to be challenged. Indira Gandhi successfully revived the electoral fortunes of the Congress, but only after it had revamped its identity. The old Congress split into two parties, with one branch—the Congress(O)—dying, leaving the other, Congress(I)—the 'I' standing for Indira Gandhi—to inherit the position of the old, undivided Congress. Except for two interludes when the Janata Party formed governments—during 1977–1980, following the national Emergency and during 1989–1991—all national governments in independent India have been led by the Congress.

Prior to Indira Gandhi, rank-and-file party members elected the lowest-level Congress Party officers, who in turn elected the officers at higher levels of the party organization, up to the position of the party leader who was also the prime minister. In effect, the prime minister was elected from below and by the party. Indira Gandhi reversed this "bottom up" party structure.[14] She gained immense personal popularity by populist appeals to the masses and subsequently created a "top-down" party in which party officers were appointed by the leaders. With some modifications, including some limited internal party elections, this is basically how the contemporary Congress Party is organized. The top-down structure enables the leaders to control the party, but it is a major liability when grassroots support is necessary. As the nation's oldest party, the Congress still continues to attract substantial electoral support. However, if this support ever declined sharply, most likely the party rank and file would demand its reorganization.

Whereas Congress during the 1970s had a left-of-center, pro-poor political platform, beginning in 1984, it moved toward the ideological center under Rajiv Gandhi (Indira Gandhi's son). (See Section 2 for the reasons behind this shift.) Today the current Congress Party tilts right-of-center, championing issues of economic efficiency, business interests, and limited government spending, over the rights of the poor and the working people, and over social questions of health, education, and welfare. Whether this political shift will cost the Congress the support of poor Indians is not fully clear as yet. As a nationalist party, the Congress Party is intimately associated with the stability of the Indian nation and the state in Indian political culture. Irrespective of its economic program, therefore, the Congress has always attracted support from diverse social groups: rich and poor, upper and lower castes, Hindus and Muslims, northerners and southerners. Nevertheless, elections in the 1990s indicate that Congress may be losing some of its traditional constituencies among the poor, lower castes, as well as among such minorities as Muslims. If these trends are not reversed, they could spell considerable political trouble for the Congress.

The Janata Party, India's other centrist party, formed short-lived national governments in 1977 and 1989. The Janata Party, however, is not so much a political party as an umbrella for various parties and factions who move in and out depending on political circumstances. The Janata Party was created in 1977 when several smaller parties, who opposed Indira Gandhi's Emergency, hurriedly united to contest her and, much to their own surprise, won the national elections. This loose coalition, however, lasted only for a little over two years, when conflicting leadership ambitions tore apart the fragile veneer of a party. Subsequently, several political groups, many of whom were at one time or another part of the Congress, attempted to rejuvenate the Janata Party, with mixed results.

During the late 1980s, the Janata Party enjoyed another brief term as a national government, under the leadership of a breakaway Congress leader, V. P. Singh, who championed himself as an honest, native son, battling the corrupt and westernized Rajiv Gandhi. Gandhi was associated with the "Bofors scandal," so-called because the Swedish arms manufacturing company Bofors apparently bribed senior Congress officials in Rajiv Gandhi's government to obtain a lucrative arms contract. With these appeals, the Janata Party won enough seats in the national parliament to form a minority government in 1989. Once again, however, factionalism overwhelmed any attempt at a stable government, and this second attempt with a non–Congress-led government also collapsed after a little over two years. This brought about national elections in 1991 during which Rajiv Gandhi was assassinated during a campaign rally and Narasimha Rao was elected.

The Janata Party has a very weak organizational structure and lacks a distinctive, coherent political platform. To distinguish itself from the Congress, it claims that it is more Gandhian—a reference to the decentralized, village-oriented vision of Mahatma Gandhi for modern India—more rural-oriented, and less pro-Brahmin. Although most efforts at political self-definition have not been very successful, while in power, V. P. Singh undertook one major policy initiative that identified the Janata Party with a progressive cause. This was the acceptance of the Mandal Commission's recommendations that India's backward castes—generally, the middle, rural castes who constitute a near majority in the Indian countryside—be provided substantial reservations (or reserved access) in government jobs and educational institutions. The acceptance of this recommendation produced a nationwide outburst of riots and violence, led by members of upper castes who felt threatened and squeezed. The uproar eventually contributed to the downfall of V. P. Singh's government. Nevertheless, the acceptance of "Mandal" by V. P. Singh associated the Janata Party with the interests of the backward castes. How strongly backward castes will continue to identify with the Janata in the future is unknown. For now, the Janata Party is viewed, especially in north-central India, as a party of small, rural agriculturalists, who generally fall somewhere in the middle of the rigid caste hierarchy—between Brahmins and the untouchables.

The major political challenger of the Congress in contemporary India is the BJP.[15] Although only recently formally constituted in the early 1980s, the party is a direct descendant of the Jana Sangh, an older political party that entered the Indian political scene in 1951. The BJP is a right-leaning, Hindu-nationalist party, the first major party to mobilize explicitly on the basis of religious identity; it is also exclusionary because of appeals to Hindu identity that vilify Muslims. In comparison to both the Congress and the Janata, the BJP is highly organized; it has disciplined party members, who after a prolonged apprenticeship become party cadres, and the authority lines within the party are relatively clear and well respected.

The party is closely affiliated with many related political organizations, the most significant of which is the Rashtriya Sevak Sangh (Association for National Service), known as the RSS. Most BJP leaders were at one time members of the RSS, which recruits youth (especially educated youth in urban areas), and involves them in a fairly disciplined set of cultural activities, including the study of a chauvinistic reinterpretation of India's "great Hindu past." These youth, uniformed in khaki shorts and shirts, can often be seen in Indian cities, doing group exercises in the mornings and evenings, and singing songs glorifying India's Sanskritic civilization (Sanskrit is a classical language in which some of the ancient Hindu scriptures are written). Reminiscent of right-wing fascist groups of interwar Europe, these seemingly innocent youth, involved in an activity no more harmful than a disciplined inculcation of cultural pride, send shivers down the spine of many non-Hindu minorities and many Indian liberals. They recognize the havoc that cultural pride as a mobilized political force has unleashed historically, as for example in Nazi Germany, and may do again in a different setting.

Those traditionally attracted to the Jana Sangh and the BJP were mainly urban, lower-middle-class groups, especially small traders and commercial groups. As long as this was their main source of support, the BJP remained a minor actor on the Indian political scene. Since the mid-1980s, however, the BJP succeeded in dramatically widening its support base using the theme of Hindu nationalism, especially in north-central India. The decline in Congress's popularity created a vacuum that the BJP was well positioned to fill. Moreover, the BJP found in Indian Muslims a convenient scapegoat for the frustrations of various social groups and successfully mobilized Hindus in an attempt to create a religiously oriented political force where none had existed before. The electoral success of the BJP in the 1989 and 1991 elections underscores the party's early success. The Ayodhya incident was a culmination of such efforts by the BJP. However, the BJP fared poorly in elections held in four states in November 1993; whereas they ruled all four until 1993, they failed to elect a parliamentary majority in three of the four in 1993 and thus lost control of these state governments. What these results indicate about the future of the BJP is not clear. There are many poor or otherwise frustrated social groups in India whose anger is available for political mobilization. Whether the BJP will succeed in tapping this anger cannot be predicted. What can be said is that democracy and large pockets of social frustration provide a combustible mix that will continue to generate unexpected outcomes in Indian politics.

The fourth major political party is the Communist Party of India (Marxist), or the CPM. The CPM is an offshoot of the Communist Party of India that was formed during the colonial period and has existed nearly as long as the Congress Party. Though the contemporary CPM has a national presence—that is, it nearly always elects representatives to the *Lok Sabha*—its political base is concentrated in two of India's states, West Bengal and Kerala. These states have often been ruled by the CPM, and they often elect *Lok Sabha* members who run on a CPM ticket.

The CPM is a disciplined party, with party cadres and a sharply hierarchical authority structure. Other than its name and internal organization, however, there is nothing communist about the CPM; it is instead more of a social-democratic party, along the lines of the British Labour Party or the German Social Democratic Party. The CPM accepts the framework of democracy, regularly participates in elections, and often tends to win them in West Bengal and Kerala.

Village women wait in line to get voting slips inside a polling booth in a village in India's Orissa state, March 7, 1995. Source: Reuters/Bettmann.

Within these two states, the CPM enjoys the support of the lower-middle and lower classes, both factory workers and poorer groups of peasants. Within the national parliament, CPM members often strongly criticize government policies that are likely to hurt the poor, though they also on occasion provide support to the Congress against potential threats from the BJP. When the CPM runs state governments, for example in West Bengal and Kerala, it has provided a relatively honest and stable administration. It has also pursued a moderate but effective reform program, ensuring the rights of agricultural tenants (such as preventing their evictions), providing services to those living in shanty towns, and encouraging public investments toward the rural areas.

These four major parties, along with several other minor parties, periodically compete for the votes of the Indian electorate. Elections in India are a colossal event. Nearly 500 million people are eligible to vote in India today and close to 300 million actually vote. The turnout rate in recent elections (1991 and 1989) has been over 60 percent, a level considerably higher than that in the United States. The level of technology that is used both in campaigning and in the conduct of elections is fairly low. Television plays an increasingly important role, but much campaigning still involves face-to-face contact between politicians and the elec-

torate. Senior leaders fly around the country, making speeches to millions of potential supporters at political rallies held in tiny villages and district towns. Lesser politicians and thousands of their party supporters travel the dusty streets, liberally blaring music and political messages from loudspeakers mounted on their vehicles.

Given the high rate of illiteracy, pictures of party symbols become critical: a hand for the Congress(I); a lotus for the BJP; a peasant with a hoe for the Janata; a hammer and sickle for the CPM. The way many voters signify their vote for a candidate in the polling booth is to put their thumb mark on one of these symbols. During the campaign phase, therefore, parties and their representatives work very hard to associate certain individuals and election platforms with specific symbols. A typical election slogan, for example, is, "Vote for the hammer and sickle because they stand for the rights of the working people."

India's electoral system, like the British system, is a first-past-the-post system. A number of candidates compete in an electoral district; the candidate who has the most votes wins. For example, if the Congress candidate wins the most votes, say 35 percent of the vote from a district, and the candidates of other parties split the remaining votes, the Congress candidate is victorious. This system privileges the major political parties, especially the Congress, which typically secured around 40 percent of the popular vote in India's national elections in the past but won more than 60 percent of the seats in the *Lok Sabha*. This system generates considerable pressure for opposition parties to work together so as to not split the non-Congress votes. In practice, however, given the differences between opposition parties and the considerable clash of leadership ambitions, many parties frequently compete, enabling Congress candidates to squeeze by as winners.

POLITICAL CULTURE, CITIZENSHIP, AND IDENTITY

The only generalization that can be made about Indian political culture is that, in such an incredibly large and culturally diverse country, no single set of cultural traits is shared by the entire population. Nevertheless, three important political cultural tendencies—or habits of mind, produced by repeated practice—are worth noting. These political cultural traits reflect India's hybrid political style, as a rigid, hierarchical, and village-oriented old civilization adapts itself to modern socioeconomic changes, especially to the introduction of democratic politics.

Elite factionalism: India's political elite often have difficulty working and cooperating with each other, so a factionalized elite is a well-known characteristic of Indian politics. The roots of such behavior are complex, reflecting India's fragmented social structure; that is why it is considered an aspect of Indian political culture, implying that this style of politics is by now deeply ingrained in India. Although some important exceptions exist, generally the personal political ambitions of Indian leaders frequently prevent them from pursuing such collective goals as forming cohesive political parties, running a stable government, or focusing on problems of national development. An additional consequence is that intra-elite disagreements give Indian politics a "noisy," conflictual quality. In contrast to many East Asian countries, where norms of consensus are powerful and much of politics is conducted behind closed doors, politics in India veers toward the other extreme, with open disagreements and conflicts nearly the norm.

Weak public-private divisions: A related political cultural trait is that India's political and public spheres of activity are not sharply divided from personal and private spheres of activity. India is not unique in this; this is an issue in most developing countries and, in some respects, given its long history of a nationalist movement and its well-established civil service, India has a much better developed sense of the public sphere than, say, many African countries. Nevertheless, the idea that a public office is not a legitimate means for personal enrichment or for furthering the interests of family members or of personal associates is not fully accepted as yet in India. One important result is a fairly widespread misuse of public resources for personal gain, or more directly, widespread corruption in political life.

Social fragmentation: The third political cultural tendency that deserves attention concerns fragmentation of political life in India. Indian society is highly segmented: Different regions have different languages and cultures; within regions, villages are poorly connected with each other; and within villages, different castes often live in isolation from one another. As this segmented and localized society has been drawn into a more homogenizing democratic politics, the results have often been unexpected. For example, there is an expectation in democratic politics that those sharing similar interests may unite politically to pursue collective interests. Following this logic, one may expect the poor in India to come together politically to make collective demands on the state. However, the "habits of mind" in India have inhibited any such group formation based on class, at least so far. Instead, politics is often fragmented along caste lines and even caste grievances tend to remain local, rather than accumulate nationally, or even regionally. Some observers of India find this segmented quality of Indian politics a blessing, because it localizes problems, facilitating political stability; by contrast, others find the same tendency a curse because it stymies the possibility of pursuing reforms to improve the lot of the poorest members of Indian society.

Democracy is relatively well established in India. Most Indians value their citizenship rights and, in spite of poverty and illiteracy, exercise them with vigor. One of the four core themes of this volume is that the urge to control one's government is a powerful force promoting the global spread of democracy. This can certainly be applied to India. However, the spread of democratic politics can simultaneously fuel political conflicts. In India, this spread of democracy is undermining many of India's political givens, including some of the most rigid hierarchies, and has begun to produce new political patterns.

The most significant of these recent developments concerns identity politics, whereby the dynamics of democratic politics mobilizes latent identities to produce powerful collective identities. Region, language, religion, and caste, for example, all help Indians define who they are and, as a result, help them categorize who is a "we" and who is a "they" in political associations and conflicts. Such differences have for some time generated political cleavages in India, underlining both the importance and yet malleability of collective identities; recall the Hindu-Muslim conflict at the time of independence. Some of these identity conflicts remained dormant when Nehru's secular nationalism and Indira Gandhi's poor-versus-rich cleavage defined the core political issues. Over the last ten to fifteen years, however, with the relative decline of the Congress Party and its hold over India's political imagination, and with developments in communications and transportation making people much more aware of each other and their differences, identity-based political conflicts have mushroomed in India. Two of the more significant conflicts deserve mention.

First, caste conflicts, though usually confined to local and regional politics, have taken on a national dimension in recent years. Recall the discussion concerning the acceptance of the recommendations of the Mandal Commission by India's former prime minister, V. P. Singh. These recommendations were meant to benefit India's backward castes, who are numerically significant and who generally tend to be rural agriculturalists by occupation and somewhere in the middle of the caste hierarchy. Groups of backward castes have been politically significant in many states but prior to Mandal, they were seldom a cohesive factor in national politics. In all probability, V. P. Singh, by approving pro–backward caste policies, hoped to create a powerful support base out of disparate groups that could bolster his future electoral prospects. However, the move backfired. The threatened upper or forward castes reacted sharply to V. P. Singh's actions with demonstrations, riots, and considerable political violence. Not only did this disruption contribute to the downfall of V. P. Singh's government, it also converted the conflict between forward and backward castes from a perennial local- and state-level issue to an important and divisive national issue.

The second significant identity-based political conflict that has reemerged in recent years pitches Indian Hindus and Muslims against each other. Tensions between these religious communities have a deep history in India that goes back several centuries to when Muslim rulers from Central Asia conquered and established the Moghul dynasty in India. Stories and memories of the relative greatness of one community over the other, or of atrocities and injustices unleashed on one community by the other, abound in India's popular culture. For the most part, these legends and the related social exclusiveness of the two religious communities create low-level, latent hostilities that do not prevent peaceful coexistence. However, political circumstances, especially political machinations by ambitious leaders, can unleash these latent tendencies and instigate overt conflict. This is what has happened since the mid-1980s as the BJP has whipped up anti-Muslim sentiments in an effort to unite disparate Hindu groups into a united political force. The resulting victimization of Muslims in acts of political violence, including destruction of life, property, and places of worship, emphasizes the dangers of identity-based political passions.

INTERESTS, SOCIAL MOVEMENTS, AND PROTEST

India's democracy is an active one. At any time, numerous groups are demanding a greater share of wealth, status, and/or power from a state or the national government. How business and other elite groups influence the government was discussed above. In addition, organized labor is politically quite active in India. However, labor unions in India are politically fragmented: Instead of the familiar model of one factory/one union, within one factory in India competing unions can be organized by different political parties. Above the factory level, numerous labor organizations compete for labor's support. While unions can bring considerable pressure to bear on both management and politicians, for the most part, they also do not act as a well-organized, national-level political group. The government generally stays out of labor-management conflicts; India's industrial relations are thus closer to the pluralist model practiced in Anglo-American countries than to the corporatist model, say, of Mexico. The political energies of fragmented unions, however, are channeled into frequent local battles involving strikes, demonstrations, and a peculiarly Indian protest institution called *gherao.** Labor politics in India is thus active but not coherent.

Except for big business groups and unionized labor, most demand groups unite mainly for a specific purpose and then often disband. Peasant or farmer groups are a good example of the latter. The better-off peasantry periodically organize in one state or another—and, on occasion, even nationally—to make such demands as higher support prices for agricultural products or increased subsidies for inputs such as fertilizer. As discussed earlier, numerous noneconomic groups, such as those formed around caste and religion, are also very active in Indian politics. The plethora of such political activities underlines the health of Indian democracy, and highlights a central tension in it: Namely, how does any government in such a setting simultaneously accommodate multiple demands and focus on facilitating a coherent program for national development?

There are several active women's movements in India, especially in urban areas but sometimes in rural settings too.[16] These movements may bring together educated, middle-class women and, at other times, poor women. The movements comprised of middle-class women tend to be more durable because they usually aim to alter deeply held attitudes, whereas others are likely to be a protest against an immediate injustice like rape, dowry deaths (a murder or suicide because of a perceived inadequate marriage dowry), or the unrestricted sale of alcohol, which is viewed as responsible for alcoholism among husbands.

A number of environmental movements have also sprouted across India in recent years. These are often led by educated, urban environmentalists who mobilize victims of development projects. For example, the movement against deforestation, called the "Chipko" movement, has been fairly successful. More recently, a movement against a very large project sponsored by the World Bank—construction of a dam over the river Narmada—created quite a stir.

The construction of the dam would have wrought environmental problems, including the displacement of thousands of families who currently live where the dam is planned. The protest was sufficient to cause the World Bank to rescind its support. The Indian government, however, still hopes to pursue the project, despite the possibility of continuing conflict with environmentalists.

A variety of poor people's movements flourish. Most tend to be local and short-lived, but they can mobilize quickly and have considerable political impact. For example, there are a variety of "tribal" groups, often ethnically distinct, who live in remote areas, tend to be very poor, and are categorized as tribals because the government chooses to label them as such. Many of these groups organize political protest, demanding a greater share of public resources, preservation of the meager resources they control, or the like. India's untouchable castes also organize politically to protest caste injustices. In some states, like Bihar, such movements have in recent years become very violent, with various caste groups arming themselves in private armies. At times, issues of caste, tribe, and poverty overlap to produce a highly volatile mix. In the southern state of Andhra Pradesh, for example, poor tribals have been organized by armed revolutionaries who hang village landlords and other perceived exploiters to achieve a measure of local justice. Even though such movements regularly confront the police, usually losing in the resulting encounters, their proliferation illustrates the considerable activism and dissatisfaction in India's political society.

To review, political participation in India has over the years broadened in scope and deepened in intensity. As more and more groups demand a share of power, it can be suggested that forces of democratization in India have spread wide and deep. A single-party dominant system led by the Congress Party has thus slowly been supplanted by a multiparty system in which parties on both the left and the right of the Congress now pose a significant political challenge. Similarly, old hierarchies of caste have eroded in Indian society; upper castes cannot readily control the political behavior of those below them. The result is that many groups in society increasingly feel empowered and hope to translate this new consciousness and sense of cohesiveness into material gains by influencing government policies. The challenge for any

---

* The word *gherao* literally means encirclement. Unhappy labor groups using this protest technique will generally encircle a member of management and will not let him go—sometimes for days—until management meets their demands.

government in India is how to respond to these growing demands; the dilemma is how to promote economic efficiency and growth while channelling resources to these newly empowered groups.

Indian Politics at the Crossroads

POLITICAL CHALLENGES AND CHANGING AGENDAS

Elections were held in several key Indian states between 1993 and 1995. Two of these states were Uttar Pradesh (U.P.) and Bihar, two of India's largest states with populations at nearly 100 million each—larger than Britain, France, or Germany and nearly the size of Brazil. The party in power in U.P. prior to elections, the BJP, failed to recapture power. This was a notable event because it curbed the growing popularity of the Hindu-nationalist party. More significant was who won the elections in these two states. In U.P., it was not the Congress but a coalition of lesser-known parties that garnered the support of the state's middle and lower castes; in Bihar, the Janata Party with a similar caste coalition was elected to power. Whether these specific coalitions hold or not (in U.P. the coalition came undone in the middle of 1995), these developments in India's most populous states help focus attention on some important emerging trends in Indian politics.

Victories by middle and lower caste coalitions in U.P. and Bihar represent the culmination of a trend that began in other regions of India as early as the 1960s and has spread to much of India during the intervening decades. As democracy has established roots, the hold of such dominant castes as Brahmins on Indian politics is fast vanishing, probably forever. Accompanying this change is the parallel loss of Congress's hegemony, which often rested on the power of the dominant castes. These changes have led parties, including the Congress, to forge new coalitions with the result that politics in India are likely to remain fluid and difficult to predict. However, two trends are emerging: (1) Indian democracy in the near future is likely to be characterized by considerable political ferment, with a variety of dissatisfied groups making demands on parties and governments; and (2) India's major political parties will continue to feel the pressure to broaden their electoral appeal to include these disadvantaged groups, especially those belonging to the middle and lower strata, many of whom are very poor.

Political parties make both material and symbolic promises to mobilize political support. The prospect of a better economic future and/or pride in group membership—whether the group is the whole country or some subset of it—are recurring themes in political party platforms. With the spread of democracy in India, many dissatisfied groups are finding their voice and becoming politically mobilized. These circumstances are favorable for leaders and parties willing to make populist and/or nationalist appeals to mobilize support. Populist leaders promise quick economic improvement to the poor masses, and nationalist parties offer ready national greatness if their political platform is implemented. These are strong appeals, especially in a poor democracy like India with considerable political discontent and an insecure national image. India's political leaders in the near future will thus continue to experience expansionary pressures, that is, pressures to expand their support base by promising economic improvements and/or by manipulating nationalist symbols.

Following major electoral losses in state-level elections (late 1994 and early 1995), Prime Minister Rao lays out his electoral strategy for the future.
Source: Courtesy R. K. Laxman, *The Times of India.*

If the pressures of electoral politics in India are likely to encourage an expansion of government programs in response to discontented groups, government efforts to promote an efficient economy are likely to run in nearly the opposite direction. Because the collapse of communism is fresh in memory and, rightly or wrongly, the confidence in the capacity of governments to generate economic prosperity is low, India's economic policy-makers believe that the way to create a healthy economy is to provide an attractive business climate for private entrepreneurs, both national and global. This policy often implies governmental austerity: curtailing government expenditures so as to control inflation and opening national economies to foreign capital and competition. Restricting government's role, however, conflicts with implementing distributive or populist programs, just as opening national economies to foreign economic actors and products is likely to aggravate nationalist sentiments. One central political tension that will certainly continue to characterize India is a product of these two competing tendencies—expansionary electoral pressures on the one side, and on the other, the preferred liberal economic approach of the elites, emphasizing governmental austerity and economic openness.

Related to this central tension between distributive and efficiency policies are three other sources of tension, all likely to influence the future patterns of political change in India. One is created by the growing pressures on political institutions from a more demanding Indian society and from the actions of threatened leaders. Second, the weakness of political institutions has become and is likely to remain a source of yet newer political problems in India. Because the ruling party, the Congress, does not practice intraparty democracy, dissatisfied groups often look to other parties for a political outlet. Some of these parties, like the BJP, border on extremism. The increased popularity of the more extreme parties, in turn, becomes a source of growing political tensions. Similarly, a government presiding over a fairly mobilized political society needs to respond effectively to a variety of demands. The government may thus be required to provide better education, better health services, better police protection, better run cities, better irrigation services, and on and on. Growing politicization of the bureaucracy has made it difficult in India, especially

below the level of the central government, to provide public services to the society, adding to India's political tensions.

A third inevitable source of tension in Indian politics will continue to be politicization of ethnic identities. Because large amounts of economic resources are controlled by the government and those who control governments have access to these resources, many groups mobilize politically to gain this access for themselves. Caste, language, and religion all provide identities around which political mobilization can be galvanized. Identification with a group, in turn, is further heightened in a democratic context in which parties and leaders freely choose to manipulate such symbols. Mobilized ethnic groups seeking access to state power and state-controlled economic resources are thus a basic component of the contemporary Indian political scene.

To summarize, there are three major contemporary political tensions within India. The first is the *political economy* tension. The challenge this poses is how to reconcile the creation of an efficient, growing economy with distributive political pressures from India's middle and lower strata. The second challenge is that of *governability:* That is, how to create effective political institutions that can both accommodate diverse interests and provide effective government. And the third source of tension in contemporary India arises from politicized *ethnic* identities. The challenge this poses is how to accommodate diverse ethnic demands without obliterating differences among groups while maintaining a degree of coherent government. These three sources of tensions and challenges are interrelated and are likely to influence the future path of Indian politics.

Indian Politics in Transition

The future of Indian politics appears to offer more of the same: India will continue to muddle through as a democracy, ruled by one centrist party or another, successfully accommodating some demands, repressing others, and ignoring still others. However, three alternative scenarios for the future cannot be ruled out: (1) the emergence of the Hindu-nationalist BJP as India's ruling party, which may create an India ethnically intolerant at home and aggressive toward external powers; (2) substantial political disintegration, which would endanger democracy; and (3) high economic growth resulting from liberalization, which would create favorable conditions for more consensual politics.

Muddling Through

Two important factors indicate why Indian politics in the near future is likely to resemble Indian politics of the recent past. First and foremost, democracy is now relatively well established in India, having sustained numerous stresses, strains, and defects. The ongoing practice of democracy has made it very difficult in contemporary India to gain and exercise legitimate power without winning elections. Regular elections, the hallmark of all democracies, will likely remain an integral feature of Indian politics in the near future. Although the possibility that power may be usurped by illegitimate means (such as a military coup) can never be fully ruled out, that scenario is unlikely in India.

Given its democratic history, political compulsions within India will continue to nudge leaders away from narrow political extremes, towards the broad political middle. Winning elections, for example, requires substantial political support, which pressures leaders to adopt broad platforms that appeal to a number of diverse groups. No democracy is immune to appeals from the extreme left or right, but parties with narrow platforms risk being marginalized, especially within India's heterogeneous society. It is likely, therefore, that governing parties in India will continue to be centrist parties.

If India continues to be a democracy, ruled by one centrist party or another, dramatic political changes in the near future are not likely. What is likely instead is more of the same: muddling through at a relatively low level of political effectiveness, coping with some problems, ignoring many others, and acting decisively only when faced with a crisis. Three challenges were identified earlier in this section as significant for India's political future: reconciling growth with distribution; providing effective government; and dealing with ethnic conflict. If both government and politics in India tend to muddle through, most likely such challenges will not be met head on; the political capacity to do so in India is and will remain low. It is more likely that these challenges will be met, if they are met at all, incrementally; that is, the government will first attack one problem, find a partial solution, and then move on to deal with other pressing problems. The danger of such incrementalism is that problems accumulate, overwhelming the already low governmental capacity to deal with them.

The BJP Triumphant

One alternative to the muddling through scenario is an electoral victory by India's right-leaning, Hindu-nationalist party—the BJP replaces the Congress (and other centrist parties) as India's ruling party. If the BJP comes to power without changing its current political platform, most likely the new government would be hostile to India's minorities, especially Muslims, and relatively aggressive toward India's neighbors, especially Pakistan. However, the prospects are slim that the BJP can win national elections without diluting its militant Hindu platform. Hinduism is a highly diverse religion, not easily unified politically. Moreover, India's caste, class, and regional identities will continue to militate against the BJP's attempts to redefine Indian nationalism along pro-Hindu lines. If the BJP succeeds electorally, therefore, it is only likely to do so by diluting some of its exclusiveness and militancy, that is, by moving toward the political center.

Political Disintegration

It is conceivable that India's problems could overwhelm India's ruling institutions and lead to a political breakdown in the near future. A breakdown could occur along one of two lines: one or more of India's regions secede to form separate nation-states; or democracy is suspended by a civilian or a military ruler who initiates an authoritarian regime. Neither of these outcomes is very likely in the near future. Regarding secession, India has a powerful and united armed force that is loyal to the elected national government and that provides a ready check against extreme secessionist militancy. Because moderate demands for greater regional autonomy can, at least in principle, be accommodated within the framework of India's democratic constitution, the Indian political system encourages politics of compromise over politics of confrontation. It is possible that ambitious leaders will tamper with the scope of India's democracy, that is, narrow its scope so as to protect their own political positions. It is also possible that India's economic elite will demand and succeed in limiting the role of labor and peasant groups in the political economy. Such creeping authoritarian tendencies, however, would fall far short of major political disintegration.

A Benign Political Realignment

A last possible scenario to be considered is one in which high economic growth relieves distributional tensions along class, region, and caste lines, facilitating more consensual politics. India's economic policy-makers believe that recent liberalization will generate strong economic growth. If this happens, it is likely to have a positive political impact, mainly because conflicts are more readily resolved when more resources are available. Such a scenario is unlikely, though, for the following reasons. First, no observer expects India's growth rate to be as high as South Korea's or China's was over the last two decades. A sustained annual growth rate of 5–6 percent is the best India may achieve. With India's population growing at just under 2 percent a year, the annual per capita income growth rate of 3 to 4 percent is not likely to provide a dramatic relief from poverty and distress. More important, the distribution of gains from growth is likely to be skewed, benefiting some more than others. Further maldistribution of wealth is hardly a recipe for relieving distributional pressures.

To summarize, predicting the political future of a country as complex as India is risky. Of the four plausible future scenarios, logic and evidence suggest that Indian politics is likely to continue along its present path of muddling through. However, there are important new tendencies within India that should not be ignored: a Hindu-nationalist party has gained popularity; numerous dissatisfied groups continue to demand more from the government; and India's future economic growth is likely to be higher than in the past. The long-term implications of these new trends are hard to predict.

INDIA IN COMPARATIVE PERSPECTIVE

Because India is a large developing country and a democracy, a study of Indian politics sheds light on more general issues of comparative politics. In this chapter, India's development has been examined in light of four comparative themes: democracy, economic development, ethnic politics, and the global position of a state. How well do these themes help illuminate Indian politics and, in turn, what does Indian politics teach us about comparative assumptions concerning these themes?

Some comparative scholars suggest that the widespread desire of citizens to exercise some control over their government is a potent force encouraging democracy. This assumption is clearly illustrated in Indian political trends. Even though democracy was introduced to India by its elites, the democratic tendency has permeated society, helping democracy put down firm roots in India.[17] A clear example supporting this view was India's experience with Emergency rule, when Indira Gandhi curtailed democratic freedoms from 1975 to 1977. In the next election in 1977, Indian citizens decisively voted Indira Gandhi out of power, clearly registering their preference for democratic over authoritarian tendencies. Moreover, although India is challenged with numerous strains and stresses, no widespread anti-democratic movement exists. On the contrary, most Indians value democracy and use its institutions to advance their claims, at times even excessively, with disquieting consequences.

Comparativists also debate the conditions that promote economic development. India is a difficult country to use for examining this theme, mainly because India's economic experience constitutes neither a case of clear success nor of clear failure. If many African countries have done rather poorly economically and many East Asian countries have been dramatic successes, India falls somewhere in the middle. Three conditions may explain this middling outcome. First may be the nature and the quality of the government for promoting economic growth. In this, India has been fortunate to have enjoyed relatively good government since independence: its democratic system is mostly open and stable; its most powerful political leaders are public spirited; and its upper bureaucracy is well trained and competent. These positive attributes truly stand out when India is compared to such African countries as Nigeria.

The second condition concerns India's strategy for economic development. As noted previously, India in the 1950s chose to insulate its economy from global forces, limiting the role of trade and foreign investment, and emphasizing the role of government in promoting self-sufficiency, both in heavy industry and in agriculture. The positive impact of this strategy was that India now produces enough food to feed its large and growing population while it simultaneously produces a vast range of industrial goods. This strategy, however, was not without costs. The protective atmosphere reduced competition to the extent that most of India's manufactured goods are now produced rather inefficiently by global standards. Additional economic growth that may have come from competing effectively in the global markets and by selling its products abroad was sacrificed. India also gave up another area of potential economic growth by discouraging the additional investment that foreign companies would have brought. And last, during the phase of protective industrialization, India did little to alleviate its staggering poverty: land redistribution failed, job creation by heavy industries was minimal, and investment in the education and health of the poor was minuscule in relation to the magnitude of the problem. The poor also became a drag on economic growth because they were unable to buy goods and stimulate demand for increased production and because an uneducated and unhealthy labor force is not a productive labor force.

A stable government and an emphasis on self-sufficiency have promoted modest economic growth in India; higher rates of growth, however, have been difficult to achieve without greater links to the outside world and with the staggering numbers of poor people. This leads to the third condition regarding India's middling political economy—it concerns the emerging trends. India has in recent years liberalized its economy, integrating it more and more into the global arena. This trend reflects a growing confidence and an awareness that sustained and higher rates of growth necessitate such a shift. The results of this shift will become clear only in the next century. Meanwhile, the continuation of staggering levels of poverty in India is a disturbing problem. If India is to achieve sustained levels of high economic growth, the Indian government must address the issues of literacy, health, and welfare for the poor, enabling them to join the economy as truly productive participants.

India also provides a rich case for studying a third area of comparative interest, namely, the growing political impact of ethnic identities. When studying Indian politics, it is difficult to neatly separate interest- and identity-based politics. For example, caste struggles in India are simultaneously struggles for identity, for power, and for wealth. Similarly, the roots of religious and linguistic movements can often be traced back to struggles over power and resources. Once mobilized, political divisions along ethnic lines, especially along religious lines, take on an intense power: Hindu-nationalist forces are not likely to be readily satisfied by subsidies or wage concessions. So, two conclusions follow. First, proliferation of identity politics in contemporary India has its roots in the manipulation of symbols by ambitious leaders seeking access to the state and its resources. Second, once mobilized, ethnic and religious identities in India, as in many other countries, become powerful political forces.

The last comparative theme to consider concerns the factors that help nations deal with global forces. As a large country with a legitimate government and a sizable armed force, India is not readily influenced by external forces. During the last four to five decades, India mostly withdrew from both global economic integration and the Cold War. However, India's continuing economic weakness and recent changes in the global political economy, have made its autarkic approach very costly. India's economic crisis in the early 1990s exposed its vulnerability and provided an occasion for a major shift in its approach to the global economy. How India reconciles domestic political demands for greater economic redistribution with global pressures for an efficient economy will generate some of the more important future trends in India's evolving political economy.

In conclusion, a simple but important fact needs to be reiterated. By the year 2015 or so, India will be the largest country in the world, surpassing China in total population. How such a country is governed will remain an issue of considerable significance, not only for the large segment of humanity that resides within India's boundaries, but also for India's neighbors and for other concerned citizens worldwide. A democratic and prosperous India could be an enormously stabilizing force; by contrast, a nationalist and angry India, poor but powerfully armed, could not be considered a positive development. Similarly, a turbulent India, driven by ethnic and class turmoil, and with a collapsing authority structure, will have profound negative consequences, not just for Indians, but globally. The study and understanding of evolving political trends in India will remain matters of continuing significance.

Key Terms

Hindus

Muslim(s)

caste system

Brahmin(s)

untouchables

Maharajas

zamindars

satyagraha

Emergency (1975–1977)

economic liberalization

Sikh(s)

green revolution

nonaligned bloc

Indian Administrative Service (IAS)

Suggested Readings

Section 1

Brass, Paul. *The New Cambridge History of India.* Vol. 4, bk. 1, *The Politics of India since Independence.* New York: Cambridge University Press, 1994 (rev.).

Sarkar, Sumit. *Modern India: 1885 to 1947.* Madras: Macmillan, 1983.

Section 2

Bardhan, Pranab. *The Political Economy of Development in India.* Oxford: Basil Blackwell, 1984.

Nayar, Baldev Raj. *India's Mixed Economy.* Bombay: Popular Prakashan, 1989.

Section 3

Hardgrave, Robert L., Jr., and Stanley A. Kochanek. *India: Government and Politics in a Developing Nation.* 4th ed. New York: Harcourt Brace Jovanovich, 1986.

Misra, B. B. *Government and Bureaucracy in India: 1947–1976.* Delhi: Oxford University Press, 1986.

Section 4

Kohli, Atul. *Democracy and Discontent: India's Growing Crisis of Governability.* New York: Cambridge University Press, 1991.

Rudolph, Lloyd I., and Susanne Hoeber Rudolph. *In Pursuit of Lakshmi: The Political Economy of the Indian State.* Chicago: University of Chicago Press, 1987.

Endnotes

[1] For an accessible account of the transition to colonialism, see C. A. Bayly, *The New Cambridge History of India: Indian Society and the Making of the British Empire,* vol. II, no. 1 (Cambridge: Cambridge University Press, 1988).

[2] For a thorough discussion of how India was unified under the British, see B. B. Misra, *The Unification and Division of India* (New Delhi: Oxford University Press, 1990).

[3] A synthetic account of the Indian economy during colonial period can be found in Dietmar Rothermund, *An Economic History of India: From Pre-Colonial Times to 1986* (London: Croom Helm, 1988).

[4] For an account of India's nationalist movement, including Gandhi's role, see Sumit Sarkar, *Modern India: 1885 to 1947* (Madras: Macmillan, 1983).

[5] A good but detailed account of Nehru's role in independent India is found in Sarvepalli Gopal, *Jawaharlal Nehra: A Biography* (New Delhi: Oxford University Press, 1984), vols. II and III.

[6] For a solid political biography, see Mary C. Carras, *Indira Gandhi: In the Crucible of Leadership* (Boston: Beacon Press, 1979); for a critical discussion of her role in Indian politics, see Paul R. Brass, *The New Cambridge History of India: The Politics of India Since Independence,* vol. IV, no. 1 (Cambridge: Cambridge University Press, 1990).

[7] Two books that review India's political economy are Francine Frankel, *India's Political Economy, 1947–1977* (Princeton: Princeton University Press, 1978); and Baldev Raj Nayar, *India's Mixed Economy* (Bombay: Popular Prakashan, 1989).

[8] For a good discussion of the factors leading up to this shift, as well as of the issues involved, see Bimal Jalan, *India's Economic Crisis: The Way Ahead* (New Delhi: Oxford University Press, 1991).

[9] An excellent brief account of the political and economic role of these groups in Indian politics and economics can be found in Pranab Bardhan, *The Political Economy of Development in India,* (Oxford: Basil Blackwell, 1984).

[10] For further discussion, see Atul Kohli, *The State and Poverty in India: The Politics of Reform* (Cambridge: Cambridge University Press, 1987).

[11] A helpful study of this issue is Myron Weiner, *The Child and the State in India* (Princeton: Princeton University Press, 1992).

[12] A more detailed and readable account of India's political institutions is Robert L. Hardgrave, Jr., and Stanley A. Kochanek, *India: Government and Politics in a Developing Nation,* 4th ed. (New York: Harcourt Brace Jovanovich, 1986).

[13] A somewhat dated but still the best-known work on Indian military is Stephen P. Cohen, *The Indian Army: Its Contribution to the Development of a Nation* (Berkeley: University of California, 1971).

[14] For a detailed account of the causes and consequences of this shift, see Atul Kohli, *Democracy and Discontent: India's Growing Crisis of Governability* (Cambridge: Cambridge University Press, 1991).

[15] For a historical account of movements and parties leading up to the formation of the BJP, see Bruce Graham, *Hindu Nationalism and Indian Politics* (Cambridge: Cambridge University Press, 1990); for a more recent account, see Tapan Basu, et al., *Khaki Shorts and Saffron Flags: A Critique of the Hindu Right* (New Delhi: Orient Longman, 1993).

[16] See, for example, Amrita Basu, *Two Faces of Protest: Contrasting Modes of Women's Activism in India* (Berkeley: University of California Press, 1992).

[17] For essays that explore why India, despite numerous strains, continues as a functioning democracy, see Myron Weiner, *The Indian Paradox: Essays in Indian Politics* (New Delhi: Sage Publications, 1989).

CHAPTER 9

Mexico

U N I T E D   M E X I C A N   S T A T E S

Land and Population

Capital	Mexico City
Total Area (square miles)	761,602 (about three times the size of Texas)
Population	90 million
Annual Projected Population Growth Rate (1993–2000)	1.8%
Urban Population (% of total)	74%

Ethnic Composition		
Ethnic Groups	Mestizo (Indian-Spanish)	60%
	Amerindian	30%
	Caucasian	9%
	Other	1%
Languages	Spanish	92%
	Various Amerindian	8%
Religions	Catholic	90%
	Protestant	5%
	Other and nonreligious	5%

Economy

Domestic Currency	Peso
GNP (US$)	$324.9
GNP per capita (US$)	$3,610
Purchasing Power Parity GDP per capita (US$)	$6,810
Average Annual GNP Growth Rate (1980–1993)	1.6%

Structure of Production (% of GDP)	Agriculture	8%
	Industry	28%
	Services	63%
Labor Force Distribution (% of total)	Agriculture	23%
	Industry	29%
	Services	48%
Women as % of Total Labor Force	27%	

Income Distribution (1984)	% of Population	% Share of Income or Consumption
	Richest 20%	55.9%
	Poorest 20%	4.1%
Total Foreign Trade (exports plus imports) as % of GDP	23%	

Society

Life Expectancy	Female	74
	Male	68
Population per Doctor	1,850	
Infant Mortality (per 1,000 live births)	35	
Adult Literacy	Female	86%
	Male	91%
Average (Mean) Years of Schooling (of adults 25+)	Female	4.8
	Male	5.0
Communications (per 100 people)	Radios	25
	Televisions	15
	Telephones	12
1995 Human Development Index (1 = highest)	Ranks 53 out of 174	

Political Organization

Political System   Federal republic

Regime History   Current form of government since 1917.

Administrative Structure   Federal, with 31 units of subnational government called states and a federal district.

Executive   President, elected by direct election with a six-year term of office; reelection not permitted.

Legislature   Bicameral; upper and lower house elections held every three years. There are 128 senators, four from each state, elected for six years to serve in the upper house. Three senators from each state are elected by simple majority vote, the fourth is assigned to the largest minority party. There are 500 deputies elected every three years to serve in the lower house: 300 are elected by simple majority; 200 by proportional representation.

Judiciary   Independent supreme court with 21 justices and 5 auxiliary judges.

Party System   Multiparty system, with the Institutional Revolutionary Party (PRI) dominating elections after 1929; other important parties are the National Action Party (PAN) and the Democratic Revolutionary Party (PRD).

SECTION 1
The Making of the Modern Mexican State

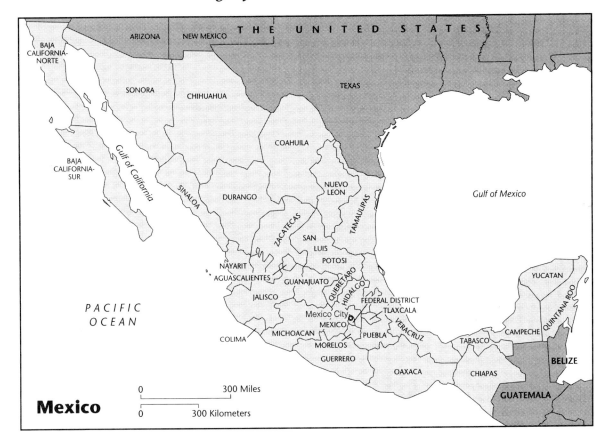

Mexico

Mexico at the Crossroads

On March 23, 1994, presidential candidate Luis Donaldo Colosio finished a campaign speech in the northern border city of Tijuana. Then, as he struggled through the noisy crowd greeting his supporters, an unknown assailant approached quickly, drew a gun, and shot Colosio in the head and torso. The candidate for Mexico's highest office died a few hours later. A suspect was immediately apprehended, along with several other people who had been in the immediate vicinity of the shooting. The ensuing investigation raised concerns about a possible conspiracy implicating party and law enforcement officials, and rumors circulated about a cover-up scandal. Eventually, skep-

ticism about the integrity of the inquiry was so great that President Carlos Salinas de Gortari called for a new investigation.

The assassination of Colosio, the candidate of the Institutional Revolutionary Party (PRI, pronounced "pree"), which had governed the country without interruption since 1929, shocked Mexico's 90 million citizens and shook its political elite deeply. Mexicans at all levels of society pondered the meaning of this violent act. Not since 1924, when a military revolt threatened to displace presidential elections, had there been such uncertainty about who would lead the government for the next six years. Not since 1928, when Alvaro Obregón was assassinated, had a presidential candidate met with violent death. Not since 1929,

Acronyms Used in This Chapter

CNC	National Confederation of Peasants
CNOP	National Confederation of Popular Organizations
CTM	National Confederation of Workers
EZLN	Zapatista National Liberation Army
FDN	National Democratic Front
ISI	Import Substituting Industrialization
NAFTA	North American Free Trade Agreement
PAN	National Action Party
PEMEX	Petroleum Company of Mexico
PMR	Mexican Revolutionary Party
PNR	National Revolutionary Party
PRD	Democratic Revolutionary Party
PRI	Institutional Revolutionary Party
UNE	Citizens in Movement

when the PRI was founded, had there been such fear that the political elite was so divided that violence, not accommodation and compromise, might be used openly to resolve disputes.

The assassination came on the heels of another deeply disturbing event. On January 1, 1994, a rural rebellion in the southern state of Chiapas challenged the Mexican political system to respond to extensive evidence of inequity and injustice. The Zapatista National Liberation Army (EZLN), named after one of the country's great revolutionary heroes, Emiliano Zapata, took over military control of four towns in the state and captured national and international attention. The EZLN demanded "jobs, land, housing, food, health, education, independence, freedom, democracy, justice and peace."[1] The peasant army also called on the government to repeal the North American Free Trade Agreement (NAFTA), which went into effect on the day the uprising started. These demands and the progress of the rebellion were immediately transmitted throughout Mexico and around the globe by domestic and international media as camera crews and reporters flocked to this remote and poverty-stricken state.

The EZLN's call for an end to exploitation at the hands of voracious landowners and corrupt bosses of the PRI, as well as for social services and citizenship rights, resonated deeply throughout the country. Soon, a broad spectrum of local, regional, professional, and human rights groups took up the banner of the Chiapas rebels and called on the government to open the political system to more just and democratic elections, decision-making processes, and policies. By calling in the army to suppress armed peasants, most of whom were Mayan Indians, the government only increased sympathy for the impoverished **indigenous groups** that had been marginalized from the country's development. The Chiapas rebellion symbolized for many the reality of Mexico's political, economic, and social inequalities.

For many citizens, the assassination of a presidential candidate and a rural rebellion were reasons to be concerned about the future of Mexican politics. During the 1980s and 1990s, many openly questioned the right of the PRI to continue to monopolize political power. They organized to press for fairer elections and more responsive public officials. They demanded the right of opposition parties to compete for power on an equal basis with the PRI. They argued that the president had too much power and that the PRI was riddled with corruption. So great was their disenchantment with the existing system that the PRI presidential candidate in the 1988 elections barely won, presenting the narrowest margin of victory since the party's creation. Many argued that Carlos Salinas de Gortari only won because of widespread fraud practiced by party and government officials. Then, in 1994, Ernesto Zedillo Ponce de Leon was elected with an even narrower margin, although allegations of fraud were less insistent than they had been in 1988. Then, a high-level PRI official was assassinated on a street in Mexico City, and the man's brother was later accused of covering up leads implicating the brother of the president in the murder. By 1995, the PRI was deeply divided. Did waning PRI influence, which had contributed centrally to the long tradition of political stability in the country, presage a new era of instability while the country struggled to build more open and democratic political institutions?

The events of early 1994 raised equally puzzling questions about Mexico's economic development. Mexico was just emerging from the most profound crisis since the depression of the 1930s. Renewed possibilities for growth were dashed by a major economic crisis at the end of the year. Beginning in the mid-1980s, the government introduced major policy changes that affected virtually every aspect of the country's economy. Reformers wanted Mexico to have a market-oriented economic system to replace one in which the state played a major role in guiding the process of development. They wanted to see the country's industry and agriculture thrive in a competitive global market. The depth and duration of the crisis and the new policies affected many people adversely, however. Incomes fell, businesses went bankrupt, jobs were lost, and government services were cut back. Were these changes related to the outbreak of violence in Tijuana and Chiapas? Would the reformers' dreams be thwarted by an inability to adjust to a market-oriented economy?

Events in Tijuana and Chiapas also drew attention to deep inequalities among social classes in the country. While modern commercial farmers prospered, the country's large peasant population faced increasing insecurity. In the cities, where 74 percent of the population lived, gradually improved living standards for those with steady jobs contrasted sharply with the growth of the **informal sector,** an underground economy in which even small children were forced to struggle daily for survival. The impressive academic credentials of the country's elites could be seen as an indictment of a system that was providing only minimal education to the poor majority, just as knowledge of those who flew to New York, Houston, and Paris for open-heart surgery called into question a public health system that struggled to provide even basic medical care to large portions of the population. Increasingly, crime, corruption, drugs, and urban violence became facts of life for all Mexicans. How would such conditions, and the government's capacity to address them, affect the ability to achieve economic and political reform?

Thus, the assassination of a presidential candidate and a rebellion in a poor and distant region drew attention to ongoing and interrelated challenges of Mexico's development.

• Would a country with a long tradition of authoritarian government be able to move toward the more open and democratic political system being demanded by its citizens?

• Would a country that had long sought economic development through government activism and the growth of a domestic market be able to compete effectively in an increasingly competitive and market-driven global economy?

• Would a country long noted for severe inequalities between the rich and the poor be capable of providing better living standards for its growing population?

CRITICAL JUNCTURES

In coming to terms with these challenges, Mexicans are deeply affected by the legacies of their collective past, particularly the central formative event in the country's modern history, the Revolution of 1910. Mexico experienced the first great social revolution of the twentieth century, a conflict that lasted for almost a decade and claimed the lives of as many as 2 million people. Some died in violent confrontations, but the majority lost their lives through the massive destruction, dislocation, and famine caused by the shifting and sporadic nature of the conflict. The revolution was fought by a variety of forces for a variety of reasons. Indeed, the consolidation of power that followed the violence was as important as the revolution itself. The institutions and symbols of the current political regime emerged out of these complex conflicts.

The Porfiriato

The roots of the Revolution of 1910 are embedded in the country's long history. They lie in an era prior to the beginning of the conquest by Spanish forces under Hernán Cortés in 1519, with the rise and subsequent decline of sophisticated Amerindian civilizations. And they lie in the interaction between Spanish and indigenous cultures and in the struggle for independence that began in 1810 and lasted until independence was won in 1821, as well as in the chaotic years that followed, as issues of centralism or federalism, republic or empire, secularism or religion were debated and fought over. The most direct roots of the revolution, however, are found in the dictatorship of President Porfirio Díaz, who ruled the country from 1876 to 1911.

When Díaz came into power, Mexico had been experiencing decades of political and economic turmoil. Díaz imposed a highly centralized authoritarian system to create political order and advance economic progress.[2] In time, he relied increasingly on a small clique of advisers, known as *científicos* (scientists), who wanted to adopt European technologies and values to modernize the country, forcefully if necessary. Deeply disdainful of the vast majority of the country's population, Díaz and the *científicos* eagerly encouraged foreign investment and amassed huge fortunes, which they used to support lavish lifestyles and to copy the latest European styles. During this period, known as the Porfiriato, this small elite successfully monopolized positions of political power and reserved

General Porfirio Díaz in 1908.
Source: From *Un Siglo de Caricaturas en México* by
Eduardo del Rio, Editorial Grijalbo, 1984.

lucrative economic investments for themselves and
their allies. Economic and political opportunities were
closed off for new generations of middle- and upper-
class Mexicans, who became increasingly sensitive to
the rapaciousness of the Porfirians and their own lack
of opportunities.

The Revolution of 1910

In 1910, conflict erupted as young reformers sought to
open up the political and economic systems in order to
gain greater opportunities for themselves. Díaz had
pledged himself to an open election for president, and,
in 1910 Francisco I. Madero, a landowner from the
northern state of Coahuila, presented himself as a candidate. Despite being imprisoned by Díaz, Madero
rapidly found himself at the front of a movement to
displace the dictatorship. The slogan "Effective Suffrage, No Reelection" summed up the reformers'
goals in creating opportunities for politically ambitious people to move into positions of power.

Their challenge to the decrepit regime—Díaz was
eighty-one at the time—escalated rapidly, and, by
May of 1911, the dictator was on a ship bound for
Europe and exile. As he left the country, Díaz is reported to have said, "Madero has unleashed a tiger; let
us see if he can control him."[3] His words proved pro-
phetic. Madero was elected president in 1911 but soon
proved to be a poor leader and administrator; protest
and opposition plagued his government. Within
months, the new president was using the military to
put down revolts of reformers and reactionaries alike.
In 1913, Madero was assassinated by leaders of the
army he had called on to repress opposition. Struggles
for political and military leadership continued and political order in the country virtually collapsed.

At the same time that middle-class reformers
struggled to displace Díaz, a peasant revolt erupted,
centered in the southern states of the country and focused on land claims. This revolt had roots in legislation introduced in the 1850s, 1880s, and 1890s that
made it easy for wealthy landowners and ranchers to
claim the lands of peasant villagers; other land was
simply stolen from them. By 1910, 90 percent of Mexican peasants were landless and only 15 percent of all
villages still had claim to their traditional communal
lands; many peasants were virtual slaves on the haci-
endas and plantations of wealthy landowners.[4]

Encouraged by the weakening of the old regime
and driven to desperation by increasing landlessness,
villagers armed themselves and joined forces under a
variety of local leaders. The most famous of these was
Emiliano Zapata, who amassed a peasant army from
Morelos, a state in southern Mexico. Peasant battal-
ions swept through the countryside and grew in numbers; women as well as men flocked to fight under
Zapata and other revolutionary leaders. Their common
goal was to reclaim the lands lost to large landowners
under the Porfiriato. An Indian peasant woman recalled the day that Zapata and his revolutionaries came
to her village.

> One day a great man by the name of Zapata
> arrived from Morelos. . . . All his men were
> dressed in white—white shirts, white pants,
> and they all wore sandals. All these men
> spoke Nahuatl [an Indian language] more or
> less as we spoke it. Señor Zapata also spoke
> Nahuatl. . . . Zapata stood in at the head of
> his men and addressed the people of Milpa

Conquest or Encounter?

There is in Mexican society a pervasive awareness of the ancients. The Indian presence intrudes on the national psyche; it suffuses the art, philosophy, and literature. It is stamped on the face of Mexico, in the racial features of the sturdy *mestizo*. It lies within the marvelous prehistoric ruins.*

The year 1519, when Hernán Cortés arrived on the shores of the Yucatán Peninsula, is often considered the starting point of Mexican political history. But the Spanish explorers did not set off across an uninhabited land waiting to be excavated for gold and silver. Instead, the land that was to become New Spain and then Mexico was home to extensive and complex indigenous civilizations that were advanced in agriculture, architecture, and political and economic organization—civilizations that were already over a thousand years old. The Mayans of the Yucatan and the Toltecs of the central highlands had reached high levels of development long before the arrival of the Europeans. By 1519, diverse groups had fallen under the power of the militaristic Aztec Empire, which extended throughout what is today central and southern Mexico.

The encounter between the Europeans and these indigenous civilizations was marked by bloodshed and violence. The great Aztec city of Tenochtitlán—the site of Mexico City today—was captured and largely destroyed by the Spanish conquerors in 1521. Cortés and the colonial masters who came after him subjected indigenous groups to forced labor, robbed them of gold, silver, and land, and introduced flora and fauna from Europe that destroyed long-existing aqueducts and irrigation systems. They also brought alien forms

of property rights and authority relationships, a religion that viewed indigenous practices as the devil's own work, and an economy based on mining and cattle—all of which soon overwhelmed existing structures of social and economic organization. Within a century, wars, savage exploitation at the hands of the Spaniards, and the introduction of European diseases reduced the indigenous population from an estimated 25 million to a million or less.

Passionate debate surrounds the issue of whether the Spaniards' arrival should be considered a conquest of one culture by another or an encounter between two cultures that provided opportunities for economic, religious, cultural, and linguistic evolution, resulting in a diverse and dynamic culture that is uniquely Mexican. It is certainly difficult to escape reminders of the rich indigenous past in today's Mexico—the bright colors and rich embroideries of traditional dress; the temples and cities preserved in numerous archeological zones; the use of indigenous language by more than 8 percent of the population; the exquisite crafts, music, and art representing traditional themes, forms, and colors; and national symbols such as the flag. It is also hard to escape reminders of the unequal interaction of European and indigenous cultures—those with strongest links to the precolonial past live in the most remote areas of the country and suffer from the harshest conditions of poverty, disease, illiteracy, and isolation.

---

*Michael C. Meyer and William L. Sherman, *The Course of Mexican History* (New York: Oxford University Press, 1979), 3. *Mestizo* refers to people of mixed European and Amerindian heritage.

Alta in the following way: "Come join me! I have risen in arms, and I have brought my countrymen with me. . . . Join the Revolution with us since we are tired of the few cents the rich pay us. There isn't enough to eat or to buy clothes. I want every man to have his own plot of land. He will sow it and reap corn, beans, and other grains. What do you people say? Will you join us?"[5]

Zapata's Plan de Ayala, first announced in 1911 and agreed to at a national meeting of revolutionary leaders in 1915, became the cornerstone of the radical agrarian reform that was incorporated into the Constitution of 1917.

In yet another focal point of the revolution, Francisco (Pancho) Villa led his own army of workers, small farmers, and ranch hands in northern parts of the country. He presented a major challenge to the national army,

now under the leadership of Venustiano Carranza, who had inherited Madero's middle-class reformist movement and eventually became president. Villa's forces recognized no law but that of their chief and combined military maneuvers with banditry, looting, and warlordism in the territories under their control. In 1916, Villa and his guerrillas crossed into the United States, raided a border town, and killed eighteen U.S. citizens. President Woodrow Wilson, responding to domestic pressure for retaliation and concerned about violence and instability in the neighboring country, ordered General John J. Pershing to hunt down Villa and punish him for this incursion. But the U.S. military operation was badly planned and poorly executed. Villa was never located and Mexican hostility toward the United States, already running high because of an invasion and seizure of the port city of Veracruz in 1914, increased.

The Constitution of 1917 was forged out of this diverse and often conflicting set of interests. It

Conflicts of the Past: Independence, Church and State, and Centralization

Spain ruled Mexico for three centuries, administering a vast economic, political, and religious empire in the interest of the imperial country, its kings, and its representatives in North America. Colonial policy was designed to extract wealth from New Spain and to limit the possibilities for Spaniards in the New World to benefit from agriculture, commerce, or industry without at the same time benefiting Spain. It was also designed to ensure commitment to the Catholic religion.

In 1810, Miguel Hidalgo, a parish priest in central Mexico, proclaimed the famous Grito de Dolores to a group assembled in a parish church in the town of Dolores. He called for an end to Spanish misrule. At the head of a motley band of rebels, he began the first of a series of wars of independence that pitted rebels against the Spanish crown until 1821. When Hidalgo was executed in 1811, José María Morelos became the leader of the insurgency. Later, Agustín de Iturbide, who defected from the Spanish military after fighting the rebels for almost ten years, assumed leadership and brought an end to the wars, but not to the violence and dissent they had unleashed. For several decades after independence was gained in 1821, Mexico struggled to create stability and a legitimate and respected government.

Liberals and conservatives, federalists and centralists, those who sought to expand the power of the church and those who sought to curtail it, and those who wanted a republic and those who wanted a monarchy were all engaged in the battle for Mexico's soul during the nineteenth century. Stability was elusive. Between 1833 and 1855, thirty-six presidential administrations came to power. During this disorganized period, Mexico lost half its territory to the United States.

Mexico's northern territory of Texas proclaimed and then won independence in a war ending in 1836. The Lone Star Republic was annexed to the United States by Congress in 1845, and claims on Mexican territory north of the Rio Grande were increasingly heard from Washington. On the basis of a very dubious claim that Mexico had invaded U.S. territory, the United States declared war on its southern neighbor. The war was first fought along what was later to become the border between the two countries and then, in 1847, the U.S. army invaded the port city of Veracruz. Causing considerable loss of civilian lives, this army marched toward Mexico City and the final battle at Chapultepec Castle. An 1848 treaty gave the United States title to Texas, California, and New Mexico for about $18 million and left a legacy of deep suspicions about U.S. imperialism.

Throughout this period, liberals and conservatives continued their struggle to resolve issues of political and economic order and, in particular, the power of the Catholic church. The Constitution of 1857 incorporated many of the goals of the liberals, such as republican government, a bill of rights, abolition of slavery, and limitations on the economic and political power of the church. Benito Juárez, who occupied the presidency on three separate occasions, continues to be revered in Mexico today as an early proponent of open and republican government.

The Constitution of 1857 did not guarantee stability, however. In 1861, Spain, Great Britain, and France occupied the coastal town of Veracruz to collect customs claims from the government, providing the French army an opportunity to march on Mexico City and establish the government of Emperor Maximilian and Empress Carlota from 1864 to 1867. Conservatives and Catholic loyalists welcomed this respite from the liberals. But Juarez was back in office in 1867, again spearheading reforms in economic, social, and political arenas. It was these reforms that set the stage for the dictatorship of Porfirio Díaz, which began in 1876 and lasted until 1911, and which brought sustained stability to the country.

established a formal set of political institutions and guaranteed a range of progressive social and economic rights to citizens—agrarian reform, social security, the right to organize in unions, a minimum wage, an eight-hour work day, profit sharing for workers, and universal secular education. In an effort to limit the power of foreign investors, the constitution declared that only Mexican citizens or the government could own land or rights to water and other natural resources. It also contained numerous articles that severely limited the power of the Catholic church, long a target of liberals who wanted Mexico to be a secular state. The signing of the document signaled the formal end to the revolution and an agreement among contending parties of their intention to form a new political regime. Despite such noble sentiments, violence continued as competing leaders sought to assert power and displace their rivals. Political assassinations were common through the 1920s, as were regional skirmishes among local warlords. Zapata, Villa, and presidents Carranza and Obregón were all assassinated.

Despite this violence, power was gradually consolidated in the hands of a group of revolutionary leaders from the north of the country. Known as the Sonoran Dynasty, after their home state of Sonora, these leaders were committed to a capitalist model of economic development. During the 1920s, they skillfully outmaneuvered those who wished to see a socialist economy rise from the ashes of civil war. Eventually, one of the Sonorans—Plutarco Elías Cal-

In 1914, Pancho Villa (right) met with Emiliano Zapata in Mexico City to discuss the revolution and their separate goals for its outcome.
Source: Freck/Odyssey, Chicago.

les—emerged as the *jefe máximo,* or supreme leader. Elected president in 1924, Calles managed to select and dominate his presidential successors from 1929 to 1934. The consolidation of power under his control was accompanied by extreme **anticlericalism** that eventually resulted in warfare between conservative leaders of the Catholic church and their followers and the government.

In 1929, Calles managed to bring together the most powerful contenders for leadership, many of them regional warlords who were fighting over the spoils of victory, to create an umbrella political party. The bargain he offered was simple. Contenders for power and spoils would agree to forgo violence against each other and accommodate to each others' interests in the expectation that, in the end, they would all be richer and more powerful through such behavior. Named the National Revolutionary Party (PNR), the party they created was the precursor to the PRI.* For the next 65 years, Calles' bargain was effective in ensuring a tradition of nonviolent conflict resolution among elites and the uninterrupted rule of the PRI in national politics.

Although the revolution was complex and the interests contending for power in its aftermath were numerous, there were five clear results of this protracted conflict. First, the power of traditional rural landowners was undercut. In the years after the revolution,

wealthy elites would again emerge in rural areas, but they would never again be so powerful in national politics, nor could their power be so unchecked in local areas. Second, the power of the Catholic church at the national level was firmly destroyed. While the church remained important at regional and local levels in many parts of the country, it no longer figured among the interests that participated openly in national political debates. Third, the power of foreign investors was severely limited; prior to the revolution, foreign investors owned much of the country's land, as well as many of its railroads, mines, and factories. Henceforth, a clear sense of Mexican nationalism would shape economic policy-making. Fourth, a new political elite consolidated power and agreed to resolve conflicts through accommodation and bargaining, rather than violence. And fifth, the new constitution and the PNR laid the basis for a strong central government that could assert its power over the agricultural, industrial, and social development of the country. Modern Mexican government and the country's economic development were profoundly affected by these accomplishments.

Lázaro Cárdenas, Agrarian Reform, and the Workers

In 1934, Plutarco Calles again handpicked his successor to the presidency. He fully anticipated that candidate Lázaro Cárdenas, a revolutionary general and governor of the state of Michoacán who had been part of the elite coalition of the PNR, would continue to bow to Calles' behind-the-scenes management of the country and continue the economic policies of the postrevolutionary coalition. To his great surprise, Cárdenas executed a virtual coup that established his own supremacy and sent Calles packing to the United States for an "extended vacation."[6] Even more unsettling to the coalition, often referred to as the "Revolutionary Family," Cárdenas set out to mobilize peasants and workers in pursuit of the more radical goals of the revolution. He encouraged peasant syndicates to petition for land and claim rights promised in the Constitution of 1917. He eventually superintended the distribution of more than 17 million hectares of land (1 hectare = 2.471 acres). Most of these lands were distributed as *ejidos,* or land grants to peasant groups who would be jointly responsible for them. *Ejidatarios* (those who acquired *ejido* lands) became

---

* The PNR was renamed the Mexican Revolutionary Party (PMR) in 1939 and acquired its current name in 1946.

one of the most enduring bases of support for the government because of the redistribution of lands that was so forcefully pursued in the 1930s. Cárdenas also encouraged workers to form unions and demand higher wages and better working conditions. He established his nationalist credentials when he nationalized the petroleum industry in 1938, wresting it from U.S. and British investors.

The Cárdenas years (1934–1940) were a period in which the bulk of the Mexican population was incorporated into the political system. Organizations of peasants, workers, middle-class groups, and the military were added to the party, and the voices of the poor majority were heard within the councils of government, reducing the risk that they would become radicalized outside them. In addition, the Cárdenas years witnessed a great expansion of the role of the state as the government set up a powerful investment bank to encourage industrialization, provided credit to agriculture, invested in infrastructure, and nationalized the petroleum industry.

As with all great political leaders in pursuit of political and economic change, Cárdenas's motives were mixed. As a politician, he sought a base of support among the working classes in rural and urban areas to free himself from reliance on the capitalist-oriented Sonoran Dynasty. In addition, he sought to bring life to his vision of a prosperous country whose wealth was generated and shared by organized groups of peasants and workers. At another level, his actions clearly indicated his concern to control all economic groups in the interest of a larger development role for the state and a dominant position for the PRI in national politics. By encouraging extensive organization of peasants and workers into national confederations, he provided later political leaders with a set of institutions that could be used to control participation and enhance authoritarian and centralized government.

Lázaro Cárdenas continues to be a national hero to Mexicans, who look back on his presidency as a period when government was clearly committed to improving the welfare of the country's poor majority. His other legacy was to institutionalize patterns of political succession and presidential behavior that continue to set standards for Mexico's leaders. He campaigned extensively, even though he was not seriously challenged by other candidates, and his campaign travel took him to remote villages and regions, where he listened to the demands and complaints of

humble people. Cárdenas served a full six-year term and relinquished political power when his term of office was officially completed to allow the new president, Manuel Avila Camacho, to assume fully the mantle of presidential authority. Cárdenas's conduct in office created hallowed traditions that all subsequent PRI presidents have observed.

Industrialization: The 1940s and the 1980s

Although Cárdenas directed a radical reshuffling of political power in the country, leaders who succeeded him were able to use the institutions he created to counteract his reforms. Ambitious local and regional party leaders and leaders of peasants' and workers' groups began to use their organizations as pawns in exchange for favors from the political system. Gradually, the PRI developed a huge patronage machine, providing union and *ejido* leaders with jobs, opportunities for corruption, land, and other benefits in return for delivering their followers' political support. Extensive chains of personal relationships based on the exchange of such favors allowed the party to amass far-reaching political control and limit opportunities for organizing independently of the PRI. These exchange relationships, known as **clientelism,** became the cement that built loyalty to the PRI and the political system.

This kind of political control translated into the capacity of post-Cárdenas presidents to reorient the country's development away from the egalitarian social goals of the 1930s toward a development strategy in which the state actively encouraged the accumulation of wealth and investment in industrialization. Initially, industrialization created jobs and made available a wide range of basic consumer goods to Mexico's burgeoning population. Growth rates were high during the 1940s, 1950s, and 1960s, and Mexicans flocked to the cities to take advantage of the jobs created in the manufacturing and construction industries. By the 1960s, however, the policies that had encouraged industrial development were no longer generating rapid growth and could not keep pace with rapidly rising demands for jobs. The basis for Mexico's economic growth was "becoming weaker, not stronger, with the passage of time."[7]

The country's economy was in deep crisis by the mid-1970s. Just as policymakers began to take actions to correct the problems, however, vast new amounts of oil were discovered in the Gulf of Mexico. Soon, rapid

Painted in 1947–1948 by Diego Rivera, this mural at the Hotel del Prado in Mexico City depicts well-known personages from Mexico's political, military, economic, and cultural history.
Source: Diego Rivera, *Dream of a Sunday Afternoon in the Alameda* from the Hotel del Prado, Mexico City, photo by Schalwijk/Art Resource, NY.

economic growth was refueled by extensive public investment programs in virtually every sector of the economy. Based on the promise of petroleum wealth, the government and private businesses borrowed huge amounts of capital from foreign lenders who were, of course, eager to do business with a country that had so much oil. Unfortunately for the country, however, international petroleum prices plunged sharply beginning in 1981. Almost overnight, there was no more credit to be had and much less money from petroleum to pay for economic expansion or the interest on the debts incurred in preceding years. Mexico plummeted into a deep economic crisis that affected many countries around the world.

In fact, this crisis helped two presidents, Miguel de la Madrid (1982–1988) and Carlos Salinas (1988–1994), introduce the first major reversal of the country's development strategy since the 1940s. New policies were put in place to limit the government's role in the economy and to make it easier for Mexican producers to export their goods. This period clearly marked the beginning of a new effort to become more important in international economic affairs. In signing NAFTA, which commits Mexico, the United States, and Canada to eliminating trade barriers among them, Mexico's policymakers signaled the extent to which they envisioned the future prosperity of their country as tied to that of other states in the region. Efforts to increase trade and investment to Latin American, European, and Asian countries also emphasized Mexico's new commitment to competitiveness in a global economy. The economic reforms of the 1980s, and 1990s were a turning point for the country's development, even though they left unresolved issues of dem-

ocratic and social reform, and meant that Mexico's future development would be closely tied to conditions in the international economy. A major economic crisis at the end of 1994, in which billions of dollars of foreign investment fled the country, was indicative of this new international vulnerability.

Nationalism and National Identity

The myths, legends, symbols, and realities of the Porfiriato, the Revolution of 1910, the struggles of the Cárdenas years, and the process of industrialization are deeply embedded in the images that Mexicans have of themselves as a nation. In addition, national interpretations of the pre-Hispanic past, the conquest of indigenous people by Spanish colonizers, and the struggle for independence are important in the widely shared belief that Mexico is a unique and special nation. The mural art that flourished in the years after the revolution reflects the ways in which historical experiences have been claimed as part of the collective identity that defines Mexicans.

In the Hotel del Prado in Mexico City, for example, a mural by Diego Rivera painted in 1947–1948 but destroyed in an earthquake in 1985, provided a panorama of the devils and heroes of Mexican history. At the extreme left of the mural are figures from the conquest and colonial past—Hernán Cortés, the conqueror, and Spanish and Catholic officials who reigned supreme during the colonial period. Leaders of the independence movement mingle with French and U.S. soldiers who invaded the country in the mid-nineteenth century, and Emperor Maximilian and Empress Carlota, who ruled the country briefly in the 1860s. President Benito Juárez holds the Constitution of 1857. In the center of the mural, Porfirio Díaz, in uniform and plumed hat, watches over the pillars of his dictatorship—the military, the wealthy, foreign investors, *científicos,* and a deathlike parody of their social and economic vices. Rivera depicts himself as a child in front of his famous artist wife, Frida Kahlo, to the skeleton's right. To its left, José Guadelupe Posada, a political satirist much admired by Rivera, appears. On the right are Emiliano Zapata on horseback and Francisco Madero, tipping his hat.

Supporting these and many other important historical figures are the common people of Mexico—a poverty-striken pickpocket and street vendors on the left, a prostitute and a peasant family being roughed up by police in the center, indigenous peasant villagers, workers, street hawkers, and revolutionaries on the right. Behind them are the factories and skyscrapers that Rivera pictured emerging from the revolution. In the faces of many are strong reminders that Mexicans have their roots in the indigenous precolonial past as well as in Europe. The Mexican flag and a balloon depicting the Mexican Republic (RM) suggest the extent to which these symbols and historical myths serve to unite a society marked by deep political, economic, and social inequalities.

Mexico's sense of national identity has been strengthened by the proximity of the United States. Facing each other across a 2,000-mile border, the two countries have a history that is rife with violence, hostility, and suspicion as well as trade, tourism, and cultural interaction. Mexico has frequently been on the losing end of the relationship. "Poor Mexico," Porfirio Díaz is reported to have said. "So far from God and so close to the United States."[8] A peace treaty in 1848 ended a war with the United States that erupted when the United States annexed Texas, which had once belonged to Mexico. Mexico lost the war and half its territory to the United States. U.S. troops occupied Mexico City in 1847. An impressive monument in Mexico City commemorates the six young cadets who jumped to their deaths rather than surrender to the invading U.S. troops. Invasion during the Revolution of 1910 also contributed to deep suspicion of the "Colossus of the North." The great economic power of its northern neighbor and the potential for "cultural imperialism" as U.S. life-styles and values are spread by the mass media have also concerned Mexican nationalists.

Mexicans from widely diverse backgrounds and status share a deep sense of nationalism based on these historical experiences and symbols. But Mexicans, like citizens of many other countries, are also critical of their country's past and present. They are well aware that the noble goals of the revolution—democracy, social justice, and nationalism—have been sacrificed to political order and the economic advancement of some at the expense of many others. Their sense of national uniqueness and pride coexists with deep cynicism about a system in which electoral results are predetermined and social class divisions are extensive. In the 1980s, concerns about the widening gap between national ideology and national realities increased the willingness of many Mexicans to organize in opposition to the PRI-dominated system. They did so, however, out of a desire to see their country fulfill its historical commitments, not because they had lost their sense of national identity.

Mexicans share a deep sense of national identity, but they also recognize distinctions based on their affiliations to region, class, and special interests. They will, for example, identify themselves as northerners or southerners, cityfolk or villagers, Yucatecans or Tamaulipans, just as people in the United States identify with distinct regions of the country, types of lifestyles, and particular states. Mexico's middle class is large by developing country standards and increasingly, many identify themselves with this label. The revolutionary heritage of the country also means that many identify themselves proudly as workers or peasants. The same revolutionary heritage discourages people from openly claiming title to aristocratic or highly elite backgrounds, but there is little question that such distinctions are important socially. Traditionally, political activity has been organized around class identities, even within the PRI. Currently, just as in other countries, groups based on common values or shared concerns such as community, the environment, gender, or specific economic and political issues are becoming more prevalent. None of these identities threatens the overall sense of national belongingness, however.

Another ingredient in the collective identity of Mexicans is less easily incorporated into their sense of historical uniqueness. In their aspirations for the future of their country, Mexicans increasingly share the image of a prosperous and modern population living in cities full of skyscrapers and enjoying the latest communications technologies, consumer fashions, and musical fads. They desire to live in a country that is important and powerful in international debates, that benefits from international trade, that is open and democratic, and that is part of a world of states. These images portray a nation that resembles the industrialized countries of North America and Western Europe. Can this new image be widely shared without destroying so much that has traditionally made Mexicans believe they have a unique heritage and culture?

State and Society in Modern Mexico

The Mexican state emerged out of a popular revolution, proclaiming goals of democratic government, social justice, and nationalism. In the chaotic years after the revolution, this state effectively created conditions for political and social peace. By incorporating peasants and workers into party and government institutions and providing benefits to low-income groups in the 1930s, it became widely accepted as legitimate. In encouraging considerable economic growth in the years after 1940, it also encouraged belief in its ability to provide material improvements in the quality of life of large portions of the population. These factors worked together to create a strong state capable of guiding economic and political life in the country. Despite the fact that many remained marginal to full participation in the country's economic, political, and social life, most Mexicans agreed—at least until the 1980s—that the state was legitimate and nationalist.

The relationship between state and society has also been shaped by a strong belief that capitalism, unless carefully monitored by government, creates economic injustice because the private sector's pursuit of profit causes it to exploit workers and disregard the good of the community for its own advantage. Such beliefs derive in part from traditional Catholic social philosophy and in part from the ideology of the revolution and the reforms of the 1930s. In this view, the state has an obligation to protect and provide for the poor and to champion their rights in order to counterbalance the power of the rich. Within this tradition, many Mexicans believe that the state also has an obligation to ensure peace and order by determining the rights and obligations of various groups—peasants, workers, the military, merchants, clergy, and industrialists, for example—to one another. This **corporatist philosophy,** which contrasts strongly with the deep distrust of the state and the strong sense of individualism that is characteristic of U.S. citizens, contributes

to the increased importance and power of the state in Mexico.

The factors that encouraged the development of a strong state also increased its power in relation to civil society. The Mexican state has been able to determine how citizens would interact with government and how much government would respond to their needs. The state has taken the lead in defining goals for the country's development and, through the school system, the party, and the media, has inculcated a broad sense of its legitimate right to set such goals. In addition, the state has had extensive resources at its disposal to control or co-opt dissent and to purchase political loyalty. The PRI has been an essential mechanism through which material goods such as jobs, the distribution of land, and the allocation of development projects have been used to increase popular support for the system or to buy off opposition to it. Citizens wishing to have greater input into national decision making have long faced an uphill battle in doing so.

This does not mean that Mexican society is unorganized or passive. Indeed, many Mexicans are actively involved in local community organizations, religious activities, unions, and public interest groups. But traditionally, the scope for challenging the government, for insisting on basic civil rights, or for demanding an open and responsive government has been very limited.[9] Nor does Mexico's strong state mean that the government is openly repressive or brutal. On the contrary, officials in the government and the party work hard to find ways to resolve conflicts peacefully and they maintain the belief that the state represents the aspirations of all Mexicans. In fact, most Mexicans pursue their daily lives without feeling directly threatened by the power of the state. Open use of force is widely considered to be a sign of the government's failure to maintain an effective state-society relationship. State and local officials who have asked that the army be called in to deal with rebellious students or to manage other conflicts, for example, characteristically lose their jobs after the disturbance is dealt with. The norm in Mexico's state-society relationship is peaceful resolution of conflict and behind-the-scenes accommodation of conflicting interests.

By the 1980s, however, cracks began to appear in the traditional ways in which Mexican citizens interacted with the government. As the PRI began to lose its capacity to control political activities, and as civic groups increasingly insisted on their right to remain independent from the PRI and the government, the terms for the state-society relationship were clearly in need of redefinition. Developing a new relationship, however, would be largely a result of the capacity of civil society to become stronger in insisting that government be more responsive, fair, democratic, and effective. At the same time, a philosophical tradition supporting the notion of a strong and protective state was in some tension with the more market-oriented development strategy that was adopted in the 1980s and 1990s. State-society relations were changing because of the political and economic conflicts of the 1980s and new development strategies, but how they would be redefined was still an open question in the mid-1990s.

IMPLICATIONS FOR CONTEMPORARY MEXICAN POLITICS

The political regime that emerged in Mexico in the early twentieth century and continues today is civilian and authoritarian. In contrast to many other developing countries, Mexico's leaders successfully established political order and developed a set of institutions that have been widely regarded as legitimate. They were also successful in diminishing the political relevance of the military, an accomplishment that few other states have been able to achieve. Administrations change with regularity, and conflicts over political succession, which lead to bloodshed and coups in many developing countries, have not been violent in Mexico, at least not until 1994. This regime has become more open and more accepting of criticism and dissent in recent years, but it is still far from providing full democratic institutions or choices to its citizens. Power is highly centralized in the executive branch of government, state and local governments are dependent on the national government, and campaigns and elections are carefully orchestrated to limit threats to the power of government or the PRI.

This description of a civilian and authoritarian regime contrasts markedly with what is written in the constitution. The Mexican government, on paper, is structured like that of the United States. But Mexico differs strongly from its neighbor in terms of how its institutions actually function. Its presidency is one of the strongest in the world in terms of how much power a president can command; U.S. presidents are extremely weak in comparison. The congress, by contrast, is among the weakest in the world, and the judiciary is far from independent. Even though they hold elective office, most state governors serve at the pleasure of the president, and local officials must have both state- and national-level support from political leaders if they are to remain in office.

The relationship between the party and the government also strengthens the power of the executive branch. It is based on a consistent division of labor in which the PRI focuses on mobilizing political support, controlling participation, and resolving conflicts. Its purpose, in other words, is to bring in the votes and keep the political peace. The government bureaucracy and the president focus primarily on policy development and implementation. Their role is to direct the course of national development. Even if in the future the PRI loses elections from time to time and opposition strength grows stronger in the legislature and captures more state and local governments, the power of the executive branch to make and implement policy is likely to remain very strong.

There are controls on the power of Mexico's president, however, the most important of which is the constitutional provision that denies presidents and other high-level officials the right to run for reelection. The writers of the constitution made this rule as a way of preventing dictators like Porfirio Díaz from controlling the country for long periods of time. The six-year term of office, called the *sexenio,* means that there are periodic opportunities to adjust public policy to new interests and exigencies when presidential administrations change. At the same time, presidents need to accommodate powerful economic groups, pay at least lip service to the historic myths of the revolution, recognize that a large and inefficient government bureaucracy can stymie the plans of even the most committed reformers, and respond to the realities of domestic and international economic conditions.

Mexican Politics in Comparative Perspective

The Mexican political system is unique among developing countries in the extent to which it has managed to institutionalize and maintain civilian political authority for a very long time. In a world of developing nations that are wracked by political turmoil, military coups, and regime changes, this regime has managed to establish enduring institutions of governance and conditions for ongoing political stability. Other countries have sought to emulate the Mexican model of stability based on an alliance between a dominant party and a strong development-oriented state, but most have lacked the legitimacy to cement the relationship between state and society that is characteristic of Mexico. The regime's revolutionary heritage as well as its ability to maintain a sense of national identity are important factors in accounting for its political continuity. Its future stability, however, will be significantly affected by its ability to adapt to the demands for greater democracy that Mexican citizens believe are part of being a truly modern country.

Mexico has enjoyed considerable economic advancement since the 1940s, although a number of other countries in the developing world have been equally or more successful in generating sustained economic growth and providing for improved standards of living. The country has moved significantly toward industrialization and, in the 1990s, acquired aspirations to be considered one of the "newly industrializing countries" (NICs) of the world, similar in stature to countries such as South Korea, Malaysia, and Taiwan. It was certainly facing up to many of the problems of the more advanced industrial nations—trying to achieve international competitiveness for its products, dealing with problems of air and water pollution, and managing the growth of its megacities. The decision to promote a free trade agreement with its northern neighbors clearly indicated the government's recognition of the need to become integrated into a wider world of states. The larger questions of whether a new development strategy can generate growth, whether Mexican products can find profitable markets overseas, and whether investors can create extensive job opportunities for millions of unemployed and part-time workers continue to challenge the country.

Improving social conditions is an equally important challenge. While elites enjoy the benefits of sumptuous life-styles, education at the best U.S. universities for their children, and luxury travel to the capitals of the world, large numbers of Mexicans remain ill-educated, poorly served with health care, and distant from the security of knowing that their basic needs for food, shelter, and employment can be met. Many have sought such goals in the United States and other countries as they have migrated for jobs and opportunities for personal advancement. The country will not be able to achieve its desired NIC status unless it can ensure greater equity and provide jobs for a better-educated and healthy workforce. Gaps in income and lifestyles also threaten political stability. Indeed, the myths and symbols of the revolution and the PRI are increasingly less meaningful to average citizens in the absence of opportunities for political participation, economic advancement, and social equity.

SECTION 2
Political Economy and Development

Mexico has been categorized as an upper-middle-income developing country, along with countries such as Argentina, Portugal, South Korea, and Venezuela.[10] It has made significant strides in industrialization, which accounts for about 28 percent of the country's gross domestic product (GDP). Agriculture contributes about 8 percent to GDP, and services contribute some 63 percent. This structure is very similar to the economic profiles of Brazil, New Zealand, and Hungary. But, unlike these other countries, Mexico is an oil-rich country, a fact that gives the government a ready source of revenue and foreign exchange at the same time that it makes the country extremely vulnerable to changes in international prices for this commodity.

Mexico's industrial and petroleum-based economy means a higher per capita income than most other developing countries. If income were spread evenly among all Mexicans, each would receive $3,030 annually (1991)—far more than the per capita income of India ($330 in 1991), China ($370), and Nigeria ($340), but considerably less than that of Britain ($16,550), France ($20,380), and Germany ($23,650).[11] Of course, income is not spread evenly. Mexico suffers from great inequalities in how wealth is distributed, and poverty continues to be a grim reality for millions of Mexicans. The way Mexico promotes economic growth and industrialization is important in explaining why widespread poverty has persisted and why political power has not been more equitably distributed.

More than many other countries, Mexico adopted a development strategy in which the government guided the process of industrial and agricultural development and set the political conditions for its success. Often referred to as **state capitalism,** this strategy for development relied heavily on government actions to encourage private investment and to lower risks for private entrepreneurs.[12] Through a variety of policies and investment programs, the government stimulated economic growth over several decades and encouraged the emergence of powerful groups of entrepreneurs, who eventually had the capacity to insist on policies to increase the benefits they were receiving. Unions and party and government officials also developed vested interests in the perpetuation and expansion of existing policies. In the 1980s, however, these groups were weakened by economic crisis; the government took the opportunity to make new policies that were expected to rekindle the country's economic potential.

Among the important objectives of Mexico's efforts to industrialize has been the desire to become less vulnerable to international economic conditions and less dependent on foreign capital, particularly from the United States. At times, this has resulted in policies to limit and control foreign investment and to rely on domestic markets for the goods and services the country was producing. Presently, along with many other countries, the effort to become less dependent has taken the form of working to increase the international competitiveness of Mexican products and diversifying its trade relations with other countries so that it becomes less vulnerable to economic conditions in any one of them. Despite such initiatives, Mexican economic development is becoming more, not less, tied to the economic future of the United States.

STATE AND ECONOMY

Mexico's economic development has been characterized by recurring efforts to encourage rapid industrialization. During the Porfiriato, the country began to produce some textiles, footware, glassware, paper, beer, tiles, furniture, and a few other simple products. At that time, however, policymakers were convinced that a developing country such as Mexico could grow rich by exporting its raw materials to more economically advanced countries. Their efforts to attract domestic and international investment encouraged a major boom in the production and export of products such as henequin (for making rope), coffee, cacao (cocoa beans), cattle, silver, and gold. Soon, the country had become so attractive to foreign investors that large amounts of land, the country's petroleum, its railroad network, and its mining wealth were largely controlled

by foreigners. Nationalist reaction against the power of these foreign interests played a significant role in the tensions that produced the Revolution of 1910.

Some years after the revolution, many of those concerned about the country's development became convinced that economic growth would not occur unless Mexico could industrialize more fully. They argued that reliance on exports of agricultural products, minerals, and petroleum forced the country to import manufactured goods and, over the long term, these would always cost more than what was earned from exports.* In addition, critics of the earlier agro-export model of development argued, prices of primary products shifted greatly from one year to the next and countries that produced them were doomed to repeat boom/bust cycles as their domestic economies reflected sharp fluctuations in international prices for the goods they exported. Mexico, they believed, should begin to manufacture the goods that it was currently importing.

Import Substitution and its Consequences

For several decades, Mexico pursued a model of industrialization known as import substitution, or **import substituting industrialization (ISI)**. Under this strategy, manufacture of previously imported goods is encouraged. In Mexico, ISI policies emerged piecemeal. "Mexico slipped into [import substitution] when war-imposed restrictions on exports to Mexico created a sizable market for Mexican manufacturers in Mexico and the United States. When the end of World War II destroyed this natural protection, the regime of Miguel Alemán Valdés (1946–1952) instituted tariffs and import licenses to protect the nation's fledgling manufacturing sector."[13]

Through policies to encourage domestic and international investment, provide credit and tax incentives to industrialists, maintain low rates of inflation, and keep wage demands low through subsidized transportation, housing, and health care for workers, the government continued to promote industrialization to provide goods for a domestic market. It also helped this process along by investing in state-owned steel mills, electric power generators, ports, and petroleum. Between 1940 and 1970, in fact, over 40 percent of all

---

* This argument became extremely influential in policy-making circles throughout Latin America in the 1950s and 1960s.

fixed capital investment came from the government. These policies had considerable success. Initially, the country produced simple products (shoes, clothing, and processed foods) but then began to produce consumer durables (refrigerators, automobiles, trucks, and so on), intermediate goods (steel, petrochemicals, and other products used in the manufacturing process), and capital goods (heavy machinery to produce manufactures) by the 1960s and 1970s.

Mexican agriculture was also affected by this drive to industrialize. Under Lázaro Cárdenas, a massive agrarian reform was carried out and the *ejido* became an important structure in the rural economy, accounting for half the cultivated area of the country and 51 percent of the value of agricultural production by 1940. After Cárdenas left office, however, government policymakers moved rapidly away from the economic development of the *ejidos*. Instead, they became committed to developing a strong, entrepreneurial private sector in agriculture. For them, "the development of private agriculture would be the 'foundation of industrial greatness.' "[14] They wanted agriculture to provide foodstuffs for the growing cities, raw materials for industry, foreign exchange from exports, and a supply of labor for new factories. To encourage these goals, the government invested in transportation networks, irrigation, and storage facilities for agricultural commodities. It provided extension services and invested in research. It encouraged imports of technology to improve output and mechanize production. Policymakers believed that modern commercial farmers would respond more to these investments and services than would peasants on small plots of land, so it provided most of its assistance to large landowners.

The government's generous encouragement of industry and agriculture set the country on a three-decade path of sustained growth. Between 1940 and 1950, gross domestic product grew at an annual average of 6.7 percent, while manufacturing increased at an average of 8.1 percent. In the following two decades, GDP growth rates remained impressive and manufacturing growth continued to outpace overall growth in the economy. In the decade of the 1950s, manufacturing achieved an average of 7.3 percent growth annually, and between 1960 and 1970, it averaged 10.1 percent annually. Production of a wide range of agricultural commodities, particularly export products, also grew rapidly as new areas were brought

under cultivation and the new green-revolution technology (scientifically improved seeds, fertilizers, and pesticides) was extensively adopted on large modern farms. These were, indeed, years for great optimism as foreign investment increased, the middle class grew larger, and indicators for health and welfare steadily improved. Between 1940 and 1970, Mexico City grew from a modest-sized city of a million and a half people to a major metropolis of over 8 million inhabitants. This was a period in which even the poorest Mexicans believed that their lives were improving. Table 1 on the following page presents data that summarize a number of advancements during this period. So impressive was Mexico's economic performance that it was referred to internationally as the "Mexican Miracle."

U.S. private investment was an important source of capital for the country's effort to industrialize; in the twenty years after 1950, it grew at an average of over 11 percent a year. In 1962, the United States accounted for 85 percent of all foreign investment in Mexico. Moreover, U.S. exports to Mexico typically constituted two-thirds of the country's imports. Mexico regularly sent two-thirds of its exports to the United States. At the same time, Mexican policymakers viewed the closeness and size of the U.S. economy as a significant threat, and many policy initiatives—restricting foreign investment in industries considered important to national development and seeking to diversify trade relationships with other countries, for example—were undertaken to lessen the country's dependence on the United States.

While the government took the lead in encouraging industrialization, it was not long before a group of domestic entrepreneurs developed a special relationship with the state. Government policies protected the market for their products through high tariffs or special licensing requirements, limiting imports of competing goods. Business elites in Mexico received subsidized credit to invest in equipment and plant facilities, and they benefited from cheap energy—subsidized by the government—and rarely had to pay taxes. Inflation was kept in check and the government helped ensure that investors would have access to cheap labor by providing workers' housing, transportation, and medical coverage.

Through the impact of such policies, an elite of protected businesses emerged as powerful players in national politics. In the 1940s and 1950s, they strengthened a set of industry-related interest groups

---

TABLE 1   Mexican Development, 1940–1990

	1940	1950	1960	1970	1980	1990
Population (thousands)	19,815	26,282	38,020	52,771	70,416	88,598
Life Expectancy[a] (years)	—	51.6	58.6	62.6	67.4	68.9
Infant Mortality[a] (per 1,000 live births)	—	—	86.3	70.9	49.9	42.6
Illiteracy (% of population age 15 and over)	—	42.5	34.5	25.0	16.0	12.7
Urban Population (% of total)	—	—	50.7	59.0	66.4	72.6
Economically Active Population in Agriculture (% of total)	—	58.3	55.1	44.0	36.6	22.0

	1940–1950	1950–1960	1960–1970	1970–1980	1980–1990
GDP Growth Rate (average annual percent)	6.7	5.8	7.6	6.7	1.6
Per Capita GDP Growth Rate	—	—	3.7	3.7	−0.7

[a]Five-year average

Sources: *Statistical Abstract for Latin America,* United Nations, Economic Commission for Latin America; Roger Hansen, *The Politics of Mexican Development.* Baltimore: The Johns Hopkins University Press, 1971; *Statistical Bulletin of the OAS.*

---

that worked to promote and sustain favorable policies. With this organizational base, groups like the chambers of industry, commerce, and banking began to play increasingly important roles in government policymaking. They were able to veto efforts to the government to cut back on their benefits and to lobby for even more advantages. The government remained the source of most policy initiatives, but generally it was not able to move far in the face of opposition from those who benefited most from its policies. Perhaps as important, business elites became adept at sidestepping government regulations, paying bribes to acquire licenses, credit, permits, and exemptions, and working out deals with officials on a one-to-one basis. In these ways, the government's activities became an embedded aspect of the relationship between the state and the economic elites, and the capacity of government to initiate policies in the face of elite opposition weakened.[15]

Workers also became more important players in national politics. As we saw in the previous section, widespread unionization occurred under President Lazaro Cárdenas, and workers won many rights that had been promised in the Constitution of 1917. Cárdenas organized the unions into the National Confederation of Workers, the CTM, which became the most powerful official voice of organized labor within the PRI. The policy changes initiated in the 1940s, however, made the unions more dependent on the government for benefits and protection. The government provided benefits to workers but also limited the right to strike. Wage standards were set through active annual negotiation between the CTM and the government, with employer groups largely sitting on the sidelines. Despite the fact that unions were closely controlled, organized workers continued to be an elite within the country's working classes. Union membership meant job security and important benefits such as housing subsidies and health care for families. These factors helped compensate for the lack of democracy within the labor movement. Moreover, the labor leadership had privileged access to the country's political leadership and was able to benefit personally from its control over jobs, contracts, and working conditions. In return, it guaranteed labor peace.[16]

In agriculture, those who benefited from government policies and services were primarily farmers who had enough land and economic resources to irrigate and mechanize and who had the capacity to make technological improvements in their farming methods and crops. By the 1950s, a group of large, commercially oriented farmers emerged to dominate the agricultural economy.[17] They, like their urban counterparts in business, became rich and powerful. Industrialization also created a powerful class of government employees and officials. Many of them were able to benefit from their ability to dispense jobs, licenses and permits for a variety of activities, public works projects, and government investments by selling such favors in return for *mordidas* (bites, or bribes) or political support. They also became firm supporters of the continuation of government policies that provided them with special advantages.

There were significant costs to this pattern of economic and political development. Most important, government policies eventually limited the potential for further growth. Industrialists, who received extensive subsidies and benefits from government, had few incentives to produce efficiently. High tariffs kept out foreign competition, further reducing incentives for efficiency or quality in production. Importing technology to support industrialization eventually became a drain on the country's foreign exchange. In addition, government helped the industrialists by providing subsidies to workers in terms of benefits such as housing, social security, and transportation; the costs of providing such benefits increased beyond the capacity of the government to generate revenue, especially because tax rates were kept extremely low as a further incentive to investors. Mexico's tax rates, in fact, were among the lowest in the world, and opportunities to avoid payment were extensive. Eventually, the ISI strategy became less effective in generating new jobs as industrialists moved from investing in labor-intensive industries such as processed foods and textiles to capital intensive industries such as the production of automobiles, refrigerators, and heavy equipment. As a result, cities began to fill up with underemployed and unemployed workers. Mexico's development strategy had "generated growth, but at increasingly higher costs."[18]

Moreover, as the economy grew, and with it the power of industrial, agricultural, and urban interests, many were left behind. The ranks of the urban poor grew steadily, particularly from the 1960s on. Mexico developed a sizable informal sector—workers who produced or sold goods and services at the margin of the economic system and who faced extreme insecurity. Living in squatter settlements, most lacked access to even the most basic of public health facilities such as sewerage and potable water. By 1970, a large proportion of Mexico City's population lived in inner city tenements or in squatter settlements surrounding the more established parts of the city.[19]

Also left behind in the country's development after 1940 were the country's peasant farmers. Their lands were often the least fertile, plot sizes were minuscule, and access to markets was impeded by poor transportation and exploitive middlemen who trucked products to markets for exorbitant fees. The 1940s and 1950s were important years for increasing the gap between commercial agriculture—largely centered in the north and northwestern regions of the country, where much of Mexico's political elite originated—and subsistence agriculture, largely made up of small private farmers and *ejidatarios* who lived in central and southern parts of the country. Farming and surviving in the *ejido* communities, where land was held communally, was particularly difficult. Because *ejido* land could not be sold or (until the early 1980s) rented, *ejidatarios* could not borrow money from private banks because they had nothing to pledge as collateral if they defaulted on their payments. Government banks provided credit to them, but usually it was given only to those who had the right political connections. The government invested little in small infrastructure projects throughout the 1960s, and because they did not have individual title to their land, *ejidatarios* had little incentive to provide their own infrastructure. Agricultural research and extension focused on the large farm sector. Controlled prices for basic foodstuffs rounded out the lack of incentives for the *ejidos* to invest in farming. Not surprisingly, the *ejido* sector consistently reported low productivity.

Increasing disparities in rural and urban incomes, coupled with high population growth rates, contributed to the emergence of rural guerrilla movements and student protests in the mid- and late-1960s. The government was alarmed by this evidence of opposition, particularly when, in 1968, a student movement openly challenged the government on the eve of the Olympic games, which were being hosted by Mexico City. Moreover, by the early 1970s, it was becoming evident that the size of the population, growing at a rate of some 3.5 percent a year, and the structure of income distribution impeded the effective pursuit of further industrial development. The domestic market for goods produced in the country was limited by poverty; many Mexicans could not afford to buy the more sophisticated manufactured products the country would need to produce in order to continue to grow under the import substitution model.

Early hopes that the process of industrialization would free the Mexican economy from excessive dependence on the industrialized world, and particularly on the United States, and make the country less subject to abrupt swings in the prices for primary commodities, were counterbalanced by evidence of new sources of vulnerability. Manufacturing required foreign investment and imported technology. The more advanced the process of industrialization, the greater the needs. Concerns about powerful multinational companies, which had invested heavily in the country in the 1960s, grew, as did the need to spend scarce foreign exchange for foreign technology. Moreover, the country was increasingly unable to meet domestic demand for basic foodstuffs and, by the late 1960s, increasingly large quantities of food had to be imported, costing the government precious foreign exchange that it could have used for better purposes. By the 1970s, some policymakers had become convinced that industrialization had actually increased the country's dependence on advanced industrialized countries and particularly on the United States.

Sowing the Oil and Reaping a Crisis

In the early 1970s, the policy response to emergent economic and political problems was to increase the role of government in the economy through investment, control over foreign capital, and greater attention to escalating social needs. Under the leadership of President Luis Escheverría (1970–1976), the state expanded development expenditures and rapidly became the principal supplier of goods and services not only in urban but also in remote rural areas. "The belief at the time was that a country in which the state controlled a larger share of investment, owned more 'strategic' sectors (energy, steel, and so on), and regulated more of the price-setting mechanism would be more prosperous, more equitable, and less vulnerable to the political pressures of the business sector at home and abroad."[20]

Increased government expenditures and activities were not supported by increased concern for tax revenue or greater economic growth, however. The government was spending much more than it generated, and as the public internal debt grew rapidly, the government began borrowing abroad heavily. Echeverría's outspoken criticism of the private sector discouraged its willingness to invest significantly during his adminis-

tration. Between 1971 and 1976, inflation rose from an annual average of 5.3 percent to almost 16 percent and the foreign debt more than tripled. In response to mounting evidence that current policies could not be sustained, the government devalued the peso in 1976 and signed a stabilization agreement with the International Monetary Fund (IMF) to reduce government spending, increase tax collection, and control inflation. Little progress was made in changing the existing set of policies, however, because, just as the seriousness of the economic situation was being recognized, major new finds of oil were reported.

Between 1978 and 1982, Mexico was transformed into a major oil exporter. As international oil prices rose rapidly—from $13.30 per barrel in 1978 to $33.20 per barrel in 1981—so did the country's fortunes, along with those of other oil-rich countries such as Nigeria, Iran, Indonesia, and Venezuela. Moreover, estimates of Mexico's reserves were adjusted upward. The administration of President José López Portillo (1976–1982) embarked on a policy to "sow the oil" in the economy and "administer the abundance," with vast investment projects in virtually all sectors and major new initiatives to reduce poverty and deal with declining agricultural productivity. Public spending increased at dramatic rates and economic growth was unprecedented, reaching a four-year average of 8.6 percent. Oil revenues paid for much of this expansion, but the foreign debt also mounted rapidly as both public and private sectors borrowed heavily to finance investments and lavish consumer spending. Mexico, like many other countries, was able to borrow so extensively because international financial markets were flush with so-called petrodollars.

In 1982, Mexico's foreign debt was $86 billion and the exchange rate was seriously overvalued.* Oil accounted for 77.2 percent of the country's exports, causing the economy to be extremely vulnerable to changes in oil prices. And change they did. In 1983, the international price for Mexican petroleum dropped precipitously to $26.3 a barrel. Resources from exports declined dramatically. At the same time, the United States tightened its monetary policy, and ac-

---

* An overvalued exchange rate makes imports cheaper and exports more expensive, generally limiting their attractiveness in foreign markets. Overvalued exchange rates can easily lead to foreign exchange crises because countries are using foreign exchange more rapidly than they are generating it from exports.

cess to foreign credit dried up rapidly. Wealthy Mexicans responded by sending vast amounts of capital out of the country just as the country's international creditors demanded repayment on their loans. In August 1982, the government announced that the country could not pay the interest on its foreign debt. This announcement triggered a debt crisis that reverberated around the world.

The impact of these conditions on the Mexican economy was devastating. GDP growth in 1982 was −0.6 percent and fell to −4.2 percent in the following year. New policy measures were put in place by the administration of Miguel de la Madrid (1982–1988) to deal with the economic crisis, but they were repeatedly overtaken by escalating inflation, financial sector panic, depleted foreign reserves, severe trade imbalances, and debt renegotiations. Because of these problems, "Mexico experienced an increasingly heated national debate over development strategy, a widening rupture in the state-private sector relationship, and a shift from traditional negotiation strategies to public confrontation by key opposition groups. . . ."[21] In 1985, just as another agreement to reschedule debt repayments was concluded with the IMF, massive earthquakes rocked Mexico City on September 19 and 20, causing 8,000–10,000 deaths, $4–5 billion in damage, and incalculable loss through the destruction of communication networks, chaos in the physical infrastructure, and disorientation among citizens and officials alike. As if the earthquakes were not devastating enough, in 1986, petroleum prices dropped to $12 a barrel. In the following year, inflation exceeded 130 percent. Only at the end of the de la Madrid administration did the government begin to gain control of the problems facing the country's economy.

The economic crisis had several important implications for structures of power and privilege in Mexico. First, faith in import substitution was firmly destroyed. While criticism of this strategy for industrialization had been increasing since the 1970s, the crisis of the 1980s convinced even the most recalcitrant that import substitution created inefficiency in industrial and agricultural production, failed to generate sufficient employment, cost the government far too much in subsidies, and increased economic dependency on industrialized countries. By the mid-1980s, few policymakers or informed citizens argued strongly for the traditional highly interventionist state or for its protectionist and social welfarist role.

In addition to the final undermining of what had been considered an appropriate development strategy for the country, the power of economic interest groups and their ability to influence government policy were profoundly altered. Prolonged economic crisis hit the business sector particularly hard. When the economy stagnated, declined, and failed to recover rapidly, private debts could not be repaid, inflation and rising unemployment diminished domestic demand, government subsidies were repeatedly cut back through austerity measures, and most public investment plans were put on hold. The inevitable result was the loss of economic viability of many of the country's domestic businesses. Bankruptcy and recession exacted their toll on the fortunes of even large entrepreneurs. As economic hardship affected their members, the traditional business organizations lost their ability to put strong pressure on the government.

Similarly, the country's relatively privileged unions lost bargaining power with government over the issue of wages and protection. Inflation focused many of the country's workers on day-to-day survival rather than on union militancy, and a shift in employment from the formal to the informal sector further fragmented what had once been the most powerful sector of the PRI. Austerity affected subsidies for public transportation, food, electricity, and gasoline and increased economic pressure on workers. The combination of these factors weakened the capacity of labor to resist policy changes that affected the benefits they received.

New voices also emerged to demand that the government alter its policies. Throughout the years of deep economic hardship, in which wages lost between 40 and 50 percent of their value, increasingly large numbers of people became unemployed, inflation cut deeply into middle-class incomes, and budgets for health and education services were severely cut back, Mexico's citizens demanded that the government do something to alleviate the hardship. During the 1980s, a wide variety of interests began to organize outside the confines of the PRI. In fact, the earthquake of 1985 was a watershed for Mexican society. Severely disappointed by the government's failure to respond to the problems created by death, destruction, disorientation, and homelessness, hundreds of communities organized rescue efforts, soup kitchens, shelter, and rehabilitation initiatives. A surging sense of political empowerment developed, as groups long accustomed to dependence on government learned that they could deal with basic social and economic problems better without government than with it.[22]

In addition, the PRI was challenged by the increased popularity of opposition political parties, one of them headed up by the son of the country's most revered president, Lázaro Cárdenas. The elections of 1988 became a focus for protest against the economic dislocation caused by the crisis and the political powerlessness that most citizens felt. When the votes were counted for Carlos Salinas, the PRI candidate received a bare majority of 50.7 percent even while opposition parties claimed widespread electoral fraud.

A New Strategy and Emergent Political Voices

Thus, when Carlos Salinas de Gortari assumed the presidency in late 1988, the authority and legitimacy of the Mexican state was at its lowest point in decades. Government claims that inflation was being controlled and economic recovery was on the way were met with skepticism. Among the principal challenges to the Salinas administration were basic questions about the capacity of the Mexican government to define a development strategy that was appropriate for the country and to rebuild political support for the government and the PRI.

Demands on the Salinas administration to deal with the economic and political crisis were extensive. At the same time, the weakening of the old centers of political power provided it with a major opportunity to reorient the country's strategy for economic development, as President Salinas suggested in his inaugural address. "This is a singular moment in history, weighted with risk, yet rich in opportunities."[23] His administration acted on these words. Between 1988 and 1994, the dependency relationship between industry and government was weakened when new free-market policies were put in place. Decreasing regulation of economic interactions was an important part of this restructuring of state-economy relationships. Deregulation meant that the private sector had more freedom to pursue economic activities and less reason to seek special favors from government. A number of large government industries, such as the telephone company, the banking sector, the national airlines, and steel and sugar mills, were reorganized and sold to private investors. This privatization re-

duced government activities and expanded the private sector. A constitutional revision made it possible for *ejidatarios* to become owners of individual plots of land, thus making them less dependent on government. In addition, financial sector reform, such as changing laws about banking and establishing a stock exchange, encouraged the emergence of new banks and brokerage and insurance firms.

Among the most far-reaching initiatives carried out by the Salinas administration was the negotiation and eventual signing of the North American Free Trade Agreement with Canada and the United States. This agreement created the basis for gradual introduction of free trade among these three countries. These changes were a major reversal of import substitution and economic intervention that had marked government policies in the past. In the future, the Mexican state would continue to be a regulator of the economy, but it would be much less directly involved in economic activities than it had been in the past. Mexican industrialists and farmers would have to work much harder to make their businesses internationally competitive. As we will see, liberalizing the Mexican economy and opening up its markets to foreign competition increased the vulnerability of the country to changes in international economic conditions. These factors, as well as mismanaged economic policies, led to a major economic crisis for the country at the end of 1994.

Questions remain about the future relationship between economic interest groups and the government. Under the country's new development strategy and policies, banking and insurance industries will no doubt become more powerful, as will export industries that could capture new opportunities in international markets. How will they organize themselves to represent their interests to the government in the future? How effective will they be in developing the capacity to influence government policies?

ECONOMY AND SOCIETY

Mexico's economic development has had a significant impact on social conditions in the country. Overall, the standard of living has improved markedly since the 1940s. Rates of infant mortality, literacy, and life expectancy have steadily improved. Provision of health and education services expanded until the government cut back on social expenditures in the early 1980s in response to the economic crisis. Among the most important consequences of economic growth was the development of a large middle class, most of whom live in Mexico's numerous large cities. By the 1980s, a third or more of Mexican households could claim a middle-class lifestyle—that is, steady income, secure food and shelter, access to decent quality education and health services, a car, some disposable income and savings, and some security that their children would be able to experience happy and healthy lives.

Achieving these goals reflects well on the ability of the economy to increase social well-being in the country. However, the impressive growth rates that the economy achieved prior to the early 1970s and then between 1978 and 1982 could have produced greater social progress. In terms of standard indicators of social development—namely, infant mortality, literacy, and life expectancy—Mexico falls behind a number of Latin American countries that have grown less rapidly but have provided more effectively for their populations. Countries such as Costa Rica, Colombia, Argentina, Chile, and Uruguay had less overall growth but greater social development in the period after 1940. These countries paid more attention to the distribution of the benefits of growth than did Mexico. Moreover, in its pursuit of rapid industrialization, Mexico City has become one of the largest, most congested, and most polluted cities in the world. "Near lethal levels of pollution from industrial firms that had made the industrialization miracle possible were strangling the local population. . . . The overcentration of vehicles, population, and industry also produced severe scarcities in urban services."[24] A leading Mexican intellectual called Mexico City a "monstrous inflated head, crushing the frail body that holds it up."[25] In some rural areas, oil exploitation left devastating environmental damage, destroying also the life-styles and opportunities of *ejidatarios* and small farmers.

Mexico's economic development has also resulted in a widening gap between the wealthy and the poor and among different regions in the country. Although the poor in rural and urban areas are better off than they were in the early days of the country's drive toward industrialization, they are worse off when compared to middle- and upper-income groups. In 1950, the bottom 40 percent of the country's households shared about 14 percent of total personal income, while the upper 30 percent shared 60 percent of income.[26] By 1984, it was estimated that the lowest 40 percent shared about 12 percent of income, while the top 30 percent shared almost 68 percent.[27] This is a profile of a country in which, relatively speaking, the rich are growing richer and the poor are growing poorer.

Among the poorest are those in rural areas who have little or no access to productive land and those in urban areas who do not have steady jobs. Harsh conditions in rural areas have fueled a half-century of migration to urban areas, as the poor have abandoned the land in search of jobs and better opportunities. Nevertheless, some 25 million Mexicans continue to live in rural areas, many of them in deep poverty. Large numbers of them must work for substandard wages and migrate seasonally to search for jobs in order to sustain their families. Traditionally, those who have crossed the border to the United States—legally and illegally—in search of jobs have come from depressed rural areas. It is not unusual to find some villages inhabited by children, women, and elderly people for six to eight months of every year as able-bodied men make the hazardous journey to the United States to find work as farm laborers and workers in low-skill service industries. Studies have documented that in some villages, 60–80 percent of all household income is from the remittances of these seasonal migrants.

Among those rural inhabitants who have access to land, almost half can count on five hectares or less. Almost all of this land is unirrigated and dependent on erratic rainfall. The land is often bleached of nutrients as a result of centuries of cultivation, population pressure, and erosion. A 1983 study characterized many of the country's farms as infrasubsistence, that is, plots of land that were insufficient to provide even for the subsistence needs of a household. The crops grown on such farms, primarily corn and beans, are poor people's crops and do not bring high prices in the markets. To improve production, peasant farmers would have to buy fertilizer, improved seeds, and insecticides, and they would have to find ways to irrigate their plots. But they generally have no money to purchase these inputs or invest in irrigation. In many areas, farm production provides as little as 20–100 days of employment each year. Not surprisingly, underemployment is high in rural Mexico, as are rates of seasonal migration. It is also not surprising to learn that the incidence of disease, malnutrition, and illiteracy is much higher in Mexico's rural areas than in urban areas. When the rebels in Chiapas called for jobs, land, education, and health facilities, they were clearly reflecting the realities of life in much of the country.

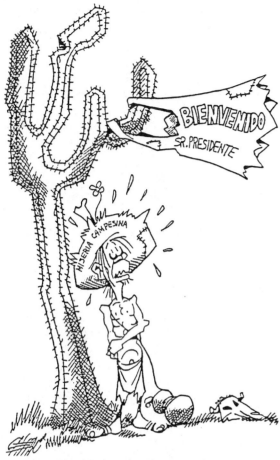

Among those who have benefited least from the
government's development policies are the rural poor.
Source: *Ausencias y Presencias Gente de Ayer y Hoy en
su Tinta: Problematica Politica, Social, Vista por un
Cartoonista Potosino* by Luis Chessal, Universidad
Autonoma de San Luis Potosi, Mexico, 1984.

Poverty has a regional dimension in Mexico. The
northern areas of the country are significantly better
off than southern areas and central areas also demonstrate a high incidence of poverty. Much of the regional distribution of poverty is related to conditions
in the agricultural sector. In the north, large commercial farms grow fruits, vegetables, and grains for export using modern technologies. The U.S. border, the
principal destination of agricultural products, is close
at hand, and transportation networks are extensive and
generally in good condition. Moreover, industrial cities such as Monterrey and Tijuana provide steady jobs
for skilled and unskilled labor. Along the border, a
rapidly growing band of manufacturing and assembly

plants has provided numerous jobs, particularly for
young women who are seeking some escape from the
burdens of rural life or the constraints of traditional
family life.

In southern and central regions of the country,
however, the population is denser, the land poorer, and
the number of *ejidatarios* eking out subsistence is
greater. Transportation is often difficult and, during
parts of the year, some areas may even be inaccessible
because of heavy rains and flooding. In addition, most
of Mexico's remaining indigenous groups live in
southern regions, often in very remote areas where
they have been forgotten by government programs and
exploited by regional bosses for generations. The conditions that spurred the Chiapas rebellion are found
throughout the southern states.

The economic crisis of the 1980s had an impact
on social conditions in the country. Wages declined by
about half and unemployment soared as businesses
collapsed and the government started laying off workers in public offices. The informal sector expanded
rapidly. Here, people eke out a living by hawking
chewing gum, umbrellas, sponges, candy, shoelaces,
mirrors, and a variety of other items in the street,
jumping in front of cars at stoplights to wash wind-
shields and sell newspapers, producing and repairing
cheap consumer goods such as shoes and clothing, and
selling services on a daily or hourly basis. While the
informal sector often provides important goods and
services as well as jobs for low-income people, conditions of work are often dangerous and insecurity about
where the next peso will come from, and when, is
endemic.

In addition to a decline in wages and jobs, the
economic crisis of the 1980s also meant that social
services were under extreme pressure and generally
declined in availability and quality. Expenditures on
education and health declined after 1982 as the government imposed austerity measures. Salaries of primary school teachers declined by 34 percent between
1983 and 1988 and many began working second and
even third jobs in order to make ends meet. Per capita
health expenditures declined from a high of about 150
pesos in 1980 to under 90 pesos in 1990. Hospitals,
clinics, and schools were left in disrepair for a good
part of the decade, and obtaining equipment and supplies became almost impossible given diminished
budgets. Although indicators of mortality did not rise
during this troubled decade, the incidence of diseases

associated with poverty—namely, malnutrition, cholera, anemia, and dysentery—increased. The diet of most Mexicans became less rich in protein as they ate less meat and drank less milk because of the crisis. The crisis began to ease in the early 1990s, however, and many came to believe that conditions would improve for the poor. Government began investing in improving social services. Then, in late 1994, a new economic crisis emerged, marking 1995 with rapidly rising levels of unemployment and austerity measures that severely limited investments.

Questions remain about how well the voices of Mexico's poor will be heard in the future. This is particularly true of *ejidatarios.* Despite the poor economic performance of the *ejidos,* they were little short of sacred cows in Mexican politics because of their ties to the symbolism of the revolution, the radical reform years of the Cárdenas administration, and political support for the regime. Under the Salinas administration, however, a reform of the constitution of 1917 made it possible for *ejidatarios* to obtain private title to their plots and to buy and sell land for the first time since the revolution. Henceforth, peasants would no longer be so dependent on the government for access to land, credit, and markets, and the PRI and the National Confederation of Peasants (CNC) would no longer have such power over them. As small farmers, would they be able to organize effectively and demand effective rural development policies and investment from government? Would they give support to opposition parties when the government was unresponsive to their needs?

MEXICO AND THE INTERNATIONAL POLITICAL ECONOMY

Under the import substitution strategy in effect until the 1980s, Mexico steadily increased the extent to which it protected its domestic producers. High tariff barriers and import license requirements severely restricted the extent and efficiency of its trade relationships with other countries. In 1982, for example, all imports had to have a special license to enter the country. This acted as a considerable constraint on any activity that required imported goods because of the cost and delay involved in acquiring a permit. The average tax on imports was 27 percent and, for some goods, it was as high as 100 percent. The crisis that began in 1982 clearly indicated that a policy of encouraging

more Mexican exports and opening up its markets to foreign goods was essential. In the years after 1982, the government relaxed restrictions on the ability of foreigners to own property, reduced and eliminated tariffs, and did away with most of the licenses that importers were required to obtain from the government. Foreign investment was courted with the intent of increasing the manufacture of goods for export. The government also introduced a series of incentives to encourage the private sector to produce goods for export. In 1986, the country joined the General Agreement on Tariffs and Trade (GATT), a multilateral agreement that attempts to promote freer trade among countries.

Each of these changes signaled the government's effort to encourage Mexico to pursue a more outward-oriented development strategy, in which the country was actively engaged in trade with other industrial nations. Mexico was responding to evidence, much of it based on the experience of the rapidly growing economies of East and Southeast Asia, that export-oriented development could fuel sustained economic growth. The government believed that, along with many other countries in the world, Mexico had to become part of a global economy. President Salinas signaled the importance of this goal in a speech to business leaders. "Mexico does not want to be late for the world's appointment with the twenty-first century."[28]

In the 1990s, many countries were trying to form regional trade organizations such as the European Union. In 1990, Mexican and U.S. citizens learned that their governments were exploring possibilities for a free trade agreement. In 1991, Canada joined these discussions. The chief executives of the three countries signed an agreement in August 1992 and Mexico moved rapidly to ratify it. The government, which had pinned its hope for renewed economic growth on the possibility of greater trade and investment among the three countries, had to endure a cliff-hanging debate in the United States before the agreement was ratified by Congress in 1993. The Canadian government followed suit shortly thereafter and NAFTA was born. On January 1, 1994, its gradual implementation was initiated.

This agreement is important to Mexico. In 1990, 64.6 percent of the country's exports were sent to the United States and 69.7 percent of its imports came from that country. The next most active trading country with Mexico was Japan, which received only 5.7

percent of its exports and accounted for only 4.7 percent of its imports. Access to the U.S. market is thus of considerable economic interest to Mexico's government and to domestic and foreign investors. Foreign investment grew significantly in Mexico during the period when the agreement was being negotiated because investors anticipated that numerous business opportunities would develop in the country once it was signed. The agreement did not make trade among the three countries completely free, but it lowered many tariffs and made it easier to resolve disputes among them when allegations of unfair trade practices arise. The agreement will be implemented gradually over fifteen years to allow industries time to adapt to new regulations and become more competitive.

NAFTA entails risks for Mexico also. Domestic producers worried about competition from U.S. firms. Farmers were concerned that Mexican crops could not compete effectively with those grown in the United States. Many were particularly worried that peasant producers of corn and beans would be destroyed when U.S.-grown grains became widely available at much lower prices. In addition, many people believed that embracing free trade with Canada and the United States indicated a loss of sovereignty, and that Mexico's economic situation would be much more vulnerable to the ebb and flow of economic conditions in the much larger U.S. economy. NAFTA is also a very long and complicated document, with numerous regulations and technical details. After it had been in effect for only a few months, exporters and importers on both sides of the border began to complain about the cumbersome, confusing, and time-consuming process for assessing duties and tariffs that it introduced. Nevertheless, NAFTA signaled a new period in U.S.-Mexican relations by making closer integration of the two economies a certainty.

As in the past, renewed efforts to diversify economic relationships are seen as one way to manage the increasing integration with the other economies of North America. Presidential candidate Ernesto Zedillo announced that diversification of economic and political relationships was one of the planks of his 1994–2000 foreign policy platform. "The strategic interest of Mexico demands that we strengthen our ties with all the regions of the planet. . . . In its economic aspect, diversification will be aimed at increasing Mexican exports, better participation in financial resource flows, and new markets. We will also seek to attract

capital, to modernize the productive apparatus, and technology transfer."[29] At the same time, the speech confirmed the investment Mexico had in the success of stronger trade relations with the United States and Canada.

The fears of those who questioned the rapid opening up of the Mexican economy to international competition became greater at the end of 1994. In the preceding years, massive amounts of foreign and domestic investment had spurred a major boom in the Mexican stock market. Much of this investment was in bonds that had short-term maturities and that could be rapidly converted to dollars. In the summer and fall of 1994, investor confidence began to wane somewhat as political violence increased, as the conflict in Chiapas defied solution, and as the government allowed the peso to become overvalued in order to control inflation. The newly installed administration of Ernesto Zedillo then mismanaged a devaluation in mid-December, and investor confidence in the country plummeted. In the ensuing weeks, massive amounts of capital flowed out of the country, and the peso rapidly lost much of its value against the dollar. The United States, newly aware of the importance of the Mexican economy to its own economic growth and concerned about the impact of economic and political instability on its southern border, hammered together a $50 billion economic assistance program composed of U.S., European, and IMF commitments to allow Mexico to meet the demands of its external creditors. The Mexican government imposed a new stabilization package that contained austerity measures, higher interest rates, and limits on wages. This new economic crisis raised questions throughout the globe about the growth potential of emerging markets in countries as diverse as Mexico, Argentina, Malaysia, Thailand, Brazil, Indonesia, and India.

The incorporation of Mexico into NAFTA introduced novelties in economic and political relationships. During negotiations, new international political alliances developed. Environmental groups from the United States sought support in Mexico and Canada for fighting the agreement, and labor groups also looked across both borders for allies in opposing new trade relations. Environmental and labor groups united around concerns that Mexico would not enforce environmental protection and fair labor legislation. Some business interests allied across countries in supporting the agreement, anticipating oppor-

Mexicans are very conscious of the disparities of wealth and power between the United States and their country.
Source: From *Un Siglo de Caricaturas en México* by Eduardo del Rio, Editorial Grijalbo, 1984.

tunities for larger markets, cheaper labor, or richer sources of raw materials. As economic relationships develop around freer trade in the region, these political alliances may grow in influence and raise questions about traditional notions of sovereignty, particularly in the discussion of domestic economic policies. For Mexico, which has traditionally feared the power of the United States in its domestic affairs, internationalization of political and economic relationships poses particularly difficult problems of adjustment.

Such concerns are heightened because of the expansion of modern means of communication, which have stripped Mexico of some of the secrecy that traditionally surrounded government decision making, electoral processes, and efforts to deal with political dissent. More than ever before, the 1980s and 1990s focused international attention on the country. The government could no longer respond to events such as the peasant rebellion in Chiapas, the questioned honesty of the 1994 elections, or the management of exchange rates without considering how such actions would be received in Tokyo, New Delhi, Nairobi, London, or Washington.

SECTION 3
Governance and Policy-Making

ORGANIZATION OF THE STATE

According to the supreme law of the land, the Constitution of 1917, Mexico's political institutions resemble those of the United States. There are three branches of government, and a set of checks and balances limits the power of each. The congress is composed of a senate and a chamber of deputies. One hundred twenty-eight senators are elected, four from each of the country's thirty-one states and an additional four from the federal district (capital).* Five hundred deputies are elected from 300 electoral districts, 300 by simple majority vote and 200 by proportional representation. The states and local governments are also elected. The president, governors, and senators are elected for six years, and deputies and municipal officials are elected for three.

In practice, the Mexican system is very different from that of the United States. The constitution is a very long document, especially when compared to that of the United States. It lays out the structure of government and guarantees a wide range of human rights, including familiar ones such as freedom of speech and protection of the law, but also economic and social rights such as the right to a job and the right to health care. The political system is highly centralized and presidentialist, a moderate authoritarian system governed by a civilian elite that shares membership in a dominant party and commitment to political stability and economic development. Although the system has made a series of pragmatic adjustments to pressures for greater democracy and electoral honesty, it remains far from the electoral democracy familiar to U.S. citizens. Its policy-making processes are also very distinct from those in the United States, even though the constitutional arrangement of powers is superficially similar.

THE EXECUTIVE

The Presidency

"The political sun rises and sets every six years on the presidency."[30] This statement by an observer of Mexican politics suggests the importance of the presidency

* Until 1993, two senators were elected from each state.

to the political system. The Mexican presidency is the central institution in a centralized system of governance and policy-making. The president selects a successor, appoints officials to all positions of power in the government and the PRI, and often names the PRI candidates who, in the past, almost automatically won elections as governors, senators, deputies, and local officials. The president sets the broad outlines of policy for the administration and has numerous resources to ensure that those policy preferences are adopted. Until the mid-1970s, Mexican presidents were considered above criticism in national politics and revered as symbols of national progress and well-being. While economic and political events of the 1980s and 1990s diminished the prestige of incumbent presidents, the extent of their power remains impressive. In fact, some have argued that Mexican presidents are little short of dictators during their six years in office.

Mexican presidents have a set of formal powers that allows them to initiate legislation, lead in foreign policy, create government agencies, make policy by decree or through administrative regulations and procedures, and appoint a wide range of public officials. More importantly, informal powers provide them with the capacity to centralize control in the executive—that is, the president is head of the PRI, manager of a vast patronage machinery for filling positions at all levels of government and the party, initiator of legislation and policies that are routinely approved by the congress, and the designator of his own successor. His preferences determine who will rise and fall in political fortune and how government resources will be spent. When the president makes his first state-of-the-nation address, Mexicans listen avidly to learn "what's going to happen for the next six years [as he] tells them what to believe in and how to behave," as one observer of Mexican politics stated.[31]

In the last year of an administration, a sitting president selects his own successor through a process known as the ***destape*** (unveiling). This continues to be a mysterious process.[32] It is generally assumed that the president consults with leaders of business and labor and with top-level chiefs in the PRI as well as with his own close advisers, but there is no requirement that he do so and no evidence that it is regularly done. Among the factors that political commentators believe are considered in the selection are pressures to accommodate important political interests and the president's desire to see his own policy preferences maintained.

Mexican presidents select their own successors. The chosen candidate waits to be unveiled.
Source: *Ausencias y Presencias Gente de Ayer y Hoy en su Tinta: Problematica Politica, Social, Vista por un Cartoonista Potosino* by Luis Chessal, Universidad Autonoma de San Luis Potosi, Mexico, 1984.

Once the president has made his choice, it is normally announced by the leadership of the PRI, often by the head of the CTM. Immediately, the candidate is acclaimed as the unanimous and most popular choice by all sectors of the party and by politically ambitious officials all over the country.

The PRI presidential candidate has almost always been a member of the outgoing president's cabinet. In past years, several had been minister of the interior, the person responsible for maintaining internal law and order. This was true of Miguel Alemán (1946–1952), Adolfo Ruiz Cortines (1952–1958), Gustavo Díaz Ordaz (1964–1970), and Luis Echeverría (1970–1976). With the expansion of the government's role in economic development, candidates in the 1970s and 1980s were selected from the ministries that manage

TABLE 2   **Mexico's Presidents, 1884–2000**

Porfirio Díaz (1876–1880)	1884–1911
Francisco Léon de la Barra (interim)	1911
Francisco I. Madero	1911–1913
Pedro Lascurain (interim)	1913
Victoriano Huerta (interim)	1913–1914
Francisco S. Carbajal (interim)	1914
Venustiano Carranza	1914; 1915–1920
Eulalio Gutiérrez (interim, named by Convention)	1914
Roque González Garza	1914
Francisco Lagos Cházan	1915
Adolfo de la Huerta (interim)	1920
Alvaro Obregón	1920–1924
Plutarco Elías Calles	1924–1928
Emilio Portes Gil (interim)	1928–1930
Pascual Ortiz Rubio	1930–1932
Abelardo L. Rodríguez (interim)	1932–1934
Lazaro Cárdenas	1934–1940
Manuel Avila Camacho	1940–1946
Miguel Alemán Valdés	1946–1952
Adolfo Ruiz Cortines	1952–1958
Adolfo López Mateos	1958–1964
Gustavo Díaz Ordaz	1964–1970
Luis Echeverría Alvarez	1970–1976
José López Portillo	1976–1982
Miguel de la Madrid	1982–1988
Carlos Salinas de Gortari	1988–1994
Ernesto Zedillo Ponce de Léon	1994–2000

the economy. José López Portillo (1976–1982) had been minister of finance, and Miguel de la Madrid (1982–1988) and Carlos Salinas (1988–1994) had served as ministers of budgeting and planning prior to being selected as candidates. The selection of Luis Donaldo Colosio, who had been minister of social development and welfare, was thought by political observers to signal renewed concern with problems of social development. When Colosio was assassinated, the selection of Ernesto Zedillo, who had first been minister of budgeting and planning and then minister of education, was interpreted as an ongoing concern with social problems of the country and as an effort to maintain the policies of economic liberalization that Salinas had introduced. Table 2 lists Mexico's presidents since 1884.

Those selected to run for president under the banner of the PRI have all had long public careers. Until Luis Escheverría was selected in 1969, candidates had usually held elective positions, often as state governors, as well as positions within the PRI and in the government. Echeverría and his successors, however, never held elective positions. In addition, party activism became much less important as a criterion for high-level office; recent presidents have gained party credentials by serving as directors of the PRI's policy think tank or as campaign managers rather than by working their way up from the ranks of the party. They were assigned these activities after they had become prominent enough to be among the handful of hopefuls for the *destape*. Luis Colosio had been the campaign manager for Carlos Salinas. He was then selected to head the party prior to being brought into the cabinet. Ernesto Zedillo never held any elective or important party positions until he was chosen as campaign director for Colosio.

Moving away from the tradition of extensive experience in the party and regional politics, candidates since the mid-1970s have spent more of their careers in Mexico City and have tended to be trained in economics and public management rather than in the traditional field of law. Presidents since López Portillo

Mexican presidential
candidates are expected to
campaign hard, traveling to
remote locations, making
rousing campaign speeches,
and meeting with citizens
of humble origins. Here,
presidential candidate Ernesto
Zedillo is on the campaign trail
in 1994.
Source: AP/Wide World
Photos.

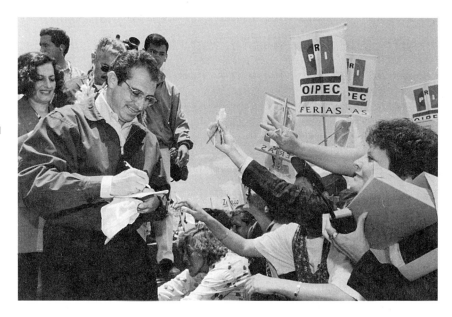

have had postgraduate training at elite institutions in the United States. Miguel de la Madrid held a master's degree in public administration from Harvard; Carlos Salinas received a Ph.D. in political economy and government from Harvard; Luis Colosio studied for a Ph.D. in economics from the University of Pennsylvania; and Ernesto Zedillo had a Ph.D. in economics from Yale. Some have argued that because of their tendency to come from more urban and elite backgrounds, recent presidents have lost touch with the masses and with the traditional politicians of the PRI who have their roots in regional, labor, or rural politics. By the 1980s, a topic of great debate in political circles was the extent to which a divide between *políticos* and *técnicos* (technocrats) had emerged within the national political elite. Among the old guard of the PRI, there was open skepticism about the ability of young technocrats like Carlos Salinas and Ernesto Zedillo to manage political conditions in the country. During the presidential campaign of 1994, considerable efforts were made to stress the more humble beginnings of Colosio and Zedillo and the fact that they had had to work hard to get an education.

Once selected as the official candidate, the future president must campaign widely and exhaustively, sometimes for as long as a year prior to the August elections. He is expected to put on rousing campaign appearances, making speeches that remind voters of the heroic traditions of the revolution and the PRI's

agenda for bringing social and economic justice to the country. In a tradition set by Lázaro Cárdenas, he must take time to listen to the grievances of ordinary citizens in remote villages and dusty urban squatter settlements. He is expected to pay particular attention to the poor and marginalized to whom he will promise assistance once elected. This kind of campaigning helps elevate the president to the level of a national symbol of unity and promise, a person who, though elected as the supreme leader, is able to speak with common people and share their concerns, dreams, and aspirations. In his travels, the candidate must also meet extensively with local and regional politicians and PRI operatives and work to strengthen the PRI networks throughout the country.

Once elected, the president moves quickly to name a cabinet. Generally, he selects as his closest advisers those with whom he has worked over the years as he has risen to political prominence. He may also use cabinet posts to make certain he has a broad coalition of support; in this regard, he may appoint people with close ties to the labor movement, or to business interests, or to some of the regional strongholds of the party. Under Carlos Salinas, for example, the president's closest advisers assumed leadership of important economic ministries such as finance, industry and commerce, and planning and budgeting. Ministries that were less central to his policy concerns, such as interior, labor, and transportation and communication, were awarded to those who had strong links to the old guard of the PRI—often to those who had strong skills in negotiating political deals and resolving conflicts within the party. During his administration, cabinet changes signaled the emergence of new president priorities when Luis Colosio, a very close ally of President Salinas, was moved to the Ministry of Education. Most took this as a signal that education would be the next sector to be reformed by the Salinas technocrats.

The president also selects the head of the party and heads of important state-owned companies such as the national electricity board and PEMEX, the petroleum company. He has numerous appointments to fill high-level positions in the office of the president, which allows him to provide policy direction and keep tabs on what is occurring throughout the government and the party. These appointments help the president build a team of like-minded officials within the government and ensure that those who hold the most important positions are personally loyal to him. In turn, high-level appointees have numerous jobs that they fill in their organizations. Like the president, they use this patronage power to put together personally loyal teams of officials whose career advancement is tied to their own political fate. These officials, in turn, build their own teams, and so on down through middle levels in the bureaucracy.

The initiation of each new administration is therefore characterized by extensive turnover of positions, although many of the newly appointed officials served in other positions in prior administrations. This giant patronage system has the potential to be extremely inefficient. And, indeed, little happens in government in the year prior to an election as officials bide their time or jockey for positions in the next administration, or in the year following an election as newly appointed officials learn the ropes and assemble their own teams. Nevertheless, when a president has set clear goals and expects high performance from his personally chosen officials, these people in turn must expect good performance from their staffs if they are to produce for the president. In many situations, then, the patronage system results in the potential for increased presidential leadership and effective performance, at least at high levels in government, as officials seek to do well by their superiors and therefore advance their careers. Many middle- and high-level officials hope that their performance will be noticed by their minister, espe-

cially if that person has the potential to be selected as the PRI's presidential candidate. If this should happen, they could expect to be appointed to a higher-level office in the next administration.

Once the newly appointed officials are in office, the president is in a position to set and carry out important policy measures. Together with the bureaucracy, the president is the focal point of all policy formulation and political management. The legislature has always had a PRI majority and has acted as a rubber stamp on presidentially sponsored legislation. In 1988, the PRI lost enough seats in the chamber of deputies that it no longer had the two-thirds majority needed to pass amendments to the constitution. Carlos Salinas therefore had to wait until the midterm elections of 1991 returned this majority before he introduced amendments that made significant changes in such important areas as rights to land in rural areas and church-state relations.

Mexican presidents, though powerful, are not omnipotent. They, must, for example, abide by a deeply held constitutional norm—fully adhered to since 1940— to step down at the end of their term, and they must honor the political norm to step out of the political limelight to allow the successor to assume full presidential leadership. In addition, several factors tend to limit the extent of presidential discretion. Mexican presidents are always "creatures of the system," selected because they have proved themselves adept at understanding and playing by the rules of the existing system. Through their careers in politics or government, they have become familiar with the range of interest groups in the country and have demonstrated a willingness to compromise on policy and political issues so that these interests do not unduly challenge the government. They have also proved themselves to be skillful in the fierce bureaucratic politics that surround career advancement and in guessing about who the next candidate for president is likely to be. In addition, presidents must demonstrate their loyalty to the myths and symbols of Mexican nationalism such as the indigenous roots of much of its culture, the agrarian origins of the revolution, commitment to social justice, and sovereignty in international affairs.

One of the most effective constraints on presidential power is the limited ability to ensure that policies are actually implemented. At times, policies are not implemented because public officials at lower levels in government disagree with the policies or make deals with affected interests so they can benefit personally. This is the case, for example, with taxes that remain uncollected because individuals or corporations bribe officials to overlook them. In other cases, lower-level officials may lack the capacity or skills to implement some policies, such as those directed toward improving education or rural development services. For whatever reasons, Mexican presidents cannot always deliver on their intentions. Traditionally, they have been above criticism when this has occurred because of the willingness of Mexican citizens to blame lower-level officials for such "slippage." However, exempting the president from responsibility for what occurs—and what does not occur—during his watch became much less common in the 1980s and 1990s.

The Bureaucracy

Mexico's executive branch is large and powerful. Almost a million and a half people work in the federal bureaucracy, most of them in Mexico City. An additional million work in the national education system, and yet another million work for the large number of state-owned industries and semiautonomous agencies of the government. State and local governments employ over 600,000 people. Pay scales are usually low and, in the past, the number of people filling lower-level positions such as drivers and messengers and clerical and maintenance jobs far exceeded demand for them. In the 1980s, austerity measures cut down on some of this overstaffing.

Officials at lower levels in the bureaucracy are unionized and protected by legislation that gives them job security and a range of benefits. At middle and upper levels, most officials are called "confidence" employees; that is, they serve as long as their bosses have confidence in them. These are the officials who are personally appointed by their superiors at the outset of an administration. Their modest salaries are compensated for by the prospect of career mobility and by the significant power that they can have over the course of public events. For aspiring young professionals, a career in government is often very attractive because of the challenge of dealing with important problems on a daily basis and being part of the process of finding solutions. Some employees also benefit from opportunities to take bribes or use insider information to promote private business deals.

From the 1980s on, the Mexican government became famous for the large number of young techno-

crats who were attracted to public office, many of them trained in economics and public policy at major U.S. universities. In fact, 59 percent of the cabinet members selected by Carlos Salinas held degrees in economics, and many of them had advanced degrees from universities such as MIT, Yale, the University of California at Berkeley, the University of Pennsylvania, Stanford, and Harvard. These officials filled their ministries with young and well-trained appointees, further reinforcing the technocratic image of this administration. Echoing some of the concerns about the political inexperience of recent presidents, such officials were criticized for being remote from the life experiences of the significant number of people living below the poverty line and the large number who do not have access to decent public services or normal protection of the law. Some confirmation of this perspective came in the wake of the Chiapas rebellion, when high-level officials seemed caught off guard by the demands of those participating in the rebellion.

Policy initiative is routinely taken by the central ministries in direct response to the president's policy priorities. Ministries headed by the most likely presidential candidates and staffed by people closest to the president are the ones that respond with greatest zeal to the president's lead. Ministries that have been awarded to groups or interests that are important to the PRI's coalition are more likely to be less activist in following presidential preferences if these have any negative consequences for those interests. Thus, for example, during the Salinas administration, many ministries were called upon to eliminate a wide range of the regulatory functions they had traditionally performed. Some ministries were slow to respond, however, because deregulation threatened the convenient relationships they had developed with the industries they were charged with regulating and eliminated many opportunities for collecting bribes.

The Legislature and the Executive

Students in the United States are frequently asked to study complex charts explaining how a bill becomes a law, because the formal process of lawmaking affects the content of legislation. In Mexico, while there are formal rules that prescribe such a process, studying them would not be useful for understanding the legislature or for policy-making. For almost sixty years, Mexico's two-chamber legislature was fully dominated by the PRI. Because of the overwhelming presence of this political party, opposition to presidential initiatives was rarely heard. To the extent that representatives did not agree with policies they were asked to rubber stamp, they counted on the fact that policy implementation would be flexible and would allow for after-the-fact bending of the rules or disregard of measures that were harmful to important interests.

As we have seen, almost total control of the legislature by the PRI was destroyed, at least temporarily, in 1988. The growing strength of opposition parties, combined with legislation that provided for greater minority representation in the congress, led to the election of 240 opposition deputies that year. After that, when presidential legislation was sent to the chamber, real debate about issues often ensued and the opposition challenged the tradition of legislative passivity in the face of presidential initiatives. Because the Salinas administration was engaged in introducing major policy reforms, some of which required constitutional amendments in order to be implemented, some initiatives were not brought to congress, and the reform process was slowed. In other cases, the president pursued policy initiatives through decree laws and administrative measures rather than through the legislature where they might be questioned even when they would certainly be approved by the PRI delegates. The two-thirds PRI majority was returned in 1991—amid allegations of significant voter fraud—and presidentialism was reasserted. Nevertheless, the strong presence of opposition parties encouraged the legislature to become more of a forum for debate than it had been traditionally, and PRI delegates were challenged to defend legislative initiatives. The 1994 elections returned a clear PRI majority of 300 deputies and 64 senators. Opposition parties will be heard, but they will not be able to stop firm presidential leadership in legislation, unless the PRI becomes significantly fragmented and its legislators cease to vote as a block.

The Military

Mexico is one of only a few countries in the developing world that have successfully depoliticized the military. Much of the credit for this process belongs to Plutarco Calles, Lázaro Cárdenas, and subsequent presidents who introduced mechanisms to rotate regional commands among the military brass so that none could build up regional bases of power. In addition, postrevolutionary leaders made an implicit bargain with the military leaders by providing them with

opportunities to engage in business so that they did not look to political power as a way of gaining economic power. Salaries and benefits for the military have been kept at adequate levels to limit possibilities that such conditions could become politicized. After 1946, the military, which originally formed one of the pillars of the PRI, no longer had institutional representation within the party and became even more marginalized from the centers of power. Since that time, the military has been kept poor, small, and subordinate to civilian leadership.

Nevertheless, the military has, from time to time, been called in to deal with situations of domestic unrest—in rural areas in the 1960s, in Mexico City and other urban areas to repress student protest movements in 1968, in 1988 in the arrest of a powerful labor leader, in 1989 to break a labor strike, in 1990 to deal with protest over electoral fraud, and, most recently, in Chiapas in 1994. The military was also called in to deal with the aftermath of the earthquake in Mexico City in 1985, but its poor ability to respond to the emergency and its lack of capacity to assist citizens in need did little to enhance its already low esteem in the eyes of the public. The military has also been heavily involved in efforts to manage drug trafficking in recent years, and rumors abound about deals struck between military officials and drug barons. How the institution really operates and the extent to which such rumors reflect reality, however, remain "one of the great mysteries of modern Mexico."[33]

When the military is called in to resolve domestic conflicts, some observers of Mexican politics become concerned that the institution is becoming politicized and may begin to play a larger role in political and policy decision making. From time to time, rumors of preparations for a coup are heard, as during financial panics in the 1980s and in the aftermath of the assassination of candidate Colosio. Thus far, however, such fears have not been realized and many believe that as long as civilian administrations are able to maintain the country's tradition of stability, the military will not intervene directly in politics. Mexican politics, for all its authoritarianism and abuses of power, continues to be firmly civilian.

The Para-Statal Sector

The para-statal sector—composed of semiautonomous or autonomous government agencies, many of which produce goods and services—has been extremely large and powerful in Mexico. Because the government provided significant support for the development of the private sector as part of its post-1940 development strategy, numerous activities were assumed by the government that in other countries are carried out by the private sector. Thus, until the Salinas administration, the country's largest steel mill was a state-owned industry, as were the nation's largest fertilizer producer, sugar mills, and airlines. In addition, the national electricity board produces energy and supplies at subsidized prices to industries. PEMEX grew to enormous proportions in the 1970s and 1980s under the impact of the oil boom. NAFIN, a state investment corporation, provides a significant percentage of all investment capital in the country. A state marketing board, CONASUPO, was responsible for the importation and purchase of the country's supply of basic staples and, in the 1970s, played a major role in distributing food, credit, and farm implements in rural areas. In 1970, there were 391 para-statal organizations in Mexico. By 1982, their number had grown to 1,155, in part because of the expansion of government activities under presidents Echeverría and López Portillo and in part because of the nationalization of private banks carried out in 1982 by President López Portillo. In the 1980s and 1990s, concerted efforts were made to privatize many of these industries, the largest of which were the telephone company, the national airline, and the nationalized banks. By 1990, only 280 state-owned industries remained and efforts continue to sell or liquidate many of them. Para-statals such as PEMEX and the electricity board are likely to remain in government hands, however, because they are considered too important to national interests to be entrusted to the private sector.

These para-statal industries have often been powerful players in national politics, none more so than the national petroleum company, which set national policies about exploration, exploitation, and exportation of oil. Historically, much of PEMEX's power came from a large and extremely powerful organization, the petroleum workers' union. For many years, this union was headed by a powerful and corrupt boss, known as La Quina, who sold jobs and dictated the terms of all contracts that were let by PEMEX. The coffers of the union and pocketbooks of its leaders grew extremely large under his leadership. It was widely believed that not even the president could challenge his control over the petroleum industry. In a

striking move only weeks after he assumed the presidency, however, Carlos Salinas had La Quina arrested for corruption and thrown in jail, destroying his reputation for invincibility.

OTHER STATE INSTITUTIONS

The Judiciary

Like other political institutions in Mexico, the judiciary is politically, though not constitutionally, subordinate in the presidentialist system. On most issues, the courts rule on the basis of established law. They can occasionally slow the actions of government by issuing a writ of protection *(amparo)* to individuals who claim that their rights are being violated by specific government actions. Although such writs are issued from time to time, they are not generally used to restrain presidential power or intentions. On almost all issues in which the power of government or presidential interests are at stake, the courts can be counted on to rule on the side of the government. In this sense, the courts are not independent voices within the political system, even though the principle of judicial review is accepted. They are instead part of a structure of power that makes it difficult for opposition voices to be heard or protected.

With the increasing interest in human rights issues in recent years, the courts are under added pressure from the media and citizens groups to play a stronger role in protecting basic freedoms. Concern about confidence in the legal system figured in the presidential campaign in 1994, when the PRI candidate argued that "citizens do not feel that the authorities are on their side. There are cases of police and law enforcement agencies corruption almost every day."[34]

States and Municipalities

Regional and local government in Mexico is similar to other aspects of the political system in that what is described in the constitution is far from reality. Mexico has a federal system and each state has its own constitution, executive, unicameral legislature, and judiciary. Municipalities (equivalent to U.S. counties) are governed by popularly elected mayors and councils. But state and municipal governments are poor and are subordinate to Mexico City economically and politically. Most of the funds they command are transferred to them from the central government, and they have little legal or administrative capacity to raise their own revenue.

The president selects or approves the PRI candidates for governor and, until 1988, all governors were from the PRI. Not all candidates selected to run for governorship are part of the personally loyal group *(camarilla)* supporting the president. Some are selected because they are regional strongmen whose fiefdoms, controlled by their own loyalists at the local level, are important to maintaining the political peace and electoral dominance of the PRI. The governor of the state of Chiapas under the Salinas administration, for example, was nationally known to be a regional boss who ruled the state autocratically and often brutally, as if it were his private hacienda. His predecessor, who enjoyed a similar reputation, became minister of the interior under Salinas. Both had regularly returned massive majorities for the PRI. Nevertheless, popular wisdom has it that the political life of a governor who defies the president is over with one phone call from Los Pinos, the presidential residence in Mexico City, to the governor's office. In the absence of political unrest or scandal, however, governors are often allowed considerable autonomy. They play a central role in the selection of mayors and councilors at the municipal level.

States and localities suffer greatly from the lack of well-trained and well-paid public officials. As at the national level, many jobs are distributed as political patronage, but even officials who are motivated to be responsive to local needs are generally ill-equipped to do so. Several presidents have sought to decentralize public sector activities to the state level, but most such initiatives have sought to decentralize the central government rather than delegate powers to subordinate levels of government. For example, in the early 1970s, regional headquarters of the national ministry of agriculture were established in the states rather than improving the capacities and responsibilities of the state-level ministries of agriculture. A similar effort to decentralize the ministry of health was undertaken in the early 1980s. In a break with this tradition, the Salinas administration delegated powers over education to ministries of education at the state level. Henceforth, the state bureaucracy was to assume responsibility for the schools, teachers, and administration of education. Interestingly, many governors resisted this initiative because it meant that they would have to deal with the powerful teachers' union and because they did not have the administrative capacity to handle such a large and complex responsibility. Moreover, they

worried that they would be unable to acquire the budgetary resources necessary to carry out their new responsibilities.

There are exceptions to this picture of regional and local government impoverishment and lack of capacity. State governments in the north of the country, such as Nuevo Leon, have been more responsive to local needs and better able to administer public services. In such states, local municipalities have become famous for the extent to which they differ from the norm in most of Mexico. Monterrey, in Nuevo Leon, for example, has a reputation for efficient and forward-looking city government. Much of this local capacity can be credited to a regional political tradition that has stressed independence from—and even hostility to—Mexico City and the PRI and to entrepreneurial groups that have invested time and resources in local government.

The governance of states and localities in Mexico is yet another area in which transition is occurring. In 1986, many believe that only electoral fraud kept two governorships out of the hands of an opposition party. In 1989, a non-PRI governor assumed power in Baja California Norte. Also, municipalities have increasingly been the focus of authentic party competition. By the early 1990s, some 5 percent of them were no longer run by the PRI. In 1995, state-level elections placed opposition governors in control of some large and important states. As opposition parties come to control these levels of government, they will be challenged to improve services such as police protection, garbage collection, sanitation, and education. PRI-dominated governments will also be pressured to improve their performance because they are more threatened by the possibility of losing elections. Whoever controls these governments, however, will be operating under considerable financial constraint and with public institutions that have rarely been well managed. Despite these handicaps, their ability to perform better will be critical to them in consolidating and expanding their electoral support for the future.

THE POLICY-MAKING PROCESS

This section has outlined a policy process that is fully dominated by Mexico's president. In fact, the Mexican system is enormously dependent on the quality of its leadership and presidential understanding of how economic and social policies can affect the development of the country. Broad changes in the scope and direction of policies conform to presidential administrations because each president has considerable capacity to introduce such changes. In selecting their successors, of course, presidents try to ensure that the candidate agrees with and will continue their policy initiatives, but there is no assurance that this will happen. New presidents often wish to distance themselves from their predecessor and to ensure their own place in history by enunciating new policies and development goals. In a rare example of the tensions that can occur in the transition from one *sexenio* to the next, in early 1995 the administration of Ernesto Zedillo openly blamed the outgoing administration of Carlos Salinas for mismanaging economic policy.

As indicated throughout this chapter, the *sexenio* is an extremely important fact of political life in Mexico, calibrating the basic rhythm of public life. New presidents introduce extensive change in positions within the government and the PRI. They are able to bring in "their" people who, in turn, build teams of "their" people within ministries, agencies, and party networks. This generally provides the president with a group of high- and middle-level officials who share a general orientation toward public policy and who are highly motivated to carry out his goals. They also believe that, in doing so, they enhance their own opportunities for upward political mobility in the future. In such a context, it is possible to introduce changes in public policies every six years.

Of course, under most conditions, the extent of change is limited by the resources the government has and by elite support for such changes. Presidential skills in negotiating, managing opposition, using the media to acquire public support, and maneuvering within the bureaucracy can be important for ensuring that a presidential vision is fully endorsed. Under extraordinary conditions such as the deep and sustained economic and political crisis faced by Carlos Salinas, it is even possible to introduce major reversals in national development strategies. The first months of Ernesto Zedillo's administration were marked by considerable conflict with disaffected elements in the PRI, and many questioned the president's political skills and ability to build support for his agenda.

Significant limits on presidential power also occur when policy is being implemented. In fact, in areas as diverse as the regulation of working conditions, antipollution laws, tax collection, election monitoring, and provision of basic health care in remote rural areas, Mexico often has extremely advanced legislation on the books. Even cursory familiarity with factory conditions, pollution in Mexico City, tax evasion, election fraud, and poor health care suggests that in many cases legislation remains on the books rather than being translated into practice. Because of this tendency, it is important to treat many government claims about its accomplishments with some skepticism. There are frequently large gaps between what is announced as policy and what is accomplished in fact.

The dynamics of the policy process in Mexico clearly indicate that the government, not the PRI, is the principal source of policy leadership. Of course, the president is elected as the standard bearer of the PRI, but he has traditionally dominated the party from the time he sets the party platform for the elections to the time he selects the head of the party after taking office to the time he chooses a successor as he gets ready to step down from power. As we will see in the next section, the PRI is much more a mechanism for political mobilization and support than for policy leadership.

SECTION 4

Representation and Participation

How do citizen interests get represented in Mexican politics, given the high degree of centralization, presidentialism, and PRI domination? Is it possible for ordinary citizens to make demands on government and to influence public policy? In fact, Mexico has achieved over seventy years of relatively stable and peaceful political interactions in part because the political system offers some channels for representation and participation. Through its long history, the political system has emphasized compromise among contending elites, behind-the-scenes conflict resolution, and distribution of political rewards to those willing to be patient and to play by the formal and informal rules of the game. It has also responded, if reluctantly and defensively, to demands for political and policy change.

These characteristics do not mean that Mexico has an open, pluralist democracy, however. Although challenged to become more democratic, it continues to be a political system in which power is concentrated and participation is limited. In order to understand how Mexican citizens participate in their government and how they represent their interests in this centralized system, it is important to understand the way the party system works, the extensive networks of personal relationships that cement political loyalties, and the importance of accommodation to diverse interests that helps maintain the political peace. It is also important to understand the sources of pressures for change and the increasing vulnerability of the system to those pressures.

Often, these aspects of Mexican politics indicate that citizens are best able to interact with the government through a variety of informal means rather than by expressing their interests and concerns through formal processes such as elections, campaigns, and interest-group lobbying. Interacting with government through the personal and informal mechanisms of clientelism usually means that the government retains the upper hand in deciding which interests to respond to and which to ignore. Thus, although the political system incorporates a wide range of interests, it does not provide for full democracy. For many interests, it has been "incorporation without power."[35] Increasingly, however, Mexican citizens are organizing to alter this situation.

THE LEGISLATURE

The congress has not been an important location for representation and participation in Mexico since the PRI was created. The reason for this is simple: The legislature has always had a PRI majority and the PRI has always acted as a rubber stamp to presidential decisions. Until the late 1980s, neither the senate nor the chamber of deputies had been a forum for discussing alternatives to presidentially initiated policies or even for seriously questioning such initiatives. Because important policy decisions are not made—only approved—in congress, interest groups do not pay much attention to the deputies or senators or to the process of legislation. The senate has even been called "a kind of political museum" to empha-

size its irrelevance to government decision making.[36] Groups wishing to influence policy prefer to focus their attentions on the president and the executive branch, where policies are formulated and interests accommodated.

These characteristics may be changing, however. As discussed in the previous section, the Mexican congress may be becoming a more important forum for a variety of political voices and points of view to be heard. PRI candidates are facing more competitive elections in many locales, and the number of "safe seats" for party stalwarts is declining. Greater opposition party representation in the legislature in the future could easily translate into greater importance for the legislature, at least as a forum for debating government policy and representing a more diverse set of interests than those traditionally represented by the PRI. If the congress does increase in importance as a place where legislation is debated and shaped, interest groups will begin to pay it greater attention and focus more of their lobbying activities on it.

The real importance of the legislature, at least until recently, has been largely a result of the informal aspects of Mexican politics that emphasize the exchange of political rewards for loyalty to the system. The PRI provides positions as deputies and senators for politicians who help maintain support for the system. While the situation may be undergoing significant change, it is still the case that "the main role of the national legislature remains that of providing another source of sinecures, a place for young politicians to pause on the way up or for old ones to rest on the way down; of providing another salary for a deserving political worker or cold storage for one for whom an appropriate job cannot at the moment be found."[37] Becoming a senator or a deputy is a way of accumulating local or regional political power and being able to benefit from and distribute jobs, development projects, contracts and licenses for businesses, and other "goodies." However, because the top political elites no longer need party service for upward mobility, legislative positions are most attractive to local and regional politicians and to those who do not have the elite educational credentials necessary for moving into important positions in the bureaucracy. The use of these positions as rewards, however, is being threatened by the declining ability of the PRI to win elections.

THE PARTY SYSTEM AND ELECTIONS

The PRI

Mexico's Institutional Revolutionary Party is the result of a coalition of political elites who agreed that it was preferable to work out their conflicts within an overarching structure of compromise than it was to continue to resort to violence. In the 1930s, the PRI incorporated a wide array of popular interests into the regime, transforming it into a mass-based party that drew support from all classes in the population. Its principal activities were—and continue to be—generating support for the government, organizing the electorate to vote for its candidates, and distributing jobs and development resources in return for loyalty to the system.

Until the 1990s, party organization was based largely on the corporate representation of class interests—the pillars of the party that were referred to in earlier pages. Labor was represented within party councils by the National Confederation of Labor (CTM), a sector organization made up of industry-based unions at local, regional, and national levels. Peasants were represented by the National Confederation of Peasants (CNC), a peak organization of *ejido* and peasant unions and regional syndicates. The so-called popular sector, comprising small businesses, community-based groups, and public sector workers, had less internal cohesion, but was represented by the National Confederation of Popular Organizations (CNOP). Of the three, the CTM was consistently the most organized and powerful. Its venerable leader, Fidel Velásquez, who was ninety years old in 1990, was for decades one of the most powerful people in the country.

Within these corporate structures, the PRI functioned through extended networks that distributed public resources—particularly jobs, land, development projects, and access to public services—to lower-level activists who controlled votes at the local level. This form of informal political organization, known as clientelism, works through multiple chains of patron-client interaction that culminate at the highest level of political decision making within the PRI and the office of the president of the country. In this system, those with ambitions to public office or to positions within the PRI put together networks of supporters from above (patrons), for whom they deliver the vote, and supporters from below (clients), who

trade allegiance to the politicians for access to public resources. Traditionally, the PRI's strongest support has come from the countryside, where *ejidatarios* and other peasants have been the most grateful for and dependent on rewards of land or jobs from the political bosses. As the country has become more urbanized, the support base provided by rural communities has remained important to the PRI, but has meant less in terms of overall electoral support.

For well over half a century, this system worked extremely well. Figure 1 demonstrates that PRI candidates won by overwhelming majorities until the 1980s. Of course, electoral fraud and the ability to distribute government largesse are central explanations for these numbers, but they also attest to an extremely well-organized party. Indeed, although the PRI became much weaker in the 1980s and 1990s, it was still the only political party that could boast a nationwide network of constituency organizations in virtually every village and urban community in the country. Through the patron-client networks, it continues to provide means for people of humble origin, especially those living far from the center of political power, to interact with the political system in ways that allow them some access to benefits, however meager. Its vast political machinery allows it to monitor events, even in remote areas, and to manage political tensions at the local level.

Within the PRI, power was centralized and the sector organizations (the CTM, the CNC, and the CNOP) responded primarily to elites at the top of the political pyramid rather than to member interests. Over time, the corporate interest-group organizations, particularly the CTM and the CNC, became widely identified with corruption, bossism, centralized control, and lack of effective participation. By the 1980s, however, the PRI was facing increasing difficulties because of the way in which such characteristics limited effective representation of interests. New generations of voters were less beholden to patronage-style politics and much more willing to question the party's dominance. When the administrations of de la Madrid and Salinas imposed harsh austerity measures, the PRI was held responsible for the resulting losses in incomes and benefits. Simultaneously, as the government cut back sharply on public sector jobs and services, the PRI had far fewer resources to distribute to maintain its traditional bases of support. Moreover, it began to suffer from increasing internal dissention

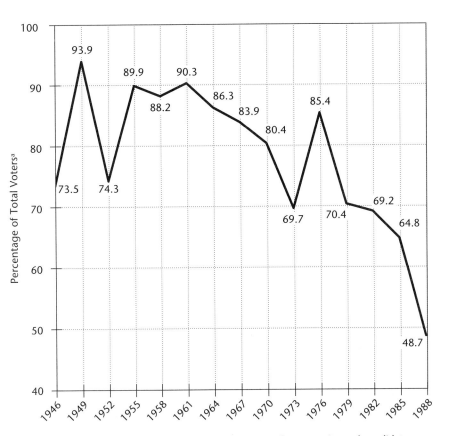

[a]Percentage base includes annulled votes and those cast for nonregistered candidates.

Figure 1   PRI Support in Congressional Elections, 1946–1988
Source: Juan Molinar Horcasitas, *El tiempo de la legitimidad: Elecciones, autoritarismo y democracia en México* (México, D.F.: Cal y Arena, 1991).

between the old guard and those who wanted to reform the party. In the aftermath of the election of 1994, these tensions resulted in open conflict between the modernizers and the so-called dinosaurs. Most significantly, many of the groups that became politically active during the 1980s, fiercely resisted traditional methods of control used by the party.

Until the elections of 1988, there was no question that the PRI candidate would be elected president. Until then, the lowest percentages of the total vote recorded for PRI candidates were 71 percent for Miguel de la Madrid in 1982 and 74.3 percent for Adolfo Ruiz Cortines in 1952. Victories recording 85–95 percent of the total vote for the PRI were much more the norm (see Table 3). In 1988 and again in 1994, however, PRI candidates were challenged by parties to the right and

left, and outcomes were hotly contested by the opposition, which claimed fraudulent electoral practices. In 1994, the PRI candidate won primarily because the opposition was not well organized and failed to present a program beyond that of opposition to the PRI.

As the PRI faced greater competition from other parties and continued to suffer from declining popularity, efforts were made to restructure and reform it. Reformists were appointed by Carlos Salinas to head the party in 1989. The CNOP was replaced by another organization, the UNE (Citizens in Movement), which sought to incorporate a wide array of nonclass-based citizen and neighborhood movements. In 1990, membership rules were altered to allow individuals and groups not identified with its corporate sector organizations to join. In addition, regional party organizations

TABLE 3   **Voting in Presidential Elections, 1934–1994**

Year	Votes for PRI Candidate[a] %	Votes for PAN Candidate %	Votes for All Others[b] %	Turnout (% Voters Among Eligible Adults)[c]
1934	98.2	—	1.8	53.6
1940	93.9	—	6.1	57.5
1946	77.9	—	22.1	42.6
1952	74.3	7.8	17.9	57.9
1958	90.4	9.4	0.2	49.4
1964	88.8	11.1	0.1	54.1
1970	83.3	13.9	1.4	63.9
1976[d]	93.6	—	1.2	59.6
1982	71.0	15.7	9.4	66.1
1988	50.7	16.8	32.5[e]	49.4[f]
1994	50.2	26.1	23.7	—

[a]From 1958 through 1982, includes votes cast for the Partido Popular Socialists (PPS) and the Partido Auténtico de la Revolución Mexicana (PARM), both of which regularly endorsed the PRI's presidential candidate. In 1988, they supported opposition candidate Cuauhtémoc Cárdenas.
[b]Excludes annulled votes; includes votes for candidates of nonregistered parties.
[c]Eligible population base for 1934 through 1952 includes all males ages 20 and over (legal voting age: 21 years). Both men and women ages 20 and over are included in the base for 1958 and 1964 (women received the franchise in 1958). The base for 1970–1988 includes all males and females ages 18 and over (the legal voting age was lowered to 18, effective 1970).
[d]The PRI candidate, José López Portillo, ran virtually unopposed because the PAN failed to nominate a candidate. The only other significant candidate was Valentín Campa, representing the Communist Party, which was not legally registered to participate in the 1976 election. More than 5 percent of the votes were annulled.
[e]Includes 31.1 percent officially tabulated for Cuauhtémoc Cárdenas.
[f]Estimated using data from the Federal Electoral Commission. However, the commission itself has released two different figures for the number of eligible voters in 1988. Using the commission's larger estimate of eligible population, the turnout would be 44.9 percent.

Source: Cornelius and Craig, "Politics in Mexico," in Almond, *Comparative Politics Today,* 4th ed. Copyright © 1988. Reprinted by permission of HarperCollins College Publishers. 1994 figures are unofficial election results.

gained representation at the national level. Party conventions were introduced in an effort to democratize the internal workings of the party, although they appeared to have little impact. In addition, some states and localities began to hold primaries to select PRI candidates, a significant departure from the old system of selection by party bosses. Additional efforts were made to undercut regional bosses who had been closely allied with the patron-client system of the past.

In addition, in an effort to give the appearance of a modern party system in the country, electoral reforms were introduced by the López Portillo, de la Madrid, Salinas, and Zedillo administrations to make it easier for opposition parties to contest elections and win seats in the legislature. The Salinas administration also marginalized PRI operatives from the resource distribution networks that had been so central in the past. The government continued to distribute resources through patronage networks, but they were networks that flowed directly from the president's office to re-

gional and local levels, generally bypassing PRI officials in the process, particularly ones who did not support the president's modernization plans. This helped weaken the traditional bosses of the party at the same time it helped centralize power in the president's office. A national program known as Solidarity, run first out of the president's office and then out of a newly formed ministry of social development, provided extensive resources for local development initiatives that were allocated with an eye for political support building. Much of the political violence of the 1994 election was credited to the traditional party bosses who were reacting to their loss of power.

The PRI continues to face a difficult future. The Mexican electorate is now predominantly urban. Voters are also younger, better educated, and more middle-class than in the days of the PRI's greatest success—the 1940s, 1950s, and 1960s. In 1990, only 27 percent of the population lived in rural areas, but 32 percent of the population lived in cities of one million or more, and 25

TABLE 4 **Support for the PRI by Type of Congressional District (percentage of total vote)**

Districts	1979	1982	1985	1988	Average 1979–1988
Federal District (Mexico City)	46.7	48.3	42.6	27.3	41.2
Other Urban[a]	53.4	56.2	51.1	34.3	48.8
Mixed[b]	67.9	66.2	59.2	46.4	60.0
Rural[c]	83.5	80.9	77.3	61.3	75.8

[a]Urban districts are those in which 90 percent or more of the population live in communities of 50,000 or more inhabitants. Total number: 40 in the Federal District and 56 in other urban areas.
[b]Districts in which more than 50 percent but less than 90 percent of the population live in communities of 50,000 or more inhabitants. Total number: 44.
[c]Districts in which less than 50 percent of the population live in communities of 50,000 inhabitants. Total number: 160.

Sources: Molinar Horcasitas, *El tiempo de la legitimidad;* Cornelius and Craig, "Politics in Mexico," in Almond, *Comparative Politics Today,* 4th ed. Copyright © 1988. Reprinted by permission of HarperCollins College Publishers.

percent of the population lived in Mexico City, which has become one of the world's largest megacities. The 1988 elections demonstrated the relevance of these demographic conditions for the PRI when only 27.3 percent of the population of Mexico City voted for the PRI candidate and only 34.3 percent of the population in other urban areas supported him. While rural support for the party had remained strong, it had also clearly diminished since the 1970s (see Table 4).

The PRI divided over how to respond to its declining base of support. Some, particularly party activists who were brought in by the Salinas administration and others who were sympathetic to its young and technocratic image, have promoted reforms in the party. Others have favored holding onto political power by whatever means necessary. Elections in Mexico have always had a reputation for fraud, but those of 1988, and a series of state and local contests before and after them, broke new ground in terms of allegations of "electoral alchemy," ballot box stuffing, and altering of voter registration lists. Heightened concern about such practices was magnified by national and international media drawn to the contest because of the novelty of the PRI's vulnerability. The struggle between the old guard and reformists continues in Mexico, although the 1994 elections were notably cleaner than those of 1988. The assassination of the secretary general of the PRI, José Francisco Ruiz Massieu, in Mexico City in September 1994 raised serious questions

about the extent of old guard opposition to the modernizers, represented by the party leadership.

The PAN

Several opposition parties compete in elections. Two of them have the potential to contest the dominance of the PRI in the future. The National Action Party (PAN) is the oldest. Founded in 1939 to represent pro-business interests that were firmly opposed to the centralization and anticlericalism of the PRI, its strength is centered in northern states where the tradition of resistance to Mexico City is strong. The PAN has traditionally campaigned on a platform endorsing greater regional autonomy, less government intervention in the economy, reduced regulation of business, clean and fair elections, rapprochement with the Catholic church, and support for private and religious education.

In the past, the PAN was usually able to elect 9–10 percent of all deputies to the national congress and to capture control of a few municipal governments. Then, in the early 1980s, and especially after President López Portillo nationalized the country's private banks, opposition to centralism and statism grew more popular. The PAN began to develop greater capacity to contest elections at higher levels of government. In particular, the party grew in popularity among urban middle-class voters, captured leadership in several provincial cities, and came close to winning governorships in two states

This cartoon suggests the "arrogance of power" that has resulted from almost seventy years of uninterrupted PRI government.

Source: From *Un Siglo de Caricaturas en México* by Eduardo del Rio, Editorial Grijalbo, 1984.

Despite such victories, the PAN will find it difficult to displace the PRI, or even to challenge it significantly on a national level. Until the 1980s, voting at the national level for the PAN was generally interpreted as a protest vote against the PRI rather than as a vote for the program of the PAN. Moreover, much of its program became official policy in the 1980s and 1990s, robbing the party of its capacity to argue against government regulation of business, excessive intervention in the economy, and hostility to the Catholic church. Although support for the PAN expanded to urban areas of some central states, it remained primarily a party identified with the northern region of the country. It was as factionalized as the PRI about its program and electoral strategy and compared very unfavorably with the PRI in terms of its ability to organize at the grassroots level throughout the country.

The PRD

Until the 1994 elections, a more significant challenge to the PRI came from the National Democratic Front (FDN), which became the Democratic Revolutionary Party (PRD) in 1988. The FDN presented Cuauhtémoc Cárdenas as its candidate in the 1988 elections. He ran again under the banner of the PRD in 1994. Cárdenas was not only the son of Mexico's most famous and revered president, but also a PRI insider until party leaders virtually ejected him and other reformers for demanding internal democratization of the party and commitment to a platform emphasizing social justice. In the 1988 elections, Cárdenas was officially credited with winning 31.1 percent of the vote, and the party captured 139 seats in the chamber of deputies. He benefited from massive political defection from the PRI and garnered support from workers who were disaffected with the boss-dominated unions and peasants who saw in him a reflection of his father's concern for the agrarian reform and investment in the poor. Mexico City gave him 50.4 percent of the vote, which represents some middle-class support for this populist and nationalist alternative to the PRI.

Even while the votes were being counted, the party began to denounce widespread electoral fraud and to claim that if the elections had been honest, Cárdenas would have won. The PRD challenged a number of vote counts in the courts and walked out of Salinas' inauguration speech. Considerable public opinion supported the party's challenge. In the aftermath of the 1988 elections, then, it seemed that the

in the early and mid-1980s. In 1988, it captured 16.8 percent of the vote for president, 101 congressional seats, and 1 senate seat. The following year, it won the governorship of the state of Baja California Norte. For the first time since the PRI was founded, the dominant party did not control all governorships in the country. The PAN's candidate for the presidency in the 1994 elections, Diego Fernández de Cevallos, became a nationally popular figure, capturing as much as 30 percent of votes in public opinion polls prior to the elections.[38] He garnered 26 percent of the presidential vote, and the PAN captured 119 seats in the chamber of deputies and 25 in the senate. In a closely watched election after Ernesto Zedillo became president, the PAN won the governorship of the large and important state of Jalisco.

PRD was a strong contender to become Mexico's second most powerful party. It was expected to have a real chance in future years to challenge the PRI's "right" to the presidency. The popularity of Cárdenas as a candidate demonstrated the possibility that an opposition party could seriously challenge the PRI.

However, in the years leading up to the 1994 elections, the party was plagued by internal divisions over its platform, leadership, organizational structure, and strategy for winning votes. By 1994, it was still lagging far behind the PRI in its ability to establish and maintain the local constituency organizations needed to mobilize votes and monitor the election process. In addition, the PRD found it difficult to define an appropriate left-of-center alternative to the market-oriented policies carried out by the Salinas administration. While the claims that such policies ignored the need for social justice were popular, policies to respond to poverty that did not imply a return to unpopular government intervention were difficult to devise. In the aftermath of the Colosio assassination, citizens also became more alarmed about violence, and some were concerned that the level of political rivalry represented by the PRD threatened the country's long-term political stability. In the immediate aftermath of a nationally televised debate among the leaders of the three main parties, Cárdenas's performance was so weak that only 11 percent of respondents in a poll indicated that they would vote for him, compared with 48 percent for the PRI candidate and 26 percent for the PAN candidate.[39] In the elections, Cárdenas won only 17 percent of the votes; the PRD elected 71 deputies and 8 senators.

Elections and Support for the PRI

Each of these three political parties draws voters from a wide and overlapping spectrum of the electorate. Nevertheless, a typical voter for the PRI is more likely to be from a rural area or small town, to have less education, and to be older and poorer than voters for the other parties. A typical voter for the PAN is more likely to be from a northern state, to live in an urban area, to be a middle-class professional, to have a comfortable lifestyle, and to have a high school or even a university education. A typical voter for the PRD is more likely to be young, to be a political activist, to have an elementary or high school education, to live in one of the central states, and to live in a small town or an urban area.

In terms of future elections, the support base for the PRI is the most vulnerable to economic changes

occurring in the country. Voting for opposition parties is an urban phenomenon, and the country continues to urbanize at the rate of 3 percent a year. This means that, in order to stay competitive in elections, the PRI will need to garner more support from such areas. It must also be able to appeal to younger voters, especially the large numbers who are attracted to the PRD and the PAN. The cost of acquiring such support, however, may be willingness to democratize its internal decision-making processes and to desist from blatant acts of electoral fraud. Voters in Mexico's elections are becoming more independent; the easy assumption of PRI victory can no longer be made.

But the opposition parties face a difficult task in attempting to upset the PRI. The official party, although weaker and less legitimate in the mid-1990s than it had ever been, continued to have a stronger organization than either of the two opposition parties. It has a centralized national structure that is experienced in the art of electoral mobilization and it continues to have an extensive network of party loyalists and clients. Opposition parties lag far behind in these organizational characteristics. Moreover, pollsters continue to disagree about whether voting for the PAN or the PRD represents approval of their platforms and candidates or simply a vote of opposition to the PRI. Party identification remains weak for the opposition.

Elections are becoming more competitive in Mexico, as Table 3 indicates. The government is also under tremendous pressure to make them fairer. In characteristic fashion, it has accommodated these pressures, if only reluctantly and partially. In the 1990s, laws to limit campaign spending and campaign contributions and to mandate greater media coverage of opposition parties and candidates were part of the response to the demand to "level the playing field" between the PRI and the other parties. Voter registration was reformed to ensure that fraud would be more detectable. Election monitoring was also strengthened and another reform increased the chances for opposition parties to win representation in the senate. Along with these reforms, however, went others that encouraged splintering of opposition parties.

In an extensive effort to encourage greater confidence in the honesty of elections, the Mexican government invested $1 billion in "the design of an elaborate computer system capable of keeping track of almost 45 million names, one of the world's largest computerized voter registration lists."[40] It was thought to be the

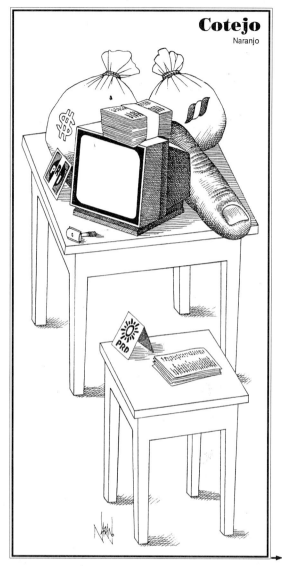

Cotejo
Naranjo

This cartoon suggests the unequal access to resources that favors the PRI. The second bag of "goodies" refers to the National Solidarity Program, which disburses money for local development projects.
Source: © Naranjo, courtesy of *Proceso.*

lowed to register with the Federal Election Commission. Domestic observers were also encouraged because "citizen observation . . . directs sunshine on the process, minimizes fraud, and reduces post-electoral violence by enhancing the credibility of the results."[41]

In the 1994 elections, however, citizens continued to be skeptical about the honesty of elections. An opinion poll carried out during the first week of June 1994 indicated that only 50.4 percent of respondents were "confident that the upcoming presidential election [would] be clean."[42] In the same poll, 37.9 percent thought the elections would not be honest. The PRI's candidate, Ernesto Zedillo, was chosen by 41.1 percent of respondents as the person they would vote for, although 76.1 percent of the respondents believed that the PRI would win the election. Despite continued emphasis on the commitment of the government and the PRI to clean, democratic elections, and despite candidate Zedillo's claim that "my party not only wants the vote of the Mexican people, but also legality, credibility and legitimacy," many had a wait-and-see attitude about whether the system was capable of delivering honest elections.[43] The governor's race in Chiapas left many accusing the PRI of extensive fraud, but observers of the election generally concluded that "while not perfect, the election was free from the kind of widespread fraud that would have changed the results."[44]

POLITICAL CULTURE, CITIZENSHIP, AND IDENTITY

Most citizens in Mexico have long believed that their political institutions are legitimate and nationalist in that they represent and protect the ideals of the Revolution of 1910. They are not blindly loyal, however. Citizens demonstrate overall commitment to the system while expressing considerable criticism—and often cynicism—about how it works and how equitable it is. A survey of almost any *ejido,* for example, will uncover lengthy local histories of how *ejidatarios* have been mistreated, "given the runaround" by bureaucratic organizations, and cheated by local, regional, and national leaders of the CNC, the PRI, and government agencies. The survey will reveal deep commitment to the country's heroes, the president, and the institutions of government along with anger, distrust, frustration, and biting jokes told at the ex-

most advanced system in the world. Some 43 million Mexicans, 86 percent of the eligible voters, carried computerized voter identification cards with their pictures, fingerprints, magnetic strips, and eighteen-digit identification numbers on them. And, in a further effort to demonstrate that the elections were clean, virtually anyone who wished to come to Mexico as an international observer of the election process was alpense of the rich and powerful. However, the extent to which citizens feel distanced from their government while believing deeply in its legitimacy actually increases the power of the government. According to some analysts, "apathy and marginalization did not always constitute clear and present dangers to the regime—indeed, it often permitted the government to do what it wanted."[45]

Along with commitment and cynicism, most Mexicans have a deep familiarity with how the political system works and the ways in which they might be able to extract benefits for themselves from the system. This involves understanding the informal rules of the game in Mexican politics that help keep the system in place, despite extensive inequalities in economic and political power. A brief story demonstrates how these informal rules operate as a kind of cement to maintain citizen tolerance for the system.

> Juan López, the mayor of a small municipality in a southern state, has visitors. Carmen Morales and her daughter, Evelina, have been sitting outside his office in the rundown town hall since 6:30 in the morning, over five hours ago. Carmen has journeyed to the mayor's office from her village, where her husband is an *ejidatario.* As the mayor is leaving his office for the day, Carmen advances quickly and tells him she is the daughter of a former leader of the *ejido,* a person known to López. The mayor becomes attentive, inquiring about the father. Carmen then explains respectfully that she has come for assistance. Her daughter is ill and needs medical attention. Would the mayor please help her get attention from the local public health clinic? The line is long and the doctor and nurse refuse to attend to any more than twenty patients a day. López scribbles a few lines on a scrap of paper and sends Carmen away with it. She will take it to the clinic the next day.

This scene provides valuable clues as to how the Mexican political system works through informal means at the grassroots level. The mayor, undoubtedly an PRI supporter, is emphasizing his power by letting Carmen wait outside his office such a long time. When she approaches him, however, and explains about her father, he becomes more attentive

because she has indicated a link to his patronage network. She asks the mayor for a very concrete and personal favor—to use his position to gain preferential access to services that are strictly rationed. Carmen will take the child to the clinic the following day, push her way to the head of the line, and present the paper she has been given to an aloof attendant. She will be told to wait. Eventually, however, she will be granted an audience with the doctor, who will prescribe medicine. Carmen will explain that she has no money for medicine. Depending on his relationship to the mayor, the doctor may shrug his shoulders and explain that there is nothing he can do or he may give her one of the free samples of medicine that vendors leave with him on their rounds. Carmen will return to her village and extol the mayor for his kindness to the poor and downtrodden. When the next election occurs, she will vote for the people the mayor supports. So will her husband, her three sisters, and numerous other relatives. The mayor will continue to be influential, even when he has left office, because the state governor will know that he has been able to deliver the vote for the PRI.

Exchanges like these happen thousands of times each day and probably millions of times during each presidential administration in Mexico. Clientelism, or the exchange of favors among people of different status or degrees of power, extends from the very top of the political system to the most remote and poverty-stricken village. It is a form of participation in the sense that many people, even the poorest, are able to interact with public officials and, frequently, to get something out of the political system. This kind of participation emphasizes how limited resources—such as access to health care—can be distributed in a way that provides maximum political payoff.

This informal system is a fundamental reason why many Mexicans, despite their increased cynicism about the political system, continue to vote for the PRI. Carmen and Juan were engaged in a political ritual practiced effectively by a wide spectrum of the population. In the past, for the poor and rural, it was a ritual they had to learn if they were to survive because government controlled so much that was central to their lives, particularly land. So pervasive is the idea that the personal relationships of the patron-client networks are the key to getting response from government that it has been called the "myth of the right connection."[46]

However, new ways of interacting with government are emerging and they coexist along with the clientelistic style of the past. An increasing number of citizens are seeking to negotiate with the government on the basis of citizenship rights; they conspicuously refuse the temptations of traditional patron-client methods of resolving problems. They also resist the tradition of federation into large national organizations that could be easily manipulated by government. Instead, the movements that emerged in the 1980s sought to form broad but loose coalitions with other organizations and attempted to identify and then work with reform-oriented public officials. Their suspicion of traditional political organizations such as the PRI or the CNC and the CTM also carried over to suspicion of close alliances with the PAN and the PRD.

As politics and elections become more open and competitive, the role of public opinion and the mass media in the political process is also becoming more important. Public opinion polling in Mexico has been contaminated by the dominance of the PRI, and some polling organizations are even subsidized by the party or the government. Increasingly, however, even the PRI and the government are more interested in objective information and analysis of public opinion. These data have become important in influencing the content and timing of government decisions and in developing strategies about election campaigns. In 1994, politicians, citizens, and political activists closely followed the popularity polls for the three major candidates for president, and party officials monitored how the image of their contender could be molded to capture higher voter approval ratings.

Extensive public opinion polling is also comparatively new in the country, so it is difficult to assess how attitudes have changed over time toward the regime. However, data from surveys in the 1980s and 1990s indicate that confidence in the regime fell extensively during the 1980s but then rose somewhat in the 1990s. Fewer Mexicans claim a party preference today than did so in the past, and the percentage of citizens who identify with the PRI has fallen sharply. According to one analyst, "The average Mexican regards participation in electoral campaigns, attendance at rallies, voting, and affiliation with political parties as ritualistic activities. He or she believes that engaging in such activities may be necessary to extract benefits from the system, but they have little effect on the shape of public policy or the selection of public officials."[47]

The media play an important role in public opinion formation in Mexico. In the past, although there was some scope for criticizing the government and presenting opposition views, it was not easy for newspapers, magazines, or radio and television stations to be openly opposed to the government. For many years, the government used access to newsprint, which it controlled, to reward sympathetic news coverage and to penalize coverage considered hostile. In addition, the government subsidized the salaries of some reporters, and politically ambitious public and PRI officials paid stipends to those who covered their activities sympathetically. A considerable amount of the revenue of newspapers and other media organizations came from advertising placed by the government. Each of these mechanisms was used to encourage positive reporting of government activities, strong endorsement of presidential initiatives, and quashing of stories that reflected ill on the party or the government, all without resorting to outright control of the media by the government. This resulted in considerable cynicism about the media.

As with other aspects of Mexican politics, the media are also in a period of transition, enjoying a "spring" of greater independence and diversity of opinion. There are currently several major television networks in the country, and many citizens have access to CNN and other global networks. The number of newspapers is expanding, as is their circulation, and news magazines such as *Nexos* and *Proceso* play the same role in Mexico that *Time* and *Newsweek* play in the United States. While there continues to be some reticence on the part of the media to take on full independence—in part because some channels and newspapers are owned or managed by those with close ties to the government—citizens in Mexico today clearly hear a much wider range of opinion and much greater reporting of opposition to government and the PRI than at any time previously.

INTERESTS, SOCIAL MOVEMENTS, AND PROTEST

As we have seen, clientelism is a way for individuals to participate in a political system that limits the power

Mexico's press has often been better at providing propaganda services to the government and the PRI than at reporting the truth.
Source: Courtesy of Hector Aguilar Camin and Lorenzo Meyer, *Historia Grafica de Mexico 1968–1984*, Instituto Nacional Antropologia e Historia, 1988.

of citizens to have a voice in national policy-making, allowing them to acquire some concrete benefits from a system that is controlled from the top. The Mexican system also responds to broader groups of citizens through pragmatic accommodation to their interests. This is one important reason why political tensions among major interests have not often escalated into the kind of serious conflict that can threaten stability. Where open conflict has occurred, it has generally been met with efforts to find some kind of compromise solution, even in cases in which the government has repressed opposition. Accommodation serves to respond to interests as diverse as business, labor, and rebellious students.

Accommodation has been particularly apparent in response to the interests of business. As we have seen, Mexico's development strategy encouraged the growth of wealthy elites in commerce, finance, industry, and agriculture. Although these elites have been primary beneficiaries of the country's development, they were never incorporated into the PRI. Instead, they represent themselves through a set of business-focused interest groups and through personal relationships with influential people in public office. Through networks that tie them to the political elite, business organizations and individuals have a long history of seeking policies that are favorable

to their interests and seeking accommodations when policies are not favorable to them. Under the import substituting model, for example, they sought to raise tariff levels and acquire special advantages to protect their products from foreign competition. They frequently bribed officials to obtain licenses, permits, and exemptions from inconvenient rules and regulations.

Labor is similarly accommodated within the system, although it is much more closely controlled by government than are business interests. Wage levels for unionized workers grew fairly consistently in the period between 1940 and 1982, when the economic crisis caused a significant drop in wage income. Wage rates and employment benefits result from negotiations between the government and union leaders—not between labor and management—and are a central means for limiting wage demands. In addition, the government controls the right to strike. Despite these controls, labor interests have been attended to in terms of concrete benefits and limitations on the rights of employers to discipline or dismiss workers. Labor union leaders play a dual role in the relationship between the government and the workers. They control the rank and file of the labor unions in the interest of their own power to negotiate with government but, at the same time, they seek benefits for workers who continue to provide support for the PRI. In this dual role, they work to maintain authoritarian control of the unions. Nevertheless, the power of the union bosses is declining, in part because the unions are weaker than in the past, and in part because there are demands for greater democratization from members.

Accommodation of this sort is often coupled with **cooptation** as a means of incorporating dissidents into the system so that they do not threaten its continuity. In 1968, for example, students protesting against authoritarianism and the failure of the regime to address deep issues of poverty and inequity challenged the government just prior to the opening of the Olympic games. The government responded with force—in one instance killing several hundred students in Mexico City—and in so doing, sparked even greater animosity toward the regime. When Luis Echeverría became president in late 1970s, however, he used his control of the patronage machinery to recruit large numbers of the student activists into his administration. He also dramatically increased spending on social services, putting many of the young people to work in expanding antipoverty programs in the countryside and in urban slums. Through these actions, a generation of political and social activists was incorporated into the system at the same time that there was some accommodation to their concerns.

Despite the strong and controlling role of the PRI in Mexico's political history, the country also has a tradition of civic organizations that operate at community and local levels with considerable independence from politics. Local village improvement societies, religious organizations, sports clubs, and parents' organizations are widespread. Many activities of these organizations are not explicitly political, although they may have political implications in that they encourage individuals to work together to find solutions to common problems or to organize around common interests. Other organizational experiences are more explicitly political. In the 1930s, for example, locally organized groups of peasants and workers, responding to encouragement from the government of Lázaro Cárdenas, initiated massive efforts to expand syndicates and unions in support of revolutionary goals to redistribute property and social rights. Business groups initiated organizations in the 1930s in order to represent their interests in gov-

ernment and became very powerful during the import substitution years. The student movement of 1968 provided additional evidence that civic society in Mexico had the potential to contest the power of the state. The emergence of independent unionism in the 1970s was another indication of renewed willingness to question the right of the state to stifle the voices of dissent and the emergence of demands for greater equity and participation.

The economic crisis of 1982 combined with this civic tradition to heighten demands for assistance from the government and to increase skepticism about its ability to respond to citizen needs. As official unions declined in power and influence, many workers joined community-based organizations. The urban middle class, hard hit by high rates of inflation, likewise turned to old and new organizations to demand response from government. In October of 1983, as many as 2 million people participated in a civic strike to call attention to the crisis and demand government response to the dire situations of average citizens. A less successful strike in June 1984 made the same point to the government. One Mexican newspaper reported 1,448 demonstrations, strikes, and other kinds of protest activities in the country between 1985 and 1987.[48]

In urban areas, citizen groups demanded land rights in squatter settlements, as well as housing, infrastructure, and urban services, as rights of citizenship rather than as a reward for political loyalty to the PRI. In the aftermath of the 1985 earthquake, citizen groups became especially vociferous in demanding that government respond to the needs of citizens without reference to their history of party loyalty. Residents of Mexico City demanded that the government let them decide how to rebuild and relocate their neighborhoods and choose who would serve as mayor and represent them.[49] Many have also become active in groups that share concerns about quality-of-life issues such as clean air and safe neighborhoods.

In rural areas, peasant organizations demanded greater independence from government and the leaders of the PRI and the CNC.[50] In addition to greater access to land, they also demanded better prices for the crops they produced, access to markets and credit, development of better infrastructure, and the provision of better education and health services in

Urban Popular Movements

In October 1968, hundreds of students and people of humble origin took to the streets of Mexico City to protest high rates of unemployment and the authoritarianism of the government. What began as a peaceful rally in Tlatelolco Plaza ended in rout when government troops opened fire on the crowd and killed an estimated 200 people.

The political activism of the students heralded the birth of urban popular movements in Mexico. The "Massacre in Tlatelolco" became a symbol of a government that was unwilling or unable to respond to citizen demands for economic and political equity. The protest movements sparked by the events of 1968 sought to transcend class boundaries and unite voices around a range of urban issues—from housing shortages to inadequate urban services to lack of land to centralization of government decision making. Such social movements forged new channels by which to express the immediate needs of poor and middle-class urban residents. They also helped spread demands for more democratic government when other channels of protest and reform, such as political parties, were not available to represent such concerns. In May 1980, the first national congress of urban movements was held in Monterrey in northern Mexico.

Urban popular movements—referring to activities of low- and modest-income (popular) groups—were given renewed vitality in the 1980s. When the economic crisis of that

decade resulted in drastic reductions of social welfare spending and cutbacks in the services available to urban residents, coalitions among working- and middle-class neighborhoods were forged and national discussions of the problems of urban communities were greatly expanded. The Mexico City earthquake of 1985 encouraged unprecedented numbers of grassroots movements to coalesce in response to the slow and poorly managed relief efforts of the government. Turning to each other, earthquake victims organized to provide shelter, food, and relocation. The elections of 1988 and 1994 provided these groups with significant opportunities to press parties and candidates to respond to their needs. They insisted on their rights to organize and protest without fear of repression or co-optation by the government or the PRI.

Urban popular movements bring citizens together around needs and ideals that cut across class boundaries. Neighborhood improvement, the environment, local self-government, economic development, feminism, and professional identity have been among the factors that have forged links among these groups. As such identities have been strengthened, the need of the political system to negotiate and bargain with a more independent citizenry has increased. Urban popular movements are one reason the PRI has become less certain that it can maintain its hold on political power in the future.

rural communities. They began to share interests with other groups and to form alliances with them. For example, in the Yucatán peninsula in the late 1970s and 1980s, PEMEX's exploration and production of oil caused massive ecological damage and was carried out with complete disregard for the rights of local *ejidatarios.* Environmental groups joined peasant organizations and student activists in protesting against the power and depredations of PEMEX. The rebels in Chiapas became a focal point for broad alliances of those concerned about the rights of indigenous groups (ethnic minorities) and rural poverty. Indigenous groups have also emerged to demand that government be responsive to their needs and respectful of their traditions.

A variety of groups are also becoming organized around issues that are traditionally associated with middle-class and urban interests. Among the most noticeable are environmental concerns. In Mexico City, community groups and broader citizen alliances have

been active in calling attention to the disastrous levels of air, water, and noise pollution in the capital city. Increasingly, concerns about the environment and natural resource management are bringing people together across class boundaries and even across the urban-rural divide. Women have begun to mobilize in urban areas around demands for equal pay, legal equality, and opportunities in business traditionally denied to them.[51] Religious groups, both Catholic and Protestant, have begun to demand greater government attention to problems of poverty and inequity as well as more government tolerance of religious education and religious practices. The government's social adjustment program, Solidarity, helped organize thousands of grassroots organizations around local development projects and possibly contributed to a trend in broader mobilization independent of the PRI clientelist networks.[52]

Civic society in Mexico is becoming more pluralist and less easily controlled. There is broader scope

Rebellion in Chiapas

In the months after January 1994, indigenous women set out daily for the tourist-infested zones of central Mexico City to sell handmade dolls. These dolls, dressed in brightly colored costumes, also sported black ski masks. They represented a symbolic connection to the rebels of the Zapatista National Liberation Front (EZLN) in the southern state of Chiapas, who wore such ski masks to avoid identification by the government. The street vendors found an active market for their wares. Images of the ideological leader and public spokesperson of the Zapatista movement, Subcomandante Marcos, also appeared throughout the country, and people of diverse ethnic, class, and political backgrounds began expressing affiliation with the goals of the rebels.

The rebellion by some 2,000 members of the EZLN broke out on January 1, 1994, the day that NAFTA went into effect. The Zapatista army captured four towns in the state. Media attention was intense, and the Zapatista leadership used it to express demands for the termination of the NAFTA agreement and for land and economic and social assistance from the government. The EZLN sought to use its military movement for strategic and tactical ends—to bring public attention to extensive evidence of social, economic, and political inequity in Mexico.

In their struggle, the Zapatistas did not seek an overthrow of the Mexican political system. They believed, however, that the system created and maintained by the PRI had become very much like the dictatorship of Profirio Díaz, which, because of extensive inequity, collapsed in the Revolution of 1910. They were united by their demand that indigenous groups throughout Mexico be granted fair treatment and means to escape the poverty, powerlessness, and hopelessness of their current conditions. They resorted to violence because they believed the government would not otherwise attend to their demands.

The Zapatista rebellion presented a major challenge to Mexico's image of political stability. It brought international attention to the fact that "two Mexicos" exist—one representing a stable, prosperous, and educated country and another representing a poor, indigenous, undereducated, and politically disenfranchised country.

The Chiapas uprising had a profound effect on the election of 1994, as competing political parties and candidates sought to identify with rebel demands for indigenous rights, economic justice, and honest elections. The rebels rejected a peace treaty that would have encouraged the electoral fortunes of the PRI, arguing instead for increased space for political debate and dialogue. The government spent over $200 million on social programs and infrastructure projects in the state in the months leading up to the election, a 44 percent increase over what had been budgeted. Just weeks before the elections, however, the EZLN hosted a National Democratic Convention of a large number of diverse groups committed to pressuring the government to undertake fundamental political reform.

The rebels insisted that economic assistance alone would not solve the problems that plague the southern part of the country. They expressed disdain for government efforts to avoid addressing the deeper causes of injustice—namely, concentration of wealth in the hands of a local and brutal elite and concentration of power in a government that values stability and compromise with local elites above all else.

In the aftermath of the rebellion, Mexican officials sought to erase the impression that the insurgency was an Indian uprising. They pointed out that many indigenous groups rejected the EZLN. Yet major indigenous organizations across Mexico and elsewhere in Latin America expressed solidarity with the Chiapas rebels and with the decision to take up arms. While some argued that the Chiapas rebellion was a local phenomenon and an isolated set of incidents, others predicted the spread of the Mexican example of armed uprisings by indigenous groups. The roots of such insurrections are in economic and social exploitation, they argued, not in specific ethnic identities.

---

for legitimate protest, opposition, and dissent from government. In predicting change for the future, however, it is important to remember that Mexico has achieved over seventy years of relative stability because its political system offered some channels for representation and participation, despite a high degree of centralization, presidentialism, and PRI domination. It has responded—if reluctantly, slowly, and defensively—to demands for political and policy change and has emphasized compromise, accommodation, and piecemeal distribution of political rewards in order to keep the political peace.

Although the Chiapas rebellion reminded the country of the potential for violent opposition to the regime, particularly if social inequities are not addressed, there is little evidence that large numbers of people in Mexico prefer opposition outside the regime to peaceful change from within. The assassination of Luis Donaldo Colosio appears to have increased citizen fear of civil unrest and violence. This is a lesson that the PRD learned during the 1994 presidential elections when many Mexicans indicated skepticism about the party because they feared that its campaign and electoral tactics might incite

Mexicans demonstrate for better housing in Mexico City's central plaza.
Source: Freck/Odyssey, Chicago.

violence. After the elections, the assassination of PRI Secretary General Ruiz Massieu raised even more concern about incipient violence. The Mexican political system is highly centralized, and political and economic power are very inequitably distributed. Nevertheless, Mexicans are engaged in an increasingly open discussion about how to reform it rather than how to overthrow it.

SECTION 5
Mexican Politics at the Crossroads

If the artist Diego Rivera were alive in the mid-1990s, he might wish to update the Hotel del Prado mural he painted in the late 1940s (see page 497). Many of the changes considered earlier in this chapter happened after he finished the mural—namely, the emergence of Mexico as an urban and industrial country, the success of the PRI in managing political conflict in the interests of government and business elites, the dramatic boom and bust of the Mexican economy that did so much to destroy the country's faith in import substitution, its effort to become more fully integrated into the global economy, and the struggle to become more democratic. How might such events be interpreted by Rivera?

Rivera might agree with many other Mexicans and portray a country that had gradually reverted to the economic, political, and social inequities that characterized the era of Porfirio Díaz. He might paint greedy PRI politicians, union bosses, and *ejido* officials grinning wickedly as they trampled on humble citizens, workers, and peasants. He might paint a background of giant factories occupied by rich businessmen, deal-making public officials, powerful drug dealers, and investors from the United States wielding dollars and large sticks to subdue the country's economy. He might paint a large landowner driving his tractor while an *ejidatario* and his family starve by the roadside. He would portray the rich and powerful with

European features while the faces of the poor and downtrodden would remind onlookers of Mexico's indigenous past. And he might paint recent presidents such as Miguel de la Madrid, Carlos Salinas, and Ernesto Zedillo surrounded by young technocrats and foreign intellectuals in a fashion that would recall the *científicos* who surrounded Porfirio Díaz. PRI banners would be hoisted aloft by politicians, the military, government officials, and foreign investors. On a more positive note, Rivera would probably include the portrait of Cuauhtémoc Cárdenas waving the PRD banner and supported by the orphans of the revolution, the peasants and workers.

Indeed, the revolution betrayed is a strong theme in current discussions of Mexican politics. But so is the theme of progress and stability. An artist more sympathetic to the regime might emphasize the strong national identity of the Mexican population, its relatively high achievement in terms of life expectancy and health statistics, its access to urban and modern amenities, and the subordinate role of the military in politics. A painting along these lines would no doubt portray airplanes, trucks, trains, and ships carrying Mexican goods abroad and citizens proudly welcoming tourists and investors to their progressive land. A banner would proclaim "Peace and Stability" and groups of citizens would be working together to find solutions to common problems.

These conflicting images of Mexico suggest alternative possibilities for the future. One envisions a quasi-dictatorship limping into the future to the benefit of political and economic elites, eventually to be challenged by another revolution. The other envisions a political and economic system that is capable of gradually transforming itself into an open, modern, and prosperous democracy. Both visions acknowledge the heritage of the past and recognize the challenge of becoming more global and democratic in the future.

POLITICAL CHALLENGES AND CHANGING AGENDAS

Considerable disagreement surrounds concerns about the country's political future. Central among them is the degree to which the PRI-dominated government will cede power to other political parties. Embedded in this debate is an implicit recognition that the government continues to have great power to set the terms for the interaction of state and civil society. The ability of citizen groups and opposition parties to resist manipulation and control by government and to sustain pressure on the regime over an extended period is still untested. The PRI and the government have responded to political pressures for reform, but with reluctance and always with an eye to maintaining the upper hand. Thus, for example, while it has become easier for opposition parties to gain representation in congress, until recently the rules continued to favor the ruling party by limiting the extent to which challengers could become the majority. Campaign reforms limit spending by candidates, but because these limits are very high, the party with the greatest access to resources, the PRI, continues to benefit. And, as long as the PRI elects the president, enormous government resources are available for shoring up the PRI's electoral support base.

Political reform will not come easily to Mexico. As discussed in previous sections, historical trends in demographics—the youth of the population, its increasing education level, and its concentration in urban areas—is working against the continued dominance of the PRI. Nevertheless, the party continues to have access to extensive resources for buying political support, and its activities continue to be carried out by some who are skilled in the arts of electoral manipulation and fraud. There is an ongoing struggle for the "soul" of the PRI between those who would like to see it become more modern and democratic and those

who recognize that in following such a path, the party would inevitably lose some of its power.

If the modernizers are successful, the changes they favor will increase the likelihood that the PAN or the PRD will install a president in Los Pinos. For many party loyalists, this outcome is almost unimaginable. The modernizers retort that the failure to become more democratic will doom the party to increased loss of legitimacy and push the opposition to violent tactics in its efforts to acquire access to power. They do not welcome the possibility that other parties might capture the presidency from time to time, but they believe that the only way the PRI can continue to be relevant to the country's future is to accept more democratic processes and win elections in ways that are accepted as fair by most citizens. The PRI modernizers may face real dilemmas in the future, however, because it is as yet unclear whether their commitment to democracy is strong enough to enable them to step down from the presidency gracefully should an election go against them. This untested commitment stands in considerable contrast to the deep commitment of the old guard to hold onto political power by whatever means necessary.

Other political changes must be considered. The Mexican government is highly centralized. Increasingly, however, countries around the globe are recognizing that the solutions to large numbers of policy problems lie at regional and local levels. Issues such as how to ensure that children are receiving a high-quality education that will prepare them adequately for the challenges of modern life, how to make sure that commerce is not brought to a standstill by massive traffic congestion, how to collect and dispose of garbage in ways that do not threaten public health and convenience, and how to monitor and resolve problems like air and water pollution require state and municipal governments that have money, authority, and capable public officials—precisely the conditions that only a very few regional and local governments in Mexico have ever had.

MEXICAN POLITICS IN TRANSITION

In addition to these institutional factors, the future of Mexican politics will be significantly shaped by the ability of the government to stimulate economic development and address serious problems of economic and social inequity. Currently, Mexico's population of 90 million people is a young one, with about half under the age of sixteen. The rate of population increase has slowed considerably since the early 1970s and is now growing at less than 2 percent a year. Nevertheless, high birthrates in earlier decades mean that the labor force is growing faster than the population. According to some estimates, 1 million new jobs need to be created every year just to keep up with increasing demand. The demand for jobs for new entrants into the labor market, of course, must be added to existing demand from large numbers of unemployed and underemployed people. Some estimates suggest that as much as one-quarter to one-third of the labor force falls into these categories.

New development policies for the 1990s and after need to be designed with employment creation in mind. As we have seen, a significant problem with the import substitution strategy was its failure, after an initial "exuberant" phase, to create sufficient jobs for the rapidly expanding and urbanizing population. Demand for urban jobs will be particularly strong because of changes in property rights on agricultural lands. In the past, the stipulation that *ejidatarios* could maintain claim to *ejido* plots only if they cultivated them two out of three years kept many *ejidatarios,* even those with the smallest and least productive land, in the countryside. Under the new legislation, many of these peasants are likely to sell or abandon their land and migrate to urban areas in search of jobs. Experts estimate that the 23 percent of the labor force engaged in agriculture in 1990 will shrink to about 16 percent within a few years because of such changes.

The issue of temporary labor migration to the United States is deeply related to the inability of the Mexican economy to create enough jobs. Extensive migration to the United States has been occurring since the 1880s, when Mexican workers were recruited to help build railroads. In the 1920s and between 1942 and 1964, special bilateral agreements existed between Mexico and the United States to provide workers to help the United States meet labor shortages. When such programs ended, a greater proportion of the labor migrants crossed the border into the United States illegally. Differences in wage levels—as high as 13:1 during the 1980s—and the jobs lost during the economic crisis, added to the number of workers seeking employment in the United States. It is estimated that at any given time, there are between half a million and a million temporary labor migrants from Mexico in the United States. In the past,

many of these migrants came from Mexico's poor rural areas. In the United States, they play an important role in providing low-wage and unskilled labor for agricultural and service industries. Stiff legislation to contain illegal migration to the United States was passed by Congress in 1986, but considerable evidence suggests that legal restrictions are not particularly effective if people really need jobs and believe they can find them across the border. Thus, the problem of illegal migration to the United States can only be effectively resolved by generating good jobs in Mexico.[53]

There is disagreement about how to respond to the economic challenges the country faces. Much of the debate surrounds the question of what integration into a competitive international economy really means. For some, it represents the final abandonment of Mexico's sovereignty. For others, it is the basis on which future prosperity must be built. Those who are critical of the market-based and outward-oriented development strategy introduced by presidents de la Madrid and Salinas and NAFTA are most concerned about their impact on workers, peasants, and national identities. They argue that the state has abandoned its responsibilities to protect the poor from the vicissitudes of the market and to provide for their basic needs. They believe that U.S. and Canadian investors will come to Mexico only to find low-wage labor for industrial empires located elsewhere. They see little benefit in further industrial development based on importation of foreign-made parts, their assembly in Mexico, and their export to other markets. This kind of development, they argue, has been prevalent in the *maquila,* or assembly, industries located along the U.S.-Mexico border.

Critics of the new development strategy also believe that NAFTA will bring the final demise of the peasant population because the corn and beans that most *ejidatarios* produce will not be able to compete with the technologically advanced high-productivity crops from the north that will be available and cheap. While some peasants will be able to transform themselves into productive small farmers, most do not have land that can become profitable nor the economic resources to invest in it. Many will be forced to migrate to already overcrowded cities or to the countries to the north.

Those who favor closer integration with Canada and the United States acknowledge that some foreign investment will not contribute directly to Mexico's ability to benefit from technological advances and move its workforce into higher-paying and more skilled jobs. They emphasize, however, that most investment will occur because the country has a relatively well-educated population, the capacity to absorb modern technology, and a large internal market for industrial goods. They acknowledge that the future is grim for many *ejidatarios,* but they tend to see their displacement as an inevitable cost of modernization and further industrialization. They expect that, eventually, growth in industry and on large modern farms will create enough jobs for those forced to abandon their traditional lifestyles in the countryside.

After the Chiapas rebellion in January 1994, Mexicans were much more aware that conditions of social welfare for many of the country's citizens were far behind what they should be. Increasingly, many spoke of the necessity to address a social agenda in health, education, public sanitation, and income distribution. Chiapas made the social agenda a topic of everyday conversation by reminding Mexicans at all levels that some people lived in appalling conditions with little hope for the future. Indeed, the average schooling received is still under five years, and only about half of the eligible students are enrolled in secondary school.

Debate surrounds what to do about these conditions. As in the United States, some argue that economic growth and the expansion of employment that would accompany it will resolve the major problems of poverty in the country. They believe that prosperity, tied to Mexico's economic future internationally, will benefit everyone eventually. For this to occur, however, they insist that education will have to be improved and made more appropriate for developing a well-educated workforce. They also believe that improved education will come about when local communities have more control over schools and curriculum and when parents have more of a choice between public and private education for their children. From this perspective, the solution to poverty and injustice is fairly clear—more and better jobs and improved education.

For those critical of the development path that Mexico embarked upon in the late 1980s and early 1990s, the solution to problems of poverty and inequity are more troubling. They involve understanding diverse causes of poverty, including not only lack of

jobs and poor education but also exploitation, geographical isolation, discriminatory laws and practices, and families disrupted by migration, urbanization, and the tensions of modern life. Answers also involve a difficult analysis of the role of government in the provision of social welfare. In the past, Mexicans regularly looked to government for such benefits. But their provision was deeply flawed by inefficiency and political manipulation. The government and the PRI consistently used access to social services as a means to increase its political control and limit the capacity of citizens to demand equitable treatment. Thus, while many continue to believe that it is the responsibility of government to ensure that citizens are well educated, healthy, and able to make the most of their potential, the populace is deeply suspicious of its capacity to provide such conditions fairly and efficiently. Decentralization, local control, and active community organizations might provide an answer to how public goods such as social services and basic infrastructure could be provided more effectively, but each of these factors would be difficult to achieve, given the history of the country.

MEXICO IN COMPARATIVE PERSPECTIVE

Mexico faces many of the same challenges that beset other countries—creating equitable and effective democratic government, becoming more integrated into a global economy, and responding to increasingly complex social problems. Indeed, these were precisely the challenges that the United States faced in the mid-1990s—along with India, Nigeria, China, Japan, and Germany, among others. Like these other countries, Mexico confronts these challenges within the context of a unique historical and institutional evolution. The legacies of its past, the tensions of the present, and the innovations of the future will not doubt evolve in ways that continue to be uniquely Mexican, even though global economic trends and communication technologies bring countries closer together in many ways.

The pressure for change in Mexico and many other countries is accelerating as modern technology increases the extent to which people in one country are aware of what is occurring in others and the degree to which citizens are able to communicate their concerns and interests among themselves and to the government. The current government has been very successful at dealing with demands on a piecemeal basis and keeping interests from becoming broadly mobilized but is under extensive pressure to respond more quickly to more wide-ranging demands and interests. Groups in Mexico have begun to organize regionally and nationally and to demand that government not respond through the old clientelist mechanisms but instead recognize citizenship claims for equitable treatment and open discussion and debate. Like many other countries, then, Mexico is being pressured by the people to make its political processes more democratic and responsive.

Above all, Mexico's political system is being pressured by large numbers of its citizens to become open and democratic, to allow political opposition, and to ensure that public officials can be held accountable for their actions. The democratic ideas of citizen rights to free speech and assembly, free and fair elections, and responsive government are major reasons why the power of the PRI is under attack by so many in Mexico. Inevitably, the PRI will be forced to accommodate greater opposition as its support base wanes in size and importance. Political parties such as the PAN and the PRD will need to learn how to govern effectively as they begin to win elections.

At the same time, like other countries, Mexico must address its international position, particularly in terms of relationships with its neighbors. Many Mexicans see NAFTA as the beginning of closer integration with trading partners in Latin America, Asia, and Europe. For all countries, economic integration raises issues of national sovereignty and identity. Of special concern to many Mexicans is what economic integration means for the country's sense of citizenship, historical uniqueness, and nationalism. Mexicans define themselves in part through a set of historical events, symbols, and myths that focus on the country's troubled relationship with the "Colossus of the North." Among numerous national heroes and martyrs are those who distinguished themselves in confrontations with the United States. The myths of the Revolution of 1910 emphasize the uniqueness of the country in terms of its opposition to the capitalists and militarists of the northern country. In the 1970s, Mexicans were encouraged to see themselves in the leadership of Third World countries arguing for increased bargaining positions vis-à-vis the industrialized countries of the north. This view stands in strong contrast to more recent perspectives touting the benefits of an internationally oriented economy.

The sense of national identity is also affected by international migration. Of particular importance in the Mexican case is labor migration. Every year, as we have seen, large numbers of Mexicans enter the United States as workers. Others live in the United States for several years at a time and, like their more temporary fellow citizens, return to their towns and villages either temporarily or permanently, with new values and new views of the world shaped by their sojourn in the United States. While most continue to believe that Mexican culture is preferable to that in the United States, which they see as unintegrated, excessively materialistic, and violent, and while most believe that Mexico is a better place to nurture strong family life and values, they are nevertheless strongly influenced by United States mass culture—including popular music, movies, television programs, fast foods and junk foods, and consumer goods. Over time, it is inevitable that Mexico's sense of uniqueness will be diluted through closer integration with neighboring countries.

Given these internal and external pressures, will Mexico in the future look significantly different from Mexico in the past? How much will the pressures for change and the potential loss of national identity affect the nature of the political system? It is, of course, difficult to predict what particular changes will occur in Mexico in the coming decade or two. Indeed, at the outset of the 1980s, few people in the world could have predicted the extensive economic policy reforms and pressures for democracy that Mexico faced in that decade. Economic and political crisis catapulted the country toward economic policies and compromises with opponents of the PRI that took most people by surprise. Considering the pace and dimensions of political change in the future, it is important to remember that Mexico has a long tradition of relatively strong institutions. It is not a country that will easily slip into sustained political instability. In this regard, it is a country that is significantly different from many others in the developing world. A tradition of constitutional government, a strong presidency, a political system that has incorporated a wide range of interests, a weak tradition of military involvement in politics, and a strong sense of national identity—these are among the factors that need to be considered in predicting the political consequences of democratization, economic integration, and greater social equality. In many ways, these institutional advantages make these challenges less intractable for Mexico than they are for many other countries that are more divided by political instability and lack of institutional legitimacy and longevity.

Key Terms

indigenous groups	*sexenio*
informal sector	state capitalism
anticlericalism	import substituting
ejidos	industrialization (ISI)
ejidatarios	*destape*
clientelism	cooptation
corporatist philosophy	

Suggested Readings

Section 1

Cornelius, Wayne A. "Nation-building, Participation, and Distribution: The Politics of Social Reform under Cárdenas." In *Crisis, Choice, and Change: Historical Studies of Political Development,* edited by Gabriel A. Almond et al. Boston: Little Brown, 1973.

Hamilton, Nora, *The Limits of State Autonomy: Post-Revolutionary Mexico.* Princeton, N.J.: Princeton University Press, 1982.

Meyer, Michael C., and William L. Sherman. *The Course of Mexican History.* 2d ed. New York: Oxford University Press, 1983.

Paz, Octavio. *The Labyrinth of Solitude: Life and Thought in Mexico.* New York: Grove Press, 1961.

Womack, John, Jr. *Zapata and the Mexican Revolution.* New York: Vintage Books, 1968.

Section 2

Baer, M. Delal, and Sidney Weintraub. *The NAFTA Debate: Grappling with Unconventional Trade Issues.* Boulder, Colo.: Lynne Rienner, 1994.

Collier, Ruth Berins. *The Contradictory Alliance: State-Labor Relations and Regime Change in Mexico.* Berkeley: University of California Press, 1992.

Grindle, Merilee S. *Challenging the State: Crisis and Innovation in Latin America and Africa.* London: Cambridge University Press, 1995.

Hansen, Roger. *The Politics of Mexican Development.* Baltimore, Md.: Johns Hopkins University Press, 1971.

Lustig, Nora. *Mexico: The Remaking of an Economy.* Washington, D.C.: Brookings Institution, 1992.

Section 3

Bailey, John. *Governing Mexico: The Statecraft of Crisis Management.* New York: St. Martin's Press, 1988.

Grindle, Merilee S. *Bureaucratics, Politicians, and Peasants in Mexico: A Case Study in Public Policy.* Berkeley: University of California Press, 1977.

Roett, Riordan, ed. *The Challenge of Institutional Reform in Mexico.* Boulder, Colo.: Lynne Rienner, 1994.

Ronfeldt, David, ed. *The Modern Mexican Military: A Reassessment.* San Diego: Center for U.S.-Mexican Studies, University of California, 1984.

Smith, Peter. *Labyrinths of Power: Political Recruitment in Twentieth-Century Mexico.* Princeton, N.J.: Princeton University Press, 1979.

Section 4

Cornelius, Wayne A., Judith Gentleman, and Peter H. Smith, eds. *Mexico's Alternative Futures.* San Diego: Center for U.S.-Mexican Studies, University of California, 1989.

Eckstein, Susan, ed. *Power and Popular Protest: Latin American Social Movements.* Berkeley: University of California, 1989.

Fowerake, Joe, and Ann L. Craig, eds. *Popular Movements and Political Change in Mexico.* Boulder, Colo.: Lynne Rienner, 1990.

Stevens, Evelyn Huber. *Protest and Response in Mexico.* Cambridge, Mass.: MIT Press, 1974.

Section 5

Cook, Maria Lorena, Kevin J. Middlebrook, and Juan Molinar, eds. *The Politics of Economic Restructuring in Mexico.* San Diego. Center for U.S.-Mexican Studies, University of California, 1994.

Cornelius, Wayne A., Ann L. Craig, and Jonathan Fox, eds. *Transforming State-Society Relations in Mexico: The National Solidarity Strategy.* San Diego: Center for U.S.-Mexican Studies, University of California, 1994.

Cornelius, Wayne A, and Philip Martin. *The Uncertain Connection: Free Trade and Mexico-U.S. Migration.* San Diego: Center for U.S.-Mexican Studies, University of California, 1993.

Mumme, Stephen, C. Richard Bath, and Valerie J. Assetto. "Political Development and Environmental Policy in Mexico." *Latin American Research Review* 23, no. 1 (1988).

Sklair, Leslie. *Assembling for Development: The Maquila Industry in Mexico and the United States.* San Diego: Center for U.S.-Mexican Studies, University of California, 1993.

Endnotes

[1] As cited in Neil Harvey, *Rebellion in Chiapas: Rural Reforms, Campesino Radicalism, and the Limits to Salinismo* (La Jolla, Calif.: University of California at San Diego, Center for U.S.-Mexican Studies, 1994), 1.

[2] A useful history of the Díaz period and the political instability that preceded it is found in Michael C. Meyer and William L. Sherman, *The Course of Mexican History,* 2d ed. (New York: Oxford University Press, 1983).

[3] Porfirio Díaz, 1911, as he boarded a ship for exile. Charles Cumberland, *Mexico: The Struggle for Modernity* (London: Oxford University Press, 1968), 241.

[4] For a history of the agrarian revolution and the role of Emiliano Zapata in that conflict, see especially John Womack, *Zapata and the Mexican Revolution* (New York: Vintage Books, 1968).

[5] "Doña Luz Jiménez," in *Life and Death in Milpa Alta: A Nahuatl Chronicle of Díaz and Zapata,* ed. and trans. Fernando Horcasitas (Norman, OK: University of Oklahoma Press, 1972), 127.

[6] An excellent history of this event is presented in Wayne Cornelius, "Nation-building, Participation, and Distribution: The Politics of

Social Reform under Cárdenas," in *Developmental Episodes in Comparative Politics: Crisis, Choice and Change,* eds. Gabriel Almond and Scott Flanagan (Boston: Little Brown, 1973).

[7]Raymond Vernon, *The Dilemma of Mexico's Development* (Cambridge, Mass.: Harvard University Press, 1963), 180.

[8]Quoted in Daniel Levy and Gabriel Székely, *Mexico: Paradoxes of Stability and Change* (Boulder, Colo.: Westview Press, 1983), 171.

[9]For how protest and dissent were dealt with traditionally in Mexico, see, for example, Evelyn P. Stevens, *Protest and Response in Mexico* (Cambridge, Mass.: MIT Press, 1974).

[10]According to World Bank, *World Development Report, 1994* (New York: Oxford University Press, 1994).

[11]Figures are taken from World Bank, *World Development Report, 1993* (New York: Oxford University Press, 1993).

[12]One of the best analyses of this development process is Roger Hansen, *The Politics of Mexican Development* (Baltimore: The Johns Hopkins University Press, 1971). See also Vernon, *The Dilemma of Mexico's Development.*

[13]Douglas C. Bennett and Kenneth E. Sharpe, *Transnational Corporations Versus the State* (Princeton, N.J.: Princeton University Press, 1985), 27.

[14]Merilee S. Grindle, *State and Countryside: Development Policy and Agrarian Politics in Latin America* (Baltimore: The Johns Hopkins University Press, 1986), 63, quoting President Avila Camacho (1940–1946).

[15]*Ibid.*

[16]Kevin J. Middlebrook, ed., *Unions, Workers, and the State in Mexico* (San Diego: Center for U.S.-Mexican Studies, University of California, 1991).

[17]Grindle, *State and Countryside.*

[18]Carlos Bazdresch and Santiago Levy, "Populism and Economic Policy in Mexico," in *The Macroeconomics of Populism in Latin America,* eds. Rudiger Dornbusch and Sebastian Edwards (Chicago: University of Chicago Press, 1991), 72.

[19]For an assessment of the mounting problems of Mexico City and efforts to deal with them, see Diane E. Davis, *Urban Leviathan: Mexico City in the Twentieth Century* (Philadelphia: Temple University Press, 1994).

[20]Nora Lustig, *Mexico: The Remaking of an Economy* (Washington, D.C.: Brookings Institution, 1992), 18.

[21]Wayne A. Cornelius, *The Political Economy of Mexico under de la Madrid: The Crisis Deepens, 1985–1986* (San Diego: University of California, Center for U.S.-Mexican Studies, 1986), 2.

[22]Joe Foweraker and Ann L. Craig, eds., *Popular Movements and Political Change in Mexico* (Boulder, Colo.: Lynne Rienner Publishers, 1989).

[23]Carlos Salinas de Gortari, Inaugural Address, December 1, 1988.

[24]Davis, *Urban Leviathan,* 2–3.

[25]Octavio Paz, quoted in Davis, *Urban Leviathan,* 2.

[26]Hansen, *The Politics of Mexican Development,* 75.

[27]Lustig, *Mexico: The Remaking of an Economy,* 64.

[28]Carlos Salinas, "Presidency of the Republic," Speech to the Business Roundtable, date not given.

[29]Ernesto Zedillo, Address on Foreign Policy, June 26, 1994.

[30]Frank Brandenburg, *The Making of Modern Mexico* (Englewood Cliffs, N.J.: Prentice Hall, 1964), 141.

[31]Merilee S. Grindle, *Bureaucrats, Politicians, and Peasants in Mexico: A Case Study in Public Policy* (Berkeley: University of California Press, 1977), 81.

[32]For a description of this process, see Peter Smith, *Labyrinths of Power: Political Recruitment in Twentieth-Century Mexico* (Princeton, N.J.: Princeton University Press, 1979).

[33]David F. Ronfeldt, "The Modern Mexican Military: An Overview" in *The Modern Mexican Military: A Reassessment,* ed. David Ronfeldt (San Diego: Center for U.S.-Mexican Studies, University of California, 1984), 1.

[34]Ernesto Zedillo, Presidential Candidates' Debate, May 12, 1994.

[35]Levy and Szekely, *Mexico: Paradoxes of Stability and Change,* 100.

[36]Smith, *Labyrinths of Solitude,* 226.

[37]Martin Needler, *Mexican Politics: The Containment of Conflict* (New York: Praeger Publishers, 1993), 86.

[38]El Norte de Monterrey/Reforma Opinion Poll on Mexico's Presidential Race, June 1–6, 1994, gave Diego Fernández de Cevallos 29.1 percent of responses to the question, "If presidential elections were held today, which candidate would you vote for?"

[39]Covarrubias y Asociados Poll of Mexican Presidential Preferences, May 13–17, 1994.

[40]*The New York Times,* June 22, 1994, D5.

[41]See the *Wall Street Journal,* June 3, 1994, A15.

[42]El Norte de Monterrey/Reforma Opinion Poll on Mexico's Presidential Race, June 1–6, 1994.

[43]Zedillo, Presidential Candidates' Debate, May 12, 1994.

[44]*The New York Times,* September 8, 1994, A11.

[45]Wayne A. Cornelius, Judith Gentleman, and Peter H. Smith, "Overview: The Dynamics of Political Change in Mexico," in *Mexico's Alternative Political Futures,* eds. Wayne A. Cornelius, Judith Gentleman, and Peter H. Smith (San Diego: Center for U.S.-Mexican Studies, University of California, 1989), 9.

[46]Stevens, *Protest and Response in Mexico,* 94.

[47]Wayne A. Cornelius and Ann L. Craig, "Politics in Mexico," in *Comparative Politics Today,* 5th ed., eds. Gabriel Almond and G. Bingham Powell, 1992, 502.

[48]*La Jornada,* May 5, 1988, reported in Alberto Aziz Nassif, "Regional Dimensions of Democratization," in *Mexico's Alternative Political Futures,* 1989, 94.

[49]Susan Eckstein, *Power and Popular Protest: Latin American Social Movements* (Berkeley: University of California Press, 1989).

[50]Jonathan Fox and Gustavo Gordillo, "Between State and Market: The Campesinos' Quest for Autonomy," in *Mexico's Alternative Political Futures,* 1989.

[51]Foweraker and Craig, *Popular Movements and Political Change in Mexico.*

[52]Wayne A. Cornelius, Ann L. Craig, and Jonathan Fox, eds., *Transforming State-Society Relations in Mexico: The National Solidarity Strategy* (San Diego: Center for U.S.-Mexican Studies, University of California, 1994).

[53]Merilee S. Grindle, *Searching for Rural Development: Labor Migration and Employment in Mexico* (Ithaca, N.Y.: Cornell University Press, 1988). Presents a discussion of the issues of rural poverty, employment, and migration.

CHAPTER 10

Brazil

FEDERATIVE REPUBLIC OF BRAZIL

Land and Population

Capital	Brasilia
Total Area (square miles)	3,286,470 (slightly larger than continental U.S.)
Population	156 million
Annual Projected Population Growth Rate (1993–2000)	1.6%
Urban Population (% of total)	71%

Ethnic Composition

Major Ethnic Groups	White	54%
	Mulatto and Mestizo	39%
	Black	6%
Major Language	Portuguese	
Major Religions	Catholic	76%
	Evangelical Protestant	11%

Economy

Domestic Currency	Cruzeiro real	
GNP (US$)	$464.8 billion	
GNP per capita (US$)	$2,980	
Purchasing Power Parity GDP per capita (US$)	$5,370	
Average Annual GDP Growth Rate (1980–1993)	2.1%	
Structure of Production (% of GDP)	Agriculture	11%
	Industry	37%
	Services	52%
Labor Force Distribution (% of total)	Agriculture	28%
	Industry	25%
	Services	47%
Women as % of Total Labor Force	28%	

Income Distribution (1989)	% of Population	% Share of Income or Consumption
	Richest 20%	67.5%
	Poorest 20%	2.1%

Total Foreign Trade (exports plus imports) as % of GDP	13%

Society

Life Expectancy	Female	69
	Male	64
Population per Doctor	670	
Infant Mortality (per 1,000 live births)	57	
Adult Literacy	Female	81%
	Male	84%
Average (Mean) Years of Schooling (of adults 25+)	Female	3.9
	Male	4.1
Communications (per 100 people)	Radios	38
	Televisions	22
	Telephones	9
1995 Human Development Index (1 = highest)	Ranks 63 out of 174	

Political Organization

Political System Federal republic, presidential with separation of powers.

Regime History Democratic since 1946 with brief periods of military authoritarianism.

Administrative Structure Federal, with 27 units of subnational government called states, and the Federal District, which also functions as a state. Its legislatures are unicameral. The states are divided into municipalities (over 5,000), with mayors and councillors directly elected.

Executive President, vice president, and cabinet. The president and vice president are directly elected by universal suffrage in a two-round run-off election for four-year terms.

Legislature Bicameral: The Senate is made up of three senators from each state and from the Federal District, elected by plurality vote for an eight-year term; the Chamber of Deputies consists of representatives from each state and from the Federal District, elected by proportional vote for a four-year term.

Judiciary Supreme Court, High Tribunal of Justice, regional courts, labor courts, electoral courts, military courts, and state courts. Judiciary has financial and administrative autonomy. Judges are nominated for life.

Party System Multiparty system includes PMDB, PFL, PSDB, PPR, PT, PTB, and PDT. There is no restriction to creating or merging parties.

SECTION 1
The Making of the Modern Brazilian State*

BRAZIL AT THE CROSSROADS

In October 1992, Brazil's president, Fernando Collor, was impeached. Just three years earlier, his victory had symbolized a fresh start in Brazil's quest for democracy and social equality in the country. The reinstatement of civilian rule in 1985, after twenty-one years of a repressive military regime, had appeared to create favorable political conditions for solving Brazil's grave social problems. A new constitution was enacted in 1988 guaranteeing direct elections at all levels and confirming the principle of separation between executive, judicial, and legislative powers. Political and civil rights were restored, and a broad spectrum of parties, including those on the left, were given legal status. Collor's inauguration as the first president elected by universal suffrage since 1964 seemed finally to confirm the long-awaited return to democracy. Unfortunately, subsequent events raised questions about whether Brazil's restoration of democracy would prove durable. Long-standing problems and their effects in the post-1985 period are highlighted by Collor's rise and fall.

*Grateful acknowledgment is made to Alfred P. Montero for his assistance in the preparation and writing of this chapter.

Rising from political obscurity, Collor fought a grueling campaign against his rival, the left-wing labor leader and head of the Workers' Party (*Partido dos Trabalhadores,* or PT), Luis Inacio "Lula" da Silva. Business elites opposed to the Workers' Party gave Collor their support. They viewed him as their best bet to reduce Brazil's large public sector and promote the private sector according to free market principles.

Collor's campaign strategy was to depict himself as the only leader capable of overcoming the corruption and inefficiency of Brazilian politics. His goal was to appeal to the millions of Brazilians frustrated with the country's economy and the inertia of federal and state bureaucracies. Though born to a wealthy and politically powerful family from a poor state in the northeast, Collor was presented to voters as the voice against corruption and "old politics." Labeled by the media as the "hunter of maharajahs"—the highly paid political appointees who benefited greatly from bureaucratic corruption—Collor surpassed his competitors for the presidency within the first months of campaigning.

The candidate's rhetoric was welcomed by the *descamisados*—literally, the "shirtless," poor, who were attracted by his attacks against politicians and the social problems caused by bureaucratic inefficiency. Collor took on the image of a Don Quixote battling everything and everybody: from greedy entrepreneurs who received special protection and subsidies from their political friends, to corrupt politicians who practiced graft on an everyday basis or ran powerful political machines at the state level. As a skillful performer on television, Collor mobilized the people's frustration and resentment, at once symbolizing opposition to the state, politics, and politicians.

Collor's victory, however, did not extend to members of his practically unknown party, the National Renovation Party (*Partido Renovador Nacional,* or PRN), who failed to win election to Congress. Lacking the support of a partisan majority and facing severe opposition from his many political rivals in the legislature, Collor implemented policy through a number of top-down "emergency" methods. His favorite instruments were executive decrees and provisional acts which bypassed most forms of congressional oversight. Often, Collor justified these measures by going directly to the public via the mass media. By gathering popular support outside the legislature, Collor be-

lieved that he could effectively railroad his policies through Congress.

The centerpiece of Collor's economic policies was an anti-inflationary provision in 1990 which froze most of the country's financial assets. This measure severely penalized the upper and middle classes, many of whom could not protect their savings from the freeze. To the *descamisados,* such a policy meant long-awaited justice and vengeance against the elite. However, Collor's failure to achieve inflation control, state reform, and social reform precipitated his fall. By the end of 1990, Collor's popularity was rapidly declining. He tried to renew his image as a resolute savior of the country by acting audaciously on a number of public occasions, but he was never able to reclaim the degree of popular support he enjoyed immediately following his election. High levels of continuing poverty and corruption made Collor's image as a warrior against injustice and crime an object of public mockery.

Ironically, the mobilization of public opinion against corruption triggered by his own electoral campaign eventually turned against him. Shortly after evidence emerged in 1992 that the president and a number of his closest relatives and friends were involved in the embezzlement of public funds and other corrupt acts, a public campaign to oust Collor was launched. By the end of 1992, mass demonstrations had succeeded in pressing the legislature to impeach the president.

Collor's story reveals much about the obstacles facing the consolidation of democracy in Brazil. As in recent Indian and Russian history, social inequalities, weak political parties, the abuse of executive powers, inflation, and a general incapacity for policy-making have lowered the prospects for democracy in Brazil. Above all, Collor's presidency illustrates the political elite's incapacity, or lack of will, to deal with the miserable socioeconomic conditions of large segments of the Brazilian population.

Brazil's political history demonstrates that democracy must be based on a host of political and social institutions and not simply on periodic elections. Since 1891, the country has had many institutional features of a modern democracy. However, it has been democratic mostly in name because important conditions which promote a durable democracy—a substantial measure of social equality and justice—have not existed. States must be capable of

OLÁ! EU SOU O MAIS NOVO
PERSONAGEM DE FICÇÃO: MUITO
EFEITO ESPECIAL, DISPENDIOSA
PRODUÇÃO... MAS SÓ FUNCIONO
NA TELEVISÃO...

"Hey! I am the latest fictional personality: lots of special effects, lavish production . . . but it all just works on television."
Source: © Chico Caruso, from *O Globo.*

implementing economic and political reforms for democratic elites to be truly responsive to their constituencies. The subjugation of state organizations to private networks of interests in Brazil—as in Russia, Mexico, and Nigeria—have weakened the state's capacity to engage in reform. As a result, the interests of weaker social actors—the poor in particular—are not addressed. Assumptions that industrialization would, by itself, minimize inequality were, and still are, widespread in the world. Since the 1930s, these assumptions strongly inspired Brazilian decision makers. The military governments were champions of this view. Waving the banner of "Great Brazil," they advocated the principle of attaining economic growth at all costs as a sufficient condition for future social equality. Brazil's appalling levels of poverty and inequality vividly challenge such assumptions: Sadly, the country is a world showcase of how, in the absence of a responsive democracy, the benefits of stunning economic development, industrialization, and modern production methods can be badly distributed.

The nation's poor democratic development has not destroyed Brazilians' hopes. The 1994 election of Fernando Henrique Cardoso, a political figure known for his honesty, sensibility to social problems, and support for democratic principles has partially renewed the optimism which had been shattered by Collor's fiasco. Moreover, the rise of new social movements in the country has reinforced the hopes of improving both political and social conditions.

This chapter explores these problems and analyzes them in comparative perspective. Section 1 discusses the historical dilemmas of Brazilian state-making. The section emphasizes how, from very early in the country's history, the building of state organizations weakened democratic institutions, political representation, and the organization of civil society. But it also shows that this formula for state-building could not be sustained. Section 2 discusses how the economic development of the country failed to distribute the benefits of industrialization to the majority of Brazilians, although it did transform Brazil from an agricultural economy into an industrialized one active in international trade by the late twentieth century. Section 3 describes the causes of weakness among the institutions historically associated with democratic government and competent policy administration—that is, the formal institutions of the state. Section 4 discusses how the evolution of political representation failed to accommodate changes in the country's class structure, political culture, and collective identities. Thus those institutions that regulated citizenship and the larger social and cultural ideas communicating the concept of the "Brazilian nation" incorporated some segments of society while disorganizing and repressing others. Section 5 analyzes the present period and suggests future trends in Brazilian politics. We begin with a brief overview of the country.

Brazil Today

By almost any standard, Brazil is an impressive country. In land surface it is larger than the continental United States and occupies nearly half of South America. With the exception of Chile and Ecuador, its territory has borders with all the other countries of South America. Its most urbanized regions are located in the southern and southeastern regions. More than 15 million inhabitants live in Greater São Paulo alone. This density contrasts with the northern, largely uninhabited, rainforest regions of the Amazon.

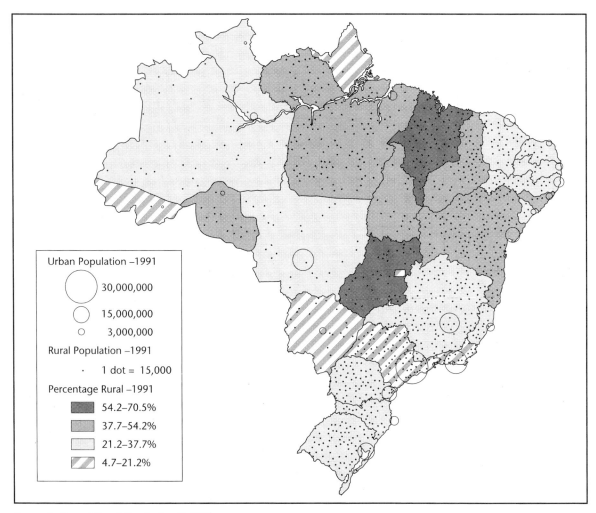

Concentration of Population in Brazil, 1991

Brazil is an immigrant country of varied ethnic makeup. In this sense, Brazil is like many of the ethnically plural societies such as India, Mexico, Nigeria, Russia, and Iran. Unlike India, Iran, and Nigeria, however, Brazilians are not greatly divided over religious differences. Catholicism was imposed by Portuguese colonial rule in Brazil, then reinforced by immigration from Catholic Italy, Spain, and Portugal after the end of colonial rule in the nineteenth and twentieth centuries. Some African-based religious beliefs and rituals, first brought to Brazil by slaves, also coexist with Catholic observance.

Centuries of voluntary and involuntary immigration of Europeans and Africans contributed to the emergence of an ethnically mixed society. Mixtures of

Europeans, Africans, and Indians produced hundreds of distinct colors of people. Different cultural influences also entered this ethnic melange. European values and rituals were likewise mixed with African and Indian traditions and images. The offshoots of these cultural interrelations took on distinct regional identities over time. This chapter does not attempt to describe each of these influences, but it should be noted that Brazil has a single dominant religious influence but is ethnically heterogeneous.

The country enjoys a highly diversified economy. After four or five decades of an industrial development policy aimed at achieving economic self-sufficiency, the country now produces and exports a highly diversified range of industrial goods from shoes and textiles to small aircraft. Brazilian contractors have become successful competitors for international engineering and construction jobs, especially in the developing countries of Africa, the Middle East, and Asia.

Because of its size, population, natural resources, and sustained economic growth, Brazil could potentially be a substantial force in international politics. With its large internal market for foreign and domestic industry, its dominance over a majority of the rainforests contained within the Amazon (the so-called green lung of the planet), Brazil possesses resources that could make it a global superpower. This fact is not lost on its neighbors, on the great powers of the world, nor even on Brazilians themselves. But this is yet another anomaly in Brazilian history—its capacity for acting on the world stage as a superpower was never actualized as it was by the Great Powers of Western Europe (Britain, France, and Germany).

Unfortunately, Brazil is also impressive for many negative reasons. Although it is one of the world's ten wealthiest economies with an industrial production base worth $410 billion, social indicators such as income distribution, infant mortality, and nutrition show that it ranks near the bottom in the world of states. A profound dualism, both regional and social, characterizes Brazilian society. Unemployment and underemployment, poverty, malnutrition, and disease contrast with the ostentation and arrogance of the wealthy few. Income disparities also generally mirror racial differences as the poor are represented by mostly blacks and mulattoes (as offspring of racially mixed marriages are called in Brazil), whereas the rich are invariably mostly white. The poverty of the north and northeast also contrasts with the more industrialized and prosperous southeastern and southern states.

The country's perverse socioeconomic inequality is a direct consequence of its historic choice of economic development strategies and of its shallow experiences with democracy. For most of its almost two centuries as an independent country, Brazil has enjoyed many aspects of a liberal democracy. Since the country became independent from Portugal in 1822, the Brazilian elite has usually espoused liberal ideas, inspired by the French Revolution and the United States Constitution: separation of powers between executive, legislative, and judiciary; freedom of speech, and the right to vote. These ideas were expressed in most of the Brazilian constitutions enacted during the nineteenth and twentieth centuries. Nevertheless, such liberal ideas were not often synonymous with true democracy in Brazil. Equality of opportunity and citizenship did not historically include the majority of Brazilians.

As we shall explain later, the integration of the popular sectors was established through institutions considered inimical to democracy: **state corporatism** and **populism.** The Brazilian experience with such institutions throughout much of the twentieth century became a basis for the establishment in 1964 of military **authoritarianism.** The circumstances involved in the transition from a military regime and the institutional legacies inherited from Brazil's past made clear that the way to a true democracy would be more difficult than initially envisioned.

Considering the many challenges facing Brazil, it would be an understatement to say that the country is "at the crossroads." The political turbulence and despair induced by the fiasco of Collor's presidency made unmistakably clear to all Brazilians that perhaps now, more than ever, change is essential.

To understand the problems that have afflicted Brazil and still persist to this day, we now turn to a historical analysis of the most important points—the critical junctures—of Brazilian politics that have helped to determine the development of the modern state and democracy.

CRITICAL JUNCTURES

The Emergence of a Central Bureaucratic Power

Brazil was discovered in 1500 by Pedro Alvares Cabral. Unlike the other countries of Latin America, Brazil was a Portuguese colony, not a Spanish one. Thus, it was spared the devastatingly violent wars of independence that afflicted its neighbors. Instead, Brazil gained its independence peacefully in 1822 when Dom Pedro I, the son of the Portuguese king Dom João VI, declared himself emperor of Brazil with the support of Brazilians and Portuguese residents in the country. Dom Pedro I was succeeded by his son, Dom Pedro II, who reigned as emperor from 1840 to 1889. The sole hereditary constitutional monarchy in Latin America, the Brazilian Empire remained in power for sixty-seven years.

Brazil's postindependence state-building was driven primarily by the need to maintain both territorial integration and the slave labor on which its

Brazil's Independence

João VI and his son had previously been exiled in Brazil in 1808 as the result of Napoleon Bonaparte's campaigns in Spain and Portugal. The eventual defeat of Napoleon forced Dom João to reclaim his throne in Portugal, but his son Dom Pedro was left behind in Rio de Janeiro as prince regent to watch over the empire's colony. In September 1822 the prince declared Brazil's independence and became its first emperor. The Portuguese monarchy did not strongly object to the independence declared by the prince regent because control of the colony would still be in the hands of the monarchy.

export-based economy depended. From a very early point in Brazilian history, national political power was centralized. Although a modern, bureaucratic state had yet to be formed, the early experience of the empire had a tremendous influence on the character of subsequent state formation. The 1824 Constitution conferred specific reserved powers on the monarchy that continued to the empire's end. These powers transformed the monarchy into a *poder moderador* (moderating power) destined to stand above and harmonize the executive, legislative, and judicial branches of government, to arbitrate party conflicts, and to fulfill the responsibilities of government when nonroyal agents failed. The emperor had the authority to appoint ministers and dismiss legislative assemblies.

The early centralization of authority was a key factor differentiating the Brazilian experience from that of the other postcolonial Latin American states. Whereas the former Spanish colonies suffered from conflicts among many provincial, territorially dispersed strongmen called *caudillos,* Brazilian state-building overcame the challenges of governing a large territory with economically and socially diverse regions.

On the eve of independence (1822), Brazil was already becoming economically diverse. The sugar economy of the northeastern region—dominant in the eighteenth century—was a mere shadow of what it had once been. Its slave and freed population, however, continued to have an important socioeconomic impact on the northeast and other regions. The migration and sale of labor from the declining sugar region to the

central-south region and the ranch economy of the southern region expanded the labor pool southward.

The existence of a national slave economy had direct effects on the centralization of national power. In 1819, there were 1.1 million slaves, which corresponded to 30 percent of the population; in 1872, there were 1.5 million slaves, which represented 15.2 percent of the population. British pressure during mid-century to end the international slave trade led the Brazilian imperial state to take a strong international position in favor of slavery. A combination of the continued reliance on slave labor and the perceived need to rebuff British interventionism in imperial policy compelled the empire to oppose external pressures. However, the regional **oligarchy** was far too fragmented politically and geographically to present a unified front to Britain's influence. Thus they relied on the central government to confront international opposition to the slave economy. This event marked a pivotal moment in Brazilian state development: The central government reaffirmed its authority over a fragmented rural oligarchy by standing up to an external power of considerable military capabilities.

By the mid-nineteenth century, the empire had built a state and firmly established its territorial unity despite many obstacles—inadequate means of communication and transportation, the fragmentation of the national economy into regional economies, and the absence of a strong sense of national identity. Over the course of the century, the centralizing authority of the *poder moderador* and the development of a bureaucratic structure made the Brazilian imperial state, along with the Chilean state, one of the two most institutionally developed states on the continent.

The early pattern of imperial state formation was marked by several key strengths and weaknesses. Both the relative territorial unity achieved under the empire and an executive with command over the formal mechanisms of government were among the strengths. Among the weaknesses, a crucial one was the early formation of an administrative bureaucracy, long before most Brazilians could participate in politics, with the effect that the provincial elites who had access to positions of power within the bureaucracy would come to dominate Brazilian politics. Because Brazil's export-based economy produced cycles of economic growth and recession, upper-class unemployment was common. An expanding bureaucracy created jobs for members of the higher social strata. In the nineteenth century, the general underdevelopment of the country, the crisis in the northeast sugar economy, and the monopoly of trade by foreigners in the largest municipalities led many members of the landowning class to take positions in the bureaucracy. The expansion of citizenship and the political participation of other segments of Brazilian society would make other groups more significant much later. But from a very early time in the history of Brazilian state-building, provincial elites, who often represented powerful economic interests, dominated the national bureaucracy.

The constitutional empire marked the birth of Brazilian liberal institutions. In stark contrast with its neighbors, the country enjoyed several features of a functioning representative democracy: regularity of elections, the alternation of parties in power, and scrupulous observation of the constitution. In substance, however, liberal institutions only regulated political competition among the rural, oligarchical elites, reflecting the interests of a privileged minority and not the larger Brazilian population. The social reality of the country was an agrarian and illiterate slave society governed by a cosmopolitan elite that mimicked European civilization.

The Coming of the Liberal Republican Order (1889)

The next critical juncture in Brazilian history occurred in 1889 with the peaceful demise of the empire and the emergence of an oligarchical republic commanded by landowning elites from Brazil's coffee regions. Many causes led to the end of the empire. The institutions of slavery and the monarchy were topics of heated debate among landowners, politicians, and commercial elites. In the mid-nineteenth century, worldwide abolitionist movements brought pressure upon the Brazilian monarchy to end slavery. These pressures resulted in governmental measures which freed slaves over sixty years of age and children of slaves not yet born. Full abolition occurred only when it became clear to the powerful coffee elite of the state of São Paulo that the institution could not provide them with enough cheap labor. By 1888, all slaves were formally freed from bondage.

Among the expanding bureaucratic, commercial, and professional middle classes, republican ideas circulated widely during the last decade of the empire,

creating a growing receptivity for alternative forms of government. The landowning oligarchy, mainly from the coffee regions, advocated more decentralized government with more influence over policy-making. Liberalism was considered consistent with these interests because it was opposed to the despotic rule of a centralized government.

Apart from the larger social and ideological beliefs that supported the end of the empire, the church and the military played instrumental roles in actually making the political transition happen. After a church-state conflict in which Dom Pedro II imprisoned two bishops, the church ceased to back the monarchy. The military became discontented with the empire after internal divisions over the abolition issue and the advancement of junior and middle-level officers. After a brief military plot that forced the second emperor, Dom Pedro II, to exile in Portugal, the republic was proclaimed on November 16, 1889.

The Old Republic (1889–1930) that replaced the empire reflected a shift of political power and economic vitality from the northeast to the south and south-central coffee regions. By the end of the nineteenth century, coffee had become the main economic commodity with Brazil supplying most of the world's demand. Railroads linked coffee growers and markets from the rural areas of the state of São Paulo with the urban commercial elites of Rio de Janeiro and contributed further to the development of the south-central region. These structural changes in the economy accentuated the political influence of coffee elites.

Many political institutions from the monarchy were replaced by new institutions after the end of the empire in 1889. The liberal Brazilian constitution of 1891, which was closely inspired by the U.S. constitutional model, established a directly elected president as the head of the government, separated the state from the Catholic church, and expanded the franchise to include all literate males. The legitimacy of the republican political system was thus formally established on the principle of equal political rights for everyone rather than, as previously, on the hereditary rights of the emperor. The states were granted autonomy, extensive fiscal rights, and the right to contract foreign loans without the federal government's endorsement. They also had the authority to levy export taxes on products destined for other states and maintain militias stronger than the local contingents of the federal army.

Although the republican elite went further than the empire's elite in expressing liberal ideas in the constitution, to the majority of Brazilians, republican liberalism was a sham. Brazil continued to be a predominantly rural society. In 1890, only six cities had more than 50,000 inhabitants out of a population of 14 million. The landed oligarchy vigorously suppressed dissent in the rural areas and labor associations and urban interests were excluded from any meaningful participation. The patron-client ties that continued to keep poor people from mobilizing politically were widespread. The abolition of slavery did not significantly change the position of freed slaves in Brazilian society. Although the elites of the Old Republic claimed that liberal institutions made "citizens" of previously enslaved Africans, the fact that only literate males could vote kept many nonwhites imprisoned in poverty and politically unorganized. The poor Brazilians composed a majority of the population, but the electorate continued to average less than 3 percent of the population.

The solution offered by the republican government to the slavery problem is one of the primary causes of the social disparity between whites and blacks to this day. The Brazilian elite believed that the abolition of slavery would be sufficient to resolve all the harm it had inflicted. Therefore, the elite did not offer education, health, or jobs to incorporate the one-time slaves into society as full citizens. The abolitionist demand for grants of land to freedmen was forgotten. Coffee barons replaced slaves with immigrants, and urban black artisans lost their jobs to immigrants. Nor did the abolition of slavery place the "race question" on the national political agenda. Inequalities between blacks and whites did not become the basis for a political movement or a major political issue because either would have threatened the numerically small oligarchy's control over national politics.

The sociopolitical context eventually changed with the large influx of European and Asian immigrant laborers to replenish labor shortages induced by the end of slave traffic in 1851. From 1881 to 1930, almost 4 million Portuguese, Italian, Spanish, and German immigrants entered the country. The two largest European groups were Italian (36 percent of all immigrants during the period) and Portuguese (29 percent). From 1925 onward, Japan subsidized Japanese immigration. These immigrants established themselves as small proprietors and played an important role in the diversi-

fication of agricultural production in Brazil. Between 1931 and 1940, the Japanese were the second largest group of immigrants to enter Brazil. Despite the diversity of the immigration experience, immigrants tended to settle in the richer southern half of Brazil. In 1920, 93.4 percent of all foreigners lived in the center-south, south and south-eastern regions. Fifty-two percent of all foreign residents in the country lived in the state of São Paulo.

European immigrants with socialist and radical trade union backgrounds were the first organizers of the Brazilian labor movement during the Old Republic and often provided leadership in the newly formed trade unions. As a result of the large numbers of European workers entering Brazil at the turn of the century, their brand of trade union politics quickly dominated Brazilian trade union organization. In 1900, 92 percent of the workers in São Paulo factories were foreign. The effect of European immigration on the early development of trade unions was also evident in other countries of the hemisphere that experienced a wave of immigration during the late nineteenth century. The United States and Argentina, the two other great immigrant societies in the Americas, stand out in this regard.

The Old Republic proved to be a watershed for the evolution of state formation and Brazilian politics into the next century. First, it institutionalized the process known as *coronelismo*—the national government's grant of extensive extralegal authority to local, rural bosses in exchange for electoral support. The rural population's electoral loyalty to local authorities was manipulated by wealthy landowning oligarchs who easily influenced politics by mobilizing the weak and poor. Oligarchs could simply gather their labor force and "vote them" (using their votes to guarantee the election of local "colonels"). Ties between the patron (the landowners) and the client (the peasant) became the basis of Brazilian politics. In return for protection and occasional favors, the client would do the bidding of the patron. As urbanization and the growth of the state's administrative and bureaucratic agencies proceeded, the process of trading favors and demanding action was transformed and became known as **clientelism.** *Coronelismo* in rural areas and clientelist relations in urban areas were extended to the politics of the national state. In this way, the state was dominated by **patrimonialism**—the injection of private interests into public policy-making. Corruption, pervasive graft, and outright bribes developed as a parallel means of reinforcing patrimonialism.

Second, the Old Republic established within the central state the power of governors. The local "colonels" who exercised political control in villages and counties came to depend exclusively on the regional governors who became the chief controllers of the electoral process and local politicians. Perhaps at no time in Brazilian political history was the "politics of the governors"—the hegemony of the so-called barons of the republic—as blatant as it was during the years of the Old Republic. Regional elites, mainly from the coffee and cattle regions, dominated national politics, with three states in particular emerging as key players: São Paulo (coffee), Minas Gerais (coffee and ranch economy), and Rio Grande do Sul (ranch economy). These states profoundly influenced economic policy-making and the choice of presidential candidates. The presidency alternated almost on a regular basis between São Paulo and Minas Gerais. The pattern was so obvious that this period of Brazilian political history is popularly referred to as the rule of *"café com leite"* (" coffee with milk"), reflecting the dominance of São Paulo coffee and Minas Gerais cattle elites. The power of state government during the Old Republic created tremendously powerful political legacies. Even today, governors continue to play a key role in national agenda setting and they virtually dominate party politics. The regional governors continue to be at the center of federal and regional patrimonialism. Decentralized posts of political power still weaken the national Congress as a center of party development and policy-making.

A third, but no less important, development during the Old Republic was the emergence of the national military as a key actor in Brazilian politics. After the military revolt that precipitated the fall of the monarchy, the military underwent a process of continued professionalization and modernization. These developments would prove critical to Brazilian politics during much of the twentieth century.

The upsurge in European immigration, the beginnings of industrialization, and the modernization of the national military proved essential for the expansion of the middle class composed of artisans, professionals, politicians, civil servants, and military officers. With increased urbanization, these groups tended to weaken the political monopoly of the rural oligarchy and its clientelist order. Increased demands for expanded suffrage, urban political power, and the frustrations of young military officers would culminate in the third critical moment of Brazilian political history.

The 1930 Revolution

The 1930s were another watershed period for all Latin American countries. A worldwide depression had hit the region's economies, and markets for exported crops such as coffee collapsed. In Brazil this change threatened the traditional export-based pattern of economic development. Suddenly, social contradictions that had been simmering since World War I exploded. Political attacks by new generations of middle-class professionals and young military officers against the existing oligarchical political system soon revealed the weaknesses in the Old Republic.

A series of military revolts in 1922 and 1924 led by junior officers, the *tenentes,* convinced the upper classes that the institutions of the Old Republic could not hold together much longer. Worker demonstrations and the rise of the Brazilian Communist Party suggested that the end of the Old Republic was at hand. From the ranks of discontented political elites a figure emerged who would change the shape of Brazilian politics for the rest of the century—Getulio Vargas. The events around the presidential campaign and the effects of the 1929 crisis led to the 1930s' revolution that brought Vargas to power.

As the head of the new "revolutionary" government, Vargas gained legitimacy and authority to redesign the political system to expand the power of the central government and thus lessen that of the regional oligarchies. He moved swiftly to crush middle-class and popular dissent and to build a political coalition around a new economic project of industrialization, led by the central government and based on central state resources. Vargas was often ruthless, employing the federal military to coerce regional elites into obeying national directives. In 1932, federal troops became engaged in the most deadly of these episodes. A four-month-long rebellion by São Paulo's traditional social forces and its state militia resulted in hundreds of deaths and the capture of the city of São Paulo by federal troops. Vargas further solidified his control over the regional governments by replacing all governors with hand-picked allies *(interventores).* As a result, Vargas consolidated his authority and the centrality of the national state.

Getulio Vargas

Getulio Vargas came from a wealthy family in the cattle rich southernmost state of Rio Grande do Sul. Vargas began his political career as a district attorney and soon became a federal deputy for the state. His political acumen quickly made him the leader of his state's contingent in the Congress. Vargas became minister of finance during the Washington Luis administration (1926–1930). The 1929 international economic crisis compelled several regional economic oligarchies to unite in opposition to the coffee and financial policies of the government. The states, including the state of São Paulo, divided their support between two candidates for the presidency: one, Julio Prestes, supported by President Luis, and the other, Vargas, head of the opposition. The two states of Minas Gerais and Rio Grande do Sul voted as a bloc in favor of Vargas, but he lost the 1930 election. Immediately after this loss, a conspiracy among discontented military and political leaders led to the coup of October 1930, which installed Vargas in power. Once on top, Vargas remained for fifteen years, first as the chief of the provisional government (1930–1934), next as the indirectly elected president (1934–1937), and last (1937–1945) as the dictator. In 1945, he was obliged to renounce the presidency, only to return as a directly elected president in 1950. Defiant opposition from strong segments of the civilian and military elites led to his suicide in 1954.

Getulio Vargas, with whom modern Brazil started, as president in 1952.
Source: Photoworld/FPG

Previously, social rights issues were treated by political elites as a mere security issue, in which the police were considered more effective for securing "social peace" than for ensuring social rights. However, during the 1930s the government began developing policies to treat social rights' concerns as more than security issues. This acknowledgment took on particular characteristics, such as the abandonment of the liberal ideas that had guided the previous regimes. For the elite in power during Vargas's regime, the masses were considered, but their demands were met by voluntary concessions from a paternalistic state. People were to participate, not via party membership, elections, or representation in congress, but through state-created and state-regulated unions or associations. Moreover, only members of these state-sponsored unions and associations could enjoy the new social rights. These values and structures formed the body of what has been called state corporatism.

Corporatism refers to a method of organizing public-private relations and participation. It rejects the idea of competition among social groups by having the state deliberately organize political activity and settle conflicts. In state corporatism the state dominates both labor and business, turning unions and associations into little more than vehicles for transmitting orders from the executive powers. In Brazil, this concept was inspired by the Iberian and Eastern European corporatist Catholic right during the 1920s and the 1930s.

Liberal ideas were set aside and replaced by the establishment of a political dictatorship in the period 1937–1945 known as the *Estado Novo* (New State). By 1937, Vargas had achieved a position of virtually uncontested power. From such a vantage point, he implemented a series of reforms whose influence is still felt. During his eight-year dictatorship, Vargas consolidated his project into what could be called the *"Vargas Paradigm."*

The components of the Vargas Paradigm were: (1) an irreversible increase in central authority along with a high degree of state intervention in the economy for the purpose of promoting industrialization; (2) the creation of symbols of national identity, with the adoption of a cultural policy based on both nationalism and the charisma of the presidential office; (3) implementation of welfare policies and concession of workers' rights intended to draw the growing urban working class into a network of state-controlled labor unions; and (4) a low level of legitimacy for political parties and for Congress who were depicted as beholden to oligarchical interests.

The first and second elements reinforced each other in a clear manner. The symbolism of the New State conveyed the image of the national state as the protector of all Brazilians. Vargas was called the *pai do povo* (literally, the "father of the people"). The new regime expanded a few rudimentary social insurance and pension programs into a broad welfare and health care system for urban workers. Although unemployment insurance was not envisaged by the new laws, workers were provided with insurance against occupational accidents, illness, and death. A Ministry of Labor was created and labor courts were instituted to regulate and solve conflicts between employers and labor.

The state also expanded its interventionist role in the area of welfare through state agencies created to handle subsidized housing, food, and education for specific sectors of the urban working population. These policies increased the dependency of workers and even the middle class on federal subsidies and the provision of public sector jobs. The corporatist structure of interest mediation and representation reinforced the idea, central to the New State, that the federal government was the key mobilizer, provider, and protector of the Brazilian nation. One important element of this national project was the close identification of the worker with citizenship. Based on what was called the *estatuto do trabalhador* (worker's statute), the Brazilian state gave social and political identity to the common man. The statute claimed that workers who were members of official unions were guaranteed full Brazilian citizenship.

As a complement to the state-centered and state corporatist character of the New State, element (4) proved pivotal. Vargas's position as father of the people could not be questioned by competing political images and organizations. Parties and congressional politicians became mere outsiders. Vargas coined a phrase that best expressed the illegitimacy of representative bodies: "from now on there are to be no middlemen between the President and the people." One of the key thinkers of the New State coined another, even more dramatic phrase: "the new regime can have only one party, namely that of the state, which is at the same time the party of the nation."

The state became virtually the sole mediator of industrial relations. Business was often asked to participate in the various national councils that Vargas created to study and plan industrial development. Together with union leadership, these councils also dealt with social welfare issues and workers' rights. In this way, the two social classes mainly responsible for political change in Western Europe and Latin America, namely labor and the bourgeoisie, were incorporated into the political system through bureaucratic politics. That is, bureaucratic agencies, not workers or capitalist organizations, determined both the issues for government involvement and the options for their solution. The bourgeoisie and urban workers were induced to participate in politics before democratic representative institutions had been developed. The state, not political parties, projected those segments into the political arena.

The particular legacy of state centralism in Brazil contrasted significantly with what happened in other Latin American countries. Brazil was not the only country in South America to have adopted corporatism. Chile took this path in the 1920s, Mexico in the 1930s, and Argentina in the 1940s. But in contrast to Brazil, these countries, at the time corporatism took hold, had already developed political parties based mainly on the urban middle class. When Argentine urban workers were incorporated by state corporatist structures, they were linked to a party (the Justicialist Party) under the leadership of Juan Perón. At the time, industrial business leaders, agrarian interests, and even the military were already integrated into politics through national parties.

Brazil's political development evolved in clear contrast to the Mexican experience. Whereas the Mexican Revolution of 1910 turned rural workers into political actors, in Brazil these social segments remained politically marginal, non-citizens, up to the late 1950s.

More importantly, the Mexican state incorporated segments of the rural poor and the urban working class into a party, the Institutional Revolutionary Party (*Partido Revolucionario Institucional,* or PRI) after 1929. Brazil presented nothing similar, merely a patchwork of local oligarchical organizations that had been parties only in name during the Old Republic.

The growth of a powerful and centralized bureaucracy *before party and suffrage development* weakened the role of the party system that was eventually created after World War II. When national parties finally emerged, they were powerless to modify the vision of the state as a private, inherited property owned both by the bureaucracy and by the landed powers—in short, a patrimonial state. Furthermore, the parties soon realized that their chances for survival as organizations rested on the privileged access to benefits granted by the bureaucracy. Electoral and party politics became secondary institutions in the decision-making process.

The military was another important focus of Vargas's reforms. Under the New State, the armed forces experienced massive improvements in armament production and recruitment. Professional standards of promotion, conduct, and the use of force were codified in the establishment of the Superior War College (*Escola Superior de Guerra*). The military had been an important political actor since the proclamation of the republic. But it was during the New State that the military established itself as a policymaker and developed new doctrines for inspiring the crucial role the military should play in Brazilian politics. The military's linkage of industrialization and national security was a hallmark of these doctrinal changes. The ideology of the military regimes that dominated Brazil from 1964 to 1985 emerged directly from these earlier experiences.

The Rise of the Populist Republic (1945)

The political transition that began in 1945 was smooth and peaceful. The defeat of Nazi-fascism in Europe, the ever-growing mobilization of segments of the working and middle classes, and U.S. diplomatic pressure forced Vargas to consider democratization by calling for general elections. Despite the movement toward democracy, the presidential election of 1945 was won by one of the architects of the New State, General Eurico Dutra of the Social Democratic Party (PSD) in alliance with the Brazilian Labor Party

(PTB). Vargas played the key role in constructing the party-based corporatism of the post-1945 period. The Social Democratic Party was founded through organizing the "lords" of political machines across the country—the appointed state and municipal officers of the previous dictatorship (*interventores*). The other party, the Brazilian Labor Party, arose from the system of official unions that had been sponsored by the state. Both parties were wholly dependent upon the state and supporters of nationalism and state-led industrialization. The sole significant opposition party to emerge, the National Union Democratic Party (UDN), was created by regional leaders who had been outsiders during the New State; however, they also shared the interests of pro-Vargas forces in maintaining state-centered industrialization. Both electoral and party laws discouraged the rise of organizations independent of the state and linked to the lower or middle classes. The exception was granting legal status in 1945 to the Communist Party, which backed Vargas's economic projects and continued to do so even after it was declared illegal in 1947.

The transition process lacked a clear break with the past. The 1946 Constitution combined a liberal framework with core elements of Vargas's brand of authoritarianism. State corporatism, the vast concentration of power in the presidency, was retained along with many of Vargas's state-centered policies. The previous centralization of authority and policy-making in the hands of the state sapped the vitality of party-parliamentary politics. The divorce of party-electoral processes from the bureaucratic arena, where the most important economic and social issues were decided, boded ill for any experiment with democratic institutions, which was in fact attempted from 1945 onward.

Populism, not democracy, became the defining characteristic of the new political order after the end of World War II. The term *populist* or *populism* refers to politicians, programs, or movements that seek to expand citizenship to previously disenfranchised sectors of the society without organizing these sectors. An effective strategy employed by populist governments is to grant benefits while discouraging lower-class actors from formally organizing to express their demands. Although populism may bring lower-class citizens into politics for the first time, often populists use their support in a narrow way, failing to address the larger social and economic causes of poverty among the lower classes.

Critical Junctures in Brazil's History

1822	Dom Pedro I declares himself emperor of Brazil, peacefully ending 300 years of Portuguese colonial rule.
1888	Abolition of slavery
1889	Dom Pedro II is forced to exile; landowning elites establish an oligarchical republic.
1891	A new constitution establishes the office of an elected president.
1930	Getulio Vargas gains power after a coup led by military and political leaders. His period of dictatorship (1937–1945) is known as the New State.
1945	Vargas calls for general elections. General Eurico Dutra of the Social Democratic Party wins.
1950	Vargas is elected president. Scandals precipitate his suicide in 1954.
1956	Juscelino Kubitschek becomes president.
1960	Jânio Quadros becomes president.
1961	Quadros resigns. João Goulart gains presidency despite an attempted military coup.
1964	A military coup places power in the hands of successive authoritarian regimes.
1985	*Diretas Já*, a mass mobilization campaign, calls for direct elections.
1985	Vice presidential candidate José Sarney becomes president upon the sudden death of elected president Trancredo Neves.
1989	Fernando Collor is elected president.
1992	Collor is impeached; Vice president Itamar Franco assumes presidency.
1994	Fernando Henrique Cardoso is elected president.

In other parts of the world the term *populism* is used to describe movements with a strong agrarian character, as in Russia and the United States in the first decades of this century, although in Brazil and elsewhere in Latin America, populism generated a broad degree of mass support within the urban working and middle classes. Its leaders, around whom personality cults formed, came mostly from the ruling class and advocated what appeared to be anti-establishment policies. Perón in Argentina, Cárdenas in Mexico, and Vargas in Brazil were prototypical populist politicians. Recognition of labor organizations, provisions of social insurance and health care, and compulsory improvements in working conditions were the sorts of measures that earned them substantial backing from the working classes.

Brazilian populism was based on nationalist political movements that developed in the 1940s and 1950s when industrialization created rapid urbanization and social change. Through nationalism (the ideological core of most forms of Latin American populism), governments sought to erase the conflicts between the working class, the poor in general, and business owners. Their common enemies were the foreign interests and domestic rural landowners whose alliance was perceived to be the root cause for delayed industrial development. Nationalism, state-led industrialization, and anti-imperialism became rallying points for political mobilization during this period.

Vargas was elected to the presidency in 1950 and took power in 1951 sustained by his two parties (PSD and PTB). To win working-class support, the government promised periodic increases of the minimum wage, improvements to the social insurance system, subsidies for public transportation and basic foodstuffs. Industry was granted state subsidies and protective tariffs. The broad spectrum of wide-ranging, multiclass, populist alliances was not without internal tensions. In the early 1950s, when faced with severe economic problems—inflation, declining real wages, flagging exports—Vargas doubled the minimum wage. Such actions added to the inflationary pressures on the economy, confirming the opposition's view that Vargas could no longer promote the country's development. He was soon swept up by a cyclone of political intrigue and conflicts among members of his cabinet with the bureaucracy and the opposition UDN party. A bizarre scandal involving the attempted assassination of a popular journalist finally drove Vargas to suicide on August 24, 1954.

The ultimate crisis of multiclass populism was delayed until the beginning of the 1960s by rapid economic expansion. As a result of the developmentalist policies launched by Vargas's eventual democratic successor, Juscelino Kubitschek (1956–1960),

Brazilian industry expanded tremendously in the 1950s. Kubitschek's administration was filled with symbols of a new and bigger Brazil, perhaps the chief of which was Brasilia, the futuristic new capital started during the Kubitschek administration.

Although Kubitschek was successful in accelerating the pace of industrial development, spearheaded by the arrival of several automobile manufacturers and their suppliers, his tenure witnessed little in the way of political institutional development. Centralization of decision-making power in the hands of the executive remained unchanged. The role of government agencies continued to expand. As a counterweight to the old clientelistic bureaucracy, Kubitschek raised professional standards in recently created institutions involving, for example, regional and federal planning and finance for industrial development. Such efforts professionalized some bureaucratic agencies but left a vast array of other agencies largely unaffected.

Party-based populism finally ended in the early 1960s when Jânio Quadros, a populist antiparty maverick secured the presidency. Anti-establishment populist rhetoric may have elected him, but it failed to help him govern. The incapacity to govern was, among other factors, a consequence of the growing split between the two parties (PSD and PTB) on which the multiclass populist strategy of his two predecessors, Vargas and Kubitschek, had rested. A generalized economic crisis brought high inflation and diminishing rates of growth and also exacerbated the political conflicts that emerged in the early 1960s. Quadros's tenure in office ended abruptly with his sudden resignation, bringing João Goulart, Vargas's former minister of labor and Quadros's acting vice president, to the presidency. This occurred despite an attempted military coup in 1961—an omen of things to come.

Although Goulart had inherited Vargas's populist outlook, he lacked Vargas's charisma and, like Quadros, he was unable to run the Congress. Goulart embarked on an ill-fated campaign for structural reforms (the so-called *reformas de base*), mainly of the educational system and the federal administration, and a progressive agrarian policy *(reforma agraria).* The growing radicalization—both left and right—within the Brazilian polity, the differing attitudes of the PTB and PSD toward strikes, peasants league movements *(Ligas camponesas),* and illegal land occupation, increasingly fragmented the PTB-PSD party coalition.

Legislative stalemate added to policy-making paralysis. Unable to form a coalition capable of shepherding his reforms through Congress, Goulart was driven to construct a left-leaning political alliance. With the support of labor organizations, PTB leftist groups, and the semilegal Communist Party, the government began to mobilize urban groups, lower ranking military officers, and rural workers in an attempt to garner political capital outside institutionalized processes. The president's gamble soon proved costly as it convinced powerful upper- and middle-class interests, the upper ranks of the military, and the international business community that populism had given way to communism in a replica of what had happened in Cuba following the revolution of 1959. Industrial and landowning elites promptly rose in opposition to Goulart's reforms. Ad hoc right-wing organizations brought hundreds to the streets of the main capitals. Given such conditions, the military intervened in 1964, putting an end to an experiment in democratic populism that had lasted for almost two decades.

The Coup of 1964 and the Rise of Bureaucratic Authoritarianism

The professionalization of the Brazilian military during the New State and the period from 1945 to 1964 made the armed forces one of the most advanced in the region. Not only did the military possess sophisticated equipment and well-trained personnel, it was also advanced politically and organizationally. Instruction at the Superior War College involved comprehensive curricula in decision-making skills, economics, and administration. Additionally, the national security doctrine of the armed forces defined economic development as an integral part of domestic security. As such, the economic crisis that plagued Goulart's administration was viewed as a threat to the country. These developments provided the armed forces with the motive and the capability to overthrow Goulart and govern the country directly.

The military period (1964–1985) ranged from combinations of mild forms of authoritarianism that constricted civil rights and other political freedoms and harsher forms of authoritarianism, including wholesale censorship of the press through Institutional Acts, torture of civilians, and imprisonment without trial. The first and last two military rulers, Castelo Branco (1964–1967), Ernesto Geisel (1974–

The Role of the United States in the 1964 Military Coup

Brazilian-American relations during João Goulart's presidency were mixed from the start. In November 1961, the Chamber of Deputies passed a strict profit-remittance bill, limiting the extent to which American companies and other multinationals could take money out of the country. Washington considered retaliating by cutting off an aid program mandated by President John Kennedy's Alliance for Progress. With great concern about the spread of the Cuban Communist revolution throughout Latin America, Washington feared that Goulart's land reform policies would incite peasant revolt in the northeast. Lincoln Gordon, the U.S. ambassador to Brazil (1961–1966), warned that if Washing-ton did not support "democratic islands of sanity" in Brazilian politics—namely, civilian politicians like Carlos Lacerda who bitterly opposed Goulart—Brazil would go the way of Cuba. The American embassy proceeded to support anti-Goulart politicians like Lacerda and their clandestine operations to unseat Goulart with military support. The embassy channeled information about Goulart's whereabouts to the conspirators, thus facilitating military actions on March 31, the first day of the 1964 coup. As a sign of Washington's tacit consent for the conspiracy against Goulart, a contingent of U.S. Marines was stationed offshore in Rio.

1979), and João Figueiredo (1979–1985) presented less violent forms of authoritarianism, whereas the rule of Costa e Silva and of Emilio Médici (1968–1974) witnessed the worst forms of authoritarian crackdowns.

The Main Characteristics of the Period Although professing adherence to liberal economic principles of free markets, the military reinforced the previous pattern of bureaucratic expansionism and state interventionism in the economy. These governments actively promoted state-led industrialization by creating hundreds of state corporations.

Unlike the Argentine and Chilean military regimes, those in Brazil retained, albeit in a limited form, the national Congress, elections, and the party system. Though the Congress remained in operation, two new processes weakened its character. First, the creation of "institutional decrees" took important areas of legislation out of the jurisdiction of Congress, thereby reinforcing the impotence of the national legislature as a policy-making body.

Second, the purging of legislators who threatened the designs of the military reduced the possibility that a popular civilian would take the spotlight away from the military. The restructuring of the multiparty system into a two-party system (the National Alliance for Renovation, or ARENA, and the Brazilian Democratic Movement, or MDB) with numerous restrictions on the activities of the "official" opposition party also severely limited the potential of party-based politics. Direct elections for the presidency and for governorships were abolished. Electoral politics continued but were divorced from policy-making and from the suc-cession of the most powerful executive positions within the Brazilian state.

Another characteristic of the military period was the growth of a coercive, paramilitary apparatus with strong, anticommunist ideologies. A formidable repressive apparatus, independent of the judiciary, was created that practiced censorship, illegal imprisonment, and torture of suspected dissidents. The National Information Service (SNI) headed the various organizations that engaged in torture, systematic roundups of political dissidents, and executions of members of underground left-wing organizations. Once organized, these organizations were difficult to eliminate, even when it was clear that they had exceeded the authority delegated to them by the military chain of command.

Under military leadership, Brazil implemented one of the most successful economic development programs in the Third World. Nonetheless, as we will see later in this text, the deepening of socioeconomic inequalities and a staggering external debt were intricately linked to the military's development paradigm.

The Transition to Democracy and the Rise of the New Republic (1974–1985)

From 1974 onward, the economy began to falter; growth slackened and inflation increased. As a result, business groups gradually joined the opposition, thus adding powerful voices to those already complaining about the military's administration of the economy and protesting against repression. The increasing criticism from members of the social classes which had benefited the most from the military's economic policies led the military governments of Ernesto Geisel

(1974–1979) and João Figueiredo (1979–1985) to commit to gradual democratization. The worst abuses of human rights decreased in frequency, and controls over the press and public debate had relaxed enough by 1980 to permit the emergence of widespread opposition to military rule. The Brazilian transition was gradual and negotiated from above by civilian and military elites. It was not precipitated by dramatic, external events as in Portugal or Argentina, where transitions occurred abruptly after military governments were defeated in war.

The last two military governments had envisioned only a liberalizing, or "opening" *(abertura),* of the regime that would allow civilian politicians to contest for political office. As was the case with Gorbachev's glasnost, however, control over the process of liberalization gradually slipped from the fingers of authoritarian figures to be captured by organizations within civil society.

In retaining the trappings of the previous populist-democratic regime—particularly the Congress, periodic elections, and parties—the post-1964 military governments had gambled that they could somehow exploit these institutions to legitimize their rule. This gamble did not pay off as the military would have liked. Electoral competition between the two official parties, the ARENA (promilitary) and the opposition MDB (Brazilian Democratic Movement), did not always provide the military with a clear mandate. Particularly damaging to the political hegemony of military candidates were the 1974 electoral results in São Paulo for the Senate. The state of São Paulo, both the economic center and the largest electoral body of the country, gave the opposition party a stunning victory. Although the military government fixed electoral rules intended to severely handicap MDB candidates, ARENA failed to garner a landslide victory and for the first time since the military coup in 1964, the MDB channeled popular preferences.

Abertura grew as the resistance of civil society was channeled into the electoral process. The opposition made successive electoral gains and used them to get concessions from the government. The most important of these concessions was the reestablishment of direct elections for governors in 1982, political amnesty for dissidents, the elimination of the government's power to oust legislators from political office, and the restoration of political rights to those who had previously lost them.

The negative legacies of Brazil's economic miracle—high inflation, concentration of wealth and income, and high external debt—emerged clearly in the 1980s. The ensuing economic downturn gradually enabled the opposition forces to prevail against authoritarianism. Rising international criticism of human rights abuses during the military rule, a concern of the Carter administration in the United States, also began to resonate domestically. The gubernatorial elections of November 1982 sealed the fate of promilitary candidates. Opposition gubernatorial candidates won landslides, capturing the most developed states—Minas Gerais, São Paulo, and Rio de Janeiro. The 1982 elections were a crucial event that made the process of liberalizing the authoritarian regime irreversible.

The pressures against the military climaxed in 1985 when a mass mobilization campaign for direct elections—the *Diretas Já* (Direct Elections Now!)—took the country by storm.

The opening up of the electoral process was not entirely complete by 1985. The *Diretas Já* campaign had largely failed to reverse military-imposed constitutional directives that called for indirect elections of the new civilian president. Nevertheless, the military's fight to retain these prerogatives cost them dearly by alienating civilian supporters. Confronting direct elections for governorships in the context of greatly increased opposition, a key group of politicians and regional governors who had previously supported the military broke with the regime and forged an alliance (the Liberal Front) with Tancredo Neves, the candidate of the opposition MDB. Neves's victory in 1984, however, was short-lived. His sudden death on the eve of his inauguration left Vice President José Sarney as the first civilian president of Brazil since 1964.

The bizarre sequence of events which led to Sarney's presidency made the transition to democracy disappointing to all those who hoped for deeper institutional ruptures with the authoritarian past. Sarney had been an important supporter of the military and was viewed by most Brazilians as an illegitimate president. The armed forces viewed him as a traitor for helping to precipitate the military's exit from power. At the same time, many of the organizations that promoted the transition, including labor unions, distrusted Sarney as an old political hack of the military. Such divisions weakened his government. He became embroiled in conflicts with unions, business organizations, the church, and international financial

Diretas Já campaign crowds fill the streets just as at Carnival time.
Source: AP/Wide World Photos.

institutions. More importantly, as the first civilian government of the democratic transition, the Sarney administration failed to significantly reform the old authoritarian modes of policy-making, among them corporatist institutions and military prerogatives over civilian government.

Brazilian society, however, had developed substantially during the years of authoritarian rule. To continue authoritarian forms of policy-making would no longer serve social demands. In comparison with other worldwide democratic transitions, the Brazilian one is frequently praised for its gradual development and its lack of serious conflicts. However, the "mild rupture" with militarism involved in Brazil's path to democratization brought about a highly explosive mixture inimical to democratic stability: widely discredited parties, politicians, legislature, and other institutions of representation combined with an otherwise highly mobilized society. Fernando Collor's administration did not change this legacy.

Collor's impeachment brought to power Itamar Franco, Collor's little-known vice president. Franco's presidency seemed ill-fated at first because he was considered unprepared and illegitimate because he had not been elected as president. Although Franco had to cope with the same institutional problems that had plagued previous administrations, he achieved a stunning success: the reduction of inflation from 26 per-

cent in October 1992 to 2.82 percent in October 1994. From that time, most of his previous defects were forgiven. Franco was portrayed by the media as a "common man" who was thrust into power unexpectedly and had done well. He finished his term as one of the most popular Brazilian presidents in recent memory. His success was complete in 1994 when his minister of the economy, Fernando Henrique Cardoso, the man responsible for the anti-inflationary plan, was elected president of the republic.

IMPLICATIONS FOR CONTEMPORARY BRAZILIAN POLITICS

Although there have been improvements in the Brazilian political context since Collor's fall, the historical legacies of economic distortions and weak democratic institutions continued to weigh heavily upon Brazilian society past the mid-1990s. The legacies that persist on the national stage can be categorized into five areas.

First, for more than half a century, Brazilian development took a form that has left the country with among the most highly skewed income distribution in the world. Social welfare and educational standards, in comparison with those of Argentina, Uruguay, and Chile, where the transition to democracy also took place recently, are unacceptably low. Brazil's large population intensifies the pressure on already frayed resources. Even worse, insufficient state revenues

Favelas in Rio de Janeiro, another aspect of Brazilian modernization.
Source: © Richard Wilkie, FPG.

have necessitated severe cuts in social spending. The still feeble capacity of the state to tax the upper class and segments of the middle class makes it increasingly impossible to provide basic services to all its citizens. Urban decay and the rings of squatter settlements *(favelas)* around the major cities thus continue to grow. Significant segments of the country's largest cities live in these *favelas*—7 percent in São Paulo, 12.4 percent in Rio de Janeiro, and 42.2 percent in Recife.

Second, for low income Brazilians, the right to vote is regarded as secondary to mere survival, at whatever cost. Violence, corruption, and crime, inevitable by-products of urban decay and poverty, have reached levels that threaten political stability and democratic equity. Official violence, unequal access to judicial resources, and violations of worker rights are still a part of life in Brazil. Most abuses of citizens' individual rights go untried. Seldom are violent police officers or military officials put on trial for their crimes. The rights of children and indigenous peoples also continue to be trampled on regularly by government officials and unscrupulous capitalists. Little has been done in this area beyond the official rhetoric that shrouds the occasional atrocity reported in the international press. Society at large has the clear perception that neither state nor government is able to make its decisions stick. Feelings of vulnerability and social

isolation extend to public cynicism of politics and politicians. The rise of right-wing extremist elements in the 1989 and 1994 elections greatly exacerbated this cynicism. All these issues have convinced many that Brazil is undergoing a dangerous moral crisis.

Third, Brazil is experiencing great difficulty in consolidating its democracy because it has failed to maintain a political coalition capable of backing social and economic reform. Democratic consolidation requires (at least in part) a reasonably stable and workable party system. It is generally agreed, for example, that the early creation and significant role of the Congress Party was a solid foundation for democratic consolidation in India, despite that country's formidable socioeconomic problems. The history of Brazil, however, has witnessed the state playing the key political role throughout postindependence at the expense of political institutions such as parties and Congress. Brazilian political parties are short-lived and the party system tends to fragment, thus undercutting the capacity of major parties to assemble viable legislative alliances. Regional politics decisively mark the configuration of the Brazilian party system, thus making it difficult to characterize the political parties as national organizations. The proliferation of parties in Brazil is in sharp contrast with the situation in most other Latin American countries where the number hardly ever exceeds three or four major parties. The contrast is even sharper when one considers that in Mexico a single party (the Institutional Revolutionary Party, or PRI) has controlled electoral life (albeit often through pervasive fraud and coercion).

The disagreement among parties and between parties and the government marks two characteristics of the Brazilian decision-making process: decision-making paralysis in some areas of policy-making and precipitous decision making in others. It is no wonder the legacy of executive discretion extends to Brazil's present. The first three civilian presidents since 1985—Sarney, Collor, and Itamar Franco—all employed executive, discretionary authority that bypasses congressional oversight.

Fourth, a key explanation for the apparent weakness of the Brazilian state in preparing the economy for technological growth is, paradoxically, the state-centered character of the country's institutional development ever since its formative period. The result is a weak and dependent bourgeois class and a state bureaucracy riddled with political appointees catering to special interests. This kind of excessive state control over the economy and society tends to feed corruption. Evidence accumulating throughout the world shows that huge public sectors and pervasive state subsidies can hamper economic efficiency and become major obstacles to vigorous economic growth. This has become increasingly apparent in India, Mexico, Nigeria, and Eastern European countries where state ownership has led to the waste of capital, to corruption, and to a heavy drag on the economy from unprofitable and inefficient state enterprises. The Nigerian case graphically portrays how the scale and extension of corruption can delegitimize the entire political system, not just particular leaders or parties.

Each of these aspects has a corrosive effect on the rule of law and on respect for the constitution. The current high degree of ambivalence with respect to democracy is not found in any of the other Southern Cone countries (Argentina, Paraguay, Uruguay, and Chile).

Finally, Brazil has developed economically and politically at the periphery, or better yet—considering the relatively more underdeveloped Latin American and African states—at the semiperiphery of the world economy. Although Brazil is not so weak that it depends tremendously upon the United States for economic aid, as does Mexico, it has been more a follower of North American economic and foreign policies than other states such as France and Iran. The recent dominance of free-market policies in Brazil has strengthened the country's pursuit of ideas that are not

its own—constructed instead in policy laboratories in North America and Western Europe. This will have serious implications for Brazil if it means that domestic elites lose sight of the limitations of imported ideas and the need to innovate against ever-changing economic and political realities.

There is some hope that Brazil may be developing this capacity. Several analysts suggest that the greatest opportunities to improve the country may rest on the rise of political awareness and the organization of the Brazilian society. Issues that were once taboo are rapidly becoming topics of national debate and self-examination. New political identities, unimaginable even a decade ago, have been forged. Many domestic and international actors have begun to play interesting new roles in political mobilization at all levels, local, state, and national. Nongovernmental organizations (ngos) active in the field of human rights, environmental issues, poverty, and violence, have bridged the gap between international and domestic politics. Domestic groups, feminists, unions, ethnic organizations, and church-based movements have mobilized resources and have been important catalysts for change.

The immensity of Brazil's problems and the many perverse political legacies of state building cannot be appreciated without a study of the country's economic development. State-centered politics often accompanied a variant of state-centered economic development. It is to this crucial area of study that we now turn.

SECTION 2
Political Economy and Development

Brazil's struggle for economic and social development is shaped by a combination of state intervention in domestic markets and the effects of external economic fluctuations. These two factors are interrelated and influence each other. External economic crises—world depressions, fluctuations in the price of exported goods, upsurges in the prices of imported goods—increasingly compelled the Brazilian state to intervene in the domestic economy, through protection, subsidies, and even the production of goods that were previously imported.

Like its Latin American neighbors, Brazil's early economic development was based on **export-led growth,** that is, on the export of agricultural, or primary, products such as sugar, cotton, coffee, and for a short time at the turn of the century, rubber. Under the Old Republic, export was structured by Brazil's monopolistic position in the coffee market, which allowed producers to determine supply and prices in the world market. Under these conditions, coffee quickly became Brazil's main export product. High demand for Brazilian coffee in Europe and North America made it extremely competitive. Cotton and sugar continued to be important export products, but they were clearly secondary to coffee.

Up to the turn of the century, export-led growth depended on minimal state intervention. In 1906, however, governmental policies called "valorization coffee schemes" were launched, inaugurating the interventionist role in the economy that the Brazilian state continued in the years to come. With the shift to higher levels of protection during the 1930s, the state increased its involvement in the economy. The Brazilian state financed large investments, both industrial and infrastructural, gave protection to national and international capital, and used fiscal and monetary policies to foster investment and ensure profitability. Industry thus became the dominant segment of the economy. In the process, the state itself became a major industrial investor. The relative weight of the state-owned sector continued to grow until the end of the military regime in the mid-1980s. Nationalism and state-led industrialization formed the ideological core that sustained the course taken by the country's political economy. Both the political left and Vargas's supporters based their mobilization upon this orientation.

During the 1950s, Latin American academics and policymakers widely proclaimed that Latin America had to solve its problems by reordering its economic relations with the major powers, particularly the United States. In response, various military and civilian governments attempted to diversify Latin American economies with the goal of reducing their dependency on the U.S. market by broadening the region's trading partners. Beginning in the late 1960s, Brazil succeeded in these efforts by expanding the range and depth of its international diplomatic contacts, export markets, sources of imports, and investments and financing.

Although the military governments claimed to be against nationalism and state-led industrialization, the military only stripped nationalism of its leftist tones and expanded the model of state-led growth. Although nationalist rhetoric during the 1950s and early 1960s linked welfare, the demands of popular sectors, and the growth of industry, nationalism during the military period became extremely patriotic as the "nation" was urged to make efforts to transform Brazil into a great power.

The major emphasis of Brazil's current political economy is to reduce the state's economic role and to open up the domestic economy to international market forces. The idea of free markets has taken Brazil and the entire region by storm. Today, the so-called Washington Consensus, an epithet for the United States' support for liberal market policy in the region, is the

General Médici, military repression at its peak.
Source: AP/Wide World Photos.

dominant political economic paradigm in Brazil among policymakers.

Both state-led and market-oriented policies have had costly effects for most Brazilians. Social welfare for the poor sectors has suffered under all development alternatives. The Brazilian elite's preference for economic development at all costs and the restrictive aspects of political institutions on participation and political organization by the poor has led to the slow development of an extended welfare system.

In order to fully understand the ways that political and economic development have been intertwined in Brazil, the first section, "State and Economy," explores the state-led model of development. In the second section, "Society and Economy," we consider how the domestic effects of the state-led model of development have generated enormous social costs alongside high growth levels. Finally, in the third section, "Brazil and the International Political Economy," we will investigate the international capitalist forces that shaped domestic economic policy and its social implications.

STATE AND ECONOMY

As already noted, international prices were the crucial factors in determining how well the export economy would function. Although the Brazilian state could not directly determine the value of the domestic coffee economy, it did limit the effects of the deterioration of coffee prices in the international market through policies that were launched during the first decades of the twentieth century.

As long as the coffee economy did well, domestic industrialists could afford to import machines for domestic production and pay their labor force. According to Celso Furtado, an expert on Brazilian economic development, the coffee economy contributed to the early development of small industries. Salaried European immigrants would work the coffee plantations, earn enough to invest in a small business, and in time, would become entrepreneurs themselves. Coffee growers often diversified their own assets, investing in the new industries that produced for the growing consumer market of salaried workers. The vitality of coffee exports ensured the growth of a domestic market for domestically produced industrial goods. The growth of exports, however, made the vitality of the domestic economy dependent upon fluctuations in international prices. Brazil's capacity to import depended on its ability to obtain foreign exchange from exporting coffee. Without these reserves, Brazilians could not purchase manufactured goods.

Brazil's use of its export income to industrialize was not typical of other Latin American export-led economies. The latter required foreign capital and other resources. These conditions often benefited the foreign investor and left little room for the emergence of domestic entrepreneurs. In contrast, the Brazilian pattern was based on the control of coffee production by domestic producers, the abundance of natural resources, the availability of labor, and, last but not least, given the nation's large size and population, *the potential of a large internal market.* The growing size of the internal market for industrial products enabled Brazil's industrialization to be largely self-sufficient. The absence of an excessive reliance on foreign capital also allowed the pattern of domestic industrialization to stay largely confined to the growing internal market.

The dominance of coffee and small industry faded in the 1930s when the Great Depression caused a precipitous fall in the international demand for coffee. As a result, the influx of foreign exchange earnings declined rapidly. Both the stagnation of European and North American manufacturing and the decreasing ability of Brazilian

entrepreneurs to import decimated the older model of industrialization.

Import Substituting Industrialization

During the 1930s, a process of **import substituting industrialization (ISI)** developed alongside export-led growth. Through this process, the economy gradually developed domestic industries that would produce previously imported goods. By 1937 this industrial growth trajectory, which now relied heavily on state intervention, emerged along with Vargas's New State. At first, large doses of state intervention were not necessary. The initial phase of ISI—the so-called light or easy phase—was dominated by the substitution of manufactured imports that required little capital or sophisticated technology. Most of these industries, such as textiles and food processing, were labor intensive and thus created jobs. Although these conditions did not require large infusions of state capital, the New State provided limited subsidies and tariff protection to nascent ISI sectors.

At the end of World War II, new ideas about Third World development began to be adopted by various international agencies and regional ministries. In Brazil, as in Argentina, Mexico, and India, a new generation of state technocrats emerged during the 1950s. These new technocrats advocated economic growth based on domestic industrial capacity and internal markets. Latin American governments became more active in the promotion of ISI, inspired by the texts of the United Nations Economic Commission for Latin America (ECLA) and backed by loans from sources like the World Bank. This time, however, the goal was to move out of the easy phase of ISI and "deepen" the model by promoting heavy industry and capital-intensive production. Industrial planning and targeting became the new tools of ECLA "developmentalists" throughout the region.

Brazil was the epitome of ECLA-style **developmentalism** during the 1950s. More than any other Latin American state, the Brazilian state was organizationally capable of implementing industrial policies to deepen ISI. New bureaucratic structures, like a national development bank and national public firms, were built during the first and second Vargas governments. PETROBRAS, the state oil firm, quickly became one of the earliest examples of what the Brazilian state wanted to become—a state that could produce as well as regulate. The "producer state" promoted the expansion of private investment by producing and distributing raw materials for domestic industrialization at prices well below the international market level. These lower prices were in effect subsidies to domestic industry. In this way, subsidized steel and subsidized credit from the national development bank would fuel domestic industrialization. Secondary producers linked to targeted sectors would benefit in a chain reaction fashion.

Brazilian developmentalism came to its fullest fruition between 1955 and 1960 during the presidency of Juscelino Kubitschek. President Kubitschek's ambitious industrialization plan sought, in his words, to foster "fifty years of development in five" (the five years of his presidential term). Under "JK," the Brazilian state subsidized industrial production in capital-intensive sectors like automobiles and in the production of input commodities like steel.

Although growth rates achieved impressive levels during the 1950s and early 1960s, it was during this period that the first serious contradictions of ISI emerged. Protection fostered noncompetitive industrial structures and inefficient production. High inflation accompanied each upsurge in growth. As domestic industrialists became increasingly dependent on imports to satisfy the growing domestic demand for manufactured goods, the Brazilian currency became overvalued. As the need for imports grew, export earnings to pay for them simultaneously declined because their competitiveness suffered due to the overvaluation of the currency. The export sector could not supply the state with much-needed revenues to sustain growth, prompting the government to print money which in turn led to inflation. Under the Goulart government (1961–1964), the economy's capacity to import and export dwindled and stagnation set in. The economic crisis which soon followed contributed to the coup of 1964 and Goulart's fall.

The military's usurption of power in 1964 did not mean either the end of ISI or its continued deepening according to the older developmentalist route. The state retained its role as the main planner and coordinator of domestic industry, but its functions and the political structures that would manage it changed irrevocably between 1964 and 1985 under military rule.

The pattern of industrialization intensified around the production of consumer durable goods for the domestic market such as automobiles, televisions, refrigerators, and machinery. This pattern of industri-

TABLE 1	**GDP Growth Rates, 1950–1993**

Year	GDP Rate (percentage)
1940–1950	5.6
1950–1960	6.1
1960–1970	5.4
1970–1980	12.4
1980–1990	1.5

Source: Brazilian Institute of Geography and Statistics (IBGE).

alization involved domestic entrepreneurs in the transfer of technology from foreign investors, particularly during the 1970s and 1980s when they participated in joint ventures in pharmaceuticals and, later, in computers.

State firms played an important role in the military's development model. Large-scale projects in shipbuilding, mining, steel, oil, bauxite, and aluminum were financed and managed by bureaucratic agencies and state firms. These projects often operated in conjunction with larger development plans designed to attract domestic and foreign entrepreneurs. Peter Evans, an American specialist on Brazilian political economy, characterized these complex relations among the state, foreign investors, and domestic capitalists as a triple alliance. The state, however, remained the dominant partner. Table 1 shows the rate of GDP growth and Table 2 shows the sector composition of the GDP.

The military played a significant role in Brazil's domestic expansion after 1964 through the growth of the defense industry. The military's desire to free the country from its reliance on military imports was reinforced by the government's belief that building a strong defense industry would enhance Brazil's influence among less developed countries in Latin America, Africa, and Asia. Moreover, the building of a sound defense industry would demonstrate the competence of the military ruling elite.

After the military seized power, an important shift in ideas related to exporting primary products to foreign markets occurred among economists and government planners. Previously, the export of primary products was considered to be a symbol of delayed development typical of Third World countries. In the

TABLE 2 **Sector Composition of the GDP, 1970–1990**

Year	Agriculture	Industry (percentages)	Services
1970	11.55	35.87	52.59
1980	10.16	40.99	48.84
1990	9.26	34.20	56.54

Source: Brazilian Institute of Geography and Statistics (IBGE).

1970s and 1980s, propelled by the decrease of revenues and the payment of foreign debt services, the military once again emphasized primary exports alongside consumer durable exports. Policies to increase agricultural productivity and technological modernization, which had already been implemented in the first years of military rule, were expanded and agriculture began to be integrated with industrial production.

Previously, the vitality of the agricultural sector was measured by its capacity to generate foreign reserves through exports and to supply inexpensive foodstuffs for the internal market. During the 1970s and 1980s, this older pattern changed. The export of agricultural surplus and the sale of food products in the internal market were increasingly facilitated by a growing agro-industry sector. Spurred on by state subsidies, the agro-business complex supplied new resources and management for inefficient agriculture. Agricultural production in the agro-business sector employed heavy machinery and advanced technologies that increased the size of the average yield. One of the most outstanding and successful agro-business ventures occurred in the 1970s when the military government introduced a plan to use sugarcane alcohol as a fuel source. Northeast agro-business boomed during these years as the sugar economy became tied to the dynamic industrial economy of the south and southeast.

The Tax System

Before the military took over the government, the Brazilian tax system was notoriously weak. Tax evasion was rampant. The number of tax exemptions and low tax rates combined to bring only modest revenues to the federal government. To ensure that the central state had the necessary funds to command the new project of national development, the military regime, via the 1967 constitutional reform and several administrative changes, expanded the state capacity to tax, created new taxes, and centralized fiscal policy and the control of revenues. Changes to the tax system brought immediate results. From 1965 to 1975, tax revenues as a percentage of gross domestic product (GDP) increased from 19.1 to 25.2 percent. However, because one of the military's primary objectives was to stimulate private savings and to increase capital formation, it meant that exemptions, as well as transfers of resources to upper middle classes and firms, were given privileged status. Thus tax burdens on the middle classes and salaried workers were maintained, largely sparing the higher-income sectors and the profits of business and rural landowners.

From 1980 to 1984, total tax revenues fell 12.7 percent and the tax on manufactured products went down 53.3 percent, forcing the military to adopt various schemes to increase state revenues from income tax by elevating the tax on profits. The upper classes fervently opposed the increase of their tax contribution. But their opposition was not the only factor that eventually made increased taxes ineffectual at increasing revenues. The early 1980s experienced a world recession that forced unemployment to rise. All these factors led to an overall decline in tax revenues.

These processes resulted in the emergence of an informal market, or "invisible economy," as people sought to avoid what they believed to be strangling taxes. Backyard small firms, domestic enterprises, street vendors, and unregistered employees proliferated. Legally registered companies began to subcontract unregistered professionals to render services beyond the reach of the tax system. Although reliable information is lacking, economists estimate that the informal economy represents close to half of Brazil's GDP and employs about 30 million people.

Figure 1   1991 Federal Budget*
*Numbers are estimates. Most of these categories
cross-over regularly.

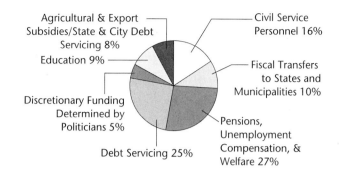

Agricultural & Export
Subsidies/State & City Debt
Servicing 8%

Education 9%

Discretionary Funding
Determined by
Politicians 5%

Debt Servicing 25%

Civil Service
Personnel 16%

Fiscal Transfers
to States and
Municipalities 10%

Pensions,
Unemployment
Compensation, &
Welfare 27%

Due in part to the weakness of the tax system, public financing for industry and infrastructure depended upon foreign lending and taxes on export receipts. After 1980, foreign loans played a larger role in financing state-led industrialization once internal resources became insufficient to finance investments in the three spheres of government. By relying on foreign creditors, the Brazilian state could overcome the problem of depending solely on export revenues and taxation to finance development projects.

Since the government of Itamar Franco, important trends began to emerge: an attempt to shift the income tax base from the low and middle classes to the upper classes, capital, and the financial market; and an effort to obtain resources to finance new social projects. Nevertheless, as the director of the federal tax system admitted, only middle-class and salaried people pay taxes in Brazil. Although the profile of the taxed population did not evolve much, the efforts launched by the Cardoso government achieved some substantial results in curbing tax evasion.

Regarding the distribution of revenues between the three spheres of government, Brazil has the highest level of fiscal decentralization among the Third World countries, a tendency accentuated in the last fifteen or twenty years. The 1988 Constitution accelerated fiscal decentralization by allowing states and municipalities to keep a larger share of tax revenues. Additionally, the states also retained a high level of autonomy in administering their own state and local taxes. In 1993, states and municipalities collected 34 percent of the country's total revenues, but retained 44 percent of the total. That is, the states collected more of Brazil's tax money and spent even more than they collected of total public revenue.

The division of resources between the federal government and the states has produced definite ten-

dencies in the fiscal structure of the country. On the one hand, the regional states were provided with larger shares of resources without a complementary expansion of their obligations. On the other hand, the amount of issues and areas accountable to the federal government was maintained. More money flowed to the states, leaving less for the federal government. The result was a federal government forced to spend more than it collected in taxes in order to pay for its administrative costs (see Figure 1).

The Welfare System

Brazil supports a public school system, as well as a health, retirement, and social assistance system that includes funds for unemployment relief. Salaried workers are entitled to such benefits as medical care, work accident insurance, retirement pensions, paid vacations, and extra working hours. Although welfare and education expenditures constitute a significant portion of the federal budget, the overall performance of the Brazilian welfare state is mediocre and well below the needs of the population. Unlike many countries in Western Europe and even in South America, Brazil's welfare system does not alleviate high levels of poverty or help the majority of the poor. Vast sectors of the population, deprived of credits, titles, and jobs, remain totally outside the reach of these welfare services. Corruption and waste of resources makes the welfare system incapable of delivering benefits to the people that need them the most.

Part of the problem is that more people need welfare than actually contribute to the welfare state. Today only half of the 65 million people who are economically active contribute to the welfare system. In the last eleven years, for instance, while the population doubled, the number of retired people multiplied elevenfold, thus adding to the roster of those depending on public welfare spending. In 1995, the welfare system received $3.5 billion less than was needed to pay the retirement pensions of the 15.2 million inactive workers and 3 million new beneficiaries.

During the military period, important changes were made both in welfare administration and in the extension of social rights to segments outside the domain of welfare services. To make the system more efficient, the resources and the control over the implementation of social policies were centralized in the hands of the federal executive to reduce the effects of clientelism at the local level. Similar reasoning justified the expulsion from existing welfare agencies of all representatives from unions and employers' organizations.

One of the first of the military governments' welfare reforms was to make job stability obsolete. Since the 1930s, welfare provisions guaranteed that an employee working for a firm or business for a period of ten years could not be dismissed thereafter without compensation. Instead, an insurance fund (FGTS) was created that adjusted proportionally to the years of employment. The elimination of job stability compensation affected the lives of millions of workers and, despite military repression, led to mass protests by the opposition and labor unions.

Second, social rights were extended to several sectors that previously had been outside of the welfare benefits system: rural workers, domestic workers, and professionals. In 1974, the Ministry of Welfare was created to administer these new programs. As a whole, social expenditures constituted an increasingly significant portion of the national fiscal budget during the military period. In some years, welfare expenditures reached 15 to 18 percent of the GNP.

Third, the proliferation of state agencies and companies swelled the number of civil servants and workers who were directly linked to state enterprises. This led to a huge expansion of state benefits and services. These state-linked sectors along with members of the legislature, the judiciary, and executive branches of government continued to benefit the most from the state welfare system. In addition to health and medical care, they were granted generous retirement pensions, subsidized housing, and a vast array of fringe benefits.

The economic crisis of the early 1980s, which limited even further the extent to which the state

could attack social problems, made budget austerity more important than expanding social welfare programs. Unfortunately, the demands on the welfare system proliferated along with the expansion of the public deficit, but now cuts in welfare programs were quickly engineered to reduce the budget deficits for the long term. Welfare expenditures did not reach 1981 levels again until 1989. During the first civilian government, the only positive result concerning welfare policy was its inclusion in the 1988 Constitution. This document established new social rights and expanded unemployment benefits. Between 1988 and 1989, Congress began a discussion of the complementary legislation required to implement the constitutionally set welfare principles. The legislative debate continues to this day.

During Collor's tenure, under the label of administrative reform, the state welfare system began to be dismantled precipitously. Welfare policies and public services deteriorated to levels never seen in the contemporary history of the country. The federal funds for health care, for example, were reduced by 50 percent after Collor took office in 1990. In 1988, the welfare system transferred 25 percent of its revenues to health welfare; in 1990, that number was only 15 percent. In 1993 *no funds* were transferred.

Simultaneous with the reduction in total welfare payments was the concentration of social expenditures in "privileged sectors"—namely, civil servants and politicians. The latest figures show that the welfare system pays $35.2 billion to 15 million inactive workers in the private sector. Inactive public sector workers, who number 404,000 receive $10.5 billion. That means that the average retired or unemployed civil servant received $2,188 monthly as compared to an average of $194 for private workers.

Forced to confront these problems, the present government has increased its efforts to control tax evasion and to reform the welfare system. A large campaign has been launched to make private employers as well as some state companies (among the worst offenders) pay their share of social welfare contributions. The debate over the role of the state in social welfare as well as over the need to prioritize the beneficiaries of state policies has intensified. The dilemmas between state-sponsored welfare policies versus privatization and the expansion of existing programs for salaried workers, or the expansion of welfare coverage for those who are not receiving regular salaries, were on the agenda for the scheduled revision of the 1988 Constitution.

The Problem of Inflation

The process of redemocratization after 1985 brought increased pressure from various sectors of the society for something to be done about income differentials and their social consequences. The deficit, inflation, and pressure to alleviate the socioeconomic conditions of the poor led the civilian governments of Sarney, Collor, and Franco, to launch several economic packages. Their purpose was both to undercut the sources of inflation (which were primarily government deficits and the insolvency of the state sector) and to renew productive investments in the private sector. All these packages were based on the assumption that stabilization measures would not lead to a recession, even though classical stabilization policies produce declines in output and employment and hence assume the inevitability of recession.

From 1986 to 1990, all stabilization packages involved the use of controls to arrest price and wage increases. Nonetheless, real wages were allowed to rise and there was virtually no effort to limit subsidies to private firms or to control public spending. A new spiral of inflation began when pressures on prices ultimately forced the relaxation of government controls. Overall, the stabilization packages proved unable to sustain the fiscal and monetary discipline necessary for their success, leading to an economic deterioration and four-digit inflation. The climate of uncertainty fostered by the swings in government policies was extremely negative for the credibility of Brazilian governments domestically and abroad.

The record of Brazil's anti-inflation policies was abysmal. Although the country underwent at least six successive plans during the period 1986–1993, no lasting reduction of inflation was achieved. Figure 2 illustrates this terrible track record.

One of the first complications in anti-inflation policy was a conflict between Brazil and the International Monetary Fund (IMF) over the nature of this policy. The IMF advocated an orthodox anti-inflation policy that included reductions in fiscal deficits and tight monetary policy through increases in interest rates. Such prescriptions promised recession and severe budget cuts in welfare and industrial promotion. In response, Sarney and his team of economic advisers advocated a heterodox policy. Although heterodoxy

also embraced tight monetary policy and some fiscal restraint, it adamantly opposed provoking recession to control inflation. Price controls, mechanisms totally rejected by orthodoxy, were employed to gradually eliminate expectations that prices would rise.

The first of a series of anti-inflationary policies, the Cruzado Plan, was launched in 1986. The plan employed a combination of price and wage controls to combat inflationary pressures. Although the Cruzado Plan succeeded in arresting large upsurges in inflation for an eight-month period, prices eventually returned to their previous upward climb. Part of the problem was that the plan allowed real wages to rise and did little to limit subsidies or to control public spending. When pressure on prices eventually forced the relaxation of controls, a new spiral of inflation began. Stabilization packages such as the Cruzado Plan proved unable to sustain the fiscal and monetary discipline necessary for their success.

After a bout with hyperinflation during the last two years of Sarney's mandate, Collor took a more direct approach to inflation. The Collor Plan was launched in 1990 as a heterodox shock program that ended up more shocking than heterodox. Savings accounts were frozen nationally. Inflation fell, but by the end of the year there was another upsurge in prices. The most aggressive of Brazil's homespun anti-inflation plans proved disastrous. Combined with the global recession, inflation and credit scarcity discouraged investment. A climate of extreme uncertainty chilled the entrepreneurial fervor that had been at the core of Brazil's past experience with high growth.

The failures of the previous plans prompted the ministers of finance under the Itamar Franco government to refuse to launch any economic packages that included wage and price freezes or other shock policies. His policies tried to reduce inflation through budget cuts, tax increases, curbing tax evasion, stabilizing the currency by indexing it to the dollar, and privatization. This approach to reducing inflation had a promising beginning with the launching of the *Plano Real* (Real Plan) at the beginning of July 1994.

Like its predecessors, the Real Plan changed the name of the national currency in an attempt to eliminate the memory of inflation associated with the older currency. But unlike the previous plans, it attempted to anchor the Real, the new currency, in a Unit of Real Value (URV) which was itself indexed to the dollar. Yet unlike similar plans in Mexico and Argentina, the

Figure 2   Annual Inflation, 1970–1993
Source: DIEESE and Indicadores DESEP.

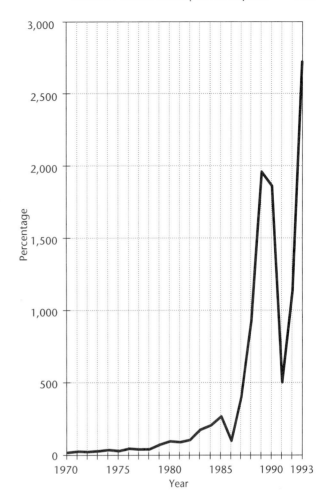

Real Plan did not fix the Real to the dollar strictly, but allowed it to float within "bands," thus allowing for more flexibility in the exchange rate.

One of the essential weaknesses of the Real Plan was made clear soon after the crisis of the Mexican maxi-devaluation of December 1994. The dollar anchor overvalues the currency, making exports more expensive abroad, raising the costs of production, and making imports cheaper. If this trend is maintained, trade deficits begin to appear because imports grow faster than exports. Over the long term, the country's large foreign reserves may dwindle as import consumption is financed with reserves and not export earnings. When that occurs, the government may not be able to preempt speculators who bet against the Real. A run on the Real in regional stock markets may cause a Mexican-style maxi-devaluation (with its in-

flationary effects) down the road. With this question hanging over the Real Plan, it is too early to be applauding the strategy.

SOCIETY AND ECONOMY

Brazil's astounding levels of industrialization during the 1950s, 1960s, and 1970s had lasting effects on the urban social structure. Urbanization and the percentage of the economically active population employed in industry increased while those employed in primary productions declined (see Table 3 on the following page). Import substitution had created these jobs by expanding the domestic market. ISI led to a jump in the size of both the working class and the middle class. Service sector professionals like lawyers, doctors, and private teachers soon found clients as the domestic consumer market grew along with the working class.

TABLE 3	**Changes in Brazilian Urbanization and the Job Market: 1950, 1980**	
Urbanization (%)	c. 1950	c. 1980
Population living in cities	36.20	67.70
Sectors of Employment (%)		
Primary sector	59.90	29.93
Industry	14.18	24.37

Source: Adapted from Vilmar Faria. "Desenvolvimento, Urbanização o e Mudanças na Estrutura do Emprego: a Experiência Brasileira dos últimos Trinta Anos." In Bernardo Sorj, et al., eds. *Sociedade e Política no Brasil Pós-64.* São Paulo: Brasilense, 1983, 120.

Nevertheless, the number of jobs created in the industrial sector did not even begin to absorb the number of unemployed Brazilians in the job market. Many of the new jobs were in sectors that required skilled and semiskilled specialized labor. Metallurgy, automobile production, and mining did not provide many opportunities for the large numbers of unskilled workers in the Brazilian labor market. The growth of the service sector also provided social mobility to only a small percentage of the labor market. In short, Brazilian industrialization ended up adding to income disparities and class inequalities.

As a result, it became clear that the earlier assumptions that industrialization would contribute significantly to eradicating the racial inequalities inherited from slavery were unduly optimistic. The industrialization experience since the turn of the century in the state of São Paulo had led many to believe that racial distinctions would be subsumed under class considerations. But recent studies have shown that for Afro-Brazilians, factors related to occupation and social mobility remained relatively stagnant in comparison to white Brazilians. In Bahia (northeast Brazil), which industrialized much later than the south, the profile of race and class relations remained much as it was before World War II. Despite some evidence that more blacks are entering the ranks of the middle classes in poor states like Bahia, whites still hold most positions of political power and social status in these predominantly black populations.

Afro-Brazilian women, who are doubly disadvantaged by race and gender, are in a particularly precarious situation. It is impossible to discuss industrialization without factoring in both the role of race and of women in society. Women are believed to constitute at least 28 percent of the economically active population in Brazil. Although overall unemployment has increased as a result of the economic recession, available evidence suggests that women continue to be absorbed by the labor market. This is because women in the economically active population have more years of schooling than men and are therefore better prepared to meet the demands of an increasingly technological economy. Despite such developments, women receive lower salaries than men employed at the same job. Table 4 illustrates income disparities by race and gender.

The restructuring of the rural economy into a more modern and capitalist sector radically altered the rural social structure during the 1960s and 1970s. The growth of agro-business during the military period marked a clear contrast with the previous pattern of agricultural production, traditionally defined by great landed estates. These *latifundios* were based on backward agricultural practices, including labor often in a state of partial servitude and absentee landowners. This image changed as agricultural modernization and agro-business promoted a regionally diverse and complex pattern of agricultural production. Thousands of *latifundios*, mostly in the southeast and centerwest, were transformed into capitalist enterprises. New business groups soon began to compete for a share of the productive and dynamic agro-business.

The growing role of agro-business and the capitalization of agricultural production created a rural working class that no longer depended upon the protection and patrimonialism of a landed oligarchy. During the 1970s and 1980s, rural workers were increasingly organized into rural unions that received welfare transfers from the state—medical plans, job security, and protection of wages against inflation. After 1964, various state welfare programs were launched in the agricultural sector: retirement policies for low-income producers, pension plans for rural workers, and financial support to community rural associations. These policies had implications far beyond organized labor. They played a prominent role in breaking the traditional landowners' political and economic control of the rural population. The erosion of the traditional *latifundios* and the transfer of capital to the rural sector worked together with state welfare and corporatist rural unions to reduce the influence of the landed oligarchy.

TABLE 4   **What Women and Racial Minorities Make Compared to White Men, 1990**

Indices of Average Annual Income by Race[a] and Gender (percentage)

White	100.0	Men	100.0
Black	41.0	Women	57.5
Mulatto	47.0		

	Men	Women
White	100.0	100.0
Black	40.7	45.0
Mulatto	46.6	48.8

[a]Breakdown for other racial categories not available. Note: In Brazil, for each $1 of average annual income that a white man makes, a woman makes 57.5 cents; but for each $1 that a white woman makes, a black woman makes 45 cents.

Source: Calculated from IBGE, Anuário Estatístico Brasileiro, 1992.

Nonetheless, the expansion and protection of the rural working class did not encompass all rural workers, most of whom were not represented by unions. This mass of impoverished and largely illiterate people could only trade their rural misery for the misery of urban poverty. The growth of industry in the south and southeast enticed millions to migrate to the states of São Paulo, Minas Gerais, and Rio de Janeiro in the hopes of finding new economic opportunities. Economic stagnation in the large rural areas of the northeast also encouraged rural-urban migration, much of which was seasonal. Rural workers, called *boias frias,* built small villages from which landowners would contract migrant workers on a daily basis to harvest during the season.

The rapidity of rural-urban migration was striking. In the 1960s, over 13.8 million people (about 36 percent of the rural population in 1960) migrated to the cities of the south and southeast. In 1970, 17 million (approximately 42.2 percent of the rural population in 1970) were rural-urban migrants. It took migrations in the United States eight decades to reach the same number of migrants as went from rural to urban areas in Brazil during the 1960s and 1970s. By the early 1980s, 68 percent of Brazil's total population lived in urban areas. Between 1960 and 1980, rural-urban migration accounted for 58 percent of urban population growth.

The flood of rural migrants to urban areas and the growth of urban populations created terrible social problems. The pressures on Brazilian cities for basic services such as sanitation, education, and transportation soon overwhelmed the budgets of municipalities and state governments. Migration quickly outpaced the capacity of local and state politics to respond to the problem. Government ineffectiveness left poor people to their own devices. Squatters soon took government land, settling on the outskirts of the major cities. Millions of these *descamisados* built "homes" out of cardboard, wood from dumps, and blocks of mortar and brick. Huge shanty towns began to create rings of extreme poverty around cities like Rio and São Paulo. These *favelas* are now part of Brazil's identity as a nation. In Rio, they form the backdrop to every beautiful site and tourist attraction the city has to offer. Set alongside the prosperity of industry and a growing middle class, Brazil's squalid *favelas* highlight the country's many contradictions.

Income disparities among the regions are also stark, but efforts have been made to redistribute wealth to less developed regions. Because the military governments believed there was too much income and wealth disparity among the regions, various funds financed by percentages of the collected income tax and tax on manufactured products were established. The criteria for the allocation of resources in those funds were three: land surface, population, and per capita income. As a result, the north and the northeast were provided with a large share of resources for investments and income was transferred from the industrial centers to the underdeveloped areas. The federal government granted fiscal incentives and direct investments to expand the economy of the north, northeast and centerwest. Communication and transportation for these regions were subsidized by the federal government and several state agencies were created to implement regional developmental projects. In 1992–1993, the south and southeastern regions contributed 87 percent of all tax revenues; São Paulo alone was responsible for 50 percent of total tax revenues. Nevertheless, São Paulo and the other states of the south and southeast do not receive the lion's share of federal funding to the states and municipalities. Over 85 percent of this funding is transferred to the less developed regions in the north, northeast and centerwest regions.

TABLE 5   **Brazilian Income Distribution in Comparative Perspective**

Country	Year	10% Richest	20% Richest	40% Poorest	20% Poorest
Brazil	1989	51.3	67.5	7.0	2.1
Chile	1989	48.9	62.9	10.5	3.7
Mexico	1984	39.5	55.9	11.9	4.1
Peru	1985	35.4	51.4	14.1	4.9
India	1989	27.1	41.3	21.3	8.8
United Kingdom	1988	27.8	44.3	14.6	4.6
France	1989	26.1	41.9	17.4	5.6
United States	1985	25.0	41.9	15.7	4.7
China	1990	24.6	41.8	17.4	6.4
Germany	1988	24.4	40.3	18.8	7.0
Poland	1989	21.6	36.1	23.0	9.2

Source: World Bank, 1994.

The policies regarding the less developed regions brought both positive results and negative outcomes. The contribution of these regions to the gross domestic product increased. The rate of growth of the centerwest turned out to be among the highest in the country during the period, spearheaded by regional agro-industrial activities, by mineral exploration, a large number of financial institutions, and the creation of a significant inter-regional economic flux. The economic disparity between regions also declined as a result of the economic crisis which hit hardest in the south and southeast where capital goods and consumer goods were concentrated.

Nonetheless, although the economic gap between regions decreased as the concentration of industries in the southeast diminished during the 1980s, social and income disparities *within* the underdeveloped regions increased. One reason for this unevenness is that the industrialization process in the northeast was capital-intensive. The benefits of industrialization, particularly jobs, became concentrated in that segment of the labor market with the most skilled workers. Second, incentives favored the concentration of industry in midsize and large enterprises, but the resources generated by such industries did not stay in the region because the industrial inputs and consumer markets for their manufactured products were located far away in the south and southeast. Competitiveness with the more advanced regions had to be maintained through new government investments. Several evaluations of these kinds of regional development projects were re-

cently publicized. The plans for agriculture in the northern states were deemed disastrous in terms of job creation, ecological destruction, the murder of native Brazilians, and the great waste of resources as a result of official corruption.

The shrinking labor market for unskilled workers, the rapidity of rural-urban migration, and the regional disparities that add to poverty have all limited income distribution in Brazil. Compared with other developing countries, including Mexico and India, Brazil has one of the worst structures of income distribution in the world (see Table 5).

BRAZIL AND THE INTERNATIONAL POLITICAL ECONOMY

The financing needs of the state-led pattern of industrialization in Brazil soon outstripped the resources of the national development bank and domestic bankers. The deepening of ISI into capital-intensive industries substantially increased the pressure on the state and private bankers to supply high amounts of finance. With domestic industrialists importing more and more technology and input products, new financing sources were needed for these purchases. During the 1960s, this need coincided with the need of European and North American banks to lend money. Brazil was one of many developing countries that began to depend on loans from private international creditors to finance its expenditures. After 1973, the rate and scope of lending and borrowing changed radically. The first oil price crisis in 1973 generated tremendous amounts of petro-

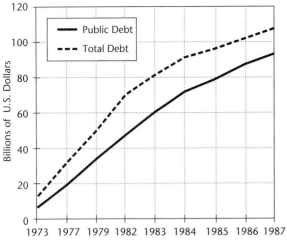

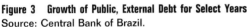

Figure 3 Growth of Public, External Debt for Select Years
Source: Central Bank of Brazil.

leum profits that European and North American banks then circulated. Lenders were eager to provide financial capital and lesser developed countries like Brazil were eager to borrow and pay for industrialization. The stage was set for the cataclysm known as the "debt crisis."

Brazil became increasingly dependent upon foreign finance, rather than on foreign reserves earned through exports. Figure 3 demonstrates the tremendous growth of foreign debt, and it points to the growing composition of the total debt by the public sector. This illustrates the connection between the fiscal crisis of the state and the external debt crisis.

The growth of the public sector debt was also propelled by the growth of the internal debt, money owed to Brazilian citizens as a result of the sale of government bonds and treasury stock. In 1980, the Brazilian state owed $16.8 billion in public titles (4.2 percent of the GDP). But that amount had shot up to $63.7 billion by 1989 (13.1 percent of the GDP). Thus strapped by both an external and an internal debt, the Brazilian state entered a profound fiscal crisis in the 1980s.

External events also propelled the Brazilian fiscal crisis. Between 1980 and 1985 the vulnerability of the economy increased dramatically after a second round of oil shocks and a world recession caused interest rates in Europe and the United States to soar to unprecedented levels. The jump in interest rates in London and New York ratcheted the total Latin American

debt. The full scope of the disaster for countries in Brazil's situation became clear in 1982 when Mexico, one of the largest debtors, announced that it could no longer make payments on its debt. The "debt crisis" had begun.

During the ensuing crisis, the World Bank and the International Monetary Fund became the key negotiator of foreign debt. They began surveillance of exchange rate policies and macroeconomic policies to ensure that national adjustment efforts did not conflict with the purposes of the organizations or the repayment of debt. These functions relied on a bargain negotiated between debtors and foreign creditors known as a conditional agreement. The IMF and World Bank would extend additional credit only to debtors who took steps to reduce inflation, open their domestic markets to foreign competition, promote exports, and privatize state industries. Each of these areas of policy became defining elements of a regional attempt to return Latin American economies to free-market principles.

The Sarney government rejected the free-market policies of the IMF and World Bank. In 1987, his government took the ultimate gamble in resisting creditors by declaring a moratorium on debt repayment, only to be forced to lift it a few months later, under intense pressure from the international financial community. Opposition to the moratorium within the country was also great among the business community, which feared such aggressive action would scare away foreign investors and ruin the country's already tattered credit rating. Collor turned more explicitly to free-market policies, both as a result of leverage by international creditors and as a reaction to the continued failure of alternative policies pursued under Sarney.

The first, and perhaps, the most critical of Brazil's problems was inflation. Stabilizing inflation and reducing the balance of payments deficits (the consequence of importing more than the economy's exports could pay for) were clearly related to servicing the debt. Both of these problems had been exacerbated by the large influx of private bank loans during the 1970s and early 1980s. Excess liquidity in the economy produced spiraling inflation and encouraged upsurges in imports versus exports. After 1982, when the permissive international financial environment became more restrictive, international pressures demanded both stabilization policies and the servicing of the debt. The main idea was that macroeconomic stability (controlling inflation and the balance of payments) would generate a more viable investment climate that would return Brazil to creditworthiness. As already noted, in practice anti-inflation efforts proved to be very unsuccessful.

The dismal failure of the heterodox plans has renewed demands by the IMF and World Bank, as well as by some bureaucrats in the Ministry of the Economy, that Brazil should turn to orthodoxy. Brazil's position has been a sticking point in negotiations over the conditions set by foreign funding institutions. Some economists suggest that this is not as important an issue as returning the country to high growth. Since Brazil had virtually always experienced high inflation along with high growth rates, several economists and politicians do not fear the prospect of continued 40 percent monthly inflation rates as long as growth is also high. There is, however, plenty of evidence to suggest that such views today are only held by a minority of economists and policymakers. Orthodox prescriptions were given much consideration during the government of Itamar Franco with the launching of the Real Plan. Nevertheless, Brazil's version of orthodoxy is still much more restrained than that of countries like Chile.

The real crisis in Brazil was the continued low growth rates throughout the end of the 1980s and into the 1990s. A fundamental reason for low growth was that the Brazilian state could no longer play the key role that it had played in the past as an articulator and

mobilizer of the country's productive resources. The state underwent a severe fiscal crisis that limited its capacity for subsidizing and financing domestic industry. At the heart of this dilemma was a combination of service payments on the foreign debt and the internal fiscal deficits. By commanding large percentages of revenues, these deficits generated serious fiscal limitations on economic policies designed to promote private sector growth.

The IMF's response to the Brazilian fiscal crisis was clear (as it has been everywhere in Latin America): open domestic markets to foreign competition, privatize state firms, and reform the tax system to raise revenues. In practice, however, these prescriptions required not *less* state intervention in the economy but *new* ways for the state to promote industrial exports. The first priority was returning Brazilian industry to high growth. This was a real challenge. Overall in the period from 1981 to 1990, domestic industrial production stagnated and only returned to its 1979 levels in 1990. Industrial production showed a growth of 3.6 percent as a result of the performance of extractive industries (oil and mining products for export) and the incipient computer industry.

The emphasis of economic policy on liberalization of markets opened Brazilian industry to higher degrees of foreign competition. As a result, the productivity of domestic firms quickly emerged as a core problem. Brazilian industrial productivity reached its lowest levels in 1992, when Brazil was ranked just ahead of Pakistan. The productivity problem undermined the rationale of IMF-style free-market policies, precisely because free markets alone could not guarantee growth. As the East Asian examples show, growth in newly industrialized countries requires the active participation of domestic industry and the state in the promotion of productive technologies and labor retraining.

Privatization is also causing political problems for IMF-style policies because it is opposed by those who see it as "selling out the national patrimony" to foreign interests. Thus far, privatization has been proceeding at a slow pace. State mining and metallurgical industries have been sold off and appear to be successful as private firms. But the political backlash from the auctions of these firms is a clear threat to the progress of privatization.

The nationalist concern with privatization should not, however, obscure the fact that Brazil maintains

TABLE 6	Brazilian Trade Data, 1980–1993 (in $ billions)			
Year	Exports	Imports	Surplus	Reserves
1980	20.1	22.9	–2.8	5.9
1990	31.4	20.7	10.7	10.0
1993	38.9	25.7	13.1	32.2

Source: Central Bank of Brazil.

the most vibrant domestic industrial sectors in the region. Most of the capital going into the purchase of privatized state firms is local, not international. Foreign investors, however, have increasingly become a significant part of Brazilian industrialization. As in the past, direct foreign investment tends to be concentrated in a few highly advanced sectors—pharmaceuticals, computers, and automobiles. These firms often complement domestic industrialization by transferring technology and creating new jobs. It should be noted that Brazil has a long experience with foreign investment. Under both Kubitschek's civilian management in the 1950s and the military governments' subsequent stewardship, foreign investment was skillfully directed into high-growth sectors that depended on foreign technology. Although all the evidence is not in, it appears that today foreign investment is returning to Brazil and once again becoming one of the prime movers of domestic industrialization.

If foreign investment often has positive effects on the domestic economy, the same cannot be said for foreign trade competition. As Brazil's gradual liberalization of its domestic markets continues, foreign imports have crowded out some national producers. Collor's ill-advised and largely indiscriminate slashing of import duties devastated many domestic capital goods industries that could not compete with foreigners. Once again, it might be too early to tell, but the prospect of further liberalization has created strong incentives among domestic industries to restructure production and increase the productivity of their labor force.

Taking a more cross-regional and historical perspective, Brazil is still a very closed economy. The country imports only about 8 percent of its GDP, whereas during the 1970s it imported 15 percent of its GDP. Currently, Chile imports 15 percent of its GDP.

More advanced economies like Germany and Belgium import upward of 30 to 40 percent of their GDP. A more striking comparison for Brazil is that of India, considered one of the most closed economies in the world—Brazil imports less than India. These comparisons suggest that, although recent liberalization has made the economy more open, there is still much to be done.

Exports continue to be Brazil's strong suit, and the country has maintained an export surplus since 1980. Much of that gain has been the direct result of the international competitiveness of the country's commodity and raw materials exports: steel, food products, ores, paper, and some consumer manufactured goods. The maintenance of this positive trade balance explains how Brazil retains one of the largest reserves of foreign earnings in the world. Table 6 illustrates this impressive record.

The continued positive performance of Brazilian exports partially depends on the trade practices of other countries. Recent conflicts with the United States over Brazilian steel exports (one of Brazil's most export-competitive industries) have involved the threat of U.S. protectionism. This problem speaks to the larger question of what kind of trade policy the United States will pursue in Latin America. The North American Free Trade Agreement addresses the willingness of the United States to negotiate regional integration with all its neighbors, but in practice, that rhetoric has thus far only included Mexico and Canada.

A more immediate concern is trade with Brazil's closest neighbors—the countries of the Southern Cone. In the past, Brazil has kept a certain distance from its continental neighbors and shown little interest in economic integration schemes. More recently, however, Brazil's trade with South American countries has increased. Much of this increase can be credited to the country's participation in the MERCOSUL free trade agreement with its Southern Cone neighbors. The possibilities for the agreement depend on the ability of the participating countries to agree on exchange standards, timetables, and resolutions of conflicts over priorities.

Perhaps a more ambitious idea is the so-called Latin American free trade zone. Such an accord would provide for a region-wide integration of markets which could have mixed consequences for the Brazilian economy. Brazil would benefit from regional integration because of its large volume of exports to the United States. Still, the agreement might hurt Brazil more than any other Latin American country by limiting Brazil's exports to Europe, its largest export market. According to 1992 data, the European Union absorbs 30 percent of Brazilian exports compared to Latin America (22 percent), the United States (20 percent) and Asia (16 percent). Regional integration would also impose additional pressures to domestic producers trying to survive the onslaught of more productive U.S. exporters.

Both Brazil's economic past and its economic future are linked by the country's inclusion in international markets. The vitality of Brazilian industrialization will depend increasingly on the actions of the citizens and the policymakers of other economies. As in other recently reestablished democracies of Latin America or the liberalizing regime of Mexico, Brazil's democracy is also deeply threatened by urgent economic crises, the relief of which depends in part on a host of factors such as trade barriers, interest rates, and levels of economic assistance, over which Brazil itself has at most only limited influence.

SECTION 3
Governance and Policy-Making

ORGANIZATION OF THE STATE

Brazil's constitutional rules have undergone many rapid changes over the last forty-five years. Judged by the standard of two decades of authoritarianism, the 1988 Constitution presents some impressive changes. Still, core institutions and practices inherited from the past have been grafted onto contemporary organizations of the state. Important limitations to democracy in Brazil remain: the longstanding preeminence of the executive powers, military prerogatives over policy-making, retention of bureaucratic discretion in policy formation, state monopolies in several sectors, and corporatist union representation.

The 1987 Constituent Assembly that drafted the 1988 Constitution reexamined the Vargas institutional legacy as a whole. The debates among the delegates highlighted a new and crucial development in Brazilian politics: the erosion of elite consensus concerning the viability of older institutions inspired by the Vargas Paradigm. At the same time, no clear alternative to old institutions emerged. The drafting of the new constitution might have been an opportunity for redressing some of Brazil's many institutional problems. Instead, it became an arena of confusion and uncertainty about which institutions should accompany democracy.

Debates and political conflict also swirled around the 1988 Constitution's many controversial provisions concerning presidentialism, division of resources and obligations between the union and the states, privatization, and the increase in the number of social

rights. The 1988 Constitution was simultaneously the focus of much hope and the object of intense attack. As such, it became too diffuse and too mired in politics to provide a coherent vision of precisely how the country's political institutions should be structured and what functions they should serve. The relative incoherence of the 1988 Constitution means that power, notably the separation of powers, is less important than ad hoc arrangements in determining power relations among the branches of government and between the federal and state governments. Informal relations and "understandings" still play a major role in the interpretation of law and authority.

Certain generalizations, however, about the organization of the Brazilian state can be made. First, the church and state are officially separated. The Catholic church has never controlled any portion of the state apparatus or maintained a direct influence on national politics to the extent that it did in other Catholic countries such as Spain. This does not mean, however, that the Catholic church plays no role in Brazilian politics as we will see in the next section.

Second, Brazil has a presidential system of government in which the directly elected president is the head of state, the head of government, and the commander-in-chief of the armed forces. The Brazilian state was organized to assure vast power in the hands of the executive. In theory, it comprises a balance of powers between the executive, legislative, and judicial branches, but traditionally, Brazilian presidents have been freer of judicial and legislative constraints than their European or North American counterparts. Not only have past Brazilian constitutions granted the executive more discretion in enforcing laws or in making policy, but in actual practice, presidents have exercised more authority than the other branches of government. The legislature and the judiciary historically have played secondary functions.

The organization of the Brazilian state defies the checks and balances that work relatively well in the United States presidential system. It differs also from the semipresidentialism of France in which the directly elected president, although dominant over the legislature and judiciary, faces broader constraints to the abuse of executive power (both constitutional and de facto) than the Brazilian president. The French Parliament has a stronger presence in the pattern of executive-legislative relations. Although its prime minister is appointed by the executive and not elected by the legislature, as in other parliamentary systems, he or she is chosen from the party with the majority of elected representatives in parliament, which is not necessarily the president's party. Moreover, the French party system is more organized and less fragmented than its counterpart in Brazil, making the legislature more efficient and capable of checking executive actions.

The presidency remains very powerful. The executive and the bureaucracy contain most of the policy-making and implementation functions. Both the federal legislature and the state governments look to the presidency and, in economic matters, to the minister of the economy, for leadership on policy. At times, the ministers of the economy, of planning, and the president of the central bank retain more discretion over the details of policy than the president. This is a function both of the different styles and expertise of the presidents and of the needs of the moment. Inflationary crises have often forced a shifting of discretionary power over price controls and interest rates to the ministers of the economic bureaucracy (economy, industry and planning). The minister of justice has recently retained sweeping powers over tax reform and the judiciary.

Third, various institutions in Brazilian history have constrained the power of the executive. In the wake of the transition to democratic rule in 1985, these institutions have become critical to democracy. The 1988 Constitution gave many oversight functions to the legislature and judiciary so that presidential discretion in economic and social policy is now largely subject to approval by either the legislature or the judiciary or both. This gives them some independence and leverage over the presidency, although often they are not employed effectively. Creating democratic institutions and maintaining them are not similar processes. Traditions carry weight and the obstacles to the decentralization of executive power are still enormous.

The powers and resources still held by the president, combined with the expansion of the powers of the legislature, resulted in the current form of government, which many authors label "quasi-presidentialist" or "quasi-parliamentary," depending on their point of view. At the core of this term is the concept that the authority of each main branch of government—the legislature and the executive—overlaps so that neither branch clearly understands its role and power. Despite the fact that some political scientists have argued that mixtures of presidentialism and parliamentarism are best for the survival of democratic institutions and economic policy effectiveness, Brazil's uncertain mixture of these forms leaves much room for doubt. Conflicts between the presidency and Congress over competencies have politicized and complicated the everyday flow of legislation.

It is too early to say if any issue on the nation's political agenda was solved by the 1988 Constitution. The most disputed decisions made by the Constituent Assembly can be changed. In fact, the constitutional text as a whole was open to revision in 1995 when deputies and senators decided by a majority of 60 percent which changes should be engineered. Constitutional revision is a continuing debate in Congress, although certain issues remain "untouchable": the federal structure, secret and direct vote, the formal separation of power, and individual rights. Despite divergent evaluations of the constitution, clearly it has already promoted important incentives to transform the redistribution of power at several levels and branches of the government.

THE EXECUTIVE

The delegates to the 1987 Constituent Assembly opted to preserve the presidential system of government. The continuation of presidentialism in 1988 was assured by an odd coalition that included the extreme left, heirs of Vargas populism, various business sectors, and the military. Support for the presidential system was based mainly on the view that decision-making functions should be centralized in the chief of state. For many Brazilians, governmental effectiveness has historically been identified with presidential supremacy. Also for a large number of politicians, the presidential office became the ultimate distributor of clientelism, credits, public investments, and the arbiter among regional interests. For the popular sectors it has been the focus of demands for improvement in living conditions and better wages. For the military, the president is the very embodiment of national security.

The 1988 Constitution granted citizens the right to vote by plebiscite on the system of government. In reality, the issue was not resolved in 1988, but deferred for a plebiscite held in 1993, which reaffirmed the presidential system, thus eliminating parliamentarism. The issue continued to cut across all parties, from the left to the right. The preference for presidentialism over parliamentarism was based on two major factors: widespread suspicion of legislative politics and the belief, made popular by campaigns to retain presidentialism, that the parliamentary option was little more than a trick to "take the right to vote away from the people." The concept of a parliamentary system that would allow a prime minister to be elected by legislative elites and not directly by the citizenry seemed contrary to what Brazilians had fought for during the long struggle for democracy. The ultimate check upon the presidency, direct elections by voters every four years, is retained as the core institution of Brazilian democracy. Similar to the French system, should no candidate win an absolute majority of votes on the first ballot, a runoff election follows between the two leading candidates.

Because one of the opposition's most important demands against authoritarian governments involved the reduction of the federal executive's power, the 1988 Constitution reinstated some important checks on executive supremacy. Congressional prerogatives that had existed prior to 1964 were reinstated and new ones were granted. Oversight of economic policy and rights of consultation concerning executive appointments were among the additions to the legislative branch. Executive decrees were abolished and in their place provisional measures were established, which must be voted on by the Congress under certain conditions. The provisional measures are weaker instruments because unlike executive decrees they can be modified in Congress. In the case of macroeconomic policies,

for example, a two-thirds vote of both houses may override a provisional measure. These measures nonetheless still provide much leeway (if not a virtual monopoly) for executive initiatives and were abusively used by all presidents since Sarney's administration. Based on the argument that the Brazilian economy is passing through a major crisis characterized by spiraling inflation and industrial stagnation, provisional measures were enacted with the intent of hastening decision making.

Collor's anti-inflation policy dramatically illustrated the dominance of the presidency over the Congress and the judiciary. Through provisional measures he was able to freeze the nation's financial assets as an anti-inflationary measure. Collor severely abused these powers, handing down 150 "provisional measures" in the first year of his presidency. Technically, this meant that the country experienced a "crisis situation" every forty-eight hours. The Supreme Tribunal, the highest court in Brazil, did little to curb this obvious abuse of the constitutional authority by the president. Although the effects upon the economy are debatable, the concentration of discretionary authority over economic policy-making in the executive is a clear result of the frequent employment of "provisional" decree powers.

The presidential election is a great political event because much is at stake: especially appointments to powerful executive positions and the shape of policy in key areas like economic reform. The Brazilian president has broad powers to select and dismiss close associates. He or she selects ministers for the armed forces according to the merit system prevailing in their respective branches. Usually the president appoints other ministers from groups of his longtime cronies and collaborators or from any of the existing parties. Until recently, appointment choices did not need to be sanctioned by any other governmental authority. Rigorous oversight and approval functions were considerably weakened because the Brazilian president could name thousands of public officials, making Brazil one of the world's most blatant examples of the "power of appointments." Currently, the president must negotiate with Congress and some powerful groups (business associations, labor unions, bar associations, and so on) over certain positions in the cabinet, mainly those responsible for economic policy-making. Even so, the president currently maintains impressive powers of appointment.

A certain hierarchy of influence among ministries can be identified according to the command over resources each enjoys. Since the military period, the heads of the Ministry of Economy have had more authority than other cabinet members. Especially with the country's recent economic problems, the preeminence of this ministry is currently at its height. Recent ministers of the economy have had levels of authority typical of a prime minister in a parliamentary system. Authority over the federal budget and economic policy enables the minister of economy to influence all significant foreign and domestic economic policies. As a recent indicator of the power of this cabinet position, Fernando Henrique Cardoso, a former minister of the economy in the Itamar Franco government, won the 1994 presidential election based largely on his claim that his anti-inflation reform had proven successful.

The Bureaucracy, State and Semipublic Firms

The 1988 Constitution failed to alter significantly the concentration of power in the federal bureaucracy, especially in the economic bureaucracy. Although it was hoped that the constitution would give incentives to expand private initiative or to set only general guidelines for the operation of the economy, the main instruments of economic regulation created during the military period and concentrated in the federal bureaucracy were retained. The 1988 Constitution actually codified bureaucratic monopolies over policy formulation and monopolies by state firms in basic economic sectors such as oil, gas production and refining, the exploration of minerals, nuclear energy, and telecommunications. Although these agencies are still in place, the 1988 Constitution did include mechanisms to limit their proliferation and fiscal independence. The authority of bureaucratic agencies to incur debt was severely curtailed. Most important, the 1988 Constitution forbids the executive from creating new state agencies or corporations without Congress's approval.

Since 1940, the government has created a huge number of bureaucratic agencies independent of the central ministries in order to free the latter from undue political manipulation and to increase their effectiveness for the implementation of various developmental projects. Some of these agencies have been granted fiscal autonomy and have accumulated most of the current public debt. The economic weight of the public sector in the overall economy has grown progressively since the New State. An annual ranking of Brazil's largest 500 corporations in 1981 revealed that ten of the top twenty-five firms were owned by the federal government and eight belonged to state governments. The sectors dominated by these public firms include aluminum, petroleum, chemical, electrical power, iron mining, and finance. Public expenditures as a share of GDP increased from 16 percent to 27 percent from 1947 to 1964. By 1969, this percentage exceeded 32 percent of GDP, a far higher rate than any other Latin American country, with the exception of socialist Cuba.

In the 1950s, the main developmental projects were hydroelectric plants and the building of Brasilia. State firms like PETROBRAS (petroleum) and USIMINAS (metallurgy and mining) have dominated Brazil's development, and account for much of the country's exports and industrial production. PETROBRAS, for example, continues to be one of the largest corporations in the world and VALE DO RIO DOCE, a mining and metallurgy operation, continues to figure prominently in Brazil's export statistics. Under the three last military presidents (Medici, Geisel, and Figueiredo), numerous projects were developed: the Trans-Amazonian highway, the northeast petrochemical industrial district, the largest hydroelectric plant in the world (Itaipú), railroads, the Tucuruí hydroelectric plants, the AçoMinas metallurgy park, and the National Nuclear Reactor Program, to name just a few. Before the debt crisis in 1983, a private research organization called IBASE *(Instituto Brasileiro de Análises Sociais e Economicas)* identified thirty-three huge state projects, some already in operation, that would absorb $88 billion in external debt, would employ 1.5 million people, and would add $47 billion to annual production. The external debt crisis caused some of these projects to be abandoned; others, however, continued to be developed.

The National Bank for Economic and Social Development (*Banco Nacional de Desenvolvimento Economico e Social,* or BNDES), founded by Vargas in the early 1950s played a key role in channeling public funds to industrial projects. Among many projects, the BNDES financed the expansion of automobile production during the 1950s, public works in mining and metallurgy during the 1970s, and is still the center of a debate on the role of public financing and industrial policy in Brazil.

The military's Itaipú dam
project scars the landscape.
Source: UPI/Bettmann.

Semipublic firms, state firms, and public finance were also a common source of patronage in Brazilian politics. Both civilian and military leaders often appointed close political supporters as the heads of semipublic and state firms. In these positions, many exercised immense authority over astounding resources, doling out rich government projects to associates and even companies owned by officials of the semipublic firms.

Nonetheless, the Brazilian bureaucracy also has a technocratic and professional side. The technocratic tendency was especially evident in state agencies that retained autonomy from powerful capitalist interests and placed much emphasis on efficiency. These agencies were often considered "islands of efficiency" in a state apparatus characterized by organizations riddled with patronage. The BNDES, the national development bank, was the archetypal case. Its professional hiring and advancement practices, its logical, hierarchical structure, and its code of civil service made it an efficient and remarkable resourceful targeter of public sector finance to industry.

The capacity of state agencies to set priorities for stabilization and growth in the 1980s and 1990s has been seriously hindered by the old politics of clientelism and the mercurial politics of Brazil's civilian presidents. The current emphasis on cutting the wages of

public employees has bled the bureaucracy of its most talented personnel. Cuts in retraining and education have diluted the technocratic and professional strains within the state bureaucracy by reducing the recruitment pool. Once again, patronage has become a mechanism for advancement and protecting one's own job. Professionals who had never concerned themselves with politics are increasingly cultivating political ties in order to keep their jobs.

The recent privatization of USIMINAS by the Collor administration and the promise of the new Cardoso administration to privatize VALE DO RIO DOCE, clearly mark the end of development via state firms in Brazil. Due to growing fiscal burdens and macroeconomic problems, political pressure has intensified from the IMF and domestic business to downsize state agencies and semipublic firms and sell off their assets at public auctions. This is partly because they no longer offer the rich patronage they once did. Fiscal cutbacks have left many agencies a mere shadow of what they were in the 1960s and 1970s.

Nevertheless, the public firms continue to be significant economic actors in Brazil. The office of the presidency reports that there are today 149 state enterprises with 661,000 employees. The public firms have a $25 billion payroll and a debt of $96.7 billion. As a whole, the public firms make approximately $50 bil-

TABLE 7   **Brazil's Ten Largest State Firms, 1994**

Rank	Company	Sector	Net Worth (in billions)
1	Eletrobras	Utilities	$44.6
2	Telebras	Telecommunications	16.2
3	RFFSA	Railroads	13.5
4	Petrobras	Petroleum	12.5
5	BNDES	Finance	8.4
6	CESP	Electricity	7.5
7	VALE DO RIO DOCE	Mining	6.6
8	Banco do Brasil	Finance	6.5
9	CEMIG	Utilities	4.2
10	BANESPA	Finance	1.3

Source: *Gazeta Mercantil, 1994–1995,* Balanço Anual.

lion in profits a year and retain assets in excess of $318 billion (see Table 7).

The Military

The military is another significant and powerful arm of the state. Like many other Latin American militaries, the Brazilian armed forces still retain a substantial degree of independence from civilian presidents and legislators. This is in contrast to the Mexican situation where the military has for most of the twentieth century been subordinated to command by the presidency. Mexico has suffered no coups, or even serious threats of coups, as has been the case in Brazilian politics. In addition, the Mexican military has not acted as a powerful interest group blocking policies it does not like and dictating those it favors, as has been true in Brazil.

Military participation in Brazilian politics changed from near dominance during the authoritarian period to a more limited role in support of the civilian regimes. Some qualifications, however, should be emphasized. As in previous constitutions enacted after World War II, the recent transition to democracy also granted the armed forces a broad mandate to guarantee "internal order." This principle allows the military to play a "tutelary role": democracy and civilian governance exist only at the sufferance of the military. Civilians fear that any action which might be seen as a threat to the military may induce a coup.

During the 1988 constitutional review, the military ministers, their official representatives on constitutional commissions, and the military lobbies launched an extensive campaign to neutralize their opponents and win allies to retain the traditional constitutional role for the military in domestic affairs. In 1987 and 1988, the ideological climate and civil-military relations were such that more than half of the members of the assembly said they were in favor of some internal defense role for the military. As a result, the military had a significant impact in some of the most important decisions made by the Constitutional Assembly. Their interference was crucial in securing votes against parliamentarism, land reform, and changes in corporatist representation.

One of the key indicators of the military's continued freedom from civilian control is that, although not prescribed by the constitution, the minister of defense remains a military position, not a civilian one. Although precise figures are lacking, many middle- and lower-level positions of bureaucratic agencies are occupied by members of the armed forces in practically all agencies of the federal government.

The military was influential in obtaining amnesty for members of past military governments who perpetrated human rights abuses—torture, killings, and illegal imprisonments. The Congress in 1979 voted for an amnesty on crimes practiced between 1964 and 1979. This measure was interpreted by civilians and military officials as a mutual amnesty. Nevertheless, it was hoped that the new democratic regime would remove torturers from important positions and possibly bring the worst offenders to justice. Military pressure, in the form of direct lobbying of the president and veiled threats through the media, were crucial in preserving the amnesty. During the first two years of civilian government, not one conviction for terrorism committed by security forces after 1979 was handed down by any court. This largely contrasts with what happened in Argentina, where several military offenders were convicted and imprisoned. Even in Chile, where the treatment of such issues was delayed by the overbearing presence of General Pinochet, Chileans took to the streets to demand justice. In Brazil, only a few intellectuals and opposition leaders manifested concern about these issues.

Lately, the military's changing views on national security have caused the armed forces to seek a less interventionist role in civilian politics. External threats, rather than internal security matters, have become their primary concern. For example the interests and pressures of nongovernmental organizations and foreign powers regarding the environmental issues in the Amazon are viewed with dismay by military planners. The deeply ingrained nationalism among the military prompt them to view international demands as threats to Brazil's sovereignty and security, particularly in the Amazon region. Whether this will mean more or less military intervention in executive politics in the long run is merely speculation.

The military and civil police of each major municipality are formally under the command of the military hierarchy and the local government, respectively. In practice, however, the military and civil police in many cities of the northeast and Rio de Janeiro have acted independently of the chain of command. Publicized instances of corruption and systematic killings committed by military and civil police forces have received much international attention. One recent example occurred during the summer of 1993, when four military police officers were convicted of killing eight street children in Rio de Janeiro. Widespread corruption among the Rio police forces prompted Itamar Franco to sign an accord with the Rio state government to allow the national military to occupy the city's *favelas* during late 1994 and early 1995 in order to combat Rio's infamous drug gangs. Military intervention was justified, according to the government, because the city's drug gangs often pay off the police.

The federal police operates much like a combination of the U.S. Federal Bureau of Investigation, Secret Service, Drug Enforcement Agency, and Immigration and Naturalization Service. Under the authority of the executive, this police force of 3,000 is charged with the responsibility of providing security to public officials, cracking down on drug rings, administering federal law at customshouses, and investigating federal crimes. Considering the demands placed on this single agency's resources, many have considered splitting up the federal police and making it more specialized, much like the U.S. system. This type of reform, however, is only under consideration.

OTHER STATE INSTITUTIONS

The Judiciary

The Brazilian judiciary is composed of a network of state courts with jurisdiction over state matters and a federal court system, not unlike the one in the United States, which maintains jurisdiction over federal crimes. A Supreme Court (the Supreme Federal Tribunal), similar in jurisdiction to the U.S. Supreme Court but lacking authority over the other branches of government, stands as the final judicial arbiter of court cases. It is composed of eleven justices, each appointed by the president and approved by an absolute majority of the Senate. The military maintains its own court system.

As in the rest of Latin America, the penal codes govern the powers of judges. This makes the judiciary less flexible than its North American counterpart, but it also provides a more effective barrier against "judicial activism"—the tendency of the courts to render broad interpretations of the law.

Since the 1940s, the judicial branch of government in Brazil has been formally entitled to high degrees of independence from the executive power. On many occasions, however, and especially under authoritarian rule, the judiciary was dictated to by the executive branch. More recently, President Collor exercised sweeping executive powers without much judicial review. The Supreme Court was viewed as ceding to the new president significant extra-constitutional authority by not challenging Collor's rule by fiat. One year after the economic megashock of the asset freeze launched by Collor, some of the country's renowned jurists finally decided to oppose further blockage of financial assets on the ground that it was unconstitutional. Although opposition came late, it began a national debate concerning the jurisprudence of executive provisional measures which continues to this day.

Recently, the judiciary has been under serious attacks. The main criticisms are directed against its lack of political sensitivity to the real problems of the country and to the sweeping corruption infesting the lower levels of the court system. The Supreme Tribunal's reluctance to act on these matters leaves little hope for change in the short term. Judicial reform has thus far focused upon speeding up the Supreme Tribunal's judicial review functions, avoiding for the moment the trickier question of restructuring the judiciary to eliminate corruption.

The future constitutional revision may provide a key step in the much needed restructuring of the judiciary by subjecting judges to external control through periodic elections, although members of the judiciary deeply resent and fear such a prospect. They argue that such a move would push the institution into the kind of partisanship that has mired policy debates on key social and political issues. However, others consider the structure of the judiciary and its approach to interpreting and implementing laws to be central obstacles in accomplishing policy goals. And yet others argue that court-bashing is simply an attempt to reinforce the supremacy of the executive.

The judiciary is designed to adjudicate political conflicts as well as civil and social conflicts. The Electoral Supreme Tribunal (TSE) has exclusive responsibility for the organization, direction, and vigilance of acts related to suffrage. Among the key powers of the TSE are the power to investigate charges of political partiality by public employees, to file criminal charges against persons violating electoral laws, and to scrutinize and validate electoral results. In addition to these constitutional provisions, under electoral law and its own regulations, the TSE monitors campaign compliance with the law and executive neutrality in campaigns. The integrity of the tribunal in the conduct of elections has remained very high, virtually eradicating fraud in national elections.

Subnational Government

Brazil has a federal structure with twenty-seven states and the Federal District (Brasilia). The state political structures parallel the national government except that their legislatures are unicameral. States are, in turn, divided into municipalities (close to 5,000 throughout Brazil).

Compared with their counterparts in Latin America, the states and municipalities enjoy much more autonomy from the central government. Although state governments do not retain the leverage

over national policy that they enjoyed at the beginning of the century, they still have a great deal of influence. In Mexico, the president has the authority to depose troublesome governors. This, however, is unthinkable in Brazil. Governors, especially from the most populated and industrialized states, acquire broad influence in the capital, Brasilia, due to their vast electorates and dynamic economies. State-based influence pervades the legislature and is a crucial factor in presidential appointments. Usually, powerful state-based figures, political and economic, are given prime appointments in the federal bureaucracy.

Throughout the country's political development, Brazilian municipalities have been largely dependent upon state and federal funds. The 1988 Constitution, however, granted them a larger share of financial resources. Since 1946 and even during the military regimes, mayors and city councilors have been directly elected, not appointed by national political authorities as in Venezuela. In contrast to Mexico where political careers are made in the capital, political careers in Brazil are made at the grassroots level. Moreover Brazil's midsize cities can constitute solid bases for opposition parties, as was the case even during the military period. In contrast, the dominant party in Mexico (the PRI) continuously holds the overwhelming majority of municipalities and risks a national political catastrophe if its dominance at the municipal level slips.

THE POLICY–MAKING PROCESS

The country's policy-making is an embodiment of what Douglas Chalmers has called the "politicized state," that is, a state in which political exchanges govern each stage of the policy-making process: formulation, decision making, and implementation. One of the main characteristics in the overall process of policy-making is the divorce between the levels at which policies are *formulated* and the formal channels to *implement* them.

Two features dominate Brazilian policy-making: (1) an executive power that holds broad autonomous powers to formulate policies without following regular procedures with representative institutional bodies; and (2) the permeability of the bureaucracy to clientelist interests.

Overall, the formulation of social and economic policy has consistently been made within the national and state executive branches. Foreign policy remains an object of exclusive decision by a few ministries, military representatives, and the president. Also, the bargaining arena where the decisions regarding investment policies and overall capital accumulation take place are only marginally open to political parties or to the Congress. It's fair to say that for most of Brazilian business, bureaucratic politics are more accessible to entrepreneurial lobbying. Brazilian business prefers not to be formally identified with any political party in the policy-making process.

A complex network of informal and formal relations within the bureaucratic hierarchy dominates virtually all significant decision-making processes. Consequently, the role of the Congress in the decision-making process has been historically far from crucial in Brazil. During the democratic period (1945–1964), presidents and politically adept bureaucrats often struck bargains with local elites in order to establish policies. Under military rule, central ministries took a more pivotal role in the construction of political coalitions in favor of economic policy. Relations between governors and the national bureaucracy are the cornerstone of these coalitions.

Since 1985, one widely discussed possibility regarding policy-making was the use of neocorporatist pacts, negotiated agreements, among state officials and the leaders of labor and business peak associations. Because the new democratic regime provided for representation by business and labor groups in administrative agencies and regulatory bodies, there was much hope that such pacts could serve to mitigate the dilemmas of policy-making by developing interactions among the principal economic actors. Shortly after Sarney took power in 1986, for example, talks were initiated between business, government, and representatives of one or two of the major labor federations. These quickly broke down. The cleavages within the Brazilian union movement indicated that some sector of organized labor always manifested its refusal to be bound by any agreement. After the talks failed, the government launched, by decree, the Cruzado Plan. A new round of negotiations started, failed once more, and a new executive decree launched still another economic plan a few months later.

Whereas these pacts have undoubtedly been a factor contributing to successful economic management in small European countries, in most of Latin America they have achieved virtually nothing. Conditions in most of Latin America differ sharply from the developed world: high levels of income inequality, the partial functioning of market economies, the lack of strong social democratic parties, and unified labor movements. These factors greatly limit the possibility of reaching credible agreements between political forces.

Policy Implementation

Debate and lobbying do not stop in Brazil once laws are enacted. Policy implementation is a subject of perpetual bargaining. In this sense, there is always *a jeito brasileiro* (the "Brazilian way") around the law. Politics and patronage have played the central role in "getting things done" in Brazil.

The trading of local support for national resources, the essence of what Americans call "pork-barrel politics" has been perfected in Brazil during decades of practice. An essential element of pork-barrel politics in Brazil is the permeability of the structure of the federal bureaucracy, which is highly fragmented and colonized by elite interests. State bureaucrats are often linked with politicians and capitalists in an institutionalized form some scholars call "bureaucratic rings"—small sets of individual bureaucrats connected with small sets of individual industrialists, usually through some pivotal officeholder. These rings are ardent defenders of their own interests. Because they are entrenched and well connected throughout the Brazilian bureaucracy, few policies can be implemented without the resources and political support of the most powerful bureaucratic rings.

Organized private interests have, more often than not, opposed executive policies or sought to turn these policies to collective or individual advantage. One prominent example is the influence of the Federation of São Paulo Industries (*Federação das Industrias do Estado de São Paulo,* or FIESP). Few major economic policies are passed without changes from the lobbying efforts of the FIESP. Only recently have such interests begun to coordinate their demands in the form of public demonstrations and statements or unified lobbying strategies.

As a result of the huge expansion of the state apparatus and of the clientelism within it, the private sector has captured many state units. Various bureaucratic agencies and politicians in the executive and legislative are interested in the maintenance of such dynamics only for the benefits and profits resulting from it. Politicians, both central and regional/state elites, function as brokers between the bureaucracy and private interests, and the opportunities for illegal enrichment through bribes and graft help to maintain the system. Politicians are driven to buy political support, which becomes increasingly more expensive, through the manipulation of public policies that benefit the groups they serve. Recent scandals surrounding the malfeasance of the federal legislature uncovered the extent of these clientelist relations in the organizations formulating the national budget.

Since decisions about the most important policies still remain a monopoly of the bureaucracy, the majority of legislators do not feel responsible for the course of public policies. Each action, each project, each measure to be implemented is preceded by numerous bargains with political leaders. Such pork-barreling grossly distorts the intent and substance of what was originally intended by legislation. Each stabilization plan, for example, from Cruzado I to the Real Plan, involved political bargains with affected groups. The

result in most cases was that those with influence avoided paying the brunt of austerity, thus maintaining high public spending and oligopolistic competition—two factors at the core of Brazil's horrible inflation record.

Another aspect related to the implementation of public policies is the lack of information that policy-makers have about how citizens will react to state policies. The inputs to policy-making are not generated through the action of organized political groups but are instead a product of the bureaucrats' qualifications, peer group pressures, and the ideologies or fads they follow. Because the formulation of policies is not subjected to a broad, societal debate, through parties or Congress, popular views often go unheard. But not heeding public opinion has spelled the demise of many a social and economic policy in Brazil. In this sense, the implementation of the policy-making process is self-defeating.

SECTION 4

Representation and Participation

Since the 1940s, there has been a marked expansion of the electorate and a proliferation of political organizations, institutions, and movements. The capacity of these new institutions to represent the demands of society at large, however, is still severely limited. Urbanization, modernization, and diversification of the economy naturally brought about a process of transformation within the political parties. Mass appeal became an important element in campaigns and political alliances. New unions and special interest organizations emerged, making new organizational ties possible. Despite this richer political, organizational life, the state continued to structure and control political participation and representation. State-structured corporatist unionism remained.

Industrialization, urbanization, increasing literacy, and efforts by the parties to expand voting registration also increased the number of citizens eligible to vote. The vote is compulsory for all but illiterates. Voting rights were granted in 1981 to anyone eighteen or older and, in 1988, to anyone over sixteen years of age (see Table 8 on the following page).

The continued predominance of older, largely corporatist, forms of political participation and the fragmentation of societal associations share a common

root. Until the liberalization period of the 1970s, Brazil rarely experienced the autonomous growth of political organizations capable of representing a segment of the country's society. Corporatist forms of representation, primarily of workers in official unions, were the foundation of Brazilian populism. The combination of a long history of restricted participation and strong tendencies toward the centralization of representation in official parties and unions are today the core obstacles to building viable representative democratic institutions.

When civilian rule was reestablished in 1985, many of the authoritarian institutions of the past persisted. They might have been eliminated by the continued vibrancy of a new Brazilian society, but the groups who had fought for democracy could not sustain the push for deepening democratic values, practices, and institutions. With the exception of rural and urban unions, many political organizations experienced internal divisions and fragmentation.

THE LEGISLATURE

The national legislature (594 members) is bicameral, consisting of a Senate and a Chamber of Deputies. Each state elects three senators, to make a total of

TABLE 8   **Evolution of Brazilian Electorate**

Eligible Voting Population					
1945	1950	1955	1960	1989	1994
7,459,849	11,455,149	15,243,246	15,543,332	82,074,714	94,782,410
Total of Voters as a Percentage of the National Population					
16.2	22.0	24.8	21.9	55.0	60.0
Level of Abstention as Percentage of Eligible Voters					
16.88	27.94	40.32	19.02	11.93	17.7
Invalid (Null or Blank)[a] Votes as Percentage of Total Votes Cast					
5.3	4.32	5.19	7.21	6.43	18.7

[a]Null votes refer to destroyed ballots or those for noncandidates like popular television personalities. Blank votes contain insufficient information or are simply without information.

eighty-one senators. The Chamber of Deputies is made up of 513 members. Each state is allowed a minimum of eight deputies, regardless of population or size of the electorate, and a maximum of eighty deputies. The seats over twenty are allocated by population using a formula clearly unfavorable to the most populated states. This system was designed to overrepresent the least populated and rural states, generally the poorest. Conversely, the system underrepresents the most populous, industrialized, and urbanized states, especially the state of São Paulo. In the legislature (1990–1994) the north region had 4.85 percent of the voters but elected 11.33 percent of the deputies. The more populous southeastern region had 46 percent of the electorate but only 33.59 percent of the seats in the Chamber of Deputies. The northern, northeastern and center-western regions together have 49.4 percent of the seats in the Chambers of Deputies. This imbalance has existed since the birth of the republic but was reinforced after 1964. In order to pack the Congress with supporters and cronies, military and civilian governments alike granted statehood to sparsely populated territories. As a result, a voter can increase the value of his or her vote several times by moving from the state of São Paulo to Acre, a state in the poor north.

The Brazilian legislature was rarely a significant arena for representing the majority of Brazilians. First, because throughout most of Brazilian history the legislature was clearly submissive to the power of the presidency. Second, elite patronage was more important and powerful than mass representation. With elitist patronage a key factor in policy-making and clientelism the preeminent motive for getting elected, representatives in the Congress were never driven to organize their parties or large segments of the population in support of national policy. After the working class became more organized and politicized, official unions, not legislative parties, became the key representatives of labor interests. Between official unions, official parties, and elitist policy-making fraught with patronage, legislative procedures were reduced to mere redundancies throughout Brazilian history.

Other problems related to the particular character of the legislature also limit the representative capacity of the body. For many members of the Brazilian elite, election to the federal legislature is often only a stepping-stone in their political careers. The presidency and the governorships of the industrialized states are the most coveted positions in the country's political landscape. Appointment to head any of the premier ministries and state firms also ranks high. The narrowness of interests for a large part of the legislature makes it less likely to be concerned with the broad claims of national constituencies. This profile has led several journalists to describe the Congress as no more than a huge debating society for city councillors.

Although the 1988 Constitution granted more powers to Congress, Congress has largely failed to use them. Lack of a legislative quorum to vote is a frequent problem, and recently acquired powers have provided greater opportunities for some legislators to practice corruption and backroom dealing. A recent event is illustrative. Congressional oversight regarding the federal budget was granted by the 1988 Constitution. Instead of debating the proposed budget offered by the executive, a majority of legislators were more concerned with offering a vast number of clientelist amendments or in hindering the budget's final approval. The 1994 federal budget was not approved until the end of that year!

The Brazilian legislature's many deficiencies were magnified in the mid-1990s by several corruption scandals. Perhaps the most serious of these involved a handful of senators and deputies accused of embezzling from the national treasury. When the scandal first broke in late 1993, few Brazilians were surprised at the extent of the corruption. The scandal was yet another vindication for those citizens who distrusted everything congressional politicians said or did.

The role of the Congress has not always been so insignificant. There are several moments in Brazilian history when it *has* met the expectations of what an autonomous legislative power ought to be. For example, after the resignation of President Quadros in 1961, Congress was able to resist an attempted military coup by reaching a short-lived compromise among key politicians. Other examples can be mentioned, such as the resistance of several legislators to the enactment of highly repressive Institutional Acts designed by the military to limit civil and press freedoms. More recently, Congress sustained Collor's impeachment and headed an inquiry into corrupt practices by important leading congressional members, some of whom lost their seats, either voluntarily or forcibly.

THE PARTY SYSTEM AND ELECTIONS

The Brazilian political party system is one of the most mercurial in the world. Party names, the party affiliations of politicians, and the structure of interparty alliances are all constantly in flux. Brazilian political history is marked by the discontinuity of party systems and of political groups within each party. Not only do parties disappear with each new regime, but the regional elites, in a dance of frightening speed, may

change from one party organization to another even during a single, short presidential term.

Parties today differ from their predecessors in name, size of constituency, and degree of militancy among their cadres. Yet they still form a fragile system responsible for governing, policy-making, and representing the interests of the majority of the population. The consensus among political analysts is that the organization of the Brazilian party system has always presented one of the most serious obstacles to the functioning of a stable democratic system. No doubt this is still true.

The deficiencies of the political party system have deep roots in Brazilian political history. Like many of the country's current problems, they stretch back to the New State of Getulio Vargas and the increasing centralization of politics in the Brazilian state. During the 1930s and 1940s, Brazil bore a certain resemblance to the majority of other countries in Latin America: the political incorporation of the masses preceded by many years the establishment of stable rules for ordering political competition. However, in Brazil the centralization of decision-making power in the state during the 1930s occurred in a polity without any institutional channels for union representation or viable political parties. This institutional vacuum facilitated the rise of Vargas and the establishment of the New State. Any incipient political parties were destroyed in the process. Thus, very early in modern Brazilian history, the state, rather than a political party system, took responsibility for incorporating social groups into national politics.

A second factor reinforcing the centrality of the state and the weakness of the party system was employing redistribution to garner the political support of the emerging middle and working classes. The incorporative and distributive characteristics of populism were achieved through the extreme centralization of policy-making in the state. This tendency retarded the development of viable institutions for representing members of the polity. The bureaucratic monopoly over decision making was buttressed by a series of corporatist institutions that incorporated workers and even industrialists in vast interest networks presided over by the Brazilian state. Participation, in this sense, was engineered by the state and not by political action initiated by autonomous segments of civil society.

The nature of electoral procedures is yet another key factor weakening the party system. Since the

1930s, Brazilian electoral laws have been structured to encourage antiparty behavior and reinforce the self-interest patronage networks that have damaged national party development.

The proportional representation system, first introduced in 1932, was reaffirmed in 1950 and 1965. It remains substantially unchanged as the system that regulates elections for the federal chamber of deputies, state assemblies, and municipal councillors. According to the system, voters must select a single candidate from a list established by each party in contention, for each of the three legislatures: municipal, state, and federal. The distribution of seats is based on several mathematical calculations to assure proportionality among political parties. The number of seats obtained by each party is determined by multiplying the ratio between party and total valid votes by the total number of seats.

Some facts about the actual functioning of the proportional representation system might be helpful. It can be said that, overall, the system helped to erode the monopoly of representation by rural oligarchies because it allowed various political currents to be expressed. Nonetheless, severe distortions in the representation of deputies occur as a result of the multiplicity of parties, the unbalanced apportionment of seats among the states, and even the sheer geographic size of the electoral territories. First, as hundreds of candidates and parties canvass for votes in large states, the votes obtained by each candidate are often highly scattered, limiting the accountability of those elected. This outcome is reversed when each seat corresponds to a particularly small district and a final runoff is held among two or three candidates. Second, because the electoral and party quotients are lower in the less populated states, candidates often alter their legal place of residence immediately before an election in order to run for a safer seat, thus further compounding the lack of accountability. Electoral laws are highly permissive regarding the candidate's change of residence. For example, ex-president Sarney, realizing that he would not be eligible to run for a Senate seat in his home state, successfully changed his residence only a few months before the 1990 elections.

There are no legal rules preventing elected representatives from switching parties. The excessive party switching that occurs in Brazil continues to reduce political parties to mere labels for individual politi-

cians. For example, more than one-third of all federal deputies who were elected in 1986 changed their party for the 1990 elections! After the 1994 elections, this same pattern continued. Ad hoc electoral coalitions in municipalities and states are frequent, often among parties in opposite fields at the federal level.

Under the New Republic, the party system was further weakened. Soon after Sarney became president, a constitutional amendment abolished virtually all restrictions on the formation of political parties—today, the presentation of a program and a list of 101 individuals supporting the creation of a party are sufficient to obtain preliminary registration. Definitive registration requires that within a year, conventions must be held in a certain number of municipalities in nine states to create municipal electoral committees. While filling the requirements for definitive registration, the party can present candidates for elections at all levels. If the party fails to meet all the requirements needed for definitive registration, that party's candidates can retain the advantages of a political party by switching to another party within sixty days. Recent laws provide other incentives for party formation. A party with even one representative in Congress is entitled to virtually all the privileges accorded to the major parties.

An extremely important feature of this fluid electoral system was established during the military period, namely, free electoral propaganda on radio and TV. All radio stations and TV channels are required to broadcast, at no charge, two hours of party propaganda each day during a campaign season. The parties are entitled to an amount of time on the air proportional to their respective number of votes from the previous election. Often some candidates have no more than a few seconds to present themselves and their platform to the public.

The almost mindboggling proliferation of parties in Brazil was the product of this short-sighted electoral legislation. The democratic opening *(abertura)* led to an indiscriminate growth in the number of parties (twenty-nine registered parties for the 1986 elections). The proliferation of minority parties and the growth of small party coalitions inject a great deal of instability and uncertainty into electoral contests. No less than twenty-one parties existed in Brazil in 1995, making the electoral process exceedingly confusing for many voters and even political specialists. Although the Constituent Assembly of 1987 provided an opportunity for addressing these problems, the opportunity was ignored. Neither the 1988 Constitution nor specific party laws have altered in any significant way the laws guiding the functioning of the party system.

Current Parties

Before 1979, under military rule, only two parties existed: the Brazilian Democratic Movement (MDB) and the National Renewal Alliance (ARENA). The former was a conglomerate of associations affiliated with the political opposition. The latter was the official party of military-supported candidates. In 1979, the military revised the electoral laws, allowing for a larger number of parties. The Party of the Brazilian Democratic Movement (*Partido do Movimento Democratico Brasileiro,* or PMDB) evolved from the MDB, a party that opposed the military during the authoritarian period. The Party of the Liberal Front (*Partido da Frente Liberal,* or PFL) emerged as a dissident of the ARENA party. These two parties became allies during the indirect elections of Tancredo Neves in 1985. The ARENA party changed its name to the Social Democratic Party (PDS) in the early 1980s. Recently the PDS again changed its name, to the Progressive Renewal Party (*Partido Progressista Renovador,* or PPR).

The potential for the emergence of new parties based upon more programmatic and ideological lines was already evident at the end of the military period. By the early 1980s, several of these parties garnered national significance. Among the most prominent were the Workers' Party (PT), the Democratic Labor Party (PDT), and the Brazilian Labor Party (PTB).

The creation of the PT was a remarkable innovation in Brazilian political party history. It was founded in the early 1980s by workers who had defied the military government and engaged in strikes in São Paulo's metalworking and automobile industries during 1978 and 1979. Although the PT began with a working-class message and leftist platform, its identity broadened during the course of the 1980s and early 1990s. The party and its leader, Inacio "Lula" da Silva, increasingly campaigned for the support of the middle class, the rural and urban poor, and even segments of the business and upper classes. Unlike previous "leftist-populist" parties in Brazil, the PT aimed both to integrate previously excluded sectors of the population into the political arena and to change substantively the status quo.

As Margaret Keck, a U.S. scholar of the PT, argues, the Workers' Party was a novel development among Brazilian political organizations. First, it aimed to be a party that expressed the interests of the workers and the poor. This had never before been attempted by any political organization that operated independently from the state. Second, the PT sought to be an internally democratic party. Third, the PT was accountable to its rank and file, often conducting national meetings in which a diversity of views were heard.

Soon after José Sarney became president, a large group of politicians discontented with PMDB politics broke off from the party and formed the Party of Brazilian Social Democracy (PSDB) in 1987, which became the sustaining force behind Presidents Itamar Franco and Fernando Henrique Cardoso.

Since 1988, various parties have been created, others have disappeared, and some have been co-opted. Two of the new parties enjoyed some remarkable electoral success. The National Renovation Party (*Partido Renovador Nacional,* or PRN), founded by Fernando Collor in 1989 as part of his campaign for the presidency, had its leader elected. Also in 1989, the neofascist Party of the Reorganization of the National Order (*Partido da Reorganização da Ordem Nacional,* or PRONA), led by Enéas Ferreira da Silva, garnered many more votes than some observers expected during the 1989 and 1994 elections.

Political Parties and Ideologies

It is difficult to generalize about the organizational structure and the ideological content of Brazil's party system today. With political loyalties in Brazilian politics always changing, the platforms, personalities, and organizations associated with each party are hard to identify. However, a few broad statements can be risked about the period and after 1984.

Political parties on the right currently defend neoliberal economic policies designed to shrink the size of the public sector. They support the reduction and partial privatization of the welfare state. A majority advocate a liberal trade policy, but a substantial minority press for protectionism. In terms of foreign economic policy, political parties on the right favor MERCOSUL; on constitutional reform, they are fairly united in favor of curtailing the number and range of social rights granted by the 1988 document; they also advocate electoral legal reform—specifically, the establishment of a majority or mixed, rather than a purely proportional, district voting system.

Political parties on the left currently advocate state reform, but also seek to maintain the public sector in public hands and improve the welfare state. Left-oriented parties want to expand the state's role in promoting and protecting domestic industry. On constitutional reform, they support the social rights guaranteed by the 1988 Constitution.

Right and left alike are fragmented into several political parties. A loose set of conservative parties currently struggle for the mantle of the right. In front of the pack are the PPR and the PFL. Many wildcard parties, with low to moderate levels of representation in Congress, often ally themselves with right-wing parties or advocate right-wing issues: the PTB, the Progressive Party (PP), and the Liberal Party (PL) are examples. Various microparties also comprise the right-wing side of the ideological spectrum. The PRN, PRONA, the Christian Social Party (PCS), the Social Democratic Party (PSD—no relation to the Vargas-era PSD), and the Republican Progressive Party (PRP) are examples. The PMDB and the PSDB dominate the center and center-left segment of the ideological spectrum. Nevertheless, certain groups within both of these parties also identify with the positions that define the political right or the political left.

The Workers' Party (PT) has garnered much of the left's political space, further marginalizing already peripheral parties such as the Brazilian Communist Party (PCB) and the Communist Party of Brazil (PC do B). The PDT is also a leftist party, but it maintains a very specific identity. Its leader, Leonel Brizola, the ex-governor of Rio de Janeiro, advocates Vargas-era nationalism and state-led development. The Brazilian Socialist Party (PSB) and the Green Party (PV) add to the left-wing segment of the ideological spectrum.

The increased representation of the left and right has been accompanied by the growing fragmentation of party representation in Congress. Table 9 demonstrates that no party has more than 30 percent of the seats in either house of Congress.

The place occupied by the large parties (PMDB and PFL) fell from 76 percent in 1986 to 46 percent in 1990 and to 38 percent in 1994. The number of parties represented in Congress grew from thirteen to nineteen between 1986 and 1991 but has not increased since 1991. Although the PSDB is not large, it made the greatest headway in gaining seats in the Chamber of Deputies. The PT grew at a high rate in the Senate. The PTB, PDT, and PPR also hold a moderate repre-

sentation in the legislature. Another batch of minuscule organizations, such as the PRN, manage to fragment support for legislative action even further. The proliferation of parties in Congress increases the number of diverse interests that must be considered to pass legislation and reduces the possibility of building majority parties. Also state patronage, not party loyalty, remains one of the key instruments for gaining congressional support.

An outstanding aspect of recent Brazilian politics is the schizophrenic structure of the party-government relationship. Until the end of the Franco government, the so-called governing parties did not govern, nor did they clearly oppose the government. Even the largest parties in the legislature exempted themselves from any responsibility for government policies. The role of parties in Congress was largely characterized by a tendency to move ideologically toward the center, but it was a fuzzy center lacking clear boundaries and "backbone" concerning specific issues, policies, or presidents. Congress portrayed the image of an arena in which everyone seemed to be potentially in alliance with everyone else, yet each was actually alone. In such a context, it is easy to understand why civilian governments had such a difficult time building congressional support.

POLITICAL CULTURE, CITIZENSHIP, AND IDENTITY

The notion of national identity describes a sense of national community that goes beyond mere allegiance to a state, to a set of economic interests, regional loyalties, or kinship affiliations. The cultivation of a national identity occurs through a process of "nationbuilding" during which a set of national symbols, cultural terms and images, and shared myths consolidate around historical experiences that define the loyalties of a group of people. Although states influence and are influenced by the process of nation formation, as in the construction and usage of nationalist political symbols and rhetoric, not all nations are created by states. In Brazil, the early existence of the state as a central source of authority and the establishment of uncontested territorial boundaries by the end of the eighteenth century were not enough to establish a lasting national identity in the nineteenth century. The birth of a Brazilian nation had to wait for the evolution of citizenship and political participation by more than an elitist class.

TABLE 9   **Party Representation in Congress: 1990, 1994**

	Chamber of Deputies		
	Number of Seats		
Party	1990	1994	1994 Percentage
PMDB	96	107	20.8
PFL	89	90	17.5
PSDB	48	62	12.0
PPR	66	53	10.3
PT	36	49	9.5
PP	45	37	7.2
PDT	35	34	6.6
PTB	38	30	5.8
PSB	11	14	2.7
PL	16	13	2.5
PC do B	6	10	1.9
Others	—	14	3.2

	Senate		
	Number of Seats		
Party	1990	1994	1994 Percentage
PMDB	25	22	27.1
PFL	14	17	20.9
PSDB	10	11	13.5
PPR	5	7	8.6
PT	1	6	7.4
PDT	6	5	6.2
PTB	8	5	6.2
PP	4	5	6.2
Others	—	3	3.9

Several historical events and processes made Brazilian nationbuilding possible. Unlike the early process of nation formation in culturally, linguistically, and geographically diverse Western Europe, Africa, and Asia, Brazil enjoyed a homogeneous linguistic and colonial experience. As a result, Brazilian history largely avoided the ethnic conflicts that have recently become obstacles to nationbuilding in Eastern Europe and India. Immigrants added their ideas and value systems at the turn of the century, but they brought no compelling identities that could substitute for an overarching national consciousness. Regional secessionist movements were scarce in Brazilian history and did not last into the twentieth century, so that subnational loyalties remained insubstantial.

As already discussed, racial identities in Brazil were seldom the basis for political action. This was partly the result of the historical myth that the country was racially mixed, thus devoid of a diversity of ethnic identities, so there was a singular racial consciousness. Clearly the economic and political realities of the country oppressed Indians and Africans, but the myth of racial democracy had a power and resonance that persisted in the national consciousness. Brazilian literature, political discourse, and history texts used in education reinterpreted the importance of ethnic identities to boost the myth that Brazil was a racial democracy. The unique contributions of different ethnic groups were not appreciated. The famous Brazilian anthropologist and sociologist, Gilberto Freyre in his *Casa Grande e Senzala (Master and Slaves)* discloses the peculiarities of social relations among blacks and whites since colonial times, but he seems to treat the underlying reality of racial conflict as an issue of

Carnival in Brazil is the world's largest floor show.
Source: Reuters/Bettmann.

secondary importance. Brazilian literature and history texts convey the relations between Indians and whites in unrealistic, idealistic tones. One of the best known stories regards the Portuguese Diogo Alvares *(Caramuru)* and the Indian woman *Paraguaçu.* Their amorous relations led to many racially mixed children who became simply known as Brazilian. Such works argue that miscegenation diminished racial differences and unified what were once antagonistic polarities between white lords and black or Indian slaves. This thinking buttressed the false belief that prejudice and discrimination were lacking among whites, blacks, Indians, and mulattoes.

Brazilian literature and culture also attempted to address the idea of the nation as something that was more than the sum of the country's ethnic character. In these writings and discourses there is a search for a national character that lies somewhere between the European culture and the indigenous culture represented by the Indians. Oswald de Andrade's well-known question: "Tupi or not Tupi? [Tupi is the name of an Indian tribe], that is the question," is a vivid and ironic illustration of this cultural search in the 1920s. Over time, the search for the Brazilian national character has been transformed into an analysis and treatment of social, political, and economic structures, thus taking the search well beyond the cultural realm.

The process of state-building, with its centrality in Brazilian history, invaded the process of nation-building. The construction of a national state apparatus coincided with the use of symbols and rhetoric that married the nation and the state. For example, Getulio Vargas's building of the New State in the 1930s was punctuated with Vargas's image as the father of the people. Much later, Juscelino Kubitschek's project of accomplishing "fifty years of development in five" took on the character of a national mission.

Like the myth of racial democracy, these political articulations defining the nation often sought to hide or negate the real conflicts that existed among political factions. The symbols and images of political nationalism tended to boost the quasi-utopian visions of the country's future development through a national project on which all elites could agree. Although optimistic, this conceptualization of nation exceeded mere optimism as it imbued political relations with "elite conciliation" and "political flexibility."

Political articulations of the nation often reflected attempts to integrate previously excluded segments of Brazilian society. Vargas's populism, Kubitschek's developmentalism, and Goulart's leftist alliances all articulated a concept of the nation that sought to validate extensions of the status of citizenship. As we have already seen, citizenship in Brazil was determined by an interdependent set of processes: the extension of local patrimonial relations into the formation of a strong, central state; the expansion of the electorate; the enfranchisement of segments of society through populist programs; the evolution of a class structure that provided impetus to the rise of political organizations and the incorporation of such organizations into the state through corporatist institutions. Since the 1980s, the notion of Brazilian citizenship continues to expand to include groups that were rarely, if ever, incorporated by these processes: illiterate voters, *favelados,* and political organizations no longer controlled by the state's corporatist institutions.

Despite the importance of both the cultural and political articulations of the Brazilian nation and the continued evolution of citizenship, these processes do not completely determine the political orientations of Brazilians. A few general points about Brazilian political culture can be made. Citizens often exhibit the most extreme forms of discontent with their government while still embracing patriotic visions of the country's future. New leaders tend to inspire confidence until that confidence is worn away by the frustration of Brazil's massive problems or by the specter of corruption. In this context, it is difficult to put one's finger on the pulse of the electorate. Given the frenetic nature of Brazilian political change, it is difficult even to discern continuous political identities among the citizenry. Perhaps the ultimate reflection of these contradictory tendencies is the well-known joke among Brazilians that "Brazil is the country of the future and will always be."

The political sentiments and orientations of Brazilian society are actually quite static because most Brazilians feel powerless and incapable of changing their destiny. One offshoot of this perspective is that Brazilians have always considered liberal democratic institutions, particularly individual rights, as artificial or irrelevant. Although this view may appear cynical, it is a deeply ingrained notion in Brazilian political culture. Since the end of the nineteenth century, Brazilians have made a distinction between the "legal" Brazil and the "real" Brazil. The former involves the formal laws of the country, the latter refers to what actually occurs. One prime example was the "façade" of liberal democracy concealing the patronage-ridden interior of Brazilian politics. This notion is actually quite popular throughout much of Latin America. The phrase *"para ingles ver"* ("for the Anglos to see") refers to the notion that liberal democracy was implanted to impress foreign observers, hiding the fact that true Latin American politics would be conducted by other means.

One of the key conclusions of the generalized sense of powerlessness among the majority of Brazilians was the notion that the state should organize society. This belief helped to justify both the Vargas dictatorship in 1937 and the military authoritarianism that followed the coup of 1964. The primacy of the state manifested itself in several ways in the political culture of the Brazilian citizenry. The notion that the state had a duty to provide for its citizens' welfare clearly placed the state at the center of the Brazilian polity. An offshoot of this belief in the importance of the state was the primacy of the president, the embodiment of centralized power.

The Left

The dominance of the developmentalist state and a politically powerless citizenry are not the only elements of Brazilian political culture. A rather vibrant ideological left existed for many years. Before 1964, leftist politics, as elsewhere in Latin America at the time, were predominantly focused on anti-imperialism. But unlike the Cuban or Nicaraguan variety, the Brazilian anti-imperialist left did not advocate class warfare and peasant revolution; instead, it focused its attention on social reform and an aggressive foreign policy. This more moderate position was reinforced by the Brazilian Communist Party. The Communists tended toward populism and nationalism rather than toward Marxist-Leninism. Foreign policy, the United States, and foreign multinationals were more often the target of the party's campaigns than the country's oppressive class structure.

Leftist nationalism fit neatly into the political discourse of the 1950s and 1960s when economic development was established as the primary goal of the country's political leadership. The ideology of developmentalism that existed at the time was often buttressed by nationalist arguments. In this way, the Brazilian left became one of the strongest supporters of the development of the internal market, land reform, and state-led industrialization. However, this made it more of a follower than a leader of already established populist programs. Populism had not required a leftist party nor the revolutionary rhetoric of the left.

Although the cultural presence of the left was not extinguished after the 1964 coup d'état, it was severely weakened. During the military period, the leftist intelligentsia was pressured both from the right and from the radical left. The right, represented in its most extreme form by the military government of Emilio Médici, engaged in systematic torture and imprisonment of intellectuals, artists, and political activists viewed as leftist. From the left, more radical tactics, supported by Cuba and inspired by the rhetoric of Ernesto "Che" Guevara, pressed segments of the Brazilian left into disastrous guerrilla activities which ended in the deaths of hundreds of leftists. Both pressures severely hurt the Brazilian left, but did not eliminate it. Although torture and repression were widespread, leftists successfully infiltrated unions and social movements during the transition to democracy. Despite the fact that the guerrilla campaigns during the late 1960s were summarily crushed by the military, segments of the left continued, albeit more subdued, in their rhetoric to bring about civilian government.

The end of the military regime revealed splits among the Brazilian Left. Both repression and the failure of the guerrilla option had severely fragmented leftist organizations. Trotskyites, Maoists, unionists, liberation theologians, and a host of other factions often opposed each other within the same organizations, making impossible a cohesive national left-wing movement. The crisis of Soviet and Eastern European socialism together with the continuing problems of the Cuban experiment, further hindered prospects for a "Project of the Left" outside that already represented by Lula and the PT.

The Right

The politics of the Brazilian right have historically been associated with the business community and the military. Brazilian business was perennially a weak political power. The right was a follower of state-led developmentalism rather than a key decision maker. This weakness within the state structure, however, did not prevent Brazilian business from having a significant influence on the political right during times of crisis. During the 1964 coup, key leaders of the political right, many of them prominent business people and journalists, joined the military in denouncing João Goulart and the "street radicals" that supported him.

In recent years, the political right, especially that portion composed of business interests, has been concerned with the promotion of market-oriented economic policies and the emphasis on increasing competitiveness. These positions have been channeled into politics as business associations support politicians who agree with these policy prescriptions.

During the redemocratization process and in the New Republic, new trends in Brazilian political culture flourished. Each trend accepted the language of "modernization with democracy," not that of revolution or of coups d'état. One new trend was stimulated by the Catholic church, which argued that the myriad political organizations and movements that had stimulated the transition to democracy should remain active. This argument was based on the idea that representative democracy was too limited and civil society must continue to participate actively in the evolution of a democratic order.

A second trend that developed during and after the New Republic was a profound sense of antistatism. This sense pervaded not just the sphere of economic policy but also other areas such as social policy. One popularized component of this view blamed the Brazilian state for all the nation's political maladies.

A third salient trend in Brazilian political culture occurs among segments of the elite, particularly intellectuals, politicians, journalists, and entrepreneurs. It maintains that tinkering with national institutions—what some call "institutional engineering"—is needed to consolidate democracy. Advocates of this trend argue that to consolidate democracy, formal institutions must be reformed to allow civil society to organize and participate. The recent emphasis on constitutional reform, which prioritizes legislative mechanisms in the consolidation of Brazilian democracy, is an example.

Overall, the identities, political culture, and notions of citizenship that exist in Brazil are all highly factionalized. Although Brazilian civil society has grown and become more dynamic in the past three decades, coalitions and alliances among the various sectors are rare. Civil society in Brazil thus shows much dynamism but lacks strong democratic institutions to link interests.

Political Culture and the Media

As common everywhere, the media, particularly radio and television, have in many ways displaced the political parties in shaping public opinion and identity, often turning politics into just another form of show business. Brazil appears to have many requisites for media freedom. The great majority of the media are privately owned. Although there is significant government influence over the resources necessary for media production and the advertising revenue from governmental campaigns, there is no overt government censorship, and freedom of the press is widely and constitutionally proclaimed.

Although private ownership may constitute a hedge against government control, it does not necessarily imply free coverage of the news by competitive organizations. First, there is less competition among media organizations than the high number of publishers and broadcasters might imply. Many newspapers belong to media conglomerates, a few of which dominate the industry. The Globo network, for example, is Brazil's preeminent media empire and one of the five largest television networks in the world. It has been formidable in shaping public opinion; some believe it played a prominent role in Collor's election in 1989.

The media's independence from government interference varies according to the particular medium in question. The print media is generally less restrained in its criticism of politicians and governments than broadcast media. Though television newscasts, which attract millions of viewers, continuously cover events embarrassing to the government or criticize government policies, the majority of viewers hear woefully little information on how and why political decisions are made, why one policy is favored over another, and the ultimate results. Domestic broadcast news coverage in Brazil is often merely the broadcasting of official government versions.

The media played a key role in selling the positive nature of free markets to the Brazilian people. In particular, television has molded public opinion in recent years to favor competition within an open market as a national priority. Broadcasters told the public that the premises of liberal economic thinking were the only realistic and sensible choice for Brazilian development. The uncritical exaltation of free-market economics, the confidence that social equity can be achieved through the operation of the market, and the naive belief that the state is the source of all evils, have influenced not only the middle classes, but even the working class, which increasingly shares these opinions.

The media has sometimes taken more critical positions. Recently, the media performed a crucial role in denouncing the blatant privileges, arbitrariness, and corruption pervasive in the activities of Brazilian government officials. Nevertheless, the positive effect of the media in revealing the networks of corruption entrenched in the country's political system has produced some unwanted consequences for the legitimation of Brazil's new democracy. The selective character of information and the continuous partiality regarding the persons and institutions targeted by the media's anticorruption campaign are reinforcing a traditional aspect of Brazil's political culture: a deep-seated mistrust of politics and politicians. Despite the evident involvement of bureaucrats in the emergence of recent episodes of corruption and waste of resources, the mass media have constantly placed the blame primarily upon politicians, Congress in particular. Parties and representatives are pictured as a homogeneous group, forming a sort of "kleptocracy." At the same time, however, the criticism and denunciations seem to spare other leading government figures, some of them prominent during the preceding military regime. These figures are frequently praised for their efficacy in achieving economic development while in power. Their unpublicized, but nevertheless widely recognized, acts of corruption are implicitly forgiven, and their policies, although largely to blame for the present situation, are rarely denanced.

INTERESTS, SOCIAL MOVEMENTS, AND PROTEST

Large segments of the population, although having a class or a socioeconomic identity, also engage in collective actions on the basis of communal, kin, ethnic, and/or gender identities. The role these collective actors play in supporting and changing political institutions may be interpreted by political activists and policymakers as both a source of political support and of potential opposition. These groups may also be perceived as the proponents of progressive social action or as conservative forces bent on impeding real socioeconomic change.

The centrality of the Brazilian state does not mean that other organizations, movements, and institutions in civil society do not have a significant effect on politics. One need not look further than the Catholic church as a prime example. From the early 1930s until recently, the church cooperated intimately with the Brazilian state. Its basic goal was the formal conversion of the entire society through Catholicism. Until the mid-1950s, the church continued this mission with the cooperation of the state and with the assistance of European Catholicism. However, after 1955, Brazilian society began to change very rapidly. Labor movements emerged in urban and rural areas and new political parties were formed to contest for state power. These political developments and the larger social changes which undergirded them presented new challenges and opportunities for the Catholic church.

Among the changes in Catholic doctrine that accompanied the Second Vatican Council in the early 1960s, the Catholic church in Brazil was to become more directly active in supporting social and political reform. The church formed the National Conference of Brazilian Bishops (CNBB) to govern the new mission within Brazil. By means of the Basic Education Movement (MEB), the church promoted literacy and greater political awareness. In both rural and urban areas, the church formed links to the unions and worked to help mobilize workers, to establish their legal rights, and to improve workplace conditions. This reformist drive was not supported by all church members. Conservative segments and laypersons sometimes reacted violently to the church's "messing in politics," and protests against the new mission were common in the 1960s. But such demonstrations could not stop the changes that were already rocking the Catholic church both in Brazil and internationally.

Not long after the military took power, sectors of the Brazilian church started denouncing the military regime and its economic model. The so-called theology of liberation, developed by Frei Leonardo Boff, became a popular alternative. "Liberation theology," as it came to be known, attempted to relate theology to Brazilian reality. This doctrinal shift profoundly changed the role of the Catholic church in Brazil. A number of factors spurred on these changes. First, the reality of Brazilian poverty and the mounting social dilemmas of the country were subjects that Catholic priests could not ignore. Segments of the church began to view themselves as responsible for directly improving the lot of the majority of Brazilians. Second, the mounting evidence of torture and killings under military auspices convinced Catholics throughout Brazil that the church should take a more active role in ending these practices. Finally, the church diversified its role in society and politics to counteract competition

from evangelical groups that attempted to mobilize believers in both politics and religion.

In rural areas, the new role of the church was evident with the formation of church-sponsored activist organizations. The ecclesiastical Native Missionary Council (CIMI) was founded in 1972 to defend the few remaining indigenous Brazilians from the threat of extinction. In 1975, a conference was called to discuss the issue of land tenure. The participants took steps to promote agrarian reform through a *Comissão Pastoral de Terras* (Pastoral Land Commission).

By 1976, the conflict between the church and the military government became acute. Religious protests against authoritarianism increased. In 1978, the CNBB issued a major document for the General Assembly of the Latin American Episcopal Conference in Puebla, Mexico. This document argued that the church could not afford to ignore the injustices of poverty or government brutality. The CNBB also took a more active role by smuggling reports of human rights violations out of the country. Confirmed stories of mutilations, torture, and secret killings were made available by the Catholic church to the international community. They were subsequently published as a book, *Nunca Mais (Never Again).* Through a series of national meetings, the church also drew attention to the land tenure issue. Often, church officials went so far as to openly endorse physical resistance on the part of squatters and peasants.

This activist position also extended to urban areas. The progressive sectors of the church encouraged the formation of grassroots or base communities (CEBs) that urged and often organized poor people to participate in politics. One of the principal functions of the CEBs was the development of a popular political consciousness and the awakening of the lower classes to their rights. CEBs organized inhabitants of Brazil's many *favelas* to lobby state and local bureaucracies for sanitation facilities, squatters' rights, and education. Many continue the fight today. According to Ralph Della Cava, a specialist on the Brazilian church, there is no doubt that in the early and mid-1970s the church played a crucial role in augmenting democratic pressures in Brazil.

In the mid-1970s, Brazil witnessed a historic awakening of new forms of social and political organization: grassroots popular movements; new forms of trade unionism; neighborhood movements; professional associations of doctors, lawyers, and journalists; entrepreneurs; and middle-class organizations. At the same time, a host of nongovernmental organizations (ngos) became more active in Brazil. Examples included Amnesty International, Greenpeace, and native Brazilian rights groups. Domestic groups active in these areas increasingly turned to the ngos for resources and information, adding an international dimension to what was previously solely within the realm of domestic politics.

Women's organizations played a significant role in popular urban social movements in the context of noninstitutional politics during the 1970s. By the 1980s, women participated in and even led popular initiatives on a wide variety of issues relating to employment and the provision of basic services. Many of these organizations have gone on to enlist political parties and trade unions in battles concerning women's wages, birth control, rape, and violence in the home. The 1988 Constitution reflected the importance of the issues championed by women's groups. For example, its provisions for maternity leave make it more progressive on women's issues than the U.S. Constitution, which still lacks an Equal Rights Amendment.

Women's issues have become more salient in Brazil mostly because of the greater role of women in Brazilian society and the economy. Women working outside the home constitute 39 percent of the female population. That figure is higher than in Mexico (22 percent) and Argentina (33 percent). More than 20 percent of Brazilian families are supported exclusively by women. Of 5,000 ngos in Brazil, 115 have projects directed toward women's issues. Three thousand separate organizations have been created by women. Although practically absent in employers' organizations, women are highly active in urban unions. Out of the country's 5,324 urban unions, 14.8 percent have elected women directors. Women are less involved in the management of rural unions (6.6 percent), but they compose 78 percent of active membership. The share of domestic help in the female workforce has declined from 32 percent to 20 percent over the last ten years, suggesting that traditional roles for women have not absorbed the increase in the female workforce.

Despite improvements in women's participation and organization, much remains to be done. Labor laws determine that women and men should receive equal pay for equal work, but men invariably earn higher salaries. On average, women earn 43 percent less than men. Only 7 percent of women with university degrees earn more than twenty times the minimum wage, as compared to 28 percent of men. Thirty-four percent of illiterate women earn the minimum salary or less versus 5 percent of illiterate males.

Recent indicators suggest that the increased impact of women's issues is creating change. The average number of births per woman of childbearing age fell from 6.28 in 1960 to 2.7 in 1991. As of 1994, 86 percent of all fertile women used birth control pills, the IUD, or sterilization as forms of contraception, twice the proportion for several other developed countries.

Despite the rise of movements dedicated to human rights, the environment, and women's issues, a politically significant organization dedicated to addressing the pivotal questions of racial discrimination has not emerged. This fact is especially surprising since Brazil is one of the world's most racially mixed countries. Only during the 1940s did some public officials and academics acknowledge that prejudice existed against blacks. At that time, however, the problems of race were equated with the problems of class. Prejudice came to be viewed as a class-based, not a race-based, phenomenon. Attacking class inequality was thus considered a way to address prejudice against blacks. This belief seemed plausible because most poor Brazilians are either mulatto or black. But this is no coincidence. It might be just as logical to suggest that they are poor because they are black.

In the 1950s some intellectuals finally began to address the issue of prejudice as racial discrimination. Although academic attitudes changed in this regard, social attitudes remained hostile to the notion that Brazil had a "race question" or a "race problem." From the colonial era to the present, the articulation of race as part of any political program was taboo among the political elite. Such a position threatened the power of the largely white elite—from the white landowner with black slaves during colonial and imperial times to the white entrepreneur and his predominantly mulatto *pardo,* or black workers. These sentiments did not remain in the domain of class relations but became popularized among all Brazilians. Roberto DaMatta, a well-known Brazilian anthropologist, explained that even today whites and blacks may disagree, but when a decision must be made, whites need just utter the words, "Do you (the black) know who you're talking to?" and the argument ends. Such patterns are deeply rooted in Brazilian history, development, and culture.

Some analysts believe in a gradual and peaceful evolution of race relations. Others believe that, as a consequence of white economic and political domination, blacks still lack the collective identity and political organization necessary to make race relations a viable issue on the political agenda. Both sides seem to agree, however, that although poverty and color are significantly correlated, overt race confrontation is uncommon. Ironically, this may be precisely why no serious national discussion of race relations has ever emerged in Brazil. Should black and mulatto Brazilians develop their own politically significant organizations and, like women, place the issue of race on the national agenda, attitudinal changes are likely to follow. Already there are signs that Brazilians are organizing politically around issues of race. Since 1985, various small antiracist movements have gathered allies; over fifty of these groups now exist in sixteen states, but they are small and politically marginalized.

As a corollary to the race issue, the rights of indigenous peoples, namely the Indians of the Amazon, continue at the center of Brazil's most pressing social problems. Over the past half century, the development of the Amazon has directly threatened the cultures and lives of Indians. Members of the Ianomamis, one of Brazil's largest Amazon tribes, are frequently murdered by miners just to acquire access to mines in Indian territory. Many such massacres have occurred in territories legally provided by the central state to the Ianomamis. Without more federal protection, Amazonian Indians will continue to be threatened.

Aside from the thorny issues of race, the question of the relationship between human beings and the environment has challenged the very way that Brazilians live. When the volume of evidence increased during the 1970s on the link between the destruction of the Amazon and higher carbon dioxide levels in the world's atmosphere, greater attention was placed on the environment as a major national issue. Yet only recently has the environment become a political issue around which Brazilians have mobilized. As discussion of environmental problems evolved at the national level during the 1980s, an environmental movement emerged composed of intellectuals, middle-class professionals, students, and ngos. The movement soon became involved in the municipal elections of 1985 and organized a conference that gathered 2,000 urban and rural ecologists. As the environment increasingly became an unavoidable issue in Europe and North America, external resources, both funding and information, became more available to Brazilian ecologists. In the summer of 1992, international and domestic concern for the environment reached a high point with the World Ecology Conference in Rio de Janeiro.

Urban and rural unions have channeled the frustrations and represented the positions of workers. Between 1960 and 1992, an immense upsurge in labor organization occurred in Brazil. Sixty-four percent of the unions that currently exist were created between 1960 and 1990. Rural unions expanded in size and number as issues of land ownership concentration and rural workers' rights increased in significance. The number of rural unions grew from 625 in 1968 to 2,852 in 1989, representing more than 5 million rural workers. From 1964 to 1988, 96 percent of the current rural employee unions and 76 percent of rural employer federations were created.

The expansion of capitalist agriculture based on export crops at the expense of food crops for the local population led to increasing conflicts over land ownership. Between 1970 and 1980, 50.4 percent of the agro-business properties had less than 10 hectares and corresponded to 2.4 percent of the occupied land; 0.9 percent of the properties with areas of more than 1,000 hectares corresponded to 45 percent of the occupied land. Data for 1994 show that there are 4.8 million rural workers without land; whereas the wealthiest 1 percent of the proprietors have 44 percent of the rural properties, 67 percent of the proprietors have only 6 percent of the land. Political confrontation over land property led to the establishment of the Catholic church's Land Pastoral Commission *(Comissão Pastoral da Terra)* and to rural activism. The CONTAG (National Confederation of Rural Workers) began to play a larger role in national labor politics as these issues achieved greater visibility.

Urban unions witnessed a similar rise to national political prominence. The growth of industry and the service sector since the 1950s has greatly expanded the resource and organizational base of labor unions. The most profound change in urban labor's political role took place at the end of the 1970s when a movement known as the "new unionism" *(Novo Sindicalismo)* emerged in the industrial heartland of São Paulo. Based primarily in the metalworking and auto industries, the "new union" movement campaigned on behalf of union autonomy from state corporatism, collective bargaining, and the right to strike. Illegal strikes in 1978 and 1979 challenged the military government and employers. The movement succeeded in defying state authority and in forcing employers to deal directly with independent union leaders.

The success of the "new union" movement led to an upsurge in the number and organizational strength of independent, national labor organizations. The 1980s and 1990s witnessed the rise of several national labor organizations in addition to the CONTAG: the United Workers Organization (CUT), the National Coordination of the Working Class (CONCLAT), the General Confederation of Workers (CGT), and Union Force *(Força Sindical)*.

Throughout the 1980s and 1990s, labor unions in Brazil succeeded in garnering many benefits through pressure on the legislature, mobilization of public opinion, and strikes. Among the major achievements were numerous wage concessions, workweek time agreements, job safety provisions, and parental leave. Many of these issues were even codified into the 1988 Constitution, but other work-related issues remained to be settled, including the thorny question of job security.

Beyond issues of the workplace, Brazilian unions have also been politically active on larger questions. Some of the most ardent opponents of military rule in the late 1970s were union members. During the transition to civilian governance, urban unions organized in support of direct presidential elections and individual rights. Labor organizations such as CGT and CUT have become involved in issues of national importance such as privatization and anti-inflation policies.

Brazilian employers also have their own organizations on both the national and the state level. A prominent example is the Federation of São Paulo Industries (FIESP), which has extended its interests to states other than São Paulo. Organizations like FIESP have been key proponents of such market-oriented policies as privatization of state corporate investments. Economic elites have engaged in a wide range of political activities, including political parties and presidential task commissions.

Brazil lacks a single political party that speaks for the interests of business. After they outline a position on a given economic policy issue, business organizations like FIESP may form alliances with any number of parties advocating a similar stand. This contributes even further to the uncertainty of Brazilian politics inasmuch as business may swing support to virtually any political organization.

The recent sprouting of movements, associations, and interest groups may seem impressive, but they represent specific constituencies. Most Brazilians do not participate in parties, movements, and unions because often the basic functions of a competent government such as security, justice, education, and health care simply do not reach most Brazilians. Economic recession, unemployment and the distrust and fear of police forces nurture a feeling that nothing is stable or sure in the immediate future. When the belief system about public power and the society where people live is undermined by insecurity, the majority of the population comes to expect little from government or from other political organizations. In this sense, many Brazilians eschew organized and peaceful political action, often taking to the streets in sporadic riots, or, in the case of impoverished young *favelados,* mass stealing sprees called *arrastões.* Such events demonstrate that many Brazilians perceive only two choices in the face of impersonal and unresponsive political and state organizations: violent protest or isolationism.

SECTION 5

Brazilian Politics at the Crossroads

POLITICAL CHALLENGES
AND CHANGING AGENDAS

During the summer of 1993, Fernando Collor's attorney was busily at work filing documents with the courts to protect his client. The much-vilified ex-president was not attempting to defend himself from a legislature bent on trying him for crimes and misdemeanors stemming from his corrupt actions as president. Nor was Collor enduring this legal process to protect his family from a series of injunctions against its property. Rather, Collor's attorney was desperate to defend his client from a soon-to-be-released soap opera ironically entitled *"O Maraja"* ("The Maharaja").

The soap opera, as advertised, was to detail (with fictional embellishments) all the corrupt and "perverted" practices of the Collor presidency. Surprisingly, Collor was victorious in his request and the series was not run. A year after his ouster, the ex-president who had been the focus of so much scorn and outrage was still able to force a national network to pull a soap opera from the air waves.

In an October 1993 press interview, a former director of the department of the federal budget described the existence of a huge corruption ring in the Brazilian bureaucracy. The accusations directly incriminated incumbent ministers, ex-ministers, deputies, senators, construction firms, governors, sectors of the judiciary, and the core of the two largest parties in the Congress, the PMDB and PFL.

A month before the polls opened in the 1994 presidential elections, Finance Minister Ricupero, who replaced the candidate Cardoso as the manager of the Real Plan, was inadvertently caught speaking informally by homeowners with satellite dishes. The flap that subsequently exploded revolved around Ricupero's admission that he regularly manipulated price statistics to help Cardoso's claim that the Real Plan was bringing down inflation. "I have no scruples," he confided. "What is good news we exploit; what is bad, we hide."

These and similar stories lead to a widespread feeling that not much has changed in Brazilian politics. These events, however, do not fully illustrate the contemporary situation. The scale of the social and institutional problems facing the new administration frequently hides the progress the country has made toward democracy. It is often forgotten that Brazilian institutions exhibited an unexpected vigor during the impeachment of President Collor, which was a victory for the rule of civilian law. At no time during these proceedings did any significant political force attempt to involve the military in changing democratic procedures.

Similarly, the media's airing of corruption charges and the response from the Congress in carrying out a full investigation was promising for continued civilian control over politics. For the first time in Brazilian history, the Congress took decisive measures in 1993 to investigate the entrenched corruption rings in its own quarters. Although the inquiries resulted in mixed outcomes, several national leaders were forced to resign and others were stripped of their seats.

Democratic success may be traced both to the growth of democratic values and their roots in a country's historical and cultural traditions. One can detect a strong ambivalence toward democracy in Brazilian political culture similar to that of many other recently established democracies. The country has often been torn between a consensus on the legitimacy of popularly elected government on one hand, and an excessive fear of division stemming from class warfare, on the other. Nonetheless, a strong liberal-democratic current permeates Brazil's political culture, which made it difficult for the military regime to consolidate and perpetuate authoritarian rule. Today, among the elites, there is a general willingness to compromise and to moderate demands so that relapses into authoritarianism are avoided. A key indication of this transition in Brazilian politics is that the two main candidates in the 1994 presidential race were far more to the left than other Latin American candidates in recent years.

In addition to representative institutions valued by the society and relatively independent of the state, a critical and active society is also necessary for the consolidation of democracy. The proliferation of associations and political organizations and the autonomy of such groups from the state can be effective mechanisms for fostering democracy. The number and vitality of associations in India have become crucial resources for democratic expression and accountability as formal political institutions have deteriorated in the past two decades. In Nigeria, the efforts of the military regime to deepen its repressive character from 1984 to 1985 were frustrated by the organizational strength of civil society. This popular resistance proved crucial in precipitating the downfall of General Buhari.

The absence of a vigorous sector of voluntary associations and interest groups, or the control of such organizations by a corporatist state, may obstruct the development of democracy. In Mexico, the early incorporation of peasants' and workers' organizations into a dominant corporatist party created obstacles for more contemporary organizations to break free of corporatist controls and call for the democratization of the Mexican state. Although corporatist restrictions on participation are nonetheless still felt, a similar struggle has already been successful in Brazil. Moreover, it has not produced the wave of political murders that recently swept Mexico in the course of dismantling the PRI and corporatism.

Fernando Henrique Cardoso

In the early 1950s, Fernando Henrique Cardoso studied at the University of São Paulo where he soon earned a teaching position. By the late 1950s, his major intellectual positions were inspired by Marxist studies. During the 1960s and 1970s, Fernando Henrique became one of the key authors in the "dependency literature" movement, which sought to explain how Third World development was affected by an international economic system created by First World countries. Cardoso co-authored *Dependency and Development in Latin America*, one of the most influential texts in this genre. When the Brazilian armed forces seized power in 1964, he went into exile in Chile. During his years in exile, Cardoso worked as a professor at the Sorbonne in Paris and at Oxford University. In 1969, Cardoso returned from exile only to be fired from his professorship at the University of São Paulo. He subsequently founded CEBRAP, a research institute in São Paulo dedicated to conducting research on Brazilian society under dictatorship. When the military began

For Fernando Henrique Cardoso, victory is within reach as he casts his ballot in the 1994 presidential elections. Source: Reuters/Bettmann.

the gradual transition to democratic civilian rule, Cardoso ran for senator on the opposition party (PMDB) ticket in São Paulo. He lost the election but later, when the other candidate on the same ticket was elected governor, Cardoso slipped into his vacant seat. In 1985, he ran for mayor of São Paulo and lost. In 1986, he was re-elected senator; in 1988 he and a group of colleagues seceded from the PMDB to found the Brazilian Social-Democratic Party (PSDB). Later, in 1993, Cardoso was named foreign minister in Itamar Franco's administration. In early 1994, Franco made him minister of the economy. Cardoso assembled a group of gifted economists and long-time friends to prepare the Real Plan. His candidacy to the presidency was supported by a wide ideological coalition of center and left forces and his close competitor Luis Inacio "Lula" da Silva from the Workers' Party was sustained by socialist-left currents. Cardoso was elected by a landslide on the first ballot, winning 34 million votes.

Last but not least, Fernando Henrique Cardoso, the new president inaugurated in 1995, arrives with impressive power credentials: a mandate based on a landslide electoral victory, broad congressional support, and respect among academics and foreign dignitaries; he is arguably one of the most intellectually sophisticated heads of any contemporary state. His track record on social questions indicates that social welfare will remain a key issue in the next administration.

BRAZIL'S TRANSITION IN COMPARATIVE PERSPECTIVE

Few observers would deny the improvements toward the consolidation of democracy in Brazil, nor the faults of the new democracy and the challenges to be overcome.

Compared with countries such as Nigeria, Mexico, Iran, and China, Brazil can claim several positive achievements. Freedom of political organization, expansion of political rights, lack of censorship, and honest elections are guaranteed in the present regime. Clearly, Brazil does not suffer the degree of electoral fraud seen in Mexico, nor the harsh authoritarian rule of Iran or China. Also, despite the existence of military prerogatives over civilian administration, the armed forces have abandoned their traditional threats when there are civilian decisions which they oppose. This contrasts with the persistent militarism of Nigeria. Moreover, another positive feature regarding the country's future is that, despite the socioeconomic disparities, the idea of a single nation in Brazil contrasts strikingly with Russia, Nigeria, Iran, and India, which are dealing with fragmentation over ethnic and religious differences.

The depth and value that Brazil's democratic institutions have acquired might not be enough to ensure them safe passage through severe difficulties. First, the country continues to suffer from weak political institutions in the channeling of interests, in the arbitration of conflicts, and in the guarantee of a moderate degree of predictability in making and implementing decisions. Second, egregious income, regional, gender, and racial inequalities still plague Brazilians. Third, the economy still faces macroeconomic instability and fiscal crises. Finally, the Brazilian state is itself weak and fragmented.

To the extent that the transitions failed to reverse the concentration of executive power by previous rulers, a new hybrid regime looms in contemporary democratization processes. The difficulties of Brazilian democracy are better understood in comparison to other countries that have recently undergone a similar transition. Since the mid-1970s, other authoritarian and communist regimes in southern Europe, Latin America, Eastern Europe, and the former Soviet Union have been replaced through largely nonviolent transitions. One of the main obstacles to democratic governance in most of these newly established democracies is the persistence of powerful institutional instruments and routines of previous authoritarian and totalitarian periods. In all of these countries, the central challenge is to combine the advantages of a strong executive power that provides efficiency of action with institutional checks that guarantee accountability and oversight. These problems are faced by all democracies, but they are particularly acute in new ones.

A common solution has been to grant the executive emergency powers that supersede the normal channels of representation and decision making. The costs of granting executives emergency powers are often compared to the costs of prolonged political gridlock and/or rapid economic deterioration. When such powers have been backed by broad political support, they have at times contributed to successful economic management as many observers say happened in Chile and Korea. However, the potential for abuse of emergency powers can provide opportunities for "soft coups," as was the case in India in 1977. Also, granting the executive the authority to legislate, especially in presidential systems, can undermine the incentives of party leaders to reach compromises. This is

dangerous to polities in which the party system is characterized both by sharp political cleavages and a high level of party fragmentation, as in Brazil.

Since redemocratization, the Brazilian presidency has appeared to be a weak institution. The 1988 Constitution gave greater powers to the Congress and reduced the federal executive's share of public revenues. Although these changes severely restricted the president's powers, the perception of feebleness is due to the quality of the men in office. Sarney was not elected directly by the people, Collor had no party behind him and was corrupt, and Itamar Franco was regarded as an interim president. The performance of these men obscured the reality that the president is far more powerful juridically and politically than the U.S. president.

Despite the poor history of the concentration of executive power in decision making, Cardoso's record as an individual dedicated to democratic principles may turn the still powerful office of the presidency into an asset. Ironically, the most direct path to asserting the oversight role of the Congress and strengthening the judiciary through a constitutional reform may require the short-term use of the executive's authority to simply get these jobs done.

Reform of the federal and state judiciary is another crucial area in which democratic safeguards must be asserted. The construction of a viable set of juridical institutions capable of providing effective judicial review has become an issue of national importance. If the current governmental attention to this issue manifests itself as concrete policy or constitutional law, then Brazil may begin to develop a system of checks and balances—the best remedy for official corruption. Of course, political practice would have to follow suit by accommodating itself to rule changes.

To be stable, democracy requires a widespread belief among elites and masses in the legitimacy of the democratic system. This legitimacy, in turn, is buttressed by the performance of the democratic regime in achieving social equity, maintenance of both individual and social rights, civil order, and personal security. No matter how one measures them, levels of income inequality and mass poverty in Brazil are among the worst in the world. The deep and cumulative social inequalities provide a poor foundation for democracy. Any other developed and stable democracy would suffer when confronted with the sharp inequalities and major social strains that are manifest in

Brazil. In this regard, the present regime may be seen by a majority of Brazilians to lack legitimacy.

These desperate times seem to cry out for a political remedy—something akin to a social democratic, high-growth project. In response, Cardoso has come the closest to formulating of this type of project. His party (the PSDB) clearly seeks to become a Brazilian version of the Spanish Socialist Party of Felipe Gonzalez or the French Socialists of François Mitterrand. The PSDB Manifesto declares that "Brazil is no longer an underdeveloped country, it is simply an unjust country." Increasingly, the motto of "equity with growth" is finding resonance in Brazilian political circles.

The building of a social-democratic project in Brazil confronts several obstacles. The most urgent is the need to bring the economy back to high growth with low, manageable rates of inflation. Since 1985, Brazilians have experienced price controls, savings account freezes, and wage restrictions, all for the purposes of controlling inflation. Even after all of these measures, the country continued to suffer from inflation rates of 30–50 percent per month.

The backbone of current efforts to fight inflation is the Real Plan of former minister of finance and current president of the republic, Fernando Henrique Cardoso. Since it was implemented in July 1994, inflation rates have fallen from 40 or 50 percent a month to 2 percent in January 1995. However, the Mexican currency crisis which erupted in late 1994 and threatened to destabilize financial markets throughout Latin America, Asia, and Europe—the "tequila effect"—threatens the current plan. Although Brazil has a larger reserve of foreign currencies to prevent the kind of speculation which fueled the Mexican crisis, the Real Plan did overvalue the Brazilian currency. Of course, only the long-term results of the plan will determine whether Brazil is headed down the same path as Chile, which effectively brought down inflation and returned to growth, or Mexico, which suffers from an economic meltdown.

The building of a social-democratic project in Brazil confronts other obstacles. Even where organized labor remains politically strong, as in Brazil, its potential role as the foundation for a social-democratic pact is uncertain. As in Mexico and many ex-communist countries, some of the most organized segments of the Brazilian union movement are located in sectors of the economy—the public sector and state-owned enterprises—which stand to lose from the current agenda focused on both privatization and an open economy. What will be the role played by organized labor in the context of a more open, export-oriented economy which faces substantial pressures to contain wage costs? Also, since the 1980s, Brazil's economy has been characterized by high levels of underemployment, unemployment, and large informal sectors. These sectors are fragmented and difficult to organize. Finally, it remains unclear how organized labor will respond to new gender, environment, and race movements, whose objectives are often in disagreement with the labor movement.

In contrast with other countries which are going through democratic transitions, Brazil is characterized by an extraordinary fragmentation of political parties. Previous experiences of pact-building were unsuccessful because the major governing parties, which were little more than an undisciplined amalgam of political bosses and self-concerned leaders, showed a limited capacity to reach a solid agreement around governmental policies. In Mexico, on the contrary, the existence of a dominant corporatist party played an important role in implementing economic and state reforms.

Although political reform seems a difficult issue for Brazilian politicians to tackle, several changes have already been proposed by the Cardoso government. They aim to restrict the number of parties, to enforce the loyalty of politicians to their parties, and to implement an electoral system similar to the present German one that mixes features of proportional and majority-based systems. These reforms will assure better representation and strengthen the accountability of representatives. In turn, the reforms will enhance the chances of building stable majorities in Congress.

The economic performance of developing countries depends on many factors beyond the control of national governments, including the availability of international finance and changing trade balances. Policy choices within the constraints set by these international parameters influence the prospects for democratic consolidation. Now more than ever, what occurs outside Brazil will have a direct influence on domestic politics and economic development. In the current era of free markets and ceaseless flow of information, Brazilian policymakers, business people, workers, and consumers must think globally. Brazil has several productive and competitive economic sectors that may be the harbingers of a future economic powerhouse. Chemicals, pharmaceuticals, metallurgy, biotechnology, paper, and aeronautics top the list of leaders. Global investments in these sectors, technology transfer, and expectations of future trading opportunities are beginning to dominate the current talk in policy and business circles. Once again, Brazilian elites are talking about industrial policy, export promotion, and "Brazil as the country of the future."

Brazil's position in world markets, now more than ever, has been emphasized by policymakers as the linchpin of the country's future. Exports of Brazilian manufactured goods to Europe, Asia, North America, and the rest of Latin America hold out the promise of achieving the perennial Brazilian dream of Brazil as a global, productive powerhouse.

However, poverty and social inequality are not problems easily addressed by simplistic prescriptions for opening markets or expanding exports. The benefits of such actions do not automatically trickle down to those who continue to suffer the indignity of being down and out in the Third World. Cardoso is well aware of these limitations to neoliberal economic policy. In his inaugural address, he noted that the ultimate criteria for judging the efficacy of neoliberal policy will be whether such prescriptions improve the economic and social status of the poorest Brazilians.

At the top of the agenda for addressing Brazil's poverty is reform of the welfare state: The challenges presented by the erosion of the welfare system are many and not easily solved. The first one concerns the narrow social base of contributions used to finance social policies. Social welfare funds remain scarce because workers with low wages do not contribute enough tax revenues and the upper classes engage in tax evasion. Second, the large pool of potential welfare recipients makes for an unwieldy fiscal burden in the absence of fixed priorities. For example, a program to provide lunch to elementary school children 200 days a year would require the provision of meals for a clientele of 30 million on a daily basis—the equivalent of the entire population of Argentina! With Brazil's current fiscal difficulties, such action is financially impossible.

This brings us to the last and more important factor: the Brazilian state. Without the emergence of a state with the capacity to govern, no social democratic project will survive the light of day. It is evident that the state, due to corruption and poorly implemented development policies, has drained away much of the economic resources necessary for recovery. Similar urgent and difficult problems must be confronted by countries such as Russia, Poland, Nigeria, and Mexico where the preeminence of the state over the economy has nurtured a vast corruption network. Also, like Brazil, those countries have been forced to address their economic woes amidst a general crisis resulting from poor economic management, high inflation, and deterioration in the quality of the civil service. The choices facing these states have narrowed dramatically.

The country's fiscal crises and the threat of renewed inflation have chilled support for grand socialist schemes. Nevertheless, the present government appears to believe that a "fiscally responsible," social democratic project is viable. Having brought down inflation, the government has concentrated its efforts on reducing fiscal deficits through drastic cuts in state expenditures, reforming the tax, welfare and administrative systems, and advancing privatization. The fiscal system is notoriously chaotic and regressive—only 7 million out of an economically active population of 65 million pay income tax! The obvious need for tax reform, however, contrasts with the slow pace adopted by the government in solving the problem. This may well be wise from a strategic point of view since any full tax reform package would likely split the party coalition that elected Cardoso. Thus, although the government has already presented Congress with a seemingly radical reform regarding corporate income taxes, reform of the personal income tax system has been postponed. Because a full package is unlikely in the short term, the emphasis is on emergency tax adjustment (mostly reforms to import and export taxes) and on the expansion of privatization. The sale of state assets is expected to create a compensation fund for social investment and reform. The successful management of fiscal crises and some stability in macroeconomic and regulatory policies do not in themselves guarantee the resumption of growth. But they may provide more realistic options about the precise role the state can play in the economy.

It is still difficult to predict how the new democratic systems will perform because current institutional arrangements are not fully consolidated. Several observers tend to focus their analysis on the party coalition that brought Cardoso to power, the coalition of the PFL and the PSDB. Among the more frequently

Cardoso's Proposed Revisions to the 1988 Constitution*

The Public Sector

1. Omit the distinction between national and foreign enterprises. All firms investing in Brazil are to be considered Brazilian, regardless of the national origin of their investors.
2. State firms must be subjected to the same market-imposed criteria of efficiency and solvency as private firms. Public firms that are unable to compete must declare Chapter 11 and be placed in bankruptcy.
3. Foreign firms will be allowed to invest in the mining and energy sectors, including natural gas.
4. Although PETROBRAS, the state oil company, will not be privatized, its monopoly in the domestic petroleum sector will be eliminated. Foreign and domestic private firms will be allowed to engage in joint ventures and unilateral investments in refining, petroleum transport, and drilling.
5. The public monopoly in telecommunications will be broken up, and concessions will be sold to private domestic and foreign firms.
6. Foreign firms will be allowed to purchase shares of state banks undergoing privatization.

The Tax System

1. The ICMS, the state taxes, will be unified into a single national tax system that integrates each state tax with national taxes on industrial products and income.

2. The ITR, or Rural Propriety Tax, will be transferred from the federal government to the municipalities. Local officials will be granted more autonomy over the collection of the ITR.
3. All current taxes on trade, export and import, will be unified into a single national tax on commerce.

The Welfare System

1. The creation of a singular national welfare system that would guarantee a minimum retirement pension to *all* workers—private, public, civilian, and military.
2. The elimination of all state and local welfare programs for civil servants and the establishment of the exclusivity of national welfare policy-making.
3. The establishment of a "floor" on time and amount already paid in to qualify for a public pension.
4. The elimination of "special retirement pensions" for the judiciary, congressional support staff, university professors, journalists, and civil servants.
5. Unification of the system currently administering retirement pensions for rural and urban workers.

*These are *some* of Cardoso's proposals as presented in February 1995. Congress has already approved items 1, 3, 4, 5, and 6 regarding reform of the public sector.

---

heard criticisms of this alliance is that it makes for very odd political bedfellows. The mixture of the social-democratic PSDB with the conservative PFL is strange given that these two ideological tendencies tend to be in opposite political camps in other countries such as Germany, Britain, and France.

The PFL is fundamentally a conservative party dominant in the agricultural northeast, the PSDB is from the industrial southeast. Many observers argue that the PSDB-PFL alliance resembles Getulio Vargas's formula based on a dual system of support: traditional *coronelismo* in the countryside and industrial populism in the cities. There are, however, limits to how far this type of coalition can succeed in Brazil, so long after the death of Vargas and his PSD-PTB alliance. Today the relative weight of rural and urban groups has been altered completely and the mechanisms of political control are no longer the same. Patron-client relations have lost ground to the powers of advertising and television. The kind of nationalism and paternalism that sustained past populism have

eroded. Ironically, Cardoso may be assembling a similar kind of alliance to undo the very institutions built by the Vargas Paradigm. Yet there are many obstacles to that operation. Whereas Vargas did not have to confront any significant force to his left, Cardoso has to confront the PT. In the last elections, more than 17 million people voted for Lula, whose strength lies in his party's grassroots support among thousands of unions. CUT, the workers' confederation with the closest ties to the PT, is composed of two thousand unions with 16 million members. CUT unions organize diverse segments across the public and private sectors, including the federal police, dockworkers, hospital workers, banking employees, oil workers, and rural labor. Cardoso still lacks any base of his own in organized labor and other labor federations; CGT and the Union Force, although often sympathetic to the new president, are independent from him. Lacking his own organized base of support while facing an opposition that *is* organized, presents some imposing obstacles for the new president's reforms.

CHICO CARUSOAG. O GLOBO

Strange Political Bedfellows—The Alliance Between the PSDB and PFL: Fernando Henrique Cardoso (representing the PSDB) as the groom and Luis Eduardo Margulhães (Speaker of the Chamber of Deputies, PFL) as the not-so-submissive bride.
Source: © Chico Caruso, from *O Globo*.

It is too early to talk about whether Cardoso will be successful in updating the *Getulista* formula. Everything is still in play—he is one of the most promising presidents to appear in a long time and most opposition groups have yet to make any challenge. It is also difficult to predict how long Brazilian democracy will endure. There may, however, be grounds for cautious optimism. During recent history, Brazilians have experienced the worst conditions—authoritarianism, official corruption, poverty, and hyperinflation—and yet democracy has survived and grown.

Key Terms

state corporatism
populism
authoritarianism
poder moderador
oligarchy
clientelism

patrimonialism
export-led growth
import substituting
   industrialization (ISI)
developmentalism

Suggested Readings

Section 1

Baretta, Silvio, R. Duncan, and John Markoff. "Brazil's Abertura: A Transition From What to What?" In *Authoritarians and Democrats: Regime Transition in Latin America,* edited by James Malloy and Mitchell Seligson. Pittsburgh: University of Pittsburgh Press, 1987.

Cardoso, Fernando Henrique. "Entrepreneurs and the Transition Process: The Brazilian Case." In *Transitions from Authoritarian Rule: Comparative Perspectives,* edited by Guillermo O'Donnell, Philippe Schmitter, and Laurence Whitehead. Baltimore, Md.: Johns Hopkins University Press, 1986.

Cohen, Youssef. "Democracy From Above: The Political Origins of Military Dictatorship in Brazil." *World Politics* (1988).

Lamounier, Bolivar, Dionisio Carneiro, and Marcelo Abreu. *Fifty Years of Brazil.* Rio de Janeiro: Fundação Getulio Vargas, 1995.

Merquior, J. G. "Patterns of State-Building in Brazil and Argentina." In *States in History,* edited by John Hall. New York: Basil Blackwell, 1986.

Roett, Riordan. *Brazil: Politics In a Patrimonial Society.* 4th ed. New York: Praeger, 1992.

Stepan, Alfred, ed. *Democratizing Brazil: Problems of Transition and Consolidation.* Oxford: Oxford University Press, 1989.

Viotti, Emilia. *The Brazilian Empire—Myths and Histories.* Chicago: Chicago University Press, 1985.

Section 2

Baer, Werner. *The Brazilian Economy: Growth and Development.* 3d ed. New York: Praeger, 1989.

Bethell, Leslie. *The Abolition of the Brazilian Slave Trade.* Cambridge: Cambridge University Press, 1970.

Evans, Peter B. *Dependent Development: The Alliance of Multinational, State, and Local Capital in Brazil.* Princeton, N.J.: Princeton University Press, 1979.

Furtado, Celso. *The Economic Formation of Brazil.* Berkeley: University of California Press, 1966.

Geiger, Pedro P., and Fany R. Davidovich. "The Spatial Strategies of the State in the Political-Economic Development of Brazil." In *Production, Work, Territory: The Geographical Anatomy of Industrial Capitalism,* edited by Allen J. Scott and Michael Storper. Boston: George Allen & Unwin, 1986.

Graham, Richard, ed. *Brazil and the World System.* University of Texas Press, 1991.

Kaufman, Robert R. "Stabilization and Adjustment in Argentina, Brazil, and Mexico." In *Economic Crisis and Policy Choice: The Politics of Adjustment in the Third World,* edited by Joan M. Nelson. Princeton, N.J.: Princeton University Press, 1990.

Section 3

Collier, Ruth Berins, and David Collier. *Shaping the Political Arena.* Princeton: Princeton University Press, 1991. (chapters 3–5.)

Geddes, Barbara. "Building 'State' Autonomy in Brazil, 1930–1964." *Comparative Politics* 22, no. 2 (January 1990).

Lamounier, Bolivar. "Brazil towards Parliamentarism?" In *The Failure of Presidential Democracy,* edited by Juan Linz and

Valenzuela Arturo. Baltimore, Md.: Johns Hopkins University Press, 1994.

Mainwaring, Scott. "Brazilian Party Underdevelopment in Comparative Perspective." *Political Science Quarterly* 107, no. 4 (1993).

Power, Timothy J. "Politicized Democracy: Competition, Institutions, and 'Civic Fatigue' in Brazil." *Journal of Interamerican Studies & World Affairs* 33, no. 3 (Fall 1991).

Schneider, Ben Ross. *Politics Within the State: Elite Bureaucrats and Industrial Policy in Authoritarian Brazil.* Pittsburgh: University of Pittsburgh Press, 1991.

Stepan, Alfred. *Rethinking Military Politics: Brazil and the Southern Cone.* Princeton, N.J.: Princeton University Press, 1988.

Section 4

Alvarez, Sonia. *Engendering Democracy in Brazil.* Princeton: Princeton University Press, 1990.

Candido, Antonio. *On Literature and Society.* Princeton: Princeton University Press, 1995.

Fontaine, P. M., ed. *Race, Class, and Power in Brazil.* Los Angeles: Center for Afro-American Studies/UCLA, 1985.

Gomes, Paulo E. Salles. "Cinema: A Trajectory Within Underdevelopment." In *Brazilian Cinema,* edited by Randal Johnson and Stan Robert. Associated University Presses, 1982.

Johnson, Randel. "Regarding the Philanthropic Ogre: Cultural Policy in Brazil, 1930–1945/1964–1990." In *Constructing Culture and Power in Latin America,* edited by Daniel H. Levine. Michigan: Michigan University Press, 1993.

Matta, Roberto da. *Carnivals, Rogues, and Heroes: An Interpretation of the Brazilian Dilemma.* Notre Dame, Ind.: University of Notre Dame Press, 1991.

Schwarz, Roberto. *Misplaced Ideas: Essays on Brazilian Culture.* New York: Verso Publishing, 1992.

Skidmore, Thomas E. *Black Into White: Race and Nationality in Brazilian Thought.* Durham, N.C.: Duke University Press, 1993.

Section 5

Baer, Werner, and Joseph S. Tulchin, eds. *Brazil and the Challenge of Economic Reform.* Baltimore, Md.: Johns Hopkins University Press, 1993.

Chalmers, Douglas A., Maria do Carmo Campello de Souza, and Atilio A. Boron, eds. *The Right and Democracy in Latin America.* New York: Praeger, 1992.

Dean, Warren. *With Broadax and Firebrand (The Destruction of the Brazilian Atlantic Forest).* Berkeley: California University Press, 1995.

Hurrell, Andrew. "Brazil and the International Politics of Amazonian Deforestation." In *The International Politics of the Environment: Actors, Interests, and Institutions,* edited by Andrew Hurrell and Benedict Kingsbury. New York: Oxford University Press, 1992.

Lamounier, Bolivar, and Edmar Bacha. "Democracy and Economic Reform in Brazil." In *A Precarious Balance: Democracy and Economic Reform in Latin America,* edited by Joan M. Nelson. Washington, D.C.: Overseas Development Council, 1994.

Scheper-Hughes, Nancy. *Death Without Weeping: The Violence of Everyday Life in Brazil.* Berkeley: University of California Press, 1992.

CHAPTER 11

Nigeria

Land and Population

Capital	Abuja*	
Total Area (square miles)	356,668 (more than twice the size of California)	
Population	90 million	
Annual Projected Population Growth Rate (1993–2000)	2.9%	
Urban Population (% of total)	38%	
Ethnic Composition Ethno-Linguistic Groups	Hausa-Fulani	32%
	Yoruba	21%
	Igbo	18%
	Ibibio	6%
	Various dialects	14%
	Other	8%
Official Language	English	
Religions	Muslim	50%
	Christian	40%
	Indigenous	10%

Economy

Domestic Currency	Naira		
GNP (US$)	$31.5 billion		
GNP per capita (US$)	$300		
Purchasing Power Parity GDP per capita (US$)	$1,400		
Average Annual GDP Growth Rate (1980–1993)	2.7%		
Structure of Production (% of GDP)	Agriculture	34%	
	Industry	43%	
	Services	24%	
Labor Force Distribution (% of total)	Agriculture	48%	
	Industry	7%	
	Services	45%	
Women as % of Total Labor Force	34%		
Income Distribution (1992)	% of Population	% Share of Income or Consumption	
	Richest 20%	49.0%	
	Poorest 20%	5.1%	
Total Foreign Trade (exports plus imports) as % of GDP	54%		

Society

Life Expectancy	Female	52
	Male	49
Population per Doctor	6,670	
Infant Mortality (per 1,000 live births)	83	
Adult Literacy	Female	41%
	Male	63%
Average (Mean) Years of Schooling (of adults 25+)	Female	0.5
	Male	1.7
Communications (per 100 people)	Radios	17.0
	Televisions	3.0
	Telephones	0.5
1995 Human Development Index (1 = highest)	Ranks 141 out of 174	

Political Organization

Political System   Military dictatorship

Regime History   Current military regime seized power in a coup in November 1993, replacing the unelected civilian regime of Edward Shonekan. Ibrahim Babangida was the military general who ruled from August 1985 until August 1993.

Administrative Structure   Power is centralized within the military governing body and the Provisional Ruling Council (PRC). However, a system of 30 federal states, plus the Federal Capital Territory (FCT) in Abuja, also exists.

Executive   General Sani Abacha, who seized power in November 1993, holds the title of President of the Federal Republic of Nigeria. Abacha has declared that he will cede power to an elected civilian president in 1998.

Legislature   A bicameral civilian legislature was elected in July 1992. The 91 senators were elected on the basis of equal representation: three from each state, and one from the FCT. The 593 members of the House of Representatives were elected from single-member districts. The legislature was dismissed in November 1993 by Abacha.

Judiciary   The Nigerian judicial system resembles that of the U.S. with a network of local and district courts as well as state-level courts. The state-level judiciaries are subordinate to the Federal Court of Appeal and the Supreme Court of Nigeria, which consists of 15 appointed associate justices and the chief justice. All levels of the judiciary have been subject to manipulation and corruption by the military regimes.

Party System   A decision by the Babangida government in 1989 established a party system consisting of only two parties, the Social Democratic Party and the National Republican Convention. Shortly after seizing power, Abacha abolished both parties.

* Nigeria's capital was officially moved from Lagos to Abuja in December 1991; however many government offices remain in Lagos pending completion of facilities in Abuja.

SECTION 1
The Making of the Modern Nigerian State

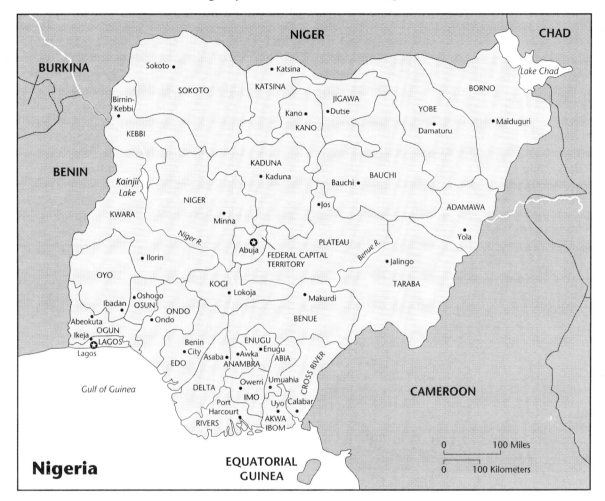

It used to be argued: "As Nigeria goes, so goes the rest of Sub-Saharan Africa." This pithy statement, oft-repeated in both policy and academic circles, reflects at least three positions of interest to this chapter and sheds light on why Africa, and Nigeria in particular, warrant study.

The first concerns Nigeria's size. With a population of almost 90 million, Nigeria is by far the largest country in Africa and among the ten most populous countries in the world. About one out of every five black Africans are Nigerians. The second reason to study Nigeria is that, unlike most other countries on the continent, Nigeria has a salutary combination of *human and material resources* to help it overcome the vicious cycle of poverty and **autocracy** that has become all too prevalent in Africa. Anticipating this breakthrough for the last thirty-five years of independence has been a source of considerable pessimism—some deserved and some not—for Nigeria as well as for all of Africa. If Nigeria, with its vast resources, cannot succeed in breaking this cycle, what does that portend for the rest of Sub-Saharan Africa?

A third reason to study Nigeria is that it is a paradox. Nigeria offers, within a single case, both the negative and positive characteristics that identify Africa. These opposing themes are symbolized by the constant struggle in Nigeria between **authoritarian** and democratic forces, the push for development and the pull of underdevelopment, the burden of public corruption and the pressure for accountability. The paradox is also symbolized by the many attempts to fashion some order out of social incoherence through the creation of a viable nation-state. There are over 250 competing nationalities—or ethnic groups—in Nigeria (largely defined by language differences), which repeatedly clash over economic and political resources. All these factors combine to produce the political entity known as Nigeria with a very low level of popular **legitimacy** and **accountability** and an increasing inability to meet the most basic of its citizens' needs.

Nigeria, therefore, provides a crucible in which to examine questions of democracy and authoritarianism, the pressures and management of ethnic conflict, and the economic underdevelopment brought about both by colonial oppression and independent Nigeria's mismanagement of its vast resources. Each of these issues contributes important lessons for understanding the themes of this book—the democratic idea, collective identities, political economy, and the world of states—particularly as they relate to the developing world. As a single case to use in studying the many issues confronting other African states as well as many developing states in Asia, Eastern Europe, and Latin America, Nigeria commends itself for careful analysis.

NIGERIA AT THE CROSSROADS

Much about Nigeria is controversial. Since gaining independence from British colonial rule in 1960, Nigeria has undergone several political transitions, from democratic governments to autocratic regimes, both military and civilian, and from one military regime to another. In the United States and most of the West, changes of government administration—that is, of the individuals who comprise it—are a regular occurrence; changes of the *type* of government are not. In established democracies, elections are held as mandated by constitutions and according to a fixed schedule: the winners assume office and the losers become the opposition until the next election.

In much of the developing world, particularly in Africa, politics seldom achieve such certainty, and the

results are striking and sometimes disastrous. In its thirty-five years as an independent nation, Nigeria has yet to witness an orderly and constitutional transition from one democratic regime to another. It has experienced six successful coups (most recently in November 1993) and many unsuccessful attempts, and was torn by three years of civil war that claimed over 100,000 military and over a million civilian casualties. Against this background, Nigeria today remains essentially an **unfinished state** characterized by instabilities and uncertainties.

Thomas Hodgkin, a highly regarded scholar of Nigerian history, once exclaimed in frustration that it was "difficult to present a coherent picture of the Nigerian past."[1] One can add that the present is even more confounding and the future very uncertain. Nevertheless, Nigerian politics *has* reached a critical turning point. What is not clear is in which direction the country is moving—toward an increasingly authoritarian future and greater underdevelopment, or toward the promise of democracy and sustainable growth. Nigeria remains a country characterized by ambiguity.

Historical Context

An examination of Nigeria's past reveals much about its development thus far and provides important clues about its future. Nigeria was a British colony from 1914 until its independence on October 1, 1960, although foreign domination of much of the territory had actually begun in the mid-nineteenth century. During that period, Nigeria's resources were extracted, and its people exploited as cheap labor, to further the growth of British society and defray administrative costs of the British Empire. To be sure, some Nigerians benefited from British occupation; some became wealthy and gained appointment to political positions within the colonial structure. For most Nigerians, however, colonialism left a bitter legacy that will be detailed in the pages that follow.

Colonialism left its imprint on *all* aspects of Nigeria's existence. It bequeathed a British political system that was inappropriate in many respects. It empowered certain individuals and groups and weakened others. It left a heritage of harsh authoritarian domination that instilled the idea that there were two sets of rules: one for political leaders and another for the citizenry. British domination left conflicting signals about the democratic idea: on one hand was the legacy of formally democratic institutions; on the other, an authoritarian political culture. Colonialism also contributed to strengthening the collective identities of Nigeria's multiple ethnic groups and fostered enduring competition among them. Most of this competition has occurred between the three largest groups: the Hausa-Fulani, Yoruba, and Igbo (sometimes spelled "Ibo" in older texts). Within the world of states, Nigeria has been a second-class nation, first as the victim of domination by a far stronger, more developed state, and today as a country with a weakening economy. However, it is important to emphasize that, although colonialism bears much of the blame for the initial retardation of the country's political, social, and economic development, Nigerians have not reversed that legacy after three and a half decades of independent rule.

Thus Nigeria's predicament cannot be blamed exclusively on colonialism. The country's economic and political potential has been squandered by a corrupt and self-seeking leadership and its poor policy decisions. Sadly, many of Nigeria's postindependence leaders have been personally more exploitative of the populace than their colonial predecessors. Most of these governments have been run by generals who have come to power via military coups and have ruled the country for all but ten years since 1960.

Nigeria and the Elusive Democratic Idea

Owing as much to the peculiarities of Nigerian politics as to the precariousness of military governments, Nigerian military leaders, despite their extensive control over the organs of the state and economy, are nevertheless influenced by, and to a certain degree susceptible to, popular opinion (a phenomenon that will be explored in greater detail in Sections 4 and 5). Military heads of state who have not *promised* to return power to civilians have seen their tenures cut short by a palace coup. General Yakubu Gowon (head of state from 1967 until 1975) wavered in his commitment to restore democracy and was deposed by a coup not unlike the one that swept him to office. Gowon's successors, first General Murtala Muhammed (who was assassinated in February 1976) and his successor, General Olusegun Obasanjo, immediately pledged to initiate a transition to civilian rule, a vow honored in 1979—Nigeria's only case of the promise fulfilled. Similarly, Major General Muhammadu Buhari, who ousted the civilian government of the Second Republic (1979–1983), refused to pledge a rapid return to democratic

Nigeria's president from 1985–1993, General Ibrahim Babangida enticed civilian politicians to participate in an ever-changing program of transition to democracy which ultimately collapsed.
Source: AP/Wide World Photos.

rule. His popular support consequently wavered, and Major General Ibrahim Badamosi Babangida seized power. It should therefore come as no surprise that Babangida announced a program of transition to democratic rule as one of his first acts as the new head of state. Through an elaborate set of stalling techniques, the Babangida regime engaged in a deliberate effort to extend its tenure. Babangida was astute in that he did not repeat the errors of Generals Gowon or Buhari before him: the promise of a civilian government was never rescinded, although it seemed increasingly distant. This so-called organized confusion involved numerous amendments, annulments, cancellations, the banning and unbanning of politicians, human rights abuses, and repeated extensions of military rule. This "transition" went on for seven years until it was finally derailed in 1993.

The critically important interruption of the transition process occurred when Babangida annulled the presidential election of June 12, 1993, which should have preceded a full withdrawal of the military from the political scene. Interestingly, that election had been widely acclaimed as free and fair, a notable observation that stands in stark contrast to all prior elections since independence, especially those of 1964, 1965, 1979, and 1983. Each of those elections was

Chronology of Major Events in Recent Nigerian Political History

Year	Event
1960	Independence. Nigeria consists of three regions under a Westminster parliamentary model. **Abubakar Tafawa Balewa,** a Northerner, is the first prime minister.
1962	Census conducted; north (Hausa-Fulani) is undercounted.
1963	Fourth region added (excised from western region). New census *over*counts north. Continuing "northernization program" favors Hausa-Fulani.
January 1966	Civilian government deposed in coup. **General Aguiyi Ironsi,** an Igbo, becomes head of state.
July 1966	Countercoup led by **General Yakubu Gowon** (an Anga, from the "Middle-Belt") with aid from northern groups.
1967	Biafran secession (primarily Igbo groups)/civil war begins.
1967	Eight more states created to dilute Biafran regional support and give more power to eastern minorities.
January 1970	Biafran civil war ends.
July 1975	Military coup deposes Gowon; led by **General Murtala Muhammed,** a northerner.
February 1976	Murtala Muhammed assassinated in failed coup led by "Middle Belt" minorities. Muhammed's second-in-command, **General Olusegun Obasanjo,** a Yoruba, assumes power.
1976	Seven more states created, for a total of nineteen.
September 1978	New constitution completed, marking the adoption of the U.S. presidential model.
October 1979	Elections held. A majority in both houses is won by NPN, led by Northern/Hausa-Fulani groups. **Alhaji Shehu Shagari** is elected Nigeria's first executive president.
October 1983	Elections. The NPN landslide victory is marred by widespread accusations of electoral fraud.
December 1983	Military coup led by **General Muhammadu Buhari,** a northerner.
August 1985	Buhari is overthrown by **General Ibrahim B. Babangida,** a northerner, in a palace coup. Promises a return to democracy.
1987	Two new states created (for a total of twenty-one states).
1987	Constituent Assembly convened to write a new constitution.
1988	First round of elections are scheduled for December 1989.
October 1989	Babangida introduces two-party system with designated parties, the NRC and SDP. Elections previously scheduled for December 1989 are postponed to December 1990.

marred by accusations (most subsequently proven) of massive election fraud, vote rigging, and registration tampering. The annulment of the June 12, 1993, election, which was apparently won by southern businessman Moshood Abiola, provoked an angry reaction from a population weary of postponed transitions, military rule, and deception. Was the Babangida regime's program of change at best a transition to nowhere, or at worst, a transition to increased authoritarianism? Although the ultimate intentions of the Babangida regime may never be known, so far the Abacha regime seems to be following the pattern set by its predecessors.

General Sani Abacha seized power in November 1993 from Ernest Shonekan, whose civilian puppet government was selected and supported by Babangida. Abacha, who had held top military positions in both the Buhari and Babangida regimes, including

minister of defense under Babangida, seized the reins of power from the tepid and ineffectual Shonekan. Shonekan's government, never regarded as legitimate because it was literally installed in August 1993 by Babangida, was vulnerable to increasing agitation from both civilian and military ranks. As the head of state, General Abacha prolonged the now established tradition of military dominance and combines increased repression with frequent public commitments to restore a constitutional democracy. As his predecessor Babangida had done nine years earlier, in April 1994, Abacha announced a new program of transition to civilian rule. Nigeria's penchant for such transitions will be discussed in Section 5.

By its very nature, military rule is oppressive and stifling. Under military rulership, political and social liberties are restricted and constitutional rights are limited or nonexistent. In Nigeria, as elsewhere, one of the

Chronology of Major Events in Recent Nigerian Political History (continued)

Year	Event
April 1990	An attempted coup against Babangida fails.
December 1990	Local government elections held.
1991	Nine new states created, for a total of thirty (plus the Federal Capital Territory in Abuja).
December 1991	State governor elections; NRC wins sixteen states, SDP fourteen. State legislative elections are also held.
April 1992	New (1991) census results released. Population figures revised downward to 88.5 million from previous estimates of 100+ million.
July 1992	Federal legislative elections held: 593 representatives; 91 senators. Turnout is 25 percent nationally.
September 1992	Presidential primaries; results are annulled by Babangida for alleged impropriety.
December 1992	Original date for presidential elections; postponed (for the third time) until June 1993.
March 1993	Party conventions are held and party candidates for president are elected. The NRC chooses **Bashir Tofa** (Hausa-Fulani); the SDP selects **Moshood Abiola** (Yoruba).
June 12, 1993	Presidential elections held. The SDP's Abiola is the nominal winner. (General assessment by Nigerian and international monitors: "free and fair.")
June 15, 1993	Restraining order issued to prevent publication of voting results.
June 23, 1993	Annulment of election.
August 27, 1993	Original date for Babangida to leave office and cede power to civilian government. Instead, **Ernest Shonekan** is installed as "civilian president."
November 1993	Defense Minister **General Sani Abacha** seizes power in coup.
June 1994	Moshood Abiola declares himself president and is charged with treason.
July 1994	Convened by Abacha, a new constitutional conference begins its deliberations.
July–Sept. 1994	Pro-democracy strike by the major oil union, NUPENG, cuts Nigeria's oil production by an estimated 25 percent. Sympathy strikes ensue followed by arrests of political and civic leaders.
June 1995	Secret trials of former military ruler **O. Obasanjo** and others accused of planning a coup d'état.
October 1, 1995	General Abacha announces three-year transition to civilian rule to end in 1998.

first acts of every military regime has been the suspension of the constitution. But Nigerians are tired of the pervasive public corruption that has hampered economic growth and threatened personal and social well-being. The effects of corruption coupled with military rule have been economic collapse and the revocation of political liberties. Military government has failed repeatedly to deliver on the promises made to justify seizing power. Beginning in the late 1980s, democratic transitions have swept the globe, including Africa, as populations rally against military, one-party, and dictatorial rule. As more states embrace constitutional democracy, why does Nigeria turn its back on these historic trends? More importantly, after so many false starts and frustrated hopes, when will Nigeria finally be on the path that leads to stable civilian government?

Although Nigerians have been governed by military regimes for twenty-five of the thirty-five years since independence, they have demonstrated a strong tradition of activism and an anti-authoritarian ethos. In times of crises or in the face of tyranny, that activism is often manifested in negative and destructive movements against all forms of authority, including those that are apparently democratic. For example, street protests as well as university and school-based demonstrations have all too frequently degenerated into riots and violent confrontations with the authorities.

It is important to point out that anti-authoritarianism does not necessarily translate into democratic political culture. It is obvious that the complex reality of Nigerian society also includes undemocratic elements. History shows that there has been a low quotient of tolerance, patience, compromise, and respect for the rule of law among political leaders and the general population. More important, the plural nature of Nigerian society could be and has been manipulated to generate social tensions that facilitate the retention of power by autocratic regimes. Indeed, Nigeria's multiethnic society—which has failed in many respects to achieve a truly "collective" identity—adds a substantial degree of complexity to its political puzzle, an aspect that will be revisited throughout this discussion.

Domestic and foreign observers reported the June 1993 presidential election to have been the most peaceful and orderly Nigeria has experienced in three decades.
Source: Reuters/Hulton Deutsch.

Nigeria's Fragile "Collective" Identity

Given the potential explosiveness of ethnic conflict, therefore, it is an irony of history that the Babangida regime sought to manipulate ethnoregional fears and set different sections of the country against one another as part of its survival strategy to resist mounting challenges to its continued stay in office, especially after June 12, 1993. Thus, a quarter-century after a thirty-month bloody civil war to preserve the country's unity was successfully completed, Nigeria stands divided as it has not been since 1970. The Nigerian civil war (also referred to as the Biafran War) began in 1967 and had its origins in ethnic and regional tensions whose roots can in part be traced back to the colonial management of Nigeria's diverse ethnic populations.

In 1967, the predominantly Igbo population of eastern Nigeria attempted to secede and form its own independent nation, which they called "Biafra." The Igbo-dominated Biafran secessionists wanted to break free from Nigeria and its government, which, except for a brief occupation of the central government by Igbo general Ironsi from January to June 1966, had

This cartoon appearing in a Nigerian magazine illustrates the penchant of Nigeria's military leadership to promise civilian rule repeatedly, but to keep it constantly out of reach.
Source: Courtesy *Newswatch Magazine*, Newswatch Communications, Ltd.

been dominated by northerners. Many northern officials had been killed in the coup that brought General Ironsi to power. After Ironsi himself was killed in a countercoup, there was a tremendous backlash against Igbos throughout Nigeria. Igbo migrant laborers were persecuted in the north prior to the war and many fled to their "home" region in the east following the outbreak of violence. The Igbo separatists believed there was no place for them in a Nigeria that would continue to be controlled by ethnic groups from the north by virtue of their greater number. Moreover, since the northern region was less developed economically and educationally than the East and West, there was a fear that the country's progress would continue to be hampered by northern dominance of the federal government. Eventually, the rest of Nigeria was brought together under a government of national unity led by Yakubu Gowon, and in January 1970, Biafra was defeated. Although the war was settled and a lasting peace quickly established, its prosecution exacted a heavy and indelible toll on Nigeria's populace.

Today, the fear of another civil war has led to mass migrations of Nigerians across ethnoregional boundaries, in response to the military regime's handling of mass protests arising from the annulment of the June 12, 1993, election. In fact, ethnic politics remains so potentially volatile that individuals from minority groups in one region have reason to fear for their safety outside their home region.

Nigeria in the World of States

In the modern world, a country's position in the world of states is determined largely by its power, which can be understood either in terms of economic resources or military capabilities, or both. Although Nigeria meets these criteria within the West African region, on a global level, Nigeria has become increasingly marginalized. In Section 2, its political economy is more thoroughly examined. Readers should recognize, however, that Nigeria's position in the world of states is inextricably linked to its political economy, and vice versa. In many respects, the course of Nigeria's political economy has been determined by its global position, as a source first of slaves and harvested natural products such as palm nuts, then of colonial extraction, and finally, of oil exports.

Resource-rich, Nigeria has long been regarded as a potential political and economic giant of Africa. With its large population, extensive oil and natural gas reserves, and a broad agricultural and small industrial base, the country has a solid foundation for the achievement of self-sustaining growth. Yet Nigeria is listed in the UNDP *Human Development Report, 1995* as among the poorest 20 percent of the countries of the world, with a GNP per capita of just $330. Instead of

independent growth, today Nigeria depends on oil revenues, external loans, and aid, a victim of its leaders' bad policies and poor management. Owing to underinvestment in and neglect of agriculture, in the mid-1960s Nigeria moved from self-sufficiency in the production of basic foodstuffs to heavy dependence on imports of those goods less than twenty years later. Rapid population growth (3.3 percent per year), which is outstripping economic growth and agricultural production, further complicates development efforts. Already inadequate health care and social services become even more strained under pressure from population increases. Nigeria's total reliance on oil as a source of foreign earnings has made it vulnerable to price fluctuations in that market. Drastic oil price declines in the 1980s led to a severe shortage of funds and a need to borrow heavily from international lenders.

As the economic crises in Africa and the rest of the developing world began to accelerate in the early 1980s, the International Monetary Fund (IMF) and the World Bank (also known as the International Bank for Reconstruction and Development, or IBRD) were increasingly called on to provide funds necessary for countries to import goods and make their external payments. Though more and more funds were provided, the economic condition of many countries failed to improve, resulting in higher debt levels, increasing debt service (interest and principal payments), and a deepening cycle of decline. Faced with this hardship, the IMF and the Bank designed plans for reorganizing and revitalizing economies called **structural adjustment programs (SAPs),** which will be discussed in greater detail in Section 2.

In many ways, despite the SAPs, the cycle of economic decline has continued in many countries, with general modest recovery in only a handful. Many scholars argue that the cycles of international debt, and the often harsh terms that countries must accept in adopting SAPs, often worsen the dependence of indebted countries on their Western creditors.

Although several of the developed nations and the IFIs have lent financial and other assistance, Nigeria cannot rely solely on outside intervention to address its many problems. Despite its oil resources, Nigeria is increasingly vulnerable and weakened within the world of states. The relative abundance of oil globally further weakens Nigeria's position. The end of the Cold War diminished the strategic significance of Nigeria in the standoff between the Soviet Union and the West, thus decreasing any financial or military benefits that might accrue from such significance. Finally, Nigeria finds itself increasingly isolated in the world community. More and more frequently, international groups such as Amnesty International and Human Rights Watch/Africa accuse it of widespread human rights abuses associated with the military regime. Nigeria's recent addition to the U.S. government's list of countries making insufficient efforts to combat the illegal drug trade, and a growing belief that Nigeria is a way station for international drug trafficking to the United States, has only intensified that isolation. Nigerian officials vehemently object to this classification; still, its imposition and continuation provides yet another indication of Nigeria's declining position. The arrest and secret trials of many former and current military officials in 1995, including Olusegun Obasanjo and his former deputy, Shehu Yar'Adua have provoked widespread condemnation of the Abacha government.

In short, Nigerian politics is precarious, characterized by political and economic corruption, mismanagement, and social strife. What does this portend for the future? If Nigerian politics is truly "at the crossroads," what lies ahead: continued military authoritarianism or participatory democracy? Will the country continue its economic decline or will it witness an economic recovery? Some of these questions will be addressed in the following sections. Next, we identify some of the critical junctures, beginning in the precolonial period, that helped shape the political and socioeconomic landscape of modern Nigeria. An in-depth look at Nigeria's past should provide important clues to its future direction.

CRITICAL JUNCTURES

A number of critical junctures helped shape the character of the Nigerian state. The four identified in the section that follows illustrate the difficult path that Nigeria has taken during the past century. These junctures occurred in the precolonial period, in the imposition and aftermath of British colonialism, in the alternation of military and civilian rule, and in the post-1980 economic collapse precipitated internally by both Nigeria's political corruption and overreliance

on its petroleum industry and externally by its declining position in the world of states.

The Precolonial Period

State Formation The process of state formation in Nigeria precedes the imposition of British colonial rule or any form of European influence. This was a time when the various states, peoples, and societies engaged in social and economic interaction. They included such collectivities as Kanem-Bornu, the Hausa States, Nupe, Igala, Oyo, Benin, the Delta States, and the Igbo communities. The interactions took various forms, including "war and enslavement, diplomacy, treaties, the visits of wandering scholars, the diffusion of political and religious ideas, the borrowing of techniques, and above all trade."[2]

One major element that shaped the course of events in the savannah area was trade with northern Africa across the Sahara Desert. Trade brought material benefits as well as Arabic education and Islam, which gradually replaced traditional, spiritual, political, and social practices in what is now northern Nigeria. Islam's impact was so extensive that, by the first few decades of the nineteenth century, an Islamic theocratic empire had been created through holy war (**jihad**) in much of the territories of the northern savannah. Some regions, such as the area to the south now known as the Middle Belt, peopled by the Tiv, were able to repel jihadist attacks. From the time of its founding, the Fulani empire sought to use a common religion (Islam) and a common language (Hausa) to forge a unity out of the disparate groups in that area of what later became Nigeria. The Fulani empire held sway until British colonial rule was imposed on northern Nigeria around 1900.

Much of Nigeria's precolonial history, including the first thousand years A.D., has had to be reconstructed from oral history because, with few exceptions, a literate culture evolved much later. Evidence from about 1,000 A.D. shows that the first major division between the peoples in this area was neither linguistic nor cultural but geographic. These geographic distinctions had implications for state formation among the peoples of the forest belt to the south as compared to those of the more open savannah to the north. The more open terrain in the north, with its need for irrigation, encouraged the early growth of centralized states. Such states from the eighth century A.D.

Precolonial Polities and
Societies
Source: K. Michael Barbour,
Julius Oguntoyinbo, J. O. C.
Onyemelukwe, and James C.
Nwafor, *Nigeria in Maps*
(New York: Africana
Publishing Company,
1982) 37.

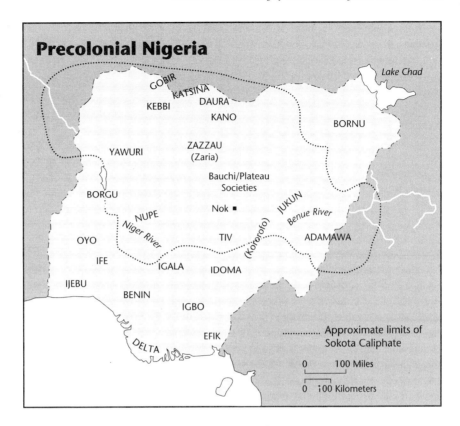

included Kanem-Bornu in the northeast and the Hausa states in the west. The more prominent Hausa states that included walled cities were Kano, Katsina, Zazzau (also called Zaria), Rano, Daura, Gobir, and Biram. Still another attempt at state formation led to the emergence of Jukun kingdom; however, by the end of the seventeenth century, the Jukun became a tributary state of the Bornu empire. An unconsolidated Islamic state (caliphate) with its center in Sokoto and headed by the Sultan of Sokoto, has exercised religious and some political authority since the early nineteenth century.

Toward the southern edge of the savannah lived such groups as the Tiv, whose political organizations seldom extended beyond the village level. Within such societies, politics was generally conducted along lineage and kinship lines. Political authority was diffused rather than centralized. Considering their loose political structures, it is not surprising that they were later described by Western contacts as "stateless societies." Years later, these societies escaped much of the

upheaval experienced by the centralized states and retained much of their autonomy.

The development of collective identities was equally complex in the area now called southern Nigeria. This ranged from the highly centralized empires and kingdoms of Oyo and Ife (now identified with the Yoruba), and Benin in the west to the fragmentary, **acephalous societies** to the east (now identified with the Igbo), and the trading city states of the Niger Delta and its hinterland.

The growth of the kingdoms of Oyo, Ife, and Benin is not attributable to specific external factors as was the case with northern state formation (through Islam) or in the Niger Delta (through European slave trading and subsequently "legitimate" trade). Contact with Europeans along the coast and the hinterland generated social conflicts and tensions and provoked the subsequent loss of autonomy for these polities. External factors led to the eventual disintegration of the Oyo empire in the early nineteenth century through attacks from the Dahomey kingdom to the west (now in the neighboring country of Benin) and Islamic jihadists from the Fulani empire to the north.

The general scenario at the time colonial rule was fully imposed was, however, one in which social conflicts tended to occur more frequently *within* ethnoregional constituencies than between them. War, trade, and other interaction notwithstanding, there was considerable isolation and thus limited contact and conflict across ethnolinguistic lines. Fulani empire-building in much of northern Nigeria involved a holy war on the Hausa States and other political communities from 1804 to around 1830. In the same way, following the decline of the Oyo empire, much of the area now called Yorubaland was the scene of rivalries and warfare from the late eighteenth century through much of the nineteenth century. In the Igbo areas of the east, prior to colonial rule, there was no overarching political authority and therefore little sense of a common history. The intensity of divisions within the fiercely independent Igbo communities was as strong, if not stronger, than those between them and their more hierarchically organized neighbors of the delta.

In conclusion, state formation in Nigeria predates the colonial period although it was either blocked or diverted along a different course as a result of colonial rule. Even after the imposition of the colonial state, these precolonial formations continued to exercise a parallel authority over Nigerians, especially in the Hausa-Fulani areas of the north and among the Yoruba.

The Emergence of the Democratic Idea   Colonialism was a major disruptive force in the development of the democratic idea in Sub-Saharan Africa. Several precolonial societies had democratic elements that may have led to more open and more participatory societies had they not been interrupted by colonialism. Although such a conclusion is necessarily speculative, it is clear that where the more nearly democratic societies existed, particularly in the east, the institutions of colonialism strengthened the authority of traditional chiefs and kings in relation to subjects and weakened the rulers' accountability to the ruled.

Colonialism represented an exclusive control over political and economic resources: The rulers profited at the expense of the ruled. By restricting or barring indigenous popular participation and implementing a policy of divide and rule, the colonial regime was able to limit threats to its preeminent position. Thus Nigeria and many other African states were steeped in these authoritarian traditions for several decades. As Peter Ekeh, a leading Nigerian political sociologist contends:

> The main characteristics of modern African politics . . . would appear to have been fashioned by the colonial experience of the nineteenth and twentieth centuries. If there is any continuity in African political structure—comparable to the continuity which de Tocqueville . . . saw between the old regime and modern Europe—it is not between precolonial and colonial Africa, but between colonial and postcolonial Africa.[3]

In Nigeria, particularly in the Yoruba (west) and Igbo (east) communities, as in much of the rest of Sub-Saharan Africa, one of the two major features of governance in the precolonial era was the doctrine of *accountability:* Rulers could not disregard the views and interests of the governed or they would risk revocation of that consent and loss of their positions. The second element was *representation,* defined less in terms of procedures for selecting leaders and more in terms of the representativeness of those who governed. The overall purpose was to ensure that the ruler and ruled adhered to culturally mandated principles and obligations.

Among the shared traits of many precolonial African societies were tales of origin that traced their political communities to a particular god, heaven, or a mythical ancestor. The pervasive role of religion in the theory and practice of governance ensured that the use of social power was legitimized by divine and supernatural forces. This tendency had further implications. It ensured that most precolonial African political systems were theocratic and, in that regard, absolutist in their demand for loyalty. At the same time, however, these theocratic elements provided important limits to the exercise of power. These limits were further strengthened by additional social structures such as councils of chiefs, secret societies, warrior bands, and age-grade associations.

Among the Jukun in the northeast, for example, "when a new king has been installed, he is told of his power; how he is to use it to benefit the people; and the threat of popular rebellion against his regime and assassination if he deviates from this duty."[4] Similarly, among some Yoruba groups, the Oba (king) could be forced to commit ritual suicide if he was found to be acting in a way inconsistent with the best interests of his people. In other words, it was not uncommon in precolonial societies to find a "use-of-power" contract in which the people could invoke ancestral spirits against a ruler who had abused his power. In societies with strong theocratic elements, such threats would be taken quite seriously. Moreover, the rulers were not exempt from the principle of community. Rights of both the ruler and the ruled were defined in communal rather than in personal terms. The dominant perspective placed more emphasis on the individual's *membership* in various groups and subgroups and the community at large than on individuality *per se.* The survival of the individual, therefore, depended on the survival of the community. On the whole, power was fragmented—in some areas seldom concentrated in the hands of an individual—and there were deeply rooted cultural mechanisms to check the potential for abuse of power. In the same vein, justice was used primarily to enhance the moral fabric of social and political life. Crimes against society often attracted more severe punishment than crimes against the individual.

Modes of participation in decision making in precolonial societies also reflected aspects of the democratic idea. For example, popular discussions preceded public policy decisions in the acephalous societies of the Middle Belt as well as among the Igbos in the east. The age-based system of rule often meant that popular discussions occurred in councils of elders and similar institutions, thereby conferring on older persons greater powers to influence decisions.

Although not indigenous to Nigeria, Islam first appeared around the eleventh century and later spread throughout much of what is now Northern Nigeria through the jihad of the great Fulani leader Uthman dan Fodio in the early nineteenth century. Among the Islamic communities that eventually emerged, political society was highly structured, as dictated by Islamic principles established in the Qur'an, or Holy Book. The leadership structures were considerably hierarchical, dominated by a few educated elites in positions of authority. In addition, although some of the pre-Islamic indigenous beliefs showed deference to important women spirit leaders, under Islam women were consigned to a subordinate position in systems of governance.[5] The Islamic Fulani empire was a confederation in which the rulers (**emirs**) of constituent units

(called emirates) owed allegiance to the *sultan,* who was the temporal and spiritual head of the empire, The sultan's powers, in turn, were circumscribed by the obligation to observe the principles of Islam in fulfilling his duties.

For their part, the empires and kingdoms in the forest belt to the south combined elements of monarchy with checks on power not unlike those monarchies in other countries during the same period. Within this framework, the ruler was essentially a constitutional monarch whose authority depended on the council of chiefs, the deities, and various corporate bodies that could articulate public views.

Impact of Colonial Rule

Colonial Rationale Perhaps no words capture the process that led to Nigeria's present geographic identity better than these three: recent, accidental, artificial. The facts about Nigeria's creation are clear. Before 1900, and specifically from the middle of the nineteenth century, parts of what later became known as Nigeria had come under the British colonial sphere of influence through charters granted to British companies. Initially, there were three territories that were treated as separate entities: the Lagos Colony, the Oil Rivers Protectorate (from 1893 known as the Niger Coast Protectorate), and the Royal Niger Protectorate.

Nigeria as a future nation was a product of the competition for African territories by European imperial powers. The "scramble for Africa" occurred after the 1884–1885 conference in Berlin, at which the conditions for Africa's colonization were worked out, especially the principle of "effective occupation." Under this principle, the "effective occupation" of considerable portions of the Nigerian territory enabled the British to claim Nigeria during the scramble. What were the Europeans scrambling for? A full explanation of European colonization in Africa is an amalgam of interstate rivalries, the pursuit of material gains by trading firms, and the ambitions of particular individuals to achieve military conquests. In general, Europe needed raw materials to fuel the rapid industrialization taking place in the late nineteenth century, which in turn would keep their respective empires afloat. In short, much of British initiative in Nigeria with regard to territorial and other acquisitions was driven by competition for trade and empire in Africa with other European imperial powers, particularly France and

Germany. The same dynamics were duplicated in other parts of the continent and the world.

In 1900, Britain revoked the company charters so that it could administer each of these territories more directly, and separately, from London as part of the British colonial empire. The territories were now known as the Lagos Protectorate, the Protectorate of Southern Nigeria, and the Protectorate of Northern Nigeria. In 1906, the Protectorates of Lagos and Southern Nigeria were brought under a single administration. Nigeria's identity took its final geographic form (at least in terms of its *external* borders) in 1914 following the amalgamation of the Northern and Southern Protectorates by the British colonial administration. This step was accomplished under the leadership of the colonial governor-general, Sir (later Lord) Frederick Lugard. Interestingly, even the name "Nigeria," by which the amalgamated territory came to be known, was first suggested in 1898 by Flora Shaw, who later became Lugard's wife.

Foundations of Nigeria's Political Economy   Even before colonial rule, contacts between communities in what is now Nigeria and the international environment were dominated by commerce. Trade flourished between coastal territories and various European principalities by sea and between northern territories and North Africa and Arabia through the Sahara Desert. Colonial rule strengthened the former channels while it redirected the flow of trade to North Africa along the coast. Beginning in the mid-nineteenth century, commercial interaction was dominated by Western Europe, especially Britain. In the case of Nigeria, this overseas exchange of commodities greatly influenced the evolution of the economy. The terms of trade were unfavorable to Nigeria because its major trading partner, Britain, was also its colonial master. That Nigeria was inserted into the modern international economy when it was a subordinate, colonial territory has meant that it has had to operate within terms designed by the more dominant and experienced members of the international system. Nigeria has since found it difficult to overcome the initial tilt toward commerce, especially in primary products, in its political economy.

At a second level, the colonial experience helped shape the character of the Nigerian state in its relation to the international capitalist system. The concept of the state introduced into the colony was a set of administrative, legal, and coercive systems whose over-riding purpose was to restructure relationships within and between civil society and public authority in order to integrate the local economy with metropolitan (that is, European) capitalism. This highly circumscribed concept of the state was imposed on the colony at a time when Europe was developing a more varied concept of the state. The Nigerian colonial state was conceived and fashioned as **interventionist.** In contrast to Britain, where political freedoms and free-market capitalism limited state action, in Nigeria the colonial state was unhindered in the policies it pursued to achieve its economic objectives. Why were European powers inconsistent in their approaches to state and economy in Europe as opposed to the colonies? It is important to realize that Europe was not interested in creating economic competitors. The principal goals of the British colonial enterprise were to maintain tight control over the pattern of economic growth in Nigeria and the flow of resources from the colonies to the metropole. Of secondary concern was the creation of an economic environment driven by free markets and private enterprise.

Colonial policy thus helped to create a particular perception of the relationship between state and economy. It fostered an interventionist state, defined as one that intrudes into the major sectors of the economy and society. To a certain degree, most states get involved in the provision of infrastructure and the establishment of public enterprises within their domestic economies (the establishment of the federally financed interstate system of highways in the United States is one example). But an interventionist state goes far deeper into the management of the economy, tightly controlling and frequently establishing significant ownership positions in areas as diverse as agriculture, banking, commerce, manufacturing, transportation, mining, education, health, and employment. Nigeria has conformed to this characterization from the early days of the colonial administration. The problems caused by massive state intervention have continued to plague Nigeria to the present, a subject that will be discussed in Section 2.

Impact of Colonialism on Democratic Ideas   Colonialism introduced a cultural dualism—a clash of cultures, values, and political systems—between the traditions of precolonial society and the dictates of the West. Although colonialism was unsuccessful in its attempts to supplant traditional values (particularly in the north) with western ones, the result of its efforts was frequently a moral disorientation. Traditional cultural traits, which had ensured accountability in society, were gradually replaced with the ideas of individualism. The religious beliefs of traditional society, particularly as they pertained to governance and accountability, were also altered by colonialism. As Christianity spread throughout southern Nigeria, it carried with it a monistic and abstract view of a universal, remote god who was not directly concerned with issues of daily governance—as were the deities of traditional beliefs—and who could be approached only through specific practices and observances.

The marginalization of traditional norms and practices early in the colonial regime caused a weakening of the indigenous basis for the accountability of rulers and the social responsibility of the governed. These tendencies were complicated by the weakening of traditional checks on abuse of office, such as those outlined above. Traditional religion was condemned as paganism; age-old checks on monarchies were selectively tampered with, and pseudomonarchical systems of authority were introduced into acephalous societies, such as those of the Igbo, which had a long tradition of consensual or participatory modes of government. Notably, the British appointed **warrant chiefs,** who were entrusted with "executive" authority where no such authority had been conferred on an individual in precolonial society. In the north, the British employed a system of rule that left many of the traditional leaders in place, many of them agents of the colonial regime or whose areas of autonomy did not challenge British interests.

The Culture of Colonialism. Colonial rule left Nigeria with institutions that required a "participant" political culture—that is, it provided Nigeria with the machinery of parliamentary democracy following the Westminster model—but it had the effect of socializing the local population to be passive subjects rather than responsive participants. In other words, even as colonial rule sought to implant democracy in principle, in practice it was a form of military rule that bequeathed an authoritarian legacy to independent Nigeria.

Colonialism also led to the development of two public realms. The first, following a now classic essay by Peter Ekeh, can be described as the "communal realm"—derived from membership in an ethnic or subethnic group—in which an individual is identified as Igbo, Tiv, or Yoruba, for example.[6] The second was a "civic realm" derived from the colonial administration and its imposed institutions in which citizenship was universal. Both realms fed on each other, though the communal realm was often stronger in certain respects than the civic realm. Contrast this dichotomy with more settled sociopolitical societies in which the national civic realm tends to prevail over all others. The direct result of this dichotomy in Nigeria is that the citizen functioned simultaneously in two different publics—the communal (parochial) and the civic (national)—and this development has had major consequences. For the populace, there are unresolved questions as to how one's citizenship is defined and to which group one owes primary loyalty. Likewise, for those in government, there are persistent questions about whose interests should be served at any given time, the national or the parochial? In fact, the advent of the colonial civic realm and the colonial state itself (as well as the successor postcolonial state) was seen as an alien, exploitative force from which rights were to be extracted and to which duties and taxes were to be withheld.

The colonial enterprise bequeathed a state-centered and state-directed economic system for the extraction of agricultural produce for overseas export. However, as colonial powers did elsewhere in Africa, Britain severely limited government expenditures in Nigeria with the result that the colonial administration was overstretched and overcommitted. To perform its functions, therefore, the colonial administration had to build up a support system of Nigerians who would be incorporated into the management structure of the colony. These individuals were carefully selected by the colonialists, and initially were the traditional elite and rulers who were willing to work with the colonial government under a system of governance that was known as **"indirect rule."** In the south, where Christianity and Western education had penetrated, the British were able to create such offices as warrant chiefs. In the north, where more developed, hierarchical political structures already were present, and the British had significantly less penetration, they utilized indigenous structures. During the period of decolonization initiated after 1950, a select group of educated elites, most of them southern, were employed to stabilize the colonial enterprise.

The evolving state system was therefore one with ambitions that exceeded its abilities. It nevertheless became a large and cumbersome entity with a penchant for intervention in both society and economy. The emerging Nigerian state was built on the exploitative logic of the colonial enterprise and required an intrusive political apparatus that the emerging indigenous elite learned to use to their advantage. The net result was that leaders of the anticolonial movement developed a view of the state that regarded control of the state as a means to pursue personal and group interests rather than broad collective, national interests. It further cemented among the elite, according to Larry Diamond (citing Mosca) a perspective that "all moral and material advantages depend on those who hold power . . . [and] there is no act of chicanery that will not be resorted to in order to attain power."[7] The emergent quest for power and material advantage among African elites was at odds with many of the precolonial society's more democratic traditions, as discussed earlier. Futhermore, it discouraged grassroots participation in governance, accountability, and public service.

This approach to political and economic life by the elite essentially drained the democratic process of much of its substance. The culture of venality among the indigenous elite fostered a respect for only the trappings, but not the substance, of democracy. This emerging elite increasingly focused on the rituals of periodic participation in elections during the first few years following independence. Eventually, however, they became so arrogant and dismissive of elections, and they had perfected election-rigging devices to such an extent, that they could boast on the campaign trail (even while in opposition strongholds) that whether or not the people voted for them, they would surely be returned to power.

Un-Collective Identities: Ethnic Politics Under Colonialism   At least since the late 1940s, politics in Nigeria has been characterized by competition for access to public resources. This competition has developed along societal cleavages often defined in ethnic terms and can be explored along a number of different dimensions. Among ethnic groups, the three largest—the Hausa-Fulani, Igbo, and Yoruba, which together comprise approximately 65 percent of contemporary Nigeria's population—have come to dominate the political process. The irony is that these group identities were clearly delineated only in the context of colonial rule and did not exist in their contemporary

forms in the precolonial era. Although the most crucial and obvious defining characteristic of these ethnic groups is language, it is instructive to note that the majority of Nigeria's inhabitants belong to a *single* group of languages called the Niger-Congo family. This language group covers the entire southern part of modern Nigeria as well as the major part of the Middle Belt peopled by minority groups. The next most extensive language group is called Afro-Asiatic and covers much of the far and central north, followed by the smaller Nilo-Saharan group in the northeast.

The notion that Nigerian history is one of interethnic conflict is largely an invention of the colonial rulers. What happened in the latter part of colonial rule, especially with the emergence of the now dominant Hausa-Fulani, Igbo, and Yoruba ethnic groups, can be described as a classical case of an "invention of tradition" in the context of colonial rule. To manage the colonial enterprise, the British needed to establish boundaries and administrative areas. They also had concerns about their own security. The documentation of interethnic conflict was part of the effort to divide and rule. If the indigenous groups could be pitted against one another, there would be no unified threat of opposition to British authority. One way in which this objective was achieved was by providing resources to some groups—albeit limited resources—such as missionary education and lower-level civil service jobs, while depriving others, thus fostering an environment of envy and mistrust.

Though the colony was unified officially in 1914, colonialism had profoundly different effects on the northern and southern regions. The southern Nigerian coastal cities of Lagos and Calabar, and the regions that encompass them, experienced both the benefits and burdens of colonial occupation. The proximity of these capitals to the Atlantic Ocean made them important hubs for trade and shipping activity, around which the British built the necessary infrastructure—schools, roads, ports, and the like—in order to facilitate the colonial enterprise and resource extraction. In addition, a large African civil service developed in the south: labor was needed for resource extraction as well as various colonial projects. Northern Nigeria, which was administered in a less intrusive manner (that is, in regard to direct contact with British personnel), received few of these benefits. It was remote from the shipping capitals of the south and, though home to the most populous ethnic group in Nigeria, the Hausa-

Fulani, it possessed fewer resources of interest to the colonialists. Thus a pattern of uneven development was established whereby the basis for modern economic development was laid in the south, whereas the north was deprived of similar benefits.[8] The disparities between northern and southern Nigeria that were exacerbated by colonial rule would remain a source of discord after independence. Instead of fostering an environment of cooperation and conciliation—arguably essential in multiethnic societies—colonial rule fostered ethnoregional distinctiveness and rivalry.

Note from the foregoing discussion that many of the traditional ethnic groups overlapped and experienced some precolonial interaction, and they broadly shared common linguistic origins. There were also important differences among them, as outlined above, which have been emphasized throughout the twentieth century. Reinforced by colonial authorities and championed by local educated elites, these groups began to propound tales of origin that provided the bases for wider self-definition and a more exclusivist identity and heritage. Simply put, indigenous elites were able to rally followers based on notions of common identity. The self-declared representatives for these groups mobilized popular support, then constantly lobbied and challenged the colonial administration. Extensive attempts were made to develop standardized and written forms of the languages and histories of these groups where few had existed previously.

The three large groups did not begin to mobilize for political purposes until the late 1940s, when independence for Nigeria became a distinct possibility. Beginning in 1922, the colonial regime had acceded to a very restricted form of electoral representation for inhabitants of two southern cities, Lagos (three seats) and Calabar (one seat), in the colonial legislative council. Importantly, electoral contests for those seats were not conducted along racial, ethnic, or cultural lines. Even foreigners, as long as they were citizens of the British Commonwealth (made up of Britain and its colonial territories), could participate as voters or candidates. By the early 1940s, however, Nigerians began to consider this arrangement inappropriate and opposed the election of foreigners, black or white, into the council.

The early ethnic-based associations were initially concerned with nonpolitical issues: promoting mutual aid for housing and education, as well as sponsoring cultural events. With the encouragement of ambitious leaders, however, these groups took on a more political character.[9] As the prospects for independence increased, indigenous elites began to divide along ethnic lines because the appeal to ethnic identities was an effective means of mobilizing support. It was in this context that such pan-ethnic cultural groups as the *Jamaar Mutanen Arewa* (for the Hausa-Fulani in the north), *Egbe Omo Oduduwa* (for the Yoruba in the western part of the south), and the Igbo State Union (for the Igbo in the east) were formed. These groups subsequently served as the nuclei of the parties that succeeded the colonial regime after independence (namely, the Northern Peoples Congress, or NPC, in the north, and the Action Group, or AG, in the west) or took over effective control of the party (as in the National Council for Nigerian Citizens, or NCNC, in the east). This development was enhanced by the way federalism was introduced to Nigeria in 1954, six years before independence.

As independence approached, the British began to make provisions to bring Nigerians into the administration of the country. As shown on the map on the following page, in 1954 Nigeria became a federation of three states (actually referred to as regions until 1967). However, each of the federated units soon fell under the domination of one ethnic group and one party. The Northern Region came under the control of the NPC, associated with and dominated by Hausa-Fulani elites. In the southern half of the country, the Western Region was controlled by the AG, which was associated with and controlled by the elites of the Yoruba group. Likewise the Igbo, the numerically dominant group in the Eastern Region, were closely associated with the NCNC, which became the ruling party there. Thus the distinctive and often divisive ethnic and regional characteristics of modern Nigeria were reinforced during the transition to independence.

This amalgamation of territories, each with a distinct culture and history (and frequently language), was to have severe and complex implications for Nigeria that have continued to the present day. Consider that in a celebrated statement made in 1947, one of the first generation of indigenous Nigerian political leaders, Chief Obafemi Awolowo, argued that "Nigeria is not a nation. It is a mere geographical expression. There are no 'Nigerians' in the same sense as there are 'English,' 'Welsh,' or 'French.' The word 'Nigerian' is merely a distinctive appellation to distinguish those who live within the boundaries of Nigeria from those who do

Nigeria in 1955: Divided into Three Federated Regions
The administrative division of Nigeria into three regions
later became the basis for ethnoregional conflicts.
(Note: At the time of independence, the southeastern
part of the country, which had been governed as a trust
territory, opted to become part of independent
Cameroon; two northern trust territories opted to
become part of independent Nigeria.)
Source: K. Michael Barbour, Julius Oguntoyinbo,
J. O. C. Onyemelukwe, and James C. Nwafor, *Nigeria in
Maps* (New York: Africana Publishing Company,
1982) 39.

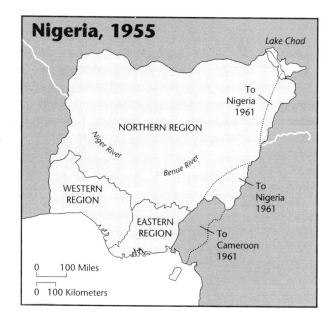

not."[10] One of Awolowo's contemporaries, Alhaji Abubakar Tafawa Balewa, also warned in 1948, "Since 1914 the British Government has been trying to make Nigeria into one country, but the Nigerian people themselves are historically different in their backgrounds, in their religious beliefs and do not show themselves any sign of willingness to unite . . . Nigerian unity is only a British creation for the country."[11]

Interestingly, in 1959, a year before the country achieved independence, Chief Awolowo emerged as the head of government in one of the regions that subsequently constituted Nigeria's fledgling federal arrangement. And Balewa, a Hausa, became head of the federal administration that would oversee the end of colonial rule, and subsequently led the first independent Nigerian government as its prime minister. These influential leaders, and others like them, helped entrench the belief that Nigeria was a mere "geographical expression." The proliferation of these views made the task of governing an independent Nigeria, ostensibly concerned with national unity, all the more difficult.

A confluence of factors accelerated the move to independence in the years following World War II. In addition to increased nationalism, influenced in part by the success of Indian and Pakistani nationalism in winning independence from Britain in 1947, the British faced many structural pressures. The establishment

of the United Nations in 1945 was based in part on principles calling for the self-determination of peoples and the eventual end of colonial rule. More importantly, Britain was weakened severely by the war and could no longer maintain the expense of its far-flung empire.

When the British finally gave up their colony and granted Nigeria independence in 1960, the new central government came to be dominated by northerners by virtue of their greater population. Finally in control of the developmental resources and distributive capabilities of the state apparatus (jobs, finances, and other forms of patronage), the government instituted a process of "northernization" whereby the previously underprivileged north would be granted jobs, investments, and other political favors. This policy was implemented often at the expense of southerners who had achieved a position of relative strength under British rule.

Postindependence: Alternating Governments but Consistent Themes

The postindependence period is, in actuality, a *collection* of junctures. Although many events have occurred in the postindependence period, it is treated here as one juncture because the year 1960 marked a significant break with the colonial past: It signaled the initiation of self-government and a new set of problems. The importance of this juncture is that it captures a persistent phenomenon in Nigerian politics, namely, the alternation between military and civilian rule and, significantly, the alternation between different military regimes. This roller coaster of regimes and transitions has meant that independent Nigeria has experienced little stability and constancy and, as a result, has been unable to institutionalize political norms or even to establish the "rules of the game" that provide the foundation for democratic governance.

Rather than a detailed discussion of the specific characteristics of each government that has been part of this alternating pattern, it will be more useful to discuss the central themes that led to the pattern of alternation and the key issues that precipitated the downfall of each successive government. With every change in government has come a change in regime, with distinct differences between the patterns of military rule. These have ranged from the relatively consensual and ultimately productive Murtala/Obasanjo government, to the civilian regime of Shagari, to the increasingly harsh authoritarian rule of Sani Abacha. Even though the governments and regimes have changed with alarming frequency (and only once via electoral transfer), the themes have remained remarkably consistent.

Three principal themes have been apparent in the postindependence juncture. The first is the ever-present bane of Nigerian development: corruption and clientelism. The second theme is concerned with Nigeria's ethnic conflict and its embrace of a distinctive federalism, which has been proposed as a means of mitigating and diffusing ethnic conflict. Finally, the pervasive role of the highly politicized Nigerian military warrants attention. Each of these themes is closely interrelated and can be said to have played a significant role in the downfall of each successive postindependence regime.

The First Republic   In many ways, the First Republic embodied each of the critical issues introduced above. Its government's inability to deal effectively with the problems of collective identity, federalism, corruption, and the military set the stage for the cycle of alternating governments which followed. Nigeria's postindependence juncture essentially began poorly when the early politics of independence became defined by resource competition and its concomitant, control of the state. The Nigerian civilian government

which held power from 1960 until 1966 was a study in violently partisan and ultimately failed governance. The ruling coalition for the first two years, ostensibly an alliance between the predominantly Igbo NCNC and the Hausa-Fulani dominated NPC, quickly turned into a northern-only coalition when the NPC achieved an outright majority in the legislature.

Corruption. Having benefited less from the positive economic, educational, and infrastructural aspects of colonialism, the northerners who dominated the First Republic set out to redistribute resources in their own direction. A policy of "northernization" ensued, which brought them into direct conflict with their southern counterparts, particularly the Yoruba-based Action Group in the early days of independent rule, but later with the Igbo-dominated NCNC as well.

In 1962 the leader of the Action Group, Obafemi Awolowo, became embroiled in an ideological dispute with his associate, Chief Samuel Akintola, then AG premier of the Western Region. When this internal conflict led to a political crisis in the regional assembly, the NPC-led national government immediately seized the opportunity and declared a state of emergency in the region. The NPC government used the pretext of the crisis to marginalize its old adversary Awolowo, eventually trying and convicting the Yoruba leader on questionable charges of treason for which he served a prison sentence from 1962–1966. By most accounts, Awolowo's trial and subsequent detention were based more on the desire to silence a political rival than on legal procedures, for which the NPC, with support from the NCNC and the Akintola faction of the AG, showed little regard. This early lack of respect for the rule of law set a significant precedent for Nigerian politics.

Akintola, meanwhile, remained western premier, though he allied himself with the NPC government, causing a split in the AG. With the influential Awolowo sidelined, the NPC-led national government subdivided the Western (largely Yoruba) Region into West and Mid-West, making the subsequent dilution of Yoruba political power considerably easier. However, the violence escalated, especially among the Yoruba factions in the west, between supporters of Awolowo and those of Akintola.

The NPC-dominated government engaged in additional acts of political corruption as well. Although both the 1962 and 1963 versions of the census were attempts to inflate artificially the ranks of northern versus southern constituencies (in order to receive a larger allocation of parliamentary seats), the 1963 results, which blatantly overcounted the north, were used as the basis for allocating seats after the 1964–1965 elections. Earlier, defections from several minority parties to the NPC coalition had left the NPC a majority in the legislature and removed the need to have the NCNC as its junior partner. Thus shut out from the ruling coalition, the NCNC and its leader, Nnamdi Azikiwe, allied with Awolowo's wing of the Action Group to form the United Progressive Grand Alliance to contest the elections. However, those elections were based on a fraudulent census and falsified ballots, together with violence against and intimidation of supporters and candidates alike. With all the resources at its disposal, an NPC "victory" was assured.

Enter the Military. As the rivalries intensified, Azikiwe, who was also president in the First Republic (then a largely symbolic position), and Tafawa Balewa, the prime minister, separately approached the military to ensure that, if it came to conflict, they could count on its loyalty. Thus, in the words of Billy Dudley, "In the struggle for personal survival both men, perhaps inadvertently, made the armed forces aware that they had a political role to play."[12] In doing so, Nigerian politicians found themselves on the slippery slope of a politicized military, a move that has proved irreversible during the subsequent thirty years.

The first military coup, in January 1966, was led largely by Igbo officers. Aguiyi Ironsi, also an Igbo, became head of state by dint of being the highest ranking officer rather than a coup plotter. The announced aim was to end violence and unrest in the Western Region and stop political corruption and the abuse of the political process by the northern-dominated government by *centralizing* the state apparatus. Although Ironsi claimed to be multiethnic in his perspective, other Nigerians, particularly northerners, were deeply suspicious of his pledges and his attempted revocation of federalism. Indeed, those suspicions were bolstered by the fact that several northerners were killed in the coup, including Tafawa Balewa and the premier of the Northern Region, Sardauna of Sokoto, Sir Ahmadu Bello. The coup was seen as antinorthern and, predictably, the countercoup plotting began almost immediately. A coup of July 1966 brought Yakubu Gowon to power as head of state.

Gowon successfully prosecuted the Biafran War, and when it was over, he presided over national reconciliation with the mostly Igbo separatists, which pro-

ceeded fairly smoothly. He also oversaw an increase in the armed forces from about 10,000 men in 1966, to nearly 250,000. These men in uniform reaped the benefits of the oil boom and corruption was widespread. Influenced by the unwillingness of the military elite to relinquish power and the spoils of office, Gowon opted to postpone the return to civilian rule from his original schedule of 1976. He was overthrown in 1975 by Murtala Muhammed, who promptly reactivated the transition program.

Military Rule Through its extensive and unrestrained use of the coup d'état, the highly politicized Nigerian military has often justified its takeover and stay in power as a corrective for civilian government corruption. Not surprisingly, the military itself has not only indulged heavily in such behaviors, it also has fomented corruption and clientelism among civilians.

In addition, the military has proclaimed itself a force for the "restoration of democracy," although the cause of democracy has been subverted by the long periods of military rule. The distinctive characteristics of military rule, however, go well beyond the disruption and erosion of the social infrastructure of democracy. Military governments cannot be held accountable to an electorate. They show disdain for human rights and political freedoms, and though the threat of a "barracks coup" is always present, military rulers cannot be removed by the ballot box if they will not leave voluntarily. The strength of the Nigerian military as an institution, and of the individuals who control it, was fundamentally enhanced after its first taste of power. Following the first coup in 1966, and such developments as centralized planning of the war economy during the civil war and, importantly, federal control of petroleum revenues after the war, the central government became much more powerful than the states. The access to and control of this source of wealth makes a military return to the barracks difficult. The combination of greed and arrogance induce military rulers to find ways to cling to power. The only exception was Murtala Muhammed's successor, General Obasanjo, who also allowed considerable social freedoms and political liberties before peacefully ceding power in 1979.

Nigerian Federalism and the Politics of Collective Identity In the period after independence, the number of federated states was increased through the division of existing ones. Initially, this was done to undermine the control of the Yoruba Action Group and the influence of Awolowo, as well as to respond to long-standing demands of local communities, through the creation of the Mid-West Region in 1963. As more ethnic groups became politically active, they also pressured the central government for greater autonomy and for their "own" states. Thus the number of subnational units increased from three at independence in 1960 to thirty by 1991.

The successive exercises in remolding the federation have had three major effects. First, they have diluted the power of the states as compared to the central government. Second, they have given minority groups greater political space (in terms of new states). Third, these actions have provoked subethnic rivalries among the various ethnic groups. The issues and problems associated with Nigerian federalism are addressed in Section 3, "Organization of the State." For now it is important to recognize that these developments have not altered the dominant framework of Nigerian politics inherited at independence: north versus south and sectional competition among the Hausa-Fulani, Igbo, and Yoruba. Adding to this precariousness is the fact that the federation continues to be perceived as politically imbalanced in favor of the larger and more populous north, and educationally and economically in favor of the south.

In addition, other types of cleavages, particularly those of a religious nature, have had the effect of further dividing Nigerian society. The country today shows rough parity between two world religions (50 percent Muslim; 40 percent Christian). Often, these cleavages are perceived to be reinforcing (whether or not they are in reality), resulting in popular perceptions of a Christian south and a Muslim north, a view that tends to deepen, rather than diffuse, societal discord. Significant numbers of Yoruba in the southwest, for example, adhere to traditional religious beliefs, while the percentage of Muslims and Christians are almost equal.

The Second Republic　The president of the Second Republic, Alhaji Shehu Shagari, and his ruling National Party of Nigeria, NPN (the northern successor party to the First Republic's NPC), did little to assuage the mistrust between the various parts of the federation. Shagari's government was also perceived as a defender of northern interests, and it failed to stem the

increase in bribery, smuggling, and the diversion of government proceeds from petroleum production. The most flagrant acts of corruption in the Second Republic, however, were the methods employed by the NPN to "win" its 1983 reelection bid. Voter registration was falsified, names were added to the register in some constituencies and mysteriously deleted in the south. During the election itself, massive fraud was committed on ballots and in polling stations. When it was all over, the NPN had won an implausible thirteen of (then) nineteen state governorships and overwhelming majorities in the House and Senate elections. In a multiple-candidate race, Shagari won reelection with an equally implausible 47 percent of the vote. Led by General Buhari, the military seized power just a few months later in December 1983.

Conclusion: Corruption and Alternating Governments　The Nigerian experience, with its alternating governments, suggests several related points. The first is that **clientelism,** corruption, and authoritarian governing structures hinder economic potential. Clientelism is the practice by which a particular group receives disproportionate policy benefits or political favors from a political patron, usually at the expense of the larger society. In Nigeria, patrons are often linked to clients by ethnic, religious, or other cultural ties, and these ties have generally benefited only a small elite. The risks such clientelism and corruption pose to the broader population are enormous, and the results obvious, as presented in the preceding discussion. A more recent example of such abuse of authority is the discovery in 1994 that over $12.2 billion out of $12.5 billion of oil revenues generated during the Gulf War crisis had been disbursed clandestinely to top military and appointed officials in the Babangida administration—evidence of corruption on an unprecedented scale. Authoritarian and clientelist tendencies, therefore, coupled with a profound neglect of infrastructure, have prevented full utilization of productive capacity.

The ruling elites, whether military or civilian, have used state power to redistribute wealth in their favor, rather than toward the creation of new wealth and investment in productive assets that would benefit the country as a whole. Thus the three themes in this juncture are tightly linked. The abuse of state power through corrupt and clientelist actions has perverted federalism into a means to distribute what is euphemistically called "the national cake" to explicitly ethnic clients rather than using federalism to mitigate conflict. The ethnic basis of political power, compounded by corruption, is inherently unstable, always opening the door for a military seizure of power. By engaging in the same corrupt behavior as their civilian counterparts, however, military rulers leave themselves vulnerable to countercoups from within their own ranks, thus the alternation of Nigerian governments in the postindependence juncture continues.

Independent Nigeria in the World of States: Neocolonialism and Regional Leadership

In this section, we identify and discuss the stages in the building of the neocolonial political economy, Nigeria's declining strategic importance in the wake of the Cold War, and its experience with the rise and decline of oil wealth. In addressing these interrelated issues of political economy chronologically, beginning with the economic foundations laid in 1939, we can trace Nigeria's economic slide. Ironically, despite its diminished position globally, Nigeria remains a regional leader, both economically and militarily.

The foundations of the postcolonial economy were established in several stages after 1939, and since that time the main focus of economic activity has remained the import-export trade, despite changes in the composition of that trade from slaves, to agricultural produce, and finally, to petroleum. In recent periods, the inability and unwillingness of Nigeria to diversify its exports beyond oil, coupled with unabated corruption, have helped precipitate the economic collapse that became plainly evident in the 1980s. Thus, in part due to its own failed policies and the continuation of neocolonial practices by Western states in the world economy, Nigeria's economic position in the world of states remains marginal.

Neocolonialism   **Neocolonialism** refers to the policies implemented by the departing European powers to retain their economic influence in, and economic benefits from, their colonies even while relinquishing political control. The reins of the colonial enterprise were transferred to African elites and groups on whom the Europeans could rely to protect their economic interests. Further, unequal and restrictive trading agreements bound the nominally independent states to their former colonial powers. Thus the pattern of economic and resource exploitation continued, and

African exporters were tied to the markets of the metropole. Although the French version of neocolonialism is widely regarded as more extensive than that of the British, Nigeria nevertheless experienced a similar relationship.

An important step in the construction of the neocolonial economy in Nigeria was the establishment of marketing boards as state monopolies for agricultural produce by the colonial regime in 1939. Under this scheme, peasant farmers were required to sell their products to these state agencies. Because prices paid to producers were well below world market prices, these arrangements guaranteed a capital windfall for the state. Initially this surplus was used to finance British trade balances. Later, it was used to finance the administration of the colonial state and the creation and expansion of a bureaucratic and commercial bourgeoisie in the colony. As independence approached, the marketing boards were transferred to the regional governments created in 1954.

The Africans who inherited access to the Nigerian economy from the British wanted to keep the spoils for themselves. The process of transferring political power to the local elite, which began in 1948 and concluded at independence, created a class of politicians committed to protecting existing arrangements, including the pattern of competition for the spoils of office.

After 1947, foreign firms resident in Nigeria shifted their activities from the purchase of locally produced goods and concentrated on importing and distributing consumer goods. These imports were facilitated by Greek and Levantine (Middle Eastern) traders who controlled the lucrative intermediary trade between local entities and foreign companies. A related development was the expansion of the state bureaucracy with the creation between 1954 and 1966 of several major regulatory institutions such as the Central Bank, as well as the introduction of a complex regime of state regulations covering taxation, foreign trade and foreign exchange, licenses, loans, and contracts. These developments expanded the state's role in managing the economy without significantly altering the structure of the economy inherited from the colonial era.

The Cold War   Another factor directly affecting Nigeria's position was the politics of the Cold War. In the period immediately following independence, Nigeria's foreign economic and political relations were mainly with Western powers. Even up to the outbreak of the civil war in 1967, official contacts with the communist world were discouraged. It was only after that war, in which the federal cause was strongly supported by the Soviet Union, that Nigeria expanded relations with communist nations. Of course, the central component of U.S. foreign policy during that period was preventing the spread of communism. Intensifying Cold War competition allowed Nigeria to benefit materially as the superpowers competed for perceived strategic advantage.

Oil Reserves Beginning in 1970, with the country reunified following the defeat of Biafra, Nigeria emerged as a major exporter of petroleum products. The central government under General Yakubu Gowon managed the oil reserves and collected **rents** from foreign oil companies that moved to expand operations in Nigeria. Access to this huge revenue stream increased the powers of the central government, and revenues from oil were used to fund a rapid expansion of the state. The economy, not surprisingly, came to depend on oil as the major export earner, and other sectors, including agriculture, declined in relative importance.

The global oil crisis of 1973–1974, following the Middle East war of 1973, resulted in a further dramatic increase in oil revenue. In the early 1970s, an abundant supply of oil kept international oil prices low. The members of the Organization of Petroleum Exporting Countries (OPEC), which Nigeria joined in 1970, gradually emerged as a powerful cartel. By controlling the level of oil production, they could demand higher prices and guarantee increased profit margins. The oil-dependent nations, however, were adversely affected as the price of their primary energy source—oil imports—soared.

Regionalism During the 1970s, Nigeria became increasingly active in international affairs, drawing on the new status derived from the successful prosecution of the civil war and the financial revenues from oil exports. In 1975, the Gowon government played a major role in the formation of a subregional organization, the **Economic Community of West African States (ECOWAS).** The goals of ECOWAS, following the example of the European Union, were initially quite modest. The announced aim of ECOWAS was to strengthen and broaden the economies in the region. Its members are the sixteen governments in West Africa and its highest authority is the annual meeting of the heads of state from member countries. Specific long-term goals include the removal of all barriers to trade among its members (such as import quotas and domestic content laws), freedom of movement for their citizens, and monetary cooperation. Although ECOWAS has achieved some of these goals, such as enhanced freedom of movement through the removal of visa requirements, the general weakness of the economies of its member states is reflected in the very limited progress made in promoting economic cooperation and integration.

Nigeria also gained visibility in the 1970s in other bodies such as the regional Organization of African Unity (OAU), the Commonwealth, the Nonaligned Movement, and the United Nations, where it played a prominent part in the UN anticolonial and anti-apartheid programs. By the late 1970s, however, Nigeria's domestic and external gains began to erode.

Decline After another international oil crisis in 1979, the unified front of OPEC unraveled through a combination of factors, both external and internal. Although worldwide demand for oil remained strong, non-oil producing states, especially the industrialized nations, found new ways to conserve petroleum; high-efficiency cars proliferated in the United States, for example. In addition, vast deposits of oil were discovered in the North Sea in the mid-1970s, creating an alternative source of supply from nations, notably Britain and Norway, outside the OPEC domain. By the late 1970s and early 1980s, oil flowing from North Sea reserves began to exert pressure on the OPEC cartel.

As the 1980s began, some OPEC members consistently exceeded their production quota in order to generate increased revenue. This failure to act collectively increased the oversupply of oil and led to sharp declines in world prices of petroleum. Beginning in 1979, Nigeria could no longer rely on increased earnings from oil exports, and it was forced to begin borrowing heavily to maintain consumption levels and to sustain numerous major construction projects. Eventually, as a result of the growing **balance-of-payments** deficit and its inability to meet debt servicing payments, Nigeria was forced to adopt structural adjustment programs under the aegis of the World Bank and IMF. In twenty-five years, therefore, this potential giant of Africa had gone from colonial dependence to dependence on international financial institutions largely as a result of its political instability and mismanagement.

IMPLICATIONS FOR CONTEMPORARY NIGERIAN POLITICS

This review of the making of the Nigerian state shows that contemporary Nigeria is a product of influences from the precolonial, colonial, and postcolonial periods. It is clear, for instance, that Nigeria's adoption of a federal arrangement has been a strategy to ensure "unity in diversity" with the objective of building a coherent nation-state out of over 250 different nationalities. In reality, however, and thanks to many years of military rule after independence, a *unitary* system has emerged in a federal disguise; it is a system with an all-powerful center surrounded by weak and economically insolvent states.

Another consequence of military rule, whose roots must be traced to the colonial era, is the relative overdevelopment of the executive arm at all levels of government—federal, state, and local—at the expense of weak legislative and judicial institutions. Executive superiority, a key feature of the colonial era, has been strengthened by each period of military rule. This unchecked executive power has encouraged a web of patron-client networks that sap the economy of its vitality, prevent accountability, and undermine the rule of law. The dominance of the executive has also ensured that the vitality of institutions and processes crucial to a democratic system—elections, electoral institutions, an independent judiciary, and a free press—would be in constant jeopardy. The result: a spate of electoral failures and cycles of civil and political instability culminating in periodic military coups d'état.

Nevertheless, Nigeria remains the oldest surviving federation in Africa. At a time when other federations are dissolving, whether peacefully as in the former Czechoslovakia or violently as in the former Yugoslavia, Nigeria manages to maintain its fragile unity. That unity has come under increasing stress, and a major challenge is ensuring that Nigeria does not go the way of Yugoslavia. One fact is certain: Military dominance and northern dependence on revenues generated in the south would certainly prevent a peaceful dissolution of the federation.

Nigeria remains a major, if increasingly cash-strapped, actor in the international arena on issues of concern to black and African peoples the world over. As indicated earlier, Nigeria is the most populous country in Africa. It is also a country rich in human and material resources, although its failure to sustain democracy and economic development makes it an important case for the study of resource competition and the perils of corruption. Further, its multiethnic, multireligious, multiclass, and multiregional nature make it an especially valuable case for the study of social cleavages in conflict and cooperation.

Nigeria's experience has also shown the interrelationship between democracy and development. Clearly, democracy and development also depend on other factors, including leadership, mass culture, the level of institutional autonomy, and the external economic climate. A long-standing debate among political scientists suggested that authoritarian regimes—because they lack legislative opposition and can force uncomfortable changes on society without fear of electoral reaction—are better able to accelerate economic growth and development. More recent research has shown, however, that democracies are no less likely to foster economic development and, in fact, may even allow for predictable norms and respect for property rights that will foster economic development. The history of independent Nigeria suggests that a combination of authoritarian government and widespread corruption has thwarted sustained development. Moreover, the Nigerian experience points to the need to pursue, with conviction, both economic and political liberalization. The latter process would open up society to democratic and developmentalist tendencies, while the former would provide the material bases (across a wider spectrum of society) for democratic consolidation. The boost to individual initiatives from both processes, together with confidence in law-based governance, are now regarded as imperatives for national recovery.

As a new century approaches, there are major challenges shaping the political agenda in Nigeria. Each of these challenges reflects the four principal themes of this book: the democratic idea, political economy, collective identities, and the world of states. Foremost among Nigeria's challenges is the maintenance of the country's unity in its present form while ensuring progress in the pursuit of political and economic liberalization as dictated by the world of states of which it is part. The goal must be to fashion a widely shared national agenda out of contending and often antagonistic religious, regional, ethnic, class, and corporate interests. Other aims would be the encouragement of accountability within the state bureaucracy, the further entrenchment of developmentalist and democratic tendencies in civil society, and the expansion of the material bases for sustaining democracy. Yet another challenge is the need for the political system to overcome its authoritarian legacies, especially those arising from military rule. Nigeria must find ways to restore civilian control of the military. A related challenge is to develop the anti-authoritarian aspects of civil soci-

ety to provide a firm rampart for democracy and development.

Ultimately, the most crucial challenge Nigeria faces is the pervasive condition of uncertainty. At this stage, it is uncertain whether Nigeria is traveling decidedly down the path of autocracy, underdevelopment, and disintegration, or if, out of the deepening crisis, a great reversal will occur, as happened at the end of Gowon era in 1975–1976, catapulting Nigeria onto the course of democratic renewal and vigorous national construction. In the following sections we will explore a number of these key issues and evaluate how they may shape Nigerian politics in the years ahead.

SECTION 2

Political Economy and Development

Politics and economics have become so inseparable in Nigeria that neither political nor economic development can be seriously addressed independent of the other in theory, policy, or practice. In this section, we will explore the domestic and international contexts of Nigeria's political economy and the role of the state and how it has intervened in Nigeria's economy. This active role of the state is consistent with the legacy established by the colonial regime as discussed in Section 1.

The state came to occupy center stage in Nigeria with regard to the extraction, deployment, and regulation of scarce economic resources. This tendency has led to what observers describe as the "overpoliticization" of economic and social life as individuals, groups, and communities jostled for control of or access to the state. In this context, the state has evolved beyond the role of regulator and licenser as it would be in a more laissez-faire, less interventionist environment described in Section 1. In Nigeria, the state is perceived as the greatest economic resource. Although in most societies access to the state and its leadership confers economic advantages (in the United States until recently, the access of the defense industry to Washington resulted in contracts, jobs, and other perks), this observation applies even more to developing countries.

At the international level, the state has remained weak and dependent on Western industrial and finan-

cial interests three and a half decades after Nigeria became a full-fledged member of the international community. The country suffers from an increasing debt burden. In addition, Nigeria is dependent on the developed industrial economies for finance capital, production and information technologies, as well as for basic consumer items and raw materials. As highlighted at the end of the preceding section, despite its lack of influence on a global scale, Nigeria strives to provide leadership at the continental (African) and subregional (West African) levels. Most of its policy and intellectual elites support this self-image.

In Section 1, we argued that understanding the making of modern Nigeria requires an examination of both its colonial and precolonial histories. Much of the blame for Nigeria's path of underdevelopment and authoritarianism was placed on foundations laid during the colonial period. However, in many parts of Nigeria the pervasive role of the state is traceable to the colonial period. The basic features of the interventionist state were introduced by the colonial authorities.

In the period since independence, state intrusion into the economy and society has been strengthened by the control over rents accruing from agricultural, then petroleum, exports. The exigencies of the civil war and the consequences of prolonged military rule contributed to the centralized and intrusive approach to economic affairs. At the same time, the state has become a theater of struggles for ascendancy among groups and interests in civil society. To that extent, the state simultaneously affects and reflects forces in the political economy, an issue we examine in greater detail below.

STATE AND ECONOMY

Origins of Economic Decline

As described in Section 1, Nigeria's overreliance on oil as a source of export revenues, together with the decline in world petroleum prices, were major contributing factors to the weakness of the Nigerian economy by the early 1980s. Now we turn to Nigeria's economic decline and how the state has attempted to address it. First, however, several of the root causes of Nigeria's poor economic performance require elaboration.

In the colonial and immediate postcolonial periods, Nigeria's economy was centered on agricultural production for domestic consumption as well as for export.[13] Peasant producers were "induced" by the colonial state to produce the primary export commodities—cocoa in the west, palm oil in the east, and ground nuts and cotton in the north—through direct taxation, forced cultivation, and the presence of European agricultural firms.[14] Despite the emphasis on exports, Nigeria was self-sufficient in food production at independence, and vital to this effort was small scale local production of sorghum and maize in the north and cassava and yams in the south. Some rice and wheat were also produced. It was not until the 1960s that emphasis shifted to the development of nonfood export crops through large-scale enterprises.

Near-exclusive state attention to large-scale, nonfood production meant that small farmers were left out and received scant government support. Predictably, food production suffered, and food imports were stepped up to meet the increasing needs of a burgeoning population. Nevertheless, agriculture was the central component of the national economy. Watts points to a combination of three factors that effectively undermined the Nigerian agricultural sector. The first was the Biafran War, which drastically reduced palm oil production in the east where the war was concentrated. Second, severe drought in 1969 produced a famine in 1972–1974. Finally, the development of the petroleum industry caused a total shift in economic focus away from agriculture in terms of both labor and capital investment. Instead, resources went into petro-

Since 1974, oil shipments have accounted for over 90 percent of Nigeria's export earnings.
Source: Topham Picture Library/Image Works.

leum production, which increased from 5 million barrels in 1960 to 325 million barrels by 1970. In contrast, agricultural export production plummeted from 80 percent of exports in 1960, to just 2 percent by 1980. To fill the gap, imports of food exploded by 700 percent between 1970 and 1978.[15]

With revenue from oil, Nigeria greatly increased its expenditures on education, defense, and infrastructure throughout the 1970s. The university system was expanded, roads and ports were built, and industrial and office buildings were constructed. Imports of capital goods and raw materials required to support this expansion rose by over 700 percent between 1971 and 1979. Similarly, imports of consumer goods also rose dramatically (600 percent) in the same period, as an increasingly wealthy Nigerian elite developed a taste for expensive imported goods.[16] By 1978, the Nigerian government could no longer finance many of its ambitious projects; consequently, the government was forced to borrow money to make up the deficit. Be-

TABLE 1   **Oil Sector Statistics, 1970–1989**

	Annual Output (million barrels)	Average Price Index	Oil Exports as Percent of Total Exports	Government Oil Revenue (N million)	Percent of Total Revenue
1970	396	5.3	58	166	26
1971	559	7.2	74	510	44
1972	643	7.8	82	767	54
1973	750	11.2	83	1,016	60
1974	823	31.7	93	3,726	82
1975	651	33.5	93	4,271	77
1976	756	36.3	94	5,365	79
1977	761	40.9	93	6,081	76
1978	692	39.5	89	4,556	62
1979	840	58.5	93	8,881	81
1980	753	100.0	96	12,353	81
1981	525	108.4	97	8,563	70
1982	470	99.4	99	7,814	66
1983	451	84.6	96	7,253	69
1984	508	83.3	97	8,268	74
1985	544	79.9	97	10,915	75
1986	534	42.4	94	8,107	66
1987	464	52.1	93	19,027	76
1988	507	41.1	91	20,934	77
1989	614	49.5	95	41,334	82

Sources: Output is from *Petroleum Economist* (1970–1989); price index and exports are from IMF, *International Financial Statistics* (1970–1984) and from Central Bank of Nigeria, *Annual Reports* (1985–1989); revenues are from Central Bank of Nigeria, *Annual Reports* (various years). From Tom Forrest, *Politics and Economic Development in Nigeria.* (Boulder: Westview Press, 1993), 134.

cause of its offsetting income from oil, Nigeria did not face great difficulty in obtaining foreign loans to finance its expansion from both bilateral and multilateral creditors, and debt levels accelerated rapidly.

As noted throughout this chapter, corruption has been an almost constant theme underlying Nigerian politics. The acceleration in oil wealth was mirrored by a corresponding increase in graft. Many public officials became very wealthy through the oil sector by means of joint ventures with foreign firms and others from the illicit diversion of public funds for private benefit. According to Watts, "Throughout the 1970s, enormous but inestimable amounts of money capital mysteriously appeared in private European bank accounts (estimated to be between $5–$7 billion), and the level of bureaucratic malfeasance was simply stag-

gering."[17] (This was compounded by the revelation in 1994 that an estimated $12.2 billion of $12.5 billion revenues received during the Gulf crisis in 1990–1991 was similarly "disbursed.")

In sum, the oil boom was a double-edged sword for Nigeria. On one hand, it has been a tremendous source of income; on the other, a source of dependence. Nigeria has relied on oil for over 90 percent of its export earnings since the early 1970s, and in that time, the industry has accounted for about three-quarters of *all* government revenues, as shown in Table 1. As a result of frenzied and ill-managed industrial and infrastructural expansion and neglect of the vital agricultural sector during the oil boom—under both military and civilian regimes—coupled with a lack of bureaucratic safeguards against corruption, the

Nigerian economy was unable to absorb the sharp fall in world oil prices after 1981 and found itself in crisis.

1985–On: Deepening Economic Crisis and the Search for Solutions

Structural Adjustment   The year 1985 marked a major turning point for the Nigerian state and economy. It ushered in Ibrahim Babangida's eight-year rule and revealed the precarious condition of the Nigerian economy. Important decisions had to be made regarding how Nigeria would embark on efforts to strengthen its domestic political and economic power base and improve its position in the international economy.

Within a year of wresting power from General Buhari in August 1985, the Babangida military regime developed an economic structural adjustment program (SAP) with the active support of the World Bank and IMF (also referred to as the **International Financial Institutions,** or **IFIs**). The decision to embark on SAP was made against a background of increasing economic constraints arising from a combination of factors, such as the continued dependence of the economy on oil exports, a growing debt burden, balance of payments difficulties, and lack of fiscal discipline. Although the structural adjustment program is specific to Nigeria and addresses such problems as the country's overreliance on oil, the Nigerian SAP contains provisions that are similar to most economic reform programs that have been instituted in Africa and elsewhere.

Though they were used sparingly in the 1970s, SAPs became a prominent feature of economic reform programs in the 1980s. Proponents of SAPs contend that only through radical changes in the very structure of stagnant economies, from monetary policies to fiscal (budgetary) issues, can these economies rebound to become efficient and productive. In the decade since SAPs came into widespread use in Africa, however, their success rate has been decidedly mixed, and the length of time allotted to such programs has been extended because of the recognition that Africa's economic problems could not be solved through quick-fix methods.

It should be noted that SAPs, and IFI intervention in general, are often resisted for two reasons. First, states do not relish the prospect of ceding part of their economic sovereignty—decisions over policy

choices, programs, and the like—to international institutions. Second, the austerity that results from such programs, although intended and predicted to be a short-term consequence, can be destabilizing to governments and populations alike. However, because they are dependent on lenders for continued support, most African governments have felt that they had little choice but to comply with the demands of these multilateral creditors. Besides, other creditors (including private banks or foreign governments) often will not consent to provide any additional monies in the absence of an agreement with the IFIs. These plans, however, have not been easy for governments to implement nor have they always been well designed. Confronting the magnitude of economic problems like those in Africa involves experimentation, learning, and adaptation. Therefore, mistakes are made in both design and implementation of potential solutions. Such conditions would be challenge enough for the most purposeful and committed of governments. But Nigeria's government is rife with corruption, and its institutions and policies have been cynically manipulated by military and civilian leaders alike for their own personal gain, making Nigeria's task doubly difficult.

One of the first objectives of Nigeria's SAP was to restructure and diversify the economy's productive base to reduce dependence on the oil sector and on various imports. Secondly, under pressure from the World Bank and the IMF, the Babangida government sought to achieve fiscal discipline and balance of payments viability by curtailing government spending to reduce budget deficits and the rising debt. It was believed that these reforms would establish a basis for sustainable growth with minimal inflation. A third objective of the program was the **privatization** of state-owned enterprises (SOEs, or para-statals). The policies of the World Bank and the IMF are motivated by a strong commitment to free market principles and a belief in the greater efficiency of private versus public enterprise. Similarly, Nigeria's goal is to lessen the dominance of unproductive investments in the public sector, improve the sector's efficiency, and intensify the growth potential of the private sector.

Privatization   Privatization means that state-owned businesses would be sold to private (nonstate) investors, either domestic or foreign. The benefits of privatization are threefold: (1) revenue is generated for the

Structural Adjustment Programs

The solutions to Nigeria's economic woes lie first within its own people and government, but assistance must also come from outside its borders. In addition to bilateral (country-to-country) assistance, *multilateral* economic institutions also exist to provide loans, grants, and other forms of economic development aid. These institutions are sponsored by and comprised of countries in the international community whose representatives elect governing bodies and implement policy. The institutions then supply support where needed to member states. Two multilateral institutions that have become familiar players on the African economic scene are the International Monetary Fund (IMF) and the World Bank. These international financial institutions (or IFIs, for short) were established following World War II to provide short-term credit facilities to facilitate growth and expansion of trade and longer term financing packages, respectively, to rebuild the countries of war-torn Europe. Today, the functions of the IFIs have adapted and expanded to meet contemporary needs, including efforts to stabilize and restructure faltering economies. One area of emphasis by the IFIs, particularly among African countries, is the structural adjustment program (SAP).

Several requirements by the World Bank and the IMF accompany SAP facilities. These rigorous programs, which invariably extol the virtues of the liberal free-market economy, call for immediate austerity measures by recipient governments. SAPs generally begin with currency devaluation and tariff reductions. These actions are followed by measures aimed at budget deficit reductions, restructuring of the public sector (particularly employment practices), public divestitures (privatization of state-owned enterprises), and agricultural reform (which includes the reduction of consumer subsidies on staple foods, thus driving agricultural prices *up*). The results of these programs, particularly in the short term, can be severe. SAPs result in considerable economic—and frequently social—dislocation; dramatic price increases in foodstuffs and fuel, plus rising unemployment are seldom popular with the general population.

At Babangida's insistence, Nigeria's current SAP was developed and deployed in 1986 independently of the IMF and the World Bank. However, it was endorsed by the IFIs, therefore making Nigeria eligible to receive disbursements of funds from the IMF and the Bank. Ironically, Nigeria's SAP is in many regards more rigorous than those programs designed by the IFIs themselves. Like SAPs elsewhere, the Nigerian program is designed to encourage economic liberalism and private enterprise as superior to state-run and state-owned enterprises; the logic here is that competition leads to more efficient products and markets. However, there has been as yet little recovery among Africa's struggling economies. Certainly Africa's economic problems are deeply entrenched, and we now know that although stabilizing an economy may be done relatively quickly, comprehensive *structural* adjustment takes considerably longer. Thus far, Nigeria's SAP—in part because of the social reaction to austerity measures, continued corruption in its implementation, and the complicating factor of unstable military rule—has not succeeded in revitalizing the Nigerian economy. The final years of the Babangida administration (1983–1993) saw a marked slippage in the reform program; and the Abacha regime has enhanced that trend.

state upon sale of the enterprise; (2) there is a substantial reduction in state expenditure because the state no longer finances operating costs of money-losing operations; and (3) there is an implicit assumption that the private sector can run businesses more efficiently than the government sector. However, there are also risks involved for the government. Privatization usually means that jobs will be lost: A private company cannot afford to maintain a bloated payroll and retain unqualified staff if it hopes to survive. The government is often reluctant to swell the ranks of the unemployed and to confront the consequent political opposition that such actions usually provoke. Nevertheless, a component that seeks to commercialize and privatize state enterprises is central to Nigeria's economic adjustment program.

Although the declared intentions of the SAP since 1986 have been to limit the role of the state, expand the sphere of private initiative, and strengthen market forces in the economy and society, the reality has been quite different. Government has successfully divested itself of shares in such areas as banking and finance, but it has proceeded much more slowly regarding most of the key para-statals such as the National Petroleum Corporation (NNPC), the National Electric Power Authority (NEPA), the Nigerian Ports Authority (NPA), and Nigerian Airports Authority (NAA). It has proposed making such para-statals more commercially viable without taking them fully out of state control.

Paradoxically, the state's role in the economy and society has become *more* pronounced. The state and its managers have played a crucial role in determining the timing and direction of what was portrayed as the withdrawal of the state from the economy. By definition, the objective of privatization is to promote a style of management concerned with generating profits through efficient production; however, in Nigeria, commercialization and privatization of many parastatals have been pursued for the benefit of state managers and their associates. Those in public office or those with access to the state have been able to invest in privatized companies at insider prices. At the same time, the deregulation of previous licensing arrangements, designed to simplify business investment and management, has fostered new sets of regulations as burdensome as those scrapped.[18]

Most signs reveal that the Nigerian economy remains as interventionist and as state-centralized as ever. One example of Nigeria's illiberal economic practices is that the so-called national plan remains the central focus of economic rationalization and forecasting. Beginning in 1946, when the colonial administration announced a ten-year Plan for Development and Welfare, national plans have been prepared by ministries of finance, economic development, and planning. The innovation introduced by the Babangida regime was to create a permanent National Planning Commission and to extend the duration of national plans from four years to fifteen-to-twenty years. However, the national plan, pervasive as an instrument of policy, has not been an effective management tool. The reason for this disparity is the absence of an effective data base for planning as well as a great lack of discipline in plan implementation. As a leading Nigerian economist stated in 1992,

> Planning for economic development in Nigeria is like a giraffe. The closer you get to the giraffe the less of it you see.— Similarly, it appears that the more we planned the less wealth or health per head of the population we seemed to have been achieving.[19]

The picture that emerges, therefore, is one of a state striving to control and dictate the pace and direction of economic development but lacking the tools and the political will to deliver effectively on the obligations which it has itself defined! Those who control the state in Nigeria control the major access to wealth. Competition for control of the state, therefore, is predictably intense and unrelenting.

Various indicators show that the situation has remained the same even under the apparent free-market regime introduced with SAP in 1986. In an illustrative essay, Dele Olowu, a Nigerian professor of public administration, has highlighted the growing evidence of political, administrative, and economic centralization in Nigeria, each of which is interwoven and mutually reinforcing.[20] There has been a concentration of power and experience in the hands of the executive at all levels of government, a tendency that has created a sense of virtually unlimited power in the executive branch of government.

At the economic level, federal control of earnings from oil and other mining rights has enabled the state to increase its involvement in direct production through the creation of para-statals and the acquisition of large shares in major banks and other financial institutions, manufacturing, and construction companies. This practice has ensured that the state remains the biggest employer as well as the most important source of revenue, even for the private sector.

It is not unusual in many developing countries for the state to become the primary employer; the civil service payroll swells as a result of government patronage. However, when the state is unrestrained, vital resources are diverted to nonproductive activities and available funds must increasingly be used to pay the salaries of the civil service and other government employees. By the 1980s, the public service bureaucracy in Nigeria had swollen to over 3 million employees (most employed by the federal and state governments), representing more than 60 percent of employment in the modern sector of the economy.

The question of how private the Nigerian private sector really is has provoked sharp debate. The dominant perspective appears to be that much of the distinction between the public (governmental) and private sectors of the economy is artificial. The share of the private sector in the economy has actually been falling in recent years. According to one analysis, the private sector contribution to investment was approximately 45 percent during the first national development plan (1962–1968). By contrast, the fifth national development plan (1981–1985) anticipated just a 14 percent contribution from the private sector.[21] At the same time, the public sector share has witnessed continued growth. Moreover, much of the private sector enjoys a parasitic

TABLE 2   **Selected Economic Indicators, 1970–1989 (annual percentage change)**

	GDP	Manufacturing	Government Expenditure[a]	CPI Price[b]	Food Price
1970	29.8	11.4	105.6	13.8	22.9
1971	18.4	5.7	−11.4	16.0	28.5
1972	7.3	6.3	46.5	2.8	2.5
1973	−2.7	23.0	4.5	5.4	3.2
1974	12.1	−3.3	100.5	12.8	16.9
1975	−3.0	23.6	104.0	33.6	40.6
1976	10.9	23.4	28.8	21.9	26.3
1977	8.1	6.2	14.9	15.8	19.6
1978	−7.3	13.9	6.5	16.6	17.7
1979	2.5	48.0	2.7	11.7	8.0
1980	5.3	5.3	72.7	9.9	7.6
1981	−8.4	14.6	8.0	20.8	25.2
1982	0.1	9.6	21.9	7.7	8.9
1983	−4.1	−26.3	−19.5	23.2	23.2
1984	−6.8	−11.9	0.5	39.6	42.9
1985	7.9	19.9	23.1	5.5	3.9
1986	−3.2	−3.8	7.9	5.4	0.1
1987	1.8	33.6	46.8	10.2	8.6
1988	4.0	12.8	29.2	38.3	52.2
1989	4.0	2.1	38.0	40.9	39.1

[a]Government expenditure is federal current and capital expenditure including statutory appropriations to state and local governments.
[b]Price indices are lower-income urban group (1970–1976) and composite covering all income groups in urban and rural areas (1977–1987).

Sources: Manufacturing index, government expenditure, money supply, and prices are from Central Bank of Nigeria, *Annual Reports* (various years); GDP is from IMF, *International Financial Statistics* (various years). From Tom Forrest, *Politics and Economic Development in Nigeria* (Boulder: Westview Press, 1993), 135.

relationship to the public sector. That is, it derives its income mainly from government expenditures and patronage. Even attempts in the 1970s to widen indigenous participation in business life and reduce the foreign presence enhanced state involvement because government had to take over shares and businesses when local bids were not made or were inadequate.

The political economy, therefore, remains crisis-prone. Analyses show that it is still characterized by low investment, low capacity-utilization, unreliable distribution, stifling corruption, and overregulation. Average annual GDP growth rates have been negative in several years since the early 1980s. Consumption and investment have also recorded negative growth, indicating that both purchases and new investments are in decline (see Table 2).

Finally, exacerbating Nigeria's economic decline is its heavy foreign debt. The total debt to bilateral and

---

TABLE 3   **Nigeria's Total External Debt (millions of US$; current prices and exchange rates)**

										Average Annual		
1980	1981	1982	1983	1984	1985	1986	1987	1988	1989	1975–79	1980–85	1986–Most Rec.
8,934	12,136	12,954	18,540	18,537	19,551	24,043	31,193	31,947	32,832	3,304	15,109	30,004

Source: UNDP, World Bank, *African Development Indicators* (Washington, D.C.: World Bank, 1992), 159.

TABLE 4   **Index of Real Household Incomes of Key Groups 1980/81–1986/87**
(Rural self-employed in 1980/81 = 100)

	1980/81	1981/82	1982/83	1983/84	1984/85	1985/86	1986/87
Rural self-employed	100	103	95	86	73	74	65
Rural wage earners	178	160	147	135	92	95	84
All rural households	105	107	99	89	74	84	74
Urban self-employed	150	124	106	94	69	69	61
Urban wage earners	203	177	164	140	101	101	90
All urban households	166	142	129	109	80	80	71

Sources: National Integrated Survey of Households (NISH), Federal Office of Statistics (FOS) consumer price data, and World Bank estimates. As found in Paul Collier, *An Analysis of the Nigerian Labour Market,* Development Economics Department Discussion Paper (Washington, D.C.: World Bank, 1986). From Tom Forrest, *Politics and Economic Development in Nigeria* (Boulder: Westview Press, 1993), 214.

---

multilateral lenders, as well as international commercial banks, exceeded $34 billion in 1991, and is now estimated to be over $40 billion. Debt service charges, that is, the amount of interest and principal Nigeria is expected to pay each year on its outstanding loans, exceeds current capacity. Total debt service as a percentage of exported goods and services jumped five-fold from 4.2 percent in 1980 to 20.3 percent in 1990. This means that of every dollar Nigeria earns from its exports, 20 cents must go to service the debt. Nigeria, once considered a country likely to achieve self-sustaining growth, now ranks among the debt-distressed countries in the developing world that cannot earn enough from the export of goods to service its foreign debt and meet the basic needs of the population (see Table 3).

Social Welfare

Given the continued decline in its economic performance since the early 1970s, it is not surprising that Nigeria's social welfare has suffered greatly as well. Since 1986, there has been a sharp decline in the quantity and quality of social services, complicated by a marked decline in household incomes as seen in Table 4. The problem has not been an inability to establish policy guidelines, but the absence of concrete initiatives at the level of policy execution and a lack of commitment to allocate already scarce resources to social welfare projects. In addition, the SAP program, with its emphasis on austerity and the reduction of state expenditures, has not provided a fertile environment for costly programs designed to boost social welfare.

A major criticism of the SAP program has been its impact on marginal and vulnerable groups such as the urban and rural poor, women, the young and the elderly. Indeed, Nigeria performs poorly in meeting basic needs: Life expectancy is barely above fifty years and infant mortality is estimated at more than 85 deaths per every 1,000 live births. Nigeria's provision of basic education is also inadequate. To make matters worse, there has been no tradition in independent Nigeria of direct government contribution to social security support, such as that found in the United States and elsewhere. Even in the best of times, there has always been a tendency for growth in public social spending to lag behind growth in the economy. Much of the resulting gap has traditionally been filled by culturally based networks of extended families. Furthermore, the scant social spending that does exist is often manipulated for partisan political purposes by both civilian and military governments. Public spending on housing, for example, represents less than 1 percent of the federal budget[22] and is often diverted to meet the needs of the military.

The provision of health care and other social services—water, education, food, and shelter—remains woefully inadequate in both urban and rural areas. Rural areas are doubly burdened by their relative isolation because of poor roads, transportation, telecommunication facilities, and erratic electrical power.[23] In all parts of Nigeria, health care facilities, for example, lack equipment, drugs, and doctors—there is only one doctor for every 6,000 people. With economic decline, health standards have also dropped. Malnutrition, especially in women and infants, is on the rise, as is susceptibility to malaria, dysentery, and other potentially deadly diseases because drugs, most of which are produced abroad, are increasingly scarce. The devaluation of the Nigerian currency, the naira, in accordance with the provisions of SAP, sent imported drug prices soaring. However, even traditional healers, on whom many rural dwellers rely, have raised their prices as well. As a result, it is reported that "most government hospitals are just consulting clinics, and the private hospitals are so expensive that only the rich patronize them."[24]

It has also been noted that although the national leadership gives lip service to the importance of social welfare in general, health care has received repeatedly low priority in Nigeria's national development plans. The funding allocated to social spending is made even more stark in comparison to expenditure on the military, which has received higher priority. To illustrate, "military expenditure [barracks, training, schools, equipment, and personnel expense] accounted for 10.3 percent of the allocation of development funds in the Second National Development Plan [1970–1974]. . . ." The comparable figure for health care was 4.6 percent.[25]

It is perhaps not surprising that the disparities between social and military spending have continued in subsequent national development plans. Given Nigeria's propensity for military coups, one can see why the national leadership—whether military or civilian—would try to accommodate the often unpredictable armed forces. This shortsighted pragmatism has occurred, however, at the expense of the needs of the majority of Nigeria's 90 million people.

It should be clear at this point that the Nigerian state, and especially the central government, controls access to available capital resources. As a result, the state has become the major focus for competition among sectional and associational groups (of an ethnic, regional, religious, or class nature) for access to these resources. In such an environment, elite members of these groups become "conflict generators" rather than "conflict managers."[26] It is to the social bases of this conflict that we now turn.

SOCIETY AND ECONOMY

A major assumption underlying the Babangida regime's economic adjustment program was that deregulation would encourage increased investment in manfuacturing by both Nigerians and foreign interests. These expectations have not been fulfilled. For instance, whereas the annual growth rate in gross domestic investment between 1965 and 1980 was positive (14.7 percent), it was negative for the period 1980 to 1900 (–10.2 percent). For potential foreign investors, uncertainties about Nigeria's future have become so prevalent that the country hardly offers an attractive environment for new long-term investment. New investors are hesitant to risk significant capital in an environment characterized by political and social instability, an inert economic adjustment program, and unpredictable military regimes. On a domestic level, Nigerian entrepreneurs have found that trading and government contracting always offer more attractive and quicker yields than productive enterprises such as manufacturing. The service sector, as a consequence, had positive annual growth rates between 1980 and 1990 whereas manufacturing and industry recorded a decline. Furthermore, a partial explanation for the failure of economic strategies can be found within Nigerian society itself—a complex mix of contending, often hostile, ethnic, religious, and regional constituencies.

Ethnic and Religious Cleavages

The structure of Nigeria's ethnic relations has generated tensions that sap the country's economy of much needed vitality. This structure falls within a category Donald Horowitz has described as centralized, in which a few groups "are so large that their interactions are a constant theme of politics at the center."[27] Competition takes place regarding national economic and political resources. The dominance of the Hausa-Fulani, Igbo, and Yoruba in the country's national life, and the conflicts among political elites from these groups, flow over into economic affairs as policy decisions are made less on their merits and more on how they impact perceptions of group strength, a subject reviewed below.

Religious cleavages have also affected economic and social stability. Some of the federation's states in the far north are populated mainly by Muslims, whereas others, particularly in the middle and eastern parts of the south, are predominantly Christian. The imagery in popular (and often academic) discourse often simplifies the more complex reality by juxtaposing a so-called Christian south with a Muslim north (the Yoruba people in the southwest, for example, are almost equally divided between Muslims and Christians and with many adherents of Yoruba traditional beliefs). This simplification exacerbates ethnoregional conflicts by superimposing Nigeria's religious conflicts on them. Religious harmony has thus been elusive.

A combination of inept government actions and a worldwide upsurge in Islamic militancy has heightened conflicts between adherents of Christianity and Islam. Christians have perceived the northern-dominated federal government as being too pro-Islam in its management and distribution of scarce resources as well as in its policy decisions. Christians fear that government actions are jeopardizing the secular nature of the state and putting the country on the path to an Islamic theocracy. In response, Muslims have questioned the secular nature of the Nigerian state. Muslims insist that colonial rule, under the tutelage of the church-state of England, created a state more Christian than secular in Nigeria, and one that is unable to provide a suitable environment for the proper observance of Islam. The consequence of these disputes throughout the 1980s and early 1990s was a series of clashes along religious lines in various parts of the country, often accompanied by extensive loss of life and property damage.

Further complicating matters, the 1980s witnessed an increase in social disturbances associated mainly with the extremist fringes of Islamic groups in some parts of the north. The decline in the Nigerian economy also contributed to the rise of fundamentalism. As elsewhere in the world, Islamic leaders have increasingly blamed secular governments for the rise in poverty and social dislocation. In northern Nigeria, disputes over economic issues have sometimes escalated into physical attacks on Christians and members of southern ethnic groups residing in the north. Occasionally, it is religious revivalism among some of the various Christian sects (which include Anglicans, Methodists, Baptists, and Catholics) that has provoked violent protests by Muslims.

In addition to economic decline, two other inter-related factors have heightened religious and ethnic tensions in Nigeria. The first concerns imbalances in the structure and management of the federation; the second, the impact of military rule, especially since 1985. In popular imagery, Nigerian federalism is perceived as politically tilted in favor of states in the former Northern Region. As discussed earlier, this region is larger and more populous than the south. Conversely, the southern states rest on a stronger educational and economic base. (Refer to the discussion of federalism and federal character in Section 3.) Furthermore, the recurring intrusion of the military into the political arena has tended to erode the social and physical infrastructure for democracy and development. It has often arrested, and even reversed, any positive gains made during periods of civilian rule.

Based on general perceptions that the south fears "northern political domination—the tyranny of population," while the north fears a "southern tyranny of skills,"[28] it is often argued that the north must continue to control political power at the central government level—again, through military or civilian means—so as to neutralize the south's perceived advantages. Such attitudes degenerated into open controversy during the Babangida regime, which was perceived as a northern-dominated administration. Moreover, Babangida earned the dubious distinction of appearing more willing to manipulate Nigeria's ethnic divisions than any of his predecessors. Under General Abacha, since November 1993, the perception of an overlap between northern and military dominance has grown.

Abacha's Provisional Ruling Council is tilted overwhelmingly in favor of northerners, specifically Hausa-Fulani, in its membership. Any appearance of regional representation in the council was shattered when, in August 1994, Abacha replaced the only non-northern senior staffers with his Hausa co-ethnics. It is also worth noting that since Abacha's seizure of power, numerous attacks have been perpetrated against southerners, particularly Yoruba, and many suspect government complicity. The government has also closed universities and detained a number of activists, particularly in the south. Further, the constitutional conference, part of Abacha's "transition" initiative, was held despite widespread protest, most marked among the Yoruba, thus further undermining the already dubious legitimacy of the conference and threatening the remaining unity of the country.

But it is not only Yoruba groups that have been adversely affected by Abacha's rule. Recent reports show that the Ogoni and other southern minority groups, who are heavily represented among oil industry workers, have been brutalized by military and police forces because of their participation in protests against the regime. Finally, the Abacha regime has fomented ethnic tensions by deliberately using northern police and military units to put down forcibly pro-democracy demonstrations in the south since 1993. These divide and rule tactics are reminiscent of the practices employed by the British colonialists. But a more accurate picture of Nigerian cultural cleavages suggests that such tactics may have limits. What is also often overlooked is that none of Nige-

ria's main ethnic or religious groups is itself internally coherent and cohesive. Each is split by class, ideological, regional, linguistic, and sublinguistic considerations which also serve to mitigate the emergence of confrontations along purely ethnic and religious lines. Indeed, this pluralism encourages a residual optimism that only an institutionalized democracy will enable Nigeria to achieve political stability and create an environment for resumed economic growth.

Demonstrating a propensity similar to that of their military counterparts, political and business elites have also accentuated these sectional cleavages. Culture or ethnicity is used to fragment, rather than to integrate the country, with grave consequences for the economy and society. It is therefore not surprising that these divisive practices overshadow certain positive aspects of sectional identities. For example, associations based on ethnic and religious affinities often serve as vehicles for mobilizing savings, investment, and production, such as informal credit associations. In addition, professional associations—comprised of lawyers, doctors, journalists, business and trade groups, academics, trade unions, or students' organizations—have played a prominent role in the anti-colonial struggle. These groups, which form the core of civil society, have continued to provide a vehicle for political expression while also reflecting the divisive pressures of Nigeria's cultural pluralism. It should be noted, however, that the most political of these groups traditionally have been dominated by men. Although women form a vital part of the economic sector, gender has not yet emerged as a major basis of social conflict in Nigeria.

Gender Cleavages

A final cultural element that needs to be highlighted is unequal gender access to communal resources. Although the Land Use Act of 1978 vests land ownership in government, land tenure in southern Nigeria is still governed by traditional practice, which is basically patriarchal. Thus women have been the victims of discriminatory cultural practices. Despite the fact that women, especially from the south and Middle Belt areas, have traditionally dominated agricultural production and form the bulk of agricultural producers, they are generally prevented from owning land, which is the major means of production. Trading, in which women also feature prominently, is also controlled in many areas by traditional chiefs and local government councillors who are overwhelmingly male.

Women have not succeeded in transforming their economic importance into political clout. Their inability to achieve direct access to state power is also a reflection of several factors. Women's associations have tended to be elitist, urban-based, and mainly concerned with issues of trade, welfare, and religion. The few that do have a more political orientation have been largely token appendages to the male-dominated political parties or instruments of the government. An example of the latter was the "Better Life Program" directed by the wife of Babangida and its successor, the "Family Support Program," directed by the wife of Abacha. Finally, women are grossly underrepresented at all levels of the governmental system. For instance, when Chief Ernest Shonekan announced the names of his thirty-two-person interim government that succeeded the Babangida regime in August 1993, only one was a woman. Following the removal of Shonekan three months later, the Sani Abacha regime has steadily replaced civilians by military personnel throughout the governmental apparatus, thereby also accentuating its male-dominated character.

Prebendalism

Simply put, **prebendalism**—the peculiarly Nigerian version of corruption—is an extreme form of clientelism that refers to the practice of mobilizing cultural and other sectional identities through corrupt inducements and behavior by political aspirants and officeholders. Prebendalism is an institutionalized pattern of political behavior that justifies the pursuit of and the use of public office for the personal benefit of the officeholder and his clients; the official public purpose of the office is a secondary concern. As with clientelism, the officeholder's "clients" are comprised of a specific set of elites to which he is linked, typically by ethnic or religious ties, and this linkage is key to understanding the concept. There are thus two sides involved in prebendalism, the officeholder and the client; and expectation of benefits by the clients (or supporters) perpetuates the prebendalist system. Prebendalism explicitly involves the abuse of the public realm, and therefore its inevitable consequence is the bankrupting of the state's coffers.[29] In the context of prebendalism, a civilian or military officeholder, for example, might award state contracts to clients solely on the basis of their financial support, without regard to merit or due

consideration of more qualified proposals. As practiced in the Babangida era, when official corruption occurred on an unprecedented scale, prebendalism deepened sectional cleavages and eroded the resources of the state. It has also discouraged genuinely productive activity in civil society and expanded the class of individuals who live off state patronage.

As long as prebendalism remains the norm of Nigerian politics, a stable democracy will be elusive. What prebendalism underscores is that these practices are now deeply embedded in Nigerian society and, therefore, are more difficult to uproot. The corruption resulting from prebendalist practices is blamed in popular discourse for the enormous flight of internally generated capital into numbered accounts in overseas banking institutions. The squandered $12.2 billion Gulf War windfall, the lion's share of which is believed to have accrued directly to Babangida and senior members of his regime and the Central Bank, is but one example—albeit exceptional in its magnitude—of the systematic pilfering of public resources. It is this type of massive unbridled corruption that led to the United Nations Development Program's 1992 call for an "Honesty International" to combat these practices.[30]

NIGERIA AND THE INTERNATIONAL POLITICAL ECONOMY

Nigeria and the Regional Political Economy

Nigeria has aspired to be a regional leader in Africa, and those aspirations have not been dampened by its declining position in the global political economy, even if it has lost prestige in regional and international forums. For example, Nigeria was a major actor in the formation in 1975 of the Economic Community of West African States (ECOWAS) and has carried a disproportionately high burden for keeping that troubled regional organization afloat. Nigeria has also been the largest contributor of troops to the West African peacekeeping force in Liberia, the ECOWAS Monitoring Group, known as ECOMOG. Nigeria had also initiated and borne the brunt—in terms of personnel and financial commitment—of that regional intervention force. ECOMOG troops were dispatched to Liberia in August 1990 by ECOWAS countries to restore order and to prevent the Liberian civil war from destabilizing the subregion. While retaining its commitment to ECOMOG, in 1994 Nigeria gradually began reducing its force level in Liberia.

Because it is the largest economy in the West African subregion, Nigeria has been adversely affected by a wave of smuggling and illegal immigration. At the height of the 1970s oil boom, many West African laborers, most of them Ghanaians, migrated to Nigeria for work, which was plentiful at that time. When the oil-based expansion ceased and jobs became scarce, Nigeria sought to protect its indigenous labor force. Despite its commitment, through the principles articulated in the ECOWAS agreement, to the free movement of peoples in the region, Nigeria expelled thousands of West Africans in early 1983.

On balance, ECOWAS has not accomplished much in pursuit of its goal of economic integration. The region is riven by jealousies and rivalries still largely organized around French- and English-speaking blocs. Each of these blocs maintains closer ties to its former colonial masters (France and Britain) economically and culturally than with each other. France, in particular, has tried to undermine ECOWAS to protest its privileged neo-colonial relationship with its former colonies.

In the years following independence, Nigeria has also been active in the Organization of African Unity (OAU), the Commonwealth (composed of former British colonies), the Nonaligned Movement, and the United Nations. In recent years, Nigeria played a major role in reorienting the focus of the Nonaligned Movement toward issues of economic development and cooperation. In bodies such as the OAU and the UN, Nigeria generally took firm positions to promote decolonization and the development of the Third World, and against the apartheid regime in the Republic of South Africa. But times have changed for Nigeria even within Africa. Ironically, the government of national unity in South Africa led by the African National Congress under President Nelson Mandela, which came to power in 1994, has been one of the leading critics of the Abacha regime. President Mandela, himself a former political prisoner, has been prominent among world leaders calling for the immediate release of Moshood Abiola and has sent Nobel peace laureate Archbishop Desmond Tutu to present this request to General Abacha in person.

Nigeria and the Political Economy of the West

The link between internal and external (in this case, Western) factors in Nigeria's political economy is best reflected in the interplay of forces that eventually drove General Babangida from power on August 26, 1993. This action followed his cancellation of the June 12 presidential election that should have been the final event in the full military withdrawal from governance on August 27 of that year.

Pro-democracy groups in Nigerian society were strengthened in their anti-Babangida campaign by the pressure being applied by external donors and creditors, especially the United States, Britain, and the European Union. Thus, under increasing pressure from external sources, and an increasingly outspoken and hostile domestic opposition to his continuation of the status quo, Babangida stepped aside on August 26. However, it is yet another irony of the Nigerian situation that Babangida was still able to install an unelected and handpicked interim government, again postponing the inauguration of the Third Republic.

It was not an easy task to dislodge a Nigerian ruler, especially one with considerable resources at his disposal. First, Babangida was a military dictator commanding one of the largest armed forces in Sub-Saharan Africa. Second, with a population of nearly 90 million, Nigeria possesses the region's biggest potential market. Third, Nigeria remains a highly visible and powerful member of OPEC, selling on the average 2 million barrels of petroleum daily, which has accounted for more than 10 percent of the United States' oil imports. Finally, Babangida presided over an economy in which each of the leading European countries such as Britain, France, and Germany has over $1 billion in investments.

However, despite these resources, there are also equally important areas of vulnerability which render Nigeria susceptible to political and economic influences from abroad. A resource-rich country, Nigeria is listed very close to the bottom of the UNDP's Human Development Index (HDI), just behind India and Haiti. Gross national product (GNP) per capita in 1989 was $250, less than 2 percent of which was recorded as public expenditures on education and health, respectively. Though the 1991 census adjusted the Nigerian population downward to 88.5 million from earlier estimates of over 100 million, per capita GNP still did not exceed $300 in 1991. Again, such figures compare unfavorably with the $350 per capita GNP for China and $340 per capita for India. On the basis of its per capita GNP, the Nigerian economy is the seventeenth poorest in the world in a 1992 World Bank ranking.

For comparative purposes, the same study ranks China as twenty-third poorest and India twenty-first.

Nigeria's global influence peaked in the 1970s at the height of the oil boom. Shortly after the 1973–1974 global oil crisis, Nigeria's oil wealth was perceived by the Nigerian elite largely as a source of strength. In 1975, for example, Nigeria, which at that time was selling about 30 percent of its oil to the United States,[31] was able to use these exports to apply pressure to the administration of President Gerald Ford in a dispute over Angola. Nigeria supported the communist-backed Popular Movement for the Liberation of Angola (MPLA) in the liberation struggle following the withdrawal of the Portuguese colonialists, a direct challenge to the position taken by the U.S. government. However, by the 1980s, the global oil market had become a buyer's market. Thereafter, it became clear that Nigeria's dependence on oil was a source of weakness, not strength. In addition to its dependence on oil revenues, Nigeria was dependent on Western technology and Western industrial expertise for exploration and extraction of its oil reserves.

The depth of this international weakness became clear with the adoption of structural adjustment in the mid-1980s. Since 1988, the growing economic crisis arising from dwindling oil revenues has forced Nigeria to embark on what Babangida's foreign minister, Major-General Ike Nwachukwu, branded as "economic diplomacy" to complement the SAP introduced in response to pressure from the World Bank, IMF, and major bilateral agencies in 1986. The essence of this economic diplomacy is that it seeks to subordinate other foreign policy goals to the economic imperative. It is also distinguished from the more defiant tactics employed against President Ford and Secretary of State Henry Kissinger a decade earlier. In a 1988 memo, Nwachukwu insisted that "it is the responsibility of our foreign policy apparatus to advance the course of our national economic recovery." In 1991, he further told a gathering of Nigerian ambassadors,

> The ballgame today in international relations is self-interest and economic development. In your utterances and in your behavioral patterns, please remember that Nigeria is a developing country. It needs support from the international community and that support can only come when you can win the confidence of those whose support you seek. . . .

> You begin to win that confidence through friendliness and loyalty to their cause (i.e., the cause of those whose support you seek). What matters is your ability to win for Nigeria what we cannot for ourselves, that is, the economic well-being of our people and physical well-being of Nigeria. . . . [32]

As Nigerian scholars contend, "economic diplomacy is the foreign policy component of the structural adjustment program . . . and it contains in its aspirations, at least, all the logical policy elements which flow from the submissions by Nigeria to the IMF and the World Bank."[33] There is no doubt, given the enormity of the economic crisis that has compelled it to seek IMF/World Bank support to improve its balance of payments and facilitate economic restructuring and debt rescheduling, that Nigeria has had to accept direction for the first time since gaining independence from foreign agencies. Annual budget proposals from the federal government and various government accounts have been subjected to scrutiny by these institutions.

Nigeria has had to operate under the political conditionality principle introduced to foreign aid programs by major industrial powers (the Group of Seven, or G-7) in the early 1990s. Thus, the military regime was subjected to pressures and threats of aid cutoff at crucial moments in the prolonged democratic transition under Babangida. All of these circumstances illustrate the magnitude of changes in the international arena that impinge on Nigeria's internal affairs. Some of these changes have been welcomed by Nigerians, who now applaud Western countries like the United States and Britain when they take forthright positions against corruption, human rights abuse, and military domination.

Unfortunately, unlike the situation in economically weaker African countries such as Benin, Malawi, and Zambia—where external pressures have bolstered internal demands for change, resulting in sometimes dramatic political transitions—in Nigeria, military regimes can still choose if, when, and how to accede to these pressures. It appears that the government of General Abacha is far less sensitive to international pressure than its predecessors. Limited economic sanctions and the growing threat of more severe measures have yet to influence Abacha. As it completes its second anniversary in power, the Abacha regime is more repressive than ever, and it has also decided unilaterally to stop implementing key features of the structural adjustment program.

Relations with the United States and countries of the European Union have deteriorated since the 1993 election annulment and still further under Abacha. In July 1993, the United States announced plans to suspend all commercial military sales to Nigeria and cancelled all but humanitarian aid. In July 1994, the U.S. House of Representatives passed a resolution condemning human rights abuses and advocating the restoration of democracy. Similar pronouncements

have been issued by Germany and Britain. However, Nigeria has avoided severe sanctions from the international community, because of its size, its high-grade petroleum reserves, and the significant presence (thus far, still secure) of foreign oil companies in the country.

In Section 3 we address governance and policy-making in Nigeria. As implied by the foregoing discussion of the military's control over the Nigerian state and economy, the institutions of governance and policy-making are either dormant or severely constrained by military authority.

SECTION 3
Governance and Policy-Making

The rough edges of what has been called the "unfinished Nigerian state" are very much in evidence with regard to its institutions of governance and policy-making. Nearly ten years into an elaborately sequenced transition from military to civil democratic rule—initiated years before democratization became fashionable in Africa and Eastern Europe—originally scheduled to end in 1990, Nigeria is no closer to civil or democratic rule. It is at the moment suspended in the limbo of history, saddled with a government completely lacking in legitimacy. The proposed Republic, administered by popularly elected civilians and governed by a constitution, remains elusive. Thus it is difficult to characterize and categorize precisely the institutions of governance in Nigeria as can be done for other countries. With that in mind, in this section we will present an account of how these institutions functioned in Nigeria historically, how they are intended to function in idealized form, and how they operate in practice given the vagaries of military domination in Nigeria's political processes.

We begin with a discussion of Nigerian constitutions. Constitutions are intended to form the basis of the fundamental laws and principles of modern states. The constitution establishes the legal-institutional framework for the governance of a society, the role of the state, and the rights and duties of citizens.

ORGANIZATION OF THE STATE
Constitutional Governance

Nigeria has changed its constitution often in the search for perfection, with constant constitutional engineer-

ing and the inauguration of several constitutions since colonial amalgamation in 1914. Although much attention has been focused on *making* constitutions, there has been little effort made to ensure that governments govern *according* to the constitution and that the rule of law is enforced in place of capricious governance. In short, Nigeria has produced many constitutions but it has yet to entrench constitutionalism.[34]

The reasons for this failure are not straightforward. Since 1914, Nigeria has inaugurated eight constitutions, five under colonial rule (in 1922, 1946, 1951, 1954, and 1960) and three after colonial rule: the 1963 Republican Constitution, the 1979 Constitution for the Second Republic, and the 1989 Constitution for the Third Republic. The most enduring was that of 1922 because there were few changes in the structure of colonial rule between the two world wars. None of the others lasted more than six years, and the 1989 Constitution has never gone into effect. In July 1994, Abacha convened a new constitutional conference whose decisions regarding any revisions to the 1989 document would be subject to veto by the Provisional Ruling Council.

It is important to note that none of these constitutions was initiated and drafted in a genuinely democratic environment. Of the three prepared after independence, two were engineered under military rule. Only the 1963 Constitution was initiated under an elected civilian federal administration. However, that government had lost its democratic credentials and was overthrown in the coup that terminated the First Republic in January 1966. Thus the constitution, as the notion of democracy itself, has come to be perceived in Nigeria largely as a gift bestowed by autocratic leaders. It is not surprising, therefore, that constitutions and constitutional guarantees are among the first casualities in the aftermath of a coup against elected government.

In the United States, the U.S. Constitution is often perceived as a "living document" and therefore subject to interpretation. However, whereas the U.S. Constitution has been interpreted in various ways based on legal precedent and political expedience, the document itself has endured for over 200 years with just twenty-six amendments. In contrast, Nigerian constitutions, in their various forms, have earned no such respect from leaders who are unwilling to abide by legal-constitutional constraints. Even under civilian rule, the tendency has been for the constitution to be treated in a cavalier manner by elected politicians who are impatient with its constraints and influenced by the authoritarian tradition of previous regimes.

Governance and policy-making in this context are conducted by fragile institutions that are often swamped by personal and other narrow considerations. Military rule has worked to accentuate these tendencies and to concentrate and personalize governance and policy-making, restricting the space for autonomous action. Moreover, the uncertainties caused by Nigeria's deliberately mismanaged democratic transition, first under Babangida, subsequently under the Shonekan and Abacha regimes, make it difficult to provide any definitive statements about the character of these institutions. With this in mind, we will discuss key elements of recent periods of military rule, their continued influence in the present, and the institutions projected for the future under full democratic rule.

Overview of State Structure

Nigeria's First Republic experimented with the parliamentary model in which the executive is chosen directly from the legislative ranks. The First Republic was relatively decentralized, with the locus of political power in the three federal units, the Northern, Eastern, and Western Regions. The constitution which went into effect with the advent of the Second Republic in 1979 adopted a presidential model. The consensus among Nigeria's constitutional planners for the next Republic is that the structure of the Nigerian polity today should resemble closely that of the United States of America. In this view, democratic Nigeria should

possess: a presidential system with a strong executive who is constrained by a system of checks and balances on authority; a bicameral legislature; an independent judicial branch charged with matters of law and constitutional interpretation. In addition, it should have a federal structure comprised of states and local government units empowered to enact certain laws within their individual jurisdictions, but which are ultimately accountable to central government authority. Together, these units constitute a single, national entity.

In this system the formal powers of the different levels of government would be clearly delineated, and the relationships among and between them defined. In Nigeria, by contrast, these institutions have been radically altered by military rule. The dominance of central government authority, particularly the executive, has been enhanced by military rule. So while Nigerian federalism remains a subject of political and social discourse, in large part because of its ethnic overtones and "federal character," it is necessary to point out that the military is not a unit of a federal governing structure, at least not in the traditional sense. The control of oil wealth by this centralized command structure has further cemented economic and political control in the center, resulting in a "skewed federalism" in which states enjoy nominal powers, but in reality are totally dependent on the central government. Abacha's rule has weakened the constituent units still further by abolishing all elective state and local political structures.

Nigerian Federalism and "Federal Character"

The context in which **federalism** was adopted in 1954, six years before independence, was one in which the political elite increasingly withdrew to their ethnic constituencies. Although some nationalist leaders desired a unitary republic when the marked differences among the regions began to influence political life, it became evident that only federalism, involving units organized around major ethnolinguistic groups, offered the possibility of achieving peace and stability in a multinational country. It is important to note, however, that Nigeria actually witnessed an *increase* in interethnic tension before independence. In many other African states—though ethnic tensions often did erupt following independence—the aspiring leaders were often able to put aside their ethnic differences to present a more unified front against colonial rule. In others, and Nigeria is notable among them, the prospect of a transfer of power encouraged divisive strategies that often persisted into the postcolonial era.

It was widely believed that federalism, in which the constituent units agree to subordinate their authority to a central government accorded certain powers, would be the system best suited to accommodate Nigeria's ethnic pluralism. The assumption in the 1950s, which we now know to have been overly optimistic, was that the central government would be responsible for the "equitable distribution" of resources to the constituent units. This arrangement is now referred to as "guaranteeing unity in diversity."

There are several elements of the Nigerian experience with federalism of relevance for governance and policy-making. Although organized by territorial units (states) around a central national government, Nigerian federalism since inception has operated in practice around ethnic communities. One reason for this tendency is that "African leaders are so steeped in ethnic considerations that they cannot imagine any other mode of operation."[35] This practice is also influenced by the ease with which African communities mobilize along ethnic and subethnic lines. In other words, while in Western industrialized nations, cooperation as well as conflict and political affiliation are based on cultural affinities and on divisions of economic class, or what are called "horizontal" relations, in Africa, particularly in Nigeria, the weakness of genuine class distinctions makes appeals to ethnic ties (vertical relations) more potent.

Another relevant factor is the way decisions have been made to constitute and reconstitute Nigerian federalism. These decisions have been made by the regime controlling the federal center and imposed on the country. None of various configurations of Nigerian homfederalism required input from the state and local governments. Again, because Nigeria has sought to emulate American political institutions, a comparison with the United States is helpful: unlike the United States' experience with federalism in the eighteenth century, when the states voted on the adoption of the federal structure, in Nigeria the tenfold increase in the number of federal units (from three to thirty) between 1967 and 1991 was made by the military governments of Generals Gowon, Obasanjo, and Babangida acting on their own authority (see Table 5 on the following page).

Thus virtually the entire process of constituting and reconstituting this federal arrangement, including the addition of a third level of government consisting

(in 1991) of 589 local government units, has occurred under either colonial or military rule. The initial motivation to create additional subnational units in the federation was to bring government closer to the people, foster development, and accommodate the demands of minority ethnic groups for their "own" units. It was clear by 1991, however, that adding more states to the federation was an intrinsic part of a strategy of state corporatism, designed to keep the many subnational units financially dependent on and beholden to the central government. Such practices were employed by the Babangida military regime to divide and control the Nigerian population rather than to enhance popular participation. In sum, the Nigerian experience has promoted a distributive approach to federalism.[36] The lofty claims for federalism as a way of promoting unity through diversity are lost amid the intense competition among "local communities and elites for access to national patronage in the form of oil revenues which are collected, and then appropriated or *redistributed,* by the federal [national] administration."[37] (See Table 6.)

Clearly, the long periods of military administrations, and their centralized power structure, have hindered the emergence of genuine federalism in Nigeria. Thus Nigeria has been described as "a unitary system in federal disguise." As oil revenues came to dominate the nation's finances after 1970, the fact that the lion's share went to the federal government rather than to the states or local governments accentuated the centralizing tendencies in Nigeria's federalism.

Federal Character   Numerous attempts have been made to arrive at some form of elite accommodation to moderate some of the more divisive dimensions of cultural pluralism. For example, recruitment of local elements into the army shortly after independence followed a quota system. Through such a system it was hoped the army would reflect the country's complex ethnic makeup more closely. A similar practice, reflecting what Nigerians now refer to as "federal character" was introduced into the public service and formally codified in Section 14(3) of the 1979 Constitution:

> The composition of the Government of the Federation or any of its agencies and the conduct of its affairs shall be carried out in such manner as to reflect the federal character and

TABLE 5   **Political Divisions, 1963–1991**

1963	1967	1976	1987	1991
Northern Region	North Western	Niger	Niger	Niger
		Sokoto	Sokoto	Sokoto
				Kebbi
	North Eastern	Bauchi	Bauchi	Bauchi
		Borno	Borno	Borno
				Yobe
		Gongola	Gongola	Adamawa
				Taraba
	North Central	Kaduna	Kaduna	Kaduna
			Katsina	Katsina
	Benue Plateau	Benue Plateau	Benue Plateau	Benue Plateau
	West Central	Kwara	Kwara	Kwara
				Kogi[a]
	Kano	Kano	Kano	Kano
				Jigawa
Eastern Region	East Central	Anambra	Anambra	Anambra
				Enugu
		Imo	Imo	Imo
				Abia
	South Eastern	Cross River	Cross River	Cross River
			Akwa Ibom	Akwa Ibom
	Rivers	Rivers	Rivers	Rivers
Western Region	Western	Ogun	Ogun	Ogun
		Ondo	Ondo	Ondo
		Oyo	Oyo	Oyo
				Osun
Lagos[b]	Lagos	Lagos	Lagos	Lagos
Mid-West Region	Mid Western	Bendel	Bendel	Edo
				Delta
Federal Capital Territory		Abuja	Abuja	Abuja[c]

[a]Kogi state was created by combining parts of Benue and Kwara states.
[b]Lagos was excised from the Western Region in 1954 and became the federal capital. In 1967, it also became capital of the new Lagos State, which included Badagry, Ikeja, and Epe districts from the Western Region.
[c]Abuja replaced Lagos as the federal capital in December 1991.

Source: Tom Forrest, *Politics and Economic Development in Nigeria* (Boulder, Colo.: Westview Press, 1993), 214.

the need to promote national unity, and also to command national loyalty thereby ensuring that there shall be no predominance of persons from a few states or from a few ethnic or other sectional groups in that government or any of its agencies.

Because federal character is also perceived as a tool of ethnic management, disputes about its application have tended to focus on ethnic representation rather than on representation of state interests. Although this principle was originally regarded as a positive Nigerian contribution to governance in a plural society, its application has tended to intensify rather than reduce intergroup rivalries and conflicts. In recent years there have been calls for the use of merit over federal character in awarding public sector jobs.

Despite the methods of its institution and reform, ironically, the federal system has enjoyed wide support within Nigeria historically. However, the federal structure endures increasing strain. With the conclusion of the civil war in 1970, it was assumed that the

Corporatism

There are varying definitions and interpretations of corporatism, but it may be defined broadly as a system of interest group aggregation whereby interest groups are hierarchically ordered in terms of their relationship with the state, and licensed and/or controlled by the state. European or societal corporatism allows the national government greater access to information about various groups in society. Societal corporatism usually connotes a coherent and efficient state bureaucracy and describes a set of centralized interest organizations that bargain with the state. Many Africanist scholars, however, have argued that the concept of "corporatism" as described here does not apply in Africa because the state is fragmented. That is, there is a lack of centralization and coherence; state, local, and national agencies operate at cross-purposes in pursuit of different goals. A few, notably Julius Ihonvbere and Tim Shaw (1989), have argued that a *state corporatist* model can be applied to Nigeria. The

theoretical debate notwithstanding, the Nigerian state has endeavored to institute corporatist-like controls over various societal interest groups, including labor and business, in what might be labeled *state corporatism*, a variety of corporatism consistent with the authoritarian aspects of military rule. A more blatant example of Nigeria's state corporatism was the 1994 attempt to co-opt and control organized labor by firing the union heads and replacing them with Abacha's cronies. However, unlike most environments of societal corporatism, in which labor leaders with the support of their constituents agree to cooperate with government, it is not likely that the rank and file of Nigerian labor will cooperate with the military regime.*

---

*See Ihonvbere and Shaw, "Corporatism in Nigeria" in *Corporatism in Africa: Comparative Analysis and Practice*, ed. Julius Nyang'oro and Tim Shaw (Boulder, Colo.: Westview Press, 1989).

TABLE 6   Percentage Contribution of Different Sources of Government Revenue to Allocated Revenue, 1980–1988

| Year | Oil Revenue | | Non-Oil Revenue | | |
	Petroleum Profits Tax	Mining Rents and Royalties	Customs and Excise Duties	Others	Total
1980	58.1	25.7	12.3	3.9	100.0
1981	55.5	19.6	20.4	4.5	100.0
1982	44.5	27.3	21.5	6.7	100.0
1983	35.7	33.4	18.9	12.0	100.0
1984	44.8	32.4	15.2	7.6	100.0
1985	47.8	30.0	14.7	7.5	100.0
1986	40.5	25.3	14.6	19.6	100.0
1987	50.6	25.4	14.3	9.7	100.0
1988	46.7	31.5	15.9	5.9	100.0

Source: Federal Ministry of Finance and Economic Development, Lagos. From Adedotun Phillips, "Managing Fiscal Federalism: Revenue Allocation Issues," *Publius: The Journal of Federalism*, 21, no. 4 (Fall 1991), p. 109.

---

question of national unity had been finally settled. Thus attempts to include clauses on the right to secede into the constitutions of 1979 and 1989 were roundly rejected by the drafting committees. Other widely held beliefs, although now questioned by some elements in society, is that Nigeria will continue to be a secular state as outlined in Section 10 of the 1979 Constitution and will persist as a federation to accommodate the

country's ethnic, cultural, and religious heterogeneity. Some northerners have advocated turning Nigeria into an Islamic state, prompting fear among many Christians. To resolve these issues, some Nigerians have called for a national conference to review the basis of national unity and even to consider the restructuring of Nigeria into a loose confederation of autonomous states. Such calls have been ignored by the Abacha

Nigeria's "Federal Character"

What is Nigeria's "federal character"? Federal character, in principle, is an "affirmative action" program to ensure representation of all ethnic and regional groups, particularly in the civil service. Although federal character is regarded as a euphemism for ethnic balancing, in practice it has provoked ethnic instability, rivalry, and conflict. Federal character goes beyond federalism in the traditional Western and territorial sense, although it definitely contains a territorial element. Federalism as a principle of government has a positive connotation (especially in regard to mitigating ethnic conflict); however, federal character invokes the unevenness and inequality in Nigerian politics.

Federal character connotes the need for ethnic balancing, but the pursuit of this arguably worthy goal has had numerous ill effects, several of which are identified by Nigerian scholar Peter Ekeh. First, there has been an "overgeneralization" of federal character: It has created benefit-seeking and autonomy-seeking groups in areas where they

did not previously exist. Second, the addition of more states has cemented group ties and consciousness, not the reverse. Third, federal character and federalism have overloaded the political system in terms of personnel and other costs. Fourth, federal character has "invaded the integrity of the public bureaucracy" by ignoring merit. Finally, the thirty states that currently exist in Nigeria are vying for control of the center in order to extract the greatest benefits. None of these conditions is likely to change in the near future, whether a military or a civilian government is in power, Federal character, and everything that goes with it, appears to be a permanent part of Nigeria's political and social landscape.*

------

*See Ekeh, "The Structure and Meaning of Federal Character in the Nigerian Political System" in *Federalism and the Federal Character in Nigeria*, ed. Peter Ekeh and Eghosa E. Osaghae (Ibadan: Heinemann, 1989).

regime, which refused to permit any debate on the viability of a united Nigeria in the recent Constitutional Conference, thus maintaining the geographic status quo, at least for now.

THE EXECUTIVE

Evolution of Executive Function

At independence, Nigeria inherited the British-type parliamentary system of government. The national government of the First Republic (1960–1966) was headed by a prime minister, Sir Abubakar Tafawa Balewa, a *primus inter pares* (first among equals) in his cabinet. A move toward a stronger executive type of personalized leadership followed the military coup of January 1966 and continued during the thirteen subsequent years of military rule. It was therefore not surprising that, by the inauguration of an elected administration in 1979 in the Second Republic, the parliamentary system had been dropped in favor of a presidential system based on the American model. In this system, the executive is chosen directly by the electorate rather than indirectly by the legislature. The rationale for the change was based on the experience of the First Republic; the instability and ultimate failure of that government (which was less a result of the parliamentary model *per se,* than of underlying societal cleavages), left a bitter legacy. In addition, there was a widespread belief that a popularly elected presi-

dent, a truly "national" figure, could serve as a symbol of unity. Finally, the framers of the Second Republic's constitution believed that placing the election of the president in the hands of the electorate, rather than parliament, would mitigate the effects of a lack of party discipline in the selection of the executive.

In rejecting British parliamentarism for American-style presidentialism, the framers of the 1979 Constitution of the Second Republic argued that the new arrangement would lead to a more focused executive authority and facilitate the effective use of that authority. According to them, the American model would also ensure (through the exercise of checks and balances and separation of powers) that no single arm of government would gain so much power as to put the liberties of citizens at risk. It was argued also that presidentialism would promote political integration since it authorized the head of the executive branch to appoint individuals from outside the legislature to the cabinet.

Powers were consolidated within the executive, however, and the checks and balances and separation of powers central to the proper running of a presidential system in a constitutional government were gradually eliminated. Of course, as students of American constitutional history will readily recall, the reason given for checks and balances is to prevent the domination of any one branch of government over the oth-

General Sani Abacha, a prominent member of Nigerian military regimes since December 1983, took over the government in November 1993, disbanded all elective institutions, and has since suppressed all opposition forces. On October 1, 1995, he announced a plan to transfer power to civilians by 1998.
Source: AP/Wide World Photos.

ers. The effective removal of legislative opposition has contributed to the unchallenged power of the executive branch in Nigeria.

The Second Republic's experiment with presidentialism lasted for only four years before it was ended by the 1983 coup. Although there is a continuing debate among political scientists over the relative merits of parliamentarism versus presidentialism,[38] that coup did not indict the presidential model as such. Instead, the coup was justified by citing corrupt political practices, including massive vote-rigging by the civilian regime of the elections in December 1983 as well as economic mismanagement. Once again, however, the reality of military rule further concentrated power in the hands of the chief executive, first head of state Major-General Muhammadu Buhari, until the 1985 palace coup. His successor, General Babangida, although obviously unelected, assumed the title of president, the first Nigerian military ruler to do so, as if to

confer some sort of popular legitimacy on his seizure of power. After ousting Shonekan in November 1993, Sani Abacha reverted to the title of head of state.

The Executive Under Military Rule and Future Civilian Governments

There has been a wide variation in the styles and leadership approaches among Nigeria's seven military heads of state. The military regime of General Gowon (1966–1974) was consensual, endeavoring to include a range of groups in positions of authority. In the aftermath of the Biafran War, Gowon presided effectively over the reuniting of the warring factions and the country in a lasting settlement. Although all have talked of "transitions to democracy" at one point or another, only one, General Olusegun Obasanjo, successfully fulfilled the pledge. As head of state from 1976–1979, General Obasanjo was able to make good on the promise of democracy. Buhari's coup in 1983 was initially welcomed by popular support in the wake of the abuses during the Second Republic. However, Buhari was intensely authoritarian in his methods, suspending political liberties, outlawing political activities, and extensively using the security services to repress political opposition. Similarly, Abacha's harsh authoritarian style is reflected in the 1994 suspension of *habeas corpus* and numerous brutalities.

Under both civilian and military administrations, appointments to the highest (and not so high) offices of the state are made, and restrained, at the whim of the president, without the need for legislative approval for most senior appointments. Following a 1988 reform of the civil service carried out by the Babangida administration, even middle-level appointees were transformed from career bureaucrats to purely political officeholders, a change scrapped by Abacha in 1995. Both leaders, however, have consolidated one-person rule which rests "on a clientelist system that runs from the head of state down to rural villages and urban wards."[39]

Even with the tumultuous events in Nigeria since Babangida stepped aside in August 1993, the form and function of Nigeria's politics remain basically the same. It is not surprising, therefore, that ethnic, religious, and regional constituencies pay close attention to the pattern of appointments to the executive branch and the higher echelons of the national bureaucracy. This scrutiny has intensified since 1983 under the

General Olusegun Obasanjo was the Nigerian head of state who supervised the transition of civil rule from 1976 to 1979. In 1995 he was arrested and convicted in a secret trial in connection with an alleged attempt to overthrow the regime of General Abacha.
Source: Reuters/Bettmann.

Buhari and Babangida military regimes, both of which were headed by northern Muslim military officers. They have been criticized for inattention to southern and Christian interests in making appointments and for their policies in general. As discussed in Section 2, General Abacha, also a northerner and a Muslim, has attracted even greater criticism than his predecessors.

Under the 1989 Constitution, the proposed Third Republic would have included an executive similar to the American model with the required checks and balances. The American presidential model is expected to be included once again in the recommendations of the Constitutional Conference of 1994–1995. However, it remains to be seen whether these provisions will be included in the revised document, and if they are, will

they be respected through implementation? Nigeria's political history and recent experience suggest that the country will again experience the unchallenged neo-patrimonial rule of an executive president and his handpicked cabinet, ineffectually checked by a weak legislature and judiciary, both vulnerable to executive and clientelist pressures.

The Military as Executive Branch

As a result of its long years in power, the military has emerged as a central component of executive authority in Nigeria. As a consequence, the institution of military service has itself been weakened for, unlike professional (nonpoliticized) militaries, Nigeria's military lacks camaraderie, discipline, a clear command structure, and unity of purpose. It has become evident since 1966, and it was increasingly so under Babangida's rule, that a distinction has developed between the *military-in-government* and the *military-in-barracks.* A difference has emerged between military officers appointed to political posts and those who perform traditional military duties. Officers in the latter group have increasingly called for a withdrawal of the armed forces from politics and a return to military professionalism. Military coups against military-run governments have often resulted from this intramilitary tension. Several such attempts have not been successful, resulting in the execution or dismissal from office of those officers implicated or suspected of disloyalty. Keenly aware of this, Babangida displayed a readiness to divide and rule within the military as well as within civil society. Command and other major postings were dictated largely by questions of loyalty to his regime, ensuring a highly visible profile for northern officers like himself and a lower profile for the others. Increasingly, under Sani Abacha, there is a widening gulf between junior officers and the inner circle of northern military elites. The former are beset by a lack of prestige and inadequate pay, whereas many of the latter, including Abacha himself, are known to have profited greatly from their control of the state.

A final point to note is that the Nigerian military appears to have lost its political neutrality. In 1966, the military was perceived as a temporary alternative to misrule by civilian politicians. Subsequently, the military as an institution was transformed from an instrument to assure national defense into a permanent alternative to political parties. Three decades after the first military coup, Nigerians believe that the armed forces have compounded Nigeria's political and economic problems. During the last few years, there have been concerted attempts by groups in civil society to achieve the military's withdrawal from public life. Clearly, the Nigerian armed forces, in view of the number of years they have been in office, have primary responsibility for the country's failure to achieve economic growth, social peace, probity in government, and political development.

The Bureaucracy

The bureaucracy is related to and affects all aspects of Nigerian governmental institutions. Although we referred to the Nigerian bureaucracy in the previous two sections, it is necessary to explain further how the Nigerian bureaucracy came to be bloated, inefficient, and corrupt. The colonial system relied greatly on an expanding bureaucracy to govern Nigeria. As structures of governance and society were increasingly "Africanized," the bureaucracy became a means of rewarding individuals in the patrimonial system. Bureaucratic growth was then no longer determined by function and need; increasingly, individuals were appointed on the basis of patronage, ethnic group, and regional origin rather than merit. Administration departments also became structures that the government could use to insulate and protect itself by installing civil servants who were loyal to and beholden to the state. As successive military governments since 1967 increased the number of states, while also taking on grandiose public projects, the capabilities of the bureaucracy declined, while its size steadily increased. Conservative estimates of federal and state government personnel increased from a modest 72,000 at independence to well over 1 million by the mid-1980s. The largest component of the national bureaucracy in Nigeria are the state-owned enterprises (SOEs), or para-statals, which increased from 75 entities to 500 over the same period.[40]

Para-statals **Para-statals** in Nigeria are corporate enterprises owned by the state and established to provide specific commercial and social welfare services. They can be regarded as situated between institutions that engage in traditional government operations, such as customs or the postal service, and those in the private sector that operate primarily for profit. In organizational terms, such para-statals are similar to private

enterprises in that they have their own boards of directors to which management is directly answerable. To this extent, they are autonomous of the government that established them. In reality, however, such autonomy is limited since their boards are appointed by, and ultimately answerable to, the government through the supervising government department (in Nigeria called a ministry).

In general, para-statals are established for the following reasons. First, they are created as public utilities to provide services that government departments cannot handle effectively. In such cases, private business cannot fully provide these services because the capital investment required is too great, or national security implications may be involved (as in the case of ports, waterworks, telecommunications, defense industries, hydroelectric power, petroleum exploration and extraction). A second rationale for the establishment of para-statals is the need to accelerate economic development. This justification has been advanced for establishing para-statals in such large-scale industries as steel production, public transportation, petroleum, and certain areas of agriculture. Third, para-statals are intended to provide basic utilities and services (water, electricity, agricultural support) to citizens at a low cost. These costs are held below the level needed to generate a profit if the same services were provided by private firms.

Finally, there is a nationalist dimension that relates to issues of sovereignty over sectors perceived to be "sensitive." Para-statals are intended to provide services in economic areas that could fall under the control of foreign capital and expertise. The para-statal structure is seen as a way to reduce dependence on foreign multinational firms in such industries as air transportation, seaport management, steel and petroleum production, power generation, and mass communication.

In Nigeria, para-statals such as commodity boards and the Nigerian National Petroleum Corporation (NNPC) have served as major economic instruments of the interventionist state. They have been used to co-opt and hierarchically order business and societal interests within the state for the purpose of controlling both society and economy—a form of governance usually called **state corporatism.** Because they are not motivated by profit, are protected by the state, and are frequently managed by administrators whose jobs are based on their personal connections rather than on managerial ability, the track record of Nigerian para-statals is littered with inefficiency, cronyism, and various forms of corruption. Instead of providing economic benefits, most para-statal enterprises in Africa as a whole, and in Nigeria specifically, are a tremendous drain on the economy. It is not surprising, therefore, that one of the major requirements of the economic structural adjustment program discussed in Section 2 is the privatization of most of these enterprises, especially those that would interest private capital. Although laudable in principle, in practice the frequently mismanaged privatization program has meant a continuation of all the problems identified above and in Section 2. Without concerted and genuine efforts at privatization, therefore, the indications are that Nigerian para-statals will continue to fall far short of the original expectations that they would contribute to economic development and efficient provision of services. What is more likely is that para-statals will remain central to the politics of patronage and resource allocation conducted along class and ethnic lines. In this regard, their role as vehicles for venality and instruments of gross inefficiency will remain largely unchanged.

OTHER STATE INSTITUTIONS

Other institutions of governance and policy-making, including the federal judiciary and subnational governments (incorporating state and local courts), operate within the context outlined above of a strong central government dominated by an all-powerful chief executive.

The Judiciary

At one time, the Nigerian judiciary enjoyed relative autonomy from the executive arm of government. Aggrieved individuals and organizations could take the government to court and expect a judgment based on the merits of their case. This situation changed as each successive military government demonstrated a profound disdain for judicial practices, and eventually undermined not only the autonomy but also the very integrity of the judiciary as a third branch of government.

The principal instrument used by the Babangida and Abacha regimes to achieve this outcome has been a spate of repressive decrees that contain ouster clauses disallowing judicial review. Such clauses are regularly inserted in government decrees barring

("ousting") any consideration of their legality by the courts, as well as any actions taken by government officials under them. Other methods include intimidation by the security services, the creation of parallel special military tribunals that could dispense with various legal procedures and due process, and disrespect for courts of record. Through the executive's power of appointment of judicial officers to the high bench as well as the executive's control of funds required for the running of the judiciary, the government can manipulate and dominate the courts at all levels. Even in more routine civil and criminal actions, the courts are subject to political interference. In addition, what was once regarded as a highly competent judiciary has been undermined severely by declining standards of legal training as well as bribery. Deprived of adequate resources and the protections afforded the judiciary in Western societies, the judiciary has become more of an instrument of military regimes than an independent branch of government.

Any remaining doubts about this development were dispelled on July 22, 1993, when, in what analysts labeled "judicial terrorism," the Supreme Court endorsed a government position that literally placed all actions of the executive beyond the pale of judicial review. In a landmark judgment on a suit which sought judicial review of Babangida's decision to annul the June 12 election, the court ruled that it lacked jurisdiction, thereby bowing to the government lawyer's argument that any decree of the military government is the law of the land and that such decrees cannot be challenged.[41]

The judiciary in Nigeria has effectively ceased to be the last hope of Nigerian citizens. The prolonged detention of Moshood Abiola, after he declared himself president in June 1994, and the multiple changes in presiding judges hearing challenges to his detention, has further eroded public confidence in the judiciary. By the end of 1994, Abiola had received four rulings in his favor declaring that he should be released on bail. The Abacha regime has steadfastly refused to comply and ultimately responded by revoking the writ of *habeas corpus.* State Security Decree Number Two effectively prevents courts from ordering the government to produce political detainees in court who wish to challenge their detention.

It is hoped that some of the professionalism and dignity engendered by independence will revert to the judiciary in the next Republic, especially if provisions

Federal Courts

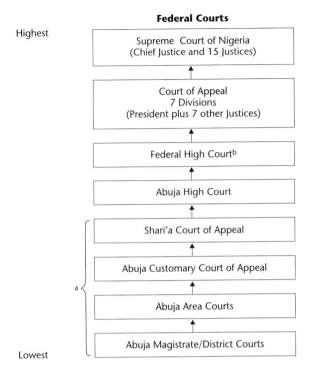

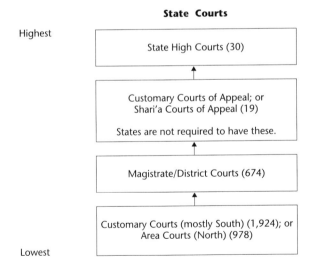

aFederal Capital Territory (FCT) Courts. Same functions as state courts, but under federal court system.
bHears mostly revenue cases; no appellate jurisdiction; same rank as state high courts.

Figure 1 The Nigerian Court System
Source: Adapted from Clement Nwankwo, Basil Ugochukwu, and Dulue Mbachu, *Nigeria: The Limits of Justice* (LAGOS: 1993).

regarding its functions and authority in the 1989 Constitution are unchanged. That document calls for judicial autonomy—a true separation of powers—judicial review, due process, and provisions for the appointment, tenure, and removal of judges. Even so, new budgetary arrangements will be needed to protect the institutional interests of the judiciary vis-à-vis the executive. Moreover, the executive will need to be encouraged to respect judicial autonomy as a vital component of democratic governance. Unfortunately, the experience of the judiciary during periods of civilian party politics, although not as devastating as during military rule, does not bode well for the restoration of an autonomous judiciary and respect for the rule of law in the near future.

Subnational Government

Nigeria operates a federal system with three levels of government: the first or highest is the national government (which we also refer to as the central or federal government), and, as in the U.S. federal system, there are also state and local levels of government. Like the national government, each of the thirty state governments and 589 local governments in Nigeria has an executive branch and a legislative branch, though all were dismissed by Abacha when he seized power. The judicial system also resembles that of the United States with a network of local and district courts as well as state-level courts.

State and Local Judiciaries The judiciaries at the state level are subordinate to the Federal Court of Appeal and the Supreme Court. Some of the states in the northern part of the country with high Muslim populations maintain a parallel court system based on the Islamic **shari'a** (divine law). Similarly, some states in the Middle Belt and southern part of the country have subsidiary courts based on customary law. Each of these, in turn, maintains an appellate division, as shown in Figure 1. Otherwise, all courts of record in the country are based on the English common law tradition, and all courts are ultimately bound by decisions handed down by the Supreme Court. As noted earlier, however, the decisions of all courts may be effectively overruled by the military government.

Because it has been a source of continuing debate in Nigerian politics, the subject of *shari'a* deserves mention. For several years, some northern groups have participated in a movement to apply *shari'a* to all

TABLE 7   **Share of Total Government Expenditure, in Million Naira (percentages)**

	1961	1965	1970	1975	1980	1987
Federal Government	49	53	73	72	66	75
State Government	51	47	27	28	34	25
Total Expenditure	336	445	1,149	10,916	21,349	29,365

Sources: Central Bank of Nigeria, *Annual Report and Statement of Accounts;* Federal Office of Statistics, *Abstract of Annual Statistics* (Lagos: Federal Government Printer, 1961, 1965, 1970, 1975, 1980, and 1987). From Izeubuwa Osayimwese and Sunday Iyare, "The Economics of Nigerian Federalism: Selected Issues in Economic Management," *Publius: The Journal of Federalism,* 21, no. 4 (Fall 1991), p. 91.

of Nigeria, and some even advocated that it be made the supreme law of the land. In 1977, northern groups led a boycott of the Constituent Assembly when it began drafting the Second Republic Constitution, demanding stronger emphasis on *shari'a* in that national document. Although the military government of Obasanjo blocked the expansion of *shari'a,* provisions were made that allowed the appointment of several judges qualified in Islamic personal law to the federal Court of Appeal and the Supreme Court. Demands for a broader application of Islamic law were made during the drafting of the 1989 Constitution, but these were again thwarted. At present, *shari'a* courts have jurisdiction only in civil proceedings and in questions of Islamic personal law.

The application of *shari'a* has sparked heated debate. On the one hand, Muslims view the *shari'a* as a way of life. On the other, southerners and Christians consider the very presence of *shari'a* on a national level as threatening to their own interests and beliefs, and another example of northern domination. The attempt under Babangida to alter Nigeria's status from observer to full membership in the Council of Islamic States also prompted fears that the secular nature of the state was endangered.

State and Local Governments   State governments are generally weak and dependent on federally controlled revenues. Most of them would be insolvent and unable to sustain themselves without substantial support from the central government, because of the states' weak resource and tax base. In the same way that states depend on federal handouts, local governments have remained dependent on both state *and* federal governments. This practice has continued

despite reforms of the local government system initiated by the Babangida regime in 1988 supposedly to strengthen that level of government. The weakness and dependence of all subnational governments lies in their inability to raise sufficient financial resources of their own through taxation and other means. This obstacle to subnational development persists despite constitutional and legal powers of the states and local governments to raise funds through taxes. There is a pronounced unwillingness among Nigerians, especially those in self-employment, trade, and other informal sector activities, to pay taxes and fees to a government with such a poor record of delivering basic services to the people. Moreover, it is often believed that most funds paid to governments, at all levels, will be misused or simply stolen. The result is a vicious cycle: Government is sapped of resources and legitimacy and cannot adequately serve the people. Communities, in turn, are compelled to resort to self-help measures to protect these operations and thus withdraw further from the reach of the state. One can imagine if such a scenario unfolded in the United States, or any other nation that requires taxation as a major source of government revenues: If very few individuals and organizations paid taxes, even the most basic government functions could not be performed (see Table 7).

Finally, although elected civilian governors had replaced military governors in 1992 following elections in December 1991 as part of the program of democratic transition, the elected governors were treated by the Babangida regime just as military governors were treated; their administrations were wholly dependent on, and therefore subservient to, the military administration at the center. General Abacha went even further, dismissing the civilian governors and state legislators shortly after he seized power in November 1993 and replacing them with military administrations.

Although intergovernmental relations tend to be less confrontational under military rule because of its unitary command structure, it is obvious that the situation just described leaves much room for conflict between subnational and national governments, whether the context is military rule or civilian rule and multiparty politics. In the civilian Second Republic, some conflicts did develop between the federal and state governments, mostly over access to economic resources. About 90 percent of state incomes were received directly from the federal government, which includes a lump sum based on oil revenues, plus a percentage of oil income based on population.[42] With power in Nigeria concentrated at the political center, competition for scarce resources also takes place at the center. Many of the states have a predominant ethnic identification. Consequently, the struggle for national resources among states takes on an ethnoregional cast that has weakened Nigerian federalism in the First and Second Republics.

THE POLICY-MAKING PROCESS

Nigeria's prolonged experience with military rulers has resulted in a policy process based on top-down directives rather than on consultation, political debate, and legislation. Under Babangida, the concentration of power reached its highest level since independence because Babangida was the sole center of the policy-making process in the military administration. The period from 1985 until 1993 witnessed a concentration of policy-making powers in his hands, and in the hands of those answerable to him, and a corresponding weakening of the authority of the formal institutions of governance, namely the federal and state legislatures.

Formal powers are concentrated in the military ruler. Much of the policy input process (to the extent it exists) comes to the president and his "cabinet" through informal channels and networks where clientelist practices flourish. Babangida created this system in various ways. His penchant for making cabinet changes (his cabinet consisted of both military officers and civilians) gave the impression that only one man could provide consistency in making decisions. He adopted the same approach within the highest organ of his administration, the Armed

Forces Ruling Council (AFRC, later called the National Defense and Security Council, NDSC, and now known as the PRC, which has no civilian members), composed mainly of senior military officers. This body performed both executive functions (by reviewing the work of the cabinet office) and legislative ones. Babangida dismissed the original members of the AFRC until they were all replaced by his own men. He was able to do this because he closely monitored appointments to all command and staff positions in the armed services, ensuring that officers who advanced in the system and controlled strategic units remained loyal to him.

Another tactic Babangida successfully employed was to neutralize or marginalize information networks that he could not control within Nigerian society. He then used divide-and-rule tactics as well as state largesse to nurture his vast informal network. He successfully marginalized such groups as the Kaduna mafia and the Langtang mafia. Note that the term *mafia* in this context refers less to a notion of organized crime and more to political machines that have a distinctive social and regional cast. The Kaduna mafia, made up of northern technocrats who formed a powerful network centered on the northern city of Kaduna, and the Langtang mafia, composed of military officers from Langtang in the minority area of the Middle Belt, had been significant players in political and social life. Interestingly, the latter group had played a major role in the coup that brought Babangida to power. Their ranks, however, were gradually depleted and sidelined following a purported coup plot against Babangida in 1986 in which officers from the Middle Belt were implicated.

In place of these networks, Babangida put together a network consisting of academics, especially political scientists, and middle-ranking military officers united by loyalty to his person and administration. Soon the policy-making process took place within these informal channels. The formal structures, including the higher civil service, the cabinet, and the AFRC served mainly as coordinating centers, sounding boards, and rubber stamps for Babangida's decisions and initiatives.

Babangida, always a skillful politician, never overlooked the importance of public opinion in the policy-making process. The frequent reversals reflected his tendency to want to satisfy as many informal constituencies as possible. Indeed, he was quite

General Sani Abacha forces the head of the "interim" civilian government, Edward Shonekan, overboard.
Source: Courtesy *West Africa Magazine*, West Africa Publishing Co., London.

sensitive to public disenchantment. His long stay in power—particularly when contrasted with both his military and civilian predecessors—reflects his ability to defuse potential sources of opposition, suppressing some while placating others, and his ability to reverse course when necessary.

Military regimes are not voted out of office. They either engineer a transition to a civilian government or are forcibly removed by coups similar to the ones that brought them to power. Although never enjoying the legitimacy of popularly elected democratic governments, military rulers must be sensitive to opinion within the military establishment and civil society. It is a precarious existence, certainly, and military leaders must placate the public while acting to prevent the emergence of a unified opposition front. The *tactics* do not differ that substantially from civilian politics, but the stakes are considerably higher. Some semblance of policy-making, therefore, becomes an impor-

tant political function in military regimes, although the methods chosen hardly guarantee effective policy outcomes.

In the short life span of the interim government under Ernest Shonekan (August 1993–November 1993), policy-making was suspended while attention was focused on elections to complete the project of democratic transition. Because the interim regime lacked legitimacy as an unelected government chosen by Babangida, its policy capabilities were limited. These factors facilitated the government's overthrow by Abacha in November 1993. The military regime of Abacha is also sensitive, to a degree, to public opinion. In April 1994, Abacha announced the first phase of a *new* transition to democracy program, convened a Constitutional Conference, and permitted politicians to form associations to discuss political issues, presumably as a prelude to lifting the ban on party politics.

SECTION 4

Representation and Participation

In the last section, we examined the organization of the Nigerian state and its chief institution of governance (particularly under military rule), the executive branch. This section focuses on official representation through another state institution, namely, the legislature, and the official means of participation through

the party system. Representation and participation are two vital components in modern democracies; however, Nigeria clearly is not a democracy. As noted above, Nigerian legislative bodies, though "representative" of constituencies in a literal sense, have been ineffectual in practice; the party system and elections have been marred by fraud, elite manipulation, and military interference. Nevertheless, there exist other modes of participation in Nigerian society *outside* the official structures.

Another important focus of this section will therefore be unofficial (that is, nongovernmental) methods of representation and participation through the institutions of civil society. Whereas the institutions of political society include such entities as parties, constitutions, and legislatures, those of **civil society** include professional associations, trade unions, religious groups, and various interest groups.

The Nigerian experience described in this section emphasizes the complex nature of the relationship between representation and participation. It shows that formal representation does not necessarily enhance participation; neither is participation always channeled through electoral representation. In fact, there are situations in which the most important modes of political participation are found outside of and in opposition to the institutional modes such as elections and legislatures, as well as in the institutions and organizations of civil society.

THE LEGISLATURE

Not surprisingly, Nigeria's legislature has been a victim of the country's political instability and its history of disorderly and unpredictable change. Legislative structures and processes have not operated free of abuse, neglect, or peremptory suspension by the executive arm for any appreciable length of time since independence. As such, the history of the legislature lacks any continuity, and thus has not been able to develop and function effectively as a vital component of a democratic system. For analytical purposes, there has been minimal progress in general understanding of the functions, duties, and responsibilities of the legislature.

As discussed earlier, until the first coup in 1966, Nigeria operated its legislature along the lines of the British Westminster model with an elected lower house and a smaller upper house composed of individuals selected by the executive. Then for the next thirteen years under military rule, legislative functions were performed by an unelected military council that initiated and passed decrees at will, the more important of which contained clauses forbidding judicial review. Between October 1979 and the coup of December 1983 that terminated the second attempt at

civilian democratic rule, the legislature operated similar to the United States system. As in the United States, Nigeria employed a bicameral structure, with both houses (the smaller Senate and the larger House of Representatives) consisting of elected members. Unlike in the United States, however, the vice president did not preside over Senate sessions. This role was filled by a Senate president chosen by his peers. It is assumed that the recommendations of the Constitutional Conference of 1994–1995 will be to maintain the American-inspired legislative system and a separately elected president and vice president. (Babangida had a nominal vice president while Lt. General Oladipo Diya serves as Abacha's second-in-command under the largely ceremonial title of chief of general staff.)

Beginning with the 1983 coup led by Muhammadu Buhari, Nigeria has witnessed a succession of military councils under different names (the Supreme Military Council, or SMC; the Armed Forces Ruling Council, or AFRC; the National Defense and Security Council, or NDSC; and most recently, the Provisional Ruling Council, or PRC, under Abacha) that perform the function of approving decrees issued by the military administrations. It would be inaccurate and misleading to call these institutions "legislatures" because they do not initiate legislation independently. Instead, they have provided a rubber stamp for decisions made by the head of state and his closest advisers.

As part of the Babangida regime's transition program, the civilian members of the National Assembly, elected under the 1989 Constitution in July 1992 for the Third Republic, actually held meetings until mid-1993. Once seated, however, they were barred by military decree from deliberating on issues other than those dealing with such relatively benign and noncontroversial topics as the national museum. Part of the interim national government arrangement in 1993 was that full powers of legislation were to be granted to the elected 91-member Senate and 593-member House of Representatives. The arrival of the Abacha regime in November 1993 eliminated this possibility with the dismissal of both houses.

The composition of the assembly was overwhelmingly male: only one of the 91 senators and two of the 593 representatives were female. This reflects the limited formal political role of women in Nigeria, as discussed in Section 2. Election to the Senate is on the basis of equal state representation, with three senators from each of the thirty states, plus one senator from the federal capital territory, Abuja. For purposes of comparison, the practice of equal representation in the upper house of the legislature is identical to that of the United States, except that Nigerian states elect three senators instead of two. Another difference is the election of a senator from Abuja Capital Territory, whereas Washington, D.C., has no such representation. Election to the Nigerian House of Representatives was also based on state representation but weighted to reflect the relative size of each state's population, again after the U.S. example. The release of provisional figures from the 1991 census brought with it expectations that it will form the basis of state representation in future elections rather than the inaccurate 1963 census previously used.

An innovation made in the halting transition to the Third Republic is that *local* government structures are to be granted greater autonomy from state control, another emulation of the American model. The lessons from Nigeria's past, however, will weigh on future developments. As indicated earlier, the most important of these lessons is that, on the whole, the executive has been overdeveloped compared to other branches of the government. It must be stressed again that subordination of the legislature to the executive is partially a consequence of the frequency of military coups. It is standard practice among coup leaders to replace civilian, elected legislatures with ruling councils, handpicked by the military executive. Indeed, as noted previously, General Abacha's first act as head of state in November 1993 was to abolish *all* political institutions, including the duly elected national and state legislatures.

To summarize, Nigerian legislatures under military government can be described as powerless or nonexistent. However, even under elected civil administrations, Nigerian legislatures have been subjected to such executive pressure that they have been little more than rubber stamps themselves. Because the executive and majority interests in the assembly have belonged to the same party, this influence has been easily exercised through the actions of strong party machines, as well as the executive branch's use of its resources to bribe legislators. In either case, the history of independent Nigeria is the story of a national legislature that has been subverted and its ability to represent its constituencies faithfully and adequately greatly under-

mined. Underlying all this is a political economy skewed in favor of an executive branch that dominates state resources and of legislators who depend on their allowances from the executive and who are overwhelmed by relentless demands for jobs, contracts, and other favors from members of their constituencies.

THE PARTY SYSTEM AND ELECTIONS

As discussed throughout this chapter, the unfortunate legacy of the party and electoral system bequeathed at independence in 1960 was that political parties were associated with certain regions and ethnic groups. Given the plural nature of Nigerian society, this extreme factionalization was further encouraged by most Nigerians' tendency to perceive politics as a desperate *zero-sum struggle* (or winner-take-all) for access to state resources. Unlike Mexico and, to some extent India, Nigeria did not develop an authoritarian de facto single-party system after independence that might have transcended some of these social cleavages. Instead, the multiparty system reinforced and deepened existing social segmentation and polarization. Although the four-year experiment with a two-party system from 1989 to 1993 demonstrated some positive features, it eventually succumbed to the familiar north-south schism in Nigerian political life.

One legacy of the zero-sum approach to electoral politics became evident two years after independence when the western and predominantly Yoruba Action Group (AG) was in opposition. Following political strife in the Western Region, the central government (at that time dominated by the Northern Peoples' Congress, or NPC) imposed a state of emergency on the Western Region and ruled it directly until 1963. Through a series of legislative maneuvers and by virtue of its greater numbers, the majority NPC was able to wrest temporary control of the Western Region from its rival the AG. During the state of emergency, the federal government used the opportunity to create Nigeria's fourth region, the Mid-West, in a successful effort to dilute the national power of the AG.

In general, such chicanery and desperation in electoral behavior has been aided by the use of a "first-past-the-post" plurality electoral system as in Britain and the United States which, in Nigeria, has awarded legislative majorities to ethnic-based parties on the basis of population. All of the parties of the First Republic, and arguably throughout Nigeria's history, were less concerned with the development of

Nigeria as a whole than with the well-being of their home region's clients. Control of the center, or at least access to it, ensures access to resources. In a polity as potentially volatile as Nigeria, however, this structure can create considerable political fragmentation and, of major importance, lingering ill will among the losers (see Table 8 on the following page).

The Nigerian parties that were involved in the politics of the First Republic were dominated by certain groups and interests. As Nigeria has engaged in subsequent democratic experiments, many of the more recent parties can trace their "roots" to their predecessors in the First Republic. Although the name of a given party may have changed, the leadership, participants, and supporters of the party generally have not. For example, the victorious NPN of the Second Republic, under the leadership of Shehu Shegari, was the political heir to the northern-dominated NPC of the First Republic. Similarly, the runner-up UPN of the Second Republic can be traced to the western-based Action Group of the First Republic. The Second Republic's NPP drew on the legacy of the NCNC of the First Republic, the strongest party of the former Eastern Region. The presence of these strong roots in parties of failed attempts at civilian rule was a significant factor in the Babangida regime's attempt to construct a two-party system.

The Two-Party Mandate

In its wavering steps toward the civilian Third Republic, General Babangida's administration in October 1989 announced a landmark decision to establish, by decree, two political parties. The state provided initial start-up funds, constitutions, manifestos, and infrastructure for these parties. According to the government, its decision to form the parties followed the failure of various political associations to meet the requirements set by the government for registration as political parties. From this controversial decision, the National Republican Convention (NRC) and the Social Democratic Party (SDP) emerged, designed by the government to be a little to the right and a little to the left, respectively, on the political-ideological spectrum.

The NRC and SDP were the only two parties allowed to operate legally as parties for the Third Republic, in accordance with Section 220(1) of the 1989 Constitution. Again, it is significant that the NRC and SDP are plainly modeled after their Western counterparts, the Republican and Democratic parties in the

United States and the Conservative and Labour Parties in Britain. There are, however, two vital differences between the American and British institutions and the Nigerian design. First, the American and British party structures emerged after years of voluntary interaction and evolved through the convergence of popular ideals and attitudes. They were not decreed into existence by the state, as in Nigeria. Second, although two parties dominate the political arena in the United States and Britain, they are not the sole parties and, significantly, there are no legal restrictions on the formation of additional parties. In Nigeria, however, the two-party limitation was explicit. Furthermore, Section 220(2) of the 1989 Constitution established requirements for party registration by the electoral commission, while Section 219 barred any association other than the two recognized parties from canvassing for votes for candidates in any election or from contributing to party funds or election expenses of such candidates.

Interestingly, the results of those elections which took place between 1990 and 1992 at local, state, and federal levels indicate that, despite their inauspicious beginnings, the two parties cut across the cleavages of ethnicity, regionalism, and religion in their membership and electoral performance in a way never before observed in Nigerian politics. Results from these elections also suggest that some of the old interethnic factionalism was reappearing, although a substantial measure of interethnic cooperation seems to have contributed to the victory of Moshood Abiola, a southern Muslim, in the June 12 presidential election. As shown in Table 8, northern-based parties clearly dominated the first and second experiments with civilian rule. Given this historical trend, it is significant that a southerner was able, apparently, to win the presidency in 1993—the first time in Nigeria's history that a southerner defeated a northerner in elections to lead the nation. The decision by the northern-dominated Babangida regime to annul the June 12 elections, rather than release the results, was perceived as a deliberate attempt by the military and northern interests to maintain their decades-long domination of the highest levels of government.

The Annulment

The decision to annul the election, and the subsequent heightened regional and ethnic tension, provided reinforcement for the belief that Nigerian party and

TABLE 8 Federal Election Results in Nigeria's First and Second Republics

1959 Federal Parliamentary Election[1]

	Number of Seats	NPC	NCNC/NEPU Alliance	AG	Others
Total	310	134	89	73	14
Percent	100	43.2	28.7	23.6	4.5

Distribution of Parliamentary Seats after 12/64 and 3/65 Elections[2]

	Number of Seats	NPC	NNDP	NCNC	AG	NPF	Independent
Total	312	162	36	84	21	4	5
Percent	100	51.9	11.6	26.9	6.7	1.3	1.6

1979 General Election, House of Representatives[3]

	Number of Seats	GNPP	UPN	NPN	PRP	NPP
Total	449	43	111	168	49	78
Percent	100	9.6	24.7	37.4	10.9	17.4

1979 Senate Election[4]

	GNPP	UPN	NPN	PRP	NPP
Seats won out of 95	8	28	36	7	16
Percent	8.4	29.5	37.9	7.3	16.9

1979 Presidential Election[5]

		Waziri Ibrahim (GNPP)	Obafemi Awolowo (UPN)	Shehu Shagari (NPN)	Aminu Kano (PRP)	Nnamdi Azikiwe (NPP)
Actual Vote	16,846,633	1.68 million	4.92 million	5.69 million	1.74 million	2.81 million
Percent	100	10.0	29.2	33.8	10.3	16.7
No. States won > 25%	—	3	6	12	2	3

Requirements for victory: Plurality of popular vote, plus at least 25 percent of the vote in two-thirds (66.66 percent) of the nineteen states. Note that Shagari reached this level in just twelve of nineteen states (63.16%); however, a favorable ruling by the Federal Elections Commission (FEDECO) ensured his victory.

1983 House of Representatives Election[6]

	Number of Seats	NAP	GNPP	UPN	NPN	PRP	NPP
Total	450[a]	—	—	33	264	41	48
Percent	100	—	—	7.3	58.7	9.1	10.7

[a]One seat added for FCT.

TABLE 8   Federal Election Results in Nigeria's First and Second Republics (continued)

1983 Senate Election[7]

	NAP	GNPP	UPN	NPN	PRP	NPP
Seats won out of 96[a]	0	1	16	61	5	13
Percent	0.0	1.0	16.7	63.6	5.2	13.5

[a]One seat added for FCT.

1983 Presidential Election[8]

		Tunji Braithwaite (NAP)	Waziri Ibrahim (GNPP)	Obafemi Awolowo (UPN)	Shehu Shagari (NPN)	Hassan Yusuf (PRP)	Nnamdi Azikiwe (NPP)
Actual Vote	25,454,967	.289 million	.641 million	7.91 million	12.05 million	1.04 million	3.53 million
Percent	100	1.1	2.5	31.1	47.3	4.1	13.9
No. States won (25%)	—	NIL	NIL	7	16	1	4

Requirements for victory: Plurality of popular vote, plus at least 25 percent of the votes in two-thirds of the nineteen states.

Notes:
1. Adapted from Richard Sklar, *Nigerian Political Parties: Power in an Emergent Nation* (New York: NOK Publishers, 1983), 36.
2. Adapted from Larry Diamond, *Class, Ethnicity and Democracy in Nigeria: The Failure of the First Republic* (Syracuse: Syracuse University Press, 1988), 227.
3. Figures from Richard A. Joseph, *Democracy and Prebendal Politics in Nigeria* (London: Cambridge University Press, 1987), 126.
4. Figures from Joseph, 125.
5. Adapted from Joseph, 127.
6. Adapted from Toyin Falola and Julius Ihonvbere, *The Rise and Fall of the Second Republic* (London: Zed Books, 1985), 221.
7. Adapted from Falola and Ihonvbere, 22.
8. Adapted from Falola and Ihonvbere, 220.

List of Acronyms Used in Table 8

AG	Action Group
GNPP	Great Nigerian Peoples' Party
NAP	Nigerian Advance Party
NCNC	National Convention of Nigerian Citizens (formerly, National Council of Nigeria and the Cameroons)
NEPU	Northern Elements Progressive Union
NNDP	Nigerian National Democratic Party
NPC	Northern People's Congress
NPF	Northern Progressive Front
NPN	National Party of Nigeria
NPP	Nigerian People's Party
NRC	National Republican Convention
PRP	People's Redemption Party
SDP	Social Democratic Party
UPN	Unity Party of Nigeria

electoral processes could not overcome its ethnic and cultural cleavages. Although the SDP was linked in terms of its membership and leadership to a southern-dominated Second Republic alliance of the Unity Party of Nigeria, UPN (mainly Yoruba), and the Nigerian Peoples Party, NPP (mainly Igbo), it had also attracted splinter elements of the Second Republic's Peoples Redemption Party, PRP (organized and located around Kano city in northern Nigeria) and the Great Nigeria Peoples Party, GNPP (organized around the Kanuri northeast). Similarly, the NRC was seen as having its roots in northern forces that were the core of the National Party of Nigeria (NPN), the party that dominated the central government in the Second Republic under the leadership of Shehu Shagari. Thus, even before the 1993 election debacle, and despite statistics indicating a fairly diverse support base for each party (especially for Nigeria), the public perceived the SDP as the *Southern* Democratic Party and the NRC as the *Northern* Republican Convention.

Whether tensions had really subsided, the decision to annul the election of June 12, 1993, and to organize a new one brought ethnoregional factors to the fore again in Nigeria's party and electoral system. Even before that decision, it was clear that, given their linkages with predecessor parties, the SDP and NRC had not made a clean break with the party politics of the First and Second Republics. Moreover, by annulling the June 1993 election, judged by local and foreign monitors to be the freest and fairest in Nigeria's political history, the military has undermined any lingering confidence that the will of the electorate will be respected in future elections.

Analysis

Military rule has shown its tendency to exacerbate ethnoregional and clientelist factionalization and corruption of the party and electoral system. A hallmark of military rule is that it hinders the development of the infrastructure and skills needed for improved governance. One of the first acts of the military in government is to disband and ban civilian parties and to weaken other aspects of the constitutional system. Clearly, military intervention in politics has retarded the development of a party and electoral system in Nigeria.

In fairness, not all blame for Nigeria's anemic electoral system rests with the military. As we know, the civilian-instituted party and electoral system at the time of Nigeria's independence were ethnically-based and prone to factionalism. Nevertheless, as Larry Diamond has argued, progress toward the evolution of genuine multiethnic parties and an electoral system evolving through the process of bargaining within and between the parties *was being made* during both the First and the Second Republics. In each case, that progress was terminated by military intervention. Although Diamond agrees that the party system has traditionally "tended to reflect ethnic and regional particularities too closely to provide a fresh, crosscutting basis for political conflict," for him,

> This has been the characteristic problem of Nigerian politics, but it was beginning to change in the Second Republic as a result of the nineteen-state structure and various electoral provisions requiring broad ethnic representation in parties as a condition for registration. Still, the party system of Nige-

ria's Second Republic was victimized by a lack of time, in advance of the full onset of electoral competition, to develop fresh leaderships, new and coherent identities, and broad constituencies. As a result, the new parties were weak and extraordinarily volatile, and politics were greatly destabilized by the chaos of their divisions, defections, expulsions, and permutations.[43]

Looking to the future, the question that arises is how the party and electoral system can be given sufficient breathing space by the political elite and the military. The former has tended to turn parties into privatized and sectional bodies while the latter has displayed a penchant for plotting coups against constitutional government. A number of changes can be suggested.

The introduction of some elements of a **proportional representation (PR)** system, in which parties gain representation in direct relation to the percentage of the popular vote, would encourage power sharing in government. A number of scholars of Africa have argued recently that more attention should be devoted to PR systems in African constitutional drafting. Interestingly, PR systems have rarely been applied in Africa.[44] The problem that is often associated with PR, creating a fragmented legislature (that is, one with many small ineffectual parties), could be avoided by the establishment of minimum electoral requirements for parties, as in Germany. Another change in Nigeria's party structure could occur if nascent parties and party leaders were encouraged to appeal to social issues and to organize parties based on interests that cut across lines of ethnicity and region. This was one of the stated objectives of the two-party system created by Babangida. The cancellation of the 1993 presidential elections ended that unorthodox experiment. Consequently, it will never be known if the mandated two-party system would have eventually forced political aspirants to build coalitions around specific policy issues rather than around the traditional magnets of ethnicity and region.

POLITICAL CULTURE, CITIZENSHIP, AND IDENTITY

Traditionally, institutions that help to represent and mobilize society in the political sphere include legislatures, political parties, and trade unions. In the process, they help to shape, organize, and express political culture and identities, thus nurturing qualities of citizenship. For all but ten years since independence in 1960, however, these institutions in Nigeria have either been proscribed and disbanded (in the case of legislatures and political parties) or muzzled (in the case of labor unions) under military rule. Their roles, therefore, have been largely assumed by other groups and institutions, including ethnic and religious organizations, the mass media, and professional and trade groups.

The basic units of socialization are mainly family, community, and peer groups; thus it is not surprising that ethnic, religious, and educational institutions have assumed a greater role in the organization and expression of political attitudes and culture. Although these institutions can be a positive force, they often possess elements that can contribute to the distress of the political process. In many of these circles, the state (federal government) is regarded as an amoral entity. The state's unwillingness or inability to deliver appropriate services to the populace, its rampant corruption, and the frequency of military coups have fostered a political culture of apathy and alienation.

Modernity versus Traditionalism

The terrain of political culture, citizenship, and identity remains incoherent and discontinuous for several reasons. First, the interaction of modern (colonial, Western) elements with traditional (precolonial, African) practices has created the duality of a modern sociopolitical system with traditional foundations. In other words, it has led to a situation in which traditional elements have been modernized and modern elements traditionalized, so that individual Nigerians straddle two worlds, each of which lacks internal coherence. On one hand, the strong elements in communal societies that promoted accountability have been weakened by a Western culture oriented toward individuality and the marginalization of traditional institutions and practices. On the other hand, the modern state has been unable to free itself from rival ethnic claims organized around narrow, exclusivist constituencies.

One consequence of these tensions is that such exclusivist identities have come to dominate the political culture and to define the nature of citizenship. Individuals identify first with their immediate ethnic, regional, and religious (or subethnic, subregional and subreligious) groups before identifying with the more universal modern state, especially in moments of crisis. Individuals seek to extract as many benefits as possible from the modern state but hesitate when it comes to performing such civic duties as paying taxes or taking care of public property. Indeed, as Billy Dudley has demonstrated, nonpayment of taxes is a regular method of Nigerian popular protest.[45] In short, entirely missing from the relationship between state and citizen in Nigeria is a fundamental reciprocity based on the belief that there is a common interest that binds them.

Religion

As this chapter has stressed repeatedly, religion has been a persistent theme and frequent basis of conflict in Nigerian history. Islam first began to filter into Nigeria in the eleventh and twelfth centuries, spread to Hausaland by the fifteenth century, and greatly expanded in the early nineteenth century largely through the jihad of Usman Dan Fodio, the great Fulani leader. In the north, Islam first coexisted with, then gradually supplanted, indigenous religions. Christianity arrived later but it expanded rapidly through missionary activity in the south dating from the early nineteenth century. The amalgamation of northern and southern Nigeria in 1914 brought together the two regions in which different world religions had become predominant.

It is easy to understand how these religious cultures came to clash; indeed, notions of oppression, religious persecution, and divine inspiration have been at the core of many religious conflicts throughout history. We have already discussed the debate over *shari'a:* For most Muslims it represents a way of life and supreme (personal) law that transcends secular and state law; for many Christians it threatens the secular nature of the Nigerian state and their position within it. The strong pull of religious versus national identity becomes even more alluring in times of economic and social hardship: Today strong ethnoreligious nationalism threatens the stability of a number of states, including Bosnia, Northern Ireland, and Israel. In Nigeria, as elsewhere, religious-based clashes have intensified where different religious communities came into contact. The Babangida period corresponded with a rise in both Islamic fundamentalist movements and evangelical Protestant fundamentalism. Where significant numbers of southern Christians are living in predominantly Muslim states (for example, Kaduna state), many clashes have erupted.

The continued political prominence of ethnicity, religion, and regionalism has both positive and negative consequences. On the positive side, the pluralities of ethnic, regional, and religious loyalties have made it difficult for authoritarian rule to be sustained in Nigeria and have, therefore, provided space for continued agitation for a more democratic polity. On the negative side, the depth of communal divisions continues to undermine state coherence and stability and calls into question the survivability of Nigeria as one nation. The plural nature of Nigerian society, rather than the emergence of a shared political culture, is now manifested in virtually all aspects of public life. The Nigerian press, for instance, has long been the liveliest and most irreverent in Africa. The Abacha regime has moved to stifle its independence, banning several publications and threatening suspension of others. It is significant to note that most of the Nigerian press has been based in a Lagos-Ibadan axis in the western part of Nigeria and it has frequently been labeled "southern." In 1994, Abacha closed several of the most influential and respected southern Nigerian newspapers and magazines, including *The Guardian, Concord* (owned by Abiola), the *Punch,* leaving less critical and more biased publishers intact. A northern paper, the *New Nigerian* published in Kaduna, fell victim to overt sectionalism. The fact that the media is regarded as a captive of ethnic and regional constituencies has weakened its capacity to resist onslaughts against its rights and privileges.

Government Efforts to Foster Citizenship

There have been periodic attempts by Nigerian governments, including, ironically, the Babangida regime, to launch programs of mass mobilization intended to alter the political attitudes and identification patterns of Nigerians. The emphasis has been on how to use the modern state to fashion a new, all-inclusive sense of belonging that would weaken close identification with the claims of subnational groups and strengthen affinity and loyalty to the nation-state. Ways have been explored that would build loyalties across cleavages of ethnicity, religion, region, and class. Given the tragic history of the Nigerian state, however, it is not surprising that the government's achievements have not only fallen far short of these objectives, but its actions have

tended to polarize further an already fragmented nation. Under the Babangida regime, vast sums were spent on sponsoring activities designed to foster a greater sense of national citizenship, but these were eventually dismissed by much of the population as a smokescreen to divert attention away from issues of governmental corruption and regime hegemony. The resulting cynicism is reflected in the desultory voter turnouts toward the end of the Babangida regime.

A final point needs to be made here. Issues relating to political attitudes, political culture, and identities are still dominated and defined largely by elite and male urban-based interests. These interests include ethnic as well as professional and associational groups. The few nonelite groups encountered in this sphere, such as urban-based market women's associations, often serve as conduits for the decisions and agendas of male-dominated groups. In essence, nonelite and rural elements continue to be marginalized and manipulated by elites and urban groups. Lacking competence in the language of public discourse, namely English, and access to financial networks, it is difficult for sectors of society other than elites to engage, on their own, the decision-making centers of the state and society.

Interests, Social Movements, and Protest

One of the ways that Nigerians participate is through membership in civic organizations, interest groups, and other society-based organizations. Such groups include labor unions, business associations, student groups, and similar organizations. Because the political machinery has usually been in the hands of the military, Nigerian citizens have sought alternative means of representation and protest in an effort to impact political life. Historically, labor has played a significant role in Nigerian politics as have student groups and various radical and populist organizations. Business groups, on the other hand, have frequently supported and colluded with corrupt civilian and military regimes. More recently, however, there have been calls from the business class for an end to such arbitrary rule. Finally, as with all aspects of Nigerian political, economic, and social life, there is the familiar reliance on ethnic, religious, and regional symbols by activists; and given the manipulation of ethnoregional

A demonstration for better schools and salaries by members of the Nigerian Union of Teachers (N.U.T.) in Onitsha in eastern Nigeria.
Source: Keystone/Popperfoto.

and religious divisions by Generals Babangida and Abacha, this tendency has grown in recent years.

Labor

Over the years, there has been a decline in the role of organized labor in Nigerian politics and in the use of socialist rhetoric, which reached its peak in the late 1970s. Socialist discourse in Nigeria can be traced back to the nationalist period. However, with the ending of the Cold War, the once-fashionable Third World anti-Americanism and anti-imperialism also declined. By the late 1980s, the socialist model was still being promoted by only a small number of intellectuals, mostly on university campuses. The collapse of communism worldwide, and the deliberate attempt of the Babangida regime to co-opt some socialist activists into its administration, effectively blunted the appeal socialist ideas once enjoyed in certain Nigerian circles.

The Babangida regime also implemented strategies of state corporatism to control and co-opt various social forces such as labor. Organized labor, which has played an important role in challenging governments during both the colonial and postcolonial eras in several African countries, is now unable to sustain such actions in Nigeria. Whenever the leadership of the Nigerian Labour Congress (NLC), to which all unions belong, takes a vigorous stand against the government (as happened in the strike action against the Abacha regime in summer 1994), the government merely sacks the leaders and appoints its own replacements.

Despite its important role in aggregating interests and conducting protest campaigns, the Nigerian labor movement has been vulnerable to reprisals by the state and private employers. To begin with, the state has always been the biggest single employer of labor in Nigeria. In addition, the state is the recognized regulator of industrial relations between employers and employees. Another factor is the division along ethnic, regional, and religious lines that have always hampered labor solidarity; these divisions are readily exploited by the state.

The first attempt to establish a corporatist structure for organized labor was made in 1978 under the military government of Olusegun Obasanjo. It used a conflict within the labor movement to restructure it completely by creating a single central labor organization, the NLC. This policy of centralization and co-optation was carried further under Babangida, who ensured that only candidates endorsed by the government won elections into the leadership of the more powerful unions. The government applied coercion, financial inducements, and divide-and-rule tactics, as required. The result has been a waning of trade union militancy, the abandonment of socialist pronouncements, and a steady decline in the importance of the labor movement as a political and social force.

If allowed to function without such manipulation and control by the government, however, the labor movement can regain its vitality. That potential was demonstrated during the summer of 1994 when pro-democracy strikes by the National Petroleum Employees Union (NUPENG) and other sympathetic labor groups significantly reduced oil production and nearly brought the country to a halt before the Abacha regime arrested and disbanded its leadership.

The corporatist proclivities of the Babangida regime were also evident in other areas. Its programs of economic liberalism and political democratization, for example, were pursued under very strict state control and manipulation. The limit of state corporatism is set, however, by its rising costs, especially in an underdeveloped economy presided over by a state with limited legitimacy.

Associations

The Business Community Given this background, associational and professional life has remained vibrant. Nigeria has a long history of entrepreneurialism and business development. However, it also has a history of rent-seeking capitalism; its business class is often characterized as "pirate capitalists" because of their corruption and interests in accumulating wealth, not through the provision and operation of productive capital, but by means of state largesse. The business community includes a number of wealthy individuals,

many of whom have served in the military or civilian governments (for instance, Moshood Abiola, who made a fortune in communications and other activities). Nevertheless, as the economic and political conditions in Nigeria deteriorate, the state can offer fewer avenues for businesspeople and cannot provide the necessary infrastructure for business development.

Private interests have proved surprisingly resilient, though, as business groups have emerged to represent the interests of the business class and to promote development. Increasingly, this is done without state support and through groups of enterprising capitalists organized into business associations. Business associations have proliferated throughout Nigeria, and in many areas, separate associations can be found that represent everything from butchers, to manufacturers, to car-hire owners. In a number of cases these groups have benefited both their communities *and* the government by building roads, schools, market stalls, and similar infrastructure, all of which reduce the burden on the government's limited resources.

Many local or regional groups are also members of national ones. Lately, national business associations, such as the Nigerian Association of Chambers of Commerce, Industry, Mines, and Agriculture (NACCIMA), the largest in the country, have taken an increasingly political stance, pressing the military leadership for a resolution of the crisis. Given the intransigence of the Babangida and Abacha regimes, such pressure has had limited impact. But it is significant that although the objective of most businesspeople is to reduce the uncertainty and halt the decline of the economy in order to preserve and protect their economic positions, the effect has been that large, influential organizations increasingly serve what are clearly *political* roles.

Other Social Groups Student activism has continued to be an important feature of political life. University and other higher-level students—and occasionally, as in the period following the annulment of the June 12 election, primary and secondary school students—play an important political role. Along with their teachers, they have withstood government harassment, banning, and attempts to engineer divisions in their unions and associations. As a result, they have endured countless closings of the universities by military authorities. Many professional associations of doctors and lawyers have also become champions of human rights. They often bolster campaigns conducted by social rights organizations that have proliferated since the first, the Civil Liberties Organization (CLO), was founded in 1987.

The activities of these social groups have increased in the context of the harsh conditions associated with the economic structural adjustment program (SAP). Marginal groups, including women and the young, the urban poor, and people in rural areas, have perceived an imbalance in the distribution of the benefits and burdens produced by the SAP program. Not surprisingly, the flagrant display of wealth by senior members of the military has alienated these groups and has encouraged a "growing culture of rage"[46] among youths, unorganized labor, artisans, the urban poor, and the unemployed. As has been argued,

> While similar tendencies in other Third World countries such as Brazil and India have not put in serious jeopardy the project of nationalist reconstruction, the very strong appeals of competing loyalties coupled with the relative absence of a visible, disciplined and nationalistic group within the Nigerian ruling class itself have strengthened these tendencies for mass alienation from the Nigerian state. The result has been that, in the period of transition to the liberal state and market, organized and unorganized contact between these groups and state managers has increasingly assured a confrontational stance.[47]

A major consequence of the increasing alienation among these social groups is the use of ethnic, religious, and regional symbols to mobilize particular constituencies. The military has contributed to this polarization within Nigeria by its insensitivity to the need to allow the plural aspects of the society to be manifested in nonconfrontational ways.

One should not conclude this section with the impression that these ethnic and religious cleavages are reified or immutable entities. In fact, these cleavages appear to be an immutable fact of Nigerian political and social life because of the ways in which they are deliberately heightened. Political and economic elites act to create the perception that current social cleavages are fixed and immutable. By fostering divisions among the population, these elites deflect popular scrutiny of their own actions. Simply put, Nigerian elites maintain power by exploiting differences among ethnic groups, even as they promote cultural uniformity and homogeneity within their own specific groups. In many respects, therefore, governance in contemporary Nigeria is a throwback to the colonial era when, as indicated earlier, it was in the interest of the colonial authorities to emphasize *inter*tribal disharmony while encouraging *intra*tribal unity. The critical question is whether the Nigerian elite will continue to sacrifice the long-term advantages of development and democracy in the pursuit of their short-term interests in the form of unstable fiefdoms based on ethnic, religious, and regional intolerance.

SECTION 5

Nigerian Politics at the Crossroads

Nigeria remains today an unfinished state characterized by uncertainties and contradictions. The original promise to establish democracy was made by General Ibrahim Babangida in August 1985, on the day he announced a palace coup against the military regime led by General Muhammadu Buhari. Babangida not only accused Buhari of failing to make a similar pledge to support democracy but also of having a poor record in human rights and economic management, as well as gross insensitivity to the plural nature of Nigerian society.

Babangida's promise was made long before such promises of democratization became fashionable

among African leaders and before it became an element of the political conditionality imposed by international financial institutions and major bilateral donors. After a decade following this highly guided and unpredictable transition, however, Nigeria remains far from the goal of constitutional and democratic rule. When he was forced to step aside in August 1993, Babangida left behind a tense political situation. The interim administration of Ernest Shonekan was still essentially Babangida's regime. Conditions of tension and uncertainty have only increased under the military administration of General Sani Abacha who seized power in November 1993. Despite ten years of promises—while many other Sub-Saharan African countries, much less endowed with human and material resources, have either fully moved to a pluralist democratic system or achieved significant progress in that direction—Nigeria has experienced further erosion of existing freedoms and political institutions. Such countries include Benin, Cape Verde, Eritrea, Ghana, Madagascar, Malawi, Mauritius, Mozambique, Namibia, Niger, São Tomé and Principe, and Zambia. The most bitter and striking irony of all, however, is the transition to a popularly elected government in South Africa in April 1994. Nigeria had contributed substantial funds to support anti-apartheid organizations and had played a leading role in criticizing the policies of South African governments in a number of international arenas. It was therefore a source of great anguish for Nigerians to witness the historic steps being taken toward constitutional democracy in South Africa as their own country slipped back into military dictatorship.

The Nigerian transition has been halting in part because it has been planned and directed solely from above. This approach contrasts sharply with the popular-based, "people-propelled" movements that unseated autocracies in Central and Eastern Europe beginning in the spring of 1989. However, a top-down depiction of Nigeria's transition reflects only the dynamics of the official program and overlooks other significant developments.

Promises of democratic transition have been made periodically during Nigeria's political history as a ploy by the military aimed at stabilizing and legitimizing their governments. It is interesting to note that the two transitions to democratic rule in Nigeria's political history since independence were initiated by military regimes which themselves came to power by ousting other military regimes. The ousted regimes made similar missteps: They either reneged on an earlier promise to transfer power to elected civilians (as the Gowon regime did in the early 1970s, paving the way for its overthrow in 1975 by the Murtala/Obasanjo regime), or they refused to make a firm pledge to restore democratic rule as in the case of the Buhari administration of 1984–1985. What has existed in Nigeria, therefore, is a two-track policy. On one track is the "official," announced program of transition, on the other, a military strategy to extend its stay in power as long as possible. Although the military has governed Nigeria for all but ten years since

independence, only once has the oft-repeated promise of a transition to civilian rule resulted in an actual transition, namely that under General Obasanjo in 1979. If General Abacha were forced to give way to an elected government, as many civilian politicians have demanded, it would represent a major breakthrough for a people who have lost confidence in the military and civilian political class. Abacha, however, is proving as adept as Babangida at engineering an illusory transition.

POLITICAL CHALLENGES AND CHANGING AGENDAS

We will consider the following "tale of three cities": Abuja, the new federal administrative capital; Sokoto, a bastion of tradition and the precolonial capital of the Fulani empire; and Lagos, the former federal administrative capital and still the commercial and financial center of the country. The following examination of recent occurrences reported in each city—three events in the life of a nation—can be read as scenes from a one-act play whose director does not know when to draw the curtain. These events and the views they reflect help to illuminate the lines of tension that run through contemporary Nigerian politics. They also highlight potential openings for change in the future.

Scene One: Abuja. General Babangida has just finished a meeting with his senior military commanders drawn from all military formations in the country. The meeting is held on June 25, 1993, at Aso Rock, the president's highly fortified official residence in Abuja, after mass protests over his decision two days earlier to annul the June 12 presidential election. Although the election was judged by local and foreign observers to be free and fair, it is widely believed that the election was annulled for two main reasons. First, although the results were not released officially, indications are that the candidate from the south, Moshood Abiola, is the winner, and powerful northern interests, including Babangida, do not want power to be handed to a southerner. Second, it is widely believed that Babangida does not want to leave office and is only trying to engineer a crisis that will give him an excuse to stay in power. At the end of the meeting, surrounded by his military colleagues, Babangida announces to journalists and the nation: "We, members of the armed forces . . . are committed to democracy, to the democratic process, and to *our* transition program. What we did was to annul the election, not the transition program. I have been mandated by this distinguished gathering . . . to let you know that . . . we shall *install* a democratically elected government on the 27th of August."[48] Not surprisingly, public reaction remains skeptical and disturbed, noting the possessive tone Babangida uses to talk about democratization and his plan to install a "democratically elected" president by August 27.

In the face of unrelenting criticism, Babangida finally steps aside on August 26, but only after he had threatened to abolish, with a stroke of a pen, all democratic institutions he had put in place at the local, state, and federal levels between 1986 and 1993. These bodies would have included elected executives and legislatures in 589 local councils, four area councils in the federal capital, thirty states, the bicameral National Assembly, and the two political parties. Notably, Babangida leaves office without installing an elected president as promised but instead a handpicked civilian successor. The entire transition has thus turned into a charade. The people are bitterly disappointed.

Scene Two: Sokoto. It is December 1992 at the royal palace of the Sultan of Sokoto, Alhaji Ibrahim Dasuki, who exercises temporal and traditional authority over much of northern Nigeria. In addition, as president of the Supreme Council of Islamic Affairs (SCIA), he is the spiritual head of all Nigerian Muslims. The sultan has decided to respond to two developments. The first is a government program of mass mobilization for which an agency was established in 1987 and given considerable state resources. In a challenge to the state's costly initiative, he notes with pride: "If you want to mobilize people in this country . . . , it is far easier and cheaper than any other method . . . to work through the traditional institution. For instance, if I want all the district heads, all the village heads, and elders in the Emirate, all I do is to send for them and they will turn up. I don't pay them. At best I may give them a grand lunch or dinner. That's all."[49] In short, the appeal of traditional institutions, such as the sultanate, is stronger and fosters a greater sense of duty and obligation than expensive state-run efforts.

The other development to which Alhaji Dasuki responds are the mounting calls for a review of the role traditional institutions play in the country's public affairs. He declares that anybody who tries to ridicule

traditional institutions, which are the "symbol of our identity," will face the people's wrath. He also notes with derision that calls for a diminution of the role of traditional institutions are usually disingenuous and intended to serve some ulterior political aim. "All this hue and cry about the traditional institutions are coming from the elite, but one irony is that even all those elites, after they will have finished all their *bariki* [roughly, "elitism"], they come back home and the next thing they want is one [traditional] title or the other. Whether you are a policeman, or a businessman, or a school teacher, the radicals, all these, after they have finished all their radicalism, the next thing they come looking for are titles. . . . So there must be something in the traditional institutions which attracts them."[50] The sultan's observation that traditional institutions remain a powerful and positive force in Nigeria was well taken. The question is whether this authority and influence sustains, parallels, or undermines Nigerian cohesiveness.

Scene Three: Lagos. In the most exclusive part of Lagos, and before a gathering of Nigeria's captains of industry, leading academics, private professionals, and key public figures, a respected Nigerian professor of economics recalls a conversation he once had with his "most powerful" ambassador friend. According to the professor, his friend told him that "Nigeria is the only place where you can have a multimillionaire who has no industry, who does nothing other than dance around."[51] There is considerable applause and nodding of heads in agreement among the crowd, and no voice is raised in dissent.

Taken together, these three events illustrate the societal issues that remain unresolved at the political, social, and economic levels. The events in Abuja in 1993 clearly reveal the arbitrary and unnatural nature of a transition imposed and manipulated from above by one man, a military ruler. The scene depicted in Sokoto reminds us of two significant facts about Nigerian society. First, the continuing strength and influence of traditional society cannot be disregarded; collective identities defined on the basis of religion or ethnicity are often more binding than "national" (that is, all-Nigerian) ones. Second, these traditional identities can be, and have been, used to mobilize support at the local level to foster divisive politics at the federal center. Finally, the unanimity of opinion reached in the

Lagos scene suggests the parasitic nature of much of the Nigerian economy. Rent-seeking and other unproductive, often corrupt, business activities are today accepted norms of wealth accumulation.

In each of these events, however, the seeds of change can be found. Nigerians became fed up with the deceptions of Babangida; the political role of traditional institutions is believed to be excessive; and there is a recognition, at least by some elites, that "dancing around" is not the way to build a viable economy.

There has also been a dramatic shift in attitude toward the military as an alternative to elected civilians in government. Nigeria has undergone six successful military coups d'état, two against elected civilian republics (in January 1966 and December 1983), three by factions of the military against military regimes (in July 1966, July 1975, and August 1985), and one of an indeterminate nature, in which a puppet civilian government was overthrown by the military (November 1993). In all of these instances, except the most recent, military intervention was applauded by significant sections of the population. The Nigerian experience demonstrates that military coups are not simply self-propelled events on the part of the military but involve civilians who, directly or indirectly, encourage the army to intervene. From this perspective, a military coup is often meant to rein in the state that has distanced itself from vital interests in civil society, and bring it back into line with those interests. In this regard, therefore, Nigeria's coups have been prompted by the previous regime's loss of legitimacy, whether a military or civilian government, and a temporary assertion of the power of public opinion.

The Nigerian military has been held in relatively high esteem for much of the postcolonial period. The experiences since 1985 have, however, greatly diminished the image of the Nigerian military, perhaps irreversibly, in the public eye. The decline in the appeal of military rule can be attributed to the abysmal performance of the Babangida regime in economic policies, governance, and its interactions with society. It is now generally recognized that the military, despite its important contributions to national security and unity, is incapable of achieving economic and social progress in Nigeria. In fact, military rule has resulted in the greatest erosion of national cohesion since the civil war in the late 1960s.

The school system from the primary to the tertiary levels has deteriorated, as have health care, public transportation, many sectors of the economy, and public morality and ethics. Simultaneously, there has been a marked increase in the abuse of fundamental rights and liberties, misuse of public trust by those in government, social tensions over policy disputes, and official corruption. Unfortunately, popular exhortation by Nigerians to ensure that the Babangida regime would be "the last military government we shall have"[52] has failed to prevent the rise of another, even more authoritarian, regime under General Abacha.

Events since the annulment of the June 12, 1993, election further underscore the extent to which civil society is no longer willing to be a passive vehicle for elite intrigue. The Babangida regime, accustomed to having its way, was unprepared for the widespread condemnation of this action and the unprecedented demonstrations and riots. The administration resorted to divide and rule tactics to split the ranks of party leaders and portray the ensuring conflict as one fueled by ethnic and regional sentiments. In brief, it sought to pit the Yorubas from Moshood Abiola's home area against the rest of Nigeria. Nevertheless, public pressure on Babangida to quit office as scheduled on August 27, 1993, did not relent. He eventually stepped aside on August 26, 1993, but not before co-opting a number of leaders of the SDP and NRC into adopting his plan to hand over power to a handpicked interim administration that would, in turn, conduct a new election and inaugurate the Third Republic.

But the pressure for a complete transition to democratic rule did not cease when Babangida tapped Edward Shonekan to lead an interim "civilian" administration. Attempts by the military to attract the support of powerful traditional chiefs, senior elected and party officials and respected members of society were countered by mass resistance. For the first time in independent Nigeria's history, the elite had lost control of street-level politics—the concept of "people power" in Nigeria had suddenly been unleashed. This was the culmination of a process that had become noticeable around 1990, when the effort to establish democracy, good government, and development began to shift from its traditional location in the state to activities within civil society. The series of demonstrations, strikes, and passive civil disobedience following the 1993 annulment (and again in the summer of 1994), organized to force the military from office, demonstrated to Nigerians, long intimidated by the threat of military violence, the potential power of mass action. Indeed, the massive labor strikes in the summer of 1994 led by the petroleum workers' union, NUPENG, and quickly joined by other groups, provided alarming evidence of this people power. However, Abacha did not back down. He eventually broke the unions by detaining activists and then dismissing their leadership. Nevertheless, by demonstrating the deep revulsion felt toward military misrule, the unions and other groups sent a powerful message. The strikes forced a 25 percent reduction in Nigeria's vital oil production for nearly two months. They also attracted international attention to the cause of ordinary Nigerians and their determination to throw off the yoke of military rule.

One commentator has noted that if a democratic resolution to Nigeria's political crisis is ever reached, it will not originate in the political class—those politicians who allowed their ranks to be split by Babangida and Abacha. Instead, "credit will belong largely to the man in the street. I mean the man (and woman too) who came out to cast his vote on June 12, 1993 and who has said in more ways than one that his vote was a message to Abuja (the seat of government) that change was long overdue."[53] The Nigerian elite is in disarray and the people were obliged to fill the void by supporting greater militancy on the part of union and civic leaders. As a respected former federal minister of petroleum in the 1970s, Shettima Ali Monguno, warned recently: The people are preparing for a revolution in which the common man will be its champion.[54]

The institutional network needed to channel civil society's energies into pro-democratic behavior is already being built, and it worked dramatically during the confrontations with the government over the June 12 election annulment. This network consists of a group of human rights organizations that operate under the collective name the Campaign for Democracy (CD). There are also other human rights and pro-democracy bodies outside this network, including organized labor, students, and professional associations. The operations of the CD and its allies, however, have had more impact in the south, especially in Lagos, Nigeria's industrial, commercial, and financial center. Not coincidentally, Lagos has served as the center of activity for human rights organizations since they began to emerge on Nigeria's sociopolitical scene in 1987.

As a consequence of Babangida's and Abacha's willingness to exploit the deep divisions in Nigeria,

and to make these the basis of public policy, it was perhaps inevitable that much of the gains recorded since independence in nation-building have been dissipated since 1985. The popular vote on June 12, 1993, which provided a radical departure from the sectionalism of the past and offered a refreshing opportunity to develop a more national political agenda, was used by the Babangida regime to rekindle north-south sectionalism. The June 12 vote was as much a protest against the military as a ruling group, and against Babangida as a discredited leader, as it was an endorsement of Moshood Abiola for president. In the words of Claude Ake, a noted Nigerian political economist,

> June 12 was a historical breakthrough, the day the ordinary people of Nigeria rose against the ethnic, religious and regional prejudices and the divisive politics with which colonialism and the political class had oppressed them for a half-a-century. In doing this, they took a great step towards making Nigeria a truly viable and democratic polity. Already this historical opportunity is slipping away on account of the cynical campaign by those who created the political impasse to ethnicize and regionalize it. This campaign has put ethnicity, religion and regionalism back on the agenda. They return with a vengeance because our hapless political class has now seen how fragile their parochial political base is. The interim [Shonekan] government arrangement gives them another chance of reinforcing their regression strategies of power and their parochial constituencies, a change they will embrace heartily because it is the only one they have, being in no position to mobilize political support by appealing to personal integrity, ideology or principle.[55]

On the positive side, civil society's success in forcing military strongman Babangida to step aside, despite his extensive efforts to penetrate and subvert society through co-optation, bribery, and divide-and-rule strategies, underscored the resilience and vitality of Nigeria's democratic forces. Moreover, the failure of Babangida's tactics—tactics that reflect the essence of **neopatrimonial rule** (or **patrimonialism),** in which "the chief executive maintains authority through personal patronage, rather than through

After trying to arrange international support in August 1993, Moshood Abiola returned to Nigeria to try and negotiate a peaceful transfer of power.
Source: AP/Wide World Photos.

ideology or law"[56]—reveals that neopatrimonialism is not inevitably bound to succeed in countries like Nigeria. However, the long history of patrimonial rule and prebendal politics in Nigeria does not bode well for economic, nor for democratic political, reform. As Goran Hyden has argued, "While patrimonialism may provide stability in the short-run, it tends to block the road to constitutional development and reform. . . . As a result, changes in the system are difficult without resorting to unconstitutional means."[57]

Nevertheless, the prospect of an eventual return to constitutional rule was enhanced by the concerted efforts within civil society to pressure Babangida to step down, even though this victory was followed by Abacha's harsh rule. Some additional observations are prompted by these developments. The first is that the emergence of a particular type of state seems to be responsible for much of Africa's predicament. Again, in Hyden's words, "It is less the state—as the current neo-liberal emphasis suggests—than politics *writ large* that is at the root of the crisis in Africa. It is the 'rolling back' of patrimonialism that constitutes the ultimate challenge."[58] The nature and outcome of the battle against patrimonialism will help to determine the direction of political and economic change in Nigeria. For now, it is enough to note that the political crisis since 1993 provided the opportunity for an embattled people to challenge patrimonial rule by attack-

ing its very lifeline; earnings from oil exports that go directly to the state's coffers.

Second, foreign pressure has played a visible and decisive role in maintaining the quest for democracy and sustainable development. Unlike the experiences of the past, in recent years major external forces have been more forthright and decisive in supporting civil society and democratization in Nigeria. The United States, Britain, and some member states of the European Union were very visible in exerting pressure on Babangida to leave and in showing a willingness to apply sanctions in support of democracy. This has been made possible, in part, by a changing international environment, especially the willingness of the major industrial countries and the international financial institutions to support democracy in the Third World. Nigeria's increasingly weak economy and enormous debt, now estimated at $40 billion, has made it susceptible to this kind of pressure. It is important to note, however, that although diplomatic pressures were applied to the Abacha regime, economic sanctions were never seriously threatened by the international community, allowing Abacha the breathing room he needed to obstruct, at least for a time, civil society's efforts to avoid another extended period of military rule.

Paradoxically, such pressures on the Babangida regime might have elicited a negative reaction from the Nigerian public, ordinarily determined to defend Nigeria's sovereignty and leadership against perceived imperialist acts emanating from Western countries. However, Babangida's misrule brought together what were traditionally ideologically opposed interests—the major Western powers and Nigeria's militant pro-democracy activists, many of whom have been staunch anti-imperialist radicals.

Foreign support of Nigeria's (and indeed much of Sub-Saharan Africa's) search for democracy and development, reflects two conflicting moralities associated with the so-called new world order. One is a new morality of good governance that seeks to strengthen pro-democratic and developmentalist forces in the Third World. The other is what might be called a new "morality of greed," which emphasizes the profit motive in the interaction between developed and underdeveloped economies. To many observers in the developing world, the economic adjustment programs imposed in the 1980s appeared to have the ultimate goal of enabling Third World countries to repay debts, rather than enabling them to strengthen capacities to meet popular needs. Rather than ministering to public needs, debtor governments have had the latitude to increase authoritarianism and decrease internal accountability, especially when confronted with public reactions that threaten those objectives, such as popular demonstrations against the austerities of adjustment. At the same time, Third World economies have been forced to endorse trade liberalization, even though their counterparts in the developed world did not always embrace free-trade practices.

This new morality of greed is not limited to the developed nations; it also has an internal component in poor countries. It has worked to deepen corruption among Third World leaders and accelerate capital flight from their economies into numbered bank accounts in Western financial centers. Much of the official corruption in Nigeria has been unwittingly underwritten by aid from foreign governments and international agencies because of the inadequate mechanisms to ensure accountability in applying aid monies. A complicating factor is that banking practices in the West often encourage and thrive on corrupt capital flight from underdeveloped economies such as Nigeria's through guarantees of anonymity and unimpeded future access to such wealth. Foreign bank accounts and the holding of other assets abroad are common among Nigeria's ruling military elite. The UNDP's call for an "Honesty International" to police such illicit activities is therefore very welcome.

Beyond this, there is also the question of the consistent and long-term commitment of the G-7 nations to the political conditionalities that link economic development to democratization. There is a very real risk that, given the vagaries of their own domestic politics and the absence of Cold War strategic concerns, the developed world, particularly the G-7, will lose interest in Africa. Western commitment to development and democracy in Africa is not guaranteed. Much of the initiative for Africa's growth, therefore, still needs to emerge from within. In Nigeria, such initiatives will depend on substantial changes in the way Nigerians do business. As Larry Diamond has warned, "If there is to be any basis for self-sustaining growth and peaceful, democratic politics, there must be a transition . . . from pirate capitalism to a more sophisticated and effective nurture capitalism. Nigeria must develop, for the first time, a basis of production and accumulation outside of oil and outside the state."[59] In other words,

there must be a gradual replacement of the current political, economic, and social elite that derives its power and resources from state patronage and remains committed to this closed and exclusive order. They must be replaced by an elite which derives its economic power from diversified sources and through private initiatives *outside* the state system. Indeed, as Hyden has indicated, it is becoming increasingly clear that constitutional governance will be difficult to enthrone in much of Africa "without a concomitant rise of a bourgeoisie ready to defend those principles."[60]

In addition, the project of building a coherent nation-state out of competing nationalities remains largely unfinished and under constant siege by resurgent ethnonationalism and religious fundamentalism. The challenge here is to achieve a proper balance between ethnic-based symbols and institutions and those of a "transethnic" nature. Ethnic consciousness cannot—and arguably, *should not*—be eliminated from society, but ethnicity also cannot become the main basis for political competition. Although the events before and immediately after the historic June 12, 1993, election pointed to an emerging national consensus, Babangida's decision to annul the election and his regime's inciting of divisive emotions in an unsuccessful attempt to cling to power, has unraveled a generation of nationbuilding efforts in Nigeria.

The country remains locked into military rule, pervasive social tension, and economic paralysis. Even though the opposition activities by human rights and pro-democracy activists in 1993 and 1994 were remarkable, they never coalesced into a truly national movement. These urban-based efforts did achieve a measure of success in their efforts to link up with mass associations, including some trade unions, market women, artisans, and other guild associations. And it was the actions of these latter elements that paralyzed the economy after the arrest and detention of Moshood Abiola in June 1994.

Nevertheless, the reach of most civic groups in Nigeria pales in comparison with the obtrusive state security apparatus put in place by Babangida and still used effectively by Abacha. Babangida's security forces have ensured that Nigerian politics resembles that of several Latin American countries in the 1960s and 1970s with its recourse to state terrorism, disappearances, and the penetration of educational, associational, and opposition groups by security services. In the later months of 1994, Nigeria's security services

"Are you down there?"

After declaring himself president in June 1994, one year after the historic election, Moshood Abiola was arrested and charged with treason by the Abacha government. Despite numerous requests from world leaders, court orders, and domestic protests, the regime has kept him imprisoned. Source: Courtesy *West Africa Magazine,* West Africa Publishing Co., London.

were responsible for an unprecedented wave of political terror as militant trade unionists and pro-democracy activists were harassed, detained, and subjected to the torching of their properties. In retaliation, the homes of government supporters, or "fence sitters," were similarly attacked.

Although there was some optimism when Babangida left office, the Abacha coup reignited grave doubts within the international community and in Nigeria as to whether Nigeria can escape the military's firm hold on power. One question continues to be asked: Can an army that has enjoyed the spoils of uncontested power for most of the period of independent nationhood, that has its own university and is planning its own bank, voluntarily relinquish power?

A review of Nigerian politics up to the fall of the Second Republic lamented that "since a democratic route to nationhood, in the context of Nigeria's social pluralism, is a parlous one, and an authoritarian route has not . . . been seriously attempted, Nigerian society is left to oscillate between the broadening of democratic participation and the freezing of such practices with the reimposition of military rule."[61] That statement was made, however, before the dark days of au-

thoritarianism under Babangida and his successor, Abacha, which have witnessed the closing of Nigeria's universities, independent newspapers, and magazines, and the 1994 suspension of *habeas corpus* and other civil rights.

When the Second Republic collapsed in December 1983, the smug assumption among Nigerians was that Nigeria could never produce a dictator in the fashion of Togo's Eyadema, Uganda's Idi Amin, the Central African Republic's Bokassa, or Zaire's Mobutu Sese Seko. Although they came very close to that reality under Babangida, Nigerians have now confronted it head on under Abacha. Here is a pertinent remark made in 1993 by a Nigerian businessman:

> The silence of an elite too anxious to protect what little gains they have made, caused us to so severely jeopardize the future of our children. We cannot abandon the conscience of society to a few professional iconoclasts and some human rights advocates. Voices must rise from boardrooms, chambers of commerce and other citizen groups, if we are to prevent these things from repeating themselves. For now we have to pay tribute to the activists, for it could have been worse without them. . . . We must dedicate ourselves to preventing this from happening again. . . . Unless we say never again, we will wake up one day and a psychopath in uniform will usurp authority, use and abuse power to plunder the nation and dare us speak.[62]

The emerging consensus is still very much tentative, and its resolve has been weakened—at least in the form of public criticism of the regime—since Abacha successfully broke the labor strikes, ended the mass demonstrations in September 1994, and closed a number of prominent newspapers. The Constitutional Conference that he appointed defiantly established a firm date of January 1996 for the transition process leading to the replacement of military rule by an elected civilian government. As he has demonstrated in his ability to manipulate the courts and other state institutions, Abacha has pressured enough of the delegates to allow him an "indefinite" tenure. Even if elections are held, however, no one can guarantee if the outcome will be respected by the military officer corps, or for how long.

NIGERIAN POLITICS IN TRANSITION

As indicated in the first section, Nigerian politics has been characterized by turmoil and periodic crises since the British relinquished colonial power in 1960. Thirty-five years later, the country still lacks a stable and orderly political system. In fact, over the past two decades Nigeria has retrogressed, as evidenced by the stagnation and decline of major productive sectors, infrastructure and institutions, the heightened sociopolitical tension, an increasingly irresponsible elite, and an expanding mass culture of despondency and rage. What, it must be asked, is the likely future of Nigerian politics?

There appear to be two possible scenarios. The first scenario envisions the completion of the transition process begun a decade ago by Ibrahim Babangida. After initially refusing to commit itself to a specific date by which power would be transferred to a civilian government, General Abacha announced in April 1994 a new transition program, the first phase of which would be completed in early 1995 with the lifting of the ban on political parties. Neither his Nigerian critics nor international observers were impressed by the vagueness of the commitment. It seemed to open the way for another round of years spent, and wasted, on constitution drafting and revisions, the emergence and then dissolution of political associations and parties, and costly electoral exercises that kept civilian politicians busily engaged while the military continued to rule and despoil the country. The Babangida regime revised its own transition program four times, extending its projected tenure with each change. The Abacha regime must still convince a deeply skeptical Nigerian public that the farcical "transition" routines of the 1980s will not be repeated in the 1990s, this time as a grave tragedy. The political activism that nearly brought the country to a screeching halt in 1994 could give way to cathartic and unfocused violence. Simply put, the "rage against inept authoritarianism [could be] transformed into a mindless anger against all forms of government, including democracy."[63]

It is a variety of that rage that informs our second possible scenario: the possible collapse of Nigeria in its present form. Pressure for full democratization is increasingly exerted by social groups who see their realization of "a Nigerian dream" as inextricably bound up with the victory of Abiola and what they consider as his rightful ascension to the presidency. Although the experience of Yugoslavia is a frightening reality to both sides of the crisis, even more relevant is Nigeria's own ethnic civil war which claimed an estimated 1 million lives by the time it ended in January 1970. The persistent manipulation of sectional and ethnic sentiments during the long crisis since Babangida annulled the elections has raised fears of Nigeria's descent into the nightmare of another civil war.

The only alternative to such a tragedy is steady progress toward renewed democratic rule. Nigeria's complex problems can be resolved within the existing parameters of its statehood if the avenues of participation and accommodation of all sections of the population are reopened through a democratic system. As we know from the analysis of recent events, embarking on such a path is an enormous challenge. The unanswered question is: What will induce the ruling alliance of northern military officers and conservative politicians to agree to such a transition? Of obvious relevance to Nigeria are the "foundational pacts" among political actors in Latin America that allowed entrenched military regimes to gradually relinquish power through negotiated settlements with their civilian successors.[64] In addition, the recent experience of South Africa, in which such a process of "transition by transaction" was consummated, challenges Nigerian political and military leaders, both in and out of office, to demonstrate that they can also arrive at a negotiated exit from their country's ruinous confrontations and divisions.

NIGERIA IN COMPARATIVE PERSPECTIVE

It is seldom the case that theoretical insights from the historical experiences of one country or region are fully applicable to another; and political scientists are wary about stretching concepts so far as to suggest that one polity can be modeled after another. Nigeria's current crisis is the result of a specific set of historical circumstances, some avoidable and perhaps preventable, such as the extensive misuse of oil revenues, some not, such as the imposition of European colonial domination. In short, a unique combination of factors has contributed to Nigeria's present deplorable condition. Given these caveats, the study of Nigeria has important implications for the study of African politics and, more broadly, of comparative politics.

The Nigerian case embodies a number of key themes and issues that can be generalized to increase social science knowledge, and these themes deserve careful consideration. We can learn much about how democratic regimes are established and achieve stability by understanding the pitfalls Nigeria has encountered. By analyzing the historical dynamics of Nigeria's ethnic conflict, for example, we can identify institutional mechanisms that may be effective in mitigating ethnic conflict in plural states. We can also learn much about how viable and sustainable economies are developed by contrasting their evolution with Nigeria's. Each of these issues, in turn, offers comparative lessons for the major themes explored in this book: the democratic idea, collective identities, political economy, and the world of states.

The Democratic Idea

As was mentioned at the beginning of this chapter, many African countries are undergoing transitions from authoritarian rule. With the end of superpower competition in Africa, and the consequent withdrawal of the support from both the former Soviet Union and the United States to Africa's despots, many African societies have experienced a resurgence of popular pressures for greater participation in political life and more transparent forms of governance. Decades of authoritarian, single-party, and military rule in Africa have left a dismal record: arbitrary imprisonment and silenced political opposition; harassment of civic, professional, and religious institutions; stifled public discourse and free speech; and bankrupted treasuries and mismanaged economies. At the same time, a handful of elites have acquired large fortunes through wanton corruption. The examples, sadly, are plentiful. Consider Nigeria's "missing" $12.2 billion windfall in oil revenues after the Gulf War in 1991; or the fact that Zairian president Mobutu Sese Seko's "personal" wealth is estimated to be several billion—perhaps as much as half the external debt of the entire country. Or that Kenya's president Daniel Arap Moi is considered among the richest men in Africa, a group to which Ibrahim Babangida and Sani Abacha of Nigeria now certainly belong. The devious ways in which these fortunes are acquired and stashed in banks and property abroad make it difficult to give concrete figures. They do, however, suggest convincingly that the exercise of postindependence authoritarian rule in Africa has contributed to economic stagnation and decline and, simultaneously, to the enrichment of a handful of "big men." The difficulty that such countries as Kenya, Cameroon, Togo, and Nigeria have experienced in moving to democratic systems is a reflection, among other factors, of the ruling elites' unwillingness to lose control of the political instruments of self-enrichment.

Nigeria exemplifies the harsh reality of authoritarian and unaccountable rule and the urgent need for society to be freed from it. Corruption, fraud, and mismanagement, even the restriction of political liberties, are often tolerated by populations long accustomed to the misuse of power by their governments. Nigeria has endured six military regimes, countless attempted coups, and a bloody civil war that claimed over 1 million lives. Promises of change have been made and repeatedly broken. Yet the democratic idea remains strong among many Nigerians. As socioeconomic conditions worsen, democracy becomes even more of an imperative because it would provide mechanisms for limiting abuses of power and for holding governments accountable. It is not clear how long the Abacha regime will endure and whether its promised "transition" will materialize, but the forces in support of Abiola and against the regime remain strong throughout the country, perhaps illustrating the resilience of the democratic idea. Indeed, even the Constitutional Conference Abacha has been able to manipulate in December 1994 voted for a return to civilian rule by January 1996. Abacha, however, used all the means at his disposal to reverse this critical decision and allow the regime to set its own termination date of 1998.

Collective Identities

Nigeria presents an important case in which to study the dangers of ethnic-based nationalism in a society with deep cultural divisions. How can multiethnic countries manage their diversity? What institutional mechanisms can be employed to avert ethnic-based tragedies such as the 1967–1970 civil war, or the continuing conflicts that have brought so much suffering to the former Yugoslavia and Rwanda? This chapter has suggested electoral system tools, such as proportional representation, that may present one such solution. Others must be identified.

Insights from the Nigerian experience may, for example, explain why some federations persist and identify the factors likely to bring about their collapse. Nigeria's complex social situation and its varied attempts to create a nation out of its highly diverse population enhance our understanding of the politics of cultural pluralism,[65] and the difficulty of accommodating sectional interests under conditions of political and economic insecurity. As described in this chapter, federal character in Nigeria has been abused and distorted into a form of ethnic and regional favoritism and a tool for dispensing patronage. Yet, the country has benefited in some ways from the attention devoted to creating state and local governments and giving people in different regions a sense that they are stakeholders in the entity called "Nigeria." Such gains, unfortunately, have been severely diluted in the Babangida-Abacha era.

Political Economy

Nigeria provides insights into the political economy of underdevelopment. At independence in 1960, Nigeria was stronger economically than its Southeast Asian counterparts. Independent Nigeria appeared poised for growth, with a wealth of natural resources, a large, if undereducated, population to provide labor resources, and the presence of highly entrepreneurial groups in all regions of the country. Today, Nigeria is among the poorest countries in the world in terms of per capita income, while many of its Asian counterparts have joined the ranks of the "newly industrializing nations" (NICs). Much of this chapter has been devoted to understanding what went wrong in Nigerian economic development. One critical lesson Nigeria teaches us is that a rich endowment of resources is not enough to ensure economic development. Even the bonus of mineral wealth could be mismanaged rather than used to alleviate underdevelopment.

Other variables are critically important, notably, political stability (if not necessarily democracy), and a strong developmentalist ethic. Such a developmentalist ethic, and an institutional structure to enforce it, would set limits to corrupt behavior and constrain the pursuit of short-term personal gain at the expense of national economic growth. Institutions that appear critical are a professional civil service, an independent judiciary, and a vigorous free press. Nigeria has had each of these, and each was undermined and corrupted. As we know, the "ethic" that has come to dominate Nigerian political economy has been prebendalism. Where corruption is unchecked, as in

Nigeria, the Philippines under Ferdinand Marcos, or in many states of Latin America, such as Mexico before recent economic and political reforms, economic development will remain elusive.

Nigeria also demonstrates that sustainable economic development requires sound economic policy, something it has painfully lacked. Without export diversification, commodity exporting countries are buffeted by the price fluctuations of one or two main products. This situation, of course, can be traced back to overreliance on primary commodity export-oriented policies bequeathed by the British colonial regime. Yet other former colonies have managed to diversify their initial export base successfully, such as Malaysia and Indonesia. Nigeria, in contrast, has substituted one form of commodity dependence for another: It has allowed its petroleum industry to overwhelm completely all other sectors of the economy. Nigeria even became a net importer of products (for example, of palm oil and palm nuts) for which it was once a leading world producer. In comparative perspective, we can see that natural resource endowments such as those enjoyed by Nigeria can be tremendously beneficial. The United States, for example, has parlayed its endowments of agricultural, mineral, and energy resources into one of the world's most diversified modern economies. Meanwhile Japan, which is by comparison poorly endowed with natural resources, has one of the strongest economies in the world, achieved in large part through its unique developmental strategies. Each of these examples illustrates the primacy of sound economic policies. Nigeria's three and a half decades since independence, in contrast, can be studied to show how a nation's enormous economic potential could be undermined by unstable politics, prebendalist attitudes, and unsound economic policies.

A World of States

Nigeria exists in two "worlds" of states—one in the global political economy and the other within Africa. We have addressed at length Nigeria's position in the world. Economically, Nigeria was thrust into the world economy in a position of weakness, first as a British colony and later as an independent nation. Despite its resources and the potential of oil to provide the investment capital needed to build a modern economy, Nigeria has grown weaker. It has lost much of its international clout and, in place of the respect it once enjoyed in diplomatic circles, Nigeria is now regularly criticized for persistent human rights abuses. Although calls for stringent sanctions have been loud, these have elicited mainly symbolic actions, such as the denial of visas to government officials.

In the mid-1990s, the desire of the United States to intervene—whether economically, politically, or militarily—in Third World nations has diminished, as has that of many European countries. Further, given recent experiences in Bosnia, Somalia, and Rwanda, as long as military regimes retain effective political control in Nigeria, it is unlikely that more drastic steps—such as an embargo on oil purchases will be taken.

In comparative politics courses and textbooks alike, Africa is usually neglected or consigned to brief remarks in the section covering the "developing world." Yet Africa is an important region to study and to understand, especially because many problems encountered there, as well as successes, are comparable to those occurring elsewhere. But there is a deeper significance to Africa as well. Archeological research and recent genetic studies confirm that Africa is the birthplace of humanity. It has been the home of great civilizations—in Mali, Songhay, Zimbabwe, and ancient Egypt, for example.

Africa has also known centuries of depredation and exploitation. Between the sixteenth and the nineteenth centuries, the slave trade bled it of human resources. Later, as the victim of colonial domination and division, its economies were structured to meet the Western industrializing nations' need for primary products and raw materials. In the postcolonial period, Africa became an arena in which the West and Eastern bloc initiated bloody proxy wars, such as in Angola, and manipulated and corrupted African regimes for their own strategic geopolitical ends. In addition, Africa was exploited by its own opportunistic and frequently vicious indigenous elites and leaders. The hopes raised that the end of colonial rule would usher in decades of sustained development were quickly dashed, except in a few small countries like Botswana and Mauritius. By the mid-1980s, it became clear that new pathways had to be blazed. Economic reform programs were adopted, and after 1989, a wave of democratization movements led to the emergence of pluralist political systems in well

over half the continent. The irony of Nigeria today is that it was an early leader in both the economic *and* political spheres.

In a continent that comprises more than 10 percent of the world's population, there remain vast resources (for indigenous consumption and export), large potential markets, and many opportunities to achieve greater prominence in the world of states. This chapter began by quoting the statement, "As Nigeria goes, so goes the rest of Sub-Saharan Africa." However, as the African historian Achille Mbembe has written, Africa is "going in several directions simultaneously." Instead of leading the continent, Nigeria is being left behind in such respects as national cohesion, state capabilities, economic growth and, of course, democratization. Rather than serving as a positive model in matters of economic and political reform, the three military regimes since December 1983 have used tactics designed to prolong their hold on power. Only diehard authoritarian regimes on the continent can derive encouragement from the course of events in Nigeria since 1983. For example, soon after the annulment of the June 12 election in Nigeria, the president of the Central African Republic tried to nullify his own country's presidential election when it became apparent that he would be defeated. He reluctantly agreed to allow the election results to be completed and announced when France, the country's major external supporter, threatened to sever all assistance.

The future of democracy, political stability, and economic renewal in other parts of Africa, and certainly in West Africa, will be greatly influenced, for good or ill, by unfolding events in Nigeria. Beyond the obvious demonstration effect, the economy of the West African subregion can be revitalized by resumed growth of the Nigerian economy just as the states of southern Africa hope to benefit from the enormous international interest in postapartheid South Africa. International political, scholarly, and business attention has shifted steadily to the south of the continent, focusing chiefly on South Africa and its stable neighboring states of Botswana and Namibia. That shift portends a greater danger of marginalization, as Africa becomes divided into a zone of prosperity that attracts investment and loan capital and other resources, and a zone of decay.

Therefore, the challenges that Nigeria will face in the remaining years of this century concern not only its peoples' frustrated hopes for a better life, stable government, and a democratic political order, but also the potential contributions that this giant of Africa could still make to the entire continent, and to the world at large, if only an exit can be found from the cycle of endless woe.

Key Terms

autocracy
authoritarian
legitimacy
accountability
unfinished state
structural adjustment
  program (SAP)
jihad
acephalous societies
emirs
interventionist
warrant chiefs
indirect rule
clientelism
neocolonialism
rents
Economic Community
  of West African
  States (ECOWAS)

balance of payments
International Financial
  Institutions (IFIs)
privatization
prebendalism
federalism
para-statals
state corporatism
shari'a
civil society
proportional
  representation (PR)
neopatrimonial rule
  (patrimonialism)

Suggested Readings

Section 1

Diamond, Larry. *Class, Ethnicity and Democracy in Nigeria: The Failure of the First Republic.* London: Macmillan, 1988.

———. "Nigeria's Search for a New Political Order." *Journal of Democracy* 2, no. 2 (Spring 1991): 54.

Forrest, Tom. *Politics and Economic Development in Nigeria.* Boulder, Colo.: Westview Press, 1993.

Hodgkin, Thomas. *Nigerian Perspectives.* London: Oxford University Press, 1975.

Joseph, Richard A. *Democracy and Prebendal Politics in Nigeria: The Rise and Fall of the Second Republic.* Cambridge: Cambridge University Press, 1987.

Lewis, Peter M. "Endgame in Nigeria? The Politics of a Failed Democratic Transition." *African Affairs* 93 (1994): 323–340.

Oyediran, Oyeleye, ed. *Nigerian Government and Politics Under Military Rule.* London: Macmillan, 1979.

Section 2

Horowitz, Donald L. *Ethnic Groups in Conflict.* Berkeley: University of California Press, 1985.

Joseph, Richard A. *Democracy and Prebendal Politics in Nigeria: The Rise and Fall of the Second Republic.* Cambridge: Cambridge University Press, 1987.

Ogwu, U. Joy, and Adebayo Olukoshi, eds. "Special Issue: The Economic Diplomacy of the Nigerian State." *Nigerian Journal of International Affairs* 17, no. 2 (1991).

Onoge, Omafume. *Nigeria: The Way Forward.* Ibadan: Spectrum Books, 1993.

Turok, Ben, ed. *Alternative Development Strategies for Africa.* Vol. 3: *Debt and Democracy.* London: Institute for African Alternatives, 1991.

Watts, Michael, ed. *State, Oil, and Agriculture in Nigeria.* Berkeley: University of California Press, 1987.

Wunsch, James S., and Dele Olowu, eds. *The Failure of the Centralized State: Institutions and Self-Governance in Africa.* Boulder, Colo.: Westview Press, 1990.

Section 3

Adamolekun, L. *Politics and Administration in Nigeria.* London: Hutchinson, 1986.

Achike, Okay. *Public Administration: A Nigerian and Comparative Perspective.* London: Longman, 1978.

Ekeh, Peter P., and Eghosa E. Osaghae, eds. *Federal Character and Federalism in Nigeria.* Ibadan: Heinemann, 1989.

Nyang'oro, Julius, and Tim Shaw, eds. *Corporatism in Africa: Comparative Analysis and Practice.* Boulder, Colo.: Westview Press, 1989.

Oyovbaire, Sam E. *Federalism in Nigeria: A Study in the Development of the Nigerian State.* London: Macmillan, 1985.

Rothchild, Donald, and Victor Olorunsola, eds. *State Versus Ethnic Claims: African Policy Dilemmas.* Boulder, Colo.: Westview Press, 1983.

Section 4

Agbaje, Adigun. *The Nigerian Press: Hegemony and the Social Construction of Legitimacy, 1960–1983.* Lewiston, N.Y.: Edwin Mellen Press, 1992.

Crook, Richard, and A. M. Jerve, eds. *Government and Participation: Institutional Development, Decentralization and Democracy in the Third World.* Bergen, Norway: Chr. Michelsen Institute, 1991.

Sklar, Richard L. *Nigerian Political Parties: Power in an Emergent African Nation.* New York: NOK Publishers, 1983.

Section 5

Agbaje, Adigun. "Twilight of Democracy in Nigeria." *Africa Demos* 3, no. 3:5. Atlanta: The Carter Center of Emory University, 1994.

Bienen, Henry. *Political Conflict and Economic Change in Nigeria.* London: Frank Cass, 1988.

Healey, J., and M. Robinson. *Democracy, Governance and Economic Policy: Sub-Saharan Africa in Comparative Perspective.* London: Overseas Development Institute, 1992.

Jackson, Robert H., and Carl G. Rosberg. *Personal Rule in Africa.* Berkeley: University of California Press, 1982.

Young, Crawford. *The Rising Tide of Cultural Pluralism: The Nation-State at Bay?* Madison: University of Wisconsin Press, 1993.

Endnotes

[1] Thomas Hodgkin, *Nigerian Perspectives* (London: Oxford University Press, 1975), 2–3; also C. S. Whitaker, "The Unfinished State of Nigeria," *Worldview* 27, no. 3 (March 1984): 6.

[2] Hodgkin, *op. cit.,* 2.

[3] Peter P. Ekeh, "Colonialism and the Development of Citizenship in Africa: A Study in Ideologies of Legitimation," in *Themes in African Social and Political Thought,* ed. Onigu Otite (Enugu: Fourth Dimension Publishers, 1978), 308.

[4] Okello Oculi, "The Limits of Power: Lessons from Egyptology," in *African Traditional Political Thought and Institutions,* ed. John A. Ayoade and Adigun A. B. Agbaje (Lagos: Center for Black and African Arts and Civilization, 1989), 47.

[5] Caroline Dennis, "The Role of Religious Ideas in Social Change," in *Social Change in Nigeria,* ed. Simi Afonja and Tola Olu Pearce (Essex: Longman, 1984), 147.

[6] Ekeh, "Colonialism and the Two Publics in Africa: A Theoretical Statement," *Comparative Studies in Society and History,* 17, no. 1 (January 1975).

[7] Larry Diamond, "Class Formation in the Swollen African State," *Journal of Modern African Studies* 25, no. 4 (1987): 592.

[8] Donald Horowitz, *Ethnic Groups in Conflict* (Berkeley: University of California Press, 1985).

[9] Basil Davidson, *Modern Africa,* 3d ed. (London: Longman Group, 1994).

[10] Obafemi Awolowo, *Path to Nigerian Freedom* (London: Faber and Faber, 1947), 47–48.

[11] Quoted in Nigeria, *Legislative Council Debates,* March 4, 1948, 227.

[12] Billy Dudley, *An Introduction to Nigerian Government and Politics* (Bloomington: Indiana University Press, 1982), 71.

[13] The following discussion is based on Michael J. Watts, *State, Oil and Agriculture in Nigeria* (Berkeley: University of California Press, 1987), 61–84.

[14] *Ibid.,* 61.

[15] *Ibid.,* 71.

[16] *Ibid.,* 66.

[17] *Ibid.,* 69.

[18] Adigun Agbaje, "Adjusting State and Market in Nigeria: The Paradoxes of Orthodoxy," *Afrika Spectrum* 27, no. 2 (June 1992): 123–137; Pita O. Agbese, "Moral Economy and the Expansion of the Privatization Constituency in Nigeria," *Journal of Commonwealth and Comparative Politics* 30, no. 3 (November 1992): 335–357.

[19] Sam Aluko, "Planning for Economic Development in Nigeria," in *Nigeria: The Way Forward,* ed. Omafume F. Onoge (Ibadan: Spectrum Books, 1993), 6.

[20] Cited in Richard A. Joseph, *Democracy and Prebendal Politics in Nigeria: The Rise and Fall of the Second Republic* (Cambridge: Cambridge University Press, 1987), 75.

[21] Dele Olowu, "Centralization, Self-Governance, and Development in Nigeria," in *The Failure of the Centralized State: Institutions and Self-Governance in Africa,* ed. James S. Wunsch and Dele Olowu (Boulder, Colo.: Westview Press, 1991), 211.

[22] Central Bank of Nigeria: Federal Budget Estimates, 1987 and 1988.

[23] Ben O. Nwabueze, *Military Rule and Social Justice in Nigeria* (Ibadan: Spectrum Law Publishing, 1993), 21.

[24] *West Africa,* April 13–19, 1992, 620.

[25] Nwabueze, *Military Rule and Social Justice in Nigeria,* 22–23.

[26] Billy J. Dudley, *Instability and Political Order: Politics and Crisis in Nigeria* (Ibadan: Ibadan University Press, 1973), 35.

[27] Donald L. Horowitz, *Ethnic Groups in Conflict* (Berkeley: University of California Press, 1985), 39.

[28] J. Isawa Elaigwu, "The Nigerian Federation and Future Prospects," in *Nigeria: The Way Forward,* ed. Onoge, 32 33.

[29] Joseph, *Democracy and Prebendal Politics.*

[30] UNDP, "Honesty International," in *Human Development Report, 1992* (New York: Oxford University Press, 1992), 89.

[31] Douglas Rimmer, "External Trade and Payments," in *Nigeria Since 1970: A Political and Economic Outline,* ed. Anthony Kirk-Greene and Douglas Rimmer (London: Hodder and Stoughton, 1981), 136.

[32] Cited in U. Joy Ogwu and Adebayo Olukushi, "Nigeria's Economic Diplomacy: Some Contending Issues," *Nigerian Journal of International Affairs* 17, no. 2 (1991): 5–6.

[33] *Ibid.*

[34] Victor A. Olorunsola, "Questions on Constitutionalism and Democracy: Nigeria and Africa," in *Democracy and Pluralism in Africa,* ed. Dove Ronen (Boulder, Colo.: Lynne Rienner, 1986).

[35] K. B. Hadjor, *On Transforming Africa: Discourse with Africa's Leaders* (New Jersey: Africa World Press, 1987), 60.

[36] D. C. Bach, "The Mamman Dike Challenge: Ethnicity, Nationality and Federalism in Nigeria," paper presented to the Conference on Democratic Transition and Structural Adjustment in Nigeria (Stanford: Hoover Institution, August 1990), 15.

[37] Rotimi T. Suberu, "Problems of Federation in the Second Nigerian Republic and Prospects for the Future," *Africa* (Roma) 47, no. 1 (March, 1992): 31. (emphasis added)

[38] See Juan Linz, "The Perils of Presidentialism," *The Journal of Democracy* 1, no. 1 (1990): 51–69; and responses in "Debate—Presidents vs. Parliaments," *The Journal of Democracy* 1, no. 4 (1990): 73–91.

[39] Richard Joseph, "Nigeria: The War Forward," testimony before the Subcommittee on Africa, House Committee on Foreign Affairs, Washington, D.C. (August 4, 1993), 7.

[40] William D. Graf, *The Nigerian State: Political Economy, State Class and Political System in the Post-Colonial Era* (London: James Currey, 1988), 205.

[41] *The (Lagos) Guardian,* July 22, 1993, 4.

[42] *Ibid.,* 139.

[43]Larry Diamond, "Introduction: Roots of Failure, Seeds of Hope," in *Democracy in Developing Countries,* Vol. 2: *Africa,* ed. Diamond et al. (Boulder, Colo.: Lynne Rienner, 1988), 10.

[44]Goran Hyden, "The Electoral System: The Forgotten Factor in Africa's Political Transitions," *The Democratic Challenge in Africa* (Atlanta: CCEU, 1994), 169.

[45]Billy Dudley, *An Introduction to Nigerian Government and Politics* (Bloomington: Indiana University Press, 1982).

[46]Adigun Agbaje, "Adjusting State and Market in Nigeria: The Paradoxes of Orthodoxy," *Afrika Spectrum* 27, no. 2 (1992): 132.

[47]*Ibid.*

[48]*The Guardian (Lagos),* June 26, 1993, 1.

[49]*Citizen* (Kaduna, Nigeria), December 14, 1992, 14.

[50]*Ibid.,* 2.

[51]Omafume F. Onoge, ed., *Nigeria: The Way Forward—Proceedings and Policy Recommendations of the First Obefemi Awolowo Foundation Dialogue* (Ibadan: Spectrum Books, 1993), 105.

[52]Olukunle Iyanda, "A Nation of Compromisers," *The Guardian,* August 31, 1993, 27.

[53]Yemi Kayode-Adedeji, "Thoughts on the Political Class," *The Guardian,* August 18, 1993, 27.

[54]*The Guardian,* September 9, 1993, 3.

[55]Claude Ake, "Our Interim Future," *The Guardian,* September 9, 1993, 13.

[56]Michael Bratton and Nicolas van de Walle, "Neopatrimonial Regimes and Political Transitions in Africa," *World Politics,* vol. 46 (July 1994): 453–489.

[57]Goran Hyden, "Reciprocity and Governance in Africa," in *The Failure of the Centralized State: State Institutions and Self-Governance in Africa,* ed. James S. Wunsch and Dele Olowu (Boulder, Colo.: Westview Press, 1990), 265.

[58]Goran Hyden, "The Role of Aid and Research in the Political Restructuring of Africa," in *Government and Participation: Institutional Development, Decentralisation and Democracy in the Third World,* ed. Richard Crook and A. M. Jerve (Bergen, Norway: Chr. Michelsen Institute, 1991).

[59]Larry Diamond, "Nigeria: Pluralism, Statism and the Struggle for Democracy," in *Democracy in Developing Countries,* Vol. 2: *Africa,* ed. Diamond, Lipset, and Linz (Boulder, Colo.: Lynne Rienner, 1988), 85.

[60]Hyden, "Reciprocity and Governance," 263.

[61]Joseph, *Democracy and Prebendal Politics,* 185.

[62]*The Guardian,* July 16, 1993, 17.

[63]Adigun Agbaje, "Twilight of Democracy in Nigeria," *Africa Demos* 3, no. 3 (Atlanta: The Carter Center of Emory University, 1994): 5.

[64]Terry Lynn Karl and Philippe C. Schmitter, "Modes of Transition in Latin America, Southern and Eastern Europe," *International Social Science Journal* 1, no. 28 (May 1991).

[65]See Crawford Young, *The Politics of Cultural Pluralism* (Madison: University of Wisconsin Press, 1976), and Crawford Young, ed., *The Rising Tide of Cultural Pluralism: The Nation-State at Bay?* (Madison: University of Wisconsin Press, 1993).

CHAPTER 12

Iran

ISLAMIC REPUBLIC OF IRAN

Land and Population

Capital	Tehran	
Total Area (square miles)	636,293 (slightly larger than Alaska)	
Population	61.6 million	
Annual Projected Population Growth Rate (1993–2000)	3.0%	
Urban Population (% of total)	58%	
Ethnic Composition		
Ethnic Groups	Persian	51%
	Azerbaijani	24%
	Gilaki and Mazandarani	8%
	Kurd	7%
	Arab	3%
	Other	7%
Major Languages	Farsi (Persian)	59%
	Turkic	27%
	Kurdish	7%
	Arabic	1%
	Other	6%
Religions	Shi'i Muslim	90%
	Sunni Muslim	9%
	Other	1%

Economy

Domestic Currency	Rial	
GNP (US$)	$148.4 billion	
GNP per capita (US$)	$2,410	
Purchasing Power Parity GDP per capita (US$)	$4,670	
Average Annual GDP Growth Rate (1980–1993)	2.6%	
Structure of Production (% of GDP)	Agriculture	24%
	Industry	29%
	Services	47%
Labor Force Distribution (% of total)	Agriculture	25%
	Industry	26%
	Services	49%
Women as % of Total Labor Force	9%–19% (varies widely according to source)	

Income Distribution (Urban)	% of Population	% Share of Income or Consumption
	Richest 20%	48.0%
	Poorest 40%	14.6%

Total Foreign Trade (exports plus imports) as % of GDP	39%

Society

Life Expectancy	Female	68
	Male	67
Population per Doctor	3,140	
Infant Mortality (per 1,000 live births)	35	
Adult Literacy	Female	45%
	Male	67%
Average (Mean) Years of Schooling (of adults 25+)	Female	3.1
	Male	4.6
Communications (per 100 people)	Radios	23
	Televisions	.7
	Telephones	5
1993 Human Development Index (1 = highest)	Ranks 70 out of 174	

Political Organization

Political System   Theocracy (rule of the clergy) headed by a cleric with the titles of Supreme Jurist and Supreme Leader. The clergy rule by divine right.

Regime History   Islamic Republic since the 1979 Islamic Revolution.

Administrative Structure   Centralized administration with 24 provinces. The Interior Minister appoints the provincial governor-generals.

Executive   President and his cabinet. The president is elected by the general electorate every four years. The president chooses his cabinet ministers, but they need to obtain the approval of the *Majles* (parliament).

Legislature   Unicameral. The *Majles,* formed of 270 seats, is elected every four years. It has multiple member districts with the top runners in the elections taking the seats. Bills passed by the *Majles* do not become law unless they have the approval of the clerically dominated Council of Guardians.

Judiciary   A Supreme Judge and a Supreme Court independent of the executive and legislature but appointed by the Supreme Leader.

Party System   The ruling clergy restrict all party and organizational activities.

SECTION 1
The Making of the Modern Iranian State

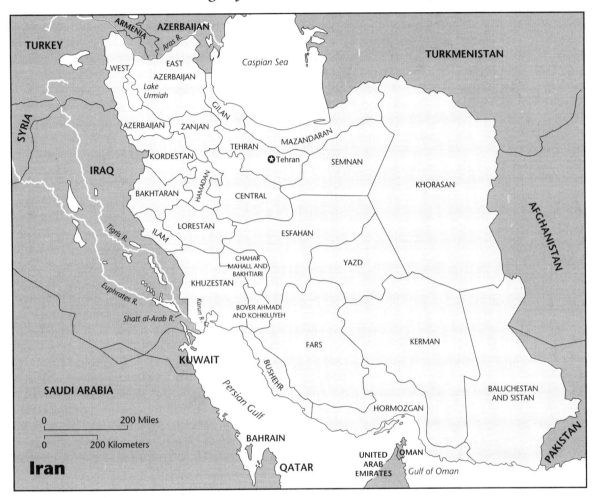

IRAN AT THE CROSSROADS

On January 16, 1979, Mohammad Reza Pahlavi, the Shah-in-Shah (King of Kings), the Commander of Imperial Iran, the Shadow of God on Earth, Light of the Aryan Race, and Guide to the Great New Civilization, flew into exile never to return. Two weeks later, **Ayatollah** Ruhollah Khomeini, a prominent cleric, triumphantly returned home from exile to claim his Islamic Revolution. He promptly replaced the Pahlavi monarchy with an Islamic Republic dominated thoroughly by the clergy. For this reason alone, the Islamic

Republic can be described as a true theocracy—one of the few in world history. The new regime hailed Khomeini as the Great Leader of the Islamic Revolution, the Founder of the Islamic Republic, the Guide for the Oppressed Masses, and, most potent of all, the **Imam** (Infallible Leader)—a title Iranians had never before bestowed on a living person.

Khomeini followed up the Islamic Revolution with an incessant propaganda war against the United States. Accusing the United States of being a "satanic" power and setting up a "den of spies" inside its Tehran embassy, Khomeini incited university students

At first glance this poster appears to be religious with the angels in the background. A more careful scrutiny reveals Maoist and Stalinist influences.

to occupy the embassy grounds and incarcerate American diplomats. Thus began the famous U.S. hostage crisis, which lasted 444 days and contributed to President Jimmy Carter's failure to be reelected. Relations with the West, particularly the United States, deteriorated even further when Iran launched a project to develop a nuclear bomb, assassinated émigrés living in Europe, and, most sensational of all, issued a death warrant against the Muslim-born British writer Salman Rushdie for his alleged blasphemy of Islam in his controversial book *Satanic Verses.*

The Islamic Revolution is a landmark in contemporary politics for a number of reasons. First, it is comparable to the other classic revolutions—notably, the French, Russian, and Chinese. It exploded like a volcanic eruption, suddenly and dramatically, utterly destroying the age-old monarchy. Although the last dynasty was only a half-century old, the Iranian monarchy as a whole boasted 2,500 years of history, leading some to claim that it had become part and parcel of the "Iranian mentality." The revolution blew away the society's upper levels, drastically changing the social

landscape, scattering debris into the neighboring regions, and affecting the political climate even on the other side of the globe. By the early 1990s, Western governments feared similar Islamic Revolutions would erupt not only in neighboring Turkey, Iraq, Afghanistan, Saudi Arabia, and Central Asia, but also in such faraway areas as Gaza, Egypt, Algeria, Nigeria, and even Indonesia. In fact, this event introduced into our contemporary language the term "Islamic fundamentalism."

Second, it occurred in one of the most important states in the Middle East. On the eve of the revolution, Iran had nearly 36 million people, making it one of the most populous nations in the region. It had one of the area's largest and fastest-growing economies. It was one of the most developed and industrialized societies in the region, with nearly 50 percent of its total population living in urban centers. It was the world's fourth-largest oil producer and second-largest oil exporter, thus making it highly important to such oil-importing countries as Japan, France, Germany, Italy, and the United States. It possessed the world's fifth-largest army, one of the most up-to-date air forces, and by far the largest navy in the Persian Gulf. The United States had appointed the Shah to be its main policeman in the Persian Gulf. Thus, the revolution had drastic repercussions on America's strategic position in the Persian Gulf.

Third, the Islamic Revolution raised theoretical questions about modernization in general and revolutions in particular. Social scientists have often argued that modernization, especially urbanization and industrialization, inevitably produces secularization—the marginalization of religion in public life. Some have even argued that modernization inevitably relegates the clergy to the dustbin of history. Yet in Iran, fifty years of substantial modernization had enhanced the role of the clergy to the point where they could establish a full-fledged **theocracy.** Furthermore, political scientists have often pointed out that revolutions usually follow defeats in war or peasant rebellions and bring to power the intelligentsia at the head of disciplined political parties. Yet in Iran, the revolution occurred with no foreign wars, no peasant revolts, no triumphant intelligentsia, and no highly organized political parties.

Few observers in 1979–1980 expected the Islamic Republic to last long. They considered a clerical state in the twentieth century to be an anachronism. After all,

Islam

Islam, with some 1 billion adherents, is one of the largest religions in the world. *Islam* means literally submission to God, and a Muslim is someone who has submitted to God—the same God that Jews and Christians worship. Islam has one central tenet: "There is only one God, and Mohammad (d. A.D. 632) is His last Prophet." Muslims, in order to consider themselves faithful, need to perform the following four duties to the best of their abilities: give to charity; pray every day facing Mecca, where Abraham is believed to have built the first place of worship; make a pilgrimage to Mecca at least once; and fast during the daytime hours in the month of Ramadan to commemorate God's revelation of the Qur'an (Koran, or Holy Book) to Mohammad. These four, together with the central tenet, are known as the "Five Pillars of Islam."

From its earliest days, Islam has been divided into two major branches—the Sunnis and the Shi'is. The Sunnis, which means literally the followers of tradition, are by far the majority. The Shi'is, which means the followers of Ali, constitute less than 10 percent of Muslims. They are concentrated in Iran, southern Iraq, eastern Turkey, and southern Lebanon. Although both accept the five pillars, the Shi'is believe that after the Prophet's death his authority should have been passed to Imam Ali—his cousin, son-in-law, and early disciple. The Sunnis, on the other hand, recognize the legitimacy of Caliphs (Deputies of the Prophet) appointed by the community notables after Mohammad's death. Since then, the Sunnis and Shi'is have developed slight variations in their interpretations of the law, theology, history, and political theory.

theocracy appeared incompatible with democracy and the modern demand for popular representation and mass political participation. The clergy, steeped in theology and history, were dismissed as inherently incapable of dealing with the challenges of the contemporary world—that is, with rival states, ultrasophisticated weaponry, the information superhighway, modern mass media, and complex international organizations. Despite predictions of imminent demise, the Islamic Republic of Iran survived to emerge in the 1990s as one of the major threats to U.S. interests in the Middle East—at least in the eyes of U.S. policymakers.

The Islamic Revolution was carried out under the banners of anti-imperialism, republicanism, and Islam—especially Shi'i Islam. We can better understand the potency of these three ideas by considering the legacy of the three important dynasties that have shaped modern Iran*: the Safavids (1501–1722), the Qajars (1796–1925), and the Pahlavis (1926–1979). Throughout this chapter, we will also examine four important influences on Iran's development: its power relative to other states, especially the Western industrialized nations; its economic status as a developing country almost solely dependent on oil revenues; its attempts to develop democratic institutions; and its collective identity as an Islamic and Iranian nation-state.

---

* Iranians have traditionally referred to their country as Iran, and to their main language as *Farsi* (Persian). But Europeans since the Middle Ages have referred to Iran as Persia. In the 1930s, Iran formally asked the international community to cease using the term *Persia*.

CRITICAL JUNCTURES

The Safavids

The development of the Iranian state has been profoundly influenced by Islam, especially by the division of Islam into two main branches—the Sunnis and the Shi'is—soon after the religion was founded. The Sunnis recognized the legitimacy of the early dynasties that ruled the Islamic Empire with the exalted title of Caliph (the Prophet's Deputy). The Shi'is, however, argue that as soon as the Prophet Mohammad died in A.D. 632 his political and religious authority should have been passed on to Imam Ali, the Prophet's close companion and disciple. They further argue that Imam Ali passed this authority on to his direct male heirs, the Third of whom, Imam Husayn, had been martyred fighting the Sunnis in A.D. 680, and the Twelfth of whom had supposedly gone into hiding in A.D. 941. Furthermore, the Shi'is argue that after this disappearance, the Imam's religious authority as shepherds of the flock and the rightful interpreters of the *shari'a* (divine law) had been handed down to the high-ranking clerical scholars. Thus, from the beginning, the Shi'is harbored ambivalent attitudes toward the state, especially if that state was led by Sunnis or if its rulers lacked genealogical links to the Twelve Imams.

Although small Shi'i communities existed in Iran from the earliest decades of Islam, Shi'ism did not become the dominant religion until the sixteenth century when the Safavid family conquered much of what is present-day Iran. Thus, the boundaries of the modern state were set some 400 years ago. A

Turkic-speaking family from Azerbaijan, the Safavids adopted Shi'ism and boasted descent from the Imams. Their adherents were fellow Turkic tribes.

Taking the titles of Shah-in-Shah and the Shadow of God on Earth, the Safavids declared Shi'ism to be the state religion, imported Shi'i clerics from abroad, purged the country of Sunni scholars, and forcefully converted their subjects to the new official religion. Whatever their motives, Shi'ism helped create homogeneity against the surrounding Sunni powers—namely, the Ottomans in the west, the Uzbeks in the north, and the Afghans in the east. The Safavids, however, failed to capture from the Ottomans the two most holy Shi'i centers: Karbala and Najaf. Karbala was the sight of Imam Husayn's martyrdom. Najaf was the location of the main Shi'i seminaries. Thus, the Iranian state never gained control over the most senior Shi'i clergy. This was to have important implications for state-clerical relations in later centuries, especially in the twentieth century.

By the mid-seventeenth century, over 90 percent of Iran was Shi'i. Sunnism survived only among tribal groups in the periphery—namely, the Kurds in the northwest, the Turkomans in the northeast, the Baluchis in the southeast, and the Arabs in the southwest. In addition, there were communities of Jews, Zoroastrians, and Christians (Armenians and Assyrians) in Isfahan, Shiraz, Kerman, Yazd, and Azerbaijan. The Safavids—like most Muslim rulers, but unlike medieval Christian kings—tolerated these religious minorities as long as they paid special taxes and accepted royal authority. According to Islam, Christians, Jews, and Zoroastrians were to be tolerated as legitimate "People of the Book."

The Safavids established their capital in Isfahan, a Persian-speaking city, and recruited Persian scribes into their court administration. Such families had helped administer the ancient Iranian Empires. They proceeded to govern not only through these Persian scribes and Shi'i clerics, but also through local magnates—tribal chiefs, large landowners, religious notables, city merchants, guild elders, and urban ward leaders.

The Safavid army was formed mostly of tribal cavalry officered by local chieftains. Financial restraints prevented the Safavids from creating either a large bureaucracy or an extended standing army. Their revenues came mostly from land taxes levied on the peasantry. In theory, the Safavids claimed absolute

power. In actual fact, they had no choice but to seek the cooperation of many semi-independent local leaders. The central government was linked to the general population not so much through the coercive institutions as through provincial and hereditary notables. It survived for the most part because the society below was sharply fragmented—by lack of communications, by geographical barriers (especially inaccessible mountains), and by regional, tribal, communal, and ethnic differences. The monarch did not control society. Rather, he hovered over it, systematically orchestrating its many existing rivalries. For Westerners, the Safavids were typical "Oriental despots" with unlimited powers. In reality, their writ often ran no further than their capital. They survived only because their society was so fragmented.

The Qajars

The Safavid dynasty collapsed in 1722 when Afghan tribesmen invaded the capital. The invasion was followed by a half-century of civil war until the Qajars—another Turkic tribe—reconquered much of Iran. The Qajars moved the capital to Tehran and recreated the Safavid system of central manipulation and court administration, including the Persian scribes. They also declared Shi'ism to be the state religion even though they could not boast of any genealogical links with the Twelve Imams. This was to have far-reaching repercussions. Since these new shahs did not pretend to wear the Imam's mantle, the Shi'i clerical leaders could claim to be the main interpreters of Islam.

The Qajar century coincided with the peak of European imperialism, especially the age of concession-hunting. The Russians seized parts of Central Asia and the Caucasus from Iran. They also extracted a series of major economic concessions, which later became known as "The Capitulations." These included the Caspian fisheries; the right to open commercial offices; and the exemption of their merchants from import duties, from internal tariffs, and from the jurisdiction of Iranian law courts.

The British obtained even more important concessions. The British Imperial Bank won the monopoly to issue paper money. The Indo-European Telegraph Company got a contract to extend communication lines through the country. A British citizen named D'Arcy bought the exclusive right to drill for oil in the southwest. The Qajars also constantly borrowed from European banks to meet their lavish court expenses. By the end of the century, these loans had become so heavy that the Qajars were obliged to guarantee repayments by placing the country's entire customs service under European supervision. Not surprisingly, Iranians felt that their whole country had been auctioned off to the West and that their merchants faced unfair competition from abroad.

These public resentments culminated in the Constitutional Revolution of 1905–1909. The revolution began with shopkeepers and moneylenders demonstrating against the Europeans being placed in charge of the custom collections. They suspected that the Shah would renege on local debts in favor of repaying his foreign loans. They also protested that the government was not doing enough to protect native merchants and local industries. The protests intensified when the government tried to lower sugar prices by publicly whipping two major merchants after sugar prices rose out of control as a result of the disruptions of the 1905 Russian revolution.

The protests peaked when leading clerics took sanctuary in Qom, a major Shi'i center outside Tehran. Meanwhile, in Tehran, some 14,000 guildsmen and merchants set up camp inside the compounds of the British legation, demanding a written constitution. After weeks of haggling, the Shah conceded in part because the British legation advised compromise and in part because the unpaid Cossack Brigade—the regime's sole standing army—threatened to join the protesters. Officered by Russians and named after the Tsar's praetorian guards, the Cossack Brigade was the only force in Iran resembling a disciplined army. A British diplomat commented, "The Shah with his unarmed, unpaid, ragged, starving soldiers, what can he do in face of the menace of a general strike and riots?"[1]

The 1906 constitution was modeled after the Belgian one. While retaining the monarchy, it introduced the parliamentary system of government, sharply separating the legislature from the executive and the judiciary. Parliament, termed the *Majles,* was hailed as "the representative of the whole People." Four seats were guaranteed for the recognized religious minorities—the Jews, Zoroastrians, Armenians, and Assyrians. But no seats were given to the Bahais—a recent offshoot of Shi'ism—whom the clerical leaders considered to be a "sinister heresy linked to the imperial powers."

The constitution gave the *Majles* final say over all laws, budgets, treaties, loans, concessions, and, of course, the composition of the cabinet. The ministers

were accountable to the *Majles,* not to the shah. "Sovereignty," declared the constitution, "is a trust confided (as a divine gift) by the People to the person of the Shah." The constitution also included a bill of rights guaranteeing citizens equality before the law, protection of life and property, safeguards from arbitrary arrest, and freedom of expression and association.

Although the constitution was modeled on the liberal secular system of government, it made some concessions to Shi'ism. Shi'ism was declared Iran's official religion. Only Shi'is could hold cabinet posts. Clerical courts retained the right to implement the divine law *(shari'a),* especially in family matters. A **Guardian Council** formed of senior clerics was given the authority to veto parliamentary bills deemed to be un-Islamic. In short, popular sovereignty was to be restricted by a clerical veto power. In actual fact, this Guardian Council was not convened until the 1979 Islamic Revolution. Divisions within the clerical establishment as well as opposition from parliament prevented the convening of this Guardian Council.

Although euphoria greeted the Constitutional Revolution, deep disillusionment set in during the subsequent decade—disillusionment caused in part by internal conflicts, in part by continued pressures from the imperial powers, and in part by the worsening economic crises, particularly the devastating post–World War I famine, which took some 1 million lives, or almost 10 percent of the total population. Internal conflicts polarized the *Majles* into warring liberal and conservative factions. The former, mostly members of the intelligentsia, championed social reforms, especially the replacement of the *shari'a* with a modern law code. The latter, led by landlords, tribal chiefs, and senior clerics, vehemently opposed such reforms, particularly land reform, women's rights, and the granting of full equality to the religious minorities.

Meanwhile, the central government, lacking any real army, bureaucracy, or tax-collecting machinery, was unable to administer the provinces—especially the regions inhabited by such armed tribesmen as the Kurds, Turkomans, and Baluchis. Some tribes, equipped with modern breach-loading European rifles, had more firepower than the central government. What is more, Russia and Britain during World War I implemented their 1907 agreement carving up Iran into three separate zones. Russia occupied the north; Britain the south. Iran was left with a small "neutral zone" in the middle.

Reza Shah's coronation as depicted
on a stamp.

By 1920–1921, Iran was in complete disarray. The Shah was gathering his crown jewels to flee south. The British, in their own words, were hoping to "salvage" some "healthy limbs" in their southern zone. Left-wing rebels, helped by the young communist regime in Russia, had taken over the Caspian province of Gilan and were threatening nearby Azerbaijan, Mazandaran, and Khurasan. According to a British diplomat, the propertied classes, fearful of bolshevism, were anxiously seeking a savior on horseback.[2]

The Pahlavi Dynasty Under Reza Shah

The savior appeared in February 1921 in the shape of Colonel Reza Khan, the recently appointed Iranian commander of the Cossack Brigade. Carrying out a typical military coup, he replaced the cabinet and, while paying lip service to the Qajar monarch, consolidated in his own hands all real power, especially the post of army commander-in-chief. Six years later, he emerged from behind the throne, deposed the Qajars, crowned himself Shah-in-Shah in the style of his hero Napoleon, and established his own Pahlavi dynasty, adopting a name associated with the glories of ancient Iran. This was the first nontribal dynasty to rule the whole of Iran. To forestall opposition from Britain and Russia, Reza Shah assured both countries that he would remain strictly nonaligned and would give no military bases to any foreign power.

Reza Shah spent much of his reign building a highly centralized state—the first in Iran. He was able to do so in large part because the British-owned petroleum refinery was beginning to yield some revenues. The new state rested on three pillars: the military, the bureaucracy, and royal patronage. The central pillar

grew from a motley collection of cossacks, city policeman, and *gendarmes* (rural policemen)—altogether totaling no more than 40,000 men—to a conscript army of 124,000 equipped with rapid-fire rifles, tanks, armored vehicles, and, most important of all, machine guns. It was not for naught that the new Shah was labeled the "machine-gunner." These weapons drastically shifted the balance of power away from the tribes to the central government. For the first time in living history, the central government had the military means to impose its will on the provinces.

The bureaucracy expanded from a haphazard collection of hereditary scribes—some without fixed offices—into ten full-fledged ministries employing over 90,000 civil servants. The top civil servants were drawn mostly from the ranks of the landed aristocracy. The Interior Ministry (the main bureaucracy) appointed the provincial governors, town mayors, district superintendants, village headmen, and electoral supervisors. It could thus rig *Majles* elections, provide the Shah with rubber-stamp parliaments, and cover up the military monarchy with the fig leaf of constitutional law. The constitutional laws of 1906–1909 survived—at least in theory.

The Education Ministry grew from administering 600 primary schools, 58 secondary schools, and 6 small colleges to 2,300 primary schools, 245 secondary schools, and 1 large university. Its aim was not only to broaden educational opportunities, but also to train future civil servants and Persianize the non-Persians who constituted over half the total population.

The Justice Ministry drafted a new civil code based on European law and supplanted the clerical courts with a modern judicial system. This went all the way up from district courts through provincial courts to a Supreme Court. To practice in these courts, lawyers and judges had to pass government-administered exams based on European jurisprudence. In effect, the legal system was secularized.

The Transport Ministry completed an impressive array of bridges, ports, and asphalt roads, and launched the ambitious Trans-Iranian Railway. As part of his modernization drive, Reza Shah established a National Bank; raised protective tariff barriers; set up factories, particularly for light industrial goods; and annulled most of the foreign economic concessions, with the notable exception of the British oil agreement.

Reza Shah also bolstered his regime with court patronage. The son of a modest landowner, Reza Shah soon became the largest landowner in all of the Middle East. He did so by rechanneling irrigation systems, confiscating land, and making offers that neither rich nor poor could refuse. In the words of a British diplomat, Reza Shah had an "unholy interest in property"—especially other people's property.[3] This wealth transformed the court into a large military-landed complex providing patronage for the thousands employed in its numerous palaces, hotels, casinos, charities, companies, and foundations.

Although the new state looked impressive, it lacked foundations in the larger society. The drive for secularization, centralization, industrialization, tribal pacification, railway construction, educational expansion, and national self-assertion won some favor from the urban propertied classes—especially the aristocracy, the new industrialists, and the prosperous merchants. But arbitrary rule, tacit alliance with the upper class, disregard for constitutional liberties, and stifling of independent newspapers, political parties, and professional associations all produced widespread resentment—particularly among the clergy, the intelligentsia, and the masses. In short, this state was strong in the sense that it controlled new instruments of coercion and administration. But it was weak in terms of its failure to link the new state institutions to the country's social structure. The Pahlavi state—like the Safavids and the Qajars—hovered over, rather than embedding itself into, the society.

Mohammad Reza Shah: The Last Shah

The Pahlavi drive to create a centralized state was interrupted by the Anglo-Soviet invasion of Iran during World War II. The Allies invaded in 1941 to secure the oil installations, open a land corridor to the Soviet Union, and forestall any pro-German military coup in Iran. The invasion forced Reza Shah to abdicate and obliged his heir, Mohammad Reza Shah, to open up the political arena to opposition parties and independent politicians. In the words of the U.S. ambassador, "no one" regretted Reza Shah's fall and subsequent death in exile, for the simple reason that he had been a "brutal, avaricious, and inscrutable despot."[4]

In the years between Reza Shah's fall in 1941 and the establishment of Mohammad Reza Shah's absolutism in 1953, the Pahlavi dynasty faced two major challenges: one from the communist Tudeh Party, which led a militant trade union movement, and one from Mohammad Mosaddeq (1882–1967), a charismatic aristocrat who enjoyed extensive middle-class support mainly because he campaigned vigorously for the nationalization of the British-owned oil industry. Mosaddeq denounced court corruption, took the Shah to task for interfering in politics, and argued that the monarchy was supposed to reign symbolically—not actually rule the country. Elected prime minister in 1951, Mosaddeq nationalized the oil company and confronted the Shah over various constitutional issues, especially the control of the military. Mossadeq's premiership, however, was cut short in 1953 when the CIA, fearful of his toleration of the Tudeh, joined the British and some royalist officers to overthrow him. After 1953, Mohammad Reza Shah ruled autocratically, much as his father Reza Shah had done.

Mohammad Reza Shah spent the next quarter-century fulfilling his father's mission of creating a strong and highly centralized state. The task was made infinitely easier by the impressive growth of the oil revenues produced by the signing of a more favorable oil agreement with a consortium of American and British companies in 1955; by the drilling of new wells in the 1960s; and, most important of all, by the quadrupling of world petroleum prices in 1974.

The Shah once again gave priority to the military. By the mid-1970s, Iran's armed forces numbered 410,000 men with 25,000 in the navy, 100,000 in the air force, and some 1,800 ultramodern tanks in the regular army. There was also an omnipotent secret service known as SAVAK—the Persian acronym for the state's Security and Information Organization. Huge amounts of ultrasophisticated weapons necessitated the employment of thousands of American advisers.

This 1935 stamp series depicts the Pahlavi ideology—stressing military strength, industrialization, railway construction, social services, and ancient glories of Iran. The image of a woman representing "justice" (bottom, center) comes from the West.

The Shah granted these advisers special privileges, such as immunity from Iranian laws. Not surprisingly, this reminded many Iranians of the humiliating nineteenth-century Capitulations.

The growth of the bureaucracy was no less remarkable. By 1977, the cabinet had grown to 21 full ministries employing some 300,000 civil servants and over 1 million white- and blue-collar workers. The Ministries of Education and Higher Education together administered 28,600 schools and 13 universities, totaling 5 million pupils and 154,000 college students.

The Agricultural Ministry experienced a dramatic growth—especially after the 1962 land reform through which the state bought land from aristocratic families and gave it to peasant cultivators. By the mid-

This 1978 stamp set honors Reza Shah and his son Mohammad Reza Shah. Note Reza Shah checking his watch to make sure his train has arrived on schedule.

1970s, this ministry administered cooperatives and state farms, distributed seeds and fertilizers, sprayed fields and fruit gardens, fixed agricultural prices, constructed irrigation works, and helped set up literacy classes and health clinics, including birth-control clinics.

In addition to the twenty-one ministries, the state established a number of large institutions: the Plan Organization, the Central Bank, the National Iranian Oil Company, the Industrial and Mining Development Bank, and the National Radio-Television Network. By the mid-1970s, most urban households had access to television and most rural households had access to transistor radios.

The royal patronage system also experienced remarkable growth, especially after the creation of the supposedly charitable Pahlavi Foundation. By the 1970s, the Pahlavi Foundation controlled 207 large companies active in tourism, insurance, banking, agribusiness, mining, construction, and manufacturing. In the words of the *New York Times:* "Behind the facade of charitable activities, the foundation is a source of funds for the royal family; a means of exerting influence on large sectors of the economy; and a conduit for rewarding the supporters of the regime."[5] A U.S. government report argued that court corruption was reaching new peaks and that large industrialists and

export-importers could not do business unless they placed members of the royal family on their boards and gave them as much as 10–40 percent of their profits.[6]

As if the Pahlavi state did not control enough of society, the Shah in 1975 announced with much fanfare the formation of the Resurgence Party. Iran was now to be a one-party state. "Those reluctant to join this organization," the Shah declared, "are communists who should go to jail or exile." The rest of the population was invited to join this party. Until then, the Shah had permitted the handpicked *Majles* deputies to have two separate parties. Because of their subservience to the Shah, they were known as the "yes" and the "yes sir" parties. To underline the importance of the Resurgence Party, the Shah replaced the traditional Islamic calendar with a new royalist one, jumping from the Muslim year 1355 to the royalist year 2535; 2,500 years were allocated to the monarchy in general and 35 years for the Shah's own reign.

The Resurgence Party was designed to create yet another organizational link with society—especially with the traditional marketplaces called **bazaars.** Until then, the bazaars—in sharp contrast to professional associations and trade unions—had escaped direct state control and had retained their own merchant, trade, and craft guilds. The Resurgence Party promptly established bazaar guilds as well as newspapers, women's organizations, professional associations, and labor unions. The state was venturing into areas where previous rulers had feared to tread.

The Resurgence Party promised to establish an "organic relationship between rulers and ruled"; "synthesize the best of capitalism and socialism"; chart the way toward the future Great Civilization; and help the Great Commander complete his reforms known as the *White* Revolution to differentiate it from the *Red* communist revolutions. The party also praised the Shah for curbing the power of the "medieval clergy," eradicating vestiges of "class warfare," and having the authority of a "Spiritual Guide" as well as a world-renowned statesman. For his part, the Shah told an English-language newspaper that the party's philosophy was "based on the dialectical principles of the White Revolution" and that nowhere in the world was there such a close relationship between a ruler and his people. "No other nation has given its Commander such a *carte-blanche* [blank check]."[7] The terminology, as well as the boast, revealed much about the Shah at the height of his power.

Khomeini versus the Shah

The critical junctions in history created acute tension between the Pahlavi state and the Iranian society. On one hand, the state—financed largely by oil—appeared to be omnipresent, omnipotent, and totally independent of the society below. The Shah, with the huge military, bureaucracy, court patronage, and now the one-party state, could well imagine himself to be the master of his empire. He acted as if he was entirely separate from society and powerful enough to rule without regard for public support.

Society, on the other hand, was full of an ever-increasing list of economic, social, and political grievances. An article entitled "Fifty Marks of Treason in Fifty Years of Treason," which appeared in an émigré paper on the bicentennial of the Pahlavi dynasty in 1976, succinctly summed up these grievances.[8] The article denounced the Pahlavis for establishing a dictatorship; benefiting from the 1953 CIA coup; trampling over the 1905–1909 constitution; creating a "cult of personality"; using terror, especially SAVAK, to silence the opposition; rigging parliamentary elections; organizing a "fascistic" one-party state; stifling intellectual activities; shooting down unarmed demonstrators; torturing and murdering political prisoners;

making a mockery of the judiciary; taking over seminaries, clerical endowments, and religious publishing houses; and fostering "cultural imperialism" to undermine Iran's national identity.

It also accused the regime of neglecting agriculture; enducing millions of landless peasants to migrate into the cities; creating huge sprawling shantytowns; widening the already wide gap between rich and poor; funneling money away from the small bourgeoisie into the pockets of the wealthy comprador bourgeoisie (the entrepreneurs linked to foreign companies and multinational corporations); bloating the already overbloated bureaucracy; wasting national resources on unnecessary military expenditures; and granting capitulations to the West, especially to the United States. It further accused the regime of betraying the nation, violating Mosaddeq's policy of neutralism, and siding with the West against the nonaligned bloc and with Israel against the Arab World.

These grievances were given greater articulation in the mid-1970s when Ayatollah Khomeini began to formulate a new version of Shi'ism from his exile in Iraq. Khomeini's version of Shi'ism has often been labeled "Islamic fundamentalism," but would be better described as Shi'i populism. The term **fundamentalism** implies religious inflexibility, intellectual purity, political traditionalism, social conservatism, rejection of the modern world, and the centrality of scriptural texts on such issues as the earth being flat and the center of the universe. Khomeini, however, was less concerned about literal interpretations of the Qur'an (Koran) than about championing grievances against the elite and national resentments against the United States.

Khomeini began to denounce monarchies in general and the Pahlavis in particular as part of the exploiting elite arrayed against the oppressed masses. The oppressors, in his words, were formed of the feudal landowners, the high-ranking military officers, the wealthy foreign-connected capitalists, the corrupt courtiers, and the millionaire palace dwellers. The oppressed, on the other hand, were the masses, especially the wretched of the earth and the hardworking people of shantytowns.

In calling for the overthrow of the Pahlavi monarchy, Khomeini began to give a radically new meaning to the old Shi'i term *Velayat-e Faqih* (**jurist's guardianship**). He argued that the term gave the senior clergy all-encompassing authority over the whole

Ayatollah Khomeini (1902–1989)

Ruhollah Khomeini was born in 1902 into a landed clerical family well known in central Iran. During the 1920s, he studied in the famous Fayzieh Seminary in Qom with the leading theologians of the day—most of whom were scrupulously apolitical. He taught at the same seminary from the 1930s through the 1950s, avoiding politics, even during the mass campaign in the early 1950s to nationalize the British-owned oil company. His real entry into politics did not come until 1962 when he, along with most other clerical leaders, denounced the Shah's White Revolution. Forced into exile,

Khomeini taught at the Shi'i center of Najaf in Iraq from 1964 until 1978. During these years, he developed his own novel version of Shi'i populism. Returning home triumphant in the midst of the Iranian revolution, he was declared the Supreme Leader, the Founder of the Republic, the Guide of the Islamic Revolution, and the Imam of the Shi'i community. In the past, Iranian Shi'is had reserved the term "Imam" for only Imam Ali and his direct heirs, whom they considered to be semidivine. Khomeini ruled as Supreme Leader of the Islamic Republic until his death in 1989.

community—not just over widows, minors, and the retarded, as had been the interpretation in previous centuries. He insisted that only the senior clerics had the competence to understand the *shari'a;* that the divine authority given to the Prophet and the Imams had been passed on to their spiritual heirs—the clergy; and that throughout history the clergy had championed the rights of the people against bad government and foreign powers. He further insisted that the clergy were the people's true representatives since they lived among them, listened to their plight, and shared their everyday joys and pains. He also warned that the Shah intended to confiscate religious endowments, replace Islamic values with "cultural imperialism," and force women to go "unveiled" and "naked" into the streets. In actual fact, the last Shah had merely encouraged women to unveil; he had never banned the use of the full covering known as the *chador.*

Khomeini's concept of jurist's guardianship resonated well among theology students. But none of the other senior ayatollahs at Qom and Najaf subscribed to it. For them, as for their predecessors, the proper function of a clerical leader was to keep a safe distance from politics, sometimes accommodating the authorities, sometimes mediating between them and the religious constituents, but never actually seeking state power nor calling for the overthrow of the monarchy. Even in the Constitutional Revolution, they had merely sought to reform rather than destroy the monarchy.

Khomeini also targeted the regime's most visible socioeconomic failures: unemployment, rural illiteracy, peasant land hunger, mass migration into the cities, lack of low-income housing, glaring inequalities, squandering of oil revenues on the ever-expanding army and bureaucracy, nepotism and court corruption,

and the bazaar's inability to compete with foreign companies and wealthy entrepreneurs. "The duty of the clergy," Khomeini declared, "is to liberate the hungry from the clutches of the rich." Thus, Khomeini transformed Shi'ism from a pious, apolitical, and conservative monarchical religion into a highly political, revolutionary, and republican ideology.

The Islamic Revolution

By the mid-1970s, Iran was ripe for revolution. The Pahlavi state claimed absolute power backed by a huge bureaucracy and an impressive military. Yet this seemingly strong state had feet of clay. It not only lacked organic links with the general population but had managed to alienate most sectors of the country, particularly the intelligentsia, the industrial working class, and, with the creation of the Resurgence Party, the clergy and the bazaar middle class. It ruled without regard for, or consultation with, the key groups in society. What is more, some clerics were now expounding a new dynamic version of Shi'ism—demanding the establishment of a republic, the elimination of imperialist influences, the overthrow of the existing social structure, and the radical redistribution of wealth. Only a few sparks were needed to set off the revolutionary explosion.

The sparks came in the form of minor economic difficulties and intermittent external pressures to curb SAVAK's gross abuses of human rights. In 1977–1978, the Shah tried to deal with a 20 percent rise in prices and a 10 percent decline in oil revenues by cutting construction projects and declaring war against "profiteers," "hoarders," and "price gougers." Not surprisingly, shopkeepers felt that the Shah was diverting attention from court corruption, planning to replace them with government-run department stores, and that he intended to destroy once and for all the bazaar, which some felt was the "the real pillar of Iranian society."[9]

The pressure to curb SAVAK came from Amnesty International, the United Nations, and the Western press, as well as from the recently elected Carter administration in the United States. In 1977, after meeting with the International Commission of Jurists, the Shah permitted Red Cross officials to visit prisons and allowed defense attorneys to attend political trials. In the words of Khomeini's first prime minister, this international pressure allowed the opposition to "breathe" again after decades of "suffocation."[10]

This slight loosening of the reins, coming in the midst of the economic recession, proved to be explosive. Political parties, labor organizations, and professional associations—especially lawyers, writers, and university professors—regrouped after years of being banned. Bazaar guilds regained their independence from the government party. What is more, college, high school, and seminary students, especially in the religious center of Qom, took to the streets to protest the quarter-century of repression. For some, the regime was "despotic," "autocratic," and "fascistic." For others, it was "paganistic" and "anti-Islamic."

Once the regime resorted to force, the situation turned more intense and confrontational, especially after a violent incident on September 8, 1978, known as Bloody Friday, when martial law authorities in Tehran fired into a crowded square, killing hundreds of unarmed demonstrators. By late 1978, a general strike brought the whole economy to a grinding halt, paralyzing not only the oil industry, the factories, the banks, and the transport system, but also the civil service, the media, the bazaars, and the whole educational establishment. The oil workers vowed that they would not export any petroleum until they had exported the "shah and his forty thieves."[11]

Meanwhile, in the urban centers, local committees attached to the **mosques** (Muslim places of worship) and financed by the bazaars were distributing food to the needy, organizing militias known as revolutionary guards, and setting up ad hoc courts to retain some semblance of law and order because the whole judicial structure, including the police, had melted away. Equally significant, the anti-regime rallies were now attracting as many as two million protesters. The largest of them, held in Tehran in December 1978 to commemorate the martyrdom of Imam Husayn at

Woman in the Cemetery for Martyrs of the Revolution, 1980.
Source: ©Abbas/Magnum Photos.

Karbala, demanded the abolition of the monarchy, the return of Khomeini, and the establishment of a republic that would preserve national independence from imperialism and give workers and peasants social justice in the form of decent wages, land, and a proper standard of living.[12] Propagandists later forgot these economic demands, claiming that the Islamic Revolution was made purely for "fundamentalist" reasons.

Although these rallies were led by pro-Khomeini clerics, they had valuable support from a broad spectrum of organizations: Mosaddeqite nationalists; Marxists, including Maoists and the Tudeh; liberal lawyers, writers, and women's organizations; and, of course, the many well-financed bazaar merchants and guilds. A secret Revolutionary Committee set up by the pro-Khomeini clerics in Tehran tried to coordinate the many strikes and protests that erupted—mostly spontaneously—in the provincial cities. This Revolutionary Committee was in daily phone contact with Khomeini in exile and could easily disseminate Khomeini's speeches through clandestine tape cassettes. This was a revolution made in the streets and inspired by audiotapes.

After a series of such mass rallies in late 1978, the *Washington Post* concluded that the "disciplined and well organized marches lent considerable weight to the opposition's claim of being an alternative government."[13] Similarly, the *Christian Science Monitor* reported that the "giant wave of humanity sweeping through the capital declared louder than any bullet or bomb could the clear message, 'The Shah must go.'"[14]

Chronology of Pahlavi Iran

1921	Colonel Reza Khan's military coup
1926	Establishment of the Pahlavi dynasty
1941–1945	Allied occupation of Iran
1951	Nationalization of the oil industry
1953	Coup against Mosaddeq
1956	Establishment of SAVAK
1963	White Revolution
1971	Celebrations for the 2,500-year-old monarchy
1974	Quadrupling of world oil prices
1974	Amnesty International criticizes Iran for human rights violations
1975	Establishment of the Resurgence Party
September 1978	Bloody Friday
December 1978	Demonstrations begin
January 1979	Shah leaves
February 1979	Islamic Revolution

Confronted by this opposition and aware that increasing numbers of soldiers were deserting to the opposition, the Shah decided to leave Iran and permit Khomeini to return. A year later, when the Shah in exile was dying of cancer, some claimed that he would have weathered the upheavals if he had been healthy. But even a healthy man with an iron will would not have been able to deal with 2 million demonstrators, a massive general strike, and defections in the army rank and file.

On February 11—only three weeks after the Shah's departure and ten days after Khomeini's return—armed groups supported by air force cadets broke into the large barracks in northern Tehran, promptly distributed arms, and then assaulted the main police stations, the jails, and eventually the national radio-television station. That same evening, the radio station made the historic announcement: "This is the voice of Iran, the voice of true Iran, the voice of the Islamic Revolution." A few hours of street fighting had completed the destruction of the 53-year-old dynasty and the 2,500-year-old monarchy.

Implications for Contemporary Iran

The euphoria surrounding the Islamic Revolution was in many ways deceptive. It hid from public view the serious problems that would inevitably confront the future Islamic Republic. It was true that the Islamic Republic was the product of democratic aspirations, mass participation, and popular outcry for social justice. But these democratic features contradicted Khomeini's theory that the senior "jurists" were the people's ultimate "guardians." For Khomeini, sovereignty lay not in the people, but in God and the high-ranking clergy, God's sole interpreters in this world. Democracy and theocracy were bound to collide. In addition, the *shari'a*—as interpreted by Khomeini—conflicted with the concept of equality in a number of significant ways. It placed women in inferior positions vis-à-vis Muslim males. Religious minorities were assigned lower status. And it placed Muslims who lost their faith or adopted another one—such as the Bahais—in the highly precarious position of being prosecuted as "heretics," "apostates," and "blasphemers."

It was true that the revolutionaries, in denouncing the Shah's economic policies, had called for more industrialization, more rapid modernization—especially in public education and social services—and more independence from both the oil revenues and the imports from the West. Demanding economic self-sufficiency, they had criticized the Shah for modernizing too slowly rather than too quickly. Despite these aspirations, the Islamic Republic soon discovered harsh economic realities: heavy dependence on oil revenues, erratic fluctuations in the world oil markets, agriculture with limited potentials, a population explosion, and, consequently, a dwindling per capita national income.

It was true that the revolutionaries had accused the Shah of wasting scarce resources on a gigantic military, thereby alienating the neighboring Persian Gulf states. But the Islamic Republic soon discovered

The Shah's statue on the ground, February 1979.
Source: ©Abbas/Magnum Photos.

that in the world of *real politique,* especially when it tired to export the Islamic Revolution, military expenditures were not a luxury but a dire necessity. The Iraqi invasion—prompted by Saddam Hussein's ambition to gain territory—and the subsequent Iran-Iraqi War that lasted from 1980 until 1988 forced the Islamic Republic to match the Shah's huge military expenditures. Iran ceased to be viewed as the United States' local "policeman." Instead, it became feared as the regional bully and troublemaker.

It was true that the Islamic Republic began with a broad collective identity since Muslims formed 99 percent of the population. This asset, however, soon withered away. The stress on Shi'i Islam naturally alienated the Sunnis, who constituted some 9 percent of the population. The insistence on clerical Shi'ism inevitably antagonized not only the traditional clerical hierarchy, who rejected Khomeini's theory of government, but also the lay secular Muslims, who led most of the political parties. Similarly, the association of Shi'ism with the central Persian-speaking regions carried with it the potential danger of alienating the important Turkic minority in Azerbaijan. Finally, the Islamic Republic had to formulate policies that would favor either the bazaar middle class or the shantytown poor. Populist rhetoric could not permanently bridge the gap between these two classes who together had made the Islamic Revolution.

SECTION 2
Political Economy and Development

STATE AND ECONOMY

In 1993, billboards appeared all over Tehran announcing the triumphant return to Iran of Coca-Cola after a fourteen-year absence. In its initial enthusiasm for economic self-sufficiency and self-reliance, the Islamic Republic had ousted Coca-Cola and many other multinational corporations. Although some leaders continued to warn against Western consumerism and cultural imperialism, the regime as a whole was now more than eager to market this and other hallmarks of American capitalism. It was living proof that Iran, despite its anti-Western stance, had been integrated into the world economy. This section will analyze how Iran under the Pahlavis became drawn into the Western-dominated global economy. Section 5 will analyze why the Islamic Republic has failed to end this dependency and create a more self-sufficient economy.

The integration of Iran into the world system began in a modest way in the latter half of the nineteenth century. Before that time, there had been some commercial contact with the outside world, as in the famous medieval "Silk Route to China," but this had been confined mostly to transit trade and to such luxury goods as raw silk, precious stones, carpets, perfumes, porcelain, and prized horses. The Safavids, for example, had tried unsuccessfully to raise money by encouraging the export of raw silk to Europe.

A number of factors account for this nineteenth-century integration: the economic concessions granted to the European powers; the improvements made in the transport systems—namely, the opening of the Suez Canal and the building of the Trans-Caspian and the Batum-Baku railways; the laying of telegraph lines across Iran to link India with Britain; the outflow of capital from Europe after 1870; and, most important of all, the Industrial Revolution in Europe and the subsequent export of manufactured goods to the rest of the world.

In the course of the nineteenth century, Iran's foreign trade increased tenfold. In 1800, it had been insignificant. By 1900, it had reached the modest sum of 8 million pounds sterling. Over 83 percent was with Russia and Britain; 10 percent with Germany, France, Italy, and Belgium; and less than 7 percent with the rest of the Middle East. Exports were mostly carpets and agricultural products, including silk, raw cotton, opium, dried fruits, rice, and tobacco. Imports were mostly tea, sugar, kerosene, and such industrial products as textiles, glassware, guns, and other metal goods. Also in this period, foreign investment increased from nothing to some 12 million pounds sterling. It was confined to banking, fishing, carpet weaving, transport, and telegraph communications.

Contact with the West had far-reaching repercussions. It produced what later became known as economic dependency: the overreliance of the underdeveloped world on the developed; the vulnerability of the poor countries to the sudden fluctuations in the rich economies; and the export of raw materials, whose prices often stagnated or declined, in return for the import of finished products, whose value invariably increased. Not surprisingly, many in the Third World now argue that this dependency is the root cause of economic underdevelopment in much of Africa, Latin America, and Asia (including the Middle East).

The nineteenth-century influx of mass-manufactured goods devastated traditional handicrafts, espe-

cially cotton textiles. In the words of a tax collector in Isfahan, the import of cheap, colorful, cotton piece goods damaged not only the local weavers, dyers, and carders, but also the thousands of housewives who in the past had subsidized their family incomes with their cottage industries and home spindles.[15] They naturally blamed foreign imports for their plight.

Moreover, the introduction of cash crops—especially cotton, tobacco, and opium—reduced the acreage available for wheat and other cereals. Many landowners ceased growing food and turned to commercial export crops. This paved the way for a series of disastrous famines in 1860, 1869–1872, 1880, and 1918–1920. Opium cultivation was particularly encouraged by British merchants eager to meet the ever-rising demands of the Chinese market brought about by the notorious Opium Wars.

Furthermore, the competition from foreign merchants, together with the introduction of the telegraph and the postal systems, brought the many local merchants, shopkeepers, and workshop owners together into a national middle class aware for the first time of their common statewide interests against both the central government and the foreign powers. In short, the bazaars were transformed into a propertied middle class conscious of its national grievances. This awareness played an important role in the Constitutional Revolution.

However, the real integration of Iran into the world system did not come until the twentieth century. Its main engine was oil. This oil income started in trickles in 1904 when British prospectors struck oil in Khuzistan, and the British admiralty soon after decided to fuel its ships with petroleum rather than coal. The British government also decided to buy most of this fuel from the Anglo-Iranian Oil Company in which it was a major shareholder. The oil revenue for Iran increased modestly in the next four decades to reach $16 million in 1951. After the 1955 agreement with a consortium of U.S. and British companies, oil revenues rose steadily—from $34 million in 1955 to $715 million in 1962, to $5 billion in 1973, and, after the quadrupling of oil prices in 1974, to over $23 billion in 1976. Between 1953 and 1978, the cumulative oil income came to over $100 billion (see Table 1 on the following page).

Oil became known as Iran's "black gold," financing over 90 percent of the imports and 80 percent of the annual budget, and far surpassing all of the tax receipts combined. In contrast, domestic

TABLE 1   **Oil Revenues**

Year	In Millions (US$)
1954–1955	34
1956–1957	181
1958–1959	344
1960–1961	358
1962–1963	437
1964–1965	555
1966–1967	715
1968–1969	958
1970–1971	1,268
1971–1972	2,114
1972–1973	2,536
1973–1974	5,066
1974–1975	18,000
1975–1976	20,488
1976–1977	23,000
1977–1978	21,867

Sources: F. Fesharaki, *Development of the Iranian Oil Industry* (New York: Praeger, 1976), 133; H. Amirahmadi, *Revolution and Economic Transition* (Albany: State University of New York, 1990), 225.

taxation provided 75 percent of the revenues of the Japanese government. Oil also enabled Iran to undertake ambitious development programs. Other countries, such as the Soviet Union and China, were able to undertake similar projects only by squeezing resources out of their populations. In fact, the oil revenue created what is known by French political scientists as a typical "*rentier* state"—the government obtains a lucrative income merely by exporting petroleum or renting out oil wells. Iran, as well as Iraq, Algeria, and the Gulf states, received enough money from their wells to be able to disregard their internal tax bases. It meant that the state became relatively independent of society. In turn, the society had few inputs into the state. Little taxation meant little representation. It also meant that the state was totally reliant on one commodity, oil, whose price it could not control.

Mohammad Reza Shah tried to diminish oil dependency by encouraging other exports and attracting foreign investment into non-oil ventures. Neither policy succeeded. Despite some increase in carpet and pistachio exports, oil continued to dominate, and on the eve of the revolution, it still provided 97 percent of the country's foreign exchange. The new industries faced difficulties finding export markets.

At the same time, Iran failed to draw external capital despite the much-publicized 1955 Law for the Attraction and Protection of Foreign Investments. Even after the oil boom, foreign firms—mostly U.S., European, and Japanese—invested no more than $1 billion. Much of this was not in industry, but in banking, trade, and insurance. In Iran, as in the rest of the Middle East, Western companies were weary of investing fixed assets, in part because of government corruption, in part because of high labor costs, in part because of the limitations of the internal market, and in part because of the fear of potential instability and outright confiscations. Apparently, the companies did not share their governments' confidence that Iran was an "island of stability."

The oil revenues financed all of Mohammad Reza Shah's development projects. It is true—as the opposition liked to publicize—that some revenue was squandered on palaces, royal extravagances, bureaucratic waste, outright corruption, ambitious nuclear projects, and ultrasophisticated weapons too expensive even for many NATO countries. But it is also true that even larger sums were channeled into economic and social development. Iran's gross national product (GNP) grew at the average rate of 9.6 percent every year in the period between 1960 and 1977. It grew at the annual rate of 8 percent in 1962–1970, 14 percent in 1972–1973, and 30 percent in 1973–1974. Overall output rose from $4 billion in 1960–1961 to more than $77 billion in 1977–1978—at current prices and the official dollar exchange rates. This made Iran one of the fastest-developing countries in the Third World at that time. However, this brought little popularity for the regime. On the contrary, the way development was carried out made it even more unpopular.

Oil resources were put into development through both direct and indirect channels. They were put directly into the Land Reform Program and the Five-Year Plans, and indirectly into banks, notably, the Industrial and Mining Development Bank, which extended low-interest loans to court-connected entrepreneurs, industrialists, and agribusinessmen. Over $50 billion was injected into the economy through such channels. The Shah, like most advocates of conservative economics, believed that if enough benefits were extended to the rich, some of them would gradually but inevitably filter down into society's middle and lower ranks. But in Iran, as elsewhere, the benefits got stuck at the top.

TABLE 2 Land Ownership in 1977	
Size	Number of Owners
200+ hectares	1,300
51–200 hectares	44,000
11–50 hectares	600,000
3–10 hectares	1,200,000
landless	700,000

Note: 1 hectare is approximately 2.47 acres.

Source: E. Abrahamian, "Structural Causes of the Iranian Revolution," *Middle East Research and Information Project*, no. 87 (May 1980), 23.

The 1962–1963 land reform program—the White Revolution's linchpin—transferred land from large owners to small family farmers. The program was followed by the construction of large dams and irrigation canals, the setting up of farm cooperatives and tractor stations, and the distribution of seeds, pesticides, and fertilizers. Between 1963 and 1978, agricultural production grew by 4.8 percent per year.

Land reform itself was launched in part because of pressures from the Kennedy administration. The Shah also hoped that his land reform would steal the main plank of the radical intelligentsia. He had concluded that it was better to lead a White Revolution from above than to be swept away by a Red one from below. The whole venture, however, had the unintended consequence of further undermining him. Previous rulers had been able to rely on the support of large landowners and tribal chiefs, but when the Islamic Revolution began, no such class existed to extend a helping hand to the Shah in his hour of greatest need.

Even more dangerous, land reform on the whole failed to win over the peasantry. The government gave the vast majority of peasants either no land at all or too little for them to become viable farmers. In most regions, a farmer needed at least 10 hectares (approximately 24.7 acres) of land to survive. The government also failed to follow up land reform with agricultural credits to the smaller farmers, forcing many to sell their small parcels to agribusinesses and then move into the cities in search of work. The countryside became sharply divided between, on one hand, a few large and medium-size landowners, and, on the other hand, a mass of landless and near landless peasants (see Table 2).

The regime also invested considerable sums in infrastructure. The Trans-Iranian Railway was completed, fulfilling Reza Shah's dream of linking Tehran with Tabriz, Mashad, and Isfahan, and the Caspian Sea with the Persian Gulf. The roadways were extended, connecting Tehran to the provincial capitals, and the large villages to their local market towns. This further integrated the outlying villages into the world economy. What is more, port facilities in Enzeli, Bandar Shapour, Bushire, and Khorramshahrs were improved to handle the ever-increasing importation of consumer and capital goods.

Investments in modern factories brought about a minor industrial revolution. Between 1963 and 1977, the manufacturing share of the GNP rose from 11 to 17 percent. By 1977, the country had 159 large factories (each with over 500 workers) producing steel, aluminum, fertilizers, machine tools, textiles, cars, trucks, tractors, and petrochemicals. It also had 830 medium-size factories manufacturing such consumer goods as canned food, soap, beverages, paper, glass, sugar, clothes, matches, and refrigerators (see Tables 3 and 4 on the following page). The opposition complained that most of these factories were not real manufacturing industries but merely assembly plants owned by the elite and employing few workers while the mass of the labor force was left untouched and even illiterate.

At the same time, substantial sums went into human resources. Between 1963 and 1977, enrollment nearly tripled in primary schools, doubled in secondary schools, and increased sixfold in the universities. There was also a huge increase in technical training and in adult literacy classes. The expansion is even

---

TABLE 3   Industry (number of factories)

	1953	1977
Small (10–40 workers)	Less than 1,000	More than 7,000
Medium (50–500 workers)	300	830
Large (over 500 workers)	19	159

Source: E. Abrahamian, "Structural Causes of the Iranian Revolution," *Middle East Research and Information Project,* no. 87 (May 1980), 22.

TABLE 4   Industrial Production

	1953	1977
Coal (in tons)	200,000	900,000
Iron ore (in tons)	5,000	930,000
Steel (in tons)	—	275,000
Cement (in tons)	53,000	4,300,000
Sugar (in tons)	70,000	527,000
Tractors	—	7,700
Motor vehicles	—	109,000

Source: E. Abrahamian, "Structural Causes of the Iranian Revolution," *Middle East Research and Information Project,* no. 87 (May 1980), 22.

TABLE 5   Educational Growth

	Number of Schools (number of students)			
	1953		1977	
Universities	4	(14,500)	16	(154,315)
Technical schools	36	(2,538)	800	(227,507)
Secondary schools	527	(121,772)	1,714	(741,000)
Primary schools	5,956	(746,473)	23,476	(4,078,000)

Source: E. Abrahamian, "Structural Causes of the Iranian Revolution," *Middle East Research and Information Project,* no. 87 (May 1980), 22.

---

more impressive if one compares the 1977 statistics with those of 1953 (see Table 5).

The expansion of health services was equally dramatic. Between 1963 and 1977, the number of hospital beds increased from 24,126 to 48,000; the number of medical clinics went from 700 to 2,800; nurses went from 1,969 to 4,105; and doctors from 4,500 to 12,750. These improvements, together with the elimination of epidemics and famines—mainly due to substantial food imports—lowered infant mortality and led to a population explosion. In the two decades prior to the revolution, the overall population doubled from 18 million to nearly 36 million. This explosion gave the country a predominantly youthful age structure.

Figure 1   Iran's Class Structure in the Mid-1970s
The society was divided sharply not only into horizontal classes, but also into vertical sectors—the modern and the transitional, the urban and the rural. This is known as a dual society.

Upper Class

Pahlavi Family; Court-Connected Entrepreneurs; Senior Civil Servants and Military Officers	0.1%

Middle Class

Traditional (Propertied)	13%	Modern (Salaried)	10%
Clerics Bazaaris Small Factory Owners Commercial Farmers		Professionals Civil Servants Office Employees College Students	

Lower Classes

Rural	45%	Urban	32%
Landed Peasants Near Landless Peasants Landless Peasants Unemployed		Industrial Workers Wage-Earners in Small Factories Domestic Servants Construction Workers Peddlers Unemployed	

By the mid-1970s, half the populace were under sixteen years of age, and two-thirds were under thirty. This was to have repercussions in the street politics of 1977–1979.

SOCIETY AND ECONOMY

These expenditures produced in Iran—as in other oil-rich countries—what is known as a dual society. On one side was the modern sector, headed by the elites with close ties to the state. On the other side was the traditional sector comprising the clergy, the bazaar middle class, and the rural masses. Each sector, in turn, was sharply stratified into unequal classes. Thus, Iranian society was divided vertically into the modern and the traditional, and horizontally into a number of urban as well as rural classes (see Figure 1).

The upper class—the Pahlavi family, the court-connected entrepreneurs, the military officers, and the senior civil servants—constituted less than 0.01 percent of the population. The modern middle class—namely, professionals, civil servants, salaried personnel, and college students—formed as much as 10 percent of the population. The bottom of the modern sector—that is, the urban working class, which included factory workers, construction laborers, peddlers, and unemployed—constituted over 32 percent. The traditional middle class, particularly bazaar merchants, small retailers, shopkeepers, workshop owners, and well-to-do family farmers, made up another 13 percent. Finally, the rural masses, including landless and near landless peasants, as well as nomads and village construction workers, made up as much as 45 percent of the nation.

The 1970s oil boom widened these divisions. The state expanded the central bureaucracy, putting more resources into Tehran and the provincial capitals. It built factories in Tehran, in Mazandaran, and in the central cities of Isfahan, Shiraz, Kashan, and Semnan. It tried to control urban food costs by importing cereals and placing ceilings on agricultural prices, which inevitably discriminated against the countryside. It gave out low-interest loans not to the small entrepreneur, but to the business elite, prompting the bazaars to denounce the whole banking system as un-Islamic. To

TABLE 6   **Measures of Inequality of Urban Household Consumption Expenditures: 1972, 1977**

Year	Percentage Share in Total Expenditures		
	Bottom 40%	Middle 40%	Top 20%
1972	16.7	36.2	47.1
1977	11.7	32.8	55.5

Source: V. Nowshirvani and P. Clawson, "The State and Social Equity in Postrevolutionary Iran," in *The Politics of Social Transformation in Afghanistan, Iran, and Pakistan,* ed. M. Weiner and A. Banuazizi (Syracuse: Syracuse University Press, 1994), 248.

compound these inequities, the population explosion forced some 1 million landless peasants a year to move out of their villages into new shantytowns.

Government statistics show the rising inequality—both between classes and between regions. In 1972, the richest 20 percent of the urban households accounted for 47.1 percent of the total urban family expenditures. By 1977, they accounted for as much as 55.5 percent. In 1972, the poorest 40 percent accounted for 16.7 percent of the urban family expenditures. By 1977, they accounted for as little as 11.7 percent (see Table 6). According to the International Labor Office, Iran had one of the most lopsided income distributions in the world.[16]

Regional inequality between town and country and between the central and the outer provinces was no less marked. Tehran got many of the new factories and over 60 percent of the loans handed out by the Industrial and Mining Development Bank. By 1975, Tehran manufactured over 50 percent of the country's industrial goods. According to one comparative study, the per capita regional product in the richest areas was ten times more than in the poorest areas. This meant that Iran—after Brazil—had the highest regional disparity in the developing world.[17] According to another study, the ratio of urban to rural incomes was 5 to 1—again making it one of the worst in the world.[18]

The literacy rate was as high as 62 percent in Tehran. It was as low as 25 percent in Kurdestan, Sistan, and Baluchestan. Tehran had 5,000 doctors—half of the country's total of 10,000. Another 3,500 lived in the other major cities. Only 1,500 doctors served the entire rural population. Tehran had one dentist per 5,626 residents, and one nurse per 1,820 residents. On

the other hand, Kurdestan had one doctor per 6,477 people, one dentist per 57,294 people, and one nurse per 46,552. Sistan and Baluchestan had one doctor per 5,311 people, one dentist per 51,663 people, and one nurse per 27,064 people. The mortality rate was 8 per 1,000 in the towns and 16 per 1,000 in the villages. Infant mortality was 61 per 1,000 in the towns and 116 per 1,000 in the villages.

These inequalities fueled resentments against the ruling elite. These resentments, however, were expressed more in cultural and religious, rather than economic and class, terms. The poet laureate of these resentments was a gadfly writer named Jalal al-Ahmad (1923–1969). A former communist who had rediscovered his Shi'i roots in the 1960s, al-Ahmad shook his contemporaries by publishing a polemical pamphlet entitled *Gharbzadegi* ("The Plague from the West"). Al-Ahmad argued that the ruling class was destroying Iran by blindly imitating the West, neglecting the peasantry, showing utter contempt for popular religion, worshipping mechanization, regimentation, and industrialization, and flooding the country with foreign ideas, tastes, luxury items, and mass-consumption goods. He stressed that Third World countries such as Iran could survive this "plague" of Western imperialism only by returning to their cultural roots and developing a self-reliant society—especially a fully independent economy. Al-Ahmad began the long search for cultural authenticity and economic self-sufficiency.

These themes were developed further by another young intellectual named Ali Shariati (1933–1977). Studying in Paris during the turbulent 1960s, Shariati was influenced by Marxist sociology, Catholic liberation theology, the Algerian revolution, and, most im-

Poverty in the slums of southern Tehran (right) juxtaposed
against consumer activity in the Central Bazaar of
Tehran (below).
Source: AP/Wide World Photos.

portant of all, Frantz Fanon's theory of Third World
revolutions as laid out in his famous book, *Wretched of
the Earth*. Shariati returned home with what can be
defined as a fresh and revolutionary interpretation of
Shi'ism, echoes of which would later appear in
Khomeini's writings.

Shariati argued that history was a continuous struggle between oppressors and oppressed. Each class had

its own interests, its own interpretations of religion, and
its own sense of right and wrong, justice and injustice,
morality and immorality. To help the oppressed,
Shariati believed, God periodically sent down prophets,
such as Abraham, Moses, Jesus, and Mohammad. In
fact, Mohammad had come to launch a dynamic community in "permanent revolution" toward the ultimate
utopia—a perfectly classless society in this world.

Stamps of the Islamic Republic honoring Jalal al-Ahmad and Ali Shariati, the two main critics of "cultural imperialism" and advocates of a return to Shi'i roots.

Although Mohammad's goal had been betrayed by his illegitimate successors, the Caliphs, his radical message had been preserved for posterity by the Shi'i Imams—especially by Imam Husayn who had died to show future generations that human beings had the moral duty to fight oppression in all places at all times. He equated Imam Husayn with Che Guevara of Latin America. According to Shariati, the contemporary oppressors were the imperialists, the feudalists, the corrupt capitalists, and their hangers-on, especially the "tie-wearers" and "the palace-dwellers," the carriers of the "Western plague." He also criticized the conservative clerics who had tried to transform revolutionary religion into an apolitical public opiate. Shariati died on the eve of the revolution, but his prolific works were so widely read and so influential that many felt that he rather than Khomeini was the true theorist of the Islamic Revolution.

Iran and the International Political Economy

The oil boom gave the Shah the opportunity to play a significant role in regional and international politics. As the second-most important member of the Organization of Petroleum Exporting Countries (**OPEC**), Iran could cast decisive votes for raising or moderating world oil prices. At times, the Shah curried favor in the West by moderating prices. At other times, needing larger sums to finance ambitious projects, he pushed aggressively for higher prices despite his overall dependency on the West. Angered by this aggressiveness, one U.S. cabinet member went so far as to publicly label him "a nut case."

The oil revenues transformed Iran into the major power in the Persian Gulf. Iran's GNP, human resources, and military capabilities soon dwarfed those of its neighbors—Afghanistan, Pakistan, Iraq, Kuwait, and the other Gulf sheikhdoms. Its position was strengthened by three concurrent events. In the early 1970s, the British decided to close down their bases east of the Suez Canal. For the first time since the eighteenth century, the British navy would not dominate the Persian Gulf. At the same time, President Richard Nixon encouraged America's Asian allies to strengthen their military forces to safeguard their own security. This became known as the Nixon Doctrine. Moreover, his secretary of state, Henry Kissinger, openly argued that the United States should finance its ever-increasing oil imports—much of them coming from the Persian Gulf—by exporting more military hardware. The Shah was now able to buy from the United States almost any ultrasophisticated weapon he desired. Arms dealers began to jest that the Shah read their technical manuals in the same way that other men read *Playboy*.

The Shah's arms buying from the United States jumped from $135 million in 1970 to a peak of $5.7 billion in 1977. Between 1955 and 1978, Iran spent more than $20.7 billion on U.S. arms alone. Weapons were also purchased from Britain, France, Italy, and the Soviet Union. By 1977, Iran had by far the largest tank and ground forces as well as the most up-to-date air force and navy in the Gulf.

This military might gave the Shah a reach well beyond his immediate boundaries. He invaded and occupied three small but strategically located Arab islands in the Straits of Hormuz, thus controlling the oil lifeline through the Persian Gulf. He talked of estab-

TABLE 7   Iran's Foreign Trade, 1971–1977 (in millions of US$)

Exports	1971	1972	1973	1974	1975	1976	1977
United States	136	199	344	2,133	1,398	1,483	2,756
West Germany	300	340	582	1,126	1,334	1,807	1,696
Japan	1,241	1,376	1,754	4,331	4,526	4,049	3,881
United Kingdom	242	282	532	1,093	1,412	1,709	1,245
France	136	174	284	651	1,150	1,309	998
Imports							
United States	530	614	474	974	2,051	2,133	3,004
West Germany	403	459	655	991	1,824	2,304	3,014
Japan	262	360	484	847	1,662	2,098	2,136
United Kingdom	209	318	338	450	877	992	1,256
France	101	135	163	217	415	630	751

Source: Congressional Report, *Economic Consequences of the Revolution in Iran* (Washington, D.C.: U.S. Government Printing Office, 1979), 11–15.

lishing a presence well beyond the Gulf on the grounds that Iran's "national interests" reached into the Indian Ocean. "Iran's military expenditures," according to a 1979 U.S. Congressional Report, "surpassed those of the most powerful Indian Ocean states, including Australia, Indonesia, Pakistan, South Africa, and India."[19]

In the mid-1970s, the Shah dispatched troops to Oman to help the local sultan fight rebels. He offered Afghanistan $2 billion to break its ties with the Soviet Union, a move that probably prompted the Soviets to intervene militarily in that country. The Shah, after supporting Kurdish rebels in Iraq, forced Baghdad to concede to Iran vital territory on the Shatt al-Arab estuary. This had been a bone of contention between the two countries ever since Iraq had come into existence after World War I. A U.S. Congressional Report summed up Iran's overall strategic position:

> Iran in the 1970s was widely regarded as a significant regional, if not global, power. The United States relied on it, implicitly if not explicitly, to ensure the security and stability of the Persian Gulf sector and the flow of oil from the region to the industrialized Western world of Japan, Europe and the United States, as well as to lesser powers elsewhere.[20]

These vast military expenditures, as well as the oil exports, tied Iran closely to the industrial countries of the West, as well as to Japan. Trade with neighboring

and other Third World countries was insignificant. In 1977, 43 percent of Iran's imports came from the European Economic Community (now the European Union); 13 percent from Japan; and another 19 percent from the United States. Less than 25 percent came from the rest of the world, including, Turkey, India, and the Soviet Union (see Table 7).

By the mid-1970s, Iran was importing millions of dollars worth of wheat, rice, industrial tools, construction equipment, pharmaceuticals, tractors, pumps, and spare parts for the new assembly plants. The bulk of the rice and wheat, and a substantial portion of the tractors, medicines, and construction equipment, came from the United States. In the words of the Department of Commerce in Washington, "Iran's rapid economic growth" has provided America with "excellent business opportunities."[21]

The oil revenues thus had major consequences for Iran's political economy, all of which helped pave the way toward the Islamic Revolution. They allowed the Shah to pursue ambitious programs that inadvertently widened class and regional divisions within the dual society. They drastically raised public expectations without necessarily meeting them. They made the *rentier* state independent of society. They also made the state highly dependent on oil prices and imported products. Iran was no longer a simple *rentier* state, but an oil-addicted one, vulnerable to the vagaries of the world petroleum market. Economic slowdowns in the industrial countries could lead to a decline in their oil demands, which, in turn, could diminish Iran's ability to buy such essential goods as food, medicine, and industrial spare parts. One of the major promises made by the Islamic Revolution was to end this economic dependency on oil and the West. As Section 5 will show, such promises are not easy to fulfill. The Pahlavi monarchy and the Islamic Republic may differ in many ways, but they nevertheless have a similar political economy.

SECTION 3
Governance and Policy-Making

ORGANIZATION OF THE STATE

A decade after the revolution, a junior deputy from the provinces created a major uproar in parliament, known as the Islamic *Majles,* by inadvertently mentioning that the constitution of the Islamic Republic was built on two contradictory principles—jurist's guardianship and popular sovereignty. The former, he went on, was derived from Islam, Imam Khomeini, and the Twelve Shi'i Imams. The latter came from the West, and thus by implication from the Enlightenment, Montesquieu, and de Gaulle's Fifth Republic. It was as if a child had pointed out that the emperor had no clothes on. He had exposed the core problem of the Islamic constitution, that is, the attempt to reconcile theocracy with democracy, clerical authority with popular sovereignty, and the clergy's divine mandate with the modern concept of inalienable human rights. While some deputies threatened to beat up and expel their simple-minded colleague, others reminded him that such inappropriate questions had already destroyed many a promising career.[22]

The constitution was drafted shortly after the revolution by an Assembly of Religious Experts. It was ratified in December 1979 by a nationwide referendum held in the midst of the American hostage crisis. In fact, the occupation of the U.S. Embassy was, for the most part, motivated by Khomeini's desire to undermine the provisional premier, Mehdi Bazargan, who had criticized the proposed constitution for giving too much power to the clergy. During the referendum, anyone faulting the constitution was denounced by Khomeini as favoring the Shah and America. The 1979 constitution was amended in April–June 1989 during the very last months of Khomeini's life by a Council for the Revision of the Constitution handpicked by Khomeini himself. These amendments, in turn, were ratified by a nationwide referendum in July 1989, immediately after Khomeini's death. The final document, totaling 175 clauses and some 40 amendments, is a potpourri of theocracy and democracy with a dash of populist autocracy.

The constitution institutionalized clerical power, creating a full-blown theocracy. It affirmed faith in God, Divine Justice, the Qur'an, the Resurrection, Mohammad, the Twelve Imams, the eventual return of the Hidden Imam (the Mahdi), and, of course, Khomeini's doctrine of the jurist's guardianship. All laws, institutions, and state organizations were to be based on these "divine principles."

It named Khomeini to be the Supreme Jurist for life on the grounds that the public overwhelmingly respected him as the "most just, pious, informed, brave, and enterprising" of the very senior clerics. It further described him as the Leader of the Revolution, the Founder of the Islamic Republic, and, most potent of all, the Imam (Infallible Leader) of the whole community. It furthermore stipulated that if no single Supreme Jurist emerged after Khomeini's death then all his authority would be passed on to a Leadership Council of two or three senior jurists. After Khomeini's death, however, his disciples so distrusted the surviving senior jurists that they did not set up such a council. Instead, they elected one of their own, Hojjat al-Islam Khamenei, a medium-ranking cleric, to be the new Supreme Leader. All of Khomeini's titles, with the exception of Imam, were bestowed on Khamenei. The Islamic Republic has often been described as the regime of the ayatollahs (high-ranking clerics). It would be more aptly described as the regime of the *hojjat al-Islams* (medium-ranking clerics).

The constitution gave wide-ranging authority to the Supreme Leader. Described as the "link" between the branches of government, he could mediate between the legislative, the executive, and the judiciary. He could "determine the interests of Islam," "supervise the implementation of general policy," and "set

---

Chronology of the Islamic Republic, 1979–1989

February 1979	The Islamic Revolution
August 1979	Elections for the Assembly of Religious Experts
November 1979	Students take over the U.S. Embassy
December 1979	National referendum on the constitution
March 1980	Elections for the First Islamic *Majles*
July 1980	Shah dies in exile
September 1980	Iraq invades Iran
December 1980	Amnesty International lists 1,000 executions since February 1979
January 1981	U.S. hostages released
June 1981	Large demonstrations against the regime
	President Bani-Sadr ousted
July 1982	Iranian troops cross border into Iraq
October 1982	Khamenei elected president
February 1983	Amnesty International lists 5,000 executions since February 1979
April 1983	Elections for Second Islamic *Majles*
April 1988	Elections for Third Islamic *Majles*
August 1988	Cease-fire with Iraq
September 1988	Mass executions in prisons
February 1989	Khomeini calls for Rushdie's death
April 1989	Khomeini appoints committee to amend the constitution
June 1989	Khomeini dies
	Khamenei appointed Supreme Leader
	Rafsanjani elected president

---

political guidelines for the Islamic Republic." He could eliminate presidential candidates as well as dismiss the duly elected president. He could grant amnesty. As commander-in-chief, he could mobilize the armed forces, declare war and peace, and convene the Supreme Military Council. He could appoint and dismiss the chief of joint staffs as well as the commanders of the army, navy, air force, and revolutionary guards.

The Supreme Leader could nominate and remove the chief judge, the chief prosecutor, and the revolutionary tribunals. He could also remove lower court judges. He could appoint six clerics to the highly important Guardian Council. He could also fill a number of influential nongovernment posts: the preachers (**Imam Jum'ehs**) of the main mosques, the director of the National Radio-Television Network, and the head of the main religious foundations, especially the **Foundation of the Oppressed,** which now dwarfed the previous Pahlavi Foundation. This foundation administers the real estate confiscated from the old elite. The Supreme Leader had obtained more constitutional powers than the Shah had ever dreamed of.

The later constitutional amendments transformed the Assembly of Religious Experts, which had origi-

nally been convened as a constituent assembly to draft the constitution, into a permanent body. Packed by clerics, the assembly not only elected Khamenei as Khomeini's successor, but also reserved the right to dismiss him if it found him "mentally incapable of fulfilling his arduous duties." In effect, the Assembly of Religious Experts became the second-chamber equivalent of a clerical upper house above the Islamic *Majles.* Figure 2 on the following page illustrates the hierarchy established by the constitution.

Since the whole constitution was based on Khomeini's' theory of the jurist's guardianship, it gave wide-ranging judicial powers to the Supreme Jurist in particular and to the clerical strata in general. Laws were supposed to conform to the *shari'a,* and the clergy, particularly the senior jurists, were regarded as the ultimate interpreters of the *shari'a.* In fact, the constitution made the judicial system the central pillar of the state, overshadowing the executive and the legislature. Bills passed by the Islamic *Majles* were to be vetted by the Guardian Council to insure that they conformed to the *shari'a.* All twelve members of this Guardian Council were to be clerics, with six appointed by the Supreme Leader and six

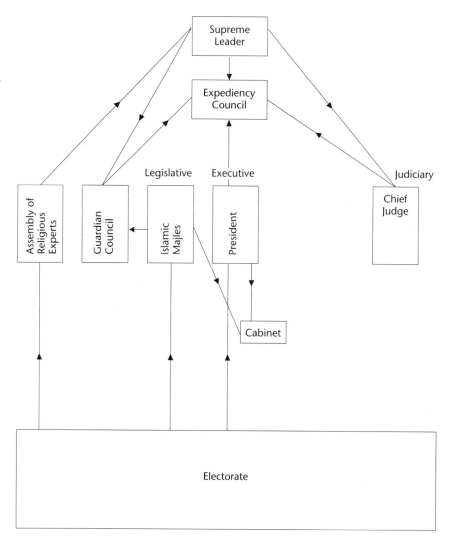

Figure 2 The Islamic Constitution
The general public elects the *Majles*, the president, and the Assembly of Religious Experts. But the Supreme Leader and the cleric-dominated Guardian Council decide who can compete in these elections.

appointed jointly by the Supreme Judge and Islamic *Majles*. The justice minister was to be chosen by the president and the Islamic *Majles* from a list drawn up by the Supreme Judge. The judicial system itself was Islamized all the way down to the district courts with seminary-trained jurists replacing university-educated judges. The Pahlavis had purged the clergy from the judicial system. The Islamic Republic now proceeded to purge the university-educated from the same judiciary.

To further Islamize the judiciary, the regime enacted a penal law based on an extremely narrow reading of the *shari'a*—so narrow that it prompted many modern-educated lawyers to resign in disgust charging that it contradicted the UN Charter on Human Rights.

It permitted injured families to demand blood money. It mandated the death penalty for a long list of "moral transgressions," including adultery, homosexuality, apostasy, drug trafficking, and habitual drinking. It sanctioned stoning, live burials, hand amputations, and physical gouging, citing the Qur'anic principle "an eye for an eye, a tooth for a tooth." It divided the population into male and female, Muslim and non-Muslim, and treated them unequally. For example, in court, the evidence of one male Muslim was equal to that of two female Muslims.

Significantly, the law was Islamized, but the modern centralized judicial system was not dismantled. For years, Khomeini argued that in a truly Islamic society the local *shari'a* judges would pronounce final

Ali Khamenei (1939–   )

Ali Khamenei succeeded Khomeini as Supreme Leader. He was born in 1939 in Mashed into a minor clerical family originally from Azerbaijan. He studied theology with Khomeini and was briefly imprisoned in 1962. Active in the opposition movement in 1978, he was given a series of influential positions immediately after the revolution even though he held only the medium rank of hojjat al-Islam. He became Friday prayer leader of Tehran, head of the revolu-

tionary guards, and, in the last years of Khomeini, president of the republic. After Khomeini's death, he was elevated to the rank of Supreme Leader even though he was not a Grand Ayatollah or a recognized senior expert on Islamic law—two constitutional prerequisites. The government-controlled media, however, began to refer to him as an ayatollah. Some ardent followers even referred to him as a Grand Ayatollah qualified to guide the world's whole Shi'i community.

---

verdicts without the intervention of the central authorities. Their verdicts would be swift and decisive. This, he insisted, was the true spirit of the *shari'a*. After the revolution, however, he discovered that the central state needed to retain ultimate control over the justice system, especially over life and death. Thus, the new regime retained the appeal system, the hierarchy of state courts, and the power to appoint and dismiss all judges. State interests took priority over the spirit of the *shari'a*.

Although the Islamic Republic is a full-fledged theocracy, some supporters of the regime have argued that it is nevertheless compatible with democracy. According to the constitution, the government represents the "general" electorate. The Supreme Leader is chosen by the Assembly of Religious Experts, who, in turn, are elected by the general population. This is viewed as a two-stage popular election.[23] As will be discussed in Section 4, the legislature also has a considerable constitutional role. According to Rafsanjani, previously the legislature's speaker, "the Islamic *Majles* is the centerpiece of the Islamic Constitution. It has many prerogatives, including that of enacting or changing ordinary laws [with the approval of the Guardian Council], investigating and supervising all affairs of state, as well as approving and ousting the cabinet ministers."[24] Finally, some also argue that the public, by voting with their feet in the mass demonstrations of 1978–1979, had implicitly favored a type of democracy that would be confined within the boundaries of Islam. One architect of the constitution argued that the Iranian people, by carrying out an Islamic Revolution, had determined for the future generations that democracy in Iran should be placed within the rubric of the jurist's guardianship.[25] Another declared that if he had to choose between the people and the jurist's guardianship, he

would not hesitate to choose the latter since it came directly from God.[26] On the eve of the initial referendum for the constitution, Khomeini himself insisted that democracy and the jurist's guardianship in no way contradicted each other:

> This constitution, which the people will ratify, is in no way a contradiction with democracy. Since the people love the clergy, have faith in the clergy, want to be guided by the clergy, it is right that the supreme religious authority oversee the work of the Prime Minister or of the President, to make sure that they don't make mistakes or go against the law: that is the Koran.[27]

The Executive

The constitution—particularly after the amendments—concentrates a considerable amount of power in the presidency. The president is described as the chief executive and the highest state official after the Supreme Leader. He is chosen every four years through a national election. He must be a "pious" Shi'i and faithful to the principles of the Islamic Republic. He cannot be elected to more than two terms. He chairs and selects the cabinet. He draws up the annual budget and supervises economic matters by chairing the Plan and Budget Organization. He can propose legislation to the *Majles*. He conducts the country's internal and external policies. He signs all international treaties, laws, and agreements. He also chairs the National Security Council, which is responsible for all defense matters, including intelligence.

The president, moreover, appoints most of the senior officials, that is, the provincial governors-general,

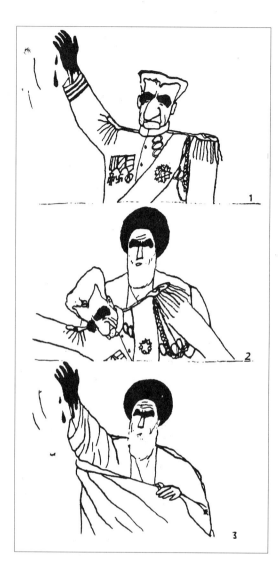

Cartoon of the Shah turning into Khomeini, from an émigré newspaper.
Source: Courtesy Nashriyeh.

reaucracies. In fact, these ministries continued to prolif-erate after the revolution despite Khomeini's earlier denunciations of the Shah's bloated bureaucracy. They expanded, for the most part, to provide jobs for the many college and high school graduates. On the eve of the revolution, Iran had 21 ministries with 300,000 civil servants and 1 million employees. By the early 1990s, it had 23 full ministries with over 600,000 civil servants and 1.5 million employees. The Iranian revolution, like many others, started by attacking the state as being too big, but ended up creating an even bigger one.

The Ministry of Public Guidance censors the me-dia and enforces "proper conduct" in public life. The Ministry of Heavy Industries manages the recently na-tionalized factories. The Ministry of Construction Crusade has the dual task of expanding social services and "true Islam" into the countryside. Its mission is to build bridges, roads, schools, libraries, and mosques in the villages so that the peasantry will learn the basic principles of Islam. "The peasants," declared one cleric, "are so ignorant of true Islam that they even sleep next to their unclean sheep."[28] For the first time in Iranian history, the state is taking Islam into the countryside.

Although Khomeini went out of his way during the revolution to promise that in the new regime the task of actual administration—as opposed to overall guid-ance—would be given to the professionally trained technocrats, the clergy have ended up influencing the executive as much as the judiciary and the legislature. As of 1995, two of the three presidents have been cler-ics—Khamenei and now Rafsanjani. The most sensi-tive ministries—Intelligence, Interior, Justice, and Public Guidance—have invariably gone to clerics.

The other ministers, even those with Ph.D.'s from the West, are often related by birth or marriage to the clerical families. They appear to be highly trained technocrats but, in fact, are technocrats cho-sen by, trusted by, and related to, the ruling clergy. What is more, the clergy have controlled the armed forces, both the regular army and the new revolu-tionary guards, through a network strikingly similar to the communist commissar system. Military officers cannot move their contingents without the knowledge and approval of their clerical supervisors. Abol-Hasan Bani-Sadr—the Islamic Republic's first president, whose tenure was cut short in 1981 because he had dared criticize the clergy—called the new regime a "dictatorship of the

regional governors, town mayors, and ambassadors. Furthermore, as head of the executive, he names the directors of the many large public organizations—the National Iranian Oil Company, the National Electric-ity Board, and the main banks, airlines, mines, insur-ance companies, and shipping firms—most of which were nationalized immediately after the revolution.

What is more, the president, as chief executive, heads the government ministries with their huge bu-

Revolutionary Guards

The Army for the Guarding of the Islamic Revolution, better known as the revolutionary guards, originated in late 1978 when the old regime was crumbling. The more active city mosques armed local volunteers to keep law and order as well as to protect their neighborhoods against government reprisals. Immediately after the revolution, Khomeini placed these local militias under central control and assigned them the task of policing the whole country. In the early 1980s, the revolutionary guards were drastically expanded to control street protests, arrest dissidents, and repel the Iraqi invasion. By the end of the 1980s, the revolutionary guards were a parallel organization to the regular Iranian military—especially the infantry—and had their own officers, uniforms, budgets, recruitment centers, and even munitions factories. According to the constitution, the main task of the regular army is to defend the country's borders, while the task of the revolutionary guards is to protect the Islamic Revolution.

mullahtariat" modeled on the communist "dictatorship of the proletariat."[29]

OTHER STATE INSTITUTIONS

The Islamic Republic has set up a number of semipublic institutions: the Foundation for the Oppressed, the Alavi Foundation (named after Imam Ali), the Martyrs Foundation, the Pilgrimage Foundation, the Housing Foundation, the Foundation for the Publication of Imam Khomeini's Works, and the Fifteenth of Khordad Foundation, which commemorates Khomeini's 1963 denunciation of the White Revolution. These organizations are supposedly autonomous, but their directors are invariably prominent clerics appointed by the Supreme Leader. According to one conservative estimate, the annual budget of these foundations may be as much as half of the government's budget.[30]

The largest of these institutions, the Foundation for the Oppressed, administers some 203 mining and manufacturing enterprises, 470 agribusinesses, 100 construction companies, and over 2,700 urban real estate properties. Much of these businesses had previously belonged to entrepreneurs, senior bureaucrats, and high-ranking officers who had either fled the country after the revolution or had been judged by the clerical courts to be "active counterrevolutionaries." This foundation also owns the country's two leading newspapers, *Ettela'at* and *Kayhan*. The London *Guardian* estimated that in 1993 the foundation employed some 65,000 and had an annual budget of $10 billion.[31] According to an Iranian economist, this was as much as 10 percent of the government budget.[32]

The Alavi Foundation, the second largest of these institutions, is the direct heir to the Pahlavi Foundation and administers the vast assets that had belonged to the previous Shah. The Martyrs Foundation, in charge of helping war veterans, controls the property of the old elite that was confiscated in 1979 but not handed over to the Foundation for the Oppressed. It also receives an annual subsidy from the government. These three foundations together own some 20 percent of the country's private assets, employ over 150,000, and administer vast economic empires including 7,800 hectares of farmland, 270 orchards, 230 commercial companies, 130 large factories, and 90 cinemas. They can be described as "states within a state," but with the important caveat that the same clerical elite that controls the state also controls these foundations.

The other major foundations—those for Pilgrimage, Housing, War Refugees, Fifteenth of Khordad, and Publication of Imam Khomeini's Works—are also headed by clerics even though most of their funding comes directly from the government. As their names imply, they are assigned specific tasks, but their jurisdiction often infringes on state matters. For example, the annual pilgrimage to Mecca has direct bearing on Iran's foreign policy. If its organizers insist on openly denouncing the Saudi royal family, who are Sunni Muslims, as "oppressive blood-sucking exploiters," then obviously Iran's relations with Saudi Arabia suffer. Similarly, the head of the Fifteenth of Khordad Foundation decided in 1989 that the best way to keep the Islamic Revolution alive was to double the $1 million bounty offered for Rushdie's assassination. At the time, it was generally felt that President Rafsanjani was eager to forget the Rushdie affair for the sake of normalizing economic relations with the West. Such problems continue to plague Iran's policy-making process.

LOCAL GOVERNMENT

Iran is divided into provinces, districts, subdistricts, townships, and villages. Provinces are headed by governor-generals, districts by governors, subdistricts by lieutenant governors, towns by mayors, and villages by headmen. All are appointed by the Interior Ministry.

The Islamic constitution promised popularly elected councils *(showras)* on each level of administration. The constitution declares that the "management of local affairs" in every village, town, subdistrict, district, and province will be "under the supervision of councils whose members will be elected by the people of the locality." It also declares that "governor-generals, governors, mayors, and other local officials appointed by the government have an obligation to abide by the decisions of the local councils." These clauses were incorporated because of mass demonstrations organized in late 1979 by the left—notably the Mojahedin and the Fedayi—demanding the formation of elected councils. The word *showra* had radical connotations, the soviets' setup in the Russian revolutions of 1905 and 1917 were known in Iran by that same term.

Despite the promises, the councils have not been convened, leaving local administration in the hands of government officials. Although these officials do not have to contend with elected councils, they do have to oblige local notables—especially revolutionary guard officers, court judges, and *Imam Jum'ehs* (town preachers) with their mosque pulpits. Each can cause headaches for local officials.

THE POLICY-MAKING PROCESS

The revolutionary clerics remained united while building a new order. After all, they were convinced that they alone had the divine mandate to govern. They formed a distinct social stratum as well as a cohesive political group. They followed the same leader, admired the same texts, cited the same potent symbols, remembered the same real and imaginary indignations under the Shah, and, most important of all, shared the same vested interest in preserving their Islamic Republic. What is more, most of them had studied at the same seminaries and had come from the same lower-middle-class backgrounds. Some were even related to each other through marriage and blood ties.

But once the Islamic constitution was in place, the same clerics drifted into two loose but identifiable blocs: the statists, who favored a government-directed economy; and the free-marketers, who preferred to limit the economic and social activities of the state. The statists hoped to consolidate their lower-class support by redistributing wealth, nationalizing more

A Mojahedin cartoon depicts Khomeini and the two warring clerical factions.
Source: Courtesy Mojahed (in exile).

enterprises, confiscating more large estates, implementing ambitious social programs, rationing and subsidizing essential goods, and placing price ceilings on many consumer commodities. In short, they espoused the creation of a comprehensive welfare state. The free-marketers, on the other hand, hoped to retain middle-class support, especially in the bazaars, by removing price controls, lowering business taxes, cutting red tape, encouraging private entrepreneurs, opening up the market, and balancing the budget—even at the cost of sacrificing subsidies and social programs.

The free-marketers were labeled "middle-roaders" and "traditionalists." The statists were labeled "progressives," "fast-walkers," "seekers of new ideas," "clergy favoring the oppressed," and "Followers of the Imam's Line." The free-marketers often denounced their rivals as "extremists," "leftists," and "pro-Soviet Muslims." The statists countered by denouncing the free-marketers as "medievalists," "rightists," "capitalist jurists," "mafia bazaaris," and "pro-American Muslims." In the euphoria of 1979, Khomeini had declared that economics was a subject worthy of donkeys. He had also argued that the many who had sacrificed their lives for the revolution had not done so merely to lower the price of melons. But it was precisely such mundane issues that eventually polarized his followers.

This polarization produced a major political gridlock. Between 1981 and 1987, over 100 bills passed by the Islamic *Majles*—some with much fanfare—were vetoed by the Guardian Council on the grounds that they were un-Islamic and unconstitutional. During these years, the *Majles* was dominated by the statists, but the Guardian Council was packed with conservative free-marketer jurists. Khomeini had appointed such jurists to the Guardian Council to curry favor in the bazaars and build bridges to some of the highly conservative grand ayatollahs who distrusted the whole revolutionary movement. The vetoed legislation included a labor law, land reform, nationalization of foreign trade, progressive income tax, control over urban real estate transactions, and confiscation of the property of émigrés (whom the courts had not yet found guilty of counterrevolutionary activities). These bills were introduced into the *Majles* by individual members. They received quick passage because the statists controlled the crucial *Majles* committees and held a majority on the *Majles* floor.

In their polemics, both sides could cite the Islamic constitution to support their positions. The free-marketers referred to the long list of clauses protecting private property, promising balanced budgets, and placing agriculture, small industry, and retail trade in the private sector. The statists referred to an even longer list promising education, medicine, jobs, low-income housing, unemployment benefits, disability pay, interest-free loans, and the predominance of the public sector in the economy, especially in heavy industry, banking, and large mines.

To ease the constitutional gridlock, Khomeini set up a special Expediency Council for Determining the Public Interest of the Islamic Order. Khomeini himself was eager to remain above the fray so as not to be identified too closely with either side. He assigned to the Expediency Council the task of resolving the conflicts between the Islamic *Majles* and the Guardian Council. He packed it with thirteen clerics, including the president, the Supreme Judge, the speaker of the Islamic assembly, the six jurists from the Guardian Council, and his own son Hojjat al-Islam Khomeini. The Expediency Council passed the more moderate bills favored by the statists—notably the much-disputed labor law, which provides a minimum wage and some semblance of job security for workers in large factories.

After Khomeini's death, the constitutional amendments institutionalized this Expediency Council. The Supreme Leader was authorized to name all of its members and to determine its size, tenure, and jurisdiction. No restrictions were placed on the council—especially on whether it had to publish its reports and deliberations. The new Supreme Leader packed the council with eight of his own clerical supporters—none of them prominent ayatollahs. He also extended its jurisdiction, allowing it to initiate entirely new laws and not restrict itself to resolving the existing differences between the *Majles* and the Guardian Council. The amendments have made the cumbersome constitution even more cumbersome. In effect, the Expediency Council is now a secretive supraconstitutional body accountable only to the Supreme Leader. In this sense, it has become the most powerful policy-making body in the Islamic Republic.

SECTION 4

Representation and Participation

THE LEGISLATURE

The Islamic Republic's constitution is undoubtedly a theocratic document. Nevertheless, it recognizes the importance of democracy and popular participation. It stipulates direct elections for the presidency, for the Assembly of Experts, and, most important of all, for the Islamic *Majles,* which is defined by the constitution as the "Legislative Branch." In describing this branch of government, the constitution uses the term *qanun* (statutes) rather than *shari'a* (divine law) so as to gloss over the fundamental question of whether law is derived from God or the people. The pretense is kept up that divine law comes from above, but statutes are made by the elected representatives of the people.

The Islamic *Majles*—described by the constitution as "representing the nation"—contains 270 deputies elected every four years through secret and direct balloting. All adults over the age of fifteen, including women, can vote. The *Majles* has wide-ranging authority. It can pass *qanuns* (laws), as long as these laws conform to Islam and as long as the approval of the Guardian Council is obtained. It can interpret the laws, as long as these interpretations do not contradict the judicial authorities. It can choose six jurists for the twelve-man Guardian Council, but this choice is limited to a list drawn up by the Supreme Judge.

It can investigate at will cabinet ministers, "all affairs of state," and public complaints against the executive and the judiciary. It can remove cabinet members—with the exception of the president—through a parliamentary vote of no confidence. It can withhold approval for government budgets, foreign loans, international treaties, and cabinet appointments. It can hold closed debates, provide its members with immunity from arrest, and regulate its own internal workings, especially its committee system.

Although the 1989 constitutional amendments weakened the *Majles* vis-à-vis the presidency and the Expediency Council, it nevertheless remains highly important. In recent years, the *Majles* has revamped the annual budget, criticized government policies, modified the Five-Year Plan, and forced the president to replace his cabinet ministers as well as the director of the National Radio-Television Network. At one point, 217 deputies circulated an open letter that explicitly emphasized the prerogatives of the *Majles,* and thereby implicitly downplayed those of the Supreme Leader. The latter's supporters promptly issued a counterblast reminding the *Majles* that the Islamic Republic was based on Khomeini's concept of the jurist's guardianship.

THE PARTY SYSTEM AND ELECTIONS

The constitution promises that all elections, including those for the Islamic *Majles,* will be entirely free. In practice, however, elections have become increasingly more regulated, manipulated, and controlled. The Guardian Council eliminates candidates on the grounds that they are not sufficiently committed to the "principles of the Islamic Republic." The National Radio-Television Network, the main source of information for the vast majority of people, favors some candidates, ignores others, and denounces yet others. The Interior Ministry bans opposition groups with the claim that they are anti-Islamic and antirevolutionary. Ballot boxes are invariably placed in mosques. Revolutionary guards supervise the voting. Neighborhood clerics are on hand to help illiterates complete their ballots. Club-wielding gangs assault opponents of the regime. Elections are timed to coincide with high religious holidays. The Supreme Leader inevitably denounces those tempted to abstain

as "secret agents of the devil." The electoral law, based on a winner-take-all majority system rather than proportional representation, which guarantees some seats to any party that wins a certain percentage of the vote, was designed to minimize the voice of the opposition, particularly in the early days of the republic when there *was* such a thing as an opposition.

The Islamic Republic has so far had four *Majleses* (1980–1984), (1984–1988), (1988–1992), and (1992–present). *Majles* elections have gone from being relatively free to being completely controlled.

The First Majles

In the election for the First *Majles* in 1980, there were over 4,400 candidates, over 40 parties, over 200 dailies and weeklies, and thousands of workplace organizations in the bazaars, campuses, high schools, factories, and offices. The parties represented the whole range of the political spectrum   from the far right, through the center, to the extreme left. The revolution had shattered the state, liberating scores of social and political groups. It was as if, after years of silence, every professional and occupational association, every political party and ideological viewpoint, and every interest and pressure group rushed into the open to air its views, print its newspapers and broad sheets, and, of course, field its parliamentary candidates.

On the right was the Islamic Republican Party (IRP). It was founded immediately after the revolution by Khomeini's closest disciples. The IRP had the support of two highly conservative religious groups that had survived the old regime: the Fedayan-e Islam and the Hojjatieh Society. It also had the support of the Islamic Association of Bazaar Guilds, the Islamic Association of Teachers, the Islamic Association of University Students, the Association of Seminary Teachers of Qom, and, most important of all, the Association of Militant Clergy in Tehran. The Islamic Republican Party openly favored Khomeini's notion that the clergy had a divine mandate to rule.

At the center was the Liberation Movement, headed by Mehdi Bazargan. Bazargan had been appointed prime minister in February 1979 by Khomeini himself, but had resigned in disgust ten months later when the revolutionary guards had permitted the students to take over the U.S. embassy. The Liberation Movement favored free markets, limited government, nonalignment without bellicose attacks on the United States, and a pluralistic political system in which all

Political Parties

Political parties cannot function in Iran without a license from the Interior Ministry. As of 1995, no real party had succeeded in obtaining a license. The following five parties, however, function in exile—especially in Europe.

The Liberation Movement. Established in 1961 by Mehdi Bazargan, who later became Khomeini's first premier, the Liberation Movement is a moderate Islamic party similar in some ways to the Western European Christian Democrats. Since 1981, the regime has tightly controlled its activities, in part because it opposed continuation of the war with Iraq, in part because it criticized the arbitrary confiscation of private property, and, for the most part because it denounced the clergy for interfering in politics. The Liberation Movement, despite its religiosity, advocates secularism and the strict separation of mosque and state.

The Mojahedin. Formed in 1971 as a guerrilla organization to fight the old regime, the Mojahedin tried to synthesize Marxism and Islam. It interpreted Shi'i Islam to be a radical religion favoring equality, social justice, martyrdom, and redistribution of wealth. Immediately after the revolution, the Mojahedin attracted a large following among college and high school students, especially when it began to denounce the clergy for establishing a new dictatorship. The regime retaliated with mass executions and forced the Mojahedin to move their base of operations into Iraq. Not unexpectedly, the Mojahedin became associated with the national enemy and thereby lost much of its appeal within Iran.

The Fedayi. Formed in 1971, the Fedayi modeled itself after the Marxist guerrilla movements of the 1960s in Latin America—especially those inspired by Che Guevara and the Cuban revolution. Losing more fighters than any other organization in the guerrilla war against the Shah, the Fedayi came out of the revolution with much revolutionary mystique and popular urban support. But it soon lost much of its strength, in part because of massive government repression and in part because of a series of internal splits.

The Tudeh. Established in 1941, the Tudeh is the mainstream communist party of Iran, fully supporting the policies of the former Soviet Union. Although the Tudeh supported the Islamic Republic as a "popular anti-imperialist state," it was banned, and most of its organizers were executed in 1983 when it criticized the regime for continuing the war across the Iraqi border.

---

parties—religious and nonreligious, right and left—would be able to function and compete in fair and open elections. The Liberation Movement also favored a regime built on its own liberal interpretation of Islam—one in which the clergy would guide and advise rather than rule and dominate the community. Bazargan was a former member of Mosaddeq's National Front—the organization instrumental in nationalizing the oil industry in 1951. But Bazargan, unlike Mosaddeq, liked to sprinkle his speeches and bolster his ideas, concepts, and arguments with choice quotations from the Qur'an, the Prophet, and the Twelve Imams.

Closely allied with the Liberation Movement was the National Front, a mere shadow of its former self, and its offshoots, the National Party and the Democratic National Front. These parties, like the Liberation Movement, favored liberal democracy and were led by western-educated, middle-aged professionals and technocrats. But, unlike the Liberation Movement, they avoided making use of Islam. Like their deceased mentor Mosaddeq, they preferred to separate politics from religion and to treat the latter as primarily a private matter. The Liberation Movement can be defined as a liberal Muslim party, and the National Front and its offshoots as liberal secular parties.

The left was fragmented even more into religious and nonreligious radical groups. The religious groups included such Muslim yet anticlerical ones as the People's Mojahedin, the Movement of Militant Muslim, and the Movement for the Liberation of the Iranian People. The nonreligious groups included a number of Marxist and ethnic parties: the Tudeh, the Majority and Minority factions of the Fedayin guerrillas, the Kurdish Democratic Party, the Maoist Paykar Organization, and at least ten smaller Marxist-Leninist parties. To complicate matters further, Bani-Sadr, who had been elected president in January 1980, was distancing himself from the Islamic Republican Party by fielding a number of his own candidates.

Many of these political parties had their own student, labor, professional, and women's organizations. For example, in the early years of the revolution, there were over a dozen women's organizations in Tehran alone. Among them were the Society of Militant Women, the Islamic Association of Women, the Union of National Women, the Union of Women Lawyers, the Union of Democratic Women, the Women for Justice, and the Society of Islamic Revolutionary Women. Each was affiliated with one of the two main political parties.

Not surprisingly, the elections for this First *Majles* were extremely lively, even though the IRP manipulated the state machinery, especially the Interior Ministry and the National Radio-Television Network. On the eve of the voting, the interior minister forthrightly declared that all were free to run but that only "true Muslims" would have their credentials accepted in the forthcoming parliament.[33] Some 80 percent of the electorate participated in the first round.

The main contestants were, on the one hand, the IRP and its clerical and bazaar affiliates and, on the other hand, President Bani-Sadr, the Mojahedin, and their secular-leftist allies. The competition was so intense in some constituencies—particularly Kurdestan, Kermanshah, West Azerbaijan, and the Caspian provinces—that the Interior Ministry stepped in, impounded the ballot boxes, harassed candidates, and postponed the second round indefinitely. The second round was not held until late 1981. By then, the regime had cracked down on the opposition, forcing Bani-Sadr into exile, banning many leftist parties, and executing hundreds of Mojahedin organizers.

Of the 216 deputies elected in 1980, 120 were supporters of the IRP, 33 of Bani-Sadr, and 20 of the Liberation Movement, while 33 described themselves as "independent." The independents included two Kurdish Democrats and five National Front leaders. The latter five had their parliamentary credentials promptly rejected on the grounds that documents found in the recently occupied U.S. Embassy "proved" them to be "U.S. spies." The IRP had won only 35 percent of the popular vote, but had collected over 60 percent of the filled seats. The Mojahedin, on the other hand, had won 25 percent of the popular vote, but had not obtained a single seat. The electoral law based on majority rather than proportional representation had paid off for Khomeini.

Once the IRP carried out the second round and replaced the purged members, including Bani-Sadr's supporters, it gained a solid majority.[34] This included 105 clerics—more than 50 percent of the *Majles*—making it by far the highest clerical representation in Iran's parliamentary history. Most were medium-ranking clerics serving as court judges and town preachers *(Imam Jum'ehs)*. The others were white-collar employees and high school teachers, some of whom were seminary graduates. Over 90 percent came from the propertied middle class. Their fathers had been clerics, bazaar merchants, guild elders, or small farmers.

The Second Majles

The elections for the Second *Majles* in 1984 were carried out under very different circumstances. The "Spring of the Iranian Revolution" was over. The opposition—including the Liberation Movement—was now banned. The IRP monopolized the political scene, manipulating the state and controlling a vast array of organizations, including large foundations, local mosques, revolutionary guards, and thousands of town preachers. Not surprisingly, it won a landslide victory, leaving a few seats to independent-minded clerics with their own local followings. Also not surprisingly, voter participation fell sharply to less than 60 percent, even though the voting age was reduced from 16 to 15 and even though Khomeini declared that abstaining was tantamount to betraying Islam.

Over 54 percent of the 270 deputies were clerics, almost all medium-ranking.[35] Most of the nonclerics had Ph.D.'s, M.A.'s, B.A.'s, associate degrees, or high school diplomas. Only 11 had not completed high school. Twenty-seven of the lay members had at one time or another attended a seminary. As before, most were in their late thirties or early forties.

In 1987, Khomeini dissolved the IRP in preparation for the Third *Majles*. No reason was given, but the decision was probably prompted by the conflict between the statists and the free-marketers. The party's central committee was divided sharply into radicals demanding land reform, progressive income tax, and more nationalization, on the one hand, and conservatives favoring the bazaar, the industrial employers, and the reduction of state expenditures, on the other. One radical deputy claimed that "the party had been infiltrated by opportunistic time-servers pretending to be devout followers of the Imam's Line."[36] In the *Majles,* the radicals could muster 120 votes; the conservatives some 90; the remainder moved back and forth between these poles.

Moreover, the IRP's monopoly of power had aroused concern. Some drew parallels with the Resurgence Party and remembered how the clergy had unanimously denounced the Shah's "totalitarian" drive to take over the whole society. Furthermore, provincial clerics with their own power bases lobbied Khomeini against the IRP. They feared the party not only for its economic radicalism but also for its drive to centralized power. Finally, as far as Khomeini himself was concerned, the IRP had accomplished its main purpose: eliminating the Mojahedin, the National Front, the Tudeh, and the Liberation Movement.

In dissolving the IRP, Khomeini declared the clergy to be free to establish two competing organizations as long as both remained diligent against imperialism, advocated neither communism nor capitalism, and agreed to preserve Islam, the Islamic Revolution, the Islamic Republic, and the jurist's guardianship. "Political differences," he commented, "are natural. Throughout history our religious authorities have differed among themselves. . . . Besides," he added, "Iranians should be free to express themselves."[37] He could have added, "within reason and the context of Islam, as defined by myself."

In preparation for the Third *Majles* elections in 1988, the statist clerics left the Association of Militant Clergy *(Jameh-e Ruhaniyat-e Mobarez)* to form their own Society of Militant Clergy *(Majm'eh-e Ruhaniyun-e Mobarez)*. From then on, there were two rival clerical organizations: on one side, the radical statists with their association and five major newspapers, including the two largest national papers named *Kayhan* and *Ettela'at;* on the other side, the conservative free-marketers with their society and at least two affiliated newspapers. This was political pluralism, but a pluralism limited to the Khomeinist clergy and their protégés who subscribed fully to their interpretation of Shi'ism.

The Third and Fourth Majleses

The radicals won the lackluster elections. In the new parliament, there were 86 clerics—a 23-percent decline from the previous assembly.[38] This, however, did not signify the demise of clerical power. Some prominent clerics had gone on to higher positions, especially to the Assembly of Religious Experts. Many of the new lay deputies were young protégés of the clerics recruited into their fold from the students who had taken over the U.S. Embassy. The conservative clerics who did not run in these elections went on to occupy other influential positions—as heads of religious foundations, preachers in the city mosques, and editors of mass newspapers.

Although the radical clergy began the Third *Majles* with a clear majority, this dominance soon evaporated, in part because of Khomeini's death in 1989, and in part because Khamenei and Rafsanjani,

the new Supreme Leader and president, respectively, began to adopt free-market policies soon after the end of the war with Iraq. During the war, these two had been vocal advocates of price controls, rationing, high taxes, nationalization, and large government budgets. Now, with the cease-fire, they argued that the only way to revive the war-torn economy was to encourage private enterprise, open up the market, and cut government expenditures.

In giving the eulogy for Khomeini, Rafsanjani launched the new course.[39] He played down Khomeini's role as a charismatic revolutionary who had led the downtrodden. Indeed, the word "oppressed" was hardly mentioned. Instead, he praised Khomeini as a world-famous statesman who had restored Iran's national sovereignty. He also praised him as a highly reputable scholar-theologian who had intellectually "awakened the moribund seminaries" from their "Medieval graves." This ran counter to the prevailing notion that Shi'i Islam was by definition a revolutionary creed against all forms of despotism and exploitation.

To ensure that the change of economic course would go smoothly, Khamanei handed over the two main newspapers—*Kayhan* and *Ettela'at*—to the conservative free-marketers. He also authorized the Guardian Council to oversee the 1992 elections for the Fourth *Majles*. The Guardian Council announced that all candidates had to prove their "practical commitment to the Supreme Leader and the Islamic Republic." The Guardian Council further restricted the campaign to one week, permitting candidates to speak in mosques and run newspaper advertisements, but not to debate each other in open forums. The head of the Guardian Council announced that he would use pesticides to cleanse parliament of anyone with "difficult attitudes." Seventy-five radical candidates withdrew. Forty were disqualified by the Guardian Council. Only a handful of radicals were allowed to be elected. Voter participation dropped to a new low after the revolution. In Tehran, less than 55 percent of the eligible voters bothered to cast ballots despite Khamenei's pronouncement that it was the "religious obligation of everyone to participate."[40]

Ayatollah Khalkhali, a vocal radical, was barred from running on the grounds that he did not have appropriate theological training. Yet the same Khalkhali had been considered qualified enough in 1978–1987 to sit as a high court judge dispatching hundreds of political prisoners to their deaths. Khalkhali retorted that his candidacy had been rejected by rightists who had sat out the revolution but were now weaseling their way into the Guardian Council. The former minister of heavy industries warned that "true servants of the revolution, like himself, had been subjected to a political purge as a prelude to a future physical purge." Another disqualified candidate, who had earlier dismissed any talk of human rights as a "'foreign conspiracy," now complained that the Guardian Council had grossly violated the UN Charter on Human Rights. It had failed to inform him of the charges brought against him; it had given him insufficient time to respond; and it had denied him the right to defend himself in a proper court of law.

The Guardian Council responded that its decisions had been kept out of the mass media in order to protect "state secrets" and the "public reputations" of the unqualified. The purged were expected to be grateful for this sensitivity. It also argued that it had followed precedent, reminding the radicals that they themselves had used similar procedures to keep out "undesirables" from the previous three parliaments—undesirables such as the Mojahedin, the Fedayin, the Tudeh, the National Front, the Liberation Movement, and the "pseudo-clerics" who did not believe in the jurist's guardianship.

The purge was relatively easy to carry out. For one thing, the extensive powers entrusted to the Supreme Leader by the Islamic constitution left the radicals vulnerable. As Hojjat al-Islam Mohtashami, a leading radical, complained, the institution of the jurist's guardianship was now being used to clobber revolutionary heads. When radicals complained that they were being slandered as "traitors" for merely questioning free-market economics, their opponents countered that disobedience to the Supreme Leader was tantamount to disobedience to God. They argued that only proponents of "American Islam" would dare question the decisions of the Supreme Leader. They also reminded them that the new oath of office required parliamentary deputies to obey the Supreme Leader as "the Vice-Regent of the Hidden Twelfth Imam." Khamenei may not have inherited Khomeini's title of Imam, but he had obtained the new exalted position of the Hidden Imam's Spokesman.

What is more, the conservatives effectively used populist rhetoric against the radicals. They described them as the "newly moneyed class" and the "Mercedes-Benz clerics." They accused them of misusing official positions to line their own pockets, open slush funds and secret foreign accounts, give lucrative contracts to their friends, sell contraband, and deceive the masses with unrealistic promises. "They," exclaimed one, "act like a giant octopus, giving with one tentacle but taking away with the others." They also placed the responsibility for the country's economic malaise squarely on the shoulders of the radicals. They argued that a decade of statist policies had further increased poverty, illiteracy, inflation, unemployment, and slum housing. Before the revolution, these problems were blamed on the Pahlavis. Now they were blamed on the "extremist pseudo-clerical radicals."

The purge was so decisive that the radicals dissolved their Society of Militant Clergy in 1992 soon after the convening of the Fourth *Majles*. Some went to head foundations and libraries. Some took up seminary positions. Others began to write for newspapers, occasionally arguing that the public should choose its Supreme Leader and that the Guardian Council should stay out of the whole electoral process. Yet others remained active in national politics, mildly criticizing the regime and quietly awaiting the day when free-market economics would fail. As Section 5 will show, this expectation was not entirely unrealistic. The Fourth *Majles* continues to be divided into clerical factions, especially conservative free-marketers and radical statists.

POLITICAL CULTURE, CITIZENSHIP, AND IDENTITY

In theory, the Islamic Republic should be highly viable since Shi'ism is the religion of both the state and the vast majority of the population. Shi'ism can be described as the central component of popular culture. The Islamic constitution also guarantees basic rights to religious minorities as well as individual citizens. All citizens, regardless of "race, color, language, and religion," are promised the rights of expression, worship, and organization. They are guaranteed freedom from arbitrary arrest, torture, and police surveillance. In short, the Islamic constitution has incorporated the concept of individual rights as developed in the West and as introduced into Iran during the 1905 revolution.

The constitution gives specific guarantees to the recognized religious minorities. Although the Armenians, Assyrians, and Jews form 1 percent of the total population, they are allocated five *Majles* seats. They are permitted their own places of worship, their own community organizations, including schools, and their own marriage, divorce, and inheritance laws. The constitution, however, is ominously silent about the Bahais, whom the clerics view as "apostates" linked to the West.

The constitution also gives guarantees to the non-Persians who, together, form about half of the total population. No accurate figures exist for the simple reason that all censuses taken in Iran have avoided the sensitive issue of language and ethnicity. The constitution promises that "local and native languages [can] be used in the press, media, and schools." It also promises extensive jurisdiction to local councils—to be elected on the provincial, town, and village levels. These councils, which could not be dismissed by the central government, were to supervise the governors-general and town mayors and watch over educational, cultural, and social programs. In effect, the linguistic minorities were promised a level of autonomy unprecedented in Iran's history.

These generous promises are honored more in theory than in fact. The local councils—the chief institutional safeguard for the provincial minorities—have yet to be convened, creating a potentially explosive issue in Kurdestan, Baluchestan, and Azerbaijan. Subsidies to non-Persian publications and radio stations are meager. Jews have been so harassed as "pro-Israeli Zionists" that more than half of them—20,000 out of 40,000—have left the country. Armenians have had to accept Muslim principals in their schools, end coeducational classes, adopt government curriculum, abide with Muslim dress codes, including the veil, and close their community clubs to Muslims. Christians, on the whole, have been distrusted for being sympathetic to the West and contaminated by "imperialist culture." The Christian population has declined under the Islamic Republic from over 300,000 to less than 150,000.

The Bahais, however, have borne the brunt of religious persecution. Their leaders have been executed as "apostates" and "imperialist spies." Their adherents have been fired from their jobs, had their property confiscated, and been imprisoned and tortured to pressure them to convert to Islam. Their schools have been closed, their community property expropriated, and their shrines and cemeteries bulldozed. It is estimated that since the revolution one-third of the 300,000

Bahais have left Iran. The Bahais, like the Jews and Armenians, have migrated mostly to Canada and the United States, especially to New York and California.

The constitution's grand promises on individual rights have also been flagrantly violated. The regime has closed down newspapers, professional association, labor unions, and political parties. It has banned demonstrations and public meetings. It has incarcerated tens of thousands without due process. It has systematically tortured prisoners to extract false confessions and public recantations. And it has executed some 25,000 political prisoners. In the summer of 1988 alone, over 100 Marxists—some of whom had already completed their prison terms—were executed simply on the grounds that they refused to pray and answer questions such as whether they believed in the afterlife, in God, and in Mohammad. As Marxists, they were declared to be apostates from Islam. The United Nations, Amnesty International, and Human Rights Watch have all strongly criticized Iran for violating the UN Charter on Human Rights as well as the Islamic constitution itself.

Although these violations affect the whole population, they arouse special resentments among four large sectors of the country: the intelligentsia, the Sunnis, traditionally minded Shi'is, and, last but not least, women. The modern middle class, which forms as much as 10 percent of the total population, has been secular and even anticlerical ever since the 1905 revolution. Little love is lost between it and the Islamic Republic. Not surprisingly, most of those executed have been teachers, engineers, professionals, and college students. Members of the intelligentsia who join the regime are regarded by their colleagues as betrayers of their class.

The Sunnis, who form as much as 9 percent of the population, naturally feel alienated from a regime that stresses its Shi'i identity. The Sunnis include many of the 3,800,000 Kurds, 700,000 Baluchis, 700,000 Arabs, and 600,000 Turkomans. In 1979 to 1981, the regime crushed major uprisings in these communities with thousands of revolutionary guards recruited from the central Shi'i Persian provinces. In more recent years, especially since the establishment of the independent Republic of Azerbaijan, the ethnic issue has threatened to spill over to the large Azeri population, which forms as much as 24 percent of Iran. Section 5 will have more to say about this potential time bomb.

The more traditionally minded Shi'is had difficulty accepting Khomeini's populist version of Islam, including his concept of the jurist's guardianship. At the time of the revolution, none of the grand ayatollahs subscribed to this theory of government. After the revolution, few of them were willing to be associated with the Islamic Republic. And after Khomeini's death, even fewer were willing to give his successor a helping hand. The grand ayatollahs—some residing in Iraq, others in Iran—could still influence large numbers of pious Muslims, especially from the older generation. Just because the state was Shi'i did not automatically mean it enjoyed the allegiance of all Shi'is. The new theocracy is haunted by the old Shi'i distrust of the state.

Finally, women harbor a long list of grievances against the Islamic Republic. Although the Western press has largely dwelled on the veil, Iranian women consider the veil as one of their lesser problems. If given a free choice, they would most likely continue to wear the veil since they consider it practical and customary. More important to women are their work-related grievances. They have been purged from some offices and occupations. They are the last hired and the first fired. They are discriminated against in pay scales. They are encouraged to stay home, have babies, raise children, and do housework. To add insult to injury, the law treats them as the wards of their male relatives, requiring them to have legal guidance from their fathers, husbands, or brothers. As a result of all these disaffections, Bazargan in 1995 told a foreign correspondent that the Islamic Republic had become so unpopular that even its own ministers and civil servants were complaining to the Liberation Movement.[41]

INTERESTS, SOCIAL MOVEMENTS, AND PROTESTS

Although the Islamic Revolution was made through mass participation, and although the Islamic constitution guarantees political liberties, the Islamic Republic has become increasingly theocratic and autocratic. There are several explanations for the failure of democracy in Iran.

First, Iran has a long history of autocracy. Like its predecessors, the Islamic Republic claims wide-ranging authority, especially the authority to decide which interest groups can and cannot function. In fact, no political party, professional association, student organization, trade union, or even athletic club can function unless it first obtains government permission. No state recognition—no existence. In this sense, the Islamic Republic operates like a communist state, such as China, with the notable difference that it has no ruling party. By 1994, the Iranian government had recognized some 100 organizations, and boasted of political pluralism. However, the organizations are all noncritical of the regime. The licensed organizations include clubs belonging to the recognized minorities, bazaar guilds and chambers of commerce, the Islamic Association of Students, the Islamic Women's Association, and the Worker's House—a center in Tehran for factory employees who support the regime. These organizations are all controlled by clerics. Other state-approved organizations include the Teachers of the Qom Seminaries, the Society of Militant Clergy, and the Association of the Militant Clergy. At most, less than 1 percent of the population belong to these organizations.

Second, Khomeini and his successors have frequently argued that organizational competition was permissible and even "healthy" as long as all groups pledged allegiance to the Islamic Republic and its Supreme Leader. Any questioning, even of economic policies, could easily be construed as "religious betrayal," "deviation from the correct path," "heresy to Islam," and even as "acts against God Almighty." Such a restriction is hardly conducive to political pluralism.

Third, the legacy of foreign imperialism in Iran has further stifled political pluralism. Since the Western powers have frequently manipulated indigenous forces to undermine national sovereignty—such as the 1953 coup that overthrew Mosaddeq—many have concluded that liberalism gives too much leeway to "dubious" organizations and thus too many opportunities for the "foreign hand" to interfere in Iranian affairs. As Khamenei boasted on the anniversary of Mosaddeq's death, "we are not liberals like Mosaddeq willing to be snuffed out by the CIA."[42] In light of twentieth-century Iranian history, this paranoia is understandable. The clerical elite equates policy differences with foreign intrigue, liberalism with weak-mindedness, and political toleration with permissiveness toward real and imagined "traitors." In their view, there is no compromise with "traitors"; you either lock them up or shoot them.

The increasing distrust of the public is reflected in the official stamps issued to commemorate the revolution. In the early 1980s, the commemorative stamps were full of energy and even depicted real demonstrators. By the late 1980s, the commemorative stamps were highly abstract and stylized. The crowds have become calligraphic as well as regimented and controlled.

Finally, public disillusionment with the Islamic Republic, especially because of the failure to deliver its grand economic promises, has fueled resentment from below and has even sparked some spontaneous strikes and shantytown protests. To prevent such incidents, the regime has increasingly tightened its controls in colleges, high schools, factories, and shantytowns. No organizations, even if pro-regime, are permitted to hold street meetings unless they first obtain government permission, even though the constitution explicitly guarantees the right to assemble.

Although the regime has become more autocratic, it has permitted the two clerical factions—the conservative free-marketers and the radical statists—and their allied associations to function. This, in turn, has permitted a modicum of interest group politics. The conservatives have been able to obtain financial and electoral support from bazaar guilds, chambers of commerce, and farmers' associations. The radicals have obtained assistance from the Islamic Association of Students, the Islamic Association of Teachers, the Islamic Women's Association, and the Worker's House.

The extent, as well as the limitations, of these interest group politics can be seen in the passage of the labor law, which took a full eleven years. Immediately after the revolution, the labor minister, who was a free-marketer conservative, drafted a bill that proposed that almost all labor issues be resolved by employers and employees themselves. His attitude was that the state should not be involved in "private contracts," and that good Muslim employers did not need government regulations to tell them how to treat their employees. Besides, a society that had the Qur'an, the *shari'a,* and the jurist's guardianship did not require a Western-style labor law. He even proposed to do away with child labor restrictions, the minimum wage, mandatory holidays, and the weekly day of rest. This draft caused such an outrage that it had to be withdrawn. Most of the outrage came from the radical clerics in parliament and their friends outside, especially the Worker's House and Islamic Workers' Associations. The head of the Worker's House warned that such a retrogressive bill would drive factory employees into the arms of the Marxist parties.

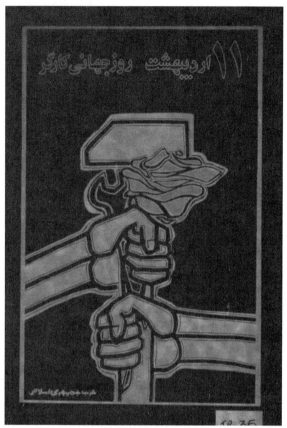

May Day poster issued by the Islamic Republic, 1980.
Source: Poster Collection, Hoover Institution Archives,
Stanford University.

The radical clerics came up with their own fairly comprehensive labor law, which guaranteed pensions, disability pay, health insurance, annual holidays, maximum work hours, minimum wages, job security, and government arbitration. The bill, however, made no mention of independent labor unions. The Worker's House helped pass the bill through the *Majles* in 1986 by holding a series of mass rallies—especially on May Days, celebrating the international Worker's Day. This bill, however, was promptly vetoed by the Guardian Council on the grounds that it was un-Islamic and violated the sanctity of private property. It was precisely this veto that prompted Khomeini in 1987 to create the Expediency Council. He also declared that an Islamic government had absolute rights—even the right to suspend central features of Islam, such as daily prayer and property rights—in order to protect the long-term interests of Islam. The labor minister who had drafted this bill later admitted that the Expediency Council eventually endorsed the legislation in 1989 because of the direct intervention of Hojjat al-Islam Ahmad Khomeini, the Imam's son.[43] The regime that claims to represent the oppressed masses had taken a full decade to enact a fairly mild labor law. But the fact that it had been enacted against the opposition of the employers and the bazaars was clear indication that interest group politics existed within the Islamic Republic.

SECTION 5

Iranian Politics at the Crossroads

POLITICAL CHALLENGES AND CHANGING AGENDAS

In 1995, Bazargan—Khomeini's first prime minister and a man not given to hyperbole—estimated that no more than 5 percent of the population continued to back the Islamic Republic.[44] This was a far cry from the days when millions of people had poured into the streets to support the revolution and over 90 percent of the electorate had endorsed the abolition of the monarchy.

The loss of support is due to the republic's failure to deliver the socioeconomic promises it made during the revolution. The revolution had promised to make Iran fully independent, particularly from the West, and

to lessen the country's heavy reliance on oil exports. It had further promised to lead the nation into the modern world by raising the standard of living, and by providing the masses with jobs, schools, housing, and medical facilities. Furthermore, it had promised to establish "social justice" by narrowing the wide gap between rich and poor, town and country, modern and traditional sectors.

By 1995, few of these promises had been met.[45] Oil continues to provide over 90 percent of the foreign exchange revenue, so that Iran remains a "*rentier* state" and a "one-commodity" exporter. The gross domestic product has fallen by 50 percent; the per capita income by 38 percent. Foreign debt has jumped from zero to

Conventional Western view of the Iranian revolution.
Source: LePelley, © The Christian Science Monitor.

over $17 billion, and the trade imbalance from zero to $6 billion. The value of the currency has plummeted. Inflation has soared to over 30 percent annually. Per capita agricultural output has fallen, causing an increase in food imports. Industry is still heavily dependent on imported raw materials and spare parts that the government can ill afford. Industrial growth has come to a standstill, shrinking the percentage of the labor force in manufacturing from 34 to 24. Unemployment has jumped to 15 percent nationally and over 25 percent in the urban centers. One-third of the entrants into the labor force every year cannot find gainful employment. Salaries and wages have not kept pace with inflation. The purchasing power of government employees has been halved; and in some occupations, such as teaching, it has been quartered.

The rural exodus has continued unabated. The urban sector has increased from 47 to 58 percent. The population of Tehran has grown from 4.5 million to over 10 million. The dismal housing problem has become worse, further expanding the sprawling shantytowns. The absolute number of illiterates has increased from 14 million to 15 million. Their numbers grow annually by 900,000. Despite larger classes and two or three shifts a day, the ratio of school enrollment to school-age population has actually fallen. The ratios of doctors, dentists, nurses, and hospital beds to the total population has also declined by more than 10 percent. The health minister has warned that the country would soon face a major catastrophe unless it took immediate measures to expand medical schools, hire foreign doctors, and attract home émigré doctors who had fled during the revolution.

Overall, the total number of people living in poverty may have increased by as much as 40 percent. Some 9 million urban dwellers earn less than the poverty level as defined by the government. Over 50 percent of the population are still deprived of essential services such as running water, electricity, and health care. According to one parliamentary deputy, 12 million live in dire poverty, 22 million live in near poverty, and another 22 million would find themselves in the same predicament if the annual inflation rate of 30 percent continued.[46]

Cartoon of the clerical regime and its two stilts—the sword and the oil wells.
Source: Courtesy Mojahed (in exile).

Income distribution remains highly unequal despite initial improvements when the new regime confiscated property, controlled prices, and subsidized a large variety of essential goods. By 1986, the richest 20 percent of the urban households accounted for 48 percent of the total urban household expenditures; the middle 40 percent accounted for 37.5 percent; and the poorest 20 percent accounted for as little as 14.6 percent—not much more than before the 1974 oil boom (see Table 8). According to one estimate, the top 10 percent received as much as 33 percent of the national income, while the bottom 10 percent obtained as little as 1.3 percent.[47] One of the clerical newspapers complained that the number of "millionaire families" had increased from 100 to 900, with most of the new rich being bazaar merchants and state-linked contractors.[48] The Pahlavis had enriched the modern industrial bour-

geoisie; the Islamic Republic has enriched the traditional bourgeoisie of the bazaars.

Regional inequalities also continue to exist, especially in per capita numbers of schools, hospitals, doctors, factories, and municipal services.[49] As before, the more developed provinces include Tehran, the Caspian, and the central region. The less developed include Sistan, Baluchestan, and Kurdestan. The only changes have been the movement up of Isfahan from middle-ranking to the more developed, and the movement down of Khurasan, Lurestan, East Azerbaijan, and West Azerbaijan to the less developed. Government investments seem to have improved the relative position of the central provinces—regions that are predominantly Shi'i and Persian-speaking. No doubt, this could have repercussions on future ethnic politics.

The regime's one notable success has been to narrow the urban-rural gap. It has brought schools, roads, clinics, electricity, television, and telephones to many villages. It has provided farmers with fertilizers, pesticides, and agricultural loans. It has raised farm prices to stimulate agricultural production. As a result, the average rural household expenditures as a percentage of average urban household expenditures rose from 47 in 1977 to 61 in 1987. But this improvement went mostly to the more prosperous landed farmers, not to the landless peasants. In 1982, the top 20 percent of the rural households had accounted for 45.2 percent of the rural household expenditures, and the bottom 40 percent for 15.8 percent. By 1986, the top 20 percent accounted for as much as 49.1 percent of the expenditures, and the bottom 40 percent for as little as 13.3 percent.

Iran's economic miseries can be largely attributed to the following four factors: the revolution itself, the Iraqi war, the world oil slump, and the population explosion. These have been compounded by erratic shifts in government policies. The Islamic Revolution, like most revolutions, wrought social havoc, forcing some 1 million professionals, managers, and businessmen to flee the country. This caused a financial as well as a managerial and brain drain. To prevent mass unemployment and industrial shutdown, the government took over their abandoned factories and companies. Between 1979 and 1985, the private sector shrunk whereas the public sector tripled.

The eight-year war with Iraq cost Iran 160,000 lives, $15 billion in lost oil revenues, $30 billion in additional arms expenditures, and $18 billion in mate-

TABLE 8   **Measures of Inequality of Urban Household Consumption Expenditures: 1979, 1980, 1986**

Year	Percentage Share in Total Expenditures		
	Bottom 40%	Middle 40%	Top 10%
1979	12.7	35.8	51.5
1980	15.2	39.9	45.0
1986	14.6	37.5	48.0

Source: V. Nowshirvani and P. Clawson, "The State and Social Equity in Postrevolutionary Iran," in *The Politics of Social Transformation in Afghanistan, Iran, and Pakistan,* ed. M. Weiner and A. Banuazizi (Syracuse: Syracuse University Press, 1994), 248.

rial damage, especially in the leveling of such important cities as Abadan and Khorramshahr. According to one economist, the direct and indirect costs of the war totaled $600 billion.[50] Some suspect that it was this financial drain that eventually forced Khomeini in 1988 to sign the cease-fire, which, in his own words, was like "drinking from the poison chalice." For years, his slogan had been "War, War Until Victory."

The oil slump was even more serious. The international price of oil, which had topped $40 per barrel in 1980, began a steep decline in 1984, hitting a low of $10 per barrel in 1986. By the early 1990s, OPEC was trying hard to prevent prices from falling below $14 per barrel. There were several reasons for this decline: the worldwide economic recession; the slackening of demand in the industrialized countries; the entry of non-OPEC countries, such as Britain and Mexico, into the international market; and the OPEC members themselves exceeding their quotas. In some years, Iran had the additional problem of not being able to meet its own quota because of technical difficulties, especially the lack of deep-drilling equipment.

The decline took a heavy toll on Iran. Its annual oil revenues, which had reached $20 billion before the revolution, fell to $6 billion in 1986. They hovered around $13 billion in the late 1980s and amounted to $12 billion in 1994. The real decline was even more serious than these figures would seem to indicate because Iran—like other OPEC members—is paid in U.S. dollars, the value of which has declined appreciably since the 1970s, especially in relationship to the price of industrial goods imported from Japan and Germany. Oil brought Iran riches in the 1970s, but it brought relative deprivation in the 1980s and 1990s.

The population explosion was equally detrimental to Iran's development. The Shah's regime had managed to lower the annual growth rate from 3.1 to 2.7 percent through birth-control measures, especially contraceptives. But the Islamic Republic, which initially associated numbers of people with national strength, dismantled these measures, prompting the annual population growth to jump at one point to 3.9 percent, one of the highest in the world. Between 1977 and the early 1990s, Iran's population doubled from 30 million to almost 60 million. This caused not only a drain on government resources, especially social services and imported foods, but also a 50-percent decline in real per capita income. The Pahlavi monarchy had faced serious economic challenges, and the Islamic Republic faced even more serious ones, especially by the time Khoemini died in 1989. His successors had no choice but to give priority to these economic problems.

IRANIAN POLITICS IN TRANSITION

The collapse of the Soviet Union, which coincided with Khomeini's death, created widespread fear in the West that Iran's brand of revolutionary Islam would sweep across Central Asia and the Middle East. Many warned that Iran was posed to "export" its revolution to neighboring Afghanistan, Iraq, Turkey, the Gulf states, and elsewhere. These fears proved to be unfounded for two major reasons.

First, the Soviet collapse created not a "window of opportunity" for Iran but a new and lethal danger: Azerbaijani nationalism. The establishment of the independent Republic of Azerbaijan right across the border endangered the very survival of Iran, for this

Ali-Akbar Hashemi Rafsanjani (1934–   )

Rafsanjani was born in 1934 into a fairly prosperous business-farming family in the heartland of the Shi'i and Persian-speaking provinces. He studied in Qom with Khomeini, found himself in prison four separate times during the 1960s, set up a number of commercial companies, including one that exported pistachios, and wrote a book praising a nineteenth-century prime minister who had made an aborted attempt to industrialize the country. Nevertheless, Rafsanjani remained active enough in clerical circles to be considered a hojjat al-Islam. After the revolution, he became a close confidant of Khomeini and attained a number of cabinet posts, culminating with the presidency in 1989.

Ali-Akbar Hashemi Rafsanjani
Source: AP/Wide World Photos.

new republic freely used pan-Turkic symbols, called for union with its "southern" compatriots, and openly courted the large Turkic-speaking Azerbaijani population within Iran. Until the Soviet collapse, the ethnic problem in Iran had been confined to the small Sunni minority and the numerically insignificant non-Muslim communities. After the collapse, the ethnic issue became a potential time bomb, especially since economic difficulties and regional inequalities continued to fuel ethnic grievances. The Islamic Republic is well aware of how ethnic conflicts destroyed the former Yugoslavia and now threaten Afghanistan, Tadzhikistan, and Russia.

Second, the economic crisis in Iran forced Khomeini's successors—Supreme Leader Khamenei and President Rafsanjani—to focus their attention on mundane, bread-and-butter questions. Having consolidated power in 1989–1990, they tried to jump-start the economy by abandoning their previous statist policies and adopting free-market measures.

They stressed that the revolution had been "guilty of excesses." They beseeched their followers to put away "childish slogans." They talked increasingly of realism, stability, efficiency, managerial skills, work discipline, expertise, individual self-reliance, modern technology, entrepreneurship, and business incentives. They warned that the worst mistake a state could make was to spend more than it earned. Rafsanjani declared:

"Some people claim that God will provide. They forget that God provides only for those willing to work." Khamenei sermonized on how Imam Ali, the founder of Shi'i Islam, had taken great care and pride in his plantations. Khomeini had depicted Imam Ali as a humble "water-carrier"; Khamenei depicted him as an entrepreneurial "plantation-owner."[51]

The new policy was not merely rhetoric. The government relaxed price controls; liberalized imports; took some goods off the rationing list; ceased fining hoarders and price gougers; returned some of the confiscated real estate; and withdrew all bills associated with land reform, income redistribution, and nationalization of foreign trade. It set up a stock exchange in Tehran and free-trade zones in the Persian Gulf. It began to privatize some 500 large enterprises nationalized during the revolution. It promised amnesty and tax holidays to émigrés who returned home with capital. It also promised to balance the budget by increasing taxes and cutting subsidies, especially for food and fuel. The president of the chamber of commerce, who was also a prominent *Majles* deputy, fully supported these measures, pointing out that the government subsidies absorbed most of the $12 billion of oil revenues.

The regime also did a complete about-face in its attitude toward foreign loans and investments. It had previously denounced all foreign investments, particularly the 1955 law permitting aliens to own as much as 49 percent of any Iranian company. The Islamic constitution had "absolutely forbidden" foreign loans, concessions, and investments. After 1989, however, Rafsanjani openly sought billions in foreign capital, amended the constitution, and replaced the 1955 law with one permitting foreigners to own as much as 100 percent of companies and to repatriate all their profits. In Rafsanjani's own words, "Our most pressing goal is to convince the world that Iran is ripe for foreign investments and loans." To meet the World Bank's and the International Monetary Fund's (IMF) conditions for future loans, Rafsanjani promised to liberalize trade further, privatize industry, trim expenditures, especially subsidies, increase interest rates, remove price controls, and water down the much-disputed labor law.

The regime did a similar about-face on the population issue. It declared that Islam required healthy rather than large families and that one literate soldier was better than ten illiterate ones. It reopened birth-control clinics, cut subsidies for large families, and announced that the ideal family should consist of no more than two children. By 1994, the government was boasting that it had reduced the annual population growth from 3.8 to 1.8 percent. Some argued that this was impossible. Others argued that the reduction was due to economic hardships that forced women to delay both marriage and pregnancy.

Closely related to the population issue was the government's changing policy toward women. The regime raised the marriage age to fifteen, implicitly contradicting the age set by the *shari'a*. It allowed women—often relatives of prominent clerics—to organize associations, publish papers, form a parliamentary lobby, and enter professions previously closed to them, such as law, geology, architecture, agriculture, and veterinary medicine. It encouraged women to include in their marriage contracts a special clause permitting divorce if their husbands took a second wife. Such suggestions had previously been considered un-Islamic. Now they were considered part and parcel of true Islam. Even more surprising, the Expediency Council in 1994 ruled that divorced women could collect as much as half of the property that the family had accumulated during the marriage. Although lower courts are unlikely to implement such progressive decisions, some observers had talked of the emergence of Islamic "feminism" and even of "fundamentalist feminism."

The economic reforms, however, have had mixed results. The opening up of trade led to a substantial influx of goods since the previous years had bottled up consumer demands. This influx led to a balance-of-trade crisis, a foreign exchange crisis, and a currency crisis. The U.S. dollar, which had equaled 80 rials before the revolution and 1,648 rials in 1989, rose to 3,000 in 1995. The foreign debt reached a new high of $17 billion with the government having serious difficulties servicing its $8 billion short-term debt. These debts, in turn, led to a further rise in prices; the closing down of factories left without foreign spare parts and raw materials; more factory layoffs; and further erosion in incomes and the standard of living. Liberalization had intensified rather than alleviated the economic crisis.

The new economic policy failed in many other ways as well. As of 1995, only 14 of the 500 largest state enterprises had been privatized. Wealthy bazaaris prefer to invest in trade, especially since these factories have never been really profitable. The labor law remains intact; talk of changing it sparked workers' petitions and demonstrations. Direct taxes, particularly on the bazaars, continue to be extremely light. Businessmen pay as little as 1 percent of their profits in taxes. Taxation provides the government with only 15 percent of its revenues.

The free-trade zones have failed to develop. Few émigrés have dared to return, and the few who have have not brought back their capital. More capital flows out than in. The wooing of foreign capital has fallen on deaf ears even though these free-market measures met the stringent IMF and World Bank requirements. Western companies prefer to invest in Eastern Europe and the Far East, where the markets are bigger and the labor forces are better trained. It should be remembered that even in the Pahlavi heyday few multinational corporations had been willing to actually invest in Iran. The paltry sums the World Bank and the IMF have voted to give to Iran—mainly for education and earthquake relief—have been blocked by the United States. The Clinton administration refuses to give any assistance until Iran lifts the death warrant on Rushdie, stops assassinating opponents abroad, scraps its nuclear-weapons program, ceases opposing the Israeli-Palestinian peace process, and cuts off assistance to Islamic movements in Algeria and Gaza.

These foreign policy problems, together with the continued economic crisis, have gradually divided the conservative free-marketers who won the 1992 elections for the Fourth *Majles*. One bloc, totaling some 175 deputies, has become more cautious in economic matters while remaining conservative in social issues. Violent riots in five cities have persuaded these deputies that subsidy cuts, especially for food, fuel, and medicine, are far too dangerous. The deputies have been instrumental in reimposing price controls, reinstalling courts to punish speculators, financing inefficient enterprises to prevent further layoffs, and protecting the large clerical foundations from government scrutiny. At the same time, they favor the continued persecution of the Bahais, the total Islamization of the mass media, the banning of satellite dishes that give Iranians access to CNN and the BBC, and the strict enforcement of the veil regulations. In foreign affairs, they want to keep the Rushdie affair alive, inflame the Palestinian conflict, and continue to denounce the United States as the Great Satan. They have the ear of Khamenei, the Supreme Leader.

The other bloc, numbering forty or so deputies, enjoys presidential support and backs Rafsanjani's policies of trying to normalize relations with the United States, woo back émigrés, relax cultural controls, and further liberalize the economy. These deputies prefer to open up the press, treat the Bahais and dissenters more leniently, build bridges to the Liberation Movement, and make more concessions to women, especially over what constitutes proper Islamic dress. They frequently warn of the "dangers of dogmatism." The first bloc can be described as the conservative free-marketers; the second as the liberal free-marketers.

The attitude of the radical clerics remains ambivalent. Even though these clerics have lost their power within the *Majles,* they remain influential outside. On the one hand, they may side with the conservatives on issues of foreign policy and state subsidies. On the other hand, they distrust Khamenei and consider cultural issues, particularly the veil, as distractions from the more important task of economic modernization. Some even advocate cultural diversity, political toleration, and free press. This belies the conventional notion that those who are radical in economics are inevitably autocratic in politics—and vice versa, that those who are liberal in economics are tolerant in politics.

The divisions among the clerics became glaringly obvious in 1994 to 1995 when Khamenei's supporters launched a campaign to portray him as the Supreme Jurist of Shi'ism as well as the Supreme Leader of the Islamic Republic. They hoped to give him scholastic authority in addition to political power. Few joined the campaign for the simple reason that Khamenei lacked the academic qualifications. He may have been qualified to be a medium-ranking teacher of theology in Mashad, but he certainly lacked the publication prerequisites to be a grand ayatollah at the main seminaries pronouncing on the intricacies of Islamic jurisprudence. Some clerics recognized as prominent jurists three grand ayatollahs who resided in Iran, all three of whom shunned politics. Others supported a grand ayatollah in Najaf who had opposed Khomeini and his concept of jurist's guardianship. Still others dared to back Grand Ayatollah Montazeri, who, at one time, had been designated as Khomeini's heir as Supreme Jurist, but had then been hastily disqualified when he had denounced the regime for gross violations of human rights. He lives in Qom under house arrest. Khomeini's disciples had gained control of the Iranian state, but not of the Shi'i establishment.

IRAN IN COMPARATIVE PERSPECTIVE

Iran is both like and unlike the rest of the Third World. Unlike most Third World countries, it is an old state with institutions that go back to the ancient Persians and Greeks. Unlike most others, it is not a newly independent country since it was never formally taken over by the imperial powers. It remained officially independent, even at the height of European imperialism. Unlike most others, it has a religion that links the elite with the masses, the cities with the villages, the state with the citizenry. Shi'ism, as well as Iranian identity, serves as social cement, giving the population a collective identity. Unlike most Third World countries, it possesses rich oil resources and thus has the potential for rapid economic development. And unlike most others, it has produced two popular upheavals in the twentieth century: the constitutional and the Islamic revolutions. In both, the citizenry actively intervened in politics, overthrowing the old regime and shaping the new. The Islamic Republic and the 1905 constitution were authentic home products, not foreign imports.

Yet Iran shares some problems with much of the Third World. It has failed to establish a viable democracy. Its economy remains underdeveloped, highly reliant on one commodity, and unable to meet the revolution of rising expectations. Its collective identity is strained by internal fault lines, especially those of class, ethnic, secular-religious, and interclerical conflicts. And its ambition to enter the world of states as an important player has been thwarted by international as well as internal and regional realities. In fact, this ambition has helped to undermine democracy, economic development, and collective identity even further.

Democracy has been replaced by theocracy. Some argue that Islam made this inevitable. But Islam, like Christianity and the other major religions, can be interpreted in ways that either support or oppose democracy. Islam stresses the importance of justice, equality, and consultation. It has a tradition of tolerating other religions. Its *shari'a* explicitly protects life, property, and honor. In practice, if not always in theory, it has separated politics from religion, statutes from holy laws, spiritual affairs from worldly matters, and the state from the clerical establishment.

Moreover, this theocracy originates not in Islam but in the jurist's guardianship, a new concept developed by Khomeini out of Shi'ism. Sunni Islam considers the clerics to be merely theological scholars, not a special stratum. This helps explain why the Iranian revolution is difficult to export to the rest of the Muslim world. The failure of democracy in Iran can be attributed less to Islam than to the confluence of the 1979–1981 crises that allowed a small group of clerics to seize power. Whether they remain in power depends no so much on Islam as on how they handle the opposition, their own differences, and, most important of all, the country's horrendous economic problems.

The Islamic Republic is sharply divided on how to manage an economy beset by rising demands, falling petroleum revenues, and the looming nightmare that in the next two generations the oil wells will run dry. Most clerics favor the conventional capitalist road to development, hoping to liberalize the market, privatize industry, attract foreign capital, and encourage the propertied classes to invest. Others envisage an equally conventional statist road to development, favoring central planning, government industries, price controls, high taxes, state subsidies, national self-reliance, and ambitious programs to eliminate poverty, illiteracy, slums, and unemployment.

As the clock ticks, the population grows, oil revenues stagnate, and the per capita national income falls. The economic problems that undermined the monar-

chy could well undermine the Islamic Republic as well. Only time will tell whether social discontent will be expressed through apolitical channels, such as drug addiction, emigration, and quietist religion; through the radical clerics remaining within the regime; through insurrectionary organizations such as the Mojahedin; or through new ethnically based movements in the provinces.

Iran's collective identity has come under great strain in recent years. The emphasis on Shi'ism has obviously alienated the Sunnis as well as the non-Muslims. The emphasis on clerical Shi'ism has further alienated all secularists, including lay liberals, radical leftists, and moderate nationalists. Furthermore, the emphasis on Khomeini's brand of Shi'ism has alienated Shi'is who reject the whole notion of the jurist's guardianship. And the elevation of Khamanei as the Supreme Leader has antagonized many early proponents of the jurist's guardianship. In short, the regime has used slicing tactics on itself, gradually reducing its social base to a bare minimum.

The recent creation of the independent Republic of Azerbaijan poses a potential problem for the long-term future of Iran. Its future hinges on the question of whether the many Turkic-speaking Azerbaijanis in Iran will continue to see themselves as Shi'is and Iranians, as they have in the past, or whether they will take on a new Turkic-Azerbaijani identity. If they do the latter, Iran will suffer either a major secession or a violent civil war like those in the Caucasus and the former Yugoslavia. It will be ironic if the Islamic Republic ends up destroying Iranian identity as well as the 2,500-year-old monarchy.

Finally, the Islamic Republic's attempt to enter the international arena as a militant force has been counterproductive. It has diverted scarce resources to the military, especially the navy and the revolutionary guards. It has frightened Saudi Arabia and the Gulf sheikhdoms into the arms of the United States. It has prompted the United States to isolate Iran, discouraging investments and preventing international organizations from extending it economic assistance. It has also frightened the neighboring secular states such as Turkey, Tadzhikistan, and Azerbaijan, not to mention Iraq. It has strained relations with some other Third World countries, including India. Moreover, Iran has discovered that its brand of Islam is not very exportable to the Sunni world. The West may perceive Iran as the vanguard of the Islamic radicalism that is spreading throughout the Middle East and North Africa. But the Sunni world sees Iran much more as a unique Shi'i phenomenon. Only the future will show whether the 1979 Islamic Revolution can be repeated elsewhere.

Key Terms

Ayatollah	jurist's guardianship
Imam	mosque
theocracy	OPEC
shari'a	*hojjat al-Islams*
Farsi	*Imam Jum'ehs*
Guardian Council	Foundation of the
bazaar	Oppressed
fundamentalism	

Suggested Readings

Section 1

Abrahamian, E. *Iran Between Two Revolutions.* Princeton, N.J.: Princeton University Press, 1982.

Arjomand, S. *The Turban for the Crown.* New York: Oxford University Press, 1988.

Bill, J. *The Eagle and the Lion.* New Haven, Conn.: Yale University Press, 1988.

Green, J. *Revolution in Iran.* New York: Praeger, 1982.

Kapuscinski, R. *Shah of Shahs.* New York: Vintage Books, 1986.

Keddie, N. *Roots of Revolution.* New Haven, Conn.: Yale University Press, 1981.

———. "The Iranian Revolution in Comparative Perspective." *American Historical Review* 88, no. 3 (June 1983): 579–598.

Mottahedeh, R. *The Mantle of the Prophet.* New York: Simon and Schuster, 1985.

Section 2

Amirahmadi, H. *Revolution and Economic Transition.* Albany, N.Y.: State University of New York Press, 1990.

Amuzegar, J. *Iran's Economy Under the Islamic Republic.* London: Taurus Press, 1994.

Foran, J. *Fragile Resistance: Social Transformation in Iran from 1500 to the Revolution.* Boulder, Colo.: Westview Press, 1993.

Katouzian, H. *The Political Economy of Modern Iran.* New York: New York University Press, 1981.

Pesaran, M. "Dependent Capitalism in Pre- and Post-Revolutionary Iran." *International Journal of Middle East Studies* 14, no. 4 (November 1982): 501–522.

Section 3

Abrahamian, E. *Khomeinism.* Berkeley: University of California Press, 1993.

Bakhash, S. *The Reign of the Ayatollahs.* New York: Basic Books, 1984.

Banuazizi, A., and M. Weiner, eds. *The State, Religion, and Ethnic Politics.* Syracuse, N.Y.: Syracuse University Press, 1986.

Milani, M. "Shi'ism and the State in the Constitution of the Islamic Republic of Iran." In *Iran: Political Culture in the Islamic Republic,* ed. S. Farsoun and M. Mashayekhi. New York: Routledge, 1993.

Saffari, "The Legitimation of the Clergy's Right to Rule in the Iranian Constitution of 1979." *British Journal of Middle Eastern Studies* 20, no. 1 (1993): 64–81.

Section 4

Abrahamian, E. *The Iranian Mojahedin.* New Haven, Conn.: Yale University Press, 1989.

Akhavi, S. "Shi'ism, Corporatism, and Rentierism in the Iranian Revolution." In *Comparing Muslim Societies,* edited by J. Cole. Ann Arbor: Michigan University Press, 1992.

———. "Elite Factionalism in the Islamic Republic of Iran." *Middle East Journal* 41, no. 2 (Spring 1987): 181–201.

Sarabi, F. "The Post-Khomeini Era in Iran: The Elections of the Fourth Islamic Majlis." *Middle East Journal* 48, no. 1 (Winter 1994): 89–107.

Siavoshi, S. "Factionalism and Iranian Politics: The Post-Khomeini Experience." *Iranian Studies* 25, nos. 3–4 (1992): 27–49.

Section 5

Aghajanian, A. "Ethnic Inequality in Iran." *International Journal of Middle East Studies* 15, no. 2 (May 1983): 211–224.

Banuazizi, A., and M. Weiner, eds. *The Politics of Social Transformation in Afghanistan, Iran, and Pakistan.* Syracuse, N.Y.: Syracuse University Press, 1994.

Behrooz, M. "Factionalism in Iran under Khomeini." *Middle Eastern Studies* 27, no. 4 (October 1991): 597–614.

Ramazani, N. "Women in Iran: The Revolutionary Ebb and Flow." *Middle East Journal* 47, no. 3 (Summer 1993): 407–428.

Ramazani, R. *Revolutionary Iran.* Baltimore, Md.: Johns Hopkins University Press, 1986.

Sharbatoghlie, A. *Urbanization and Regional Disparities in Post-Revolutionary Iran.* Boulder, Colo.: Westview Press, 1994.

Endnotes

[1] Quoted in E. Browne, *The Persian Revolution* (London: Barnes and Nobles, 1910), 137.

[2] British Financial Adviser to the Foreign Office in Tehran, *Documents on British Foreign Policy, 1919–39* (London: Government Printing Office, 1963), First Series, XIII, 720, 735.

[3] British Minister to the Foreign Office, "Report on the Seizure of Lands," Foreign Office 371/Persia 1932/File 34-16007.

[4] American ambassador to the State Department, June 26, 1945, *Foreign Relations of the United States for 1945* (Washington, D.C.: U.S. Government Printing Office, 1965), VIII, 385.

[5] *New York Times,* January 10, 1979.

[6] *Iran Times,* March 2, 1984.

[7] *Kayhan International,* November 10, 1976.

[8] Editorial, "Fifty Marks of Treason in Fifty Years of Treason," *Khabarnameh,* no. 46 (April 1976).

[9]*New York Times,* December 17, 1978; November 7, 1979.

[10]M. Bazargan, "Letter to the Editor," *Ettela'at,* February 7, 1980.

[11]*Iran Times,* January 12, 1979.

[12]"Text of the Mass Rally of Ashura," *Khabarnameh,* December 15, 1978.

[13]*Washington Post,* December 12, 1978.

[14]*Christian Science Monitor,* December 12, 1978.

[15]Mirza Hosayn Khan Tahvildar-e Isfahan, *Jukhrafiha-ye Isfahan (The Geography of Isfahan)* (Tehran: Tehran University Press, 1963), 100–101.

[16]International Labor Office, "Employment and Income Policies for Iran (unpublished report, Geneva, 1972), Appendix C, 6.

[17]A. Sharbatoghilie, *Urbanization and Regional Disparity in Post-Revolutionary Iran* (Boulder, Colo.: Westview Press, 1991), 4.

[18]*Wall Street Journal,* November 4, 1977.

[19]Congressional Report, *Economic Consequences of the Revolution in Iran* (Washington, D.C.: U.S. Government Printing Office, 1979), 184.

[20]*Ibid,* 5.

[21]U.S. Department of Commerce, *Iran: A Survey of U.S. Business Opportunities* (Washington, D.C.: U.S. Government Printing Office, 1977), 1–2.

[22]*Iran Times,* August 6, 1993.

[23]S. Najafabadi, *Velayat-e Faqeh: Hokumat-e Salihan (Jurist's Guardianship: Worthy Government)* (Tehran: Rasa Press, 1982).

[24]Hojjat al-Islam Rafsanjani, "The Islamic Consultative Assembly," *Kayhan,* May 23, 1987.

[25]S. Saffari, "The Legitimation of the Clergy's Right to Rule in the Iranian Constitution of 1979," in *British Journal of Middle Eastern Studies* 20, no. 1 (1993): 64–81.

[26]Ayatollah Montazeri, *Ettela'at,* October 8, 1979.

[27]O. Fallaci, "Interview with Khomeini," *New York Times Magazine,* October 7, 1979.

[28]Cited in *Iran Times,* July 9, 1993.

[29]E. Abrahamian, *The Iranian Mojahedin* (New Haven, Conn.: Yale University Press, 1989), 66.

[30]J. Amuzegar, *Iran's Economy Under the Islamic Republic* (London: Taurus Press, 1994), 100.

[31]Cited in *Iran Times,* July 9, 1993.

[32]Amuzegar, *Iran's Economy,* 101.

[33]*Kayhan,* March 6, 1980.

[34]Islamic Majles, *Ashna'i beh Majles-e Showraye-e Islami (Guide to the Islamic Consultative Assembly)* (Tehran: Majles Publishing House, 1982), Vols. 1–2.

[35]Islamic Majles, "Sketch of the Assembly," *Kayhan-e Hava'i,* September 18, 1985. In this sketch, the aggregate figures are reversed so as to give the clerics 45 percent and the lay members 55 percent.

[36]*Kayhan,* April 21, 1987.

[37]*Kayhan-e-Hava'i,* November 16, 1988.

[38]The Cultural Affairs Office of the Islamic Republic, *Moarefi-ye Nemayandegan-e Majles-e Islami (Introduction to the Members of the Islamic Majles)* (Tehran: Majles Publishing House, 1989).

[39]A. Rafsanjani, Friday sermon, *Kayhan,* November 4, 1989. For the sources of these quotations below see E. Abrahamian, *Khomeinism* (Berkeley: University of California Press, 1993), 131–36.

[40]F. Sarabi, "The Post-Khomeini Era in Iran: The Elections of the Fourth Islamic Majlis," *Middle East Journal* 48, no. 1 (Winter 1994): 89–107.

[41]Interview with M. Bazargan, *Iran Times,* January 27, 1995.

[42]*Ettela'at,* March 5, 1981.

[43]Interview with the former Labor Minister, *Salam,* January 9–25, 1993.

[44]Interview with M. Bazargan, *Iran Times,* January 27, 1995.

[45]Statistics in this chapter have been obtained predominantly from J. Amuzegar, *Iran's Economy Under the Islamic Republic* (London: Taurus Press, 1994); V. Nowshirvani and P. Clawson, "The State and Social Equity in Postrevolutionary Iran," in *The Politics of Social Transformation in Afghanistan, Iran, and Pakistan,* ed. M. Weiner and A. Banuazizi (Syracuse, N.Y.: Syracuse University Press, 1994), 228–332.

[46]Cited in H. Amirahmadi, *Revolution and Economic Transition* (Albany: State University of New York Press, 1990), 196.

[47]*Ibid.,* p. 201.

[48]Cited in *ibid.,* p. 201.

[49]A. Sharbatoghlie, *Urbanization and Regional Disparities in Post-Revolutionary Iran* (Boulder, Colo.: Westview Press, 1994), 117–38.

[50]Amirahmadi, *Revolution and Economic Transition,* 54.

[51]*Kayhan-e Hava'i,* October 11, 1989.

Appendix

Land and Population

Capital	Washington, D.C.
Total Area (square miles)	3,618,765 (about 2-1/2 times size of Western Europe)
Population	257.8 million
Annual Projected Population Growth Rate (1993–2000)	0.9%
Urban Population (% of total)	76%

Ethnic Composition

Ethnic and National Identity	White	75%
	Black	12%
	Hispanic	10%
	Asian and Pacific Islander	3%
	American Indian and Eskimo	1%
Major Languages	English, Spanish (spoken by sizable minority)	
Major Religions	Protestant	53%
	Roman Catholic	26%
	Other Christian	8%
	Jewish	2%
	Muslim	2%
	Other	2%
	Nonreligious	8%

Economy

Domestic Currency	Dollar
GNP (US$)	$6.4 trillion
GNP per capita (US$)	$24,740
Purchasing Power Parity GDP per capita (US$)	$24,740
Average Annual GDP Growth Rate (1980–1993)	2.7%

Structure of Production (% of GDP)	Agriculture	2%
	Industry	29%
	Services	69%
Labor Force Distribution (% of total)	Agriculture	3%
	Industry	25%
	Services	72%
Women as % of Total Labor Force	41%	

Income Distribution (1985)	% of Population	% Share of Income or Consumption
	Richest 20%	41.9%
	Poorest 20%	4.7%
Total Foreign Trade (exports plus imports) as % of GDP	16%	

Society

Life Expectancy	Female	79
	Male	73
Population per Doctor	420	
Infant Mortality (per 1,000 live births)	9	
Adult Literacy*	97%	
Average (Mean) Years of Schooling (of adults 25+)	Female	12.5
	Male	12.3
Communications (per 100 people)	Radios	212
	Televisions	81
	Telephones	79
1995 Human Development Index (1 = highest)	Ranks 2 out of 174	

Political Organization

Political System   Presidential system

Regime History   Representative democracy, usually dated from the signing of the Declaration of Independence (1776) or the Constitution (1787).

Administrative Structure   Federalism, with powers shared between the national government and the fifty state governments; separation of powers at the level of the national government among legislative, executive, and judicial branches.

Executive   President, "directly" elected (with Electoral College that officially elects president and vice president) for four-year term; cabinet is advisory group selected by president to aid in decision-making but with no formal authority.

Legislature   Bicameral. Congress comprised of a lower house (House of Representatives) of 435 members serving two-year terms and upper house (Senate) of 100 members (two from each state) serving six-year terms; elected in single-member districts (or, in the case of the Senate, states) by simple plurality.

Judiciary   Supreme Court with nine justices nominated by president and confirmed by Senate, with life tenure; has specified original and appellate jurisdiction and exercises the power of judicial review (can declare acts of the legislature and executive unconstitutional and therefore null and void).

Party System   Two-party system (Republican and Democrat), with relatively weak and fractionalized parties; more than in most representative democracies the personal following of candidates remains very important.

* Studies in the late 1980s indicate that adult "functional" literacy may not exceed 85%.

*Glossary**

accountability   a government's responsibility to its population, usually by periodic popular elections and (in **parliamentary systems**) by parliament having the power to dismiss the government by passing a motion of no-confidence. In a political system characterized by accountability, the major actions taken by government must be known and understood by the citizenry. (See **democracy.**)

acephalous societies   literally "headless" societies. A number of traditional Nigerian societies, such as the Igbo in the precolonial period, lacked executive rulership as we have come to conceive of it. Instead, the villages and clans were governed by committee or consensus.

administrative court   court that hears cases from private citizens and organizations involving allegations of bureaucratic violations of rules and laws. In Germany, the third branch of the court system, consisting of the Labor Court, the Social Security Court, and the Finance Court. In France, the highest administrative court is the Council of State.

administrative guidance   in Japan, informal guidance, usually not based on a statute or formal regulation, that is given by a government agency, such as a ministry and its subdivisions, to a private organization, such as a firm, or a lower-level government. The lack of transparency of the practice makes it subject to criticisms as a disguised form of collusion between a government agency and a firm.

amakudari   a Japanese practice, known as "descent from heaven," in which government officials retiring from their administrative positions take jobs in public corporations or private firms under their own ministry's jurisdiction.

anarchy   a condition in which government authority and social order break down and lawlessness is widespread.

ancien régime   the monarchical **regime** that ruled France until the Revolution of 1789, when it was toppled by a popular uprising. The term is used to describe long-established regimes in other countries ruled by undemocratic elites.

anticlericalism   opposition to the power of churches or clergy in politics. In some countries, for example, France and Mexico, this opposition has focused on the role of the Catholic church in politics.

Association of Southeast Asian Nations (ASEAN)   an organization formed in 1967 to promote regional economic and political cooperation. In 1995, ASEAN consisted of six member states: Brunei, Indonesia, Malaysia, the Philippines, Singapore, and Thailand. Laos, Myanmer, and Vietnam were expected to join the organization shortly.

autarky   a situation in which a country is economically self-sufficient and isolates itself from the international economic system.

authoritarian   (See **authoritarianism.**)

authoritarianism   a system of rule in which power does not depend on popular legitimacy but rather on the coercive force of the political authorities. Hence there are few personal and group freedoms. It is also characterized by near absolute power in the executive branch, and little if any legislative and judicial controls. (See **autocracy, fascism, patrimonialism.**)

autocracy   a government in which one or a few rulers has absolute power, thus, a **dictatorship.** Similar to **authoritarianism.**

autonomous region   in the People's Republic of China, a territorial unit equivalent to a province that contains a large concentration of ethnic minorities. These regions have some autonomy in the cultural sphere but in most policy matters are strictly subordinate to the central government.

autonomous republic   a territorial unit in the Soviet Union which was a constituent unit of the **union republic** within which it was located; autonomous republics were populated by a large national (**ethnic**) group, after which the autonomous republic was generally named. They enjoyed little actual autonomy in the Soviet period. Once Russia adopted its new constitution in 1993, those autonomous republics within Russian territory became constituent units (now called republics) of the Russian Federation.

Ayatollah   literally, God's symbol. High-ranking clerics in Iran. The most senior ones—often no more than half a dozen—are known as Grand Ayatollahs.

balance of payments   an indicator of international flow of funds, it shows the excess or deficit in total payments of all kinds between or among countries. Included in the calculation are exports and imports, grants, and international debt payments.

Basic Law (*Grundgesetz*)   German document establishing the founding of the Federal Republic of Germany (West Germany) in 1949. Similar to a written constitution.

bazaar   an urban marketplace where shops, workshops, small businessmen, and even export-importers are located.

Brahmin(s)   highest caste in the Hindu caste system, who traditionally dominated the Hindu society of India.

---

* Note: Boldface terms *within* a definition can be found as separate entries in the Glossary.

brain drain   the emigration of highly educated people from one country to another, particularly from Third World to the developed countries.

bureaucracy   an organization structured hierarchically, in which lower-level officials are charged with administering regulations codified in rules which specify impersonal, objective guidelines for making decisions. In the modern world, many large organizations, especially business firms and the executives of developed states, are organized along bureaucratic lines.

bushi   the warrior class in medieval Japan, known also as *samurai.* The class emerged around the tenth century A.D. and a dominant band established Japan's first warrior government in the twelfth century. The last warrior government was overthrown in the Meiji Restoration of the mid-nineteenth century.

cabinet   the ministers who direct executive departments. In **parliamentary systems,** the cabinet and high-ranking sub-cabinet ministers (also known as the government) are considered collectively responsible to parliament.

cadre   a person who occupies a position of authority in a **communist party-state;** cadres may or may not be communist party members.

capital flight   when a government adopts measures which private investors fear will harm their interests, they may send their money (capital) to other countries.

capitalism   an economic system in which productive assets (capital) are privately owned, rather than owned by the state or workers in a given firm, and in which resources are allocated primarily on the basis of supply and demand, that is, market competition. In a capitalist system, production is carried on for profit, that is, owners of capital make investment decisions on the basis of what they judge will bring them the highest profits. (See **capital flight, communism, socialism.**)

caste system   India's Hindu society is divided into castes. According to the Hindu religion, membership in a given caste is determined at birth. Castes form a rough social and economic hierarchy. (See **Brahmins, untouchables.**)

central planning   (See **command economy.**)

chancellor   the German head of government. Functional equivalent of prime minister in other parliamentary systems.

charisma   the ability of a leader to attract an intensely devoted following because of personal characteristics that supporters believe endows the charismatic leader with extraordinary and heroic qualities.

citizen action groups   formed in Germany in the 1970s, forerunner of the Greens Party.

civil servants   state employees who make up the bureaucracy.

civil society   refers to the space occupied by voluntary associations *outside* the state, for example, professional associations (lawyers, doctors, teachers), trade unions, student and women's groups and religious bodies, and other voluntary association groups. The term is similar to **society,** although civil society implies a degree of organization absent from the more inclusive term *society.*

clientelism   (or **patron-client relations**) an informal aspect of policy-making in which a powerful patron (for example, a traditional local boss, government agency, or dominant party) offers resources such as land, contracts, protection, or jobs in return for the support and services (such as labor or votes) of lower status and less powerful clients; corruption, preferential treatment, and inequality are characteristic of clientelist politics. (See **patrimonialism, prebendalism.**)

co-determination   German legal mechanism which authorizes trade union members in firms with 2,000 or more employees to have nearly 50 percent of the seats on the firm's board of directors.

cohabitation   the term used by the French to describe the situation in the Fifth Republic when a president and prime minister belong to opposing political coalitions.

Cold War   the term designates the hostile relations that prevailed between the United States and the USSR from the late 1940s until the demise of the Soviet Union in 1991. Although an actual (hot) war never directly occurred between the two superpowers, they clashed indirectly by supporting rival forces in many wars occurring in the Third World.

collective responsibility   a basic principle relating to the decision-making role and procedures of the **cabinet** in **parliamentary systems,** which requires that the cabinet—and not the prime minister alone—assume responsibility for government policy and for directing the entire executive, and that all cabinet members and senior sub-cabinet–level ministers publicly support all policy.

collectivization   a process undertaken in the Soviet Union under Stalin in the late 1920s and early 1930s, and in China under Mao in the 1950s, by which agricultural land was removed from private ownership and organized into large state and collective farms.

colonialism   the practice of establishing direct political domination over another nation or territory for the purpose of exploiting its natural resources, securing privileged access to domestic markets, and gaining geopolitical power. Similar to **imperialism,** although imperialist control of an area can occur without direct colonial (political) rule. (See **neocolonialism.**)

command economy   a form of **socialism** in which government decisions ("commands") rather than market mechanisms (such as supply and demand) are the major influences in determining the nation's economic direction; also called **central planning.**

Commonwealth   the association of independent states which evolved from the British Empire, including the United Kingdom and former British colonies or dependent territories.

communism   a system of social organization based on the common ownership and coordination of production; according to Marxism (the theory of German philosopher Karl Marx, 1818–1883), communism is a culminating stage of history, following **capitalism** and **socialism.** In historical practice, leaders of China, the Soviet Union, and other states who have proclaimed themselves seeking to achieve communism have ruled through a single party, the communist party, which has controlled the state and society in an authoritarian manner, and have applied **Marxism-Leninism** to justify their rule.

communist   (See **communism.**)

communist party-state   a type of **nation-state** in which the communist party attempts to exercise a complete monopoly on political power and controls all important state institutions. (See **communism.**)

company union   a labor union that consists of employees of one company. Japanese labor unions are largely company unions in this sense. Such unions tend to be more sensitive to the company's interests and more willing to cooperate with its management than unions organized on a craft or industrial basis, like most unions in Western Europe and North America.

comparative politics   the study of the domestic politics, political institutions, and conflicts of countries. Often involves comparisons among countries and through time within single countries, emphasizing key patterns of similarity and difference.

Confucianism   a social philosophy based on the teachings of the Chinese sage, Confucius (c. 551–479 B.C.) that emphasizes social harmony, righteous behavior toward others, and deference to one's superiors. Confucianism remains a major source of cultural values in the countries of East Asia, including China and Japan.

conservative   the belief that existing political, social, and economic arrangements should be preserved. Historically, this has involved a defense of the inequalities (of class, race, gender, and so on) that are part of the existing order; often

used to identify the economic and social policies favored by right-of-center parties.

cooptation   incorporating activists into the system while accommodating some of their concerns.

corporatism   a pattern of organizing interests and influencing public policy in which the state gives favored status to certain **interest groups;** typically involves tripartite (three-way) consultations among representatives of business, labor, and government over economic policy. Corporatism can occur in both **democratic** and **authoritarian** settings. However, it is usually criticized for the fact that it limits open debate and representative processes. (See **neocorporatism, state corporatism.**)

corporatist philosophy   (See **corporatism.**)

country   a territorial unit controlled by a single state. Countries vary in the degree to which groups within them have a common culture and ethnic affiliation. (See **ethnicity, nation-state, state.**)

coup   (or **coup d'état**) the sudden, illegal seizure of political power by a small group of people, usually military officers.

Cultural Revolution   a movement in China in 1966–1976 when Mao Zedong and other radical communist leaders sought to purge their political opponents and steer the country in the direction of what they saw as a purer form of **communism.**

danwei   a Chinese terms that means "unit" and is the basic level of social organization and a major means of political control in China's **communist party-state.** A person's *danwei* is most often his or her workplace, such as a factory or an office.

decentralization   policies that aim to transfer some decision-making power from higher to lower levels of government, typically, from the central government to subnational governments.

democracy   a political regime in which leaders are chosen by citizens in elections which are free and fair. For a regime to qualify as democratic, all citizens must possess the legal right to compete for office and vote, critics of the government must have the right to express their opposition, and the government must be accountable to the electorate, the parliament, and/or judicial authorities.

democratic   (See **democracy.**)

democratic centralism   a system of political organization developed by V. I. Lenin and practiced, with modifications, by all **communist party-states.** Its principles include a hierarchical party structure in which (a) party leaders are elected on a delegate basis from lower to higher party bodies;

(b) party leaders can be recalled by those who elected them; and (c) freedom of discussion is permitted until a decision is taken, but strict discipline and unity should prevail in implementing a decision once it is made. In practice, in all communist parties in China, the Soviet Union, and elsewhere, centralizing elements tended to predominate over the democratic ones.

democratic socialism   a form of socialism which seeks to organize the political system and economy in a participatory manner. In contrast to **social democracy,** which accepts the existence of a market or capitalist economy, and the informal pattern of **neocorporatism,** democratic socialism seeks to maximize public ownership of firms, decentralize government, and achieve grassroots democracy. In contrast to **communism,** democratic socialism emphasizes the importance of democratic processes and a private sphere outside state control.

demokratizatsiia   the policy of democratization identified by former Soviet leader Mikhail Gorbachev in 1987 as an essential component of **perestroika.** The policy was part of a gradual shift away from a vanguard party approach toward an acceptance of **liberal** democratic norms. Initially, the policy embraced multicandidate elections for the soviets and a broadening of political competition within the Communist Party itself; after 1989 it involved acceptance of a multiparty system.

destape   announcement (unveiling) of the Mexican presidential candidate by the PRI. The selection is made by the incumbent PRI president.

détente   a relaxation of tensions between formerly hostile nations that moves them toward more normal diplomatic relations. Often used to describe a thaw in the **Cold War** beginning in the 1960s.

developmental state   a **nation-state** in which the government carries out policies that effectively promote national economic growth.

developmentalism   an ideology and practice in Latin America during the 1950s in which the state played a leading role in seeking to foster economic development, through sponsoring vigorous **industrial policy.** [See **import substituting industrialization (ISI).**]

dictatorship   (See **autocracy, authoritarianism, totalitarianism.**)

dictatorship of the proletariat   a concept of **Marxism-Leninism** that describes a system in which industrial workers (the **proletariat**) become the ruling class and, led by the communist party, use their power to suppress all opposition and to build **socialism** and ultimately **communism.**

dirigisme   a French term denoting that the state plays a leading role supervising the economy. *Dirigisme* differs from **socialism** or **communism** in that, under a system of *dirigisme,* firms remained privately owned. At the other extreme, *dirigisme* differs from the situation where the state has a relatively small role in economic governance.

dirigiste   (See *dirigisme.*)

dual-structure system   a structure of an industrial economy characterized by a sharp division between a modern corporate sector composed of large and powerful enterprises on the one hand and a traditional small-business sector, on the other. The latter tend to be dependent on and often controlled by the former. The pre–World War II Japanese economy was characterized by such a structure.

Economic Community of West African States (ECOWAS)   the organization established in 1975 among the sixteen governments in West Africa. The goals of ECOWAS are to strengthen and broaden the economies in the region through the removal of trade barriers among its members (such as import quotas and domestic content laws) and freedom of movement for their citizens and monetary cooperation.

economic liberalization   attempts to dismantle government controls on the economy.

Economic Miracle   denotes a period of rapid economic growth, such as occurred in France, Germany, and Japan during the 1950s and 1960s (and, for Japan, through the 1980s).

ejidatario   recipient of *ejido* land grant in Mexico.

ejido   land granted by Mexican government to organized group of peasants.

Emergency (1975–1977)   the period when Indian Prime Minister Indira Gandhi suspended many formal democratic rights and ruled in an **authoritarian** manner.

emirs   traditional Islamic ruler. The emir presides over an "emirate," or kingdom, in Northern Nigeria.

ethnic identity (ethnicity)   allegiance or association based on real or imagined ancestry and common historical experience, often distinguished by common cultural practices and language.

European Union   an economic organization created in 1957 (formerly known as the European Community) grouping the industrialized democracies of Western Europe to further their economic integration by seeking to reduce tariffs and other restrictions on the free movement of capital, trade, and populations among member countries.

export-led growth   economic growth generated by the export of a country's commodities. Export-led growth can occur at an early stage of economic development, in which case it involves primary products, such as the country's mineral resources, timber, and agricultural products; or at a later stage, when industrial goods and services are exported.

Farsi Persian word for the Persian language. Fars is a province in central Iran.

fascism an **authoritarian** form of political ideology and practice in which power is exercised in a repressive and undemocratic way by a single political party, usually led by one who claims supreme power. Fascist regimes often use racist or ethnically based appeals to justify their claim to rule.

fascist (See **fascism.**)

federal system (See **federalism.**)

federalism a system of governance in which political authority is shared between a central government and regional or state governments. The powers of each level of government are usually specified in a federal constitution.

Fiscal Investment and Loan Program (FILP) known also as Japan's "second budget," FILP draws its funds mainly from deposits collected by the national postal savings system, premiums paid into the public life insurance program, and contributions to public pension programs. The funds are allocated to public and semipublic enterprises, and amounted to nearly two-thirds of Japan's regular annual budget in 1993.

Foundation of the Oppressed a clerically controlled foundation set up after the revolution in Iran. It owns much of the confiscated assets of the old elite. Its profits are supposed to go to charity and education.

framework regulation German style of regulation in which the general patterns of public policy are outlined, but specific details of policy are left to policy-makers' discretion as long as they remain within the general framework.

fundamentalism a term recently popularized to describe radical religious movements throughout the world. It is widely believed that these movements interpret the fundamental texts of their religion literally and intend to recreate their religion's early societies. Iranian leader Khomeini hardly fits this definition of fundamentalism.

fusion of powers a constitutional principle that merges the authority of branches of government, in contrast to the principle of **separation of powers.** In Britain, for example, Parliament is the supreme legislative, executive, and judicial authority; the fusion of legislature and executive is also expressed in the function and personnel of the cabinet.

Gastarbeiter guestworkers from Southern Europe, especially Turkey, first recruited ("invited") to work in Germany during labor shortages in the 1960s. Although many *Gastarbeiter* and their families have remained in Germany since then, Germany's severe naturalization law has prevented most from attaining German citizenship.

gender social division based on the cultural and political significance ascribed to sexual difference.

genro a reference to an informal group of nine senior statesmen who acted as the emperor's advisers in pre–World War II Japan. Members of the group were responsible, above all, for the selection of a new prime minister and members of his cabinet.

gerontocracy a **political system** governed by elderly people; the term is often applied to China from the late 1980s through the mid-1990s, when elderly Communist Party leaders, including Deng Xiaoping (b. 1904), were the most powerful figures in the **regime.**

glasnost Gorbachev's policy of "openness" or "publicity," which involved an easing of controls on the media, arts, and public discussion, leading to an outburst of public debate and criticism covering most aspects of Soviet history, culture, and policy.

grassroots democracy term used to describe activist, local political action, and community control. Used frequently by the Greens Party in Germany and many **social movements** elsewhere.

Great Leap Forward a movement launched by Mao Zedong in 1958 to industrialize China very rapidly and thereby propel it toward **communism.** The Leap ended in economic disaster in 1960, causing one of the worst famines in human history.

green revolution a strategy for increasing agricultural (especially food) production, involving improved seeds, irrigation, and abundant use of fertilizers.

gross national product (GNP) a measure of a country's total economic output. It includes the goods and services produced within the country's borders (the gross *domestic* output) plus income earned abroad by the country's residents.

guanxi a Chinese term that means "connections" or "relationships," and describes personal ties between individuals based on such things as common birthplace or mutual acquaintances. *Guanxi* are an important factor in China's political and economic life.

Guardian Council a committee of twelve jurists created by the Iranian constitution. It has the authority to veto any parliamentary bill it considers to be un-Islamic and against the constitution.

guerrilla warfare a military strategy based on small bands of soldiers (the guerrillas) who use hit-and-run tactics to attack a numerically superior and better-armed enemy.

health insurance funds a semipublic system in Germany that brings all major health interests together to allocate costs and benefits by way of consultation and group participation.

hegemonic power a state that can control the pattern of alliances and terms of the international order, and often shapes domestic political developments in countries throughout the world.

Hindus India's main religion is Hinduism, and its adherents are called Hindus.

hojjat al-Islams literally, the proof of Islam. Medium-ranking clerics in Iran.

household responsibility system the system put into practice in China beginning in the late 1970s in which the major decisions about agricultural production are made by individual farm families based on profit motive rather than by a **people's commune** or the government.

Human Development Index (HDI) a measure used by the United Nations to rank and compare the overall quality of socioeconomic life in the world's countries. A country's HDI ranking is based on three factors: *longevity* (**life expectancy** at birth), *knowledge* (literacy and average years of schooling), and *income* [according to **purchasing power parity (PPP)**].

Hundred Flowers a movement in China during 1956–1957 when the communist party invited public criticism of its policies; the movement ended in a vicious crackdown against critics of the regime.

ideology a relatively coherent, comprehensive political doctrine or set of beliefs which seeks to explain how the political world is constituted, how it should be improved, and a strategy for achieving desired changes. Examples of ideologies are **communism, conservatism,** and **social democracy,** although these terms are also applied both to more overarching political philosophies and concrete systems of social organization, as distinct from political doctrines or value preferences.

illiteracy the lack, among people over the age of fifteen, of basic reading and writing skills.

Imam leader. Iranians traditionally used this title only for the twelve early Infallible Leaders of Shi'ism. During the Islamic Revolution, this title was used for Khomeini to elevate him above the other Grand Ayatollahs.

Imam Jum'ehs prayer-leaders in Iran's main urban mosques on Fridays. Appointed by the clerical hierarchy in Qom, these prayer-leaders enjoy considerable authority in the provinces of Iran.

imperialism the domination and exploitation of a weaker nation by a stronger one, usually for the purpose of economic gain; can also refer to the policies of imperial powers such as Britain and Japan to extend and maintain their empire. (See **colonialism.**)

import substituting industrialization (ISI) strategy for industrialization based on domestic manufacture of previously imported goods to satisfy domestic market demands. (See **developmentalism.**)

Indian Administrative Service (IAS) India's civil service, a highly professional and talented group of administrators who run the Indian government on a day-to-day basis.

indicative planning a term used to describe the development of a national economic plan which *indicates* what the plan specifies as desirable priorities for economic development. Indicative planning can be distinguished from plans developed under **command economies.**

indigenous groups population of Amerindian heritage in Mexico.

indirect rule a term used to describe the British style of colonialism in Nigeria in which local traditional rulers and political structures were used to help support the colonial governing structure.

industrialists an informal elite lobbying group in Russia made up of the heads or top executives of large state-owned or formerly state-owned enterprises to represent their interests. Elsewhere, the term refers to top executives of industrial firms.

industrial policy a generic term to refer to a variety of policies designed to shape leading sectors of the economy and enhance competitiveness, especially for industries that are considered strategic to national interests. Countries differ substantially regarding the degree to which their states consciously pursue industrial policies.

infant mortality rate the annual number of children in a particular country who die between birth and age one.

informal sector (economy) an underground economy.

insider privatization a term used in relation to Russia to refer to the transformation of formerly state-owned enterprises into **joint-stock companies** or private enterprises in which majority control of the enterprise is in the hands of employees and/or managers of that enterprise.

interest groups organizations that seek to represent the interests—usually economic—of their members in dealings with the government. Important examples are associations of occupational groups, such as farmers, or business firms in a particular sector (for example, steel producers or aircraft manufacturers).

International Financial Institutions (IFIs) generally refers to the International Bank for Reconstruction and Development (The World Bank) and the International Monetary Fund (IMF), but can also include other international lending institutions. [See **structural adjustment program (SAP)**.]

interventionist an interventionist state acts vigorously to shape the performance of major sectors of the economy.

jihad Islamic "holy war" against nonbelievers. One of the fundamental duties required of Muslims, although its interpretation varies widely.

joint-stock company a business firm whose capital is divided into shares which can be held by individuals, groups of individuals, or governmental units. In Russia, formation of joint-stock companies has been the primary method for privatizing large state enterprises.

judicial review the prerogative of a high court (such as the U.S. Supreme Court) to nullify actions by the executive and legislative branches of government that, in its judgment, violate the constitution.

Junkers reactionary land-owning elite in nineteenth-century Prussia. Major supporters of Bismarck's attempts to unify Germany in 1871.

jurist's guardianship Khomeini's concept that the Iranian clergy should rule on the grounds that they are the divinely appointed guardians of both the law and the people. He developed this concept in the 1970s.

keiretsu a group of closely allied Japanese firms that have preferential trading relationships, and often interlocked directorates and stock-sharing arrangements. The relationships among *keiretsu* member firms have been regarded as collusive and harmful to free trade by some of Japan's principal trading partners.

Keynesian demand management named after the British economist John Maynard Keynes, an approach to economic policy in which state economic policies are used to regulate the economy in an attempt to achieve stable economic growth. During recession, state budget deficits are used to expand demand in an effort to boost both consumption and investment (and create employment); during periods of high growth, when inflation threatens, cuts in government spending and a tightening of credit are used to reduce demand.

Keynesianism (See **Keynesian demand management**.)

koenkai usually translated as "support association," *koenkai* is a Japanese campaign organization for a particular candidate, consisting mainly of the candidate's relatives, friends, alumni, coworkers, and their acquaintances. Networks of *koenkai* organizations are far more important and effective than political parties in assisting politicians' election campaigns. Since it costs politicians a great deal to maintain these networks, *koenkai*-centered elections thus encourage corruption.

kolkhoz large collective farms formed after the collectivization campaign of the late 1920s and early 1930s in the Soviet Union. While formally defined as run by the collective of peasants employed there, the *kolkhoz* in fact differed little from the state farm, or *sovkhoz.*

krai one of the six territorial units in the Russian Federation which are defined by the constitution of 1993 to be among the 89 members of the federation, with a status equal to that of the republics and *oblast'*. Like the *oblasts'*, during the Soviet period, the *krai* were defined purely as territorial-administrative units within a particular **union republic** of the Soviet Union. A *krai* differed from an *oblast'* in that part of its border was on an external boundary of the USSR and/or it included a mixture of diverse ethnic territories. Generally a *krai* is a geographically large unit, but relatively sparsely populated.

Kulturkampf "cultural struggle" between Protestant and Catholic forces in late-nineteenth-century Germany.

land reform the process of reducing gross inequalities in the ownership of farm land by either confiscating or buying it from large owners and redistributing it to those who have little or no land.

law-based state a state where the rule of law prevails, so that actions of the government as well as of nongovernmental actors are subject to the requirements of the law. The creation of a law-based state in the Soviet Union was one of the explicit goals of Gorbachev's reform process, thus limiting the ability of state agencies or the Communist Party of the Soviet Union arbitrarily to circumvent laws or legal provisions.

legitimacy a belief by powerful groups and the broad citizenry that a state exercises "rightful" authority. In the contemporary world, a state is said to possess legitimacy when it enjoys consent of the governed, which usually involves democratic procedures and the attempt to achieve a satisfactory level of development and equitable distribution of resources. (See **democracy**.)

liberal (See **liberalism**.)

liberalism an ideology that gives priority to individual liberty over other values, such as equality, and seeks a limited role for government. When applied to the economy, liberalism is synonymous with free-market **capitalism;** when applied to the international order, liberalism supports free trade among countries. In the United States, liberalism involves advocating left-of-center social and economic positions, whereas in Europe liberalism represents a centrist alternative to the **conservative** right and **socialist** left. (See **economic liberalization, neoliberalism.**)

life expectancy the number of years that a newborn child can normally be expected to live.

lifetime employment the practice common among Japanese government agencies and large business firms to keep newly hired high school and university graduates on payroll until they reach mandatory retirement age. As a rule, however, the practice applies only to male employees and, moreover, is on the decline in contemporary Japan, where both the general population and workforce are rapidly "graying" and the ratios of temporary, part-time, and female employees are rising.

luan a Chinese term meaning "chaos." It conveys the fear of China's leaders and many of its people that without strong central leadership the country would collapse into **anarchy.**

mafia a term borrowed from Italy and widely used in Russia to describe networks of organized criminal activity that pervade both economic and governmental structures in that country and that involve activities such as the demanding of protection money, bribe-taking by government officials, contract killing, and extortion.

Maharajas India's traditional rulers—monarchs—who retained their positions under British tutelage during the colonial period but who were removed from power when the Indian **republic** was established.

Maoism a Chinese variant of **Marxism-Leninism** that incorporates the ideas of Mao Zedong (1893–1976). Maoism emphasizes the importance of mobilizing the masses in pursuit of communist objectives and the need for a continuing struggle against the enemies of **communism** even after the communist party has come to power; also called Mao Zedong Thought.

market reform a strategy of economic transformation embraced by the Yeltsin government in Russia and the Deng Xiaoping government in China that involves reducing the role of the state in managing the economy and increasing the role of market forces. In Russia, market reform is part of the transition to **post-communism** and includes the extensive transfer of the ownership of economic assets from the state to private hands. In China, market reform has been carried out under the leadership of the Chinese Communist Party and involves less extensive privatization.

martial law a declaration by a government, usually in an emergency situation, that law and order will be maintained by military force and that certain civil liberties and other legal procedures may be suspended.

Marxism-Leninism an **ideology** loosely derived from the theories of Karl Marx (1818–1883) about the superiority of **socialism** and **communism** over **capitalism,** and the theories of V. I. Lenin (1870–1924) about the need for a centralized political party needed to reach socialism and communism.

mass line a style of leadership defended by the Chinese Communist Party according to which officials are supposed to stay in close touch with the masses in order to learn from them as well as lead them.

middle-level theory seeks to explain phenomena in a limited range of cases, in particular, a specific set of countries with particular characteristics, such as parliamentary regimes, or a particular type of political institution (such as political parties) or activity (such as protest).

Minamata Disease organic mercury poisoning caused by eating contaminated river fish and clams, which produces paralysis of limbs and speech impairment. Occurred in Japan in the 1950s and 1960s as a result of industrial firms' discharge of toxic wastes. The disease is regarded as one of the most tragic examples of the widespread industrial pollution that characterized postwar Japanese society at the height of its dramatic economic growth.

mir a traditional form of communal peasant organization in Russia that survived until the collectivization campaign of the late 1920s and which involved a periodic redistribution of strips of land among families of the commune.

monetarism an approach to economic policy that assumes a natural rate of unemployment determined by the labor market, and rejects the instrument of government spending to run up budgetary deficits for stimulating the economy.

mosque Muslim place of worship, equivalent to church, temple, or synagogue.

Muslim(s) followers of Islam.

nationalism an ideology that seeks to create a **nation-state** for a particular community; a group identity associated with membership in such a political community. Nationalists often proclaim that their **state** and **nation** are superior to others.

nationalization the take-over by the government of privately owned business firms.

nations political communities with common historical and cultural characteristics that inhabit clearly defined territories.

nation-state distinct, politically defined territory with its own **state,** relatively coherent culture, economy, and ethnic and other social identities. (See **country.**)

neocolonialism   a system in which the more powerful developed countries continue to control and exploit the **Third World** after the era of formal colonial rule has ended, often through nonpolitical mechanisms such as multinational corporations; also referred to as neo-imperialism.

neocorporatism   in **democratic** regimes, governments may grant an **interest group** official recognition to represent its members in dealing with the government, for example, by assisting the government in setting policy for the sector in which the interest operates. Neocorporatism is often criticized as undemocratic because leaders of the interest group are not democratically elected nor **accountable** by democratic procedures yet nonetheless participate in government policy-making. Neocorporatism can be distinguished from **corporatism, state corporatism,** and **pluralism.**

neocorporatist   (See **neocorporatism.**)

neo-imperialism   (See **neocolonialism.**)

neoliberalism   a term used to describe government policies aiming to promote free competition among business firms within the market, notably, **liberalization** and **monetarism.**

neopatrimonial rule   (See **patrimonialism.**)

new right   a conservative political perspective which emphasizes individual and market-based freedoms and minimalist government, and often appeals to traditional social and family values.

new social movements   grassroots associations that may be differentiated from more established **social movements** and from **interest groups** by their greater tendency to raise basic questions about social values, social goals, and political styles; examples include environmentalism, women's rights, peace, and gay rights.

newly industrializing country (NIC)   a country that is experiencing a rapid growth of industrial output and economic modernization based largely on the expansion of the export sector; the term refers most explicitly to a small group of East Asian economies (Hong Kong, Singapore, South Korea, and Taiwan).

nomenklatura   a system of personnel selection utilized in the Soviet Union and China under which the Communist Party maintains control over the appointment of important officials in all spheres of social, economic, and political life. The term is also used to describe individuals chosen through this system and thus refers more broadly to the privileged circles in the Soviet Union and China.

nonaligned bloc   a group of countries that refused to ally with either the United States or the USSR during the **Cold War** years.

nongovernmental organization (ngo)   a private group that seeks to influence public policy and deal with certain problems that it believes are not being adequately addressed by governments; examples include Amnesty International (human rights), Oxfam (famine relief), and Greenpeace (the environment).

oblast'   one of 49 territorial units in the Russian Federation which are defined by the constitution of 1993 to be among the 89 members of the federation, with a status equal to that of the republics and **krai.** An *oblast'* generally lacks a non-Russian national/ethnic basis. During the Soviet period, the *oblasts'* were defined purely as territorial-administrative units located within a particular **union republic** of the Soviet Union.

official international currency exchange rates   the rate at which the national banks of different countries (such as the Federal Reserve Bank of the United States) exchange the currency of one country for that of another.

oligarchy   narrowly based, undemocratic government, often by traditional elites. (See **autocracy, authoritarianism.**)

OPEC   Organization of Oil Exporting Countries. Iran is one of its leading members.

Ostpolitik **(eastern policy)**   initiated by West German Chancellor Willy Brandt in the 1970s as the first step toward dialogue between the Federal Republic of Germany with East Germany and the Soviet Union.

overlapping responsibilities (policy)   refers to the unique pattern of German federalism in which federal and state governments share administrative responsibility for implementation of public policies.

para-statals   state-owned, or at least state-controlled, corporations, created to undertake a broad range of activities, from control and marketing of agricultural production to provision of banking services, operating airlines, and other transportation facilities and public utilities. (See **interventionist.**)

parliamentary sovereignty   a constitutional principle of government (principally in Britain) by which the legislature reserves the power to make or overturn any law without recourse by the executive, the judiciary, or the monarchy; only parliament can nullify or overturn legislation approved by parliament; and parliament can force the cabinet or the government to resign by voting a motion of no-confidence.

parliamentary system   a form of representative government in which the executive is drawn from and **accountable** to an elected legislature.

patrimonialism   (or **neopatrimonialism**) a system of governance in which a single ruler treats the state as personal property (patrimony). Appointments to public office are made on the basis of unswerving loyalty to the ruler. In turn, state officials exercise wide authority in other domains, such as the economy, often for their personal benefit and that of the ruler, to the detriment of the general population. (See **authoritarianism, autocracy, prebendalism.**)

patrimonial state   (See **patrimonialism.**)

patron-client relations   (or **network**) (See **clientelism.**)

people's communes   large-scale rural communities that were in charge of nearly all aspects of political, social, and economic life in the Chinese countryside from the late 1950s until the early 1980s when they were disbanded and replaced by a system of household and village-based agricultural production.

perestroika   the policy of "restructuring" embarked upon by Gorbachev when he became head of the Communist Party of the Soviet Union in 1985. Initially, the policy emphasized decentralization of economic decision-making, increased enterprise autonomy, expanded public discussion of policy issues, and a reduction in the international isolation of the Soviet economy. Over time, however, restructuring took on a more political tone, including a commitment to **glasnost** and *demokratizatsiia.*

physical quality of life (PQLI)   a measure of the noneconomic standard of living in a country based on three factors: **life expectancy, infant mortality rate,** and literacy (see **illiteracy**). Now largely replaced by the **Human Development Index (HDI).**

planning (See **command economy, indicative planning.**)

pluralism   a pattern of interest representation in **democratic** regimes where, in contrast to interest representation within **neocorporatism, interest groups** organize freely, there is typically a plurality of interest groups in a given economic sector, the government does not recognize any one of them as uniquely qualified to represent the sector's interests, and groups do not have official and privileged status to participate in government policy-making.

poder moderador   used in Brazilian politics to refer to the situation following the 1824 constitution in which the monarchy was supposed to act as a *moderating* power, standing above and harmonizing the executive, legislative, and judicial branches of government, arbitrating party conflicts, and fulfilling governmental responsibilities when nonroyal agents failed.

political culture   the attitudes, beliefs, and symbols that influence political behavior; often defined in terms of specific national political-cultural orientations.

political development   the stages of change producing more modern and effective political institutions.

political economy   the study of the interaction between the state and the economy, that is, how the state and political processes affect the organization of production and exchange (the economy), and how the organization of the economy affects political processes.

political institutions   the formal rules, structured relationships, and organizations within the state, and, more broadly, within the political sphere. Some key examples are the executive, legislature, judiciary, military, and political parties.

political system   the pattern of political institutions and processes that form a relatively coherent, durable, and unified whole. Political systems may be identified by one of their dominant characteristics, as in a **presidential system** or **communist** system.

populism   gaining the support of popular sectors. When used in Latin American politics, this support is often achieved by manipulation and demagogic appeals.

post-communism   the period after the collapse of a **communist party-state.** Most post-communist states face the twin challenges of replacing a dictatorial regime with a democratic political system and **central planning** with a market-based economy. (See **communism.**)

prebendalism   patterns of political behavior that rest on the justification that official state offices should be competed for, and then utilized for the personal benefit of office holders as well as of their support group or clients. Thus, prebendal politics is sustained by the existence of **patron-client networks.** (See **patrimonialism, clientelism.**)

presidential system   a pattern of **state** institutions in which there is a **separation of powers** between the executive and legislature. Typically, the president is directly elected and supervises the executive. The president is neither selected by parliament nor directly **accountable** to it. (See **semipresidential system, cabinet, parliamentary system.**)

privatization   the sale of state-owned enterprises to private companies or investors. Those who support the policy claim that private ownership is superior to government ownership because for-profit entities promote greater efficiency. Privatization is a central component of **structural adjustment programs (SAPs)** to curtail the losses associated with these enterprises and generate state revenue when they are sold. For Russia, see **spontaneous privatization.**

privatization voucher   a certificate worth 10,000 rubles issued by the government to each Russian citizen in 1992 to be used to purchase shares in state enterprises undergoing the process of privatization. Vouchers could also be sold for cash or disposed of through newly created investment funds.

proletariat the industrial working class which, according to Marxism-Leninism, is destined to seize power and replace capitalism with socialism.

proportional representation (PR) a system of political representation in which seats are allocated to parties within multimember constituencies, roughly in proportion to the votes each party receives. PR usually encourages the election to parliament of more political parties than single-member district winner-take-all systems.

purchasing power parity (PPP) a method used to compare income levels (and total production) among nations that takes into account the actual cost of living in a particular country by figuring what it costs to buy the same bundle of goods in different countries.

regime a form of government or a government with a distinctive ideological orientation or leadership style that has been in power for a long time.

relative deprivation describes a situation in which people feel deprived because they are no longer able to fulfill their rising political, economic, or social expectations. If it becomes strong enough, relative deprivation can lead to individual or collective violence directed against the state or other perceived causes of frustrated expectations.

rents above-market returns to a factor of production. Pursuit of economic rents (or "rent-seeking") is profit-seeking that takes the form of nonproductive economic activity.

republic in contemporary usage, a political regime in which leaders are not chosen on the basis of their inherited background (as in a monarchy). A republic may but need not be **democratic.** For Russia, see **autonomous republic.**

revolution the process by which an established political regime is replaced (usually by force and with broad popular participation) and a new regime established that introduces radical changes throughout society. Revolutions are different from **coups d'état** in that there is widespread popular participation in revolutions, whereas coups d'état are led by small groups of elites.

satyagraha a form of nonviolent protest, perfected by Mohandas Gandhi to help India attain independence from Britain.

Self-Defense Forces (SDF) inaugurated in Japan as a Police Reserve Force with 75,000 recruits in August 1950, following the outbreak of the Korean War. Known by the present name since 1954, the SDF today consists of approximately 250,000 troops equipped with sophisticated modern weapons and weapons systems. The constitutional status and operational mandates of these forces are controversial.

semipresidential system (regime) a regime which combines elements of a **presidential system** and a **cabinet** or parliamentary government. In a semipresidential regime there is neither a complete separation of powers between executive and legislature, as in a presidential system, nor a **fusion of powers,** as in a **parliamentary system.** The elected president exercises extensive power but shares control of the executive and policy-making powers with a prime minister and government responsible to parliament.

seniority-based wages a pay system in which an employee's pay is determined on the basis of length of service, largely independent of ability or performance. The practice has been common among Japanese companies but, like **lifetime employment,** has been on the decline since the 1970s when the Japanese economy entered an era of slow growth.

separation of powers an organization of **political institutions** within the **state** in which the executive, legislature, and judiciary have autonomous powers and no one branch dominates the others. This is the common pattern in **presidential systems,** as opposed to **parliamentary systems,** in which there is a **fusion of powers.**

sexenio six-year administration of Mexican presidents.

shari'a Islamic law derived mostly from the Qur'an and the examples set by the Prophet Mohammad, but more broadly, the totality of **Muslim** belief and practice; the legal foundation of Islamic theocracy.

shock therapy a variant of **market reform** which involves the state simultaneously imposing a wide range of radical economic changes, with the purpose of "shocking" the economy into a new mode of operation. Shock therapy can be contrasted with a more gradual approach to market reform.

Sikh(s) an important religious minority group in India.

social class common membership in a group whose boundaries are based on a common economic location, notably, occupation and income. Members of the same social class often share similar political attitudes.

social democracy the political orientation which most **socialist** parties have advocated within democratic political systems. Social democracy seeks to extend the sphere of state control over the **capitalist** economy and to expand the **welfare state.** Unlike **democratic socialism,** social democracy accepts the existence of a capitalist economy and, generally, the existing centralized, **bureaucratized** institutions of the state.

Social Market Economy   term describing the German economy which combines an efficient competitive economy with generous welfare state benefits for large segments of the population.

social movements   grassroots associations which demand reforms of existing social practices and government policies. Social movements are less formally organized than **interest groups.** (See **new social movements.**)

socialism   in a socialist regime, the state plays a leading role in organizing the economy and most business firms are publicly owned. A socialist regime, unlike a **communist party-state,** may allow the private sector to play an important role in the economy and be committed to political pluralism. In **Marxism-Leninism,** socialism refers to an early stage in development of **communism.** Socialist regimes can be organized in a **democratic** manner, in that those who control the state may be chosen according to democratic procedures (see **social democracy, democratic socialism**). They may also be governed in an undemocratic manner, when a single party, not chosen in free competitive elections, controls the state and society.

socialist democracy   a term that communist party-states apply to themselves, which is meant to convey that their type of political system is superior to capitalist democracies which are based on economic inequality and exploitation. Not to be confused with **social democracy.** (See **socialism, democratic socialism.**)

society   the totality of private individuals, citizens, and groups within a country. Society is usually defined by distinguishing it from the **state** or **political institutions.** (See **civil society.**)

soviet   elected councils that existed at all levels of the state structure during the Soviet period to represent the population. Although formally legislative bodies, these councils were largely rubber-stamp organizations which unanimously approved policies determined by the Communist Party. Until the late 1980s elections were noncompetitive, with only one candidate running for each seat.

sovkhoz   large state farms formed in the Soviet Union after the **collectivization** campaign of the late 1920s and early 1930s.

spontaneous privatization   a process, which occurred in the late 1980s and early 1990s in Russia, in which existing managers or ministry bureaucrats transformed promising state-owned enterprises into privatized entities in their own hands, without the existence of a clear legal framework for doing so. (See **privatization.**)

spring labor offensive   an annual event in Japan since 1955, the spring labor offensive refers to a series of negotia-

tions between labor unions in major industries and management that take place each spring. The wage increases and changes in working hours and working conditions negotiated in this manner set the standards for management-union negotiations in other industries in the given year.

state   a unified political entity; the state comprises a country's key political institutions that are responsible for making, implementing, enforcing, and adjudicating important policies in that country. States have also been defined as those institutions within a country that claim the right to control force within the territory comprising the country and to make binding rules (laws) which citizens of that country must obey. (See **civil society, society.**)

state capitalism   strategy in which government guides industrial and agricultural development and sets political conditions for its success.

state corporatism   an **authoritarian regime** in which the **state** requires all members of a particular economic sector to join an officially designated **interest group.** Such interest groups thus attain public status and they participate in national policy-making. The result is that the state has great control over the groups, and groups have great control over their members. (See **corporatism, neocorporatism.**)

state formation   the historical development of a **state,** often marked by major stages, key events, or turning points (critical junctures) which influence the contemporary character of the state.

structural adjustment program (SAP)   medium-term, generally 3–5 year, programs (which include both action plans and disbursement of funds) established by the World Bank intended to alter and reform the economic structures of highly indebted, **Third World** countries as a condition for receiving international loans. SAPs often involve the necessity for **privatization,** trade **liberalization,** and fiscal restraint. [See **International Financial Institutions (IFIs).**]

succession   the process by which one political leader takes over from, or succeeds, another, particularly when death, physical incapacity, or forced resignation causes a sudden and unexpected vacancy in a high-level position. In democracies, the rules for succession are prescribed by law, whereas in dictatorships, the passing of a leader often leads to a period of uncertainty and instability.

Supreme Commander for the Allied Powers (SCAP)   the official title of General Douglas MacArthur during 1945–1951, when he led the Allied Occupation of Japan.

tacit social contract   a term used to refer to an unwritten and implicit agreement between the Soviet leadership and the Soviet population which involved the party/state making concessions to various social groups in exchange for political compliance.

Taisho Democracy   a reference to Japanese politics in the period roughly coinciding with Emperor Taisho's reign, 1919–1925. The period was characterized by the rise of a popular movement for democratization of government by the introduction of universal manhood suffrage and the reduction of the power and influence of authoritarian institutions of the state.

theocracy   a state dominated by the clergy who rule on the grounds that they are the only interpreters of God's will and law.

Third World   a term used to refer to the developing countries of Asia, Africa, and Latin America to distinguish them from the more economically developed countries of the world such as the United States, Japan, and the nations of Western Europe.

totalitarianism   a political system in which the state attempts to exercise total control over all aspects of public and private life, including the economy, culture, education, and social organizations, through an integrated system of ideological, economic, and political control. The term has been applied both to **communist party-states** and **fascist** regimes such as Nazi Germany.

unfinished state   a **state** characterized by instabilities and uncertainties that may render it susceptible to collapse as a coherent entity.

union republic   one of fifteen territorial units which constituted the **federal system** of the Soviet Union and which subsequently became independent states with the break-up of the Soviet Union in December 1991.

unitary state   by contrast to the **federal systems** of Germany, India, Canada, or the United States, where power is shared between the central government and state or regional governments, in a unitary state (such as Britain) no powers are reserved constitutionally for subnational units of government.

untouchables   the lowest caste in India's **caste system,** whose members are among the poorest and most disadvantaged Indians.

vanguard party   a political party that claims to operate in the ''true'' interests of the group or class it purports to represent, even if this understanding doesn't correspond to the expressed interests of the group itself. The communist parties of the Soviet Union and China are good examples of vanguard parties.

warrant chiefs   employed by British colonial regime in Nigeria: A system in which ''chiefs'' were selected by the British to oversee certain legal matters and assist the colonial enterprise in governance and law enforcement in local areas.

welfare state   not a form of state, but rather a set of public policies designed to provide for citizens' needs through direct or indirect provision of pensions, health care, unemployment insurance, and assistance to the poor.

Westminster model   a form of **democracy** based on the supreme authority of parliament and the **accountability** of its elected representatives; named after the parliament building in London.

works councils   legally mandated workplace organizations that provide collective representation for workers with their employers. Separate organization from the trade unions.

zaibatsu   giant holding companies in pre–World War II Japan, each owned by and under the control of members of a particular family. The largest were divided into a number of independent firms under the democratization program during the postwar occupation but were later revived as *keiratsu,* although no longer under the control of any of the original founding families.

zamindars   landlords who acquired private property rights during British rule of India and retained their property in the modern period.

Zollverein   1834 Customs Union among various pre-unification German states. Fostered economic cooperation which led to nineteenth-century German unification (1871).

About the Editors and Contributors

Ervand Abrahamian is Professor of History at Baruch College and the Graduate Center of the City University of New York. His recent publications include *Khomeinism: Essays on the Islamic Republic* (University of California Press, 1993). He is currently working on a book entitled *Tortured Confessions: Prisons and Public Recantations in Iran.*

Adigun Agbaje is Senior Lecturer in Political Science at the University of Ibadan (Nigeria). His research interests include the role of political parties and civil society in Nigeria's efforts toward a democratic transition. He is the author of *The Nigerian Press, Hegemony, and the Social Construction of Legitimacy, 1960–1983* (Edwin Mellen Press, 1992).

Christopher S. Allen is an Associate Professor at the University of Georgia where he teaches courses in comparative politics and political economy. He has had Research Fellowships at the Harvard Business School, Johns Hopkins University, and from the German Marshall Fund. He is currently writing a book on democratic politics and capital investment in industrial societies.

Joan DeBardeleben is a professor in and director of the Institute of Central/East European and Russian-Area Studies at Carleton University (Canada). Her present research involves social effects of the economic transformation in Russia, developments in Russia's regions, and Russian elections. She recently co-edited (with John Hannigan) *Environmental Security and Quality After Communism: Eastern Europe and the Soviet Successor States* (Westview, 1995).

Maria do Carmo Campello de Souza is a Senior Researcher at the São Paulo Institute of Economic, Social, and Political Studies. She has been Professor of Political Science at the University of São Paulo (Brazil) and also an Adjunct Professor at the Institute of Latin American and Iberian Studies at Columbia University. She recently co-edited *The Right and Democracy in Latin America* (Praeger Publishers, 1992).

Shigeko N. Fukai is Professor of Political Science in the Faculty of Law at Okayama University (Japan). She has written on Japan's land problems and policy-making, Japan's role in emerging regional economic order in East Asia, and Japan's electoral and party politics.

Haruhiro Fukui is Professor Emeritus at the University of California, Santa Barbara, from which he retired in 1994. He is currently Professor of Political Science at the University of Tsukuba (Japan) where he is engaged in research on Japanese electoral politics and on security and economic relations in East Asia. He is co-editor of *The Politics of Economic Change in Postwar Japan and West Germany* (St. Martin's Press, 1993).

Merilee S. Grindle is Edward S. Mason Professor of International Development at the John F. Kennedy School of Government, Harvard University. She is a specialist on the comparative analysis of policy-making, implementation, and public management in developing countries and has written extensively on Mexico. Her most recent book is *Challenging the State: Crisis and Innovation in Latin America and Africa* (Cambridge University Press, 1996).

Richard A. Joseph is Asa G. Candler Professor of Political Science at Emory University and a Visiting Professor of Political Science (1995–1997) at the Massachusetts Institute of Technology. He has written extensively on Nigerian politics and governance in sub-Saharan Africa in general. He is the author of *Democracy and Prebendal Politics in Nigeria: The Rise and Fall of the Second Republic* (Cambridge University Press, 1987).

William A. Joseph is Professor of Political Science and chair of the department at Wellesley College and an Associate of the Fairbank Center for East Asian Research at Harvard University. His research focuses on contemporary Chinese politics and ideology. He is co-editor of *New Perspective on the Cultural Revolution* (Harvard University Press, 1991), and editor of *The Oxford Companion to Politics of the World* (Oxford University Press, 1993) and the Asia Society's China Briefing series.

Mark Kesselman is Professor of Political Science at Columbia University. A specialist on the French and European political economy, he is co-editor of *European Politics in Transition* (D. C. Heath, 1987, 1992). His recent publications include contributions to *The Mitterrand Era: Policy Alternatives and Political Mobilization in France* (Macmillan, 1995) and *Mitterrand's Legacy, Chirac's Challenge* (St. Martin's Press, 1996).

Atul Kohli is Professor of Politics and International Affairs at Princeton University. His principal research interests are in the comparative political economy of developing countries and India in particular. His recent publications include *Democracy and Discontent: India's Growing Crisis of*

Governability (Cambridge University Press, 1990). His current research involves a comparative analysis of industrialization in South Korea, Brazil, India, and Nigeria.

Joel Krieger is the Norma Wilentz Hess Professor of Political Science at Wellesley College. His work on British politics includes *Reagan, Thatcher and the Politics of Decline* (Oxford, 1986) and *Undermining Capitalism: State Ownership and the Dialectic of Control in the British Coal Industry* (Princeton, 1983). In addition, he was editor-in-chief of *The Oxford Companion to Politics of the World* (Oxford University Press, 1993) and is co-editor of *European Politics in Transition* (D. C. Heath, 1987, 1992).

Scott Taylor is a doctoral candidate in political science at Emory University. His dissertation focuses on the impact of business groups on government economic policy-making in Africa and is entitled, "Economic Growth and Political Change in Africa: The Role of Business Associations in Zimbabwe and Zambia."

Index*

Abacha, Sani, 618, 647, 657, 664, 666, 672, 678, 683
Abertura, 562
Accountability, Nigeria, **616,** 624
Acephalous societies, **623**
Adenauer, Konrad, 179
Administration, 5
Administrative Court, **201**
Administrative guidance, **248**
Advisory bodies or agencies, 68
Africa, 686
Ake, Claude, 679
Akintola, Samuel, 631
Al-Ahmad, Jalal, 712
Alavi Foundation, 721
All-China Federation of Trade Unions, 422
All-China Women's Federation, 423
Alliance, 82
Allied Occupation, Japan, 241–243
Amakudari, **262**
Anarchy, **378**
Ancien régime, 107–**108**
Anticlericalism, **495**
Aristotle, 4
Assembly of Religious Experts, 717
Association of Southeast Asian Nations (ASEAN), **285**
Autarky, **381**
Authoritarian, **616**
Authoritarian government, **370**
Authoritarian Vichy regime, **105**
Authoritarianism, **9, 551**
Autocracy, **615**
Autonomous regions, **400**
Autonomous republics, **325**
Awolowo, Obafemi, 629, 631
Ayatollah, **693**
Azerbaijan, 739
Azikiwe, Nnamdi, 632

Babangida, Ibrahim, 617, 640–641, 657, 663, 665, 675
Bahais, 729
Balance-of-payments, **635**

Balewa, Alhaji Abubakar Tafawa, 630, 632, 656
Bani-Sadr, Abol-Hasan, 720
Barraclough, Geoffrey, 173
Basic Law, 192–193
Bastille Day, 103
Bazaars, **701**
Bazargan, Mehdi, 724
Bharatiya Janata Party (BJP), 443–444, 473, 475, 482
Biafra, 620–621
Bicameralism, France, 141–143
Bismarck, Otto von, 169–172
Blair, Tony, 94
Block grants, 72
Boff, Frei Leonardo, 600
Bolshevik Revolution, 297–298
Bonaparte, Napoleon, 109
Brahmins, **445**
Brain drain, **393**
Brandt, Willy, 179
Brazil, 546–610; bureaucracy, 551–553, 583–585; citizenship, 594–599; contemporary politics, 563–565; coup of 1964, 560–561; economy, 546, 566–576; elections, 591–594; executive power, 581–586; history, 551–553; ideologies, 593–594; import substituting industrialization, 567–569; inflation, 572–573; interests, 599–603; international political economy, 576–580; judiciary, 586–587; labor unions, 602–603; land and population, 546; legislature, 589–591; liberal republican order, 553–555; military, 585–586; modern state, 547–565; national identity, 594–599; new republic, 561–563; 1930 Revolution, 555–558; parties, 593; policy-making, 587–589; political culture, 594–599; political economy and development, 565–580; political left, 597–598; political organization, 546; political right, 598; political

transition, 605–610; populist republic, 558–560; protest movements, 599–603; racial issues, 595–596, 601–602; religion, 599–600; representation and participation, 589–603; social movements, 599–603; society, 546, 573–576; state, 566–573, 580–581; state and semipublic firms, 583–585; subnational government, 587; taxes, 569–570; trade, 579–580; welfare system, 570–572; women, 574, 601
Brazilian Democratic Movement (MDB), 593
Brazilian Social Democratic Party (PSDB), 605, 607
Brezhnev, Leonid, 302–303
Britain, 9, 11, 30–96; bureaucracy, 65–67; cabinet government, 62–65; citizenship, 83–85; civil service, 65–67; constitution, 93; democratic idea, 41–43; economic management, 50–52; economy, 30, 48–50, 57–59; elections, 79–83; ethnicity, 45–46, 57–58; and Europe, 59–60, 89–90; executive power, 62–70; formation of U.K., 37–39; governance, 60–72; interests, 85–87; international dimension, 44–45, 59–60, 93; judiciary, 71–72; land and population, 30; legislature, 74–79; military and police, 70; modern state, 31–46; national identities, 43–44, 83–85; nationalized industries, 67–68; nondepartmental public bodies, 68–69; parliament, 77–78; policy-making, 72–73; political challenges, 87–91; political culture, 83–85; political economy and development, 46–60; political organization, 30; political parties, 79–83; proceedings, 74; protest movements, 85–87; representation and participation, 73–87; rule of India, 447–449;

---

* Numbers in boldface indicate the page where a key term is defined.

A19